lonely planet

Vietnam, Cambodia, Laos & Northern Thailand

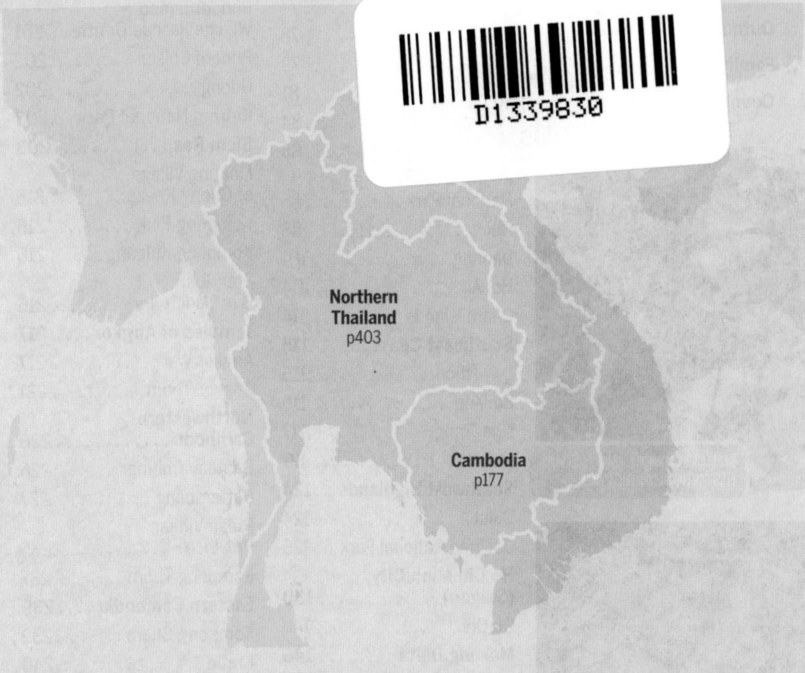

Greg Bloom, Austin Bush, David Eimer, Nick Ray, Iain Stewart, Bruce Evans, Paul Harding, Damian Harper, Ashley Harrell, Mark Johanson, Anirban Mahapatra, Bradley Mayhew, Daniel McCrohan

PLAN YOUR TRIP

CATHERINE SUTHERLAND/LONELY PLANET ©

LOTUS FLOWERS, SUKHOTHAI HISTORICAL PARK P481

KELLY CHENG TRAVEL PHOTOGRAPHY/GETTY IMAGES ©

FLOWER HMONG WOMAN, BAC HA MARKET P79

ON THE ROAD

Contents

COVID-19

We have re-checked every business in this book before publication to ensure that it is still open after the COVID-19 outbreak. However, the economic and social impacts of COVID-19 will continue to be felt long after the outbreak has been contained, and many businesses, services and events referenced in this guide may experience ongoing restrictions. Some businesses may be temporarily closed, have changed their opening hours and services, or require bookings; some unfortunately could have closed permanently. We suggest you check with venues before visiting for the latest information.

Right: Preah Khan (p224), Temples of Angkor, Cambodia

NIDO HUEBL/SHUTTERSTOCK ©

WELCOME TO

The Mekong Region

My affair with the Mekong region began in 1997. An overnight bus from Bangkok and the next morning I'm in Vientiane. It's traffic- and tourist-free, and it's surely the most relaxed place on earth. The next month is a somnolent journey north along misty mountain roads and rivers coloured caramel by the monsoon. A decade later I returned, this time to live in Cambodia, where the icons of Mekong life – exuberant temples, radiant green rice fields, glistening water buffalo – became part of my daily life, and continue to draw me back to this day.

By Greg Bloom, Writer
For more about our writers, see p576

Vietnam, Cambodia, Laos & Northern Thailand

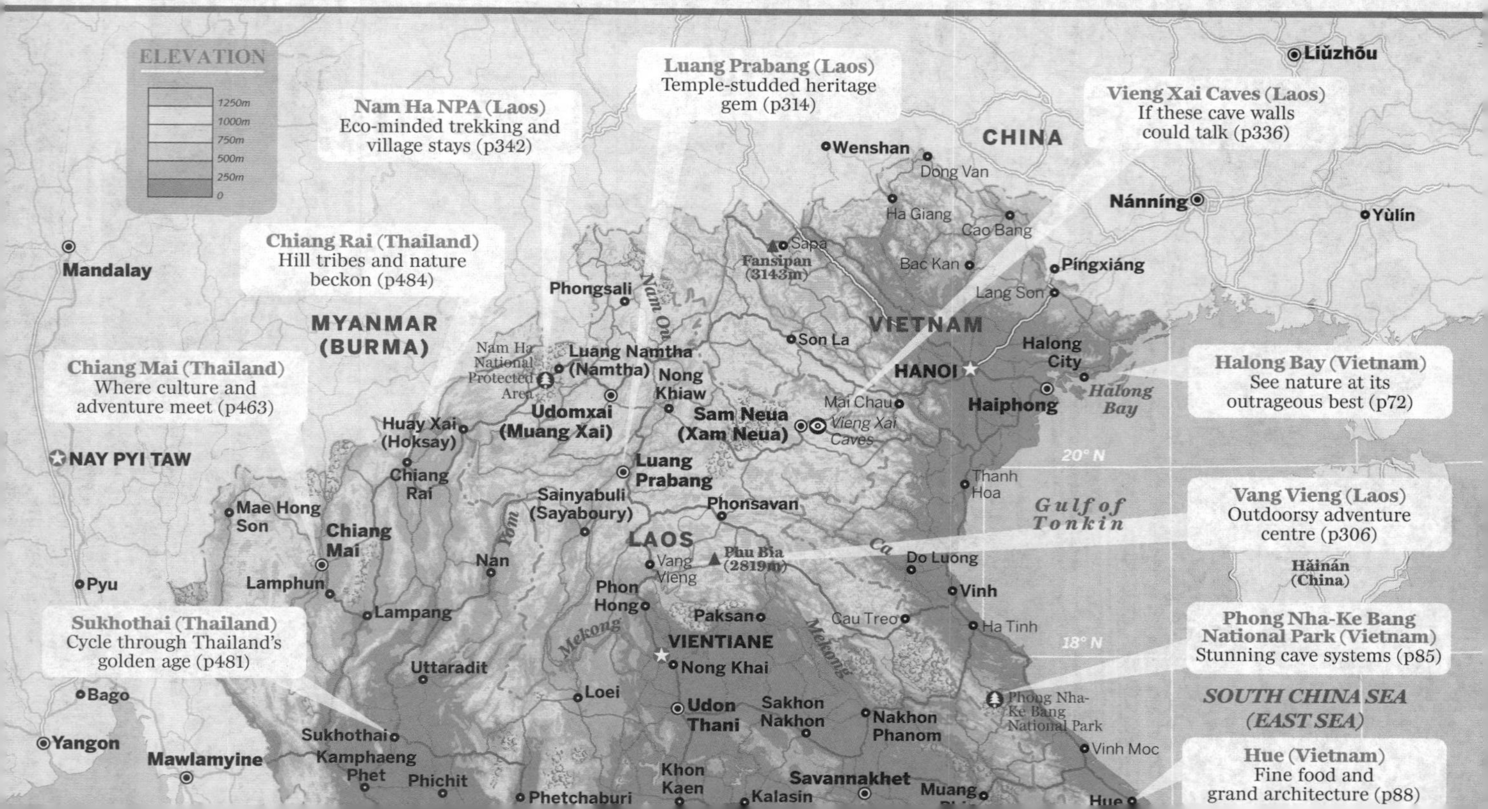

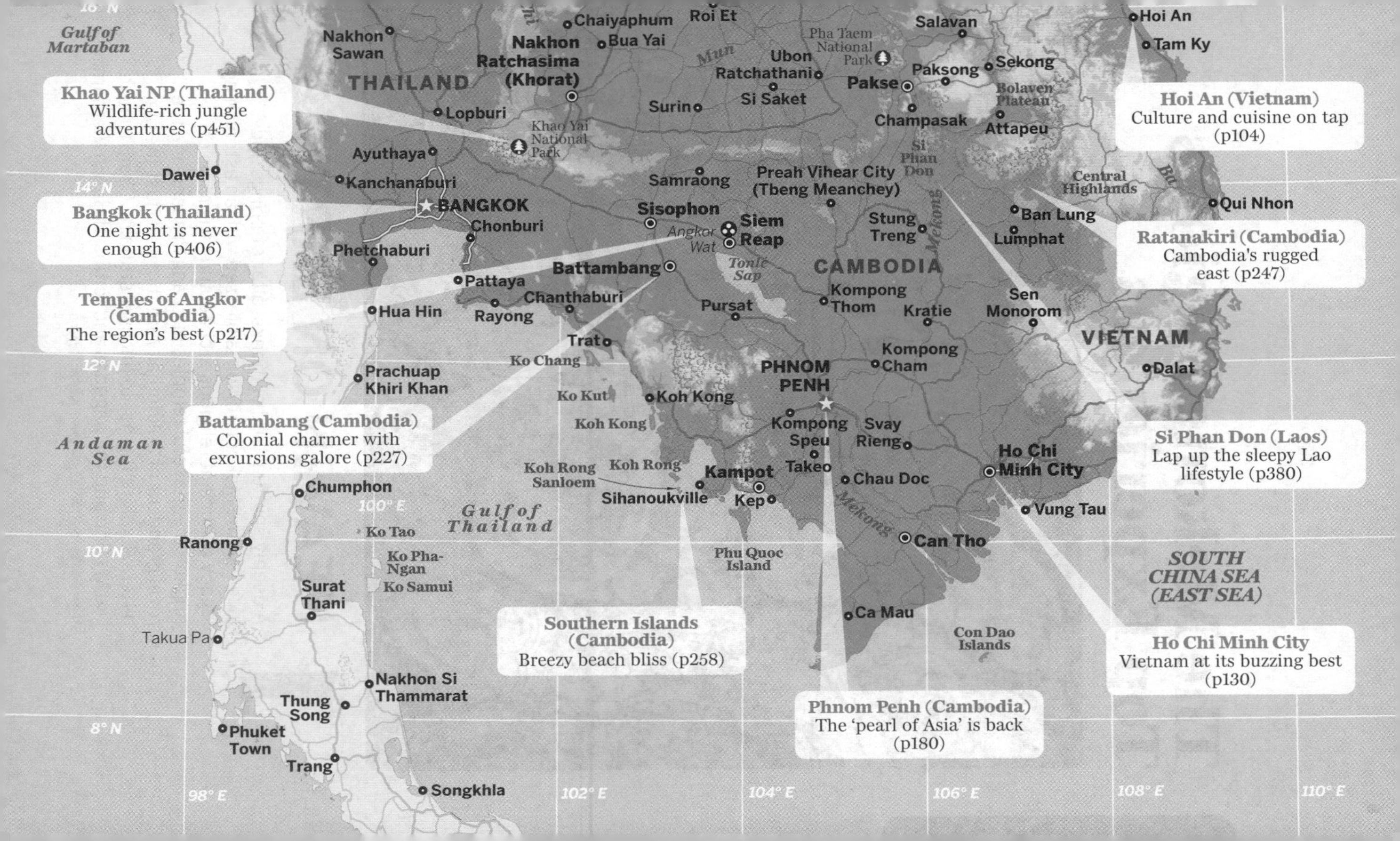

Khao Yai NP (Thailand)
Wildlife-rich jungle adventures (p451)
Bangkok (Thailand)
One night is never enough (p406)
Temples of Angkor (Cambodia)
The region's best (p217)
Battambang (Cambodia)
Colonial charmer with excursions galore (p227)
Southern Islands (Cambodia)
Breezy beach bliss (p258)
Phnom Penh (Cambodia)
The 'pearl of Asia' is back (p180)
Ho Chi Minh City
Vietnam at its buzzing best (p130)
Si Phan Don (Laos)
Lap up the sleepy Lao lifestyle (p380)
Ratanakiri (Cambodia)
Cambodia's rugged east (p247)
Hoi An (Vietnam)
Culture and cuisine on tap (p104)
Gulf of Martaban
Andaman Sea
Gulf of Thailand
SOUTH CHINA SEA (EAST SEA)
THAILAND
CAMBODIA
VIETNAM
BANGKOK
PHNOM PENH
Nakhon Sawan
Chaiyaphum
Nakhon Ratchasima (Khorat)
Bua Yai
Roi Et
Ubon Ratchathani
Si Saket
Surin
Pha Taem National Park
Pakse
Salavan
Paksong
Sekong
Bolaven Plateau
Champasak
Attapeu
Hoi An
Tam Ky
Lopburi
Khao Yai National Park
Ayuthaya
Dawei
Kanchanaburi
Chonburi
Phetchaburi
Pattaya
Rayong
Chanthaburi
Hua Hin
Trat
Ko Chang
Prachuap Khiri Khan
Ko Kut
Koh Kong
Koh Rong
Koh Rong Sanloem
Sihanoukville
Kampot
Kep
Chumphon
Ko Tao
Ko Pha-Ngan
Ko Samui
Ranong
Surat Thani
Takua Pa
Nakhon Si Thammarat
Thung Song
Phuket Town
Trang
Songkhla
Samraong
Sisophon
Angkor Wat
Siem Reap
Battambang
Tonlé Sap
Pursat
Preah Vihear City (Tbeng Meanchey)
Si Phan Don
Stung Treng
Mekong
Kompong Thom
Kratie
Kompong Cham
Kompong Speu
Takeo
Svay Rieng
Chau Doc
Can Tho
Ca Mau
Phu Quoc Island
Ban Lung
Lumphat
Central Highlands
Ba
Qui Nhon
Sen Monorom
Dalat
Ho Chi Minh City
Vung Tau
Con Dao Islands
Mun
Chi
14° N
12° N
10° N
8° N
98° E
100° E
102° E
104° E
106° E
108° E
110° E

The Mekong Region's Top Experiences

1 HEAVEN ON EARTH

A deeply spiritual land of monks, altar offerings and incense, the Mekong region is blessed with an astonishing legacy of ancient religious architecture: the ruins of Angkor, the graceful temples of Luang Prabang and the royal grandeur of Sukhothai. And those are just the big hitters. Explore further to uncover stunning Cham ruins like My Son and the pagodas and tombs of Hue in Vietnam.

Above: Banteay Srei (p225), Temples of Angkor, Cambodia

ARTIE PHOTOGRAPHY (ARTIE NG)/GETTY IMAGES ©

Temples of Angkor (Cambodia)

Perhaps the greatest cultural monument in the world, this extraordinary temple complex includes incomparable Angkor Wat; wonderfully weird Bayon; and Ta Prohm, where nature runs amok. p217

Right: Bayon (p221), Temples of Angkor, Cambodia

BEIBAOKE/SHUTTERSTOCK ©

PIKOSO.KZ/SHUTTERSTOCK ©

Luang Prabang (Laos)

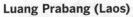

Hemmed in by the Mekong River and Nam Khan (Khan River), this timeless city of temples is a traveller's dream: rich in royal history, saffron-clad monks, stunning river views, world-class French cuisine and the best boutique accommodation in Southeast Asia. p314

Above: Buddhist monks collecting alms, Luang Prabang, Laos

Sukhothai Historical Park (Thailand)

This majestic former capital (pictured above) is best explored by bicycle, as you wind your way around crumbling temples, graceful Buddha statues and fish-filled ponds. Worthwhile museums and some of the country's best-value accommodation round off the experience. p481

2 LESS IS MORE

The Mekong region has its share of megacities that are certainly dynamic and exciting to experience, but many travellers revel in the slower pace of life found in smaller cultural hubs such as Hoi An, Chiang Mai and Battambang. All these rewarding destinations boast fantastic dining scenes, cooking schools and independent stores focusing on local crafts.

Below: Assembly Hall of the Chaozhou Chinese Congregation, Hoi An (p104), Vietnam

MIKEPHOTO/SHUTTERSTOCK ©

AOYA/SHUTTERSTOCK ©

Hoi An (Vietnam)

Immerse yourself in history in the beautiful, ancient port of Hoi An, which contains a warren-like Old Town replete with temples and pagodas, cafes and restaurants. Then hit glorious An Bang Beach, wander along the riverside and bike the back roads. p104

Left: Thu Bon River, Hoi An, Vietnam

Battambang (Cambodia)

Unfurling along the banks of the Sangker River, Battambang is one of the best-preserved colonial-era towns in Cambodia. Streets lined with graceful old shophouses host art galleries and social enterprises ranging from fair-trade cafes to tour agencies peddling bike excursions. In a word? Charming. p227

Top left: Colonial-era architecture, Battambang, Cambodia

Chiang Mai (Thailand)

The cultural capital of Northern Thailand, Chiang Mai is beloved by culture geeks, temple-spotters, families and foodies. Loaded with monuments from the once-independent Lanna kingdom, the old city's evocative winding side roads are a delight to explore, as is the city's market. p463

Left: Wat Phra That Doi Suthep (p467), Chiang Mai, Thailand

3 BEACH BLISS

If you're in search of a tropical beach where the crowds are thin, coconuts are plentiful and the water aquamarine, you've come to the right place. Vietnam's coastline has near-endless options, Cambodia and Thailand's islands offer coral reefs and scuba dreams, while even land-locked Laos has some fine hammock-swinging spots. Yes, you're never far from a beach haven in the Mekong region.

Below: Koh Rong (p259), Cambodia; Right: Kayaking the Mekong near Don Det (p383), Laos

MATTHEW MICAH WRIGHT/GETTY IMAGES ©

DITTY_ABOUT_SUMMER/SHUTTERSTOCK ©

ALEKSANDAR TODOROVIC/SHUTTERSTOCK ©

Ko Kut (Thailand)

Ko Kut (pictured above) has beautiful stretches of sand, fine snorkelling and hidden waterfalls. Best of all, the island retains a supremely unhurried pace of life that visitors soon find themselves imitating. p447

Si Phan Don (Laos)

These idyllic tropical islands, bounded by the waters of the Mekong, are known for sun worshipping, kayaking, and boat trips to see the Irrawaddy dolphin. p380

Cambodia's Southern Islands

A secret no more, the islands of Koh Rong and Koh Rong Sanloem fulfil lost paradise fantasies while ensuring enough buzz to keep the party people happy. p258

4 EATS & TREATS

There's no surer way to spice up your life than with a culinary odyssey through the Mekong region. Delve a little into the region's history and it's easy to appreciate the influence of India in Cambodian *amok* and the presence of China in soy-sauce-soaked noodles and hotpots of Northern Vietnam. Cooking schools offer the chance to learn a new skill, while street food treats are ubiquitous and delicious.

ASIA IMAGES/SHUTTERSTOCK ©

SOPHIE LENOIR/SHUTTERSTOCK ©

Street Food

Virtually every town and city will have a zone where street vendors serve up sizzling regional dishes. Hanoi is a mecca, famous for specialities like *bun cha* (barbecued pork). p61

Top left: *Bun cha*, Vietnam

Seafood

Head to Kep in Cambodia for special dishes like succulent fresh crab with Kampot pepper at the iconic Crab Market. p273

Bottom left: Stir-fried crab, Cambodia

Fine Dining

For memorable home cooking with Gallic flare, book ahead for Laos' top restaurants. HCMC, Phnom Penh and Bangkok are other key foodie destinations.

Above: Quail dish at L'Elephant (p323), Luang Prabang, Laos

5 BIG NATURE

CPM PHOTO/SHUTTERSTOCK ©

LENA SERDITOVA/SHUTTERSTOCK ©

MATTHEW WAKEM/GETTY IMAGES ©

The Mekong region offers nature on a very grand scale indeed, particularly in Northern Vietnam and Eastern Laos, home to limestone peaks, colossal caves and thousands of craggy karst islands. Elsewhere, Thailand's best scenery is in its far north, where you'll find superb road trip potential; the landscape a cascade of forested mountains and plunging river valleys, lonely hill tribe villages and breathtaking vistas.

Phong Nha-Ke Bang National Park (Vietnam)

Perhaps the world's most exciting caving destination, Phong Nha-Ke Bang has cathedral-like chambers to explore, including Hang Toi (Dark Cave) and the other-worldly beauty of Paradise Cave. p85

Top left: Paradise Cave (p86), Phong Nha-Ke Bang National Park, Vietnam

Halong Bay (Vietnam)

Halong Bay's stunning combination of karst limestone peaks and sheltered, shimmering seas (pictured left) is one of Vietnam's top draws, and with more than 2000 islands, there's plenty of superb scenery to go around. p72

Vieng Xai Caves (Laos)

This is history writ large in stone. Vieng Xai was home to the Pathet Lao leadership, who burrowed into these natural caves for protection. A superb audio tour brings the experience alive. p336

6 WILD AT HEART

National parks offer the best opportunity for wildlife encounters. Flora and fauna is incredibly exotic and varied, with species new to science being discovered every year. Highlights include kayaking trips to see the freshwater Irrawaddy dolphin on stretches of the Mekong, pre-dawn hikes to see gibbons, birdwatching in wetlands (including Cambodia's Prek Toal) and visiting elephant sanctuaries.

Khao Yai National Park (Thailand)

Wildlife-spotting is excellent in this vast Unesco-listed reserve, home to elephants, monkeys, gibbons, amazing birdlife (including hornbills), pythons, bears, a million bats and even a few wily tigers. p451

Below: Great hornbill, Khao Yai National Park, Thailand

SUN_SHINE/SHUTTERSTOCK ©

Gibbon Experience (Laos)

Realise your inner Tarzan as you whiz above the forest floor attached to a zipline (pictured above). These cables span valleys in the Bokeo Nature Reserve (habitat of the black-crested gibbon). p350

Cat Tien National Park (Vietnam)

Set on a bend in the Dong Nai River, there is something vaguely *Apocalypse Now* about Cat Tien (pictured right). Popular activities include cycling, trekking and wildlife spotting. p129

7 ADVENTURE SPORTS

PATRIK DIETRICH/SHUTTERSTOCK ©

The Mekong region has outstanding outdoor appeal. There's outstanding kite-surfing, a myriad of great kayaking options plus decent scuba diving and snorkelling around the Cambodian and Thai islands. Inland, there's amazing rock climbing in Vietnam's Cat Bat Island and Lan Ha Bay and near-endless hiking and biking routes – hotspots include the highlands of Northern Vietnam and Laos.

Nam Ha National Protected Area (Laos)

Ecotreks in this wonderland in northern Laos, where clouded leopards still roam, are deeply rewarding and controlled to minimise pressure on local hill tribes. Other activities include rafting, mountain biking and birding. p342

Vang Vieng (Laos)

The riverine jewel in Laos' karst country, Vang Vieng offers well-organised ziplining, trekking, caving and climbing – and not forgetting the main draw: river trips by kayak or longtail boat. p306

Mui Ne (Vietnam)

A kitesurfing capital (pictured above), with world-class wind and more than 20km of palm-fringed beachfront that stretches invitingly along the shores of the South China Sea. Sailing, windsurfing and hot-air ballooning are also possible. p121

8 BIG CITY BUZZ

Prime your senses, loosen your collar and enter the dragon: the region's megacities are as dynamic and exciting as anywhere on planet earth. Grand thoroughfares are graced with historical sites, fine museums, fascinating galleries, chic boutiques and imposing colonial-era edifices. Yet explore more and you'll encounter tradition and street life just a step or two away; in areas such as Hanoi's Old Quarter, lanes are thick with street kitchens and craft industries.

VASSAMON ANANSUKKASEM/SHUTTERSTOCK ©

LE QUANG PHOTO/SHUTTERSTOCK ©

Bangkok (Thailand)

The original City of Angels more than lives up to its hype. Traffic jams and humidity aside, Bangkok is now tidier and easier to navigate than ever. p406

Top left: Chatuchak Weekend Market (p416), Bangkok, Thailand

Hanoi & HCMC (Vietnam)

Vietnam's two metropolises both have a visceral energy: Ho Chi Minh City is raucous and thrilling while Hanoi (pictured above left) is a little more reserved. p52 & p130

Phnom Penh (Cambodia)

Cambodia's capital (pictured above) is a chaotic yet charming city that has thrown off the shadows of the past to embrace a brighter future. p180

9 HILL TRIBE CULTURE

TOPTEN22PHOTO/SHUTTERSTOCK ©

GIL.K/SHUTTERSTOCK ©

The mountainous north of the region is deeply diverse and home to over a hundred ethnic groups. Laos and Vietnam are famous for community-based treks, many of which include a stay in a minority village. Luang Namtha (in Laos) and Bac Ha (in Vietnam) are popular bases. Northern Thailand has a very multicultural feel too and here, Burmese, Chinese and Shan influences are evident.

Chiang Rai Province (Thailand)

The days of the Golden Triangle opium trade are over, but intrigue still lingers at Chiang Rai in the form of trekking and self-guided exploration. Visit an Akha village or stay at the Yunnanese-Chinese hamlet of Mae Salong. p484

Top left: Doi Mae Salong (p489), Thailand

Bac Ha (Vietnam)

From the sleepy village of Bac Ha you can hike to Tay, Flower Hmong and Dzao homestays on treks and explore bucolic rural lanes on two wheels to minority markets. p79

Left: Flower Hmong woman, Bac Ha Vietnam

Mondulkiri & Ratanakiri (Cambodia)

The rolling hills of the nation's wild northeast offer trekking amid threatened forests and ethnic-minority villages where animism and ancestor worship are still practised. Elephant sanctuaries are another draw. p245 & p247

Need to Know

For more information, see Survival Guide (p533)

Currency

Cambodia Riel (r)
Laos Kip (K)
Thailand Baht (B)
Vietnam Dong (d)

Languages

Cambodia Khmer
Laos Lao
Thailand Thai
Vietnam Vietnamese

Visas

Cambodia US$30 (on arrival)
Laos US$30 to US$42 (on arrival)
Thailand Waivers (on arrival)
Vietnam US$20 (in advance; some countries exempt)

Money

ATMs are widely available in Thailand and Vietnam, and in most Cambodian and Lao provincial capitals. Credit cards are accepted at most midrange and top-end hotels throughout.

Mobile Phones

Roaming is possible in all countries, but it's expensive. Local SIM cards and unlocked mobile phones are available.

Time

Indochina Time (GMT/UTC plus seven hours)

When to Go

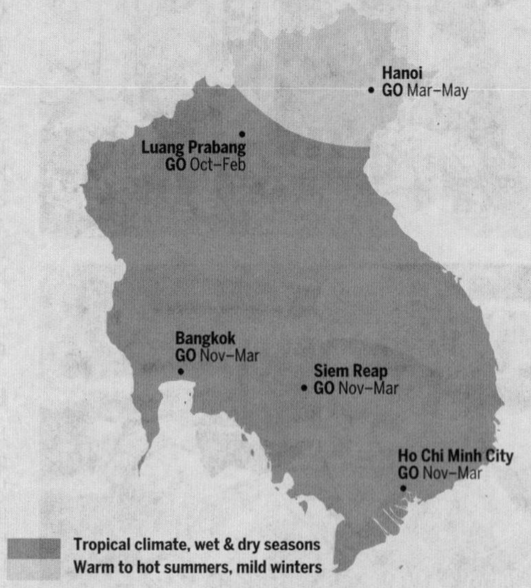

High Season (Dec–Mar)

- Cool and dry in the southern Mekong region.
- Cold in Hanoi and the mountains of Laos and Vietnam.
- Watch out for Chinese New Year in January/February, when everyone is on the move.

Shoulder (Apr, May, Oct & Nov)

- April to May is sweltering hot in the lowlands.
- October and November offer good trekking, lush landscapes and a pleasant climate.
- Songkram (April) is a blast, albeit Laos, Thailand and Cambodia shut down for business.

Low Season (Jun–Sep)

- Wet season means emerald-green landscapes and respite from the searing sun.
- Big hotel discounts at beaches and in touristy spots such as Siem Reap.
- Thailand remains busy as Western visitors flock there for summer holidays.

Useful Websites

Lonely Planet (www.lonelyplanet.com) Destination information, hotel bookings, traveller forum and more.

Travelfish (www.travelfish.org) Opinionated articles and reviews about the region.

Mekong Tourism (www.mekongtourism.org) Updated links to latest regional travel news and trends.

Golden Triangle Rider (www.gt-rider.com) The motorbiking website for the Mekong region.

Important Numbers

Always remember to drop the initial 0 from the mobile prefix or regional (city) code when dialling into Cambodia, Laos, Thailand or Vietnam from another country.

Cambodia	☎855
Laos	☎856
Thailand	☎66
Vietnam	☎84

Exchange Rates

Cambodia	US$1	4000r
Laos	US$1	9000K
Thailand	US$1	31B
Vietnam	US$1	23,000d

For current exchange rates, see www.xe.com.

Daily Costs

Budget: Less than US$50

- Dorm bed: US$2–3
- Cheap guesthouse room: US$10–15
- Local meals and street eats: US$1–2
- Local buses and trains: US$2–3 per 100km

Midrange: US$50–150

- Air-con hotel room: US$15–50
- Decent local restaurant meal: US$5–10
- Short taxi ride: US$2–3
- Local tour guide per day: US$20

Top End: Over US$150

- Boutique hotel or resort: US$50–500
- Gastronomic meal with drinks: US$25–75
- 4WD rental per day: US$60–120
- Upmarket adventure tour: US$100–200

Getting Around

Trains, planes, automobiles and boats are equally viable options in the Mekong region.

Bus The reliable warhorse of the region; will likely be your main form of transport.

Plane Plenty of interregional and domestic routes between major cities. Domestic routes in Cambodia and Laos are more limited.

Train Alternative to buses in Thailand and Vietnam; relaunched in 2016 after decades of dormancy in Cambodia; just about ready for prime time in Laos.

Boat Losing popularity as roads improve.

Car Private vehicle hire affordable for those who prefer private transport. Self-drive rentals becoming more popular.

Motorbike Great for localised travel; rentals cheap and widely available.

Local transport Cheap tuk-tuks and motorcycle taxis are ideal for short hops.

Etiquette

Individual countries have their own rules and taboos, but the following apply for pretty much the entire Mekong region:

Arguments Do not lose your temper. This will lead to a loss of face. Smile through conflict instead.

Chopsticks Don't leave a pair of chopsticks sitting vertically in a rice bowl – they can look like the incense sticks that are burned for the dead.

Feet Avoid pointing your feet at people or sacred objects (eg Buddhas); if you can't control your feet, tuck 'em behind you, like a mermaid.

Food Don't turn down food placed in your bowl by your host.

Heads Considered sacred: don't touch anyone on their head.

Monks They are not supposed to touch or be touched by women.

Nude sunbathing Considered totally inappropriate.

Shoes Remove them when entering a temple or home.

Temples Don't bare too much skin; remove any hat or head covering before entering.

For much more on **getting around**, see p546

What's New

Change is happening at a breakneck pace in the Mekong region. Countering global trends, all countries (except Thailand) boasted growth figures in pandemic-hit 2020, and regional hubs like Phnom Penh, Hanoi, Vientiane and Chang Mai are emerging as truly cosmopolitan cities.

Aerial Adventures

Bird's-eye views are all the rage these days. Perched atop Thailand's tallest building, SkyWalk at King Power Mahanakhon (p416) offers a nerve-jangling 360-degree view of Bangkok. Mekong Fly (p385) on Don Khon, Laos, traverses the raging torrent of the Tat Somphamit waterfall. Soaring high above the An Thoi Islands off Phu Quoc, Vietnam, the Hon Thom Cable Car (p154) is the world's longest over-sea cable car. Nong Khiaw Jungle Fly (p339) in Laos throws down ziplines, 'Tarzan swings', canopy walks and abseiling as part of its adventure package. In Vietnam, Ba Na Hill Station's Golden Bridge offers astonishing panoramas (though working around the crowds of Instagrammers isn't easy).

Righting Animal Wrongs

Some rare good news for animals – both wild and domestic. The latest census of Irawaddy dolphins along the Mekong River in Cambodia found the population has risen for the first time in years.

Officials in Hanoi have urged city dwellers to not eat dog meat in a bid to make the city free of the canine meat trade.

ChangChill (p469) has become the only elephant reserve in Northern Thailand to be designated elephant-friendly by World Animal Protection.

Can Tho Takes Off

Long the unofficial capital of the Mekong Delta on account of its sophisticated hotels and restaurants and nearby floating markets, Can Tho is now well and

LOCAL KNOWLEDGE

WHAT'S HAPPENING IN VIETNAM, CAMBODIA, LAOS & NORTHERN THAILAND

Greg Bloom, Lonely Planet Writer

Long a conduit for trade, the Mekong River has increasingly become a source of tension. Laos' campaign to build up to nine dams has downriver folk in Cambodia and Vietnam genuinely worried about its potential effects on fish stocks and the supply of water.

The elephant in the room continues to be China, which has been pouring billions of dollars in investments and loans into Cambodia and Laos through its 'Belt and Road' initiative, while legitimising one-party elites. The geopolitical entanglements and long-term costs are a cause of concern.

Meanwhile, traditionally neutral Thailand has remained that way. The Thais have enough to worry about on the home front, with a military junta overseeing politics and angry protests calling for reform of the monarchy.

Certain sectors, including manufacturing and agriculture, faired well during 2020, though tourism in the Mekong region was hit particularly hard as international visitor arrivals plummeted.

truly on the map thanks to a network of domestic flights that connect it to the blissful beaches of Phu Quoc and Con Dao, as well as Dalat, Danang, Haiphong and Hanoi. International budget airlines offer direct connections to Bangkok and Kuala Lumpur.

Rail Buffs Rejoice

Train service continues its slow proliferation throughout the Mekong region. The major intra-regional railway linking Kunming in China to Vientiane, begun in late 2016, is scheduled for completion in 2021. Cambodia's long-mothballed rail system saw the reopening of its pre–WWII northern line in 2018 after the southern line opened in 2016. Hanoi's first metro line is set to commence service in late 2021 or 2022. Progress on HCMC's metro remains slow, but trains should start rolling in 2022 or 2023. Bangkok's new Bang Sue Grand Station will open in 2021 as the nation's new rail hub.

Luang Prabang Branches Out

Several interesting activities have sprouted up outside Laos' boutique capital. Try your hand at milking a buffalo on a tour of Laos Buffalo Dairy (p328). Verdant Nahm Dong Park (p328) features waterfalls, swimming holes, ziplines, a treetop walk and trekking. Rural e-mountain-biking excursions with E-bike Adventures (p320) can be combined with kayaking on the Nam Khan River.

Sihanoukville on the Slide, Southern Islands on the Rise

Well-documented in the international press, former party mecca Sihanoukville, Cambodia, is a development disaster with chaotic construction, terrible traffic and numerous casinos. Luckily the surrounding islands are taking up the slack thanks to beautiful beaches and a great range of accommodation.

Waste Not ...

Grassroots projects aim to lead the climate-change-vulnerable Mekong region toward greener pastures. Refill Not Landfill (https://refilltheworld.com) works with hotels, restaurants and shops across the region to provide refillable water bottles and drinking-water refill stations. Trash Heroes (https://trashhero.org) is a growing initiative that sees volunteers picking up rubbish around the beaches of Thailand and Cambodia.

Bangkok Biennale

Running from October to February in alternate years, the Bangkok Biennale (www.bkkartbiennale.com) is a new mega-festival that started in 2018–19, showcasing the works of some of Asia's biggest and trendiest artists at public spaces across the metropolis. The next edition is scheduled for 2022–23.

LISTEN, WATCH & FOLLOW

For inspiration, visit www.lonelyplanet.com/vietnam/articles, www.lonelyplanet.com/cambodia/articles, www.lonelyplanet.com/laos/articles and www.lonelyplanet.com/thailand/articles.

Bangkok Post (www.bangkokpost.com) Bastion of independent, English-language reporting in the region; covers Thailand and beyond.

RFA (Radio Free Asia; www.rfa.org/english/news/laos) Unbiased, censorship-free news on the region from Asia-based journalists.

The Bureau (https://thebureauasia.com) Fine restaurant and bar reviews, plus a good podcast.

Vietcetera (https://vietcetera.com/en) Great cultural, travel and cuisine content. Based in HCMC.

FAST FACTS

Food trend Contemporary street food

Highest peak Mt Fansipan, Vietnam (3143m)

Tigers remaining in the wild 180

Population 196 million

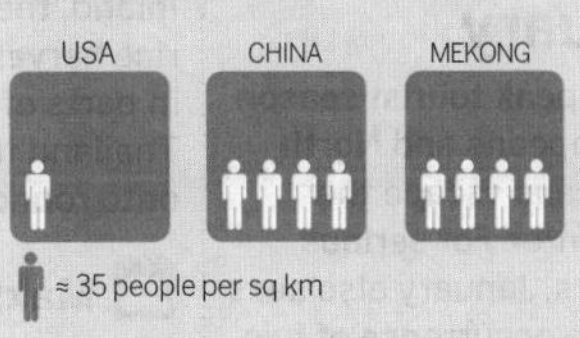

Month by Month

TOP EVENTS

Tet/Chinese New Year, January/February

Khmer/Lao/Thai New Year, April

Rocket Festival, May

Pchum Ben, September/October

Loi Krathong, November

January

This is peak tourist season as Europeans and North Americans escape the cold winter. For serious revellers, January also sees the rare occurrence of two new-year celebrations in a month.

Tet

The Big One! Vietnamese Lunar New Year is Christmas, new year and birthdays all rolled into one. Travel is difficult at this time, as transport is booked up and many businesses close. Falls in late January or early February.

Chinese New Year

Always occurring in January or February, at the same time as Vietnamese New Year (Tet), these festivities are headline news in major cities such as Phnom Penh and Bangkok. Expect businesses to close for a few days and dragon dances to kick off all over town.

February

Still peak season for the region, and the coastline is busy with sun-seekers. Inland, the first round of rice harvesting is over, but in parts of Vietnam and Thailand they are already onto round two.

Makha Bucha

One of three holy days marking important moments of Buddha's life, Makha Bucha falls on the full moon of the third lunar month and commemorates Buddha preaching to 1250 enlightened monks who came to hear him 'without prior summons'. Celebrations are most fervent in Laos and in Thailand, where it is a public holiday.

Flower Festival

Chiang Mai displays its floral beauty during this three-day event. The festival highlight is the flower-decorated floats that parade through town.

April

The hottest time of year, so book an air-con room. New year is ushered in all over the region. The accompanying water fights in Laos and Thailand are a guaranteed way to keep cool.

Songkran

Songkran, the Thai New Year, is a no-holds-barred countrywide water fight that has to be seen to be believed. Bangkok and Chiang Mai are some of the most raucous battlegrounds. Like Lao and Khmer New Year, it always falls in mid-April.

Bun Pi Mai

Lao New Year is one of the most effusive, fun-splashed events in the calendar as houses and Buddha statuary are cleaned, and the country has a weeklong national water fight with water pistols and buckets of H_2O. Protect your camera and join in the fun.

Top: Chiang Mai Flower Festival (p470)

Bottom: Preparations for Tet (Vietnamese Lunar New Year)

Chaul Chnam

Khmer New Year is a more subdued event than in neighbouring Laos and Thailand, but water fights still kick off in much of the countryside. It's mainly a family holiday, when city dwellers return to the place of their ancestry to meet distant relatives.

Liberation Day

Saigon fell to the north on 30 April 1975 and was renamed Ho Chi Minh City. It's celebrated by the Communist Party; expect the reaction to be more subdued in the south.

Hue Festival (Biennial)

Vietnam's biggest cultural event (www.huefestival.com) is held every two years, including 2022 and 2024. Most of the art, theatre, music, circus and dance performances, including many international acts, are held inside Hue's Citadel.

May

The hottest time of year in many parts of the region; escape to northern Vietnam for springlike weather. This is low season, when visitor numbers drop and prices follow.

Chat Preah Nengkal

Led by the royal family, the Royal Ploughing Ceremony is a ritual agricultural festival held to mark the traditional beginning of the rice-growing season. It takes place in early May in Phnom Penh. If the royal oxen eat, the harvest will be bountiful; should they refuse, it may spell drought. Also celebrated at the Royal Palace in Bangkok.

Visakha Bucha

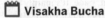

The holy day of Visakha Bucha (Phong Sinh in Vietnam) falls on the 15th day of the waxing moon in the sixth lunar month and commemorates Buddha's birth, enlightenment and *parinibbana* (passing away). Activities centre on the temple.

Rocket Festival

The Rocket Festival is a pre-Buddhist rain ceremony celebrated alongside Visakha Bucha. Villagers craft bamboo rockets *(bang fai)* and fire them into the sky to provoke rainfall to bring a bountiful rice harvest. Mainly celebrated in northeastern Thailand and Laos, where it can get wild with music, dance and processions. Dates vary from village to village.

June

The wet season begins in much of the Mekong region. Expect a daily downpour, but much of the time it should be dry. River levels begin to rise again.

Phi Ta Khon

The Buddhist holy day of Bun Phra Wet is given a Carnival makeover in Dan Sai village in northeastern Thailand. Revellers disguise themselves in garish 'spirit' costumes and parade through the village streets wielding wooden phalluses and downing rice whisky. Dates vary between June and July.

July

The wet season is in full swing in much of the Mekong region and rivers begin to swell. Many Europeans head to the region to coincide with long summer holidays back home, creating a mini-high season in the midst of the low season.

Danang International Fireworks Festival

The riverside of Danang (Vietnam) explodes with sound, light and colour during this spectacular event, which features competing pyrotechnic teams from around the world and is spread over five weekends in June and early July.

Asahna Bucha

The full moon of the eighth lunar month commemorates Buddha's first sermon, in which he described the religion's four noble truths. It is considered one of Buddhism's holiest days.

Khao Phansaa

The day after Asahna Bucha, Buddhist monks retreat into monasteries in Cambodia, Laos and Thailand – the traditional time for young men to enter monasteries or when monks begin a retreat for study and meditation. Worshippers offer candles and donations to the temples and attend ordinations.

September

The height of the wet season: if places like Bangkok or Phnom Penh are going to flood this is when it usually happens. Occasional typhoons sweep in across Vietnam, wreaking havoc.

Vietnam National Day

Big parades and events are held across Vietnam on 2 September. Celebrated with a rally and fireworks at Ba Dinh Sq, Hanoi (in front of Ho Chi Minh's mausoleum), and there are also boat races on Hoan Kiem Lake.

Pchum Ben

A sort of Cambodian All Souls' Day – respects are paid to the dead through offerings made at wat to resident monks. Often falls in October. Trung Nguyen is a similar festival celebrated in Vietnam, usually in the preceding month.

Vegetarian Festival

Thailand takes a holiday from meat for nine days in adherence with Chinese beliefs of mind and body purification. Generally held late September/early October.

October

The rains are easing off and farmers prepare for the harvest season. A series of festivals fall around this time and the temples are packed as monks emerge from their retreat.

Bon Om Tuk

Cambodia's raucous Water Festival celebrates Jayavarman VII's victory over the Chams in 1177 and the reversal of the Tonlé Sap river. It's celebrated mainly in Phnom Penh, where tens of thousands watch boat races and colourful fluvial processions.

Ork Phansaa

The end of the Buddhist Lent (three lunar months after Khao Phansaa) is marked by the *gà·tĭn* ceremony, in which new robes are given to monks by merit-makers. The peculiar phenomenon known as the '*naga* fireballs' coincides with Ork Phansaa.

November

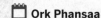

The cool, dry season begins and is an ideal time to visit for lush landscapes. In the far north of the region, temperatures begin to drop.

Loi Krathong

Join Thais in launching floating candles during the festival of Loi Krathong, usually held in early November. If you happen to be in Chiang Mai, the banana-leaf boats are replaced by *yêe peng* (floating paper lanterns).

Bun Pha That Luang

That Luang Festival is tied to the November full moon. Based in Vientiane and lasting a week, this celebration involves music, a lot of drinking, processions to That Luang, fireworks and a cast of many thousands who flock to the Laos capital.

Ramadan

Observed in southern Thailand and the Cham areas of Cambodia and Vietnam during October, November or December, the Muslim fasting month requires that Muslims abstain from food, drink, cigarettes and sex between sunrise and sunset.

December

Peak tourism season is back and the weather is fine, so the chances of a white Christmas are very slim unless you happen to be climbing Vietnam's highest peak, Fansipan.

Christmas

Most of the region has adopted Christmas in some shape or form, and while not a national holiday, it is celebrated throughout Vietnam particularly, by the sizeable Catholic population. It's a special time to be in places like Phat Diem and HCMC, where thousands attend midnight Mass.

Lao National Day

This 2 December holiday celebrates the 1975 victory over the monarchy with parades and speeches. Lao national and communist hammer-and-sickle flags are flown all over the country. Celebration is mandatory.

Angkor Wat International Half Marathon

Held the first weekend in December amid the incredible backdrop of the temples of Angkor, with 3km and 10km events complementing the 21km main event, which draws big crowds to cheer on participants from all over the world.

Plan Your Trip
Itineraries

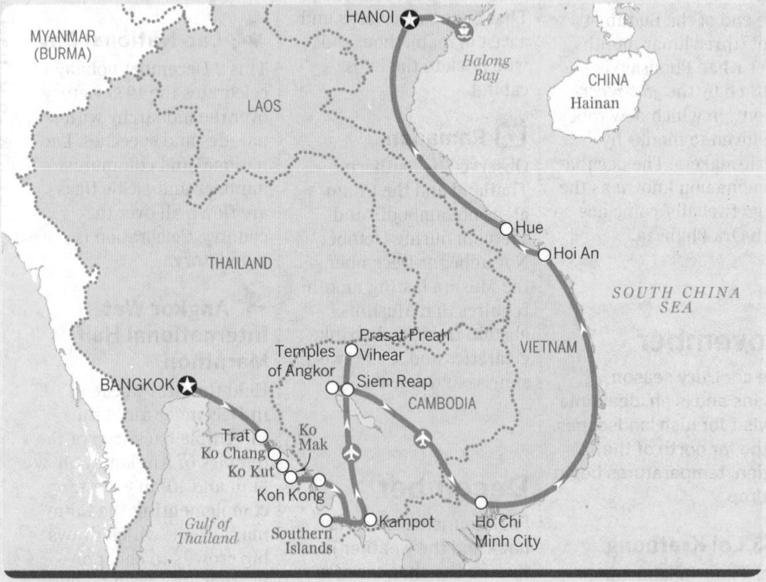

3 WEEKS Greatest Hits

Traverse the fertile belly of the region, taking in the Mekong's main metropolises, idyllic islands and its most iconic sight, Angkor Wat.

Like so many Southeast Asian journeys, yours begins in **Bangkok**. Acclimatise with the sights, sounds, smells and divine culinary flavours of the City of Angels before boarding a bus to **Trat**, the jump-off point to the underrated islands off Thailand's eastern seaboard. Jungle-covered **Ko Chang** is loved for its tropical ambience and thriving party scene, while quiet **Ko Kut** excels in seaside seclusion and **Ko Mak** boasts a chill island vibe.

Cross the border into Cambodia at **Koh Kong**, where jungle adventures await in the Koh Kong Conservation Corridor, then head to the **Southern Islands** off Sihanoukville for more fun in the sun, or to **Kampot** for good food and indolent river vibes. Cheap flights link Sihanoukville with **Siem Reap**, the gateway to the incredible **Temples of Angkor**. See the mother of all temples, Angkor Wat, the world's largest religious building; the Bayon, with its enigmatic

Ko Kut (p447), Thailand

faces; and jungle-clad Ta Prohm. Set aside a day to visit a remote temple like **Prasat Preah Vihear**, a mountain temple perched precariously atop a cliff on the Thai border.

Fly or take a bus to **Ho Chi Minh City** to spend a day or two hitting the markets, browsing museums and eating some of Asia's best cuisine. Then it's a plane or train up to Danang to access the cultured charmer and culinary hot spot that is **Hoi An**. Enjoy Hoi An's unique ambience, touring its temples and Old Town, and visit the nearby beach of An Bang. Then it's on to the old imperial capital of **Hue** for two to three nights to explore the citadel, pagodas and tombs.

Next it's a long journey by train to **Hanoi** to check out the capital's evocative Old Quarter, munch some street food and view the city's elegant architecture and cultural sights. From Hanoi book a tour to incomparable **Halong Bay**, which boasts more than 2000 limestone islands, before returning to Hanoi for your flight home.

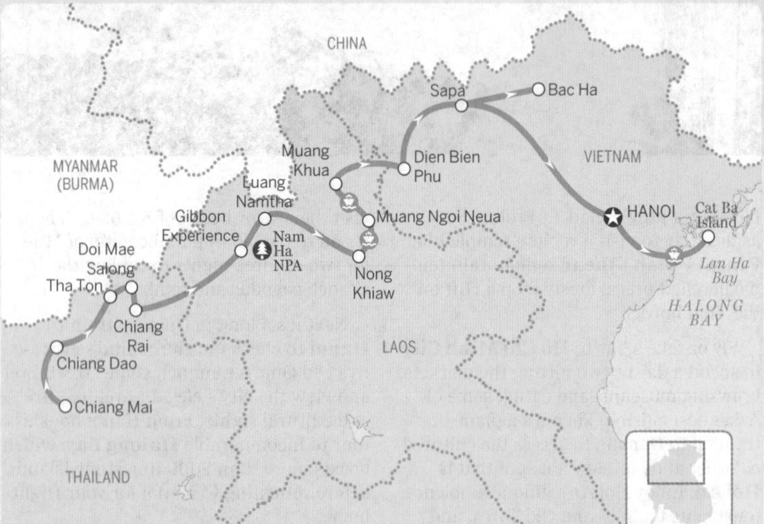
CHINA
Sapa
Bac Ha
Muang Khua
Dien Bien Phu
VIETNAM
MYANMAR (BURMA)
Luang Namtha
Gibbon Experience
Nam Ha NPA
Muang Ngoi Neua
HANOI
Cat Ba Island
Lan Ha Bay
HALONG BAY
Doi Mae Salong
Tha Ton
Chiang Rai
Nong Khiaw
Chiang Dao
Chiang Mai
LAOS
THAILAND

MATT MUNRO/LONELY PLANET ©

ANDREA PISTOLESI/GETTY IMAGES ©

Top: Sapa (p81), Vietnam
Bottom: Akha woman, Luang Namtha (p342), Laos

4 WEEKS Highland Adventure

This itinerary takes you from northern Thailand to Halong Bay, Vietnam, via the rugged and thrilling northern route. Traversing the Mekong's highest mountains, you'll get up close and personal with colourful hill tribes and have a range of outdoor adventures at your disposal.

Start in **Chiang Mai**, where adventure activities abound: mountain biking, kayaking, abseiling, trekking and ziplining. Next head north to **Chiang Dao**, where plenty of mountains await, and on to the charming riverside village of **Tha Ton** before zigzagging up to **Doi Mae Salong**, a mountain town inhabited by ethnic Chinese. Slide into **Chiang Rai** for a hill-people homestay and culturally sensitive treks.

Cross into Laos at Huay Xai and check out the **Gibbon Experience** before continuing east to **Luang Namtha** for trekking, cycling, or rafting in and around the Nam Ha National Protected Area (NPA). Veer southeast to **Nong Khiaw** on the banks of the Nam Ou, with striking limestone crags looming all around. Board the adventurous boat trip to **Muang Khua** in Phongsali Province with a stop in sublime **Muang Ngoi Neua**. If you have time, spend some days exploring the authentic hill-tribe settlements of Phongsali before crossing into Vietnam at historic **Dien Bien Phu**.

There's plenty of incredible scenery and some of the country's most dramatic mountain passes around Dien Bien Phu. Once you've had your fill, head up to **Sapa**, an old French hill station and popular gateway to the region's minority communities. Spend at least a few days in and around **Bac Ha**, home to the colourful Flower Hmong folk and great walking country. Head south to **Hanoi** to check out the capital's evocative Old Quarter, munch some street food and view the city's elegant architecture and cultural sights.

Still seeking adventure? Set off for **Halong Bay**, or detour to **Cat Ba Island**, the jumping-off point for Lan Ha Bay, the 'new' Halong Bay without the tourists. Boating, kayaking and Robinson Crusoe–style camping are possible here, and there are some beautiful hidden coves. Experienced craggers will find challenging routes on the Cat Ba's spectacular limestone outcrops, and there's instruction available for novice climbers as well.

6 WEEKS Mekong River Meander

This trip follows the mother river downstream from northern Laos all the way to its terminus in Vietnam's Mekong Delta. En route you'll encounter a wide range of landscapes, cultures and adventures as you slice through all four countries of the Mekong region.

Leave behind the bustle of **Bangkok** and make a beeline for **Chiang Rai** near the Golden Triangle, where the borders of Laos, Myanmar (Burma) and Thailand converge. Crossing the Mekong into Laos at **Huay Xai** is like stepping back in time. Slowboat down the Mekong to **Luang Prabang**, overnighting in **Pak Beng**. Soak up the magic before leaving the river for kayaking and rock-climbing mecca **Vang Vieng**.

Continue to **Vientiane** and reunite with the mighty waterway. Laos' capital is a sleepy place with some great cafes, restaurants and bars – which you won't be encountering for a while after here. Board a bus and follow the river southeast, stopping in **Tha Khaek**, **Savannakhet** and **Pakse**, old river trading centres that encapsulate the spirit of the Mekong. Visit the imposing Khmer sanctuary of **Wat Phu Champasak**, in the shadow of Lingaparvata Mountain; explore the waterfalls and villages of the **Bolaven Plateau**; or enjoy some hammock and tubing time in **Si Phan Don** (10,000 Islands).

Cross into Cambodia. If you missed the Irrawaddy dolphins near Don Khon in Si Phan Don, you can see them further south in the laid-back Mekong riverside town of **Kratie**. From Kratie, consider peeling off to visit the mountains of **Mondulkiri Province**, home to elephants, hill tribes and pristine nature.

Weeks in rural provinces will have you happy to see **Phnom Penh**, where the Mekong merges with another vital regional waterway, the Tonlé Sap. Take a sunset boat cruise or participate in an aerobics session on the riverfront promenade. When you're recharged, board a fast boat downstream to **Chau Doc**, Vietnam, gateway to the Mekong Delta. Check out **Can Tho**, the delta's commercial heart, or delve deeper into the delta with a homestay around **Vinh Long**. Hotfoot it to **Ho Chi Minh City** for a night out, or make for the tropical retreat of **Phu Quoc Island**, a well-earned reward for following the mother river.

CUONGVND/GETTY IMAGES ©

PENG_CH/SHUTTERSTOCK ©

Top: Mekong Delta (p146), Vietnam
Bottom: Wat Phu Champasak (p373), Laos

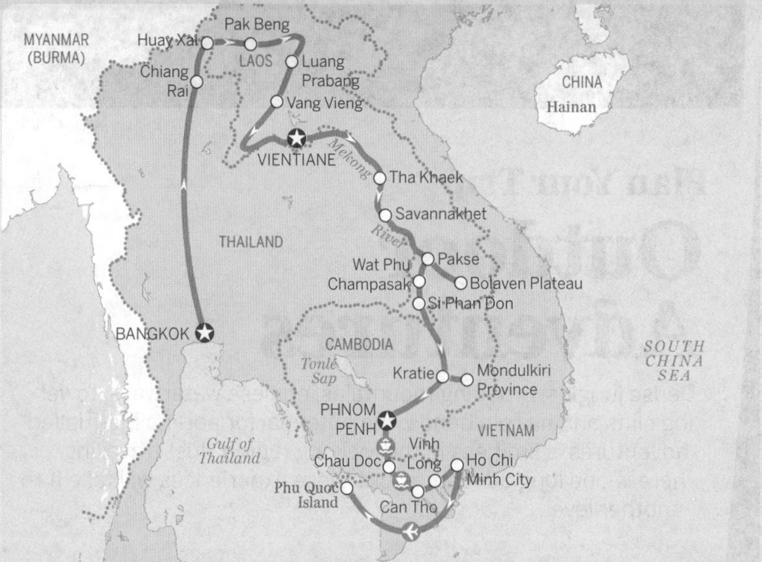
MYANMAR (BURMA)
Huay Xai
Pak Beng
LAOS
Luang Prabang
Chiang Rai
Vang Vieng
CHINA
Hainan
VIENTIANE
Mekong River
Tha Khaek
Savannakhet
THAILAND
Pakse
Wat Phu Champasak
Bolaven Plateau
Si Phan Don
BANGKOK
CAMBODIA
SOUTH CHINA SEA
Tonle Sap
Kratie
Mondulkiri Province
PHNOM PENH
VIETNAM
Gulf of Thailand
Vinh Long
Chau Doc
Ho Chi Minh City
Phu Quoc Island
Can Tho

Divers, Nha Trang (p117), Vietnar

Plan Your Trip

Outdoor Adventures

Dense jungles, brooding mountains, endless waterways, towering cliffs and hairpin bends: the potential for adrenaline-fuelled adventures is limitless in the Mekong region. Just travelling here is one long adventure, but these experiences will take it to another level.

Best Outdoors

Trekking

Cat Tien National Park Accessible park that is chock-full of wildlife.

Nam Ha National Protected Area (NPA) Responsible treks in old-growth forest.

Chiang Rai Fascinating hill-tribe terrain.

Koh Kong Conservation Corridor Experience raw nature in the Cardamoms.

Cycling

Mekong Delta Ride the back roads through Vietnam's rice bowl.

Sukhothai Pedal into Thai history.

Nong Khiaw Adventure cycling trips led by responsible operators.

Angkor Free-wheel past ancient wonders.

Diving & Snorkelling

Con Dao Islands Remote underwater adventures.

Nha Trang Vietnam's most popular diving.

Koh Rong Sanloem In range of most of Cambodia's best dive sites.

Ko Rang Thai marine park that's the best in the western gulf.

Trekking

Trekking is a huge draw in all four countries. Hike one to several days to minority hill-tribe villages, walk a half-day through the jungle to pristine waterfalls, or launch an assault on Fansipan (3143m), the region's highest mountain. The scenery – think plunging highland valleys, tiers of rice paddies and pulsating rainforests – is often remarkable.

Prices for organised treks usually include all food, guides, transport, accommodation and park fees, and start at around per day per person US$25 for larger groups. For more specialised long treks into remote areas, prices can run into several hundred US dollars. It may be necessary to arrange special permits for some treks, especially if you plan to spend the night in remote mountain villages in parts of Laos and Vietnam.

Cambodia

Trekking in northeast Cambodia has traditionally been centred in the provinces of Mondulkiri (p245) and Ratanakiri (p247) thanks to their wild natural scenery, abundant waterfalls and ethnic minority populations. Remote Virachey National Park (p248) in Ratanakiri offers the possibility of multiday trips. The tremendous Cardamom Mountains near Koh Kong (p253) are teeming with wildlife.

Laos

Trekking through the mountains and forests of Laos is almost a mandatory part of any visit to the country. Luang Namtha (p342) has developed an award-winning ecotourism project for visits to local ethnic-minority villages in Nam Ha National Protected Area (NPA). In southern Laos, Se Pian NPA (p375), close to Pakse, is a great option for multiday treks combined with traditional canoe rides or birdwatching. Tha Khaek (p355) is a base for trekking and climbing trips into Phu Hin Bun NPA (p358), with stunning karst formations and caves.

Thailand

The northern Thai cities of Chiang Mai (p463) and Chiang Rai (p484) are very popular for treks, often in combination with white-water rafting and elephant experiences. Pai (p478) has also emerged as an alternative hub for treks, many of which are run by ethical operators with sustainable trips to help disadvantaged minority peoples, but there are also a lot of cowboys out there. Doi Phu Kha National Park (p493) presents endless opportunities for day and longer treks in the northern province of Nan, passing waterfalls, caves and ethnic minority villages along the way.

Vietnam

Vietnam's traditional trekking mecca is Sapa (p81), with its remarkable tableau of mountains, rice paddies and tribal villages, but it has become crowded. Bac Ha (p79), at a lower elevation, is less rainy and the trails not as heavily tramped. Some outstanding treks and numerous trails have been developed amid the limestone scenery of Phong Nha-Ke Bang National Park (p85). Adventure-tour operators in Hoi An (p104) offer some intriguing treks in the tribal areas west of town.

Safety Guidelines for Trekkers

- Don't stray from established paths, as there are landmines and unexploded ordnance (UXO) in parts of Cambodia, Laos and Vietnam.
- Guides are worth hiring; they're inexpensive, speak the language and understand indigenous culture.
- Dogs can be aggressive; a stout stick may come in handy.
- Carry a mosquito net if trekking in malarial zones of the region.
- Consider quality socks and repellent to reduce the likelihood of leeches.
- Carry water-purification tablets if you have a weak constitution.
- Invest in some snack bars or energy snacks to avoid getting 'riced out' on longer treks.

Cycling

For hard-core cyclists, the mountains of northern Vietnam and northern Laos are the ultimate destination. The trails of Doi Suthep-Pui National Park in northern Thailand offer adrenaline-charged descents, with mountain-bike gear and guides available for hire in Chiang Mai (463). In Cambodia, mountain-bike rental and guided tours are available out of Chi Phat (p255) in the Southern Cardamom Mountains, or out of Kampot (p267). Dalat (p124) in Vietnam's southwest highlands is another good base for mountain-bike tours.

For those who like a more gentle workout, meandering along Mekong villages is memorable, particularly around Luang Prabang (p314) and Vientiane (p292) in Laos, the Mekong Delta (p146) in Vietnam, and Koh Dach (p201) and Kratie (p240) in Cambodia. Hoi An's Old Town (p105) is closed to motorised traffic during the daytime these days, allowing cyclists to take over. Biking around Angkor (p217) is a great way to get around. And Thailand's northeast can be rewarding thanks to good roads and light traffic.

Bou Sraa Waterfall (p245), Cambodia

Throughout the region, basic bicycles can be rented for US$1 to US$3 per day and good-quality mountain bikes for US$10 to US$25. When it comes to cycling tours, Bangkok-based Spice Roads (www.spiceroads.com) is the acknowledged expert for the Mekong region and Asia beyond, but there are good local operators in each country.

Motorbiking

For those with a thirst for adventure, motorbike trips into remote areas of the region are unforgettable. All four countries offer prime off-road territory for motorcyclists: 'the Loop' in central Laos; the highlands of north Vietnam and northern Thailand; and forgotten temple trails in Cambodia.

And it hardly stops there. The old Ho Chi Minh Trail, a symbol of war's futility to some, is a holy grail of sorts to trail bikers: a network of rugged dirt paths

Vang Vieng (p306), Laos

that criss-cross the border of Laos and Vietnam. Cambodia's mazelike Cardamom Mountains (p253) are legendary – just don't get lost or you may end up spending a cold night in the jungle (a fate met by at least one Lonely Planet writer). Want something a bit easier (ie paved) but still plenty adventurous? The Southern Swing around Laos' Bolaven Plateau (p376) is one of many options.

Specialist motorcycle-touring companies can organise multiday trips into remote areas using the roads less travelled. Costs for these trips start from US$50 per day, going up to US$150 or more for the premium tours, depending on accommodation. Most tours are confined to a single country. Hanoi-based Explore Indochina (www.exploreindochina.com) is one company that does cross-border trips into Laos and sometimes Cambodia.

Based in Vientiane, the Midnight Mapper (www.laosgpsmap.com) is a GPS service that hires out satellite navigation machines with your route especially pre-programmed. Golden Triangle Rider (www.gt-rider.com) is an excellent source for exploring the more remote bits of the Mekong region, including the Golden Triangle area and the Ho Chi Minh Trail.

Motorbikes are widely available for rent (p547) throughout the region; hiring usually requires a licence (p547) in Thailand but you rarely need to show one in Laos, Cambodia and Vietnam.

Boat Trips

With the Mekong cutting a swath through the heart of the country, it is hardly surprising to find that boat trips are a major drawcard here. There are also opportunities to explore small jungled tributaries leading to remote minority villages.

Kayaking & Rafting

Though white-water rafting and kayaking is in its infancy in the Mekong region and the rivers are fairly tame most of the year, things can get a little more vigorous in the wet season. White water can be found in Vietnam on the Langbian River near

Dalat (p124), with class II, III or IV rapids. Companies based in Nha Trang (p117) also offer trips.

In northern Thailand, the rivers around Chiang Mai (p463) have white water from July to March (class II to class V). There is a short season (September to December) for white-water rafting in Nan (p491), with trips passing through scenic forests and remote villages.

Note that rivers are prone to flash-flooding after heavy monsoon rain and can be dangerous at this time. When choosing a white-water operator take a careful look at their safety equipment and procedures.

Mellower river-rafting and kayaking trips are a hit throughout the region. In Thailand you can try a two- to three-day rafting trip out of Pai (p478). In Laos you'll find similar trips offered around Luang Namtha (p342) in the north. In the south, paddling around Si Phan Don (p380) is a must. The Song River in Vang Vieng (p306) is a hotspot for kayaking and tubing, while the extraordinary Tham Kong Lor (p359) cave in Khammuan Province is navigable by kayak.

In Vietnam you can explore the rivers and cave systems around Phong Nha (p85) by kayak, and the Hoi An (p104) region also has delightful rivers for kayaking. In Cambodia, use Stung Treng (p243) as a base to paddle from the dolphin pools on the Lao border downstream through bird-infested flooded forests, where the Mekong River is at its most brilliant. Mellow river paddling trips are also offered in the Cambodian towns of Kratie (p240), Battambang (p227) and Kampot (p267).

Sea kayaking is a popular diversion in coastal areas. In Vietnam, many standard Halong Bay (p72) tours include kayaking through the karsts, or you can choose a kayaking specialist and paddle around majestic limestone pinnacles, before overnighting at a remote bay. Nearby in less touristed Lan Ha Bay (p73) you can kayak to hidden coves and sandy beaches. Sea-kayaking opportunities abound on Cambodia's Koh Rong (p259), Koh Rong Sanloem (p263) and Koh Ta Kiev (p266), and over the border on Ko Chang (p444), Thailand.

Diving & Snorkelling

Compared with destinations like Indonesia and the Philippines, diving and snorkelling opportunities in the Mekong region are limited. Southern Thailand has great diving for those heading south from Bangkok. Vietnam, and to a lesser extent Cambodia, have growing dive industries.

The Con Dao Islands (p157) offer unquestionably the best diving and snorkelling in Vietnam, with bountiful marine life, fine reefs and even a wreck dive, though it's much more costly than the rest of Vietnam. The most popular place to dive in Vietnam is Nha Trang (p117), which has plenty of reputable dive operators – as well as several dodgy dive shops, some of which have fake PADI credentials, so stick to reputable, recommended dive schools with qualified instructors and well-maintained equipment. Phu Quoc Island (p153) has some beautiful coral gardens full of marine life, although visibility can be a challenge. Dive trips out of Hoi An head to the lovely Cham Islands (p114), where the focus is on macro life.

In Cambodia, the best diving is in the Southern Islands, particularly around Koh Rong Sanloem (p263) and the Koh Sdach Archipelago (p266). Long day trips head further offshore to remote Koh Tang and Koh Prins. Just over the border in Thailand, uninhabited Ko Rang (p444) has the best diving in the vicinity of Ko Chang.

Costs

Typical costs are as follows:

Discover Scuba US$70–90

Two fun dives US$85–95 (US$160 in Con Dao Islands)

PADI Open Water US$400–500

Snorkelling day trip US$20–40

Kitesurfing & Windsurfing

In Vietnam, Mui Ne (p121) is the undisputed top spot for Asian wind chasers. You can kitesurf in Mui Ne year-round (rare for Southeast Asia), although it's best in the dry season (November to April); Nha Trang (p117) and Vung Tau (just outside HCMC) are other possibilities.

If you've never kitesurfed before, go for a taster lesson (one/two hours US$60/100) before you enrol in a lengthy course – a three-day (nine-hour) course costs around US$500.

Above: Tree house, Gibbon Experience (p350), Laos

Right: Ziplining, Chiang Mai (p463), Thailand

AOUNPHOTO/SHUTTERSTOCK ©

Surfing

Unfortunately, that wave scene in *Apocalypse Now* was shot in the Philippines. The Mekong region is hardly known for surfing, but if you need your fix you can find some swell at certain times of the year – finding a board can be decidedly more problematic, however.

With a 3000km coastline, Vietnam is the obvious top candidate. Your best bet is Danang (p101), where there's a small scene and some surf shops with boards for hire. Board hire costs US$5 to US$20 per day, while a two-hour surfing lesson will set you back about US$25. Mui Ne (p121) and Vung Tau also have occasional waves and board rental available. The peak season is December to March, when the waves are small but steady. July to November is fickle, but occasional typhoons passing offshore can produce clean peaks over 2m (though watch out for pollution after heavy rains).

Rock Climbing & Canyoning

When it comes to organised climbing, Chiang Mai (p463) in Thailand has the most on offer, but the region is liberally peppered with karsts and climbing options are plentiful. Don't compromise on safety; only book canyoning trips through reputable, well-established companies.

In Vietnam, the acknowledged specialists are Langur's Adventures (p74), a highly professional outfit based on Cat Ba (p73) that offers rope climbing on karst hills, deep-water soloing and climbing/kayaking combo excursions. In Dalat (p124) there are a couple of good adventure-tour operators offering climbing and canyoning, which mixes rappelling, scrambling, hiking and swimming. Over the border in southern Cambodia, Climbodia (p270) runs courses and guided climbs in karst-laden hills around Kampot (p267).

In Laos, Vang Vieng (p306) has some of the best climbing in Southeast Asia, with 200 routes – many of them bolted – up the limestone cliffs (most are rated between 4a and 8b). Adam's Rock Climbing School (p309) has excellent instructors and safe equipment. Tha Khaek (p355) is home to the Green Climbers Home (p357), a climbing school in range of some 250 routes from beginner to expert level.

Climbing costs start from about US$25 to US$30 and rise for more specialised climbs in the Halong Bay area or for instruction.

WHEN TO GO

For most activities, the dry season (November to May in most of the region) is the best time to visit. Trekking during the wet season can be particularly difficult, and leeches are all but guaranteed. On the other hand, swollen rivers make for great kayaking and scenic boat trips during this time. Cycling is doable year-round, but can be challenging in September and early October when the rains really pick up.

Wildlife-Watching

While wildlife-spotting may not be quite as straightforward as in the Serengeti, it is still possible to have some world-class encounters in the Mekong region.

Gibbons are the big draw. You'll need to arrive at a gibbon colony super early – before dawn in most cases – to have a chance of seeing them, so sleep on-site the night before if it's an option. Good spots for seeing gibbons include Cat Tien National Park (p129) in Vietnam, with its Wild Gibbon Trek; and Cambodian Gibbon Ecotours (p248) and the Jahoo Gibbon Camp (p246), both in eastern Cambodia. Also in Cambodia, the Cardamom Tented Camp (p254) makes a wonderful base for spotting gibbons and scores of other wildlife. Back in Vietnam, Cat Ba Island (p73) is home to one of the world's most endangered primates, the Cat Ba langur, as well as rare waterfowl.

At Thailand's remote Khao Yai National Park (p451), the massive jungle is home to one of the world's largest monsoon forests. Wildlife here includes more than 200 elephants and countless birds. Laos has plenty of wildlife, including the region's largest population of wild elephants, but spotting them is difficult to impossible.

Bar-bellied pitta bird, Cat Tien National Park (p129), Vietnam

Birdwatching is also popular throughout the region. Cambodia is the best place in the world to spot six critically endangered species: the giant ibis, white-shouldered ibis, Bengal florican and three species of vulture. The Prek Toal Bird Sanctuary (p216) is a premier wetland birdwatching spot. The award-winning Sam Veasna Center (p207) runs trips to all the best sites. Off land, the freshwater Irrawaddy dolphin is one of the rarest mammals on earth, with fewer than 100 inhabiting stretches of the Mekong. Kayak with a small pod on the Laos–Cambodia border, or further south near Kratie (p240) in eastern Cambodia.

Lastly, interacting in a natural environment with retired domesticated elephants (p541) is possible here, with a few dozen sanctuaries set up for this purpose across the region.

Ziplining

Ziplining has, well, taken off in the Mekong region. Laos was the pioneer and is still the undisputed king. The Gibbon Experience (p350) in Laos pioneered the use of ziplines to explore the jungle canopy. Visitors hang from a zipline and glide through the forest where the gibbons roam, then overnight in tree houses.

In nearby Udomxai, **Nam Kat Yorla Pa Adventure Park** (☎020-55564359, 081-219666; www.namkatyorlapa.com; Faen village, Xay District) offers similarly thrilling ziplines and tree-house lodging, as does Green Discovery (p367) down south in Pakse. Adventure hotbed Vang Vieng (p306) has several options, including the pulsating Vang Vieng Challenge (p309). Green Jungle Park (p329) near Luang Prabang features monkey bridges and rope courses in addition to ziplines.

Flight of the Gibbon (p468) is a thrilling treetop zipline course in Chiang Mai, while Angkor Zipline (p225) offers similar aerial thrills in the jungle near Angkor Wat. Both programs have a forest-conservation component and are run in tandem with programs to reintroduce gibbons to the surrounding forest.

Plan Your Trip

Family Travel

Children can live it up in the Mekong region, as they are always the centre of attention and almost everybody wants to play with them. This goes double for exotic-looking foreign children from faraway lands, who become instant celebrities wherever they go.

Keeping Costs Down

Accommodation

Many hotels and guesthouses offer family rooms that can sleep four comfortably, sparing you the expense of paying for another room. Some hotels will provide baby cots (cribs) on request, although not always for free.

Activities/Sightseeing

Some attractions and museums offer half-price tickets for children under 12. Kids under three usually enter for free. Consider boat trips as a way to double down on transport and fun.

Eating

Children are always welcomed in restaurants (and even bars). But few offer a children's menu outside the cosmopolitan main cities. Although kids might find the region's generally spicy food challenging, there's an entire repertoire of inexpensive, non-spicy menu items (sticky rice, anyone?).

Transport

In general, public land transport is so cheap that you won't even feel the need to ask about child discounts. Discounted tickets for kids on Thai trains and on Bangkok's Skytrain and subway systems network are useful, as are 50% discounts for kids under 10 on some Vietnamese trains.

Children Will Love...

Adventures

Tham Kong Lor, Laos (p359) A family-friendly boat trip to the centre of the earth through this 7km river cave system.

Hang Toi, Vietnam (p86) Cave in Phong Nha-Ke Bang National Park combines into-the-water and above-water zipline thrills with spelunking.

Angkor Zipline, Cambodia (p225) Ziplining through the treetops around Angkor Wat, with an abseil to finish the course.

Flight of the Gibbon, Thailand (p468) The original Thai zipline experience, in a splendid patch of preserved rainforest east of Chang Mai.

Nong Khiaw Jungle Fly, Laos (p339) Kids will love the 'Tarzan swings' and gliding over the bamboo forests around Nong Khiaw.

Local Fruits

Durian This might not be the most popular fruit for visiting children thanks to the noxious smell, but they won't forget it soon.

Mango Mangoes are available year-round across the region, but are simply out of this world during the heatwave of April and May.

Mangosteen Queen Victoria supposedly offered 100 pounds to anyone who could deliver her a ripe mangosteen, so it is now known as the queen of fruit.

Rambutan Its sea-urchin-like appearance makes it a hard sell for some children, but it is a great travel snack and available year-round.

Jackfruit Weighing up to 20kg, the world's largest fruit will fascinate kids whether or not they enjoy the sweet, gum-like pulp.

Animal Encounters

Phnom Tamao Wildlife Rescue Centre, Cambodia (p201) Learn how to be a 'bear keeper' or 'elephant keeper' for a day at this world-class centre outside Phnom Penh.

Thai Elephant Care Center (p468) Elderly elephants retired from logging camps and elephant shows receive care at this centre northwest of Chiang Mai.

Endangered Primate Rescue Center, Vietnam (p71) Teaming up with the adjoining Turtle Conservation Center to give kids an educational animal experience.

Laos Buffalo Dairy (p328) Kids can learn to milk a buffalo, help feed and wash buffaloes and meet the resident rabbits at this working farm in Luang Prabang.

ChangChill, Thailand (p469) A highly authentic, educational and ethical elephant experience that promotes the safety and happiness of both the elephants and their handlers.

Beaches

Koh Rong Sanloem, Cambodia (p263) White sand and shallow waters characterise Saracen Bay on the east coast, while family haven Lazy Beach awaits on the west coast.

Ko Chang, Thailand (p444) Easy ocean entry points for swimmers and you might even spot elephants being bathed on certain beaches.

Phu Quoc, Vietnam (p153) The white sands of gorgeous Sao Beach and graceful Long Beach are dreamscapes for tots.

Koh Tonsay, Cambodia (p273) A short boat ride from Kep, 'Rabbit Island' offers a real beach and delicious fresh seafood, including the legendary Kep crab.

Con Dao Islands, Vietnam (p157) It's cheaper than ever to bring the family to these dreamy isles marooned in the South China Sea.

Region by Region

Vietnam

Children will have a good time in Vietnam, thanks to its wealth of beaches and child-friendly cities. Hoi An (p104) combines culture with cavorting on the sand, Nha Trang (p117) has fun boat trips, and older kids can windsurf or sandboard in Mui Ne (p121). Watch out for rip tides along the main coastline. Some popular beaches have warning flags and lifeguards.

Halong Bay (p72) will stun children of any age, as the scenery is simply out of this world. Big cities usually have plenty to keep kids interested, though traffic safety and pollution are serious concerns.

Breastfeeding in public is perfectly acceptable in Vietnam.

Cambodia

Siem Reap (p203) is ground zero for travelling families. The Temples of Angkor (p217) are the headline act, but there is a whole range of activities beyond the temples, including mountain biking, ziplining, escape rooms, crazy golf, cooking and pottery, plus plenty of child-friendly dining spots.

Phnom Penh (p180) offers some good accommodation with swimming pools, plus home comforts like cinemas, bowling and shopping malls. Out of town, the gentle back roads of Koh Dach (Silk Island; p201) make for a great family excursion.

Laos

Kids love Pi Mai (Lao New Year), when the entire country turns into a benign battleground for water fights.

Most families swarm to Luang Prabang (p314), which has a wealth of kid-friendly experiences, including ziplines and swimming holes such as Tat Kuang Si (p328), which also offers a fascinating glimpse of Asiatic Wild Moon bears. Boat trips on the Mekong, such as to the Pak Ou Caves (p327), are a nice diversion for budding explorers.

Vientiane (p292) offers child-friendly restaurants and some good accommodation with swimming pools, while a bit north the Vang Vieng (p306) area has river fun and several natural pools among the karsts. Around the country there are ziplines galore. The many islands of Si Phan Don (p380) are great for relaxing riverside fun.

Northern Thailand

When it comes to travelling with kids, Thailand has it all. It starts with Bangkok (p406), which has parks, markets and many air-conditioned shopping malls with cinemas and restaurants. Outside Bangkok, Khao Yai National Park (p451) has elephants and gibbons.

The overnight train journey from Bangkok to Chiang Mai is a hit with children, and Chiang Mai is also home to child-friendly treks. Both towns are especially fun places to spend Songkran (Thai New Year), when jovial water fights erupt.

Ko Chang (p444) has shallow and gentle seas that are ideal for kids, plus a zipline and jungle fun.

Good to Know

Transport Safety is very much an afterthought in most of the Mekong region. Bring your own car seat if you think you might need one, or request one in advance via a tour operator. Laos has a poor record on domestic flight safety, but Vietnam, Cambodia and Thailand fare better. Flying is always safer than driving.

Walking In the cities, footpaths can be crowded with vendors, making it tricky to navigate a larger pushchair or pram, so something more compact or a back carrier is smarter.

Nappies Bring a supply of nappies if your child wears size 3 or larger.

Changing facilities In public restrooms are rare, limited to a few tourist-friendly establishments in the big cities.

Health Regular handwashing is important to head off potential medical problems. Children should not play with animals, as rabies is common.

Sleeping Cots are not that common outside of the smarter hotels in the main centres, so prepare to share double or twin beds or plan ahead for rooms with connecting doors or adjacent rooms.

Cycling Increasing numbers of cycle shops in tourist centres rent bikes and helmets for kids, and you may even be able to find child seats.

Useful Resources

Lonely Planet Kids (www.lonelyplanetkids.com) Activities and great family-travel blog content.

Childsafe (www.thinkchildsafe.org) Global movement to protect children that certifies hotels and restaurants as child-safe.

Wild Junket (https://www.wildjunket.com) A mum making her way to every country in the world – including the Mekong countries.

World Travel Family (https://worldtravelfamily.com) With specific advice for Southeast Asia.

Family Fun Thailand (http://familyfun.tourismthailand.org) Discount deals for families on hotels, activities and restaurants in Thailand.

Kids' Corner

Say What?

Hello.	*xin chào* (Vietnam) *sour sdey* (Cambodia) *sábai-děe* (Laos) *sà·wàt·dee* (Thailand)
Goodbye.	*tạm biệt* (Vietnam) *lia suhn hao-y* (Cambodia) *sábai-děe* (Laos) *lah gòrn* (Thailand)
Thank you.	*cảm ơn* (Vietnam) *aw kohn* (Cambodia) *kòrp jai* (Laos) *kòrp kun* (Thailand)

Did You Know?

- Giant Mekong catfish can grow to 600 pounds and 3m.
- Vietnam has around 60 million motorbikes.

Have You Tried?

NICEMYPHOTO/SHUTTERSTOCK ©

Deep-fried crickets
Crunchy!

Countries at a Glance

Many a Mekong adventure begins or ends in Bangkok. It works as a convenient launch pad into hilly northern Thailand, Thailand's eastern seaboard, or Laos and Cambodia to the east.

Laos is the remote backwater of Indochina, but diverse minorities and national parks have made it the ecotourism darling of the region. Cambodia is best known for the Angkorian temples around Siem Reap, but also features outstanding beaches on the south coast, fine food in Phnom Penh and wildlife-watching opportunities in the mountainous east. A range of excellent community-based ecotourism initiatives bring much-needed income to more remote areas.

Vietnam is catching up with Thailand fast. Spiralling cities, designer dining and ultra-luxury beach resorts point to the future, while war relics and traditional minority lifestyles are reminders of the past.

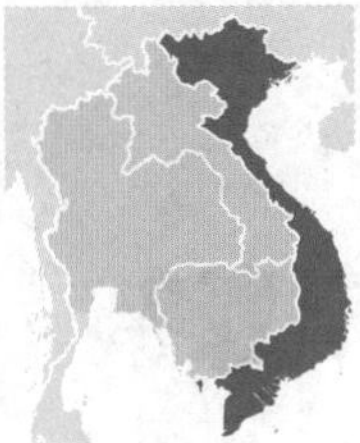

Vietnam

Beaches
Food
History

Coastal Retreats

Vietnam has a voluptuous coastline. Hoi An, Mui Ne and Nha Trang are the big hitters, but there are hundreds of kilometres of empty beaches to discover, including islands such as Phu Quoc and Con Dao.

Culinary Delights

You don't have to be a gastronome to experience the culinary delights of Vietnam. Surf the streets for sumptuous local snacks, discover the bounty of the sea along the lengthy coastline or learn the secrets of the kitchen with a cooking class.

Old Cities

Explore the bustling Old Quarter of 1000-year-old Hanoi, discover the tombs and royal relics of imperial Hue, and browse the backstreet galleries, cafes and bars of delightful Hoi An – in Vietnam you are literally spoilt for choice when it comes to cities with a story to tell.

p49

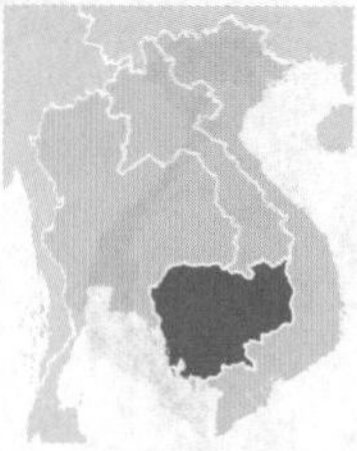

Cambodia

Architecture
Giving Back
Nature

Ancient Temples

Heard enough about Angkor Wat? Well, don't forget the pre-Angkorian capital of Sambor Prei Kuk, the region's first temple city, or the jungle temples of Preah Vihear Province.

Good Causes

There are many ways to give something back to the communities you visit in Cambodia. Dine at sumptuous training restaurants that lend a helping hand to ex-street kids, buy designer dresses stitched by disabled seamstresses or try a community homestay deep in the countryside.

Ecotourism

While it's best known for temples, Cambodia offers a rich array of pursuits for nature addicts, including jungle trekking, rare-primate-spotting and world-class birdwatching. Near Siem Reap you can zipline through the jungle or boat into remarkable Prek Toal Bird Sanctuary, while further south the wildlife-rich Cardamom Mountains await.

p177

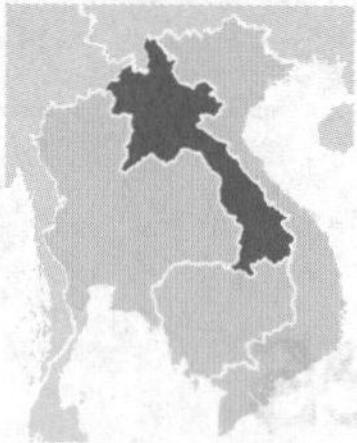

Laos

Nature
Hill Tribes
Activities

Protected Forests

With around 20 National Protected Areas, Laos has more dense forest per square kilometre than anywhere else in Southeast Asia and is begging to be explored. Award-winning ecotreks take you deep into the jungle realm of the clouded leopard, wild elephant and Asiatic black bear.

Minority Cultures

More than 65 tribes compose Laos' colourful ethnic quilt. In the rugged north, rural homestay programs allow you to encounter animism and observe cultures that have changed little in the last century.

Ziplines

Glide like gibbons on one of a number of tree-canopy ziplines that take you up close to nature and offer jaw-dropping jungle views. By night, sleep in a treehouse and listen for the predawn call of gibbons.

p289

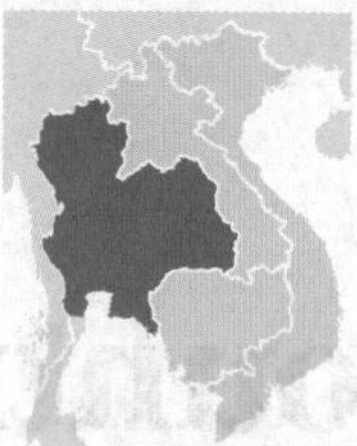

Northern Thailand

Food
Shopping
Communities

Taste Sensations

Start getting your taste buds in shape – everything you've heard about Thai food is true. From spicy stir-fries to sadistic salads, chillies form their own food group for Thais.

Retail Therapy

Believe us, you've never encountered commerce the way they do it in Thailand. From the megamalls of Bangkok to Chiang Mai's more sedate Saturday and Sunday Walking Streets, you'll inevitably leave Thailand with a souvenir or five.

Local Experiences

Provincial Thailand invites you to see the countryside from the saddle of a motorcycle, live in a homestay in rice-growing country or trek to a remote hill-tribe village; prerequisites include a Thai phrasebook and a willingness to live like a local. You'll leave with unforgettable memories.

p403

On the Road

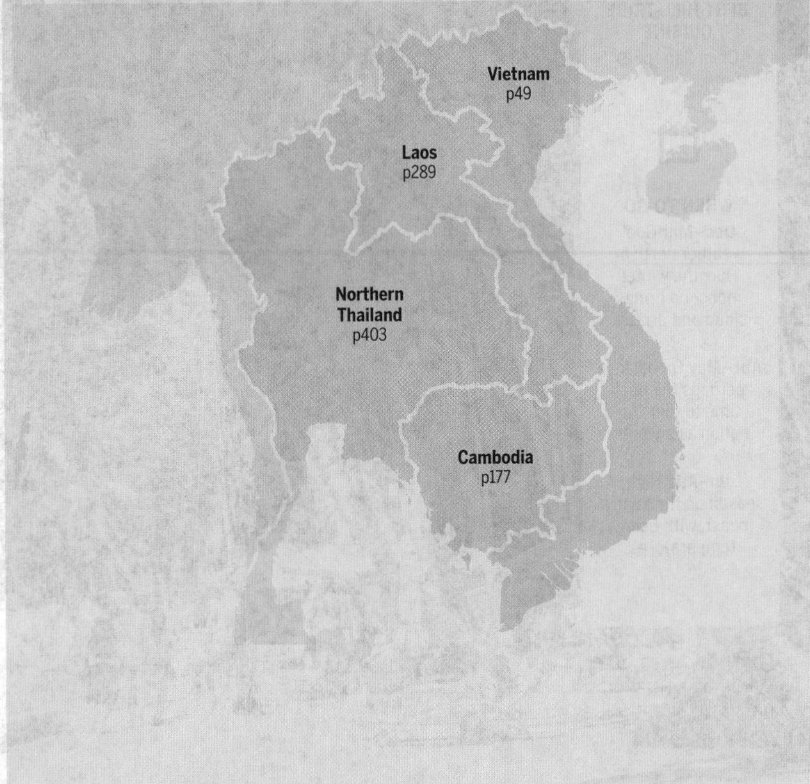

Vietnam
p49
Laos
p289
Northern
Thailand
p403
Cambodia
p177

AT A GLANCE

POPULATION
98.7 million

CAPITAL CITY
Hanoi

BEST HOT-STONE MASSAGE
Aveda (p135)

BEST COCONUT COFFEE
The Sound of Silence (p114)

BEST HILL-TRIBE CUISINE
Chim Sao (p62)

WHEN TO GO

Dec–Mar Cool weather north of Hue; the winter monsoon brings cloud and drizzle.

Apr–May On balance perhaps the best time to tour the nation as a whole.

Jul–Aug High season on the central coast, with balmy temperatures.

Sao Beach, Phu Quoc Island (p153)

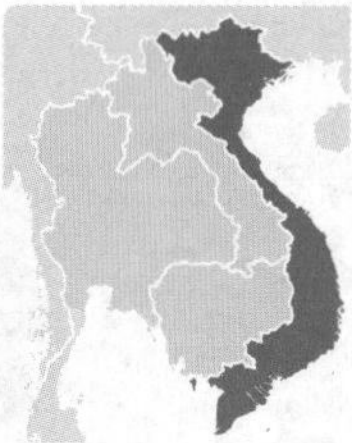

Vietnam

Astonishingly exotic and utterly compelling, Vietnam is a kaleidoscope of vivid colours and subtle shades, grand architecture and deeply moving war sites. Nature has blessed Vietnam with soaring mountains in the north, emerald-green rice paddies in the Mekong Delta and a sensational, curvaceous coastline with ravishing sandy beaches. Travelling here you'll witness children riding buffalo, see the impossibly intricate textiles of hill-tribe communities, hear the buzz of a million motorbikes and eat some of the world's greatest food. This is a dynamic nation on the move, where life is lived at pace. Prepare yourself for the ride of your life.

INCLUDES

Vietnam Highlights

1 Hoi An (p104) Taking a trip back in time in a maze of cobbled lanes.

2 Phong Nha-Ke Bang National Park (p85) Discovering limestone highlands riddled with extraordinary cave systems.

3 Hue (p88) Following in the footsteps of emperors in this majestic city.

4 Ho Chi Minh City (p130) Delighting in Saigon's visceral energy and vibrant nightlife.

5 Halong Bay (p72) Cruising the bay and being spellbound by the natural wonder.

6 Northwest highlands (p81) Exploring the dramatic landscape, dotted with tribal villages.

7 Hanoi (p52) Getting seduced by a blend of Parisian-style grace and Asian pace.

8 Con Dao Islands (p157) Visiting idyllic, remote beaches and dive sites.

9 Mui Ne (p121) Lying back on the pristine beach or kitesurfing sick waves.

10 Phu Quoc Island (p153) Searching for that perfect tropical shore.

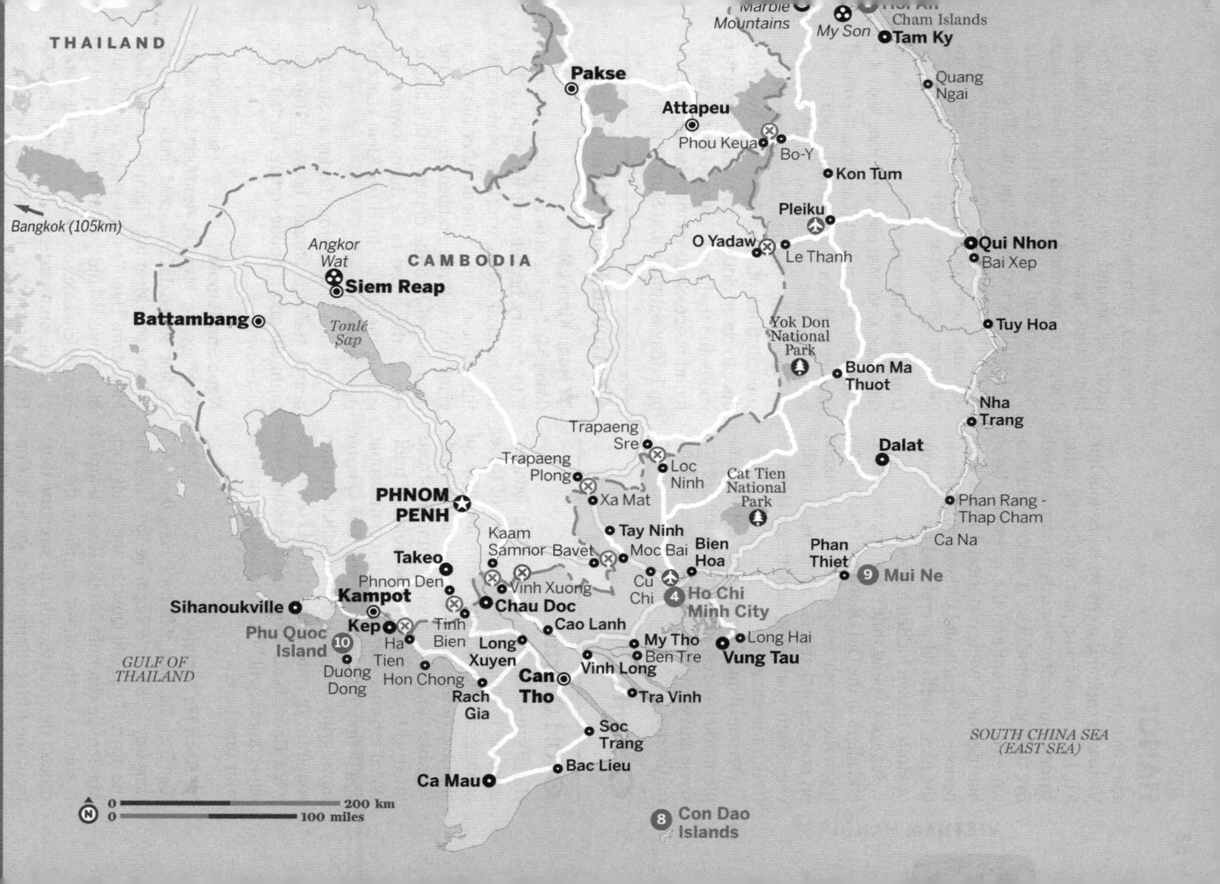

HANOI

POP 8 MILLION / ☎024

Vietnam's capital is a city with one foot buried in a fascinating past, while the other strides confidently towards tomorrow. With five million motorbikes, it surges with two-wheeled mayhem and the incessant din of blaring horns, while historical nuggets from periods of French and Chinese rule glint in the haze, overlooking crowded intersections or stuffed down hidden alleyways.

It pays to spend time exploring the streets and alleys of the Old Quarter, where farmers hawk their produce while city folk breakfast on noodles, practise t'ai chi at dawn or play chess with goateed grandfathers: Hanoi at its most fascinating.

Devour divine food at every corner, sample market wares, uncover an evolving arts scene and witness the awakening of a Hanoi on the move.

Sights

Old Quarter

Hanoi's historic heart, 'The Old Quarter', is home to more than 1000 years of trade, commerce and activity, with no signs of slowing down. Although its name tends to evoke images of ancient lamp-lit streets lined with the wooden storefronts of traditional artisans, merchants and craftspeople, you'll find the reality of the Old Quarter more gritty (congested and polluted) than romantic. In spite of this, the Old Quarter is what Hanoi is all about and adjusting your expectations will help you make the most of your time here.

★Bach Ma Temple TEMPLE

(Den Bach Ma; Map p58; cnr P Hang Buom & P Hang Giay; 8-11am & 2-5pm Tue-Sun) FREE In the heart of the Old Quarter, the small Bach Ma Temple (literally 'White Horse Temple') is said to be the oldest temple in the city, though much of the current structure dates from the 18th century and a shrine to Confucius was added in 1839. It was originally built by Emperor Ly Thai To in the 11th century to honour a white horse that guided him to this site, where he chose to construct his city walls.

★Heritage House HISTORIC BUILDING

(Ngoi Nha Di San; Map p58; 87 P Ma May; 10,000d; 9am-noon & 1-6pm) One of the Old Quarter's best-restored properties, this traditional merchants' house is sparsely but beautifully decorated, with rooms filled with fine furniture set around two courtyards. Note the high steps between rooms, a traditional design incorporated to stop the flow of bad energy around the property. There are crafts and trinkets for sale here, including silver jewellery, basketwork and Vietnamese tea sets, and there's usually a calligrapher or another craftsperson at work too.

Dong Xuan Market MARKET

(Cho Dong Xuan; Map p58; cnr P Hang Khoai & P Dong Xuan; 6am-7pm) The largest covered market in Hanoi was originally built by the French in 1889 and almost completely destroyed by fire in 1994. Almost everything you can think of, from fresh (and live) produce to cheap clothing, souvenirs, consumer goods and traditional arts and crafts, can be found inside. Stalls continue selling outside on Friday, Saturday and Sunday nights.

Around Hoam Kiem Lake

★Hoan Kiem Lake LAKE

(Map p54) Legend claims that, in the mid-15th century, heaven sent Emperor Ly Thai To a magical sword, which he used to drive the Chinese from Vietnam. After the war a giant golden turtle grabbed the sword and disappeared into the depths of this lake to restore the sword to its divine owners, inspiring the name Ho Hoan Kiem (Lake of the Restored Sword).

The area is best from Friday to Sunday: nearby traffic is banned between 7pm and midnight and a public-square, funfair vibe takes over.

Ngoc Son Temple BUDDHIST TEMPLE

(Den Ngoc Son; Map p54; Hoan Kiem Lake; adult/student 30,000/15,000d, child under 15yr free; 8am-6pm) Meaning 'Temple of the Jade Mountain', Hanoi's most visited temple sits on a small island in the northern part of Hoan Kiem Lake, connected to the lakeshore by an elegant scarlet bridge (called Cau The Huc), constructed in classical Vietnamese style. The temple is dedicated to General Tran Hung Dao (who defeated the Mongols in the 13th century), La To (patron saint of physicians) and the scholar Van Xuong.

★Hoa Lo Prison Museum HISTORIC BUILDING

(Map p54; ☎024-3934 2253; cnr P Hoa Lo & P Hai Ba Trung; adult/child 30,000d/free; 8am-5pm) This thought-provoking site is all that remains of the former Hoa Lo Prison,

Hanoi

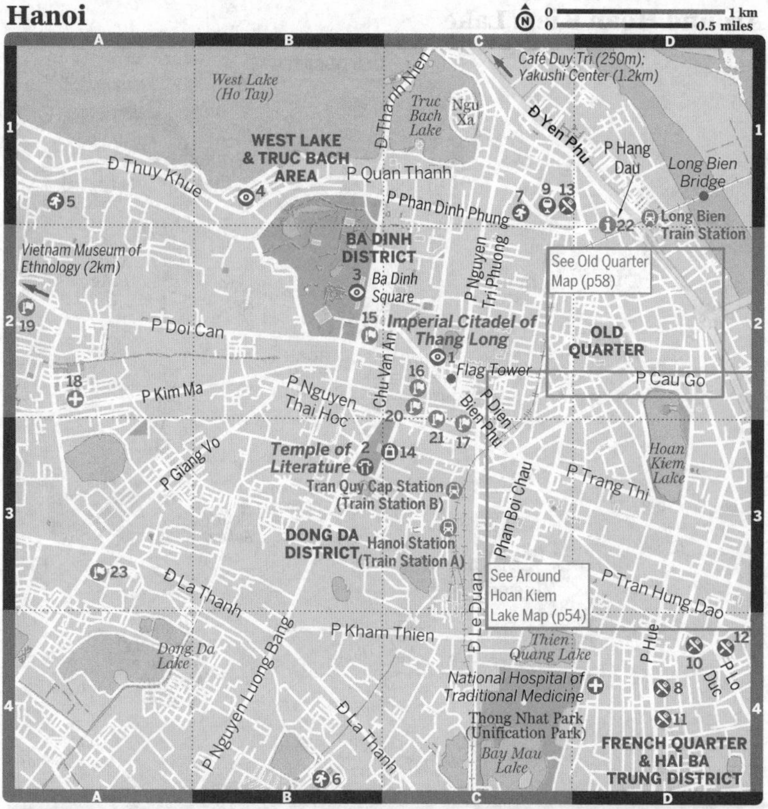

Hanoi

Top Sights
1 Imperial Citadel of Thang Long C2
2 Temple of Literature B3

Sights
3 Ho Chi Minh's Mausoleum B2
4 West Lake B1

Activities, Courses & Tours
5 Dao's Care A1
6 NGO Resource Centre B4
7 Omamori Spa C1

Eating
8 Banh Mi Pho Hue D4
9 Bun Cha 34 .... C1
10 Bun Cha Huong Lien D4
11 Chim Sao D4
12 Pho Thin D4

Drinking & Nightlife
13 Manzi Art Space C1

Shopping
14 Craft Link C3

Information
15 Canadian Embassy B2
16 Chinese Embassy C2
17 German Embassy C3
18 Hanoi Family Medical Practice A2
19 Japanese Embassy A2
20 Singaporean Embassy C2
21 Thai Embassy C2
22 Tourist Information & Support Center D1
23 US Embassy A3

ironically nicknamed the 'Hanoi Hilton' by US prisoners of war (POWs) during the American War. Most exhibits relate to the prison's use up to the mid-1950s, focusing on the Vietnamese struggle for independence from France. A gruesome relic is the ominous French guillotine, used to behead Vietnamese revolutionaries. There are also

Around Hoan Kiem Lake

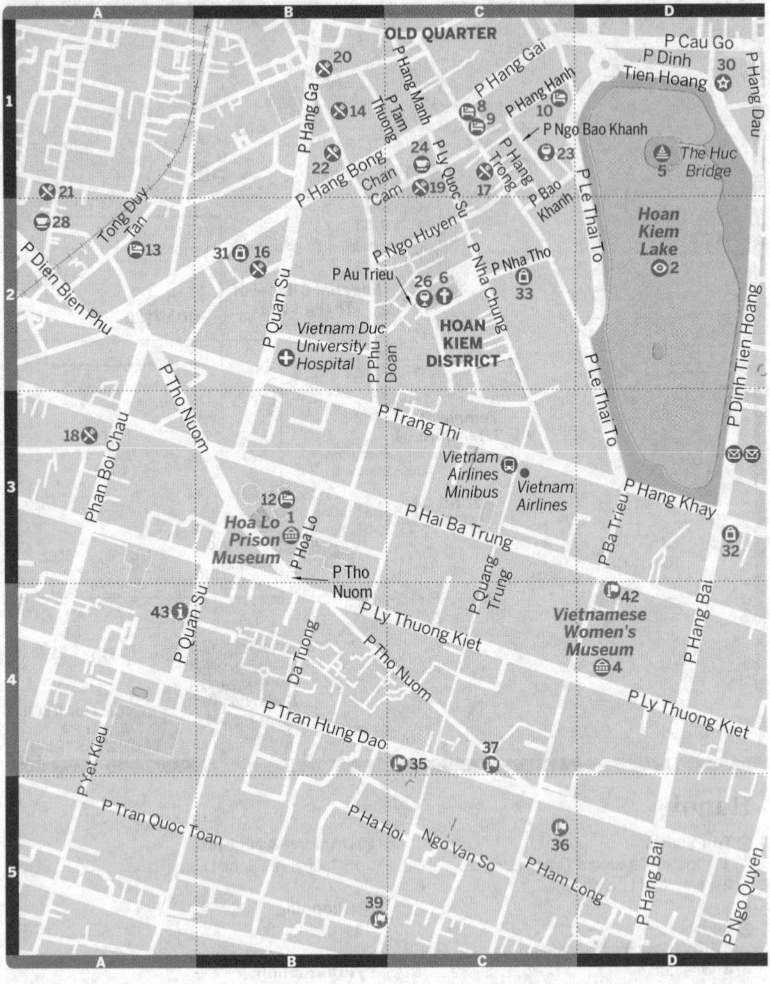

displays focusing on the American pilots who were incarcerated at Hoa Lo during the American War.

★**Vietnamese Women's Museum** MUSEUM

(Bao Tang Phu Nu Viet Nam; Map p54; ☎024-3825 9936; www.baotangphunu.org.vn; 36 P Ly Thuong Kiet; adult/student 30,000/15,000d; ⏰8am-5pm) This excellent and highly informative museum showcases the roles of women in Vietnamese society and culture. Labelled in English and French, exhibits cover everything from marriage customs to child-birth, but it's the memories of the wartime contribution by individual heroic women that are most poignant. If the glut of information sometimes feels repetitive, for visual stimulation there is a stunning collection of propaganda posters, as well as costumes, tribal basketware and fabric motifs from Vietnam's ethnic minority groups. Check the website for special exhibitions.

The audio guide is 30,000d.

★**National Museum of Vietnamese History** MUSEUM

(Bao Tang Lich Su Quoc Gia; Map p54; ☎024-3825 2853; www.baotanglichsu.vn; 1 P Trang Tien; adult/student 40,000/10,000d, camera 15,000d; ⏰8am-noon & 1.30-5pm, closed 1st Mon of month) Built

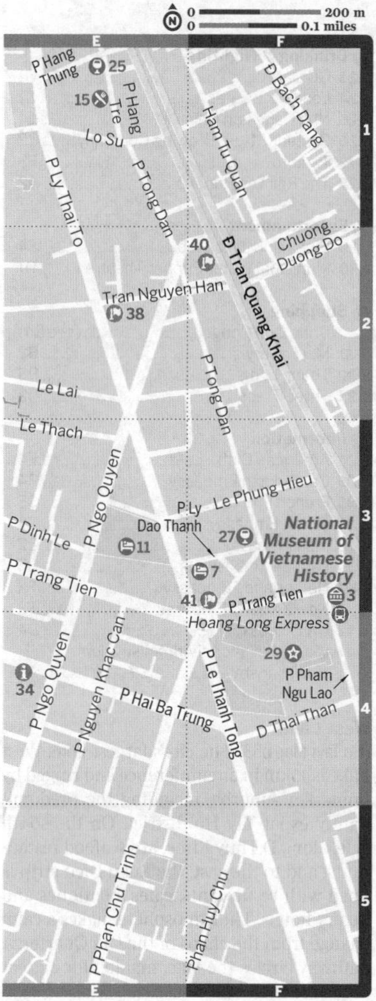

between 1925 and 1932, this architecturally impressive museum was formerly home to the École Française d'Extrême-Orient. Its architect, Ernest Hebrard, was among the first in Vietnam to incorporate a blend of Chinese and French design elements. Exhibit highlights include bronzes from the Dong Son culture (3rd century BCE to 3rd century CE), Hindu statuary from the Khmer and Champa kingdoms, jewellery from imperial Vietnam, and displays relating to the French occupation and the Communist Party. The audio guide is free.

St Joseph Cathedral CHURCH

(Nha To Lon Ha Noi; Map p54; P Nha Tho; ⏲8am-noon & 2-6pm) **FREE** Hanoi's neo-Gothic St Joseph Cathedral was inaugurated in 1886, and has a soaring facade that faces a little plaza that's usually stuffed with selfie sticks and posses of preening photographers. The church's most noteworthy features are the looming twin bell towers, elaborate altar and fine stained-glass windows. Entrance via the main gate is only permitted during Mass: times are listed on a sign on the gates to the left of the cathedral.

Other Areas

★Temple of Literature CONFUCIAN TEMPLE

(Van Mieu; Map p53; ☎024-3845 2917; P Quoc Tu Giam; adult/student 30,000/15,000d; ⏲8am-6pm) A rare example of well-preserved traditional Vietnamese architecture, the Temple of Literature honours Vietnam's finest scholars. Founded in 1070 by Emperor Le Thanh Tong, the attractive complex is dedicated to the Qufu-born philosopher Confucius (Khong Tu) and was the site of Vietnam's first university, Quoc Tu Giam (1076). The altars are popular with students praying for good grades, while the halls, ponds and gardens of the five courtyards make picturesque backdrops for student graduation photos. It is depicted on the 100,000d note.

★Vietnam Museum of Ethnology MUSEUM

(☎024-3756 2193; www.vme.org.vn; Đ Nguyen Van Huyen; adult/concession 40,000/15,000d, guide 100,000d; ⏲8.30am-5.30pm Tue-Sun) This fabulous collection relating to Vietnam's ethnic minorities features well-presented tribal art, artefacts and everyday objects gathered from across the nation, and examples of traditional village houses. Displays are well labelled in Vietnamese, French and English. If you're into anthropology, it's well worth the Grab motorbike-taxi fare (approximately 40,000d each way) to the Cau Giay district, about 7km from the city centre, where the museum is located.

★Imperial Citadel of Thang Long HISTORIC SITE

(Hoang Thanh Thang Long; Map p53; www.hoangthanhthanglong.vn; 19c P Hoang Dieu; adult/child 30,000d/free; ⏲8am-5pm Tue-Sun) Added to Unesco's World Heritage List in 2010, Hanoi's Imperial Citadel was the hub of Vietnamese military power for over 1000 years. Ongoing archaeological digs continue

Around Hoan Kiem Lake

Top Sights
1 Hoa Lo Prison Museum B3
2 Hoan Kiem Lake D2
3 National Museum of Vietnamese History F3
4 Vietnamese Women's Museum D4

Sights
5 Ngoc Son Temple D1
6 St Joseph Cathedral C2

Sleeping
7 Conifer Boutique Hotel F3
8 Golden Lotus Hotel C1
9 Golden Lotus Luxury Hotel C1
10 Madame Moon Hotel C1
11 Sofitel Legend Metropole Hotel E3
12 Somerset Grand Hanoi B3
13 Tomodachi House A2

Eating
14 Bun Cha Nem Cua Be Dac Kim B1
15 Bun Rieu Cua E1
16 Hanoi Social Club B2
17 Jalus Vegan Kitchen C1
18 La Badiane A3
19 Madame Hien C1
20 Mien Xao Luon B1
21 Old Hanoi A1
22 V's Home B1

Drinking & Nightlife
23 GC Bar C1
24 Loading T Cafe C1
25 Nha Hang Lan Chin E1
26 Pasteur Street Brewing Company C2
27 Tadioto F3
28 The Railway Hanoi 2 .... A2

Entertainment
29 Binh Minh Jazz Club F4
30 Municipal Water Puppet Theatre D1

Shopping
Chan Con Cong .... (see 24)
31 Mai Gallery B2
32 Thang Long D3
33 Three Trees C2

Information
34 American Club E4
35 Cambodian Embassy C4
36 French Embassy C5
37 Indian Embassy C4
38 Irish Embassy E2
39 Laotian Embassy B5
40 Netherlands Embassy F2
41 New Zealand Embassy F3
42 UK Embassy D4
43 Vietnam National Administration of Tourism A4

on-site, revealing remains of ancient palaces, grandiose pavilions and imperial gates. The **main gate** (Doan Mon) is named after one of the gates of the Forbidden City in Beijing. Further back is the imposing and colonnaded French **Caserne de la Compagnie d'Ouvriers**. At the rear is the **Princess Pagoda** (Hau Lau), which probably housed imperial concubines.

Lotte Observation Deck VIEWPOINT

(☎ 024-3333 6016; www.lottecenter.com.vn; 54 P Lieu Giai, Ba Dinh; adult/student day 230,000/170,000d, night 130,000/110,000d; ⏲ 9am-10pm) The city's best views can be found on the 65th-floor 360-degree Observation Deck of the landmark Lotte Center in the western corner of Hanoi's Ba Dinh district. From this uninterrupted vantage point, high above Hanoi's hustle and bustle, you can compare the size of the Old Quarter relative to the sheer scale of Hanoi's voracious growth. Glass-floor sky walks allow you to walk out over the precipitous drop. There's also a rooftop bar on the same floor as an alternative.

West Lake LAKE

(Ho Tay; Map p53) The city's largest lake, West Lake is 15km in circumference and ringed by upmarket suburbs, including the predominantly expat Tay Ho district. On the south side, along Đ Thuy Khue, are seafood restaurants, and to the east, the Xuan Dieu strip is lined with restaurants, cafes, boutiques and luxury hotels. The atmosphere makes a calm change from the chaos of the Old Quarter. A pathway circles the lake, making for a great bicycle ride.

Ho Chi Minh's Mausoleum MAUSOLEUM

(Lang Chu Tich Ho Chi Minh; Map p53; ☎ 024-3845 5128; www.bqllang.gov.vn; Ba Dinh Sq; ⏲ 7.30-10.30am Tue-Thu, 7.30-11am Sat & Sun Apr-Oct, 8-11am Tue-Thu, 8-11.30am Sat & Sun Nov-Mar) FREE In the tradition of Lenin, Stalin and Mao, Ho Chi Minh's Mausoleum is a monumental marble edifice. Contrary to Ho Chi Minh's desire for a simple cremation, the mausoleum was constructed from materials gathered from all over Vietnam between 1973 and 1975. Set deep in the bowels of the building in a glass sarcophagus is the frail, pale body of Ho Chi Minh. The mausoleum is usually closed from 4 September to 4 November while his embalmed body goes to Russia for maintenance.

Activities

★Omamori Spa MASSAGE
(Map p53; ☎024-3773 9919; www.omamorispa.com; 52a P Hang Bun, Ba Đinh; 1hr massage from 300,000d) This wonderful spa is operated by a not-for-profit organisation that provides training and employment opportunities for the blind. Masseuses here are vision impaired and speak excellent English. The trained therapists give massages with a level of gentleness and body awareness that differs from traditional practitioners. Tips are not accepted; pricing and service are excellent. There are three branches in town, including this one.

Dao's Care SPA
(Map p53; ☎024-3722 8316; www.daoscare.com; 351 Đ Hoang Hoa Tham; herbal bath from 150,000d; ⏲9am-9pm) This welcoming and friendly spa is a very therapeutic experience, with well-trained therapists who are either visually impaired or blind. There's a caring family feel here that customers respond well to, with options from herbal baths to Dao, Swedish or foot massage and much more. The spa supports members of the Red Dao ethnic minority in Sapa. A 'no tips' policy is in effect.

Yakushi Center MASSAGE
(☎024-3719 1971; www.yakushicenter.com; 20 P Xuan Dieu, Quang An, Tay Ho; treatments from 250,000d; ⏲8.30am-8pm) In the fashionable expat-centric suburb of Tay Ho you'll find this fabulous clinic that specialises in a range of traditional Vietnamese and Chinese medicine practices, as well as therapeutic and relaxing massages, including Swedish massage. Bookings are essential: your English-speaking practitioner conducts a brief consultation with you prior to commencing your treatment.

Tours

★Hanoi Free Tour Guides WALKING
(☎0988 979 174; www.hanoifreetourguides.com) There's no better way to experience the real Hanoi than with this not-for-profit organisation run by volunteer staff and guides comprising students and ex-students, speaking a multitude of languages. A variety of suggested tours is available, or you can work with your guide to tailor an itinerary. Although the service is free, you pay the small cost of the guide's transport, admission fees and meals. Book online.

★Gay Hanoi Tours WALKING
(☎0947 600 602; www.facebook.com/gayhanoitour; tours from US$65) The inimitable Tuan offers personal and small-group walking (or scooter) tours exploring lesser-known, real-life corners of the ancient city. Popular tours cover food, architecture, design, classic sights and night tours. While tours aren't gay themed, Tuan, a gay Hanoian man, offers a unique perspective on his beloved home town and Vietnamese food, regardless of your sexuality.

Hanoi Street Food Tours WALKING
(☎0904 517 074; www.streetfoodtourshanoi.blogspot.com.au; tours from US$75) There's a local company running tours under the same name, but we continue to recommend this pricier, private option, run by Van Cong Tu and Mark Lowerson, a couple of passionate Hanoi foodies. Whet your appetite with their individual social-media photos. Tours can be customised to different interests.

Festivals & Events

Vietnam's National Day CULTURAL
(⏲2 Sep) Celebrated with a rally and fireworks at Ba Dinh Sq, in front of Ho Chi Minh's Mausoleum. There are also boat races on Hoan Kiem Lake.

Sleeping

Most budget and midrange visitors make for the busy Old Quarter and neighbouring Hoan Kiem Lake area for a glut of options. For luxury stays in calmer surrounds, continue south to the French Quarter or venture further afield.

Old Quarter

★Tomodachi House HOSTEL $
(Map p54; ☎024-3266 9493; 5a Tong Duy Tan; dm/d from US$9/27; ❄@📶) This quiet and clean Japanese-styled flashpacker sits on the snazzier western edge of the Old Quarter, near hip all-night eating and drinking. Large, restful dorm beds have their own USB charging, shelf space, privacy curtain and chunky locker. A great breakfast

Old Quarter

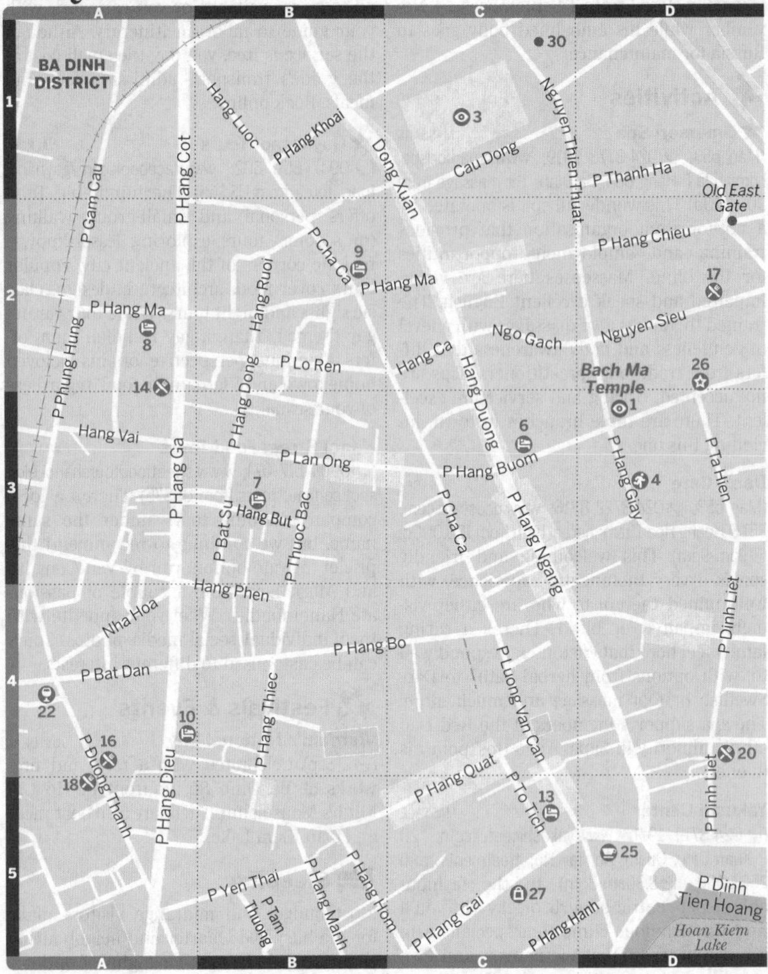

(included) and very friendly, welcoming and helpful staff seal the deal.

Cocoon Inn HOSTEL $

(Map p58; ☎024-3885 3333; www.cocooninn.com; 116-118 P Hang Buom; dm US$8-10, tw US$38-45; ❄@📶) This attractive, resourceful hostel has good dorms, a decent cocktail bar and a lovely rooftop terrace on the 7th floor. Privacy curtains indeed create a cocoon around plush, clean beds that come with personal lamps, fans and power points. An entourage of helpful staff can organise tours, airport transfers and visa extensions. It's on a busy street full of restaurants and bars.

Hanoi Hostel HOSTEL $

(Map p58; ☎0462 700 006; www.vietnam-hostel.com; 91c P Hang Ma; dm/d US$5.50/25, homestay US$30; ❄📶) This small, quiet, privately owned hostel is nicely located away from Hanoi's conglomeration of hostels. It's popular, well run and clean, with tours on tap and plenty of information about onward travel to China or Laos. The homestay option puts you in a family-owned house in the Old Quarter.

★La Beauté de Hanoi HOTEL $$

(Map p58; ☎024-3935 1626; www.la-beautehanoihotel.com; 15 Ngo Trung Yen; d/ste from

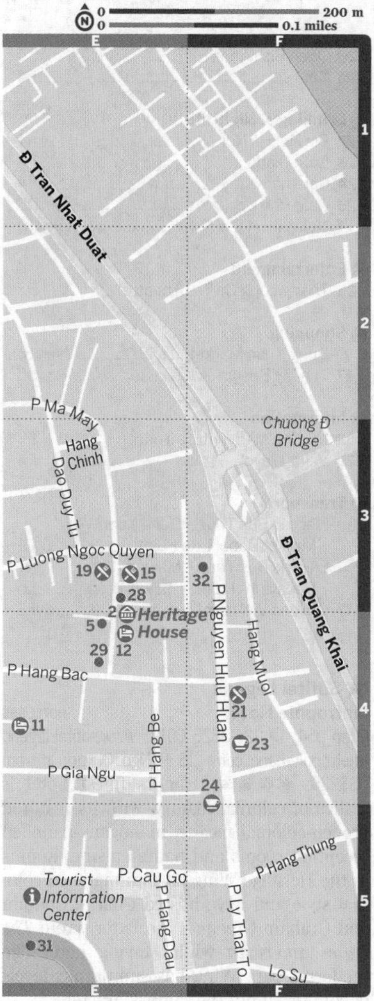

US$60/96; ❄ 📶) Renovated in 2019, this very pleasant and stylish 35-room boutique hotel has a fresh white-and-cream palette with red accents, and small private balconies attached to larger suites and family rooms. It's in an excellent location on a quiet lane just a hop, skip and a jump from all the action on P Ma May.

★Golden Art Hotel HOTEL $$
(Map p58; ☎024-3923 4294; www.goldenarthotel.com; 6a P Hang But; d & tw US$45, s $75; 🚭 ❄ @ 📶) Golden Art enjoys a quiet location on the western edge of the Old Quarter. Well-equipped rooms are stylish and relatively spacious, with a work desk and clean shower; there's a can-do attitude from the friendly staff too. Breakfast (included in the price) features warm baguettes, omelettes, *pho* (noodle soup) and fresh fruit. Nab a room here in the low season for US$30.

Hanoi Little Town Hotel HERITAGE HOTEL $$
(Map p58; ☎024-3828 3525; www.hanoilittletown.com; 77 P Hang Luoc; d & tw US$35, tr US$65, f US$85; ❄ @ 📶) Little Town has kept things old-fashioned. Dark, ornate furniture, some massive rooms, white cotton bedding, high ceilings and spacious bathrooms seem from another era. English-speaking staff also display classic good service, but with youthful enthusiasm, and breakfast is excellent. Front rooms have balconies; quieter rear rooms look to nearby Dong Xuan Market. There's a huge family room on the top floor.

Hanoi Rendezvous Hotel HOTEL $$
(Map p58; ☎024-3828 5777; www.hanoirendezvoushotel.com; 31 P Hang Dieu; d/tw/tr US$37/37/50; ❄ 📶) Deliciously close to several brilliant street-food places, Hanoi Rendezvous is a very solid choice, with huge old rooms, friendly staff and good breakfasts. It organises well-run tours to Halong Bay, Cat Ba Island and Sapa. Good deals are often available.

★La Siesta Classic Ma May Hotel BOUTIQUE HOTEL $$$
(Map p58; ☎024-3926 3641; www.lasiestahotels.vn/mamay; 94 P Ma May; d/tw US$135, tr US$195, ste from US$235; ❄ 📶) La Siesta is a top choice for its excellent service and elegant rooms, which come in a wide variety of sizes (including some snazzy bi-level suites), while its cracking location on P Ma May means that scores of restaurants, bars and things to do are right on your doorstep. If that's all a bit too hectic for you, chill out in the day spa.

Around Hoan Kiem Lake

★Nexy Hostel HOSTEL $
(Map p58; ☎024-7300 6399; www.nexyhostels.com; 12 P To Tich; dm/tw/tr from $7/35/40; ❄ 📶) Flashpackers Nexy has modern, clean dorms and bathrooms, soft beds with privacy curtains, quality linen and ample locked storage, plus staff who speak excellent English and are helpful with travel tips. This boutique hostel is also in a standout location near Hoan Kiem Lake, and has a calm bar, a games room, a small lounge and rooftop zones.

Old Quarter

Top Sights
1 Bach Ma Temple D3
2 Heritage House E4

Sights
3 Dong Xuan Market C1

Activities, Courses & Tours
4 Ethnic Travel D3
5 Handspan Adventure Travel E4

Sleeping
6 Cocoon Inn C3
7 Golden Art Hotel B3
8 Hanoi Hostel A2
9 Hanoi Little Town Hotel B2
10 Hanoi Rendezvous Hotel A4
11 La Beauté de Hanoi E4
12 La Siesta Classic Ma May Hotel E4
13 Nexy Hostel C5

Eating
14 Banh Cuon A2
15 Blue Butterfly E3
16 Cha Ca Thang Long A4
17 Com Pho Co D2
18 Grandma's Restaurant A5
19 New Day E3
20 Quan Bia Minh D4
21 Xoi Yen F4

Drinking & Nightlife
22 Bia Hoi Ha Noi A4
23 Cafe Giang F4
24 Cafe Lam F4
25 Cafe Pho Co D5
Nola (see 15)

Entertainment
26 Thang Long Ca Tru Theatre D2

Shopping
Dong Xuan Market (see 3)
27 Tan My Design C5

Information
28 Mr Linh's Adventure Tours E3
29 Vega Travel E4

Transport
30 Electric Bus Tour – Dong Xuan Market Departure Point C1
31 Electric Bus Tour – Main Departure Point E5
32 Offroad Vietnam F3

★Golden Lotus Luxury Hotel HOTEL $$
(Map p54; 024-3828 5888; www.goldenlotushotel.com.vn; 53-55 P Hang Trong; d/ste from US$55/100;) Rooms at this stylish, atmospheric hotel have attractive wooden finishes, fine silk trims, local art and high technology. Standard rooms lack natural light, but oversized suites have generous terraces. And there's a rooftop pool! Its older sister property, the **Golden Lotus Hotel** (Map p54; 024-3938 0901; www.goldenlotushotel.com.vn; 39 P Hang Trong; d/ste from US$45/89;), is marginally cheaper, and you can still use the pool here if staying there.

Madame Moon Hotel GUESTHOUSE $$
(Map p54; 024-3938 1255; www.madammoonguesthouse.com; 17 P Hang Hanh; d & tw from US$30;) Keeping it simple just one block from Hoan Kiem Lake, Madame Moon has surprisingly chic rooms and a (relatively) traffic-free location in a street filled with local cafes and bars. Note that there are three hotels belonging to Madame Moon (this review is for the property on P Hang Hanh).

★Sofitel Legend Metropole Hotel HOTEL $$$
(Map p54; 024-3826 6919; www.sofitel-legend-metropole-hanoi.com; 15 P Ngo Quyen; r from US$220;) Hanoi's finest hotel is a slice of colonial history, with its restored French-colonial facade, mahogany-panelled reception rooms and haute cuisine. Rooms in the Heritage Wing have unmatched colonial style and have hosted Charlie Chaplin and Graham Greene – the latter wrote *The Quiet American* while staying here. The modern Opera Wing has sumptuous levels of comfort, if not the same character.

Other Areas

★Somerset Grand Hanoi APARTMENT $$
(Map p54; 024-3934 2342; www.somerset.com; 49 P Hai Ba Trung; apt from US$130;) Rates vary dramatically due to the nature and location of this sprawling apartment-hotel tower, but bargains can be found if you book ahead. For the central location and amenities alone, the selection of studio to three-bedroom apartments with full kitchen and laundry facilities can't be beat. Outside high season the rates drop to

around US$100 for a one-bed 64-sq-metre apartment.

★Conifer Boutique Hotel HOTEL $$$
(Map p54; ☎024-3266 9999; www.coniferhotel.com.vn; 9 P Ly Dao Thanh; d/ste from US$95/140; ❄📶) This is a fantastic little hotel tucked away on a pleasant French Quarter side street, opposite a wonderfully dilapidated French-colonial mansion. Rooms are on the smaller side but are functional and well thought out. Be sure to pay extra for a street-facing room with a generous, enclosed balcony: perfect for watching afternoon storms. Otherwise, aim for one of the suites.

Fraser Suites Hanoi APARTMENT $$$
(☎024-3719 8877; http://hanoi.frasershospitality.com; 51 Xuan Dieu, Tay Ho; apt from US$187; ❄📶🏊) These sumptuous, fully equipped serviced apartments in buzzing lakeside Tay Ho are the perfect choice for the discerning traveller staying a few days or more. There's a gym and children's play areas, and the gorgeous, landscaped outdoor pool is the city's most alluring.

Eating

Old Quarter

★Bun Cha 34 VIETNAMESE $
(Map p53; ☎0948 361 971; 34 P Hang Than; meals 35,000d; ⏰8.30am-5pm; 📶) Best *bun cha* in Vietnam? Many say 34 is up there. No presidents have eaten at the plastic tables, but you get perfectly moist chargrilled pork, zesty fresh herbs and delicious broth to dip everything in. The *nem* (seafood spring rolls) are great too. Aim for noon for patties straight off the coals.

New Day VIETNAMESE $
(Map p58; ☎024-3828 0315; 72 P Ma May; meals 50,000-100,000d; ⏰9.30am-11pm) Busy New Day attracts locals, expats and travellers alike with its broad menu. The eager staff always find space for new diners, so look forward to sharing a table with some like-minded fans of Vietnamese food. It's not advertised, but evening diners can point and choose from selections for a mixed plate for about 100,000d.

Com Pho Co VIETNAMESE $
(Map p58; ☎024-2216 4028; 16 Nguyen Sieu; meals 60,000-140,000d; ⏰10am-9.30pm) This large, bustling restaurant attracts a mixed crowd for its long menu of simple, good Vietnamese dishes such as *ga nuong xa* (lemongrass chicken) and Hanoi *pho cuon* (steamed rice rolls filled with mango, vegetables and shrimp). The four-course set meals (US$6) are good value and can include surprisingly tasty crème caramel. Choose the internal leafy courtyard for some peace.

★Blue Butterfly VIETNAMESE $$
(Map p58; ☎0944 852 009, 024-3926 3845; www.bluebutterflyrestaurant.com; 69 P Ma May; meals 195,000-400,000d; ⏰9.30am-11pm) Blue Butterfly floats above its weight with the lamp-lit dark-wood stylings of a heritage house and a good-value menu of Vietnamese classics, from *bun cha* (barbecued pork) to duck with tamarind sauce. Staff offer knowledgeable suggestions and demonstrate how to tackle dishes such as *nem lui* (pork grilled on lemongrass skewers, wrapped in rice paper and dipped in peanut sauce).

★Cha Ca Thang Long VIETNAMESE $$
(Map p58; ☎024-3824 5115; www.chacathanglong.com; 19-31 P Duong Thanh; cha ca fish meals 180,000d; ⏰10am-3pm & 5-10pm) Bring along your DIY cooking skills and grill your own succulent *cha ca* fish dish in a pan with a little shrimp paste and plenty of veggies, herbs and peanuts. *Cha ca* is an iconic Hanoi dish heavy on turmeric and dill; staff will show you what to do. You may get taken across the road to the overspill restaurant.

Grandma's Restaurant VIETNAMESE $$
(Map p58; ☎024-3537 8666; www.grandmarestaurant.com; 6a P Duong Thanh; meals 300,000d; ⏰11am-2pm & 5-10pm; 📶) With dark-wood furniture, concrete walls and lanterns, staff dressed in white and a limited menu of artfully presented dishes, Grandma's is worth savouring for its ravishing beef, chicken, duck and seafood dishes. The sea bass with pepper sauce sounds spicy, but is actually quite sweet, and lovely. Finish with the excellent handmade coconut ice cream. There's a good wine list too. Reserve ahead.

Quan Bia Minh VIETNAMESE $$
(Map p58; 7a P Dinh Liet; meals 90,000-130,000d; ⏰7.30am-late) This *bia hoi* joint has evolved into an Old Quarter favourite, with well-priced Vietnamese food and excellent service led by the eponymous Mrs Minh. Grab an outdoor table and a cold beer and watch the beautiful chaos unfold below.

Around Hoan Kiem Lake

★Chim Sao VIETNAMESE $

(Map p53; 024-3976 0633; www.chimsao.com; 63-65 Ngo Hue; meals 45,000-120,000d; 9.30am-11pm;) Sit at tables downstairs or grab a more traditional spot on the floor upstairs and discover excellent Vietnamese food, with some dishes inspired by the ethnic minorities of Vietnam's north. Definite standouts are the hearty and robust sausages, zingy and fresh salads, and duck with star fruit (carambola). Even simple dishes are outstanding. Come with a group to sample the full menu.

Jalus Vegan Kitchen VEGAN $

(Map p54; 024-3266 9730; 2nd fl, 46 Hang Trong; meals 30,000-60,000d; 10am-10pm Tue-Sun;) Pull up a pine table at this modern, comforting and quiet hidden-away gem to sink a delicious blueberry smoothie and feast on veggie burgers, vegan soup of the day, potato curry with red rice, spinach pasta and more. There are definite Vietnamese twists, with lemongrass and spice, and sometimes special all-Vietnamese menus.

★Hanoi Social Club CAFE $$

(Map p54; 024-3938 2117; www.facebook.com/TheHanoiSocialClub; 6 Hoi Vu; meals 95,000-175,000d; 8am-11pm;) On three levels with retro furniture, the Hanoi Social Club is an artist hub and the city's most cosmopolitan cafe. Dishes include potato fritters with chorizo for breakfast, and pasta, burgers and wraps for lunch or dinner. Vegetarian options feature a tasty mango curry, and the quiet laneway location is a good spot for an egg coffee (60,000d), beer or wine.

The Hanoi Social Club also hosts regular gigs and events.

V's Home VEGETARIAN $$

(Map p54; 0888 011 074; P Duong Thanh; meals 125,000d; 10am-10pm;) Blink and you'll miss the slim alleyway opening leading to this excellent upstairs restaurant, with diners attended to by hearing- and speech-impaired staff. The relaxing space is elegant and charming, with a gorgeous tiled floor, graceful arches and green foliage. The dishes with organic ingredients are lovely and there's a good vegan selection. Profits are contributed to community initiatives.

The restaurant also purveys various goods – soaps, handmade gifts – all made with environmentally friendly ingredients.

Madame Hien VIETNAMESE $$$

(Map p54; 024-3938 1588; www.facebook.com/madamehienrestaurant; 15 Chan Cam; meals 100,000-350,000d, set menus from 397,000d; 11am-2pm & 5-10.30pm;) Housed in a restored 19th-century villa, Madame Hien is a tribute to French chef Didier Corlu's Vietnamese grandmother. Look forward to elegant versions of traditional Hanoi street food, with the '36 Streets' fixed menu (595,000d) an easygoing place to kick off your culinary tour of the city.

Other Areas

Oasis DELI $

(024-3719 1196; www.oasishanoi.net; 24 P Xuan Dieu; pizza slices 25,000d; 7am-8pm) This Italian-owned deli has excellent bread, cheese and salami, as well as homemade pasta and sauces and other items. It's north of central Hanoi in the Tay Ho restaurant strip on P Xuan Dieu. It delivers too (20,000d between 8am and 7pm).

Bun Cha Huong Lien VIETNAMESE $

(Map p53; 0966 962 683; 24 P Le Van Hu; meals from 40,000d; 10am-8pm) Bun Cha Huong Lien was launched into stardom thanks to Barack Obama, who dined here with celebrity chef Anthony Bourdain in May 2016. Customers fill the four storeys to sample the grilled-pork-and-noodle delicacy while staff call out 'Obama *bun cha*!' to passers-by. The 'Combo Obama' gets you a bowl of *bun cha*, a fried seafood roll and Hanoi beer for 90,000d.

★Old Hanoi VIETNAMESE $$

(Map p54; 024-3747 8337; www.oldhanoi.com; 18 Ton That Thiep; meals 90,000-179,000d; 10am-2pm & 5-10pm) This sophisticated eating spot in a restored French-colonial villa has a pleasant casual courtyard outside and starched white tablecloths inside. Once host to celebrity chef Gordon Ramsay, it serves traditional Hanoian and Vietnamese specialities with aplomb; you'll enjoy the selection and find the best value for money if you dine in a group.

★Tim Ho Wan DIM SUM $$

(024-3333 1725; 36th fl, Lotte Center, 54 P Lieu Giai, Ba Dinh; dim sum 69,000-95,000d; 11.30am-10pm) Do yourself a favour and reserve a window table at the Hanoi branch of this legendary Hong Kong dim sum chain, high above the city on the 36th floor of the Lotte Center. Bring a friend or six and an

TOP HANOI STREET EATS

Deciphering Hanoi's street-food scene can be bewildering, but it's worth persevering and diving in. The city's best food definitely comes from the scores of vendors crowding the city's pavements with smoking charcoal burners, tiny blue plastic stools and expectant queues of canny locals. Many of the stalls have been operating for decades, and often they offer just one dish. After that long perfecting their recipes, it's little wonder the food can be sensational. Note that opening hours may change and prices vary. Expect to pay 25,000d to 75,000d, depending on what you devour.

Old Quarter

Bun Cha Nem Cua Be Dac Kim (Map p54; 67 P Duong Thanh; bun cha 60,000d; ⏲11am-7pm) Visiting Hanoi and not eating *bun cha* (barbecued pork with rice vermicelli) with a side of *nem cua be* (sea-crab spring rolls) should be classed as a capital offence. This is an excellent spot to try this street-food classic.

Bun Rieu Cua (Map p54; 40 P Hang Tre; bun rieu 25,000d; ⏲7-9:30am) Get to this incredibly popular spot early, as its sole dish of *bun rieu cua* (noodle soup with beef in a spicy crab broth) is only served for a couple of hours from 7am. A Hanoi classic.

Banh Cuon (Map p58; 14 P Hang Ga; meals from 35,000d; ⏲8am-3pm) Don't even bother ordering here; just squeeze in and a plate of gossamer-light *banh cuon* (steamed rice crêpes filled with minced pork, mushrooms and shrimp) will be placed in front of you.

Xoi Yen (Map p58; cnr P Nguyen Huu Huan & P Hang Mam; sticky rice from 10,000d; ⏲7am-11pm) Equally good for breakfast or as a hangover cure, Xoi Yen specialises in sticky rice topped with goodies, including sweet Asian sausage, gooey fried egg and slow-cooked pork.

Mien Xao Luon (Map p54; 87 P Hang Dieu; meals from 25,000d; ⏲7am-2pm) Head to this humble stall trimmed with mini-mountains of fried eels for three different ways of eating the crisp little morsels. Try them stir-fried in vermicelli with egg, bean sprouts and shallots.

Other Areas

Banh Mi Pho Hue (Map p53; 118 P Hue; banh mi 25,000-55,000d; ⏲6.30am-7pm) *Banh mi* (sandwich) vendors abound in Hanoi, although the phenomenon is less popular than in Ho Chi Minh City. This place is usually packed with locals, which is always a good sign.

Pho Thin (Map p53; 13 P Lo Duc; pho 50,000d; ⏲6am-8.30pm) Negotiate your way to the rear of this narrow, rustic establishment and sit down to some excellent *pho bo* (beef noodle soup). A classic Hanoi experience that hasn't changed in decades.

empty stomach – we guarantee you won't regret it.

Maison de Tet Decor CAFE **$$**
(☎0966 611 383; www.tet-lifestyle-collection.com; 156 Tua Hoa, Nghi Tam, Tay Ho; meals from 120,000d; ⏲7am-10pm) Sumptuous, healthy and organic (when possible) wholefoods are presented with aplomb in one of Hanoi's loveliest settings, an expansive, airy villa overlooking West Lake.

★**La Badiane** INTERNATIONAL **$$$**
(Map p54; ☎024-3942 4509; www.labadiane-hanoi.com; 10 Nam Ngu; meals from 280,000d; ⏲11.30am-2pm & 6-10pm Mon-Sat) This stylish bistro is set in a restored, whitewashed French villa arrayed around a breezy central courtyard. French cuisine underpins the menu – La Badiane translates as 'star anise' – but Asian and Mediterranean flavours also feature. Menu highlights include sea-bass tagliatelle with smoked paprika, and prawn bisque with wasabi tomato bruschetta. Two-/three-course lunches (395,000/485,000d) are on the menu along with an evening degustation (1,890,000d).

Drinking & Nightlife

Hanoi's eclectic drinking scene features grungy dive bars, Western-style pubs, sleek lounge bars, cafes and hundreds of *bia hoi* (draught beer) joints.

Travellers flock to noisy P Ta Hien in the Old Quarter, and Ngo Bao Khanh near the northwest edge of Hoan Kiem Lake. Expect more activity Friday to Sunday, when the Old Quarter is allowed to stay open beyond midnight, until 2am.

★The Railway Hanoi 2 CAFE

(Map p54; www.therailwayhanoi.com; 65 P Ton That Thiep; ⏲9am-9pm) Choo-choo! Thao and her fun and exceedingly amiable staff woo-woo passers-by to this stand-in for the owner's other cafe by the railway line (shut at the time of research). The cafe serves excellent egg coffee, craft beer and food, teaches English to local kids (which you can join in with) and runs food tours.

★Nola BAR

(Map p58; 89 P Ma May; ⏲10am-11.30pm Mon-Sat, to 11pm Sun) Retro furniture and art are mixed and matched in this bohemian multilevel labyrinth tucked away from Ma May's tourist bustle. Pop in for a coffee and banana bread in a quiet section, or return after dark to one of Hanoi's best little bars.

Tadioto BAR

(Map p54; ☎024-6680 9124; www.facebook.com/tadiotohanoi; 24b P Tong Dan; ⏲9am-11.45pm Sun-Thu, from 8am Fri & Sat; 📶) Attracting a well-dressed clientele, Nguyen Qui Duc's unofficial clubhouse for the underground art and literary scene is this dark, quirky colonial bar in the French Quarter. Obligatory red accents (seat covers, wrought-iron grille on the doors), reworkings of art-deco furniture and plenty of recycled ironwork feature heavily. The highlight of the cool cocktail list is the sweet mojito.

Loading T Cafe CAFE

(Map p54; ☎0903 342 000; 2nd fl, 8 Chan Cam; ⏲8am-10pm; 📶) Architecture lovers will appreciate this charmer of an upstairs cafe converted from a room in a crumbling French-colonial house. The ornate tiled floor, vintage fans, huge window, mismatched furniture and other design gems capture Hanoi's faded glamour. Homemade cakes, fresh juices and coconut or yoghurt coffee are on the menu. The egg coffee is a winner, while the music is all French ballads.

HANOI'S CAFFEINE SCENE

Western-style cafes and coffee shops are widespread in Vietnamese cities, but many pale in comparison to traditional Vietnamese family-run cafes dotted around central Hanoi. Here's where to go and what to order for an authentic local experience. Most cafes are open from around 7am to 7pm, but hours sometimes vary. On the eastern edge of the Old Quarter, P Nguyen Huu Huan is lined with good cafes, most with free wi-fi.

Cafe Duy Tri (☎024-3829 1386; 43a P Yen Phu; ⏲8am-6pm) In the same location since 1936, this caffeine-infused labyrinth is a Hanoi classic. You'll feel like Gulliver as you negotiate the tiny ladders and stairways to reach the 3rd-floor balcony. Delicious *caphe sua chua* (iced coffee with yoghurt) may be your new favourite summertime drink. It's a couple of blocks east of Truc Bach Lake.

Cafe Pho Co (Map p58; ☎024-3928 8153; 4th fl, 11 P Hang Gai; ⏲8am-11pm) One of Hanoi's most hidden cafes, this place has plum views over Hoan Kiem Lake. Enter through the silk shop, and continue through the antique-bedecked courtyard up to the top floor for the mother of all vistas. You'll need to order coffee and snacks before tackling the final winding staircase. Try sweet *caphe trung da* (40,000d), coffee topped with silky-smooth beaten egg yolk.

Cafe Lam (Map p58; ☎024-3824 5940; www.cafelam.com; 60 P Nguyen Huu Huan; ⏲6.30am-7.30pm) A classic multi-room cafe and beautiful space of wooden tables that's been around for years – long enough to build up a compact gallery of modern and traditional paintings left behind by talented patrons who couldn't afford to pay their tabs during the American War. These days you might spy Vespa-riding youth refuelling on wickedly strong *caphe den* (black coffee).

Cafe Giang (Map p58; 39 P Nguyen Huu Huan; ⏲7am-10pm) The originator of Hanoi's egg coffee is still running in this time-worn family establishment, serving the best in town since 1946 at *egg-sellent* prices… Head upstairs and order up a superb regular egg coffee (25,000d), or varieties of egg coffee with chocolate, cinnamon, coke, rum or beer. Other non-egg coffees and teas are available. You get a plastic tab and pay downstairs.

Manzi Art Space BAR

(Map p53; ☎024-3716 3397; www.facebook.com/manzihanoi; 14 Phan Huy Ich; ⊙8am-10.30pm) Part cool art exhibition space, part chic cafe and bar, Manzi is worth seeking out north of the Old Quarter. A restored French villa hosts diverse exhibitions of painting, sculpture and photography, and the compact courtyard garden is perfect for a cup of coffee or glass of wine. There's also a small shop selling works by contemporary Vietnamese artists.

Pasteur Street Brewing Company BAR

(Map p54; ☎024-6294 9462; www.pasteurstreet.com; 1 P Au Trieu; ⊙11am-midnight; 📶) A curious lack of character stalks this two-floor bar, although the terrace is good. The beer menu is pricey, but the superb choice of IPAs, fruity ales, Belgian-style ales and stouts is the draw if you need to flush the ever-present taste of Hanoi beer from your palate. Try the Double IPA, a hoppy brew with a 8.7% ABV (alcohol by volume) punch.

GC Bar GAY & LESBIAN

(Map p54; ☎024-3825 0499; 5 P Ngo Bao Khanh; ⊙5pm-midnight Sun-Thu, to 2am Fri & Sat; 📶) Hanoi's long-standing (25-plus years), only established gay bar – and unofficial LGBT HQ – might seem small and vanilla midweek, but it gets pumped on weekend nights. Reasonably priced drinks make it popular with a mixed local crowd and it's easy for gay visitors to drop by. It's casual, so shorts and smoking indoors are common.

Bia Hoi Ha Noi BIA HOI

(Map p58; 2 P Duong Thanh) A *bia hoi* junction that is local in flavour is where P Nha Hoa meets P Duong Thanh on the western edge of the Old Quarter. Bia Hoi Ha Noi does superb spare ribs for a little something to go with the flow of beer.

Nha Hang Lan Chin BIA HOI

(Map p54; ☎024-3824 1138; cnr P Hang Tre & P Hang Thung; ⊙9.30am-10pm) A good spot to sample a local brew is Nha Hang Lan Chin, one of the most popular local lunch spots in town. It's busy, noisy, cheap and very local, though with chairs, not stools. It's famed for its *vit quay* (roast duck).

☆ Entertainment

★Binh Minh Jazz Club JAZZ

(Map p54; ☎024-3933 6555; www.minhjazzvietnam.com; 1a P Trang Tien; ⊙performances 9pm-midnight) This atmospheric venue tucked behind the Opera House is the place in Hanoi to catch live jazz. There's a full bar, a food menu and high-quality gigs featuring father-and-son team Minh and Dac, plus other local and international jazz acts. There's no cover charge, so the small, smoky venue fills quickly – get there early.

★Thang Long Ca Tru Theatre LIVE MUSIC

(Map p58; ☎0122 326 6897; www.catruthanglong.com; 28 P Hang Buom; ⊙8pm Thu & Sat) Concerts of traditional Vietnamese music are held in this intimate restored house in the Old Quarter. *Ca tru* is indigenous to the north of Vietnam, and concerts feature a selection of the 100 or so *ca tru* melodies. The art form has also been recognised as an endangered 'intangible cultural heritage' by Unesco.

Municipal Water Puppet Theatre PUPPET THEATRE

(Map p54; ☎024-3824 9494; www.thanglongwaterpuppet.org; 57b P Dinh Tien Hoang; tickets 100,000-200,000d) Water-puppetry shows are a real treat for children. Multilingual programs allow the audience to read up on each vignette as it's performed. Although there are five afternoon performances daily, book well ahead, especially from October to April. The first/last performances are at 3pm/8pm.

🔒 Shopping

The Old Quarter is brimming with temptations: T-shirts, musical instruments, herbal medicines, jewellery, spices, propaganda art and much, much more.

Hanoi has a burgeoning art scene and you can pick up an original work on canvas by a local artist from as little as US$40 in any one of the private galleries concentrated on P Trang Tien, between Hoan Kiem Lake and the Opera House.

For Vietnamese handicrafts, including textiles and lacquerware, head to the stores along P Hang Gai, P To Tich, P Hang Khai and P Cau Go. P Hang Gai and its continuation, P Hang Bong, are good places to look for embroidered tablecloths, T-shirts and wall hangings.

★Craft Link ARTS & CRAFTS

(Map p53; ☎024-3733 6101; www.craftlink.com.vn; 43-51 P Van Mieu; ⊙9am-6pm) A not-for-profit organisation near the Temple of Literature that sells quality tribal handicrafts, textiles and weavings at fair-trade prices. The bags are quite beautiful and richly coloured – explore them over two floors. There's another branch a little further down the road.

Chan Con Cong VINTAGE
(Map p54; www.facebook.com/chan.con.cong; 8 Chan Cam; ⏲8am-8pm) This charmingly small vintage shop stuffed away beneath Loading T Cafe sells delightful vintage long dresses and classic togs. There's another, larger branch at 14 Đ Thanh.

Tan My Design CLOTHING
(Map p58; ☎024-3938 1154; www.tanmydesign.com; 61 P Hang Gai; ⏲8am-8pm) Stylish clothing, jewellery and accessories, with the bonus of a cool cafe when you need a break from shopping. The homewares and bed linen are definitely worth a look.

Dong Xuan Market MARKET
(Map p58; Dong Xuan; ⏲6am-7pm) This large, non-touristy market is located in the Old Quarter, 900m north of Hoan Kiem Lake. There are hundreds of stalls here and lots of the goods are household items or tat, but it's a fascinating place to explore to catch the flavour of local Hanoian life. The area around it also has loads of bustling shops, and more stalls appear at night.

Mai Gallery ART
(Map p54; ☎0936 368 367, 024-3938 0568; www.maigallery-vietnam.com; 113 P Hang Bong; ⏲9am-7pm) With some very attractive, elegant and thought-provoking art hanging from its walls, this gallery, run by resident artist Mai, is a good place to learn more about Vietnamese art before making a purchase.

Three Trees FASHION & ACCESSORIES
(Map p54; ☎024-3928 8725; www.threetrees.com.vn; 15 P Nha Tho; ⏲9am-7pm) Stunning, very unusual designer jewellery, including many delicate necklaces and beautiful brooches of insects and animals wrought from silver and opals: they make for special gifts.

Thang Long BOOKS
(Hieu Sach Thang Long; Map p54; ☎024-825 7043; 53-55 P Trang Tien; ⏲9am-6pm) One of the biggest bookshops in town, with some English and French titles, international newspapers and magazines, and a good selection of titles on the history of Hanoi plus a large choice of books in Vietnamese.

ℹ Information

INTERNET ACCESS

Wi-fi access is virtually ubiquitous in the city's cafes and bars, and pretty much every hotel offers fast, free access.

MEDICAL SERVICES

Viet Duc Hospital (Benh Vien Viet Duc; Map p54; ☎024-3825 3531; http://benhvienvietduc.org; 40 P Trang Thi; ⏲24hr) Old Quarter unit for emergency surgery; the doctors here speak English, French and German.

MONEY

Hanoi has many ATMs, and on the main roads around Hoan Kiem Lake are international banks where you can change money.

POST

International Postal Office (Map p54; ☎024-3825 2030; cnr P Dinh Tien Hoang & P Dinh Le; ⏲7am-8pm) The entrance is to the right of the Domestic Post Office.

TOURIST INFORMATION

Tourist Information & Support Center (Map p53; ☎24hr English hotline 0941 336 677, Vietnamese 0911 081 968; 28 P Hang Dau; ⏲8am-5pm Wed-Sun) Hanoi finally has an official tourist information desk, although the location near the Long Bien Bridge might put off those staying south around Hoan Kiem Lake. It offers four free walking tours, themed by architecture, history, Hoan Kiem Lake and Hanoi's craft streets.

TRAVEL AGENCIES

Hanoi has hundreds of travel agencies and plenty are of ill repute. The agencies we recommend have professional, knowledgeable staff and coordinate well-organised trips. Most run smaller groups and use their own vehicles and guides.

Beware of clones of popular agencies; check addresses and websites carefully.

It's not advisable to book trips or tickets through guesthouses and hotels.

Vega Travel (Map p58; ☎024-3926 2092; www.vegatravel.vn; cnr P Ma May & 24a P Hang Bac; ⏲8am-8pm) This family-owned-and-operated company offers very well-run and popular tours around the north of the country and throughout Vietnam. Excellent guides and drivers, and Vega Travel also financially supports ethnic-minority kindergartens and schools around Sapa and Bac Ha. Great Halong Bay tours on a private cruise ship are very good value and bespoke touring is also available.

Ethnic Travel (Map p58; ☎024-3926 1951; www.ethnictravel.com.vn; 35 P Hang Giay; ⏲7am-8pm Mon-Sat, 7am-7pm Sun) Off-the-beaten-track trips across the north in small groups. Some trips are low impact, using public

STAYING SAFE

Many scams in Hanoi are linked to budget hotels and tours. We've received reports of verbal aggression and threats towards tourists who've decided against tours sold by pushy hotel staff.

Taxi swindles are also quite common. Try to avoid the taxis loitering at Hanoi's bus stations; many have superfast meters. Similarly, be careful at the airport; using the app-based Grab is a good taxi alternativecuc .

Watch out for friendly, smooth-talking strangers approaching you around Hoan Kiem Lake (but don't confuse them with the legitimate students out practising English!). Be very wary, though, if they suggest a drink or a meal, as the bill might be for hundreds of dollars.

Keep your wits about you, and try to stay in a group if you're returning from a bar late at night.

transport and homestays, others are activity based (including hiking, cycling and cooking). Offers Bai Tu Long Bay tours and also has an office in Sapa.

Handspan Adventure Travel (Map p58; ☎024-3926 2828; www.handspan.com; 78 P Ma May; ⏲9am-8pm) Sea-kayaking trips in Halong Bay and around Cat Ba Island, plus 4WD, mountain-biking and trekking tours. Other options include remote areas such as Moc Chau and Ba Be National Park, community-based tourism projects in northern Vietnam, and the *Treasure Junk*, the only true sailing craft cruising Halong Bay. Handspan also has offices in Sapa and Ho Chi Minh City.

Ocean Tours (☎024-3926 0463; www.oceantours.com.vn; 82 Ma May, Hanoi) Professional tour operator based in Hanoi, with Ba Be National Park, Halong Bay tours and excellent road trips around the north including a six-day trip that includes Dong Van (US$1158 based on two people).

Marco Polo Travel (☎0913 571 687; www.marcopoloasia.com; Rm 107b, N14-49 Nguyen Khoai; ⏲9am-5pm) Runs kayaking trips around Halong Bay and Ba Be Lakes. Also has good mountain-biking trips and hiking expeditions around the north of Vietnam.

Mr Linh's Adventure Tours (Map p58; ☎024-3642 5420; www.mrlinhadventure.com; 83 P Ma May) A professional, friendly outfit specialising in off-the-beaten-track and adventure travel in Vietnam's remote north. Ba Be Lakes homestay trips are recommended.

Getting There & Away

AIR

Hanoi has fewer direct international flights than Ho Chi Minh City, but with excellent connections through Singapore, Hong Kong or Bangkok you can get almost anywhere easily.

Vietnam Airlines (Map p54; ☎1900 545 486; www.vietnamair.com.vn; 25 P Trang Thi; ⏲8am-5pm Mon-Fri) Links Hanoi to destinations throughout Vietnam. Popular routes include Dalat, Danang, Dien Bien Phu, Ho Chi Minh City, Hue and Nha Trang, all served daily.

BUS

Hanoi has three main long-distance bus stations of interest to travellers: Giap Bat, Gia Lam and My Dinh. They are fairly well organised, with ticket offices, fixed prices and schedules, though they can be crowded and at times chaotic. Consider buying tickets the day before you plan to travel on the longer-distance routes, to ensure a seat. It's often easier to book through a travel agent, but you'll obviously be charged a commission.

Tourist-style minibuses can be booked through most hotels and travel agents. Popular destinations include Halong Bay and Sapa. Prices are usually about 30% to 40% higher than the regular public bus, but include a hotel pickup.

Many open-ticket tours through Vietnam start or finish in Hanoi.

Gia Lam Bus Station (☎024-3827 1569; 132 P Ngo Gia Kham) Has buses to regions north and northeast of Hanoi. It's located 3km northeast of the city centre, across the Song Hong (Red River).

Giap Bat Bus Station (☎024-3864 1467; Đ Giai Phong) Serves points south of Hanoi. It is 7km south of Hanoi Train Station.

My Dinh Bus Station (☎024-3768 5549; Đ Pham Hung) This station 7km west of the city provides services to the west and the north, including sleeper buses to Dien Bien Phu for onward travel to Laos. It's also the best option for buses to Ha Giang, Mai Chau and Lang Son.

Nuoc Nam Bus Station This small terminal services Cat Ba Island. On Đ Ngoc Hoi in Hoang Mai District, about 2km south of Giap Bat.

CAR & MOTORCYCLE

Car rental is best arranged via a travel agency or tour operator. The roads in the north are in pretty good shape, but expect an average speed of 35km/h to 40km/h. You'll definitely need a 4WD. Daily rates start at about US$110 a day (including driver and petrol).

Offroad Vietnam (Map p58; ☎ 024-3926 3433, 0913-047 509; www.offroadvietnam.com; 36 P Nguyen Huu Huan; ⏰ 8am-6pm Mon-Sat) For reliable Honda off-road bikes (150cc from US$20, 250cc from US$40 daily) and 150cc road bikes (US$15). Booking ahead is recommended. Offroad's principal business is running excellent tours, mainly dealing with travellers from English-speaking countries. Tours are either semi-guided, excluding meals and accommodation, or all-inclusive and fully guided.

TRAIN

Trains depart from four main stations in Hanoi, where you can purchase tickets. We recommend buying your tickets at least a few days before departure to ensure a seat or sleeper; the website www.baolau.vn is a very useful booking engine, though you can go to the station for the lowest fares. For full departure times and at-counter ticket prices, consult the website of the **Vietnam Railway Corporation** (www.dsvn.vn).

Tickets can also be purchased from most travel agencies (their commission may be worth it to avoid the language hassle of buying tickets at the train station, though there is a booth at the station where English is spoken). Travel agencies often have preferential access to tickets to popular destinations such as Hue, Ho Chi Minh City (HCMC) and Lao Cai (for Sapa).

The main **Hanoi Train Station** (Ga Hang Co, Train Station A; ☎ 024-3825 3949; 120 Đ Le Duan; ⏰ ticket office 7.30am-12.30pm & 1.30-7.30pm) is at the western end of P Tran Hung Dao; trains from here go to southern destinations.

BUSES FROM HANOI

Gia Lam Bus station

DESTINATION	DURATION (HR)	COST (D)	FREQUENCY
Bai Chay (Halong City)	4-4½	110,000-130,000	frequent 6am-6pm
Hai Phong	1½	100,000	every 40min 6am-7pm
Lang Son	4	100,000	every 45min 8am-8.30pm
Lao Cai	4-5	250,000	6 daily 8am-7pm
Mong Cai	7	200,000	irregular, no fixed times
Sapa	6	250,000	8pm & 9pm

Giap Bat Bus Station

DESTINATION	DURATION (HR)	COST (D)	FREQUENCY
Danang	13-14	350,000	4pm & 5pm
Dong Ha	9	300,000	4pm & 5pm
Dong Hoi	8	250,000	4pm & 5pm
HCMC	36-38	920,000	1.30pm, 3pm, 6pm & 6.30pm
Hue	12	350,000	4pm & 5pm
Nha Trang	24-28	700,000	4pm & 6pm
Ninh Binh	2	70,000	frequent 6am-6pm

My Dinh Bus Station

DESTINATION	DURATION (HR)	COST (D)	FREQUENCY
Cao Bang	7-8	180,000-200,000	hourly to 1pm, sleeper at 9pm
Dien Bien Phu	9-9½	320,000-415,000	7am, 7.30am, 1.30pm, 4pm & 5.45pm
Ha Giang	7½	200,000	hourly 5.30am-9pm
Hoa Binh	2	47,000-90,000	hourly 4am-6pm
Lang Son	4	100,000	frequent to 6pm
Son La	5½	220,000-270,000	10.45am & 4.45pm

Eastbound (Haiphong) trains depart from **Gia Lam Train Station** on the eastern side of the Song Hong (Red River), or **Long Bien** on the western (city) side of the river. Be sure to check which station. Trains to Nanning, China, also depart from Gia Lam station.

To the right of the main entrance to Hanoi Train Station is a separate ticket office for northbound trains to Lao Cai (for Sapa) and China. Tickets to China must be bought from counter 13. Note that all northbound trains leave from a separate station (just behind) called **Tran Quy Cap Station** (Train Station B; ☎ 024-3825 2628; P Tran Quy Cap; ⏲ ticket office 4-6am & 4-10pm).

Getting Around

TO/FROM THE AIRPORT

Hanoi's **Noi Bai International Airport** (☎ 024-3827 1513; www.hanoiairportonline.com) is about 35km north of the city, around 45 minutes away by car/taxi along a modern highway. There are several transport options:

Airport Taxi (☎ 024-3873 3333) US$20 for a door-to-door taxi ride.

Public bus 17 (9000d, 1½ hours) To/from Long Bien Bus Station.

Express bus 86 (35,000d, one hour) To/from north side of Hoan Kiem Lake and Hanoi Train Station.

Vietnam Airlines minibus (Map p54; 1 P Quang Trung; 40,000d) (1 P Quang Trung; 40,000d; every 45min 5am-7pm) To/from the Vietnam Airlines office on Quang Trung. Departs when full and can be unreliable.

BUS

Hanoi has an extensive public bus system, though few tourists take advantage of the rock-bottom fares (3000d).

CYCLO

A few cyclo (pedicab) drivers still frequent the Old Quarter, but they tend to charge more than taxis: around 50,000d for a shortish journey.

ELECTRIC BUS

Hanoi's golf-buggy-esque ecofriendly **Electric Bus** (Dong Xuan; per buggy of 6 passengers per hour 300,000d; ⏲ 8.30am-10pm) tour is actually a pretty good way to get your bearings in the city. It traverses a network of 14 hop-on, hop-off stops in the Old Quarter and around Hoan Kiem Lake, parting the flow of motorbikes and pedestrians like a slow-moving white dragon.

METRO

A nine-line metro system is under development, though work is proceeding at a very slow pace. The first line, elevated Line 2A linking Cat Linh and Ha Dong, was due to commence operations by mid-2021. The largely underground Line 2 will be of most use to visitors, but this is many years away from entering service.

MOTORBIKE TAXI

You won't have any trouble finding a *xe om* (motorbike taxi) in Hanoi, though much of their market share has been usurped by the rather handy green-jacketed Grab drivers; download the Grab app (www.grab.com). You can pay in cash.

An average journey by *xe om* in the city centre costs 15,000d to 20,000d, while a longer trip from the Old Quarter to Ho Chi Minh's Mausoleum is 35,000d to 40,000d.

TAXI

App-based Grab (www.grab.com/vn/en/transport/taxi) operates taxi-like cars in Hanoi, including from the airport, offering good rates and reliability. Avoid freelance taxi drivers as rip-offs are common.

AROUND HANOI

Ninh Binh

POP 160,000 / ☎ 0229

Bustling Ninh Binh City is lacking in sights, but makes a good base for exploring quintessentially Vietnamese limestone scenery including Tam Coc, Cuc Phuong National Park, the Van Long Nature Reserve and the Unesco World Heritage–listed Trang An grottoes. Note that the region is very popular with domestic travellers and many attractions are commercialised, with an abundance of hawkers.

TRAINS FROM HANOI

DESTINATION	HARD SEAT (D)	SOFT SEAT (D)	HARD SLEEPER (D)	SOFT SLEEPER (D)
Danang	from 412,000	from 554,000	from 751,000	from 804,000
HCMC	from 695,000	from 1,049,000	from 1,410,000	from 1,580,000
Hue	from 358,000	from 438,000	from 707,000	from 799,000
Nha Trang	from 607,000	from 905,000	from 1,209,000	from 1,305,000

Sleeping & Eating

Go Ninh Binh Hostel HOSTEL $

(☎0229-387 1186; www.goninhbinhhostel.com; 1 Đ Hoang Hoa Tham; dm US$5, weekday/weekend d US$20/24; ❄@🛜) In the city's former railway station, Go Ninh Binh has OK dorms, doubles with en-suite bathrooms, and plenty of shared areas including hammocks. A library, bar, pool table and dartboard are also popular, and the team at reception can help with ideas for exploring the broader Ninh Binh area.

★ **Friendly Home** HOTEL $$

(☎0229-388 3588; 5 60/45 Đ Hai Thuong Lang On; s US$16, d US$22-35, f $42; ❄@🛜) This excellent, very friendly and tidy hotel has six spotless en-suite rooms, buffet breakfasts and free use of bicycles. It's owned and operated by local guide Truong Nguyen, so handy information is available on local sights, bus timetables and tours around the Ninh Binh region. Motorbikes can be hired if you're keen to explore the region independently.

Nguyen Shack BUNGALOW $$

(☎0229-361 8678; www.nguyenshack.com; near Mua Cave, Hoa Lu district; bungalows US$22-45; 🛜) With a riverside setting around 5km from Tam Coc, Nguyen Shack's easygoing, lazy-days thatched bungalows are the perfect antidote to the bustle of Hanoi. Lie in a hammock, drop a fishing rod off your rustic terrace, or grab a bicycle and go exploring. There's an on-site restaurant and bar, too.

★ **Tam Coc Garden** BOUTIQUE HOTEL $$$

(☎024 6273 3615, 037 825 3555; www.tamcocgarden.com; Hai Nham village, Hoa Lu district; d US$145-175; 🚭❄🛜🏊) The most Zen place to stay around Ninh Binh is this lovely boutique hotel. In a private location with a sea of rice paddies at your balcony, it has eight stone-and-timber 50-sq-metre bungalows set in a luxuriant garden, as well as other hotel rooms. Following a day of cycling or exploring nearby attractions, there's a swim in the compact pool to look forward to.

Chookie's Hideaway CAFE $

(☎0919 103 558; www.chookiestravel.com; 147 Đ Nguyen Hue; meals 40,000-70,000d; ⏰9am-10pm; 🛜🌿) This vast place with a pool table and beer on tap serves good-value Vietnamese and Western food and has plenty of local information on what to do and see in the region as the company runs tours. Burgers, wood-fired pizzas, wraps and a few vegetarian options all feature, along with smoothies, cocktails, craft beers and a wine and gin menu.

Trung Tuyet VIETNAMESE $

(14 Đ Hoang Hoa Tham; meals 60,000-100,000d; ⏰8.30am-9.30pm; 🌿) Expect very large portions, options for vegetarians, and a warm welcome from the host family at this busy little place that's popular with travellers. The owners will even drop you off at the nearby train station if you're moving on after your meal.

Tours

Chookie's Tours OUTDOORS

(☎0229-361 8897; www.chookiestravel.com; per person 400,000-1,500,000d) Regular departures exploring the area's attractions by motorbike, with tours to the Trang An grottoes, photogenic sunset scooter tours and the Cuc Phuong National Park. Chookie's also does day tours (US$70) of Tam Coc from Hanoi, with pickup from your hotel.

Truong Nguyen TOURS

(☎0915 666 211, 0165 348 8778; truong_tour@yahoo.com) Freelance guide Truong offers escorted motorbike trips around Ninh Binh using country back roads, and trekking in Pu Luong Nature Reserve, a forested area across two mountain ridges, where you can stay in Thai and Hmong homestays. He also runs trips to the northern Ha Giang province, and operates the excellent Friendly Home hotel in town.

Information

Ninh Binh General Hospital (Benh Vien Da Khoa Ninh Binh; ☎0229-387 1030; Đ Tue Tinh; ⏰24hr) Main city hospital.

Vietin Bank & ATM (Đ Tran Hung Dao; ⏰7am-2.30pm Mon-Fri, 7.30am-noon Sat) One of two branches on this street.

Getting There & Away

Ninh Binh's **bus station** (Đ Le Dai Hanh) is located near Lim Bridge. Public buses leave every 15 minutes until 7pm for the Giap Bat Bus Station in Hanoi (from 75,000d, 2½ hours), and there are regular buses to Hai Phong (95,000d, three hours, every 1½ hours) and twice-daily connections to Halong City (140,000d, 3½ hours).

Ninh Binh is also a stop for open-tour buses between Hanoi (US$7, two hours) and Hue (US$15, 10 hours). Hotel pickups and drop-offs are available.

The **train station** (Ga Ninh Binh; 1 Đ Hoang Hoa Tham) is a scheduled stop on the main north–south line between Hanoi and HCMC.

Around Ninh Binh

At **Trang An** (⏲7.30am-4pm), 7km west of Ninh Binh, rowboats (200,000d per person, or 800,000d for your own boat) bob along the Sao Khe River through **limestone caves**.

Famed for huge limestone rock formations that loom over rice paddies, **Tam Coc** is a famous, though touristy, site 9km southwest of Ninh Binh. **Tam Coc Boat Trips** (Dinh Cac Pier, Ninh Hai village; boat base fare 150,000d, plus entry adult/child 120,000/60,000d; ⏲7am-3.30pm) take in some breathtaking scenery, passing through karst caves on the beautiful two-hour tour. Boats seat two passengers (and have no shade). Prepare yourself for pushy vendors.

The **Van Long Nature Reserve** (entry 20,000d, boat 60,000d; ⏲7am-5pm), 19km from town, offers more rowboat rides as well as glorious limestone scenery and reedy wetlands popular with birdwatchers.

Trips to all the above sights are offered by tour operators in Ninh Binh and Hanoi.

Cuc Phuong National Park

One of Vietnam's most important protected areas, **Cuc Phuong** (☎091 566 6916, 0229-384 8018; www.cucphuongtourism.com.vn; adult/child 60,000/30,000d) spans two limestone mountain ranges and three provinces. In 1962 Ho Chi Minh declared this Vietnam's first national park, saying: 'Forest is gold'. Wildlife is notoriously elusive, so manage your expectations accordingly.

The park is home to the minority Muong people, whom the government relocated from the park's central valley to its western edge in the late 1980s.

Sights & Activities

Cuc Phuong offers excellent **hiking**. Short walks include a 220-step trail up to the **Cave of Prehistoric Man**. Human graves and tools found here date back 7500 years, making it one of Vietnam's oldest sites of human habitation.

Popular hikes include a 6km-return walk to the massive 1000-year-old **'old tree'** *(Tetrameles nudiflora)*, and a longer four-hour (around 12km) walk to **Silver Cloud Peak**.

A guide is recommended for day trips and is mandatory for longer treks. See the park's website for other one-day and overnight options.

Endangered Primate Rescue Center WILDLIFE RESERVE
(☎0229-384 8002; www.eprc.asia; 30,000d; ⏲9-11am & 1.30-4pm) The Endangered Primate Rescue Center is supervised by the Frankfurt Zoological Society, and is home to around 180 primates (15 species in total), including 12 kinds of langur, plus three species of gibbon and two loris. All the centre's animals were either bred here or rescued from illegal traders. Tours with a nature-conservation focus are on offer. Volunteers (experience not necessary, just enthusiasm) are encouraged to get in touch; tasks include preparing animal feed and cleaning enclosures. Your entry ticket also allows access to the Turtle Conservation Center.

Turtle Conservation Center (TCC) WILDLIFE RESERVE
(☎024 7302 8389, 030 384 8090; www.asianturtleprogram.org; 30,000d; ⏲9-11am & 2-4.45pm) The Turtle Conservation Center houses more than 600 terrestrial, semiaquatic and aquatic turtles representing 19 of Vietnam's 25 native species. Many have been confiscated from smugglers who have been driven by demand from the domestic and Chinese markets – eating turtle is thought to aid longevity. Visitors can see turtles in tanks and incubators, as well as in ponds in near-wild settings. Signs in English about the endangered turtles are informative. Your entry ticket also allows access to the Endangered Primate Rescue Center.

Sleeping & Eating

There is accommodation in the **park headquarters** (s US$16-35, d US$27-50, stilt houses US$14, bungalows US$23), and at the **Cuc Phuong Resort** (☎030 384 8886; www.cucphuongresort.com; Dong Tam village; bungalows/villas from US$108/167, s/d from US$97; ❄@🛜🏊) nearby. It's advisable to book for weekends and public holidays.

You'll find simple restaurants and snack shops at the park headquarters and Mac Lake.

Getting There & Away

Cuc Phuong National Park is 45km west of Ninh Binh. A direct bus from Hanoi's Giap Bat southern bus station departs at 3pm, with a return bus to Hanoi at 9am. From Ninh Binh, catch a *xe om* or taxi to the park.

Hanoi tour companies offer trips to Cuc Phuong, usually combined with other sights in the Ninh Binh area.

NORTHERN VIETNAM

Vistas. This is Vietnam's big-sky country; a place of rippling mountains, cascading rice terraces and the winnowed-out karst topography for which the region is famed.

Halong Bay's seascape of limestone towers is the view everyone's here to see, but the karst connection continues inland, to Ba Be National Park, until it segues into the evergreen hills of the northwest highlands.

Not to be outdone by the scenery, northern Vietnam's cultural kaleidoscope is just as diverse. In this heartland of hill-tribe culture, villages snuggle between paddy-field patchworks outside of Sapa, and the scarlet headdresses of the Dzao and the indigo fabrics of the Black Hmong add dizzying colour to chaotic highland markets.

The twisting roads winding north from Hanoi reveal a rural world far removed from Vietnam's big-city streets. If you're up for some rural road tripping or a motorbike adventure, this is the region for you.

Halong Bay

Majestic and mysterious, inspiring and imperious, Halong Bay's 3000 or more incredible islands rise from the emerald waters of the Gulf of Tonkin. This mystical seascape of limestone islets is a vision of breathtaking beauty.

Halong City

POP 221,580 / ☎0203

Halong City (Bai Chay) is primarily a transit point. Despite enjoying a stunning position on the cusp of Halong Bay, where its high-rise hotel developments dot the shoreline, most travelers opt to skip Halong City, preferring to spend a night out in the bay itself or to head straight to Cat Ba Island, which is far less commercialised. If you're here, however, **Sunworld** (☎0203-223 8888; www.halongcomplex.sunworld.vn/en; Đ Halong; cable car adult/child 350,000/250,000d; ⏲2-10pm Mon-Fri, 9am-10pm Sat & Sun) cable car is worth a trip for the dramatic bay view.

DON'T MISS

CRUISING THE KARSTS OF HALONG BAY

The most popular way to experience Halong Bay's karst scenery is on a cruise. It can be a false economy to sign up for an ultracheap tour. Spend a little more and enjoy the experience a whole lot more. At the very least, check basic on-board safety standards. Life jackets should be provided.

Most cruise-tours include return transport from Hanoi, Halong Bay entrance fees and meals. A decent overnight tour usually includes kayaking with a guide. Drinks and even water are extra, payable in cash only.

Tours sold out of Hanoi start from a rock-bottom US$60 per person for a dodgy day trip, and can rise to around US$220 for two nights. For around US$110 to US$130, you should get a worthwhile overnight cruise, though you need more time to stray far from Halong City.

Cruising the karsts aboard a luxury Chinese-style junk is hard to beat. But be aware that paying top dollar doesn't necessarily mean you'll head away from the crowds. If you want to experience less-crowded karst views, consider cruises focussed on Lan Ha Bay, near Cat Ba Island. These operators are recommended:

Handspan Adventure Travel (p67) Operates the only true sailing ship on the bay.

Indochina Sails (☎0982 042 426; www.indochinasails.com) Cruise Halong on a traditional junk with great viewing decks and cabins kitted out to a three-star standard.

Vega Travel (p66) Good-value overnight tours of Halong Bay, with comfortable cabins. Two-night tours also explore Lan Ha Bay and Cat Ba Island, including kayaking, cycling and hiking.

Activities

Boat Day Trips BOATING

(Đ Halong; 100,000-150,000d; ⏲7am-6pm) From Tuan Chau Pier two types of boat day trips head around Halong Bay's islands and caves, but they are aimed squarely at Vietnamese tourists, so expect lots of ear-splitting karaoke. Choose between a four-hour or six-hour tour. Admission costs to the national-park attractions not included.

Sleeping

★Light Hotel HOTEL $

(☎0203-384 8518; www.thelighthalong.vn; 108a Đ Vuon Dao; r incl breakfast 220,000-400,000d; ❄📶) The good-sized, modern and super-clean rooms here are excellent value, especially the spacious triples with one large and one small bed. Chuck in the fact that the extremely helpful staff speak English and you've got Halong City's best budget find. Laundry service and motorbike rental available.

Novotel HOTEL $$$

(☎0203-384 8108; www.novotelhalongbay.com; 160 Đ Halong; r US$74-120; 🅿❄@📶🏊) The Novotel fuses Asian influences with contemporary details, resulting in stunning rooms with teak floors, marble bathrooms and sliding screens to divide living areas. Facilities include an oval infinity pool and a good restaurant. It's a great place to start or finish a top-end cruise.

Getting There & Away

All buses leave from Bai Chay bus station, 6km south of central Bai Chay. Destinations include Hanoi (120,000d, frequent, three hours) and Ninh Binh (120,000d, frequent, four hours).

Note that many buses to Halong City will be marked 'Bai Chay' rather than 'Halong City'.

Cat Ba Island

POP 13,500 / ☎0225

Rugged, craggy and jungle-clad Cat Ba, the largest island in Halong Bay, has experienced a tourism surge in recent years. The central hub of Cat Ba Town is now framed by a chain of concrete hotels along its once-lovely bay, but the rest of the island is largely untouched and as wild as ever. With idyllic Lan Ha Bay just offshore you'll soon overlook Cat Ba Town's overdevelopment.

Almost half of Cat Ba Island (with a total area of 354 sq km) and 90 sq km of the adjacent waters were declared a national park in 1986 to protect the island's diverse ecosystems. Most of the coastline consists of rocky cliffs, but there are some sandy beaches and tiny fishing villages hidden away in small coves.

> **WORTH A TRIP**
>
> **BAI TU LONG BAY**
>
> The spectacular islands of Bai Tu Long Bay, immediately northeast of Halong Bay, form **Bai Tu Long National Park** and are every bit as beautiful as its famous neighbour. In some ways it's actually more stunning, since it's only in its initial stages as a destination for travellers. The bay and its islands are still unpolluted and relatively undeveloped. As with Halong Bay, the best way to experience the full limestone-pinnacle-scattered seascape is by cruise.
>
> Hanoi travel agencies, including Vega Travel (p66) and Ethnic Travel (p66), run boat trips into the Bai Tu Long from US$120.

Sights

★Lan Ha Bay BAY

(40,000d) Lying south and east of Cat Ba Town, the 300-or-so karst islands and limestone outcrops of Lan Ha are just as beautiful as those of Halong Bay but feel more isolated and untouched, and have the additional attraction of numerous white-sand beaches. Sailing and kayak trips here are easily organised in Cat Ba Town.

★Cannon Fort HISTORIC SITE

(40,000d; ⏲sunrise-sunset) For one of the best views in Vietnam, head to Cannon Fort, where there are astounding panoramas of Cat Ba Island's jungle-clad hills, the harbour and the karst-punctuated sea. The entrance gate is a steep 10-minute walk from Cat Ba Town, and it's then another stiff 20-minute walk to the fort, or take a *xe om* from town (15,000d). Well-labelled paths guide visitors past underground tunnels and two well-preserved gun emplacements.

Cat Ba National Park NATIONAL PARK

(☎0225-216 350; 80,000d; ⏲sunrise-sunset) Cat Ba's beautiful national park is home to 32 species of mammal, including most of the world's 65 remaining golden-headed langurs, the world's most endangered primate.

There are some good hiking trails here, including a two-hour return trip to Ngu Lam peak and a day-long hike to Viet Hai village. To reach the roadside **park headquarters** at Trung Trang, hop on the Song Tung bus from Cat Ba Town, or hire a *xe om* (around 80,000d one way) or a car (US$30 return).

Hospital Cave HISTORIC SITE
(40,000d; ⌚8am-5pm) Hospital Cave served both as a secret bomb-proof hospital during the American War and as a safe house for Viet Cong (VC) leaders. Built between 1963 and 1965 (with assistance from China), this incredibly well-constructed three-storey feat of engineering was in constant use until 1975.

The cave is about 10km north of Cat Ba Town, on the road to Cat Ba National Park entrance.

Activities

Cat Ba is a superb base for adventure sports – on the island, and in, on and over the water.

Mountain Biking

A few hotels can arrange bicycles for around US$6 per day. Blue Swimmer offers better-quality mountain bikes for US$15 per day.

One possible bicycle (or motorbike) route traverses the heart of the island, past Hospital Cave and the entrance to Cat Ba National Park, down to the west coast's mangroves and crab farms, and then in a loop back to Cat Ba Town past tidal mud flats and deserted beaches. Figure on half a day with stops for the 32km cycle.

Rock Climbing

If you've ever been tempted to climb, Cat Ba Island and Lan Ha Bay are superb places to go for it – the karst cliffs here offer exceptional climbing amid stunning scenery. The limestone is not too sharp and quite friendly on the hands, and climbing is almost always possible, rain or shine.

Experienced operator **Langur's Adventures** (☎0225-388 7789; www.langursadventures.com; Đ 1-4; ⌚8am-9pm) offers half-day climbing trips including instruction and gear starting at US$39 per person.

Sailing & Kayaking

Kayaking among the karsts is one of the highlights of Lan Ha Bay and most cruises offer an hour's paddling through limestone grottoes or to a floating village in the bay.

Due to shifting, strong currents, more intrepid exploring is best done with a guide, particularly if you're not an experienced kayaker.

Plenty of places have kayaks for hire (half-day around US$8) that are ideal for exploring the coastline independently; guided kayak trips cost from US$29; check out **Cat Ba Kayak Adventures** (☎0976 713 082; www.catbakayakadventures.com; Cai Beo; kayak rental single/double US$35/45).

Trekking

Most of Cat Ba Island consists of protected tropical forest. Cat Ba National Park has the most hiking opportunities.

Tours

Boat trips around Lan Ha Bay are offered by nearly every hotel on Cat Ba Island. Typical prices start at around US$25/80 for a day/overnight tour that takes in some swimming, kayaking and a visit to Monkey Island. A two-day trip allows you to get to the remoter, less-visited islands and hidden beaches of northern Lan Ha Bay.

★**Cat Ba Ventures** ADVENTURE
(☎0912 467 016, 0225-388 8755; www.catbaventures.com; 223 Đ 1-4, Cat Ba Town; overnight boat tour per person from US$136; ⌚7.30am-8pm) Locally owned and operated company offering boat trips around Lan Ha and Halong Bays, one-day kayaking trips (US$29) and guided hikes in Cat Ba National Park (US$18 to US$29). Excellent service from Mr Tung is reinforced by multiple reader recommendations.

Blue Swimmer ADVENTURE
(☎0225-368 8237, 0915 063 737; www.blueswimmersailing.com; Ben Beo Harbour; overnight sailing trip per person from US$190; ⌚8am-8pm) This environmentally conscious outfit was established by Vinh, one of the founders of respected tour operator Handspan Adventure Travel (p67). Superb sailing and kayaking trips, and trekking and mountain-biking excursions (some with overnight homestay accommodation), are offered. Enquire at the office just before Ben Beo Harbour.

Sleeping

Most basic hotels are clustered on (or just off) the waterfront in Cat Ba Town. There are also some interesting options on other parts of Cat Ba Island and offshore on isolated islands in Lan Ha Bay.

Room rates fluctuate wildly; from June to August they can double.

Cat Ba Town

Most basic hotels are clustered on (or just off) the waterfront in Cat Ba Town. Nearby Đ Nui Ngoc lacks the views but is quieter, with good-value accommodation

Central Backpackers Hostel HOSTEL $
(0225-627 4888; www.centralbackpackershostel.com; Dap Nuoc Lake; dm 117,500d, r 423,000d;) One of a new breed of modern hostels, this well-run and spotlessly clean place on the western edge of town has dorms and a few comfortable private rooms. The garden area and small pool provide a social hub, or take the evening shuttle bus to party in town (returning at 1am).

Cat Ba Tropicana Homestay GUESTHOUSE $
(0938 934 338; 21 Alley 1, Đ Nui Ngoc; r US$13;) Clean, good-value rooms and a quiet but central location away from the busy coastal strip are a great start, but what really elevates this place is the unbelievably helpful owner Tien, who can arrange anything from bus tickets and motorbike rental to cruises.

Thu Ha HOTEL $
(0225-388 8343; www.thuhahotel.com; 205 Đ 1-4; s/d 250,000/300,000d;) This small family-run place has basically furnished, clean rooms, some boasting four beds (600,000d). Negotiate hard for a front room and wake up to sea views; otherwise, head to the 11th-floor shared balcony.

Sea Pearl Hotel HOTEL $$
(0225-368 8567; www.seapearlcatbahotel.com.vn; 219 Đ 1-4; r incl breakfast 600,000-1,000,000d; @) The Sea Pearl is a solid if somewhat old-fashioned choice. Deluxe rooms are comfortable and spacious and have fine bay views (standard rooms are smaller with no view), and staff are professional and helpful. Views from the 13th-floor Sky Bar and pool are excellent.

Hung Long Harbour Hotel HOTEL $$
(0225-626 9269; www.hunglonghotel.vn; 268 Đ 1-4; r 900,000-1,500,000d;) At the quieter southeastern end of Cat Ba Town, the towering, three-star Hung Long Harbour has spacious rooms, many with excellent harbour views. Don't bother upgrading to a superior room, as the standards are the ones with balconies.

Around Cat Ba Island

Woodstock Beach Camp HOTEL $
(0225-388 599; www.facebook.com/woodstockbeachcamp; Phu Cuong; dm 80,000-150,000d, tr/q 350,000/400,000d;) As the name might suggest, basic Woodstock has some dirt under its fingernails, but if you want a uniquely old-school hippie backpacker crash pad, there's no better place. Dorm beds can be as simple as a mattress on the balcony or a tent on the beach, but there are a few air-con-cooled rooms in the main structure.

It's located on the main road, 9km west of Cat Ba Town, with a free daily shuttle into town.

Cat Ba Sunrise RESORT $$$
(0225-388 7360; www.catbasunriseresort.com; Cat Co 3; r US$95-108; @) This beachfront resort is tastefully planned, with low-rise, tiled-roofed blocks sitting below green cliffs. The rooms are relatively spacious and smart (more expensive rooms come with sea-view balconies), but the real highlights are the beachside facilities, including a swimming pool and beach bar.

Eating & Drinking

You can't beat the ambience factor for feasting on seafood at a floating restaurant. For a cheap feed, head to the food stalls in front of the market.

★ **Casa Bonita** INTERNATIONAL $
(www.facebook.com/casabonita.vn; 82 Đ Nui Ngọc; meals from 85,000d; 7am-11pm;) This is one of our Cat Ba favourites for its combination of good service, tasty mains (try the seafood curry or fish in a clay pot), lighter options such as the chicken, avocado and mango salad, plenty of vegetarian and vegan choices, and a lovely rooftop garden. Start the day right with a smoothie bowl with house-made granola.

Little Leaf INTERNATIONAL $
(91 Đ Nui Ngoc; meals 70,000-120,000d; 7am-11pm;) Attentive service and smart decor, set around a central cafe counter, are the draws here, with tasty Chinese-style dishes (try the braised mushroom and pepper) and Vietnamese-style grilled fish with lemongrass and chilli, plus crunchy *banh mi* for lunch and sweet mango crêpes for dessert.

Yummy 2 INTERNATIONAL $

(7 Đ Nui Ngoc; meals 40,000-80,000d; 8am-10pm;) This backpacker-oriented family restaurant serves a menu of pan-Asian dishes – think Indian curries, pad thai and Vietnamese standards. Not exceptional, but capable and convenient. There's a more ramshackle **branch** (www.facebook.com/yummycatba; meals 40,000-80,000d; 8am-10pm) a block nearer to the sea, serving an identical menu.

Vien Duong SEAFOOD $$

(12 Đ Nui Ngoc; meals 150,000-200,000d; 11am-11pm) Justifiably one of the most popular of the seafood spots lining Đ Nui Ngoc, and often heaving with Vietnamese tourists diving into local crab, squid and steaming seafood hotpots. Definitely not the place to come if you're looking for a quiet night.

Bigman BAR

(www.facebook.com/thebigmanbar; Noble House, Đ 1-4; noon-late;) This bar has a real vibe and goes until late most nights, making it probably the most popular nightspot in town. It comes fully equipped with pool tables and harbour views.

Information

For tourist information, Cat Ba Ventures (p74) is helpful. Most hotels and travel agencies sell bus tickets to Hanoi.

Getting There & Away

There are reduced services on many routes in the low season (November to February/March).

Haiphong-bound **hydrofoils** depart Cat Ba Town Pier at 10am and 2pm (180,000d, one hour). Buses are more frequent, running direct every hour or so from Cat Ba to Haiphong (100,000d, two hours) from the square in front of Cat Ba pier.

Companies such as **Daiichi Travel** (www.daiichitravel.com; 19 Đ Nui Ngoc), **Cat Ba Discovery** (0988 558 392; www.catbadiscovery.com; 5 Tung Dinh), **Good Morning Cat Ba** (www.goodmorningcatba.com) and **Cat Ba Express** (www.catbaexpress.com) each offer four or five comfortable direct services from Hanoi's Old Quarter (four hours, between 7.30am and 4pm) a day, making this the easiest way to get to/from Cat Ba. Coming from Hanoi the companies will pick you up anywhere in the Old Quarter. Fares vary from 200,000d to 270,000d, depending on the season. Your hotel in Cat Ba can book any of these.

Daiichi and Cat Ba Discovery offer sleeper-bus connections to other destinations in Vietnam, including Ninh Binh (250,000d, 8am, 9am, 12.30pm and 4pm, five hours), Sapa (450,000d, 8am and 4pm, 11 hours), Ha Giang (400,000d, 4pm, 12 hours) and Hue (450,000d, 4pm, 16 hours).

Getting Around

Bicycle and motorbike hire (both around 150,000d per day) are available from most Cat Ba hotels.

Haiphong

POP 2 MILLION / 0225

Northern Vietnam's most approachable city centre has a distinctly laid-back air, with its tree-lined boulevards host to a bundle of graceful colonial-era buildings. The central area buzzes with dinky cafes where tables spill out onto the pavements – perfect for people-watching. Most travellers only use Haiphong as a transport hop between the bus from Hanoi and the ferry to Cat Ba Island.

Sleeping

May Hostel HOSTEL $

(0866 777 436; www.facebook.com/may.hostel; 35 P Le Dai Hanh; dm 160,000d;) This modern hostel hits all the right notes, with a central location, a good rooftop bar, gated motorcycle parking and everything you need from a dorm bed – from bathrooms and air-con in the rooms to plugs and lights by each bed. Prices fluctuate throughout the week by 40,000d or so, peaking on Saturday.

Eating & Drinking

★ **Nam Giao** VIETNAMESE $$

(22 P Le Dai Hanh; meals from 180,000d; 8am-11pm) Haiphong's most atmospheric dining choice is hidden within this colonial building. Rooms are an artful clutter of Asian art, old carved cabinets and antiques, with a cool bar area, while the small but well-executed menu includes a tangy sea bass in a passion-fruit sauce and a succulent caramelised pork belly cooked in a clay pot.

★ **Haiphong Brewery Beer Club** BEER HALL

(16 Đ Lach Tray; 10am-10pm) Picture an open-air German beer hall with a rowdier crowd, and you've got the vibe of this fun venue. Couple the surprisingly tasty draught brews (7000d to 25,000d; try the Amber Ale) with a menu of Vietnamese drinking snacks, and remember that *tuoi* means 'draught' in Vietnamese.

Getting There & Away

Cat Bi International Airport (☎0225-397 6408; www.haiphongairport.com; Đ Le Hong Phong) is 6km southeast of central Haiphong; a taxi to the centre is around 80,000d. Bamboo Airways, Jetstar, Vietnam Airlines and the largest carrier at Cat Bi, VietJet, offer flights to most cities in central and southern Vietnam. International destinations include Bangkok, Kunming, Seoul and Shenzhen.

Boats to Cat Ba (180,000d, one hour) depart from Haiphong's **Ben Binh Pier** (Đ Ben Binh) at 9am and 1pm, arriving at Cat Ba Town Pier. The frequency of boat departures increases from May to August.

Haiphong has three long-distance bus stations, but **Lac Long Bus Station** (P Cu Chinh Lan), the closest to Haiphong city centre, has departures for most destinations. Buses to Hanoi's Giap Bat station (100,000d, two hours) leave frequently.

The exception is buses to Cat Ba (100,000d, two hours), which depart from nearby Đ Ben Binh. **Cat Ba Travel** (☎0769 206 069; Đ Ben Binh) and **Hadeco** (☎0912 810 555; www.hadeco.vn; Đ Ben Binh) each have a half-dozen departures between 6am and 4pm.

A spur-line service travels three times daily between **Haiphong Train Station** and Hanoi's Long Bien station (75,000d to 85,000d, 2½ to 3½ hours, 9.05am, 3pm and 6.40pm). Some trains continue to Hanoi's central train station.

Ba Be National Park

Boasting mountains high, rivers deep, and waterfalls, lakes and caves, **Ba Be National Park** (☎0281-389 4721; entry 46,000d; ⏰5am-9pm) is an incredibly scenic spot. The region is surrounded by steep peaks (up to 1554m), while the park contains tropical rainforest with hundreds of plant species. Wildlife in the forest includes bears, monkeys, bats and lots of butterflies. The region is home to 13 tribal villages, most belonging to the Tay minority, who live in stilt homes, plus smaller numbers of Dzao and Hmong.

Often referred to as the Ba Be Lakes, Ba Be National Park was established in 1992 as Vietnam's eighth national park. The scenery here swoops from towering limestone mountains down into plunging valleys wrapped in dense evergreen forests, speckled with waterfalls and caves, with the lakes themselves dominating the very heart of the park.

The park entrance fee is payable at a checkpoint about 15km before the park headquarters, just past the town of Cho Ra.

Ba Be (meaning Three Bays) is in fact three linked lakes, which have a total length of 8km and a width of about 400m. More than a hundred species of freshwater fish inhabit the lake. Two of the lakes are separated by a 100m-wide strip of water called Be Kam, sandwiched between high walls of chalk rock.

The park is a rainforest area with more than 550 named plant species, and the government subsidises the villagers not to cut down the trees. The hundreds of wildlife species here include 65 (mostly rarely seen) mammals, 353 butterflies, 106 species of fish, four kinds of turtle, the highly endangered Vietnamese salamander and even the Burmese python. Ba Be bird life is equally prolific, with 233 species recorded, including the spectacular crested serpent eagle and the oriental honey buzzard. Hunting is forbidden, but villagers are permitted to fish.

Most travellers come to Ba Be on prearranged private tours organised through Hanoi-based travel agencies. But the enthusiastic local **tourist office** (☎0209-389 4721; www.babenationalpark.com.vn; Bo Lu village) can arrange kayaking, boating, hiking and cycling trips (or a combo of all four) that work out at around US$50 per day. Multiday treks (from $83 for two days) and camping trips are offered too.

Homestays in Pac Ngoi village are very popular with travellers; there's also accommodation near the national-park entrance. **Mr Linh's Homestay** (☎0209-389 4894, 0989 587 400; www.mrlinhhomestay.com; Coc Toc village; dm US$8, r with shared bathroom US$25-30, r US$30-40; ❄📶) in Coc Toc village is a step up from most and has kayaks for hire.

Getting There & Away

Ba Be National Park is 240km from Hanoi, 61km from Bac Kan and 18km from Cho Ra.

Most people visit Ba Be as part of a tour, or by chartered vehicle from Hanoi (a 4WD is not necessary).

Mai Chau

POP 12,000 / ☎0218

Set in an idyllic valley, hemmed in by misty mountains, the Mai Chau area is a world away from Hanoi's hustle. Here the rural soundtrack is defined by gurgling irrigation streams and birdsong.

Dozens of local families have signed up to a highly successful homestay initiative, and for visitors the chance to sleep in a traditional stilt house has real appeal – though note that the villages are on the tour-group agenda.

The villagers are mostly White Thai. Most no longer wear traditional dress, but the women are masterful weavers, producing plenty of traditional-style textiles. Locals do not employ strong-arm sales tactics here: polite bargaining is the norm.

Mai Chau is an extremely popular weekend getaway for locals from Hanoi; try to come midweek if possible.

Sights & Activities

Most visitors come simply to stroll (or cycle) the paths through the rice fields to the surrounding villages. Homestays rent bikes to explore the valley at your own pace.

Many hotels offer guided day-hiking options that take you by motorbike to **Pa Co market** (6-10am Sun) or southeast to Pu Luong Nature Reserve to spend a half-day exploring rural paths and remote villages.

Many travel agencies in Hanoi run inexpensive trips to Mai Chau.

Sleeping

Most visitors stay in **Thai stilt houses** (Lac village; per person 100,000-250,000d) in the villages of Lac or Pom Coong. All homestays have electricity, running water, hot showers, mosquito nets and roll-up mattresses.

★ **Little Mai Chau Homestay** GUESTHOUSE $
(0973 849 006; littlemaichauhomestay@gmail.com; Na Phon village; dm 100,000d, r 300,000-500,000d) It's hard to beat this collection of thatched bamboo bungalows, backing onto karst cliffs, with balconies overlooking the paddy fields, 2km west of Mai Chau. The secluded family bungalow in particular is perfect for couples. It's very well set up, with free bicycles, motorbike rental (150,000d per day) and sociable shared dinners (80,000d). Owner Heung speaks English and can arrange anything.

★ **Mai Chau Eco Lodge** RESORT $$$
(0218-381 9888; www.maichau.ecolodge.asia; Na Thia village; bungalows incl breakfast 2,900,000-3,430,000d) Located on a slight hill surveying the surrounding rice fields is this village-like compound. Step inside the thatched-roof bungalows and you'll find they're both modern and rustic, with attractive tiled floors, local design touches and attempts to recycle water and use solar electricity. Easily the most sophisticated place to stay in the area, so book ahead.

Getting There & Around

Direct buses to Mai Chau (90,000d, 3¾ hours) leave Hanoi's My Dinh Bus Station (p67) at 6am, 8.30am and 11am. You'll be dropped off at the crossroads, just a short stroll from Lac village.

To Hanoi and Hoa Binh (50,000d, two hours), buses leave from along Hwy 15 every hour or so until 5pm. One limousine minivan (US$12) runs directly to Hanoi's Old Quarter at 3.30pm. **Thai's Travel Bus** (0972 058 696; www.thaitravelbus.com) operates a daily tourist bus to Ninh Binh/Tam Coc (285,000d, 3½ hours) at 8.30am. Homestay owners can book these and arrange for you to be picked up from your guesthouse.

For Son La or Dien Bien Phu you'll have to take a *xe om* to the main road, 5km north, and flag down a through bus.

Several guesthouses rent out bicycles for free; others charge 40,000d per day.

Lao Cai

POP 98,360 / 0214

For travellers, Lao Cai is the jumping-off point when journeying between Hanoi and Sapa by train, and a stopover when heading further north to Kunming in China. The bustling town is squeezed right next to the Vietnam–China border.

Around the train station there are ATMs, hotels, and restaurants with free wi-fi that run as one-stop traveller shops selling train tickets, cheap beds and drinks while you wait for your next ride.

Getting There & Around

TRAIN

There are two daily services (seat/berth from 150,000/385,000d, eight hours) to Hanoi (Station B) from Lao Cai. Luxury cabins are also operated on these trains by private companies such as **Livitrans** (www.livitrans.com), **Oriental Express** (www.orienttrainticket.com) and **Victoria Express** (www.victoriahotels.asia).

It's possible to transport your motorbike on the train as freight. You'll need to buy a ticket (around 240,000d, depending on the size of bike), fill out a form, show the bike's blue ownership card and get a receipt. Staff will drain your bike of fuel.

GETTING TO CHINA: LAO CAI TO KUNMING

Getting to the border The Chinese border at the Lao Cai/Hekou crossing is about 3km from Lao Cai train station, a journey done by *xe om* (around 25,000d) or taxi (around 50,000d).

At the border The border is open daily between 7am and 10pm Vietnam time. China is one hour ahead of Vietnam. You'll need to have a prearranged visa for China. China is separated from Vietnam by a road bridge and a separate rail bridge over the Song Hong (Red River). Note that travellers have reported Chinese officials confiscating *Lonely Planet China* guides at this border, so you may want to try masking the cover or take a PDF. Be wary of getting short-changed by black-market currency traders, especially on the Chinese side. If you do need to change money, just make it a small amount.

Moving on The new Hekou bus station is around 6km from the border post. There are regular departures to Kunming, including sleeper buses that leave at around 7.30pm, getting into Kunming at around 7am. There are also four daily trains.

BUS & MINIBUS

Lao Cai's **inter-provincial bus station** (off Hwy 4E; ⏲24hr) is a whopping 10km southeast of town; a taxi there will cost about 150,000d. Most people avoid it by travelling direct to other destinations from Sapa. If you do head out there, destinations include the following:

Dien Bien Phu (200,000d to 250,000d, eight hours, four daily)

Ha Giang (130,000d, five to six hours, two daily)

Halong City (Bai Chay) (360,000d, 12 hours, three daily)

Hanoi (230,000d, 10 hours, frequent departures)

Yellow-and-red minibuses for Sapa (30,000d, 45 minutes) leave every 30 minutes between 5.10am and 6pm from the car park in front of Lao Cai train station.

Minibuses to Bac Ha (70,000d, 2½ hours) leave from the minibus terminal next to the Song Hong (Red River) bridge; there are seven daily services at 6.30am, 8.15am, 9am, 11.30am, noon, 2pm and 3pm.

Bac Ha

POP 7400 / ☎0214

Sleepy Bac Ha wakes up for the riot of colour and commerce that is its Sunday market, when the lanes fill with villagers who flock into town from the hills and valleys. Once the barter, buy and sell is done and the day-tripper tourist buses from Sapa have left, the town rolls over and goes back to bed for the rest of the week. If you can, overnight in Bac Ha on Saturday and get to the market early before the day trippers start arriving.

Despite being surrounded by countryside just as lush and interesting as Sapa's, Bac Ha has somehow flown under the radar as a trekking base. That's one reason we prefer it.

Sights & Activities

Beyond town lie several interesting markets; tour operators in Bac Ha can arrange day trips to surrounding markets in villages including **Coc Ly** (⏲8.30am-1.30pm Tue) (Tuesday), **Sin Cheng** (⏲5am-2pm Wed) (Wednesday), and **Lung Phin** (⏲6am-1pm Sun) (Sunday).

★**Bac Ha Market** MARKET

(off Đ Tran Bac; ⏲sunrise-2pm Sun) This Sunday market is Bac Ha's big draw. There's an increasing range of handicrafts for sale, but it's still pretty much a local affair. Bac Ha Market is a magnet for the local hill-tribe people, above all the exotically attired Flower Hmong.

Flower Hmong women wear several layers of dazzling clothing. These include an elaborate collar-meets-shawl that's pinned at the neck and an apron-style garment; both are made of tightly woven strips of multicoloured fabric, often with a frilly edge. Highly ornate cuffs and ankle fabrics are also part of their costume, as is a checked headscarf (often electric pink or lime green).

Vua Meo NOTABLE BUILDING

('Cat King' House; ĐT 153; 20,000d; ⏲7.30am-5pm) The outlandish Vua Meo, built in 1921 by the French to keep the Tay chief Hoang A Tuong happily ensconced in style, is a bizarre palace constructed in a kind of 'Eastern baroque' style on the northern edge of

OFF THE BEATEN TRACK

EXPLORING HA GIANG PROVINCE

Ha Giang province's secret is well and truly out of the bag, and visitor (and motorcycle) numbers running 'the Loop' via Dong Van have gone through the roof in the last few years. That said, there are plenty of quiet back roads and stunning corners to explore. The province is definitely best visited with your own wheels, as bus links are poor.

Ha Giang town is a provincial capital and the place to organise your trip to Dong Van, though there's little to keep you in the town itself. Check out **Vision Travel** (0902 093 223; www.visiontravelagent.com; 50 Đ Hai Ba Trung; 8am-8pm) for excellent motorbike and car tours (from US$57 per day with driver) and local information, while **QT Motorbikes & Tours** (0975 278 711, 0365-506 9696; www.qtmotorbikesandtours.com.vn; Lam Dong, Phuong Thien) offers reliable rental bikes. **Bong Hostel** (0888 526 606; www.bongbackpacker.com; 9a Nguyen Thai Hoc; dm/d 90,000/300,000d;) and **Huy Hoan Hotel** (0219-386 1288; www.huyhoanhotel.com; 395 Đ Nguyen Trai; r 350,000-600,000d;) are good cheap places to stay. From Ha Giang bus station there are buses to Hanoi (200,000d, six hours, eight daily) as well as connections to Sapa (from 200,000d, seven hours, three daily), Dong Van and Meo Vac.

North of Ha Giang town, it's 40km to the small town of **Tam Son**, which lies in a valley at the end of the **Quan Ba Pass**, one of the region's most dramatic sights. On Sundays there's a fascinating **market** in Tam Son with various ethnic minorities, including White Hmong, Red Dzao, Tay and Giay people.

Dong Van, tight by the Chinese border, is a popular overnight stop with solid accommodation and food choices. Here the excellent **Lam Tung Hotel** (0219-385 6789; lamtunghotel@gmail.com; Đ Vao Cho; r 350,000-450,000d;) overlooks the town's famous **Sunday market**, one of the region's biggest and most colourful. The town is also a fine base for day treks around nearby minority villages.

South of Dong Van the journey crosses the spectacular Mai Pi Leng Pass to charming **Meo Vac**. Here **Auberge de Meo Vac** (0219-387 1686; aubergemeovac@gmail.com; dm/r with shared bathroom 330,000/1,320,000d;) is very special indeed, a lovingly restored Hmong house dating from the 19th century. Heading south from Meo Vac, you'll soon pass the turn-off to Khau Vai and a high pass, before dropping to a new bridge across the Nho Que River at Na Phong (Ly Bon).

Around 75km from Meo Vac is the town of **Bao Lac**, with good accommodation options including **Song Gam Guesthouse** (0206 387 0269; Khu 11, Bao Lac; r 250,000-350,000d, VIP r 400,000d;). Heading on, buses pull through town every couple of hours to Cao Bang (100,000d, four hours). If you've your own wheels, it's worth stopping en route at the Mausoleum to Ho Chi Minh and the hanging valley above Tinh Tuc, and then the Dragon Back Panorama – the name given to a dramatic array of high karst peaks.

Bac Ha. There's not much to see, other than the architecture itself, but the ground floor has a shop selling excellent-quality embroideries and traditional clothes.

Ngan Nga Bac Ha HIKING
(0969 658 080; www.bachatrip.com; 117 Đ Ngoc Uyen; 8am-9pm) Inside the Ngan Nga Bac Ha Hotel, Mr Dong offers a great range of day hikes and longer treks with authentic village homestays. Figure on US$55/85 for one/two people for a two-day trek. He also rents out motorbikes (120,000d to 150,000d per day) and can organise trips to outlying markets.

Sleeping & Eating

Room rates tend to increase by about 20% on Saturday nights due to the Sunday market.

Ngan Nga Bac Ha Hotel HOTEL $
(0214-880 286; www.nganngabachahotel.com; 117 P Ngoc Uyen; r incl breakfast Mon-Fri 250,000-400,000d, Sat & Sun 460,000-690,000d;) Rooms here are a solid budget deal; they are a decent size and are decked out with a few homey touches, with a good ground-floor restaurant for a post-hike beer. Bag a room on the 4th floor and above for maximum natural light.

★**Huy Trung Homestay** GUESTHOUSE $$
(☎0979 776 288; huytrung@gmail.com; r 400,000-600,000d, ste 1,200,000d;) This well-designed place is clearly signposted in a residential district to the north of town and walkable from the centre. The five rooms are immaculate, and the secure parking, rooftop viewing platform, motorbike rental and seasonal plunge pool push the place into a league of its own. The three-bed family suite with balcony is the best room in town and a worthy splurge.

Hoang Yen Restaurant VIETNAMESE $
(Đ Tran Bac; meals 60,000-120,000d; 7am-10pm;) Hoang Yen's simple menu includes decent breakfast options and a set menu for 200,000d. Cheap beer is also available.

Information

There's an **Agribank** (P Ngoc Uyen; 8am-3pm Mon-Fri, to 11am Sat, ATM 24hr) with ATM

Getting There & Away

Tours to Bac Ha from Sapa cost around US$20 per person; on the way back you can bail out in Lao Cai and catch the night train or bus to Hanoi.

Bac Ha's **bus station** (P Na Lo) is out of the town centre, across the Na Co River. Sleeper buses run to Hanoi (300,000d, eight hours) at 7am, 12.30pm, 3pm and 8.30pm.

Minibuses to Lao Cai (70,000d, two hours) depart hourly from the square just south of the Ngan Nga Bac Ha Hotel until 4pm.

Sapa

POP 9000 / ☎0214 / ELEV 1650M

Established as a hill station by the French in 1922, Sapa today is the major tourism centre of the northwest. The town is oriented to make the most of the spectacular views emerging on clear days – it overlooks a plunging valley, with mountains towering above on all sides. If you were expecting a quaint alpine town, recalibrate your expectations. Modern tourism development has mushroomed chaotically in Sapa and much of the centre is under seemingly endless reconstruction.

Sapa is northern Vietnam's premier hiking base, but ugly development and over-tourism have blighted many parts of the surrounding countryside. But if you look hard enough there are still some sublime corners of traditional village architecture framed by golden terraced fields.

Sights

Surrounding Sapa are the Hoang Lien Mountains, including **Fansipan**, which at 3143m is Vietnam's highest peak. The trek from Sapa to the summit and back can take several days, although a new **cable car** (☎0214-381 8888; www.fansipanlegend.sunworld.vn; return adult/child 700,000/500,000d; 7am-4.30pm, last car from summit 6pm) to the summit and mountain-top shopping have changed the experience forever.

Some of the better-known sights around Sapa include the epic **Tram Ton Pass**; pretty **Thac Bac** (Silver Falls); and **Cau May** (Cloud Bridge), which spans the Muong Hoa River.

Sapa Museum MUSEUM
(103 P Cau May; 7.30-11.30am & 1.30-5pm) FREE An excellent showcase of the history and ethnology of the Sapa area, including the French colonial era. Dusty exhibitions overview the various ethnic groups around Sapa, with information on the region's rich handicrafts, so it's worth a quick visit when you first arrive in town. Located above a handicrafts shop behind the Tourist Information Center (p84).

Sapa Market MARKET
(Đ Ngu Chi Son; 6am-2pm) Turfed out of central Sapa and now in a purpose-built modern building near the bus station, Sapa Market is still interesting, and hill-tribe people from surrounding villages come here most days to sell handicrafts. Saturday is the busiest day.

Activities

For longer treks with overnight stays in villages, it's important to hook up with someone who knows the terrain and culture and speaks the language. We recommend using minority guides, as this offers them a means of making a living. Always go through a reputable tour agency.

★**Sapa O'Chau** HIKING
(☎0915 502 589; www.sapaochau.org; 3 Le Van Tam; 7.30am-6.30pm) Excellent local company offering day walks (from US$30 per person), longer homestay treks (around US$38 per day), Bac Ha market trips and Fansipan hikes. It also runs culturally immersive tours that focus on handicrafts and farmstays. Profits provide training to Hmong children in a learning centre.

Sapa

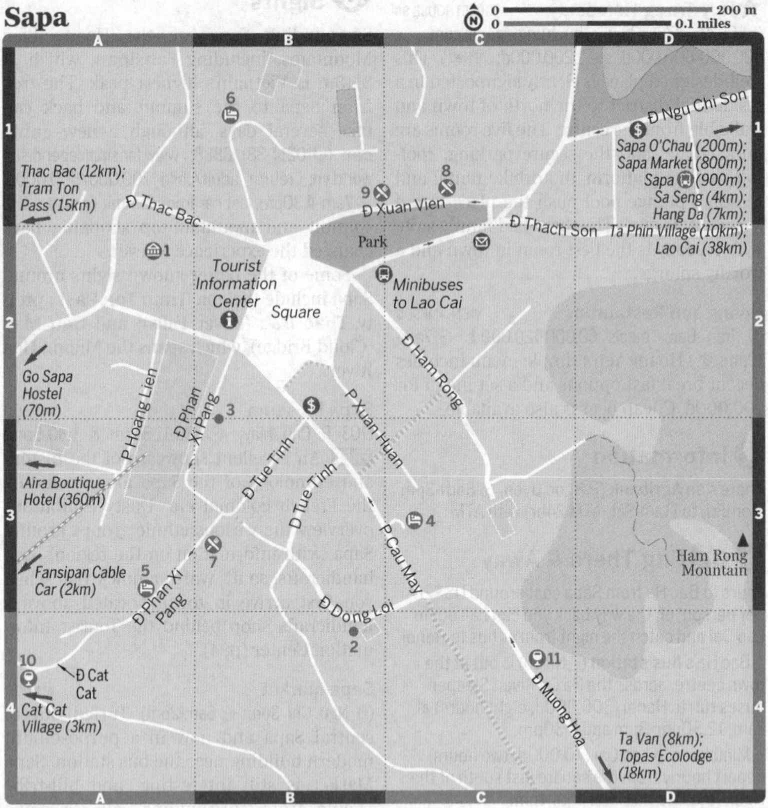

Sapa

Sights

1 Sapa Museum A2

Activities, Courses & Tours

2 Handspan Travel B4
3 Sapa Sisters B3

Sleeping

4 Auberge Hotel C3
5 Cat Cat View Hotel A3
6 Elegance Hotel B1

Eating

7 Hill Station Signature Restaurant B3
8 Hotpot & Roast Piglet Restaurants C1
9 Le Petit Gecko B1

Drinking & Nightlife

10 Cafe in the Clouds A4
11 Hmong Sisters C4

Shopping

Indigo Cat .... (see 5)

Sapa Sisters HIKING

(☎0214-377 3388; www.sapasisters.com; 9 Đ Phan Xi Pang; ⊙7am-5pm) Run by a group of savvy and knowledgeable Hmong women, Sapa Sisters offers customised private day hikes (from US$37 per person) and longer village homestay treks (from US$74), some staying in their Zao's House guesthouse in Ta Van. English and French are spoken.

Sleeping

Sapa O'Chau HOTEL $

(☎0214-387 1890; www.sapaochau.org; 3 Le Van Tam; dm US$6, r US$20-30; ❄📶) The hotel attached to the excellent tour agency (p81) exists to train locals in hotel management, so be patient. The best rooms enjoy spacious lake views and a small balcony, but even the six-bed dorms come with their own bathroom. Rates include breakfast on the rooftop, and staff rent out motorbikes. Sign up for a trek and you'll get a room discount.

Auberge Hotel HOTEL $
(☎0214-387 1243; www.aubergedangtrunghotel.com; 31 P Cau May; r incl breakfast US$15-35; 📶) An old-school yellow villa with porticos, terrace seating and a garden restaurant, the Auberge retains a vaguely colonial vibe. Rooms are comfortable but can be damp on the lower floors, so book an upper-floor or family room. It's close to the main strip but off the road, so quieter than most hotels.

Go Sapa Hostel HOSTEL $
(☎0214-871 198; www.gosapahostel.com; 25 Đ Thac Bac; dm 110,000-130,000d, r 300,000-360,000d; @📶) Up the hill from central Sapa, this well-run hostel has a multitude of six- and eight-bed dorms (with lockers) set around a communal courtyard and lots of pleasant sitting areas. The two private rooms come with their own terrace and are a great deal. Motorbike hire, bus tickets and laundry are available.

Elegance Hotel HOTEL $$
(☎0214-389 8868; www.sapaelegancehotel.com; 3 Hoang Dieu; r incl breakfast 500,000-800,000d; ❄📶) The spacious, well-furnished deluxe rooms with balcony here are one of the best deals in Sapa, especially given the perfect central location. Helpful staff can arrange bus tickets and motorbike rental, and the breakfast features deliciously crunchy baguettes. The cheapest old-block rooms in the separate villa-style back garden lack the views but are still pleasant.

Cat Cat View Hotel HOTEL $$
(☎0214-387 1946; www.catcathotel.com; 46 Đ Phan Xi Pang; r incl breakfast 500,000-1,000,000d, apt 2,000,000-3,600,000d; ❄@📶) There's plenty of choice at this rambling, family-run spot with comfortable pine-trimmed rooms over nine floors and two wings, with the upper floors opening out onto communal terracotta terraces and a restaurant. The spacious apartments are a great option for travelling families or groups of friends.

Aira Boutique Hotel HOTEL $$$
(☎0214-377 2268; www.airaboutiquesapa.com; 30 P Hoang Lien; r incl breakfast US$75-95; ❄📶🏊) Located at the edge of a cliff, and offering fantastic views of the valley below, is this fresh, modern hotel. Front-facing rooms with views are the most expensive, but all are decked out in rich chocolate-brown decor, with particularly inviting bathrooms and balconies attached to all but the cheapest rooms. Rates include afternoon tea.

Topas Ecolodge RESORT $$$
(☎0214-387 2404; www.topasecolodge.com; bungalows incl breakfast from US$235; 🏊) Overlooking a plunging valley 18km from Sapa, this resort has stone-and-thatch bungalows with front balconies to make the most of the truly breathtaking views. Bungalows don't have TVs, but a stunning infinity pool, and hiking, cycling and market tours are available.

Eating & Drinking

Hotpot & Roast Piglet Restaurants VIETNAMESE $
(Đ Xuan Vien; meals from 60,000d; ⏱11am-11pm) This strip is home to several similar places serving Vietnamese-style *lau* (hotpot; meat stew cooked with local vegetables, cabbage and mushroom) and roast piglet (a speciality of Sapa; look for the rotisserie grills).

★ **Hill Station Signature Restaurant** VIETNAMESE $$
(☎0214-388 7111; www.thehillstation.com; 37 Đ Phan Xi Pang; meals from 120,000d; ⏱11am-10pm; ❄📶🖉) A showcase of Hmong cuisine with cool Zen decor and superb views. Dishes include flash-cooked pork with lime, ash-baked trout in banana leaves, and traditional Hmong-style black pudding. Tasting sets of local rice and corn wine are also of interest to curious travelling foodies. Don't miss trying the delicate, raw rainbow-trout rice-paper rolls; think of them as 'Sapa sushi'.

Le Petit Gecko INTERNATIONAL $$
(15 Đ Xuan Vien; meals 90,000-150,000d; ⏱7am-10pm) A smaller, more intimate version of Le Gecko, just a few doors away, with cabana-style architecture and slightly cheaper prices for almost the same menu. There's more of an emphasis on Hmong dishes, such as grilled wild pork with cardamom and smoked buffalo, along with the same wonderful French-inspired desserts.

Cafe in the Clouds BEER GARDEN
(☎0214-377 1011; 60 Đ Phan Xi Pang; ⏱6am-11pm; 📶) The large upper terrace of this bar is a great corner of Sapa in which to pause and soak in the valley or, equally often, the wandering mist at eye level. Drinks are priced reasonably.

Hmong Sisters BAR
(0915 042 366; 31 Đ Muong Hoa; 4pm-1am;) With liquor sold by the bottle and shots by the metre (!), this is the place for serious late-night drinking. Earlier in the evening the spacious bar has a mellower vibe, with pool tables, an open fire and pretty decent music.

Shopping

Indigo Cat ARTS & CRAFTS
(www.indigocat.shop; 34 Đ Phan Xi Pang; 9am-9pm) This Hmong-owned, family-run handicrafts shop offers a wonderful selection of interesting local crafts, including bags, clothing, cushion covers, jewellery and a fun DIY embroidered-bracelet kit for children. Many items have hip design touches unique to the store and the set-price labels are a relief if you have haggling fatigue.

Information

There are ample ATMs in town. Sapa **tourist information center** (0214-387 3239; www.sapa-tourism.com; 103 Đ Xuan Vien; 7.30-11.30am & 1.30-5.30pm) has helpful English-speaking staff offering details of transport, trekking and weather. Head to **Handspan** (0214-387 2110; www.handspan.com; Chau Long Hotel, 24 Đ Dong Loi; 8am-8pm) for trekking and tours.

Getting There & Away

To Hanoi there are frequent sleeper buses (250,000d, six hours) between 7am and 10.30pm, as well as faster limousine vans (415,000d).

Minibuses to Lao Cai (Đ Ham Rong) Look for yellow-and-red buses with price lists in the window.

Sapa Bus Station (Đ Luong Dinh Cua) Sapa's bus station is northeast of the town centre, near the market.

Dien Bien Phu

POP 46,362 / 0215

It was in the surrounding countryside here, on 7 May 1954, that the French-colonial forces were defeated by the Viet Minh in a decisive battle, and the days of France's Indochina empire became numbered.

The town sits in the heart-shaped Muong Thanh Valley, surrounded by heavily forested hills. The scenery along the way here is stunning, with approach roads scything through thick forests and steep terrain. The city itself lies more prosaically on a broad dry plain, and boasts expansive boulevards and civic buildings. Previously just a minor settlement, DBP was elevated to provincial capital in 2004. It's a pleasant stop for fans of (predominantly French) military history or those heading to northern Laos.

Sights

There are numerous war memorials, bunkers, monuments and cemeteries around town.

A1 Hill MONUMENT
(Đ 7-5; 15,000d; 7-11am & 1.30-5.30pm) This vantage point was crucial in the battle of Dien Bien Phu. There are tanks and a monument to Viet Minh casualties on this former French position, known to the French as Eliane and to the Vietnamese as A1 Hill. The elaborate trenches at the heart of the French defences have also been recreated. Little background information is given on-site.

Dien Bien Phu Museum MUSEUM
(279 Đ 7-5; 15,000d; 7-11am & 1.30-6pm) This well-laid-out museum, contained in a space-agey modern structure, features an eclectic collection that commemorates the 1954 battle. Alongside weaponry and guns, there's a bathtub that belonged to the French commander Colonel de Castries, a bicycle capable of carrying 330kg of ordnance, and the testimony of Vietnamese who were there.

Bunker of Colonel de Castries MONUMENT
(off P Nguyen Huu Tho; 15,000d; 7-11am & 1.30-6pm) West of the Ron River, the dank command bunker of Colonel de Castries has been recreated, though there's little to actually see. A discarded tank and some mortar guns linger nearby. You might see Vietnamese tourists mounting the bunker and waving the Vietnamese flag, re-enacting an iconic photograph taken at the battle's conclusion.

Sleeping & Eating

Nam Ron Hotel HOTEL $
(0946 251 967; Đ Trang Dang Ninh; r 250,000-400,000d, VIP r 500,000d;) At the edge of the Ron River is this characterless but tidy place. By Vietnamese standards, the rooms feel tight (except for the spacious VIP rooms) but are functional and comfortable, and the VIP rooms come decked out with retro sofas. Motorbike rental is possible.

★Ruby Hotel HOTEL $$
(☎0913 655 793; www.rubyhoteldienbien.com; off P Nguyen Chi Thanh; r incl breakfast 560,000-900,000d; ❄☎) The best deal in Dien Bien Phu is this friendly hotel, down a quiet, riverside alleyway. The 31 rooms are comfortably fitted out with good beds, flat-screen TVs and bathrooms featuring rain showerheads. If you're travelling solo, treat yourself to a spacious double room as the singles are small. Online discounts of up to 50% make this a steal.

★Yen Ninh Vegetarian Restaurant VEGETARIAN $
(☎0989 887 513; www.dbpcity.wixsite.com/yenninh; 257 Group 9, Ton Thanh ward; meals 35,000-50,000d; ⊙8am-10pm; ☎✎) This is an unexpected find down a nondescript residential alley in the commercial northwest of town – a family home doubling as a bookshop that serves up light and fresh vegan food to a stream of grateful backpackers. Tuck into fresh spring rolls and banana mango smoothies, while the family goes about its daily business around you.

Ever-helpful English-speaking boss Yen also rents out motorbikes (half-day 80,000d).

Getting There & Away

DBP's **bus station** (Hwy 12) is at the corner of Đ Tran Dang Ninh. There are plentiful services heading south to Hanoi and there are early-morning services to destinations across the border into Laos.

Vietnam Airlines operates two flights daily between Dien Bien Phu and Hanoi. The office is near the airport, about 1.5km from the town centre, along the road to Muong Lay.

CENTRAL VIETNAM

The geographic heart of the nation, central Vietnam is packed with historic sights and cultural interest, and blessed with ravishing beaches and outstanding national parks.

Marvel at Hue and its imperial citadel, royal tombs and excellent street food. Savour the unique heritage grace of riverside jewel Hoi An, and tour the military sites of the Demilitarised Zone (DMZ). Check out Danang, fast emerging as one of the nation's most dynamic cities. Also established as a must-visit destination is the extraordinary Phong Nha region, home to gargantuan cave systems (including the world's largest cave), and a fascinating war history concealed amid stunning scenery.

With improving highways, and upgraded international airports at Hue and Danang, access to this compelling and diverse part of Vietnam has never been easier.

Phong Nha-Ke Bang National Park

☎0232

Designated a Unesco World Heritage Site in 2003, the remarkable **Phong Nha-Ke Bang National Park** (☎052 367 7021; www.phongnhakebang.vn/en) FREE contains the oldest karst mountains in Asia, formed approximately 400 million years ago. Riddled with hundreds of cave systems – many of extraordinary scale and length – and spectacular underground rivers, Phong Nha is a speleologists' heaven on earth.

Serious exploration only began in the 1990s, led by the British Cave Research Association and Hanoi University. Cavers first penetrated deep into Phong Nha Cave,

BUSES FROM DIEN BIEN PHU

DESTINATION	COST (D)	DURATION (HR)	FREQUENCY
Hanoi	255,000-345,000, VIP (9.30pm) 570,000	11½	7am, then frequent sleepers 4.30-9.30pm
Lai Chau	145,000	8	hourly 5am-4pm
Muong Lay	70,000	3	2.30pm & 4pm
Muong Te	150,000	6	7am & 8.15am
Sapa	230,000	8	6.30am, 9am & 11.30am, sleepers 5pm, 5.30pm & 6.30pm
Sin Ho	120,000	5	6.30am
Son La	110,000-120,000	4	9 departures 4.30am-2pm

one of the world's longest systems. In 2005 Paradise Cave was discovered, and in 2009 a team found the world's largest cave – Son Doong. In recent years access to several more cave systems has been approved.

The caves are the region's absolute highlights, but the above-ground attractions of forest trekking, the area's war history, and rural mountain biking means it deserves a stay of around three days.

The Phong Nha region is changing fast. Son Trach village (population 3000) is the main centre, with an ATM, a growing range of accommodation and eating options, and improving transport links with other parts of central Vietnam.

Sights

The Phong Nha region is exploding in popularity, and it's recommended that you book overnight caving tours in advance if possible.

Note that most of the adventure caves are closed during the wet season (around mid-September to either late November or late December).

In addition to the cave trips below, **Phong Nha Cave** (adult/child under 1.3m 150,000/25,000d, boat up to 14 people 320,000d; ⏲7am-5pm) is worth considering, a somewhat touristy, but enjoyable boat trip, while spectacular **Hang Va** (www.oxalis.com.vn; per person 8,000,000d; ⏲Feb-Aug) is a two-day expedition involving jungle camping.

★Tu Lan Cave CAVE
(www.oxalis.com.vn; 1-day tour per person 1,800,000d, 2-day tour per person 5,500,000d; ⏲mid-Nov–mid-Sep) Tu Lan cave trips begin with a countryside hike, then a swim (with headlamps and life jackets) through two spectacular river caves, before emerging in an idyllic valley. Then there's more hiking through dense forest to a 'beach' where rivers merge; this is an ideal campsite for the two-day tour. There's more wonderful swimming here in vast caverns. Moderate fitness levels are necessary. Tu Lan is 65km north of Son Trach and can only be visited on a guided tour.

★Hang Son Doong CAVE
(Mountain River Cave; ⏲Feb-Aug) Hang Son Doong (Mountain River Cave) is known as the world's largest cave, and is one of the most spectacular sights in Southeast Asia, with access only approved by the government in 2013. The sole specialist operator permitted to lead tours here is Son Trach-based Oxalis Adventure Tours. This is no day-trip destination; it's in an extremely remote area. You must book a four-day/three-night expedition with around 16 porters. It costs US$3000 per person, with a maximum of 10 trekkers on each trip.

★Paradise Cave CAVE
(Thien Dong; adult/child under 1.3m 250,000/125,000d; ⏲7.30am-4.30pm) Surrounded by forested karst peaks, this staggering cave system extends for 31km, though most people only visit the first kilometre. The scale is breathtaking, as wooden staircases plunge into a cathedral-like space with vast alien-looking stalagmites and stalactites. Get here early to beat the crowds, as during peak times (early afternoon) tour guides shepherd groups using megaphones. Paradise Cave is about 14km southwest of Son Trach. Electric buggies (per person one way/return 15,000/25,000d) ferry visitors from the car park to the entrance 1km away.

Hang En CAVE
(2-day tour per person 7,600,000d; ⏲late Dec–mid-Sep) This gigantic cave is very close to Hang Son Doong; both have been featured in a *National Geographic* photographic spread. Getting here involves a trek through dense jungle, valleys and the Ban Doong minority village, a very remote tribal settlement (with no electricity or roads). You stay overnight at a campsite in the cave or in a minority village. Tours can be booked via Oxalis Adventure Tours or local accommodation.

Hang Toi CAVE
(Dark Cave; per person 450,000d) Incorporating an above-water 400m-long zipline, followed by a swim into the cave and then exploration of a pitch-black passageway of oozing mud, it's little wonder Hang Toi is the cave experience you've probably already heard about from other travellers. Upon exiting the cave, a leisurely kayak paddle heads to a jetty where there are more into-the-water zipline thrills to be had. Don't take any valuables into the cave.

Tours

★Oxalis Adventure Tours ADVENTURE
(☎0232-367 7678; www.oxalis.com.vn; Son Trach; ⏲8am-noon & 1.30-7.30pm Mon-Sat, 10am-7.30pm Sun) Oxalis is unquestionably *the* expert in caving and trekking expeditions, and is the only outfit licensed to conduct tours to Hang

Son Doong. Staff are all fluent English-speakers, and trained by world-renowned British cavers Howard and Deb Limbert. All excursions, from day trips to Tu Lan Cave to four-night/three-day expeditions to the world's largest cave, are meticulously planned and employ local guides and porters.

★Phong Nha Farmstay Tours ADVENTURE
(☎0232-367 5135; www.phong-nha-cave.com; Cu Nam) Phong Nha Farmstay's very popular National Park Tour (per person 1,350,000d) incorporates the Ho Chi Minh Trail with Paradise Cave and Hang Toi; there's also the option of swimming in and exploring Tra Ang Cave. Ask about exciting, informative customised tours (per person 2,500,000d) in the farmstay's vintage army jeep. Guests at the farmstay also get free motorbike-sidecar jaunts.

★Jungle Boss Trekking HIKING
(☎0917 800 805; www.jungle-boss.com; Phong Nha village, Son Trach; per person from 1,350,000d) English-speaking Dzung ('Jungle Boss') is an experienced guide who runs one- and two-day tours around the Ho Chi Minh Trail and the Abandoned Valley area of the national park with a good team. An excellent option (requiring a moderate to strenuous fitness level) is exploring the remote Ma Da Valley, which includes a swim in the Tra Ang river cave and exploration of Elephant Cave.

Hai's Eco Tours HIKING
(☎0962 606 844; www.ecophongnha.com; Bamboo Cafe, Son Trach; per person adult/child under 10yr 1,450,000/1,100,000d) Rewarding day tours combine hiking in the jungle – you'll need to be relatively fit – with a visit to Phong Nha's Wildlife Rescue and Rehabilitation Centre, which rehabilitates rescued animals (mainly macaques from nearby regions, but also snakes and birds). Prices include a barbecue lunch, and there's an opportunity to cool off at the end of the day in a natural swimming hole.

Sleeping

Easy Tiger HOSTEL $
(☎0232-367 7844; www.easytigerhostel.com; Son Trach; dm from 120,000d; ❄@📶🏊) Son Trach town's first hostel, this very popular place has four- and six-bed dorms, the great **Jungle Bar** (Son Trach; ⏰7am-midnight; 📶), a pool table and excellent travel information. A swimming pool and beer garden make it ideal for relaxation after trekking and caving. Ask about the free morning talk, and free bicycles and app to explore the Bong Lai valley and surrounding region.

Central Backpackers Hostel HOSTEL $
(☎0232-6536 868; www.centralbackpackershostel.com; Son Trach; dm US$6, s/d/tr US$15/20/24; ❄📶🏊) The new kid on the block, in a new block, this place is a good-value addition to the town, with an appealing choice of clean and bright dorms, doubles and triples, an outside pool, friendly staff and free beer for an hour from 7pm.

★Phong Nha Farmstay GUESTHOUSE $$
(☎0232-367 5135; www.phong-nha-cave.com; Cu Nam; r 800,000-1,050,000d, f 2,000,000d; 🚭❄@📶🏊) The place that really put Phong Nha on the map, the relaxed Farmstay enjoys peaceful views overlooking an ocean of rice paddies. Rooms are smallish but neat, with high ceilings and shared balconies. The excellent bar-restaurant serves Asian and Western dishes, and there's a social vibe, with movies and live music several nights a week. Local tours are superb (with free sidecar rides).

Chay Lap Farmstay BUNGALOW $$
(☎0932 488 839; www.chaylapfarmstay.com; Chay Lap village; d from US$60; 🚭❄📶🏊) Accommodation in the leafy and peaceful grounds here includes an excellent variety of pleasant rooms and pine 'farmrooms' that are designed to float above floodwaters. A pool, an on-site herbal sauna and a decent restaurant and bar are welcome distractions after caving and hiking expeditions, and just a short walk away is the opportunity to kayak and paddleboard along the beautiful river at the farmstay's watersports centre.

Phong Nha Lake House Resort RESORT $$
(☎0232-367 5999; www.phongnhalakehouse.com; Khuong Ha; d US$42-60; ❄📶🏊) Owned by an Australian-Vietnamese couple, this impressive lakeside resort has excellent rooms and spacious, stylish villas. A pool and lake-view bungalows make it one of the area's most comfortable place to stay. The wooden restaurant is a traditional structure from Ha Giang province in northern Vietnam. Kayaking on the lake is included, staff are lovely and breakfast is good.

Pepper House GUESTHOUSE $$
(☎0918 745 950, 0167 873 1560; www.pepperhouse-homestay.com; Khuong Ha; d/f 950,000/1,300,000d; ❄📶🏊) Run by long-term Aussie expat Dave (aka 'Multi') and his Vietnamese wife Diem, this rural place has double rooms in attractive villas arrayed around a compact swimming pool. It's located 6km east of Son Trach en route to the Bong Lai valley. The pool is open to visitors for 50,000d (or if you purchase the same value in food and drink).

★**Victory Road Villas** VILLA $$$
(☎0232-367 5699; www.victoryroadvillas.com; 20 Victory Rd, Son Trach; villas from US$135; 🚭❄📶🏊) Effortlessly raising the bar for accommodation around Phong Nha, Victory Road Villas combines a riverside location with stunning Asian-chic decor, hip and modern bathrooms, stellar shared public spaces including an 18m lap pool, and an excellent restaurant with sublime views. Accommodation options include one-bedroom villas complete with a lounge area and fully equipped kitchen, and a river-view penthouse offering a maximum of three bedrooms.

Eating & Drinking

D-Arts Zone VIETNAMESE, BARBECUE $
(www.facebook.com/dartphongnha; Son Trach; meals 50,000-90,000d; ⏲7am-10pm) Vintage jazz and blues often feature at this interesting spot co-owned by an artist and an architect. Menu highlights include decent salads, spicy northern Vietnamese sausage infused with smoke from the restaurant's barbecue grill and excellent *bun cha* (barbecued pork). The barbecue duck is also good. Sit out front at the rustic wooden tables and watch what's happening along Son Trach's main street.

Veggie Box VEGETARIAN $
(Son Trach; meals 80,000-100,000d; ⏲7.30am-10pm; 📶🌱) This popular brick-lined vegetarian restaurant packs in a lot of flavour for those on the run from meat and dairy, with banana and mango pancakes for breakfast and delicious smoothie bowls, veggie sushi, hotpots, spring rolls, meat-free kebabs, coconut fried rice, pumpkin cake and a lot more served daily to an enthusiastic crowd.

Moi Moi VIETNAMESE $
(Bong Lai valley; snacks from 60,000d; ⏲7am-5pm) Moi Moi's super-relaxed and very rustic location is just the ticket for a lazy afternoon of playing pool, chilling in a hammock and snacking on interesting local dishes like *heo nuong cao tre* (pork barbecued in bamboo). A whole barbecued chicken is 300,000d. Pick up a Bong Lai valley map and go exploring.

Bomb Crater Bar BAR
(☎0166 541 0230; www.bombcraterbar.com; Cu Lac village; ⏲9am-7pm Nov-Sep) Ride a bike 3km from Son Trach to this riverside spot for cold beers, robust gin and tonics, and tasty Vietnamese snacks. Lying in a hammock, kayaking on the river, or chilling with the bar's resident water buffalo are all added attractions at this great place for a sundowner drink. The crater here was the result of a huge 2000lb US bomb targeting a nearby fuel depot.

Hue

POP 455,000 / ☎0234

Hue is the intellectual, cultural and spiritual heart of Vietnam. Palaces and pagodas, tombs and temples, culture and cuisine, history and heartbreak – there's no shortage of poetic pairings to describe Hue. A World Heritage Site, the capital of the Nguyen emperors is where tourists come to see the decaying, opulent royal tombs and the grand, crumbling Citadel.

Hue owes its charm partly to its location on the Perfume River – picturesque on a clear day, atmospheric even in less flattering weather. Today the city blends new and old as sleek modern hotels tower over crumbling century-old Citadel walls.

A few touts are a minor hassle, but Hue remains a tranquil, conservative city with just the right concentration of nightlife.

Sights

Most of Hue's principal sights lie within the moats of its Citadel and Imperial Enclosure. Other museums and pagodas are dotted around the city. The royal tombs are south of Hue. A good-value 'package tour ticket' (adult/child 360,000/70,000d) is available that includes admission to the Citadel and the tombs of **Gia Long** (Lang Gia Long; 100,000d; ⏲7am-5pm) FREE, Khai Dinh (p93) and Minh Mang (p93).

Inside the Citadel

Built between 1804 and 1833, the Citadel (Kinh Thanh) is still the heart of Hue. Heavily fortified, it consists of 2m-thick, 10km-long walls, a moat (30m across and 4m deep) and 10 gateways.

The Citadel has distinct sections. The Imperial Enclosure and Forbidden Purple City formed the epicentre of Vietnamese royal life. On the southwestern side were temple compounds. There were residences in the northwest, gardens in the northeast, and the Mang Ca Fortress (still a military base) in the north.

★Imperial Enclosure HISTORIC SITE
(Huang Thanh; adult/child 150,000/30,000d; ⏲7am-6pm) The Imperial Enclosure or Imperial City is a citadel-within-a-citadel, housing the emperor's residence, temples and palaces, and the main buildings of state, within 6m-high, 2.5km-long walls. What's left is only a fraction of the original – the enclosure was badly bombed during the French and American Wars, and only 20 of its 148 buildings survived. Expect a lot of broken masonry, rubble, cracked tiling and weeds as you work your way around, but it's a fascinating site and easily worth half a day.

At a leisurely stroll, many of the less-visited areas are highly atmospheric and sublime. It's best to choose a day with decent weather, with late afternoon (when there are fewer visitors and the sun is setting) a superb time to visit. There are little cafes and souvenir stands dotted around. It's best to approach the sights starting from Ngo Mon Gate and moving anticlockwise around the enclosure. Restoration and reconstruction are ongoing.

Ngo Mon Gate GATE
(Meridian Gate) The principal entrance to the Imperial Enclosure is Ngo Mon Gate, which faces the Flag Tower. The central passageway with its yellow doors was reserved for the use of the emperor, as was the bridge across the lotus pond. Others had to use the gates to either side and the paths around the pond. On top of the gate is Ngu Phung (Belvedere of the Five Phoenixes); on its upper level is a huge drum and bell.

Thai Hoa Palace PALACE
(Palace of Supreme Harmony) This 1803 palace is a spacious hall with an ornate timber roof supported by 80 carved and lacquered columns. It was used for the emperor's official receptions and important ceremonies. On state occasions the emperor sat on his elevated throne, facing visitors entering via the Ngo Mon Gate. No photos are permitted, but be sure to see the impressive audiovisual display, which gives an excellent overview of the entire Citadel, its architecture and the historical context.

Halls of the Mandarins HISTORIC BUILDING
Located immediately behind Thai Hoa Palace, on either side of a courtyard, these halls were used by mandarins as offices and to prepare for court ceremonies. The hall on the right showcases intriguing old photographs (including boy-king Vua Duya Tan's coronation), gilded Buddha statues and assorted imperial curios. Behind the courtyard are the ruins of the Can Chanh Palace, where two wonderful long galleries, painted in gleaming scarlet lacquer, have been reconstructed.

Emperor's Reading Room HISTORIC BUILDING
(Royal Library, Thai Binh Lau) The exquisite (though crumbling) little two-storey Emperor's Reading Room was the only part of the Purple Forbidden City to escape damage during the French reoccupation of Hue in 1947. The Gaudí-esque, yin-yang roof mosaics outside are in stark contrast to the sombre, renovated interior, the circular hallway of which you can walk around on the small ground level. The exterior features poems by Emperor Khai Dinh on either side; the three *chu nho* characters above the main portico translate as 'Building of Great Peace'.

Royal Theatre HISTORIC BUILDING
(Duyen Thi Duong; ☎054 352 4162; www.nhanhac.com.vn; performances 200,000d; ⏲performances 10am & 3pm) The Royal Theatre, begun in 1826 and later home to the National Conservatory of Music, has been rebuilt on its former foundations. When performances aren't on, it's free to sit in the plush chairs or examine the fascinating display of masks and musical instruments from Vietnamese theatre, with English descriptions.

Cultural performances here last 40 minutes.

Co Ha Gardens GARDENS
(Royal Gardens) Occupying the northeast corner of the Imperial Enclosure, these delightful gardens were developed by the first four emperors of the Nguyen dynasty but fell into disrepair. They've been beautifully recreated in the last few years, and are dotted with little gazebo-style pavilions and ponds. They are an absolute picture and this is one of the most peaceful spots in the entire Citadel.

Hue

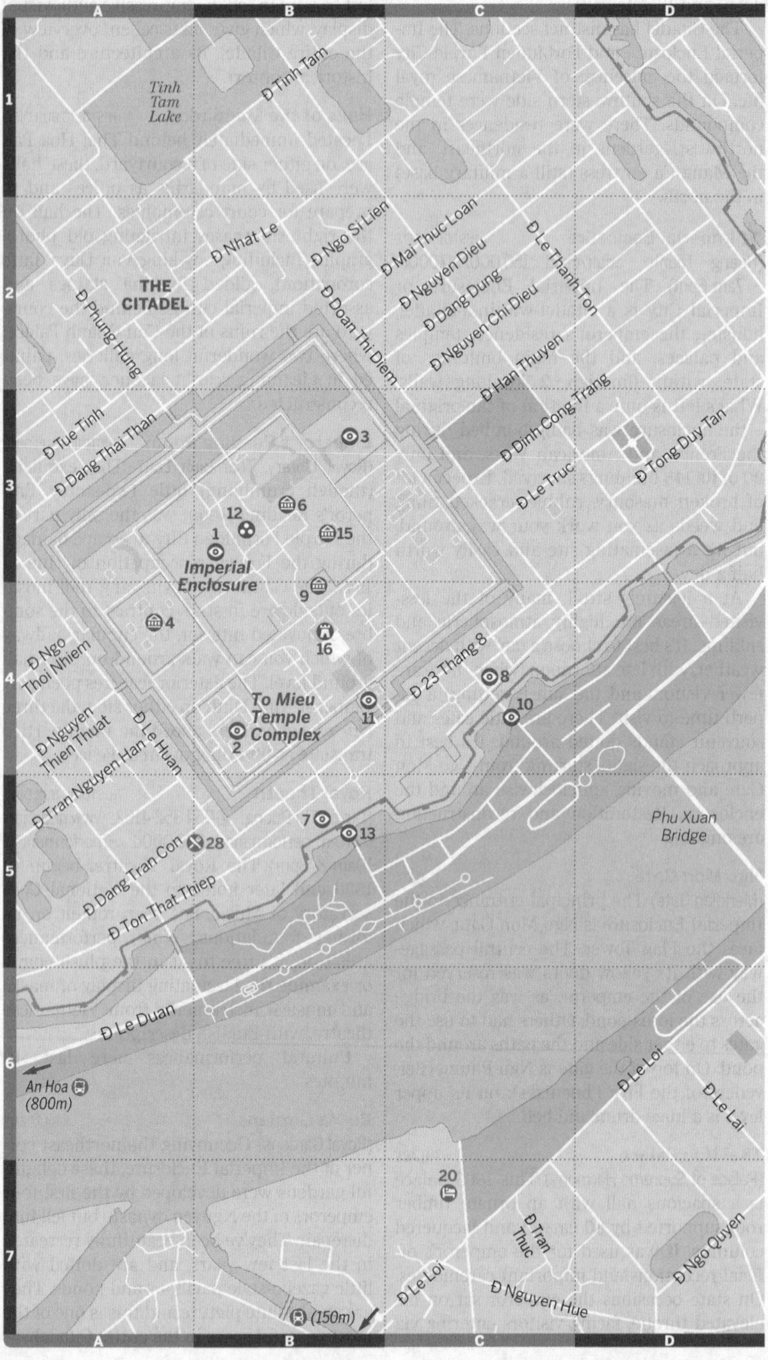
Tinh Tam Lake
Đ Tinh Tam
THE CITADEL
Đ Nhat Le
Đ Ngo Si Lien
Đ Mai Thuc Loan
Đ Le Thanh Ton
Đ Nguyen Dieu
Đ Dang Dung
Đ Doan Thi Diem
Đ Nguyen Chi Dieu
Đ Phung Hung
Đ Han Thuyen
Đ Dinh Cong Trang
Đ Tue Tinh
Đ Dang Thai Than
Đ Tong Duy Tan
Đ Le Truc
Imperial Enclosure
Đ Ngo Thoi Nhiem
Đ 23 Thang 8
To Mieu Temple Complex
Đ Nguyen Thien Thuat
Đ Le Huan
Đ Tran Nguyen Han
Đ Dang Tran Con
Đ Ton That Thiep
Phu Xuan Bridge
Đ Le Duan
An Hoa (800m)
Đ Le Loi
Đ Le Lai
Đ Tran Thuc
Đ Ngo Quyen
Đ Nguyen Hue
(150m)

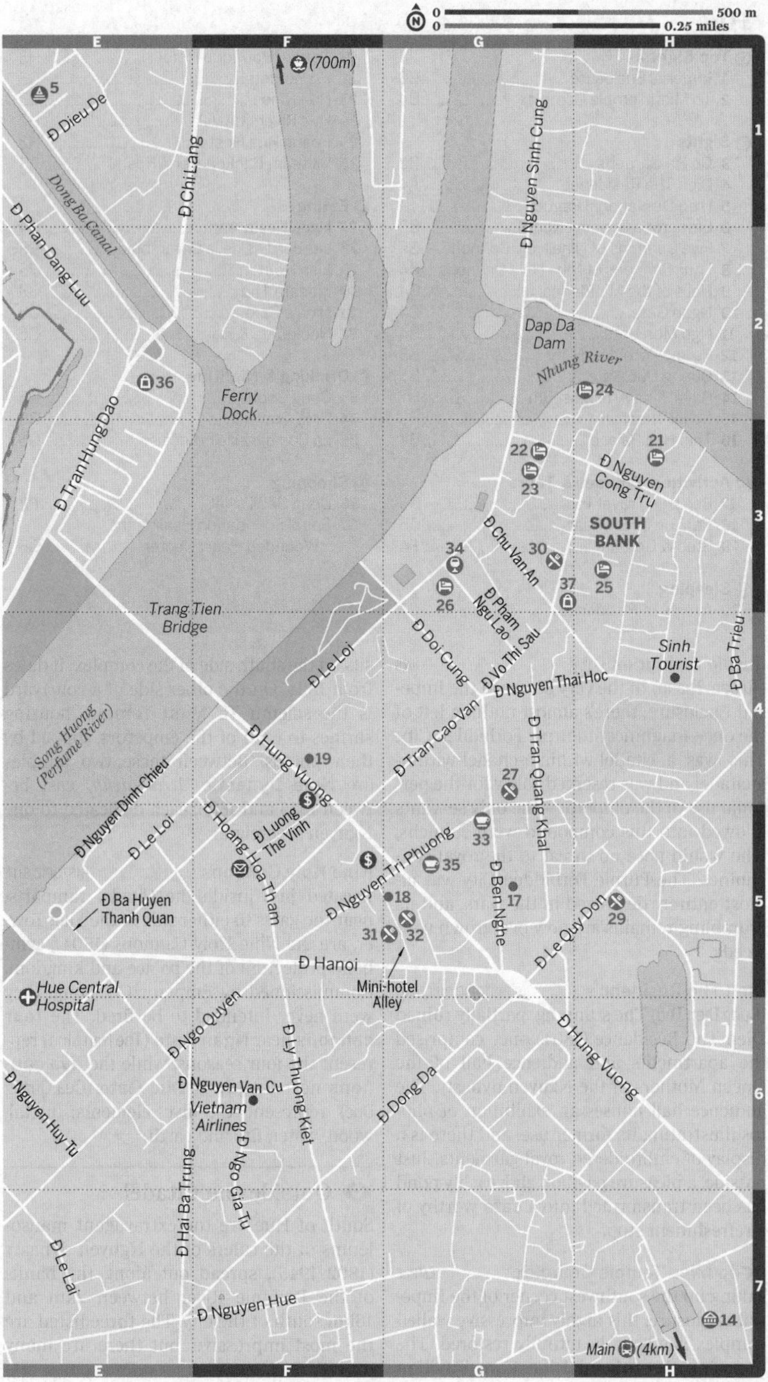
0
500 m
0
0.25 miles
E
F
G
H
1
2
3
4
5
6
7
(700m)
5
Đ Dieu De
Dong Ba Canal
Đ Chi Lang
Đ Nguyen Sinh Cung
Đ Phan Dang Luu
Dap Da Dam
Nhung River
36
Ferry Dock
24
Đ Tran Hung Dao
22
21
23
Đ Nguyen Cong Tru
SOUTH BANK
Đ Chu Van An
34
30
37
25
26
Trang Tien Bridge
Đ Pham Ngu Lao
Đ Doi Cung
Đ Vo Thi Sau
Sinh Tourist
Đ Ba Trieu
Đ Le Loi
Đ Nguyen Thai Hoc
Song Huong (Perfume River)
Đ Hung Vuong
Đ Tran Cao Van
Đ Tran Quang Khai
19
27
Đ Nguyen Dinh Chieu
Đ Hoang Hoa Tham
Đ Luong The Vinh
33
Đ Le Loi
Đ Nguyen Tri Phuong
35
Đ Ben Nghe
17
Đ Ba Huyen Thanh Quan
18
29
Đ Le Quy Don
31
32
Đ Hanoi
Mini-hotel Alley
Hue Central Hospital
Đ Ngo Quyen
Đ Hung Vuong
Đ Nguyen Van Cu
Vietnam Airlines
Đ Ly Thuong Kiet
Đ Dong Da
Đ Nguyen Huy Tu
Đ Ngo Gia Tu
Đ Hai Ba Trung
Đ Le Lai
Đ Nguyen Hue
14
Main (4km)

Hue

Top Sights

1	Imperial Enclosure	B3
2	To Mieu Temple Complex	B4

Sights

3	Co Ha Gardens	B3
4	Dien Tho Residence	A4
5	Dieu De National Pagoda	E1
6	Emperor's Reading Room	B3
7	Five Cannons of Nine Holy Cannons	B5
8	Four Cannons of Nine Holy Cannons	C4
9	Halls of the Mandarins	B4
10	Ngan Gate	C4
11	Ngo Mon Gate	B4
12	Purple Forbidden City	B3
13	Quang Duc Gate	B5
14	Royal Fine Arts Museum	H7
15	Royal Theatre	B3
16	Thai Hoa Palace	B4

Activities, Courses & Tours

17	Bee Bee Travel Tours	G5
18	Café on Thu Wheels	G5
19	Stop & Go Café	F4

Sleeping

20	Azerai La Residence	C7
21	Canary Boutique Hotel	H3
22	Home Hotel	G3
23	Hue Nino	G3
24	Hue Riverside Villa	H2
25	Poetic Hue Hostel	H3
26	Vietnam Backpackers' Hostel	G3

Eating

27	Hanh Restaurant	G4
28	Les Jardins de la Carambole	B5
29	Lien Hoa	H5
30	Madam Thu	G3
31	Nina's Cafe	G5
32	Nook Cafe & Bar	G5

Drinking & Nightlife

33	Cong Caphe	G5
34	DMZ Travel	G3
35	La Boulangerie Française	G5

Shopping

36	Dong Ba Market	E2
37	Spiral Foundation Healing the Wounded Heart Center	G3

Purple Forbidden City RUINS
(Tu Cam Thanh) In the very centre of the Imperial Enclosure, there's almost nothing left of the once-magnificent Purple Forbidden City. This was a citadel-within-a-citadel-within-a-citadel and was reserved solely for the personal use of the emperor – the only servants allowed into this compound were eunuchs, who would pose no threat to the royal concubines. The Purple Forbidden City was almost entirely destroyed in the wars, and its crumbling remains are now overgrown with weeds.

Dien Tho Residence HISTORIC BUILDING
(Cung Dien Tho) The stunning, partially ruined Dien Tho Residence (1804) once comprised the apartments and audience hall of the Queen Mothers of the Nguyen dynasty. The audience hall houses an exhibition of photos illustrating its former use, and there is a display of embroidered royal garments. Just outside, a pleasure pavilion above a lily pond has been transformed into a **cafe** worthy of a refreshment stop.

★**To Mieu Temple Complex** TEMPLE
Taking up the southwest corner of the Imperial Enclosure, this highly impressive walled complex has been beautifully restored. The imposing three-tiered **Hien Lam Pavilion** sits on the south side of the complex; it dates from 1824. On the other side of a courtyard is the solemn **To Mieu Temple**, housing shrines to each of the emperors, topped by their photos. Between these two temples are **Nine Dynastic Urns** *(dinh)* cast between 1835 and 1836, each dedicated to one Nguyen sovereign.

Nine Holy Cannons HISTORIC SITE
Located just inside the Citadel ramparts, near the gates to either side of the Flag Tower, are the Nine Holy Cannons (1804), symbolic protectors of the palace and kingdom. Commissioned by Emperor Gia Long, they were never intended to be fired. The **four cannons** near **Ngan Gate** (The Nan Mon) represent the four seasons, while the **five cannons** next to **Quang Duc Gate** (Cua Quang Duc) represent the five elements: metal, wood, water, fire and earth.

Outside the Citadel

South of Hue are the extravagant mausoleums of the rulers of the Nguyen dynasty (1802–1945), spread out along the banks of the Perfume River between 2km and 16km south of the city. The three listed are the most impressive, but there are many others.

★Tomb of Khai Dinh TOMB
(Lang Khai Dinh, Ung Lang; adult/child 100,000/20,000d; ⌚7am-5pm) This hillside monument is a synthesis of Vietnamese and European elements. Most of the tomb's grandiose exterior is covered in darkened, weathered concrete, with an unexpectedly Gothic air, while the interiors resemble explosions of colourful ceramic mosaic. Khai Dinh was the penultimate emperor of Vietnam, from 1916 to 1925, and widely seen as a puppet of the French. It took 11 years to construct his flamboyant tomb; it can be found 10km from Hue in Chau Chu village.

Tomb of Tu Duc TOMB
(Lang Tu Duc, Khiem Lang; adult/child 100,000/20,000d; ⌚7am-5pm) This tomb (completed in 1867) is the most popular, imposing and impressive of the royal mausoleums, designed by Emperor Tu Duc himself before his death. The enormous expense of the tomb and the forced labour used in its construction spawned a coup plot that was discovered and suppressed. Tu Duc lived a life of imperial luxury and carnal excess, with 104 wives and countless concubines (though no offspring). The tomb is 5km south of Hue on Van Nien Hill in Duong Xuan Thuong village.

Tomb of Minh Mang TOMB
(adult/child 100,000/20,000d) Planned during Minh Mang's reign (1820–40) but built by his successor, Thieu Tri, this majestic tomb, on the west bank of the Perfume River, is renowned for its architecture and sublime forest setting. The **Honour Courtyard** is reached via three gates on the eastern side of the wall; three granite staircases lead from here to the square **Stele Pavilion** (Dinh Vuong). Sung An Temple, dedicated to Minh Mang and his empress, is reached via three terraces and the rebuilt Hien Duc Gate.

★Thien Mu Pagoda BUDDHIST TEMPLE
FREE Built on a small hill overlooking the Song Huong (Perfume River), 4km southwest of the Citadel, this seven-storey pagoda is an icon of Vietnam and as potent a symbol of Hue as the Citadel. The 21m-high octagonal tower, **Thap Phuoc Duyen**, was constructed under the reign of Emperor Thieu Tri in 1844. Each of its storeys is dedicated to a *manushi-buddha* (a Buddha that appeared in human form). Visit in the morning before tour groups show up.

Dieu De National Pagoda BUDDHIST TEMPLE
(Quoc Tu Dieu De; 102 Đ Bach Dang) FREE Overlooking Dong Ba Canal, this pagoda was built under Emperor Thieu Tri's rule (1841–47) and is celebrated for its four low towers, one on either side of the gate and two flanking the sanctuary. The pavilions on either side of the main sanctuary entrance contain the 18 La Han *(arhat)*, whose rank is just below that of bodhisattva, and the eight Kim Cang, protectors of Buddha. In the back row of the main dais is Thich Ca Buddha, flanked by two assistants.

Dieu De was a stronghold of Buddhist and student opposition to the South Vietnamese government and the American War, and many arrests were made here when police stormed the building in 1966.

Royal Fine Arts Museum MUSEUM
(150 Đ Nguyen Hue; ⌚6.30am-5.30pm summer, 7am-5pm winter) FREE This museum is located in the baroque-influenced **An Dinh Palace**, commissioned by Emperor Khai Dinh in 1918 and full of elaborate murals, floral motifs and *trompe l'oeil* details. Emperor Bao Dai lived here with his family after abdicating in 1945. Inside you'll find some outstanding ceramics, paintings, furniture, silverware, porcelain and royal clothing, though information is a little lacking.

☞ Tours

Most hotels and travellers cafes offer shared day tours from US$5 to US$20 per person. Better ones start with a morning river cruise, stopping at pagodas and temples, then after lunch a minibus travels to the main tombs before returning to Hue. On the cheaper options you'll often have to hire a motorbike to get from the moorings to the tombs, or walk in tropical heat.

Tran Van Thinh TOURS
(☎0905 731 537; www.tranvanthinhtours.com; half-day tours per person from US$15) Thinh is a knowledgeable local motorbike guide who can arrange local city tours and explorations of the royal tombs. A long-time resident of Hue, Thinh speaks excellent English and also runs DMZ tours (US$45), tours to Hoi An (US$50) and Ho Chi Minh Trail tours (US$70).

Oriental Sky Travel ADVENTURE
(☎0985 555 827; www.orientalskytravel.com) Helmed by the experienced and friendly Shi, this Hue-based tour company arranges

Hue's Imperial Enclosure

EXPLORING THE SITE

An incongruous combination of meticulously restored palaces and pagodas, ruins and rubble, the Imperial Enclosure is approached from the south through the outer walls of the Citadel. It's best to tackle the site as a walking tour, winding your way around the structures in an anticlockwise direction.

You'll pass through the monumental ❶ **Ngo Mon Gate**, where the ticket office is located. This dramatic approach quickens the pulse as you enter this citadel-within-a-citadel. Directly ahead is the ❷ **Thai Hoa Palace**, where the emperor would greet offical visitors from his elevated throne. Continuing north you'll cross a small courtyard to the twin ❸ **Halls of the Mandarins**, where mandarins once had their offices and prepared for ceremonial occasions.

To the northeast is the Royal Theatre, where traditional dance performances are held several times daily. Next you'll be able to get a glimpse of the Emperor's Reading Room, built by Thieu Tri and used as a place of retreat. Just east of here are the lovely Co Ha Gardens. Wander their pathways, dotted with hundreds of bonsai trees and potted plants, which have been restored.

Guarding the far north of the complex is the ❹ **Tu Vo Phuong Pavilion**, from where you can follow a moat to the Truong San residence. Then loop back south via the ❺ **Dien Tho Residence** and finally view the beautifully restored temple compound of To Mieu, perhaps the most rewarding part of the entire enclosure to visit, including its fabulous ❻ **Nine Dynastic Urns**.

TOP TIPS

- Allow half a day to explore the Citadel.
- Drink vendors are dotted around the site, but the best places to take a break are the delightful Co Ha Gardens, the Tu Vo Phuong Pavilion and the Dien Tho Residence (the last two also serve food).
- Consider visiting later in the day to see the Citadel in late afternoon light.

PETER STUCKINGS/SHUTTERSTOCK ©

Dien Tho Residence
This pretty corner of the complex, with its low structures and pond, was the residence of many Queen Mothers. The earliest structures here date from 1804.

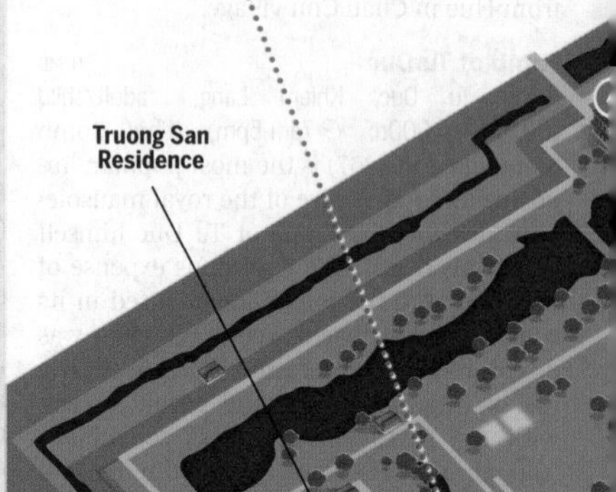

Nine Dynastic Urns
These colossal bronze urns were commissioned by Emperor Minh Mang and cast between 1835 and 1836. They're embellished with decorative elements including landscapes, rivers, flowers and animals.

LULU AND ISABELLE/SHUTTERSTOCK ©

Tu Vo Phuong Pavilion

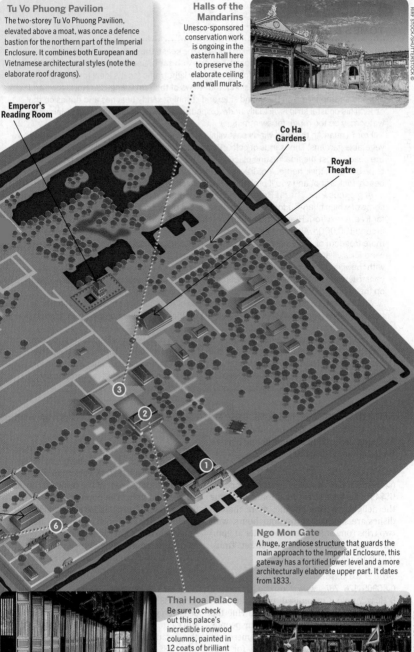

The two-storey Tu Vo Phuong Pavilion, elevated above a moat, was once a defence bastion for the northern part of the Imperial Enclosure. It combines both European and Vietnamese architectural styles (note the elaborate roof dragons).

Halls of the Mandarins

Unesco-sponsored conservation work is ongoing in the eastern hall here to preserve the elaborate ceiling and wall murals.

RIRF STOCK/SHUTTERSTOCK ©

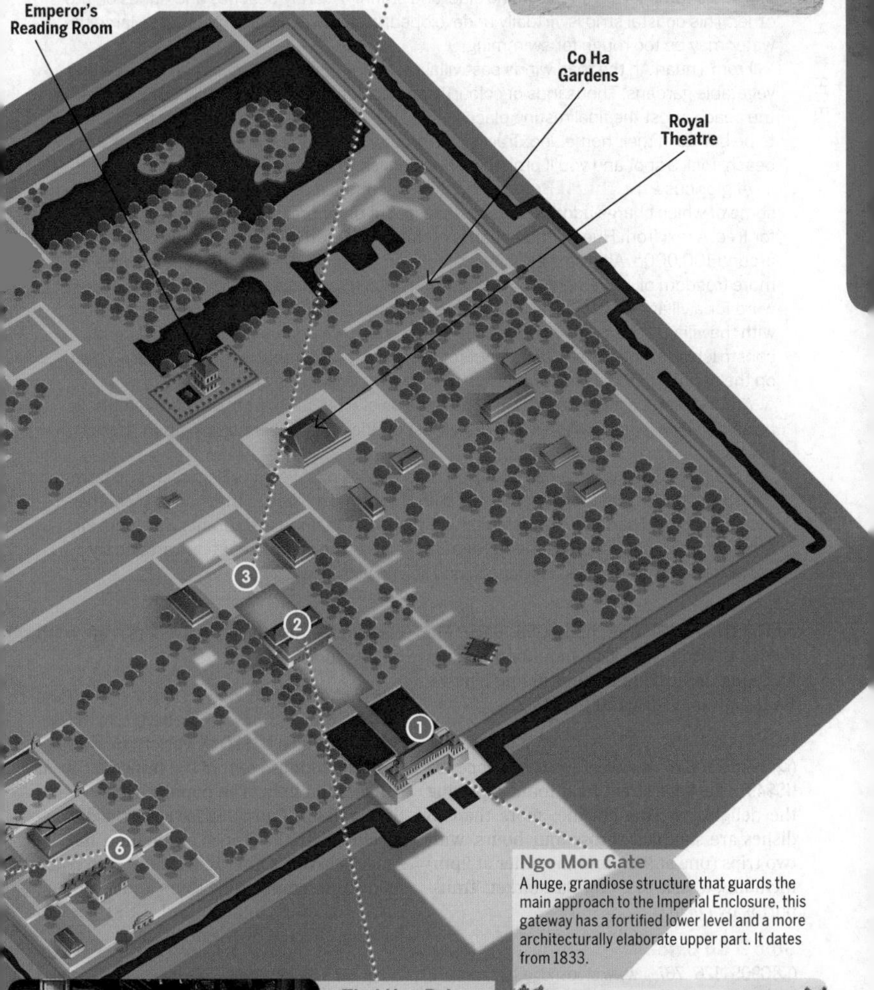

Ngo Mon Gate

A huge, grandiose structure that guards the main approach to the Imperial Enclosure, this gateway has a fortified lower level and a more architecturally elaborate upper part. It dates from 1833.

Thai Hoa Palace

Be sure to check out this palace's incredible ironwood columns, painted in 12 coats of brilliant scarlet and gold lacquer. The structure was saved from collapse by restoration work in the 1990s.

PETER STUCKINGS/SHUTTERSTOCK ©

WORTH A TRIP

TOMBS & DUNES

From the centre of Hue it's only 15km north to the coast, the road shadowing the Perfume River before you hit the sands of **Thuan An Beach**. Southeast from here there's a beautiful, quiet coastal road to follow with very light traffic (so it's ideal for bikers). The route traverses a narrow coastal island, with views of the Tam Giang-Cau Hai lagoon and fish and shrimp farms on the inland side, and stunning sandy beaches and dunes on the other. This coastal strip is virtually undeveloped, but between September and March the water may be too rough for swimming.

From Thuan An the road winds past villages, alternating between shrimp lagoons and vegetable gardens. Thousands of colourful and opulent graves and family temples line the beach, most the final resting places of Viet Kieu (overseas Vietnamese) who wanted to be buried in their homeland. Tracks cut through the tombs and sand dunes to the beach. Pick a spot and you'll probably have a beach to yourself.

At glorious **Phu Thuan Beach** (about 7km southeast of Thuan An) is a hotel or two, some of which charge admission to the beach, but other areas of beach are accessible for free. A taxi from Hue to Phu Thuan is around 250,000d and a *xe om* (motorbike taxi) around 100,000d. Alternatively, hire a scooter from your hotel or rental outlet in Hue for more freedom of movement. You can also pop into little villages at will and explore (the word for a village is *'làng'*, and you will see each settlement announced by a large gate with the village name emblazoned on it). Almost all have bright and colourful, recently constructed temples. Keep an eye out for the occasional temple with Vietnamese script on the main gate that is artfully designed to resemble Chinese characters.

Around 8km past Beach Bar Hue, the remains of **Phu Dien**, a small Cham temple, lie protected by a glass pavilion in the dunes just off the beach. There are seafood shacks here too.

Continuing southeast, a narrow paved road weaves past fishing villages, shrimp farms, giant sand dunes and the settlement of Vinh Hung until it reaches the mouth of another river estuary at Thuon Phu An, where there's a row of seafood restaurants. This spot is 40km from Thuan An. Cross the Tu Hien Bridge here and you can continue around the eastern lip of the huge Cau Hai lagoon and link up with Hwy 1.

active trips including hiking in Bach Ma National Park, and also mountain biking, kayaking and caving around Phong Nha-Ke Bang National Park and the DMZ.

Hue Flavor FOOD & DRINK
(☎0905 937 006; www.hueflavor.com; per person US$49) Excellent street-food tours exploring the delights of Hue cuisine; more than 15 dishes are sampled across four hours, with two trips (one at 9am and the other at 2pm) including a visit to Dong Ba Market. Transport is by *cyclo*.

Stop & Go Café DRIVING
(☎0905 126 767; www.stopandgo-hue.com; 3 Đ Hung Vuong) Customised motorbike and car tours: a one-day tour of three Hue top sights is US$10 per person for four people; a DMZ car tour guided by a Vietnamese war veteran costs US$59 per person for four people. Guided trips to Hoi An stopping at beaches are also recommended. Note: there are similarly named, unrelated businesses elsewhere. Also has a travellers' cafe with quality food.

Bee Bee Travel Tours WALKING
(☎0935 616 090; www.beebeetravel.com; 65 Ben Nghe; tours from US$17) A variety of walking tours, including a tour of the Imperial City at 6.30am and 2pm. The popular Hue Revolution Walking Tour (US$25) covers sights associated with the French occupation and the American War. Other tours delve into Hue's food scene, countryside tours and a cooking class. For every tour booked, US$1 goes to families affected by Agent Orange.

Café on Thu Wheels TOURS
(☎054 383 2241; 3/34 Nguyen Tri Phuong) Inexpensive cycle hire, and motorbike, minibus and car tours around Hue and the DMZ. Can also arrange transfers to Hoi An by motorbike (US$45) or car (US$55).

The establishment also serves a small selection of burgers, sandwiches and local dishes.

Sleeping

Poetic Hue Hostel HOSTEL $
(☎0918 342 138; 24/26 Đ Vo Thi Sau; dm/d/f from US$7/13/25; ⊖❄📶) In a whitewashed villa down a quiet back lane, this is a good alternative to Hue's busier hostels. Local families and birdsong give the location a neighbourhood ambience, but restaurants and bars are nearby and rooms are spacious and relaxing. Some rooms have balconies.

Canary Boutique Hotel BOUTIQUE HOTEL $
(☎0234-393 6447; www.canaryboutiquehotel.com; Lane 8, 43 Đ Nguyen Cong Tru; r incl breakfast US$18-24; ⊖❄📶) This considerably clean, budget place has professional staff, a great breakfast menu with free seconds, and competitively priced tours, with a bathtub the cherry on top after a long day at the Citadel or nearby bars. If you can't find the hotel's small lane, enquire at the sister Canary Hotel on the main road.

Home Hotel HOTEL $
(☎0234-383 0014; www.huehomehotel.com; 8 Đ Nguyen Cong Tru; r US$17-25; ❄📶) Run by a really friendly team, the welcoming Home Hotel has a youthful, hip vibe, and spacious rooms arrayed across several levels. Ask to book a room overlooking Đ Nguyen Cong Tru for a compact balcony, French doors and views of the river. The cheapest rooms come without windows. There's a gorgeous old staircase and a lovey owner, but no lift.

Hue Nino GUESTHOUSE $
(☎054 382 2064; www.hueninohotel.com; 14 Đ Nguyen Cong Tru; r incl breakfast US$18-25; ⊖❄📶) This family-owned, warm and welcoming 16-room guesthouse has an artistic flavour, with stylish furniture, artwork and smallish rooms with minibar, cable TV and quality beds. There's a generous breakfast.

Vietnam Backpackers' Hostel HOSTEL $
(☎0234-393 3423; www.vietnambackpackerhostels.com; 10 Đ Pham Ngu Lao; incl breakfast dm US$6-12, d/tr from US$15/20; ❄📶) Thanks to its central location, eager-to-please staff, good info and sociable bar-restaurant that hosts happy hour and big sporting events, this place is a backpackers' mecca. Dorms are well designed, with air-conditioning and lockers, and a mix of single and double bunk beds and female-only dorms.

★**Hue Riverside Villa** BOUTIQUE HOTEL $$
(☎0905 771 602; www.hueriversidevilla.com; 16/7 Đ Nguyen Cong Tru; tw/d incl breakfast US$70-80, f US$95; ⊖❄📶) A short walk from decent restaurants, Hue Riverside Villa combines five whitewashed and red-brick bungalows with a relaxing and breezy shared garden and a quiet, absolute edge-of-the-river location. Adorned with warm timber, the bathrooms are especially pleasant, decor is crisp and modern, and the switched-on English-speaking owner offers tours and plenty of local information. Prices can drop to around US$36 per night in the low season.

There's free bike rental.

★**Tam Tinh Vien** BOUTIQUE HOTEL $$
(☎054 3519 990, 091 4019 983; www.huehomestay.wevina.vn; Long Ha village; r US$49-56; ❄📶🏊) Around 6km from Hue in Long Ha village, tranquil and delightful Tam Tinh Vien is called a homestay but is really a delightful boutique guesthouse. Arrayed around a small pool and verdant garden, spacious villas with four-poster beds are imbued with a chic Asian aesthetic. Borrow a bike to make the 30-minute journey into Hue – a taxi is around 100,000d.

★**Azerai La Residence** HOTEL $$$
(☎0234-383 7475; www.azerai.com/la-residence-hue; 5 Đ Le Loi; r from US$240; ⊖❄📶🏊) Now extensively renovated and run by Azerai, the former 122-room residence of the French *Resident Superieur* radiates art-deco glamour, with original features and period detailing. You can gaze at the Perfume River from the 30m pool or be pampered in the heavenly spa. Rooms are sumptuously appointed, the restaurants are excellent and service is top-notch.

Ana Mandara RESORT $$$
(☎0234-398 3333; www.anamandarahue-resort.com; Thuan An; d from US$90, villas from US$169; ⊖❄📶🏊) The pleasantly breezy, naturally air-conditioned lobby is a prelude to the comforts of this seaside resort, overseen by very helpful and gracious staff. Situated by the sands of Thuan An Beach east of Hue, this is the place for sunrise views over the waves from your beachfront villa. The resort has its own long length of private beach, as well as an excellent spa.

Eating & Drinking

Vegetarian food has a long tradition in Hue. Stalls in Dong Ba Market serve it on the first and 15th days of the lunar month.

Hue also has great street food.

★**Madam Thu** VIETNAMESE $
(45 Đ Vo Thị Sau; meals 100,000d; ⏲8am-10pm) Ever-stuffed and frugal-looking Madam Thu draws in the crowds for its superb menu and lovely, very polite and helpful staff. The mushroom-and-carrot fried spring rolls (50,000d) are crispy and divine, while the peanut-topped tofu with vermicelli noodles and peanut sauce is up there with the very best. For every meal served the restaurant donates 2000d to underprivileged children in and around Hue.

★**Hanh Restaurant** VIETNAMESE $
(☎0905 520 512; 11 Pho Duc Chinh; meals 30,000-100,000d; ⏲10am-9pm) Newbies to Hue specialities should start at this busy restaurant. Order the five-dish set menu (120,000d) for a speedy lesson in *banh khoai* (savoury prawn pancakes), *banh beo* (steamed rice cakes topped with shrimp and spring onions), and divine *nem lui* (grilled pork and lemongrass skewers) wrapped in rice paper and herbs. Ask the patient staff how to devour everything.

Lien Hoa VEGETARIAN $
(☎054 381 2456; 3 Đ Le Quy Don; meals 50,000-80,000d; ⏲6.30am-9pm; ✎) This ever-popular and no-nonsense open-air vegetarian restaurant is renowned for filling food at bargain prices. Fresh *banh beo*, noodle dishes, crispy fried jackfruit and cauliflower fried with capsicum all deliver; wash it down with a *tra gung* (ginger tea). The menu has rough English translations. The restaurant name means 'Lotus'.

ROYAL RICE CAKES

These savoury Hue specialities come in different shapes and sizes, but are all made with rice flour. The most common is the crispy fried, filled pancake *banh khoai* (smaller and denser than southern Vietnam's *banh xeo* pancakes). The other variations are steamed and like sticky rice, and are usually topped with shrimp and dipped in sweet fish sauce. Look for *banh beo*, which come in tiny dishes; banana-leaf-wrapped *banh nam;* transparent dumplings *banh loc;* and the leaf-steamed pyramids *banh it*, which can come in sweet mung-bean or savoury varieties.

Nook Cafe & Bar VIETNAMESE, CAFE $
(☎0935 069 741; www.facebook.com/nookcafebarhue; 7/34 Đ Nguyen Tri Phuong; meals 50,000-120,000d; ⏲8am-10pm; 📶✎) Near a tangle of cheaper accommodation and travel agencies, Nook's breezy upstairs location is a good spot for well-executed Vietnamese dishes and Western comfort food like veggie burgers and toasted sandwiches. Top marks for the quirky decor, colourful tablecloths and lanterns, music (B-52's!), charming staff and refreshing and rejuvenating fresh juices and smoothies.

Les Jardins de la Carambole FRENCH, VIETNAMESE $$
(☎0234-354 8815; www.lesjardinsdelacarambole.com; 32 Đ Dang Tran Con; meals 120,000-300,000d; ⏲7am-11pm; 📶) This classy French restaurant occupies a gorgeous colonial-style building in the Citadel quarter. The menu majors in Gallic classics and there's a Vietnamese set menu popular with groups. Add a lengthy wine list and informed service, and it's just the place for a romantic meal – arrive by *cyclo* and it's easy to roll back the years to Indochine times.

Nina's Cafe VIETNAMESE $$
(16/34 Nguyen Tri Phuong; meals 120,000d; ⏲9am-10.30pm) Nina's is a friendly, painting-hung restaurant, around a corner at the end of an alley, where crowd-pleasing stir-fried, claypot, fried-rice and curry dishes are served to enthusiastic patrons. Top marks go to the vegetable curry loaded with tofu, carrots and potato. The vibrantly coloured Vietnamese tablecloths are for sale at the door, along with homemade chilli sauce (30,000d).

Western breakfasts are also on the menu.

★**Cong Caphe** CAFE
(www.congcaphe.com; 22 Ben Nghe; ⏲7am-11.30pm) With a lovely wood floor, concrete walls, colourful chairs and cushions and many a nook to escape to, Cong is a reassuring constant in a world of flux: here you are always guaranteed excellent service and a fun and fascinating communist-chic atmosphere, as well as grade-A coffee, thirst-busting coconut milk with peppermint, and iced coffee.

DMZ Travel BAR
(☎0234-993 456; www.dmz.com.vn; 60 Đ Le Loi; ⏲7am-2am; 📶) This always-popular bar near

the river has a free pool table, cold Huda beer, cocktails (try a watermelon mojito) and antics most nights. It also serves Western and local food till midnight, plus smoothies and juices. Happy hour is from 3pm to 8pm. Check out the upside-down map of the DMZ – complete with a US chopper – on the ceiling.

La Boulangerie Française CAFE
(☎054 383 7437; www.laboulangeriefrancaise.org; 46 Nguyen Tri Phuong; ⊙7am-8.30pm) Sit out on the slim terrace upstairs at this recently refurbished *petite boulangerie* for a delightful *petit déjeuner* with croissants, crêpes (from 20,000d) or *gaufres* (waffles), and a *café au lait* or a milkshake *glacé*. The *boulangerie* operates as a training school for young and disadvantaged Vietnamese who aspire to become bakers or chefs.

Shopping

Spiral Foundation Healing the Wounded Heart Center ARTS & CRAFTS
(☎0234-381 7643; 23 Đ Vo Thi Sau; ⊙8am-10pm) Generating cash from trash, this shop stocks lovely handicrafts – such as quirky bags made from plastic, and picture frames made from recycled beer cans – all produced by artists with disabilities. Profits aid heart surgery for children in need.

Dong Ba Market MARKET
(Đ Tran Hung Dao; ⊙6.30am-8pm) Just north of Trang Tien Bridge, this is Hue's largest market, selling anything and everything from vegetables and fruit to clothing.

Information

Hue Central Hospital (Benh Vien Trung Uong Hue; ☎0234-382 2325; 16 Đ Le Loi; ⊙6am-10pm) Well-regarded local hospital.

Post Office (8 Đ Hoang Hoa Tham; ⊙7am-5.30pm Mon-Sat)

Sinh Tourist (☎0234-384 5022; www.thesinhtourist.vn; 37 Đ Nguyen Thai Hoc; ⊙6.30am-8.30pm) Books open-tour buses, and buses to Laos and many other destinations in Vietnam.

Vietin Bank ATM (12 Đ Hung Vuong) Centrally located ATM.

Getting There & Away

Jetstar and VietJet fly to/from Ho Chi Minh City (HCMC); while **Vietnam Airlines** (☎0234-382 4709; www.vietnamairlines.com; 23 Đ Nguyen Van Cu; ⊙8am-5pm Mon-Fri) can fly you to/from Hanoi and HCMC.

The main **Phia Nam Bus Station** (57 An Duong Vuong), 4km southeast of the centre, has connections to Danang and south to HCMC. **An Hoa Bus Station** (Ly Thai To), northwest of the Citadel, serves northern destinations. Destinations include the following:

Danang (80,000d, three hours, frequent departures)

Dong Ha (60,000d, 2½ hours, every 30 minutes)

Dong Hoi (100,000d, four to five hours, frequent departures)

Hanoi (330,000d, 13 to 16 hours, nine daily)

Ho Chi Minh City (500,000d, 19 to 24 hours, nine daily)

Ninh Binh (300,000d, 10½ to 12 hours, eight daily)

For Phong Nha (around 180,000d, five hours), the Hung Thanh open-tour bus leaves 49 Đ Chu Van An between 4.30pm and 5pm, and the Tan Nhat bus leaves from the Why Not? Bar on Đ Pham Ngu Lao around 6.30am to 7am. Also convenient is a daily bus (150,000d) leaving the DMZ Travel bar at 2pm. This departure travels directly to Phong Nha.

Hue is a regular stop on open-tour bus routes. Most drop off and pick up passengers at central hotels. Expect some hassle from persistent hotel touts when you arrive.

Sinh Tourist and Stop & Go Café (p96) can arrange bookings for buses to Savannakhet, Laos.

The **Hue Train Station** (☎0234-382 2175; 2 Đ Phan Chu Trinh) is at the southwestern end of Đ Le Loi. A taxi here from the hotel area costs about 70,000d. All north–south trains stop here.

Getting Around

Hue's Phu Bai Airport is 14km south of the city. Metered **taxis** (☎0234-389 8989) cost about 220,000d to the centre, or take the Vietnam Airlines minibus service (50,000d). Pedal power is a fun way to tour Hue and the royal tombs. Hotels rent bicycles for around US$3 per day.

Around Hue

Demilitarised Zone (DMZ)

From 1954 to 1975 the Ben Hai River acted as a buffer between North and South Vietnam. The area just south of the DMZ was the scene of some of the bloodiest battles in America's first TV war, turning Quang Tri, the Rockpile, Khe Sanh, Lang Vay and Hamburger Hill into household names.

WORTH A TRIP

BACH MA NATIONAL PARK

A French-era hill station known for its cool weather, **Bach Ma National Park** (Vuon Quoc Gia Bach Ma; ☎0234-387 1330; www.bachmapark.com.vn; adult/child 40,000/20,000d) is 45km southeast of Hue. It stretches from the coast to the Annamite mountain range at the Lao border.

More than 1400 species of plants, including rare ferns and orchids, have been discovered in Bach Ma, representing a fifth of the flora of Vietnam. There are 132 kinds of mammals, three of which were only discovered in the 1990s: the antelope-like saola, the Truong Son muntjac and the giant muntjac. Nine species of primates are also present, including small numbers of the rare red-shanked Douc langur. However, wildlife is usually elusive.

There's some decent trekking in the lower levels through subtropical forest to villages on the fringes of the park. You can book village and birdwatching tours and English- or French-speaking guides (500,000d per day) at the **visitor centre** (www.bachmapark.com.vn).

Unexploded ordnance is still in the area, so stick to the trails. There are guesthouses at the park entrance.

Most travellers visit the national park on a tour from Hue; **Oriental Sky Travel** (☎0985 555 827; www.orientalskytravel.com; 2 days & 1 night per person from US$176) runs regular overnight explorations of the park.

Most sites have now been cleared, the land reforested or planted with rubber and coffee. Ben Hai, Vinh Moc and Khe Sanh have small museums. Unless you're a veteran, or a military buff, you might find it a little hard to appreciate the place – which is all the more reason to hire a knowledgeable guide.

Virtually everyone explores the DMZ on a **tour**, mostly from Hue. Standard tours are cheap (around US$15 for a group day trip). These typically take in Khe Sanh, Vinh Moc and Doc Mieu. Tours can also be arranged in Dong Ha; try **Tam's Tours** (☎0905 425 912; www.tamscafe.jimdo.com; 211 Đ Ba Trieu, Tam's DMZ Cafe & Guesthouse).

Sights

★Vinh Moc Tunnels HISTORIC SITE

(40,000d; ⏲7am-5pm) A highly impressive complex of tunnels, Vinh Moc is the remains of a coastal North Vietnamese village that literally went underground in response to unremitting American bombing. More than 90 families disappeared into three levels of tunnels running for almost 2km, and continued to live and work while bombs rained down around them. Most of the tunnels are open to visitors and are kept in their original form (except for electric lights, a more recent addition).

An English-speaking guide will accompany you around the complex, pointing out the 12 entrances until you emerge at a glorious beach that faces the South China Sea (East Sea). The museum has photos and relics of tunnel life, including a map of the tunnel network.

Khe Sanh Combat Base HISTORIC SITE

(museum 20,000d; ⏲7am-5pm) The site of the most famous siege of the American War, the USA's Khe Sanh Combat Base was never overrun, but it saw the bloodiest battle of the war. About 500 Americans, 10,000 North Vietnamese troops and uncounted civilian bystanders died around this remote highland base. It's eerily peaceful today, but in 1968 the hillsides trembled with the impact of 1000kg bombs, white phosphorus shells, napalm, mortars and endless artillery rounds, as desperate American forces sought to repel the North Vietnamese Army (NVA).

Ben Hai River MONUMENT

(museum 20,000d; ⏲7am-4.30pm) Once the border between North and South Vietnam, Ben Hai River's southern bank now has a grandiose reunification **monument**, its stylised palm leaves oddly resembling missiles. Cua Tung Beach's fine golden sands are just east of here. Ben Hai's northern bank is dominated by a reconstructed flag tower and a small **museum** full of war mementos. Ben Hai is 22km north of Dong Ha on Hwy 1.

Danang

POP 1.23 MILLION / ☎0236

Nowhere in Vietnam is changing as fast as Danang, Vietnam's fifth-most populous city. For decades it had a reputation as a quiet provincial town, but big changes have shaken things up. Stroll along the Han riverfront and you'll find gleaming new modernist hotels. Spectacular bridges span the river, and the entire Danang Beach strip is booming with tower-hotel and resort developments.

That said, the city itself still has few conventional sightseeing spots, except for a very decent museum, a handsome cathedral and a stunningly quirky bridge (or three). So for most travellers, a few days enjoying the city's beaches, restaurants and nightlife are probably enough.

Sights

★Dragon Bridge BRIDGE

(Cau Rong) The biggest show in town every Saturday and Sunday night (at 9pm), this impressive dragon sculpture spouts fire and water from its head near the Han River's eastern bank. The best observation spots are the cafes lining the eastern bank to the north of the bridge; boat trips taking in the action also depart from Đ Bach Dang on the river's western bank. The colour-changing Dragon Bridge sees selfie-takers parking their scooters on the bridge every night.

★Museum of Cham Sculpture MUSEUM

(Bao Tang; 1 Đ Trung Nu Vuong; 40,000d; ⏲7am-5pm) This small but important museum contains the world's largest collection of Cham artefacts, housed in buildings marrying French-colonial architecture with Cham elements. Founded in 1915 by the École Française d'Extrême Orient, it displays more than 300 pieces including altars, *lingas* (stylised phalluses representing Shiva), *garudas* (griffin-like sky beings), *apsaras* (heavenly nymphs), Ganeshes and images of Shiva, Brahma and Vishnu, all dating from the 5th to 15th centuries. Explanations are slim. The audio guide is 20,000d (you'll need to show ID, passport or driving licence).

Tours

Danang Free Walking Tour WALKING

(☎0905 631 419; www.facebook.com/danangfreewalkingtour; Vietnam Hostel, 22-24-26 Đ Hung Vuong; ⏲9am & 3pm) Run by local English-speaking students who are keen to practise their English, these walking tours are a decent introduction to the city. Donate what you think is appropriate at the end of the tour, and maybe sign up for one of the other (paid) specialised tours, including a street-food option. Tours leave from the Vietnam Hostel (the office is at the back).

Funtastic Danang Food Tour FOOD & DRINK

(☎0905 272 921; www.summerle.com/foodtour; per person US$45) Very popular lunch and evening street-food and restaurant tours with Danang-born food blogger Summer Le, who has been been featured in the *New York Times*. Transport is by car and tours take in five spots exploring a variety of Danang bites.

Sleeping

The sweet spot for eating and nightlife is near the river west of the Dragon Bridge; staying east across the Han River near My Khe Beach saves you short taxi trips back and forth, but things are definitely less exciting.

Danang has a rapidly expanding selection of modern hotels along the riverside, and a few much-needed new hostels.

★Vietnam Hostel HOSTEL $

(☎0236-710 9228; www.vietnamhostel.com; 22-24-26 Đ Hung Vuong; dm US$9, d/apt from US$17/65; ❄📶) With stylish brickwork and excellent service, this clean, good-looking and hip choice enjoys a very central location with a wide variety of accommodation, from neat and cool-looking dorms with sizeable bunks to comfortable doubles and snazzy, fully equipped apartments, plus a fine bar and rooftop terrace (with a cinema planned). It's also the home of the Danang Free Walking Tour.

Memory Hostel HOSTEL $

(☎0236-374 7797; www.memoryhostel.com; 3 Đ Tran Quoc Toan; dm US$7-8; ❄📶) Sweet memories are made of casual strolls to the Dragon Bridge, restaurants and nightlife, all near this hostel with a choice of four- to 12-bed dorms, as well as a female six-bed dorm. If you just want to stay in, the decor is arty and eclectic, and beds have privacy curtains. An excellent budget option. Also arranges tours.

Orange Hotel HOTEL $$

(☎0236-356 6177; https://danangorangehotel.com; 29 Đ Hoang Dieu; d US$40-85; ❄@📶) This family-owned hotel has a lemongrass aroma in the lobby and sweet service instilled

Danang

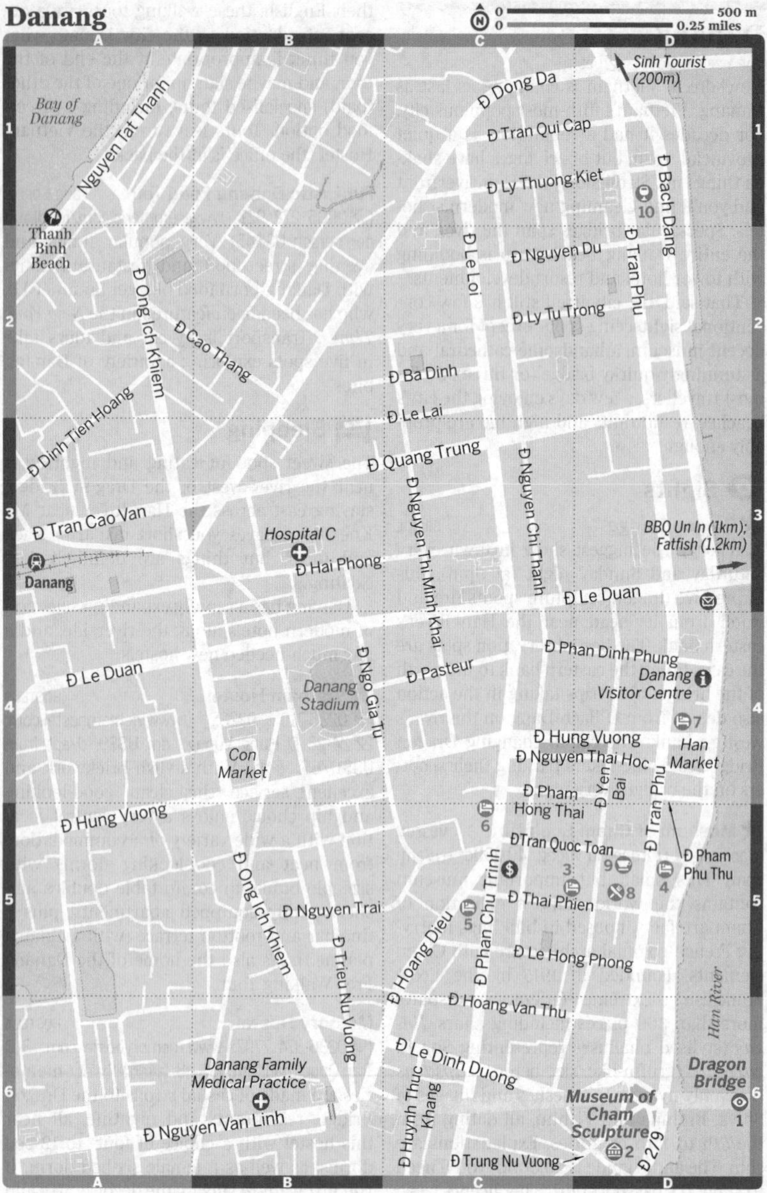

by the friendly patriarch/boss, who's sometimes on hand at reception or in the rooftop restaurant. Rooms are decorated with darkwood furniture and, despite the chintzy refrain here and there, the accommodation is very clean. The expansive weekend breakfast buffet features local dishes.

Frangipani Boutique Hotel BOUTIQUE HOTEL **$$**
(☎0236-393 8368; 8 Đ Nguyen Huu Thong; d US$45-50;) With just 11 rooms, and stylish common areas, the Frangipani is more like a classy European guesthouse. Rooms are spacious and modern with elegant decor, and it's just a short stroll to the

Danang

Top Sights
1 Dragon Bridge D6
2 Museum of Cham Sculpture D6

Activities, Courses & Tours
Danang Free Walking Tour .... (see 7)

Sleeping
3 Dong Duong Hotel C5
4 Memory Hostel D5
5 Orange Hotel C5
6 Sanouva C5
7 Vietnam Hostel D4

Eating
8 Ngoc Chi D5

Drinking & Nightlife
9 Golem Coffee D5
10 Luna Pub D1

sands of Danang Beach. There's a small indoor pool downstairs, bicycles are free to use, and there's also a pleasant on-site restaurant with courtyard seating.

Sanouva BOUTIQUE HOTEL **$$**
(☎0236-382 3468; www.sanouvadanang.com; 68 Đ Phan Chu Trinh; d from US$55;) Boutique mixes with business at the stylish Sanouva, located in a bustling commercial street just a few blocks from Danang's riverfront. An Asian-chic lobby is the introduction to relatively compact but modern rooms, and the inhouse S'Spa and S'Ngon restaurant are two good reasons to linger.

Dong Duong Hotel HOTEL **$$$**
(☎0236-363 1777; www.dongduonghotel.com.vn; 62 Đ Thai Phien; d/apt 1,800,000/3,200,000d;) The adorable staff at this large, smart hotel (with apartments) are half the appeal, while the lobby – with its classic cars (including a bright-yellow convertible VW Karmann Ghia, a scooter with sidecar and a classic Citroën) and slightly kitsch *faux* antiques – is a kind of marvel. Rooms are very comfortable, the included breakfast is superb and the service really shines.

Eating

Danang's restaurant scene is growing more cosmopolitan by the day. Street food is also great here, with copious *bun cha* (barbecued pork), *com* (rice and buffet) and *mi quang* (noodle soup) stalls. Dedicated foodies should strongly consider booking a food tour to really explore the Danang scene. Check out www.danangcuisine.com for Danang tips and tours by local blogger Summer Le.

★ **Taco Ngon** TACOS **$**
(☎0906 504 284; www.facebook.com/tacongon; 19 Đ Tu Quan; tacos 39,000d; ⏰10.30am-10pm) This small spot thrust down a back street serves quite possibly Vietnam's best tacos. Tuck into fusion flavour combos like pork with wasabi coleslaw, fish with ginger and lime, or chicken with a tamarind barbecue sauce. Cool it all down with a cheap can of La Rue beer or chuck in a tequila shot (30,000d).

There's another branch in town at 12 To Hien Thanh, also east of the Han River, to the north.

Ngoc Chi VEGETARIAN **$**
(32 Đ Thai Phien; meals 35,000d; ⏰6am-10pm;) This highly affordable and affable modern vegetarian choice enjoys a central location in the buzzing Danang downtown, with a tasty menu of classic fare from *banh canh* (noodle soup) to *banh cuon* (steamed rice rolls), *my xao mem* (fried yellow noodles), fake-meat vegan dishes or just a bowl of curry with *banh mi* bread, a winner every time.

Vegan Ramen VEGAN **$**
(34 Đ An Thuong 5; meals 100,000d; ⏰11am-11pm;) Vegans can make a beeline for this tiny one-man ramen outlet for ample and satisfying bowls of *tantan men* (dandan noodles) with shiitake mushrooms, seaweed and sweat-inducing spiciness, plus coconut curry ramen, *shoyu* ramen, cold noodles and stir-fried noodles, each dish coupled with a dessert. All ramen dishes are loaded with flavour and goodness.

★ **Fatfish** FUSION **$$**
(☎0236-394 5707; www.fatfishrestaurant.com; 439 Đ Tran Hung Dao; meals 110,000-330,000d; ⏰10am-11pm;) This stylish restaurant and lounge bar has led the eating and drinking charge across the Han River on the eastern shore. Innovative Asian fusion dishes, pizza and wood-fired barbecue all partner with flavour-packed craft beers from Ho Chi Minh City's Pasteur Street Brewing Company (p142). Fatfish is good for a few snacks or a more leisurely full meal.

BBQ Un In BARBECUE, VIETNAMESE $$
(☎0236-654 5357; www.bbqunin.com; 379 Đ Tran Hung Dao; meals 100,000-210,000d; ⏰11.30am-10.30pm) Vietnamese flavours and American barbecue combine at this fun new place along the fast-expanding restaurant strip on the Han River's eastern bank. Shipping containers daubed with colourful street art provide the backdrop for fall-off-the-bone ribs, spicy grilled sausages, and hearty side dishes including sweetcorn and grilled pineapple. Order up a good-value beer tower if you're dining in a group.

Drinking & Nightlife

Luna Pub BAR
(www.facebook.com/LunaPubDanang; 9a Đ Tran Phu; ⏰11am-2am Mon-Wed, Fri & Sat, to 1am Thu & Sun; 📶) Half bar, half Italian restaurant, this hot hang-out is a warehouse-sized space with an open frontage, a DJ booth in the cabin of a truck, cool music, an amazing selection of drinks and and some shisha-smoking action. It's also popular with the expat crowd for its authentic Italian food (pizza, pasta, salads and more). Check its Facebook page for details of regular live gigs.

Golem Coffee CAFE
(☎0915 857 079; www.facebook.com/golemdanang; 27 Đ Tran Quoc Toan; ⏰7am-10pm; 📶) Hidden away from Danang's busy streets, this leafy and quiet garden cafe with a rustic but chic vibe is popular with younger locals cooling down with smoothies and gazing into smartphones. Try the refreshing coconut-and-yoghurt smoothie, and relax in the chilled interior, or on the teak daybeds or pleasantly mismatched furniture outside. The rooftop terrace is the place to be after dark.

Information

Agribank (111 Đ Phan Chu Trinh; ⏰24hr)

Danang Family Medical Practice (☎0236-358 2699; www.vietnammedicalpractice.com; 96-98 Đ Nguyen Van Linh; ⏰8am-7pm Mon-Fri, 8.30am-5pm Sat, 8.30am-12.30pm Sun) With in-patient facilities; run by an Israeli doctor.

Danang Visitor Centre (☎0236-355 0111; www.tourism.danang.vn; 108 Đ Bach Dang; ⏰8am-9.30pm) This visitor centre is really helpful, with English spoken and good maps and brochures, while the official Danang tourism website is one of Vietnam's best. Bicycles can be rented here.

Hospital C (Benh Vien C; ☎0511 382 1483; 122 Đ Hai Phong; ⏰24hr) The most modern of the four hospitals in town.

Getting There & Around

Danang is the main gateway to Hoi An, and staff at all hotels and hostels can help arrange transport there.

AIR

Danang's large airport is 2km west of the city centre. It has international connections with China, South Korea, India, Japan, Macau, Hong Kong, Thailand, Cambodia, Singapore and Taiwan. There are also dozens of daily domestic flights to cities across Vietnam.

There is no airport bus; a taxi ride is around 60,000d to central Danang hotels.

BUS

Sinh Tourist (☎0236-384 3259; www.thesinhtourist.vn; 16 Đ 3 Thang 2; ⏰7am-8pm) open-tour buses pick up from the company office on Đ Bach Dang (near the Dragon Bridge) twice daily to both Hue (90,000d, 2½ hours) and Hoi An (80,000d, one hour); Sinh Tourist can also advise on travel to Laos.

The large **Intercity Bus Station** (☎0236-382 1265; Đ Dien Bien Phu) is 3km west of the city centre. A metered **taxi** (☎0511 356 5656) to the riverside will cost 70,000d.

TRAIN

The train ride to Hue is one of the best in the country – it's worth taking as an excursion in itself for the stunning coastline.

Services from the **train station** (202 Đ Hai Phong) go to all destinations on the north–south main line.

Hoi An

POP 152,000 / ☎0235

Graceful, historic Hoi An is Vietnam's most atmospheric and delightful town. Once a major port, it boasts the grand architecture and beguiling riverside setting that befit its heritage, and the 21st-century curses of traffic and pollution are almost entirely absent.

The face of the Old Town has preserved its incredible legacy of tottering Japanese merchant houses, elaborate Chinese guildhalls, ancestral halls and ancient tea warehouses – though, of course, residents and rice fields have been gradually replaced by tourist businesses. Lounge bars, boutique hotels, travel agents, a glut of tailor shops and vast numbers of Korean and Chinese tourists are very much part of the scene here. And yet, down by the market and over on Cam Nam Island, you'll find that life has changed little. Travel a few kilometres further – you'll find some superb bicycle, motorbike and boat trips – and some of central Vietnam's most enticingly laid-back scenery and beaches are within easy reach.

Sights

A Unesco World Heritage Site, **Hoi An Old Town** (www.hoianworldheritage.org.vn; Old Town five-attraction tickets 120,000d) levies an admission fee to most of its historic buildings, which goes towards funding the preservation of the town's architecture. Buying the ticket gives you a choice of five heritage sites to visit – Chinese Assembly Halls, pagodas and temples, historic houses and museums. Booths dotted around the Old Town sell tickets.

Tickets are valid for 10 days. You won't normally be checked if you're just dining or shopping in the area, but keep your ticket with you just in case.

Below are just a selection of Hoi An's many historic sights.

★Japanese Covered Bridge BRIDGE
(Cau Nhat Ban; entry with Old Town ticket; ⏲24hr) Emblematic of Hoi An, this beautiful bridge was first constructed in the 1590s by the Japanese community to link it with the Chinese quarters. Over the centuries the ornamentation has remained relatively faithful to the original Japanese design. When you cross using your Old Town ticket, one of the stubs will be snipped away, so if you cross the bridge again, just say your ticket stub for the bridge has been taken already, otherwise the ticket checker will remove another stub.

★Tan Ky House HISTORIC BUILDING
(101 Đ Nguyen Thai Hoc; entry with Old Town ticket; ⏲8am-noon & 2-4.30pm) Built two centuries ago by an ethnically Vietnamese family, this gem of a house has been lovingly preserved through seven generations. Look out for signs of Japanese and Chinese influences in the architecture. Japanese elements include the ceiling (in the sitting area), which is supported by three progressively shorter beams, one on top of the other. Under the crab-shell ceiling are carvings of crossed sabres wrapped in silk ribbon. The sabres symbolise force; the silk represents flexibility.

DON'T MISS

MY SON

Set under the shadow of Cat's Tooth Mountain are the enigmatic ruins of **My Son** (150,000d; ⏲6.30am-4pm), the most important remains of the ancient Cham empire and a Unesco World Heritage Site. Although Vietnam has better-preserved Cham sites, none are as extensive and few have such beautiful surroundings, with brooding mountains and clear streams running between the temples.

My Son's impressive **museum** (entry with My Son ticket; ⏲6.30am-4pm) has many statues from the site, as well as information about the carvings, statues and architecture.

The ruins are 55km southwest of Hoi An. Day tours to My Son can be arranged in Hoi An for between US$10 and US$15, not including admission, and some trips return to Hoi An by boat. Get here early in order to beat the tour groups, or later in the afternoon.

★Assembly Hall of the Fujian Chinese Congregation TEMPLE
(Phuc Kien Hoi Quan; opposite 35 Đ Tran Phu; entry with Old Town ticket; ⏲7am-5.30pm) Originally a traditional assembly hall (or guildhall), this structure was later transformed into a temple for the worship of Thien Hau, a deity who protects seafarers. The green-tiled triple gateway dates from 1975. The mural on the right-hand wall depicts Thien Hau, her way lit by lantern light as she crosses a stormy sea to rescue a foundering ship. Opposite is a mural of the heads of the six Fujian families who fled from China to Hoi An in the 17th century.

Tran Family Chapel HISTORIC BUILDING
(21 Đ Le Loi; entry with Old Town ticket; ⏲7.30am-noon & 2-5.30pm) Built for worshipping family ancestors of the Tran (陳) clan, this chapel (more accurately an ancestral hall) dates back to 1802. It was commissioned by Tran Tu, a member of the clan who ascended to the rank of mandarin and served as an ambassador to China. His picture is to the right of the chapel as you enter. The architecture of the building reflects the influence of Chinese (the 'turtle'-style roof), Japanese (triple beam) and vernacular (bow-and-arrow detailing) styles.

Hoi An

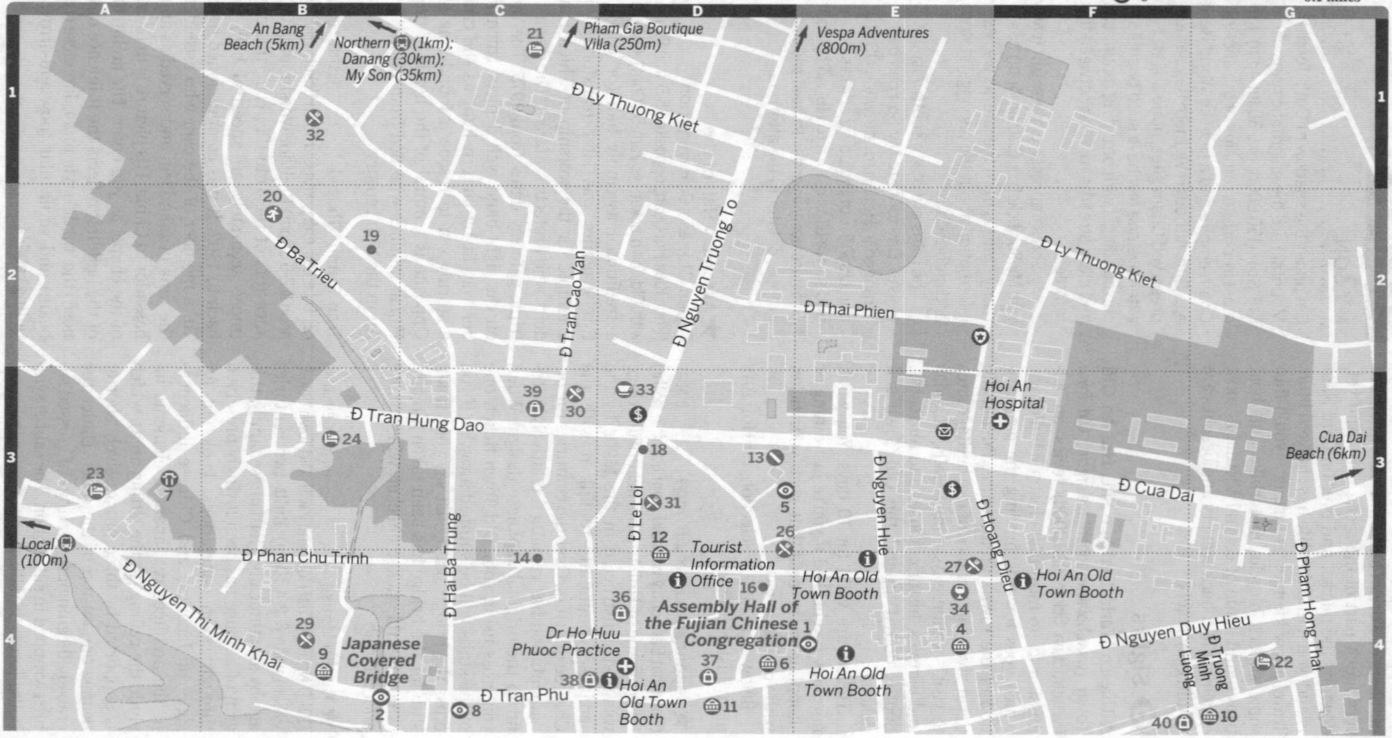
0 200 m
0 0.1 miles
A B C D E F G
1 2 3 4
An Bang Beach (5km)
Northern (1km); Danang (30km); My Son (35km)
Pham Gia Boutique Villa (250m)
Vespa Adventures (800m)
Đ Ly Thuong Kiet
Đ Ba Trieu
Đ Tran Cao Van
Đ Nguyen Truong To
Đ Thai Phien
Hoi An Hospital
Đ Tran Hung Dao
Cua Dai Beach (6km)
Đ Cua Dai
Đ Le Loi
Đ Nguyen Hue
Đ Hoang Dieu
Local (100m)
Đ Phan Chu Trinh
Đ Hai Ba Trung
Tourist Information Office
Hoi An Old Town Booth
Đ Pham Hong Thai
Đ Nguyen Thi Minh Khai
Assembly Hall of the Fujian Chinese Congregation
Dr Ho Huu Phuoc Practice
Japanese Covered Bridge
Đ Tran Phu
Hoi An Old Town Booth
Hoi An Old Town Booth
Hoi An Old Town Booth
Đ Nguyen Duy Hieu
Đ Truong Minh Luong
1 2 4 5 6 7 8 9 10 11 12 13 14 16 18 19 20 21 22 23 24 26 27 29 30 31 32 33 34 36 37 38 39 40

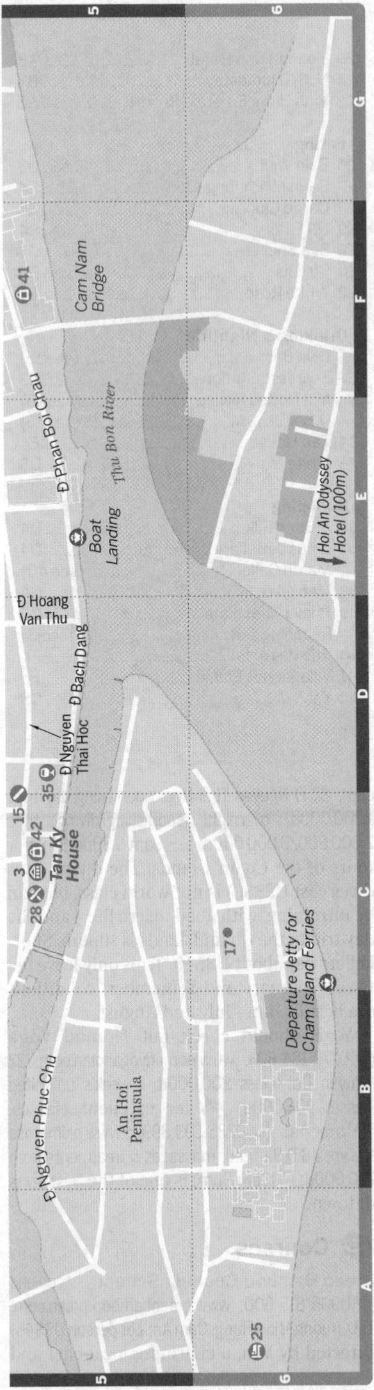

Phung Hung Old House HISTORIC BUILDING

(4 Đ Nguyen Thi Minh Khai; entry with Old Town ticket; ⏲8am-6pm) Just a few steps down from the Japanese Covered Bridge, this old house has a wide, welcoming entrance hall decorated with exquisite lanterns, wall hangings and embroidery. You can walk out onto a balcony and there's also an impressive suspended altar. Note that with all the photographing by the crowds that squeeze onto the balcony, the staff may control numbers to avoid the risk of it collapsing.

Assembly Hall of the Hainan Chinese Congregation HISTORIC BUILDING

(Hai Nam Hoi Quan; 10 Đ Tran Phu; ⏲8am-5pm) FREE Built in 1851, this assembly hall is a memorial to 108 merchants from Hainan Island who were mistaken for pirates and killed in Quang Nam province. The elaborate dais contains plaques to their memory. In front of the central altar is a fine gilded woodcarving of Chinese court life.

Confucius Temple CONFUCIAN TEMPLE

(Mieu Tho Khong Tu; Đ Tran Hung Dao) Behind an impressive gate emblazoned with Chinese *chu nho* characters that simply translate as 'Confucius Temple', this magnificent temple to the west of all the action is a colourful explosion of ceramic tiles. Look out for the spirit wall across the bridge that depicts a *ky lan,* a mythical chimerical creature often depicted in Confucian temples. At the rear is an effigy of Confucius (Khong Tu), venerated in the 'Great Achievement Hall'.

Chinese All-Community Assembly Hall HISTORIC BUILDING

(Chua Ba; 64 Đ Tran Phu; ⏲8am-5pm) FREE Founded in 1773, this assembly hall was used by Fujian, Cantonese, Hainanese, Chaozhou and Hakka congregations in Hoi An. To the right of the entrance are portraits of Chinese resistance heroes in Vietnam who died during WWII. The well-restored main temple is a total assault on the senses, with smoking incense spirals, demonic-looking deities, dragons and lashings of red lacquer – it's dedicated to Thien Hau, the goddess protector of seafarers commonly worshipped along the south coast of China.

Quan Thang House HISTORIC BUILDING

(77 Đ Tran Phu; entry with Old Town ticket; ⏲7am-5pm) This house is three centuries old and was built by a Chinese captain. As usual, the architecture includes Japanese and Chinese

Hoi An

Top Sights
1 Assembly Hall of the Fujian Chinese Congregation E4
2 Japanese Covered Bridge B4
3 Tan Ky House C5

Sights
4 Assembly Hall of the Hainan Chinese Congregation E4
5 Ba Le Well D3
6 Chinese All-Community Assembly Hall D4
7 Confucius Temple A3
8 Hoi An Old Town C4
9 Phung Hung Old House B4
10 Precious Heritage G4
11 Quan Thang House D4
12 Tran Family Chapel D4

Activities, Courses & Tours
13 Blue Coral Diving D3
14 Cactus Tours C4
15 Cham Island Diving Center D5
16 Eat Hoi An D4
17 Heaven & Earth C6
18 Herbs and Spices D3
19 Hoi An Free Tour B2
Hoi An Photo Tour ..... (see 40)
20 Palmarosa B2

Sleeping
21 Almanity Hoi An C1
22 Ha An Hotel G4
23 Hoang Trinh Hotel A3
24 Nu Ni Homestay B3
25 Vinh Hung Emerald Resort A6

Eating
26 Bale Well D3
27 Banh Mi Phuong E4
28 Cargo Club C5
29 Nu Eatery B4
30 Sea Shell C3
31 Streets D3
32 White Rose B1

Drinking & Nightlife
Dive Bar ..... (see 15)
33 Espresso Station D3
Mia Coffee House ..... (see 10)
Q Bar ..... (see 15)
34 Tap House E4
35 White Marble D5

Shopping
36 A Dong Silk D4
37 Lotus Jewellery D4
March Gallery ..... (see 40)
38 Metiseko C4
39 Pheva Chocolate C3
Reaching Out ..... (see 3)
40 Rue des Arts F4
41 Villagecraft Planet F5
42 Yaly C5

elements. There are some especially fine carvings of peacocks and flowers on the teak walls of the rooms around the courtyard, on the roof beams and under the crab-shell roof (in the salon beside the courtyard).

Cam Kim Island ISLAND

The master woodcarvers who crafted the intricate detail adorning Hoi An's public buildings and the historic homes of the town's merchants came from Kim Bong village on Cam Kim Island. Most of the woodcarvings on sale in Hoi An are produced here.

Boats to the island leave from the boat landing at Đ Bach Dang in town (35,000d, 30 minutes). The village and island, quite rural in character, are fun to explore by bicycle for a day.

Activities

Dive schools **Blue Coral Diving** (0235-627 9297; www.divehoian.com; 33 Đ Tran Hung Dao) and **Cham Island Diving Center** (0235-391 0782; www.vietnamscubadiving.com; 88 Đ Nguyen Thai Hoc; snorkelling day trips 1,200,000d, overnight snorkelling/diving trips 2,300,000/3,000,000d; 9am-9.30pm) offer tours of the Cham Islands. The diving (two dives cost US$80) is not world class, but can be intriguing, with good macro life – and the day trip to the Cham Islands is superb. Snorkellers pay about US$40. Trips only leave between February and September; conditions are best in June, July and August.

Yogis should check out **Nomad Yoga** (0777 184 604; www.nomadyogahoian.com; 22 Nguyen Du; class 200,000d, 1 week's unlimited classes 900,000d) for excellent classes. **Palmarosa** (0235-393 3999; www.palmarosaspa.vn; 48 Đ Ba Trieu; massages & treatments from 220,000d; 10am-9pm) is one of the best spas in town.

Courses

Green Bamboo Cooking School COOKING

(0905 815 600; www.greenbamboo-hoian.com; 21 Đ Truong Minh Hung, Cam An; per person US$45) Directed by Van, a charming local chef and

English-speaker, these courses are more personalised than most. Groups are limited to a maximum of 10, and classes take place in Van's spacious kitchen. Choose what to cook from a diverse menu including vegetarian choices. It's 5km east of the centre, near Cu Dai beach; transport from Hoi An is included.

Red Bridge Cooking School COOKING
(☎0235-393 3222; www.visithoian.com/redbridge/cookingschool.html; Thon 4, Cam Thanh; per person US$22-56) At this school, going to class involves a relaxing 4km cruise down the river. There are half-day and full-day courses, both of which include market visits. The half-day class focuses on local specialities, with

TOURS AROUND HOI AN

Hoi An Free Tour (www.freetour.com/hoi-an/free-bike-tours; 567 Đ Hai Ba Trung) Ride on a bike around the fringes of Hoi An with students. You get to meet the locals and see village life; they get to practise their English. Although tours are free, you will also need a reasonable 100,000d for bike rental, ferries and local community support.

Vespa Adventures (☎0938 500 997; www.vespaadventures.com; Alley 22/2, 170 Đ Ly Thai To; per person $US69-80; ⏲8am-5pm) Quite possibly the most fun and most stylish way to explore around Hoi An, Vespa Adventures offers the opportunity to ride pillion on classic retro two-wheelers with an Italian accent. There are morning and afternoon departures, and a popular after-dark 'Streets & Eats of Hoi An' option with lots of quality food and cold beer.

Phat Tire Ventures (☎0235-653 9839; www.ptv-vietnam.com; 80 Đ Le Hong Phong; per person from US$39) Offers a terrific mountain-bike trip to the My Son ruins that takes in country lanes and temple visits. Pickups from hotels are included. Also has adventure thrills via rappelling and rock climbing.

Eat Hoi An (Coconut Tours; ☎0905 411 184; www.eathoian.com; 37 Đ Phan Chu Trinh; per person US$45; ⏲7am-10pm Mon-Fri, 8am-10pm Sat, 8am-11pm Sun) Lots of really authentic cuisine and the infectious enthusiasm of host Phuoc make this an excellent choice if you really want to explore the grassroots local street-food scene. Be prepared for lots of different foods and flavours; check the website for details of cooking classes held in Phuoc's home village.

Taste of Hoi An (☎0905 382 783; www.tasteofhoian.com; per person US$70) Walk the streets to meet the vendors, then munch your lunch at an ancient (though air-conditioned) Hoi An town house on this award-winning tour.

Hoi An Photo Tour (☎0905 671 898; www.hoianphototour.com; 42 Đ Phan Boi Chau; per person from US$40) Excellent tours with experienced photographer Etienne Bossot. Sunrise and sunset tours are most popular, harnessing Hoi An's delicate light for images of fishers and rice paddies. Experienced and newbie photographers are both catered for, and specialist private and night-time workshops are also available. Check the website for details of occasional three-day photography trips uncovering more remote areas around Hoi An.

Cactus Tours (☎0235-350 5017; www.hoian-bicycle.com.vn; 66 Đ Phan Chu Trinh; tours US$29; ⏲9am-8.30pm) Has good bicycle tours along quiet country lanes, past vegetable gardens and fishing villages, as well as walking tours of Hoi An. Also uses the name 'Love of Life'.

Heaven & Earth (☎0235-386 4362; www.vietnam-bicycle.com; 61 Đ Ngo Quyen, An Hoi; tours from US$19) Heaven & Earth's cycling tours are well thought out and not too strenuous; they explore the Song Thu river delta area. Mountain-bike tours take in local dirt trails and rickety bamboo bridges.

Hoi An Motorbike Adventures (☎0905 101 930, 0235-391 1930; www.motorbiketours-hoian.com; Nguyen Chi Thanh; from US$50) Specialises in tours on hardy offroad motorbikes. The guides really know the terrain, and the trips make use of beautiful back roads and riverside tracks. Self-ride (with a licence) or back-of-the-bike pillion options are available, and some of the itineraries can also be done in a jeep.

rice-paper making and food-decoration tips thrown in for good measure. The full-day class instructs participants in the fine art of *pho* (beef noodle soup).

Herbs and Spices COOKING
(☎ 0510 393 9568, 0235-393 6868; www.herbsandspicesvn.com; 2/6 Đ Le Loi; per person US$35-58; ⏰10.30am, 4.30pm & 8pm) Set up by the owner of the Little Menu (p112) restaurant, these excellent classes have smaller, more hands-on groups than some other cookery classes, with three different menu options.

Festivals & Events

Full Moon Festival CULTURAL
(⏰5-11pm 14th day each lunar month) Hoi An is a delightful place to be on the 14th day of each lunar month, when the town celebrates a Full Moon Festival. Motorised vehicles are banned from the Old Town, while street markets sell handicrafts, souvenirs and food, and all the lanterns come out. Traditional plays and musical events are also performed.

Sleeping

Hoi An has good-value accommodation in all price categories. There are only a couple of hotels in the Old Town, but nightlife finishes early here so there is little need to be right in the middle of things. Plenty of decent sleeping options are close by.

Another option is staying at An Bang Beach, 3km away.

Lazy Bear Hostel HOSTEL $
(☎ 0905 025 491; www.facebook.com/lazybearhostel; 12 Đ Tran Quuc Toan; dm/d incl breakfast US$8/20; ❄📶) This small family-owned hostel has a good location – the Old Town and Cua Dai Beach are both around 2.5km away – and lots of free inclusions, such as breakfast, bicycles and the occasional bar crawl and food tour. A relaxing garden and modern bathrooms in the private en-suite rooms seal the deal at one of Hoi An's best-value accommodation options.

Hoi An Backpackers Hostel HOSTEL $
(☎ 0235-391 4400; www.vietnambackpackerhostels.com; 252 Đ Cua Dai; dm/tw/d incl breakfast US$12/40/40; 🚭❄@📶🏊) This purpose-built hostel – part of a hostel empire spanning the nation – offers decent and clean dorms and private en-suite rooms. A pool-side bar and restaurant and plenty of quiet common areas add kudos. It's handily located between the Old Town and the beach, and bikes for exploring are available to hire.

Hoang Trinh Hotel HOTEL $
(☎ 0235-391 6579; www.hoianhoangtrinhhotel.com; 45 Đ Le Quy Don; r incl breakfast US$20-35; ❄@📶) Well-run hotel with helpful, friendly staff who make travellers feel welcome. Rooms are quite 'old school' Vietnamese but spacious and clean. Generous breakfast. Pickup from bus station is included.

★Hoi An Odyssey Hotel BOUTIQUE HOTEL $$
(☎ 0235-391 1818; www.hoianodysseyhotel.com; Đ Xuyen Trung, Cam Thanh; d from US$55; 🚭❄📶🏊) In a semi-rural location across on Cam Thanh island – an easy 1.5km bike ride from the Old Town – the Odyssey is a great haven after a day's exploring. Rice-paddy and river views, a compact pool and stylish rooms all combine at one of Hoi An's best hotels. Bicycles and a handy shuttle to a private beach are both complimentary.

★Nu Ni Homestay GUESTHOUSE $$
(☎ 0235-392 7979; www.nu-ni-homestay.hoi-an-hotels.com/en; 131/12 Đ Tran Hung Dao; d/tr/f US$22/32/42; 🚭❄📶) Hidden down a quiet lane just north of the Old Town, the Nu Ni Homestay has seven spacious and sparkling rooms – some with large balconies – and a positive can-do attitude from the friendly family owners. Modern bathrooms and a comfortable shared downstairs area all make Nu Ni a great choice. Breakfast is not included in the price.

Ha An Hotel HISTORIC HOTEL $$
(☎ 0235-386 3126; www.haanhotel.com; 6-8 Đ Phan Boi Chau; r US$65-110; ❄@📶) Elegant and refined, the Ha An feels more like a colonial mansion than a hotel. All rooms have nice individual touches – textile wall hangings, calligraphy or paintings – and views fall over a gorgeous central garden. The helpful, well-trained staff make staying here a joy. It's about a five-minute walk from the centre of town (free bikes are available too).

The hotel has a spa, a cafe and a bar.

Vinh Hung Emerald Resort HOTEL $$
(☎ 0510 393 4999; www.vinhhungemeraldresort.com; Minh An, An Hoi; r US$50-80, ste US$95; 🚭❄📶🏊) A beautifully designed hotel with a riverside location in An Hoi, and modern-

ist rooms that represent good value for money. All rooms face the lovely central pool, or have a terrace facing the river. There's a fitness centre and small spa.

Pham Gia Boutique Villa GUESTHOUSE $$
(☎0235-396 3963, 0914 085 075; www.phamgiahoian.com; 73/1 Đ Phan Dinh Phung; d/ste from US$35/42;) Centred on its blue pool, Pham Gia edges into the boutique-guesthouse category. Blending colonial and local design, rooms are spacious and sunny, and the friendly owner is a Hoi An local with plenty of experience in the travel industry. Bikes are provided free of charge, and both the Old Town and An Bang Beach are just a short ride away.

Ivy Villa HOTEL $$
(☎0235-391 0999; www.ivyvillahoian.com; 168a Đ Nguyen Duy Hieu; r from US$32;) Out of the thick of things on the eastern edge of Hoi An, Ivy Villa is a professionally run and welcoming choice set alongside a small, blue rectangular pool. Rooms are modern, comfortable and decent value, while the breakfasts are excellent. The hotel can arrange tours and offers free bike rental.

Hoi An Beach Rentals RENTAL HOUSE $$$
(www.hoi-an-beach-rentals.com; houses US$180-200;) Asian-chic decor is the common theme of these lovely self-contained rental homes near the beach in An Bang village. Annam House (sleeps six; US$200) is a converted village home with three bedrooms and a beautiful garden. Nearby, CoChin House (sleeps four; US$180) is constructed in wood in heritage Vietnamese style, and has an expansive garden and a private lookout.

Decorated with art and antiques, the Temple Beach House (US$230) incorporates temple elements into its seductive interior.

Almanity Hoi An BOUTIQUE HOTEL $$$
(☎0235-366 6888; www.almanityhoian.com; 326 Đ Ly Thuong Kiet; d US$140-220;) With a super-breezy foyer, heritage-style and modern wellness-themed rooms, Almanity may just be the most relaxing hotel in town. Gardens and swimming pools create a laid-back haven despite the central location, happy hour in the bar often runs for three hours, and there's a full menu of spa and massage services. Check online for good-value 'Spa Journey' packages.

Eating

★ Vegan Zone VEGAN $
(☎0888 122 655; www.facebook.com/veganzonehoian; 197 Đ Nguyen Duy Hieu; mains from 60,000d; ⏲10am-9pm;) This handsome-looking restaurant in the east of town pulls out the stops with a tantalising menu of vegan dishes, from potato cake through to *bun rieu* (rice noodle soup), lemongrass tofu, delicious vegan curry or steaming mushroom hotpot. Combine these with one of Vegan Zone's thirst-busting fruit juices, satisfying smoothies or a cider. Last dinner orders are at 8.30pm.

Banh Mi Phuong VIETNAMESE $
(2b Đ Phan Chu Trinh; banh mi 20,000-30,000d; ⏲6.30am-9.30pm) What makes the *banh mi* (filled baguettes) at this cramped joint draw the stupendous crowds out front? It's the dense, chewy bread, the freshness of the greens and the generous serves of *thit nuong* (chargrilled pork), beef and other meat that seals the deal. A celebrity-chef endorsement helps too.

Streets VIETNAMESE $
(☎0235-391 1949; www.streetsinternational.org; 17 Đ Le Loi; meals from 110,000d; ⏲8am-10pm) Do the meals taste exceptional here because Streets is for a good cause? Perhaps it helps to know that the staff are disadvantaged

A HOI AN TASTER

Hoi An is a culinary hotbed and there are some unique dishes you should make sure you sample.

'White rose' *(banh vac)* is an incredibly delicate, subtly flavoured shrimp dumpling topped with crispy onions; sample it at the restaurants White Rose and Streets and at other eateries about town. *Banh bao* is another steamed dumpling, this one with minced pork or chicken, onions, eggs and mushrooms, which is said to be derived from Chinese dim sum. *Cao lau* is an amazing dish: Japanese-style noodles seasoned with herbs, salad greens and bean sprouts, and served with slices of roast pork. Other local specialities are fried *hoanh thanh* (wonton) and *banh xeo* (crispy savoury pancakes rolled with herbs in fresh rice paper). Most restaurants serve these items, but quality varies widely.

youths trained up in hospitality, but the textbook-good *cao lau* and 'white rose' dumplings deserve an A+ regardless. Although the place is busy, the service is warm and delightful.

White Rose DUMPLINGS $
(☎0235-386 2784; www.facebook.com/bonghongtrang.hoian; 533 Đ Hai Ba Trung; dishes from 70,000d; ⏲7am-8.30pm) White Rose has a menu of just two dishes, so take half of each if you want, as many diners do. The choice is the (secret recipe) *banh bao banh vac* (shrimp dumpling) – so named as it resembles a white rose – and crispy *hoanh thanh chien* (fried wonton; also nicknamed Hoi An pizza). Both are delicious and the restaurant is frequently packed.

★**Sea Shell** FRENCH, SEAFOOD $$
(☎091 429 8337; 119 Đ Tran Cao Van; meals 90,000d; ⏲noon-9pm Mon-Sat) Shaded by a decades-old banyan tree, Sea Shell is a flavour-packed offshoot of Nu Eatery in Hoi An's atmospheric Old Town. Try snacks like tempura-prawn rolls and turmeric-catfish wraps, or mains like spicy pork noodles with a refreshing calamari and green-apple salad. A decent wine list covers Australia, France, Italy and South Africa.

★**Cargo Club** INTERNATIONAL $$
(☎0235-391 1227; www.tastevietnam.asia/cargo-club-cafe-restaurant-hoi-an; 109 Đ Nguyen Thai Hoc; meals 70,000-160,000d; ⏲8am-11pm; 📶) This remarkable cafe-restaurant, serving Vietnamese and Western food, has a terrific riverside location (the upper terrace has stunning views). A relaxing day here munching your way around the menu would be a day well spent. The breakfasts are legendary (try the eggs Benedict), the patisserie and cakes are superb, and fine-dining dishes and cocktails also deliver.

Nu Eatery FUSION $$
(www.facebook.com/NuEateryHoiAn; 10a Đ Nguyen Thị Minh Khai; meals 130,000d; ⏲noon-9pm Mon-Sat) Don't be deceived by the humble decor at this compact place near the Japanese Covered Bridge; there's a real wow factor to the seasonal small plates at this Hoi An favourite. Combine the pork-belly steamed buns (35,000d) with a salad of grilled pineapple, watermelon and pickled shallots (75,000d), and don't miss the homemade lemongrass, ginger or chilli ice cream (35,000d).

Bale Well VIETNAMESE $$
(51 Đ Tran Hung Dao; meals 150,000d; ⏲11.30am-10pm) Down a little alley near the famous well, this local place is renowned for one dish: barbecued pork, served up satay-style, which you then combine with fresh greens and herbs to create your own fresh spring roll. A global reputation means it can get very busy.

Drinking & Nightlife

Hoi An is not a huge party town as the local authorities keep a fairly strict lid on late-night revelry; backstreets can be very dark after 10pm.

Espresso Station CAFE
(☎0905 691 164; www.facebook.com/TheEspressoStation; 28/2 Đ Tran Hung Dao; ⏲7.30am-5.30pm; 📶) A slice of Melbourne-style coffee culture, albeit in a heritage Hoi An residence, the Espresso Station is where to go for the best flat whites and cold-brew coffees in town. There's a compact food menu with granola, muesli and sandwiches; relaxing in the arty courtyard is where you'll want to be.

Look for the sign on the main road and venture down the alley.

Tap House CRAFT BEER
(☎0235-391 0333; 3 Đ Phan Chu Trinh; ⏲9am-11pm) Craft beers from around Vietnam are the attraction at this new Hoi An bar, but don't be surprised if you linger for the tasty charcuterie and cheeseboards as well. The Platinum pale ale is a standout, but all the brews are fine and there are a couple of ciders. The interior could do with some character, though.

White Marble WINE BAR
(☎0235-3911 862; www.facebook.com/whitemarblehoian; 99 Đ Le Loi; ⏲11am-11pm; 📶) This wine bar/restaurant in historic premises has an unmatched selection of wines; many are available by the glass. Lunch and dinner tasting menus cost from US$20, and the corner location is a great place to watch the world go by or gaze over the river.

Dive Bar BAR
(88 Đ Nguyen Thai Hoc; ⏲9am-midnight; 📶) A top bar option in Hoi An within the Cham Island Diving Center (p108), with a great vibe thanks to the welcoming service, contemporary electronic tunes and sofas for lounging. There's also a cocktail garden and bar at the rear, pub grub and a pool table.

Q Bar LOUNGE
(94 Đ Nguyen Thai Hoc; noon-midnight;) Q Bar offers stunning lighting, electronica and lounge music, and excellent (if pricey, at around 120,000d) cocktails and mocktails. Draws a cool crowd.

Shopping

Hoi An has long been known for fabric production, and tourist demand has swiftly shoehorned many tailor shops into the tiny Old Town. Shoes, also copied from Western designs, and supposed 'leather' goods are also popular, but quality is variable. Get something made to order at **Yaly** (0235-221 2474; www.yalycouture.com; 47 Đ Nguyen Thai Hoc; 8am-9pm) or **A Dong Silk** (0235-391 0579; www.adongsilk.com; 40 Đ Le Loi; 8am-9.30pm).

Hoi An also has more than a dozen art galleries; check out the streets near the Japanese Covered Bridge, along Đ Nguyen Thi Minh Khai.

★ **Villagecraft Planet** ARTS & CRAFTS
(www.facebook.com/VillagecraftPlanet; 59 Đ Phan Boi Chau; 10am-5pm Fri-Sun & Wed, to 7pm Mon, Tue & Thu) Shop here for intriguing and colourful homemade homewares and fashion, typically employing natural hemp, indigo dye and beeswax-stencilled batik, and crafted with fair-trade practices by the Hmong, Black Thai and Lolo ethnic-minority people in the north of Vietnam.

★ **Reaching Out** SOUVENIRS, CLOTHING
(0235-3910 168; www.reachingoutvietnam.com; 103 Đ Nguyen Thai Hoc; 8.30am-9.30pm Mon-Fri, 9.30am-8.30pm Sat & Sun) This excellent fair-trade gift shop stocks good-quality silk scarves, clothes, jewellery, hand-painted Vietnamese hats, handmade toys and teddy bears. The shop employs and supports artisans with disabilities, and staff are happy to show visitors through the workshop.

Rue des Arts ARTS & CRAFTS
(Đ Phan Boi Chau) This initiative focuses attention on Đ Phan Boi Chau, east of Đ Hoang Dieu, as a dedicated arts street with galleries, museums and cafes housed mainly in the heritage buildings of Hoi An's former French Quarter. Pick up a walking map from the **March Gallery** (0122 377 9074; www.marchgallery-hoian.com; 42 Đ Phan Boi Chau; 10am-6pm), **Precious Heritage** (0235-6558 382; www.facebook.com/precious.heritage.museum.art.gallery; 26 Đ Phan Boi Chau; 8.30am-8.30pm) FREE or **Mia Coffee House** (www.facebook.com/miacoffeehouse; 20 Đ Phan Boi Chau; 8am-5pm) and start exploring.

Pheva Chocolate CHOCOLATE
(0235-392 5260; www.phevaworld.com; 74 Đ Tran Hung Dao; 8am-7pm) Excellent artisan chocolate crafted from organic and free-trade cacao from Vietnam's southern Ben Tre province. The dark chocolate spiked with Phu Quoc peppercorns is especially good, but there's everything from mango to pistachio, sesame and peanuts and puffed rice.

Metiseko CLOTHING
(0235-392 9278; www.metiseko.com; 140-42 Đ Tran Phu; 8.30am-9.30pm) Winners of a sustainable-development award, this eco-minded store stocks gorgeous clothing (including kids' wear), accessories, and homewares such as cushions using natural silk and organic cotton. It is certified to use the Organic Content Standard label, and the company sources natural twill and Shantung and Habutai silk from within Vietnam.

Lotus Jewellery FASHION & ACCESSORIES
(www.lotusjewellery-hoian.com; 82 Đ Tran Phu; 8am-8pm) Lotus has very affordable and attractive hand-crafted pieces loosely modelled on butterflies, dragonflies, Vietnamese sampans, conical hats and Chinese zodiac symbols. There's another, smaller branch not far away at 53a Đ Le Loi.

Information

Hoi An is one of Vietnam's safer towns, but there are rare stories of late-night bag-snatching, pickpockets and (very occasionally) assaults on women. Many street lights are turned off from 9.30pm and it may not be advisable to walk home alone.

Agribank (12 Đ Tran Hung Dao; 8am-4.30pm Mon-Fri, 8.30am-1pm Sat) Changes cash and has ATMs.

Dr Ho Huu Phuoc Practice (0235-386 1419; 74 Đ Le Loi; 11am-12.30pm & 5-9.30pm) English-speaking doctor.

Hoi An Police Station (0235-386 1204; 6 Đ Ngo Gia Tu)

Main Post Office (6 Đ Tran Hung Dao; 6.30am-8pm) On the edge of the Old Town.

Tourist Information Office (0235-391 6961; www.quangnamtourism.com.vn; 47 Đ Phan Chu Trinh; 8am-5pm) Helpful office, with good English spoken.

Vietin Bank (0510 386 1340; 4 Đ Hoang Dieu; 8am-5pm Mon-Fri, 8.30am-1.30pm Sat) Changes cash and has an ATM.

Getting There & Away

Most north–south bus services do not stop at Hoi An, as Hwy 1 passes 10km west of the town.

More convenient open-tour buses offer regular connections for Hue and Nha Trang.

For Danang (one hour), it is much more convenient to organise a bus (around 120,000d) to pick you up at your accommodation. Yellow buses to Danang (20,000d) leave from the **Northern Bus Station** (Đ Le Hong Phong), a 15-minute walk or 20,000d taxi ride from central Hoi An. Hotels can book transfers to/from Danang airport and train station.

Getting Around

Hoi An is best explored on foot; cars and motorbikes (but not bicycles) are banned from the central Old Town streets from 8am to 11am and 3pm to 9pm. To go further afield, rent a bicycle (25,000d per day). The route east to Cua Dai Beach is quite scenic. A motorbike without/with a driver will cost around US$6/12 per day. Reckon on about 70,000d for a taxi to An Bang Beach.

Hoi An Taxi (0510-391 9919) Good local taxi operators.

Mai Linh (0235-392 5925) Local partners of a reliable Vietnam-wide taxi company.

Around Hoi An

An Bang Beach

Cua Dai Beach might be nearest to Hoi An, but its sand has largely disappeared due to coastal erosion. An Bang, 3km east of Hoi An, is one of Vietnam's most happening and enjoyable beaches. At present there's a wonderful stretch of fine sand and an enormous horizon, with only the distant Cham Islands interrupting the seaside symmetry. Staying at the beach and visiting Hoi An on day trips is a good strategy for a relaxing visit to the area.

Access to Hoi An is easy – it's just a five-minute taxi journey (70,000d) or a 20-minute bike ride.

Good sleeping options in An Bang include budget stronghold **Under the Coconut Tree** (0168 245 5666, 0235-651 6666; www.underthecoconuttreehoian.com; dm US$8, d US$25-30, f US$40;), while **An Bang Seaside Village Homestay** (0911 111 101; www.anbangseasidevillage.com; cottage & villa d US$60-115;) is a fine midrange option. Rental houses **Chi Villa** (0935 310 875; www.chivilla.com; villas from US$430;), **Hoi An Beach Bungalows** (0908 117 533; www.hoianbeachbungalows.com; Lac Long Quan; apt from US$50-150;) and Hoi An Beach Rentals (p111) offer great value for sharers and families.

Overlooking the ocean, head to the beachside **Salt Pub** (www.saltpubhoian.com; Đ Nguyen Phan Vinh; meals 120,000-180,000d; 7.30am-late) for beers and grub and the (neighbouring) sublime **Sound of Silence** (0235-386 1101; www.facebook.com/soundofsilencecoffee; 40 Đ Nguyen Phan Vinh; 7.15am-4.30pm;) cafe for coffee.

Cham Islands

POP 3000 / 0236

A breathtaking cluster of granite islands, set in aquamarine seas around 15km directly offshore from Hoi An, the Cham Islands make a worthwhile excursion. A rich underwater environment features 135 species of soft and hard coral, and varied macro life.

However, overtourism has become a problem as visitor numbers have swelled from just 17,000 in 2009 to a staggering 400,000 in 2018. A daily cap of 3000 visitors to the islands is now in effect.

The Chams have only simple guesthouses (in the main village of Bai Lang). If possible, we recommend a few nights with the **Bai Huong homestay** (www.homestaybaihuong.com; per person 120,000d) program to experience the best of the islands. Dive operators in Hoi An can also arrange overnight camping stays.

There are restaurants in Bai Lang.

Getting There & Away

Public boats to Cham Island dock at Bai Lang. There's a scheduled daily connection from a jetty on Đ Nguyen Hoang in Hoi An (two hours, departing between 7am and 7.30am), west of the Hoi An Silk Marina Resort & Spa. Foreigners are routinely charged up to 150,000d. The ferry also stops at Cua Dai Pier at 8.30am; pay your 70,000d admission fee to the islands on board the ferry. Note that boats do not sail in heavy seas. From Bai Lang, a return ferry to Hoi An leaves between 11am and 11.30am. Speedboats also make the one-way trip to Bai Lang for around 300,000d.

Alternatively, come on a day trip with an outfit such as the Cham Island Diving Center (p108).

SOUTHEAST COAST

Vietnam has an incredibly curvaceous coastline and on this coast it's defined by sweeping sands, towering cliffs and concealed bays. Nha Trang and Mui Ne are key destinations, but the beach breaks come thick and fast here. The tranquil little cove of Bai Xep is a good bet to escape the crowds.

If your idea of paradise is reclining in front of turquoise waters, weighing up the merits of a massage or a mojito, then you have come to the right place. On hand to complement the sedentary delights are activities to set the pulse racing, including scuba diving, snorkelling, surfing, windsurfing and kitesurfing. Action or inaction, this coast bubbles with opportunities.

Quy Nhon

POP 337,000 / ☎0256

A large, prosperous coastal city, Quy Nhon (hwee ngon) boasts a terrific beach-blessed shoreline and grand boulevards. Its seaside appeal and tidy, litter-free streets make it worth a stop to sample some fresh seafood.

Quy Nhon is steadily shaking off its somewhat provincial reputation, and there's an emerging cafe and bar scene worth investigating. The city is also the main gateway to the lovely cove of Bai Xep.

Other fine beaches lie east of town along the Phuong Mai Peninsula, including Ky Co.

Sights

Also check out the city's twin monuments, the **Thap Doi Cham Towers** (Đ Tran Hung Dao; 20,000d; ⏲7am-8.30pm), while you're here.

★Municipal Beach BEACH

The long sweep of Quy Nhon's beachfront extends from the port in the northeast to distant wooded hills in the south. It's a beautiful stretch of sand and has been given a major facelift in recent years. There's little rubbish in evidence and good swimming at the southern end.

Ky Co Beach BEACH

(Phuong Mai Peninsula; 100,000d) Backed by coastal cliffs, this drop-dead-gorgeous cove beach is 23km east of Quy Nhon. Ky Co's turquoise waters and fine pale sands have not gone unnoticed by the Instagram crowd, and it's wildly popular with day-tripping domestic tourists, so visit early or late in the day if possible. Note that access is tricky: from the car park above the beach via 4WD shuttle (60,000d per person), or on foot.

Binh Dinh Museum MUSEUM

(28 Đ Nguyen Hue; ⏲7-11am & 2-5pm Apr-Sep, 7.30-11am & 1.30-4.30pm Oct-Mar) FREE This small museum concentrates on regional history and has some superb Cham sculpture. The entry hall focuses on local communism, while the room to the left has a natural-history section and exhibits devoted to tribal culture. Impressive Cham relics fill the rear room, including an astonishing 12th-century statue of the Goddess Mahishasuramardini. The room to the right is devoted to the American War.

Sleeping

Kim House HOSTEL $

(☎0902 343 635; www.facebook.com/pg/den2coffee; 25 Đ Le Xuan Tru; dm 132,000d, d 297,000-330,000d; ❄📶) Fine new hostel on a side road with cosy six-bed dorms and decent private rooms that have high ceilings and solid wooden furniture. Showers are clean and there's a great cafe downstairs for your free breakfast, as well as good coffee and beers.

John & Paul Inn HOSTEL $

(☎0256-651 7770; http://johnandpaulinn.com; 63 Đ Chuong Duong; dm US$5-6, r US$16; ❄📶) Popular hostel in the south of town with clean dorms (including a female-only option) and good private rooms with cable TV and balcony. The name references the Beatles, though you're more likely to hear heavy rock and metal in the busy downstairs restobar.

Anya Hotel Quy Nhon HOTEL $$$

(☎0256-653 6728; https://en.anyahotel.com; 3 Đ Nguyen Trung Tin; r US$62-108, ste US$145; ❄📶🏊) New in 2019, this luxury hotel is set just inland from the beach. All rooms are designed in a contemporary style, with subtle greys and pale wood colour schemes. The pool area, fitness centre and spa impress too.

Eating & Drinking

Gia Vy 2 VIETNAMESE $

(14 Đ Dien Hong; meals 40,000d; ⏲7am-9.45pm) Enjoying rolling your own meal? Head to this local joint for lipsmackingly authentic *banh xeo* pancakes: grab some rice paper and make an envelope with a shrimp or beef pancake, salad leaves, green mango, sliced cucumber and a dash of chilli sauce, and savour the flavour.

★ C.ine SEAFOOD $$
(☎0256-651 2675; 94 Đ Xuan Dieu; dishes 40,000-180,000d; ⏰11am-10.30pm) Excellent seafood restaurant with gingham tablecloths and views over the bay. Prices are higher than some on this strip but worth it: try the sweet soft-shell crab, scallops with butter and garlic, grilled fish and snail dishes. There's some inaccuracy with English translations on the menu.

Den 2 CAFE
(Kim House, 25 Đ Le Xuan Tru; ⏰24hr; 📶) The original Den Coffee was closed at the time of research for rebuilding, but this branch at Kim House hostel is going strong, serving premium arabica and quality robusta beans from Vietnam, Ethiopia and around the globe. A perfect espresso is 25,000d, while a *ca phe den* (black Vietnamese drip-style coffee) costs 13,000d. Juices, snacks and meals are available.

ℹ Getting There & Away

Daily flights link Phu Cat airport (31km northwest of the city) with Hanoi and Ho Chi Minh City. Minibus transfers (50,000d) are available for airline passengers.

Quy Nhon Bus Station (☎0256-384 6246; Đ Tay Son), on the south side of town, has frequent buses to Quang Ngai (from 85,000d, 3½ hours, hourly), Nha Trang and towns in the central highlands including Pleiku (90,000d, four hours, seven daily). Son Tung operates two to three daily minibuses/buses (170,000d, six hours) between Quy Nhon and Hoi An.

The nearest mainline station is Dieu Tri, 10km west of the city. Only very slow local trains stop at **Quy Nhon Train Station** (☎0256-382 2036; Đ Le Hong Phong).

From Dieu Tri, destinations include Quang Ngai (108,000d, three hours) and all major towns on the main north–south line.

Bai Xep

POP 2500 / ☎0256

An isolated fishing village just a few years back, the pretty bay of Bai Xep now attracts a steady stream of independent travellers. It's still quite remote, 13km south of Quy Nhon, but this beach's relaxed appeal is considerable and its beauty undeniable.

Bai Xep consists of two small coves. The southern beach has an expanding range of accommodation, each place facing a stunning crescent-shaped sandy bay that offers wonderful swimming. It's easy to lose track of time here, chilling in a hammock, socialising with locals and fellow travellers.

Guesthouses can arrange island-hopping boat trips including some snorkelling (120,000d per person), cooking classes (150,000d per person) and motorbike hire. There's some surf here between October and March. In the rainy season, walks to local waterfalls are rewarding too.

🛏 Sleeping & Eating

★ Life's a Beach Backpackers HOSTEL $
(☎086-895 8843; www.lifesabeachvietnam.com; 2km north of Xuan Hai; dm/huts/r from US$5/14/18; ❄📶) This party hostel enjoys a sublime setting on a lovely, private sandy cove beach, with accommodation (good-quality dorms, bungalows and camping) scattered around a shady hillside. There's a restobar for boozing and munchies, and ample hammocks for horizontal chilling. Lots of activities are offered, from kayak hire to karaoke sing-offs. Located 5km south of Bai Xep.

Banana Sea Homestay HOMESTAY $
(☎0931 123 227; www.bananahomestay.com; Bai Sau; dm 160,000d, r 450,000d, huts 500,000-650,000d; ❄📶) Creeping up the hillside behind Back Beach, this super-hospitable Swiss-Vietnamese homestay is as welcoming a base as you could wish for. There's a selection of cute barrel-roofed huts to choose from, some with air-con and all with hot-water en suites and fine views. The clean dorm has air-con. Great food and travel info is available in the cafe below.

★ Haven GUESTHOUSE $$
(☎0982 114 906; www.havenvietnam.com; To 2, Khu Vuc 1, Bai Sau; dm 160,000d, r incl breakfast 850,000-1,200,000d; ❄📶) This homely shorefront guesthouse has undergone a serious revamp, with a new block adding an additional eight rooms and a four-bed dorm; most accommodation enjoys a sea view. The welcome and atmosphere remain as warm as ever thanks to the Australian-Vietnamese owners, who've been in Bai Xep for years and can advise about local excursions and trips.

Avani Quy Nhon Resort & Spa RESORT $$$
(☎0256-384 0132; www.avanihotels.com; 700m south of Bai Xep; r/ste incl breakfast from US$140/165; ❄📶🏊) All set up for a memorable stay, this stylish beachfront hotel

boasts well-designed rooms, all with ocean vistas, natural materials and contemporary mod cons. Tai chi, yoga, snorkelling and fishing trips are offered. There's a lovely pool, fine-dining options and the spa is the best in the region.

Big Tree Bistro INTERNATIONAL **$$**
(www.havenvietnam.com/bigtreebistro; Haven, To 2, Khu Vuc 1, Bai Sau; most mains 100,000-169,000d; 6am-9pm;) Pizza from a wood-fired oven is the speciality at this casual, sociable hotel restaurant that enjoys terrific vistas over Back Beach. You'll also find good salads and excellent barbecued meats such as whole roast chicken on the menu too.

Getting There & Away

Bai Xep is 13km south of Quy Nhon and connected by local buses: T11 (9000d) runs roughly hourly from the Metro mall in the city between 5.30am and 5pm (with a break for lunch). A taxi from Quy Nhon is 190,000d. Many travellers arrive by motorbike.

Nha Trang

POP 441,000 / 0258

Loud and proud (say it!), the high-rise, high-energy beach resort of Nha Trang enjoys a stunning setting: ringed by a necklace of hills, with a sweeping crescent beach, the city's turquoise bay is dotted with tropical islands.

Nha Trang is a party town at heart, most of it aimed directly at the many Russian and Chinese tourists. There are more sedate activities on offer too. Try an old-school spa treatment with a visit to a mudbath or explore centuries-old Cham towers still standing in the town centre.

Sights

★Nha Trang Beach BEACH
Forming a magnificent sweeping arc, Nha Trang's 6km-long golden-sand beach is the city's trump card. Sections are roped off and designated for safe swimming (where you won't be bothered by jet skis or boats). The turquoise water is very inviting, and the promenade a delight to stroll.

Two popular lounging spots are **Louisiane Brewhouse** (www.louisianebrewhouse.com.vn; 29 Đ Tran Phu; 7am-midnight;) and the Sailing Club (p121). If you head south of here, the beach gets quieter and it's possible to find a quiet stretch of sand.

★Po Nagar Cham Towers BUDDHIST TEMPLE
(Thap Ba, Lady of the City; north side of Xom Bong Bridge; admission 22,000d, guide 50,000d; 6am-6pm) Built between the 7th and 12th centuries, these impressive Cham towers are still actively used for worship by Cham, Chinese and Vietnamese Buddhists. Originally the complex had seven or eight towers, but only four remain, of which the 28m-high North Tower (Thap Chinh; AD 817), with a terraced pyramidal roof, vaulted interior masonry and vestibule, is the most magnificent.

The towers stand on a granite knoll 3km north of central Nha Trang, on the northern bank of the Cai River.

Long Son Pagoda BUDDHIST TEMPLE
(off Đ 23 Thang 10; 7.30-11.30am & 1.30-5.30pm) FREE Climb steep steps up to this striking pagoda, founded in the late 19th century. The entrance and roofs are decorated with mosaic dragons constructed of glass and ceramic tile, while the main sanctuary is a hall adorned with modern interpretations of traditional motifs. From the hilltop above, crowned with a large, white seated **Buddha** (Kim Than Phat To), there are excellent city views.

Long Thanh Gallery GALLERY
(0258-382 4875; www.longthanhart.com; 126 Đ Hoang Van Thu; 8am-5.30pm Mon-Sat) FREE This gallery exhibits the work of Long Thanh, one of Vietnam's most prominent photographers, who shoots powerful black-and-white images of everyday Vietnamese moments and compelling portraits. Prints start at around 2,000,000d.

Activities

The Nha Trang area is a prime diving, surfing, wakeboarding, parasailing, white-water rafting and mountain-biking centre. Boat trips around the bay and up the Cai River are also a great day out, and there's plenty of spa, pampering and yoga action.

★I Resort THERMAL BATHS
(0258-383 8838; www.i-resort.vn; 19 Đ Xuan Ngoc, Vinh Ngoc; packages from 300,000d; 8am-8pm) Upmarket thermal spa that's the most attractive of the mud-fests around Nha Trang, with hot mineral mudbaths (private tub 700,000d for two people), bathing pools and even nine mineral waterfalls. The rural setting is gorgeous, with distant mountain views, and there's a decent restaurant, spa/massage salon and gift shop. All kinds of mud and spa packages are available.

Nha Trang

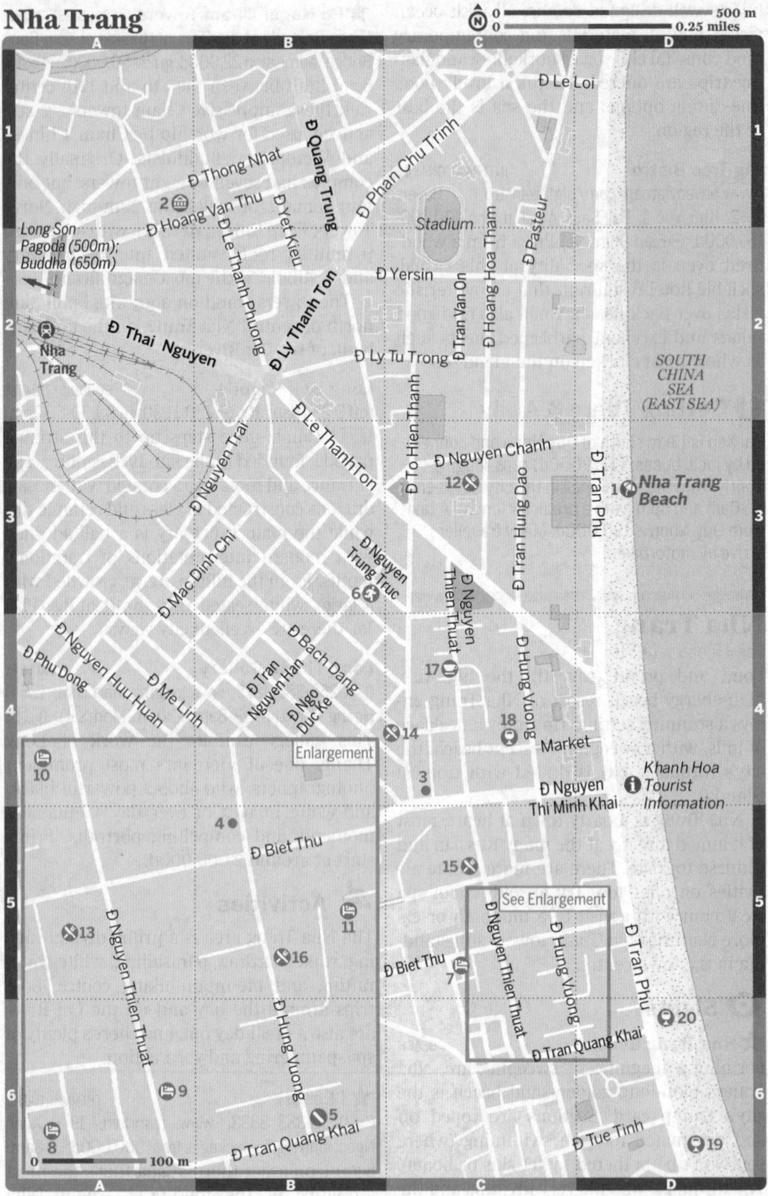

100 Egg Mud Bath THERMAL BATHS
(Tam Bun Tram Trung; ☎0258-371 1733; www.tramtrung.vn; Đ Nguyen Tat Thanh, Phuoc Trung; public/private egg per person 250,000/300,000d; ⏰8am-7pm) This place is named after its egg-shaped private pods where you can indulge in a little mud play. All kinds of mud plastering, wraps and scrubs are offered. You'll find pools and tubs (that can be filled with herbs and essential oils) scattered around this huge complex, which also has Jacuzzis, a huge swimming pool, a restaurant and a waterfall.

Nha Trang

Yoga Victoria YOGA
(☎0258-352 8119; 14 Đ Nguyen Trung Truc; per class 150,000d) Yoga Victoria has a large, air-conditioned studio and offers hatha and ashtanga classes.

Vietnam Active DIVING
(☎0258-352 8119; www.vietnamactive.com; 115 Đ Hung Vuong) Offers scuba diving (one-day trial US$70) and freediving (taster US$65).

Tours

★**Lanterns Tours** CULTURAL
(☎0258-247 1674; www.lanternsvietnam.com; 30a Đ Nguyen Thien Thuat) This nonprofit organisation offers fine-value street-food tours (250,000d per person, minimum two) of Nha Trang featuring seven dishes including *banh tai vac* (tapioca shrimp dumplings). It also offers a tour to Ninh Hoa (from US$35), a nontouristy town, which takes in a local market and lunch with a family. Cooking classes (US$27) too.

Mojzo Tours TOURS
(☎098 887 9069; www.facebook.com/pg/mojzodormhostel; 76 Đ Nguyen Thi Minh Khai) This hostel offers inexpensive tours designed for budget-watching backpackers, including a four-island bay trip (200,000d) and a snorkelling tour (350,000d).

Sleeping

★**Sunny Sea** HOTEL $
(☎090 574 6506, 0258-352 2286; www.facebook.com/nangbienhotel; 64b/9 Đ Tran Phu; r 250,000-350,000d; ❄📶) Run by a local couple (a doctor and nurse) and their staff, this very welcoming minihotel is in the heart of town and just off the beach. Rooms are in great shape: very clean, with springy mattresses, minibar and modern bathrooms (some have a balcony, though no sea views).

★**Mojzo Inn Boutique** HOSTEL $
(☎0988 879 069; www.facebook.com/mojzoInn; 120/36 Đ Nguyen Thien Thuat; dm US$7, r US$19-23; 🚭❄📶) Staff really make an effort to welcome guests at this funky hostel, providing travel tips, free local maps and transport info. There are well-designed dorms, a lovely cushion-scattered lounge area, huge breakfasts, free water refills and a cool rooftop.

iHome HOSTEL $
(☎0258-352 1239; http://ihome-nha-trang.business.site; 31e2, Đ Biet Thu; dm/d incl breakfast US$6/20; ❄📶) A hedonist's heaven, this party hostel has all bases covered with unlimited free beer during happy hour and a vibing atmosphere. Staff are lots of fun and there are tons of tours and activities, an awesome rooftop bar, a lounge for TV viewing and a good buffet breakfast.

Rosaka Hotel HOTEL $$
(☎0258-383 3333; www.rosakahotel.com; 107a Đ Nguyen Thien Thuat; r US$52-78, ste from US$90; ❄📶🏊) Offering fine value, this hotel is located 400m inland from the beach and has spacious, very well-kept rooms with wooden floors and gorgeous en suites. You'll love the stunning rooftop infinity pool and welcoming staff, gym and spa.

Summer Hotel HOTEL $$
(☎0258-352 2186; www.thesummerhotel.com.vn; 34c Đ Nguyen Thien Thuat; r US$36-82, ste incl breakfast US$96; ❄@📶🏊) The Summer is a good midranger with affordable prices. Rooms have high comfort levels and

comfortable trim, though the cheapest are windowless (or have a view of the stairwell). You'll love the rooftop pool.

★**Mia Resort Nha Trang** HOTEL $$$
(☎0258-398 9666; www.mianhatrang.com; Bai Dong, Cam Hai Dong; condos/villas from US$195/230;) Mia has an exceptional setting, on a secluded, private sandy beach, and the villas are supremely spacious and contemporary, with vast bath tubs and either ocean or garden views. There's a fine spa and a choice of great restaurants (Sandals for international fare, La Baia for Italian), while Mojito's is the perfect spot for (you've guessed it) that famous Cuban cocktail.

Champa Island Resort RESORT $$$
(☎0258-382 7827; http://champaislandresort.vn; 304 Đ 2/4, Vinh Phuoc; r/ste from US$72/96;) Spread over two islands in the Cai River, yet only 3km north of the centre, this large resort hotel makes a tranquil base and has all the facilities you could want: huge pool, large gym, ample dining options and fine spa. There's a wide choice of accommodation including two-bed suites, which are great value for families.

Eating & Drinking

Alpaca Homestyle Cafe (www.facebook.com/alpacanhatrang; 10/1b Đ Nguyen Thien Thuat; 8.15am-9.30pm Mon-Sat;) has excellent coffee, while local bars we rate include **Deja Brew** (www.facebook.com/dejabrewnhatrang; 46 Hung Vuong; 7am-10pm Mon, Tue & Thu, 9am-5pm Wed, 9am-10pm Fri-Sun;) in the centre and **Sunshine Bar** (☎0120 791 8901; www.facebook.com/sunshinebar.nhatrang; 35/48 Đ Ngo Den; 11am-9pm Tue-Sun;) by the river.

Au Lac VEGETARIAN $
(28c Đ Hoang Hoa Tham; meals 15,000-32,000d; 10am-7pm;) No-frills vegan/vegetarian place where a mixed plate (20,000d) is just about the best-value meal you can find in Nha Trang. Just point, take a seat and a plate will arrive. Surrounds are simple, with steel tables and plastic stools.

Culture Cafe CAFE $
(☎077 890 8606; www.facebook.com/pg/CafeCultureNhaTrang; 31/7a Đ Biet Thu; meals 79,000-150,000d; 8am-10pm Wed-Mon;) Owned by a welcoming Englishman, this tiny cafe down a little alley is tricky to find but well worth seeking out for fry-up breakfasts, muffins (including smoked salmon) and eggs Benedict. It also does a roaring trade in pizza (call for delivery) and serves fine espressos, coconut lattes (55,000d) and smoothies.

★**Lac Canh Restaurant** VIETNAMESE $$
(77 Đ Nguyen Binh Khiem; meals 45,000-150,000d; 11am-8.45pm) Lac Canh has shifted across the road from its original location but remains a memorable dining experience, a somewhat scruffy-looking barbecue joint filled with smoke and laughter. Locals feast on meat (beef, richly marinated with spices, is the speciality, but there are chicken cuts and seafood too), which you grill over charcoal at your table. Note: it closes quite early.

★**Mix** GREEK $$
(☎0165 967 9197; www.mix-restaurant.com; 77 Đ Hung Vuong; meals 120,000-240,000d; 11am-10pm Thu-Tue;) You will have to wait for a table at busy times, such is this bustling, sociable Greek place's popularity. Freshly prepared and beautifully presented dishes include 'mix dips' (with hummus and tzatziki), feta and watermelon salad, *patzarosalata* (beetroot salad with fresh herbs, Greek yoghurt, garlic and onion) and fine-value platters (from 190,000d).

Lanterns VIETNAMESE $$
(☎0258-247 1674; www.lanternsvietnam.com; 30a Đ Nguyen Thien Thuat; dishes 55,000-235,000d; 7am-10.30pm;) Ever-popular ethical restaurant that supports local orphanages and provides scholarship programs. Flavours are predominantly Vietnamese – order a set menu (from 140,000d) and you'll get a good selection, or try a street-food classic like *goi buoi* (pomelo salad with pork and shrimp). International offerings include pasta, salads and sandwiches, and there are several good-value breakfast combos too (from 50,000d).

★**Kiwami** JAPANESE $$$
(☎0956 130 933, 0258-351 6613; 136 Đ Bach Dang; meals 200,000-600,000d; noon-10pm Thu-Tue;) One of the best Japanese restaurants in coastal Vietnam, this is an intimate affair with a specialist sushi chef: perch on a bar stool and watch the master at work, or sit in one of the side alcoves. The sashimi and sushi sets are divine, or try some meats from the roaster grill. Sake and Sapporo beer available. Book ahead.

Sailing Club BAR, CLUB
(www.sailingclubnhatrang.com; 72-74 Đ Tran Phu; ⏲7am-2am; 📶) This beach club is a mecca for party people with DJs and bands, and draws huge crowds for its legendary Saturday-night events. Expect mainstream-chart sounds, with predictable party banter ('yo ready for dis?!') from an MC. During the week there are live bands.

Information

Though Nha Trang is generally a safe place, be careful on the beach during the day (theft) and at night (robbery). Pickpocketing is a perennial problem.

Khanh Hoa Tourist Information (☎0258-382 9357; www.nhatrang-travel.com; Đ Tran Phu; ⏲8am-5.30pm) Small office staffed by helpful English-speaking staff.

Sinh Tourist (☎0258-352 2982; www.thesinhtourist.vn; 90c Đ Hung Vuong; ⏲6am-10pm) Reliable, professional agency for inexpensive local trips, including a city tour for 649,000d as well as open-tour buses, train and flight bookings.

Getting There & Around

The **Cam Ranh International Airport** (☎0258-398 9913) is located 35km south of Nha Trang and has international connections to many Chinese cities, Seoul and Bangkok. There are also many flights to Ho Chi Minh City, Hanoi and Danang. Shuttle buses (50,000d, 45 minutes) connect the airport with Nha Trang roughly every 30 minutes between 6am and 6.30pm. They pass through the heart of town, stopping at points along the coastal road Đ Tran Phu. A taxi is around 380,000d.

Nha Trang is a major stopping point for all open-tour buses.

Nha Trang has no main bus station of much use to travellers. The smallish **Northern Bus Station** (Ben Xe Phia Bac; Dien Bien Phu) is inconveniently located 5.5km north of the centre. It's used by **Futa Buses** (☎1900 6067; https://futabus.vn; Dien Bien Phu), which provides a good service to cities including Dalat (135,000d, four hours, six daily), HCMC (225,000d, 12 hours, eight daily) and Danang (240,000d, 12 hours, two daily). Sinh Tourist is reliable and very popular with travellers; buses leave from its office in the centre. Services head north to Hoi An (250,000d, 11 hours, one daily). It also offers connections to Mui Ne (115,000d, five hours, two daily), Dalat and HCMC.

Nha Trang Train Station (☎0258-382 2113; Đ Thai Nguyen; ⏲ticket office 7-11.30am, 1.30-6pm & 7-9pm) is in the centre of town. It's on the main north–south line with good connections to destinations including Dieu Tri (for Quy Nhon), Danang and HCMC.

Mai Linh (☎0258-382 2266) is a reliable taxi company.

Mui Ne

POP 18,000 / ☎0252

Once upon a time, Mui Ne was an isolated stretch of beach where pioneering travellers camped on the sand. It's now a string of (mercifully low-rise) beach resorts set amid pretty gardens by the sea. The original fishing village is still here, but tourists outnumber locals these days. Mui Ne is definitely moving upmarket, with swish restaurants and swanky shops, but there is still a (kite) surfer vibe to the town.

Sights

Sand Dunes BEACH
Mui Ne is famous for its enormous red and white sand dunes. The 'red dunes' *(doi hong)* are conveniently located north of the main strip, but the 'white dunes' *(doi cat trang)*, 24km northeast, are the more impressive – the near-constant oceanic winds sculpt the pale-yellow sands into wonderful Saharaesque formations. But as

TRANSPORT FROM NHA TRANG

DESTINATION	AIR	BUS	CAR/ MOTORCYCLE	TRAIN
Dalat	n/a	US$7, 5hr, 11 daily	4-5hr	n/a
Danang	from US$42, 1hr, 2 daily	US$11-14, 11-12hr, 12 daily	11hr	US$14-18, 9-11hr, 7 daily
Ho Chi Minh City	from US$26, 1hr, 14-16 daily	US$9-13, 11-12hr, 16 daily	10hr	US$11-16, 7-9hr, 7 daily
Mui Ne	n/a	US$8, 5hr, 2 daily	5hr	n/a
Quy Nhon	n/a	US$6.50, 6hr, every 2hr	6hr	US$5.50-7.50, 3½-4½hr, 7 daily

Mui Ne Beach

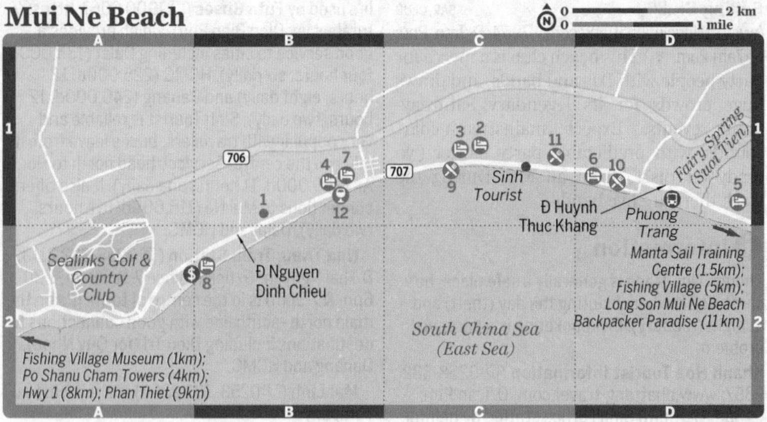

Mui Ne Beach

Activities, Courses & Tours

	Jibes	(see 12)
1	Mui Ne Cooking School	B1
	Sailing Club Kite School	(see 8)

Sleeping

2	Cargo Remote	C1
3	Cat Sen Auberge	C1
4	Coco Sand Hotel	B1
5	Duy An Guesthouse	D1
6	Minhon Hotel	D1
7	Mui Ne Backpacker Village	B1
8	Sailing Club	B2

Eating

9	Bo Ke	C1
10	Dong Vui Food Court	D1
	Sandals	(see 8)
11	Sindbad	C1

Drinking & Nightlife

12	Joe's Café	B1

this is Vietnam (not deepest Mali) there's little chance of experiencing the silence of the desert.

Fishing Village Museum MUSEUM
(☎0901 111 1666; www.seagull.vn; 360 Đ Nguyen Thong; incl guide 100,000d; ⏰9am-6pm) This new attraction is dedicated to the fishing industry in the Mui Ne and Phan Thiet region, and has 14 interactive exhibits depicting its 300-year history. The process of traditional fish-sauce-making is explained in English, Vietnamese, Russian and Chinese. It's at the western end of the main strip.

Po Shanu Cham Towers HINDU SITE
(Km 5; adult/child 15,000/7000d; ⏰7.30-11.30am & 1-4.30pm) Around 6km west of Mui Ne, these Cham towers occupy a hillside with sweeping views of nearby Phan Thiet and a cemetery filled with candy-like tombstones. Dating from the 9th century, this complex consists of the ruins of three towers, none of which are in very good shape. There's a small pagoda on site, too.

Activities

Mui Ne is the adrenaline capital of southern Vietnam. There's no scuba-diving or snorkelling to speak of, but when Nha Trang and Hoi An get the rains, Mui Ne gets the waves. Surf's up from August to December.

★ **Manta Sail Training Centre** BOATING
(☎090 840 0108; www.mantasailing.org; 108 Đ Huynh Thuc Khang; sailing instruction per hour US$66) One of Southeast Asia's best sailing schools, British-run Manta offers instruction and training (from beginner to advanced racing). Speak to staff about wakeboarding (US$100 per hour), SUP hire (US$20 half day) and boat tours. The centre also has budget rooms available right by the beach.

Sailing Club Kite School KITESURFING
(☎062 384 7440; www.sailingclubkiteschool.com; Sailing Club, 24 Đ Nguyen Dien Chieu; ⏰8am-6pm) Experienced and patient instructors and quality equipment are the draw at this fine kiting school. A two-hour Discover Kite

(Level 1) course is 2,500,000d, while the 10-hour Zero to Hero is 11,300,000d.

Jibes KITESURFING, WATER SPORTS
(☎0252-384 7405; www.jibesbeachclub.com; 84-90 Đ Nguyen Dinh Chieu; ⏰7.30am-6pm) Mui Ne's original kitesurfing school, Jibes offers instruction (US$65 per hour) and gear including windsurfs (US$55 per day), SUPs (US$20 per half-day), surfboards, kitesurfs and kayaks for hire. Catamaran sailing also offered. Accommodation deals possible too.

Courses

Mui Ne Cooking School COOKING
(☎091 665 5241; www.muinecookingschool.com; 1st fl, 85 Đ Nguyen Dinh Chieu; 2½hr class US$30-35; ⏰classes 9am-12.30pm Mon-Sat) Well-regarded Vietnamese cooking classes with two different menus, depending on the day. Dishes include *pho bo* (Vietnamese beef noodle soup) and *banh xeo*. Food tours (US$25) to Phan Thiet at night are also great fun.

Sleeping

★**Minhon Hotel** HOTEL $
(☎0252-651 5178; www.facebook.com/MiNhonMuineHotel; 210/5 Đ Nguyen Dinh Chieu; r from 260,000d;) It's difficult to find fault with this exceptional new hotel, which offers outstanding value and reflects traditional Vietnamese architecture. Staff are welcoming and helpful, and the rooms very spacious and well furnished. The location is excellent, down a little lane near the Dong Vui Food Court. It's solar powered and bikes are free for guests to use.

★**Mui Ne Backpacker Village** HOSTEL $
(☎0252-374 1047; www.muinebackpackervillage.com; 137 Đ Nguyen Dinh Chieu; dm/r from US$5/20;) More village than hostel, this huge, modern backpacking palace is very well designed around an inviting swimming pool. Thanks to the bar-restaurant, pool table, darts and table football there's a social vibe. Dorms (four to 12 beds) all have air-conditioning, while private rooms have cable TV and a balcony or patio. The hostel runs lots of good-value tours, books transport and does laundry.

Coco Sand Hotel GUESTHOUSE $
(☎0127 364 3446; www.cocosandhotel.com; 119 Đ Nguyen Dinh Chieu; r US$15-28;) Down a little lane, Coco Sand has excellent-value rooms with air-conditioning, cable TV, fridge and private bathroom. There's a shady courtyard garden (with hammocks) to enjoy and the friendly owners hire out motorbikes at fair rates.

Long Son Mui Ne Beach Backpacker Paradise HOSTEL $
(☎0252-383 6056; www.longsonmuine.com; Long Son; tents/dm from US$3/3;) Right on the beach, this travellers' delight is very well set up for long days lounging by the shore and even longer nights around the bar (it's open 24 hours!). Yes, expect lots of drinking and partying action at this social hostel. Digs consist of dorms and tents. It's 13km north-east of central Mui Ne.

Duy An Guesthouse GUESTHOUSE $
(☎0252-384 7799; www.duyanguesthouse.com; 87a Đ Huynh Thuc Khang; r 260,000-600,000d;) In a shady compound at the eastern end of the main drag, this traditional guesthouse (and restaurant) is run by friendly folk who look after their guests well. The 16 rooms include family-size options ideal for sharers.

★**Cargo Remote** BOUTIQUE HOTEL $$
(☎077 625 2825; www.facebook.com/pg/cargoremotemuine; 201/88 Đ Nguyen Dinh Chieu; s/d/tr US$50/60/70;) Eco-retreat built high on a hilltop above central Mui Ne with a stunning natural pool, al-fresco restobar and gorgeous accommodation crafted from shipping containers and kitted out with recycled furniture. Expect live music some evenings (there's a recording studio on-site). A spa and restaurant with fine local food seal the deal.

Cat Sen Auberge B&B $$
(☎0122 323 3673; http://catsen.simdif.com; 195 Đ Nguyen Dinh Chieu; r/bungalows from US$35/48;) A wonderfully relaxing place to stay, Cat Sen Auberge has well-constructed rooms and lovely bungalows dotted around extensive, coconut-tree-studded grounds. There's a great pool and lots of space, with hammocks for lounging and free drinking water.

★**Sailing Club** BOUTIQUE HOTEL $$$
(☎0252-384 7440; www.sailingclubmuine.com; 24 Đ Nguyen Dinh Chieu; r/bungalows incl breakfast from US$162/188;) An intimate beach retreat with superb attention to detail, the Sailing Club (formerly the Mia) has gorgeous bungalows built from natural materials scattered around wonderful tropical gardens. The oceanside pool is small but the

spa is one of the best in Mui Ne; staff are efficient and super-welcoming. You'll love Sandals, the in-house restaurant, for Vietnamese, Asian and Western meals.

There's a kids' club, and yoga twice-weekly.

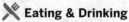

Eating & Drinking

Mui Ne is one of the most expensive places to dine in Vietnam. The incredible selection of restaurants is mostly geared to the cosmopolitan tastes of its visitors.

★Dong Vui Food Court FOOD HALL $
(www.facebook.com/DongVuiMuiNe; 246 Đ Nguyen Dinh Chieu; meals 45,000-170,000d; ⏲8am-11pm) This attractive open-air food court has loads of independently run cook stations offering everything from Punjabi cuisine to paella, German sausages and Thai curries – plus plenty of Vietnamese options. Just grab a seat and order what you fancy. There's also great craft beer on tap and live music some weekends. It's far busier in the evenings.

Sindbad MIDDLE EASTERN $
(233 Đ Nguyen Dinh Chieu; meals 50,000-120,000d; ⏲11am-10.30pm; 📶) Serves tasty, great-value Greek-ish cuisine including mean *shawarma* (beef or chicken doner kebabs), shish kebabs and great salads (Greek, Italian, garden). For a feast, order the Mediterranean Delight, which includes lots of mini plates including hummus and bruschetta.

★Sandals INTERNATIONAL $$
(☎0252-384 7440; www.sailingclubmuine.com; Sailing Club, 24 Đ Nguyen Dinh Chieu; meals 120,000-380,000d; ⏲7am-10pm; 📶) For a memorable meal in Mui Ne head straight to Sandals in the Sailing Club hotel. It's particularly romantic at night, with tables set around the shoreside pool and subtle lighting. The menu is superb, with everything from Vietnamese platters to pasta. You can enjoy wine by the glass too.

Bo Ke SEAFOOD $$
(Đ Nguyen Dinh Chieu; mains 45,000-190,000d; ⏲5-10pm) This group of seafood shacks on the shore features little more than plastic furniture and neon strip lights, but the fish and seafood are super-fresh. Check prices carefully before you eat, as billing errors are not uncommon.

Joe's Café BAR
(www.joescafemuine.com; 86 Đ Nguyen Dinh Chieu; ⏲7am-1am; 📶) This very popular pub-like place has live music (every night at 7.30pm) and a gregarious vibe. During the day it's a good place to hang, too, with seats set under a giant mango tree, magazines to browse, a pool table and an extensive food menu. Serves local, imported, draught and craft beers.

Getting There & Around

Several companies have daily bus services to/from Ho Chi Minh City (110,000d to 135,000d, six hours), Nha Trang (115,000d, five hours) and Dalat (from 118,000d, four hours). Sleeper open-tour night buses usually cost more.

Phuong Trang (http://futabus.vn; 97 Đ Nguyen Dinh Chieu) has very regular comfortable buses running daily between Mui Ne and HCMC (140,000d). **Sinh Tourist** (☎098 925 8060; 144 Đ Nguyen Dinh Chieu; ⏲7am-10pm) is another good bus company.

Open-tour buses are a good option for Mui Ne. Call **Mai Linh** (☎0252-389 8989) for a taxi.

SOUTHWEST HIGHLANDS

There's a rugged charm to this distinctly rural region, with pine-studded hilltops soaring over intensively farmed fields and remote, bumpy roads meandering through coffee plantations. Looking for big nature? Check out Cat Tien National Park, where there are gibbons, crocodiles and elusive tigers.

Dalat, a former French hill station that still boasts plenty of colonial charm, makes a great base. An adventure-sports mecca, its cool climate offers myriad biking and hiking trips for daytime thrills and atmospheric restaurants and bars for after-dark chills.

Dalat

POP 184,755 / ☎0263 / ELEV 1475M

Dalat is Vietnam's alter ego: the weather is springlike cool (daily temperatures hover between 15°C and 24°C) instead of tropical hot, the town is dotted with elegant French-colonial villas rather than stark socialist architecture, and the farms around are thick with strawberries and flowers, not rice.

The French left behind holiday homes and the vibe of a European town. Dalat is a big draw for domestic tourists – it's Le Petit Paris, the honeymoon capital. For travellers, the moderate climate makes it a superb place for adrenalin-fuelled activities or less demanding natural wonders.

Sights

There are many waterfalls in the region around Dalat.

★Hang Nga Crazy House ARCHITECTURE
(☎0263-382 2070; 3 Đ Huynh Thuc Khang; adult/child 60,000/20,000d; ⊙8.30am-7pm) A freewheeling architectural exploration of surrealism, Hang Nga Crazy House is a joyously designed, outrageously artistic private home. Imagine sculptured rooms connected by super-slim bridges rising out of a tangle of concrete greenery, an excess of cascading lava-flow-like shapes, wild colours, spiderweb windows and an almost organic quality to it all, with the swooping handrails resembling jungle vines. Think of Gaudí and Tolkien dropping acid together and designing their own version of Disneyland.

King Palace PALACE
(Dinh 1; ☎0263-358 0558; Hung Vuong; adult/child 50,000/20,000d; ⊙7am-5pm) Built by a French merchant in 1929, the surprisingly modest but attractive royal residence of Bao Dai (1913–97), Vietnam's last emperor, beckons visitors with its beautiful tree-lined avenue. It was home to Bao Dai and his family until they went into exile in France in 1954. The house was subsequently taken over by then Prime Minister Ngo Dinh Diem.

Crémaillère Railway Station HISTORIC BUILDING
(Ga Da Lat; 1 Đ Quang Trung; ⊙6.30am-5pm) FREE From Dalat's wonderful art deco train station you can ride one of the nine scheduled trains that run to Trai Mat (return from 108,000d, 30 minutes) daily between 6.55am and 4.39pm; a minimum of 25 passengers is required. A *crémaillère* (cog railway) linking Dalat and Thap Cham from 1928 to 1964 was closed due to VC attacks. A Japanese steam train is on display alongside a collection of old carriages.

Dalat Cathedral CATHEDRAL
(Đ Tran Phu; ⊙Mass 5.15am & 5.15pm Mon-Fri, 5.15pm Sat, 5.15am, 8.30am & 6pm Sun) The gingerbread-style Dalat Cathedral was built between 1931 and 1942 for use by French residents and holidaymakers. The cross on the spire is topped by a weathercock, 47m above the ground. The church is irregularly open outside Mass times.

Linh Son Pagoda ARCHITECTURE
(Chua Linh Son; 120 Đ Nguyen Van Troi; ⊙dawn-dusk) Built in 1938, the Linh Son Pagoda is a lovely ochre-coloured building that fuses French and Chinese architecture. The giant bell is said to be made of bronze mixed with gold, with its great weight making it too heavy for thieves to carry off.

WORTH A TRIP

DAMBRI FALLS

En route to Bao Loc and Ho Chi Minh City, 130km south of Dalat, Dambri Falls are one of the highest (90m), most magnificent and easily accessible waterfalls in Vietnam – they are worth visiting even in dry season. For some incredible views, ride the **vertical cable car** (5000d) or trudge up the steep path to the top of the falls.

The road to the falls branches off Hwy 20, 18km north of Bao Loc.

A second path leads down some steep stairs to the front of the falls for more great views, and carries on down to the smaller **Dasara Falls**.

Tours

★Phat Tire Ventures ADVENTURE
(☎0263-382 9422; www.ptv-vietnam.com; 109 Đ Nguyen Van Troi; ⊙8am-7pm) A highly professional and experienced operator with mountain-biking trips from US$40, trekking from US$39, kayaking from US$39 and canyoning (US$72), plus rapelling (US$57) and white-water rafting (US$67) in the rainy season. Multi-day cycling trips are available.

Pine Track Adventures ADVENTURE
(☎0263-383 1916; www.pinetrackadventures.com; 72b Đ Truong Cong Dinh; ⊙8am-8.30pm) Run by an enthusiastic and experienced local team, this operator offers canyoning (from US$55), white-water rafting (US$68), trekking (from US$35), cycling (from US$41) and some excellent multi-sport packages. A six-day bike tour from Dalat to Hoi An costs from US$650.

Dalat Happy Tours FOOD & DRINK
(☎0336 546 450; www.dalathappytours.com; street-food tour per person US$22) After all the active exertions around Dalat, replenish your calories by taking an entertaining, nightly street-food tour with friendly Lao and his guides. Start from the central Hoa Binh cinema and proceed to sample *banh xeo* (filled pancakes), buffalo-tail hotpot, delectable grilled skewers, 'Dalat pizza', rabbit

Dalat

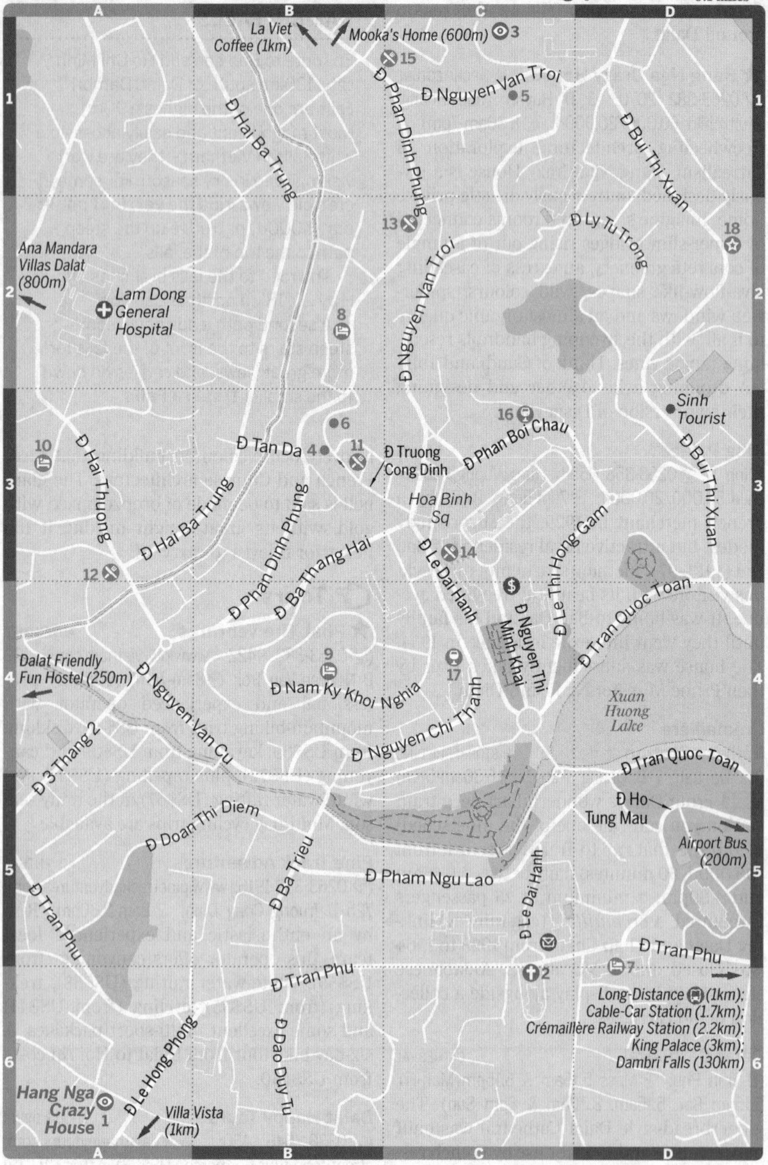

curry, hot rice wine and more. Food costs are included.

Groovy Gecko Adventure Tours ADVENTURE (0263-383 6521; www.groovygeckotours.net; 65 Đ Truong Cong Dinh; 7.30am-8.30pm) Long-running agency that offers a unique (for Dalat) canyoning adventure that includes abseiling down a remote 65m-high waterfall (US$72) at Dasar. Also does mountain-bike trips (from US$35) and day hikes (from US$28), as well as a one-day downhill cycle to Nha Trang or quieter Mui Ne (US$75).

Dalat

Top Sights
1 Hang Nga Crazy House A6

Sights
2 Dalat Cathedral C6
3 Linh Son Pagoda C1

Activities, Courses & Tours
4 Groovy Gecko Adventure Tours B3
5 Phat Tire Ventures C1
6 Pine Track Adventures B3

Sleeping
7 Dalat Hotel du Parc D5
8 Dreams Hotel B2
9 Villa Doc May B4
10 Villa Pink House A3

Eating
11 Quan Trang B3
12 Restaurant Ichi A3
13 Tau Cao Wonton Noodles C2
14 Thai Corner C3
15 Trong Dong C1

Drinking & Nightlife
16 100 Roofs Café C3
17 District I C4

Entertainment
18 Escape Bar D2

Sleeping

★ Villa Doc May GUESTHOUSE $
(☎0263-382 5754, 0363 978 225; villadocmaydalat@gmail.com; 16/3 Đ Nam Ky Khoi Nghia; r 450,000-850,000d; ❄📶) More a homestay than a guesthouse, with just four individually decorated rooms, all comfortable, as well as pleasant communal areas and an upstairs Middle Eastern–style shisha cafe. The cheaper ground-floor rooms don't have windows but are still pleasant. Owner Yom is helpful with restaurant suggestions and scooter rental. Find it up a steep alley off the street, on the left.

★ Mooka's Home HOSTEL $
(☎0932 579 752; mookahome@gmail.com; 2 Co Loa; dm 105,000d, r 290,000-400,000d; 🚭@📶) Big and light dorms come with sparkly bathrooms at this popular place, and there are five spacious private rooms. There's a roof terrace and a downstairs communal area. Group dinners or barbecues (120,000d, every other day) take place on the roof terrace. The friendly staff can arrange tours, bus tickets, motorbike rental and laundry.

Dalat Friendly Fun Hostel HOSTEL $
(☎0973 393 891; dalatfriendlyfun@gmail.com; 18 Mac Dinh Chi; dm incl breakfast US$5; 📶) This place lives up to its name with a warm welcome and helpful staff who organise nightly group dinners (US$3), as well as recommending decent tour operators. Dorms are huge and bright, with curtained beds and inside bathrooms.

Villa Pink House HOTEL $
(☎0263-381 5667; www.facebook.com/VillaPinkHouseDalat; 7/8 Đ Hai Thuong; r standard/deluxe 450,000/500,000d; @📶) A well-run, family-owned place in a quiet location down an alley across from Dalat Hospital. Rooms are comfortable, all have balconies and some have great views. It's managed by the affable Mr Rot, who can arrange day trips to the countryside around Dalat.

Dreams Hotel HOTEL $$
(☎0263-383 3748; www.dreamshoteldalat.vn; 138-140 Đ Phan Dinh Phung; r incl breakfast US$30-35; 🚭❄📶) This reliable place runs a couple of hotels in town. All rooms have high-quality mattresses and decent bathrooms, and some have balconies. There's a free Jacuzzi, a steam room and a sauna from 4pm to 7pm. The only downer is the location on a traffic-heavy street, but the double glazing works well. It also has some long-term apartments.

★ Ana Mandara Villas Dalat BOUTIQUE HOTEL $$$
(☎0263-355 5888; www.anamandara-resort.com; Đ Le Lai; r 2,000,000-3,000,000d; 🚭❄📶🏊) Elegant, secluded property spread across seven lovingly restored French-colonial villas in the peaceful western suburbs. Finished in period furnishings, which can appear a little spartan compared to modern-day ones, the villas have the option of private dining. Most come with an ornamental fireplace and all have wonderful views. The spa, pool and restaurant are all excellent.

★ Villa Vista BOUTIQUE HOTEL $$$
(☎0263-351 2468; www.facebook.com/villavistadalat; 40 Ngo Thi Sy, Phuong 4; r US$65-95; 🚭📶) Look down from this villa on the hill and the whole of Dalat opens up in the valley. There are only four rooms, decorated in

19th-century French fashion (albeit with flat-screen TVs and rain showers). Delightful owners Tim and Huong prepare remarkable breakfasts, and they can hook you up with Easy Riders or motorbike rental and will share their Dalat knowledge. Discounts of 30% in the low season.

Dalat Hotel du Parc HOTEL $$$
(☎0263-382 5777; www.royaldl.com; 15 Đ Tran Phu; r 1,000,000-2,000,000d, ste 2,500,000d; ❄📶) A respectfully refurbished 1932 building that offers a dash of colonial-era style at enticing prices. The grand lobby lift sets the tone and the rooms, while looking their age, include some period furnishings and polished wooden floors. It's bristling with facilities, from a spa and fitness centre to a decent restaurant. Deluxe rooms are worth the extra money.

Eating

★Tau Cao Wonton Noodles NOODLES $
(217 Đ Phan Dinh Phung; noodles 40,000d; ⏲6am-8pm) This humble eatery is famed throughout Dalat and is always heaving with locals, who come for the noodle wonton soup. It's served with thin slices of pork on top and a sprinkling of mincemeat. Add chilli, lime and bean sprouts to taste and you're good to go. Classic Asian street eats. No English spoken.

★Trong Dong VIETNAMESE $
(☎0263-382 1889; 220 Đ Phan Dinh Phung; meals 80,000-150,000d; ⏲11am-9pm; 📶) Intimate restaurant, run by a very hospitable team, where the creative menu includes spins on Vietnamese delights such as shrimp paste on a sugar-cane stick, beef wrapped in *la lot* leaf, and fiery lemongrass-and-chilli squid. The English menu makes life easy.

Quan Trang VIETNAMESE $
(☎0263-382 5043; 15 Đ Tang Bat Ho; dishes 35,000d; ⏲10.30am-8pm) The local speciality *banh uot long ga* here is among the best in town. The rice noodles are saucy not soupy and the fresh shredded chicken, herbs and chilli lift the dish. Delicious – people certainly aren't here for the plastic decor. Several other places nearby offer the same dish.

★Thai Corner THAI $$
(Đ Le Dai Hanh; meals 120,000-180,000d; ⏲10am-10pm) Authentic and tasty, this new place serves up a great papaya salad, tom yum soup and the best green curry we've had in Vietnam, with picturesque views over Dalat's night market below. Service is excellent. The open-air restaurant can get chilly at night, so bring a layer.

★Restaurant Ichi JAPANESE $$
(☎0263-355 5098; 17-19 Đ Hoang Dieu; rolls 60,000-130,000d, meals 150,000-260,000d; ⏲5.30-10pm Tue-Sun, closed every 2nd Tue) Dalat's only truly genuine Japanese restaurant is compact, with subdued lighting and jazz in the background. Spicy tuna rolls, chicken yakitori and tempura are all fantastic, the bento boxes are a bargain and there's even *natto* (fermented soybeans) for aficionados. Perch at the bar to watch sushi-master Tomo at work.

Drinking & Entertainment

★La Viet Coffee COFFEE
(☎0263-398 1189; www.facebook.com/coffeelaviet; 200 Đ Nguyen Cong Tru; coffee 35,000-60,000d; ⏲7am-10.30pm; 📶) Caffeine fiends will want to head to this unique mix of coffee shop, farm and factory. In a warehouse-like building with industrial design touches, and surrounded outside by coffee plants, you can either sip the excellent brews on offer at a table or go on a 10-minute tour of the facility and have the coffee-roasting and -washing processes explained to you.

District I CRAFT BEER
(34 Nguyen Chi Thanh; ⏲3pm-midnight) Opened in 2019, this two-storied bar offers a dozen craft beers on tap, mostly from Saigon's Rooster Beers, along with bottles from Belgium, Germany and the Czech Republic, in a hip, welcoming atmosphere.

100 Roofs Café BAR
(Duong Len Trang; 57 Đ Phan Boi Chau; ⏲8am-midnight; 📶) A surreal drinking experience. The owners claim Gandalf and his hobbit friends have drunk here, and the labyrinth of rooms with multiple nooks and crannies, multilevel grottoes and fantastical sculptures does resemble a Middle Earth location. A happy hour (6pm to 8pm) and Wonderland-like rooftop garden add to the wide-eyed fun.

★Escape Bar LIVE MUSIC
(☎0263-369 5666; www.facebook.com/TheEscapeBarDalat; 94 Đ Bui Thi Xuan, Golf Valley Hotel; ⏲10am-midnight; 📶) Expect top-notch improvised covers of Hendrix, the Doors and other classics at this recently relocated live-music bar owned by blues guitarist Curtis King; travelling musicians are welcome to jam.

Food is served and there's a pool table and spacious terrace. Happy hour is from 6pm to 8pm; music starts around 9.30pm.

Information

Lam Dong General Hospital (☎0263-382 1369; 4 Đ Pham Ngoc Thach; ⊙24hr) Emergency medical care.

Sinh Tourist (☎0263-382 2663; www.thesinhtourist.vn; 22 Đ Bui Thi Xuan; ⊙8am-7pm) Reliable tours, including city sightseeing trips and open-tour bus bookings.

Getting There & Around

Lien Khuong Airport is 30km south of Dalat. There are regular flights with Vietnam Airlines, VietJet Air and Jetstar, including five daily to Ho Chi Minh City, four daily to Hanoi and four flights a week to Danang. Shuttle buses (40,000d, 40 minutes) meet flights and offer connections to town.

Dalat is a major stop for open-tour buses. Sinh Tourist has daily buses at 7.30am and 1pm to Nha Trang and at 8am and 9.30pm to Ho Chi Minh City.

Dalat's long-distance **bus station** (Ben Xe Lien Tinh Da Lat; Đ 3 Thang 4) is 1.5km south of Xuan Huong Lake, and is dominated by reputable **Phuong Trang** (Futabus; ☎0263-358 5858; www.futabus.vn) buses that offer free hotel pickups and drop-offs and cover all main regional destinations.

For a taxi call **Mai Linh** (☎0263-352 1111; www.mailinh.vn) or use Grab.

Cat Tien National Park

☎0251 / ELEV 700M

Wildlife-lovers, this is the place to do your spotting. Fauna in the spectacular Cat Tien National Park includes 100 types of mammal (including the bison-like guar), 79 types of reptile, 41 amphibian species, plus an incredible array of insects, including 400 or so butterfly species. Of the 350-plus birds, rare species include the orange-necked partridge and the Siamese fireback.

Sights

Cat Tien National Park NATIONAL PARK

(Vuon Quoc Gia Cat Tien; ☎0251-366 9228; www.namcattien.vn; incl ferry ride adult/child 60,000/10,000d; ⊙7am-10pm) One of the outstanding natural treasures of the region, the 72,000-hectare Cat Tien National Park comprises an amazingly biodiverse region of lowland tropical rainforest. The hiking, mountain biking and birdwatching are the best in southern Vietnam. It's wise to book ahead for the most popular excursions, such as the **Wild Gibbon Trek** (www.go-east.org; Cat Tien National Park; per person 1,050,000d, maximum 4 people). Bear in mind that visitors rarely see the park's larger animals, which live deep in the jungle, so don't come expecting to encounter elephants or leopards.

From Ho Chi Minh City, the park is a three-hour drive northwest on Hwy 20, or a four-hour drive southwest from Dalat.

★ Dao Tien Endangered Primate Species Centre WILDLIFE RESERVE

(www.go-east.org; Cat Tien National Park; adult/child incl boat ride 300,000/100,000d; ⊙tours 8.30am & 2pm) Set on an island in the Dong Nai River, this rehabilitation centre with a stellar reputation hosts golden-cheeked gibbons, pygmy lorises (both endemic to Vietnam and Cambodia), black-shanked doucs and silvered langurs that were illegally trafficked. The eventual goal is to release the primates back into the forest. You can view gibbons in a semi-wild environment and hear their incredible calls.

Crocodile Lake LAKE

(Bau Sau; Cat Tien National Park; 140,000d) Crocodile Lake is home to 200 crocs and is one of Cat Tien National Park's highlights. Getting here involves a 9km drive or bicycle ride from the park headquarters and then a 5km hike to the swamp; the walk takes about three hours return. A vehicle to the hiking start point costs 250,000d each way. Alternatively, you can trek all the way with a guide from the park headquarters along a jungle route criss-crossed by streams.

Sleeping & Eating

Budget accommodation options include two riverside places: **Green Bamboo Lodge** (☎0973 343 345; cattien_vung@yahoo.com; Nam Cat Tien; r 150,000-350,000d, stilt houses 600,000-800,000d;) and **Green Hope Lodge** (☎0972 184 683; www.greenhopelodge.com; Nam Cat Tien; r 115,000-500,000d;). **Ta Lai Long House** (☎0974 160 827; www.talai-adventure.vn; Cat Tien National Park; dm 500,000d;) is another good cheapie, but 12km away.

Forest Floor Lodge (☎0251-669 890; www.forestfloorlodges.com; Cat Tien National Park; r or luxury tents €115;) is a classy eco-lodge 1.5km from the Park HQ. There are also small restaurants near the HQ, though most people eat at their guesthouse.

Getting There & Away

One approach to Cat Tien National Park is to take a boat across Langa Lake and then go by foot from there. Phat Tire Ventures (p125) is a reputable ecotour operator in Dalat that can offer this option.

All buses between Dalat and Ho Chi Minh City (every 30 minutes) pass the junction Vuon Quoc Gia Cat Tien on Hwy 20 for the park. The junction is around four hours' travel (190,000d to 220,000d) from both cities. From this junction, you can hire a *xe om* (around 200,000d) to cover the remaining 18km to the park. Lodges can also arrange a transfer to/from the main road.

Sinhbalo Adventures (Map p138; ☎ 028-3837 6766; www.sinhbalo.com; 283/20 Đ Pham Ngu Lao; ⏰7.30am-noon & 1.30-6pm Mon-Sat) runs recommended tours to Cat Tien from HCMC.

HO CHI MINH CITY (SAIGON)

POP 8.4 MILLION / ☎ 028

Ho Chi Minh City (HCMC) is Vietnam at its most dizzying: a high-octane city of commerce and culture that has driven the country forward with its pulsating energy. A chaotic whirl, the city breathes life and vitality into all who settle here, and visitors cannot help but be hauled along for the ride.

From the finest of hotels to the cheapest of guesthouses, the classiest of restaurants to the tastiest of street stalls, the choicest of boutiques to the scrum of the markets, HCMC is a city of energy and discovery.

Wander through timeless alleys to incense-infused temples before negotiating chic designer malls beneath sleek 21st-century skyscrapers. The ghosts of the past live on in buildings that one generation ago witnessed a city in turmoil, but now the real beauty of the former Saigon's urban collage is the seamless blending of these two worlds into one exciting mass.

Sights

Reunification Palace & Around

★ **War Remnants Museum** MUSEUM

(Bao Tang Chung Tich Chien Tranh; Map p135; ☎ 028-3930 5587; http://warremnantsmuseum.com; 28 Đ Vo Van Tan, cnr Đ Le Quy Don; adult/child 40,000/20,000d; ⏰7.30am-6pm) To understand the context of the war with the USA, and its devastating impact on Vietnamese civilians, this remarkable, deeply moving museum is an essential visit. Many atrocities documented here were well publicised, but rarely do Westerners hear the victims of military action tell their own stories. While some displays are one-sided, many of the most disturbing photographs illustrating atrocities are from US sources, including those from the My Lai massacre. Allow at least a couple of hours for your visit.

The museum primarily deals with the American War, but the French-colonial period and conflicts with China are also documented. US armoured vehicles, artillery pieces, bombs and infantry weapons are on display outside. One corner of the grounds is devoted to the notorious French and South Vietnamese prisons on Phu Quoc and Con Son islands. Artefacts include that most iconic of French appliances, the guillotine, and the notoriously inhumane 'tiger cages' used to house war prisoners.

The ground floor of the museum is devoted to a collection of posters and photographs showing support for the antiwar movement internationally. This somewhat upbeat display provides a counterbalance to the horrors upstairs.

Even those who supported the war are likely to be horrified by the photos of children affected by US bombing and napalm. You'll also have the rare chance to see some of the experimental weapons used in the war, which were at one time military secrets, such as the *flechette,* an artillery shell filled with thousands of tiny darts.

Upstairs, look out for the **Requiem Exhibition**. Compiled by legendary war photographer Tim Page, this striking collection documents the work of photographers killed during the course of the conflict, on both sides, and includes works by Larry Burrows and Robert Capa.

The War Remnants Museum is in the former US Information Service building. It was previously called the Museum of Chinese and American War Crimes. Captions are in Vietnamese and English.

★ **Reunification Palace** HISTORIC BUILDING

(Dinh Thong Nhat; Map p135; ☎ 028-3829 4117; www.dinhdoclap.gov.vn; Đ Nam Ky Khoi Nghia; adult/child 40,000/20,000d; ⏰7.30-11am & 1-4pm) Surrounded by royal palm trees, the dissonant 1960s architecture of this landmark government building and the eerie ambience of its deserted halls make it an

Ho Chi Minh City

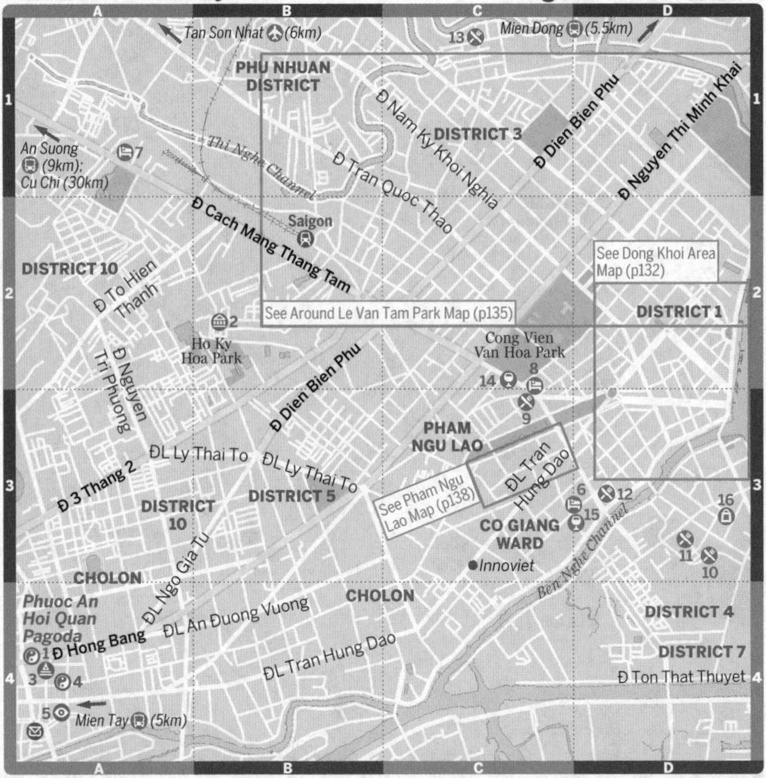

Ho Chi Minh City

Top Sights
1 Phuoc An Hoi Quan Pagoda A4

Sights
2 Museum of Traditional Vietnamese Medicine B2
3 Quan Am Pagoda A4
4 Thien Hau Pagoda A4
5 Traditional Herb Shops A4

Sleeping
6 Chez Mimosa Boutique Hotel D3
7 Ma Maison Boutique Hotel A1
8 Nguyen Shack C2

Eating
9 Banh Mi Huynh Hoa C3
10 Oc Dao 2 .... D3
11 Oc Po D3
12 Quan Ut Ut D3
13 Vegetarian Lien Huong C1

Drinking & Nightlife
14 Observatory C2
15 Tipsy Unicorn D3

Shopping
16 Xom Chieu Market D3

intriguing spectacle. The first Communist tanks to arrive in Saigon rumbled here on 30 April 1975 and it's as if time has stood still since then. The building is deeply associated with the fall of the city in 1975, yet it's the kitsch detailing and period motifs that steal the show. It's also known as the Independence Palace.

Fine Arts Museum GALLERY
(Bao Tang My Thuat; Map p132; www.baotangmythuattphcm.com.vn; 97a Đ Pho Duc Chinh; 30,000d; 8am-5pm Tue-Sun) With its airy corridors and verandas, this elegant 1929 colonial-era, yellow-and-white building is stuffed with period details; it is exuberantly tiled throughout and home to some fine

Dong Khoi Area

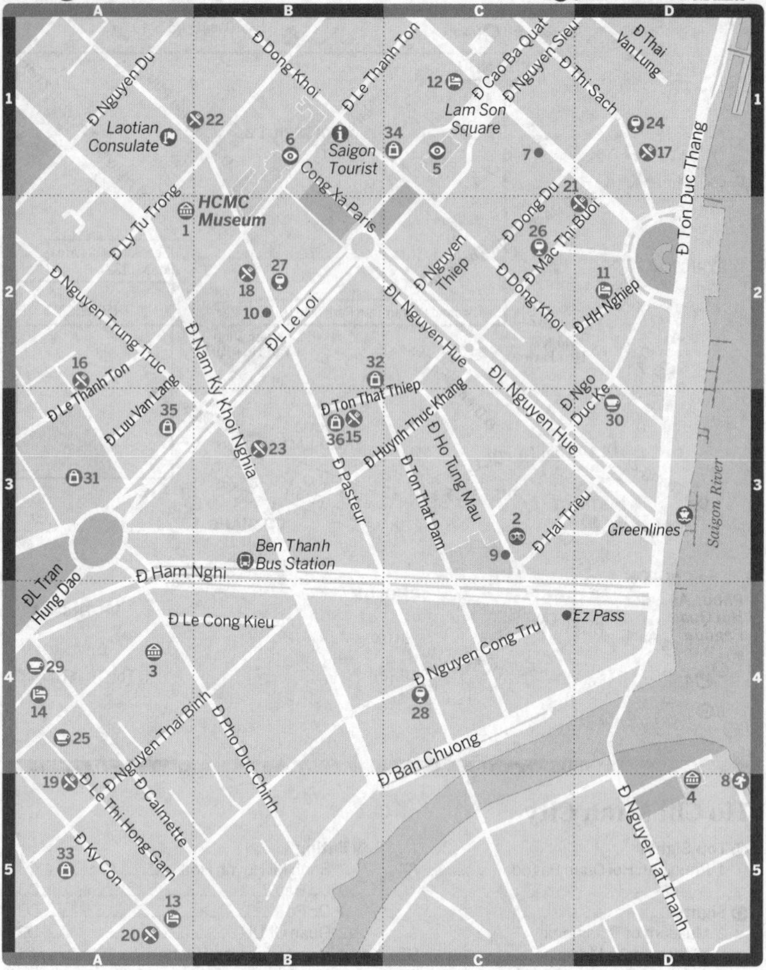

(albeit deteriorated) stained glass, as well as one of Saigon's oldest lifts. Hung from the walls is an impressive selection of art, including thoughtful pieces from the modern period. As well as contemporary art, much of it (unsurprisingly) inspired by war, the museum displays pieces dating back to the 4th century.

Dong Khoi Area

★Notre Dame Cathedral CHURCH

(Map p135; Đ Han Thuyen) Built between 1877 and 1883, Notre Dame Cathedral enlivens the heart of Ho Chi Minh City's government quarter, facing Đ Dong Khoi. A red-brick, neo-Romanesque church, it has twin bell towers that are both topped with spires and crosses that reach 60m. This Catholic cathedral, named after the Virgin Mary, was closed for renovation at the time of research, but when it reopens you'll be able to admire its stained-glass windows and interior walls inlaid with devotional tablets.

★HCMC Museum MUSEUM

(Bao Tang Thanh Pho Ho Chi Minh; Map p132; www.hcmc-museum.edu.vn; 65 Đ Ly Tu Trong; 30,000d; ⏲7.30am-5pm) A grand neoclassical structure built in 1885 and once known as Gia Long

Dong Khoi Area

Top Sights
1 HCMC Museum....A2

Sights
2 Bitexco Financial Tower....C3
3 Fine Arts Museum....A4
4 Ho Chi Minh Museum....D5
5 Opera House....C1
6 People's Committee Building....B1

Activities, Courses & Tours
7 Grain Cooking Classes....C1
8 Indochina Junk....D5
9 Les Rives....C3
10 Old Compass Travel....B2

Sleeping
11 Myst....D2
12 Park Hyatt Saigon....C1
13 Saigon Central Hostel....A5
14 Town House 23....A4

Eating
15 3T Quan Nuong....B3
16 Bep Me In....A2
17 Hum Lounge & Restaurant....D1
18 Old Compass Cafe....B2
19 Padma de Fleur....A5
20 Quince....A5
21 Racha Room....D2
22 Secret Garden....B1
23 Sky 28....B3
Square One....(see 12)

Drinking & Nightlife
Alley Cocktail Bar & Kitchen....(see 18)
24 Apocalypse Now....D1
25 Chat Coffee Roasters....A4
EON Heli Bar....(see 2)
26 Malt....C2
27 Pasteur Street Brewing Company....B2
28 Rogue Saigon....C4
29 Saigon Coffee Roastery....A4
30 Workshop....D3

Entertainment
Municipal Theatre....(see 5)

Shopping
31 Ben Thanh Market....A3
32 Chung Cu 42 Ton That Thiep....B2
33 Dan Sinh Market....A5
34 Mai Lam....C1
35 Mekong Quilts....A3
36 Saigon Kitsch....B3

Palace (and later the Revolutionary Museum), HCMC's city museum is a singularly beautiful and impressive building, telling the story of the city through archaeological artefacts, ceramics, old city maps and displays on the marriage traditions of its various ethnicities. The struggle for independence is extensively covered, with most of the upper floor devoted to it.

Central Post Office HISTORIC BUILDING
(Map p135; 2 Cong Xa Paris; ⏲7am-7pm Mon-Fri, to 6pm Sat, 8am-6pm Sun) The city's landmark French-era post office is a period classic, designed by Marie-Alfred Foulhoux (though often credited to Gustave Eiffel) and built between 1886 and 1891. Painted on the walls of its grand concourse are fascinating historical maps of South Vietnam, Saigon and Cholon, while a mosaic of Ho Chi Minh takes pride of place at the end of its barrel-vaulted hall.

Bitexco Financial Tower VIEWPOINT
(Map p132; www.bitexcofinancialtower.com; 2 Đ Hai Trieu; adult/child 200,000/130,000d; ⏲9.30am-9.30pm) This elegant 68-storey, 262m-high Carlos Zapata–designed skyscraper dwarfs all around it. It's reportedly shaped like a lotus bulb, but it also resembles a CD rack with a tambourine shoved into it. That tambourine is the 49th-floor **Saigon Skydeck**, its roof functioning as a helipad. Frankly, given the crowds and cost, the Skydeck is not that great a visitor experience; consider a drink in the **EON Heli Bar** (Map p132; http://eon51.com/eon-heli-bar; 52nd fl, Bitexco Financial Tower, 2 Đ Hai Trieu; ⏲10.30am-2am) on the 52nd floor or visit the neighbouring Sedona Suites tower instead.

Opera House THEATRE
(Nha Hat Thanh Pho; Map p132; ☎028-3823 7419; www.hbso.org.vn; Lam Son Sq) Gracing the intersection of Đ Dong Khoi and ĐL Le Loi, this grand colonial edifice with a sweeping staircase was built in 1897 and is one of the city's most recognisable buildings. Officially known as the Municipal Theatre, the Opera House captures the flamboyance of France's belle époque. Performances range from ballet and opera to modern dance and musicals. Check the website for English-language listings and booking information.

People's Committee Building NOTABLE BUILDING
(Hôtel de Ville; Map p132; ĐL Nguyen Hue) One of the city's most prominent landmarks is home to the Ho Chi Minh City People's

Committee. Built between 1901 and 1908, the former Hôtel de Ville decorates the northwestern end of ĐL Nguyen Hue, but unfortunately the ornate interior is not open to the public.

Around Le Van Tam Park

★Jade Emperor Pagoda TAOIST TEMPLE
(Phuoc Hai Tu, Chua Ngoc Hoang; Map p135; 73 Đ Mai Thi Luu; 7am-6pm daily, plus 5am-7pm 1st & 15th of lunar month) FREE Built in 1909 in honour of the supreme Taoist god (the Jade Emperor or King of Heaven, Ngoc Hoang), this is one of the most atmospheric temples in Ho Chi Minh City, stuffed with statues of phantasmal divinities and grotesque heroes. The pungent smoke of incense *(huong)* fills the air, obscuring the exquisite woodcarvings. Its roof is encrusted with elaborate tile work, and the temple's statues, depicting characters from both Buddhist and Taoist lore, are made from reinforced papier mâché.

History Museum MUSEUM
(Bao Tang Lich Su; Map p135; Đ Nguyen Binh Khiem; 30,000d; 8-11.30am & 1.30-5pm Tue-Sun) Built in 1929, this notable Sino-French museum houses a rewarding collection of artefacts illustrating the evolution of the cultures of Vietnam, from the Bronze Age Dong Son civilisation (which emerged in 2000 BCE) and the Funan civilisation (1st to 6th centuries CE) to the Cham, Khmer and Vietnamese. Highlights include valuable relics taken from Cambodia's Angkor Wat and a fine collection of Buddha statues. There's good English information. Parts of the museum are being renovated.

Cholon

★Binh Tay Market MARKET
(Cho Binh Tay; www.chobinhtay.gov.vn; 57a ĐL Thap Muoi; 6am-7.30pm) Cholon's main market has a great clock tower and a central courtyard with gardens. Much of the business here is wholesale but it's popular with tour groups. The market was originally built by the French in the 1880s; Guangdong-born philanthropist Quach Dam paid for its rebuilding and was commemorated by a statue that is now in the Fine Arts Museum (p131). Very little English is spoken but expect a friendly welcome if you take breakfast or coffee with the market's street-food vendors.

Thien Hau Pagoda TAOIST TEMPLE
(Ba Mieu, Pho Mieu, Chua Ba Thien Hau; Map p131; 710 Đ Nguyen Trai) FREE This gorgeous 19th-century temple is dedicated to the goddess Thien Hau, and always attracts a mix of worshippers and visitors, who mingle beneath the large coils of incense suspended overhead. It is believed that Thien Hau can travel over the oceans on a mat and ride the clouds to save people in trouble on the high seas.

★Phuoc An Hoi Quan Pagoda TAOIST TEMPLE
(Quan De Mieu; Map p131; 184 Đ Hong Bang) FREE Delightfully fronted by greenery and opening to an interior blaze of red, gold, green and yellow, this is one of the most beautifully ornamented temples in town, dating from 1902. Of special interest are the elaborate brass ritual ornaments and weapons, and the fine woodcarvings on the altars, walls, columns, hanging lanterns and incense coils. From the exterior, look out for the ceramic scenes, each containing innumerable small figurines, that decorate the roof.

Quan Am Pagoda BUDDHIST TEMPLE
(Chua Quan Am; Map p131; 12 Đ Lao Tu) FREE One of Cholon's most active and colourful temples, this shrine was founded in the early 19th century. It's named after the Goddess of Mercy, whose full name is Quan The Am Bo Tat, literally 'the Bodhisattva Who Listens to the Cries of the World' (觀世音菩薩 in Chinese characters), in reflection of her compassionate mission.

Traditional Herb Shops AREA
(Map p131; Đ Hai Thuong Lan Ong) While you're roaming the area, stroll over to the strip of traditional herb shops between Đ Luong Nhu Hoc and Đ Trieu Quang Phuc for an olfactory experience you won't soon forget. The streets here are filled with amazing sights, sounds and rich herbal aromas.

Greater Ho Chi Minh City

★Giac Lam Pagoda BUDDHIST TEMPLE
(Chua Giac Lam; 118 Đ Lac Long Quan, Tan Binh District; 4am-noon & 2-9pm) FREE Believed to be the oldest temple in HCMC (1744), Giac Lam is a fantastically atmospheric place set in peaceful, garden-like grounds. The Chinese characters that constitute the temple's name (覚林寺) mean 'Feel the Woods Temple' and the looming Bodhi tree (a native fig

Around Le Van Tam Park

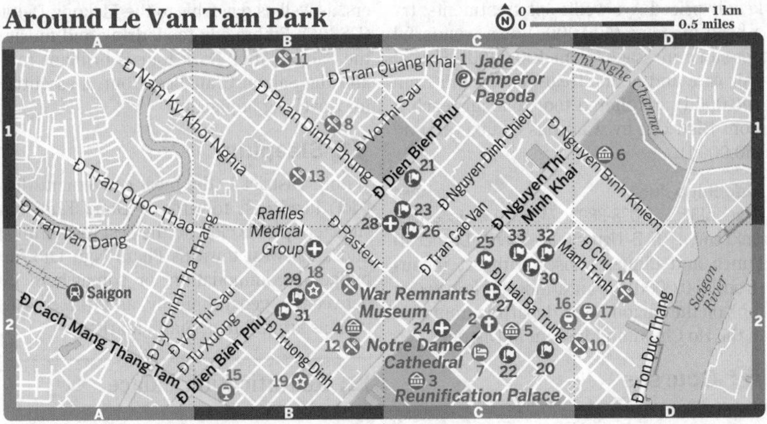

Around Le Van Tam Park

Top Sights
1 Jade Emperor Pagoda C1
2 Notre Dame Cathedral C2
3 Reunification Palace C2
4 War Remnants Museum B2

Sights
5 Central Post Office C2
6 History Museum D1

Sleeping
7 Coco Hostel C2

Eating
8 Banh Xeo 46A B1
9 Beefsteak Nam Son B2
10 Chi Hoa D2
11 Cuc Gach Quan B1
12 Hum Vegetarian Cafe & Restaurant B2
13 Pho Hoa B1
14 Quan Bui D2

Drinking & Nightlife
15 BiaCraft B2
16 Heart of Darkness C2
17 Pasteur Street Brewing Company D2

Entertainment
18 Acoustic B2
Saigon Water Puppet Theatre .... (see 6)
19 Yoko B2

Information
20 Australian Consulate C2
21 Cambodian Consulate C1
22 Canadian Consulate C2
23 Chinese Consulate C1
24 Columbia Asia C2
25 French Consulate C2
26 German Consulate C2
27 HCMC Family Medical Practice C2
28 International Medical Centre C1
29 Japanese Consulate B2
30 Netherlands Consulate C2
New Zealand Consulate .... (see 22)
31 Thai Consulate B2
32 UK Consulate C2
33 US Consulate C2

tree, sacred to Buddhists) in the front garden was the gift of a Sri Lankan monk in 1953. Prayers are held daily from 4am to 5am, 11am to noon, 4pm to 5pm and 7pm to 9pm.

Museum of Traditional Vietnamese Medicine MUSEUM
(Map p131; www.fitomuseum.com.vn; 41 Đ Hoang Du Khuong, District 10; adult/child 120,000/60,000d; ⏲8.30am-5pm) A lovely piece of traditional architecture in itself, this absorbing and very well-stocked museum with over a dozen exhibition rooms affords fascinating insights into local medical practices, which are heavily influenced by China. While you're here, catch the short film about Vietnamese medicine, *A Century of Health Care Experiences,* and be sure to delve into the world of East Asian potions and remedies through the ages. Don't miss the Cham tower at the top, equipped with a fertility symbol.

Activities

★Aveda SPA
(☎028-3519 4679; www.avedaherbal.com; Villa 1, 21/1 Đ Xuan Thuy; ⏲9am-8pm Wed-Mon) This wonderful District 2-based spa is Indian-owned and offers sublime, professional and

keenly priced Ayurvedic spa treatments: try a head massage (500,000d) or a wonderful hot-stone massage (from 400,000d). Herbal hair care and henna treatments (both from 400,000d) are offered too. You can reach it from District 1 by waterbus or taxi (around 160,000d).

Indochina Junk BOATING
(Map p132; ☎028-3895 7438; www.indochinajunk.com.vn; 5 Đ Nguyen Tat Thanh, District 4) Lunch and dinner cruises with set menus (from 350,000d) in an atmospheric wooden junk on the Saigon River, departing from next to the Ho Chi Minh Museum in District 4.

Courses

Grain Cooking Classes COOKING
(Map p132; ☎028-3827 4929; www.grainbyluke.com; level 3, 71-75 ĐL Hai Ba Trung; US$48; ⏲9am-noon & 2-5pm Mon-Sat) Cooking classes designed and coordinated by Vietnamese-Australian celebrity chef Luke Nguyen. Four-course menus change regularly to reflect seasonal produce, and Luke himself is on hand for some classes throughout the year.

Tours

★**Old Compass Travel** TOURS
(Map p132; ☎028-3823 2969; www.oldcompasstravel.com; 3rd fl, 63/11 Đ Pasteur; from US$40) Excellent city tours lead by passionate Saigon residents who are experts on Vietnamese culture and architecture. Tales of the City is a heritage walking tour that takes in many of the sights along ĐL Le Duan and into the heart of District 1. Religious Architecture and Art tours are both very rewarding too. Based at the excellent Old Compass Cafe (p139).

Consider their 'alternative' Cu Chi Tunnels tour too (which is not the typical tourist experience) or owner Mark Bowyer's superb 15-day Vietnam tours.

Back of the Bike Tours TOURS
(☎028-2221 5591; www.backofthebiketours.com; from US$42) Cheaper than other scooter tours, this outfit offers a wildly popular four-hour Street Food tour and a good Night Rider tour that takes in seven districts. The speedboat trips to Cu Chi Tunnels (per person US$80) are also great.

Vespa Adventures TOURS
(Map p138; ☎0122 299 3585; www.vespaadventures.com; 169a Đ De Tham; from US$78) Entertaining guided city tours on vintage scooters, as well as day trips to the Mekong Delta (US$95). Embracing food, drink and music, the Saigon After Dark tour is brilliant fun, and the Saigon Craft Beer Tour is essential for travelling hopheads.

Sleeping

Within District 1 (the most convenient district) head east towards Đ Dong Khoi for smarter options close to the best restaurants and bars; west towards Pham Ngu Lao for budget accommodation, or somewhere in between – geographically and price-wise, such as around Ben Thanh Market.

Reunification Palace & Around

This area boasts a lot of greenery, with Tao Dan Park at its core. There are many fine midrange options around Ben Thanh market.

Coco Hostel HOSTEL $
(Map p135; ☎090 311 8216; www.facebook.com/cocohostelbar; 178/4B Đ Pasteur; dm US$8-10, r US$27-32; ⊖❄🛜) This small hostel is run by a friendly team and has an enviable location in an upmarket corner of District 1 near parkland and the Reunification Palace. Dorm beds all have reading lights and privacy curtains, and all accommodation is air-conditioned. There's a guests' kitchen and breakfast is included.

★**Nguyen Shack** GUESTHOUSE $$
(Map p131; ☎028-3822 0501; www.nguyenshack.com; 6/15 Đ Cach Mang Thang Tam; r 900,000-1,150,000d; ⊖❄🛜) Down a quiet residential lane a shortish walk from Pham Ngu Lao and Ben Thanh Market, Nguyen Shack's first city opening incorporates a rustic look, with bamboo furniture and ample greenery, spotless and spacious rooms (some sleeping four), and a leafy, shared downstairs area. Breakfast and water refills are complimentary.

★**Ma Maison Boutique Hotel** HOTEL $$$
(Map p131; ☎028-3846 0263; www.mamaison.vn; 656/52 Đ Cach Mang Thang Tam, District 3; s US$65-75, d US$80-125; ❄@🛜) Classy Ma Maison is halfway between the airport and the city centre, and partly in the French countryside, decor-wise. Wooden shutters soften the exterior of the modern, medium-rise block, while in the rooms, painted French-provincial-style furniture and first-rate bathrooms add a touch of panache.

Dong Khoi Area

Home to Ho Chi Minh City's top-notch hotels, the Dong Khoi area is also sprinkled with attractive midrange options.

Saigon Central Hostel HOSTEL $
(Map p132; 028-3914 1107; saigoncentralhostel@gmail.com; 54/6 Đ Ky Con; dm/d US$7/27;) Friendly guesthouse located in a quiet lane in an emerging area of town – it's walking distance from Pham Ngu Lao and Dong Khoi. Dorms have decent air-con, the breakfast is good and there's a rooftop terrace.

Town House 23 GUESTHOUSE $
(Map p132; 028-3915 1491; www.townhousesaigon.com; 23 Đ Dang Thi Nhu; dm US$11, r US$32-37;) Located in a quiet cafe-lined street a short walk from the bustle of Pham Ngu Lao, Town House 23 is a modern and well-designed combination of hostel and guesthouse. The decor is particularly stylish and the team at reception is very helpful. Not all rooms have windows.

★ **Myst** BOUTIQUE HOTEL $$$
(Map p132; 028-3520 3040; www.themystdongkhoihotel.com; 6-8 Đ Ho Huan Nghiep; r US$130-180;) Very popular, this hip hotel is just a short stroll from the riverside and good shopping along Đ Dong Khoi. Decor combines retro Indochinese style with a dash of 1930s art-deco influence. The quirky exterior is enlivened by a living wall of tropical shrubbery. There's a compact rooftop lap pool, and Bar Bleu, on the 14th floor, has extensive city views.

Park Hyatt Saigon HOTEL $$$
(Map p132; 028-3824 1234; www.saigon.park.hyatt.com; 2 Lam Son Sq; r from US$320;) This recently renovated luxury hotel is one of HCMC's very best. A prime location opposite the Opera House combines with exemplary service, fastidiously attired staff and lavishly appointed rooms. Relaxation opportunities include an inviting pool and the acclaimed Xuan Spa. Highly regarded (yet affordable) restaurants include Opera, for Italian, and **Square One** (Map p132; 028-3824 1234; www.saigon.park.hyattrestaurants.com/squareOne; Park Hyatt Saigon, 2 Lam Son Sq; meals from 280,000d; noon-2.30pm & 5.30-10.30pm;), serving Vietnamese and international fare.

Pham Ngu Lao Area

Pham Ngu Lao is Ho Chi Minh City's budget zone, with more than 100 accommodation choices available. Even midrange travellers can find excellent deals here, often at budget prices.

Lily's Hostel HOSTEL $
(Map p138; 028-3920 9180; lilyhostel.hcm@gmail.com; 35/5 Đ Bui Vien; dm/d US$8/28;) Lily's has a warm and welcoming ambience courtesy of its hip, modern decor. Located in a lane just off bustling Đ Bui Vien, it easily bridges the gap between hostel and boutique guesthouse. Some private rooms have a flat-screen TV and minibar.

Diep Anh GUESTHOUSE $
(Map p138; 028-3836 7920; dieptheanh@hcm.vnn.vn; 241/31 Đ Pham Ngu Lao; r US$21-26;) A step above most PNL options, figuratively and literally (with 1000-yard stairs), Diep Anh's tall and narrow shape makes for light and airy upper rooms. Clean, safe and secure, this is very welcoming guesthouse run by a hands-on couple.

Hong Han Hotel GUESTHOUSE $
(Map p138; 028-3836 1927; www.honghanhotelhcm.com; 238 Đ Bui Vien; r incl breakfast US$25-35;) A well-run family-owned guesthouse where you can opt for front rooms with ace views, or smaller, quieter and cheaper rear options; all en suites are small and functional. There are seven floors, with no lift, however.

Hideout Hostel HOSTEL $
(Map p138; 028-3838 9147; www.hideouthostels.asia/saigon.html; 281 Đ Pham Ngu Lao; dm US$7;) A modern PNL hostel with an emphasis on good times and meeting other travellers. Dorms (one for females) are spick and span with bright colours, and a free beer per day is on offer in the rooftop bar (which has a pool table and foosball). The hostel runs bar crawls three nights a week (free for guests).

Giang Son GUESTHOUSE $
(Map p138; 028-3837 7547; 283/14 Đ Pham Ngu Lao; r US$20-32;) On a back alley off Pham Ngu Lao, tall and thin Giang Son has three rooms on each floor, a roof terrace and charming service; the sole downer is that there's no lift. Consider upgrading to a room with a window.

Pham Ngu Lao

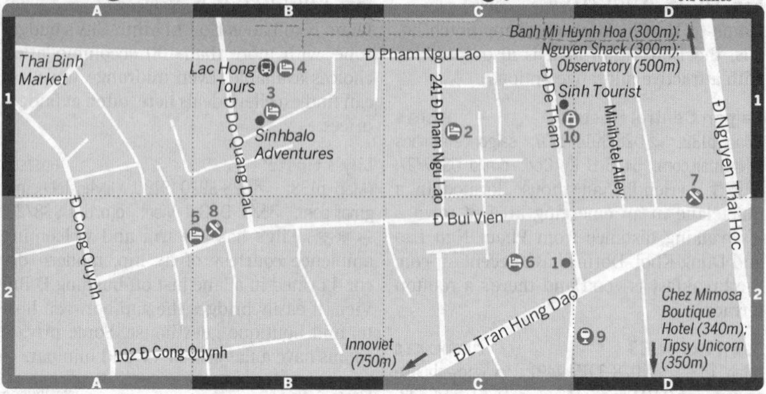

Pham Ngu Lao

Activities, Courses & Tours

1 Vespa Adventures C2

Sleeping

2 Diep Anh C1
3 Giang Son B1
4 Hideout Hostel B1
5 Hong Han Hotel B2
6 Lily's Hostel C2

Eating

7 Coriander D1
8 Five Oysters B2

Drinking & Nightlife

9 Whiskey & Wares D2

Shopping

10 Ginkgo C1

★ **Chez Mimosa Boutique Hotel** HOTEL **$$**
(Map p131; ☎028-3838 9883; www.chezmimosa.com; 71 Đ Co Giang; r 1,000,000-1,600,000d; ⊜❄⊚) Expect a warm welcome from the well-trained staff at this attractive new hotel. Rooms are light, airy and presented with white furniture and style. It's located in an interesting district that's fast becoming one of HCMC's most fashionable. Laundry is free for guests, but there's no lift.

District 2

Expat favourite District 2 is perfect if you want to escape the crowded heart of the city. It has river-bus links to the centre.

★ **River Cottage** BOUTIQUE HOTEL **$$$**
(☎028-3744 3555; www.rivercottage.com.vn; 18 Đ Duong 6; r US$90-140; ⊜❄⊚) Set in verdant gardens on the banks of the Saigon River, this hotel is a uniquely peaceful retreat from the energy of the city. Eight rooms – some riverside – blend modern design with handmade furniture, beds with luxe linen, wooden daybeds and expansive windows. There's all-day dining, with fine Western and local cuisine available.

Villa Song BOUTIQUE HOTEL **$$$**
(☎028-3744 6090; www.villasong.com; 187/2 Đ Nguyen Van Huong; r US$180-260, ste US$385-445; ⊜❄⊚≋) In a District 2 garden location with river views, this French-inspired boutique hotel is one of HCMC's most relaxing places to stay. Very romantic rooms and suites are filled with heritage Indochinese style and contemporary Vietnamese art, and the property's Song Vie bistro has an absolute riverside location. The spa is also very well regarded.

Eating

Hanoi may consider itself more cultured, but HCMC is Vietnam's culinary capital. Delicious regional fare is complemented by a well-developed choice of international restaurants, with Indian, Japanese, Thai, Italian and East–West fusions well represented. Unsurprisingly, given its heritage, HCMC has a fine selection of French restaurants, from casual bistros to haute cuisine.

The Dong Khoi area has many top-quality restaurants. Pham Ngu Lao's eating options are good value, but can attempt to satisfy every possible culinary whim, so don't expect super-authentic food.To really discover more of the city's great street food, a tour is an excellent option.

Distant District 2 scores highly for international cuisine, or for a really local experience head south to District 4, particularly for seafood and snails.

Reunification Palace & Around

Beefsteak Nam Son VIETNAMESE $
(Map p135; 157 Đ Nam Ky Khoi Nghia; meals from 50,000d; 6am-10pm;) For top-notch, affordable steak in a simple setting, this is a superb choice. Local steak, other beef dishes (such as the spicy beef soup *bun bo Hue*), imported Australian fillets and even cholesterol-friendly ostrich are on the well-priced menu.

★ **Hum Vegetarian Cafe & Restaurant** VEGETARIAN $$
(Map p135; 028-3930 3819; www.humvegetarian.com; 32 Đ Vo Van Tan, District 3; meals 130,000-240,000d; 10am-10pm;) This serene and elegant vegetarian restaurant requires your attention. Everything – from the charming service to the delightful Vietnamese dishes and peaceful outside tables – makes dining here an occasion to savour. Try the tofu in fermented bean sauce or the grilled pumpkin salad. There's also an equally laid-back and more central location.

★ **Bep Me In** VIETNAMESE $$
(Map p132; 028-6866 6128; www.facebook.com/bepmein; 136/9 Đ Le Thanh Ton; mains 60,000-150,000d; 11am-11pm;) At the rear of a nail-bar alley near Ben Thanh Market, this superb resto offers rustic, honest dishes from rural Vietnam in hip surrounds. On the ground floor there are big shared tables, and the quirky decor includes colourful wall paintings and a vintage motorcycle rickshaw doubling as a drinks station. The upstairs dining room is more quiet and refined.

Dong Khoi Area

Secret Garden VIETNAMESE $
(Map p132; 090 990 4621; www.facebook.com/secretgarden158pasteur; 4th fl, 158 Đ Pasteur; meals 70,000-120,000d; 8am-10pm;) You pass through a motorbike parking lot then negotiate the stairs of a faded HCMC apartment building to reach this wonderful rooftop restaurant. Rogue chickens peck away in the herb garden, Buddhist statues add ambience, and delicious homestyle dishes are served with city views. Service can sometimes be a little *too* casual, but it's worth persevering for the great flavours.

Chi Hoa VIETNAMESE $
(Map p135; 028-3827 3155; www.chihoacuisine.com; 31a Đ Le Thanh Thon; snacks & meals 30,000-160,000d; 7am-10pm) Vietnamese comfort food served in simple but attractive surroundings. The menu ranges widely, from lots of different sandwiches – try *banh mi bi* (shredded pork, pork skin and sticky rice powder) – to salads and rice and noodle bowls. Great breakfasts too.

★ **Old Compass Cafe** CAFE $$
(Map p132; 090 390 0841; www.facebook.com/oldcompasscafe; 3rd fl, 63 Đ Pasteur; meals 150,000d; 10.30am-10pm Sun-Thu, to 11pm Fri & Sat;) This cafe/cultural centre is a gem. It's tricky to find: off busy Đ Pasteur, along an alley and then up steep stairs in a somewhat rundown apartment building. But persevere and you'll enter a gorgeous all-day cafe that often segues into a live-music and performance space at night. Relax over coffee, wine or craft beer or opt for a fine-value lunch deal.

There are ample books to browse while you're lounging on a sofa. Check Facebook for listings of events.

★ **Quan Bui** VIETNAMESE $$
(Map p135; 028-3829 1515; www.quan-bui.com; 17a Đ Ngo Van Nam; meals 80,000-250,000d; 8am-11pm) Stylish Indochinese decor features at this slick place where the focus is on authentic local cuisine. Many dishes showcase the more hearty flavours of northern Vietnam; offerings include delicious *heo quay Quan Bui* (roasted pork served with pickle). Cocktails – from the associated bar across the lane – are among HCMC's best, and upstairs there's an air-conditioned and smoke-free dining room.

Hum Lounge & Restaurant VEGETARIAN $$
(Map p132; 028-3823 8920; www.humvietnam.vn; 2 Đ Thi Sach; meals 100,000-220,000d; 10am-10pm;) Excellent Vietnamese-inspired vegetarian cuisine in a central garden location. Settle into the elegant space with subtle lighting and classy furnishings in a lane off the riverfront. Delectable dishes include calabash and seaweed soup

(85,000d) and beetroot salad with passion fruit (140,000d).

3T Quan Nuong BARBECUE $$
(Map p132; ☎028-3821 1631; 29 Đ Ton That Thiep; meals 85,000-280,000d; ⊙5-11pm) This breezy alfresco Vietnamese barbecue restaurant on the rooftop of the Temple Club is in many a HCMC diner's diary: choose your meat, fish, seafood and veggies and flame them up right there on the table.

Sky 28 INTERNATIONAL $$
(Map p132; ☎028-3822 9888; www.sedonavietnam.com; 28th fl, Sedona Suites tower, 94 Đ Nam Ky Khoi Nghia; meals from 180,000d; ⊙7am-10.30pm;) Expect some of Saigon's best views from the tables of this 28th-floor upmarket hotel cafe-restaurant. It serves tasty international food, including burritos, club sandwiches and shawarma kebabs, and offers a three-course lunch deal for 189,000d. During happy hour (5pm to 8pm) beers cost just 40,000d. Or just grab a coffee and savour the cityscape.

★ **Quince** INTERNATIONAL $$$
(Map p132; www.facebook.com/quincesaigon; 37 Đ Ky Con; meals from 1,300,000d; ⊙5.30-11pm Mon-Sat;) Saigon's hottest ticket is a resolutely urbane, happening space with an open kitchen, distressed brick walls, cool tunes and a slightly edgy location close to the Saigon River. The vibe is reminiscent of East London or New York, with prices and a wine list to match. The regularly changing menu traverses the globe with aplomb, raiding Asia, Europe and the Americas for influence.

Racha Room THAI $$$
(Map p132; ☎0908 791 412; www.facebook.com/theracharoom; 12-14 Đ Mac Thi Buoi; meals 260,000-450,000d; ⊙3pm-midnight;) This bar-resto has cool clientele, playlists of lounge and house music and a fine layout with an elongated bar in the heart of the action. The menu features Thai street snacks (75,000d to 280,000d), shared plates (from 180,000d) and dumplings, and effortlessly

EXPLORING DISTRICT 4

Just south of the glitzy Dong Khoi area, it's a short walk over the Ben Nghe Channel to working-class **District 4**. Here the ambience is far more Saigonese, with little or no concession to tourism, and narrow lanes, street markets and shabby concrete apartment blocks. Order a coffee here and expect a drip-fed Vietnamese coffee that resembles engine oil rather than a frothy cappuccino.

District 4 is the best area in the city to sample authentic street food, with dozens of places on **Đ Vinh Khanh**. For great seafood at affordable prices, try **Oc Dao 2** (Map p131; 232 Đ Vinh Khanh; most mains 30,000-100,000d; ⊙3pm-late). HCMC is a city in love with snails, and District 4 is something of a magnet for snail eaters, with many fine places on the buzzing alley **Lo J KTT**, including **Oc Po** (Map p131; 224 Lo J KTT; dishes from 30,000d; ⊙4-11.30pm), which is always packed.

This district, bordered by canals and the Saigon River, was always one of the city's most flood-prone, until the government implemented a land-filling program that removed many small canals. A generation ago, parts of District 4 had a reputation as a hotbed for drug-dealing, illegal gambling dens and the red-light trade, and there were battles between gangsters and police for control of the streets. However, it's now considered a safe area to explore: just use your common sense, avoid dark lanes late at night and perhaps take a taxi home at the end of the evening.

Sights in D4 are few, but you will find the **Ho Chi Minh Museum** (Bao Tang Ho Chi Minh; Map p132; 1 Đ Nguyen Tat Thanh, District 4; 10,000d; ⊙7.30-11.30am & 1.30-5pm Tue-Sun) in the north of the district, while **Xom Chieu Market** (Map p131; 1 Dinh Le; ⊙5am-5pm) is a deeply traditional affair and very much geared to local tastes, especially fresh fruit and inexpensive clothing.

Tour operators use District 4 as a destination for their street-food excursions, but it's possible to investigate the area on your own and head here on foot or by cab (a taxi here from District 1 is around 45,000d). From the southern end of Đ Pasteur in District 1, cross the Ben Nghe Channel via the pedestrianised 19th-century Mong Bridge, built by the French, and you can walk along the canal bank, then south down Đ Vinh Khanh. After you've crossed the canal it's not exactly scenic, however, and traffic is heavy.

stretches to include the fare of neighbouring countries as well.

Around Le Van Tam Park

Pho Hoa VIETNAMESE $

(Map p135; http://phohoapasteur.restaurantsnapshot.com; 260c Đ Pasteur; meals 60,000-80,000d; 6am-midnight) This long-running *pho* joint is more upmarket than most but is definitely the real deal. Tables come laden with herbs, chilli and lime, as well as *gio chao quay* (fried Chinese bread), *banh xu xe* (glutinous coconut cakes with mung-bean paste) and *cha lua* (pork-paste sausages wrapped in banana leaves).

Banh Xeo 46A VIETNAMESE $

(Map p135; 028-3824 1110; 46a Đ Dinh Cong Trang; regular/extra large 80,000/120,000d; 10am-9pm;) This renowned spot serves some of the best *banh xeo* (Vietnamese rice-flour pancakes stuffed with bean sprouts, prawns and pork) in town. Vegetarian versions are available too. Other dishes include excellent *goi cuon* (fresh summer rolls with pork and prawn).

★Cuc Gach Quan VIETNAMESE $$

(Map p135; 028-3848 0144; www.cucgachquan.com.vn/en; 10 Đ Dang Tat; meals 110,000-240,000d; 9am-midnight;) It comes as little surprise to learn that the owner of this place is an architect when you step into this cleverly renovated old villa. The decor is both rustic and elegant, which is also true of the food, with many veggie options available. Despite its tucked-away location in the northernmost reaches of District 1, this is no secret hideaway: book ahead.

Pham Ngu Lao Area

Banh Mi Huynh Hoa VIETNAMESE $

(Map p131; 26 Đ Le Thi Rieng; banh mi 44,000d; 2.30-11pm) This hole-in-the-wall *banh mi* joint is busy day and night with locals zipping up on motorbikes for stacks of the excellent baguettes stuffed with pork, pork and more pork, in tasty ways you may not have known existed. Street standing room only.

Coriander THAI $

(Map p138; www.coriander-ngo-ri.com; 16 Đ Bui Vien; dishes 59,000-259,000d; 10am-2pm & 5-10pm;) The cheap decor does Coriander few favours, but the menu is stuffed with authentic Siamese delights. The lovely fried *doufu* (tofu) is almost a meal in itself, the green curry is zesty, and salads like *som tum chae* (green-papaya salad with tomato) are satisfying and authentic.

Five Oysters VIETNAMESE $

(Map p138; 090 301 2123; www.fiveoysters.com; 234 Đ Bui Vien; meals from 50,000d; 9am-11pm) With a strong seafood slant and friendly service, light and bright Five Oysters in backpackerland is frequently full of travellers feasting on oysters (25,000d to 30,000d), which are served with spring onion and garlic, wasabi, or even cheese (it works!). The octopus, shrimp dishes, seafood soup, snails, *pho* and grilled mackerel with chilli oil are also great.

Vegetarian Lien Huong VEGETARIAN $

(Com Chay Lien Huong; Map p131; 093 348 5064; 10d Đ Tran Nhat Duat; meals 60,000-120,000d; 8am-10pm;) It's moved to this new location in the north of District 1, but the creative flavours are still there. Standouts include green-banana and mushroom hotpot with lemongrass and rice noodles. The English-language menu has excellent descriptions of the health benefits of each dish. Great value.

★Padma de Fleur VIETNAMESE $$

(Map p132; 090 300 9873; www.cafe.padmadefleur.vn; 55/6 Đ Le Thi Hong Gam; meals 150,000-220,000d; 9am-10pm Tue-Sun, set meals 11.30am-2pm & 5-10pm;) This wonderful florist-cafe is run by an artistic owner who takes as much care with her bouquets as she does with her cooking. The food is healthy, nutritious and delicious, with lots of Vietnamese salad leaves and tasty morsels to savour. Located on a backstreet in an emerging hipster corner of town south of Pham Ngu Lao.

The space is open throughout the day for drinks, but food is only served at set times. Cocktails are also available in the evening (from 5pm to 10pm); reservations required.

Quan Ut Ut BARBECUE $$

(Map p131; 028-3914 4500; www.quanutut.com; 168 Đ Vo Van Kiet; meals 180,000-320,000d; 11am-10.30pm;) With a name roughly translating to the 'Oink Oink Eatery', this casual place with river views celebrates everything porcine with an American-style barbecue spin. Huge streetside grills prepare great ribs, spicy sausages and pork belly, and tasty sides include charred sweetcorn and roasted pumpkin and beetroot. The owners make their own flavour-packed craft beers.

Drinking & Nightlife

Reunification Palace & Around

★BiaCraft CRAFT BEER
(Map p135; 028-3933 0903; www.biacraft.com; 11 Đ Le Ngo Cat, District 3; 11am-11pm;) With almost 40 taps, BiaCraft is an essential destination for thirsty souls. Complementing its own creations are ales and ciders from craft breweries in Saigon and Hanoi; it's possible to take out freshly sealed cans of all available beers. Combine a tasting paddle with probably the city's best bar food, with quirky offerings like drunken baby potatoes and Nashville hot quail.

There are other BiaCrafts around town, including a (less impressive) branch in the District 2 area

★Observatory CLUB
(Map p131; www.facebook.com/theobservatoryhcmc; 85 Đ Cach Mang Thang Tam; 6pm-4am Thu, to 6am Fri & Sat;) This excellent musical cooperative now has a permanent location in a block with a skyline view for its DJ events and gigs featuring emerging electronic musicians and bands. It's one of the best places to check out the underground scene in HCMC. Check the Facebook page for listings.

Dong Khoi Area

★Heart of Darkness CRAFT BEER
(Map p135; 090 301 7596; www.heartofdarknessbrewery.com; 31D Đ Ly Tu Trong; 11am-midnight) This premier craft brewery has an always-interesting selection of innovative beers on tap. The selection varies as the Heart of Darkness brewers are always trying something, but the Dream Alone pale ale and Sacred Fire golden ale are great drops.

★Pasteur Street Brewing Company CRAFT BEER
(Map p132; www.pasteurstreet.com; 144 Đ Pasteur; 11am-10pm;) Pasteur Street Brewing turns out a fine selection of craft beer. Brews utilise local ingredients including lemongrass, rambutan and jasmine, and up to six different beers are always available (small/large beers from 45,000/95,000d). There are great bar snacks too (try the spicy Nashville fried chicken), also served in the brewery's hip space. There's a second, larger **branch** (Map p135; www.pasteurstreet.com; 26a Đ Le Thanh Ton; 11am-1am;) in District 1.

Rogue Saigon CRAFT BEER
(Map p132; 090 236 5780; www.facebook.com/roguesaigon; 11 Đ Pasteur; 4pm-midnight) Live music and Vietnamese craft beers combine on Rogue's rooftop terrace in a gritty building on the riverside edge of District 1. You'll find good beers such as Lac Brewing's Devil's Lake IPA, and music with an acoustic, blues or rock vibe. There are DJ sessions on Saturday and also jams and quiz nights.

Malt BAR
(Map p132; 091 848 4763; www.maltsaigon.com; 46-48 Đ Mac Thi Buoi; 2pm-1am Mon-Fri, noon-1am Sat & Sun;) Malt is one of the city's cosiest and most welcoming bars, and has a no-smoking policy (a rarity in HCMC). There's always a well-curated selection of local craft brews on tap – the savvy bar staff can make good beer recommendations – and there's moreish comfort food, including mac 'n' cheese and sliders. Darts and a vintage shuffleboard table are added attractions.

Alley Cocktail Bar & Kitchen COCKTAIL BAR
(Map p132; 093 565 3969; www.facebook.com/thealleysaigon; 63/1 Đ Pasteur; 5pm-midnight Mon-Wed, to 1am Thu-Sat;) Good luck finding this place (turn left just after the Liberty Central Saigon Citypoint hotel and follow the signs), but when you do discover it, celebrate with a classic cocktail, craft beer or whisky. The eclectic approach to music stretches from live music on acoustic Thursdays to DJs on Friday and Saturday nights. The generous happy hour is from 5pm to 8pm.

Apocalypse Now CLUB
(Map p132; 028-3824 1463; www.facebook.com/apocalypsenowsaigon; 2c Đ Thi Sach; 7pm-4am) 'Apo' has been around since 1991 and remains one of the must-visit clubs in town. It's a sprawling place with a big dance floor and a courtyard, and its eclectic cast combines travellers, expats, Vietnamese movers and shakers, plus the odd working girl. Expect pounding techno. There are (cheesy) live bands on Saturday nights.

Pham Ngu Lao Area

Whiskey & Wares BAR
(Map p138; 0163 279 4179; www.facebook.com/WhiskeyandWares; 196 Đ De Tham; 4.30pm-1.30am Tue-Sun;) Fine whisky, good cocktails and local craft beer all appeal at this sophisticated bar a short hop from Pham Ngu Lao. It's also a top spot to

COFFEE CULTURE

HCMC's coffee culture is deep and established, and can be witnessed (and partaken in) on most streets in the city where there's a traditional Vietnamese cafe serving treacle-thick drip coffee.

New-wave coffee shops are now mushrooming throughout the city, with **Workshop** (Map p132; www.facebook.com/the.workshop.coffee; 10 Đ Ngo Duc Ke; ⌚8am-9pm; 📶) a key venue in the centre of town. In the mean hipster streets south of Pham Ngu Lao we rate quirky independents **Chat Coffee Roasters** (Map p132; www.facebook.com/Chat-Coffee-Roasters; 55/1 Đ Le Thi Hong Gam; ⌚7am-midnight; 📶) and **Saigon Coffee Roastery** (Map p132; www.facebook.com/saigoncoffeeroastery; 12 Đ Dang Thi Nhu; ⌚7am-10pm; 📶).

Further afield, the sleek contemporary surrounds of **Bosgaurus Coffee** (www.bosgauruscoffee.com; Saigon Pearl complex, D6, off Đ Nguyen Huu Canh; ⌚7am-9pm; 📶) on the Saigon River 2km north of the centre are well worth a caffeine pilgrimage, while over in District 2 **Dolphy** (www.facebook.com/dolphycafe; 28 Đ Thao Dien; ⌚6am-10pm; 📶) is a reliable bet.

purchase local artisanal goods. It's LGBTIQ-friendly, but welcoming to all.

Tipsy Unicorn GAY & LESBIAN
(Map p131; ☎028-7307 3647; www.facebook.com/TipsyUnicornSaigon; 37 Đ De Tham; ⌚4pm-2am; 📶) One of the city's very few openly gay bars, drawing a loyal crowd of locals with a fun, welcoming vibe. There's plenty going on, with quiz nights, DJs on Saturdays, live bands and even drag-queen bingo (Sundays at 9pm).

District 2

★Saigon Outcast BAR
(www.saigonoutcast.com; 188 Đ Nguyen Van Huong, District 2; ⌚10am-11.30pm Tue-Sat, to 10.30pm Sun) This District 2 venue has a diverse combination of live music, DJs, cinema nights and good times amid street art. Cocktails, craft beer and local ciders are available in the raffish garden bar, and there are outdoor flea and farmers markets here bimonthly. There's a rock-climbing wall that will keep kids occupied for hours. Check the website for what's on.

☆ Entertainment

Consult the Saigoneer (https://saigoneer.com) to find out what's on.

Acoustic LIVE MUSIC
(Map p135; ☎028-3930 2239; www.facebook.com/acousticbarpage; 6e1 Đ Ngo Thoi Nhiem, District 3; ⌚7pm-midnight; 📶) Don't be misled by the name: most of the musicians are fully plugged in and dangerous when they take to the intimate stage of the city's leading live-music venue. And judging by the numbers that pack in, the local crowd just can't get enough. It's at the end of the alley by the upended VW Beetle.

Yoko LIVE MUSIC
(Map p135; ☎028-3933 0577; www.facebook.com/Yokocafesaigon; 22a Đ Nguyen Thi Dieu; ⌚8am-5pm Mon, 8am-midnight Tue-Sat, 4pm-midnight Sun; 📶) This live-music venue hosts anything from funk rock to metal, acoustic to indie, kicking off at around 9pm nightly. Check Facebook for what's on.

Saigon Water Puppet Theatre PUPPET THEATRE
(Map p135; History Museum, Đ Nguyen Binh Khiem; 100,000d) Within the History Museum (p134), this small theatre has performances at 9am, 10am, 11am, 2pm, 3pm and 4pm, lasting about 20 minutes.

Municipal Theatre CONCERT VENUE
(Opera House; Map p132; ☎028-3829 9976; Lam Son Sq) The landmark French-era Opera House is home to the HCMC Ballet and the Ballet & Symphony Orchestra (www.hbso.org.vn), and hosts performances by visiting artists.

Shopping

Dong Khoi Area

★Chung Cu 42 Ton That Thiep CLOTHING
(Map p132; 42 Đ Ton That Thiep; ⌚most shops 9am-9pm) Come for the apartment building partially converted into cool boutique shops, and linger for the young, social-media-savvy fashion labels that produce stylish but

affordable clothing. Triple T is a great store here selling linen menswear. Head upstairs, and also through to the back to the second building.

Mekong Quilts ARTS & CRAFTS

(Map p132; ☎028-2210 3110; www.mekongquilts.com; 68 ĐL Le Loi; ⏰9am-7pm) Beautiful handmade silk quilts, sewn by the rural poor in support of sustainable incomes. Bags, scarves, bowls and even very cool bamboo bikes are also sold.

Saigon Kitsch GIFTS & SOUVENIRS

(Map p132; 33 Đ Ton That Thiep; ⏰9am-10pm) Specialises in reproduction propaganda items, emblazoning its revolutionary motifs on coffee mugs, coasters, jigsaws and T-shirts. Laptop and tablet covers fashioned from recycled packaging, posters and Vietnamese cookbooks are also stocked.

Ben Thanh Market MARKET

(Cho Ben Thanh; Map p132; ĐL Le Loi, ĐL Ham Nghi, ĐL Tran Hung Dao & Đ Le Lai; ⏰5am-6pm) Ben Thanh and its surrounding streets comprise one of HCMC's liveliest areas. Everything that's commonly eaten, worn or used by the Saigonese is piled high, and souvenirs can be found in equal abundance. Vendors are determined and prices are usually higher than elsewhere (though restaurant stalls are reasonable), so bargain vigorously and ignore any 'Fixed Price' signs.

Mai Lam CLOTHING

(Map p132; www.mailam.com.vn; 132-134 Đ Dong Khoi; ⏰9am-9pm) Mai Lam is inspired by Vietnamese street style; head here for vibrant, innovative (but pricey) hand-stitched men's and women's clothing and accessories.

Pham Ngu Lao Area

Ginkgo CLOTHING

(Map p138; www.ginkgo-vietnam.com; 254 Đ De Tham; ⏰8am-10pm) With two branches in the PNL area, this fun upmarket shop sells exuberant, brightly coloured T-shirts and hoodies, with a quirky Asian and Vietnamese focus.

Other Neighbourhoods

Dan Sinh Market MARKET

(Map p132; 104 Đ Yersin; ⏰most stalls 7am-5pm) Also known as the War Surplus Market, head here for authentic combat boots or rusty (and perhaps less authentic) dog tags among the overflowing hardware stalls. There are also rain jackets, mosquito nets, canteens, duffel bags, ponchos and boots. Check out Steven's Shop (open 9.30am to 4.30pm) for quirky one-off and vintage discoveries.

Information

MEDICAL SERVICES

HCMC Family Medical Practice (Map p135; ☎24hr emergency 028-3822 7848; www.vietnammedicalpractice.com; rear, Diamond Department Store, 34 ĐL Le Duan; ⏰24hr) Well-run practice with branches in Hanoi and Danang.

International Medical Centre (Map p135; ☎028-3827 2366; www.cmi-vietnam.com; 30 Pham Ngoc Thach; ⏰8.30am-7pm Mon-Fri, 9am-1pm Sat) A nonprofit organisation with English-speaking French doctors.

POST

Post Office (Buu Dien Quan 5; Map p131; ☎028-3855 1763; 3 Đ Mac Cuu, District 5; ⏰7am-7pm Mon-Fri, to 6pm Sat, 8am-6pm Sun) Look for the light-yellow building with a clock.

TRAVEL AGENCIES

Ez Pass (Map p132; 89/17 Đ Ham Nghi) Run by a friendly team and specialising in visa consultant services, transport arrangements and hotel bookings. It's down a little side alley.

Innoviet (Map p131; ☎096 793 1670; https://innoviet.com; 40 Đ Tran Hung Dao; ⏰9.30am-5pm Mon-Fri) Travel agency with online booking service.

Sinh Tourist (Map p138; ☎028-3838 9593; www.thesinhtourist.vn; 246 Đ De Tham; ⏰6.30am-10.30pm) Popular budget travel agency.

Getting There & Away

AIR

HCMC is served by **Tan Son Nhat International Airport** (☎028-3848 5383; www.tsnairport.hochiminhcity.gov.vn/vn; Tan Binh District). Airlines serving around 20 domestic destinations from HCMC include Bamboo Airways, Jetstar, VietJet Air and Vietnam Airlines.

Jetstar Pacific Airlines (☎1900 1550; www.jetstar.com/vn/en/home) Flies to/from destinations including Buon Ma Thuot, Chu Lai, Dalat, Danang, Dong Hoi, Hanoi, Hue, Nha Trang, Phu Quoc, Quy Nhon, Thanh Hoa and Tuy Hoa.

Vietnam Air Service Company (Vasco; ☎028-3845 8017; www.vasco.com.vn) Flies to/from Ca Mau, Con Dao Islands and Rach Gia.

Vietnam Airlines (☎ 028-3832 0320; www.vietnamairlines.com) Flies to/from Hanoi, Hai Phong, Vinh, Dong Hoi, Hue, Danang, Quy Nhon, Nha Trang, Dalat, Buon Ma Thuot, Phu Quoc and Tuy Hoa.

BUS

Plenty of international bus services connect HCMC and Cambodia, most with departures from the Pham Ngu Lao area. Book online or check out the travel agencies at the western end of this backpacker area – especially around **Lac Hong Tours** (Map p138; ☎ 028-3920 5852; www.lachongtours.com; 305 Đ Pham Ngu Lao; ⏲ 6.30am-10pm) – for frequent bus departures to Phnom Penh (from 240,000d), Siem Reap and Sihanoukville (both from 400,000d).

An Suong Bus Station (Ben Xe An Suong; District 12) Buses to Tay Ninh, Cu Chi and other points northwest of HCMC depart from this dirty, crowded terminal, but it's not really worth using them as the Cu Chi Tunnels are off the main highway and are a nightmare to navigate.

Cholon Bus Station (District 5) Bus 1 links Ben Thanh Bus Station and Ben Thanh Market with Cholon Bus Station and Cholon's Binh Tay Market. Local bus 152 takes you to Tan Son Nhat International Airport.

Mien Dong Bus Station (Ben Xe Mien Dong; ☎ 028-3829 4056) Buses to locations north of HCMC leave from this huge and busy station in Binh Thanh district, about 5km from central HCMC on Hwy 13. Note that express buses depart from the east side, and local buses connect with the west side of the complex.

Mien Tay Bus Station (Ben Xe Mien Tay; ☎ 028-3825 5955; Đ Kinh Duong Vuong) Serves all areas south of HCMC, essentially the Mekong Delta. This huge station is about 10km west of HCMC in An Lac. A taxi here from Pham Ngu Lao costs around 210,000d. Buses and minibuses from Mien Tay serve most towns in the Mekong Delta using air-con express buses and premium minibuses.

CAR & MOTORCYCLE

Enquire at almost any hotel or tourist cafe to arrange car hire. The travel agencies in the Pham Ngu Lao area generally offer the lowest prices.

Motorbikes are available in the PNL area from US$7. However, given the insane traffic and lack of road signs, it's not a wise idea to tackle Saigon traffic.

TRAIN

Saigon Train Station (Ga Sai Gon; ☎ 028-3823 0105; 1 Đ Nguyen Thong, District 3; ⏲ ticket office 7.15-11am & 1-3pm) Trains from Saigon Train Station serve coastal cities to the north of HCMC.

ℹ Getting Around

TO/FROM THE AIRPORT

Tan Son Nhat Airport is 7km northwest of central HCMC.

Bus

There are two dedicated air-conditioned airport buses:

Route 109 (20,000d, 50 minutes, 5.30am to 1.30am, every 15 to 20 minutes) goes to the 'backpacker district' of Pham Ngu Lao via Ben Thanh Bus Station.

Route 49 (40,000d, 40 minutes, 5.30am to 1.30am, every 15 to 30 minutes) also stops at the PNL area, via Ben Thanh Market.

Taxi

Stick to either Mai Linh (p146) or Vinasun (p146) taxis.

A taxi should cost 120,000d to 170,000d to central HCMC.

TAXI

Metered taxis cruise the streets, but it is worth calling ahead if you are off the beaten path. The flagfall is around 12,000d for the first kilometre; expect to pay around 35,000d from Dong Khoi

ℹ GETTING TO CAMBODIA: HO CHI MINH CITY TO PHNOM PENH

Getting to the border The busy Moc Bai/Bavet border crossing is the fastest land route between Ho Chi Minh City and Phnom Penh. Pham Ngu Lao travel agencies sell bus tickets (US$10 to US$16) to Phnom Penh; buses leave from Pham Ngu Lao between 6am and 4pm, and again just before midnight. Allow seven to eight hours for the entire trip, including time spent on border formalities. For bus journeys to Siem Reap allow 12 to 13 hours, and 14 hours to Sihanoukville.

At the border Cambodian visas (US$30) are issued at the border (you'll need a passport-sized photo). Moc Bai is two hours from HCMC by bus and is a major duty-free shopping zone. It's a short walk from Moc Bai to Bavet (the Cambodian border) and its enclave of casinos.

Moving on Most travellers have a through bus ticket from HCMC to Phnom Penh, which is a further four-hour bus ride away.

to Pham Ngu Lao. Both **Mai Linh Taxi** (☎028-3838 3838) and **Vinasun Taxi** (☎028-3827 2727) can be trusted. Using Grab is another good option.

AROUND HO CHI MINH CITY

Cu Chi

POP 19,800 / ☎028

If the tenacious spirit of the Vietnamese can be symbolised by a place, few sites could make a stronger case for it than Cu Chi. The **tunnel network** (adult/child 120,000/35,000d) became legendary during the 1960s for its role in facilitating VC control of a large rural area only 30km to 40km from HCMC. At its peak the tunnel system stretched from the South Vietnamese capital to the Cambodian border; in the district of Cu Chi alone more than 250km of tunnels honeycomb the ground.

Two sections of the remarkable tunnel network (which are enlarged and upgraded versions of the real thing) are open to the public. One is near the village of Ben Dinh and the other is 15km beyond at Ben Duoc (admission slightly cheaper). Most tourists visiting the tunnels end up at Ben Dinh, as it's easier for tour buses to reach. Even if you stay above ground, it's still an interesting experience learning about the region's ingenious and brave resistance activities.

Both sites have gun ranges attached where you can shell out a small fortune to fire genuine AK-47s and machine guns. You pay per bullet, so be warned: if you're firing an automatic weapon, they do come out pretty fast.

ℹ Getting There & Away

As public transport to Cu Chi is a pain, by far the easiest way to get to the tunnels is by guided tour. As the competition is stiff, prices are reasonable (from US$12 per person for a standard tour).

For something different consider a tour (US$80 person, minimum two people) by Old Compass Travel (p136), which will give you far more background and takes in a Viet Cong cemetery, a war memorial and the Saigon River. Or hop on a boat to the Cu Chi Tunnels with **Les Rives** (Map p132; ☎0128 592 0018; www.lesrivesexperience.com; 4th fl, 43-45 Đ Ho Tung Mau; adult/child sunset cruise 1,399,000/980,000d, Mekong Delta cruise 2,499,000/1,799,000d); boats depart twice daily (at 7am and 11am) and rates include hotel pickup, meals, refreshments, guide and admission fees. Another option is a motorbike tour with **Saigon Riders** (☎0919 767 118; www.saigonriders.vn; from US$49), which costs US$89 per person.

MEKONG DELTA

The 'rice bowl' of Vietnam, the Mekong Delta is carpeted in a dizzying variety of greens. It's a water world that moves to the rhythms of the mighty Mekong, where boats, houses and markets float upon the innumerable rivers, canals and streams that criss-cross the landscape like arteries.

Visitors can experience southern charm in riverside homestays, while Phu Quoc is a tropical island lined with lovely beaches.

Delta tours are very convenient (book through travel agencies in Ho Chi Minh City), but independent travel is perfectly feasible, if sometimes time-consuming.

Bac Lieu

The **Bac Lieu Bird Sanctuary** (Vuon Chim Bac Lieu; ☎0291-383 5991; electric buggy 400,000d; ⏲6am-6.30pm), 6km southwest of the little-visited town of Bac Lieu, is notable for its 50-odd species of bird, including a large population of graceful white herons. Bird populations peak in the rainy season – approximately May to October – and the birds nest until about January.

Guides should be hired at the sanctuary entrance; little English is spoken. **Bac Lieu Tourist Office** (☎0291-382 4272; www.baclieutourist.com; 2 Đ Hoang Van Thu; ⏲7-11am & 1-5pm) also arranges transport and guides.

Bac Lieu is on the bus route between Soc Trang and Ca Mau.

My Tho

POP 272,000 / ☎0273

Gateway to the Mekong Delta, My Tho is the capital of Tien Giang province and an important market town – although for the famous floating markets, you'll need to continue on to Can Tho.

My Tho's proximity to Ho Chi Minh City means it's a popular day-trip destination for a taste of river life – a flotilla of boats tours the local islands and their cottage industries daily, though many bypass the town itself. The riverfront makes for a pleasant stroll and the town, including the lively **market** (Đ Trung Trac), is easily explored on foot.

Tours

Boat tours cost from 500,000 for a three-hour sightseeing trip.

My Tho Tourist Boat Station BOATING
(8 Đ 30 Thang 4) In a prominent building on the riverfront, the My Tho Tourist Boat Station is home to several tour companies offering cruises to the neighbouring islands and through the maze of small canals. Depending on what you book, destinations usually include a coconut-candy workshop, a honey farm (try the banana wine) and an orchid garden.

Sleeping

Song Tien Annex HOTEL $
(0273-387 7883; www.tiengiangtourist.com; 33 Đ Thien Ho Duong; r from 400,000d;) This place offers river views from the balconies, a central location, bathrooms with claw-foot bathtubs (rare as unicorn eggs in Vietnam) and friendly, helpful staff, but the fixtures and fittings are showing their age.

★**Island Lodge** BOUTIQUE HOTEL $$$
(0273-651 9000; www.theislandlodge.com.vn; 390 Ap Thoi Binh, Xa Thoi Son; r US$215;) It's hard to imagine a more tranquil place than this intimate island hideaway. The occupants of its 12 rooms are cheerfully attended to by professional staff, and you can watch the goings-on on the river from the pool, indulge in gourmet cuisine, or retreat to your light, bright room, complete with contemporary art and bamboo-framed beds.

Eating

My Tho is known for its vermicelli soup, *hu tieu My Tho*, garnished with fresh and dried seafood, pork, chicken, offal and fresh herbs. It's served either with broth or dry and can be made vegetarian.

Hu Tieu Chay Cay Bo De VIETNAMESE $
(24 Đ Nam Ky Khoi Nghia; mains 15,000-24,000d; 8am-9pm;) Here vegetarians can try a completely meat-free version of My Tho's vermicelli-noodle soup speciality, *hu tieu My Tho*. It's garnished with fresh herbs and served with a broth made from vegetarian stock. It's on a street with places serving meat versions of the dish and a few other vegetarian restaurants.

Chi Thanh CHINESE, VIETNAMESE $
(0273-387 3756; 279 Đ Tet Mau Than; meals 40,000-100,000d; 10am-9pm) This small but extremely popular restaurant does a steady trade in tasty Chinese and Vietnamese fare (beef, pork, squid, crab, noodles, hotpots), especially chicken with rice. There's an English menu.

Getting There & Around

If heading to Ben Tre, a taxi (around 260,000d) or *xe om* (around 120,000d) will be considerably faster than a bus. Buses head to Ben Tre (15,000d, 25 minutes, frequent), Can Tho (from 60,000d, 2½ hours, several daily) and HCMC (70,000d to 110,000d, 1½ hours, hourly).

Tien Giang Bus Station (Ben Xe Tien Giang; 42 Đ Ap Bac) is 2.3km northwest of town, on the main Hwy 1A towards Ho Chi Minh City. A *xe om* into town should cost around 40,000d.

Ben Tre

POP 260,000 / 0275

The picturesque little province of Ben Tre has a sleepy waterfront lined with ageing villas, and is easy to explore on foot, as is the rustic settlement across the bridge to the south of the centre. This is also a good place to arrange boat trips in the area, particularly for those wanting to escape the tour-bus bustle. Plus, the riverside promenade and the narrow lanes on both sides of the river are ideal for two-wheeled exploration.

Tours

★**Mango Cruises** TOURS
(0967 683 366; www.mangocruises.com) Unlike cookie-cutter tours from HCMC, Mango Cruises focuses on the less-visited back roads and canals around Ben Tre and beyond. Day tours comprise a nice mix of cycling, dining on local specialities and observing how rice paper and other local staples are made. Longer tours include outings on its day cruisers and multi-day boat trips in the delta.

Sleeping & Eating

★**Mango Home Riverside** BOUTIQUE HOTEL $$
(0275-351 1958; www.mangohomeriverside.com; d/ste from US$55/75;) Set amid coconut and mango trees along the bank of a Mekong

tributary, this delightful mango-coloured B&B, run by a Canadian-Vietnamese couple, provides a welcome place to unwind. Large, spacious rooms have air-con, some have outdoor bathrooms, and there are hammocks for lounging. The food is excellent and at night there's complete silence. It's 10km out of town; call for pickup.

Oasis Hotel HOTEL $$
(0275-246 7799; http://bentrehoteloasis.com; 151c My An C, My Thanh An; d/f US$32/48;) There's always a warm welcome at this popular, bright-yellow hotel with bar and pool, run by a very helpful Kiwi-Vietnamese couple. It's in the village south of the river and best reached by taxi. Bicycle-rental services facilitate countryside exploration.

Food Stalls VIETNAMESE $
(cnr Nguyen Binh Khiem & Đ Hung Vuong; dishes around 15,000d; 7-10pm) Sizzling meat and seafood skewers and bowls of noodles await at the market food stalls.

Ben Tre Floating Restaurant VIETNAMESE $$
(075-382 2492; near Đ Hung Vuong; meals 50,000-200,000d; 10am-10pm;) This rather grand-looking floating restaurant is set on a giant dragon boat and features three floors. The menu includes a dizzying array of Vietnamese dishes, including seafood, clay pots and hotpots. Prices are on the high side, but it's a good location to draw the river breeze.

Getting There & Away

Buses to Vinh Long drop you at Pha Dinh Kao, the ferry port across the river from town; take the ferry across.

Buses stop at the **bus station** (Ben Xe Thanh Pho Ben Tre; Đ Dong Khoi), located 5km north of the town centre. The last buses to HCMC depart at about 5pm.

Vinh Long

POP 200,000 / 0270

Plonked about midway between My Tho and Can Tho, Vinh Long is a major transit hub and the capital of the province. For travellers, it's a gateway to island life, Cai Be floating market, abundant orchards and rural homestays. The town itself, however, has little of interest to the visitor and most people are passing through on the way to aquatic adventures.

The river **market** (5am-noon) is still the principal attraction on a boat tour from Vinh Long, though it has shrunk considerably due to the building of bridges in the delta and the subsequent transportation of goods by road rather than river. The market is at its best around 6am. Wholesalers on big boats moor here, each specialising in different types of fruit or vegetable, hanging samples of their goods from tall wooden poles. It's an hour by boat from Vinh Long.

A notable sight is the huge and photogenic Catholic cathedral on the riverside.

Sleeping & Eating

Ngoc Sang HOMESTAY $
(096 936 7636; homestayngocsang@yahoo.com.vn; 95/8 Binh Luong, Dao Trinh Nhat, An Binh; per person 250,000d;) Most travellers love this friendly, canal-facing rustic homestay. The grandmother cooks up some wonderful local dishes, free bikes are available, the owner runs decent early-morning boat tours and there's a languid atmosphere about the place. The family seems shy when it comes to hanging out with guests, though. Free pickup from the ferry pier, 15 minutes' walk away.

Minh Khue Hotel HOTEL $
(0270-382 6688; minhkhuehotel.vinhlong@gmail.com; 38 Đ Trung Nu Vuong; s 250,000-350,000d, tw 400,000-500,000d, VIP from 600,000d;) Probably the friendliest and smartest among a new block of hotels near the riverfront and park on Đ Trung Nu Vuong. Rooms feature contemporary trim bathrooms and smart TVs. Some English is spoken.

Thoc Cafe CAFE $
(0270-388 7979; www.facebook.com/thoccafevinhlong; 19 Đ Le Lai; mains 20,000-75,000d; 6am-10pm;) Occupying a prime location overlooking the river and the adjacent gardens, this is an inviting al fresco cafe with an upstairs terrace for river breezes. The menu is primarily snacks and light bites, but locals flock here for coffees, shakes, juices and the views.

Vinh Long Market VIETNAMESE $
(Cho Vinh Long; Đ 3 Thang 2; meals from 20,000d; 6am-6pm) Great spot for local fruit and inexpensive street snacks, such as *nem* (fresh spring rolls).

Getting There & Around

Buses leave the **Provincial Bus Station** (Ben Xe Khach Vinh Long; Hwy 1A) hourly for Can Tho (40,000d, one hour) and Ho Chi Minh City (105,000, three hours). It's 2.5km south of town on the way to Can Tho. A taxi costs around 130,000d. Coming from HCMC, the larger bus companies Phuong Trang and Mai Linh provide a free shuttle bus to town.

Can Tho

POP 1.57 MILLION / ☎0292

The epicentre of the Mekong Delta, Can Tho is the largest city in the region and feels like a metropolis after a few days exploring the backwaters.

As the political, economic, cultural and transportation centre of the Mekong Delta, it's a buzzing town with a lively waterfront lined with sculpted gardens, and an appealing blend of narrow backstreets and wide boulevards.

Can Tho is also the perfect base for nearby floating markets, the major draw for tourists, who come here to boat along the many canals and rivers leading out of town.

Sights

★Cai Rang Floating Market MARKET

(5am-noon) FREE The biggest floating market in the Mekong Delta, Cai Rang is 6km from Can Tho in the direction of Soc Trang. There's a bridge here that serves as a great vantage point for photography. The market is best around 6am to 7am, and it's well worth getting here early to beat the boatloads of tourists and the heat. This is a wholesale market, so look at what's tied to the long pole above the boat to see what they're selling.

★Ong Temple TEMPLE

(32 Đ Hai Ba Trung; 6am-8pm) FREE In a fantastic location facing the Can Tho River and decorated with huge, constantly burning incense coils, this Chinese temple is set inside the **Guangzhou Assembly Hall**, and wandering through its fragrant, smoke-filled interior is very enjoyable. It was originally built in the late 19th century to worship Kuang Kung, a deity symbolising loyalty, justice, reason, intelligence, honour and courage, among other merits. Wait long enough and you'll see how the incense coils are lit and hung on long poles.

Phong Dien Floating Market MARKET

(5am-noon) FREE An intimate floating market, Phong Dien has more stand-up rowing boats than motorised craft, with local vendors shopping and exchanging gossip. Less crowded than Cai Rang, it has far fewer tourists and less activity. It's most bustling between 5am and 7am, with little to see later. The market is 20km southwest of Can Tho; get here by road or sign up for a six-hour combined Cai Rang–Phong Dien tour, returning to Can Tho through quiet backwaters.

Tours

★Hieu's Tour CULTURAL

(☎093-966 6156; www.hieutour.com; 27a Đ Le Thanh Ton) Young, enthusiastic, English-speaking guide Hieu and his team offer excellent, unique tours around Can Tho, from early-morning jaunts to the floating markets (US$35 per person) to cycling tours, food tours and even visits to **Pirate Island** (Quan Dao Ha Tien, Hai Tac) further afield. Hieu is keen to show visitors true delta culture, and a floating homestay is in the works.

Sleeping & Eating

Xoai Hotel HOTEL $

(☎090-765 2927; www.hotelxoai.com; 93 Đ Mau Than; r 220,000-350,000d;) This friendly, efficient hotel offers fantastic value and has bright, mango-coloured rooms – appropriate given the name means 'Mango Hotel'. Helpful staff speak excellent English and there's a roof terrace with hammocks. Budget tours are also available for those looking to band together.

Nguyen Shack Can Tho GUESTHOUSE $$

(☎0966 550 016; www.nguyenshack.com; Ong Tim Bridge, Thanh My, Thuong Thanh; d with shared bathroom 500,000d, bungalows from 1,000,000d;) Not a shack, but rather a clutch of rustic thatched bungalows with fans, this great place overlooks the Ong Tim River, 6km from Can Tho. It's the kind of place where backpackers are inspired to linger longer, thanks to the camaraderie between English-speaking staff and guests. The engaging tours and the proximity to Cai Rang floating market are bonuses.

Kim Tho Hotel HOTEL $$

(☎0292-381 7517; 1a Đ Ngo Gia Tu; r 900,000-2,100,000d;) A smart hotel, verging on the boutique, Kim Tho is decked out with attractive fabric furnishings in the foyer. Rooms are stylish throughout and include designer bathrooms. Cheaper rooms are on lower floors, but superior rooms have hardwood flooring and the pricier river-view rooms are still a great deal. There's also a rooftop coffee bar on the 12th floor.

Azerai RESORT $$$
(☎0292-362 7888; www.azerai.com; Au Island; r from 4,950,000d;) Set on a private island in the middle of the Hau River, Azerai offers the Mekong Delta's most luxurious lodgings. Rooms are set in stunning contemporary pavilions, many looking out on the river, and include a designer touch. There's an idyllic lotus pond and some iconic banyan trees – both favourites for selfie seekers – in the grounds.

Nem Nuong Thanh Van VIETNAMESE $
(☎0292-0382 7255; cnr Nam Ky Khoi Nghia & 30 Thang 4; meals 45,000d; ⏲8am-9pm) The only dish this locally acclaimed spot does is the best *nem nuong* in town. Roll your own rice rolls using the ingredients provided – pork sausage, rice paper, green banana, star fruit (carambola), cucumber and a riot of fresh herbs – then dip into the peanut-and-something-else sauce, its secret jealously guarded. Simple and fantastic!

Can Tho Night Market VIETNAMESE $
(Đ Phan Boi Chau; snacks 5000-30,000d; ⏲5-11pm) Every evening the space between Phan Boi Chau and Phan Chu Trinh streets comes alive with dozens of bustling food stalls selling grilled meats and tofu on skewers, as well as grilled rice-paper *banh trang nuong* ('Vietnamese pizza'), fresh sugar-cane juice and more.

★**Nam Bo** INTERNATIONAL $$
(☎0292-382 3908; http://nambocantho.com; 1 Đ Ngo Quyen, Nam Bo Boutique Hotel; meals 210,000-350,000d; ⏲6.30am-10.30pm;) With a charming, romantic Mediterranean feel, this restaurant does a good mix of Vietnamese and Western dishes. We're fans of the lemongrass chicken and grilled sea bass in banana leaf; bananas flambéed in rice wine add an alcoholic flourish to the meal. The six-dish set menus (from 210,000d) are a steal.

Drinking & Nightlife

1985 Cafe CAFE
(☎0292-389 2626; www.facebook.com/cafe1985cantho; 138 Đ Huynh Cuong; ⏲6.30am-10pm;) This cafe and bar stretches across a block, and its 'back door' entrance is made up of a mosaic of old shutters that gives it a dishevelled retro look. The retro theme continues inside with old motorbikes, cassette players and other '80s throwbacks on display. Live music most nights, including open mics, and chilled beers.

Information

Can Tho Tourist (☎0292-382 1852; www.canthotourist.com.vn; 50 Đ Hai Ba Trung; ⏲7am-6pm Mon-Fri, 7am-11am & 1-5pm Sat & Sun) Helpful staff speak English and French, and decent city maps are available, as well as general information on attractions in the area and bus information.

Hospital (Benh Vien; ☎0292-382 0071; 4 Đ Chau Van Liem) Offers 24-hour emergency medical care.

Getting There & Around

AIR

Can Tho International Airport (www.canthoairport.com; Đ Le Hong Phong) is served by **Vietnam Airlines** (www.vietnamairlines.com) and **Vietjet Air** (www.vietjetair.com), with flights to Con Dao, Dalat, Danang, Haiphong, Hanoi, Nha Trang, Phu Quoc, Thanh Hoa and Vinh. There are also international budget flights to Bangkok and Kuala Lumpur. There are no direct flights to HCMC, as it is a relatively easy drive.

The airport is 10km northwest of the city centre. A taxi into town will cost around 220,000d.

BOAT

Ferries across the river leave from **Xom Chai Ferry Terminal** (Ben Pha Xom Chai) for those looking to explore a more rural side of Can Tho on two wheels.

BUS

All buses depart from the main **bus station** (Ben Xe 91B; Đ Nguyen Van Linh), 2.5km southwest of the centre. A *xe om* into town costs around 50,000d, or around 75,000d in a taxi. Some bus companies will include a shuttle bus that will take you to your lodgings from the station; check when buying the ticket. Destinations include the following:

Ben Tre (70,000d, three hours, several daily)
Ca Mau (100,000d, 3¼ to four hours, hourly)
Cao Lanh (55,000d, 2½ hours, daily)
Chau Doc (65,000d, four hours, hourly)
Ho Chi Minh City (120,000d to 160,000d, 3½ hours, every 30 minutes)
Long Xuyen (50,000d, 1½ hours, hourly)
Phnom Penh (340,000d, seven hours, daily)
Soc Trang (55,000d. 1½ hours, hourly)

Chau Doc

POP 163,000 / ☎0296

Draped along the banks of the Hau Giang River (Bassac River), Chau Doc is a likeable little town with significant Chinese, Cham and Khmer communities. Cultural diversity – apparent in the mosques, temples, churches and nearby pilgrimage sites – makes Chau Doc fascinating to explore even if you're not Cambodia-bound. Taking a boat trip to the Cham communities across the river is another highlight.

Tra Su Bird Sanctuary (Rung Tram Tra Su; admission 120,000d, boat rides per person 75,000d; ⏲7am-4pm), 23km west of town, is worth a visit for avian buffs.

Sleeping & Eating

Trung Nguyen Hotel HOTEL $

(☎0296-356 1561; 86 Đ Bach Dang; s/d 300,000/400,000d; ❄📶) One of the better budget places, with something of a mid-range trim. Rooms are more decorative than the competition, with balconies overlooking the market. It's a busy corner site, so pack earplugs or ask for a room facing the rear. Excellent English spoken.

Murray Guesthouse GUESTHOUSE $$

(☎0296-356 2108; www.themurrayguesthouse.com; 11 Truong Dinh; d/f from US$32/45; 🚭❄📶) With its walls decorated with indigenous art, collected from around the world by the Kiwi-Vietnamese owners, this wonderful guesthouse outside of the centre sets a high standard. Nice touches include a guest lounge with pool table and bar, a rooftop terrace drowning in greenery, comfortable beds and a tasty *pho* for breakfast. The owners can offer travel advice and loan bicycles.

★ **Victoria Chau Doc Hotel** HOTEL $$$

(☎0296-386 5010; www.victoriahotels.asia; 32 Đ Le Loi; r/ste from US$130/175; ❄📶🏊) Chau Doc's most luxurious option, the Victoria delivers classic colonial charm, overseen by staff clad in *ao dai* (Vietnam's national dress). With a striking riverfront location, the hotel's grand rooms have dark-wood floors and furniture, plus inviting bathtubs. The swimming pool overlooks the busy river and there's a small spa upstairs. A range of tours is available to guests.

Thanh Tinh Vegetarian VEGETARIAN $

(Com Chay Tam Tinh; ☎0296-386 5064; 12 Quang Trung; meals 25,000d; 🌱) There's vegetarian and then there's exceptional smoky mock chicken, lemongrass tofu and garlic morning glory on a plate with rice, plus a sweet-and-sour soup, for a bargain price. Point and choose from the display out front.

Getting There & Away

Chau Doc Bus Station (Ben Xe Chau Doc; Đ Le Loi) The bus station is on the eastern edge of town, around 2km out of the centre, where Đ Le Loi becomes Hwy 91. All buses depart from here, with the exception of the Hung Cuong buses to Ho Chi Minh City.

Hang Chau (☎Chau Doc 0296-356 2771, Phnom Penh 855-23 998935; www.hangchautourist.vn) The Hang Chau speedboat (per person $27) departs Chau Doc at 7.30am and Phnom Penh at 12.30pm. The journey takes about five hours and the price includes a simple lunch, but not the visa.

Tourist Boats (Đ Le Loi; 2hr 100,000d) Hire a boat for a river jaunt.

Ha Tien

POP 82,000 / ☎0297

Ha Tien may be part of the Mekong Delta, but lying on the Gulf of Thailand it feels a world away from the rice fields and rivers that typify the region. There are dramatic limestone formations peppering the area, which are home to a network of caves, and the town has a languid charm, with crumbling colonial villas and a colourful riverside market.

Already bolstered by an increase in travellers bound for Phu Quoc and Cambodia, visitor numbers are set to soar further as competing ferry companies take advantage of the close proximity to Phu Quoc.

The **Thach Dong Cave Pagoda** (Chua Thanh Van; 5000d; ⏲6.30am-5.30pm) is a Buddhist cave temple 4km northeast of town. Scramble through the cave chambers to see the funerary tablets and altars to Ngoc Hoang, Quan The Am Bo Tat and the two Buddhist monks who founded the temples of this pagoda. To the left of the entrance is the Stele of Hatred (Bia Cam Thu), shaped like a raised fist, which commemorates the Khmer Rouge massacre of 130 people here on 14 March 1978.

For hotels, the **Bao Anh** (Nga Nhi Bao Anh; ☎0166 223 8440; cnr Đ Hong Van Tu & Đ Truong Sa; r Mon-Fri from 350,000d, Sat & Sun from 400,000d; ❄📶) is good value, while **Hai Van Hotel** (☎0297-385 2872; www.khachsanhaivan.com; 55 Đ Lam Son; r 180,000-350,000d; ❄📶) offers

ⓘ GETTING TO CAMBODIA FROM THE MEKONG

Visas at the border Cambodian visas officially cost US$30 at the time of writing, but be prepared to pay around US$5 extra at the border.

It's a really good idea to have US dollars on you when crossing into Cambodia; you can pay for the Cambodian visa in dong, but the exchange rate is really unfavourable. On the Cambodian side, you can withdraw dollars from ATMs.

Ha Tien to Kep

Getting to the border The Xa Xia/Prek Chak border crossing connects Ha Tien with Kep and Kampot on Cambodia's south coast. Several minibus companies leave Ha Tien for Cambodia at around 1pm, heading to Kep (US$9, one hour), Kampot (US$12, 1½ hours), Sihanoukville (US$15, four hours) and Phnom Penh (US$15, four hours). Book via **Ha Tien Tourism** (☑ 0297-395 9598; Đ Tran Hau; ⊗ 8am-5pm).

Moving on Most travellers opt for a through minibus ticket.

Chau Doc to Takeo & Phnom Penh

Getting to the border Eclipsed by the newer Xa Xia crossing, the Tinh Bien/Phnom Den border crossing is rarely used by travellers. A bus to Phnom Penh (US$25, five to six hours) passes through Chau Doc at around 7.30am; book through **Mekong Tours** (☑ 098 308 6355; 41 Đ Quang Trung) in Chau Doc.

Moving on Most travellers opt for a through bus ticket from Chau Doc.

---

smart, if featureless rooms. **River Hotel** (☑ 0297-395 5888; www.riverhotelvn.com; Đ Tran Hau; r/ste from 900,000/2,000,000d; ❄ 🕾 🏊) is the smartest in town.

For cheap grub the **night market** (Đ So 5; meals from 20,000d; ⊗ 5-9pm) can't be beat, while **Oasis Bar** (☑ 0297-370 1553; www.oasisbarhatien.com; 30 Đ Tran Hau; meals 60,000-150,000d; ⊗ 9am-9pm; 🕾) is a popular expat-run bar-restaurant; the owner provides good travel advice

Buses connect Ho Chi Minh City (165,000 to 200,000d, eight hours) and Ha Tien; they also run to destinations including Chau Doc (160,000d to 200,000d), Rach Gia (70,000d) and Can Tho (200,000d).

The bus station is located 1.5km south of the bridge, next to a hospital.

Rach Gia

Rach Gia is something of a boom town, flush with funds from its thriving port and an injection of Viet Kieu (Overseas Vietnamese) money. The population here includes significant numbers of ethnic Chinese and ethnic Khmers. If you're in town for longer than it takes to catch a boat to Phu Quoc Island, explore the lively waterfront and bustling backstreets, where you'll discover some inexpensive seafood restaurants. There is a French-colonial museum and a temple if you want to linger.

🛏 Sleeping & Eating

Thien Trang Guesthouse   GUESTHOUSE $
(☑ 094-506 5574; 24 Đ Nguyen Cong Tru; r 300,000-450,000d; ❄ 🕾) Walking distance from the ferry terminal, this is a handy place to stay before an early boat to Phu Quoc, Hon Son or Nam Du. Rooms are simple but clean and include hot-water bathrooms and TV. It has a cavernous lobby with motorbike parking – useful if you're exploring the delta on two wheels.

Quan F28   SEAFOOD $
(28 Đ Le Thanh Thon; meals from 50,000d; ⊗ 11am-10pm) Convenient for the bus-station hotels, this is lively by night and does inexpensive molluscs: shrimp, snails, cockles and the like.

ⓘ Getting There & Around

AIR

Vietnam Airlines has daily flights to and from HCMC and Phu Quoc Island (in the high-season months of November to April).

Rach Gia Airport (www.rachgiaairport.net; 418 Cach Mang Thang Tam) is around 10km southeast of the centre, along Hwy 80. A taxi into town costs around 150,000d and takes about 20 minutes.

BOAT

Ferry Terminal (Ban Tau Rach Gia Phu Quoc; Đ Nguyen Cong Tru) Fast boats to Phu Quoc Island.

Rach Meo Ferry Terminal (Ben Tau Rach Meo; ☎0297-381 1306; Đ Ngo Quyen) One speedboat daily leaves for Ca Mau (300,000d, three hours) from the Rach Meo ferry terminal, about 2km south of town.

BUS

Just north of the city centre, the **Rach Gia Central Bus Station** (Ben Xe Khach Rach Gia; Đ Nguyen Binh Khiem) primarily serves Ha Tien.

Rach Soi Bus Station (Ben Xe Rach Soi; Ben Xe Tinh Kien Giang; 376 QL63), 7km south of the city, serves Ho Chi Minh City and the majority of other delta destinations.

A taxi into town from the central bus station costs around 30,000d. From the Rach Soi bus station, fares are around 150,000d. Phuong Trang buses provides a free shuttle bus to take you from your hotel to the bus station.

Phu Quoc Island

POP 115,000 / ☎0297

Fringed with white-sand beaches and with large tracts still cloaked in dense tropical jungle, Phu Quoc has rapidly morphed from a sleepy island backwater to a must-visit beach escape for Western expats and sun-seeking tourists. Beyond the resorts lining Long Beach, the rapid development beginning on the northwest coast and the mega-resorts in sight of Sao Beach, there's still ample room for exploration and escaping the sometimes-littered waters. Dive the reefs, kayak in the bays, eat up the back-road kilometres on a motorbike, or just lounge on the beach, followed by a massage and a fresh seafood dinner.

The island's most famous, and valuable, crop is black pepper; it's also known for high-quality fish sauce (*nuoc mam*).

Sights

Duong Dong VILLAGE

The island's main town and chief fishing port on the west coast is a tangle of budget hotels catering to domestic tourists (although foreigners are allowed), streetside stalls, bars and shops. The old bridge in town is a great vantage point to photograph the island's fishing fleet crammed into the narrow channel, and the gritty, bustling produce market makes for an interesting stroll. Most visitors come for the night market, seafood and a glimpse of local life on the island.

Fish Sauce Factory FACTORY

(www.hungthanhfishsauce.com.vn; Duong Dong; 8-11am & 1-5pm) FREE The distillery of Nuoc Mam Hung Thanh is the largest of Phu Quoc's fish-sauce makers, a short walk from the market in Duong Dong. At first glance, the giant wooden vats may make you think you've arrived for a wine tasting, but one sniff of the festering *nuoc mam* essence jolts you back to reality. Take a guide along unless you speak Vietnamese.

Long Beach BEACH

(Bai Truong) Long Beach is draped invitingly along the west coast from Duong Dong to An Thoi. Development concentrates in the north, near Duong Dong, where the recliners and rattan umbrellas of the various resorts rule; these are the only stretches that are kept garbage-free. With its west-facing aspect, sunsets can be stupendous.

Although not the prettiest, Long Beach is a good budget choice for accommodation and socialising. Duong Dong and its night market are walking distance from the beach's north end.

★An Thoi Islands ISLAND

(Quan Dao An Thoi) Just off the southern tip of Phu Quoc, these 15 islands and islets are a paradise of white sand and blue waters. They can be visited by chartered boat for a fine day of sightseeing, fishing, swimming and snorkelling. Hon Thom (Pineapple Island) is about 3km in length and is the largest island in the group; it's now connected to Phu Quoc by the Hon Thom Cable Car (p154), the world's longest over-sea ride.

★Sao Beach BEACH

(Bai Sao) With picture-perfect white sand, the delightful curve of beautiful Sao Beach bends out alongside a sea of mineral-water clarity just a few kilometres from An Thoi, the main shipping port at the southern tip of the island. There are a couple of beachfront restaurants where you can settle into a deckchair (50,000d for nonguests), change into bathers (10,000d fee) or partake in water sports.

Phu Quoc National Park NATIONAL PARK

About 70% of Phu Quoc is forested and the trees and adjoining marine environment enjoy official protection. This is the last large stand of forest in the south, and in 2010 the park was declared a Unesco Biosphere Reserve. The forest is densest in the Khu Rung Nguyen Sinh forest reserve in northern Phu Quoc; you'll need a motorbike or mountain bike to tackle the bumpy dirt roads that cut through it. There are no real hiking trails.

Activities

There's plenty of underwater action around Phu Quoc, but only during the dry months (from November to May). Two fun dives cost from US$70 to US$90 depending on the location and operator; four-day PADI Open Water courses hover between US$340 and US$380; snorkelling trips are US$30 to US$35.

★**Hon Thom Cable Car** CABLE CAR
(☎088-677 8686; An Thoi; over/under 1.4m in height 150,000/100,000đ; ⏰to Hon Thom 8am-noon, to An Thoi 1.30-7.30pm) The world's longest over-sea cable car (7.9km), this is an epic ride over the An Thoi Islands to Hon Thom, with some stunning views of the fishing fleet bobbing below. The 25-minute trip is in Austrian-made Doppelmayr cars carrying up to 30 people. The cable-car embarkation point near An Thoi is designed like a faux Italian village, complete with aged Renaissance houses and a mini-Colosseum ticket office.

Flipper Diving Club DIVING
(☎0297-399 4924; www.flipperdiving.com; 60 Đ Tran Hung Dao; ⏰7am-7pm) Centrally located, multilingual PADI dive centre for everything from novice dive trips to full instructor courses. Very professional, with plenty of diving experience worldwide, and with instructors who'll put you at ease if you're a newbie.

Viet Sail BOATING
(☎077-683 0072; https://sailingschoolvietsail.business.site; Chez Carole Resort; 1-2hr 600,000-1,000,000đ; ⏰7am-7pm) Take to the high seas around Phu Quoc in a catamaran or dinghy with experienced French sailor Pierre. Snorkelling gear is included. It's located at Chez Carole Resort on Cua Can Beach.

Rainbow Divers DIVING
(☎0913 400 964; www.divevietnam.com; 11 Đ Tran Hung Dao; ⏰9am-6pm) This reputable PADI outfit was the first to set up shop on the island and offers a wide range of diving and snorkelling trips. As well as the walk-in office, it's well represented at resorts on Long Beach.

Tours

Jerry's Jungle Tours ADVENTURE
(☎093-822 6021; www.jerrystours.wixsite.com/jerrystours; 106 Đ Tran Hung Dao; day trips from US$30) Archipelago explorations by boat, with snorkelling, fishing, day and multi-day trips to islands, motorbike tours, bouldering, birdwatching, hiking and cultural tours around Phu Quoc.

John's Tours BOATING
(☎091-893 9111; www.phuquoctrip.com; 4 Đ Tran Hung Dao; tours per person US$15-35) Well represented at hotels and resorts; cruises include snorkelling, island hopping, sunrise fishing and squid-fishing trips.

Anh Tu's Tours BOATING
(☎0913 820 714; anhtupq@yahoo.com) Snorkelling, squid fishing, island tours and motorbike rental.

Sleeping

Accommodation prices on Phu Quoc yo-yo depending on the season and visitor numbers. You'll get less for your money than you'd expect for the price. Bookings are crucial for the December-to-January peak season.

Some hotels provide free transport to and from the airport; enquire when making a booking.

Duong Dong & Long Beach

★**9 Station Hostel** HOSTEL $
(☎0297-658 8999; www.9stationhostel.com; 91/3 Đ Tran Hung Dao; dm 135,000-225,000đ, r from 780,000đ; ❄📶🏊) The flashpacker hostel has arrived in Phu Quoc with 9 Station, a cracking place to stay, with a range of dorms from four to 12 beds and modern private rooms with attached bathroom. The best features are a huge reception and restaurant-bar with a helpful tour desk and a swimming pool that draws guests like moths to a light.

Langchia Home HOSTEL $
(☎093-913 2613; www.langchia-village.com; 84 Đ Tran Hung Dao; dm 165,000đ, r 600,000-1,050,000đ; ❄📶🏊) A favourite with solo travellers, this hostel gets plenty of praise for the friendliness and helpfulness of its staff, the lively bar with pool table and the swimming pool in which to cool down. Dorm beds come with mozzie nets and individual fans. It's worth paying extra for the decent breakfast.

Vida Loca Resort HOTEL $$
(☎0297-384 7583; www.vidalocaresort.com; 118/12 Đ Tran Hung Dao; r 1,200,000-2,500,000d;) This friendly place recently rebranded as Vida Loca and offers redesigned rooms and bungalows amid a leafy garden, set on a prime piece of beachfront. Splurge on a sea-view bungalow if you have the spare dong.

Sunshine Bungalow HOTEL $$
(☎0297-397 5777; www.sunshinephuquoc.com; Đ Tran Hung Dao; bungalows 300,000-700,000d;) Friendly place run by a Vietnamese family, less than 100m from the sea and sand. Large, bright rooms nestle amid lush vegetation and the owners do their best to help. Some English and German spoken.

Lan Anh Garden Resort RESORT $$
(☎077-398 5985; www.lananhphuquoc.com.vn; KP7 Đ Tran Hung Dao; r 750,000-1,450,000d;) Enticing little resort hotel with friendly, professional staff, a clutch of rooms arranged around a small pool, and motorbikes for rent. Nab an upstairs room if you can for the breezy verandas. Book on its website for discounted rates.

La Veranda RESORT $$$
(☎0297-398 2988; www.laverandaresort.com; 118/9 Đ Tran Hung Dao; r US$205-330, villas from US$445;) Shaded by palms, this Accor resort, designed in colonial style and small enough to remain intimate, is one of the most elegant places to stay on the island. There's an appealing pool, a stylish spa and rooms featuring designer bathrooms. The beach is pristine, and dining options include a cafe on the lawn and the **Pepper Tree Restaurant** (www.laverandaresort.com; 118/9 Đ Tran Hung Dao; meals 250,000-700,000d; 6am-11pm;).

Around the Island

★Bamboo Cottages & Restaurant RESORT $$$
(☎0297-281 0345; www.bamboophuquoc.com; r US$100-155;) Run by a friendly family with a coterie of cheeky dogs, Bamboo Cottages has Vung Bau Beach largely to itself. The focal point is an open-sided restaurant and bar, right by the beach. Set around the lawns, the attractive, lemon-coloured villas have private, open-roofed bathrooms with solar-powered hot water. The family supports an education scholarship for local kids in need.

★Chen Sea Resort RESORT $$$
(☎0297-399 5895; www.chensea-resort.com; villas US$199-499;) Beautiful Chen Sea has stunning villas with sunken baths (some with hot tubs) and deep verandas, designed to resemble ancient terracotta-roofed houses, all decorated with Angkorian art. The large azure rectangle of the infinity pool faces the resort's beautiful sandy beach. The isolation is mitigated by plenty of activities: cycling, kayaking, catamaran outings, in-spa pampering and fine dining.

Mango Bay RESORT $$$
(☎077-398 1693; www.mangobayphuquoc.com; bungalows 3,150,000-11,150,000d;) A romantic, if simple, getaway for those who want some romance in their life. Set around a small cove accessed from a dusty road through a mango orchard, the ecofriendly resort uses solar panels and organic and recycled building materials, and has its own butterfly garden. Strung out along the beautiful beach, airy bungalows come with delightful open-air bathrooms.

Eating

Local peppercorns and cobia fish are specialities. For local seafood. try the restaurants in Ham Ninh fishing village along the pier at the end of the main road.

Duong Dong & Long Beach

★Phu Quoc Night Market SEAFOOD $
(Cho Dem Phu Quoc; Đ Bach Dang; meals from 50,000d; 4.30pm-3am;) The most atmospheric and best-value place to dine on the island, Duong Dong's busy night market has stalls of snacks, coconut ice cream and a parade of outdoor restaurants serving a delicious range of Vietnamese seafood, grills and vegetarian options. Quality can be mixed, so follow the discerning local crowd. Riverside tables can be a bit whiffy.

A post-meal meander among the stalls of clothes, souvenirs and peppercorns is a tourist ritual.

Khanh Ly Vegetarian VEGETARIAN $
(☎0297-281 0180; 35 Đ Nguyen Trai; meals 20,000-45,000d; 8am-8pm;) Pick and choose from a buffet of Vietnamese vegan-vegetarian dishes, such as mock shrimp on sugar cane, to accompany green veg and rice for an excellent-value, delicious plate. Staff are friendly, and there are also hearty noodle soups to tempt carnivores.

Heaven Restaurant VIETNAMESE $

(☎097-554 2769; 141 Đ Tran Hung Dao; meals 40,000-90,000d; ⏲8am-11pm; ☑) You may not expect heaven to have basic wooden tables opening onto a road, but it does at this good-value family joint. With fresh, generous servings of Vietnamese dishes such as lemongrass chicken and a very long list of vegetarian options, this is paradise for every taste.

Alanis Deli CAFE $

(☎0297-399 4931; 98 Đ Tran Hung Dao; meals from 60,000d; ⏲8am-10.30pm; ☎) Fab caramel pancakes, American breakfast combos, plus good (if pricey) coffee and wonderfully friendly service. It's located near the turnoff to Ong Lang Beach, about 6km north of Duong Dong.

★ **Saigonese** FUSION $$

(☎093-805 9650; www.facebook.com/saigonese eatery; 73 Đ Tran Hung Dao; meals 150,000-220,000d; ⏲9am-1pm & 5-11pm Wed-Mon) The hippest casual dining on Phu Quoc delights with fusion dishes lifted from designer cookbooks. The seasonal appetisers excel in *bao* (steamed buns filled with pulled beef and beetroot), and squid with avocado cream. Try the caramelised shrimp clay pot and, for dessert, popcorn banana cake. Manager Thao's experiences abroad show in the chic ambience.

Spice House at Cassia Cottage VIETNAMESE $$

(www.cassiacottage.com; 100c Đ Tran Hung Dao; meals 190,000-300,000d; ⏲7-10am & 11am-10pm) Nab a sea-view table, order a papaya salad, grilled garlic prawns, *banh xeo* (Vietnamese pancake), cinnamon-infused okra, a delectable Khmer fish curry or grilled beef skewers wrapped in betel leaves and time dinner to catch the sunset at this excellent restaurant. There's even a single romantic cabana table right on the sand.

★ **Itaca Resto Lounge** FUSION $$$

(☎077-399 2022; www.itacalounge.com; 119 Đ Tran Hung Dao; tapas 90,000-195,000d, meals 170,000-550,000d; ⏲6-11.45pm Thu-Tue; ☎☑) This much-applauded restaurant has a creative Mediterranean-Asian fusion menu (with tapas), an inviting al fresco arrangement and friendly, welcoming hosts. Don't expect sea views, but do expect Wagyu beef burgers, wild-mushroom risotto, seared tuna with passion fruit and a charming ambience.

Sailing Club INTERNATIONAL $$$

(☎093-103 1035; www.sailingclubphuquoc.com; Khu Phuc Hop; meals 110,000-900,000d; ⏲10am-11pm; ☎👪) The Nha Trang institution has dropped anchor in Phu Quoc in an impressive new setting at the southern end of Long Beach, near the Intercontinental Hotel. The menu is predominantly Asian fusion, but also includes comfort food such as burgers and pizzas, plus an affordable menu for kids. A beautiful spot day or night, it tends to draw a crowd.

Around the Island

★ **So True** VIETNAMESE $$

(☎094-342 2226; Đ Le Thuc Nha, Ong Lang; mains 69,000-175,000d; ⏲1-11pm) Located in the heart of Ong Lang, this restaurant does an excellent turn at mod-Viet cuisine, with signature specialities such as *bo so tru* (beef with green-pepper sauce), squid with lemongrass and kumquat, and cobia fish with dill and turmeric. Phu Quoc draught beer is on tap and there are some interesting photographs from all over Vietnam adorning the walls.

Drinking & Nightlife

★ **House No 1** BAR

(https://houseno1phuquoc.com; 12 Đ Le Loi; ⏲5pm-1am; ☎) One of the few bars in the centre of town, House No 1 is a great spot for evening drinks, including local and craft beers, cocktails and De Spirit, a locally produced refined rice wine. Midweek live music, plus a cool rooftop cafe that's popular with a local crowd.

★ **Cheeky Traveller** BAR

(118 Đ Tran Hung Dao; ⏲4pm-1am; ☎) A great little travellers' bar run by a couple of seasoned travellers who have settled on Phu Quoc. Draught beer flows and custom cocktails are available on demand. Bar games such as Jenga towers and beer pong kick off later in the evening, plus it's been known to stay open late into the night.

Blue Bar Beach Club CLUB

(Đ Tran Hung Dao; ⏲9am-late; ☎) One of the glitziest beach clubs, with a cavernous shaded interior and a well-tended beachfront with sunbeds and beanbags.

Information

There are ATMs in Duong Dong and in many resorts on Long Beach.

Getting There & Away

AIR

From the island's **airport** (www.phuquocairport.com) there are international flights to destinations including Singapore, Bangkok, Hong Kong and Kuala Lumpur. Vietnam Airlines, VietJet Air and Jetstar between them offer daily flights to Can Tho, Danang, Hanoi, HCMC, Haiphong and Rach Gia.

BOAT

Phu Quoc Express (☎0297-628 1888; www.pqe.com.vn; 15 Đ Tran Hung Dao; ⏲7am-9pm) and **Superdong** (☎0297-398 0111; www.superdong.com.vn; 10 Đ 30 Thang 4) offer connections from Ha Tien (1½ hours) and Rach Gia (2½ hours) to Phu Quoc's **Bai Vong** (Pha Bai Vong) on the east coast. Phu Quoc Express has the smartest hydrofoils with VIP class, while Superdong is slightly cheaper but also reliable. Phu Quoc travel agents have the most up-to-date schedules and can book tickets. Seas can be rough between June and September. During peak season (December, January and national holidays), there are often extra services.

Phu Quoc Express hydrofoils to Ha Tien (standard/VIP 250,000/350,000d) depart Phu Quoc at 8am, 9.45am, 11.45am, 1.45pm and 3.30pm. From Ha Tien they leave at 6am, 7.45am, 9.45am, 11.45am and 1.45pm. Hydrofoils from Phu Quoc to Rach Gia (standard/VIP 340,000/540,000d) depart at 7.30am, 10.30am and 1.30pm. In the other direction, they depart Rach Gia at 7.20am, 11am and 1.45pm.

Superdong fast boats from Phu Quoc to Ha Tien (230,000d) depart at 8am, 9.45am, 11.45am and 1pm. From Ha Tien they depart at at 7.35am, 8am, 9.45am and 1.45pm. Fast boats between Phu Quoc and Rach Gia (330,000d) leave at 8am, 8.30am, 8.45am, 12.40pm and 1pm in both directions.

From Ha Tien there are also car ferries to Phu Quoc (passenger/motorbike/car 185,000/80,000/700,000d). Some run to Phu Quoc's Da Chong port, in the northeast of the island, with regular departures daily from 4am to 4pm from Ha Tien (3½ hours) and from 5am to 6pm from Da Chong port; some also run to Bai Vong port on the east coast. More car ferries are due to be added to meet booming demand.

To get to the ferry terminals on the east coast of Phu Quoc, Superdong runs its own shuttle buses (30,000d) from the Superdong ticket office in Duong Dong. A taxi from Duong Dong costs about 250,000d, while a *xe om* will cost about 150,000d.

There is a minimart near the ferry terminal at Bai Vong, plus local snack sellers; drinks are sold on board the ferries.

Getting Around

The island's airport is 10km from Duong Dong; a taxi costs around 110,000d to Long Beach. Bicycles/motorbikes are available through most hotels from 70,000/120,000d per day. Motorbike taxis are everywhere. Short hops cost 20,000d; figure on around 60,000d for about 5km.

Major highways run south from Duong Dong to An Thoi, the southern tip of the island, as well as to Sao Beach and north as far as Cape Ganh Dau, the northwest tip of Phu Quoc. A two-lane highway connects Duong Dong with the car-ferry port, but there are still some unsurfaced roads in the far north of the island.

Mai Linh (☎0297-397 9797) is a reliable operator. From Duong Dong it costs about 25,000d to the bars of Long Beach, 160,000d to the coast after the airport, and 250,000d to Bai Vong ferry terminal. Taxi Phu Quoc is the island's very own taxi-booking app.

Con Dao Islands

POP 7400 / ☎0254

Isolated from the mainland, the Con Dao Islands are one of Vietnam's star attractions. Con Son, the largest of this chain of 15 islands and islets, is ringed with lovely beaches, coral reefs and scenic bays, and remains partially covered in thick forests. In addition to hiking, diving and exploring deserted coastal roads and beaches, there are excellent opportunities to watch wildlife, such as the black giant squirrel and the endemic bow-fingered gecko.

Long the preserve of thousands of political prisoners in no fewer than a dozen jails during French rule and the American-backed regime, Con Son now turns heads thanks to its striking natural beauty.

Until recently, few foreigners visited Con Dao, but with the commencement of inexpensive boat connections this is changing.

Sights

Con Son Town

All the former prisons in and around Con Son Town share the same opening hours and are covered by a single ticket costing 40,000d. You can purchase this ticket in the Bao Tang Con Dao Museum (p158), which is the logical place to get some historical context before you start a tour of the prisons.

Phu Hai Prison HISTORIC BUILDING
(off Đ Ton Duc Thang; joint ticket 40,000d; ⏲7-11.30am & 1-5pm) The largest of the 11 jails on the island, this prison dates from 1862. Thousands of prisoners were held here, with up to 200 prisoners crammed into each detention building. During the French era, all prisoners were kept naked and chained together in rows, with one small box serving as a toilet for hundreds. One can only imagine the squalor and stench. Today, emaciated mannequins that are all too lifelike recreate the era.

Tiger Cages HISTORIC BUILDING
(off Đ Nguyen Hue; joint ticket 40,000d; ⏲7-11.30am & 1-5pm) The notorious cells dubbed 'tiger cages' were built in 1940 by the French to incarcerate nearly 2000 political prisoners; the USA continued using them in the 1960s and 1970s. There are 120 chambers with ceiling bars, where guards could poke at prisoners like tigers in a Victorian-era zoo. Prisoners were beaten with sticks from above, and sprinkled with quicklime and water (which burnt their skin and caused blindness).

Bao Tang Con Dao Museum MUSEUM
(Đ Nguyen Hue; 10,000d; ⏲7-5pm Mon-Sat) This impressive museum has more than 2000 exhibits, including many rare documents, dioramas and excellent photographs, which comprehensively record the island's history, including the French colonial era and of course the 'prison period'. Modern displays, including audiovisuals, are used. Entrance is free with the 40,000d Con Dao sights ticket.

Hang Duong Cemetery CEMETERY
Some 20,000 Vietnamese prisoners died on Con Son and 1994 of their graves can be seen at the peaceful Hang Duong Cemetery, located at the northeastern edge of town. Sadly, only 700 of these graves bear the name of the victim interred within.

Vietnam's most famous heroine, Vo Thi Sau, was buried here. On 23 January 1952, she was the first woman executed by a firing squad in Con Son.

Beaches & Islands

★Bai Dram Trau BEACH
Reached via a dirt track 1km before the airport on Con Son Island, Bai Dram Trau is a sublime, remote 700m half-moon crescent of soft sand, fringed by casuarina trees and bookended by forest-topped rocky promontories. It's best visited at low tide. There's snorkelling on reefs offshore and some very simple seafood shacks (all open noon till dusk only).

★Bay Canh ISLAND
Perhaps the best all-round island to visit is Bay Canh, to the east of Con Son Island, which has lovely beaches, old-growth forest, mangroves, coral reefs and sea turtles (seasonal). There is a fantastic two-hour walk to a functioning French-era lighthouse on Bay Canh's eastern tip, although it involves a steep climb of 325m. Once at the summit, the panoramic views are breathtaking.

Bai Dat Doc BEACH
This simply beautiful cove consists of a kilometre-long crescent of pale sand, fringed by wooded hills. The beach's profile is gently shelving and there's no pollution, so it's ideal for swimming. It's backed by the luxury bungalows of the Six Senses hotel. Though it's not a private beach, access is quite tricky; you can scramble down at points around the edge of the hotel grounds.

Very rarely dugongs have been seen frolicking in the water off the nearby cape.

Activities

Con Dao offers the most pristine marine environment in the country. Diving is possible year-round, but for ideal conditions and good visibility, January to June is considered the best time.

There are lots of treks around Con Son Island, as much of the interior remains heavily forested. It's necessary to take a national-park guide (180,000d to 300,000d) on some hikes when venturing into the forest.

Kitty's Tours (☎090-990 2012; www.facebook.com/tripswithkitty; Mai Homestay, Huynh Thuc Khang; half-day tour per person from 400,000d) is highly recommended for exploring the islands.

Exploring the islands by boat can be arranged through hotels and the national-park office (p160). A 12-person boat costs around 2,300,000d to 5,000,000d per day, depending on stops wanted. Local fishers also offer excursions, but be sure to bargain hard.

Bamboo Lagoon HIKING
(Dam Tre) One of the more beautiful walks on the island leads through thick forest and mangroves, past a hilltop stream to Bamboo Lagoon. There's good snorkelling in the bay

THE PRISON IN PARADISE

Occupied at various times by the Khmer, Malays and Vietnamese, Con Son Island also served as an early base for European commercial ventures in the region. The first recorded European arrival was a ship of Portuguese mariners in 1560. The British East India Company maintained a fortified trading post here from 1702 to 1705 – an experiment that ended when the English on the island were massacred in a revolt by the Makassar soldiers they had recruited on the Indonesian island of Sulawesi.

Con Son Island has a strong political and cultural history, and an all-star line-up of Vietnamese revolutionary heroes was incarcerated here (many streets are named after them). Under the French, Con Son was used as a major prison for opponents of colonialism, earning a reputation for the routine mistreatment and torture of prisoners. National heroine Vo Thi Sau was executed here in 1952.

In 1954 the island was taken over by the South Vietnamese government, which continued to use its remoteness to hold opponents of the government (including students) in horrendous conditions.

During the American War, the South Vietnamese were joined here by US forces. The US built prisons and maintained the notorious 'tiger cages' as late as 1970, when news of their existence was broken by a *Life* magazine report.

Increasing numbers of settlers from the mainland and a buoyant tourist sector in recent years are leading to population and environmental pressures.

and you may encounter black squirrels and monkeys en route. The 1½-hour trek starts from near the airport runway.

You'll need a permit (from the national-park headquarters), and the first part of the walk (along Vong beach) is very exposed so pack sun cream. A guide is not mandatory.

Ong Dung Bay HIKING

The stiff hike (about 20 minutes each way) through rainforest down to Ong Dung Bay begins 2.5km northwest of town; you pass **Ma Thien Lanh Bridge** on the way to the trail. The bay has only a rocky beach, though there is a coral reef about 300m offshore. Snorkelling gear (70,000d) is available from a shoreside lodge, and boat trips to Tre Nho Island can sometimes be arranged.

A permit is not necessary for this hike.

So Ray Plantation HIKING

It's a steep climb to the old fruit plantations of So Ray, following a slippery but well-marked trail (lined with information panels about trees and wildlife) through dense rainforest. The former plantation buildings are home to a sociable troop of long-tailed macaques and offer sweeping views over Con Son Town to the other Con Dao islands beyond.

The return hike takes about 1½ hours. A permit is necessary for this hike, but a guide is not mandatory.

Con Dao Dive Center DIVING

(☎090-3700 8483; http://divecondao.com; Bar200, Đ Nguyen Van Linh; ⏰7.30am-10pm Feb-Oct) Offers instruction and courses under the PADI umbrella (Open Water is US$550), fun dives (two-dive trips US$160), snorkelling and freediving trips. Owner Rhys is happy to chat about diving options and things to do on Con Dao. The centre is based at **Bar200** (http://divecondao.com; Đ Nguyen Van Linh; meals 120,000-220,000d; ⏰10am-2pm & 5-10pm; 📶).

Sleeping

Expect to pay about double the mainland rate here.

Con Son Town

★**Mai Homestay** HOMESTAY $

(☎096-862 0290; www.facebook.com/pg/maihomestaycondao; Huynh Thuc Khang; d 550,000d; ❄📶) Very friendly glass-fronted homestay located near the national-park office. Its eight lovely rooms have nice touches, including vintage-style tiling and a dash of art on the walls. There's a guest kitchen and areas in which to chill. The owner was born and raised in Con Dao, runs great island tours and dispenses excellent travel advice.

LoCo Home HOSTEL $

(☎097-996 4089; https://loco-home-vung-tau-vn.book.direct; Đ Le Van Luong, off Đ Huynh Thuc Khang; dm US$8, r from US$22; ❄📶) Popular new hostel-style spot with choice of female or male dorms (with shared bathrooms) or attractive, light private rooms with terrace and en suite; all accommodation is air-conditioned. It's run by a welcoming couple who offer fishing, snorkelling and camping trips. There's a guest kitchen, free drinking water and breakfast.

Red Hotel HOTEL $$
(☎096-673 0079; http://red-vn.book.direct; 17b Đ Nguyen An Ninh; r from US$24; ❄📶) This mini-hotel has a choice of rooms with hot-water en suites (though expect hard mattresses) and is close to the night market and plenty of eating options. Staff speak limited English but are eager to help and can source rental scooters for exploring the island and organise boat trips.

★Villa Maison Con Dao Boutique Hotel BOUTIQUE HOTEL $$$
(☎0254-383 0969; www.villamaisoncondaobou tiquehotel.com; 46 Đ Nguyen Hue; r incl breakfast from US$75; ❄📶) Run by a dynamic, caring young Vietnamese couple (who worked for years in five-star resorts), this outstanding hotel in a converted French-era villa offers comfort, style, space and a central location. The spectacular lobby area doubles as a dining room and bar (perfect for memorable meals and cocktails) and boasts modish furniture and contemporary art. The eight guest bedrooms are immaculately presented.

Around Con Son Island

★Six Senses Con Dao RESORT HOTEL $$$
(☎0254-383 1222; www.sixsenses.com; Dat Doc beach; villas from US$651; ❄📶) This astonishing hotel enjoys a dreamlike location on the island's best beach, 4km northeast of Con Son town. Its 50-or-so ocean-facing, timber-clad beach units fuse contemporary style with rustic chic, each with its own pool and giant bathtub. Eating options include a casual cafe and a magnificent restaurant by the shore.

Eating

All the following are in Con Son Town.

★Gia Minh VIETNAMESE $
(☎038-356 8789; www.giaminhbistro.com; Đ Nguyen Van Linh; meals 50,000-350,000d; ⏲10am-10pm; 📶) Outstanding new place on the outskirts of town run by an accomplished chef. Specialises in handmade noodles, which are available in many delicious guises, with most dishes just 50,000d or so. There are ample choices for vegetarians, who will eat very well here, and also good hotpots (starting at 180,000d), Western food (also from 180,000d) and homemade plum and pineapple wines.

★Villa Maison Con Dao Restaurant INTERNATIONAL $$
(☎0254-383 0969; www.villamaisoncondaobou tiquehotel.com; 46 Đ Nguyen Hue; mains 140,000-320,000d; ⏲10.30am-10pm; 📶) A supremely relaxing and elegant setting for a meal, this fine hotel restaurant features Asian dishes including mixed Con Dao seafood salad (320,000d) and claypots (190,000d). There's a comprehensive wine list, including options by the glass, as well as superb cocktails and mocktails and usually mellow jazz or classical music in the background.

Thu Ba SEAFOOD $$
(☎0254-383 0255; Đ Vo Thi Sau; meals 80,000-230,000d) Thu Ba is renowned for seafood (consult what's on offer from the tanks by the entrance) and hotpots. The gregarious owner speaks great English and is happy to make suggestions based on what's seasonal and fresh.

Information

National Park Headquarters (☎0254-383 0669, 098-383 0669; www.condaopark.com.vn; 29 Đ Vo Thi Sau; ⏲7-11.30am & 1.30-5pm) Located 1km northwest of Con Son Town, this office has information on island-hopping excursions and turtle-watching trips. Pick up a useful free handout on island walks – some hiking trails have interpretive signage in English and Vietnamese. There are also displays on local forest and marine life, environmental threats and conservation activities.

Vietin Bank (Đ Le Duan; ⏲8am-2pm Mon-Fri, to noon Sat) Has an ATM; does not change foreign currency.

Getting There & Around

Tiny **Con Dao Airport** (Cỏ Ống Airport; ☎090-383 1540) is 14km from the town centre. There are several daily flights between Con Son and Ho Chi Minh City, jointly operated by **Vasco** (☎038-330 330; www.vasco.com.vn; Đ Ton Duc Thang) and Vietnam Airlines. Con Son is also connected to Can Tho by a daily Vasco/Vietnam Airlines flight.

It's nearly always possible to show up and grab a seat on one of the hotel shuttle vans that meet the planes; drivers charge 50,000d and will usually drop you off at your hotel or in the town centre.

Sea connections are not reliable to Con Dao; sailings are frequently cancelled in heavy seas. All boats arrive at and depart from Ben Dam port on Con Son.

Superdong (☎ 029-9384 3888; www.superdong.com.vn; Ben Dam port) schedules one daily ferry at 7am or 8am from Tran De (adult/child 310,000/220,000d, 2½ hours), Soc Trang province, in the Mekong Delta. It returns from Ben Dam at either 1pm or 2.30pm. This crossing can be rough as the vessel is not large.

Ferry tickets can be purchased from travel agents and hotels.

Shuttle buses (50,000d per person) meet boats and connect Ben Dam with Con Son Town. A taxi costs about 260,000d.

Most hotels rent scooters for US$6 per day. Bicycles cost US$2 per day.

UNDERSTAND VIETNAM

History

The Vietnamese trace their roots back to the Red River Delta where farmers first cultivated rice. Millennia of struggle against the Chinese then followed. Vietnam only became a united state in the 19th century, but it quickly faced the ignominy of French colonialism and then the devastation of the American intervention. The nation has survived tempestuous times, but strength of character has served it well. Today, Vietnam has benefited from a sustained period of development and increasing prosperity.

Early Vietnam

From the 1st to 6th centuries AD, southern Vietnam was part of the Indianised Cambodian kingdom of Funan, famous for its refined art and architecture. Based around the walled city of Angkor Borei, it was probably a grouping of feudal states rather than a unified empire. The people of Funan constructed an elaborate system of canals both for transportation and the irrigation of rice. Funan's principal port city was Oc-Eo in the Mekong Delta, and archaeological excavations here suggest that there was contact with China, Indonesia, Persia and even the Mediterranean. Later on, the Chenla empire replaced the Funan kingdom, spreading along the Mekong River.

The Hindu kingdom of Champa emerged around present-day Danang in the late 2nd century AD. Like Funan, it adopted Sanskrit as a sacred language and borrowed heavily from Indian art and culture. By the 8th century, Champa had expanded southward to include what is now Nha Trang and Phan Rang. The Cham were a feisty bunch who conducted raids along the entire coast of Indochina, and thus found themselves in a perpetual state of war with the Vietnamese to the north and the Khmers to the south. Ultimately this cost them their kingdom, as they found themselves squeezed between these two great powers.

Chinese Occupation

The Chinese conquered the Red River Delta in the 2nd century BC. Over the following centuries, large numbers of Chinese settlers, officials and scholars moved south, seeking to impress a centralised state system on the Vietnamese.

In the most famous act of resistance, in AD 40, the Trung Sisters (Hai Ba Trung) rallied the people, raised an army and led a revolt against the Chinese. The Chinese counterattacked, but, rather than surrender, the Trung Sisters threw themselves into the Hat Giang River. There were numerous small-scale rebellions against Chinese rule – which was characterised by tyranny, forced labour and insatiable demands for tribute – from the 3rd to 6th centuries, but all were defeated.

However, the early Vietnamese learned much from the Chinese, including the advancement of dykes and irrigation works for rice cultivation, Confucianism, Taoism and Mahayana Buddhism. Monks carried with them the scientific and medical knowledge of these two great civilisations and Vietnam was soon producing its own doctors, botanists and scholars.

In 1418, wealthy philanthropist Le Loi sparked the Lam Son Uprising by refusing to serve as an official for the Chinese Ming dynasty. By 1425, local rebellions had erupted in several regions and Le Loi travelled the countryside to rally the people, and eventually defeat the Chinese, ending their 1000-year occupation.

Portuguese Catholics

The first Portuguese sailors came ashore at Danang in 1516 and were soon followed by a party of Dominican missionaries. For decades the Portuguese traded with Vietnam, setting up a commercial colony alongside those of the Japanese and Chinese at Faifo (present-day Hoi An). With the exception of the Philippines, the Catholic Church has had a greater impact on Vietnam than on any other country in Asia.

French Occupation

France's military activity in Vietnam began in 1847, when the French Navy attacked Danang harbour in response to Emperor Thieu Tri's imprisonment of Catholic missionaries. Saigon was seized in early 1859 and, in 1862, Emperor Tu Duc signed a treaty that gave the French the three eastern provinces of Cochinchina (the southern part of Vietnam during the French-colonial era).

By 1883 the French had imposed a Treaty of Protectorate on Vietnam. French rule often proved cruel and arbitrary. Ultimately, the most successful resistance came from the Communists, first organised by Ho Chi Minh in 1925.

The French-colonial authorities carried out ambitious public works, such as the construction of the Saigon–Hanoi railway and draining of the Mekong Delta swamps. These projects were funded by heavy government taxes and carried out by workers on abysmal wages who suffered appalling treatment.

During WWII, the only group that significantly resisted the Japanese occupation was the Communist-dominated Viet Minh. When WWII ended, Ho Chi Minh – whose Viet Minh forces already controlled large parts of the country – declared Vietnam independent. French efforts to reassert control soon led to violent confrontations and full-scale war. In May 1954, Viet Minh forces overran the French garrison at Dien Bien Phu. The Geneva Accords of mid-1954 provided for a temporary division of Vietnam at the Ben Hai River. When Ngo Dinh Diem, the anti-Communist Catholic leader of the southern zone, refused to hold the 1956 elections, the Ben Hai line became the border between North and South Vietnam.

The American War

Around 1960, the Hanoi government changed its policy of opposition to the Diem regime from one of 'political struggle' to one of 'armed struggle'. The National Liberation Front (NLF), a Communist guerrilla group better known as the Viet Cong (VC), was founded to fight against Diem.

An unpopular ruler, Diem was assassinated in 1963 by his own troops. When the Hanoi government ordered North Vietnamese Army (NVA) units to infiltrate the South in 1964, the situation for the Saigon regime became desperate. In 1965 the USA committed its first combat troops, soon joined by soldiers from South Korea, Australia, Thailand and New Zealand, in an effort to bring global legitimacy to the conflict. The USA had been waiting, and as early as 1954, US military aid to the French topped US$2 billion.

As Vietnam celebrated the Lunar New Year in 1968, the VC launched a surprise attack, known as the Tet Offensive, marking a crucial turning point in the war. Many Americans, who had for years believed their government's insistence that the USA was winning, started demanding a negotiated end to the war. The Paris Agreements, signed in 1973, provided for a ceasefire, the total withdrawal of US combat forces and the release of American prisoners of war.

Reunification

Saigon surrendered to the NVA on 30 April 1975; the same day, the Communists changed Saigon's name to Ho Chi Minh City (HCMC). Vietnam's reunification by the Communists meant liberation from more than a century of colonial oppression, but it was soon followed by large-scale internal repression. Hundreds of thousands of southerners fled Vietnam, creating a flood of refugees for the next 15 years. Vietnam's campaign of repression against ethnic Chinese, plus its invasion of Cambodia at the end of 1978, prompted China to attack Vietnam in 1979. The war lasted only 17 days, but Chinese-Vietnamese mistrust lasted for well over a decade.

Post–Cold War

After the collapse of the Soviet Union in 1991, Vietnam and Western nations sought rapprochement. The 1990s brought foreign investment and Association of Southeast Asian Nations (Asean) membership. The US established diplomatic relations with Vietnam in 1995, and in 2000 Bill Clinton became the first US president to visit north Vietnam. George W Bush followed suit in 2006, as Vietnam was welcomed into the World Trade Organization (WTO) in 2007; followed by Barack Obama in 2016 and Donald Trump in 2017. Relations have also greatly improved with Vietnam's historical enemy, China, barring tensions over the South China Sea. China may still secretly think of Vietnam as 'the one that got away', but Vietnam's economic boom has caught Beijing's attention, and trade and tourism are booming across mutual borders.

BEST ON FILM

The Vietnam War (2017) Definitive documentary series that examines the roots of the conflict, war itself and consequences.

Apocalypse Now (1979) The American War depicted as an epic 'heart of darkness' adventure.

The Deer Hunter (1978) Examines the emotional breakdown suffered by small-town-American servicemen.

Cyclo (Xich Lo in Vietnamese; 1995) Visually stunning masterpiece that cuts to the core of HCMC's underworld.

Vertical Ray of the Sun (2000) Exquisitely photographed family saga set in Hanoi.

People & Culture

People

The Vietnamese are battle-hardened, proud and nationalist, as they have earned their stripes in successive skirmishes with the world's mightiest powers. But that's the older generation, which remembers every centimetre of the territory for which it fought. For the new generation, Vietnam is a place to succeed, a place to ignore the staid structures set in stone by the Communists, and a place to go out and have some fun.

As in other parts of Asia, life revolves around the family; there are often several generations living under one roof. Poverty, and the transition from a largely agricultural society to that of a more industrialised nation, is changing the structure of the modern family unit as more people head to the bigger cities to seek their fortune. Today more women are delaying marriage to get an education: around 50% of university students are female and women make up 52% of the nation's workforce, but they are not well represented in positions of power.

Vietnam's population is 84% ethnic Vietnamese (Kinh) and 2% ethnic Chinese; the rest is made up of Khmers, Chams and members of more than 50 minority peoples, who mainly live in highland areas. Prejudices against hill-tribe people endure. Attitudes are changing slowly, but the Vietnamese media can still present them as primitive and exotic.

Religion

Over the centuries, Confucianism, Taoism and Buddhism have fused with popular Chinese beliefs and ancient Vietnamese animism to form what's collectively known as the Triple Religion (Tam Giao). Most Vietnamese people identify with this belief system but, if asked, they'll usually say they're Buddhist. Vietnam also has a significant percentage of Catholics (8% to 10% of the total population).

The unique and colourful Vietnamese sect Cao Daism was founded in the 1920s. It combines secular and religious philosophies of the East and West, and is based on seance messages revealed to the group's founder, Ngo Minh Chieu.

There are also small numbers of Muslims (around 60,000) and Hindus (50,000).

Arts

CONTEMPORARY ART & MUSIC

It is possible to catch modern dance, classical ballet and stage plays in Hanoi and Ho Chi Minh City.

The work of contemporary painters and photographers covers a wide swath of styles and gives a glimpse into the modern Vietnamese psyche.

Youth culture is most vibrant in Ho Chi Minh City, where there is more freedom for musicians and artists. There's a small hiphop scene, with Saigon-born Suboi acknowledged as Vietnam's leading female artist; she raps to eclectic beats including dubstep rhythms.

Popular indie acts include HCMC bands the Children and Ca Hoi Hoang ('Wild Salmon'); the latter headlined the 2019 Coracle Festival. Meanwhile, in Hanoi leading lights include the group Ngot and singer Vu.

ARCHITECTURE

The Vietnamese were not great builders like their neighbours the Khmer. Most early Vietnamese buildings were made of wood and other materials that proved highly vulnerable in the tropical climate. The grand exceptions are the stunning towers built by Vietnam's ancient Cham culture. These are most numerous in central Vietnam. The Cham ruins at My Son are a major draw.

SCULPTURE

Vietnamese sculpture has traditionally centred on religious themes and has functioned as an adjunct to architecture, especially that of pagodas, temples and tombs. The Cham civilisation produced exquisite carved sandstone figures for its Hindu and Buddhist sanctuaries. The largest single collection of Cham sculpture is at the Museum of Cham Sculpture in Danang.

LITERATURE

Contemporary writers include Nguyen Huy Thiep, who articulates the experiences of Vietnamese people in *The General Retires and Other Stories*, while Duong Van Mai Elliot's memoir, *The Sacred Willow: Four Generations in the Life of a Vietnamese Family*, was nominated for a Pulitzer Prize.

WATER PUPPETRY

Vietnam's ancient art of *roi nuoc* (water puppetry) originated in northern Vietnam at least a thousand years ago. Developed by rice farmers, the wooden puppets were manipulated by puppeteers using water-flooded rice paddies as their stage. Hanoi is the best place to see water-puppetry performances, which are accompanied by music played on traditional instruments.

BEST BOOKS

The Quiet American (Graham Greene; 1955) Classic account of Vietnam in the 1950s as the French empire is collapsing.

The Sorrow of War (Bao Ninh; 1994) A deeply poignant tale told from the North Vietnamese perspective.

Vietnam: An Epic History of a Divisive War (Max Hastings) Definitive account of the war, based on interviews with key players from both sides.

Vietnam: Rising Dragon (Bill Hayton; 2010) Candid assessment of the nation today.

The Sympathizer (Viet Thanh Nguyen) Superbly written spy novel dealing with the aftermath of the American War; 2016 Pulitzer Prize winner.

Food & Drink

Fruit

Aside from the usual delightful Southeast Asian fruits, Vietnam has its own unique *trai thang long* (green dragon fruit), a bright fuchsia-coloured fruit with green scales. Grown mainly along the coastal region near Nha Trang, it has white flesh flecked with edible black seeds, and tastes something like a mild kiwi fruit.

Meals

Pho is the noodle soup that built a nation and is eaten at all hours of the day, but especially for breakfast. *Com* are rice dishes. You'll see signs saying *pho* and *com* everywhere. Other noodle soups to try are *bun bo Hue* (combining beef vermicelli and lemongrass) and *hu tieu* (vermicelli soup garnished with fresh and dried seafood, pork chicken, offal and fresh herbs).

Spring rolls (*nem* in the north, *cha gio* in the south) are a speciality. These are normally dipped in *nuoc mam* (fish sauce), though many foreigners prefer soy sauce (*xi dau* in the north, *nuoc tuong* in the south).

Because Buddhist monks of the Mahayana tradition are strict vegetarians, *an chay* (vegetarian cooking) is an integral part of Vietnamese cuisine.

Snacks

Street stalls or roaming vendors are everywhere, selling steamed sweet potatoes, rice porridge and ice-cream bars even in the wee hours.

There are also many other Vietnamese nibbles to try:

Bap xao Made from fresh, stir-fried corn, chillies and tiny shrimp.

Bo bia Nearly microscopic shrimp, fresh lettuce and thin slices of Vietnamese sausage rolled up in rice paper and dipped in a spicy-sweet peanut sauce.

Sinh to Shakes made with milk and sugar or yoghurt, and fresh tropical fruit.

Sweets

Many sticky confections are made from sticky rice, like *banh it nhan dau,* made with sugar and bean paste and sold wrapped in banana leaf.

Most foreigners prefer *kem* (ice cream) or *yaourt* (yoghurt), which is generally of good quality.

Try *che*, a cold, refreshing sweet soup made with sweetened beans (black or green) or corn. It's served in a glass with ice and sweet coconut cream on top.

Drink

ALCOHOLIC DRINKS

Memorise the words *bia hoi,* which mean 'draught beer' – it's probably the cheapest beer in the world. It starts at around 5000d a glass, so anyone can afford a round. Places that serve *bia hoi* usually also serve cheap food.

Several foreign labels brewed in Vietnam under licence include Tiger, Carlsberg and Heineken. National and regional brands include Halida and Hanoi in the north, Huda and Larue in the centre, and BGI and 333 *(ba ba ba)* in the south of the country. There's also a large, growing craft-beer scene in all the main urban centres.

Wine and spirits are available but at higher prices. Local brews are cheaper but not always drinkable.

NONALCOHOLIC DRINKS

Whatever you drink, make sure that it's been boiled or bottled. Ice is generally safe on the tourist trail, but it's not guaranteed elsewhere.

Vietnamese *ca phe* (coffee) is fine stuff and there is no shortage of cafes in which to sample it.

Foreign soft drinks are widely available in Vietnam. An excellent local treat is *soda chanh* (carbonated mineral water with lemon and sugar) or *nuoc chanh nong* (hot, sweetened lemon juice).

> **BANH MI**
>
> A legacy of the French, *banh mi* refers to the crackly crusted rice- and wheat-flour baguettes sold everywhere (eaten plain or dipped in beef stew and soups), and the sandwiches made with them, stuffed with meats, veggies and pickles. If you haven't tried stuffed *banh mi,* you haven't eaten in Vietnam.

Environment

Environmental consciousness is low in Vietnam. Rapid industrialisation, deforestation and pollution are major problems facing the country.

Unsustainable logging and farming practices, as well as the extensive spraying of defoliants by the US during the American War, have contributed to deforestation. This has resulted not only in significant loss of biological diversity but also in a harder existence for many minority people.

The country's rapid economic and population growth over the last decade – demonstrated by the dramatic increase in industrial production, motorbike numbers and helter-skelter construction – has put additional pressure on the already stressed environment.

The Land

Vietnam stretches more than 1600km along the east coast of the Indochinese peninsula. The country's land area is 329,566 sq km, making it slightly larger than Italy and a bit smaller than Japan.

As the Vietnamese are quick to point out, it resembles a *don ganh* – the ubiquitous bamboo pole with a basket of rice slung from each end. The baskets represent the main rice-growing regions of the Red River Delta in the north and the Mekong Delta in the south.

Of several interesting geological features found in Vietnam, the most striking are its karst formations (limestone peaks with caves and underground streams). The northern half of Vietnam has a spectacular array of karst areas, particularly around Halong Bay, Tam Coc and Phong Nha.

Wildlife

We'll start with the good news. Despite some disastrous bouts of deforestation, Vietnam's flora and fauna are still incredibly exotic and varied. With a wide range of habitats – from equatorial lowlands to high, temperate plateaus and even alpine peaks – the wildlife of Vietnam is enormously diverse. There are over 300 species of mammals, over 180 reptiles, 848 birds, hundreds of fish and tens of thousands of invertebrates.

New species are regularly being discovered; the region is a biodiversity hot spot. A World Wildlife Fund (WWF) research trip in 2016 found 65 species new to science in Vietnam, including a crocodile lizard, a frog and two types of moles. And in 2019 silver-backed chevrotain, a 'mouse deer' species not seen for nearly 30 years, were found alive in southern Vietnam.

The other side of the story is that, despite this outstanding diversity, the threat to Vietnam's remaining wildlife has never been greater, due to poaching, hunting and habitat loss. Three of the nation's iconic animals – the elephant, saola and tiger – are on the brink. The last wild Vietnamese rhino was killed inside Cat Tien National Park in 2010.

And for every trophy animal there are hundreds of other less 'headline' species that are being cleared from forests and reserves for the sake of profit (or hunger). Many of the hunters responsible are from poor minority groups who have traditionally relied on the jungle for their survival.

National Parks

There are 33 national parks and over 150 nature reserves; officially, over 9% of the nation's territory is protected.

In the north, the most interesting and accessible include Cat Ba, Bai Tu Long, Ba Be and Cuc Phuong. Heading south, Phong Nha-Ke Bang, Bach Ma, Yok Don and Cat Tien are well worth investigating.

SURVIVAL GUIDE

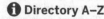

Directory A–Z

ACCOMMODATION

Accommodation is superb value for money in Vietnam. As tourism is booming it's usually best to book your accommodation a day or two in advance (most places can be booked online).

Cleanliness standards are generally very good. Communication can often be an issue (particularly off the beaten path, where few staff speak English). Perhaps because of this, service standards in Vietnam can be a little haphazard.

Homestays

Homestays are a popular option in parts of Vietnam. As the government imposes strict rules about registering foreigners who stay overnight, all places have to be officially licensed.

Areas that are well set up include the Mekong Delta, the White Thai villages of Mai Chau, Ba Be and the Cham Islands.

Some specialist tour companies and motorbike touring companies have developed excellent relations with remote villages and offer homestays as part of their trips.

Price Ranges

The following price ranges refer to a double room with bathroom in high season. Unless otherwise stated, tax is included, but breakfast excluded, from the price.

$ less than US$25 (580,000d)

$$ US$25–US$75 (580,000d–1,750,000d)

$$$ more than US$75 (1,750,000d)

CHILDREN

Children will have a good time in Vietnam, mainly because of the overwhelming amount of attention they attract and the fact that almost everybody wants to play with them.

- Big cities usually have plenty to keep kids interested, though traffic safety and pollution are serious concerns.
- Watch out for rip tides along the main coastline. Some popular beaches have warning flags and lifeguards.
- Local cuisine is rarely too spicy for kids and the range of fruit is staggering. International food (pizzas, pasta, burgers and ice cream) is available, too.
- Breastfeeding in public is perfectly acceptable in Vietnam.

Check out Lonely Planet's *Travel with Children* for more information and advice.

ELECTRICITY

Voltage is 220V, 50 cycles. Sockets are two pin, round head.

EMBASSIES & CONSULATES

Generally speaking, embassies won't be that sympathetic if you end up in jail after committing a crime. In genuine emergencies you might get some assistance.

If you have your passport stolen, it can take some time to replace it as many embassies in Vietnam do not issue new passports, which have to be sent from a regional embassy.

Australian Embassy (☎024-3774 0100; www.vietnam.embassy.gov.au; 8 Đ Dao Tan, Ba Dinh District, Hanoi; ⏲8.30am-noon & 1.30-4.30pm Mon-Fri)

Australian Consulate (Map p135; ☎028-3521 8100; www.hcmc.vietnam.embassy.gov.au; 20th fl, Vincom Center, Đ 47 Ly Tu Trong, HCMC; ⏲9am-1pm Mon-Fri)

Cambodian Embassy (Map p54; ☎024-3825 6473; camemb.vnm@mfa.gov.kh; 71a P Tran Hung Dao, Hanoi; ⏲8-11.30am & 2-5.30pm Mon-Fri)

Cambodian Consulate (Map p135; ☎028-3829 2751; camcg.hcm@mfaic.gov.kh; 41 Đ Phung Khac Khoan, HCMC; ⏲8.30-11.30am & 2-5pm Mon-Fri)

Canadian Embassy (Map p53; ☎024-3734 5000; www.canadainternational.gc.ca/vietnam; 31 Đ Hung Vuong, Hanoi; ⏲8.30-10.30am & 1.30-3.30pm Mon-Thu, 8.30-9.30am Fri)

Canadian Consulate (Map p135; ☎028-3827 9899; www.canadainternational.gc.ca; 10th fl, 235 Đ Dong Khoi, HCMC; ⏲8.30-10.30am & 1.30-3.30pm Mon-Thu, 8.30-9.30am Fri)

Chinese Embassy (Map p53; ☎024-8845 3736; http://vn.china-embassy.org/chn; 46 P Hoang Dieu, Hanoi; ⏲9am-4pm Mon-Fri)

Chinese Consulate (Map p135; ☎028-3829 2457; http://hcmc.chineseconsulate.org; 175 Đ Hai Ba Trung, HCMC; ⏲8.30-11am & 1.45-4pm Mon-Fri)

French Embassy (Map p54; ☎024-3944 5700; www.ambafrance-vn.org; 57 P Tran Hung Dao, Hanoi; ⏲8.30am-5.30pm Mon-Fri)

French Consulate (Map p135; ☎028-3520 6800; www.consulfrance-hcm.org; 27 Đ Nguyen Thi Minh Khai, HCMC; ⏲9am-noon Mon-Fri)

German Embassy (Map p53; ☎024-3845 3836; https://vietnam.diplo.de/vn-vi; 29 Đ Tran Phu, Hanoi; ⏲8.30-11.30am Mon-Fri)

German Consulate (Map p135; ☎028-3829 1967; https://vietnam.diplo.de/vn-de; 126 Đ Nguyen Dinh Chieu, HCMC; ⏲7.30am-3pm Mon-Fri)

India Embassy (Map p54; ☎024-3824 4989; www.indembassyhanoi.gov.in; Đ 58-60 Tran Hung Dao, Hanoi; ⏲9am-5pm Mon-Fri)

Irish Embassy (Map p54; ☎024-3974 3291; www.dfa.ie/irish-embassy/vietnam; 41a P Ly Thai To, Hanoi; ⏲9am-noon Mon-Fri)

Japanese Embassy (Map p53; ☎024-3846 3000; www.vn.emb-japan.go.jp; 27 P Lieu Giai, Ba Dinh District, Hanoi; ⏲9am-5.30pm Mon-Fri)

Japanese Consulate (Map p135; ☎028-3933 3510; www.hcmcgj.vn.emb-japan.go.jp; 261 Đ Dien Bien Phu, HCMC; ⏲8.30am-noon Mon-Fri)

Laotian Embassy (Map p54; ☎024-3942 4576; laoembassyhanoi@gmail.com; 40 P Quang Trung, Hanoi; ⏲8.30-11.30am & 1-4pm Mon-Fri)

Laotian Consulate (Map p132; ☎028-3829 7667; cglaohcm@gmail.com; 93 Đ Pasteur, HCMC; ⏲8-11.30am & 1.30-4pm Mon-Fri)

Netherlands Embassy (Map p54; ☎024-3831-5650; www.nederlandwereldwijd.nl/landen/vietnam; 7th fl, BIDV Tower, 194 Đ Tran Quang Khai, Hanoi; ⏲8am-5pm Mon-Fri)

Netherlands Consulate (Map p135; ☎028-3823 5932; www.nederlandwereldwijd.nl/landen/vietnam; Saigon Tower, 29 ĐL Le Duan, HCMC; ⏲8am-noon Mon-Fri)

New Zealand Embassy (Map p54; ☎024-3824 1481; www.mfat.govt.nz; level 5, 63 P Ly Thai To, Hanoi; ⏲8.30am-noon & 1-5pm Mon-Fri)

New Zealand Consulate (Map p135; ☎028-3822 6907; www.mfat.govt.nz/en/embassies; 8th fl, The Metropolitan, 235 Đ Dong Khoi, HCMC; ⏲8.30am-noon & 1-5pm Mon-Fri)

Singaporean Embassy (Map p53; ☎024-3848 9168; www.mfa.gov.sg/hanoi; 41-43 Đ Tran Phu, Hanoi; ⏲8am-noon & 1-5pm Mon-Fri)

Thai Embassy (Map p53; ☎024-3823 5092; www.thaiembassy.org/hanoi; 3-65 P Hoang Dieu, Hanoi; ⏲8.30am-noon & 1-5pm Mon-Fri)

Thai Consulate (Map p135; ☎028-3932 7637; www.thaiembassy.org/hochiminh; 77 Đ Tran Quoc Thao, HCMC; ⏲8.30-11.30am & 1.30-3pm Mon-Fri)

UK Embassy (Map p54; ☎024-3936 0500; http://ukinvietnam.fco.gov.uk; 4th fl, Central Bldg, 31 P Hai Ba Trung, Hanoi; ⏲8.30am-12.30pm & 1.30-4.45pm Mon-Thu, 8.30am-12.30pm & 1-3pm Fri)

UK Consulate (Map p135; ☎028-3825 1380; www.gov.uk/world/organisations/british-consulate-general-ho-chi-minh-city; 25 ĐL Le Duan, HCMC; ⏲8.30am-noon & 1-4.45pm Mon-Thu, 8.30am-noon & 12.30-3pm Fri)

US Embassy (Map p53; ☎024-3850 5000; https://vn.usembassy.gov; 7 P Lang Ha, Ba Dinh District, Hanoi; ⏲8am-5pm Mon-Fri)

US Consulate (Map p135; ☎028-3520 4200; https://vn.usembassy.gov/embassy-consulates/ho-chi-minh-city; 4 ĐL Le Duan, HCMC; ⏲7am-5pm Mon-Fri)

FOOD

The following price ranges refer to a typical meal (excluding drinks). Unless otherwise stated, taxes are included in the price.

$ less than US$5 (115,000d)

$$ US$5–US$15 (115,000d–340,000d)

$$$ more than US$15 (340,000d)

LGBTIQ+ TRAVELLERS

Vietnam is pretty hassle-free for gay travellers. There's not much in the way of harassment, nor are there official laws on same-sex relationships.

VietPride (www.facebook.com/vietpride.vn) marches have been held in Hanoi and HCMC since 2012. Gay weddings were officially authorised in 2015 (though their legal status has not yet been recognised). Transgender people were granted the right in 2015 to legally undergo sex-reassignment surgery and have their gender recognised.

Checking into hotels as a same-sex couple is perfectly OK. But be discreet – public displays of affection are not socially acceptable whatever your sexual orientation.

Utopia (www.utopia-asia.com) has useful gay travel information and contacts in Vietnam.

INSURANCE

Insurance is a must for Vietnam, as the cost of major medical treatment is prohibitive. A travel insurance policy to cover theft, loss and medical problems is the best bet.

Some insurance policies specifically exclude activities like scuba diving (and even trekking). Check that your policy covers an emergency evacuation in the event of serious injury.

You're highly unlikely to be driving a car, as virtually all rental options include a driver with your policy (and officially you need a Vietnamese licence and local insurance). It's also impossible to get a licence on a tourist visa.

Though many travellers drive scooters and motorbikes in Vietnam, most insurance policies will not cover you if you do not have a motorbike licence back home.

Worldwide travel insurance is available at www.lonelyplanet.com/travel-insurance. You can buy, extend and claim online anytime – even if you're already on the road.

LEGAL MATTERS

If you lose something really valuable such as your passport or visa, you'll need to contact the police. Few foreigners experience much hassle from police, and demands for bribes are rare.

The Vietnamese government is seriously cracking down on the burgeoning drug trade. You may face imprisonment and/or large fines for drug offences, and drug trafficking can be punishable by death.

MONEY

The Vietnamese currency is the dong (abbreviated to 'd'). US dollars are also widely used, though less so in rural areas.

For the last few years the dong has been fairly stable at around 22,000d to the dollar.

Tipping isn't expected, but it's appreciated, especially for tour guides.

ATMs

ATMs are very widespread. You shouldn't have any problems getting cash, but watch for stiff withdrawal charges (typically 25,000d to 50,000d) and limits: most are around 2,000,000d.

Credit & Debit Cards

Visa and MasterCard are accepted in major cities and many tourist centres, but don't expect noodle bars to take plastic. Commission charges (around 3%) sometimes apply.

OPENING HOURS

Lunch is taken very seriously and virtually everything (except restaurants) shuts down between noon and 1.30pm.

Hours vary little throughout the year.

Banks 8am to 3pm weekdays, to 11.30am Saturday; some take a lunch break

Offices and museums 7am or 7.30am to 5pm or 6pm; museums generally close on Monday; most take a lunch break (roughly 11am to 1.30pm)

Restaurants 11am to 9pm

Shops 8am to 6pm

Temples and pagodas 5am to 9pm

PHOTOGRAPHY

Camera supplies are readily available in major cities.

Avoid snapping airports, military bases and border checkpoints. Don't even think of trying to get a snapshot of Ho Chi Minh in his glass sarcophagus!

Photographing anyone, particularly hill-tribe people, demands patience and the utmost respect for local customs.

PUBLIC HOLIDAYS

If a public holiday falls on a weekend, it is observed on the Monday.

New Year's Day (Tet Duong Lich) 1 January

Vietnamese New Year (Tet) January or February; a three-day national holiday

Founding of the Vietnamese Communist Party (Thanh Lap Dang CSVN) 3 February; the date the party was founded in 1930

Hung Kings Commemorations (Hung Vuong) 10th day of the third lunar month (March or April)

Liberation Day (Saigon Giai Phong) 30 April; the date of Saigon's 1975 surrender is commemorated nationwide

International Workers' Day (Quoc Te Lao Dong) 1 May

Ho Chi Minh's Birthday (Sinh Nhat Bac Ho) 19 May

Buddha's Birthday (Phat Dan) Eighth day of the fourth moon (usually June)

National Day (Quoc Khanh) 2 September; commemorates the Declaration of Independence by Ho Chi Minh in 1945

SAFE TRAVEL

All in all, Vietnam is an extremely safe country to travel in.

- The police keep a pretty tight grip on social order and there are rarely reports of muggings, robberies or sexual assaults.
- Scams and hassles do exist, particularly in Hanoi, HCMC and Nha Trang (and to a lesser degree in Hoi An).
- Be extra careful if you're travelling on two wheels on Vietnam's anarchic roads; traffic-accident rates are woeful and driving standards are pretty appalling.

War Ordnance

Since 1975 many thousands of Vietnamese have been maimed or killed by rockets, artillery shells, mortars, mines and other ordnance left over from wars. Stick to defined paths and never touch any suspicious war relic you might come across.

TELEPHONE

International Calls

It's usually easiest to use wi-fi or 4G and an app such as WhatsApp, Skype or Viber. Mobile-phone rates for international calls can be less than US$0.10 a minute.

Local Calls

Domestic calls are very inexpensive using a Vietnamese SIM.

Phone numbers in Hanoi, HCMC and Haiphong have eight digits. Elsewhere around the country phone numbers have seven digits. Telephone area codes are assigned according to the province.

Mobile Phones

If you have an unlocked phone, it's virtually essential to get a local SIM card for longer visits in Vietnam. At around 200,000d for 5GB, 4G data packages are some of the cheapest in the world; some packages include call time, too. Many SIM card deals allow you to call abroad cheaply (from 2000d a minute) as well.

Get the shop owner (or someone at your hotel) to set up your phone in English or your native language. The three main mobile-phone companies are Viettel, Vinaphone and Mobifone.

Phone Codes

To call Vietnam from outside the country, drop the initial 0 from the area code.

Country code	✆84
International access code	✆00
Directory assistance	✆116
Police	✆113
General information service	✆1080

TIME

Vietnam is seven hours ahead of Greenwich Mean Time/Universal Time Coordinated (GMT/UTC). There's no daylight saving or summer time.

TOURIST INFORMATION

Tourist offices in Vietnam have a different philosophy from the majority of tourist offices worldwide. These government-owned enterprises are really travel agencies whose primary interests are booking tours and turning a profit. Don't expect much independent travel information.

Vietnam Tourism (www.vietnamtourism.com)

Saigon Tourist (www.saigon-tourist.com)

Online resources, travel agents, backpacker cafes and your fellow travellers are usually a much better source of information.

VISAS

The (very complicated) visa situation has recently changed for many nationalities, and is fluid – always check the latest regulations.

Firstly, if you are staying more than 15 days and from a Western country, you'll still need a visa (or an approval letter from an agent) in advance. If your visit is less than 15 days, some nationalities are now visa-exempt (for a single visit, not multiple-entry trips).

Tourist visas are valid for either one calendar month or three months. A single-entry one-month visa costs US$20, a three-month multiple-entry visa is US$70. Only US nationals are able to arrange one-year visas.

There are two established methods of applying for a visa: Visa on Arrival (VOA) via online visa agents; or via a Vietnamese embassy or consulate. E-visas are a newish third choice (for a limited number of nationalities).

Visa Extensions

Tourist visa extensions officially cost as little as US$10, and have to be organised via agents. The procedure can take seven days and you can only extend the visa for 30 or 90 days, depending on the visa you hold.

You can extend your visa in big cities, but if it's done in a different city from the one you arrived in, it'll cost you around US$30. In practice, extensions work most smoothly in HCMC, Hanoi, Danang and Hue.

Multiple-Entry Visas

It's possible to leave Vietnam and re-enter without having to apply for another visa. However, you must hold a multiple-entry visa before you leave Vietnam.

Single-entry visas can no longer be changed to multiple-entry visas inside Vietnam.

Visa on Arrival

Visa on Arrival (VOA) is the preferred method for most travellers arriving by air, since it's cheaper and faster and you don't have to part with your passport by posting it to an embassy. Online visa agencies email the VOA to you directly.

It can only be used if you are flying into one of Vietnam's international airports, not at land crossings. The process is straightforward: you fill out an online application form and pay the agency fee (around US$20). You'll then receive by email a VOA approval letter signed by Vietnamese immigration that you print out and show on arrival, where you pay your visa stamping fee in US dollars (or Vietnamese dong), cash only. The single-entry stamping fee is US$25, a multiple-entry stamping fee is US$50.

There are many visa agents, including some inefficient cut-price operators. It's recommended to stick to well-established companies; the following are very efficient:

Vietnam Visa Choice (www.vietnamvisachoice.com) Professional agency with online support from native English-speakers. Also guarantees your visa will be issued within the time specified or a refund is issued.

Vietnam Visa Center (www.vietnamvisacenter.org) Competent all-rounder with helpful staff well briefed on the latest visa situation. Offers a two-hour express service for last-minute trips (weekday business hours).

E-Visas

An e-visa program allows visitors to apply for visas online through the Vietnam Immigration Department (or visa agency). Citizens of over 80 countries are eligible, including those from the UK and the USA.

E-visas are single-entry only, valid for 30 days (non-extendable) and cost US$25 if arranged through the government website. Processing takes three to five days.

However, this government-run e-visa system has not been well implemented. The official website is glitch-prone and often fails to load. We've also heard of several cases where applications have gone AWOL and photos rejected for not being picture-perfect.

There have been reports of visitors being deported due to incorrect details (such as wrong date of birth or misspelt names) on the online application form. If you do apply for an e-visa, double-check that all the information you provide is 100% accurate. E-visas can be applied for online at https://evisa.xuatnhapcanh.gov.vn.

Some agents are now licensed to issue e-visas. The advantage of using a competent agent is that your e-visa should be processed quickly and efficiently. Agents can alert you to any potential mishaps in the application, and you'll have someone to liaise with, answer queries and guide you through the process.

Visa Works (https://visa.works) is a reputable agency run by native English speakers with a wide choice of visa options, including e-visas. Its helpful wizard guides you through the application process and communication is reliable.

Visas via Embassy or Consulate

You can also obtain visas through Vietnamese embassies and consulates around the world, but fees are normally much higher than using a visa agent and (depending on the country) the process can be slow. In Asia, Vietnamese visas tend to be issued in two to three working days in Cambodia. In Europe and North America it takes around a week.

Visa-Exempted Nationalities

At the time of research, citizens of the following countries did not need to apply in advance for a Vietnamese visa (when arriving by either air or land) for certain lengths of stay. Always double-check visa requirements before you travel, as policies change regularly.

Note that if you arrive once using an exemption and want to re-enter Vietnam, then you either have to wait 30 days (from the time of departure) or arrange a visa.

COUNTRY	VISA-EXEMPT DAYS
Myanmar, Brunei	14
Belarus, Denmark, Finland, France, Germany, Italy, Japan, Norway, Russia, South Korea, Spain, Sweden, UK	15
Philippines	21
Cambodia, Indonesia, Kyrgyzstan, Laos, Malaysia, Singapore,Thailand	30
Chile	90

VOLUNTEERING

Opportunities for voluntary work are quite limited in Vietnam as there are so many professional development staff based here. For information, chase up the full list of nongovernment organisations (NGOs) at the **NGO Resource Centre** (Map p53; ☎ 024-3832 8570; www.ngocentre.org.vn; room 201, Bldg E3, Trung Tu Diplomatic Compound, 6 Dang Van Ngu, Dong Da, Hanoi), which keeps a database of all the NGOs assisting

Vietnam. Pan Nature (www.nature.org.vn/en) has links to opportunities in the environmental sector.

WOMEN TRAVELLERS

Vietnam is relatively free of serious hassles for Western women. There are issues to consider, of course, but thousands of women travel alone through the country each year and love the experience. Most Vietnamese women enjoy relatively free, fulfilled lives and a career; the sexes mix freely and society does not expect women to behave in a subordinate manner.

Many provincial Vietnamese women dress modestly (partly to avoid the sun), typically not wearing sleeveless tops or short shorts and skirts. Women who live in big cities tend to wear what they like.

WORK

There's some casual work available in Western-owned bars and restaurants throughout the country. This is of the cash-in-hand variety; that is, working without paperwork. Dive schools and adventure-sports specialists will always need instructors, but for most travellers the main work opportunities are teaching a foreign language.

Looking for employment is a matter of asking around – jobs are rarely advertised.

English is by far the most popular foreign language with Vietnamese students. There's some demand for Mandarin, French and Russian, too.

Private language centres (US$10 to US$18 per hour) and home tutoring (US$15 to US$25 per hour) are your best bet for teaching work. You'll get paid more in HCMC or Hanoi than in the provinces.

Government-run universities in Vietnam also hire some foreign teachers.

ℹ Getting There & Away

Most travellers enter Vietnam by plane or bus, but there are also train links from China and boat connections from Cambodia via the Mekong River. Flights, cars and tours can be booked online at lonelyplanet.com/bookings.

ENTERING VIETNAM

Formalities at Vietnam's international airports are generally smoother than at land borders. Crossing overland from Cambodia and China is now also relatively stress-free. Crossing the border between Vietnam and Laos can be slow.

AIR

Airports & Airlines

The state-owned carrier Vietnam Airlines (www.vietnamairlines.com) has flights to over 30 international destinations, mainly in East Asia, but also to the USA, the UK, Germany, France and Australia.

The airline has a modern fleet of Airbuses and Boeings, and has a very good recent safety record.

There are now 17 airports deemed 'international' in Vietnam, but only eight have overseas connections (apart from the odd charter).

Vietnam Airport's main portal (www.vietnamairport.vn) has links to most of the following:

Cam Ranh International Airport Located 36km south of Nha Trang, with an expanding range of flights including to Hong Kong and Seoul.

Can Tho International Airport In the Mekong Delta, with flights to Kuala Lumpur, Bangkok and Taipei.

Cat Bi International Airport Near Haiphong, with flights to China and South Korea.

Danang Airport International flights to countries including China, South Korea, Japan, Thailand, Malaysia, Cambodia and Singapore.

Noi Bai Airport Serves the capital, Hanoi.

Phu Quoc International Airport (www.phuquocairport.com) International flights including Singapore, Bangkok and some charters to Europe.

Tan Son Nhat International Airport For Ho Chi Minh City.

Van Don Airport New airport serving Halong Bay with flights to China.

Other Vietnamese airlines include Bamboo Airways, Jetstar Airways and Vietjet Air.

LAND & RIVER

Vietnam shares land borders with Cambodia, China and Laos, and there are plenty of border crossings open to foreigners with each.

Cambodia

Cambodia and Vietnam share a long frontier with seven border crossings. One-month Cambodian visas are issued on arrival at all border crossings for US$30, but overcharging is common at all borders except Bavet. Cambodian border crossings are officially open daily from 8am to 8pm.

CROSSING	VIETNAMESE TOWN	CONNECTING TOWN
Le Thanh–O Yadaw (p250)	Pleiku	Ban Lung
Moc Bai–Bavet (p145)	Ho Chi Minh City	Phnom Penh
Vinh Xuong–Kaam Samnor (p199)	Chau Doc	Phnom Penh
Xa Xia–Prek Chak (p152)	Ha Tien	Kep, Kampot
Tinh Bien–Phnom Den (p152)	Ha Tien, Chau Doc	Takeo, Phnom Penh

China

There are three main borders where foreigners are permitted to cross between Vietnam and China: Dong Dang–Pingxiang (the Friendship Pass), Lao Cai and Mong Cai.

In most cases it's necessary to arrange a Chinese visa in advance.

Time in China is one hour ahead.

CROSSING	VIETNAMESE TOWN	CONNECTING TOWN
Lao Cai–Hekou (p79)	Lao Cai	Kunming
Mong Cai–Dongxing	Mong Cai	Dongxing
Dong Dang–Pingxiang	Lang Son	Nanning

Laos

There are seven overland crossings between Vietnam and Laos. Thirty-day Lao visas are available at all borders.

The golden rule is to try to use direct city-to-city bus connections between the countries, as potential hassle will be greatly reduced. If you travel step by step using local buses, expect transport scams (eg serious overcharging) on the Vietnamese side. Devious drivers have even stopped in the middle of nowhere to renegotiate the price.

Transport links on both sides of the border can be hit-and-miss, so don't use the more remote borders unless you have plenty of time, and patience, to spare.

CROSSING	VIETNAMESE TOWN	CONNECTING TOWN
Bo Y–Phou Keua	Kon Tum, Pleiku	Attapeu
Cau Treo–Nam Phao	Vinh	Lak Sao
Lao Bao–Dansavanh (p365)	Dong Ha, Hue	Sepon, Savannakhet
Nam Can–Nong Haet	Vinh	Phonsavan
Tay Trang–Sop Hun)	Dien Bien Phu	Muang Khua

Getting Around

AIR

Vietnam has excellent domestic flight connections, with new routes opening up all the time, and very affordable prices (if you book early). Airlines accept bookings on international credit and debit cards. Note, however, that cancellations are quite common. It's safest not to rely on a flight from a small regional airport to make an international connection the same day – travel a day early if you can. Vietnam Airlines is the least likely to cancel flights.

Bamboo Airways (www.bambooairways.com)
Jetstar (www.jetstar.com)
Vasco (www.vasco.com.vn)
VietJet Air (www.vietjetair.com)
Vietnam Airlines (www.vietnamairlines.com)

BICYCLE

Hotels and some travel agencies rent bicycles for US$1 to US$3 per day; better-quality models cost from US$6. Cycling is the perfect way to explore smaller cities such as Hoi An, Hue or Nha Trang (unless it's the rainy season!). There are repair stands along the side of roads to get punctures and the like fixed.

BOAT

Vietnam has an enormous number of rivers that are at least partly navigable, but the most important by far is the Mekong and its tributaries. Scenic day trips by boat are possible on rivers in Hoi An, Nha Trang, Danang, Hue, Tam Coc and even HCMC.

Boat trips are also possible on the sea. Cruising the islands of Halong Bay is a must for all visitors to northern Vietnam. In central Vietnam the Cham Islands (accessed from Hoi An) are a good excursion, while in the south, trips to the islands off Nha Trang and around Phu Quoc are recommended. It's possible to reach the Con Dao Islands via boat too.

Note that many boat trips are seasonal and subject to weather conditions.

BUS

Vietnam has an extensive network of buses that reach the far-flung corners of the country. Modern buses, operated by myriad companies, run on all the main highways.

Most travellers never visit a Vietnamese bus station at all, preferring to stick to the convenient, tourist-friendly open-tour bus network, or use a company like Sinh Tourist (p144), which has its own terminals.

Whichever class of bus you're on, bus travel in Vietnam is never speedy – plan on just 50km/h on major routes, perhaps 70km/h on Hwy 1 – due to the sheer number of motorbikes, trucks, pedestrians and random animals competing for space.

Bus Stations

Many cities have several bus stations – make sure you go to the right one! Bus stations all look chaotic, but many now have ticket offices with official prices and departure times displayed.

The better bus companies have their own private terminals.

Reservations & Costs

Reservations aren't required for most of the frequent, popular services between towns and cities, but it doesn't hurt to purchase your ticket the day before. Always buy a ticket online or from the office, as bus drivers are notorious for overcharging.

On some rural runs foreigners are overcharged. As a benchmark, a typical 100km ride *should* be between US$2 and US$3.

Bus Types

On most popular routes, modern air-conditioned deluxe buses offer comfortable reclining seats, while sleeper buses have flat beds for really long trips. Deluxe buses are nonsmoking. On the flip side, some are equipped with blaring TVs and even karaoke.

Connecting backpacker haunts across the nation, open-tour buses are very popular in Vietnam. These air-con buses use convenient, centrally located departure points and allow you to hop on and hop off at any major city along the main north–south route. Some open-tour buses also stop at sights along the way. The downside is that you're herded together with other backpackers and there's little contact with locals. Prices are reasonable. An open-tour ticket from Ho Chi Minh City to Hanoi costs from US$37 and US$70; the more stops you add, the higher the price. **Sinh Tourist** (www.thesinhtourist.vn) has a good reputation, with online seat reservations and comfortable buses.

Local buses in the countryside are slow and stop frequently. Conductors can overcharge foreigners on these local services.

CAR & MOTORCYCLE

Having your own set of wheels gives you maximum flexibility to visit remote regions and stop when and where you please. Car hire always includes a driver. Motorbike hire is good value, and this can be self-ride or with a driver.

Driving Licence

Unfortunately getting a valid licence to ride a motorbike in Vietnam is impossible for many. The rules and bureaucracy involved are frankly mind-boggling. Foreigners *are* permitted to ride motorbikes in Vietnam with an International Driving Permit (IDP) – you can apply for one online at www.e-ita.org/vietnam. However, this only covers countries that abide by the 1968 Convention on IDPs. There's a full list of eligible countries (which includes most EU countries, the UK and Switzerland) at https://en.wikipedia.org/wiki/International_Driving_Permit. But many other nations (including the USA, Canada, Australia and New Zealand) are not included. So if you have a 1968 IDP, you can legally ride in Vietnam.

The best source of information is available from local experts Offroad Vietnam (www.vietnammotorbikerental.com).

If you do manage to acquire a hire car without a driver, an IDP is also technically required.

Hire

The major considerations are safety, the mechanical condition of the vehicle, the reliability of the rental agency, and your budget.

Car & Minibus

Self-drive rental cars are virtually impossible in Vietnam, which is a blessing given traffic conditions. Renting a vehicle with a driver–guide is a realistic option even for budget travellers, provided there are enough people to share the cost.

Travel agencies rent vehicles with drivers for sightseeing trips. For the rough roads of northern Vietnam you'll definitely need a 4WD.

Approximate costs per day are between US$80 and US$120 for a standard car, or between US$100 and US$135 for a 4WD.

Motorbike

Many travellers hire a motorbike or scooter for a day or two when in Vietnam. However, unless you've organised an International Driving Permit you may not be covered by insurance.

Motorbikes are usually hired on a very casual basis. Scooters can be hired from virtually anywhere, including cafes, hotels and travel agencies. To tackle the mountains of the north, it is best to get a slightly more powerful model such as a road or trail bike. Plenty of local drivers are willing to act as chauffeur and guide for around US$30 per day.

The approximate costs per day without a driver are between US$5 and US$8 for a scooter or US$20 and up for trail and road bikes.

Insurance

If you're travelling in a tourist vehicle with a driver, the car-hire company organises insurance. If you're using a hired bike, consider carefully that most travel insurance policies will *not cover you* in the event of an accident if you've not got a driving licence valid for motorbike use. Many travellers wing it, but the risks are clear. The cost of treating serious injuries can be bankrupting for budget travellers.

Some policies may even exclude all cover for two-wheeled travel, so if you're riding pillion on a Grab bike or *xe om*, you may not be insured.

Road Conditions & Hazards

Road safety is definitely not one of Vietnam's strong points. Vehicles drive on the right-hand side (in theory). Size matters and small vehicles get out of the way of big vehicles. Accidents are common.

In general, the major highways are hard-surfaced and reasonably well maintained. Mountain roads are particularly dangerous: landslides, falling rocks and runaway vehicles can add an unwelcome edge to your journey.

LOCAL TRANSPORT

Cyclos

These are bicycle rickshaws. Drivers hang out in touristy areas and some speak a little English. Bargaining is imperative; settle on a fare before going anywhere. A short ride costs 12,000d to 30,000d in most towns.

Taxis

Taxis with meters, found in all major towns and cities, are very cheap by international standards. Average tariffs are about 12,000d to 15,000d per kilometre. However, dodgy taxis with go-fast meters do roam the streets of Hanoi and HCMC; they often hang around bus terminals. Only travel with reputable or recommended companies.

Two nationwide companies with excellent reputations are Mai Linh (www.mailinh.vn) and Vinasun (www.vinasuntaxi.com).

App-based taxis (both car and motorbike), including Grab, are available in several Vietnamese cities, including HCMC, Hanoi, Danang, Dalat, Hue and Haiphong. Uber is not present in Vietnam.

Xe Om

These motorbike taxis are everywhere. Fares are comparable with those for a cyclo. Drivers hang out around street corners, markets, hotels and bus stations. They will find you before you find them.

TRAIN

Operated by national carrier **Vietnam Railways** (www.vr.com.vn), the Vietnamese railway system is an ageing but pretty dependable service, and offers a relaxing way to get around the nation. Travelling in an air-conditioned sleeping berth sure beats a hairy overnight bus journey along Hwy 1. And, of course, there's some spectacular scenery to lap up, too.

It's worth consulting the excellent rail website www.seat61.com for the latest information on all trains in Vietnam.

Metro lines are under construction in both Hanoi and HCMC. The capital's first line was completed in late 2019, though testing continued through 2020; services may start in mid-2021. The HCMC metro is long-delayed.

Routes

Aside from the main HCMC–Hanoi run, three rail-spur lines link Hanoi with the other parts of northern Vietnam: one runs east to the port city of Haiphong; a second heads northeast to Lang Son and continues across the border to Nanning, China; a third runs northwest to Lao Cai (for trains on to Kunming, China).

'Fast' trains between Hanoi and HCMC take between 31 and 37 hours.

Classes & Costs

Trains classified as SE are the smartest and fastest, while those referred to as TN are slower and older.

TOURS

These Vietnam-based travel agencies offer great tours:

Buffalo Tours (www.buffalotours.com) Diverse and customised trips.

Handspan Travel Indochina (www.handspan.com) Wide range of innovative, interesting tours to seldom-visited regions.

Ocean Tours (www.oceantours.com.vn) Heads to Ba Be National Park and across the north.

Old Compass Travel (www.oldcompasstravel.com) Cultural tours led by expert guides.

Sinhbalo Adventures (www.sinhbalo.com) Heritage and cycling tours, mainly in southern Vietnam.

Vega Travel (http://vegatravel.vn). Group and bespoke tours of northern Vietnam.

Vietnam in Focus (www.vietnaminfocus.com) Photographic tours exploring Hanoi and further afield.

There are four main ticket classes: hard seat, soft seat, hard sleeper and soft sleeper. These are also split into air-conditioned and non-air-conditioned options. Hard-seat class is usually packed (and expect plenty of cigarette smoke).

Reservations

Most travellers use Bao Lau (www.baolau.vn) to book tickets, which is an efficient website with schedules and fares; it details seat and sleeper-berth availability and accepts international cards. E-tickets are emailed to you, which you show when boarding; there's a 40,000d commission per ticket.

You can reserve seats/berths on long trips 60 to 90 days in advance (less on shorter trips). Most of the time you can book train tickets a day or two ahead without a problem, except during peak holiday times. For sleeping berths, book a week or more before the date of departure.

Many travel agencies, hotels and cafes will also buy you train tickets for a small commission.

You could try to buy tickets in advance from the Vietnam Railways booking site (http://dsvn.vn); however, at the time of writing only Vietnamese credit cards were accepted.

AT A GLANCE

POPULATION
16.5 million

CAPITAL CITY
Phnom Penh

BEST KHMER CUISINE
Malis (p191)

BEST DOLPHIN TRIPS
Sorya Kayaking Adventures (p242)

BEST PARTYING
Police Beach (p262)

WHEN TO GO

Dec–Feb Cooler and windy, with almost Mediterranean temperatures.

Mar–Apr & Oct–Nov Temperatures rise and visitors melt. Rains taper off in October and November.

May–Sep Rainy season means emerald landscapes and awesome cloud formations.

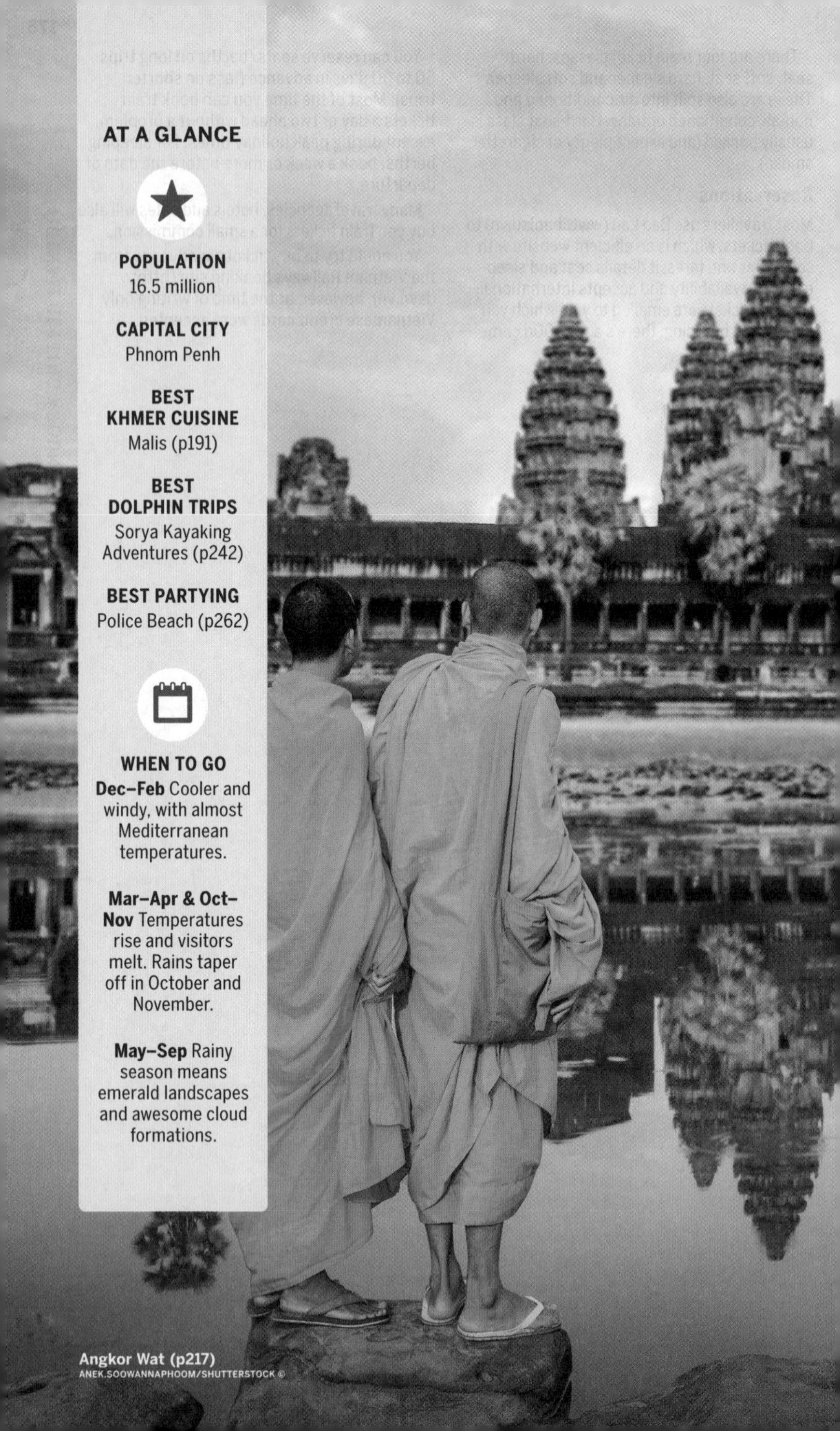

Angkor Wat (p217)
ANEK.SOOWANNAPHOOM/SHUTTERSTOCK ©

Cambodia

Fringed by beautiful beaches and tropical islands, sustained by the mother waters of the Mekong River and cloaked in some of the region's few remaining emerald wildernesses, Cambodia is an adventure as much as a holiday. This is the warm heart of Southeast Asia, with everything the region has to offer packed into one bite-size chunk. Despite the headline attractions, Cambodia's greatest treasure is its people. The Khmers have been to hell and back, but thanks to an unbreakable spirit and infectious optimism, they have prevailed with their smiles and spirits largely intact.

INCLUDES

Cambodia Highlights

❶ **Angkor** (p217) Discovering the eighth wonder of the world.

❷ **Phnom Penh** (p180) Enjoying the 'Pearl of Asia', with its striking museums, sublime riverside setting and happening nightlife.

❸ **Southern Islands** (p258) Island-hopping and soaking up the hedonistic vibes of the busier villages.

❹ **Kampot** (p267) Slipping into the soporific pace of riverside life.

❺ **Battambang** (p227) Wandering around the lush countryside, climbing to hilltop temples and exploring caves.

❻ **Mondulkiri** (p245) Exploring this wild land of rolling hills, thundering waterfalls and indigenous minority groups.

❼ **Prasat Preah Vihear** (p236) Making the pilgrimage to the awe-inspiring hilltop temple.

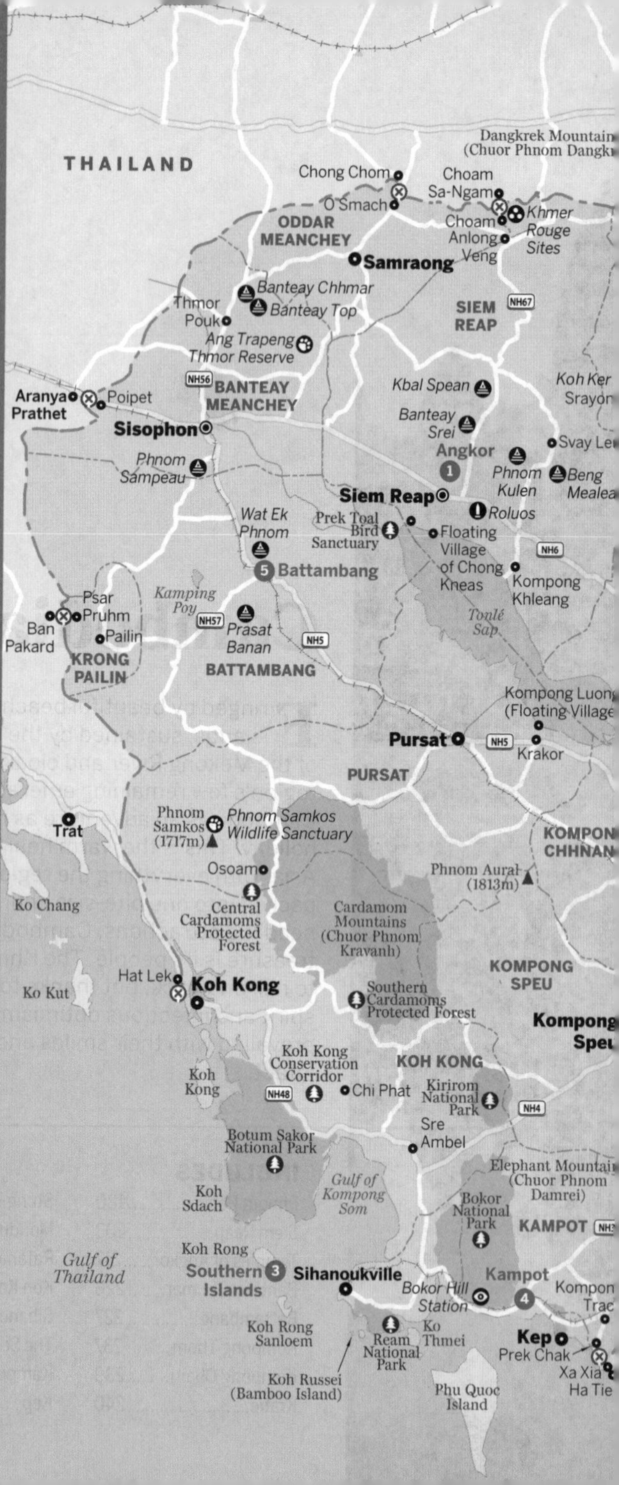

0
100 km
0
50 miles
N
LAOS
rasat
reah
hear
7
Sra Em
Muang
Khong
Siem
Pang
Virachey
National
Park
RATANAKIRI
Anlong
Cheuteal
Trapeang
Kriel
Veun Sai
Preah Vihear
City (Tbeng
Meanchey)
STUNG
TRENG
Tonlé San
Le
Thanh
Stung Treng
Ramsar Site
Preah
Rumkel
Ban Lung
Bokheo
O Yadaw
PREAH
VIHEAR
NH62
Tonlé Srepok
NH78
Thala Boravit
Stung
Treng
Lumphat
Svay Pak
O Pong
Moan
Ta Seng
Preah
Khan
Rovieng
Phnom
Dek
Rumchek
Mekong
Sen River
KOMPONG
THOM
KRATIE
MONDULKIRI
Koh Nhek
NH62
Stoeng
Mekong
Discovery
Trail
Sambor
Prei Kuk
Phnom Prech
Wildlife
Sanctuary
Dei Ey
Kompong
Thom
Phnom Santuk
Bou Sraa
Waterfall
Kampi
Mondulkiri 6
Sre Y
Phulung
Kratie
Sen Monorom
Putang
NH7
Andong Kroloeng
NH6
Keo Seima
Wildlife
Sanctuary
Kompong
Chhnang
Chhlong
Khao Seima
Kompong
Cham
KOMPONG
CHAM
Trapaeng
Sre
Skuon
Snuol
Suong
Trapaeng
Plong
Memot
Udong
Tonle Sap
Loc Ninh
Wat Maha
Leap
Xa Mat
PREY
VENG
Phnom
Penh 2
VIETNAM
Prey
Veng
Tonlé
Bati
KÂNDAL
NH1
NH11
SVAY
RIENG
Phnom Tamao
Wildlife
Sanctuary
Neak Luong
Ferry
Tay Ninh
Phnom
Chisor
Angkor
Borei
Moc Bai
ngk Tasaom
Kaam
Samnor
Svay Rieng
Bavet
Takeo
Phnom
Da
NH2
Vinh
Xuong
Ho Chi
Minh City
TAKEO
Chau Doc
Phnom
Den
Tinh
Bien
SOUTH
CHINA SEA

PHNOM PENH

023 / POP 2 MILLION

Phnom Penh (ភ្នំពេញ): the name can't help but conjure up images of the exotic. The glimmering spires of the Royal Palace, the fluttering saffron of the monks' robes and the luscious location on the banks of the mighty Mekong – this is the Asia many daydream about from afar.

Cambodia's fast-growing capital can be an assault on the senses. Motorbikes whiz down lanes without a thought for pedestrians; markets exude pungent scents; and all the while the sounds of life – of commerce, of survival – reverberate through the streets. But this is all part of the enigma.

Once the 'Pearl of Asia', Phnom Penh's shine was tarnished by the impact of war and revolution. But the city has since risen from the ashes to take its place among the hip capitals of the region, with an alluring cafe culture, bustling bars, world-class dining and a glittery new skyline growing on steroids.

Sights

★ Royal Palace — PALACE

(ព្រះបរមរាជវាំង; Map p188; Samdech Sothearos Blvd; admission incl camera 40,000r, guide per hour US$10; 8-11am & 2-5pm) With its classic Khmer roofs and ornate gilding, the Royal Palace once dominated the skyline of Phnom Penh. It's a striking structure near the riverfront, bearing a remarkable likeness to its counterpart in Bangkok. Being the official residence of King Sihamoni, parts of the massive palace compound are closed to the public. The adjacent Silver Pagoda is open to visitors.

Visitors are allowed to visit only the Throne Hall and a clutch of buildings surrounding it. All visitors need to wear shorts that reach to the knees, and a T-shirt or blouse that reaches to the elbows; otherwise you will have to buy an appropriate sarong as a covering at the ticket booth. The palace gets very busy on Sundays, when countryside Khmers come to pay their respects, but being among crowds of locals can be a fun way to experience the place.

★ Silver Pagoda — BUDDHIST TEMPLE

(ព្រះវិហារព្រះកែវមរកត; Map p188; Royal Palace compound; included in admission to Royal Palace; 7.30-11am & 2-5pm) Within the Royal Palace compound is this extravagant temple, also known as Wat Preah Keo or Temple of the Emerald Buddha. The Silver Pagoda is so named for its floor, which is covered with 5 tonnes of gleaming silver. You can sneak a peek at some of the 5000 tiles near the entrance, but most are covered for protection. Inside is a series of lavish Buddha statues made of precious metals.

The pagoda was originally constructed of wood in 1892 during the rule of King Norodom, who was apparently inspired by Bangkok's Wat Phra Kaew, and was rebuilt in 1962. It was preserved by the Khmer Rouge to demonstrate to the outside world its concern for the conservation of Cambodia's cultural riches. Although more than half of the pagoda's contents were lost, stolen or destroyed in the turmoil that followed the Vietnamese invasion, what remains is spectacular. This is one of the few places in Cambodia where bejewelled objects embodying some of the brilliance and richness of Khmer civilisation can still be seen.

★ National Museum of Cambodia — MUSEUM

(សារមន្ទីរជាតិ; Map p184; www.cambodiamuseum.info; cnr Sts 13 & 178; US$10; 8am-5pm) The National Museum of Cambodia is home to the world's finest collection of Khmer sculpture: a millennium's worth and more of masterful Khmer design. It's housed in a graceful terracotta structure of traditional design (built from 1917 to 1920) with an inviting courtyard garden, just north of the Royal Palace.

Highlights include an imposing, eight-armed Vishnu statue from the 6th century, found at Phnom Da, and a staring Harihara, combining the attributes of Shiva and Vishnu, from Prasat Andet in Kompong Thom Province. The Angkor collection includes several striking statues of Shiva from the 9th, 10th and 11th centuries; a giant pair of wrestling monkeys (Koh Ker, 10th century); a beautiful 12th-century stele (stone) from Oddar Meanchey Province inscribed with scenes from the life of Shiva; and the sublime statue of a seated Jayavarman VII (r 1181–1219), his head bowed slightly in a meditative pose (Angkor Thom, late 12th century).

Note that visitors are not allowed to photograph the collection, only the central courtyard.

★Tuol Sleng Genocide Museum MUSEUM

(សារមន្ទីរឧក្រិដ្ឋកម្មប្រល័យពូជសាសន៍ទួលស្លែង; Map p188; www.tuolsleng.gov.kh; cnr Sts 113 & 350; adult/child US$5/3, audio tour US$3, guide by donation; ⏲8am-5pm) In 1975 Tuol Svay Prey High School was taken over by Pol Pot's security forces and turned into a prison known as Security Prison 21 (S-21); it soon became the largest centre of detention and torture in the country. S-21 has been turned into the Tuol Sleng museum, which serves as a testament to the crimes of the Khmer Rouge.

Between 1975 and 1978, some 20,000 people held at S-21 were taken to the Killing Fields of Choeung Ek. Like the Nazis, the Khmer Rouge leaders were meticulous in keeping records of their barbarism. Each prisoner who passed through S-21 was photographed, sometimes before and after torture. The museum displays include room after room of harrowing B&W photographs; virtually all of the men, women and children pictured were later killed. You can tell which year a picture was taken by the style of number-board that appears on the prisoner's chest. Several foreigners from Australia, New Zealand and the USA were also held at S-21 before being murdered. It's worth hiring a guide, as they can tell you the stories behind some of the people in the photographs. An audio tour is also available, and recommended for greater insight for visitors without a guide.

Killing Fields of Choeung Ek MEMORIAL

(វាលពិឃាតជើងឯក; admission incl audio tour US$6; ⏲7.30am-5.30pm) Between 1975 and 1978, about 20,000 men, women, children and infants who had been detained and tortured at S-21 prison were transported to the extermination camp of Choeung Ek. It is a peaceful place today, where visitors can learn of the horrors that unfolded here decades ago. Admission includes an excellent audio tour, available in several languages.

The remains of 8985 people, many of whom were bound and blindfolded, were exhumed in 1980 from mass graves in this one-time longan orchard; 43 of the 129 communal graves here have been left untouched. Fragments of human bone and bits of cloth are scattered around the disinterred pits. More than 8000 skulls, arranged by sex and age, are visible behind the clear glass panels of the **Memorial Stupa**, which was erected in 1988.

The audio tour includes stories by those who survived the Khmer Rouge, plus a chilling account by Him Huy, a Choeung Ek guard and executioner, about some of the techniques they used to kill innocent and defenceless prisoners, including women and children. There's also a **museum** here with some interesting information on the Khmer Rouge leadership and the ongoing trial. A **memorial ceremony** is held annually at Choeung Ek on 20 May.

The site is well signposted in English about 7.5km south of the city limits. Figure on about US$10 for a *remork-moto* (drivers may ask for more) for a half-day. A shuttle-bus tour is available with Phnom Penh Hop On Hop Off (p185), which includes hotel pickup from 8am in the morning or 1.30pm in the afternoon.

Factory Phnom Penh CULTURAL CENTRE

(ហ្វេកធឺរីភ្នំពេញ; www.factoryphnompenh.com; 1159 NH2; ⏲7am-9pm Mon-Fri, to 7pm Sat & Sun) FREE This 3.4-hectare Levi's garment factory, 2km south of town, was completely transformed in 2018 into a graffiti-covered hub for entrepreneurs, artists and creative thinkers. On a ride through the sprawling campus (there are 50 free-to-use bikes) you'll encounter four art galleries, most run by **Kbach Arts** (វិចិត្រសាលក្បាច់; ☎031 3871444; http://kbachgallery.com; 1159 NH2; ⏲10am-6pm) FREE, as well as a skate park, trampoline park, craft brewery, cinema, stage, market and the **Workspace 1** (WS1; ☎017 999547; www.factoryphnompenh.com/workspace-1; 1159 NH2; day pass US$8; ⏲7am-8pm Mon-Sat) coworking space. It's virtually impossible to visit this aspirational complex and leave uninspired.

Psar Thmei MARKET

(ផ្សារធំថ្មី, Central Market; Map p184; St 130; ⏲6.30am-5.30pm) A landmark building in the capital, the art deco Psar Thmei (literally 'New Market') is often called the Central Market, a reference to its location and size. The huge domed hall resembles a Babylonian ziggurat and some claim it ranks as one of the 10 largest domes in the world.

The design allows for maximum ventilation, and even on a sweltering day the central hall is cool and airy. The market has four wings filled with stalls selling gold and silver jewellery, antique coins, dodgy watches, clothing and other such items. For photographers, the fresh-food section affords many

Phnom Penh

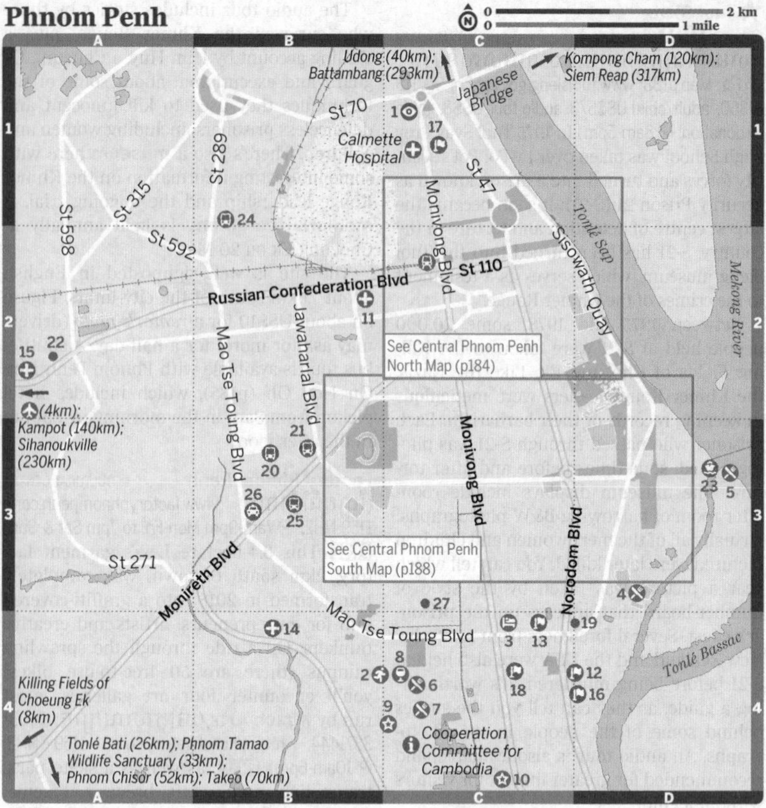

opportunities. For a local lunch, there are a host of food stalls located on the western side, which faces Monivong Blvd.

Wat Phnom BUDDHIST TEMPLE

(វត្តភ្នំ; Map p184; Norodom Blvd; US$1; ⏲7am-6pm) Set on top of a 27m-high tree-covered knoll, Wat Phnom is on the only 'hill' in town. According to legend, the first pagoda on this site was erected in 1372 to house four statues of Buddha deposited here by the waters of the Mekong River and discovered by Lady Penh. Hence the city name Phnom Penh or 'hill of Penh'.

Wat Ounalom BUDDHIST TEMPLE

(វត្តឧណ្ណាលោម; Map p184; Samdech Sothearos Blvd; ⏲6am-6pm) FREE This wat is the headquarters of Cambodian Buddhism. It was founded in 1443 and comprises 44 structures. The wat received a battering during the Pol Pot era, but today it has come back to life. The head of the country's Buddhist brotherhood lives here, along with a large number of monks.

Independence Monument MONUMENT

(វិមានឯករាជ្យ; Map p188; cnr Norodom & Sihanouk Blvds) Modelled on the central tower of Angkor Wat, Independence Monument was built in 1958 to commemorate the country's independence from France in 1953. It also serves as a memorial to Cambodia's war dead. Wreaths are laid here on national holidays.

Activities

★Grasshopper Adventures MOUNTAIN BIKING

(Map p184; ☎012 430622; www.grasshopperadventures.com; 59 St 174; tours from US$45) This recommended bike company runs half-day tours around Phnom Penh or Koh Dach, as well as a full-day cycle along back roads and an abandoned railway line out to Udong.

Phnom Penh

Sights
1 French Embassy C1

Activities, Courses & Tours
2 C4 Adventures B4

Sleeping
3 Rambutan Resort C4

Eating
4 Aeon Mall Food Court D3
5 Koh Pich Barbecues D3
6 Nesat Seafood House C4
7 Sesame Noodle Bar C4
Vibe Cafe .... (see 6)

Drinking & Nightlife
Long After Dark .... (see 6)
8 Sundown Social Club C4

Entertainment
9 Counterspace Theater C4
Prumsodun Ok & Natyarasa .... (see 9)
10 Sovanna Phum Arts Association C4

Shopping
Russian Market .... (see 8)

Information
11 Cabinet Medical Francais B2
French Embassy .... (see 1)
12 Japanese Embassy D4
13 Lao Embassy C4
14 National Blood Transfusion Centre B4
15 Royal Phnom Penh Hospital A2
16 Thai Embassy D4
17 UK Embassy C1
18 Vietnamese Embassy C4

Transport
19 Cambodia Angkor Air D4
20 Ekareach Express B3
21 Kampot Express B3
Kim Seng Express .... (see 21)
22 Lanmei Airlines A2
23 Mekong Ferry D3
24 Mey Hong Transport B1
25 Olongpich Express B3
26 Psar Dang Kor Taxi Park B3
27 Two Wheels Only C3

Also rents well-maintained bikes (US$12 for 24 hours).

★ Bodia Spa SPA
(Map p184; ☎023-226199; www.bodia-spa.com; cnr Samdech Sothearos Blvd & St 178; massages from US$35; ⏰10am-11pm) Arguably the best massages and spa treatments in town, and in a Zen-like setting just off the riverfront. All products are locally sourced and produced by the Bodia Nature team.

Samantha Spa SPA
(Map p188; ☎023-210278; http://samathaspa.com; 7CD St 278; massage from US$25; ⏰10am-11pm) One of the city's top spas, with a curvaceous design, air-con and highly professional staff. Choose your own massage oil before being led into a private room with either a bath or shower (to clean up after the treatment). Facials, scrubs and body wraps round out the menu of soothing treatments.

C4 Adventures OUTDOORS
(Map p182; www.c4-adventures.com; 12C St 444) Founded by former French legionnaire David Minetti, this adventure outfit specialises in taking thrill seekers far off the beaten path in Cambodia for kayaking, biking, canyoning and trekking. The jungles, mountains and remote islands where they lead tours are places few other agencies operate.

Boat Cruises BOATING
(Map p184) Boat trips on the Tonlé Sap and Mekong River are very popular with visitors. Sunset cruises are ideal, the burning sun sinking slowly behind the glistening spires of the Royal Palace. A slew of cruising boats are available for hire on the riverfront about 500m north of the tourist-boat dock.

Just rock up and arrange one on the spot for around US$20 an hour, depending on negotiations and numbers. You can bring your own drinks or buy beer and soft drinks on the boat.

Koh Dach Boat Trips BOATING
(Map p184; ☎012 860182; rimvuth@gmail.com; Sisowath Quay; per person US$15) Daily boat tours to Koh Dach depart at 9am and 11am from the tourist-boat dock (minimum three people).

Cambodia Cooking Class COOKING
(Map p188; ☎023-220953; www.frizz-restaurant.com; booking office 67 St 240; half-/full day US$25/35) Learn the art of Khmer cuisine through Frizz Restaurant on St 240. Classes involve a trip to the market and lots of pestle-and-mortar action. Reserve one day ahead.

Central Phnom Penh North

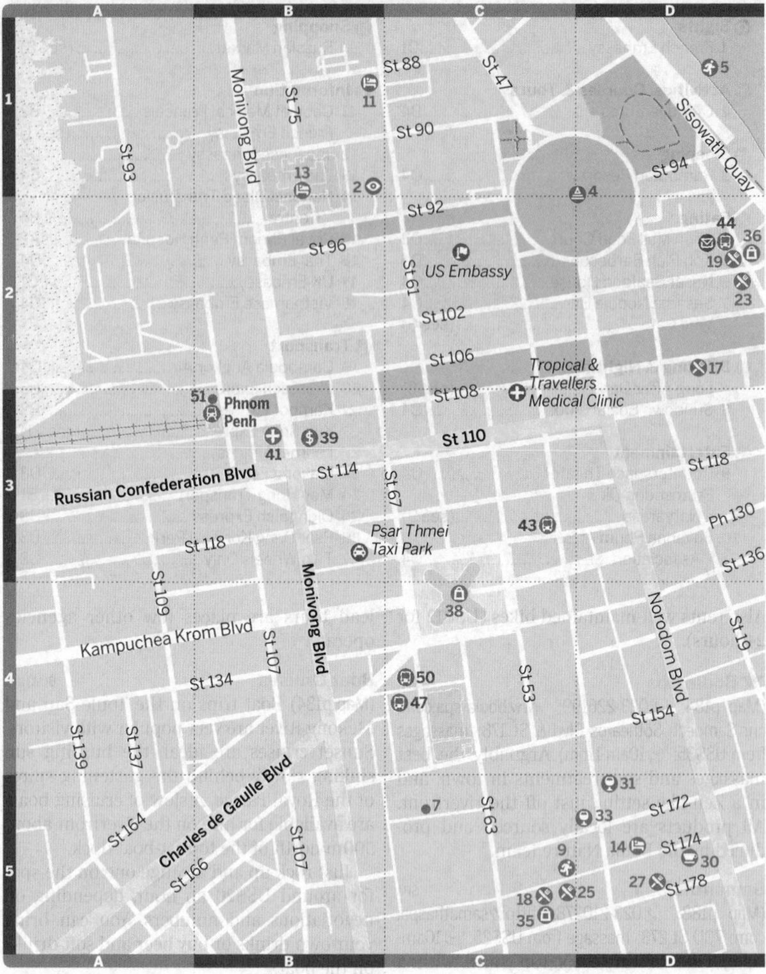

Daughters Spa SPA
(Map p184; ☎077 657678; www.daughtersofcambodia.org; 321 Sisowath Quay; 1hr foot spa US$10; ⏰9am-5.30pm Mon-Sat) Hand and foot massages are administered by participants in this NGO's vocational training program for at-risk women. Shorter (15- to 30-minute) treatments are also available.

The Place GYM
(Map p188; ☎023-999799; 11 St 51; walk-in US$15; ⏰6am-9.30pm Mon-Fri, to 9pm Sat & Sun) This is absolutely state of the art, with myriad machines, a big pool and a range of cardio classes.

FitnessOne Himawari Hotel SWIMMING
(Map p188; ☎023-214555; 313 Sisowath Quay; weekday/weekend US$9/10; ⏰6am-10pm) The Himawari has one of the best hotel pools in town. It's located near the banks of the Mekong. Admission includes use of the FitnessOne gym.

Tours

★**Lost Plate** FOOD & DRINK
(☎011 646801; http://lostplate.com; food/bar tour from US$60/50; ⏰food tour 6pm, bar tour 8pm Fri) Explore the history of Cambodia through its food on these excellent culinary

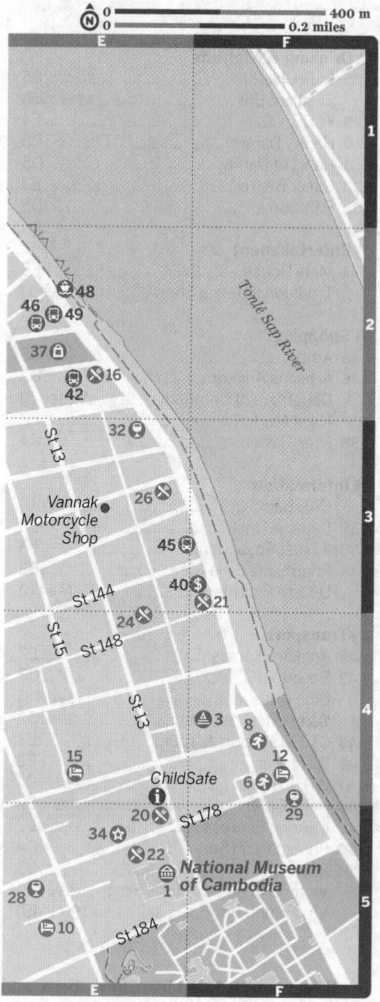

tours, which take in four off-the-beaten-path restaurants and one craft beer and cocktail bar. Just want to drink? There's a tour for that, too, where you'll visit the city's lesser-known bars and toss back unlimited craft beverages.

★Khmer Architecture Tours ARCHITECTURE
(www.ka-tours.org; 3hr tour US$15) Those interested in cycling past the colonial buildings of central Phnom Penh, diving into Cambodia's four main religions at local holy sites, or walking a circuit of new-wave Khmer architecture from the Sangkum era (1953–70) should look no further. One of these three signature tours runs each Sunday. Check the website for dates and times.

Urban Tales HISTORY
(Map p184; ☎078 911899; www.urbantales-phnompenh.com; National Library; 3hr tour adult/child US$38/28; ⏲departures 8:15am & 9:15am) City tour meets treasure hunt in this interactive adventure, where you'll follow in the footsteps of a mysterious French explorer in search of a lost Khmer antique. Tours depart from the **National Library** (បណ្ណាល័យជាតិ, Bibliothèque Nationale; Map p184; St 92; ⏲7.30-11.30am & 2-5pm Mon-Fri) and traverse about 3km of the historic centre. Bookings must be made at least 48 hours in advance.

Village Quad Bike Trails ADVENTURE
(☎099 952255; www.villagequadbiketrails.com; tours 90min/half-day/full day US$30/65/135) Offers quad biking in the countryside around Phnom Penh. The quads are automatic, and so are easy to handle for beginners (maximum two passengers per bike). Full-day tours take in Tonlé Bati (p201) and Phnom Tamao (p201); despite the area's proximity to the capital, this is rural Cambodia and very beautiful. Longer trips are also available.

Phnom Penh Hop On Hop Off CULTURAL
(☎016 745880; www.phnompenhhoponhopoff.com; half-/full day from US$15/25, excl entry fees) Offers shuttle-bus tours, which include morning or afternoon hotel pickup from 8am or 1.30pm. Routes include a half-day trip to Udong or the Killing Fields/Tuol Sleng, or a full-day city tour.

Sleeping

Accommodation in Phnom Penh, as in the rest of the country, is great value no matter your budget, with quite literally hundreds of guesthouses and hotels to choose from. There are some great boutique hotels around the city if you want to treat yourself after an upcountry adventure.

There are four popular backpacker colonies around the city, including St 172, between St 19 and St 13 (the most popular area); St 258 near the riverfront; the Psar O Russei area west of busy Monivong Blvd; and St 278 (aka 'Golden St') in the trendy Boeng Keng Kang (BKK) district south of Independence Monument.

Central Phnom Penh North

Top Sights
1 National Museum of Cambodia E5

Sights
2 National Library B1
3 Wat Ounalom F4
4 Wat Phnom D1

Activities, Courses & Tours
5 Boat Cruises D1
6 Bodia Spa F4
7 Cyclo Conservation & Careers Association C5
8 Daughters Spa F4
9 Grasshopper Adventures C5
Koh Dach Boat Trips .... (see 48)
Urban Tales .... (see 2)

Sleeping
10 Blue Lime E5
11 Eighty8 Backpackers B1
12 Panorama Mekong Hostel F4
13 Raffles Hotel Le Royal B1
14 SLA Boutique Hostel D5
15 Sundance Inn & Saloon E4

Eating
16 18 Rik Reay BBQ E2
17 Armand's The Bistro D2
18 Bouchon Wine Bar C5
19 Cam Cup Cafe D2
Daughters Cafe .... (see 8)
20 Friends E5
21 Metro Hassakan F3
22 Museum Cafe E5
23 Palais de la Poste D2
24 Psar Kandal E4
25 Romdeng C5
26 Sher-e-Punjab E3
Special Pho .... (see 6)
27 Sugar Palm D5

Drinking & Nightlife
28 Blue Chilli E5
Elephant Bar .... (see 13)
29 FCC F4
30 Happy Damrei D5
31 Heart of Darkness D5
32 Oskar Bistro E3
33 Pontoon D5

Entertainment
34 Meta House E5
Traditional Dance Show .... (see 1)

Shopping
35 Ambre C5
36 Artisans Angkor D2
Daughters of Cambodia .... (see 8)
37 Night Market E2
38 Psar Thmei C4

Information
CAB Bank .... (see 40)
39 Canadia Bank B3
40 J Trust Royal Bank F3
41 Pharmacie de la Gare B3
U-Care Pharmacy .... (see 6)

Transport
42 Angkor Express E2
43 Bayon VIP C3
Blue Cruiser .... (see 48)
44 Cambodia Post Van D2
45 CTT Transport & Tours E3
46 Giant Ibis E2
47 GTF Express C4
48 Hang Chau E2
49 Mekong Express E2
50 Phnom Penh Sorya C4
51 Royal Railways B3
Victoria Chau Doc Hotel Boat .... (see 48)
Virak Buntham .... (see 49)

Phnom Penh North

★Manor House HOSTEL $
(Map p188; ☎023-992566; www.manorhousecambodia.com; 21 St 262; dm US$5-7, r from US$25; ❄📶🏊) A villa that had a second life as a boutique hotel has transformed again into a chic hostel with some of the most luxurious dorms in town. The pool (and pool table) give it a fun atmosphere without tipping into full-on party-hostel territory. A great choice for backpacking couples!

★SLA Boutique Hostel HOSTEL $
(Map p184; ☎023-997515; www.slahostel.com; 15 St 174; dm/r from US$6.50/20; ❄📶) 🍃 This shoes-off 'poshpacker' is the cleanest hostel in the city, with hoop-like dorm beds and sleek privates – all with crisp white sheets. It's also environmentally conscious, featuring solar-powered showers, energy-saving air-con and green cleaning products. The community kitchen and stylish patio make this a no-brainer for discerning budgeteers.

Eighty8 Backpackers HOSTEL $
(Map p184; ☎023-500 2440; www.88backpackers.com; 98 St 88; incl breakfast dm US$5-7, r US$22-28; ❄📶🏊) A hostel with a swimming pool means party time, and this place hosts a big one each Saturday. The extensive property has a variety of private rooms, mixed or female-only dorms and Japanese-style sleeping pods. The courtyard boasts a central bar

with a pool table, and there are plenty of spots to lounge around the swimming pool.

Panorama Mekong Hostel HOSTEL $
(Map p184; ☎093 389336; www.facebook.com/panoramamekong178; 357 Sisowath Quay; dm US$3.50-6;) There's good news and bad news here. The good news is this place has panoramic views of the Mekong and you can even look down on the iconic Foreign Correspondents' Club (FCC), something that is unique for a backpacker pad. The bad news is there is no lift and there are four flights of stairs. Get fit and enjoy the views!

Sundance Inn & Saloon GUESTHOUSE $
(Map p184; ☎016 802090; www.sundancecambodia.com; 61 St 172; r from US$20;) A step above the guesthouse pack on St 172, Sundance has oversize beds, designer bathrooms, kitchenettes and computers that hook up to flat-screens in every room. With open-mic Tuesdays, frequent live music, all-day US$1 beers and a pool out back, it is quite the party pad. Free airport pickup with 24 hours' notice.

Blue Lime BOUTIQUE HOTEL $$
(Map p184; ☎023-222260; www.bluelime.asia; 42 St 19z; r incl breakfast US$50-115;) The Blue Lime offers smart, minimalist rooms and a leafy pool area that invites relaxation. The pricier rooms have private plunge pools, four-poster beds and concrete love seats. The cheaper rooms upstairs in the main building are similarly appealing. No children.

★**Raffles Hotel Le Royal** HOTEL $$$
(Map p184; ☎023-981888; www.raffles.com/phnompenh; cnr Monivong Blvd & St 92; r from US$235;) From the golden age of travel, this is one of Asia's grand old dames, in the illustrious company of the Oriental in Bangkok and Raffles in Singapore. This classic colonial-era property is Phnom Penh's leading address, with a heritage to match its service and style. Indulgent diversions include two swimming pools, a gym, a spa and lavish bars and restaurants.

★**Pavilion** BOUTIQUE HOTEL $$$
(Map p188; ☎023-222280; www.thepavilion.asia; 227 St 19; r incl breakfast US$60-100, apt US$120-164;) Housed in an elegant French villa, this immensely popular and atmospheric place kick-started Phnom Penh's boutique-hotel obsession. All rooms have inviting four-poster beds, stunning furniture and Bluetooth-enabled speakers, and some of the newer rooms include a private plunge pool. Guests can use bikes for free. Also free is a 25-minute welcome massage. No children allowed.

Palace Gate Hotel BOUTIQUE HOTEL $$$
(Map p188; ☎023-900011; www.palacegatepp.com; 44B Samdech Sothearos Blvd; r incl breakfast US$125-257;) Close to the riverfront, the Palace Gate has an unrivalled location overlooking the walls of, well obviously, the Royal Palace. The hotel is built around an old French colonial villa and the majority of rooms are set in a modern building behind. All are beautifully appointed with contemporary furnishings.

Plantation BOUTIQUE HOTEL $$$
(Map p188; ☎023-215151; www.theplantation.asia; 28 St 184; r incl breakfast US$80-400;) The largest and most ambitious hotel in the MAADS group of properties, Plantation ticks all the boxes with its high ceilings, stylish fixtures and fittings, open-plan bathrooms and balconies. There are two swimming pools here and a beautiful courtyard reception that hosts regular art exhibitions.

Phnom Penh South

★**Mad Monkey** HOSTEL $
(Map p188; ☎023-987091; www.madmonkeyhostels.com; 26 St 302; dm US$5-9, r US$18-32;) This colourful and vibrant hostel is justifiably popular. The spacious dorms have air-con and sleep six to 22; the smaller ones have double-width bunk beds that can sleep two. The private rooms are swish for the price, but lack TVs and, often, windows. The rooftop bar above quiet St 302 serves free beer and punch daily from 7.30pm to 8pm.

There's also a restaurant and tour desk on-site.

Top Banana Guesthouse HOSTEL $
(Map p188; ☎012 885572; www.topbananahostels.weebly.com; 9 St 278; dm from US$5, r US$16-18;) The rooms are in good shape by hostel standards, and there are some dorms available, including a four-bed female dorm. The main draw is the strategic location overlooking Wat Langka and St 278, plus the open-air chill-out area. It can get noisy, as the rooftop bar is raucous most nights. Book way ahead.

Mini Banana Guesthouse GUESTHOUSE $
(Map p188; ☎089 390379; www.facebook.com/MiniBananaGuesthouse; Langka Lane; dm US$2.50-6, r US$8-20;) It's almost a

Central Phnom Penh South

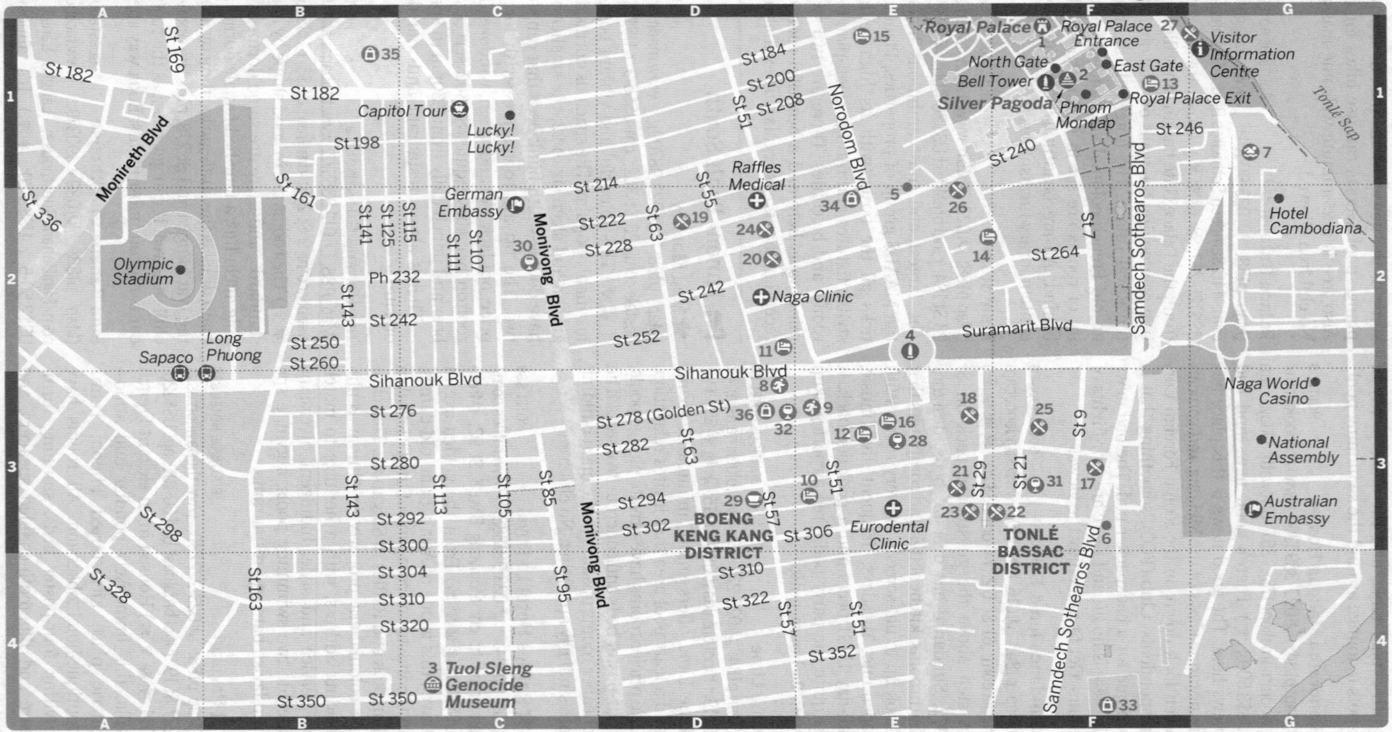

Central Phnom Penh South

Top Sights
1 Royal Palace F1
2 Silver Pagoda F1
3 Tuol Sleng Genocide Museum C4

Sights
4 Independence Monument E2

Activities, Courses & Tours
5 Cambodia Cooking Class E2
6 Cambodian Living Arts F3
7 FitnessOne Himawari Hotel G1
8 Samantha Spa D3
9 The Place E3

Sleeping
10 Mad Monkey E3
11 Manor House D2
12 Mini Banana Guesthouse E3
13 Palace Gate Hotel F1
Patio Hotel & Urban Resort ..... (see 12)
14 Pavilion E2
15 Plantation E1
Top Banana Guesthouse ..... (see 9)
16 Villa Langka E3

Eating
Bistrot Langka ..... (see 12)
17 Boat Noodle Restaurant F3
18 Feel Good Cafe II E3
19 House of Scott D2
20 Le Broken Plate D2
21 Malis E3
22 Mama Wong's F3
23 Meat & Drink E3
24 Sleuk Chhouk D2
25 Sovanna II F3
26 The Shop E2
27 Yi Sang Riverside G1

Drinking & Nightlife
28 Battbong E3
Botanico Wine & Beer Garden ..... (see 18)
29 Brown Coffee D3
30 Eclipse Sky Bar C2
Hangar 44 ..... (see 23)
Harry's Bar ..... (see 23)
31 Hub Street Cocktails F3
Library ..... (see 23)
32 Score D3
Seibur ..... (see 23)

Shopping
33 Aeon Mall F4
34 Monument Books E2
35 Psar O Russei B1
36 Smateria D3

banana republic in this part of town, with three guesthouses playing on the name. Renovated dorms with sturdy bunks, comfortable rooms with fan or air-con and a lively little bar-restaurant make this one of the most likeable of the bunch.

★Patio Hotel & Urban Resort BOUTIQUE HOTEL $$
(Map p188; 023-997900; www.patio-hotel.com; Langka Lane; s/d from US$35/60;) If you hate high-design rooms with ultra-comfy beds, rooftop bars with twinkling fairy lights, hallways lined in contemporary art and 8th-floor infinity pools with sweeping city views, then definitely steer clear of this place. It's right in the heart of the action on one of the city's hippest alleyways.

★Rambutan Resort BOUTIQUE HOTEL $$
(Map p182; 017 992240; www.rambutanresort.com; 29 St 71; r incl breakfast US$75-170;) Sixties-groovy, gay-friendly and extremely well run, this striking villa once belonged to the US embassy. The soaring original structure and a newer wing shade a boot-shaped swimming pool. Concrete floors set an industrial tone in the smart rooms, which are outfitted with top-quality furnishings.

Villa Langka BOUTIQUE HOTEL $$
(Map p188; 023-726771; www.villalangka.com; 14 St 282; r incl breakfast US$55-125;) Villa Langka was one of the first players in the poolside-boutique game and has long been a Phnom Penh favourite, even as the competition heats up. The rooms ooze postmodern panache, although there are big differences in size and style. The leafy pool area is perfect.

Eating

Phnom Penh North

18 Rik Reay BBQ BARBECUE $
(Map p184; 095 361818; 3 St 108; US$2-8; 24hr;) One of the best local barbecue restaurants near the riverfront, the Rik Reay is packed with locals every night, partly thanks to its convenient location near the Night Market, but also as a testament to the quality of its food. Choose from grilled beef, ribs, chicken, squid, shrimp and much more, all with signature dipping sauces.

Cam Cup Cafe CAFE $
(Map p184; 093 771577; Central Post Office, St 13; mains US$2-4; 6.30am-8.30pm;) This

elegant little cafe is the perfect way to make the iconic main post office relevant once more for a new generation of travellers. It offers fresh brews, herbal teas and some of the best-value Khmer dishes you can hope to find in this sort of setting. Decoration includes old postage stamps and machinery from the bygone days of the postal system.

Museum Cafe
CAFE $

(Map p184; ☑ 023-722275; National Museum, St 178; mains US$4-6; ☺ 7am-8pm; ☎) Set in the spacious grounds of the National Museum, this is a cultured place for a cuppa, but the menu includes a good selection of well-priced Khmer classics and some international wraps and salads as well.

Special Pho
VIETNAMESE $

(Map p184; ☑ 012 538904; 11 St 178; mains US$3-5; ☺ 8am-9pm) A great location near the riverfront for good pho – the noodle soup that keeps Vietnam driving forward – plus cheap fried rice and fried noodles.

★ Friends
FUSION $$

(Map p184; ☑ 012 802072; www.tree-alliance.org; 215 St 13; tapas US$4-7, mains US$6-10; ☺ 11am-10.30pm; ☎) ⦿ One of Phnom Penh's best-loved restaurants, this place is a must, with tasty tapas bites, heavenly smoothies and creative cocktails. Order two tapas or one main for a filling meal. It offers former street children a head start in the hospitality industry. Book ahead.

★ Romdeng
CAMBODIAN $$

(Map p184; ☑ 092 219565; www.romdeng-restaurant.org; 74 St 174; mains US$5-9; ☺ 11am-11pm; ☎) ⦿ Set in a gorgeous colonial villa with a small pool, Romdeng specialises in Cambodian country fare, including a famous baked-fish *amok,* two-toned pomelo salad and tiger-prawn curry. Sample deep-fried tarantulas or stir-fried tree ants with beef and holy basil if you dare. It is staffed by former street youths and their teachers.

★ Bouchon Wine Bar
INTERNATIONAL $$

(Map p184; ☑ 077 881103; 82 St 174; mains $7-25; ☺ 11am-2pm & 4pm-midnight Mon-Fri, 4pm-midnight Sat; ☎) Rehoused in a stunning French-colonial villa on St 174, Bouchon is now as much a classy restaurant as an elegant wine bar. The menu includes confit duck legs and some calorific homemade desserts. It also has a great selection of French wines by the glass, plus some of the more potent cocktails around town.

Daughters Cafe
CAFE $$

(Map p184; www.daughtersofcambodia.org; 321 Sisowath Quay; mains US$4-7; ☺ 9am-5.30pm Mon-Sat; ☎) ⦿ This fantastic air-conditioned cafe on the top floor of the Daughters of Cambodia visitor centre features soups, smoothies, original coffee drinks, cupcakes and Western mains. Diners are served by former victims of trafficking, who are being retrained with a new set of skills.

Sugar Palm
CAMBODIAN $$

(Map p184; ☑ 085 646373; www.thesugarpalm.com; 13 St 178; mains US$5-8; ☺ 11am-3pm & 6-10pm Mon-Sat) Set in an attractive French villa, the Sugar Palm is the place to sample traditional flavours infused with herbs and spices, including delicious *char kreung* (curried lemongrass) dishes. Owner Kethana showed celebrity chef Gordon Ramsay how to prepare *amok.*

Metro Hassakan
FUSION $$

(Map p184; ☑ 023-222275; www.metrokh.com; 271 Sisowath Quay; small plates US$4-10, large plates US$8-26; ☺ 9.30am-1am; ☎) Metro is one of the hottest spots on the riverfront strip thanks to its striking design and an adventurous menu. Small plates are for sampling and include beef with red ants and tequila black-pepper prawns; large plates include steaks and honey-soy roasted chicken.

Yi Sang Riverside
CHINESE $$

(Map p188; ☑ 016 320808; Sisowath Quay; dim sum US$3-5; ☺ 7am-10pm; ☎) This is one of the few places in the city where you can dine right on the riverside – perfect for a relaxing sunset cocktail. The menu includes a mix of well-presented Cambodian street flavours such as *naom banchok* (rice noodles with curry), plus plenty of dim sum.

Sleuk Chhouk
CAMBODIAN $$

(Map p188; ☑ 012 208222; 165 St 51; mains US$5-10; ☺ 10am-10pm; ☎) This place's picture-board menu may not look too appealing from the street, but venture inside for a stylish and authentic dining experience. Dishes include fish-egg soup or clay pots with zesty frogs' legs and quails' eggs in sugar palm and black pepper.

The Shop
CAFE $$

(Map p188; ☑ 092 955963; www.theshop-cambodia.com; 39 St 240; mains US$3.50-12; ☺ 7am-7pm; ☎⦿) If you are craving the local deli back home, make for this haven, which has a changing selection of sandwiches and salads with healthy and creative ingredients such as wild lentils, forest mushrooms and lamb. The pastries, cakes and chocolates are delectable and well worth the indulgence.

Sher-e-Punjab INDIAN $$

(Map p184; ☎023-216360; www.sherepunjabindianfood.com; 16 St 130; mains US$3-8; ⏲10am-11pm; ☎) This is the top spot for a curry fix according to many members of Phnom Penh's Indian community. The tandoori dishes here are particularly good, as are the excellent-value prawn curries.

★**House of Scott** FUSION $$$

(Map p188; ☎023-966895; www.houseofscott-kh.com; 29 St 228; share plates US$4-9, mains US$10-25; ⏲11am-11pm Tue-Sun; ☎) Chic and art-lined House of Scott works with the Cambodian Children's Fund by donating all proceeds towards education and job creation for Cambodian youth. The menu includes delicious shared plates, such as homemade pork and shrimp sausages or Kampot pepper beef sashimi.

Armand's The Bistro FRENCH $$$

(Map p184; ☎015 548966; 33 St 108; meals US$15-30; ⏲6pm-midnight Tue-Sun) The best steaks in town are served in Cognac flambé-style by the eponymous owner of this French bistro. The meat is simply superb, but every item on the chalkboard menu shines. Space is tight, so this is one place to book ahead.

Le Broken Plate JAPANESE $$$

(Map p188; ☎078 903335; 17 St 242; omakase menu for 2 US$80, mains US$10-15; ⏲10am-10pm; ☎) Canadian-Cambodian chef Narith Plong delivers a Khmer twist to the Japanese sushi and sashimi experience. Sourcing only the freshest seasonal ingredients, he works his magic behind the bar counter to create incredible omakase (chef's choice) tasting menus. Á la carte is also available, including fresh oysters and Mekong lobster miso soup. Bookings essential.

Palais de la Poste FRENCH $$$

(Map p184; ☎023-722282; www.palais-restaurant.com; 5 St 102; mains US$15-145; ⏲11.30am-2pm & 6.30-10pm) Located in one of the city's grandest buildings, the former Banque Indochine, Palais de la Poste features old vault doors en route to the refined dining room upstairs. Dishes are presented with a decorative flourish; menu highlights include langoustine ravioli, beef carpaccio and grilled scallops with Kampot pepper.

Phnom Penh South

★**Sovanna II** BARBECUE $

(Map p188; ☎011 840055; 2C St 21; mains US$2-8; ⏲4-11pm; ☎) Sovanna II is always jumping with locals and a smattering of expats, who have made this their barbecue of choice thanks to the huge menu and cheap local beer. **Sovanna I**, on the same street, opens from 6.30am and is as good a place as any to sample the national breakfast, *bei sait chrouk* (pork and rice).

Boat Noodle Restaurant THAI $

(Map p188; ☎012 774287; 57 Samdech Sothearos Blvd; mains US$3-7; ⏲6.30am-10pm; ☎) This long-running Thai-Khmer restaurant has some of the best-value regional dishes in town. Choose from the contemporary but traditionally decorated space at the front or a traditional wooden house behind. There are delicious noodle soups and lots of local specialities, ranging from fish cakes to spicy curries.

Feel Good Cafe II CAFE $

(Map p188; ☎078 866651; www.feelgoodcoffee.com.kh; 11B St 29; dishes US$2-6; ⏲7.30am-4.30pm; ☎) One of the only cafes in town to roast and grind its own coffee, with responsibly sourced blends that are a fusion of Cambodian, Lao and Thai coffee beans. The menu is international with influences from the Med to Mexico, including wraps and burgers.

Aeon Mall Food Court ASIAN $

(Map p182; 132 Samdech Sothearos Blvd; mains US$1-6; ⏲9am-10pm; ☎) It may be surprising to venture into the country's swankiest mall to find cheap eats, but there are two food courts here covering the best of Asia and beyond. The more local option has noodle soups, fried rice and fresh sushi. The nearby World Dining Food Court has fancier furnishings and live music some evenings.

★**Malis** CAMBODIAN $$

(Map p188; ☎015 814888; www.malis-restaurant.com; 136 Norodom Blvd; mains US$6-25; ⏲7am-10.30pm) The leading Khmer restaurant in the Cambodian capital, Malis is a chic place to dine al fresco. The original menu includes beef steamed in lotus leaf, goby with Kampot peppercorns, and traditional soups and salads. It's popular for a boutique breakfast: the breakfast sets are a good deal at US$8. Book ahead for dinner or you won't get a seat.

★Bistrot Langka FRENCH $$
(Map p188; ☎070 727233; Langka Lane; US$8-12; ⊙6-10pm; 📶) Bistrot Langka offers fine French dining in an intimate atmosphere at an affordable price. Tuna tataki and an original beef tartare are some standout moments. Book ahead, as this slick spot has only a handful of tables and is one of the city's busiest dinner destinations.

Mama Wong's CHINESE $$
(Map p188; ☎097 8508383; 41 St 308; mains US$3-7; ⊙11am-11pm; 📶) This red-lit hangout brings a contemporary touch to the city's Chinese dining scene, serving up inventive dumplings, noodle bowls and Asian tapas such as duck pancakes or chilli and garlic prawns. Good value, good fun.

Russian Market Area

★Nesat Seafood House SEAFOOD $
(Map p182; ☎077 683003; St 446; mains US$3-7; ⊙11am-11.30pm Mon-Sat; 📶) Incredibly cheap seafood cooked to perfection and served in trendy, sea-inspired surrounds. What more could you ask for? All the critters arrive fresh each day from Kampot and Kep, so you can be sure they haven't been squirming around under the sun in the nearby Russian Market. Reserve ahead.

Sesame Noodle Bar NOODLES $
(Map p182; ☎089 750212; www.sesamenoodlebar.com; 9 St 460; mains US$3.50-5.75; ⊙11.30am-2.30pm & 5-9.30pm Tue-Sun; 📶) A Japanese-American duo is behind one of the Russian Market's longest-running little diners. Cold noodles arrive in vegetarian or egg varieties and come heaped with an egg and caramelised pork or grilled tofu. Simply delicious.

★Vibe Cafe VEGAN $$
(Map p182; ☎061 764937; www.vibecafeasia.com; 26A St 446; mains US$4.50-7; ⊙7.30am-9pm Tue-Sun, to 4.30pm Mon; 📶✎) 🍃 This three-storey air-conditioned cafe sets itself out as the capital's first 100% vegan restaurant, creating original homemade superfood recipes in its laboratory-like kitchen. The signature Ritual Bowl is packed full of goodness, including quinoa, beetroot, hummus and a whole lot more. It also has innovative cleansing juices such as activated charcoal, coconut water, ginger, lemon and cayenne pepper. Detox!

LOCAL FLAVOURS

Street Fare & Markets

Street food is not quite as familiar or user-friendly here as in, say, Bangkok. But if you're a little adventurous and want to save boatloads of money, look no further. The street-side eateries really get hopping during breakfast, when many Cambodians eat out. Look for filled seats and you can't go wrong.

Phnom Penh's many markets all have large central eating areas, where stalls serve up local favourites such as noodle soup and fried noodles. Most dishes cost a reasonable US$1 to US$2. The best market for eating is the Russian Market (p195), with an interior food zone that's easy to find and has a good variety of Cambodian specialities; the large car park on the west side converts to seafood barbecues and more from around 4pm. Psar Thmei (p181) and **Psar O Russei** (Map p188; St 182; ⊙6.30am-5.30pm) are also great choices. **Psar Kandal** (Map p184; St 13 btwn Sts 144 & 154; meals 4000-6000r; ⊙market 6am-8pm), just off the riverfront, gets going a little later and is an early-evening option where Cambodians come for takeaway food.

If the markets are too hot or claustrophobic for your taste, look out for the mobile street sellers carrying their wares on their shoulders or wheeling them around in small carts.

Khmer Barbecues

After dark, Khmer eateries scattered across town illuminate their neon signs, calling locals in for fine food and generous jugs of draught beer. The speciality at most of these places is grilled strips of meat or seafood, but they also serve fried noodles and rice, curries and other pan-fried favourites, along with some veggie options.

Khmer barbecues are all over the place, so it won't be hard to find one. **Koh Pich** (Diamond Island; Map p182; US$2-6; ⊙hours vary), east of the hulking Naga World Casino, has a cluster of well-reputed barbecues.

Ten per cent of profits go to the Good Vibe Foundation (www.goodvibefoundation.org), which aims to provide 10,000 Cambodian schoolchildren with healthy daily meals.

Drinking & Nightlife

Phnom Penh has an ever-more-sophisticated bar scene, so it's definitely worth one big night out here. There are lots of late-night spots clustered around the intersection of Sts 51 and 172, nicknamed 'Area 51'. 'Golden St' (St 278) is also popular, and the riverfront has its share of bars. Bassac Lane and the Russian Market area have emerged as the hipster parts of town.

★Hub Street Cocktails COCKTAIL BAR
(Map p188; ☎017 369594; 20 St 21; ⏲6pm-1am) Cheap craft cocktails and killer street cuisine collide to great effect at this marvellous bamboo bar, beloved by expats and Cambodians alike. Arriving here feels like stumbling upon a familiar yet exotic block party, where strangers are quick friends.

★Long After Dark BAR
(Map p182; ☎093 768354; www.longafterdarkcambodia.com; 86 St 450; ⏲noon-midnight Sun-Thu, to 2am Fri & Sat; 📶) This place keeps visitors hanging around the Russian Market area long after dark with its combination of rare single-malt whiskies, Cambodian craft beers and a vinyl collection that starts a-spinnin' at weekends. Brief happy hour at 5pm on Friday and some interesting whisky flights available with Highlands or global themes. Cool and cosy all at once.

Sundown Social Club ROOFTOP BAR
(Map p182; ☎015 526373; 86 St 440; ⏲noon-11pm; 📶) Look at the Russian Market from a different angle in this funky rooftop bar on St 440. Head here for sundowners, including Club Tropicana–inspired cocktails and craft beers, and a menu of innovative pub grub and bar snacks.

Battbong BAR
(Map p188; ☎069 291643; Langka Lane; ⏲6pm-late; 📶) An always-packed speakeasy, Battbong is tricky to locate. Look out for the Coca-Cola machine at the end of Langka Lane and locate the hidden button. Inside is a decadent beatnik-style bar with signature craft cocktails, plush sofas and the kind of low lighting that makes everyone look gorgeous. Down-tempo beats set the mood when there are no live bands.

DON'T MISS

BASSAC LANE BARS

Bassac Lane is the moniker given to an alley that leads south off St 308. The brainchild of Kiwi brothers the Norbert-Munns, who have a flair for drinks and design, there are half a dozen or more hole-in-the-wall boozers in this eclectic spot. Choose from fusion wraps and burgers at the original **Meat & Drink** (Map p188; ☎089 666414; www.facebook.com/meatanddrink; mains US$4-8; ⏲5pm-midnight), tiny and intimate **Seibur** (Map p188; www.facebook.com/Seibur.pp; ⏲5pm-midnight Tue-Sun), the refined and book-filled **Library** (Map p188; www.facebook.com/TheLibraryDaiquiriBar; ⏲4.30pm-midnight; 📶), rooftop cocktail bar **Harry's** (Map p188; ☎010 275273; ⏲4.30pm-midnight) or custom-bike tribute bar, **Hangar 44** (Map p188; ⏲5pm-midnight).

Bassac Lane has cemented its reputation as the new bohemian district of Phnom Penh and is well worth a visit.

Botanico Wine & Beer Garden CRAFT BEER
(Map p188; ☎077 943135; www.facebook.com/botanicowineandbeergarden; 9B St 29; ⏲9am-10pm Sun-Thu, to midnight Fri & Sat; 📶) Bringing US-style craft brewing to Phnom Penh, this great little hideaway stocks Irish Red, IPA and other home-brewed Cerevisia beers. It is set in a verdant garden tucked down a winding alley. Live music on weekends and Tuesday trivia nights keep expats coming back for more.

Pontoon CLUB
(Map p184; www.pontoonclub.com; 80 St 172; ⏲10pm-late; 📶) After floating around from pier to pier for a few years (hence the name), the city's premier nightclub found a permanent home on terra firma. It draws top local DJs and occasional big foreign acts. Admission is US$3 to US$8 at weekends; free on weeknights. Thursday is ladies night. Adjacent Pontoon Pulse is more of a lounge club, with electronica and ambient music.

Heart of Darkness CLUB
(Map p184; http://heartofdarknessclub.com.kh; 38 St 51; ⏲9pm-late) This Phnom Penh institution with an alluring Angkorian theme has evolved into more of a nightclub than a bar

over the years, with drag shows that drop jaws Wednesday to Saturday nights. The place attracts all – and we mean *all* – sorts. Everybody should stop in at least once just to bask in the aura and atmosphere of the place.

Oskar Bistro BAR
(Map p184; www.oskar-bistro.com; 159 Sisowath Quay; ⌚5pm-2am; 📶) This upscale gastro-pub blends the bar and restaurant to perfection. Choose from creative cocktails and a huge wine list of nearly 60 tipples, while relaxing to subtle DJ beats. A top spot for a late-night feed, as the kitchen stays open until 11pm.

Elephant Bar BAR
(Map p184; Raffles Hotel Le Royal, St 92; ⌚noon-midnight; 📶) Few places are more atmospheric than this sophisticated bar at the Raffles. It has been drawing journalists, politicos, and the rich and famous for more than 90 years. Singapore slings and many more drinks are half-price during the generous happy hour (4pm to 9pm). The bar also boasts world-class G&Ts.

Brown Coffee CAFE
(Map p188; www.browncoffee.com.kh; cnr Sts 294 & 57; ⌚6.30am-9pm; 📶) The flagship outlet of a homegrown coffee chain that has outperformed all the expensive imports to produce some of Phnom Penh's most refined spaces and best coffee. There are lots of branches around town, as the company has set its sights on cracking Cambodia and, possibly, Asia.

Happy Damrei CAFE
(Map p184; ☎010 227149; 1 St 174; ⌚7am-11pm; 📶) This cool little cafe is the epicentre of board games in Phnom Penh and has everything from classics such as Risk and Cluedo to contemporary offerings including Cards Against Humanity. It's US$1.50 per hour to play. Food and drinks accompany the games.

FCC BAR
(Foreign Correspondents' Club; Map p184; 363 Sisowath Quay; ⌚6am-midnight; 📶) A Phnom Penh institution, the 'F' is housed in a colonial gem with great views and cool breezes. It's one of those Cambodian classics that's still holding onto its charm, though some needed renovations were planned at the time of writing. FCC also offers an excellent food menu both day and night.

Eclipse Sky Bar ROOFTOP BAR
(Map p188; http://eclipseskybar.business.site; Phnom Penh Tower, 455 Monivong Blvd; ⌚5pm-2am) Located on the 24th floor, this open-air venue is the dry-season venue of choice for big breezes and bigger views. The menu includes cocktails, wine by the glass and beers, but you pay a premium for the dramatic location.

Score SPORTS BAR
(Map p188; ☎078 621702; www.scorekh.com; 5 St 282; ⌚8am-2am; 📶) With its cinema-sized screen and television banks on every wall, this cavernous bar is the best place to watch a big game. It's not just the usual footy and rugby, as almost all sports are catered for here. Several pool tables tempt those who would rather play than watch.

Blue Chilli GAY
(Map p184; www.facebook.com/newbluechilli; 36 St 178; ⌚5pm-2am; 📶) The owner of this long-running gay bar stages popular drag shows from Wednesday to Saturday nights at 11pm. Sunday and Monday are karaoke nights from 8pm. The drag shows, in particular, draw a mixed crowd of gay and straight visitors.

☆ Entertainment

★Traditional Dance Show PERFORMING ARTS
(Map p184; ☎017 998570; www.experience.cambodianlivingarts.org; National Museum, St 178; adult/child from US$15/9; ⌚7pm) For this must-see performance, put on daily by **Cambodian Living Arts** (CLA; Map p188; ☎023-986032; www.cambodianlivingarts.org; 128 Samdech Sothearos Blvd), artists come from CLA's incubator program and work on specific shows for up to two years. Each is set in the attractive grounds of the National Museum. There's an optional dinner-show combo ticket (from US$30) that includes a meal at nearby Friends (p190).

★Meta House ARTS CENTRE
(Map p184; www.meta-house.com; 47 St 178; ⌚9am-11pm Tue-Sun; 📶) This German-run cultural centre screens art-house films, documentaries and shorts from Cambodia and around the world at its rooftop cinema. Films are sometimes followed by Q&As with those involved. There's also a large art gallery and on-site Art Cafe, while theatre , dance and music events round out the busy cultural calendar.

Prumsodun Ok & Natyarasa DANCE
(Map p182; www.prumsodun.com; 53 St 468; 1hr show US$25; 6.30pm Sat & Sun) Cambodia's first gay dance company infuses Khmer classics with a contemporary (and LGBTIQ+) spirit at its evocative performances in the **Counterspace Theater** (Map p182; www.javacreativecafe.com/events; Java Creative Cafe) each weekend. The works displayed here aim for high art and are more along the lines of what you'd find on the international festival circuit than the tourist-pleasing affairs elsewhere in town.

Sovanna Phum Arts Association PERFORMING ARTS
(Map p182; 010 337552; www.sovannaphumshadowpuppet.com; 166 St 99; adult/child US$10/5; performances 7pm Fri & Sat) Regular traditional shadow-puppet performances and occasional classical dance and traditional drum shows are held here every Friday and Saturday night. Audience members are invited to try their hand at the shadow puppets after the 50-minute performance. Classes are available in the art of shadow puppetry, puppet making, classical and folk dance, and traditional Khmer musical instruments (from US$20).

Shopping

★Russian Market MARKET
(Psar Tuol Tom Pong; Map p182; St 155; 6am-5pm) This sweltering bazaar is the one market all visitors should come to at least once during a trip to Phnom Penh. It is *the* place to shop for souvenirs and discounted name-brand clothing. We can't vouch for the authenticity of everything, but, along with plenty of knock-offs, you'll find genuine articles stitched in local factories.

Artisans Angkor ARTS & CRAFTS
(Map p184; www.artisansdangkor.com; 12 St 13; 9am-6pm) Classy Phnom Penh branch of the venerable Siem Reap sculpture and silk specialist, which supports some 800 craftspeople across the country.

Ambre CLOTHING
(Map p184; 023-217935; www.romydaketh.net; 37 St 178; 10am-6pm) Leading Cambodian fashion designer Romyda Keth has turned this striking French-era mansion into the perfect showcase for her stunning silk collection. There is also a wide array of stylish homewares.

Daughters of Cambodia FASHION & ACCESSORIES
(Map p184; www.daughtersofcambodia.org; 321 Sisowath Quay; 9am-5.30pm Mon-Sat) An NGO that runs a range of programs to train and assist former prostitutes and victims of sex trafficking. The fashionable clothes, bags and accessories here are made with ecofriendly cotton and natural dyes by program participants.

Night Market MARKET
(Psar Reatrey; Map p184; cnr St 108 & Sisowath Quay; 5-11pm) A cooler, al fresco version of the Russian Market, this night market takes place every evening if it's not raining. Bargain vigorously, as prices can be on the high side. Surprisingly, it's probably more popular with Khmers than foreigners.

Aeon Mall MALL
(Map p188; www.aeonmallphnompenh.com; 132 Samdech Sothearos Blvd; 9am-10pm;) The swankiest mall in Phnom Penh, this Japanese-run establishment has international boutiques, several food courts and extensive dining outlets, plus a seven-screen multiplex cinema and a bowling alley.

Smateria FASHION & ACCESSORIES
(Map p188; 8 St 57; 8am-9pm) Smateria's speciality is bags, including a line of quirky kids' backpacks, made from fishing net and other recycled materials.

Monument Books BOOKS
(Map p188; www.monument-books.com; 111 Norodom Blvd; 7am-8pm) Arguably the best-stocked bookshop in town, with almost every Cambodia-related book available and a superb maps-and-travel section.

Information

DANGERS & ANNOYANCES

Phnom Penh is not as dangerous as people imagine, but it is important to take care. Armed robberies do sometimes occur, but statistically you would be very unlucky to be a victim. However, bag and smartphone snatching is a huge problem, and victims are often hurt when they are dragged off their bicycles or motorbikes.

Do not carry a bag at night, because it is more likely to make you a target. If you ride your own motorbike during the day, some police may try to fine you for the most trivial of offences, such as turning left in violation of a no-left-turn sign. The trick is not to stop in the first place by not catching their eye.

BAG & PHONE SNATCHING

Bag snatching has become a real problem in Phnom Penh, with foreigners often targeted. Hotspots include the riverfront and busy areas around popular markets, but there is no real pattern; the speeding motorbike thieves, usually operating in pairs, can strike any time, any place. Countless expats and tourists have been injured falling off their bikes in the process of being robbed. Wear close-fitting bags (such as backpacks) that don't dangle from the body temptingly. Don't hang expensive cameras around the neck and keep mobile phones close to the body or out of sight, particularly when walking along the road, crossing the road or travelling by *remork-moto (tuk tuk)* or especially by *moto*. These people are real pros and only need one chance.

The riverfront area of Phnom Penh, particularly places with outdoor seating, attracts many beggars, as do Psar Thmei and Russian Market. Generally, however, there is little in the way of push and shove.

EMERGENCY

In the event of a medical emergency, it may be necessary to be evacuated to Bangkok.

Ambulance (☎119 in emergency; ☎023-724891)

Fire (☎118 in emergency; ☎023-723555)

Police (☎117 in emergency; ☎023-726158)

INTERNET ACCESS

Pretty much all hotels, guesthouses, cafes and restaurants offer free wi-fi connections. Local SIM cards are widely available with cheap data packages, so if you are travelling with an unlocked mobile phone or tablet, sign up soon after arrival and stay connected. Internet cafes are less common since the wi-fi explosion, but the main backpacker strips – St 258, St 278 and St 172 – have a few places.

MEDICAL SERVICES

It is important to be aware of the difference between a clinic and a hospital in Phnom Penh. Clinics are good for most situations, but in a genuine emergency, it is best to go to a hospital.

Calmette Hospital (Map p182; ☎012 772789; www.calmette.gov.kh; cnr Monivong Blvd & St 80; ⏰24hr) The best of the local hospitals, with the most comprehensive services and an intensive-care unit, but it really helps to go with a Khmer speaker.

Royal Phnom Penh Hospital (Map p182; ☎023-991000; www.royalphnompenhhospital.com; 888 Russian Confederation Blvd; ⏰24hr) International hospital affiliated with Bangkok Hospital. Boasts top facilities. Expensive.

Tropical & Travellers Medical Clinic (Map p184; ☎023-306802; www.travellersmedicalclinic.com; 88 St 108; ⏰9.30-11.30am & 2.30-5pm Mon-Fri, to 11.30am Sat) Well-regarded clinic run for more than two decades by a rather brash British general practitioner.

U-Care Pharmacy (Map p184; 26 Samdech Sothearos Blvd; ⏰8am-10pm) International-style pharmacy with a convenient location near the river.

MONEY

Visa and MasterCard are the most widely accepted cards. Cash only for street vendors. There's little need to turn US dollars into riel; greenbacks are universally accepted.

Banks with ATMs and money-changing facilities are ubiquitous. Malls and supermarkets are good bets, and there are dozens of ATMs along the riverfront. You can change a wide variety of currencies into dollars or riel in the jewellery stalls around Psar Thmei and the Russian Market.

CAB Bank (Map p184; 263 Sisowath Quay; ⏰8am-9pm) Convenient hours and location, plus there's also a Western Union office here (one of several in the city).

Canadia Bank (Map p184; cnr St 110 & Monivong Blvd; ⏰8am-3.30pm Mon-Fri, to 11.30am Sat) Has ATMs around town, with a US$5 charge. At its flagship branch you can also get cash advances on MasterCard and Visa. Also represents MoneyGram.

J Trust Royal Bank (Map p184; 265 Sisowath Quay; ⏰8.30am-4pm Mon-Fri, to noon Sat) J Trust has ATMs galore all over town, including at supermarkets and petrol stations, but there is a US$5 charge per transaction.

POST

Central Post Office (Map p184; www.cambodiapost.post/en; St 13; ⏰8am-5pm) A landmark, it is housed in a French-colonial classic just east of Wat Phnom.

TOURIST INFORMATION

Visitor Information Centre (Map p188; Sisowath Quay; ⏰8am-5pm Mon-Sat; 📶) Located on the riverfront near the Chatomuk Theatre in the Yi Sang Riverside restaurant. It doesn't carry a whole lot of information. On the other hand, it does offer free internet access, free wi-fi, air-con and clean public toilets.

Getting There & Away

AIR

Phnom Penh International Airport (PNH; ☎023-862800; http://pnh.cambodia-airports.aero) is 7km west of central Phnom Penh, via Russian Confederation Blvd. Facilities include free wi-fi, a host of internationally recognisable cafes and restaurants, and some decent handicraft outlets for last-minute purchases. There are also ATMs for US-dollar withdrawals on arrival or departure.

Domestically, there are now several airlines connecting Phnom Penh and Siem Reap. **Cambodia Angkor Air** (Map p182; ☎023-666 6786; www.cambodiaangkorair.com; 206A Norodom Blvd) flies three to six times daily to Siem Reap (from US$45 to US$110 one way, 30 minutes), while **Cambodia Airways** (☎096 8525555; www.cambodia-airways.com), **JC International Airlines** (☎018 5666888; www.jcairlines.com) and **Lanmei Airlines** (Map p182; ☎023-981363; www.lanmeiairlines.com; 575 Russian Confederation Blvd) have a few flights each week from US$35 to US$75 one way. Healthy competition has driven down prices, though crowded skies have led to a rapid turnover, with new airlines rising as others fall.

BOAT

Fast boats up the Tonlé Sap to Siem Reap and down the Mekong to Chau Doc in Vietnam operate from the tourist-boat dock at the eastern end of St 104. There are no public boat services up the Mekong to Kompong Cham and Kratie.

The fast boats to Siem Reap (US$35, five to six hours) run from roughly August through March but aren't as popular as the cheaper, more comfortable bus.

BUS

All major towns in Cambodia are accessible by air-conditioned bus from Phnom Penh. Most buses leave from company offices, which are generally clustered around Psar Thmei or located near the corner of St 106 and Sisowath Quay. Buying tickets in advance is a good idea for peace of mind, although it's not always necessary.

Not all buses are created equal, or priced the same. Buses run by Capitol Tour and Phnom Penh Sorya are usually among the cheapest, while Giant Ibis and Mekong Express buses are better and pricier.

Most of the long-distance buses drop off and pick up in major towns along the way, such as Kompong Thom en route to Siem Reap, Pursat

BUS CONNECTIONS FROM PHNOM PENH

DESTINATION	DURATION (HR)	COST (US$)	COMPANIES	FREQUENCY
Bangkok	13-17	18-25	Mekong Express, Virak Buntham	early morning & late evening
Battambang (day)	6	9-11	PP Sorya, Capitol Tour	frequent
Battambang (night)	6	10-15	Virak Buntham, Capitol Tour	4 per night
Ho Chi Minh City	6-7	9-18	most companies	frequent
Kampot (direct)	4	7-10	Capitol Tour, Giant Ibis	morning & afternoon
Kampot (via Kep)	5	8	PP Sorya	frequent
Kep	4	8-10	PP Sorya, Giant Ibis	frequent to 3pm
Koh Kong	8-9	11	Virak Buntham	7.45am
Kompong Cham	3	7	PP Sorya, Capitol Tour	hourly to 3pm
Kratie	6-7	8	PP Sorya	regularly in the morning
Poipet (day)	8	9-11	Capitol Tour, PP Sorya	hourly to 2.30pm
Poipet (night)	8	13-18	Virak Buntham, Capitol Tour	at least 1 daily
Preah Vihear City	6½	8	GTF	8.30am
Siem Reap (day)	6	7-12	most companies	frequent
Siem Reap (VIP)	6	10-15	Giant Ibis, Mekong Express	regular
Siem Reap (night)	6	12-17	Virak Buntham, Giant Ibis, Mekong Express, PP Sorya	frequent 6pm-midnight
Sihanoukville	5½	9-13	most companies	frequent
Stung Treng	9	10	PP Sorya	6.45am, 7.15am, 9.45am

on the way to Battambang, or Kompong Cham en route to Kratie. However, full fare is usually charged anyway.

Express minivans are generally faster than buses on most routes, but some travellers prefer the size and space of a large bus.

To book bus tickets online, visit www.cambo ticket.com.

Capitol Tour (Map p188; ☎023-404645; www.capitoltourscambodia.com; 14 St 182) Cheap buses to popular destinations such as Siem Reap, Sihanoukville and Battambang.

Giant Ibis (Map p184; ☎096 9993333; www.giantibis.com; 3 St 106; wi-fi) 'VIP' specialist with big buses to Siem Reap, Ho Chi Minh City (Vietnam) and Kampot. All have plenty of legroom and wi-fi. A portion of profits goes towards giant ibis conservation.

GTF Express (GST; Map p184; ☎012 434373; 13 St 142) Sleeper bus specialist with trips to secondary regional destinations.

Long Phuong (Map p188; ☎097 3110999; 315 Sihanouk Blvd) Buses to Ho Chi Minh City.

Mekong Express (Map p184; ☎098 833399; www.catmekongexpress.com; Sisowath Quay) VIP buses to Ho Chi Minh City and Bangkok, plus Siem Reap.

Phnom Penh Sorya (PP Sorya; Map p184; www.ppsoryatransport.com.kh; cnr Charles de Gaulle Blvd & St 67) Bus services all over the country.

Sapaco (Map p188; ☎023-218341; www.sapaco.net.vn; 341 Sihanouk Blvd) Buses to Ho Chi Minh City.

Virak Buntham (Map p184; ☎092 666821; www.virakbuntham.com; 1 St 106) Night-bus specialist with services to Siem Reap, Sihanoukville and Koh Kong.

EXPRESS VAN

Speedy express minivans (minibuses) with 12 to 14 seats serve popular destinations such as Siem Reap, Sihanoukville and Sen Monorom. These cut travel times significantly, but they tend to be cramped and often travel at very high speeds, so are not for the faint of heart. Several of the big bus companies also run vans, most notably Mekong Express and Virak Buntham. It's a good idea to book express vans in advance.

Angkor Express (Map p184; ☎092 966669; 5 St 108)

Bayon VIP (Map p184; ☎023-966968; www.bayonvip.com; 3 St 126)

Cambodia Post (Map p184; ☎012 931255; www.cambodiapost.post; Main Post Office, St 13)

CTT Transport & Tours (Map p184; ☎023-217217; 223 Sisowath Quay)

Ekareach Express (Map p182; ☎017 910333; 98A St 230)

Kampot Express (Map p182; ☎012 555123; 2 St 215)

Kim Seng Express (Map p182; ☎012 786000; cnr Sts 336 & 230)

Mey Hong Transport (Map p182; ☎095 777966; www.meyhongbus.com; 46 St 289)

Olongpich Express (Map p182; ☎092 868782; 70 Monireth Blvd)

Seila Angkor (☎012 766976; www.seila angkorexpress.com; 13B St 47)

SHARE TAXI

Share taxis and local minibuses leave Phnom Penh for destinations all over the country. Taxis to Kampot, Kep and Takeo leave from **Psar Dang Kor** (Map p182; Mao Tse Toung Blvd), while packed local minibuses and taxis for most other

EXPRESS VAN CONNECTIONS FROM PHNOM PENH

DESTINATION	DURATION (HR)	COST (US$)	COMPANIES	FREQUENCY
Ban Lung	9-10	10-14	Virak Buntham	2-3 daily
Battambang	5	8-12	Mekong Express, Virak Buntham, Bayon VIP, Cambodia Post	regular
Kampot	3½	7-8	Kampot Express, Ekareach Express, Mekong Express, Kim Seng Express, Cambodia Post	regular
Kep	3½	6-8	Olongpich Express, Cambodia Post	7.45am
Sen Monorom	6-7	11-12	Kim Seng Express, Virak Buntham	regular
Siem Reap	5-6	8-12	Angkor Express, Bayon VIP, Mekong Express, Mey Hong, Seila Angkor, Virak Buntham	frequent
Sihanoukville	4	7-12	CTT Transport, Bayon VIP, Olongpich Express, Cambodia Post, Mekong Express, Virak Buntham	frequent

GETTING TO VIETNAM: SOUTHEASTERN BORDERS

Some nationalities require a Vietnam visa in advance and some do not require a visa. Check with the Vietnamese Embassy (p281) in Phnom Penh to see if you need a visa or not, as visas are not available on arrival. If arriving from Vietnam, Cambodia visas are available on arrival.

Phnom Penh to Ho Chi Minh City

Getting to the border The original Bavet–Moc Bai land crossing between Vietnam and Cambodia (open 8am to 8pm) has seen steady traffic for more than two decades. The easiest way to get to Ho Chi Minh City (HCMC; Saigon) is to catch an international bus (US$9 to US$15, six hours) from Phnom Penh. There are several companies making this trip.

At the border Long lines entering either country are not uncommon, but otherwise it's straightforward provided you purchase a Vietnamese visa in advance (should you require one).

Moving on If you are not on the international bus, it's not hard to find onward transport to HCMC or elsewhere.

Phnom Penh to Chau Doc

The most scenic way to end your travels in Cambodia is to sail the Mekong to Kaam Samnor (about 100km south-southeast of Phnom Penh), cross the border to Vinh Xuong in Vietnam, and proceed to Chau Doc overland or on the Tonlé Bassac River via a small channel. Chau Doc has onward land and river connections to points in the Mekong Delta and elsewhere in Vietnam.

Various companies do trips all the way through to Chau Doc using a single boat or some combination of bus and boat; prices vary according to speed and level of service, but all boats depart from Phnom Penh's tourist-boat dock. Both Capitol Tour and **Hang Chau** (Map p184; ☎088 8787871; www.hangchautourist.vn) have services departing at 12.30pm, charging US$29 and US$25 respectively. The entire journey is by boat and lasts about five hours.

The more upmarket and slightly faster **Blue Cruiser** (Map p184; ☎016 824343; www.bluecruiser.com; US$35) departs at 1pm; **Victoria Chau Doc Hotel** (Map p184; www.victoriahotels.asia; US$95) also has a boat making several runs a week between Phnom Penh and its Chau Doc hotel. These companies take about four hours, including a slow border check, and use a single boat to Chau Doc. Backpacker guesthouses and tour companies sometimes offer cheaper bus/boat combo trips, though these are becoming increasingly less common.

Takeo to Chau Doc

Getting to the border The remote and seldom-used Phnom Den–Tinh Bien border crossing (open 6am to 6pm) between Cambodia and Vietnam lies 47km southeast of Takeo town in Cambodia and offers connections to Chau Doc. Most travellers prefer the Mekong crossing at Kaam Samnor or the Prek Chak crossing near Ha Tien to the south. Take a share taxi (US$5), a chartered taxi (US$25) or a *moto* (US$15) from Takeo to the border. Entering Cambodia from Vietnam, expect to pay US$10/20 for a *moto* from the border to Kirivong/Takeo.

At the border Several nationalities can get 15-day Vietnam visas on arrival; everyone else needs to arrange one in advance. Coming into Cambodia from Vietnam, note that e-visas are not accepted for entry here.

Moving on Travellers are at the mercy of Vietnamese *xe om (moto)* drivers and taxis for the 30km journey from the border to Chau Doc. Prepare for some tough negotiations. Expect to pay US$10 to US$12.50 for a *moto*, and US$20 for a taxi.

places leave from the northwest corner of **Psar Thmei** (Map p184; cnr Sts 120 & 126). Vehicles for the Vietnam border leave from Chbah Ampeau taxi park, on the eastern side of Monivong Bridge in the south of town. You may have to wait awhile (possibly until the next day if you arrive in the afternoon) before your vehicle fills up, or pay for the vacant seats yourself.

TRAIN

Phnom Penh's train station is located at the western end of St 106 and St 108, in a grand old colonial-era building. Passenger train services returned to Cambodia in 2016 with weekend trains from Phnom Penh to Kampot and Sihanoukville. **Royal Railway** (Map p184; ☎078 888583; www.royal-railway.com; St 106; ⏱6am-8pm) runs trains in either direction, departing Phnom Penh or Sihanoukville at 7am on Saturday and Sunday, with an additional afternoon train on Sunday at 4pm. There are also morning trains departing from Phnom Penh at 7am on Friday and from Sihanoukville at 7am on Monday. Phnom Penh to Sihanoukville is US$8, taking seven hours. Phnom Penh to Kampot is US$7, taking five hours.

Trains to Poipet, on the border with Thailand, hit the rails in 2018, with hopes of creating a seamless service from Phnom Penh to Bangkok in the near future. The trip takes 12 hours all the way to Poipet (US$7) and nine to Battambang (US$5), with departures from Phnom Penh on Friday and Sunday and departures from Poipet on Saturday and Monday. All trains leave at 7am.

ℹ Getting Around

GETTING TO/FROM THE AIRPORT

When arriving by air at Phnom Penh International Airport, there is an official booth outside the airport arrivals area to arrange taxis to the centre for US$12; a *remork* costs a flat US$9. You can get a *remork* for US$5 to US$7 and a *moto* (motorcycle taxi) for about US$3 if you exit the airport and arrange one on the street.

Even cheaper is Line 3 on the city's bus system, which passes by the airport and will take you into town, with stops at Psar Thmei and Wat Phnom (1500r, 5am to 8.30pm). It can be slow with 20 or more stops along the way, but then so can taxis with all the traffic.

The **KKStar Shuttle Bus** (☎023-688 5858; www.facebook.com/KKStarBus; US$5) is another option. It departs from the airport every 30 to 60 minutes from 9am to 7.45pm, making seven stops before terminating at the Sofitel near Aeon Mall. Royal Railways (p200) also operates a shuttle train from the airport to downtown Phnom Penh (US$2.50, 30 minutes, every 30 minutes).

Heading to the airport from central Phnom Penh, a taxi/*remork moto* will cost about US$10/6/3. The journey usually takes between 30 minutes and one hour depending on the traffic, but can take up to 90 minutes during rush hour.

BICYCLE

It's possible to hire bicycles at some of the guesthouses around town for about US$1 to US$2 a day, but take a look at the chaotic traffic conditions before venturing forth. Once you get used to the anarchy, it can be a fun way to get around.

CAR & MOTORCYCLE

Car hire is available through travel agencies, guesthouses and hotels in Phnom Penh. Everything from cars (from US$30) to 4WDs (from US$60) is available for travelling around the city, but prices rise fast once you venture beyond. Most visitors who are not used to driving in Southeast Asia opt to hire a car and driver as it's not that much more expensive.

Exploring Phnom Penh and the surrounding areas on a motorbike is a very liberating experience if you are used to chaotic traffic conditions. There are numerous motorbike-hire places around town. A 100cc Honda costs US$4 to US$7 per day and 250cc dirt bikes run from US$13 to US$30 per day. You'll have to leave your passport – a driver's licence or other form of ID isn't enough.

Lucky! Lucky! (Map p188; ☎023-212788; luckymotorcyclerental@yahoo.com; 413 Monivong Blvd) Motorbikes are US$4 to US$7 per day, less for multiple days. Trail bikes from US$13.

Two Wheels Only (Map p182; ☎012 200513; www.facebook.com/motorbikehire; 34C St 376) Has well-maintained bikes available to rent (motorbike/trail bike per day US$6/25), but call or email first as the entry gate is often closed.

Vannak Bikes Rental (Map p184; ☎012 220970; 46 St 130) Has high-performance trail bikes up to 1500cc for US$15 to US$50 per day, and smaller motorbikes for US$5 to US$7.

TUK TUK, MOTO & CYCLO

Tuk tuks come in two forms in Phnom Penh. The more traditional *remork-motos* are motorbikes with carriages. These have historically been the main way of getting around for tourists. Average fares are about double those of *motos* (motorcycle taxis): US$2 for short rides around the centre, US$3 and up for longer trips.

Newer, partly electric-powered Indian-style auto-rickshaws are now widely used on the streets of Phnom Penh. Most work for Uber-like ride-hailing apps, including **PassApp** (www.

passapptaxis.com) and **Grab** (www.grab.com/kh). These apps tend to offer cheaper rates than you'll get on your own, plus you don't have to deal with tough negotiations.

In areas frequented by foreigners, *moto* drivers generally speak English and sometimes a little French. Elsewhere around town, it can be difficult to find anyone who understands where you want to go. Most short trips are about 2000r to 3000r, although if you want to get from one end of the city to the other, you have to pay US$1 or more.

Travelling by *cyclo* (bicycle rickshaw) is less common these days. It's certainly a more relaxing way to see the sights in the centre of town, but this option doesn't work well for long distances. For a day of sightseeing, expect to pay around US$12 – find one on your own or negotiate a tour through the **Cyclo Conservation & Careers Association** (Map p184; ☎097 7009762; cyclocca@gmail.com; 9 St 158; per hour/day from US$3/12).

TAXI

At 4000r per kilometre, taxis are cheap, but don't expect to flag one down on the street. Call **Global Meter Taxi** (011 311888), **Choice Taxi** (010 888010, 023-888023) or **Taxi Vantha** (012 855000) for a pickup.

Ride-hailing apps are now widely used in Phnom Penh and can often be simpler to manage for tourists. Among the best are **PassApp** (www.passapptaxis.com) and **Grab** (www.grab.com/kh). Both can link you up with standard taxis, while PassApp also has an SUV option.

AROUND PHNOM PENH

Koh Dach

Known as 'Silk Island' by foreigners, Koh Dach (កោះដាច់) is actually a pair of islands lying in the Mekong River about 5km northeast of the Japanese Friendship Bridge. They make an easy, half-day DIY excursion for those who want to experience the 'real Cambodia'. The hustle-bustle of Phnom Penh feels light years away here.

The name derives from the preponderance of silk weavers who inhabit the islands. When you arrive by ferry, you may be approached by one or more smiling women who speak a bit of English and will invite you to their house to observe weavers in action and – they hope – buy a *krama* (checked scarf), sarongs or other silk items. If you are in the market for silk, you might follow them and have a look. Otherwise, feel free to smile back and politely decline their offer. You'll see plenty of weavers as you journey around the islands.

Tuk tuk drivers offer half-day tours to Koh Dach; US$20 should cover it (less if you just want to be dropped off at the ferry), but they have been known to charge as much as US$40. The daily boat tours (p183), departing at 9am and 11am from the tourist-boat dock, are another option (minimum three people). Cyclists can ride over with guides from Grasshopper Adventures (p182).

Tonlé Bati

Tonlé Bati (ទន្លេបាទី; incl lake & temples US$3) is the collective name for a pair of old Angkorian-era temples, **Ta Prohm** (តាព្រហ្ម) and **Yeay Peau** (យាយពៅ), and a popular lakeside picnic area. It's worth a detour if you are on the way from the capital to Phnom Tamao and Phnom Chisor.

You can eat at one of many picnic restaurants set on stilts over the water (the local delicacy is frog legs!) and hire an inner tube to float around the lake for 2000r. Just avoid Tonlé Bati at weekends, when it's mobbed with locals. Renting a motorbike or car from Phnom Penh is the easiest way to get here.

The access road heading to Tonlé Bati is signposted on the right on NH2, 33km south of Independence Monument in Phnom Penh. The entrance to the complex is 1.8km from the highway.

Most people hire private transport to get here. Figure on US$12/25 return for a *moto/remork* from Phnom Penh. Add US$5 to combine with Phnom Tamao, and more still to throw Phnom Chisor into the mix.

Phnom Tamao Wildlife Rescue Centre

This wonderful **wildlife sanctuary** (មជ្ឈមណ្ឌលសង្គ្រោះសត្វព្រៃភ្នំតាម៉ៅ; adult/child US$5/2; ⏲8.30am-4.30pm; 👪) 🍃 for rescued animals is home to gibbons, sun bears, elephants, tigers, lions, deer, enormous pythons and a massive bird enclosure. They were all taken from poachers or abusive owners and receive care and shelter here as part of a sustainable breeding program. Wherever possible, animals are released back into the wild once they have recovered.

The sanctuary occupies a vast site south of the capital and its animals are kept in excellent conditions by Southeast Asian standards, with plenty of room to roam in enclosures that have been improved and expanded over the years with help from Wildlife Alliance, Free the Bears and other international wildlife NGOs. Spread out as it is, it feels like a zoo crossed with a safari park.

The centre operates breeding and release programs for a number of globally threatened species, including pileated gibbons, smooth-coated otters and Siamese crocodiles, and provides a safe home to other iconic species, such as tigers and the gentle giants – Asian elephants. The centre is also home to the world's largest captive collection of Malayan sun bears, and you'll find a walk-through area with macaques, deer and a huge aviary.

Cambodia's wildlife is usually very difficult to spot, as larger mammals inhabit remote areas of the country, so Phnom Tamao is the perfect place to discover more about the country's incredible variety of animals. If you don't like zoos, you might not like this wildlife sanctuary, but remember that these animals have been rescued from traffickers and poachers and need a home. Visitors who come here will be doing their own small bit to help in the protection and survival of Cambodia's varied wildlife.

Both Wildlife Alliance and Free the Bears offer more-exclusive experiences at Phnom Tamao for fixed donations. **Wildlife Alliance** (☎095 970175; www.wildlifealliance.org; minimum donation US$150) offers a behind-the-scenes tour, which includes access to feeding areas and the nursery area. **Free the Bears** (☎092 434597; www.freethebears.org; per person US$90) has a 'Bear Care Tour', which allows guests to help out the on-site team for the day. These tours include transport from Phnom Penh. Otherwise, the easiest option is a rental motorbike or car from Phnom Penh in combination with Tonlé Bati or Phnom Chisor.

Phnom Chisor

A temple from the Angkorian era, **Phnom Chisor** (ភ្នំជីសូរ; US$2; ⏲7.30am-5pm) is set upon a solitary hill in Takeo Province, offering superb views of the countryside. Try to get here early in the morning or late in the afternoon, as it is an uncomfortable climb in the heat of the midday sun. Phnom Chisor lies about 55km south of Phnom Penh.

The main temple stands on the eastern side of the hilltop. Constructed of laterite and brick with carved sandstone lintels, the complex is surrounded by the partially ruined walls of a 2.5m-wide gallery with windows. Inscriptions found here date from the 11th century, when this site was known as Suryagiri.

If you haven't got the stamina for an overland adventure to Preah Vihear or Phnom Bayong (near Takeo), this is the next best thing for a temple with a view. Near the main temple is a modern Buddhist *vihara* (temple sanctuary), which is used by resident monks.

Renting a motorbike in Phnom Penh is one of the most enjoyable ways to get here in combination with Tonlé Bati or Phnom Tamao Wildlife Rescue Centre. Booking a share taxi is a comfortable option in the wet or hot seasons or you can take a Takeo-bound bus to the access road, about 49km south of Phnom Penh, and arrange a *moto* (motorcycle taxi) from there.

Udong

Another popular offering among Phnom Penh touts is a visit to Udong, which served as Cambodian capital under several sovereigns, although many people visit here for the retreats, including the **Cambodia Vipassana Dhura Buddhist Meditation Center** (☎contact Mr Um Sovann 016 883090; www.cambodiavipassanacenter.com; donation per person incl breakfast & lunch US$25).

Foreigners are welcome to practise meditation here with experienced monks or nuns for one or several days. Free meditation sessions are held daily from 7am to 9am and from 2pm to 5pm. In between you can hang out in the library, which contains scores of books on Buddhism, not to mention an impressive collection of pirated Lonely Planet books.

The en suite guestrooms are fairly comfortable by monastic standards, albeit sans mattresses (wicker mats are as good as it gets). You'll be fed breakfast and lunch, but no dinner. There is no fixed price for a meditative retreat here, so donate according to your means; US$25 per day would be considered about average.

The centre is near the base of the western staircase up Phnom Preah Reach Throap.

Kirirom National Park

You can really get away from it all at this lush, elevated national park a two-hour drive southwest of Phnom Penh. Winding trails lead through pine forests to cascading wet-season waterfalls and cliffs with amazing views of the Cardamom Mountains, and there's some great mountain-biking to be done if you're feeling adventurous.

Up in the actual national park, you'll find myriad walking trails and dirt roads that lead to small wet-season waterfalls, lakes, wats and abandoned buildings, but you'll need a map or a guide to navigate them. There's a great map of the park trails and roads made by a Phnom Penh–based mountain-bike enthusiast if you can track down a copy.

From NH4, it's 10km on a sealed road to a small village near the park entrance. From the village you have two choices: the left fork takes you 50m to the park entrance and then 17km up a fairly steep sealed road to the unstaffed Kirirom Information Centre inside the national park; the right fork takes you 10km along the perimeter of the park on a dirt road to Chambok commune, the site of an excellent **community-based ecotourism program** (CBET; ☎012 698529; touchmorn@gmail.com; adult/child US$3/1). These are two vastly different experiences, and they are nowhere near each other, so it's recommended to devote a day to each.

The easiest way to get to Kirirom National Park is via a rental motorbike from Phnom Penh or by chartering a share taxi for a day trip, which will cost in the region of US$80 round trip.

SIEM REAP

☎063 / POP 195,000 (CITY)

The life-support system and gateway for the temples of Angkor, Siem Reap (*see*-em ree-*ep;* សៀមរាប) was always destined for great things. Visitors come here to see the temples, of course, but there is plenty to do in and around the city when you're templed out. Siem Reap has reinvented itself as the epicentre of chic Cambodia, with everything from backpacker party pads to hip hotels, world-class wining and dining across a range of cuisines, sumptuous spas, great shopping, local tours to suit both foodies and adventurers, and a creative cultural scene that includes Cambodia's leading contemporary circus.

Angkor is a place to be savoured, not rushed, and this is the base from which to plan your adventures. Still think three days at the temples is enough? Think again, with Siem Reap on the doorstep.

Sights

★Angkor National Museum — MUSEUM

(សារមន្ទីរជាតិ អង្គរ; Map p204; ☎063-966601; www.angkornationalmuseum.com; 968 Charles de Gaulle Blvd; adult/child under 12 US$12/6; 8.30am-6pm May-Sep, to 6.30pm Oct-Apr) Looming large on the road to Angkor is the Angkor National Museum, a state-of-the-art showpiece on the Khmer civilisation and the majesty of Angkor. Displays are themed by era, religion and royalty as visitors move through the impressive galleries. After a short presentation, visitors enter the Zen-like Gallery of a Thousand Buddhas, which has a fine collection of images. Other exhibits include the pre-Angkorian periods of Funan and Chenla; the great Khmer kings; Angkor Wat; Angkor Thom; and the inscriptions.

Exhibits include touch-screen videos, epic commentary and the chance to experience a panoramic sunrise at Angkor Wat. Although there appears to be less sculpture on display than in the National Museum in Phnom Penh, the presentation of the artefacts here is cutting edge.

As the museum is entirely air-conditioned, plan a visit during the middle of the day to avoid the sweltering midday temperatures at the temples of Angkor. Allow about two hours to visit the museum in depth.

★Artisans Angkor – Les Chantiers Écoles — ARTS CENTRE

(អាទីសង់អង្គរ; Map p204; www.artisansdangkor.com; 7.30am-6.30pm) FREE Siem Reap is the epicentre of the drive to revitalise Cambodian traditional culture, which was dealt a harsh blow by the Khmer Rouge and the years of instability that followed its rule. Les Chantiers Écoles teaches wood- and stone-carving techniques, traditional silk painting, lacquerware and other artisan skills to impoverished young Cambodians. Free guided tours explaining traditional techniques are available daily from 7.30am to 6.30pm. Tucked down a side road, the school is well signposted from Sivatha St.

Siem Reap

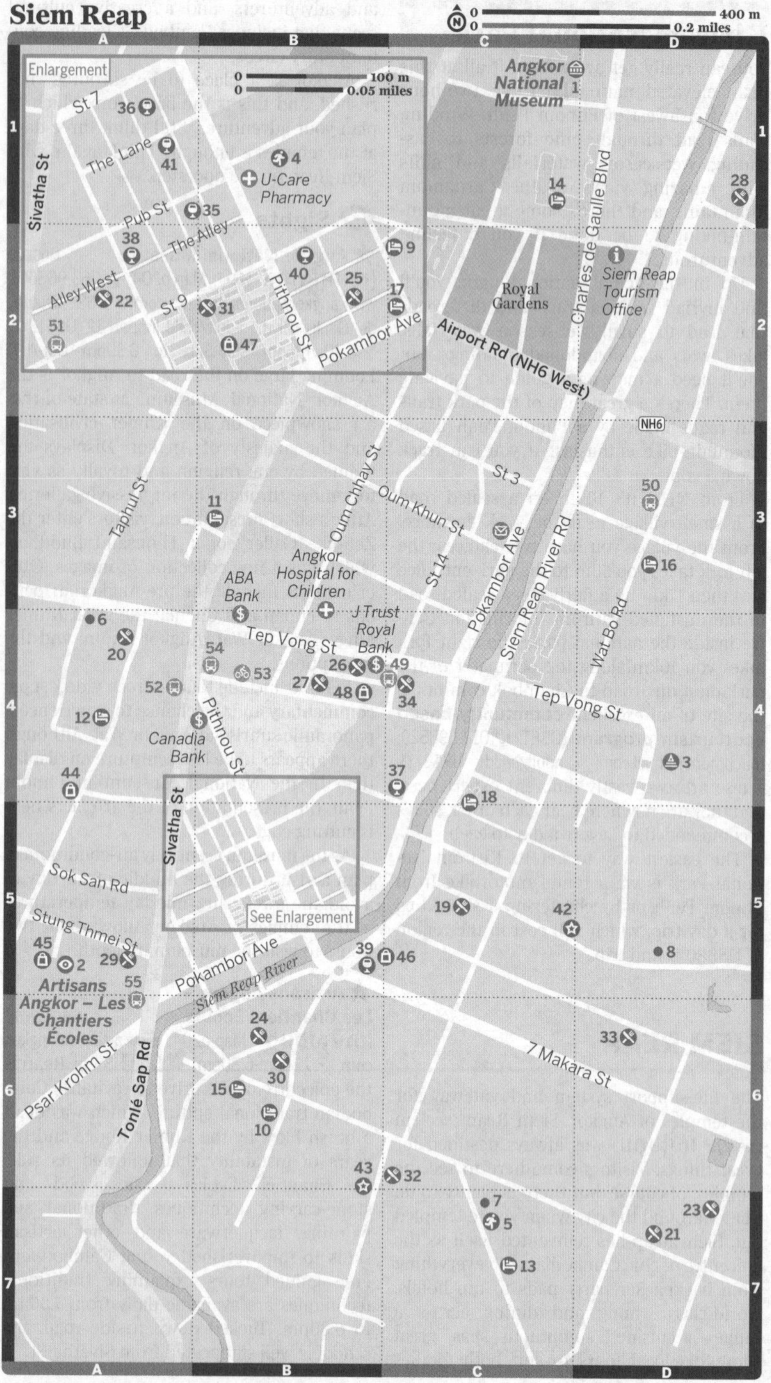
0 400 m
0 0.2 miles
Enlargement
0 100 m
0 0.05 miles
St 7
36
The Lane
41
4
U-Care Pharmacy
Sivatha St
Pub St
35
38
The Alley
40
9
25
17
Alley West
22
St 9
31
Pithnou St
51
47
Pokambor Ave
Angkor National Museum
1
14
Charles de Gaulle Blvd
28
Siem Reap Tourism Office
Royal Gardens
Airport Rd (NH6 West)
NH6
St 3
50
11
Taphul St
Oum Chhay St
Oum Khun St
St 14
16
Angkor Hospital for Children
ABA Bank
J Trust Royal Bank
Pokambor Ave
Siem Reap River Rd
Wat Bo Rd
6
20
Tep Vong St
54
53
26
49
27
48
34
52
12
Canadia Bank
Pithnou St
3
44
37
18
Sivatha St
Sok San Rd
19
42
Stung Thmei St
See Enlargement
8
45
2
29
39
46
Pokambor Ave
Siem Reap River
55
Artisans Angkor – Les Chantiers Écoles
24
33
7 Makara St
Psar Krohm St
30
15
Tonlé Sap Rd
10
43
32
7
5
23
21
13
A
B
C
D
1
2
3
4
5
6
7

Siem Reap

Top Sights
1 Angkor National Museum C1
2 Artisans Angkor – Les Chantiers Écoles A5

Sights
3 Wat Bo D4

Activities, Courses & Tours
4 Bodia Spa B1
5 Cambodia Bird Guide Association C7
6 Off Track Tours A4
7 Osmose C7
8 Sam Veasna Center D5

Sleeping
9 1920 Hotel C2
10 Downtown Siem Reap Villa B6
11 Mad Monkey B3
12 Onederz Hostel A4
13 Pomme C7
14 Raffles Grand Hotel d'Angkor C1
15 Rambutan Resort B6
16 Seven Candles Guesthouse D3
17 Shadow of Angkor Residence C2
18 Treeline Urban Resort C4

Eating
19 Banllé Vegetarian Restaurant C5
20 Bugs Cafe A4
21 Cuisine Wat Damnak D7
22 Gelato Lab A2
23 Haven D7
24 Jomno Street Food B6
25 Le Malraux B2
26 Little Red Fox B4
27 Mamma Shop B4
28 Marum D1
29 Pot & Pan Restaurant A5
30 Pou Kitchen B6
31 Psar Chaa B2
32 Spoons Cafe C6
33 Sugar Palm D6
34 Vibe Cafe C4
Village Cafe .... (see 26)

Drinking & Nightlife
35 Angkor What? A1
36 Asana Wooden House A1
37 Barcode C4
38 Beatnik Bar A2
39 Hard Rock Cafe B5
40 Laundry Bar B2
41 Miss Wong A1

Entertainment
42 Apsara Theatre C5
43 Bambu Stage B6

Shopping
44 Angkor Night Market A4
45 Artisans Angkor A5
46 Made in Cambodia Market C5
47 Psar Chaa B2
Soieries du Mekong .... (see 48)
48 trunkh B4

Transport
49 Asia Van Transfer C4
50 Bayon VIP D3
51 Capitol Tour A2
52 Giant Ibis A4
53 Green e-bikes B4
54 Mekong Express B4
55 Virak Buntham A6

★**Apopo Visitor Centre** VISITOR CENTRE
(មជ្ឈមណ្ឌលទស្សនាអាប៉ូប៉ូ; Map p218; 081 599237; www.apopo.org; Koumai Rd; US$5; 8.30am-5.30pm Mon-Sat) Meet the hero rats that are helping to clear landmines in Cambodia. Apopo has trained the highly sensitive, almost-blind Gambian pouched rat to sniff explosives, which dramatically speeds up the detection of mines in the countryside. The visitor centre gives background on the work of Apopo, with a short video and the chance to meet the rats themselves.

★**Cambodia Landmine Museum** MUSEUM
(សារមន្ទីរគ្រាប់មីនកម្ពុជា និងមូលនិធិសង្គ្រោះ; www.cambodialandminemuseum.org; NH67; US$5; 7.30am-5pm) Established by DIY deminer Aki Ra, this museum has eye-opening displays on the curse of landmines in Cambodia. The collection includes mines, mortars, guns and weaponry, and there is a mock minefield where visitors can attempt to locate the deactivated mines. Proceeds from the museum are ploughed into mine-awareness campaigns. The museum is about 25km from Siem Reap, near Banteay Srei.

Banteay Srei Butterfly Centre WILDLIFE RESERVE
(សួនមេអំបៅបន្ទាយស្រី; www.angkorbutterfly.com; NH67; adult/child US$5/2; 9am-5pm) The Banteay Srei Butterfly Centre is one of the largest fully enclosed butterfly centres in Southeast Asia, with more than 30 species of Cambodian butterflies fluttering about. It is a good experience for children, as they can see the whole life cycle from egg to caterpillar to cocoon to butterfly.

War Museum MUSEUM
(សារមន្ទីរប្រវត្តិសាស្ត្រសង្គ្រាម; Map p218; ☎097 457 8666; www.warmuseumcambodia.com; Kaksekam village; incl guide US$5; ⏲8am-5.30pm) The unique selling point here is that the museum encourages visitors to handle the old weapons, from an AK-47 right through to a rocket launcher. We're not sure what health and safety think about it, but it makes for a good photo op. Other war junk includes Soviet-era T-54 tanks and MiG-19 fighters. Former soldiers act as tour guides.

Wat Bo BUDDHIST TEMPLE
(វត្តបូណ៌; Map p204; Tep Vong St; ⏲6am-6pm) FREE This is one of the town's oldest temples and has a collection of well-preserved wall paintings from the late 19th century depicting the *Reamker,* Cambodia's interpretation of the *Ramayana*. The monks here regularly chant sometime between 4.30pm and 6pm, and this can be a spellbinding and spiritual moment if you happen to be visiting.

Activities

Foot massages are a big hit in Siem Reap – not surprising given all those steep stairways at the temples. There are half a dozen or more places offering a massage for about US$6 to US$8 an hour on the strip running northwest of Psar Chaa. Some are more authentic than others, so dip your toe in first before selling your sole.

For an alternative foot massage, brave the waters of Dr Fish: you dip your feet into a paddling pool full of cleaner fish, which nibble away at your dead skin. It's heaven for some, tickly as hell for others. The original is housed in the Angkor Night Market, but copycats have sprung up all over town, including a dozen or so tanks around Pub St and Psar Chaa.

★**Bodia Spa** SPA
(Map p204; ☎063-761593; www.bodia-spa.com; Pithnou St; 1hr massage US$24-36; ⏲10am-midnight) Sophisticated spa near Psar Chaa (the Old Market) offering a full range of scrubs, rubs and natural remedies, including its own line of herbal products.

Cambo Beach Club SWIMMING
(Map p218; ☎087 466616; www.cambobeachclub.com; Steung Thmey village; per person US$3; ⏲9am-10pm; 👪) Boasting the only beach in Siem Reap, Cambo Beach Club is a great spot to hang out day or night. The centrepiece is a huge swimming pool complete with floating beanies and a high dive pool. Dining options include lip-smackin' ribs at the Dancing Pig and there is the late-night Underdog Sports Bar for big games.

There are regular DJs for weekend parties and a whole host of special offer combinations involve booze and entry such as VIP Bubbles and Chillin & Sipping.

Angkor Wat Putt GOLF
(Map p218; ☎012 302330; www.angkorwatputt.com; Chreav District; adult/child US$5/4; ⏲8am-8pm) Crazy golf to the Brits among us, this home-grown minigolf course contrasts with the big golf courses out of town. Navigate minitemples and creative obstacles for 14 holes and win a beer for a hole-in-one. Recently relocated to a more remote location, it is well worth seeking out.

Boeng Pearaing BIRDWATCHING
(☎085 303050; www.pearaing.org; entry US$10, plus boat fees; ⏲6am-6pm) This is an up-and-coming birding site based around a natural reservoir just south of the Tonlé Sap where it's possible to spot large numbers of rare pelicans, storks and ibis. It is an affordable and accessible birdwatching alternative to Prek Toal as it lies just half an hour south of downtown Siem Reap. Entry fees go towards conservation and community support.

Peace Cafe Yoga YOGA
(Map p218; ☎063-965210; www.peacecafeangkor.org; Siem Reap River Rd East; per session US$6) This popular community centre and cafe has daily morning and evening yoga sessions, including ashtanga and hatha sessions.

Happy Ranch HORSE RIDING
(Map p218; ☎012 920002; www.thehappyranch.com; trail rides US$38-95; ⏲11am-10pm) Forget the Wild West – try your hand at horse riding in the Wild East. Happy Ranch offers the chance to explore Siem Reap on horseback, taking in surrounding villages and secluded temples. This is a calm way to experience the countryside, far from the traffic and crowds.

Courses

Lily's Secret Garden Cooking Class COOKING
(☎016 353621; www.lilysecretgarden.com; off Sombai Rd; per person US$25; ⏲9am-1pm & 3-7pm) This immersive cooking class takes place in a traditional Cambodian house on

the outskirts of Siem Reap. Morning and afternoon sessions end in a three-course lunch or dinner. The price includes pick-up and drop-off in town at the **Hard Rock Cafe** (Map p204; ☎063-963964; www.hardrock.com/cafes/angkor; Siem Reap River Rd East; ⏰11am-midnight; 📶), as the 'secret garden' cannot be revealed online.

Tours

★Siem Reap Food Tours FOOD & DRINK
(☎012 505542; www.siemreapfoodtours.com; per person US$75) Established by an American food writer and an experienced Scottish chef, these tours continue to be a recipe for engaging food encounters despite the founders having moved on. Choose from a morning tour that takes in local markets and the *naom banchok* (thick rice noodles) stalls of Preah Dak, or an evening tour that takes in street stalls and local barbecue restaurants.

★Off Track Tours CYCLING
(Map p204; ☎093 903024; www.kko-cambodia.org; Taphul St; tours US$35-60) Cycling and *moto* tours around the paths of Angkor or into the countryside beyond the Western Baray. Proceeds go towards the Khmer for Khmer Organisation, which supports education and vocational training.

★Sam Veasna Center BIRDWATCHING
(SVC; Map p204; ☎092 554473; www.samveasna.org; St 26; per person from US$100) Sam Veasna Center, in the Wat Bo area of Siem Reap, is the authority on birdwatching in Cambodia, with professionally trained English-speaking guides, powerful spotting scopes and a network of camps and bird hides scattered throughout north Cambodia. It uses ecotourism to provide an income for local communities in return for a ban on hunting and cutting down the forest.

Locally, SVC's most popular trip is to the spectacular Prek Toal Bird Sanctuary (p216) in the Tonlé Sap wetland area. All tours include transport, entrance fees, guides, breakfast, lunch and water.

Siem Reap Vespa Adventures TOURS
(☎012 861610; www.vespaadventures-sr.com; tours per person US$75-126) The modern Vespa is a cut above the average *moto* and is a comfortable way to explore the temples, learn about local life in the countryside or check out some street food after dark, all in the company of excellent and knowledgeable local guides.

Sleeping

Siem Reap has the best range of accommodation in Cambodia. A vast number of family-run guesthouses (US$5 to US$20 per room) and a growing number of hostels cater for budget travellers. In the midrange, there's a dizzying array of good-value pool-equipped boutiques (US$30 to US$70), with something of a price war breaking out in low season. High-end options abound but don't always offer more than you'd get at the midrange.

Psar Chaa Area

Downtown Siem Reap Villa HOSTEL $
(Map p204; ☎012 675881; www.downtownsiemreaphostel.hostel.com; Wat Dam Nak area; r incl breakfast US$15-35; ❄📶🏊) The hostel has been reborn as a villa and the dorms have been reinvented as rooms, but the rates here are still inviting when you factor in the swimming pool in the garden. There is also the lively little garden drinking hole called Star Bar, which pulls in an outside crowd.

★1920 Hotel BOUTIQUE HOTEL $$
(Map p204; ☎063-969920; www.1920hotel.com; St 9; r US$50-80; ❄@📶) Set in a grand old building near Psar Chaa (the Old Market) dating from, well, we'd hazard a guess at 1920, this is a thoughtfully presented budget boutique hotel with modernist touches in the rooms. The location is great for dining and drinking options in the gentrified alleys nearby.

Shadow of Angkor Residence GUESTHOUSE $$
(Map p204; ☎063-964774; www.shadowangkorresidence.com; 353 Pokambor Ave; r US$25-55; ❄@📶🏊) In a grand old French-era building overlooking the river, this friendly place offers stylish air-conditioned rooms in a superb setting close to Psar Chaa.

Sivatha St Area

★Onederz Hostel HOSTEL $
(Map p204; ☎063-963525; www.onederz.com; Angkor Night Market St; dm US$5.50-9.50, r US$20-33; ❄@📶🏊) Winner of several 'Hoscars' (Hostelworld's Oscars), this is one of the smartest hostels in Siem Reap. Facilities include a huge cafe-bar downstairs, which

acts as a giant waiting room for all those coming and going from Siem Reap. Dorms are a little more expensive than some crash pads, but prices include access to the rooftop swimming pool.

Mad Monkey HOSTEL **$**
(Map p204; www.madmonkeyhostels.com; Sivatha St; dm US$6.50-9, r US$16-26;) The Siem Reap outpost of an expanding Monkey business, this classic backpacker has deluxe dorms with air-con and extra-wide bunk beds, good-value rooms for those wanting privacy and the obligatory rooftop bar – only this one's a beach bar!

East Bank

Seven Candles Guesthouse GUESTHOUSE **$**
(Map p204; 063-963380; www.sevencandlesguesthouse.com; 307 Wat Bo Rd; r US$20-38;) Seven Candles uses profits to help a local foundation that seeks to promote education in rural communities. Rooms include hot water, TV and fridge, plus some decorative flourishes.

Rambutan Resort RESORT **$$**
(Map p204; 063-766655; www.rambutans.info; Wat Dam Nak area; r incl breakfast US$75-100;) This atmospheric, gay-friendly resort is spread over two stunning villas, each with spacious and stylish rooms and an inviting courtyard swimming pool. It also operates two chic off-site penthouses, which are like having a private apartment.

★ **Treeline Urban Resort** BOUTIQUE HOTEL **$$$**
(Map p204; 063-961234; www.treelinehotels.com; Siem Reap River Rd East; d US$100-250;) A beautiful contemporary space from the team behind the uber-successful Brown Coffee group in Cambodia, the rooms are creatively decorated with a mix of modernity and traditional items from nature. The rooftop pool above reception offers great views across the Siem Reap River. Attached is Hok, a superb, and superbly affordable, noodle bar offering Asian fusion flavours.

Riverfront & Royal Gardens

Raffles Grand Hotel d'Angkor HOTEL **$$$**
(Map p204; 063-963888; www.raffles.com; 1 Charles de Gaulle Blvd; r incl breakfast from US$250;) This historic hotel has been welcoming guests such as Charles de Gaulle, Charlie Chaplin, Jackie Kennedy and Bill Clinton since 1932. Ensconced in opulent surroundings, you can imagine what it was like to be a tourist in the early 20th century. Rooms include classic touches and a dizzying array of bathroom gifts. It recently underwent a major refurbishment.

Further Afield

★ **Hideout Hostel** HOSTEL **$**
(Map p218; 086 418606; www.hideouthostels.asia/siem-reap; Rose Apple Rd; dm US$3-6, r per person US$10-20;) One of the many 'super' hostels that have recently opened in Siem Reap, in an alternative universe it might have been a boutique hotel. Dorms are super cheap and include free access to the pool. Rooms are pretty swish for the money and some include free-standing bathtubs. Add two free beers from 7pm and it's the real deal.

★ **Pomme** HOSTEL **$**
(Map p204; www.facebook.com/pommesiemreap; Salakamreuk Rd; dm US$5-8;) Set in a spacious Cambodian wooden house with a lush tropical garden, this is one of the most welcoming hostels in town. Air-con dorms are set behind the main building and include lockers and reading lights. The restaurant and bar attract guests and residents alike, as there is some home comfort food and nightly specials.

Pavillon Indochine BOUTIQUE HOTEL **$$**
(Map p218; 012 849681; www.pavillon-indochine.com; r US$50-125;) The Pavillon offers charming colonial-chic rooms set around a small swimming pool. The trim includes Asian antiques, billowing mosquito nets and a safe. Also included in the higher rates is a *remork* driver for the day to tour the temples, making it very good value.

★ **Phum Baitang** RESORT **$$$**
(Map p218; 063-961111; www.zannierhotels.com; Neelka Way; villas US$500-720;) This beautiful resort feels like a boutique Cambodian village. Rooms are set in spacious, elegantly furnished wooden villas, some with private pools, and all connected by extensive wooden walkways over the rice fields. The decor is very designer driftwood. Angelina Jolie stayed here for three months while shooting *First They Killed My Father*, and it's not hard to see what attracted her to the place.

★Montra Nivesha BOUTIQUE HOTEL **$$$**
(Map p218; ☎063-760582; www.montranivesha.com; 5 Krom 2; r US$60-150;) A beautiful boutique hotel that gives guests a real sense of Cambodia, Montra Nivesha is set around lush gardens and offers two swimming pools, one suited to laps and one for families. Rooms are decorated with collectables but include modern touches such as smart TV, minibar and safe. The property boasts an in-house drinking water system to cut the use of plastic.

Sala Lodges BOUTIQUE HOTEL **$$$**
(Map p218; ☎063-766699; www.salalodges.com; 498 Salakamreuk Rd; r US$190-600;) An original concept, Sala Lodges offers 11 traditional Khmer houses that have been retro-fitted inside to bring them up to the standard of a rustic boutique hotel. Enter the resort and you'll think you have stumbled upon an idyllic Cambodian village; the pool and restaurant will soon confirm you have stumbled upon a gem.

Eating

Siem Reap's dining scene is something to savour, offering a superb selection of street food, Asian eateries and sophisticated international restaurants. The range encompasses something from every continent, with new temptations regularly opening up. Sample the subtleties of Khmer cuisine in town, or indulge in home comforts prior to – or after – hitting the remote provinces. Some of the very best restaurants also put something back into community projects or offer vocational training.

★Gelato Lab ICE CREAM **$**
(Map p204; www.facebook.com/gelatolabsiemreap; 109 Alley West; 1/2 scoops US$1.50/2.50; 9am-11pm;) The great ice cream scooped up here is thanks to the state-of-the-art equipment, all-natural ingredients and – most importantly – plenty of passion courtesy of the Italian owner. Also pours some of the best hand-roasted coffee in town.

Jomno Street Food CAMBODIAN **$**
(Map p204; ☎092 762539; https://jomnostreetfood.business.site; Wat Dam Nak village; dishes US$3-7.50; 11am-10pm;) Earning rave reviews for its original flavour combinations, Jomno promotes its signature platters (from US$7.50) offering a bite-size taste of a range of dishes from the Cambodian street such as *naom banchok* noodles and Battambang sausage. Twists on the classic *amok* include a crispy chicken *amok* salad and a vegan mushroom *amok*. Highly recommended.

Pot & Pan Restaurant CAMBODIAN **$**
(Map p204; ☎017 970780; www.thepotandpanrestaurant.com; Stung Thmei St; meals US$2-5; 10am-10pm;) One of the best-value Khmer restaurants in the downtown area, Pot & Pan specialises in well-presented, authentic dishes at affordable prices. The menu includes spicy soups and subtle salads, and rice is beautifully served in a lotus leaf. Some of the cheapest pizzas in town are, somewhat surprisingly, available here.

Road 60 Night Market MARKET **$**
(Map p218; Rd 60; snacks US$1-4; 4-11pm) For a slice of local life, head to the Road 60 Night Market located on the side of the road near the main Angkor ticket checkpoint. Stallholders set up each night, and it's a great place to sample local Cambodian snacks, including the full range of deep-fried insects and barbecue dishes such as quail. Plenty of cheap beer too.

Little Red Fox CAFE **$**
(Map p204; www.thelittleredfoxespresso.com; Hup Guan St; dishes US$3-8; 7am-5pm Thu-Tue;) This foxy little cafe is incredibly popular with long-term residents in Siem Reap, who swear that the regionally sourced Feel Good coffee is the best in town. Add to that designer breakfasts, bagels, salads, creative juices and air-con, and it's easy to while away some time here. The slick upstairs wing is popular with the laptop crowd.

Banllé Vegetarian Restaurant VEGETARIAN **$**
(Map p204; www.banlle-vegetarian.com; St 26; dishes US$2.50-5; 11am-9.30pm Wed-Mon;) Set in a traditional wooden house with its own organic vegetable garden, this is a great place for a healthy bite. The menu offers a blend of international and Cambodian dishes, including a vegetable *amok* and zesty fruit and vegetable shakes.

Psar Chaa CAMBODIAN **$**
(Old Market; Map p204; mains US$1.50-5; 7am-9pm) When it comes to cheap Khmer eats, Psar Chaa market has plenty of food stalls on the northwestern side, all with signs and menus in English. These are atmospheric places for a local meal at local-ish prices. Some dishes are on display, others are freshly wok-fried to order, but most are wholesome and filling.

Bugs Cafe CAMBODIAN $

(Map p204; 017 764560; www.bugs-cafe.com; Angkor Night Market St; dishes US$4-9; 5-11pm;) Cambodians were onto insects long before the food scientists started bugging us about their merits. Choose from a veritable feast of crickets, water bugs, silkworms and spiders. Tarantula doughnuts, pan-fried scorpions, snakes – you won't forget this meal in a hurry.

★Marum INTERNATIONAL $$

(Map p204; 017 363284; www.marum-restaurant.org; Wat Polanka area; mains US$4-9.75; 11am-10.30pm;) Set in a delightful wooden house with a spacious garden, Marum serves up lots of vegetarian and seafood dishes, plus some mouth-watering desserts. Menu highlights include beef with red ants and chilli stir-fry, and mini crocodile burgers. Marum is part of the Tree Alliance group of training restaurants; the experience is a must.

★Spoons Cafe CAMBODIAN $$

(Map p204; 076 277 6667; www.spoonscambodia.org; Bambu Rd; mains US$6.25-12; 11.30am-10pm Mon-Sat;) This excellent contemporary-Cambodian restaurant supports local community EGBOK (Everything's Gonna Be OK), which offers education, training and employment opportunities in the hospitality sector. The menu includes some original flavours such as *trey saba* (whole mackerel) with coconut-turmeric rice, tiger-prawn curry and *tuk kroeung*, a pungent local fish-based broth. Original cocktails are shaken, not stirred.

★Pou Kitchen CAMBODIAN $$

(Map p204; 092 262688; www.poukitchen.com; opposite Wat Dam Nak; US$3-6.50; 11am-11pm, closed Wed;) Under the direction of homegrown chef Mengly, Pou Kitchen has taken off as one of the most popular and innovative Cambodian restaurants in town. Choose from grilled beehive salad or chicken with red ant for starters, and move on to Phnom Kulen pork-belly sausage or spicy vegetable-cake curry. Simple surrounds, but far from simple flavours.

Le Malraux FRENCH $$

(Map p204; 012 332584; www.lemalraux.com; mains US$5-15; 7am-11pm;) Stunningly located in the network of alleys east of Psar Chaa, Le Malraux is one of the best French restaurants in Siem Reap, and by night this *quartier* looks like a little corner of France. Eat or drink inside at the bar or al fresco in the street. Meals include a superb *pavê* of *boeuf* and succulent fish.

Mamma Shop ITALIAN $$

(Map p204; www.facebook.com/mammashop.italian.restaurant; Hup Guan St; mains US$5-10; 11.30am-10.30pm Mon-Sat;) A compact menu of terrific homemade pasta is the signature of this bright, friendly Italian corner bistro in the bohemian Kandal village district. Add a selection of *piadina romagnola* (stuffed flatbread), a solid wine list and delicious desserts, and this place is highly recommended.

Mahob CAMBODIAN $$

(Map p218; 063-966986; www.mahobkhmer.com; near Angkor Conservation; dishes US$3.50-15; 11am-11pm) The Cambodian word for food is *mahob,* and at this restaurant it is delicious. Set in a traditional wooden house with a contemporary twist, this place takes the same approach to cuisine as it does to decor, serving up dishes such as caramelised pork shank with ginger and black pepper, or wok-fried local beef with red tree ants. Cooking classes available.

Village Cafe FRENCH $$

(Map p204; 092 305401; www.facebook.com/villagecafecambodia; 586 Tep Vong St; mains US$5-15; 5pm-late Mon-Sat;) Bar, Bites, Beats is the motto at Village Cafe, a happening little bistro that delivers on its promise. Drop in for tapas, wholesome gastropub grub and a glass of wine or four to wash it all down. Features one of the longest bars in Siem Reap. Regular DJ events at weekends draw a crowd.

Haven FUSION $$

(Map p204; 078 342404; www.haven-cambodia.com; Chocolate Rd; mains US$4.50-8; 11.30am-2.30pm & 5.30-9.30pm Mon-Sat, closed Aug;) A culinary haven indeed. Dine here for the best of East meets West; the fish fillet with green mango is particularly zesty. Proceeds go towards helping young adult orphans make the step from institution to employment.

Sugar Palm CAMBODIAN $$

(Map p204; 012 818143; www.thesugarpalm.com; St 27; mains US$6-9; 11.30am-3pm & 5.30-10.30pm Mon-Sat;) Beautiful Sugar Palm is a a popular place to sample traditional flavours infused with herbs and spices, including delicious *char kreung* dishes.

Vibe Cafe VEGAN $$
(Map p204; 069 937900; www.vibecafeasia.com; 715 St 14; mains US$3-7; 7.30am-9pm Tue-Sun, to 4.30pm Mon;) This vegan spot serves up raw organically sourced superfood bowls and cleansing juices such as the cashew, date, Himalayan salt, vanilla bean and Ayurvedic spices concoction. If that sounds too healthy for you after partying on Pub St, try the excellent vegan desserts such as raspberry cheesecake and chocolate-ganache truffle.

Mie Cafe CAMBODIAN $$
(Map p218; 069 999096; www.miecafe-siemreap.com; near Angkor Conservation; mains US$5-14; 11am-2pm & 5.30-10pm Wed-Mon;) An impressive Cambodian eatery offering a fusion take on traditional flavours. It is set in a wooden house just off the road to Angkor and offers a gourmet set menu for US$24. Dishes include everything from succulent marinated pork ribs to squid-ink ravioli.

★**Cuisine Wat Damnak** CAMBODIAN $$$
(Map p204; 077 347762; www.cuisinewatdamnak.com; Wat Dam Nak area; 5-/6-course set menu US$29/34; 6.30-10.30pm Tue-Sat, last orders 9.30pm) Set in a traditional wooden house is this highly regarded restaurant from Siem Reap celeb chef Joannès Rivière. The menu delivers the ultimate contemporary Khmer dining experience. Seasonal set menus focus on market-fresh ingredients and change weekly; vegetarian options are available with advance notice.

Drinking & Nightlife

The transformation from sleepy overgrown village to an international destination for the jet set has been dramatic and Siem Reap is now firmly on the nightlife map of Southeast Asia. For the morning after, there are lots of cafes and coffee shops, several of which operate as social enterprises to help local causes.

★**Asana Wooden House** BAR
(Map p204; www.asana-cambodia.com; St 7; 6pm-1am;) This is a traditional Cambodian countryside home dropped into the backstreets of Siem Reap, which makes for an atmospheric place to drink. Lounge on kapok-filled rice sacks while sipping a classic cocktail made with infused rice wine. Khmer cocktail classes (US$15 per person) with Sombai spirits are available at 6pm.

★**Miss Wong** BAR
(Map p204; www.misswong.net; The Lane; 6pm-1am;) Miss Wong carries you back to chic 1920s Shanghai. The cocktails are a draw here, making it a cool place to while away an evening, and there's a menu offering dim sum. Gay-friendly and extremely popular with the well-heeled expat crowd.

★**Laundry Bar** BAR
(Map p204; www.facebook.com/laundry.bar.3; St 9; 4pm-late;) One of the most chilled, chic bars in town thanks to low lighting and discerning decor. Laundry is the place to come for electronica and ambient sounds; it heaves on weekends or when guest DJs crank up the volume. Happy hour until 9pm.

Beatnik Bar BAR
(Map p204; www.facebook.com/beatniksiemreap; The Alley; 9.30am-1.30am;) A hip little bar on the corner of The Alley, it's just far enough away from Pub St not to be drowned out by the nightly battle of the bars. Cheap drinks, friendly staff and a convivial crowd add up to a great pit stop.

Barcode GAY
(Map p204; www.barcodesiemreap.com; Wat Preah Prohm Roth St; 5pm-late;) A superstylin' gay bar that's metrosexual-friendly. The cocktails here are worth the stop, as is the regular drag show at 9.30pm. Happy hour runs from 5pm to 7pm daily.

Angkor What? BAR
(Map p204; www.facebook.com/theangkorwhatbar; Pub St; 5pm-late;) Siem Reap's original bar claims to have been promoting irresponsible drinking since 1998. The happy hour (to 9pm) lightens the mood for later when everyone's bouncing along to dance anthems, sometimes on the tables, sometimes under them. Regular DJs and live music add to the party mood.

Entertainment

★**Phare the Cambodian Circus** CIRCUS
(Map p218; 015 499480; www.pharecircus.org; cnr Ring & Sok San Rds; adult/child US$18/10, premium seats US$38/18; 8pm) Cambodia's answer to Cirque du Soleil, Phare the Cambodian Circus is so much more than a conventional circus, with an emphasis on performance art and a subtle yet striking social message behind each production. Cambodia's leading circus, performing-arts and theatre organisation, Phare Ponleu

Selpak opened its big top for nightly shows in 2013, and the results are unique, must-see entertainment.

Sacred Dancers of Angkor
DANCE
(Map p218; ☑012 772641; www.nkfc.org/sacred-dancers-of-angkor; Siem Reap River Rd East; US$30; ⊙7pm Wed & Sun) There are countless *apsara* dance shows around Siem Reap, but only the Sacred Dancers of Angkor can claim royal patronage from HRH Princess Norodom Bopha Devi, one of the most accomplished classical dancers in the kingdom. The mesmerising performance takes place in the garden of the Nginn Karet Foundation, which supports the dancers' extensive training.

Bambu Stage
THEATRE
(Map p204; ☑097 726 1110; www.bambustage.com; Bambu Rd; show US$24, incl dinner US$38; ⊙shows from 7pm Mon-Sat; ☎) Bambu Stage offers an eclectic variety of traditional entertainment, including a nightly shadow puppet show that weaves a historical tale of the Cambodian civil war. Other shows include Temples Decoded (Tuesday) and Snap (Friday), a history of Cambodian photography. The venue also hosts Cambodia Living Arts' all-female drum performance, The Call, on Wednesday, Friday and Sunday at 8pm.

Apsara Theatre
DANCE
(Map p204; ☑063-963561; www.angkorvillagehotel.asia/apsara-theatre; St 26; show US$27; ⊙7.30pm) The setting for this Cambodian classical-dance show is a striking wooden pavilion finished in the style of a wat. The price includes dinner. It tends to be packed to the rafters with tour groups.

Angkor Dynasty
LIVE PERFORMANCE
(Map p218; ☑070 888900; www.angkordynasty.cn; Charles de Gaulle Blvd; US$39-49; ⊙7.30-8.45pm) Move over Macau (and Las Vegas): the Angkor Dynasty show has come to town. This is an epic multimedia performance that tells the story of Angkor through dance, song and acrobatics, involving tens if not hundreds of Cambodian and Chinese performers. With Chinese choreographers, it is not classical Khmer dance by any means, but it is entertainment.

🛍 Shopping

Siem Reap is a hub for handicrafts with stone and wood carvings, lacquerware, silk and cotton weaving and a whole lot more. Be sure to bargain at the markets, as overcharging is pretty common. Kandal village is an up-and-coming shopping destination with boutiques, galleries, cafes and restaurants.

★Artisans Angkor
ARTS & CRAFTS
(Map p204; www.artisansdangkor.com; ⊙7.30am-6.30pm; ☎) 🌱 On the premises of Les Chantiers Écoles (p203) is this beautiful shop, which sells everything from stone and wood reproductions of Angkorian-era statues to household furnishings. It also has a second shop opposite Angkor Wat in the Angkor Cafe building, and outlets at Phnom Penh and Siem Reap international airports.

All profits from sales go back into funding the school and bringing more young Cambodians into the training programme, which is 20% owned by the artisans themselves.

★Angkor Night Market
MARKET
(Map p204; www.angkornightmarket.com; Angkor Night Market St; ⊙4pm-midnight) Siem Reap's original night market near Sivatha St has sprung countless copycats, but it remains the best and is well worth a browse. It's packed with stalls selling a variety of handicrafts, souvenirs and silks. Island Bar offers regular live music and Sombai offers infused organic rice wines for those who want to make a night of it.

★Theam's House
ART
(Map p218; www.theamshouse.com; 25 Veal St; ⊙8am-7pm) After years spent working with Artisans Angkor (p203) to revitalise Khmer handicrafts, Cambodian artist and designer Theam operates his own studio of lacquer creations and artwork. Highly original, this beautiful and creative space can be tricky to find, so make sure you find a driver who knows where it is.

Eric Raisina Couture House
FASHION & ACCESSORIES
(Map p218; ☑063-963207; www.ericraisina.com; 75-81 Charles de Gaulle Blvd; ⊙store 8am-7pm, workshop 8-11am & 1-5pm) Renowned designer Eric Raisina brings a unique cocktail of influences to his couture. Born in Madagascar, partly educated in France and resident in Cambodia, he offers a striking collection of clothing and accessories. Ask one of the staff for a tour of the workshop upstairs and see where his striking, original designs are created.

AHA Fair Trade Village
ARTS & CRAFTS
(Map p218; ☑078 341454; www.aha-kh.com; Rd 60, Trang village; ⊙10am-7pm) 🌱 For locally produced souvenirs (unlike much of the

imported stuff that turns up in Psar Chaa), drop in on this handicraft market. It's a little out of the way, but there are more than 20 stalls selling a wide range of traditional items. There's a Khmer cultural show every second and fourth Saturday of the month, with extra stalls, traditional music and dancing.

Soieries du Mekong FASHION & ACCESSORIES
(Map p204; www.soieriesdumekong.com; 668 Hup Guan St; ⌚10am-7pm) Soieries du Mekong is the Siem Reap gallery for a leading handwoven silk project based in remote Banteay Chhmar, which seeks to stem the tide of rural migration by creating employment opportunities in the village. Beautiful silk scarves and other delicate items are for sale.

trunkh GIFTS & SOUVENIRS
(Map p204; www.trunkh.com; Hup Guan St; ⌚10am-6pm) The owner here has a great eye for the quirky, stylish and original, including beautiful shirts, throw pillows, jewellery, poster art and T-shirts, plus some offbeat items such as genuine Cambodian water-buffalo bells.

Psar Chaa MARKET
(Old Market; Map p204; ⌚6am-9pm) When it comes to shopping in town, Psar Chaa is well stocked with anything you may want, and lots that you don't. Silverware, silk, wood carvings, stone carvings, Buddhas, paintings, rubbings, notes and coins, T-shirts, table mats...the list goes on. There are bargains to be had if you haggle patiently and with good humour.

Made in Cambodia Market MARKET
(Map p204; www.facebook.com/madeincambodiamarket; Siem Reap River Rd East; ⌚noon-10pm) King's Road hosts the daily Made in Cambodia community market, bringing together many of the best local craftsfolk and creators in Siem Reap, many promoting good causes.

Information

Almost all accommodation providers, restaurants, cafes and bars offer free wi-fi now, so internet cafes have mostly disappeared, other than for the 24-hour use of local online gamers.

ABA Bank (Map p204; Tep Vong St; ⌚8.30am-3.30pm Mon-Fri, to 11.30am Sat) Withdrawals are limited to US$100 per transaction, and there is a US$4 transaction fee per withdrawal.

Angkor Hospital for Children (AHC; Map p204; ☎063-963409; www.angkorhospital.org; cnr Oum Chhay & Tep Vong Sts; ⌚24hr) This international-standard paediatric hospital is the place to take your children if they fall sick. It will also assist adults in an emergency for up to 24 hours. Donations accepted.

J Trust Royal Bank (Map p204; Tep Vong St; ⌚8.30am-3.30pm Mon-Fri, to 11.30am Sat) Offers credit-card cash advances. Several branches and many ATMs (US$5 per withdrawal) are located around town.

Main Post Office (Map p204; Pokambor Ave; ⌚7am-5.30pm) Services are more reliable these days, but it doesn't hurt to see your stamps franked. Includes a branch of EMS express mail.

Royal Angkor International Hospital (Map p218; ☎063-761888; www.royalangkorhospital.com; Airport Rd) This international facility affiliated with the Bangkok Hospital is on the expensive side as it's used to dealing with insurance companies.

Siem Reap Tourism Office (Map p204; ☎063-959600; Royal Gardens; ⌚7am-5pm) Check out the swanky new office in the Royal Gardens, which includes a branch of popular Thai coffee chain Inthanin.

U-Care Pharmacy (Map p204; ☎063-965396; Pithnou St; ⌚8am-10pm) Smart pharmacy and shop similar to Boots in Thailand (and the UK). English spoken.

Getting There & Away

AIR

All international flights arrive at the **Siem Reap International Airport** (Map p218; ☎063-962400; www.cambodia-airports.com), 7km west of the town centre. Facilities at the airport include cafes, restaurants, bookshops, international ATMs and money-changing services.

There are no direct flights between Cambodia and the West, so all visitors will end up transiting through an Asian hub such as Bangkok, Kuala Lumpur or Singapore.

Domestic links are currently limited to Phnom Penh and Sihanoukville. Airlines operating domestic flights include Cambodia Angkor Air (www.cambodiaangkorair.com), Lanmei Airlines (www.lanmeiairlines.com) and JC International Airlines (www.jcairlines.com). Demand for seats is high during peak season, so book as far in advance as possible.

BOAT

There are daily express boat services between Siem Reap and Phnom Penh (US$35, five to six hours) or Battambang (US$20, four to eight hours or more, depending on the season). The boat to Phnom Penh is rather overpriced these days, given it is just as fast by road and so much cheaper. The Battambang trip is seriously scenic, but breakdowns are *very* common.

BUS

Any advertised services to Ho Chi Minh City or Pakse or the Four Thousand Islands in southern Laos invariably involve a time-consuming transfer or two. For Pakse, you're best off taking a minivan to Stung Treng and changing there – Asia Van Transfer can sort you out with this. Note that any advertised *bus* trip to Laos will invariably take a six-hour detour through Kompong Cham, with a possible overnight in Kratie. You've been warned.

All buses officially depart from the **bus station and taxi park** (Map p218), which is 3km east of town and nearly 1km south of NH6. However, tickets are available at bus offices in town, guesthouses, hotels, travel agencies and ticket kiosks. Most bus companies depart from their in-town offices or send a minibus around to pick up passengers at their place of lodging. Upon arrival in Siem Reap, be prepared for a rugby scrum of eager *moto* drivers when getting off the bus at the main bus station.

Bus companies in Siem Reap:

Asia Van Transfer (AVT; Map p204; ☎063-963853; www.asiavantransfer.com; Hup Guan St) A daily express minivan departs at 8am to Stung Treng via Preah Vihear City (Tbeng Meanchey), with onward services from Stung Treng to Don Det (Laos), Ban Lung and Kratie.

Bayon VIP (Map p204; ☎063-966968; www.bayonvip.com; Wat Bo Rd) Express minivan services to Phnom Penh.

Capitol Tour (Map p204; ☎012 830170; www.capitoltourscambodia.com; St 9) Buses to destinations across Cambodia.

Giant Ibis (Map p204; ☎095 777809; www.giantibis.com; Sivatha St) Has free wi-fi on board.

Larryta Express (Map p218; ☎016 202020; www.larryta.com; 752 NH6) Smart Ford Transit minibuses to Phnom Penh hourly throughout the day.

Liang US Express (☎081 954546; Borey Seang Nam Rd) Has some direct buses to Kompong Cham.

Mekong Express (Map p204; ☎063-963662; www.catmekongexpress.com; 14 Sivatha St) Upmarket bus company with hostesses and drinks.

Mey Hong (Map p218; ☎095 777933; NH6) Express minivans to Phnom Penh.

Nattakan (Map p218; ☎070 877727; nattakan.sr@gmail.com; Concrete Drain Rd) The first operator, and still one of the most reliable, to do direct trips to Bangkok. It's out of the way, so request a free pickup.

Phnom Penh Sorya (PP Sorya; ☎063-969097; www.ppsoryatransport.com.kh; Psar Krom Rd) Most extensive bus network in Cambodia.

Virak Buntham (Map p204; ☎017 790440; www.virakbuntham.com) The night-bus specialist to Phnom Penh and Sihanoukville.

SHARE TAXI

Share taxis and other vehicles operate along some of the main routes and these can be a little quicker than buses. Destinations include Phnom Penh (US$10, five hours), Kompong Thom (US$5, two hours), Sisophon (US$5, two hours) and Poipet (US$7, three hours). To get to the temple of Banteay Chhmar, head to Sisophon and arrange onward transport there (leave very early).

Getting Around

Many hotels and guesthouses in Siem Reap offer a free airport pickup service with advance bookings. Official taxis/*remork-motos (tuk-tuks)* are available next to the terminal for US$9/7. Book using a taxi app like Grab or PassApp and the price drops to US$5.25/3.50.

Most hotels and guesthouses can organise car hire for the day, with a going rate of US$35 and up. Foreigners are technically forbidden to rent motorcycles in and around Siem Reap, but the rules have relaxed and motorbike hire is now widely available for about US$10.

Some guesthouses around town hire out bicycles, as do a few shops around Psar Chaa, usually for US$1 to US$2 a day. Also consider

TRANSPORT CONNECTIONS FROM SIEM REAP

DESTINATION	CAR & MOTORCYCLE	BUS	BOAT	AIR
Bangkok, Thailand	8hr	US$15-28, 10hr, frequent	N/A	US$50-150, 1hr, 8 daily
Battambang	3hr	US$5-8, 4hr, frequent	US$20, 6-8hr, 7am	N/A
Kompong Thom	2hr	US$5, 2hr, frequent	N/A	N/A
Phnom Penh	4-5hr	US$6-15, 5-6hr, frequent	US$35, 5hr, 7am	US$30-120, 30min, frequent
Poipet	3hr	US$5-8, 3hr, frequent	N/A	N/A

GETTING TO THAILAND: SIEM REAP TO BANGKOK

There are a few direct services to Bangkok that do not involve a change of bus at the border, but most require a change. There are some 'night' buses to Bangkok advertised, but these are pretty pointless given the Poipet border does not open until 7am!

Nattakan is the original and still one of the most reliable operators servicing Bangkok. It has direct buses to Bangkok (US$28, 7½ hours, 8am and 9am), which include fast-track immigration at the border – potentially a big advantage during peak periods to bypass long lines.

Getting to the border By far the busiest crossing between Cambodia and Thailand, the Poipet–Aranya Prathet border crossing (6am to 10pm) is the route most people take when travelling between Bangkok and Siem Reap. It has earned a bad reputation over the years, with scams galore to help tourists part with their money, especially coming in from Thailand.

Frequent buses and share taxis run from Siem Reap and Battambang to Poipet. Don't get off the bus until you reach the big roundabout adjacent to the border post. Buying a ticket all the way to Bangkok can expedite things and save you the hassle of finding onward transport on the Thai side. There are now several bus companies that offer through-buses from Siem Reap to Mo Chit bus station in Bangkok.

At the border Be prepared to wait in sweltering immigration lines on both sides – waits of two or more hours are not uncommon, especially in the high season. Show up early in the morning to avoid the crowds, but be aware that rarely does anybody get across before 6.30am. You can pay a special 'VIP fee' (aka a bribe) of 200B on either side to skip the lines, but beware of scams and realise that you are contributing to longer wait times for everybody else. There is no departure tax to leave Cambodia despite what Cambodian border officials might tell you. Entering Thailand, most nationalities are issued 15-day visa waivers free of charge.

Coming in from Thailand, under no circumstances should you deal with any 'Cambodian' immigration officials who might approach you on the Thai side – this is a scam. Entering Cambodia, the official tourist visa fee is US$30, but it's common to be charged $35. If you don't mind waiting around, you can usually get the official rate if you politely hold firm. Procuring an e-visa (US$37) before travel won't save you any money but will lower your stress levels.

Moving on Minibuses wait just over the border on the Thai side to whisk you to Bangkok's Victory Monument (230B, four hours, every 30 minutes from 6.30am to 4.30pm). Or make your way 7km to Aranya Prathet by *tuk tuk* (100B) or *sŏrngtăaou* (pickup truck; 15B), from where there are regular buses to Bangkok's Mo Chit and Eastern stations between 5am and 3pm (229B, five to six hours). Make sure your *tuk tuk* driver takes you to the main bus station in Aranya Prathet for your 100B, not to the smaller station about 1km from the border (a common scam). The 6.40am and the 1.55pm trains (six hours) are other options to Bangkok.

electric **Green e-bikes** (Map p204; ☎095 700130; www.greene-bike.com; Central Market; per 24hr US$11; ⏲7.30am-7pm).

A *moto* with a driver will cost from US$10 per day depending on the destination. The average cost for a short trip within town is 2000r or so, and around US$1 or more to places strung out along the roads to Angkor or the airport.

Tuk tuk trips around town start from US$2, but you'll need to pay more to reach the edge of town at night. Prices rise when you add three or more people. Another type of *tuk tuk* is the auto-rickshaw, and these tend to be a bit cheaper.

AROUND SIEM REAP

Floating Village of Chong Kneas

The famous **floating village of Chong Kneas** (ចុងឃ្នាស; boat trip per person US$20, entrance fee US$3) has become somewhat of a circus in recent years. Tour groups have taken over and there are countless scams to separate tourists from their money. In-the-know travellers opt for harder-to-reach but more memorable spots such as Kompong Khleang or Prek Toal.

For all its flaws, Chong Kneas is very scenic in the warm light of late afternoon and can be combined with a sunset from the nearby hilltop temple of Phnom Krom.

Boat prices are fixed at US$20 per person, plus a US$3 entrance fee (although in practice it may be possible to pay just US$20 for the boat shared between several people). Your boat driver will invariably try to take you to an overpriced floating restaurant and souvenir shop, but there is no obligation to buy anything.

One of the best ways to visit the floating village of Chong Kneas is to hook up with the **Tara Boat** (092 957765; www.taraboat.com; per person incl lunch/dinner US$29/36), which offers all-inclusive trips with a meal aboard its converted cargo boat. Prices include transfers, entry fees, local boats, a tour guide and a two-course meal.

The *moto* to Chong Kneas from Siem Reap costs US$3 each way (more if the driver waits), or US$15 or so by taxi. The round trip, including the village visit, takes two to three hours. Alternatively rent a bicycle in town and just pedal out here, as it is a leisurely 11km through pretty villages and rice fields.

Kompong Pluk

The friendly village of **Kompong Pluk** (ភូមិអណ្តែតទឹកកំពង់ភ្លុក; boat trip per person US$20, community fee US$2) is an otherworldly place where houses are built on soaring stilts about 6m high. Nearby is a flooded forest, inundated every year when the lake rises to take the Mekong's overflow. As the lake drops, the petrified trees are revealed like something out of Grimm's Tales. Exploring this area by wooden dugout in the wet season is very atmospheric.

Best visited from July to December when there is high water in the lake, it is a very different scene in the dry season months of January to June, although it it is very rewarding to explore the dry flooded forest on foot as it looks like something out of a fairy tale.

Prices to visit have been fixed rather high, and when you add up all the separate costs, it may work out cheaper to sign up to a budget tour out of Siem Reap. If you are unlucky enough to come alone, you may be charged US$30, but have the option to link up with other independent travellers.

The most popular way to get here is via the small town of Roluos by a combination of road (about US$10/15/30 by *moto/remork/*taxi) and then boat. All said, the road-and-boat route will take up to two hours, but it depends on the season – sometimes it's more by road, sometimes more by boat. The new road brings the dry season access time to around one hour.

Kompong Khleang

One of the largest communities on the Tonlé Sap, Kompong Khleang (កំពង់ឃ្លាំង) is more of a town than the other villages, and comes complete with several ornate pagodas. Most of the houses here are built on towering stilts to allow for a dramatic change in water level. There is only a small floating community on the lake, but the stilted town is an interesting place to browse for an hour or two. Fewer tourists visit here compared with the floating villages closer to Siem Reap, so that might be a reason to visit in itself.

Kompong Khleang is about 50km from Siem Reap and not difficult to reach thanks to an all-weather road via the junction town of Dam Dek. The trip takes around an hour and costs about US$60 return by taxi; it's a longer ride by *remork-moto,* but should be around US$25 to US$30.

Prek Toal Bird Sanctuary

Prek Toal is one of three biospheres on the Tonlé Sap lake, and this stunning **bird sanctuary** (ដែនជម្រកសត្វស្លាបទឹកព្រែកទាល់; US$20; 6am-6pm) makes it the most worthwhile and straightforward of the three to visit. It's an ornithologist's fantasy, with a significant number of rare breeds gathered in one small area, including the huge lesser and greater adjutant storks, the milky stork and the spot-billed pelican. Even the uninitiated will be impressed, as these birds have a huge wingspan and build enormous nests.

During the peak season (December to early February) visitors will find the concentration of birds like something out of a Hitchcock film. As water starts to dry up elsewhere, the birds congregate here. They remain beyond February but the sanctuary becomes virtually inaccessible due to low water levels. It is also possible to visit from

September, but the bird numbers may be lower. Serious twitchers know that the best time to see birds is early morning or late afternoon and this means an early start or an overnight at Prek Toal's environment office, where there is very basic accommodation (single/double bed US$15/20).

Several ecotourism companies in Siem Reap arrange trips out to Prek Toal including the Sam Veasna Center (p207), **Cambodia Bird Guide Association** (CBGA; Map p204; ☎092-657656; www.birdguideasso.org; 203 Salakamreuk Rd; ⊙8.30am-5.30pm Mon-Fri) (CBGA), **Osmose** (Map p204; ☎063-765506; www.osmosetonlesap.net; Salakamreuk Rd; per person in group of 5/2 US$95/165) and **Prek Toal Tours & Travel** (☎077 797112; www.prektoal-tours.com; birdwatching per person in group of 5/2 US$65/128), which is run by Prek Toal villagers. Tours include transport, entrance fees, guides, breakfast, lunch and water. Binoculars are available on request, plus the Sam Veasna Center has spotting scopes that they set up at observation towers within the park. All outfits can arrange overnight trips for serious enthusiasts. Day trips include a hotel pickup at around 6am and a return by nightfall.

Trips to the sanctuary also bring you up close and personal with the fascinating floating village of Prek Toal, a much more rewarding destination than over-touristed, scam-ridden Chong Kneas closer to Siem Reap. Part of your entrance to the sanctuary goes towards educating children and villagers about the importance of the birds and the unique flooded-forest environment.

TEMPLES OF ANGKOR

Welcome to heaven on earth. Angkor (ប្រាសាទអង្គរ) is the earthly representation of Mt Meru, the Mt Olympus of the Hindu faith and the abode of ancient gods. The temples are the perfect fusion of creative ambition and spiritual devotion. The Cambodian 'god-kings' of old each strove to better their ancestors in size, scale and symmetry, culminating in the world's largest religious building, Angkor Wat.

The temples of Angkor are a source of inspiration and national pride to all Khmers as they struggle to rebuild their lives after the years of terror and trauma. Today, the temples are a point of pilgrimage for all Cambodians, and no traveller to the region will want to miss their extravagant beauty. Angkor is one of the world's foremost ancient sites, with the epic proportions of the Great Wall of China, the detail and intricacy of the Taj Mahal, and the symbolism and symmetry of the pyramids, all rolled into one.

Information

Visitors have the choice of a one-day pass (US$37), a three-day pass (US$62) or a one-week pass (US$72). The three-day passes can be used over three non-consecutive days in a one-week period while one-week passes can be used on seven non-consecutive days over a month.

In 2016, the Angkor ticket booth and main entrance moved to a new location out by the Siem Reap Convention Centre, about 2km east of the old checkpoint. Tickets are not sold at the old ticket checkpoint.

Passes include a digital photo snapped at the entrance booth, so queues can be slow at peak times. The fee includes access to all the monuments in the Siem Reap area but not the sacred mountain of Phnom Kulen (US$20) or the remote complexes of Beng Mealea (US$5) and Koh Ker (US$10).

All the major temples now have uniformed staff to check the tickets, which has reduced the opportunity for scams. These days all roads into the central temples (including Angkor Wat, Angkor Thom and Ta Prohm) have checkpoints as well; foreigners who can't produce a pass will be turned away and asked to detour around the temples between 7am and 5pm. Visitors found inside any of the main temples without a ticket will be fined a hefty US$100.

The **Khmer Angkor Tour Guide Association** (☎095 828248; www.khmerangkortourguide.com) represents all of Angkor's authorised guides. English- or French-speaking guides can be booked for from US$30 per day; guides speaking other languages, such as Italian, German, Spanish, Japanese and Chinese, are available at a higher rate as there are fewer of them.

Angkor Wat

The traveller's first glimpse of **Angkor Wat** (អង្គរវត្ត; Map p218; incl in Angkor admission 1/3/7 days US$37/62/72; ⊙5am-5.30pm), the ultimate expression of Khmer genius, is matched by only a few select spots on earth. Built by Suryavarman II (r 1112–52) and surrounded by a vast moat, Angkor Wat is one of the most inspired monuments ever

Temples of Angkor

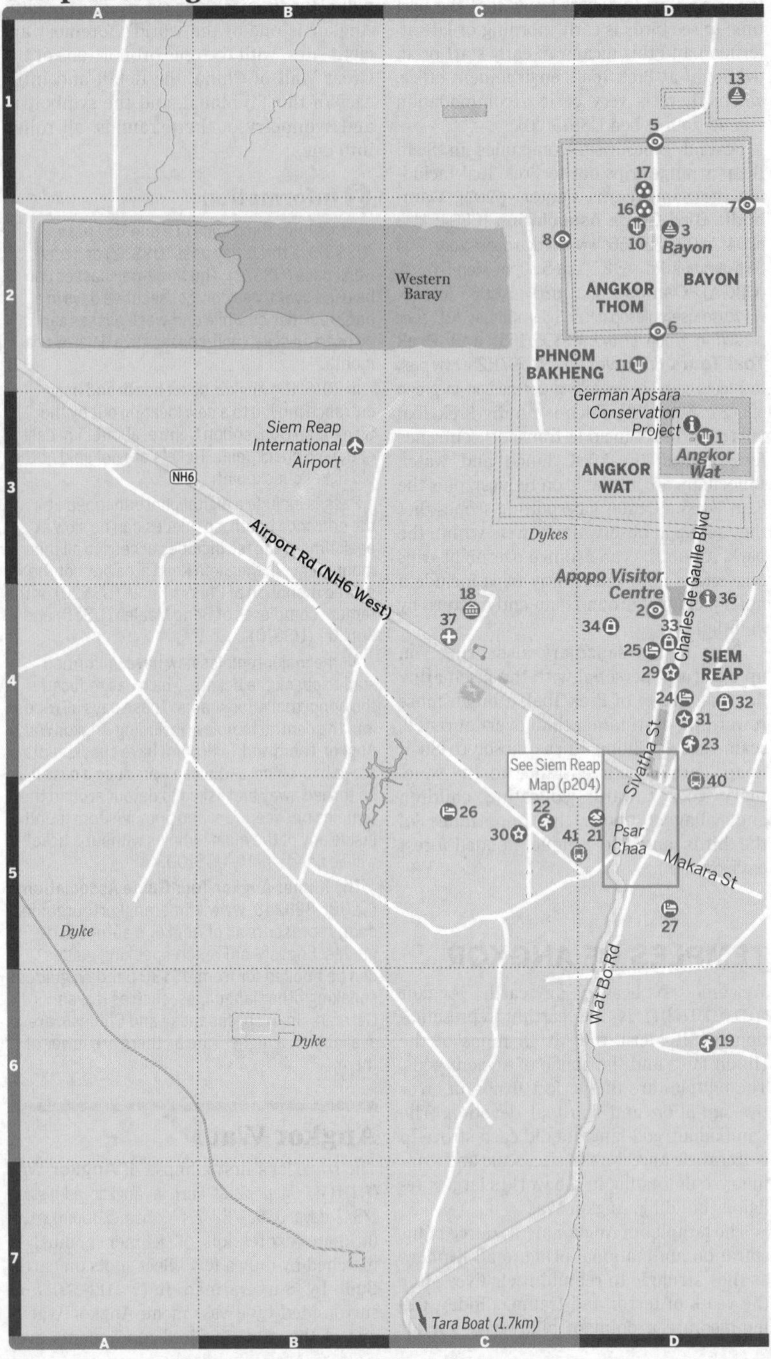

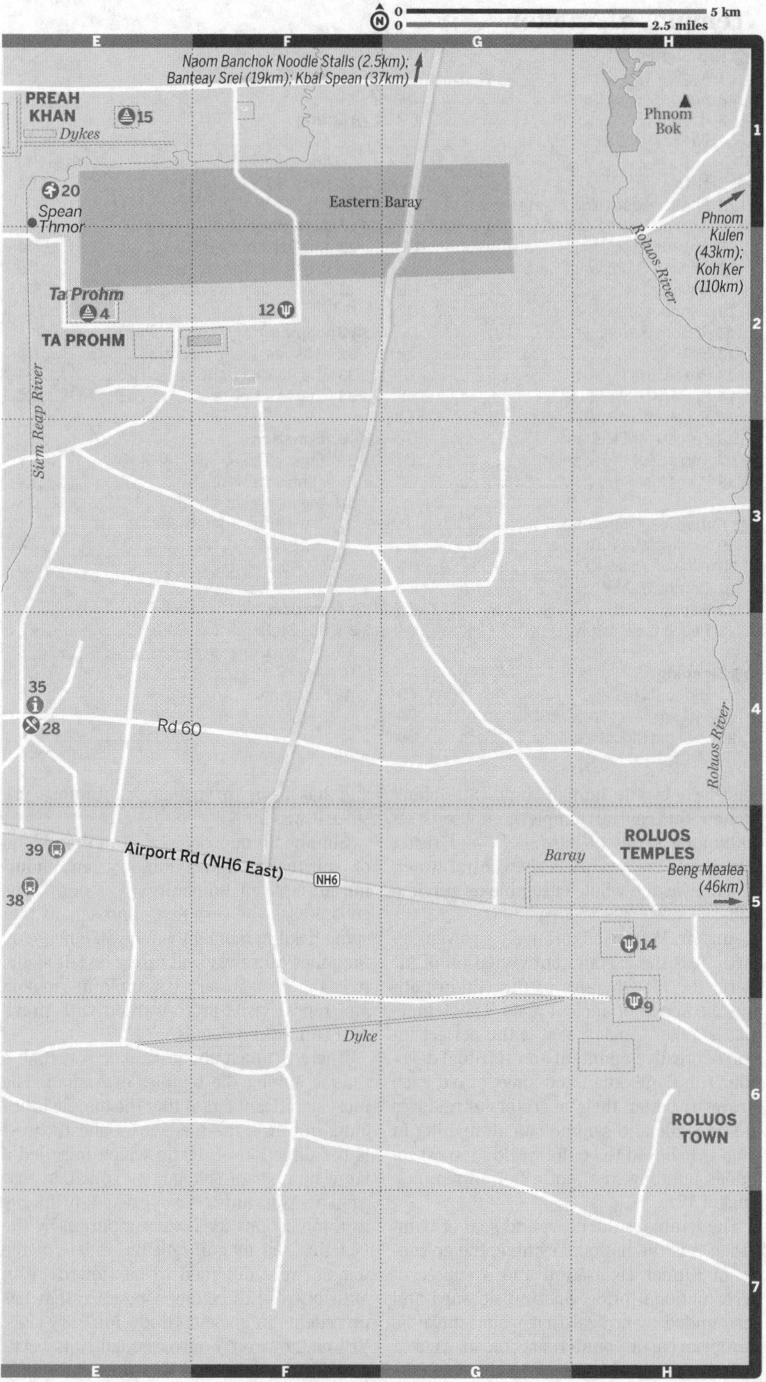
0 5 km
0 2.5 miles
E
F
G
H
Naom Banchok Noodle Stalls (2.5km); Banteay Srei (19km); Kbal Spean (37km)
PREAH KHAN
15
Dykes
Phnom Bok
20
Spean Thmor
Eastern Baray
Phnom Kulen (43km); Koh Ker (110km)
Roluos River
Ta Prohm
4
12
TA PROHM
Siem Reap River
35
28
Rd 60
Roluos River
39
38
Airport Rd (NH6 East)
NH6
Baray
ROLUOS TEMPLES
Beng Mealea (46km)
14
9
Dyke
ROLUOS TOWN
1
2
3
4
5
6
7

Temples of Angkor

Top Sights
1 Angkor Wat ... D3
2 Apopo Visitor Centre ... D4
3 Bayon ... D2
4 Ta Prohm ... E2

Sights
5 Angkor Thom North Gate ... D1
6 Angkor Thom South Gate ... D2
7 Angkor Thom Victory Gate ... D2
8 Angkor Thom West Gate ... C2
9 Bakong ... H6
10 Baphuon ... D2
11 Phnom Bakheng ... D2
12 Pre Rup ... F2
13 Preah Khan ... D1
14 Preah Ko ... H5
15 Preah Neak Poan ... E1
16 Terrace of Elephants ... D2
17 Terrace of the Leper King ... D1
18 War Museum ... C4

Activities, Courses & Tours
19 Angkor Wat Putt ... D6
20 Angkor Zipline ... E1
21 Cambo Beach Club ... D5
22 Happy Ranch ... C5
23 Peace Cafe Yoga ... D4

Sleeping
Hideout Hostel ... (see 21)
24 Montra Nivesha ... D4
25 Pavillon Indochine ... D4
26 Phum Baitang ... C5
27 Sala Lodges ... D5

Eating
Mahob ... (see 24)
Mie Cafe ... (see 24)
28 Road 60 Night Market ... E4

Entertainment
29 Angkor Dynasty ... D4
30 Phare the Cambodian Circus ... C5
31 Sacred Dancers of Angkor ... D4

Shopping
32 AHA Fair Trade Village ... D4
33 Eric Raisina Couture House ... D4
34 Theam's House ... D4

Information
35 Angkor Ticket Booth & Main Entrance ... E4
36 Angkor Ticket Checkpoint ... D4
37 Royal Angkor International Hospital ... C4
Tourist Police ... (see 35)

Transport
38 Bus Station & Taxi Park ... E5
39 Larryta Express ... E5
40 Mey Hong ... D5
41 Nattakan ... D5

conceived by the human mind. Stretching around the central temple complex is an 800m-long series of bas-reliefs, and rising 55m above the ground is the central tower, which gives the whole ensemble its sublime unity.

Angkor Wat is, figuratively, heaven on earth. It is the earthly representation of Mt Meru, the Mt Olympus of the Hindu faith and the abode of ancient gods. The 'temple that is a city', Angkor Wat is the perfect fusion of creative ambition and spiritual devotion. The Cambodian god-kings of old each strove to better their ancestors' structures in size, scale and symmetry, culminating in what is believed to be the world's largest religious building, the mother of all temples, Angkor Wat.

The temple is the heart and soul of Cambodia: it is the national symbol, the epicentre of Khmer civilisation and a source of fierce national pride. Soaring skyward and surrounded by a moat that would make its European castle counterparts blush, Angkor Wat was never abandoned to the elements and has been in virtually continuous use since it was built.

Simply unique, it is a stunning blend of spirituality and symmetry, an enduring example of humanity's devotion to its gods. Relish the very first approach, as that spine-tickling moment when you emerge on the inner causeway will rarely be felt again. It is the best-preserved temple at Angkor, and repeat visits are rewarded with previously unnoticed details.

There is much about Angkor Wat that is unique among the temples of Angkor. The most significant fact is that the temple is oriented towards the west. Symbolically, west is the direction of death, which once led a large number of scholars to conclude that Angkor Wat must have existed primarily as a tomb. This idea was supported by the fact that the magnificent bas-reliefs of the temple were designed to be viewed in an anticlockwise direction, a practice that has precedents in ancient Hindu funerary rites. Vishnu, however, is also frequently associated with the west, and it is now commonly accepted that Angkor Wat most likely served both as a temple and as a mausoleum for Suryavarman II.

Angkor Wat is famous for its beguiling *apsaras* (heavenly nymphs). Almost 2000 *apsaras* are carved into the walls of Angkor Wat, each of them unique, and there are 37 different hairstyles for budding stylists to check out. Many of these exquisite *apsaras* have been damaged by centuries of bat droppings and urine, but they are now being restored by the **German Apsara Conservation Project** (GACP; Map p218; www.gacp-angkor.de; 🕒7am-5pm).

Allow at least two hours for a visit to Angkor Wat and plan a half-day if you want to decipher the bas-reliefs with a tour guide and ascend to Bakan, the upper level, which is open to visitors on a timed ticketing system. The western causeway is currently closed to visitors for an extensive renovation and access is via a floating pontoon, which has become something of a local tourist attraction in itself.

Angkor Thom

It's hard to imagine any building bigger or more beautiful than Angkor Wat, but in Angkor Thom (អង្គរធំ, Great City; incl in Angkor admission 1/3/7 days) the sum of the parts add up to a greater whole. Set over 10 sq km, the aptly named last great capital of the Khmer empire took monumental to a whole new level.

Centred on Bayon, the surreal state temple of Jayavarman VII, Angkor Thom is enclosed by a formidable *jayagiri* (square wall), 8m high and 13km in length, and encircled by a 100m-wide *jayasindhu* (moat) that would have stopped all but the hardiest invaders in their tracks. This architectural layout is an expression of Mt Meru surrounded by the oceans.

In the centre of the walled enclosure are the city's most important monuments, including Bayon, Baphuon, the Royal Enclosure, Phimeanakas and the Terrace of Elephants. Visitors should set aside a half-day to explore Angkor Thom in depth.

Sights

★Bayon BUDDHIST TEMPLE

(បាយ័ន; Map p218; 🕒7.30am-5.30pm) At the heart of Angkor Thom is the 12th-century Bayon, the mesmerising, if slightly mind-bending, state temple of Jayavarman VII. It epitomises the creative genius and inflated ego of Cambodia's most celebrated king. Its 54 Gothic towers are decorated with 216 gargantuan smiling faces of Avalokiteshvara, and it is adorned with 1.2km of extraordinary bas-reliefs incorporating more than 11,000 figures.

The upper level of Bayon was closed for restoration when we visited and is not scheduled to reopen until 2022.

Baphuon HINDU TEMPLE

(បាពួន; Map p218; 🕒7.30am-5.30pm) Some have called Baphuon the 'world's largest jigsaw puzzle'. Before the civil war the Baphuon was painstakingly taken apart piece by piece by a team of archaeologists, but their meticulous records were destroyed during the Khmer Rouge regime, leaving experts with 300,000 stones to put back into place. After years of excruciating research, this temple has been partially restored. In the 16th century, the retaining wall on the western side of the second level was fashioned into a 60m reclining Buddha.

Terrace of Elephants ARCHAEOLOGICAL SITE

(លានជល់ដំរី; Map p218; 🕒7.30am-5pm) The 350m-long Terrace of Elephants was used as a giant viewing stand for public ceremonies and served as a base for the king's grand audience hall. Try to imagine the pomp and grandeur of the Khmer empire at its height, with infantry, cavalry, horse-drawn chariots and elephants parading across Central Square in a colourful procession, pennants and standards aloft. Looking on is the god-king, shaded by multitiered parasols and attended by mandarins and handmaidens bearing gold and silver utensils.

Terrace of the Leper King ARCHAEOLOGICAL SITE

(ព្រះលានស្តេចគម្លង់; Map p218; 🕒7.30am-5.30pm) The Terrace of the Leper King is just north of the Terrace of Elephants. Dating from the late 12th century, it is a 7m-high platform, on top of which stands a nude, though sexless, statue. The front retaining walls of the terrace are decorated with at least five tiers of meticulously executed carvings. On the southern side of the Terrace of the Leper King, there is access to a hidden terrace with exquisitely preserved carvings.

Angkor Thom South Gate GATE

(ខ្លោងទ្វារទន្លេអំ; Map p218) The south gate of Angkor Thom is most popular with visitors, as it has been fully restored and many of the

Temples of Angkor

THREE-DAY EXPLORATION

The temple complex at Angkor is simply enormous and the superlatives don't do it justice. This is the site of the world's largest religious building, a multitude of temples and a vast, long-abandoned walled city that was arguably Southeast Asia's first metropolis, long before Bangkok and Singapore got in on the action.

Starting at the Roluos group of temples, one of the earliest capitals of Angkor, move on to the big circuit, which includes the Buddhist-Hindu fusion temple of 1 **Preah Khan** and the ornate water temple of 2 **Preah Neak Poan**.

On the second day downsize to the small circuit, starting with an early visit to 3 **Ta Prohm**, before continuing to the temple pyramid of Ta Keo, the Buddhist monastery of Banteay Kdei and the immense royal bathing pond of 4 **Sra Srang**.

Next venture further afield to Banteay Srei temple, the jewel in the crown of Angkorian art, and Beng Mealea, a remote jungle temple.

Saving the biggest and best until last, experience sunrise at 5 **Angkor Wat** and stick around for breakfast in the temple to discover its amazing architecture without the crowds. In the afternoon, explore 6 **Angkor Thom**, an immense complex that is home to the enigmatic 7 **Bayon**.

Three days around Angkor? That's just for starters.

TOP TIPS

➡ To avoid the crowds, try dawn at Sra Srang, post-sunrise at Angkor Wat and lunchtime at Banteay Srei.

➡ Three-day passes can be used on non-consecutive days over the course of a week, but be sure to request this.

ADAM LAWS/SHUTTERSTOCK ©

Bayon
The surreal state temple of legendary king Jayavarman VII, where 216 faces stare down on pilgrims, asserting religious and regal authority.

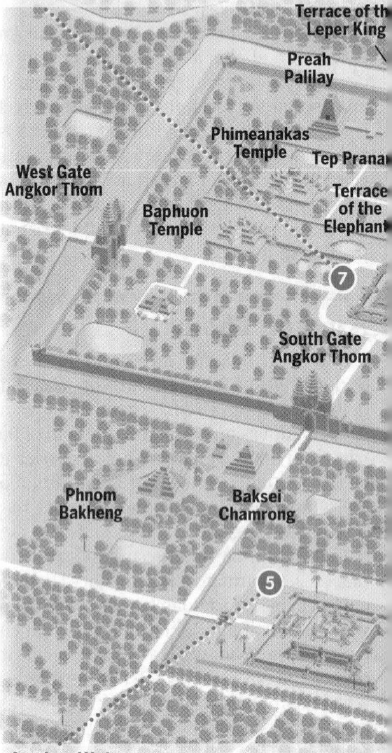

Angkor Wat
The world's largest religious building. Experience sunrise at the holiest of holies, then explore the beautiful bas-reliefs – devotion etched in stone.

TOM ROCHE/SHUTTERSTOCK ©

EFIRED/SHUTTERSTOCK ©

DREAMLOVEYOU/SHUTTERSTOCK ©

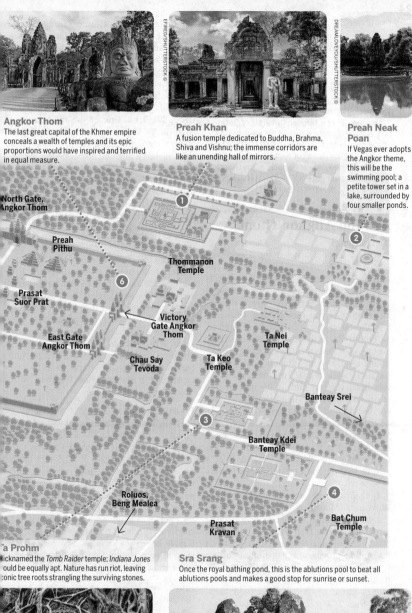

Angkor Thom
The last great capital of the Khmer empire conceals a wealth of temples and its epic proportions would have inspired and terrified in equal measure.

Preah Khan
A fusion temple dedicated to Buddha, Brahma, Shiva and Vishnu; the immense corridors are like an unending hall of mirrors.

Preah Neak Poan
If Vegas ever adopts the Angkor theme, this will be the swimming pool; a petite tower set in a lake, surrounded by four smaller ponds.

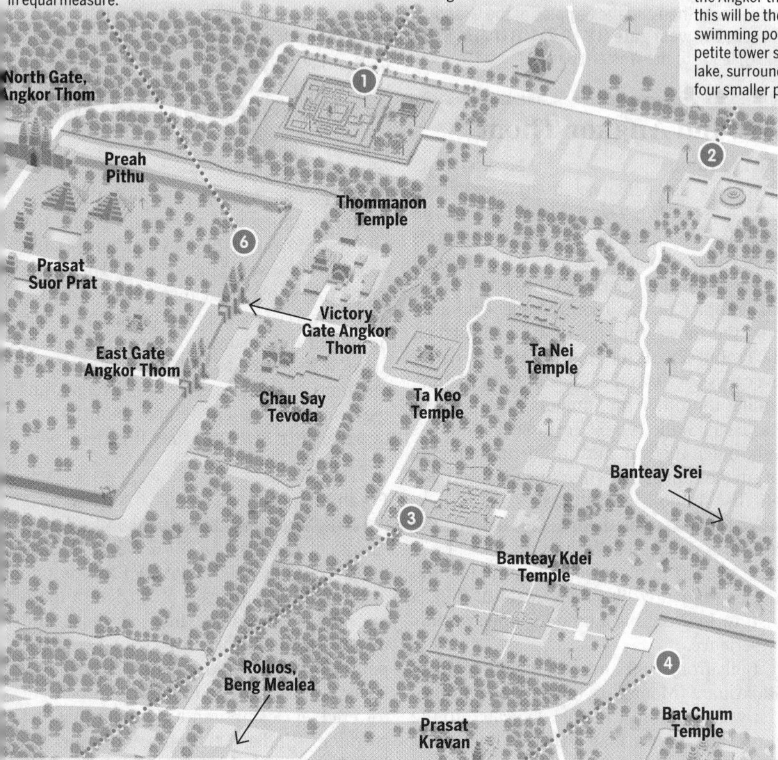

a Prohm
icknamed the *Tomb Raider* temple; *Indiana Jones* ould be equally apt. Nature has run riot, leaving conic tree roots strangling the surviving stones.

Sra Srang
Once the royal bathing pond, this is the ablutions pool to beat all ablutions pools and makes a good stop for sunrise or sunset.

PAVEL SZABO/SHUTTERSTOCK ©

heads (mostly copies) remain in place. The gate is on the main road into Angkor Thom from Angkor Wat, and it gets very busy at peak times.

Getting There & Away

If coming from Angkor Wat, you'll enter Angkor Thom through the south gate (p221). From Ta Prohm, you'll enter through the **Victory Gate** (ខ្លោងទ្វារជយ; Map p218) on the eastern side. The immense **north gate** (ខ្លោងទ្វារដីឆ្នាំង; Map p218) of Angkor Thom connects the walled city with Preah Khan and the temples of the Grand Circuit. The **west gate** (ខ្លោងទ្វារតាកៅ; Map p218) leads to the Western Baray.

Around Angkor Thom

★Ta Prohm BUDDHIST TEMPLE

(តាព្រហ្ម; Map p218; incl in Angkor admission 1/3/7 days US$37/62/72; ⏲7.30am-5.30pm) The so-called 'Tomb Raider Temple', Ta Prohm is cloaked in dappled shadow, its crumbling towers and walls locked in the slow muscular embrace of vast root systems. Undoubtedly the most atmospheric ruin at Angkor, Ta Prohm should be high on the hit list of every visitor. Its appeal lies in the fact that, unlike the other monuments of Angkor, it has been swallowed by the jungle, and looks very much the way most of the monuments of Angkor appeared when European explorers first stumbled upon them.

Well, that's the theory, but in fact the jungle is pegged back and only the largest trees are left in place, making it manicured rather than raw like Beng Mealea. Still, a visit to Ta Prohm is a unique, other-worldly experience.

Built from 1186 and originally known as Rajavihara (Monastery of the King), Ta Prohm was a Buddhist temple dedicated to the mother of Jayavarman VII. It is one of the few temples in the Angkor region where an inscription provides information about the temple's dependents and inhabitants. Almost 80,000 people were required to maintain or attend at the temple, among them more than 2700 officials and 615 dancers.

Ta Prohm is a temple of towers, closed courtyards and narrow corridors. Many of the corridors are impassable, clogged with jumbled piles of delicately carved stone blocks dislodged by the roots of long-decayed trees. Bas-reliefs on bulging walls are carpeted with lichen, moss and creeping plants, and shrubs sprout from the roofs of monumental porches. Trees, hundreds of years old, tower overhead, their leaves filtering the sunlight and casting a greenish pall over the whole scene.

The most popular of the many strangulating root formations is the one on the inside of the easternmost *gopura* (entrance pavilion) of the central enclosure, nicknamed the **Crocodile Tree**. One of the most famous spots in Ta Prohm is the so-called **Tomb Raider tree**, where Angelina Jolie's Lara Croft picked a jasmine flower before falling through the earth into...Pinewood Studios.

The temple is at its most impressive early in the day. Allow as much as two hours to visit, especially if you want to explore the maze-like corridors and iconic tree roots.

Phnom Bakheng HINDU TEMPLE

(ភ្នំបាខែង; Map p218; incl in Angkor admission 1/3/7 days US$37/62/72; ⏲5am-7pm) Located around 400m south of Angkor Thom, the main attraction at Phnom Bakheng is the sunset view over Angkor Wat. For many years, the whole affair turned into a circus, with crowds of tourists ascending the slopes of the hill and jockeying for space. Numbers are now restricted to just 300 visitors at any one time, so get here early (4pm) to guarantee a sunset spot. The temple, built by Yasovarman I (r 889–910), has five tiers, with seven levels.

Preah Khan BUDDHIST TEMPLE

(ព្រះខ័ន, Sacred Sword; Map p218; incl in Angkor admission 1/3/7 days US$37/62/72; ⏲7.30am-5.30pm) The temple of Preah Khan is one of the largest complexes at Angkor, a maze of vaulted corridors, fine carvings and lichen-clad stonework. It is a good counterpoint to Ta Prohm and generally sees slightly fewer visitors. Like Ta Prohm it is a place of towered enclosures and shoulder-hugging corridors. Unlike Ta Prohm, however, the temple of Preah Khan is in a reasonable state of preservation thanks to the ongoing restoration efforts of the WMF.

Preah Neak Poan BUDDHIST TEMPLE

(នាគព័ន្ធ, Temple of the Intertwined Nagas; Map p218; incl in Angkor admission 1/3/7 days US$37/62/72; ⏲7.30am-5.30pm) The Buddhist temple of Preah Neak Poan is a petite yet perfect temple constructed by Jayavarman VII in the late 12th century. It has a large square pool surrounded by four smaller square pools. In the middle of the central pool is a circular 'island' encircled by the two nagas whose intertwined tails give the temple its name.

Pre Rup HINDU TEMPLE
(ប្រែរូប; Map p218; ⏰5am-7pm) Pre Rup, built by Rajendravarman II, is about 1km south of the Eastern Mebon and is a popular spot for sunset. The temple consists of a pyramid-shaped temple-mountain with the uppermost of the three tiers carrying five lotus towers. Pre Rup means 'Turning the Body' and refers to a traditional method of cremation in which a corpse's outline is traced in the cinders: this suggests that the temple may have served as an early royal crematorium.

Bakong HINDU TEMPLE
(បាគង; Map p218; ⏰7.30am-5.30pm) Bakong is the largest and most interesting of the Roluos group of temples. Built and dedicated to Shiva by Indravarman I, it's a representation of Mt Meru, and it served as the city's central temple. The east-facing complex consists of a five-tier central pyramid of sandstone, 60m square at the base, flanked by eight towers of brick and sandstone, and by other minor sanctuaries. A number of the lower towers are still partly covered by their original plasterwork.

Preah Ko HINDU TEMPLE
(ព្រះគោ; Map p218; ⏰7.30am-5.30pm) Preah Ko was erected by Indravarman I in the late 9th century and dedicated to Shiva. In AD 880 the temple was also dedicated to his deified ancestors: the front towers relate to male ancestors or gods, the rear towers to female ancestors or goddesses. Lions guard the steps up to the temple. Preah Ko (Sacred Ox) features three *nandis* (sacred oxen), all of whom look like a few steaks have been sliced off over the years.

Further Afield

★Banteay Srei HINDU TEMPLE
(បន្ទាយស្រី; incl in Angkor admission 1/3/7 days US$37/62/72; ⏰7.30am-5.30pm) Considered by many to be the jewel in the crown of Angkorian art, Banteay Srei is cut from stone of a pinkish hue and includes some of the finest stone carving anywhere on earth. Begun in 967 CE, it is one of the smallest sites at Angkor, but what it lacks in size it makes up for in stature. The art gallery of Angkor, this Hindu temple dedicated to Shiva is wonderfully well preserved, and many of its carvings are three-dimensional.

DON'T MISS

ANGKOR ZIPLINE

Angkor provides the ultimate backdrop for this **zipline experience** (Map p218; ☎096 999 9100; www.angkorzipline.com; short/full course US$60/100; ⏰6am-5pm), although you won't actually see the temples while navigating the course, despite it being located inside the Angkor protected area. The course includes 10 ziplines, 21 treetop platforms, four skybridges and an abseil finish. There is a panoramic rest stop halfway, and highlights include a tandem line for couples.

Kbal Spean HINDU SHRINE
(ក្បាលស្ពាន, River of a Thousand Lingas; incl in Angkor admission 1/3/7 days US$37/62/72; ⏰7.30am-5.30pm) A spectacularly carved riverbed, Kbal Spean is set deep in the jungle to the northeast of Angkor. More commonly referred to in English as the 'River of a Thousand Lingas', the name actually means 'bridgehead', a reference to the natural rock bridge here. *Lingas* (phallic symbols) have been elaborately carved into the riverbed, and images of Hindu deities are dotted about the area. It was 'discovered' in 1969, when ethnologist Jean Boulbet was shown the area by a hermit.

Phnom Kulen MOUNTAIN
(ភ្នំគូលែន; www.adfkulen.org; US$20; ⏰6-11am to ascend, noon-5pm to descend) Considered by Khmers to be the most sacred mountain in Cambodia, Phnom Kulen is a popular place of pilgrimage on weekends and during festivals. It played a significant role in the history of the Khmer empire, as it was from here in 802 CE that Jayavarman II proclaimed himself a *devaraja* (god-king), giving birth to the Cambodian kingdom. Attractions include a giant reclining Buddha, hundreds of *lingas* carved in the riverbed, an impressive waterfall and some remote temples.

★Beng Mealea BUDDHIST TEMPLE
(បឹងមាលា; US$5; ⏰7.30am-5.30pm) A spectacular sight to behold, Beng Mealea, located about 68km northeast of Siem Reap, is one of the most mysterious temples at Angkor, as nature has well and truly run riot. Exploring this *Titanic* of temples, built to the same floor plan as Angkor Wat, is the ultimate Indiana Jones experience. Built in the 12th century under Suryavarman II,

Beng Mealea is enclosed by a massive moat measuring 1.2km by 900m.

Koh Ker HINDU TEMPLE

(កោះកេរ; US$10; ⏲7.30am-5.30pm) Abandoned to the forests of the north, Koh Ker, capital of the Angkorian empire from 928 to 944 CE, is within day-trip distance of Siem Reap. Most visitors start at Prasat Krahom where impressive stone carvings grace lintels, doorposts and slender window columns. The principal monument is Mayan-looking Prasat Thom, a 55m-wide, 40m-high sandstone-faced pyramid whose seven tiers offer spectacular views across the forest. Koh Ker is 127km northeast of Siem Reap.

ℹ Getting There & Around

The central temple area is just 8km from Siem Reap, and can be visited using anything from a car or motorcycle to a sturdy pair of walking boots. For the ultimate Angkor experience, try a pick-and-mix approach, with a *moto, remork-moto* or car for one day to cover the remote sites, a bicycle to experience the central temples, and an exploration on foot for a spot of peace and serenity.

BICYCLE

Cycling is a great way to get around the temples, as there are few hills and the roads are good, so there's no need for much experience. You take in more than you would from a car window or on the back of a speeding *moto*.

Many guesthouses and hotels in town rent bikes for around US$1 to US$2 per day. Electric bicycles hired out by Green e-bikes (p215) and others are also a very popular way to tour the temples.

CAR & MOTORCYCLE

A car for the day around the central temples is US$25 to US$35 and can be arranged with hotels, guesthouses and agencies in Siem Reap.

MOTO

Many independent travellers end up visiting the temples by *moto*. *Moto* drivers accost visitors from the moment they set foot in Siem Reap, but they often end up being knowledgeable and friendly, and good companions for a tour around the temples, starting at around US$10 per day.

TUK TUK

Remork-motos, motorcycles with hooded carriages towed behind, are more commonly known as *tuk tuks*. They are a popular way to get around Angkor as fellow travellers can talk to each other as they explore (unlike on the back of a *moto*). They also offer some protection from the rain. Some *remork* drivers are very good companions for a tour of the temples. Prices run from US$15 to US$25 for the day, depending on the destination and number of passengers. Slightly cheaper are the smaller auto-rickshaws, but they offer a little less breeze than *remorks*.

WALKING

Why not simply explore on foot? It's easy enough to walk to Angkor Wat and the temples of Angkor Thom, and this is a great way to meet up with villagers in the area. Those who want to get away from the roads should try the peaceful walk along the walls of Angkor Thom. It is about 13km in total, and offers access to several small, remote temples and some birdlife. Another rewarding walk is from Ta Nei to Ta Keo through the forest.

NORTHWESTERN CAMBODIA

POP 4.2 MILLION

Looking for temples without the tourist hordes? The remote temples of Northwestern Cambodia are a world apart. While hilltop Prasat Preah Vihear is the big hitter, the other temple complexes like Preah Khan Kompong Svay (Prasat Bakan) and Sambor Prei Kuk, wrapped in vines and half-swallowed by jungle, are fabulous to explore.

In the region's heart is Tonlé Sap, teeming with fish and a birder's paradise. Boat trips from Kompong Chhnang and Krakor (near Pursat) to the rickety floating villages that cluster along this important waterway allow you to dip your toes into life on the lake.

When forays into the region's far-flung corners are complete, the northwest has one more surprise up its sleeve. Laid-back Battambang, with its colonial architecture and burgeoning arts scene, is the main city here. There's a wealth of brilliant sights all within day-tripping distance of town, making it a worthy pit stop when all the hard travelling is done.

Banteay Chhmar

Beautiful, peaceful and covered in astonishingly intricate bas-reliefs, **Banteay Chhmar** (បន្ទាយឆ្មារ; US$5; ⏲8am-6pm) is one of the most impressive remote temple complexes beyond the Angkor area. The Global Heritage Fund (www.globalheritagefund.org) is assisting with conservation efforts here, and it is now a top candidate for Unesco World Heritage Site status.

Banteay Chhmar and its nine satellite temples were constructed by Cambodia's most prolific builder, Jayavarman VII (r 1181–1219), on the site of a 9th-century temple. The main temple housed one of the largest and most impressive Buddhist monasteries of the Angkorian period, and was originally enclosed by a 9km-long wall. Now atmospherically encroached upon by forest, it features several towers bearing enigmatic, Bayon-style four-faced Avalokiteshvara (Buddhist deities) with their mysterious and iconic smiles, and is also renowned for its 2000 sq metres of intricate bas-relief carvings that depict war victories and scenes from daily life on the exterior of the southern section of the temple's western ramparts.

Unfortunately several of these were dismantled and trucked into Thailand in a brazen act of looting in 1998; only two figures – one with 22 arms, the other with 32 – remain in situ out of an original eight, but the dazzling, intricate artistry involved in creating these carvings is still easily evoked. The segments of the looted bas-reliefs that were intercepted by the Thais are now on display in Phnom Penh's National Museum.

A wonderful **CBT Homestay Program** (☎097-516 5533, 012 435660; www.visitbanteaychhmar.org; r US$7) scheme gives visitors incentive to stay another day. The scheme includes fantastic homestays (room US$7), activities and guides for temple tours to assist with community development in the area, all booked through the **CBT Office** (Community-Based Tourism Office; ☎012 435660, 097-516 5533; www.visitbanteaychhmar.org; NH56; ⏰8am-5pm). Rooms are in private homes and come with mosquito nets, fans that run when there's 24-hour electricity, and downstairs bathrooms.

For those interested in a particularly atmospheric meal, the CBT Office can set up lunch or dinner in the main temple at Banteay Chhmar. There's an additional charge of US$10 to US$20 for the set-up, dependent on the size of your group.

Getting There & Away

Banteay Chhmar can easily be done as a day trip with private transport out of Siem Reap. Shared taxis from Sisophon, 61km south of the temple along sealed NH56, usually only go as far as Thmor Puok, although a few continue on to Banteay Chhmar (20,000r, one hour) and Samraong. A *moto* from Sisophon to Banteay Chhmar will cost US$15 to US$20 return, a taxi US$50 to US$60 return.

Battambang

☎053 / POP 150,000

There's something about Battambang (បាត់ដំបង) that visitors just love. Forget the fact that there's really not all that much to do in the city proper – the mix of architecture teetering into genteel disrepair, the riverside setting and the laid-back cafes all make up for it. It's the perfect blend of relatively urban modernity and small-town friendliness.

Outside the city's confines, meanwhile, timeless hilltop temples and bucolic villages await. Not to mention the most scenic river trip in the country, which links Battambang with Siem Reap.

That Cambodia's best-known circus (the magnificent Phare Ponleu Selpak) is here is no coincidence: the city has an enduring tradition of producing many of Cambodia's best-loved singers, actors and artists.

Sights

Much of Battambang's charm lies in its early-20th-century architecture, a mix of vernacular shophouses and French colonial construction that makes up the historic core of the city. Some of the finest colonial buildings are dotted along the waterfront (St 1), especially just south of **Psar Nath** (ផ្សារណាត់; St 1; ⏰6am-late), itself an architectural monument, albeit a modernist one.

★Romcheik 5 Artspace GALLERY

(ទីសិល្បៈរំចេក៥; ☎089 373683; St 201A; US$2.50; ⏰2-7pm) Expanded from a workshop into a bona fide gallery in 2015, this impressive space has a permanent collection upstairs displaying the edgy, contemporary works of its four founders, who in their youth were expelled from Thailand and forced to work as child labourers, before being rescued by an NGO and encouraged to express themselves through art. The results are awe-inspiring.

Wat Kor Village VILLAGE

(ភូមិវត្តគ) About 2km south of central Battambang, the village of Wat Kor is centred around the **temple** (វត្តគ) of the same name. It's a great place to wander, especially late in the afternoon when the opposite (east) bank of the Sangker River is bathed in amber tones by the sinking sun. Picturesque bridges span the river, the spires of Wat Kor glow bright platinum and Khmer village life is on full display.

Battambang

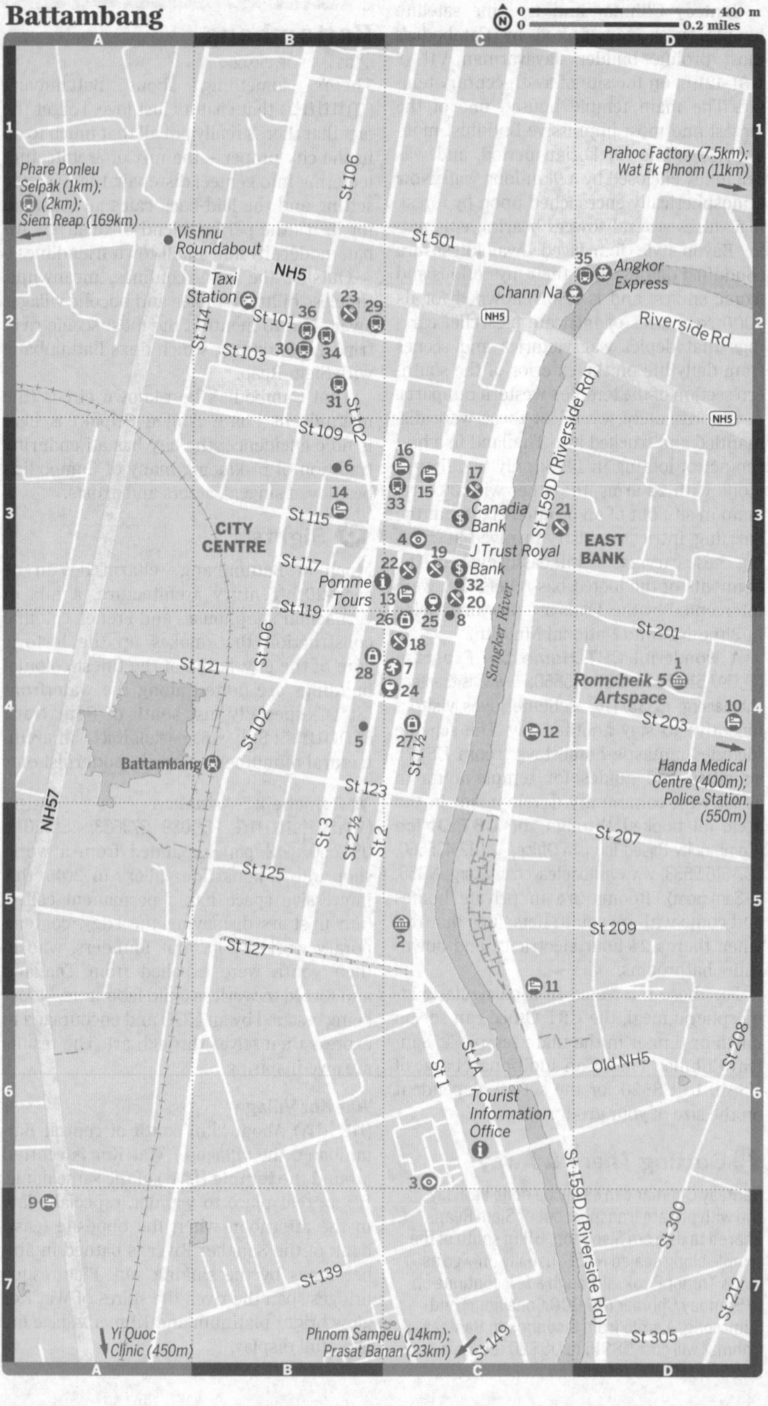
0 400 m
0 0.2 miles
Phare Ponleu Selpak (1km); (2km); Siem Reap (169km)
Prahoc Factory (7.5km); Wat Ek Phnom (11km)
Vishnu Roundabout
St 501
NH5
Taxi Station
Angkor Express
Chann Na
Riverside Rd
St 101
St 103
St 106
St 114
St 102
St 109
St 159D (Riverside Rd)
Canadia Bank
J Trust Royal Bank
St 115
CITY CENTRE
EAST BANK
St 117
Pomme Tours
St 119
Sangker River
St 201
St 121
Romcheik 5 Artspace
St 203
Handa Medical Centre (400m); Police Station (550m)
Battambang
St 1½
St 123
NH57
St 207
St 3
St 2½
St 2
St 125
St 209
St 127
St 1A
St 1
Old NH5
St 208
Tourist Information Office
St 300
St 139
St 212
Yi Quoc Clinic (450m)
Phnom Sampeu (14km); Prasat Banan (23km)
St 149
St 305

Battambang

Top Sights

1 Romcheik 5 Artspace D4

Sights

2 Battambang Museum C5
3 Governor's Residence C6
4 Psar Nath C3

Activities, Courses & Tours

5 Battambang Bike B4
6 Coconut Lyly B3
7 Nature Boutique Spa C4
8 Soksabike C4

Sleeping

9 Au Cabaret Vert A7
10 Bambu Hotel D4
11 Here Be Dragons C5
12 La Villa C4
13 Pomme C3
14 Royal Hotel B3
15 Seng Hout Hotel C3
16 The Place C3

Eating

17 Cafe Eden C3
18 Choco l'art Café C4
19 Jaan Bai C3
20 Kinyei C3
21 La Pizza C3
Lonely Tree Cafe .... (see 28)
22 Riceholic C3
23 Vegetarian Foods Restaurant B2

Drinking & Nightlife

24 Madison Pub C4
25 Miss Wong Battambang C3

Shopping

26 Bric-à-Brac C4
27 HUMAN Gallery C4
Jewel in the Lotus .... (see 13)
28 Lonely Tree Shop B4

Transport

29 Bayon VIP B2
30 Cambotra Express B2
31 Capitol Tour B2
32 Gecko Moto C3
33 Mekong Express C3
34 Phnom Penh Sorya B2
35 Rith Mony D2
36 Virak Buntham B2

About 1.5km beyond Wat Kor, you'll encounter the cluster of Khmer heritage houses that the village is known for. Built of now-rare hardwoods almost a century ago and surrounded by orchard gardens, they have wide verandahs and exude the ambience of another era.

Two of the approximately 20 heritage houses in the Wat Kor area are open to visitors: **Mrs Bun Roeung's Ancient House** (ផ្ទះខ្មែរបុរាណ លោកយាយប៊ុនរឿង; ☎017 818419; www.facebook.com/mrsbunshouse; suggested donation US$1) and neighbouring **Khor Sang House** (ផ្ទះខសង; ☎092 467264; suggested donation US$1). The owner of each will give you a short tour in French or English. They have floors worn lustrous by a century of bare feet and are decorated with old furniture and family photos.

Battambang Museum MUSEUM
(សារមន្ទីរខេត្តបាត់ដំបង; ☎012 238320; St 1; US$3; ⏲8-11am & 2-5.30pm) This petite provincial museum has been given a full makeover thanks to the generous support of Friends of Khmer Culture (FOKC; www.khmerculture.net) and now has state-of-the-art lighting and detailed signage in English and Khmer. There are some beautiful Angkorian lintels and elegant statuary from all over Battambang Province, including pieces from Prasat Banan and Sneng. There is also a detailed introduction to the pre-Angkorian Neolithic period of cave-dwelling in Laang Spean Cave.

Governor's Residence NOTABLE BUILDING
(សាលាខេត្តបាត់ដំបង; off St 139; entry by donation) The two-storey Governor's Residence, with its balconies and wooden shutters, is a handsome legacy of the early 1900s. The interior is now open to the public and has a collection of grand old furnishings, old photographs and traditional costumes inside. It was designed by an Italian architect for the last Thai governor, who departed in 1907.

Entrance is via a small gate on St 139 on the southern side of the extensive gardens.

Cambodia Peace Gallery MUSEUM
(ពិពណ៌សន្តិភាពកម្ពុជា; ☎092 455934; http://cambodiapeacegallery.org; US$5; ⏲9am-5pm) This small museum tells the big story of Cambodia's long journey from war to peace. Exhibits are well presented in a series of buildings in the spacious compound, including some original stained-glass windows showing different aspects of Cambodia's recent history. Other sections include some context on landmines in Cambodia and the

work Cambodian peacekeepers are doing all over the world.

To get here, follow the road south to Wat Banan for about 7km.

Activities

Heritage Walking Trail WALKING

(www.ka-tours.org) Phnom Penh–based Khmer Architecture Tours (p185) is highly regarded for its specialist tours in and around the capital and has collaborated with Battambang Municipality to create heritage walks in Battambang's historic centre. The walks concentrate both on the French period and on the modernist architecture of the '60s. The company's website has two downloadable PDFs including a colour map and numbered highlights.

Green Orange Kayaks KAYAKING

(☎012 720386; www.facebook.com/greenorangebtb; Ksach Poy; kayak trip US$15) Kayaks can be rented from Green Orange Kayaks, part of the Friends Economic Development Association (FEDA), a local NGO that runs a community centre in Ksach Poy village, 8km south of Battambang. Self-guided kayaking trips begin at Ksach Poy's Green Orange Cafe. From there you paddle back to the city along the Sangker River. Booking ahead is recommended.

FEDA also runs a guesthouse, the **Green Orange Village Bungalows** (☎012 736166; www.facebook.com/greenorangebtb; Ksach Poy; bungalows incl breakfast from US$20;) .

Nature Boutique Spa SPA

(☎012 251569; www.natureboutiquespa.com; St 2½; massage US$7-12, scrubs US$10, facials US$8-15; 9am-9pm) One of the most sophisticated spas in Battambang. Downstairs is a shop selling keepsakes and natural beauty products. Upstairs is the serene spa, which offers a range of very affordable rubs and scrubs.

Courses

Coconut Lyly COOKING

(☎016 399339; St 111; per person US$10) These classes are run by Chef Lyly, a graduate from Siem Reap's Paul Dubrule Cooking School. Three-hour classes (start times 9am and 3.30pm) include a visit to Psar Nath market, preparing four typical Khmer dishes (recipe book included) and then eating your handiwork afterwards. The excellent restaurant here is open from 9am to 10pm.

DON'T MISS

BATTAMBANG'S BAMBOO TRAIN

One of the world's unique rail journeys, Battambang's bamboo train has had many an obituary written about it over the years, but somehow it's still on the rails, despite the launch of proper passenger services on the line from Battambang to Phnom Penh and Poipet.

The **original bamboo train** (www.bambootrain.com; per person US$5; 6am-6pm) used to trundle from O Dambong, a few kilometres east of Battambang's old French bridge (Wat Kor Bridge), to O Sra Lav along warped, misaligned rails and vertiginous bridges left by the French. Each bamboo train – known in Khmer as a *norry* – consists of a 3m-long wooden frame, covered lengthwise with slats made of ultralight bamboo, resting on two barbell-like bogies, connected by belts to a 6HP gasoline engine. With a pile of 10 or 15 people, or up to 3 tonnes of rice, it could cruise along at about 15km/h.

The genius of the system is that it offers a solution to the most ineluctable problem faced on any single-track line: what to do when two trains going in opposite directions meet. In the case of bamboo trains, the answer is simple: one car is quickly disassembled and set on the ground beside the tracks so that the other can pass.

This original stretch of line is up and running again, albeit with new bridges and straight tracks. Encroaching foliage has been cut back along the track, so while it is a sanitised version of the old bamboo train, it is still a fun experience.

A local investor has also created a **new track** (per person US$5; 6am-6pm) about 20km away near Prasat Banan (p235), to reconstruct the bamboo-train experience. However, it is more like a kiddies' roller-coaster ride than the original bamboo train, but it does pass through some scenic rock formations around the base of Phnom Banan. There is no need to decamp from the bamboo train on this line, as the track has passing points.

DON'T MISS

PHARE PONLEU SELPAK CIRCUS

Battambang's signature attraction is the internationally acclaimed **circus** (cirque nouveau; ☎077 554413; www.phareps.org; adult/child US$14/7) of this multi-arts centre for Cambodian children. Although it also runs shows in Siem Reap, it's worth timing your visit to Battambang to watch this amazing spectacle where it began. Shows are held two to four nights per week, depending on the season (check the website), and kick off at 7pm.

Phare, as it's known to locals, is not just a circus – it's involved in lots of other projects. It trains musicians, visual artists and performing artists as well. Many of the artists you'll bump into around town, such as Ke of Choco l'art Café (p232) fame, lived and studied at Phare. Guests are welcome to take a guided **tour** (☎077 554413; https://phareps.org; US$5; ⏲9.30am, 10.30am, 2.30pm & 3.30pm Mon-Fri) of the Phare complex during the day and observe circus, dance, music, drawing and graphic-arts classes.

Tickets are sold at the door from 6pm and at many retailers around town. To get here from the Vishnu Roundabout on NH5, head west for 900m, then turn right and continue another 600m.

Tours

★Soksabike CYCLING
(☎012 542019; www.soksabike.com; St 1½; half-/full day US$27/40; ⏲departs 7.30am) Soksabike is a social enterprise aiming to connect visitors with the Cambodian countryside and its people. The half- and full-day trips cover 25km and 40km respectively, and include stops at family-run industries such as rice-paper making and the **Prahoc Factory** (ផ្សារប្រហុក), as well as a visit to a local home. Tour prices depend on group size.

It's associated with Kinyei (p232) cafe a few doors to the north.

Sleeping

Most of Battambang's budget options are clustered close to the central Psar Nath market, while midrange and luxury accommodation tends to be either on the east bank or out of the centre. South of town near Wat Kor village (p227) are some dreamy, away-from-it-all stays where Brangelina used to hang out when they were an item.

City Centre

★The Place HOSTEL $
(☎096 454 9158; https://theplacebtb.wixsite.com/theplace; 53 St 3; dm from US$4.25, r from US$9; ❄📶) Battambang's first flashpacker hostel, The Place was designed by L'Atelier Architecture & Design, who work with bamboo and other natural materials. The results are impressive with a contemporary feel in a welcoming space. Some dorms have wood-tiled walls and cubicles; others are split by a curtain. The rooftop bar is a popular spot for a sundowner.

Pomme HOSTEL $
(☎069 233620; www.facebook.com/Pommebattambang; 61-63 St 2½; s US$5, d & tw US$10; 📶) A lively little backpacker pad on popular St 2½, the accommodation here is in Japanese pod-style units. They are simple partitions and very small, but they definitely count as private rooms and are good value. The bar-restaurant downstairs is a great place to grab a meal or a drink, day or night.

Seng Hout Hotel HOTEL $
(☎012 530327; www.senghouthotel.com; St 2; r US$15-25; ❄📶🏊) Known for on-the-ball staff who are quick to help with traveller queries, the Seng Hout has a variety of nicely decorated rooms. Some are on the smaller side, so check out a few before deciding. The open-air rooftop space is a key drawcard, and the 3rd-floor pool has great views as well.

East Bank

★Here Be Dragons HOSTEL $
(☎089 264895; www.herebedragonsbattambang.com; St 159D; fan/air-con dm US$4/6, r from US$12/15; ❄📶) A stylish fun bar, leafy front garden for relaxing and free beer on arrival make Here Be Dragons a top backpacker base. Six- and eight-bed dorms come with lock-boxes, while sunny private rooms are cheerfully decked out with brightly coloured bedding. The quiet location next to the riverside park on the east bank is a bonus.

★Bambu Hotel HOTEL $$
(☎053-953900; www.bambuhotel.com; St 203; r incl breakfast US$60-90; ❄@📶≋) Bambu's spacious rooms are designed in a Franco-Khmer motif with gorgeous tiling, stone-inlaid bathrooms and exquisite furniture. The fusion restaurant is one of the best in town and the poolside bar invites lingering. Above all else, though, it's Bambu's gracious staff that set it in a category above Battambang's other boutique offerings. Book ahead, as it's deservedly popular.

La Villa BOUTIQUE HOTEL $$
(☎053-730151; www.lavilla-battambang.com; St 159D; s/d/tr incl breakfast from US$65/70/75; ❄@📶≋) For a taste of the colonial era, stay at this French-era villa renovated in vintage 1930s style. It's one of the most romantic boutique hotels in Cambodia. Gauzy mosquito nets drape over four-poster beds, original tilework graces the floors and art deco features adorn every corner, creating an old-world ambience that is hard to beat.

Further Afield

Au Cabaret Vert BOUTIQUE HOTEL $$
(☎053-656 2000; www.aucabaretvert.com; NH57; r incl breakfast US$35-90; ❄📶≋) Contemporary meets colonial at this pretty resort, a short *tuk tuk* ride southwest of the centre. Rooms are stylish and include flat-screen TV and rain shower. The swimming pool is a natural, self-cleaning pond surrounded by lush gardens, and the French-influenced food is top-notch.

★Maisons Wat Kor BOUTIQUE HOTEL $$$
(☎098 555377; www.maisonswatkor.com; Wat Kor village; r incl breakfast from US$120; ❄📶≋) About 2km south of central Battambang, Maisons Wat Kor is a secluded sanctuary of 10 rooms in traditional-style Khmer houses that once welcomed Angelina Jolie and Brad Pitt. Rooms are light-filled, spacious and come with contemporary bathrooms, and the saltwater swimming pool surrounded by lush foliage provides plenty of opportunity for chill-out time. The delightful, open-air restaurant welcomes nonguests.

Eating

★Lonely Tree Cafe CAFE $
(www.thelonelytreecafe.com; St 2½; mains US$4-5.50; ⏲10am-10pm; 📶) Upstairs from the shop of the same name, this uber-cosy cafe serves Spanish tapas-style dishes and a few Khmer options under a soaring, bamboo-inlaid ceiling. Its mascot is an actual tree on the road to Siem Reap. Proceeds support cultural preservation and people with disabilities, among other causes.

Choco l'art Café CAFE $
(☎010 661617; St 119; mains US$1.50-5; ⏲8am-11pm; 📶) Run with gusto by local painter Ke and his partner, Soline, this inviting gallery-cafe sees foreigners and locals alike gather to drink and eat Soline's wonderful bread, pastries and breakfast crêpes. Occasional open-mic nights, live painting sessions and musical performances.

Kinyei CAFE $
(www.kinyei.org; 1 St 1½; coffee US$1.50-2.50, mains US$2.75-5.25; ⏲7am-4pm; 📶) Besides having the best coffee in town (national barista champs have been crowned here), teensy-weensy Kinyei does surprisingly good Mexican food, energy salads, vegie burgers, and some of the best breakfasts in town. Aussies will appreciate the long blacks and flat whites among the coffee selection.

Vegetarian Foods Restaurant VEGETARIAN $
(St 102; mains 1500-3000r; ⏲6.30am-2pm; 🖉) This hole-in-the-wall eatery serves some of the most delicious vegetarian dishes in Cambodia, including rice soup, homemade soy milk and dumplings for just 1000r. Tremendous value.

★Jaan Bai FUSION $$
(☎078 263144; www.facebook.com/jaanbaicct; cnr Sts 1½ & 2; small plates US$3, mains US$4-10; ⏲11am-9pm; 📶🖉) Jaan Bai ('rice bowl' in Khmer) is Battambang's foodie treat, with a sleekly minimalist interior offset by beautiful French-Khmer tilework lining the wall. The menu likewise is successfully bold. Order a few of the small plates to experience the range of flavours, or go all out with the tasting menu: seven plates plus wine for US$15 per person (minimum two people).

Jaan Bai trains and employs vulnerable youth through the Cambodian Children's Trust (www.cambodianchildrenstrust.org).

★Riceholic JAPANESE $$
(☎087 483731; 39 St 2½; mains US$3.75-9.75; ⏲11.30am-2pm & 6-10pm, closed Tue; 📶) Run by a Japanese couple who operated pop-up kitchens in Australia, Riceholic specialises in making its own seasonings and a traditional koji (fermented sauce) from Battam-

bang rice. The menu offers speciality ramen with a healthy tonkotsu broth made from cashew nut, plus delicious sushi and gyoza also feature on the menu.

Cafe Eden CAFE $$
(☎053-731525; www.cafeedencambodia.com; St 1; mains US$4-7; ⏰7.30am-9pm Wed-Mon; ❄📶) This American-run social enterprise offers a relaxed space for a hearty breakfast or an afternoon coffee. The compact lunch-and-dinner menu is Asian-fusion style, with burgers, Tex-Mex tastings, some of the best fries in town and superior jam-jar shakes, all amid blissful air-con.

La Pizza PIZZA $$
(☎093 607417; St 159D; pizzas US$6-10; ⏰5-10pm, closed Thu; 📶) Pizzas come in every shape and size at this popular east-bank restaurant, including by the slice (US$1.75), half size, full size and extra large. La Pizza is set in an elegant traditional wooden house with a lantern-lit garden.

Drinking & Nightlife

Madison Pub BAR
(☎012 415513; St 2½; ⏰11am-late) Old-timer Madison Pub may no longer occupy the strategic corner it once did, but it remains one of the best late-night bars in Battambang thanks to the convivial owner Patrice. Cheap beer, homemade rice wine and a pool table keep the crowds coming, and the kitchen turns out some fusion flavours.

Miss Wong Battambang COCKTAIL BAR
(http://misswong.net; St 2; ⏰6pm-1am; 📶) A sophisticated Battambang outpost of one of Siem Reap's most popular cocktail bars, Miss Wong is situated in a characterful old shophouse on St 2 and looks like a little slice of old Shanghai. Creative cocktails and Chinese dim sum are available, including lots of seasonal favourites with fresh fruit.

Shopping

HUMAN Gallery ART
(☎096 730 0590; www.josebaetxebarria.com/human-gallery; St 1½; ⏰10am-2pm & 4-9pm Mon-Fri) Joseba Etxebarria travelled 37,000km through 29 countries on a bicycle, and took some pictures of people while he was at it. The results are stunningly displayed in this gallery, which includes portraits, postcards and books that can only be purchased here. Proceeds help educate children from Boeng Raing who live in extreme poverty.

Jewel in the Lotus ARTS & CRAFTS
(☎092 260158; 53 St 2½; ⏰8am-5pm; 📶) Jewel in the Lotus features an upstairs gallery, with paintings, prints, vintage items, unique postcards, underground comix, literature, clothing and jewellery. It holds events and workshops, offers reiki classes, and can book appointments for reiki treatments, shamanic healing, energy massage and meditation.

Lonely Tree Shop ARTS & CRAFTS
(☎053-953123; 56 St 2½; ⏰10am-10pm) Fine silk bags, chunky jewellery, fashionable shirts and skirts: definitely not your run-of-the-mill charity gift shop.

Bric-à-Brac HOMEWARES
(☎077 531549; www.bric-a-brac.asia; 112 St 2; ⏰9am-9pm) This swish store, downstairs in the bijou hotel of the same name, sells handmade *passementrie* (trimmings), textiles, antiques and accessories. It also produces some of the world's finest tassels for export.

Information

For information on what's happening in town, look out for copies of the free, biannual Battambang Buzz magazine, and visit the handy Battambang Traveller website (https://battambangtravellerposts.tumblr.com).

Free wi-fi access is the norm at hotels and most cafes and restaurants.

Canadia Bank (Psar Nath; ⏰8am-3.30pm Mon-Fri, to 11.30am Sat, ATM 24hr)

Handa Medical Centre (☎095 520654; https://thehandafoundation.org/programs/medical-center; NH5; ⏰emergency 24hr) Has two ambulances and usually a European doctor or two in residence.

J Trust Royal Bank (St 1; ⏰8am-4pm Mon-Fri, ATM 24hr)

Yi Quoc Clinic (☎012 530171, 053-953163; off NH57; ⏰24hr) The best clinic in town.

Getting There & Away

BOAT

The riverboat to Siem Reap (US$20, 7am daily) squeezes through narrow waterways and passes protected wetlands, taking from five hours in the wet season to nine or more hours at the height of the dry season. Cambodia's most memorable boat trip, it's operated on alternate days by **Angkor Express** (☎012 601287) and **Chann Na** (☎012 354344), which have informal offices on the docks at the eastern end of St 501, where the boats leave from. Buy tickets in advance.

In the dry season, passengers are driven to a navigable section of the river. The best seats are away from the noisy motor. Some travellers complain of overcrowding and safety issues, as there are rarely enough life jackets to go around.

BUS

Some buses now arrive and depart from Battambang's **bus station** (NH5), 2km west of the centre. Companies offer free shuttles for departing passengers, but arriving passengers will have to pay for a *remork* (US$3) into town. However, for departures from Battambang, most companies still use their company offices, which are clustered in the centre just south of the intersection of NH5 and St 4.

To Phnom Penh, if you're pinching pennies, **Capitol Tour** (☎ 012 810055; St 102) and **Rith Mony** (☎ 092 888847; St 1) generally have the lowest prices, followed by **Phnom Penh Sorya** (☎ 092 181804; St 106). For a quicker journey to the capital, many companies run express minivan services (US$8 to US$12, 4½ hours), including **Cambotra Express** (☎ 017 866286; St 106), Capitol Tour, **Bayon VIP** (☎ 070 968966; St 101), **Mekong Express** (☎ 088 576 7668; St 3) and **Virak Buntham** (☎ 017 333572; St 106).

Virak Buntham runs full-recline-sleeper night buses to Phnom Penh, but be aware that these, like all night buses to Phnom Penh, arrive at an ungodly hour.

The Mekong Express minibus is the most comfortable way to Siem Reap (US$7, 3½ hours, 8am and 2pm), while Bayon VIP runs a speedy minivan service (US$10, three hours, four daily).

Most buses to Bangkok involve a change at the border – usually to a minibus on the Thai side.

SHARE TAXI

At the **taxi station** (cnr Sts 101 & 110), share taxis to Phnom Penh (40,000r per person, 4½ hours) and Pursat (20,000r, two hours) leave from the southeast corner. Also here you'll find share taxis to Poipet (20,000r, 1¾ hours), Sisophon (16,000r, 1¼ hours) and Siem Reap (26,000r, three hours). Share taxis to Pailin (20,000r, two hours) and the Psar Pruhm–Ban Pakard (25,000r, 2½ hours) border leave from the corner of St 101 and St 4.

Prices are based on six-passenger occupancy; for the price of a whole taxi, multiply the per-passenger fare by six.

TRAIN

Very limited passenger **trains** (http://royal railway.easybook.com) have resumed on the Battambang–Phnom Penh (US$5 per person) line with two trains per week leaving in either direction, taking around eight hours. The train departs Phnom Penh at 7.30am on Friday and Sunday and departs Battambang at 10.05am on Saturday and Monday. There are also services to Sisophon (US$3) and Poipet (US$4) at 3.10pm on Friday and Sunday. More frequent services will eventually be introduced, but there is still ongoing renovation work on some sections of the railway.

ℹ Getting Around

English- and French-speaking *remork-moto (tuk tuk)* drivers are commonplace in Battambang, and all are eager to whisk you around on day trips. A half-day trip out of town to a single sight such as Phnom Sampeau might cost US$12, while a full-day trip taking in three sights costs US$15 to US$20, depending on your haggling skills. A *moto* costs about half that.

A *moto* ride in town costs around 2000r, while a *remork* ride starts from US$1.50.

BUSES FROM BATTAMBANG

DESTINATION	DURATION (HR)	COST (US$)	COMPANIES	FREQUENCY
Bangkok, Thailand	9	15-16	Mekong Express, PP Sorya, Virak Buntham, Capitol	7.45am, 8.30am, 10.30am, 11.30am, noon
Ho Chi Minh City, Vietnam	10-11	26	Mekong Express	7.30am
Kompong Cham	8	9	Rith Mony	9am
Pailin	1¼	4	Rith Mony	1pm, 3pm
Phnom Penh (day)	4½-7	5-12	All companies	frequent
Phnom Penh (night)	5-6	6-15	Capitol, Mekong Express, TSS, Virak Buntham	frequent 10pm-midnight
Poipet	2¼	4	Capitol, PP Sorya, Rith Mony, TSS	regular to 4pm
Siem Reap	3-4	4-10	Capitol, Bayon VIP, Mekong Express, PP Sorya, Rith Mony	regular to 3pm

Gecko Moto (089 924260; St 1; 8am-10pm) and the **Royal Hotel** (016 912034; St 115; s/d with fan US$7/10, r with air-con from US$15;) rent out motorbikes for US$6 to US$8 per day. Bicycles can be rented at the Royal Hotel, Soksabike (p231), **Battambang Bike** (095 578878; www.thebattambangbike.com; St 2½; tours half-/full day US$18/39; 7am-7pm) and several guesthouses for about US$2 per day.

Around Battambang

Phnom Sampeau BUDDHIST TEMPLE

(ភ្នំសំពៅ; combined ticket US$3) This fabled limestone outcrop 12km southwest of Battambang along NH57 (towards Pailin) is known for its gorgeous views and mesmerising display of bats, which pour out of a massive cave in its cliff face. Access to the summit is via a cement road or – if you're in need of a workout – a steep staircase. The road is too steep for *remorks*. *Moto* drivers hang out near the base of the hill and can whisk you up and back for US$4.

About halfway up to the summit, a road leads under a gate and 250m up to the Killing Caves of Phnom Sampeau, now a place of pilgrimage. A staircase, flanked by greenery, leads into a cavern, where a golden reclining Buddha lies peacefully next to a glass-walled memorial filled with bones and skulls – the remains of some of the people bludgeoned to death by Khmer Rouge cadres and then thrown through the skylight above. Next to the base of the stairway is the old memorial, a rusty cage made of chicken wire and cyclone fencing and partly filled with human bones.

On the summit, several viewpoints can be discovered amid a complex of temples. As you descend from the summit's golden stupa, dating from 1964, turn left under the gate decorated with a bas-relief of Eiy Sei (an elderly Buddha). A deep canyon, its vertical sides cloaked in greenery, descends 144 steps through a natural arch to a 'lost world' of stalactites, creeping vines and bats; two Angkorian warriors stand guard.

Back down at the hill base, people gather at dusk (around 5.30pm) to witness the spectacle of a thick column of bats pouring from a cave high up on the north side of the cliff face. The display lasts a good 30 minutes as millions of bats head out in a looping line to their feeding grounds near Tonlé Sap.

Note that there are lots of monkeys at this site, and you should not be flashy with your food, as angry monkeys have been known to become aggressive.

Prasat Banan BUDDHIST TEMPLE

(ប្រាសាទភ្នំបាណន់; combined ticket US$3; 6am-sunset) It's a 358-stone-step climb up Phnom Banan to reach Prasat Banan, but the incredible views across surrounding countryside from the top are worth it. Udayadityavarman II, son of Suryavarman I, built Prasat Banan in the 11th century; some locals claim the five-tower layout here was the inspiration for Angkor Wat, although this seems optimistic. There are impressive carved lintels above the doorways to each of the towers and bas-reliefs on the upper parts of the central tower.

From the temple, a narrow stone staircase leads south down the hill to three caves, which can be visited with a local guide.

Prasat Banan is located 23km south of Battambang.

Wat Ek Phnom BUDDHIST TEMPLE

(វត្តឯកភ្នំ; combined ticket US$3) Hidden behind a colourful modern pagoda and a gargantuan Buddha statue is this atmospheric, partly collapsed 11th-century temple. Wat Ek Phnom measures 52m by 49m and is surrounded by the remains of a laterite wall and an ancient *baray* (reservoir). A lintel showing the Churning of the Ocean of Milk can be seen above the eastern entrance to the central temple, whose upper flanks hold some fine bas-reliefs. It's about 10km north of central Battambang.

Preah Vihear Province

Vast, remote and hardly touched by tourism, Preah Vihear Province (ខេត្តព្រះវិហារ) is home to three of Cambodia's most impressive Angkorian legacies. Stunningly perched on a promontory high in the Dangrek Mountains, Prasat Preah Vihear became Cambodia's second Unesco World Heritage Site in 2008, sparking an armed stand-off with Thailand. Further south are the lonely, jungle-clad temples of Preah Khan, totally isolated and imbued with secret-world atmosphere. More accessible is 10th-century capital Koh Ker (p226), which is within day-tripping distance of Siem Reap.

Sights

★Prasat Preah Vihear BUDDHIST TEMPLE (ប្រាសាទព្រះវិហារ; adult/child US$10/free; ⏲tickets 7.30am-4.30pm, temple to 5.30pm) The most dramatically situated of all Angkorian monuments, Prasat Preah Vihear sprawls along a clifftop near the Thai border, with breathtaking views of lowland Cambodia 550m below. An important place of pilgrimage for millennia, the temple was built by a succession of seven Khmer monarchs, beginning with Yasovarman I (r 889–910) and ending with Suryavarman II (r 1112–52). Like other temple-mountains from this period, it was designed to represent Mt Meru and dedicated to the Hindu deity Shiva.

For generations, Prasat Preah Vihear (called Khao Phra Wiharn by the Thais) has been a source of tension between Cambodia and Thailand. This area was ruled by Thailand for several centuries, but returned to Cambodia during the French protectorate, under the treaty of 1907. But sovereignty over the temple has been an issue ever since, with tensions between Cambodia and Thailand flaring up from time to time – most recently from 2008 to 2011, when armed confrontations around the temple claimed the lives of several dozen soldiers and some civilians on both sides.

The temple is laid out along a north-south processional axis with five cruciform *gopura* (pavilions), decorated with exquisite carvings, separated by esplanades up to 275m long. From the parking area, walk up the hill to toppled and crumbling **Gopura V** at the north end of the temple complex. From here, the grey-sandstone Monumental Stairway leads down to the Thai border.

Walking south up the slope from Gopura V, the next pavilion you get to is **Gopura IV**. On the pediment above the southern door, look for an early rendition of the Churning of the Ocean of Milk, a theme later depicted awesomely at Angkor Wat. Keep climbing through Gopura III and II until finally you reach **Gopura I**. Here the galleries, with their inward-looking windows, are in a remarkably good state of repair, but the Central Sanctuary is just a pile of rubble. Outside, the cliff affords stupendous views of Cambodia's northern plains, with the holy mountain of Phnom Kulen (487m) looming in the distance. This is a fantastic spot for a picnic.

Prasat Preah Vihear sits atop an escarpment in the Dangrek Mountains (elevation 625m), 30km north of the town of Sra Em and about three hours by car from Siem Reap. Your first stop upon arriving should be the **information centre** (Kor Muy; ⏲7am-4.30pm), where you pay for entry, secure an English-speaking guide if you want one (US$15), and arrange transport up to the temple via *moto* (US$5 return) or 4WD pick-up truck (US$25 return, maximum six passengers). Bring your passport as you'll need it to buy a ticket. The first 5km of the 6.5km temple access road are gradual enough, but the final 1.5km is extremely steep; nervous passengers might consider walking this last bit, especially if it's wet.

★Preah Khan of Kompong Svay BUDDHIST TEMPLE (ព្រះខ័នកំពង់ស្វាយ; US$5) For tantalising lost-world ambience, this remote temple complex about 90km south of Preah Vihear City can't be beaten. It's wrapped by vines and trees, and thanks to its back-of-beyond location, the site is astonishingly peaceful. You'll very likely be the only visitor, although you'll need private transport to get here. Preah Khan of Kompong Svay is the largest temple enclosure constructed during the Angkorian period, quite a feat when you consider the competition.

Preah Khan's history is shrouded in mystery, but it was long an important religious site, and some structures here date back to the 9th century. Both Suryavarman II, builder of Angkor Wat, and Jayavarman VII lived here at various times during their lives, suggesting Preah Khan was something of a second city in the Angkorian empire.

Don't confuse Preah Khan of Kompong Svay with the similarly gargantuan Preah Khan temple at Angkor. This Preah Khan covers almost 5 sq km, and includes the main temple as well several satellite temples, including **Prasat Damrei** (ប្រាសាទដំរី), **Prasat Preah Thkol** (ប្រាសាទព្រះថ្កោល) and **Prasat Preah Stung** (ប្រាសាទព្រះស្ទឹង, Prasat Muk Buon), distinguished by four immaculately preserved Bayon-style Avalokiteshvara faces.

The main temple is surrounded by a moat (now dry), similar to the one around Angkor Thom. It consists of half-toppled *prangs* (temple towers), entangled with trees and overgrown by forest. As recently as the mid-1990s, the central structure was thought to be in reasonable shape, but at some point in the second half of the decade, looters arrived seeking buried statues under each *prang*. Assaulted with pneumatic drills and mechanical diggers, the ancient temple never stood a chance and many of the towers simply collapsed in on themselves, leaving the mess we see today.

One entry fee gains you admission to all of the temples in the enclosure. Locals say there are no land mines in the vicinity of Preah Khan, but stick to the marked paths just to be on the safe side.

Upgraded roads mean that you can now visit Preah Khan year-round, although it's still easiest in the dry season. It's an extra-long day trip from Siem Reap; to do it more cheaply, hire a *moto* or a taxi in Preah Vihear City or Kompong Thom.

To get here on your own, turn west off smooth NH62 in Svay Pak, about 60km south of Preah Vihear City and 75km north of Kompong Thom. From here an all-season dirt road (substantially pitted with potholes) takes you to Ta Seng, about 30km from the highway and just 4km from the temple. The last 4km are in surprisingly good shape.

Sleeping

★BeTreed Adventures TREEHOUSE **$$**
(☎012 765136, 078 960420; http://betreed.com; Phnom Tnout, Ta Bos village; bungalows US$60, treehouse US$60;) Secluded in the Cambodian wilderness, this eco-stay is the brainchild of two conservation-minded expats who left jobs with NGOs to save 70 sq km of forestland and all the creatures calling it home. Accommodation includes two comfy traditional wooden houses on stilts and a treehouse built from reclaimed hardwood around a wild rain tree. Book ahead as early as possible and call for detailed directions.

In addition to sleeping in the canopy, guests go on guided zipline and hiking adventures, and return to camp for delicious, mostly vegetarian meals (US$15 per day). It's US$10 for a guide, and there's also a US$15-per-person fee for community development and preservation. Note that access in the wet season can be a challenge.

★Preah Vihear Jaya Hotel HOTEL **$$**
(☎069 217571; www.preahvihearjayahotel.com; NH 26, Sra Em; r US$25-45;) One of a strip of hotels on the western edge of town, Jaya stands out for its exceptional value. Spacious rooms, all set in low-rise bungalows, include a contemporary trim and large bathrooms. There is an inviting restaurant-bar at the rear of the compound and even a swimming pool.

Getting There & Away

Liang US Express runs a 7.30am bus from the Sra Em roundabout to Phnom Penh (US$7.50, 10 hours) via Preah Vihear City and Kompong Thom. **Rith Mony** (☎092 511811) also has a 7.30am bus to Phnom Penh (US$10, 10 hours).

Kompong Thom

☎062 / POP 70,000

The friendly, bustling commercial town of Kompong Thom (កំពង់ធំ) sprawls either side of the lazy curves of the Stung Sen River, which winds its way through the centre. The town itself may be sparse on attractions, but it's a prime launching pad for exploring nearby sights. Both the serene, tree-entwined temples of Sambor Prei Kuk (p238), named a Unesco World Heritage Site in 2017, and the colourful wats of Phnom Santuk (p239) are easy half-day trips, while boutique accommodation and decent eating options make Kompong Thom a possible base for a long day trip to Preah Khan of Kompong Svay.

Sleeping & Eating

Arunras Hotel & Guesthouse HOTEL **$**
(☎062-961294; NH6; s/d with fan US$6/8, d with air-con US$10-15;) Dominating Kompong Thom's accommodation scene, this central establishment has 58 good-value rooms with Chinese-style decoration and on-the-ball staff. The popular restaurant downstairs dishes up tasty Khmer fare. The operators also run the 53-room Arunras Guesthouse in the same complex.

★Sambor Village Hotel BOUTIQUE HOTEL **$$**
(☎062-961391; www.samborvillage.asia; Democrat St; r/ste incl breakfast US$50/60;) This French-owned place brings boutique to Kompong Thom. Spacious, bungalow-style rooms with four-poster beds and chic bathrooms are set amid a tranquil and verdant garden with an inviting pool under the shade of a mango tree. The upstairs terrace restaurant has international cuisine and impressive hardwood flooring. Free use of mountain bikes. Located riverside, about 700m east of NH6.

★ Kompong Thom Restaurant CAMBODIAN $$
(NH6; mains US$3-8; ⏲7am-10pm; 📶🖉) With delightful waiters and a pocket-sized terrace overlooking the river, this restaurant is also Kompong Thom's most adventurous. Unique concoctions featuring Kampot pepper, water buffalo and stir-fried eel appear on the menu of Khmer classics, which come in generous portions.

Love Cafe & Pizza INTERNATIONAL $$
(☎017 916219; Democrat St; mains US$2.50-4.50, pizzas US$6.50-9.50; ⏲11am-9pm Mon-Sat; 📶) If you're in the mood for comfort food, this bamboo-walled place is a real gem. The big menu of pizzas and burgers is a winner, including some Tex-Mex moments, as is its fantastic selection of ice cream. The menu also includes some Cambodian favourites.

ℹ Information

Canadia Bank (NH6; ⏲8am-3.30pm Mon-Fri, to 11.30am Sat, ATM 24hr)

Im Sokhom Travel Agency (☎012 691527; St 3; ⏲8am-5pm) Runs guided tours, including cycling trips to Sambor Prei Kuk, and can arrange transport by *moto* to Sambor Prei Kuk (US$10) or Phnom Santuk and Santuk Silk Farm (US$8).

ℹ Getting There & Away

Dozens of buses travelling between Phnom Penh (US$5, 3½ hours) and Siem Reap (US$5, 2½ hours) pass through Kompong Thom. Share taxis are the fastest way to Phnom Penh (25,000r, three hours) and Siem Reap (25,000r, 2½ hours). Heading north to Preah Vihear City, share taxis cost US$5 and take two hours. Most taxi services depart from the **taxi park**, one block east of the **Tela Gas Station** on NH6; taxis to Phnom Penh depart from the Tela Gas Station.

Around Kompong Thom

Sambor Prei Kuk HINDU TEMPLE
(សំបូរព្រៃគុក; www.samborpreikuk.com; US$10; ⏲6am-6pm) Cambodia's most impressive group of pre-Angkorian monuments, Sambor Prei Kuk encompasses more than 100 mainly brick temples scattered through the forest, among them some of the oldest structures in the country. The attraction was recently named Cambodia's third Unesco World Heritage site.

A 40-minute drive from Kompong Thom, the area has a serene and soothing atmosphere, with the sandy trails between temples looping through the shady forest. A community-based tourism initiative employs local guides, organises activities and sets up homestays.

Originally called Isanapura, Sambor Prei Kuk served as the capital of Upper Chenla during the reign of the early 7th-century King Isanavarman and continued to serve as an important learning centre during the Angkorian era.

The main temple area consists of three complexes, each enclosed by the remains of two concentric walls. The principal temple group, **Prasat Sambor** (ប្រាសាទសំបូរ), dating from the 7th and 10th centuries, is closest to the entrance and is dedicated to Gambhireshvara, one of Shiva's many incarnations (the other groups are dedicated to Shiva himself). Several of Prasat Sambor's towers retain brick carvings in fairly good condition, and there is a series of large *yoni* (female fertility symbols) around the central tower.

Prasat Yeai Poeun (ប្រាសាទយាយព័ន្ធ, Prasat Yeay Peau) is arguably the most atmospheric of the three ensembles, as it feels lost in the forest. The eastern gateway is being both held up and torn asunder by an ancient tree, the bricks interwoven with the tree's extensive, probing roots. A truly massive tree shades the western gate. **Prasat Tor** (ប្រាសាទតោ, Lion Temple) is the largest of the Sambor Prei Kuk complexes. It boasts excellent examples of Chenla carvings in the form of two large, elaborately coiffed stone lions.

Community-based organisation **Isanborei** (☎017 936112; www.samborpreikuk.com) 🍃 runs an excellent homestay program and manages the guides (half/full day US$6/10), who can be easily found hanging around the old entrance near Prasat Sambor. Isanborei also offers cooking courses, rents out bicycles (US$2 per day), organises ox-cart rides and operates a stable of *remorks* to whisk you safely to/from Kompong Thom (US$15 one way).

To get here from Kompong Thom, follow NH6 north for 5km before continuing straight on NH62 towards Preah Vihear City (the paved road to Siem Reap veers left). After 11km turn right at the laterite sign, and continue for 14km on a new sealed road to the new temple entrance, which is about 500m from the Prasat Sambor group.

From Kompong Thom, a round-trip *moto* ride out here (under an hour) should cost US$10.

Phnom Santuk BUDDHIST TEMPLE

(ភ្នំសន្ទុក; US$2) Its forest-cloaked summit adorned with Buddha images and a series of pagodas, this holy temple mountain (207m) 15km south of Kompong Thom is a popular site of Buddhist pilgrimage. To reach the top, huff up 809 stairs – with the upper staircase home to troops of animated macaques – or wimp out and take the paved 2.5km road. Santuk hosts an extraordinary ensemble of colourful wats and stupas, a kaleidoscopic mishmash of old and new Buddhist statuary and monuments.

EASTERN CAMBODIA

POP 6.5 MILLION

If it's a walk on the wild side that fires your imagination, then the northeast is calling. It's home to rare forest elephants and freshwater dolphins, and peppering the area are thundering waterfalls, crater lakes and meandering rivers. Trekking, biking, kayaking and elephant adventures are all beginning to take off. The rolling hills and lush forests provide a home to many ethnic minority groups. Do the maths: it all adds up to an amazing experience.

Kompong Cham

☎042 / POP 118,240

Kompong Cham (កំពង់ចាម), an important trading post during the French period, serves as the gateway to Cambodia's northeast. Most action is on the riverfront. The surrounding province of Kompong Cham is a land of picturesque villages and quiet Mekong meanders. Some of Cambodia's finest silk is woven here.

Sights

Wat Hanchey BUDDHIST TEMPLE

(វត្តហាន់ជ័យ) This hilltop pagoda was an important centre of worship during the Chenla (pre-Angkorian) period, when, as today, it offered some of the best Mekong views in Cambodia. The foundations of several 8th-century structures, some of them destroyed by American bombs, are scattered around the compound, along with a clutch of bizarre fruit and animal statues. It's 20km north of Kompong Cham; the smooth trip out here takes about 30 minutes on a motorbike.

Koh Paen ISLAND

(កោះប៉ែន) This serene island in the Mekong River just south of town offers a slice of rural local life, with fruit and vegetable farms and traditional wooden houses. During the dry season, several sandbars – the closest thing to a beach in this part of Cambodia – appear around the island. Bicycles can be hired from some local guesthouses to explore under your own steam.

Wat Nokor Bachey BUDDHIST TEMPLE

(វត្តនគរបាជ័យ; US$3) The original fusion temple, Wat Nokor is a modern Theravada Buddhist pagoda squeezed into the walls of a 12th-century Mahayana Buddhist shrine of sandstone and laterite. It's located down a pretty dirt road just off the highway to Phnom Penh, about 2.5km west of the centre.

Sleeping & Eating

★Tmor Da Guesthouse HOTEL $

(☎011 662659; Sihanouk St; r US$15-25;) This smart place is really more of a hotel than a guesthouse, offering stylish and tasteful rooms with a contemporary wood trim. The VIP units are the best riverfront deal in town. Don't be put off by the low ceiling of the mezzanine lobby, as the rooms are really very spacious once you are inside.

★Hanchey Bamboo Resort RESORT $$

(☎076 254 2440; www.bambooresort.org; Preaek Preah Angk; dm/bungalow US$10/63;) This eye-pleasing resort built entirely from natural materials is a real stunner, perched atop a hill near Wat Hanchey, 20km north of Kompong Cham. A matrix of bamboo forms the open-air restaurant and yoga studio (daily classes are included in the rates), while the 10 bungalows have thatched roofs shaped like turtle shells. There's also a block of stylish dorms.

★Smile Restaurant CAMBODIAN $

(www.bsda-cambodia.org; Sihanouk St; mains US$3-7; 6.30am-10pm;) Run by the non-profit Buddhism for Social Development Action (BSDA), this handsome restaurant is a huge hit with the NGO crowd for its big breakfasts and authentic Khmer cuisine, such as *char k'dau* (stir-fry with lemongrass, hot basil and peanuts) and black-pepper squid. Western dishes are on the menu as well, and it sells BSDA-made *krama* (checked scarves) and trinkets.

Destiny Coffee House CAFE $
(017 860775; 12 Vithei Pasteur St; mains US$3-5; 7am-5pm Mon-Sat;) The international menu at this stylish and air-conditioned cafe breaks the mould with a delicious hummus platter, lip-smacking homemade cakes, breakfast burritos, salads and wraps. For a self-proclaimed coffee house, however, it's lacking a proper espresso machine.

★ **Moustache & Nico** FRENCH $$
(096 821 3005; 11 Vithei Pasteur St; mains 18,000-28,000r; 4pm-late, closed Mon Jun-Nov;) The best Western food in Kompong Cham by leaps and bounds, with a rotating chalkboard menu of delectable homemade specialities prepared by French chef 'Moustache' and his business partner Nico. Luxuries such as pâté, Camembert cheese and cocktail olives all make cameos.

Information

Canadia Bank (Preah Monivong Blvd; 8am-3.30pm Mon-Fri, to 11.30am Sat, ATM 24hr) ATM plus cash advances on credit cards.

J Trust Royal Bank (Preah Monivong Blvd; 8am-4pm Mon-Fri, ATM 24hr) Has an ATM.

Getting There & Away

Phnom Penh is 120km southwest of Kompong Cham. If you are heading north to Kratie or beyond, arrange transport via the sealed road to Chhlong rather than taking a huge detour east to Snuol on NH7.

Besides buses, share taxis (20,000r) and overcrowded local minibuses (12,000r) do the dash to Phnom Penh from the **taxi park** (Preah Bat Ketmealea St) near the New Market (Psar Thmei). The trip takes two hours or more, depending on traffic in the capital. Express minivans are another option to the capital (US$6, two hours); arrange these through your guesthouse.

Morning share taxis and minibuses to Kratie (US$5, 2½ hours) and Stung Treng (US$10, 4½ hours) depart when full from the **Caltex station** (NH7) at the main roundabout. There are morning minibuses from the taxi park as well.

There are no longer any passenger boats to other towns running on the Mekong from here.

Getting Around

Figure on US$10 to US$15 per day for a *moto* and US$15 to US$20 for a *remork* (slightly more if including Wat Maha Leap in your plans). Round-trip *remork* journeys to Wat Hanchey or Phnom Pros and Phnom Srei are a negotiable US$10. Most guesthouses and restaurants on the riverfront rent motorbikes (US$5 per day) and bicycles (US$2 per day).

Kratie

072 / POP 35,965

A supremely mellow riverside town, Kratie (ក្រចេះ, pronounced kra-*cheh*) has an expansive riverfront and some of the best Mekong sunsets in Cambodia. It is the most popular place in the country to see Irrawaddy dolphins, which live in the Mekong River in ever-diminishing numbers. There are also fine examples of French-era architecture, as Kratie was spared the wartime bombing that destroyed so many other provincial centres.

Many visitors are drawn to the rare freshwater Irrawaddy dolphins found in Kampi, about 15km north of the provincial capital, but Kratie itself is a little charmer and makes a good base from which to explore the surrounding countryside.

Sights & Activities

Phnom Sombok BUDDHIST TEMPLE
(ភ្នំសំបុក; 6am-6pm) FREE This small hill with an active wat offers the best views across the Mekong on this stretch of the

BUSES FROM KOMPONG CHAM

DESTINATION	PRICE (US$)	DURATION (HR)	COMPANIES	FREQUENCY
Ban Lung	11	7	Liang US Express (van)	7.30am
Battambang	7.50	8	Liang US Express, PP Sorya	7.30am & 8.30am
Kratie via Snuol	4.50	4	PP Sorya	10am & 12.30pm
Phnom Penh	4-5	3	Liang US Express, PP Sorya	hourly till 5pm
Sen Monorom	9	6	Liang US Express (van)	8am & 1pm
Siem Reap	6.50	6	Liang US Express, PP Sorya	7.30am & 8.30am
Stung Treng	7	6	Liang US Express (van), PP Sorya	7.30am & 10am

river. Located on the road from Kratie to Kampi, a visit here can easily be combined with a trip to see the dolphins for an extra couple of dollars.

★Cambodian Pride Tours TOURS
(☎088 836 4758; www.cambodianpridetours.com) Tours operated by experienced, Kratie-born guide Sithy, who is keen to promote real-life experiences, such as homestays and excursions supporting the local community. He organises single- and multi-day trips along the Mekong Discovery Trail (p243), half-day dolphin encounters or 'local living' tours and more elaborate wildlife adventures further afield to Ratanakiri.

Sleeping & Eating

Kratie offers a good selection of guesthouses and hotels, many with river views. For something even more relaxed than Kratie, consider staying directly on the island of Koh Trong, where homestays and boutique accommodation await.

★Le Tonlé Tourism Training Center GUESTHOUSE $
(☎072-210505; www.letonle.org; St 3; fan r without bathroom US$9, air-con r with bathroom US$20;) The Cambodian Rural Development Team (CRDT) runs this fantastic budget guesthouse in a beautiful wooden house in the centre. With silk pillows and bed runners, agreeable art and photos, wood floors and a great hang-out area, it puts plenty of care into the design. Rooms are somewhat dark and fan-cooled, but share boutique-quality bathrooms. It doubles as a training centre for at-risk locals.

There's a great restaurant (open 6.30am to 9pm) downstairs with delicious food prepared by program trainees. There are a few equally appealing air-conditioned rooms with private bathrooms across the street above the main CRDTours office (p243).

Koh Trong Community Homestay I HOMESTAY $
(Koh Trong; mattress per person US$4, fan r without bathroom US$8, r with air-con & bathroom US$20;) Set in an old wooden house, with dorm-style accommodation as well as proper bedrooms and fancy-pants bathrooms (that is, thrones not squats). There are two newer bungalows out back with upgraded air-con rooms. The complex is located within a pretty garden about 2km north of the island's ferry dock. Ride your bike or take a *moto* (US$1).

Kratie

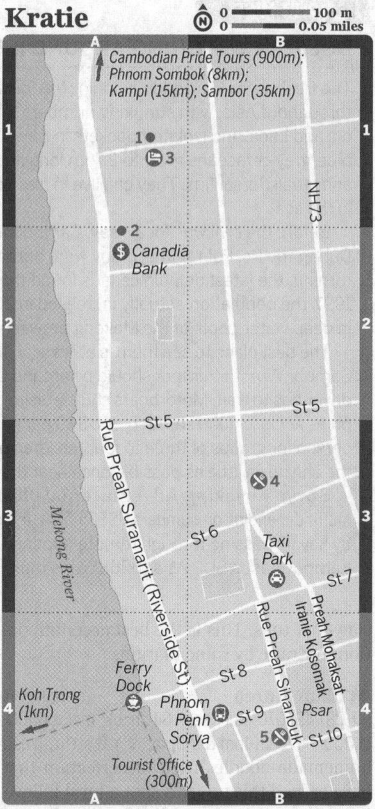

Kratie

Activities, Courses & Tours
1 CRDTours A1
2 Sorya Kayaking Adventures A2

Sleeping
3 Le Tonlé Tourism Training Center A1

Eating
4 Mlub Putrea B3
Pete's Pizza Pasta & Cafe .... (see 2)
5 Tokae Restaurant B4

★Rajabori Villas BOUTIQUE HOTEL $$$
(☎012 770150; www.rajabori-kratie.com; Koh Trong; r incl breakfast US$65-150;) A boutique lodge on the northern tip of Koh Trong island with a swimming pool and large dark-wood bungalows finished in inspired French-Khmer style. Each of the 16 rooms is uniquely designed, but all contain luxurious

DON'T MISS

DOLPHIN WATCHING AROUND KRATIE

The freshwater Irrawaddy dolphin *(trey pisaut* in Khmer*)* is an endangered species throughout Asia, with shrinking numbers inhabiting stretches of the Mekong in Cambodia and Laos, and isolated pockets in Bangladesh, Myanmar and Indonesian Borneo. The blue-grey cetaceans grow to 2.75m long and are recognisable by their bulging foreheads and small dorsal fins. They can live in fresh or salt water, although they are seldom seen in the sea.

Before the civil war, locals say, Cambodia was home to as many as 1000 dolphins. During the Pol Pot regime, many were hunted for their oils, but perhaps the tide is finally turning: the latest dolphin census found that, for the first time since counting began in 1997, the population actually increased in 2017 to 92, up from 80 in 2015. All of them live in deep water pools of the Mekong between Kratie and the Lao border.

The best place to see them is at **Kampi**, about 15km north of Kratie, on the road to Sambor. A *moto/remork* should be around US$7/10 return, depending on how long the driver has to wait. Motorboats shuttle visitors out to the middle of the river to view the dolphins at close quarters. It costs US$9 per person for one or two passengers and US$7 per person for groups of three to four (children are US$4). Encourage the boat driver to use the engine as little as possible once near the dolphins, as the noise is sure to disturb them.

Sorya Kayaking Adventures (☎010 285656; www.soryakayaking.com; Rue Preah Suramarit; depending on numbers US$25-52) runs excellent half-day trips to see the dolphins by kayak, passing through remote flooded forest and sandbars. If you prefer to stand up, Kampot-based SUP Asia (p268) runs multi-day paddleboarding tours here.

claw-foot tubs. This is the best accommodation in Kratie by some margin.

★Mlub Putrea CAMBODIAN $
(☎087 495070; Rue Preah Sihanouk; mains 6000-11,000r; ⏲6am-1pm & 3-9pm; 📶) It's the fresh homemade noodles fried to perfection that have earned this no-frills spot a loyal following among visitors and locals alike. Part of the allure is also chef Nary, the petite owner with an affinity for jumbo-sized glasses.

Pete's Pizza Pasta & Cafe INTERNATIONAL $
(☎010 285656; www.petescafekratie.com; Rue Preah Suramarit; dishes US$1-5; ⏲7am-9pm; 📶) Get your home fix of pizza, pasta, toasties and salads at this internationally run riverfront cafe. The menu includes homemade bakery items such as pumpkin bread, muffins and cookies. By night it doubles as a small bar.

Tokae Restaurant CAMBODIAN $
(☎096 742 4445; St 10; mains US$2-5; ⏲6.30am-9.30pm; 📶) Look out for Cambodia's largest *tokae* (gecko) on the wall to find this excellent little eatery. The menu offers a good mix of cheap Cambodian dishes, such as curries and *amok*, plus equally affordable Western breakfasts and comfort food. Chefs also run rooftop cooking classes (US$15), which begin with a trip across the street to the market.

ℹ Information

Canadia Bank (Rue Preah Suramarit; ⏲8.30am-3.30pm Mon-Fri, to 11.30am Sat, ATM 24hr) ATM offering cash withdrawals, plus currency exchange.

ℹ Getting There & Away

Kratie is 250km northeast of Phnom Penh (via the Chhlong road) and 141km south of Stung Treng.

Phnom Penh Sorya (☎081 908006; www.ppsoryatransport.com.kh; cnr St 9 & Rue Preah Suramarit) operates two buses per day to Phnom Penh (US$8, seven hours, 7.30am and 9.30am) along the slow route (via Snuol). Express minivans get to Phnom Penh in four hours via Chhlong (US$8, about six daily), and usually offer transfers onward to Sihanoukville.

Sorya has two daily buses to Siem Reap (US$11, nine hours, 7.30am and 9.30am). There's also an express minivan to Siem Reap (US$12, six hours, 7am). Share taxis (US$10) head to Phnom Penh between 6am and 8am from the **taxi park** (Rue Preah Sihanouk), with possible additional departures after lunch.

Local minibuses also serve Ban Lung from the taxi park (US$8, five hours, 8am and 1pm). Sorya has buses at 12.30pm and 2pm to Stung Treng (US$5, 2½ hours), and there's also a 7am minibus (US$6, two hours). There's a 7.30am minibus to Preah Vihear City (Tbeng Meanchey; US$15, five hours). To get to Laos, you must transfer in Stung Treng; Kratie guesthouses can arrange this.

For Sen Monorom, there are two daily minibuses (US$7, 3½ hours, 7.30am and noon). Alternatively, take a local minibus from the taxi park (US$5, four hours, two or three early-morning departures).

Stung Treng

☎074 / POP 35,000

Located on the Tonlé San near its confluence with the Mekong, Stung Treng (ស្ទឹងត្រែង) is a quiet town with limited appeal, but sees a lot of transit traffic heading north to Laos, south to Kratie, east to Ratanakiri and west to Siem Reap. Just north of the town centre, a major bridge across the San leads to the Lao border, while an important newer bridge traverses the Mekong south of town, connecting Stung Treng to Preah Vihear and Siem Reap.

Sights & Activities

Mekong Blue ARTS CENTRE
(មេគង្គប៊្លូ; ☎012 622096; www.mekongblue.com; ⊙7.30-11.30am & 1.30-5pm Mon-Fri) Part of the Stung Treng Women's Development Centre, this silk-weaving centre on the outskirts of town specialises in exquisite silk products for sale and export. It is possible to observe the dyers and weavers, most of whom come from vulnerable or impoverished backgrounds. The centre is about 4km east of the town centre on the riverside road that continues under the bridge.

Xplore-Cambodia ADVENTURE
(Cambodia Mekong Trail; ☎088 753 3337, 011 433836; www.cambodiamekongtrail.com) Doles out brochures, booklets and advice, and tailors one- to seven-day cycling or kayak tours along the Mekong Discovery Trail. Popular one-day trips include boating to see the dolphins, hiking near Preah Rumkel, and kayaking down the Mekong. Also rents sturdy Trek mountain bikes (US$5 per day). Multiday rides are possible with a mountain bike drop-off in Kratie.

Sleeping & Eating

★4 Rivers Hotel HOTEL $
(☎070 507822; www.fourrivershotel.com; US$15-35; ❄@📶) Stung Treng's most appealing hotel has a surprising wine cabinet in the lobby and a sky bar on the roof overlooking the Tonlé San and Mekong River. Rooms feature a contemporary trim; it's worth paying a little extra for the river-view options.

Golden River Hotel HOTEL $
(☎012 980678; www.goldenriverhotel.com; r US$15-35; ❄@📶) The best all-rounder in the town centre, the Golden River has 50 well-appointed rooms complete with hot-water bathrooms, fridges and TVs. Rooms at the front are a few dollars more thanks to panoramic views of the Tonlé San.

Blue River CAMBODIAN $
(☎088 666 6105; mains US$4-5; ⊙10am-10pm; 📶) This floating restaurant – lit by lanterns and adorned with gnarled driftwood – is the perfect place to toss back an Angkor beer

OFF THE BEATEN TRACK

MEKONG DISCOVERY TRAIL

It's well worth spending a couple of days exploring the various bike rides and activities on offer along the Mekong Discovery Trail, an initiative to open up stretches of the Mekong River around Stung Treng and Kratie to community-based tourism. Once managed by the government with foreign development assistance, its trails and routes are now being kept alive by private tour companies, such as Xplore-Cambodia in Stung Treng and **CRDTours** (Cambodia Rural Discovery Tours; ☎099 834353; http://crdtours.com; St 3; ⊙8am-noon & 2-5.30pm) and Cambodian Pride Tours (p241) in Kratie.

It's a worthy project, as it aims to offer fishing communities an alternative income, in order to protect the Irrawaddy dolphin and other rare species on this stretch of river.

There's a great booklet with routes and maps outlining excursions around Kratie and Stung Treng, but you'll be hard-pressed to secure your own copy; ask tour operators if you can photograph theirs. The routes can be tackled by bicycle or motorbike. They range in length from a few hours to several days, with optional overnights in village homestays. Routes crisscross the Mekong frequently by ferry and traverse several Mekong islands, including Koh Trong.

and watch the sun plunge into the Tonlé San. Food is standard Cambodian fare.

Ponika's Palace INTERNATIONAL **$**
(Stung Treng Burger; ☎012 916441; mains US$2-5; ⊙6am-10pm) Need a break from *laab* salad after Laos? Burgers, pizza and English breakfasts grace the menu, along with Indian food and wonderful Khmer curries. Affable owner Ponika speaks English and cold beer is available to slake a thirst.

ℹ Information

Canadia Bank (⊙8.30am-3.30pm Mon-Fri, to 11.30am Sat, ATM 24hr) Has an international ATM.

Riverside Guesthouse (☎012 257207, 097 725 7257; kimtysou@gmail.com; r with fan/air-con US$6/12; 📶) Specialises in getting people to/from Laos, Siem Reap or just about anywhere else. Also runs boat tours to the Lao border, with a trip to see the resident dolphin pod (US$100/120 for two/four people). English-speaking guides offer motorbike tours around the province.

ℹ Getting There & Away

NH7 north to the Lao border and south to Kratie is in reasonable shape these days, though it's still a bit of a bumpy ride.

Express minivans with guesthouse pickups as early as 4am are the quickest way to Phnom Penh (US$13, seven hours). A sleeper bus departs at 9pm (US$13, eight hours). Book through Riverside Guesthouse, Xplore-Cambodia (p243) or Ponika's Palace.

Phnom Penh Sorya (☎092 504066; www.ppsoryatransport.com.kh) has a 7am bus to Phnom Penh (US$10, nine hours) via Kratie (US$5, 2½ hours) and Kompong Cham (US$8, six hours). Additionally, local minibuses to Kratie depart regularly until 2pm from the riverfront bus lot (by the market).

There is a comfortable tourist van to Ban Lung (US$6, two hours, 8am and 1pm), with additional morning trips in cramped local minibuses from the riverfront bus lot (US$5, three hours).

The new highway west from Thala Boravit to Preah Vihear via Chhep is in great shape. **Asia Van Transfer** (☎071 844 3566, 012 505673; www.asiavantransfer.com; Riverside Guesthouse) has an express minibus to Siem Reap at 2pm daily (US$18, five hours), with a stop in Preah Vihear City (Tbeng Meanchey; US$12, three hours). **Virak Buntham** (☎092 222423; www.virakbuntham.com) runs the same route to Siem Reap at noon daily (US$12, five hours).

For Laos, minivans head over the border at around 1pm and 2pm, serving Pakse (US$15, six hours) and Don Det (US$12, three hours) respectively.

ℹ GETTING TO LAOS: TRAPEANG KRIEL TO NONG NOK KHIENE

Getting to the border The remote Trapeang Kriel–Nong Nok Khiene border (open 6am to 5.30pm), 65km north of Stung Treng, is a popular crossing point on the Indochina overland circuit. For many years, there was a separate river crossing here, but that's no longer open. There are also no longer any through buses between Phnom Penh and Pakse. You'll need to get yourself to Stung Treng, from where there are at least two minivans per day (at 1pm and 2pm) that run across the border and onward to the 4000 Islands and Pakse. The only other option to the border is a private taxi (around US$40) or *moto* (motorcycle taxi; around US$15) from Stung Treng.

At the border Both Lao and Cambodian visas are available on arrival (remember to bring passport photos). Entering Laos, it costs US$30 to US$42 for a visa, depending on nationality, plus a US$2 fee (dubbed either an 'overtime' or a 'processing' fee, depending on when you cross) upon both entry and exit.

Entering Cambodia, the price of a visa is jacked up to US$35 from the normal US$30. The extra US$5 is called 'tea money', as the border guards have been stationed at such a remote crossing. In addition, the Cambodians sometimes charge US$1 for a cursory medical inspection upon arrival in the country, and levy a US$2 processing fee upon exit. These fees might be waived if you protest, but don't protest for too long or your vehicle may leave without you.

Moving on There's virtually zero traffic on either side of the border. If you're dropped at the border, expect to pay 150,000/50,000 kip (US$12/4) for a taxi/*săhm-lór* (Lao *tuk tuk*) heading north to Ban Nakasang (for Don Det).

Mondulkiri Province

POP 75,000

Mondulkiri Province (ខេត្តមណ្ឌលគិរី), the original 'Wild East', is a world apart from the lowlands, with not a rice paddy or palm tree in sight.

Home to the hardy Bunong people and their noble elephants, this upland area is a seductive mix of grassy hills, pine groves and rainforests of jade green. Wild animals, such as bears, leopards and especially elephants, are more numerous here than elsewhere, although sightings are usually limited to birds, monkeys and the occasional wild pig. Conservationists have established several superb ecotourism projects in the province, but are facing off against loggers, poachers, plantations and well-connected speculators.

Mondulkiri means 'Meeting of the Hills', an apt sobriquet for this land of rolling hills. It is the most sparsely populated province in the country, with just four people per square kilometre.

Sen Monorom

073 / POP 10,000

A charming community where the famous hills meet, the area around Sen Monorom is peppered with minority villages and picturesque waterfalls, making it the ideal place to spend some time. Set at an altitude of more than 800m, the town can get quite chilly, so bring warm clothing.

Sights & Activities

★Bou Sraa Waterfall WATERFALL

(ទឹកជ្រោះប៊ូស្រា; US$2.50; 7am-5pm) Plunging into the dense jungle below, this is one of Cambodia's most impressive falls. Famous throughout the country, this double-drop waterfall has an upper tier of some 10m and a spectacular lower tier with a thundering 25m drop. Getting here involves a 33km, one-hour journey east of Sen Monorom on a mostly sealed road.

Wat Phnom Doh Kromom BUDDHIST TEMPLE

(វត្តភ្នំដោះក្រមុំ) FREE Looming over the northeast corner of the airstrip, Wat Phnom Doh Kromom has Mondulkiri's best sunset vista, where a wooden platform lets you take in the views over Sen Monorom. Continue another 5km north to the wat for **Samot Cheur** (Ocean of Trees), a viewpoint overlooking an emerald forest to the east.

★Elephant Valley Project WILDLIFE RESERVE

(EVP; 099 696041; www.elephantvalleyproject.org; Mon-Fri, Sun high season only) For an original elephant experience, visit this pioneering 'walking with the herd' project, which entices local mahouts to bring their overworked or injured elephants to this 1500-hectare sanctuary. It's very popular, so make sure you book well ahead. You can visit for a day (US$95), a half-day (US$45) or overnight.

Sam Veasna Center WILDLIFE

(SVC; 063 963710, 092 554473; www.samveasna.org) SVC works with the international NGO Wildlife Conservation Society in promoting wildlife and birdwatching tours in the nearby Keo Seima Wildlife Sanctuary (p246), including rare primate spotting at the wonderful Jahoo Gibbon Camp (p246), 30km west of Sen Monorom. Mony Sang, who runs the programme, is based in Siem Reap, so it's best to book well in advance. Hefalump Cafe (p247) provides info in Sen Monorom.

WEHH ECOTOUR

(088 613 6921; tongsamnang13@gmail.com; from US$55) The WEHH tour program offers an intimate look at Bunong culture in the Dam Dak community. Itineraries include 'life on a Bunong farm', 'the handicrafts of the Bunong' and a trek into old-growth Bunong forest. Prices start from US$55 per person, subject to the size of the group. Book at the Hefalump Cafe (p247).

Sleeping

★Nature Lodge GUESTHOUSE $

(012 230272; www.naturelodgecambodia.com; s/d/f from US$10/15/30;) Sprawling across a windswept hilltop near town are 30 solid wood bungalows with private porches, hot showers and mosquito nets. Among them are *Swiss Family Robinson*-style chalets with sunken beds and anterooms. The magnificent restaurant has comfy nooks, a pool table and an enviable bar, where guests chill out and swap travel tales.

Trek-fuelling burgers and pasta are the restaurant's speciality, plus plenty of vegetarian options. An array of tours are neatly outlined on the menu, including the affiliated **Mondulkiri Elephant & Wildlife Sanctuary** (011 494449; www.mondulkirisanctuary.org; NH76; day visits per adult US$50, child 6-14yr US$25, under 6yr free).

DON'T MISS

MONKEY BUSINESS IN MONDULKIRI

A recent Wildlife Conservation Society (WCS) study estimated populations of 23,600 black-shanked doucs and more than 1200 southern yellow-cheeked crested gibbons in **Keo Seima Wildlife Sanctuary** (ដែនជម្រកសត្វព្រៃកែវសីមា; http://cambodia.wcs.org; Andong Kroloeng; wildlife-spotting tours per person US$85-125;) , formerly Seima Protected Forest. These are the world's largest known populations of both species. **Jahoo Gibbon Camp** (community contact 088 592 8758; http://samveasna.org; Andong Kroloeng; per person incl meals US$85-200) offers the chance to trek into the wild and try to spot these primates, along with other elusive animals, thanks to an exciting project supported by the humanitarian organisation World Hope International (www.worldhope.org) in the Bunong village of Andong Kroloeng.

The Jahoo Gibbon Camp provides local villagers with an incentive to conserve the endangered primates and their habitat through providing a sustainable income. Treks wind their way through mixed evergreen forest and waterfalls, with an excellent chance of spotting the doucs and macaques along the way. Gibbons are very shy and harder to see, but thanks to recent field research by WCS and the community, the local gibbon families are more used to people than gibbons elsewhere. You'll need to be up before dawn to spot them, however, so sleeping at the camp is highly recommended.

Many other species are present in this area, including an enormous diversity of birdlife, such as the spectacular giant hornbill and peafowl. There are also chances to find the tracks and signs of more elusive species, such as bears, gaur (wild cattle) and elephants.

Registered guides, together with local Bunong guides, accompany visitors along the trails. A conservation contribution is included in the cost of the trip, which supports community development projects.

For information and booking, contact the Sam Veasna Center (p245) through the Hefalump Cafe in Sen Monorom. You can also book tours with **The Hangout** (088 721 9991; NH76) in Sen Monorom.

Indigenous Peoples Lodge BUNGALOW $
(012 471864; indigenouspeopleslodge@gmail.com; s/d/q from US$8/15/25;) Run by a Bunong family, this is a great place to stay, with a range of accommodation set in minority houses, including a traditional thatched Bunong house with an upgrade or two. The cheapest rooms involve a share bathroom, but are good value. Perks include free internet and free drop-offs in town.

Tree Lodge BUNGALOW $
(097 723 4177; www.treelodgecambodia.com; d/q/f US$7/12/15;) Sixteen bungalows of various shapes and sizes drip down a hillside at the back of the reception. Rooms have balconies and attractive open-air bathrooms, but lack any shelf space or furniture besides a bed. Hang out at the restaurant, where hammocks and tasty Khmer food await.

Green House Retreat BUNGALOW $$
(017 905659; dm US$12, bungalow US$12-45;) Opened in 2017, this lovely little resort on the edge of town offers a generous dorm and some stylish and spacious bungalows. There are extensive gardens, organic vegetables grown on-site and a restaurant-bar to soak up the views of the surrounding hills.

★Mayura Hill Hotel & Resort HOTEL $$$
(077 980980; www.mayurahillresort.com; incl breakfast r US$100-120, ste US$150;) Setting the standard for upscale accommodation in Mondulkiri, Mayura Hill is a lovely place to stay for those with the budget. The 11 villa rooms are tastefully appointed with woods and silks and the family villa includes a bunk for the children. Facilities include a swimming pool and a five-a-side football pitch! The restaurant is the most sophisticated in town.

Eating & Drinking

★Bunong Kitchen CAMBODIAN $
(097 790 4244; mains US$3-4; 6.30am-8pm;) A lovely little training restaurant for Bunong people where you can try traditional soups, such as *trav brang* (with jackfruit, pumpkin, long beans and eggplant). You'll also find locally sourced coffee and Bunong desserts including *skoo* (a boiled jungle root

with honey and sugar). All dishes are vegetarian but you can add meat to them if you like.

Hefalump Cafe CAFE **$**
(www.facebook.com/hefalumpcafe; NH76; cakes US$1-3; 6.30am-6pm Mon-Fri, 8am-4pm Sun;) A collaboration of various NGOs and conservation groups in town, this cafe doubles as a hospitality training centre for Bunong people. Local coffee or Lavazza, teas, cakes and healthy breakfasts make this a great spot to plan your adventures over a cuppa.

★ **Mondulk...Italy** ITALIAN **$$**
(096 674 2693; www.facebook.com/Mondulk.Italy; NH76; mains US$4.50-7; 10am-1.30pm & 6-10pm Mon-Sat;) When you're craving an Aperol spritz, homemade pasta or an evening glass of wine paired with a selection of fine cheeses, you never expect you'll find such things in a remote outpost like Sen Monorom. Think again! This hole-in-the-wall Italian restaurant may not be much to look at, but the cooking and ingredients are top-notch.

★ **The Hangout** BAR
(088 721 9991; 7am-late) The most happening spot in town. There are bar sports including table football, occasional jam sessions and some of Sen Monorom's best Western food to complement the Khmer menu (mains US$2 to US$7). It's run by an affable Tasmanian-Khmer couple.

MK Coffee Shop COFFEE
(www.mondulkiri-coffee.com; Market Area; 7am-8pm;) Watch out Starbucks, MK Coffee is in town. It is unlikely MK Coffee will face international competition any time soon given the remoteness of Sen Monorom, but it is ready with this contemporary cafe. This is barista-brewed coffee practically from the source – it operates a coffee plantation nearby.

Information

Acleda Bank (NH76; 8.30am-4pm Mon-Fri, to 11.30am Sat, ATM 24hr) Changes major currencies and has a 24-hour ATM.

Hefalump Cafe This NGO-run cafe doubles as a drop-in centre for Bunong people and is the best source of information on sustainable tourism in Mondulkiri Province, including the Elephant Valley Project, the Keo Seima Wildlife Sanctuary and responsible tours to Bunong communities.

Getting There & Away

The stretch of NH76 connecting Sen Monorom to Snuol and Phnom Penh (370km) is in fantastic shape and passes through large tracts of protected forest in Mondulkiri Province itself. Hardcore dirt bikers may still prefer the old French road, known as the 'King's Highway', that heads east from Keo Seima, which runs roughly parallel to NH76 and pops out near Andong Kroloeng, about 30km from Sen Monorom.

There are no longer any buses to Phnom Penh, so take an express minivan (US$10 to US$11, six hours, frequent). There are several competing companies, but local residents say Virak Buntham has the most spacious seating.

Kim Seng Express (012 790889) Up to seven minivans to Phnom Penh daily (US$10, six hours).

Rithya Express (092 963243; NH76) Minivans to Phnom Penh daily at 7am and 1pm (US$10, six hours), plus Siem Reap at 7.45am (US$18, 10 hours).

Virak Buntham Express (017 666955; www.virakbuntham.com) Two morning and two afternoon departures daily to Phnom Penh in 11-seater vans (US$11, six hours), as well as a sleeper bus at 10.30pm (US$11, eight hours). Also travels to Siem Reap at 7am and 6.30pm (US$18, 10 hours). Be sure to check in advance that the Siem Reap trip doesn't involve a bus change in Phnom Penh.

There is usually one morning and one afternoon express minivan to Ban Lung (US$7, three hours) and a noon express minivan to Kratie (US$7, three hours), which can be booked through your guesthouse.

Local minibuses, departing from the **taxi park**, are another way to Kratie (20,000r, four hours). Count on one morning departure at around 8am, with a possible second departure around noon.

Ratanakiri Province

POP 195,000

Popular Ratanakiri Province (ខេត្តរតនគិរី) is a diverse region of outstanding natural beauty that provides a remote home for a mosaic of peoples – Jarai, Tompuon, Brau and Kreung minorities, plus Lao.

Ban Lung

075 / POP 45,000

Affectionately known as *dey krahorm* ('red earth') after the distinctly red ground upon which it sits, Ban Lung (បានលុង) provides a popular base for a range of Ratanakiri romps. These days the roads are mostly surfaced and the bustling town lacks the backwater charm of Sen Monorom in Mondulkiri, but with attractions such as Boeng Yeak Lom just a short hop away, there is little room for complaint. Many of the people from the surrounding villages come to Ban Lung to buy and sell at the market.

Sights

★Boeng Yeak Lom LAKE

(បឹងយក្សឡោម; US$2) At the heart of the protected area of Boeng Yeak Lom is a beautiful, emerald-hued crater lake set amid the vivid greens of the towering jungle. The lake is about 800m across and 50m deep and is believed to have been formed 700,000 years ago. It is one of the most peaceful, beautiful locations Cambodia has to offer and the water is extremely clear. Several wooden piers are dotted around the perimeter, making it perfect for swimming. A small Cultural and Environmental Centre has a modest display on ethnic minorities in the province and hires out life jackets for children.

Virachey National Park PARK

(ឧទ្យានជាតិវីរជ័យ; ☎097 333 4775; leamsou@gmail.com; ⏲office 8-11am & 2-5pm Mon-Fri) This park is one of the largest protected areas in Cambodia, stretching for 3325 sq km east to Vietnam, north to Laos and west to Stung Treng Province. Virachey has one of the more organised ecotourism programs in Cambodia, focusing on small-scale culture, nature and adventure trekking. The program aims to involve and benefit local minority communities. All treks into the park must be arranged through the Virachey National Park Eco-Tourism Information Centre (p250) in Ban Lung.

Tours

Cambodian Gibbon Ecotours WILDLIFE

(☎097 752 9960; www.cambodiangibbons.wordpress.com; tours from US$100; ⏲tours Nov–mid-Jun) Spend the night in the jungle, then rise well before dawn to spend time with semi-habituated northern buff-cheeked gibbons at this community-based ecotourism project (CBET) set up by Conservation International (CI; www.conservation.org) just outside the border of Virachey National Park, north of Veun Sai. The high-season-only tours cost US$100 to US$200 per person for a one-night, two-day trip, depending on group size and which tour company you choose. Most companies in Ban Lung can arrange these trips on behalf of CI.

Highland Tours ADVENTURE

(☎097 658 3841; highland.tour@yahoo.com) Kimi and Horng are husband-and-wife graduates of Le Tonlé Tourism Training Center, who have moved to the highlands to run a range of tours. These include fun day trips and a multi-day tour between Veun Sai and Ta Veng that combines trekking with floating down the Tonlé San on a bamboo raft. Horng is one of the only female guides in Ratanakiri.

Sleeping

★Tree Top Ecolodge BUNGALOW $

(☎012 490333; d US$8, cottage with cold/hot water US$13/15; 📶) 'Mr T's' place is one of the best places to stay in Cambodia's 'Wild East', with oodles of atmosphere. Rough-hewn walkways lead to huge bungalows featuring thatch roofs and hammock-strewn verandahs with verdant valley vistas. Like the bungalows, the restaurant is fashioned from hardwood and dangles over a lush ravine (it's also the only place you can get wi-fi).

★Family House Homestay HOMESTAY $

(☎097 481 4444; bputhea@yahoo.com; dm/d/tr US$2.50/5/7; 📶) *Remork-moto* driver and homestay owner Bun Puthea is one of the friendliest, most knowledgeable people in town. Guests rave about his cheerful hilltop homestay, which has both rooms and detached bungalows spread around a colourful garden with mountain views. Sturdy wood-carved furniture, inviting hammocks and access to a kitchen make for a pleasant stay. Some rooms share bathrooms.

Banlung Balcony GUESTHOUSE $

(☎097 809 7036; franckburlet@outlook.com; Boeng Kansaign; dm US$2, r US$5-20, bungalow US$4; 📶🏊) Under super-friendly French management, this long-standing backpackers has upped its game with a renovation of both the atmospheric main house and the enviably placed bar and restaurant, which features sunset views over the lake and an inviting pool. The cheapest rooms share bathrooms and there's a huge public balcony. New thatched bungalows run back from the pool, but are very basic.

★Terres Rouges Lodge BOUTIQUE HOTEL $$

(☎012 660902; www.ratanakiri-lodge.com; Boeng Kansaign; r/ste incl breakfast from US$65/90; ❄📶🏊) Even as the competition kicks in, Terres Rouges remains one of the most atmospheric places to stay in provincial Cam-

Ban Lung

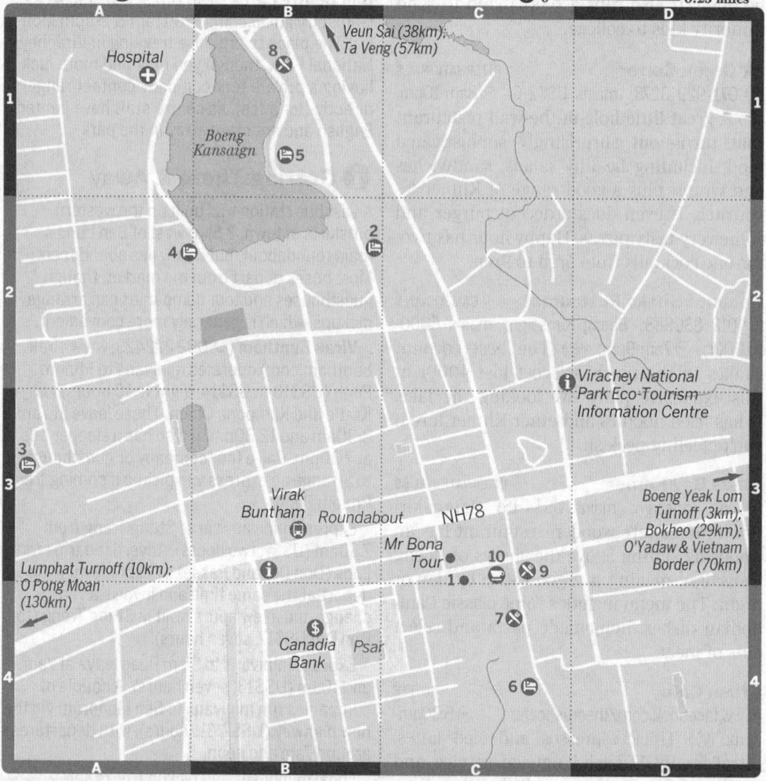

bodia. The standard rooms are small but classy, with beautiful Cambodian furniture, tribal artefacts and a long common verandah. The suites consist of spacious Balinese-style bungalows with open-plan bathrooms, set in the gorgeous garden.

Ratanakiri Boutique Hotel HOTEL **$$**
(☎070 565750; www.ratanakiri-boutiquehotel.com; Boeng Kansaign; standard/lake-view r US$19/25, ste US$60;) This smart hotel with panoramic lake views offers spry service for this remote corner of the country. With inlaid-stone bathroom walls and indigenous bed runners, the Khmer-inspired design is eye-catching, but you're mainly staying here for the combination of lake-view balconies and generous mod cons.

Eating & Drinking

★**Cafe Alee** INTERNATIONAL **$**
(mains US$1.50-7.50; 7am-9pm;) This friendly cafe has one of the more interesting menus in town, including a generous smattering of vegetarian options, a hearty lasagne and the full gamut of Khmer food. Be sure to check the exciting specials board. It

Ban Lung

Activities, Courses & Tours
1 Highland Tours ... C3

Sleeping
2 Banlung Balcony ... B2
3 Family House Homestay ... A3
4 Ratanakiri Boutique Hotel ... A2
5 Terres Rouges Lodge ... B1
6 Tree Top Ecolodge ... C4

Eating
7 Cafe Alee ... C4
8 Coconut Shake Restaurant ... B1
9 Green Carrot ... C3
Pteas Bay Khmer ... (see 4)

Drinking & Nightlife
10 Crush Cafe ... C3

often stays open later if there is drinking to be done. It also runs a scholarship to send minority kids to college.

★Green Carrot INTERNATIONAL $
(☎071 929 3278; mains US$2-6; ⏰8am-10pm; 📶) A great little hole-in-the-wall restaurant that turns out surprisingly sophisticated food, including healthy salads, sandwiches and wraps, plus a good range of Khmer favourites. It even does a decent burger and some very tasty pizzas. Happy hour has two-for-one cocktails from 5pm to 9pm.

Coconut Shake Restaurant CAMBODIAN $
(☎012 830988; Boeng Kansaign; mains 6000-16,000r; ⏰7am-9pm; 📶) The best coconut shakes in the northeast cost just 4000r at this expansive place overlooking the lake. It has fried noodles and other Khmer fare if you're feeling peckish.

Pteas Bay Khmer INTERNATIONAL $$
(Boeng Kansaign; mains US$4-15) Ratanakiri Boutique Hotel's wooden restaurant has an imposing setting above the shores of Boeng Kansaign, making it a good stop by day or night. The menu includes some classic Cambodian dishes, homemade pasta and select cuts of meat.

Crush Cafe COFFEE
(www.facebook.com/thecrushcafe; ⏰6.30am-7pm; 📶) Thick espressos and iced lattes, ultrafriendly English-language service and strong wi-fi make this cute little coffee shop the best in the region.

ℹ Information

Canadia Bank (⏰8.30am-3.30pm Mon-Fri, to 11.30am Sat, ATM 24hr) Full-service bank with an international ATM.

Virachey National Park Eco-Tourism Information Centre (☎097 730 0979, 097 333 4775; leamsou@gmail.com; ⏰8-11am & 2-5pm Mon-Fri) The place to organise trekking in Virachey National Park, though you may find more luck having a private tour company contact rangers directly (for a fee), as centre staff have limited English and are often away in the park.

ℹ Getting There & Away

A vast bus station was built on the western outskirts of town, 2.5km west of Ban Lung's main roundabout, but it now lies abandoned. Most buses depart from the market, though guesthouses and tour companies can arrange pickups, which is generally more convenient.

Virak Buntham (☎092 222423; www.virakbuntham.com) operates minivans to Phnom Penh (US$10 to US$14, eight to 10 hours) via Kratie and Kompong Cham. These leave at 7am, 8.30am and 12.30pm. It also has a sleeper bus at 7.30pm. Call a tour company or guesthouse to arrange an express van pickup if coming from Phnom Penh.

Express minivans serve Stung Treng from 7.30am (US$7, two hours). Advertised trips to Laos (Don Det and Pakse) by express minivan depart at the same time and involve a van change and a few hours' wait in Stung Treng (to Don Det US$17, seven hours).

Express minivans to Siem Reap leave at 7am and 10am (US$13, seven hours). A couple of companies run minivans to Sen Monorom via the new highway (US$7, 3½ hours), with departures around 7am and noon.

Local minibuses and pickup trucks service Lumphat (10,000r, one hour), O'Yadaw (16,000r, 1½ hours) and more remote Ratanakiri villages from the market area. Local minibuses also offer cheap transport to Kratie (25,000r) and even Phnom Penh (50,000r) for the adventurous and/or masochistic. Share taxis out of Ban Lung are rare.

ℹ GETTING TO VIETNAM: BAN LUNG TO PLEIKU

Getting to the border The O'Yadaw–Le Thanh border crossing (7am to 5pm) is 70km east of Ban Lung along smooth NH78. From Ban Lung, guesthouses advertise a 7.30am bus to Pleiku in Vietnam (US$11, five hours). The van picks you up at your guesthouse for a surcharge, which is easier than trying to arrange a ticket independently. Alternatively, take a local minibus to O'Yadaw from Ban Lung's market, and continue 25km to the border by *moto*.

At the border Formalities are straightforward and lines nonexistent, but make sure you have a Vietnamese visa if required, as visas are not issued at the border.

Moving on Once on the Vietnamese side of the frontier, the road is nicely paved and *motos* await to take you to Duc Co (20km), where there are buses to Pleiku for onward travel to Quy Nhon and Hoi An.

Getting Around

Bicycles (US$2 to US$5) and motorbikes (US$6 to US$7) are available for hire from most guest-houses in town. **Mr Bona Tour** (☎097 994 4168; mountain bike/scooter US$5/6) is a good bet for mountain bikes and scooters. Though once common, 250cc trail bikes are increasingly hard to find, due to the cost of maintenance this far from Phnom Penh.

Motos (motorcycle taxis) hang out around the market and some drivers double as guides. Figure on US$15 to US$20 per day for a good English-speaking driver-guide. A *moto* to Boeng Yeak Lom costs about US$5 return; to Veun Sai it's US$15 return; to any waterfall it's about US$7 or so return.

Remorks are expensive by Cambodian standards, about double what a *moto* costs.

SOUTH COAST

POP 2 MILLION

Cambodia's south coast is an alluring mix of clear blue water, castaway island beaches, pristine mangrove forests, time-worn colonial towns and jungle-clad mountains, where bears and elephants lurk. Adventurers will find this region of Cambodia just as rewarding as sunseekers.

Koh Kong City

☎035 / POP 36,053

Sleepy Koh Kong (ក្រុងកោះកុង) was once Cambodia's Wild West with its isolated frontier economy dominated by smuggling and gambling. Today this town is striding towards respectability as ecotourists, aiming to explore the Cardamoms, bring in alternative sources of revenue. The dusty sprawl of streets sits on the banks of the Koh Poi River which spills into the Gulf of Thailand a few kilometres south of the centre.

Sights & Activities

Koh Kong's main appeal is as a launching pad for adventures in and around the Cardamom Mountains and the Koh Kong Conservation Corridor, but there are a few diversions around town as well. If you want to take a dip, the pool at Oasis Bungalow Resort (p252) is open to nonguests (US$4) from 9am to 6pm.

Sun-worshippers will discover additional beaches further north on the Gulf of Thailand near the Thai border.

Peam Krasaop Wildlife Sanctuary NATURE RESERVE

(ដែនជម្រកសត្វព្រៃពាមក្រសោប; 5000r; ⏲7am-5pm) Anchored to alluvial islands – some no larger than a house – this 260-sq-km sanctuary's magnificent mangroves protect the coast from erosion, offer vital breeding and feeding grounds for fish, shrimp and shellfish, and are home to myriad birds. To get a feel for the delicate mangrove ecosystem, head to the park entrance, 5.5km east of Koh Kong, where a **mangrove walk** wends its way above the briny waters to a 15m observation tower. A *moto/tuk tuk* ride costs US$5/8 return.

Koh Kong Island ISLAND

(កោះកុង) Cambodia's largest island towers over seas so crystal-clear you can make out individual grains of sand in a couple of metres of water. A strong military presence on the island means access is tightly controlled. You must visit on a guided boat tour out of Koh Kong or Tatai. These cost US$21 per person, including lunch and snorkelling equipment, or US$55 for overnight trips with beach camping or homestay accommodation. The island is only accessible from October to May.

Wild KK Project OUTDOORS

(☎097 438 3772; www.wildkkproject.com) Get in touch with these guys for tours of the Areng Valley. They are a green social enterprise that is closely involved in the CBET project (p254) there, and all profits go back into protecting the forest. They also organise tours to mangrove-lined Koh Pao Island in Peam Krasaop National Park.

Ritthy Koh Kong Eco Adventure Tours ADVENTURE

(☎016 555885; www.kohkongecoadventure.com; St 1) A one-stop shop for all your tour needs in Koh Kong, this is the longest-running ecotourism operator in town. Ritthy's excursions include excellent Koh Kong Island boat tours, birdwatching, and multi-day jungle trekking and camping in the forests northeast of Koh Kong city.

Sleeping

Koh Kong is a popular holiday destination for Khmer families; hotels fill up and raise their rates during Cambodian holidays. If staying in town doesn't appeal, check out Tatai River (18km east), with its handful of fabulous eco-accommodation options.

Koh Kong City

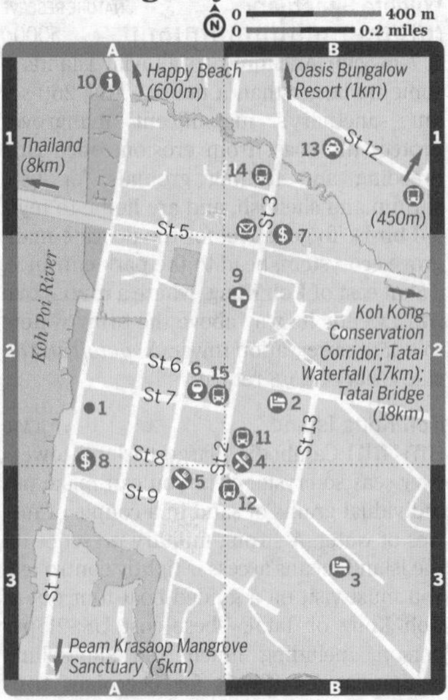

Koh Kong City

Activities, Courses & Tours
1 Ritthy Koh Kong Eco Adventure Tours A2

Sleeping
2 99 Guesthouse B2
3 Paddy's Bamboo Guesthouse B3

Eating
4 Fat Sam's B2
5 Wood House A3

Drinking & Nightlife
6 Pisey's Bar A2

Information
7 Acleda Bank B2
8 Canadia Bank A2
9 Koh Kong Provincial Hospital B2
10 Tourist Information Centre A1

Transport
11 Emerald Express B2
12 Olongpich Express B3
Rith Mony .... (see 11)
13 Taxi Station B1
14 Vibol Express B1
15 Virak Buntham A2

Hula Hula Bungalows BUNGALOW $
(071 210 7405, 016 616056; Koh Yor Beach; bungalow US$6-10;) Escapists rejoice! This place was recently taken over by a Polish couple who have created a real sanctuary for vagabonds, many of whom extend their stay indefinitely. Delightfully simple, airy bungalows sit on a windswept, sunset-facing sprawl of empty sand. The restaurant leans Asian but with some Western (including Polish) options. It usually closes during July.

Oasis Bungalow Resort BUNGALOW $$
(092 228342; http://oasisresort.netkhmer.com; d/tr US$35/40;) Nestled in a lush garden 2km north of Koh Kong centre, Oasis really lives up to its name. Five large, beautifully designed bungalows set around a gorgeous infinity pool with views of the Cardamom Mountains provide a tranquil base in which to chill out and reset your travel batteries. To get here, follow the blue signs from Acleda Bank.

Outsiders may use the pool from 9am to 6pm for US$4. Booking directly through the resort saves you US$5.

Eating & Drinking

Wood House INTERNATIONAL $
(096 864 3254; St 8; US$2.75-6.75; 9am-10pm;) A French-Khmer couple have retired to this little corner of Cambodia to cook the town's best Euro-Asian fusion food in a charming mint-green-and-yellow house marked by long wood floorboards and whirring fans. Plenty of cocktails available and French wine by the glass (US$3.50).

Happy Beach CAMBODIAN $
(Mlub Kov Su Restaurant; 097 744 4454; mains US$2.50-7; 7am-9pm) Northeast of town, this place offers a unique slice of Cambodian life with seaside, covered decks on stilts where families and friends laze about with their shoes off, taking down heaping portions of Khmer food served off a wooden block on the ground.

Fat Sam's INTERNATIONAL $
(097 737 0707; off St 3; mains US$3.50-7; 8am-1pm & 4-9.30pm Mon-Sat;) The menu at this informal bar-restaurant runs the gamut from fish and chips and chilli con carne to authentic Khmer and Thai favourites. There's also a decent beer selection and a small wine list. The English owner (*not* named Fat Sam) is a long-time Koh Kong resident and fount of information about the area. Motorbike hire is available.

Pisey's Bar BAR
(St 7; 5pm-late) Hostess Pisey is the Cleopatra of Koh Kong, and her dive bar is

where pretty much everybody ends up after everything else in town has closed (about 9.30pm). There's a pool table and guests are welcome to take control of the tunes selection. Good fun all around.

Information

Tour companies and guesthouses are the best places to get the local low-down. Thai baht are widely used so there's no urgent need to change baht into dollars or riel. To do so, use one of the many mobile-phone shops around Psar Leu.

Acleda Bank (St 3; 8am-3.30pm Mon-Fri, to 11.30am Sat, ATM 24hr)

Canadia Bank (St 1; 8am-3.30pm Mon-Fri, to 11.30am Sat, ATM 24hr)

Getting There & Away

The three main bus companies in town are **Olongpich Express** (097 505 0226; St 3), **Rith Mony** (012 640344; St 3) and **Virak Buntham** (089 998760; St 3), while **Vibol Express** (St 3) and **Emerald Express** (012 829852; St 3) run speedy minivans to Phnom Penh.

Buses drop passengers at their offices in town, or sometimes at Koh Kong's **bus station** (St 4), on the northeast edge of town, where *moto* and *tuk tuk* drivers await, eager to overcharge tourists. Don't pay more than US$1.50/3 for the five-minute *moto/tuk tuk* ride into the centre. Departures are from the company offices in town, with a stop at the bus station on the way out.

Destinations include the following:

Bangkok (US$20-22, eight hours, three daily, bus/minivan)

Phnom Penh (US$8-12, six to eight hours, several daily, bus/minivan)

Sihanoukville (US$9, five to six hours, 8am, bus)

From the bus station, share taxis head to Phnom Penh (US$15 to US$20, five hours), Kiri Sakor (for Koh Sdach; US$10, 2½ hours, 10am), Andoung Tuek (US$5, two hours), Osoam (US$12, 2½ hours, 3.30pm) and Kampot (US$20, one morning trip). Share taxis are rare to Sihanoukville so hire a private taxi (an inflated US$100 because of poor roads into Sihanoukville), or take a packed local minivan from the same lot. Guesthouses can set you up with a private taxi to Phnom Penh (US$75) or Kampot (US$75).

Getting Around

Ritthy Koh Kong Eco Adventure Tours (p251), **99 Guesthouse** (035-660 0999; 99guesthouse@gmail.com; St 6; s/d with fan US$8/10, air-con US$13/15;) and **Paddy's Bamboo Guesthouse** (015 533223; ppkohkong@gmail.com; dm with/without fan US$3/2, r US$5-10;) rent bicycles for about US$1 per day.

Short *moto* rides within the centre are 2000r; *tuk tuk* rides are double that, but overcharging is common. To hire a *moto* for the day costs about US$18.

Motorbike hire (US$4 or US$5 per day) is available from most guesthouses as well as Ritthy Koh Kong Eco Adventure Tours (p251), Wood House and Fat Sam's.

Koh Kong Conservation Corridor

Stretching along both sides of NH48 from Koh Kong to the Gulf of Kompong Som (the bay northwest of Sihanoukville), the Koh Kong Conservation Corridor encompasses the southern reaches of the fabled Cardamom Mountains, an area of breathtaking beauty and astonishing biodiversity. Part of the greater 20,746-sq-km **Cardamom Rainforest Landscape**, the corridor is the site of several groundbreaking ecotourism projects, as well as the jungle-flanked Tatai River, with its myriad eco-adventures and fairy-tale accommodation.

Sights & Activities

Tatai Waterfall WATERFALL

(ទឹកធ្លាក់តាតៃ; NH48, Km 134; US$1) Tatai Waterfall is a thundering set of rapids during the wet season, plunging over a 4m rock shelf. Water levels drop in the dry season, but you can swim year-round in the surrounding refreshing pools. The water is fairly pure as it comes down from the isolated high Cardamom Mountains. Access to the waterfall is by car or motorbike. The clearly marked turn-off is on NH48 about 15km southeast of Koh Kong and exactly 3km northwest of the Tatai Bridge. From the highway it's about 2km to the falls along a rough access road.

Botum Sakor National Park NATIONAL PARK

(ឧទ្យានជាតិបុទមសាគរ) Occupying the 35km-wide peninsula northwest across the Gulf of Kompong Som from Sihanoukville, this is one of Cambodia's largest and most biodiverse national parks. Alas, some 75% of the park has been sold off. Developments include a US$3.5 billion Chinese-run tourism project that has swallowed up roughly the park's western third. Hope has arrived in the form of Wildlife Alliance, which has a concession to manage 10% of the park and has set up the groundbreaking Cardamom Tented Camp (p254).

Stung Areng Community Based Ecotourism OUTDOORS
(☎097 355 5638; www.areng-valley.org) Another promising Wildlife Alliance community-based ecotourism (CBET) initiative in the Cardamoms, this UK-funded program offers trekking, boat trips, kayaking and homestays in the wildlife-rich Areng Valley. The area is home to Asian elephants and the last remaining wild population of Siamese crocodiles. The best way to experience the site is on a tour with Wild KK Project (p251).

Sleeping

Neptune River Bungalows ECOLODGE $$
(☎088 777 0576; www.neptuneadventure-cambodia.com; Tatai River; bungalow incl breakfast US$30-50) Want to play Robinson Crusoe? You're in the right place. German proprietor Thomas has created a jungle getaway with bags of rustic charm. The four stilted wood-and-bamboo bungalows are set amid fruit trees and have lovely bathrooms, albeit with scoop showers. Meals (US$3 to US$7), using produce from the on-site gardens, are taken right on the river.

★**Cardamom Tented Camp** TENTED CAMP $$$
(☎090 312196; www.cardamomtentedcamp.com; Botum Sakor National Park; tent from US$190;) Nestled deep in Botum Sakor National Park (p253) on the banks of the wildlife-laden Prek Tachan River, Cardamom Tented Camp is both a model ecotourism success story and one of the most unique and enchanting overnight stays you'll find anywhere. Luxurious safari tents allow guests to live in style while participating in real conservation activities like forest patrols and tree planting.

★**Rainbow Lodge** ECOLODGE $$$
(☎012 160 2585; www.rainbowlodgecambodia.com; Tatai River; s/d/f incl all meals US$89/106/140;) A slice of jungle-chic, Rainbow Lodge proves being sustainable doesn't mean having to sacrifice creature comforts. Powered by solar panels and biofuel, the bungalows here are set back from the river. They are reached by elevated walkways hugged by foliage and centred on a sleek open-air lounge with an impressive bar.

FINDING THE REAL CAMBODIA WITH MR LIM

Run by a lovely, hardworking Cambodian who calls himself Mr Lim, the **Osoam Cardamom Community Centre** (☎016 309075, 089 899895; osoamcbet@gmail.com) is an increasingly popular place to hole up in the Cardamom Mountains. Sure, you're taking bucket showers, and electricity is limited, but the isolated settlement of Osoam is true Cambodia. The local villagers long scraped out a meagre living by poaching and logging, before Lim's project began to harness the local environment sustainably by creating income-generating opportunities. The experience here is more personal than in some of Cambodia's longer-standing tourism communities – it's a spot where you end up drinking rice moonshine and eating chicken feet with locals at sundown, surrounded by livestock and happily playing puppies and children.

The stories here are endless, and Lim's personal tale is one of the most inspiring. He was born in Cambodia's dark years, and before his first birthday his family was forced to flee the Khmer Rouge into the jungle, where they lived for months before sneaking into Thailand. Despite a rough start, Lim managed to get himself an education, learn English and become a park ranger. Today, he is a self-made horticultural expert, builder and mountain guru, hellbent on saving the forest while helping his community thrive.

The centre has seven well-kept rooms (US$6) along with connections to simple guesthouses and homestays (single/double US$5/6) nearby. Lim's talented wife nails it in the kitchen (meals US$3), even inventing her own spicy 'volcano' sauce. Many a traveller who stops by opts to stay a while, volunteer and learn a few things in the garden and the kitchen.

For those interested in experiencing the natural environs of a region that has long been under the radar, the centre organises hiking, dirt-biking with **Jungle Cross** (☎097 939 8012, 015 601633; www.junglecross.com; dirt-bike rental per day US$28) and boat trips in the surrounding countryside, as well as day trips and overnights to **Phnom Samkos** (ដែនជម្រកសត្វព្រៃភ្នំសំកុស), where elephants can be spotted, and the nearby **crocodile protection sanctuary** (ដែនជម្រកការពារសត្វក្រពើរអូរសោម).

WORTH A TRIP

CHI PHAT

Once notorious for land-grabbing, illegal logging and poaching, the river village of Chi Phat is now home to a world-class community-based ecotourism project (CBET; www.chi-phat.org) launched by Wildlife Alliance (www.wildlifealliance.org). It offers travellers a rare opportunity to explore the Cardamoms ecosystems while providing an alternative livelihood to the former poachers who now act as its protectors and guides. There's a huge menu of activities on offer, from birdwatching kayak trips to combo hike-and-mountain-bike expeditions.

Note that the village only has electricity in the morning between 5am and 9am, and in the evening from 6pm to 9pm, so bring a torch (flashlight).

Many of Chi Phat's 13 homestays are in wooden, stilted Khmer houses that offer a glimpse into rural life. Rooms are all cosy and simple, and bathrooms are shared with the family. Some homestays have squat toilets and traditional shower facilities (a rainwater cistern with a plastic bucket). Dinner (US$2.50) can be provided.

Chi Phat is on the scenic Preak Piphot River, 21km upriver from Andoung Tuek, which is on NH48, 98km from Koh Kong. All buses travelling between Koh Kong and Phnom Penh or Sihanoukville pass through here.

Four Rivers Floating Lodge RESORT $$$
(☎097 643032; www.ecolodges.asia; Tatai River; d incl breakfast US$180-395;) Glamping with extra wow-factor. The 21 canvas tent-villas here, some floating on pontoons, are on Koh Andet, an island in the Tatai River 6km downstream from Tatai Bridge. The use of wicker and dark wood provides a colonial-cool ambience, topped off by the most sumptuous bathrooms you'll see under canvas anywhere. Boat transfers to/from Tatai Bridge are included (20 minutes).

Getting There & Away

Koh Kong is the main city around here, but if you're driving in from the east and heading to Chi Phat, the Tatai River area or Botum Sakor National Park, there is no need to go to all the way to Koh Kong – you can just hop off the bus on NH48 at the closest point to your destination, then take a *moto* or boat onward.

Sihanoukville

☎034 / POP 91,000

The sad story of Sihanoukville (ក្រុងព្រះសីហនុ), Cambodia's main port, is well documented. Travellers are advised to spend as little time as possible in this quagmire of construction. If you do end up here for a night, it won't be easy to find budget accommodation, as almost all the town's hostels have closed.

Of course if you are headed to the popular islands of Koh Rong or Koh Rong Sanloem, a trip through Sihanoukville is a necessary evil. The best plan is to shoot for an early arrival, then get out of Dodge on a morning or afternoon ferry. If you get stuck in town for a night, the Serendipity area near the main ferry pier has plenty of overpriced accommodation, while some cheaper, Western-run guesthouses are holding out on once-popular Otres Beach.

Sleeping & Eating

★**Sunset Lounge Guesthouse** RESORT $$
(☎097 734 0486; www.sunsetlounge-guesthouse.com; South Ochheuteal; r/bungalow from US$40/55;) Surrounded by developments at the far-south end of Ochheuteal Beach, this German-run boutique-quality resort has thick mattresses, dreamy shaded balconies, appealing bathrooms and a well-reputed restaurant. Splurge for the bungalows. The location, while a bit far from the ferry terminal, is more practical than Otres Beach as it saves you an uncomfortable and expensive *tuk tuk* ride.

Patchouly Chili House RESORT $$
(☎098 832230; patchouly.chillhouse@gmail.com; St 1033; r from US$40;) With elegantly designed rooms, attentive service, fine food and a leafy pool, this French-Khmer-run boutique is a throwback to happier times in Sihanoukville. It is also about the only affordable sleeping option left in the casino-laden Golden Lions area. That it remains open is a minor miracle; let's hope it stays that way.

Sihanoukville

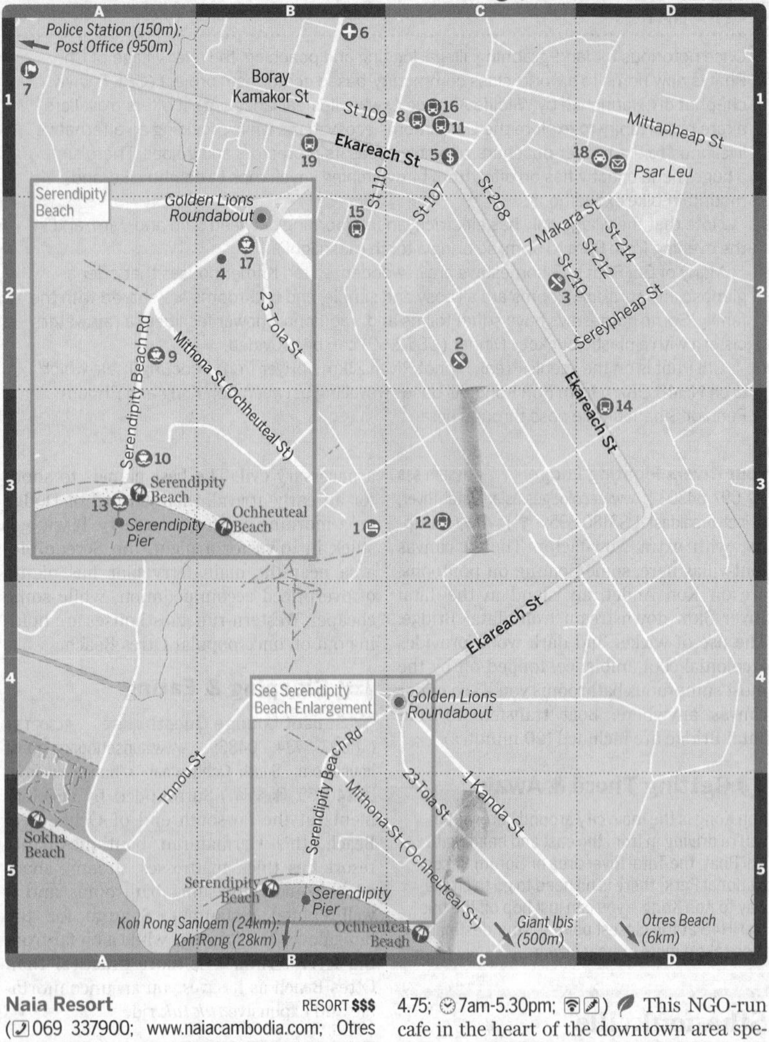

Naia Resort RESORT $$$

(☎069 337900; www.naiacambodia.com; Otres 2; r incl breakfast from US$100;) One of few Otres 2 boutique resorts to have retained both its Western management and its charm, style-conscious Naia is all about white-washed minimalism. With marvellous beds, well-furnished room terraces, a long swimming pool and a playground, it's family friendly too. The beach at **Otres 2** is nice, even if the neighbourhood isn't.

Starfish Bakery & Cafe CAFE $

(☎012 952011; www.facebook.com/thestarfishbakerysihanoukville; St 208; sandwiches US$3.50-4.75; ⏰7am-5.30pm;) This NGO-run cafe in the heart of the downtown area specialises in filling Western breakfasts, baked cakes and tarts, and healthy, innovative sandwiches heavy on Mexican and Middle Eastern flavours. Income goes to sustainable development projects. It is having trouble surviving in the new Sihanoukville, so it may be forced to move – check its Facebook page.

★ **Sandan** CAMBODIAN $$

(☎098 454400; www.mloptapang.org; St 10311; mains US$4-10; ⏰11.30am-11pm;) Loosely modelled on the beloved Phnom Penh institution Romdeng (p190), this

Sihanoukville

Sleeping	
1 Patchouly Chili House	B3
Eating	
2 Sandan	C2
3 Starfish Bakery & Cafe	C2
Shopping	
Tapang	(see 2)
Information	
4 Ana Travel	B2
5 Canadia Bank	C1
6 CT Polyclinic	B1
7 Vietnamese Consulate	A1
Transport	
8 Bus Station	C1
9 Buva Sea	A2
10 Cambodia Island Speed Ferry	A3
11 Capitol Tours & Transport	C1
12 Champa Express	C3
13 GTVC Speedboat	A3
14 Larryta	D3
15 Mekong Express	B2
16 Olongpich Express	C1
Phnom Penh Sorya	(see 8)
Rith Mony	(see 8)
17 Speed Ferry Cambodia	B2
18 Taxi Park	D1
19 Virak Buntham	B1

superb restaurant is an extension of the vocational-training programs for at-risk Cambodians run by local NGO M'lop Tapang. The menu features creative Cambodian cuisine targeted at a slightly upmarket clientele. The place is brimming with potted plants and hosts the wonderful gift shop and clothing boutique **Tapang** (www.mloptapang.org; St 10311; ⊙11am-9pm).

Information

Sihanoukville's banks – all with ATMs – are in the city centre along Ekareach St. There are plentiful stand-alone ATMs along Serendipity Beach Rd and a couple in the Otres area.

Canadia Bank (197 Ekareach St; ⊙8am-3.30pm Mon-Fri, to 11.30am Sat)

CT Polyclinic (☎034-936888, 081 886666; www.ctpolyclinic.com; 47 Boray Kamakor St; ⊙emergency 24hr) The best medical clinic in town. Can administer rabies shots, and anti-venin in the event of a snake bite.

Vietnamese Consulate (☎034-934039; 310 Ekareach St; ⊙8am-noon & 2-4pm Mon-Sat) Exceedingly speedy at issuing tourist visas.

Getting There & Away

AIR

Sihanoukville International Airport (☎012-333524; https://kos.cambodia-airports.aero; off Hwy 4) is 15km east of town, just off NH4. A taxi to town costs a fixed US$20.

Airlines serving Siem Reap and/or Phnom Penh include the following:

Cambodia Airways (www.cambodia-airways.com)

Cambodia Angkor Air (www.cambodiaangkorair.com)

Lanmei Airlines (www.lanmeiairlines.com)

Sky Angkor Airlines (www.skyangkorair.com)

Internationally, the handiest flights are AirAsia (www.airasia.com) and JC International (www.jcinternational.com) direct to Bangkok, and Cambodia Angkor Air direct to Ho Chi Minh City. In addition, a dizzying array of Chinese airlines serve several mainland China cities plus Hong Kong.

BOAT

Sihanoukville is the gateway to Cambodia's southern islands, with four main companies operating speedboats between Sihanoukville and various stops on Koh Rong and Koh Rong Sanloem.

Tickets cost US$22 and include an open-ended return. Confirm the return trip with your ferry company a day before you plan to depart from the islands. Hopping between Koh Rong Sanloem and Koh Rong (with any of the speedboats) costs an additional US$7. Schedules are unpredictable.

Most boats leave from **Serendipity Pier** in high season (October to May). During the rainy months (June to September), departures generally move to the **Sihanoukville Port Ferry Dock**. Boat companies deliver you there free of charge from the Serendipity area, but this adds at least an hour to the trip.

You can purchase tickets online via www.bookmebus.com, through your guesthouse, through a travel agent, or at ferry company offices in Sihanoukville. Ferry companies have additional ticket-sales booths at Serendipity Pier.

The four main companies, each with two to five departures daily to both Koh Rong (about one hour) and Koh Rong Sanloem (about 45 minutes):

Buva Sea (☎097 888 8950; www.buvasea.com; Serendipity Beach Rd) Runs compact speedboats to Koh Rong Sanloem and Koh Rong, including regular stops at secondary Koh Rong beaches such as Coconut Beach, Long Set Beach and Sok San Beach.

Cambodia Island Speed Ferry (TBC; ☎ 087 811711; www.islandspeedferry.com; Serendipity Beach Rd; return ticket US$20) Its blue-and-white speedboats link Sihanoukville with Koh Rong Sanloem and Koh Rong (Koh Tuch village).

GTVC Speedboat (☎ 070 221234; www.gtvcspeedboatcambodia.com; Serendipity Pier) With a booth at the Serendipity Pier, it runs fast boats to Koh Rong (Koh Tuch only) and Koh Rong Sanloem (Saracen Bay and M'pai Bay).

Speed Ferry Cambodia (☎ 081 466880; www.speedferrycambodia.com; Golden Lions Roundabout; return ticket US$20) The original Koh Rong ferry company serves secondary beaches on request on Koh Rong like Sok San Village, Love Resort, Treehouse Bungalows and Pagoda Beach, as well as Koh Rong Sanloem.

BUS

All the major bus companies have frequent connections to Phnom Penh. **Capitol Tours & Transport** (☎ 034-934042; St 109, bus station) and **Rith Mony** (☎ 081 785858; St 109, bus station) are the cheapest. The more expensive **Giant Ibis** (☎ 096 999 3333; www.giantibis.com; Ochheuteal St; 📶) 'deluxe' bus to Phnom Penh, complete with hostess and wi-fi, is well worth the splurge. It departs daily at 3.30pm. There are sleeper options to Phnom Penh but they tend to leave on the early side (around 7.30pm) and arrive in the capital at an obscenely early hour.

For minivans to Kampot (US$5) and Kep (US$7), try **Champa Express** (☎ 069 698282; Mithona St), with four daily departures, or go through **Ana Travel** (☎ 034-933929; info@anainternet.com; Serendipity Beach Rd; ⏲ 8.30am-8.30pm). Some of these trips continue to Ha Tien, Vietnam (US$13, four hours).

Other companies include the following:

Larryta (☎ 016 202020; www.larrytacarrental.com.kh; Ekareach St)

Mekong Express (☎ 012 257599; www.catmekongexpress.com; St 110)

Olongpich Express (Olympic Express; ☎ 015 540240; St 109, bus station)

Phnom Penh Sorya (☎ 034-933888; St 109, bus station)

Virak Buntham (☎ 092 222423; Ekareach St)

SHARE TAXI

Cramped share taxis (US$9 per person or US$45 per car) depart throughout the day (mornings best) while minibuses (15,000r) to Phnom Penh depart from the **bus station** (St 109) until about 8pm. Avoid the minibuses if you value things like comfort and your life.

Hotels can arrange taxis to Phnom Penh for US$50 to US$60 (about four hours). Share taxis to Kampot (US$8, four to five hours) leave mornings only from a **taxi park** (7 Makara St) opposite Psar Leu. This taxi park and the bus station are good places to look for share taxis to Koh Kong or the Thai border. If nobody's sharing, expect to pay US$75 for Koh Kong and US$80 to the Thai border.

TRAIN

Trains are a fine option to Kampot and Phnom Penh given the poor state of the road network in the south these days. Royal Railways (p200) operates trains from the **train station** (Pher St) to Phnom Penh (US$8, seven hours) via Kampot (US$6, two hours) and Takeo (US$7, five hours) at 7am on Saturday, Sunday and Monday, with an additional trip at 4pm on Sunday.

ℹ Getting Around

Sihanoukville's *moto* drivers are notorious for aggressively hassling passers-by and, more than anywhere else in Cambodia, shamelessly trying to overcharge.

Most bus companies will include free pickup from the Serendipity area. Otherwise figure on about US$5/3 for *tuk tuk*/*moto* from the bus station to the Serendipity area.

A taxi to/from the airport into town costs a fixed US$20. From the centre to the airport, figure US$10 one way for a *moto* or US$15 for a *tuk tuk* (these are hard to find if travelling from the airport).

From the train station a *tuk tuk* will cost US$6 to US$10 to the Serendipity area and US$15 or so for Otres.

Several guesthouses and travel agents in Otres Beach still rent motorbikes for US$5 to US$7 a day.

The Southern Islands

Cambodia's southern islands are the tropical Shangri-La many travellers have been seeking – as yet untouched by the mega-resorts that have sprouted across southern Thailand. Many of the islands have been tagged for major development, but developers have been slow to press go, paving the way for rustic bungalow resorts and chic Western-run boutiques to move in.

The much ballyhooed overhaul of Sihanoukville could portend darker times ahead, but for now Cambodia's islands are still paradise the way you imagined it: endless crescents of powdered-sugary-soft sand, hammocks swaying in the breeze, photogenic fishing villages on stilts, technicolor sunsets and the patter of raindrops on thatch as you slumber. It seems too good to last, so enjoy it while it does.

Getting There & Away

Scheduled boat services link Sihanoukville with Koh Rong and Koh Rong Sanloem, while other islands can be reached by private boats, usually owned by the resort you're visiting.

The Koh Sdach Archipelago is most easily accessed from Kiri Sakor, at the end of a four-lane highway that branches off NH48 and cuts through Botum Sakor National Park.

Koh Rong

Ten years ago Koh Rong (កោះរ៉ុង) was a jungle-clad wilderness rimmed by swathes of sugary-white sand, with a few beach-hut resorts speckling the shore around tiny Koh Tuch village. Today the Koh Tuch village street-strip is a bottleneck of back-to-back backpacker crash pads, restaurants and hole-in-the-wall bars. You'll either love it or hate it, but for young travellers who descend off the ferry in droves, Koh Tuch is a vital stop on any Southeast Asia party itinerary.

As roads are built and ferry companies expand their services to beaches and villages around the island, many travellers are bypassing Koh Tuch for more sedate locales. In places like Long Set Beach, Sok San village and Prek Svay, the evening frog chorus overpowers the drifting bass from the late-night raves, phosphorescence shimmers in the sea and the island's natural charms of head-turning beaches backed by lush forest interior are clear to see.

Sights & Activities

Long Set Beach BEACH

(ឆ្នេរឡុងសិន, 4K Beach) Past the Koh Tuch Beach headland (near Treehouse Bungalows (p261)) is Long Set Beach. Walk another half-hour along the sand and encounter little more than hermit crabs. A handful of hostels and boutique resorts are here, but it's still peaceful. At the extreme east end of Long Set Beach, behind Koh Rong Hill Beach Resort, a short path leads to Nature Beach. From Nature Beach, it's a 30-minute walk through the forest to **Coconut Beach** (ឆ្នេរដូង); the trailhead is behind Romduol Resort.

Sok San Beach BEACH

(ឆ្នេរសុខសាន្ត, Long Beach) On the west side of the island is Koh Rong's finest beach, a 7km, almost empty stretch of drop-dead-gorgeous white sand. Sok San village at the northern end has a cluster of local eating spots and simple guesthouses. Unfortunately the beach around the village is quite dirty; walk south for cleaner waters. Two ferry companies service Sok San village in high season (November to May). You can walk from Koh Tuch to Sok San's south end via the **jungle trail** FREE.

★ **Adventure Adam** ADVENTURE SPORTS

(☎010 354002; www.adventureadam.org; Long Set Beach) If lazing about by day and partying all night on Koh Rong seems like a missed opportunity to, you know, actually experience the island, consider booking a trip with Adventure Adam. His private day and overnight tours around Koh Rong include stops at fishing villages, remote beaches and deep jungle, and earn high marks for cultural immersion and adventure.

High Point Rope Adventure ADVENTURE SPORTS

(☎016 839993; www.high-point.asia; Koh Tuch; per person US$35; ⊙9am-6pm;) A collection of ziplines, swing bridges and walking cables takes thrill-seekers on an adrenaline-packed, 400m-long journey through the forest canopy above Koh Tuch village. Your ticket gets you unlimited access to the course for the entire day. From April to October, tickets are US$5 cheaper.

Koh Rong Dive Center DIVING

(☎096 560 7362; www.kohrongdivecenter.com; Centre Pier, Koh Tuch; ⊙9am-6pm) Koh Rong's main dive centre organises trips in the waters around Koh Rong, Koh Rong Sanloem and a few other islands nearby. Also offers boat trips to other islands, snorkelling excursions and diving courses.

Sleeping

During high season (particularly December and January), Koh Rong's accommodation fills up fast. Travellers with no bed for the night during busy periods usually end up renting a hammock. Nearly all accommodation on Koh Rong has 24-hour electricity and wi-fi. Rates drop precipitously – by 50% or more across the board – during the rainy season (June to early October).

★ **Nest Beach Club** HOSTEL $

(☎096 634 2320; www.nestcambodia.com; Long Set Beach; dm for 1/2 persons US$15/22.50;) This poshtel at the southern end of Long Set Beach is a step up from anything in Koh Tuch. The well-designed dorms are air-conditioned and feature double-wide bunks divided by walls and curtains. The restaurant

Koh Rong

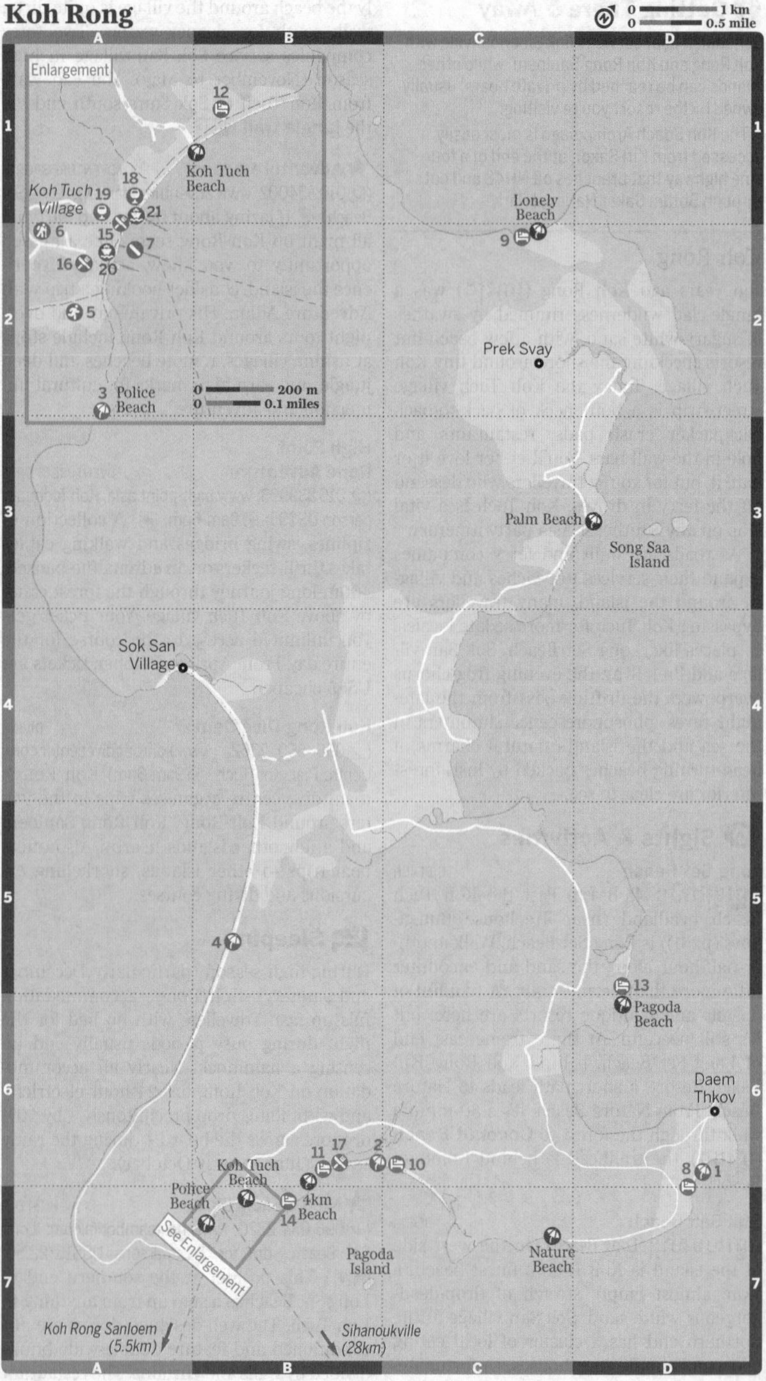
0 1 km
0 0.5 mile
A
B
C
D
1
2
3
4
5
6
7
Enlargement
12
Koh Tuch Beach
18
Koh Tuch Village
19
21
6
15
7
16
20
5
0 200 m
0 0.1 miles
3 Police Beach
Lonely Beach
9
Prek Svay
Palm Beach
Song Saa Island
Sok San Village
4
13
Pagoda Beach
Daem Thkov
11
17
2
10
8
1
Koh Tuch Beach
Police Beach
4km Beach
14
See Enlargement
Pagoda Island
Nature Beach
Koh Rong Sanloem (5.5km)
Sihanoukville (28km)

Koh Rong

Sights
1 Coconut Beach D6
2 Long Set Beach B6
3 Police Beach A2
4 Sok San Beach B5

Activities, Courses & Tours
Adventure Adam .... (see 2)
5 High Point Rope Adventure A2
6 Jungle Trail A2
7 Koh Rong Dive Center A2

Sleeping
8 Coconutbeach Bungalows D6
9 Lonely Beach C2
10 Long Set Resort C6
11 Nest Beach Club B6
12 Paradise Bungalows B1
13 Tamu Koh Rong D5
14 Treehouse Bungalows B7

Eating
Coco Hut .... (see 8)
Da Matti .... (see 20)
15 Rising Sun A1
16 Sigi N' Thai Food A2
17 White Pearl Beach B6

Drinking & Nightlife
18 Runaways A1
19 Sky Bar A1

Transport
20 Buva Sea A2
Cambodia Island Speed Ferry .... (see 21)
21 GTVC Speedboat A1
Speed Ferry Cambodia .... (see 7)

has a stunner of an open-air, oceanfront terrace with delicious sesame-battered chicken, veggie wraps and chilli-cheese fries. The all-day 'Nestival' takes place every Monday.

Coconutbeach Bungalows BUNGALOW $

(010 351248; www.coconutbeachbungalows.com; Coconut Beach; tent/r/bungalow US$5/25/40;) Coconut Beach's original guesthouse sprawls up a hillside overlooking cerulean water and powdery white sand. The owners go above and beyond for guests and have a huge library of books and games. The small semiprivate rooms have shared bathrooms, as do the basic tents atop platforms down by the ocean, or pay up for the comfortable en-suite bungalows.

★ **Lonely Beach** BUNGALOW $$

(www.lonely-beach.net; Prek Svay; dm US$12, bungalow with shared/private bathroom from US$45/60) Lonely Beach is a traveller Shangri-La hidden on a private beach along Koh Rong's northern tip. Committed to ecofriendly living, the jungle-chic bungalows and glorious open-air dorms are breeze-cooled, and all water is dispensed via coconut-shell scoop. High season sees island-hopping trips and nightly banquets on the beach. More a way of life than a resort, Lonely Beach entices many to stay for months.

Paradise Bungalows BUNGALOW $$

(093 407825; www.paradise-bungalows.com; Koh Tuch Beach; bungalows US$35-100;) The delightfully rustic bungalows at Koh Rong's original resort come in all shapes and sizes, and climb up a hill amid rambling jungle foliage. The US$35 rooms are way up the slope while more expensive options are practically lapped by waves at high tide. The loungey restaurant, with its soaring palm-leaf panel roof and shoreline panorama, is a real highlight.

Treehouse Bungalows BUNGALOW $$

(015 755594; www.treehousebungalows.com; Koh Tuch; bungalows US$30-55, tree houses US$80-85;) Nestled in a secluded cove about a 15-minute beach walk from Koh Tuch pier, Treehouse has more than a touch of the fairy tale about it. The glass-doored bungalows have balconies strung with seashells, high-raised bungalow 'tree houses' have prime vistas, and the restaurant (specialising in wood-fired pizza) is set beside a natural reservoir with an organic garden out back.

Tamu Koh Rong BOUTIQUE HOTEL $$$

(096 326 9025; www.tamucambodia.com; Pagoda Beach; r & tent incl breakfast from US$95;) Near the pier on up-and-coming Pagoda Beach, 15 minutes west of Coconut Beach by *moto*, this sleek little boutique offers a mix of luxury safari tents and concrete bungalows, all well appointed with air-con, designer furniture, private terrace and marvellous open-plan bathroom (no TV). The beach out front is exquisite, or do laps in the charcoal-toned pool.

Long Set Resort RESORT $$$

(086 796666; www.longsetresort.com; d from US$168;) In the middle of the eponymous beach, these represent by far the

classiest digs on Long Set Beach, with stylish bathrooms, minifridges, bathrobes, spa tubs and glorious beds. Active sorts will find three lap pools, a fleet of kayaks, and off-road motorbikes for rent. Two restaurants, including one with air-con.

Eating

Coco Hut CAMBODIAN $
(Coconut Beach; mains US$3.50-7; 7am-11pm;) The kitchen at this ordinary-looking beach bar surprises with some of the best Khmer food in the islands. The *amok* is spicy and delicious, and you can't go wrong with the whole steamed red snapper. Western faves and breakfasts too. Don't overlook the drinks – bartender Sopheap's margarita was wicked good (and strong).

White Pearl Beach THAI $
(096 499 0235; Long Set Beach; mains US$2.50-4; 8am-11pm) Occupying a lovely patch of Long Set Beach, this is a great place to relax and watch the waves lap the shore while enjoying splendid Thai food at rock-bottom prices. They toss a few chaise lounges in the sand and serve cocktails if you want to hang out for the day.

Rising Sun VEGETARIAN $
(Koh Tuch; mains US$4-6; 9am-9pm;) Occupying a central position on Koh Tuch Beach, Rising Sun attracts herbivores by serving vegan and vegetarian meals with a Middle Eastern flair, such as couscous salads and falafel wraps. Has a nice earthy vibe and also rents out kayaks and stand-up paddleboards for US$5 per hour, along with basic rooms from US$10.

Sigi N' Thai Food THAI $$
(Koh Tuch; mains US$4-6; 11am-2pm & 6-9pm) Pick up the unmistakable scent of Thai spices and follow your nose down an alley to this outdoor spot where authentic curries, tom yum and stir-fry are prepared right in front of you by one-man-show Sigi. A Thai native who lived for years in New York, he's a real legend and his food is the best on the island.

Da Matti ITALIAN $$
(South Pier, Koh Tuch; mains US$6-9; 8am-10.30pm) Italian food and reggae music prove to be a winning combination at Da Matti on Koh Tuch's southernmost pier. Come early for cocktails and music and stay for the pizzas, homemade gnocchi and pasta – it's all *delizioso*.

Drinking & Nightlife

Most of the action remains in Koh Tuch village, including the famous Wednesday- and Saturday-night parties on **Police Beach** (ឆ្នេរប៉ូលិស). Additional parties are added for full moons. The hostels on Long Set Beach (p259) are self-contained party units and are worth checking out. Sok San village has a mellow scene in high season.

★ Sky Bar BAR
(081 715650; Koh Tuch; 10am-last customer;) Perched way up on the hill overlooking the pier, Sky Bar is Koh Rong's most sophisticated bar, with professional cocktails, a rocking gen-X soundtrack and modern vegetarian and vegan food (raw bowls, anyone?). The views and discounted drinks make it a great happy-hour option, with the action often continuing well into the evening. The brunch is highly recommended.

Runaways BAR
(Koh Tuch; 8am-late;) Killer drinks and groovy tunes are the hallmarks of this convivial gathering spot, popular with expats and tourists alike. Positively beautiful breakfasts, too – try the stuffed avocado or the potato omelette.

Information

Bring all the cash you think you'll need with you as there are no banks or ATMs on Koh Rong. If you do run out of money, several businesses offer cash advances on credit cards for a 10% fee.

Theft can be a problem on Koh Rong. Use lock-boxes if supplied in dorms, or leave valuables in your accommodation's safe. Travellers should buddy up when walking in more isolated areas of the island, and on the beach late at night.

Getting There & Away

Fast ferries depart from one of Koh Tuch's three piers to Sihanoukville (US$15 one-way) and Koh Rong Sanloem (US$7 one-way to M'Pai Bay or Saracen Bay). The four main companies are **Cambodia Island Speed Ferry** (TBC Speed Boat; 069 811711; www.islandspeedferry.com; North Pier, Koh Tuch), **Speed Ferry Cambodia** (096 9828797; www.speedferrycambodia.com; Centre Pier, Koh Tuch), **Buva Sea** (016 888960; www.buvasea.com; South Pier, Koh Tuch) and **GTVC Speedboat** (016 331234; www.gtvcspeedboatcambodia.com; North Pier, Koh Tuch). Each runs three to six trips per day (fewer in the rainy season). There's really no telling whether a ferry will run clockwise via Sihanoukville or counterclockwise via Koh Rong. Patience is the order of the day.

Transfer from Sihanoukville to more remote resorts and beaches on Koh Rong, such as Lonely Beach and Palm Beach, is via private boat owned by the resorts.

Getting Around

Ferry companies doing the Sihanoukville–Koh Rong Sanloem–Koh Rong loop add additional stops around Koh Rong during high season and on request in low season. Regularly served destinations include Sok San Village, Long Set Pier, Coconut Beach and Pagoda Beach. Buva Sea and Speed Ferry Cambodia are the best bets for these. Hopping to another beach generally costs US$5.

Long-tail 'water taxis' are usually available to shuttle you from any of the above beaches back to Koh Tuch. Just head to the pier and ask around (there is usually a desk at the foot of the pier). Typically these cost US$5 to US$15 per person, depending on how far you are going, but if you're the only passenger expect to pay double.

Koh Rong has a small network of as-yet unsealed roads, and motorbike hire is readily available, albeit at island prices (US$15 to US$20 per day). Sections of the road dissolve into mud pits in the rainy season. This doesn't seem to deter *moto* drivers, but it might deter you. Sample prices for one-way *moto* hire from Koh Tuch: US$8 to Coconut Beach, US$15 to Sok San village, US$20 to Prek Svay and US$25 to Lonely Beach.

Koh Rong Sanloem

Blessed with endless beaches and teeming jungles, Koh Rong Sanloem (កោះរ៉ុងសន្លឹម) is many peoples' vision of tropical bliss. It has three main settlements with three distinct personalities: Saracen Bay is the beauty queen with its graceful curve of white sand; M'Pai Bay is the social butterfly with its backpacker bars and village vibe; Sunset Beach is the wild child with its arty hostels and sunset sessions.

Sights & Activities

Saracen Bay BEACH

(ឆ្នេរសារាសិន) Saracen Bay is an almost impossibly beautiful 2.5km-long crescent of white sand on the island's east coast, lined by two dozen or so resorts. Saracen Bay is under serious pressure from developers, who in 2019 clear-cut a huge swath of jungle behind the beach at the south end of the bay.

Sunset Beach BEACH

(ឆ្នេរថ្ងៃលិច) This idyllic swath of sand is home to just a few resorts that are all quite lovely. It's a 30-minute hike (sneakers necessary) here from Saracen Bay, or in high season a boat brings guests over from Sihanoukville.

Sunset Adventures ADVENTURE SPORTS

(☎088 616 6484; www.facebook.com/sunset-adventures-cambodia; Sunset Beach) Tour operator based at Sunset Beach organises all kinds of outdoor activities, including rock climbing, freediving and guided kayak trips, plus yoga and tantra sessions at nearby Robinson's Bungalows.

Scuba Nation DIVING

(☎012 604680; www.divecambodia.com; Saracen Bay; 2-dive package US$95, PADI open-water diver course US$445) A recent transplant from Sihanoukville, Scuba Nation is a PADI five-star IDC (instructor development centre) with a comfortable boat for day and liveaboard trips.

Ecosea Diver DIVING

(☎016 603400; www.ecoseadiver.com; M'Pai Bay) Another cog in the close-knit diving community of M'Pai Bay, Ecosea Diver shares a space with other dive outfits and NGO **Save Cambodian Marine Life** (☎096 224 5474; M'Pai Bay; 1-week volunteer package US$350), offering everything from discovery dives (US$70) to PADI open-water courses (US$445).

Sleeping

Cliff HOSTEL $

(☎016 329508; www.facebook.com/thecliffhostelmpaybay; M'Pai Bay; dm US$7-8, r US$30-35; 📶) The structures here – which include a 33-bed open-air dorm and a cliff-side bar and restaurant with sweeping views of the channel that separates Koh Rong Sanloem and Koh Rong – are nothing less than architectural marvels. The private rooms are compact but have plenty of rustic charm. A stairway leads down to the shore from that glorious restaurant.

My Way GUESTHOUSE $

(☎096 698 0160; www.mywaycambodia.com; M'Pai Bay; r with/without bathroom US$35/15; 📶) Well-managed My Way occupies a cute wooden house towards the south end of M'Pai Bay. The small en-suite rooms have dreamcatchers on the walls and stare at the ocean through sliding glass doors, while rooms at the back share a spotless bathroom with stone floor tiles. There's a good social vibe and wonderful French-influenced food, including brunch and daily specials.

Koh Rong Sanloem

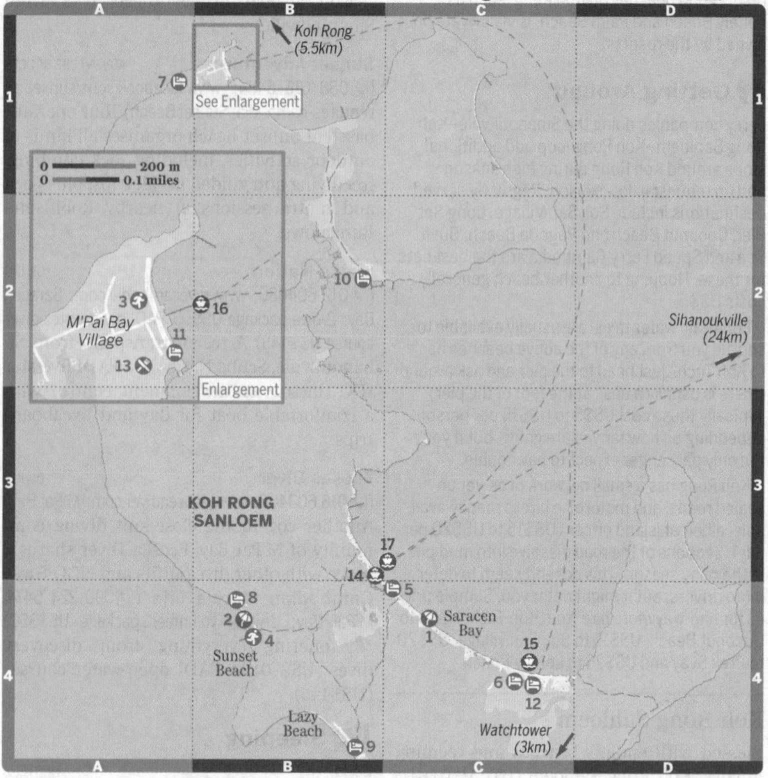

Koh Rong Sanloem

Sights

1 Saracen Bay C4
2 Sunset Beach B4

Activities, Courses & Tours

Ecosea Diver .... (see 3)
3 Save Cambodian Marine Life A2
4 Sunset Adventures B4

Sleeping

5 Big Easy C4
6 Cita Resort C4
7 Cliff A1
8 Huba-Huba B4
9 Lazy Beach B4
10 Mad Monkey B2
11 My Way A2
12 Paradise Villas C4

Eating

13 Seapony Cafe A2
Titanic .... (see 5)

Drinking & Nightlife

Tree Bar .... (see 5)

Transport

14 Buva Sea B3
15 Cambodia Island Speed Ferry C4
GTVC Speedboat .... (see 14)
16 M'Pai Bay Pier B2
17 Saracen Bay Central Pier C3
Saracen Bay South Pier .... (see 15)
Speed Ferry Cambodia .... (see 14)

Big Easy HOSTEL $
(☎071 960 0387; www.thebigeasycambodia.com; Saracen Bay; dm/bungalow from US$10/30; ❄📶) A long-time Serendipity (Sihanoukville) fave, Big Easy has brought its formula of flashy dorms and lively bar to the white sands of Saracen Bay. The air-conditioned dorm features privacy curtains and reading lights, while the bar has regular events like quiz-night Fridays and live music.

Swings in the shallow turquoise waters out front beckon passers-by.

★Lazy Beach RESORT $$
(☎016 214211; www.lazybeachcambodia.com; bungalows US$75) On the southwest coast of Koh Rong Sanloem, this idyllic getaway fronts one of the most stunning beaches you'll find anywhere. The 20 bungalows have balconies and hammocks outside, and spiffy stone-floor bathrooms and double beds inside. The combined restaurant and common area is stocked with books and board games, making the resort a good fit for families.

★Mad Monkey HOSTEL $$
(☎069 901076, 088 687 9115; www.madmonkeyhostels.com; dm US$10-11, bungalows US$50; 📶) Part of the Mad Monkey hostel empire, this edition wins big with its secluded private cove and beaches to the north of Saracen Bay. Dorms of varying size and private bungalows are oceanfront, simple and fan-cooled, and the atmosphere is laid-back and convivial. A big, open-air bar and restaurant overlooks the sea, where people laze about in hammocks all day.

Huba-Huba BUNGALOW $$
(☎088 554 5619; www.facebook.com/hubabungalow; Sunset Beach; dm US$10, tents US$20, d US$30-60, f US$90-120) Perched on secluded Sunset Beach and flanked by the jungle, this small collection of thatched-roof bungalows and glistening hardwood common spaces looks like an island fantasyland. The top-whack beachfront chalets are practically lapped by waves, as is the basic dorm. During high season, a beach restaurant with a bar constructed from the bow of a boat serves cold beers, wine, cocktails and barbecue, and everybody goes snorkelling on a nearby reef.

Paradise Villas BUNGALOW $$
(☎093 407825; www.paradise-bungalows.com; Saracen Bay; bungalows US$50-100; ❄📶) A throwback to the early days of the Southern Islands, Paradise remains a timeless testament to castaway-chic style near the far south end of Saracen Bay. Sister of Paradise Bungalows (p261) on Koh Rong, it follows similar scripts: smart, solid-wood bungalows with thick mattresses, balconies and rain showers, and a beautifully designed restaurant mixing Asian fusion with hearty European dishes.

Cita Resort RESORT $$$
(☎096 261 2418; www.facebook.com/citaresortkohrongsanloem; Saracen Bay; bungalows US$85-99; 📶) Towards the southern end of Saracen Bay, this intimate resort has about a dozen beautifully conceived raised bungalows with upper-level bedrooms fronted by sea-view balconies, open-air bathrooms and a shaded hammock-strung lounging area below. The fantastic restaurant here dishes up fresh pasta and other Italian specialities, and there's 24-hour solar power.

Eating & Drinking

Titanic SEAFOOD $
(Saracen Bay; mains US$3-6.50; ⌚8am-11pm) This place is immensely popular for all the right reasons – namely toes-in-the-sand dining on delicious, excellent-value seafood. The *amok* red curry is delicious while the mixed seafood grill with Kampot pepper is a steal at US$6. Come back for an English breakfast the next morning.

Seapony Cafe CAFE $$
(M'Pai Bay; mains US$5-6; ⌚8am-5pm Wed-Mon; 📶🖉) Run by long-time Cambodia expat Emma, this vegan-friendly little bakery behind the beach serves Aussie cafe fare like avocado on toast and flat whites. Bread is baked fresh daily and it serves yummy cakes, granola and smoothie bowls as part of the all-day breakfast.

Tree Bar BAR
(Saracen Bay; ⌚10am-late; 📶) Travellers regularly perch at this locally owned tiki bar until late into the night, playing drinking games and sizing up who might be interested in a skinny-dip in the plankton. There's also a sign for free Khmer lessons here.

Getting There & Away

The four main ferry companies serving Saracen Bay from Sihanoukville are **Buva Sea** (☎015 888970; www.buvasea.com; Central Pier, Saracen Bay), **Cambodia Island Speed Ferry** (TBC; ☎093 811711; www.islandspeedferry.com; South Pier, Saracen Bay), **GTVC Speedboat** (☎071 912 0000; Central Pier, Saracen Bay) and **Speed Ferry Cambodia** (☎070 934744; www.speedferrycambodia.com) (US$22 return, 40 minutes if direct trip). Boats use either the central pier or the south pier, so consider your resort's proximity to the respective piers when selecting a boat company.

Most ferries include M'Pai Bay on their itineraries and also do frequent trips between Koh

Rong Sanloem and Koh Rong (US$7). Note that unpredictable delays and cancellations are common.

Transport to Lazy Beach and Sunset Beach from Sihanoukville is on private boats owned by resorts, or you can take a scheduled ferry to Saracen Bay and walk.

Getting Around

To get between M'Pai Bay and Saracen Bay you can take a scheduled ferry (US$7) or hire a long-tail water taxi (US$20).

Roads linking Saracen Bay with Lazy Beach, Sunset Beach and M'Pai Bay were being built at the time of research and it may be possible to take a *moto* between these beaches by the time you read this.

Koh Sdach Archipelago

Just off the southwest tip of Botum Sakor National Park (p253), the Koh Sdach Archipelago (ប្រជុំកោះស្ដេច) is a modest grouping of 12 small islands, many of which have good snorkelling and scuba diving.

The main island, Koh Sdach (King's Island), is an authentic fishing village. It lacks beaches but is a great place to experience island life without the crowds. From here you can hire a boat to explore the other islands, including (to the north) Koh Totang, home to a single dreamy resort. At the time of research, a trio of luxury resorts were being built south of Koh Sdach on Koh Amphil Thom and Koh Amphil Touch.

Octopuses Garden Diving Centre DIVING
(086 412432; www.octopuscambodia.com; Koh Sdach; half-day 2-tank dive incl lunch US$85, Open Water Diver course US$400) Run by an expat couple, this dive shop on Koh Sdach offers snorkelling and dive trips around the archipelago. Octopuses also has laid-back waterfront digs on the nature-y, north-eastern tip of the island including a dorm (US$15) and private tree-house bungalow (US$35). Meals are communal (breakfast included, dinners US$7) and the schedule is oriented around dive trips.

★ **Nomads Land** RESORT $$$
(096 317 6267; www.nomadscambodia.com; Koh Totang; bungalows s/d incl meals from US$60/90; Nov-Aug) It's hard to imagine a more relaxed place than Nomads, the greenest resort in the islands with five funky bungalows powered by solar panels and rainwater collected for drinking. It sits on a white beach on Koh Totang and is the sole accommodation on this island speck, a 15-minute ride from the mainland's Kiri Sakor village on the resort's boat.

On the back (west) side of the island are several restaurants clustered around **Mean Chey Guesthouse** (011 979797; Koh Sdach; r from US$25;). There are local dining spots in the main village to either side of the pier. If you are invited by a local to eat fresh fish, accept.

Getting There & Away

Speedy little outboard boats with frequent departures serve the Koh Sdach village pier from Kiri Sakor village on the mainland opposite Koh Sdach (US$2.50 per person, 10 minutes). These same boats can be hired privately to take you to other islands. Nomads Land resort has its own private boat.

Share taxis serve Kiri Sakor from Koh Kong (US$10, 2½ hours, 10am departure from Koh Kong) and Sihanoukville. If you miss these, you can take a private car from Koh Kong (US$60), Sihanoukville (US$85) or Phnom Penh (US$85).

Koh Ta Kiev

If your beach-break perfection is about logging off and slothing out, this little island off Ream National Park ticks all the right boxes. Despite the fact that much of the island has been leased to developers – and a rudimentary road has recently been sliced through the jungle interior, signalling major development may not be far off – for the moment the southern tip of Koh Ta Kiev (កោះតាគៀវ) still has a clutch of delightfully bohemian and ecofriendly budget digs.

The best beach is **Long Beach**, which extends north from Ten103 Treehouse Bay. Various tracks branch off through the forest for those who want to explore. It's about a 25-minute walk from Ten103 Treehouse Bay to Last Point and Kactus Eco Village on the south tip of the island. The forest teems with wildlife and the entire island is a birdwatching mecca.

★ **Ten103 Treehouse Bay** BUNGALOW $
(097 943 7587; www.ten103-cambodia.com; hammocks US$4, dm US$6, huts with shared bathroom US$25-35, private bathroom US$40) Unplug, unwind, destress – Ten103 is a beachfront backpacker bolthole that dishes up simple beach living the way it used to be. Stilted open-air 'tree houses' have sea

views, while the towering open-air dorm and palm-thatch hammock shelters provide more basic back-to-nature options. Excellent food and drink, boat trips and kayaks available. The only place on the island open year-round.

Kactus Eco Village BUNGALOW $
(☎098 292381; www.kactusktk.com; dm US$8, bungalow US$25-45; 📶) 🍃 Under new French management, Kactus is a labyrinthine backpacker estate that hosts new-agey stuff like meditation, tantra yoga and creative art workshops using objects found on the beach. It's all part of its sustainable-living mantra, which also includes solar power, a vegan menu, detox drinks and horse riding (discovery rides US$25). A handsome beach extends 1km or so northwest.

ℹ Getting There & Away

Resorts have their own boats, and will connect you with a return trip for US$15 to US$20 (about 45 minutes). These traditionally depart from Otres Beach in the high season and from **Ream Beach** (ឆ្នេររាម; Ream National Park) in Ream National Park in the rainy season.

However, as travellers vacate Otres Beach, expect high-season departures to move to Ream Beach as well. Ream Beach is just 15 minutes from the airport by taxi. If you are arriving from the north, jumping off from Ream allows you to bypass Sihanoukville altogether – a huge relief given the sorry state of the NH4 highway between the airport and the city centre.

There is also talk of a regular ferry service from Ream Beach being launched. Watch this space.

Koh Thmei

The large island of **Koh Thmei** (កោះថ្មី) is part of **Ream National Park**. It was once slated for a major development, including a bridge to the mainland, but as projects elsewhere have taken priority, this bird-laden island has remained miraculously pristine. There's only one resort on the island, the expat-managed **Koh Thmei Resort** (www.koh-thmei-resort.com; d/f bungalow US$50/75) 🍃.

The only resort on Koh Thmei is a gem, with tidy bungalows that use solar panels and biofuel for electricity. The resort sits on a private beach, and you can easily walk to others nearby. Or go sea-kayaking, snorkelling or hiking. It's open year-round, with table football and board games to keep you entertained when it rains.

To get to Koh Thmei, make your way to Bat Kokir (Ou Chamnar), on NH4 about 12km east of Sihanoukville airport. All buses heading to or from Sihanoukville pass by Bat Kokir. Next, hire a *moto* (US$2) to take you 10km to the fishing village of Koh Kchhang. From here, Koh Thmei Resort can arrange private transport to the island, or negotiate in the village if you want to explore the island on your own.

Kampot Province

Kampot Province (ខេត្តកំពត) has emerged as one of Cambodia's most alluring destinations thanks to a hard-to-beat combination of easy-going seaside towns and lush countryside riddled with honeycombed limestone caves.

The province is renowned for producing some of the world's finest pepper. Durian-haters be warned: Kampot is also Cambodia's main producer of this odoriferous fruit.

Kampot

☎033 / POP 39,500

It's not hard to see why travellers become entranced with Kampot (កំពត). This riverside town, with streets rimmed by dilapidated shophouse architecture, has a dreamy quality, as if someone pressed the snooze button a few years back and the entire town forgot to wake up. The Prek Tek Chhouu River – more accurately an estuary – rises and falls with the moons, serving as both attractive backdrop and water-sports playground for those staying in the boutique resorts and backpacker retreats that line its banks upstream from the town proper.

Eclipsed as a port when Sihanoukville was founded in 1959, Kampot also makes an excellent base for exploring Bokor National Park (p273), the neighbouring seaside town of Kep, and the superb cave-temples and verdant countryside of the surrounding area. A growing expat community is contributing to new cultural developments and more culinary variety.

👁 Sights

Kampot is more about ambience than actual sights; the most enjoyable activity is strolling or cycling through the central old-town district where lanes are lined with crumbling shophouses, many built in the mid-20th century by the town's then-vibrant Chinese merchant population. The best streets, a couple of which have been well-restored in recent years, are between the triangle delineated by the central **Durian Roundabout**, the post office and the old French bridge.

La Plantation FARM
(☎017 842505; www.kampotpepper.com; ⏰9am-6pm) FREE This sprawling organic pepper farm offers free guided walks in French, English and Khmer, explaining how several varieties of pepper are grown, harvested and processed. The farm also grows fruits, chillis, herbs and peanuts, and there's a restaurant and shop where you can buy pepper at steep prices. (The money helps pay for children's English classes at local schools.)

Phnom Chhnork CAVE
(ភ្នំឈ្នក; US$1; ⏰7am-6pm) Phnom Chhnork is a short walk through a quilt of rice paddies from Wat Ang Sdok, where a monk collects the entry fee and a gaggle of friendly local kids offers their services as guides. From the bottom, a 203-step staircase leads up the hillside and down into a cavern as graceful as a Gothic cathedral. The view from up top is especially magical in the late afternoon, as is the walk to and from the wat.

Inside the cave you'll be greeted by a stalactite elephant, with a second elephant outlined on the flat cliff face to the right. Tiny chirping bats live up near two natural chimneys that soar towards the blue sky, partly blocked by foliage of an impossibly green hue.

Within the **main chamber** stands a remarkable 7th-century (Funan-era) **brick temple**, dedicated to Shiva. The temple's brickwork is in superb condition thanks to the protection afforded by the cave. Poke your head inside and check out the ancient stalactite that serves as a *linga* (phallic symbol). A slippery passage, flooded in the rainy season, leads through the hill.

To get to Phnom Chhnork turn left off NH33 about 5.5km east of Kampot. Look for the sign to 'Climbodia'. From the turn-off it's 6km to the cave on a bumpy road. A return *moto* ride from Kampot costs about US$6 (*tuk tuk* US$12).

Kampot Traditional Music School CULTURAL CENTRE
(☎017 726969; www.kcdi-cambodia.org; St 274; ⏰2-6pm Mon-Fri) FREE During set hours, visitors are welcome to observe traditional music and dance training sessions and/or performances at this school that teaches children who are orphaned or have disabilities. Donations are very welcome. Photos are discouraged.

Activities

★Banteay Srey Project MASSAGE
(☎012 276621; www.banteaysreyproject.org; Tek Chhouu Rd; massage from US$5; ⏰8.30am-5.30pm Wed-Mon) With an on-site women's spa and yoga studio, this social enterprise over the river empowers and generates income for local women. Daily yoga sessions on a riverfront platform are at 9am, and participants are welcome to stay and swim. Cool down with a smoothie, freshly squeezed juice or healthy meal (dishes US$2 to US$5) from its roadside Deva Vegan Cafe.

Love the River BOATING
(☎016 627410; spaceman_g@web.de; per person US$15-19) Offers long-tail-boat charters and cruises from the Green House (p270) along the river, with stops for beach swimming and exploring a durian plantation. Captain Bjorn earns high marks for local knowledge and foresight (he brings fresh fruit and cold beer to go with the sunset).

Tours

Butterfly Tours CYCLING
(☎093 775592; www.butterflytours.asia; tours per person US$17-55; ⏰7am-6pm) Take to two wheels and hit the countryside. Both cycling and motorbike tours are available through this student-run company. Destinations include pepper farms, Bokor National Park (p273) and Kampong Trach. Cycling tours emphasise interaction with local communities.

SUP Asia WATER SPORTS
(☎093 980550; www.supasia.org; 34 St 724a; 2½hr tour US$25, half-day tour US$55; ⏰8.30am-7pm Sat-Thu Oct-Aug) SUP (stand-up paddleboarding) has come to Kampot in a big way; this company offers it as an alternative form of touring the river. Daily tours depart at 8.30am, 2.30pm and 3.30pm, taking in the riverbank sights of the local area (with a SUP lesson beforehand).

Sleeping

Inside or outside town, there is accommodation for every budget, from the US$2.50 dorm bed to the US$100-plus boutique-hotel room. The further out of town you get, the quieter the atmosphere tends to be.

Kampot

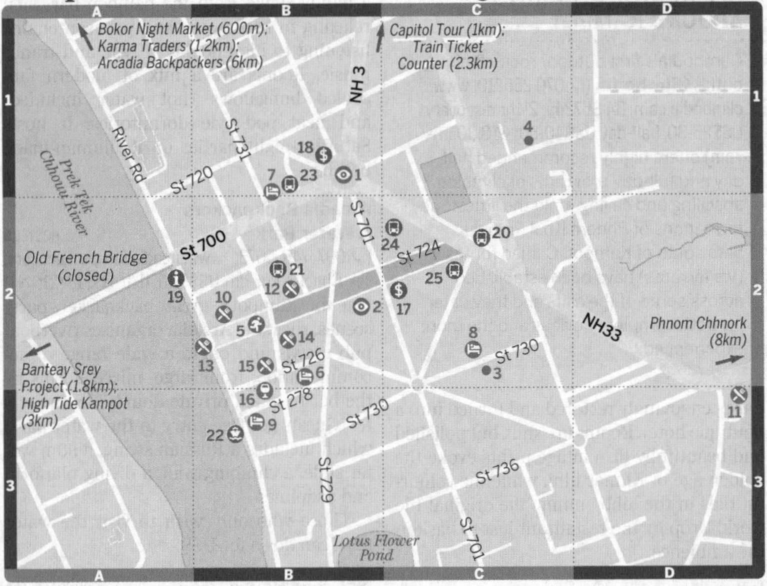

Kampot

Sights
1 Durian Roundabout B1
2 Kampot Traditional Music School B2

Activities, Courses & Tours
3 Bison Tours C2
4 Butterfly Tours C1
5 Climbodia B2
SUP Asia .... (see 5)

Sleeping
6 Columns B2
7 Hotel Old Cinema B1
8 Monkey Republic Kampot C2
9 Rikitikitavi B3

Eating
10 Armando's Food in Progress B2
11 Cafe Espresso D3
12 Epic Arts Café B2
13 Fishmarket B2
14 Kampot Seafood & Pepper B2
Tertúlia .... (see 14)
15 Twenty Three Bistro B2

Drinking & Nightlife
16 Infamata B3

Information
17 Acleda Bank C2
18 Canadia Bank B1
19 Tourist Information Centre A2

Transport
20 Bus Station C2
21 Champa Express B2
22 Crab Shuttle B3
23 Giant Ibis B1
24 Kampot Express C2
25 Phnom Penh Sorya C2

Old Town

Monkey Republic Kampot HOSTEL $
(☎012 848390; www.monkeykampot.com; St 730; dm with air-con US$5-7, r with fan US$8-12; ❄📶) This 100-bed backpacker mecca in a restored villa features Kampot's nicest dorm rooms. Choose from large dorms in the main building, or new six-bed 'pods' in the neighbouring house, with individual lockers, privacy curtains and charging stations. There's an upstairs hammock lounge, while French tiles and big booths add character to the lively bar downstairs.

★**Hotel Old Cinema** BOUTIQUE HOTEL $$
(☎095 814621; www.facebook.com/pg/oldcinemahotel; 27 St 700; r incl breakfast US$45-70; ❄📶🏊) A derelict 1930s Chinese cinema – one of Kampot's modernist architectural icons –

CLIMBING THE KARSTS AROUND KAMPOT

Cambodia's first outdoor rock-climbing outfit, **Climbodia** (☎070 255210; www.climbodia.com; 34 St 724a; 2½hr discovery US$25-30, half-day US$40-50; ⊙8.30am-7pm) offers highly recommended half-day and full-day programs of climbing, abseiling and caving amid the limestone formations of Phnom Kbal Romeas, 5km south of Kampot. Cabled routes (via ferratas) have been established across some of the cliffs and they cater for both complete novices and the more experienced.

has been lovingly restored and turned into a boutique hotel. Rooms are snug but polished and beautifully lit. Vintage prints evoke the golden age of Khmer film, while the colourful tiles in the lobby mimic the original tile work. Drop by the restaurant just to bask in the ambience.

Columns BOUTIQUE HOTEL **$$**
(☎092 128300; www.the-columns.com; St 728; r incl breakfast US$56-68; ❄📶) Set in a row of thoughtfully restored shophouses near the riverfront, this boutique hotel blends classic and modern with minimalist rooms featuring a touch of mid-century furniture, DVD player, flat-screen TV and slick modern bathrooms. Downstairs is Green's, an inviting cafe with a lovely old tile-work floor and a menu of healthy salads and shakes.

Rikitikitavi BOUTIQUE HOTEL **$$**
(☎012 235102; www.rikitikitavi-kampot.com; River Rd; r incl breakfast US$53, f from US$65; ❄📶) One of Cambodia's best-run boutique hotels, Rikitikitavi's rooms are huge and fuse Asian-inspired decor with modern creature comforts. Ceilings are graced with stunning beams, and palm panels and beautiful artwork adorn the walls. Plus you get swish contemporary bathrooms and mod-con amenities such as flat-screen TV, DVD player, fridge and kettle. Service is sublime.

On the River

★High Tide Kampot HOSTEL **$**
(☎096 416 9345; www.facebook.com/hightidekampot; Tek Chhouu Rd; hammock US$1, dm with fan/air-con US$3/7, bungalow US$15; 📶) This chill riverside spot caters to long-term backpackers who enjoy grabbing a cold one or a happy shake from the bamboo bar, then relaxing in hammocks and papasan chairs, listening to high-fidelity reggae and trance music. Rooms are a mix of modern fan-cooled bungalows (hot water included) and neat pod-style dormitories. It hosts Saturday-night parties on its human-made beach.

Arcadia Backpackers & Water Park HOSTEL **$**
(☎097 745 5073; www.arcadiabackpackers.com; Tek Chhouu Rd; dm US$5-10, d/tr US$18/21; 📶) One of Kampot's great backpacker party scenes, riverside Arcadia organises riverboat pub crawls and offers a wide range of accommodation, from large, mixed dorms by the bar to quiet, private doubles by the water. Guests get free entry to the water park, which includes a Russian swing, a 50m water slide, a climbing wall, a diving platform and a zipline.

Those who only wish to visit the water park can do so for US$7.

★Green House BUNGALOW **$$**
(☎088 886 3071; www.greenhousekampot.com; Tek Chhouu Rd; bungalows US$30-40; 📶) This gorgeously conceived riverfront pad is all about tranquillity, with the best of its palm-thatch bungalows and colourful wooden cottages (with balcony) right on the riverbank. The historic teak-wood main building, which houses the restaurant, was once home to the legendary Phnom Penh bar Snowy's (aka Maxine's), transported lock, stock and barrel here in 2011. No children under age 12.

The great restaurant is open from 7am to 8.45pm.

Sabay Beach BUNGALOW **$$**
(☎031-417 9304; www.sabaybeach.com; Ordnung Chimern village; bungalow US$25-48, d US$37-42, f US$60; 📶) Those who make it all the way to Sabay Beach will be handsomely rewarded. From the palm-tree-flanked boardwalk and the dreamy bungalows to the darling open-air restaurant and the impeccable service, this unpretentious resort is one of the finest stays in the region.

Eating & Drinking

With everything from sushi to handmade pasta to tapas, Kampot is a culinary capital full of international influences and plenty of Khmer goodness as well. Local street-food places on Old Bridge Rd between the bridge and the Durian Roundabout are great places to grab fried noodles, soups and Khmer desserts such as sticky rice with coconut sauce.

★Cafe Espresso CAFE $
(☎092 388736; NH33; mains US$4-6; ⊙8am-4pm Tue-Fri, 9am-4.30pm Sat & Sun; 📶✍) It's worth the trip to this cafe on the outskirts of town. The owners are real foodies and offer a global menu that traipses from vegetarian quesadillas to Brazilian-style pork sandwiches and has some especially tempting breakfast options. But it is caffeine-cravers who will really be buzzing, thanks to the regionally grown coffee blends, roasted daily on-site.

Khmer Roots Cafe CAMBODIAN $
(☎096 265 5171; www.khmerrootscafe.com; off NH33; mains US$2.50-3.50; ⊙11am-5.30pm) Owner Soklim's team will help you cook your own Cambodian meal at this small, family-run cafe out on Lake Tomnop Tek Krolar (aka 'Secret Lake'), near La Plantation (p268), about 45 minutes east of Kampot via dusty back roads. Or just order à la carte and kick back and enjoy the delightfully rural surroundings amid shady trees and organic vegetable gardens.

Epic Arts Café CAFE $
(www.epicarts.org.uk; St 724; mains US$2-4; ⊙7am-4pm; 📶) A great place for breakfast, homemade cakes, infused tea and light lunches, this mellow cafe is staffed by young people who are deaf or have a disability. Profits fund arts workshops for Cambodians with disabilities and there's an upstairs shop that sells art, bags, jewellery, stuffed toys and the like.

★Twenty Three Bistro INTERNATIONAL $$
(☎088 607 9731; 23 St 726; mains US$5-10; ⊙noon-9.30pm Wed-Mon; 📶) Hot damn, there's now a twice-baked cheddar soufflé in Kampot, and this is the place that loses money making it for you. We're not sure how the owners manage it, but this seems to be haute cuisine on clearance, from expats with hefty experience in world-class restaurants and a range of European cuisines. The cocktails slay, too.

Armando's Food in Progress ITALIAN $$
(St 724; mains US$5-7.50; ⊙11.30am-2pm & 5.30-10pm) Ah, the joys of skilled Italian chefs washing up in provincial Cambodia to prepare gourmet Neapolitan pizzas and Italian forest-mushroom risotto, beautifully presented and washed down with an Italian red, all for less than US$10. Kampot scores another winner. At US$5, the set lunches, which can include an entire pizza, are a steal. Exciting specials and dangerous desserts.

Kampot Seafood & Pepper INTERNATIONAL $$
(☎087 548900; St 733; US$5-10; ⊙9am-11pm) More top-notch, contemporary fusion dining has arrived in Kampot in the form of this restaurant in a beautifully refurbished old merchant house. As one might expect from the name, Kampot pepper is applied liberally to dishes as diverse as *mok cha marek chei* (sauté squid) and homemade roasted ham.

It also hosts three-hour cooking classes (per person US$20).

Fishmarket FUSION $$
(☎012 728884; River Rd; mains US$6-15; ⊙9am-11pm) The signature place of Kampot's up-and-coming dining scene lives in a restored art-deco masterpiece on the banks of the Prek Tek Chhouu River. Plop down in the breezy open-air dining area and dig into green-tea-smoked duck, a spicy beef salad or local favourites such as peppercorn crab and the baked-fish dish *amok*.

Tertúlia PORTUGUESE $$$
(☎093 375085; St 733; mains US$9-15; ⊙5-11pm; 📶) Tertúlia offers nothing less than a beautiful Portuguese dining experience, complete with a wine bar. Steaks and locally sourced seafood are slow cooked and delicious. Wash them down with port (US$2.50 to US$12) and top it off with a traditional dessert from south Portugal, such as almond pie.

★Karma Traders BAR
(☎016 556504; www.karmatraderskampot.com; ⊙8am-midnight) Reserve Tuesday nights for a visit to Karma Traders' rooftop bar, where there's live music, US$2 tacos (try the Coca-Cola pulled pork) and two-for-one drinks if you can beat the bartender in rock, paper, scissors. There's also a ping-pong room, a cinema, a pool, a slackline, a Sunday pub quiz and about a dozen rooms available (US$12 to US$16).

Infamata BAR
(☎092 821700; St 726; ⊙6pm-1am; 📶) With its shabby-chic interior and Botero-esque painting of a reclining lady behind the bar, Infamata is long on atmosphere and backs it

up with professional cocktails, craft gin and boutique beer. Live music kicks off Thursdays and Saturdays, while high season sees the opening of the gorgeous 2nd floor. Superb fusion food rounds it out.

Shopping

Bokor Night Market MARKET

(River Rd; parking 1000r; ⏲4-10pm) With about 100 stands offering things such as jewellery, karaoke, fried ice cream, sneakers and well, everything else, this nightlife experience and shopping mecca on Kampot's market circuit has loads of potential, if not many customers. The riverside setting is pleasant and family-friendly, a stage welcomes regular concerts and the aroma of tasty street food wafts on the breeze.

Information

The free and often hilarious *Kampot Survival Guide* (www.kampotsurvivalguide.com) takes a tongue-in-cheek look at local expat life.

Acleda Bank (St 724; ⏲7.30am-4pm Mon-Fri, to 11.30am Sat, ATM 24hr)

Canadia Bank (Durian Roundabout; ⏲8am-3.30pm Mon-Fri, to 11.30am Sat, ATM 24hr)

Tourist Information Centre (☎097 899 5593; lonelyguide@gmail.com; River Rd; ⏲7am-5pm) Led by the knowledgeable Mr Pov, Kampot's tourist office doles out free advice, sells tours and can arrange transport to area attractions such as caves, falls and Kompong Trach.

Getting There & Away

Kampot, on NH3, is 148km southwest of Phnom Penh, 105km east of Sihanoukville and 25km northwest of Kep. Share taxis gather near the **bus station** (St 724) to whisk passengers to Phnom Penh (US$10, three hours) and Sihanoukville (US$8, four to five hours). A private taxi to Phnom Penh costs US$45 and can be booked through your guesthouse.

BUS

If heading to Phnom Penh, be aware that a couple of the bus companies, including **Phnom Penh Sorya** (☎092 181801; NH33), go via Kep, which adds at least an hour to the trip. You're better off paying up for the more comfortable **Giant Ibis** (☎096 999 3333; www.giantibis.com; 7 Makara St) buses (US$10, 3½ hours, 8.30am and 2.45pm), or go with **Capitol Tour** (☎092 665001). Even quicker are the direct minivan services to Phnom Penh run by several companies, including **Kampot Express** (☎078 555123; NH33) and **Champa Express** (☎087 630036; St 724).

Several bus companies stop in Kep (US$3, 30 minutes) en route to Ha Tien or Phnom Penh, or you can take a *tuk tuk* (US$10, 45 minutes) or *moto* (US$6).

Guesthouses and tour agencies can arrange additional minivan transfers to Sihanoukville as well as to Koh Kong.

Destinations via bus and/or minivan include the following:

Bangkok (US$32, 14 hours, two daily, minivan)

Ha Tien, Vietnam (US$8 to US$9, 2½ hours, two daily, minivan)

Ho Chi Minh City (US$18, 12 hours, two daily, minivan)

Phnom Penh (US$5 to US$10, three to four hours, frequent, bus/minivan)

Sihanoukville (US$5 to US$6, four to five hours, several daily, minivan)

TRAIN

The rehabilitated train is a slow but scenic option to Phnom Penh (US$7, five hours), Takeo (US$6, three hours) and Sihanoukville (US$6, two hours). Departures are on Friday, Saturday, Sunday and Monday, at varying times; check the schedule at www.royal-railway.com. Kampot's **ticket counter** (☎078 888582; ⏲8am-4pm Wed-Mon) is open 8am to 4pm Wednesday to Monday; it's best to purchase tickets a few days in advance.

Getting Around

A *moto* ride in town costs around 2000r (*tuk tuk* US$1). Sometimes the driver will ask for more if it's a holiday, you're a big group, it's raining or you take a ride for longer than a few minutes.

Bicycles (US$2 per day) and motorbikes (about US$5 per day) can be rented from many guesthouses around town or from tour companies such as **Bison Tours** (☎012 442687; keusarun@yahoo.com; St 730; ⏲7am-7pm), which has the largest selection.

Bokor Hill Station

The once-abandoned French retreat of Bokor Hill Station (កស្ថានីយភ្នំបូកគោ), inside Bokor National Park, is famed for its refreshingly cool climate and creepy derelict buildings that had their heyday during the 1920s and 1930s. On cold, foggy days it can get pretty spooky up here as mists drop visibility to nothing and the wind keens through abandoned buildings. Appropriate, then, that the foggy showdown that ends the crime thriller *City of Ghosts* (2002) was filmed here.

These days the hill station is blighted by a huge development project that includes the Thansur Bokor Highland Resort & Casino and numerous holiday villas on sale at speculative prices. There's still plenty to explore, however, including the national park and the husks of several old buildings. For a history lesson on Bokor, pop into the swish **Le Bokor Palace** (www.lebokorpalace.com) hotel, which was brought back to life in 2018 after years of neglect.

Bokor National Park NATIONAL PARK

(ឧទ្យានជាតិបូកគោ, Preah Monivong National Park; motorbike/car 2000/10,000r) The dense rainforests of this 1581-sq-km park shelter an incredible array of wildlife, including the Asiatic black bear, Malayan sun bear, clouded leopard, pileated gibbon, pigtailed macaque, slow loris and pangolin. Elephants and tigers once roamed here, but the tigers were driven out long ago and the elephants are thought to have migrated north. Trekking trips up to the hill station used to be very popular, but these days most people arrive by vehicle on new roads.

Getting There & Away

You can either visit the hill station on an organised tour out of Kampot or rent a motorbike and travel under your own steam. The road up here is in excellent condition.

Kep

036 / POP 35,000

Founded as a seaside retreat by French colonisers in 1908, and a favoured haunt of Cambodian high rollers during the 1960s, sleepy Kep (កែប, Krong Kep, also spelled Kaeb) is drawing tourists back with seafood, sunsets and hikes in butterfly-filled Kep National Park. Its impressive range of boutique hotels squarely targets a more cultured beach crowd than the party-happy guesthouses of Kampot and the islands.

Some find Kep a bit soulless because it lacks a centre, not to mention a long sandy shoreline. Others revel in its torpid pace, content to relax at their resort, nibble on peppery crab at the famed crab market and poke around the mildewed shells of modernist villas, which still give the town a sort of post-apocalyptic feel.

Sights & Activities

★ **Kep National Park** NATIONAL PARK

(ឧទ្យានជាតិកែប; 4000r) The interior of Kep peninsula is occupied by Kep National Park, where an 8km circuit, navigable by foot, mountain bike, or motorbike, begins behind Veranda Natural Resort (p274). Led Zep Cafe (p275) is responsible for the quirky yellow signs that point the way to various viewpoints, sights and trailheads. The cafe, if it's open, sells a park map for 1000r. The 'Stairway to Heaven' trail is particularly worthwhile, leading up the hill to a pagoda, a nunnery and the Sunset Rock viewpoint.

★ **Sothy's Pepper Farm** FARM

(088 951 3505; www.mykampotpepper.asia; Phnom Vour, off NH33; 9am-5pm) FREE One of the friendliest farms to visit, Sothy is passionate about his product and will gladly elaborate on the history and process behind the 'champagne of pepper'. Short tours are free and there's a wonderful gift shop on the premises if you want to bring a few packs of the good stuff back home. It's about 17km northeast of central Kep. There's also an excellent restaurant, albeit pepper ripens faster than the service!

Koh Tonsay ISLAND

(កោះទន្សាយ, Rabbit Island) If you like the rustic beachcomber lifestyle, Koh Tonsay's 250m-long main beach is for you. This is a place to while away hours or days doing little but lazing on the beach, napping, reading, sipping cocktails, eating seafood and stargazing before retiring to your threadbare bungalow and drifting off to the sound of the waves. Scheduled boats to Rabbit Island (US$8 return, 20 minutes) leave from **Rabbit Island Pier** (NH33A) at 9am and 1pm and return at 3pm or 4pm.

Kep guesthouses can arrange boat tickets or you can purchase them at the Koh Tonsay Boat Ticket Office at the pier. Private boats to the island can be arranged on the spot at the ticket office and cost US$25 return for up to six people.

The main beach, rimmed by restaurant shacks and rudimentary bungalows (US$7 to US$10 per night), is nice enough, just don't expect the sparkling white sand of Koh Rong or Koh Rong Sanloem. You can walk around the island to find more isolated beaches. The island has long been tagged for development but it appears that these plans have been put off for now.

Kep Sailing Club WATER SPORTS

(078 333685; www.knaibangchatt.com/the-sailing-club; Knai Bang Chatt; 8am-5pm) Open to all, the sailing club and activity centre at the hotel **Knai Bang Chatt** (078 888554; www.knaibangchatt.com; r incl breakfast from US$209;

) hires out sea kayaks (US$10 per hour), Hobie Cats (from US$50 per hour), paddleboards (US$10 per hour) and Optimists (US$15 per hour). Optimists are small boats for children, for whom sailing lessons are available.

Decent mountain bikes are also available at US$15 per hour, as well as kayaks and stand-up paddleboards. Among Kep Sailing Club's many boat tours are a sunset cruise and a traditional fishing experience.

Kep Adventures BOATING

(015 892434; www.kep-adventures.com; per person full day US$35-65, half day US$15-40, sunset US$20; Oct-May) Take to a traditional thatched-roof long-tail boat on half- or full-day tours of a few of the less-visited islands off Kep. Sunset cruises kick off at 4.30pm and include two complimentary handmade cocktails – talk about riding in style. The full-day tour includes a BBQ lunch. All tours adhere to zero-waste principles. Highly recommended.

Sleeping

Kep meanders along the shoreline for a good 5km, with resorts and guesthouses speckled along the length of the main road and perched on the dirt tracks that wander up the hills leading to Kep National Park (p273). Prices at the classiest places can feel a bit inflated, but there are plenty of good midrange options.

★ **Khmer Hands Resort** BUNGALOW $

(088 215 0011; https://khmer-hands.business.site; r US$15-25;) Choose from sturdy, stilted, wooden bungalows and cheaper, squat, concrete huts – all with private porch – at this well-run Khmer–American venture that doubles as an arts and hospitality training school for at-risk locals. The excellent restaurant sources herbs and vegetables from a permaculture garden on the premises, and there's a cool gift shop under the restaurant selling pepper, handicrafts and more.

Bird of Paradise BUNGALOW $

(090 880413; www.birdofparadisebungalows.com; bungalows incl breakfast with fan/air-con from US$18/35;) Set in a relaxed, peaceful garden with adorable ducks roaming around, Bird of Paradise offers stupendous value and is well located just uphill from the main road, within walking distance of the crab market (p275). Simple but sweet wooden bungalows, with hammocks strung from the porch, are delightfully rustic, while the air-con concrete cottages are more spacious.

Meng Naren Guest House BUNGALOW $

(070 644321; Koh Tonsay; bungalows from US$10;) Meng Naren is the biggest and most central place on the main beach of Koh Tonsay, and also has the nicest rooms, along with a breezy restaurant and happy-hour specials galore. The roomy wooden bungalows are equipped with mozzie nets, private veranda and hammocks. It organises sunset and snorkelling boat trips and a sunset beach barbecue. Electricity runs from 6.30pm until about 11pm.

Tara Lodge GUESTHOUSE $$

(0966 866375; www.taralodge-kep.com; d incl breakfast US$55-65, f US$80;) The hugely friendly Tara Lodge gets a big tick for its split-level bungalows with wide verandas and all the mod cons, secreted within a verdant garden of palms and flowers, and set around a glistening pool. This is a secluded spot for some serious downtime. The upstairs terrace-restaurant serves excellent Khmer and French food and has views to Bokor.

Villa Kep RESORT $$

(096 967 0469; www.villakep.com; r US$50-55) This Finnish-owned complex of 18 villas sprawls across the countryside on the outskirts of Kep, with a glorious pool at the centre of it all. The spacious villas are a splendid deal, albeit they are not particularly heavy on character. They come in twin configuration or with a beautiful king-sized bed. No children allowed.

★ **Veranda Natural Resort** RESORT $$$

(012 888619; www.veranda-resort.asia; Kep Hillside Rd; r incl breakfast from US$110;) The unique hillside bungalows here are built of wood, bamboo and stone, and are connected by a maze of stilted walkways, making this a thoroughly memorable spot for a romantic getaway. Check out several rooms because the size and shape vary wildly. There are a couple of pools, the food is excellent and views from the restaurant pavilion are stunning.

Eating & Drinking

Deli's Kep DELI $

(088 470 7952; NH33A; sandwiches US$3.50-4; 7am-7pm) This gourmet food store earns high praise for its *coppa, lomo,* saucisson

and other imported meats, along with top-notch pepper (100g for US$5 to US$8), coffee and craft booze. Grab a sandwich on the way to a pepper farm, or plop down for a relaxing meal in the airy, modern space.

★Crab Market MARKET $$

(1kg crab from 50,000r) Eating at the crab market – a row of wooden waterfront restaurants by a wet fish market – is a quintessential Kep experience. Fresh crabs fried with Kampot pepper are a taste sensation. Crabs are kept alive in pens tethered just off the pebbly beach. You can dine at one of the restaurants or buy crab and have your guesthouse prepare it.

There are lots of great places to choose from at the crab market, so keep an eye on where the Khmer crowd are eating. Crab costs around US$10 a kilo at the wet market.

La Baraka INTERNATIONAL $$

(☎097 461 2543; crab market; mains US$6-10; ⏲10am-2pm & 6-10pm; 📶) A breath of fresh air from the other crab-market restaurants' identical menus, La Baraka serves a mix of European and Asian flavours with bags of seafood dishes such as sea-bass carpaccio. For non-fish-lovers there's also great pizza and pasta. The terrace, over the waves, is sunset cocktail perfection.

★Sailing Club COCKTAIL BAR

(mains US$7-12.50; ⏲10am-10pm; 📶) With a small beach, a breezy wooden bar and a wooden jetty poking out into the sea, this is one of Cambodia's top sundowner spots. The Asian-fusion food is excellent and you can get your crab fix here, too. There's an outdoor cocktail lounge and a vastly expanded seafront terrace.

Led Zep Cafe CAFE

(Kep National Park; ⏲hours vary) A lovely, secluded cafe and crêperie on the Kep National Park (p273) trail, a five-minute walk from the main entrance. Knocking back a chilled lime juice on the wide terrace with knock-out views overlooking the coast is the perfect pick-me-up after a hike. The crêpes are outstanding, but hours are sporadic, especially during low season.

ℹ Information

There's no bank in Kep but there are a couple of ATMs. One is the **ABA Bank ATM** (Kep Beach Rd; ⏲24hr) near Kep Beach.

ℹ Getting There & Around

Kep is 25km from Kampot and 41km from the Prek Chak–Xa Xia border crossing to Vietnam.

ℹ GETTING TO VIETNAM: KEP TO HA TIEN

Getting to the border The Prek Chak–Xa Xia border crossing (in theory open 6am to 6pm, though it sometimes opens late and closes early) has become a popular option for linking Kampot and Kep with Ha Tien, and then onward to either the popular Vietnamese island of Phu Quoc, or to Ho Chi Minh City.

The easiest way to get to Prek Chak and on to Ha Tien, Vietnam, is to catch a minivan from Sihanoukville (US$12, five to seven hours), Kampot (US$8, two hours), or Kep (US$7, one hour). Anny Tours (p276) and Champa Express (p276) run this service with a change of vehicles at the border.

A more flexible alternative from Phnom Penh or Kampot is to take a bus to Kompong Trach, then a *moto* (about US$3) for 15km, on a good road, to the border.

In Kep, guesthouses can arrange a *moto* (US$8, 45 minutes), *tuk tuk* (US$12, one hour) or taxi (US$20, 30 minutes). Rates and times are almost double from Kampot.

At the border Vietnam grants 15-day visas on arrival for nationals of several European and Asian countries. Other nationalities, and anyone staying longer than 15 days, must purchase a visa in advance.

At Prek Chak, a *moto* driver will ask for US$5 to take you to the Vietnamese border post 300m past the Cambodian one, and then all the way to Ha Tien (15 minutes, 7km). You'll save money walking across no-person's land and picking up a *moto* on the other side for US$2 to US$3.

Moving on From Ha Tien you can find onward transport to Ho Chi Minh City via the Mekong Delta route. To Phu Quoc island there are both slow and fast ferry departures until early afternoon.

Buses stop at Kep Beach in front of a line of travel agencies and minivan offices. You can purchase tickets here or from most guesthouses.

Most buses and minivans to Phnom Penh go via Kampot, which adds an hour or so to the trip. One exception is Phnom Penh Sorya (p198) buses, which go direct to Phnom Penh. A private taxi to the capital costs US$45 to US$50.

Anny Tours (☎096 764 6666; Kep Beach Rd; ⏲6am-9pm) and **Champa Express** (☎088 727 7277; Kep Beach Rd; ⏲6.30am-8pm) send minivans over the border to Ha Tien in Vietnam twice daily. Going the other way, the same companies serve Sihanoukville two or three times daily, with a van change in Kampot, and also serve Koh Kong with several van transfers.

For Kampot, take a *tuk tuk* (US$10, 45 minutes) or any eastbound bus or minivan. The sunset **Crab Shuttle** (☎088 829 6644; crabshuttle@gmail.com; River Rd; ⏲Oct-May) boat trip (US$10, 2½ hours, 3pm) is a nice option. There are very few *moto* drivers in town.

Motorbike rental is US$5 with **Diamond & Moon Moto Rental** (☎097 864 5062; diamondandmoon@gmail.com; scooter rental per day US$5); guesthouses and travel agencies also rent out motorbikes.

UNDERSTAND CAMBODIA

History

'The good, the bad and the ugly' sums up Cambodian history. Things were good in the early years, culminating in the vast Angkor empire, unrivalled in the region during four centuries of dominance. Then the bad set in, from the 13th century, as ascendant neighbours chipped away at Cambodian territory. In the 20th century it turned downright ugly, as a brutal civil war culminated in the genocidal rule of the Khmer Rouge (1975–79), from which Cambodia is still recovering.

Funan & Chenla

The Indianisation of Cambodia began in the 1st century AD as traders plying the sea route from the Bay of Bengal to southern China brought Indian ideas and technologies to what is now southern Vietnam. The largest of the era's nascent kingdoms, known to the Chinese as Funan, embraced the worship of the Hindu deities Shiva and Vishnu and, at the same time, Buddhism. From the 6th to 8th centuries Cambodia seems to have been ruled by a collection of competing kingdoms. Chinese annals refer to 'Water Chenla', apparently the area around the modern-day town of Takeo, and 'Land Chenla', further north along the Mekong and around Sambor Prei Kuk.

Rise & Fall of Angkor

The Angkorian era lasted from AD 802 to 1432, encompassing periods of conquest, turmoil and retreat, revival and decline, and fits of remarkable productivity. In 802, Jayavarman II (reigned c 802–50) proclaimed himself a *devaraja* (god-king). He instigated an uprising against Javanese domination of southern Cambodia and, through alliances and conquests, brought the country under his control, becoming the first monarch to rule most of what we now call Cambodia.

In the 9th century, Yasovarman I (r 889–910) moved the capital to Angkor, creating a new centre for worship, scholarship and the arts. After a period of turmoil and conflict, Suryavarman II (r 1113–52) unified the kingdom and embarked on another phase of territorial expansion, waging successful but costly wars against both Vietnam and Champa (an Indianised kingdom that occupied what is now southern and central Vietnam). His devotion to the Hindu deity Vishnu inspired him to commission Angkor Wat. The tables soon turned. Champa struck back in 1177 with a naval expedition up the Mekong, taking Angkor by surprise and putting the king to death. But the following year a cousin of Suryavarman II – soon crowned Jayavarman VII (r 1181–1219) – rallied the Khmers and defeated the Chams in another epic naval battle. A devout follower of Mahayana Buddhism, it was he who built the city of Angkor Thom. During the twilight years of the empire, religious conflict and internecine rivalries were rife. The Thais made repeated incursions into Angkor, sacking the city in 1351 and again in 1431, and from the royal court making off with thousands of intellectuals, artisans and dancers, whose profound impact on Thai culture can be seen to this day. From 1600 until the arrival of the French, Cambodia was ruled by a series of weak kings whose intrigues often involved seeking the protection of either Thailand or Vietnam – granted, of course, at a price.

French Colonisation

The era of yo-yoing between Thai and Vietnamese masters came to a close in 1864, when French gunboats intimidated King Norodom I (r 1860–1904) into signing a treaty of protectorate. An exception in the annals of colonialism, the French presence really did protect the country at a time when it was in danger of being swallowed by its more powerful neighbours.

In 1907 the French pressured Thailand into returning the northwest provinces of Battambang, Siem Reap and Sisophon, bringing Angkor under Cambodian control for the first time in more than a century.

Led by King Norodom Sihanouk (r 1941–55 and 1993–2004), Cambodia declared independence on 9 November 1953.

Independence & Civil War

The period after 1953 was one of peace and prosperity, and a time of creativity and optimism. Dark clouds were circling, however, as the war in Vietnam began sucking in neighbouring countries. As the 1960s drew to a close, the North Vietnamese and the Viet Cong were using Cambodian territory in their battle against South Vietnam and US forces, prompting devastating American bombing and a land invasion into eastern Cambodia.

In March 1970 Sihanouk, now serving as prime minister, was overthrown by General Lon Nol, and took up residence in Beijing. Here he set up a government in exile that allied itself with an indigenous Cambodian revolutionary movement that Sihanouk had dubbed the Khmer Rouge. This was a defining moment in contemporary Cambodian history: talk to many former Khmer Rouge fighters and they all say that they 'went to the hills' to fight for their monarch and knew nothing of Marxism or Mao.

Khmer Rouge Rule

Upon taking Phnom Penh on 17 April 1975 – two weeks before the fall of Saigon – the Khmer Rouge implemented one of the most radical and brutal restructurings of a society ever attempted. Its goal was to transform Cambodia – renamed Democratic Kampuchea – into a giant peasant-dominated agrarian cooperative, untainted by anything that had come before. Within days, the entire populations of Phnom Penh and provincial towns, including the sick, elderly and infirm, were forced to march into the countryside and work as slaves for 12 to 15 hours a day. Intellectuals were systematically wiped out – having glasses or speaking a foreign language was reason enough to be killed. The advent of Khmer Rouge rule was proclaimed Year Zero.

Leading the Khmer Rouge was Saloth Sar, better known as Pol Pot. As a young man, he won a scholarship to study in Paris, where he began developing the radical Marxist ideas that later metamorphosed into extreme Maoism. Under his rule, Cambodia became a vast slave-labour camp. Meals consisted of little more than watery rice porridge twice a day, meant to sustain men, women and children through a back-breaking day in the fields. Disease stalked the work camps, malaria and dysentery striking down whole families.

Khmer Rouge rule was brought to an end by the Vietnamese, who liberated the almost empty city of Phnom Penh on 7 January 1979. It is estimated that at least 1.7 million people perished at the hands of Pol Pot and his followers. The Documentation Center of Cambodia records the horrific events of the period.

A Sort of Peace

The Vietnamese installed a new government led by several former Khmer Rouge officers, including current prime minister Hun Sen, who had defected to Vietnam in 1977. In the dislocation that followed liberation, little rice was planted or harvested, leading to a massive famine. The Khmer Rouge continued to wage civil war from remote mountain bases near the Thai border throughout the 1980s. In September 1989 Vietnam, its economy in tatters and eager to end its international isolation, announced the withdrawal of all its forces from Cambodia.

In February 1991 all parties – including the Khmer Rouge – signed the Paris Peace Accords, according to which the UN Transitional Authority in Cambodia (Untac) would rule the country for two years. Although Untac is still heralded as one of the UN's success stories (elections with a 90% turnout were held in 1993), to many Cambodians who had survived the 1970s it was unthinkable that the Khmer Rouge was allowed to play a part in the process. The Khmer Rouge ultimately pulled out before polling began, but the smokescreen of the elections allowed them to re-establish a guerrilla network throughout Cambodia. Untac is also remembered for causing a significant increase in prostitution and HIV/AIDS.

The last Khmer Rouge hold-outs, including Ta Mok, were not defeated until the capture of Anlong Veng and Prasat Preah Vihear by government forces in the spring of 1998. Pol Pot cheated justice by dying a sorry death near Anlong Veng during that year, and was cremated on a pile of old tyres.

People & Culture

Population

About 16 million people live in Cambodia. According to official statistics, more than 90% of the people who live in Cambodia are ethnic Khmers, making the country the most ethnically homogeneous in Southeast Asia. However, unofficially, the figure is probably smaller due to a large influx of Chinese and Vietnamese in the past century. Other ethnic minorities include Cham, Lao and the indigenous peoples of the rural highlands. Cambodia's diverse Khmer Leu (Upper Khmer) or *chunchiet* (ethnic minorities), who live in the country's mountainous regions, probably number around 100,000.

The official language is Khmer, spoken by 95% of the population. English has taken over from French as the second language of choice, although Chinese is also growing in popularity. Life expectancy is currently 69 years.

Lifestyle

For many older Cambodians, life is centred on family, faith and food, a tradition that has stayed the same for centuries. Families stick together, solve problems collectively, listen to the wisdom of the elders and pool resources. The extended family comes together during times of trouble and times of joy, celebrating festivals and successes, mourning deaths and disappointments. A Cambodian house, whether big or small, will have a lot of people living inside.

For the majority of the population still living in the countryside, these constants carry on as they always have: several generations sharing the same roof, the same rice and the same religion. But during the dark decades of the 1970s and 1980s, this routine was ripped apart by war and ideology, as the peasants were dragged into a bloody civil war and later forced into slavery. The Khmer Rouge organisation Angkar took over as the moral and social beacon in the lives of the people. Families were forced apart, children turned against parents, brothers against sisters. The bond of trust was broken and is only slowly being rebuilt today.

For the younger generation, brought up in a postconflict, postcommunist period of relative freedom, it's a different story – arguably thanks to their steady diet of MTV and steamy soaps. Cambodia is experiencing its very own '60s swing, as the younger generation stands ready for a different lifestyle to the one their parents had to swallow. This creates plenty of friction in the cities, as rebellious teens dress as they like, date whoever they wish and hit the town until all hours. More recently this generational conflict spilled over into politics as the Facebook generation helped deliver a shock result that saw the governing Cambodian People's Party (CPP) majority slashed in half.

Cambodia is set for major demographic shifts in the next couple of decades. Currently, just 20% of the population lives in urban areas, which contrasts starkly with the country's more developed neighbours, such as Malaysia and Thailand. Increasing numbers of young people are likely to migrate to the cities in search of opportunity, forever changing the face of contemporary Cambodian society. However, for now at least, Cambodian society remains much more traditional than that of Thailand and Vietnam, and visitors need to keep this in mind.

Religion

The majority of Khmers (95%) follow the Theravada branch of Buddhism. Buddhism in Cambodia draws heavily on its predecessors, incorporating many cultural traditions from Hinduism for ceremonies such as birth, marriage and death, as well as genies and spirits, such as Neak Ta, which link back to a pre-Indian animist past.

Under the Khmer Rouge, the majority of Cambodia's Buddhist monks were murdered and nearly all of the country's wats (more than 3000) were damaged or destroyed. In the late 1980s, Buddhism once again became the state religion.

Other religions found in Cambodia are Islam, practised by the Cham community; animism, among the hill tribes; and Christianity, which is making inroads via missionaries and Christian NGOs.

Arts

The Khmer Rouge regime not only killed the living bearers of Khmer culture, it also destroyed cultural artefacts, statues, musical instruments, books and anything else that served as a reminder of a past it was trying to efface. The temples of Angkor were spared as a symbol of Khmer glory and empire, but little else survived. Despite this, Cambodia is witnessing a resurgence of traditional arts and a growing interest in cross-cultural fusion.

Cambodia's royal ballet is a tangible link with the glory of Angkor and includes a unique *apsara* (heavenly nymphs) dance. Cambodian music, too, goes back at least as far as Angkor. To get some sense of the music that Jayavarman VII used to like, check out the bas-reliefs at Angkor Wat.

In the mid-20th century a vibrant Cambodian pop music scene developed, but it was killed off (literally) by the Khmer Rouge. After the war, overseas Khmers established a pop industry in the USA and some Cambodian Americans, raised on a diet of rap, are now returning to their homeland. The Los Angeles–based sextet Dengue Fever, inspired by 1960s Cambodian pop and psychedelic rock, is the ultimate fusion band.

The people of Cambodia were producing masterfully sensuous sculptures – much more than mere copies of Indian forms – in the age of Funan and Chenla. The Banteay Srei style of the late 10th century is regarded as a high point in the evolution of Southeast Asian art.

Environment

The Land

Cambodia's two dominant geographical features are the mighty Mekong River and a vast lake, the Tonlé Sap. The rich sediment deposited during the Mekong's annual wet-season flooding has made central Cambodia incredibly fertile. This low-lying alluvial plain is where the vast majority of Cambodians live – fishing and farming in harmony with the rhythms of the monsoon.

In Cambodia's southwest quadrant, much of the land mass is covered by the Cardamom Mountains and, near Kampot, the Elephant Mountains. Along Cambodia's northern border with Thailand, the plains collide with the Dangkrek Mountains, a striking sandstone escarpment more than 300km long and up to 550m high. One of the best places to get a sense of this area is Prasat Preah Vihear.

In the northeastern corner of the country, in the provinces of Ratanakiri and Mondulkiri, the plains give way to the Eastern Highlands, a remote region of densely forested mountains and high plateaus.

Wildlife

Cambodia's forest ecosystems were in excellent shape until the 1990s and, compared with its neighbours, its habitats are still relatively healthy. The years of war took their toll on some species, but others thrived in the remote jungles of the southwest and northeast. Ironically, peace brought increased threats as loggers felled huge areas of primary forest and the illicit trade in wildlife targeted endangered species. Due to years of inaccessibility, scientists have only relatively recently managed to research and catalogue the country's plant and animal life.

Still, with more than 200 species of mammal, Cambodia has some of Southeast Asia's best wildlife-watching opportunities. Highlights include spotting gibbons and black-shanked doucs in Ratanakiri and Mondulkiri provinces, and viewing some of the last remaining freshwater Irrawaddy dolphins in Kratie and Stung Treng provinces.

Globally threatened species that you stand a slight chance of seeing include the Asian elephant, banteng (a wild ox), gaur, clouded leopard, fishing cat, marbled cat, sun bear, Siamese crocodile and pangolin. Asian tigers were once commonplace but are now considered extinct in the wild, with the last sighting back in 2007.

The country is a birdwatcher's paradise – feathered friends found almost exclusively in Cambodia include the giant ibis, white-shouldered ibis, Bengal florican, sarus crane and three species of vulture. The Siem Reap–based Sam Veasna Center (p207) runs birding trips.

Environmental Issues

Cambodia's pristine environment is a big draw for adventurous ecotourists, but much of it is currently under threat. Ancient forests are being razed to make way for plantations, rivers are being sized up for major hydroelectric power plants and the south coast is being explored by leading oil companies.

Places like the Cardamom Mountains are in the front line and it remains to be seen whether the environmentalists or the economists will win the debate.

The greatest threat is illegal logging, carried out to provide charcoal and timber, and to clear land for cash-crop plantations. The environmental watchdog Global Witness (www.globalwitness.org) publishes meticulously documented exposés on corrupt military and civilian officials and their well-connected business partners.

In the short term, deforestation is contributing to worsening floods along the Mekong, but the long-term implications of deforestation are mind-boggling. Siltation, combined with overfishing, pollution and climate change, may lead to the eventual death of Tonlé Sap lake, which would be a catastrophe for future generations of Cambodians.

Throughout Cambodia pollution is a problem, and detritus of all sorts, especially plastic bags and bottles, can be seen in distressing quantities all over the country.

The latest environmental threat to emerge are dams on the Mekong River. Environmentalists fear that damming the mainstream Mekong is disrupting the flow patterns of the river and the migratory patterns of fish (including the critically endangered freshwater Irrawaddy dolphin). The Don Sahong (Siphandone) Dam just north of the Cambodia–Laos border is now operating, and plans under consideration include the Sambor Dam, a massive 3300MW project 35km north of Kratie.

Food & Drink

Some traditional Cambodian dishes are similar to those of neighbouring Laos and Thailand (though not as spicy); others are closer to Chinese and Vietnamese cooking. The French left their mark, too.

Thanks to the Tonlé Sap, freshwater fish – often *ahng* (grilled) – are a huge part of the Cambodian diet. The great national dish, *amok,* is fish baked with coconut and lemongrass in banana leaves. *Prahoc* (fermented fish paste) is used to flavour foods, with coconut and lemongrass making regular cameos.

A proper Cambodian meal almost always includes *samlor* (soup), served at the same time as other courses. *Kyteow* is a rice-noodle soup that will keep you going all day. *Bobor* (rice porridge), eaten for breakfast, lunch or dinner, is best sampled with some fresh fish and a dash of ginger.

Beer is immensely popular in the cities, while rural folk drink palm wine, tapped from the sugar palms that dot the landscape. *Tukaloks* (fruit shakes) are mixed with milk, sugar and sometimes a raw egg.

Tap water must be avoided, especially in rural areas. Bottled water is widely available but coconut milk, sold by machete-wielding street vendors, is more ecological and may be more sterile.

SURVIVAL GUIDE

Directory A–Z

ACCESSIBLE TRAVEL

Broken pavements, potholed roads and stairs as steep as ladders at Angkor ensure that for most people with mobility impairments, Cambodia is not going to be an easy country in which to travel. Few buildings have been designed with people with a disability in mind, although new projects, such as the international airports at Phnom Penh and Siem Reap, and top-end hotels, include ramps for wheelchair access. Transport in the provinces is usually very overcrowded, but taxi hire from point to point is an affordable option.

Download Lonely Planet's free Accessible Travel guide from https://shop.lonelyplanet.com/products/accessible-travel-online-resources-2019.

ACCOMMODATION

Accommodation is great value in Cambodia, just like the rest of the Mekong region. In popular tourist destinations, budget guesthouses generally charge US$5 to US$10 for a room with a cold-water bathroom. Double rooms go as low as US$3 for a room with shared facilities. Dorm beds usually cost from US$2 to US$10 depending on hostel facilities. Rooms with air-con start at US$10. Spend US$20 or so and you'll be living well. Spend US$40 and up and we're talking boutique standard with a swimming pool. At the top end you can spend several hundred dollars a night on international-standard luxury digs in Siem Reap and Phnom Penh.

Accommodation is busiest from mid-November to March. There are substantial low-season (May to October) rates available at major hotels in Phnom Penh, Siem Reap and the islands (although you can only discount a US$5 room so much).

Homestays, often part of a community-based ecotourism project, are a good way to meet the local people and learn about Cambodian life. You can book local homestays online via Cambodia Impact Explorer (https://impactexplorer.asia/).

Price Ranges

The following price ranges refer to an en-suite double room in high season (November to February). Prices in Phnom Penh and Siem Reap tend to be a little higher.

$ less than US$25

$$ US$25–US$80

$$$ more than US$80

ACTIVITIES

Cambodia is steadily emerging as an adventure and ecotourism destination. Activities on offer include jungle trekking in Ratanakiri, Mondulkiri and the Cardamom Mountains; walking with elephants and gibbon spotting in Mondulkiri; scuba diving and snorkelling around the Southern Islands; cycling around Phnom Penh, in Mondulkiri, and around the temples of Angkor; and adventurous dirt-biking all over the country (for those with some experience).

CUSTOMS REGULATIONS

- A 'reasonable amount' of duty-free items is allowed into the country.
- Alcohol and cigarettes are on sale at well-below duty-free prices on the streets of Phnom Penh.
- It is illegal to take antiquities out of the country.

ELECTRICITY

The usual voltage is 220V, 50 cycles, but power surges and power cuts are common, particularly in the provinces. Electrical sockets are usually two-prong, mostly flat but sometimes round pin.

EMBASSIES & CONSULATES

Many countries have embassies in Phnom Penh, though some travellers will find that their nearest embassy is in Bangkok.

Australian Embassy (Map p188; ☎023-213470; www.cambodia.embassy.gov.au; 16 National Assembly St, Phnom Penh; ⊙8.30am-noon & 1.30-5pm Mon-Fri)

French Embassy (Map p182; ☎023-260010; http://kh.ambafrance.org; 1 Monivong Blvd, Phnom Penh; ⊙8.30-11.30am Mon-Fri)

German Embassy (Map p188; ☎023-216193; http://phnom-penh.diplo.de; 76-78 St 214, Phnom Penh; ⊙8.30-11.30am Mon, Wed & Fri)

Japanese Embassy (Map p182; ☎023-217161; www.kh.emb-japan.go.jp; 194 Norodom Blvd, Phnom Penh; ⊙8am-noon & 1.30-5.15pm Mon-Fri)

Lao Embassy (Map p182; ☎023-997931; 15-17 Mao Tse Toung Blvd, Phnom Penh; ⊙8.30-11.30am & 2-4.30pm Mon-Fri)

Thai Embassy (Map p182; ☎023-726306; www.thaiembassy.org/phnompenh; 196 Norodom Blvd, Phnom Penh; ⊙8.30-11am & 3-4.30pm Mon-Fri)

UK Embassy (Map p182; ☎061 300011; www.gov.uk/world/cambodia; 27-29 St 75, Phnom Penh; ⊙8.15am-noon & 1-4.45pm Mon-Fri)

US Embassy (Map p184; ☎023-728000; http://kh.usembassy.gov; 1 St 96, Phnom Penh; ⊙by appointment)

Vietnamese Embassy (Map p182; ☎097 7492430; 436 Monivong Blvd, Phnom Penh; ⊙8-11.30am & 1-4pm Mon-Fri)

FOOD

The following price ranges refer to a meal per person, including tax.

$ less than US$5

$$ US$5–US$15

$$$ more than US$15

INSURANCE

Health insurance is essential. Make sure your policy covers emergency evacuation: limited medical facilities mean evacuation by air to Bangkok in the event of serious injury or illness.

Worldwide travel insurance is available at www.lonelyplanet.com/travel-insurance. You can buy, extend and claim online anytime – even if you're already on the road.

INTERNET ACCESS

Wi-fi is pretty much ubiquitous in cafes and guesthouses across the country and is almost always free. Fast 4G access via local SIM cards is available for as little as US$1 for 4 gigabytes. 4G coverage through one or more providers is excellent in all but the most remote areas. Internet cafes are still an option in most cities. Charges range from 1500r to US$2 per hour.

LEGAL MATTERS

All narcotics, including marijuana, are illegal in Cambodia. However, marijuana is traditionally used in food preparation so you may find it sprinkled across some pizzas.

Many Western countries have laws that make sex offences committed overseas punishable at home.

LGBTIQ+ TRAVELLERS

The LGBT+ scene in Cambodia is certainly not as wild as that in Thailand, but both Phnom Penh and Siem Reap have plenty of gay-friendly establishments. Siem Reap in particular has a well-developed, if low-key, gay scene centred around its guesthouses.

As Theravada Buddhists, Cambodians are quite tolerant of homosexuality, although this applies more to foreigners than to Cambodians, who can be reluctant to come out of the closet. As with heterosexual couples, passionate public displays of affection are considered a basic no-no.

Checking into hotels across Cambodia, there is little consideration over how travelling foreigners are related. However, it is prudent not to announce your sexuality.

Recommended websites when planning a trip include the following:

Cambodia Gay (www.cambodia-gay.com) Promoting the LGBT+ community in Cambodia.

Utopia (www.utopia-asia.com) Gay travel information and contacts, including some local gay terminology.

MAPS

The best all-round map is Gecko's Cambodia Road Map at a 1:750,000 scale.

MONEY

Cambodia's currency is the riel, abbreviated in our listings to a lower-case 'r' written after the sum. The US dollar is accepted everywhere and by everyone, though change may arrive in riel (handy when paying for things such as *moto* rides and drinks). When calculating change, the US dollar is usually rounded off to 4000r. Near the Thai border, many transactions are in Thai baht. Avoid ripped banknotes, which Cambodians often refuse.

ATMs

There are credit-card-compatible ATMs (Visa, MasterCard, JCB, Cirrus) in most major cities. There are also ATMs at the Cham Yeam, Poipet and Bavet borders if arriving by land from Thailand or Vietnam. There are no ATMs on the southern islands.

Machines usually give you the option of withdrawing in US dollars or riel. Single withdrawals of up to US$500 at a time are usually possible, providing your account can handle it. Stay alert when using ATMs late at night.

Canadia Bank and ABA Bank have the most extensive network, including ATMs at petrol stations, and popular hotels, restaurants and shops. Acleda Bank has the widest network of branches in the country, including all provincial capitals, but their ATMs generally only take Visa-affiliated cards. Most ATM withdrawals incur a charge of US$4 to US$5.

Bargaining

Bargaining is expected in local markets, when travelling by share taxi or *moto* and, sometimes, when taking a cheap room. The Khmers are not ruthless hagglers, so a persuasive smile and a little friendly quibbling is usually enough to get a good price.

Credit Cards

Top-end hotels, airline offices and upmarket boutiques and restaurants generally accept most major credit cards (Visa, MasterCard, JCB, sometimes American Express), but they usually pass the charges on to the customer, meaning an extra 3% or more on the bill.

Tipping

Tipping is not traditionally expected here, but in a country as poor as Cambodia, a dollar tip (or 5% to 10% on bigger bills) can go a long way.

OPENING HOURS

Everything shuts down during the major holidays of Chaul Chnam Khmer (Khmer New Year), P'chum Ben (Festival of the Dead) and Chaul Chnam Chen (Chinese New Year).

Banks 8am–3.30pm Monday to Friday, Saturday mornings

Bars 5pm–late

Government offices 7.30am–11.30am and 2pm–5pm Monday to Friday

Local markets 6.30am–5.30pm

Museums Hours vary, but usually open seven days a week

Restaurants International restaurants 7am–10pm or meal times; local restaurants 6.30am–9pm

Shops 8am–6pm, later in tourist centres

POST

The postal service is hit and miss from Cambodia; send anything valuable by courier or from another country. Ensure postcards and letters are franked before they vanish from your sight.

Letters and parcels sent further afield than Asia can take up to two or three weeks to reach their destination. Use a courier to speed things up; EMS (www.ems.post/en/global-network/ems-operators/ems-cambodia) has branches at every major post office in the country. DHL and FedEx are present in major cities such as Phnom Penh, Siem Reap and Sihanoukville.

PUBLIC HOLIDAYS

Banks, ministries and embassies close down during public holidays and festivals, so plan ahead if visiting Cambodia during these times. Cambodians also roll over holidays if they fall on a weekend and take a day or two extra during major festivals. Add to this the fact that they take a holiday for international days here and there, and it soon becomes apparent that Cambodia has more public holidays than almost any other nation on earth!

International New Year's Day 1 January

Victory over the Genocide 7 January

International Women's Day 8 March

International Workers' Day 1 May

International Children's Day 8 May

King's Birthday 13–15 May

King's Mother's Birthday 18 June

Constitution Day 24 September

Commemoration Day 15 October

Independence Day 9 November

International Human Rights Day 10 December

SAFETY

Crime & Violence

Incidents of bag snatching in Phnom Penh and Siem Reap are common and the motorbike thieves don't let go, dragging passengers off bicycles or *motos* and endangering lives. Smartphones are a particular target, so avoid using your smartphone in public, especially at night, as you'll be susceptible to drive-by thieves.

Walking or riding alone late at night is not ideal, certainly not in rural areas. There have been several incidents of lone females being assaulted in isolated forests or rural areas, usually after dark.

Should anyone be unlucky enough to be robbed, it is important to note that the Cambodian police are the best that money can buy! Any help, such as a police report, is going to cost you. The going rate depends on the size of the claim, but anywhere from US$5 to US$50 is possible.

Violence against foreigners is extremely rare, but it pays to take care in crowded bars or nightclubs in Phnom Penh. If you get into a stand-off with rich young Khmers in a bar or club, swallow your pride and back down. Many carry guns and have an entourage of bodyguards.

Drugs

Watch out for *yaba*, the 'crazy' drug from Thailand, known rather ominously in Cambodia as *yama* (the Hindu god of death). Known as ice or crystal meth elsewhere, it's not just any old diet pill from the pharmacist but homemade methamphetamines produced in labs in Cambodia and the region beyond. The pills are often laced with toxic substances, such as mercury, lithium or whatever else the maker can find. *Yama* is a dirty drug and more addictive than users would like to admit, provoking powerful hallucinations, sleep deprivation and psychosis. Steer clear of the stuff unless you plan on an indefinite extension to your trip.

Mines, Mortars & Bombs

Never touch any rockets, artillery shells, mortars, mines, bombs or other war material you may come across. The most heavily mined part of the country is along the Thai border area, but mines are a problem in much of Cambodia. In short: *do not stray from well-marked paths under any circumstances*. If you are planning any walks, even in safer areas such as the remote northeast, it is imperative you take a guide as there may still be unexploded ordnance (UXO) from the American bombing campaign of the early 1970s.

Scams

Most scams are fairly harmless, involving a bit of commission here and there for taxi, *remorks* or *moto* drivers, particularly in Siem Reap.

There have been one or two reports of police set-ups in Phnom Penh, involving planted drugs. This seems to be very rare, but if you fall victim to the ploy, it may be best to pay them off before more police get involved at the local station, as the price will only rise when there are more mouths to feed.

There is quite a lot of fake medication floating about the region. Safeguard yourself by only buying prescription drugs from reliable pharmacies or clinics.

Beware the Filipino blackjack scam: don't get involved in any gambling with seemingly friendly folks unless you want to part with plenty of cash.

Beggars in places such as Phnom Penh and Siem Reap may ask for milk powder for an infant in arms. Some foreigners succumb to the urge to help, but the beggars usually request the most expensive milk formula available and return it to the shop to split the proceeds after the handover.

TELEPHONE

A wealth of domestic mobile providers means dirt-cheap prices for local cellular services. Calls and texts are free within the same network, and just a few a cents per minute/message to other networks.

To place a long-distance domestic call from a mobile (cell) number or a landline, or to dial a mobile number, dial zero, the area code (or mobile prefix) and the number. Leave out the zero and the area code if you are making a local call. Drop the zero from the mobile prefix or regional (city) code when dialling into Cambodia from another country.

Your home provider will charge you a fortune for roaming in Cambodia, so pick up a local SIM card as soon as you arrive. If you arrive by air, you'll find booths for all Cambodian mobile-phone providers just outside the airport exit. They stay open late and have English-speaking staff to sort you out. Around US$3 yields a generous bundle of calls and texts and several gigabytes of data. Be prepared to show your passport.

TIME

Cambodia is in the Indochina time zone, which means GMT/UTC plus seven hours. Thus, noon in Phnom Penh is midnight the previous day in New York, 5am in London, 1pm in Hong Kong and 3pm in Sydney, depending on daylight saving hours in those cities. There is no daylight saving time.

VISAS

Visas on Arrival

➡ A one-month tourist visa costs US$30 on arrival and requires one passport-sized photo. Easily extendable business visas are available for US$35.

- Most visitors to Cambodia require a one-month tourist visa (US$30). Most nationalities receive this on arrival at Phnom Penh and Siem Reap airports, and at land borders. If you are carrying an African, South Asian or Middle Eastern passport, there are some exceptions.
- One passport-sized photo is required and you'll be 'fined' US$2 if you don't have one. It is also possible to arrange a visa through Cambodian embassies overseas or an online e-visa (US$30, plus a US$7 processing fee) through the Ministry of Foreign Affairs (www.mfaic.gov.kh).
- Passport holders from Asean member countries do not require a visa to visit Cambodia.
- Travellers are sometimes overcharged when crossing at land borders with Thailand, as immigration officials demand payment in baht and round up the figure considerably. Overcharging is also an issue at the Laos border, but not usually at Vietnam borders. Arranging a visa in advance can help avoid overcharging.
- Overstaying a visa currently costs US$5 a day.

E-Visas

E-visas are only accepted at Phnom Penh and Siem Reap airports (they are not accepted in Sihanoukville), and at the two main land borders: Bavet/Moc Bai (Vietnam) and Poipet/Aranya Prathet (Thailand).

Visa Extensions

- Visa extensions are issued by the large immigration office located directly across the road from Phnom Penh International Airport.
- Extensions are easy to arrange, taking just a couple of days. It costs US$45 for one month (for both tourist and business visas), US$75 for three months, US$155 for six months and US$285 for one year (the latter three prices relate to business visas only). It's pretty straightforward to extend business visas ad infinitum. Travel agencies and some motorbike-rental shops in Phnom Penh can help with arrangements, sometimes at a discounted price.
- Those seeking work in Cambodia should opt for the business visa (US$35) as it is easily extended for longer periods, including multiple entries and exits. A tourist visa can be extended only once and only for one month, and does not allow for re-entry.

VOLUNTEERING

For volunteering with a difference, Cambodia hosts a huge number of NGOs, some of which do require volunteers from time to time. The **Cooperation Committee for Cambodia** (CCC; Map p182; ☎023-214152; www.ccc-cambodia.org; 9-11 St 476) in Phnom Penh has a handy list of all NGOs, both Cambodian and international, and is extremely helpful.

Siem Reap–based organisation ConCERT (www.concertcambodia.org) has a 'responsible volunteering' section on its website that offers advice on preparing for a stint as a volunteer.

Backpacker-oriented guesthouses, restaurants and bars are often looking for young Western faces to help out in all kinds of ways, especially during the high season (roughly November to April). The best resource for these opportunities in Cambodia is Workaway (www.workaway.info).

WOMEN TRAVELLERS

Women will generally find Cambodia a hassle-free place to travel. Foreign women are unlikely to be targeted by local men, and will probably find Khmer men to be courteous and polite, although some of the guys in the guesthouse industry can be a little flirtatious from time to time. At the same time it pays to be careful. As is the case in many places, walking or riding a bike alone late at night can be risky.

Khmer women dress fairly conservatively, in general preferring long-sleeved shirts and long trousers or skirts. In the countryside, it is quite rare for most Khmer women to wear singlet tops or very short skirts or shorts. So when travellers do, people tend to stare. If you're planning on bathing in a village or river, a sarong is essential. It is worth having trousers for heading out at night on *motos*, as short skirts aren't very practical.

Tampons and sanitary napkins are widely available in the major cities and provincial capitals, but if you are heading into very remote areas for a few days, it is worth having your own supply.

WORK

Jobs are available throughout Cambodia, but apart from teaching English or helping out in guesthouses, bars or restaurants, most are for professionals and are arranged in advance. There is a lot of teaching work available for English-language speakers and salary is directly linked to experience. Anyone with an English-language teaching certificate can earn considerably more than those with no qualifications.

ℹ Getting There & Away

ENTERING CAMBODIA

The majority of visitors enter or exit Cambodia by air through the popular international gateways of Phnom Penh or Siem Reap, and you can also fly into Sihanoukville these days if you are headed to the islands. Lots of independent travellers enter or exit the country via the numerous land borders shared with Thailand, Vietnam and Laos. There is also the option to cross via the Mekong River between Vietnam and Cambodia.

AIR

Phnom Penh International Airport (p197) is the gateway to the Cambodian capital, while Siem Reap International Airport (p213) serves visitors to the temples of Angkor. Both airports have a good range of services, including restaurants, bars, shops and ATMs. Sihanoukville International Airport (p257) serves a dozen or so Chinese cities plus Bangkok, Ho Chi Minh City and Kuala Lumpur.

Flights to Cambodia are expanding, but most connect only as far as regional capitals. **Cambodia Angkor Air** (☎023-212564; www.cambodiaangkorair.com) is the national airline and offers a handful of international flight connections to destinations around the region, including Beijing, Danang, Guangzhou and Ho Chi Minh City.

Thai Airways (www.thaiair.com) and Bangkok Airways (www.bangkokair.com) offer the most daily international flights connections, all via Bangkok. Emirates (www.emirates.com) flies daily to Dubai via Bangkok.

AirAsia (www.airasia.com) has daily flights from Phnom Penh and Siem Reap to Bangkok, while Jetstar (www.jetstar.com) connects the same two cities to Singapore. AirAsia also serves Sihanoukville from Bangkok. Other airlines connecting Bangkok to Phnom Penh and/or Siem Reap are domestic budget carriers **Lanmei Airlines** (☎023-981363; www.lanmeiairlines.com) and **JC International Airlines** (☎023-989707; www.jcairline.com), and Thai budget carrier Thai Smile (www.thaismileair.com).

From Phnom Penh JC International adds three weekly flights to Yangon and serves Bangkok and Macau. Vietjet Air (www.vietjetair.com) has a few useful routes, such as Siem Reap to Hanoi. Lanmei Airlines serves Bangkok and Hong Kong from Phnom Penh, and a host of Chinese cities from both Phnom Penh and Siem Reap.

Vietnam Airlines (www.vietnamairlines.com) has several useful connections, including from both Phnom Penh and Siem Reap to Ho Chi Minh City, as well as from Phnom Penh to Vientiane and Siem Reap to Luang Prabang, Danang and Hanoi. Philippine Airlines (www.philippineairlines.com) has four or five weekly flights to Phnom Penh from Manila.

Other regional centres with multiple daily direct flights to Cambodia include Hong Kong, Kuala Lumpur, Seoul and Taipei.

ℹ Getting Around

AIR

Domestic flights offer a great way to avoid Cambodia's often miserable roads. Cambodia's three functioning airports are all well connected to each other these days. With the exception of the Phnom Penh–Sihanoukville route, flights are very cheap. Airlines tend to come and go, with most of the newer ones existing to serve the booming Chinese market.

Cambodia Airways (☎096 852 5555; www.cambodia-airways.com) Connects Siem Reap with Phnom Penh and Sihanoukville.

Cambodia Angkor Air Offers multiple daily flights between Phnom Penh and Siem Reap and Siem Reap and Sihanoukville.

JC International Airlines Daily discounted flights between Phnom Penh and Siem Reap.

Lanmei Airlines New budget airline links Phnom Penh and Siem Reap, and links both cities to Sihanoukville.

Sky Angkor Airlines (☎063-967300; www.skyangkorair.com) Has several weekly flights between Siem Reap and Sihanoukville.

BICYCLE

Cambodia is a great country for experienced cyclists to explore. A mountain bike is the recommended set of wheels thanks to the notorious state of the roads. Most roads have a flat unpaved trail along the side, which is useful for cyclists.

Much of Cambodia is pancake flat or only moderately hilly. Safety, however, is a considerable concern on the newer surfaced roads, as local traffic travels at high speed. Bicycles can be transported around the country in the back of pickups or on the roof of minibuses.

Guesthouses and hotels in Cambodia rent out bicycles for US$1 to US$2 per day, or US$7 to US$15 for an imported brand such as Giant or Trek.

Top bikes, safety equipment and authentic spare parts are now readily available in Phnom Penh at very reasonable prices.

PEPY Tours (www.pepytours.com) is a bicycle and volunteer tour company offering adventures throughout Cambodia. PEPY promotes 'adventurous living, responsible giving' and puts funds back into community education and other projects.

BOAT

Cambodia's 1900km of navigable waterways are not as important as they once were for the average tourist, given major road improvements. North of Phnom Penh, the Mekong is easily navigable as far as Kratie, but there are no longer regular passenger services on these routes, as buses have taken all the business. There are scenic boat services between Siem Reap and Battambang, and the Tonlé Sap lake is also navigable year-round, although only by smaller boats between March and July.

Traditionally the most popular boat services with foreigners are those that run between Phnom Penh and Siem Reap. The express services do the trip in as little as five hours. The first couple of hours out of Phnom Penh along the Tonlé Sap River are scenic, but it becomes less interesting when the river morphs into the Tonlé Sap lake, which is like a vast sea, offering little scenery. It's more popular (and much cheaper) to take a bus on the paved road instead.

The small boat between Siem Reap and Battambang is more rewarding, as the river scenery is truly memorable, but it can take as long as a whole day with delays.

BUS

About a dozen bus companies serve all populated parts of the country. Comfort levels and prices vary wildly, so shop around. Booking bus tickets through guesthouses and travel agents is convenient, but often incurs a commission. Also note that travel agents tend to work with only a handful of preferred companies, thus won't always offer your preferred company and/or departure time, so it pays to shop around.

While it doesn't cover all bus companies, **bookmebus** (www.bookmebus.com) is a reliable bus-ticket booking site, including for more obscure routes (Ban Lung to Siem Reap, anyone?) and cross-border trips.

CAR & MOTORCYCLE

Car and motorcycle rental are comparatively cheap in Cambodia and many visitors rent a car or bike for greater flexibility to visit out-of-the-way places and to stop when they choose. Almost all car rental in Cambodia includes a driver, although self-drive rentals are also available in Phnom Penh.

Car hire is generally only available with a driver and is most useful for sightseeing around Phnom Penh and Angkor, and for conveniently travelling between cities. Some tourists with a healthy budget also arrange cars or 4WDs with drivers for touring the provinces. Hiring a car with a driver is about US$40 to US$50 for a day in and around Cambodia's towns. Heading into the provinces it rises to US$60 or more, plus petrol, depending on the destination. Hiring 4WDs will cost around US$60 to US$120 a day, depending on the model and the distance travelled. Self-drive car rentals are available in Phnom Penh, but think twice about driving yourself due to chaotic road conditions and personal liability in the case of an accident.

It is possible to explore Cambodia by motorbike. Anyone planning a longer ride should try out the bike around town for a day or so first to make sure it is in good health.

Motorcycles are available for hire in Phnom Penh and other provincial capitals and tourist towns. In Siem Reap motorcycle rental is still technically forbidden, but of late authorities are taking a relaxed view and a growing number of places now hire out motorbikes to tourists.

A 100cc motorbike usually rents for US$4 to US$6 per day (US$15 to US$20 on the islands). Costs are around US$15 to US$25 for a 250cc dirt bike.

LOCAL TRANSPORT

Cyclo

As in Vietnam and Laos, the *cyclo* (bicycle rickshaw or pedicab) is a cheap way to get around urban areas. In Phnom Penh *cyclo* drivers can either be flagged down on main roads or found waiting around markets and major hotels. It is necessary to bargain the fare if taking a *cyclo* from outside an expensive hotel or popular restaurant or bar. Fares range from US$1 to US$3. There are few *cyclos* in the provinces, and in Phnom Penh the *cyclo* has almost been driven to extinction by the *moto*.

Moto

Motos, also known as *motodups* (meaning *moto* driver), are small motorcycle taxis. They are a quick way of making short hops around towns and cities. Prices range from 2000r to US$1.50 or more, depending on the distance and the town; expect to pay more at night. In the past it was rare for prices to be agreed in advance, but with the increase in visitor numbers, a lot of drivers have got into the habit of overcharging. It's probably best to negotiate up front, particularly in the major tourist centres, outside fancy hotels or at night.

Taxi

Taxi hire in towns and cities is getting easier, but there are still very few metered taxis, with just a handful of operators in Phnom Penh. Guesthouses, hotels and travel agents can arrange cars for sightseeing in and around towns. Ride-hailing apps have entered the market. In the provinces they are generally used to hail *remorks* but in the main cities can be used for small or large cars.

Tuk tuk

The *remork-moto* (*remork*) is a large trailer hitched to a motorcycle and pretty much operates as a low-tech local bus with oh-so-natural air-conditioning. They are used throughout rural Cambodia to transport people and goods, and are often seen on the edge of towns ready to ferry farmers back to the countryside.

Most popular tourist destinations, including Phnom Penh, Siem Reap and the South Coast, have their very own tourist versions of the *remork*, with a canopied trailer hitched to the back of the motorbike for two people in comfort or as many as you can pile on at night. These are a great way to explore temples, as you get the breeze of the bike but some protection from the elements.

In recent years a sizable fleet of Indian-made auto-rickshaws – similar to the Indian rickshaw or the Thai *tuk tuk* – has invaded Cambodia's urban landscape. They are zippier than their *remork* cousins, but much more compact – opt for a *remork* if you are more than two or three passengers and/or have a lot of luggage.

Remorks and auto-rickshaws are interchangeably known as *tuk tuks*, and can be ordered in larger provincial capitals via ride-hailing apps **Grab** (www.grab.com) and/or **PassApp** (www.passapptaxis.com) at prices much lower than you're likely to get on the street.

SHARE TAXI

In these days of improving roads, share taxis are losing ground to express minivans. When using share taxis, it is an advantage to travel in numbers, as you can buy spare seats to make the journey more comfortable. Double the price for the front seat and quadruple it for the entire back row. It is important to remember that there aren't necessarily fixed prices on every route, so you have to negotiate. For major destinations they can be hired individually, or you can pay for a seat and wait for other passengers to turn up. Guesthouses are also very helpful when it comes to arranging share taxis, albeit at a price.

TRAIN

Mothballed for years, Cambodia's rail system has been rehabilitated in recent years and limited passenger services resumed in 2016 through national carrier **Royal Railways** (☎078 888583; www.royal-railway.com). Currently there are two lines. The southern line links Phnom Penh with Sihanoukville via Kampot and Takeo, with departures on weekend mornings. The northern line – built before WWII and reopened in 2018 – runs from Phnom Penh to Poipet on the Thai border on Friday and Sunday mornings via Pursat and Battambang. Plans call for plugging the Cambodian line into the Trans-Asian Railway network, which will link Singapore and China, but connecting Phnom Penh with Ho Chi Minh City via a Mekong bridge will take a few years yet.

AT A GLANCE

POPULATION
7.4 million

CAPITAL CITY
Vientiane

BEST YOGA CLASSES
Yoga in Vang Vieng (p310)

BEST REGIONAL DISHES
Doi Ka Noi (p300)

BEST HISTORY LESSON
Vieng Xai Caves (p336)

WHEN TO GO

Jan Cool-season breezes: even the normally sweltering south is pleasantly bearable.

Oct Mercifully cool weather. Bun Awk Phansa sees candle-bearing boats floated down rivers.

Nov–Dec Cool weather, and the best all-round time to visit. Book accommodation ahead for Christmas/New Year.

Vang Vieng (p306)
PARKERDP/SHUTTERSTOCK ©

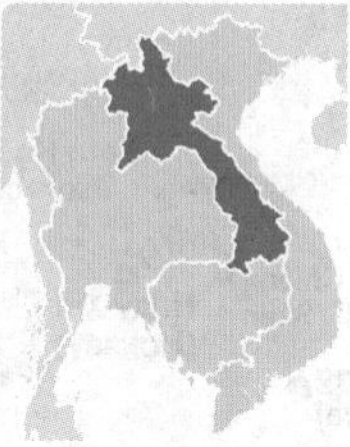

Laos

Vivid nature, voluptuous landscapes and a vibrant culture collide with a painful past and an optimistic future to make Laos an enigmatic experience for the adventurous. Thrill seekers can lose themselves in underground river caves, on jungle ziplines or while climbing karsts. Nature enthusiasts can discover brooding jungle, emerald rice fields and glistening tea plantations. Culture lovers can explore ancient temples and immerse themselves in Lao spiritual life. Foodies can spice up their lives with a Lao cooking class or go gourmand in the French-accented cities. Eclectic Laos caters for everyone.

INCLUDES

Laos Highlights

1 Luang Prabang (p314) Exploring the fabled city to find French cuisine, Buddhist temples, colonial villas, stunning river views and some of the best boutique accommodation in Southeast Asia.

2 Tham Kong Lor (p359) Taking a boat ride through the exhilarating yet spooky 7.5km-long tunnel, home to fist-sized spiders and stalactite woods, while tackling the three-day dirt-bike 'Loop'.

3 Vientiane (p292) Meandering along the banks of the Mekong in Vientiane, surely Southeast Asia's most languid capital, with wide streets bordered by tamarind trees and alleys concealing French villas, Chinese shophouses and glittering wats.

4 Nam Ha National Protected Area (p342) Taking an eco-responsible trek through some of the wildest, densest jungle in the country, home to a rich variety of ethnic tribes.

5 Si Phan Don (p380) Lowering your pulse in the travellers' mecca of Four Thousand Islands, where the Mekong turns turquoise and the night air is flecked with fireflies.

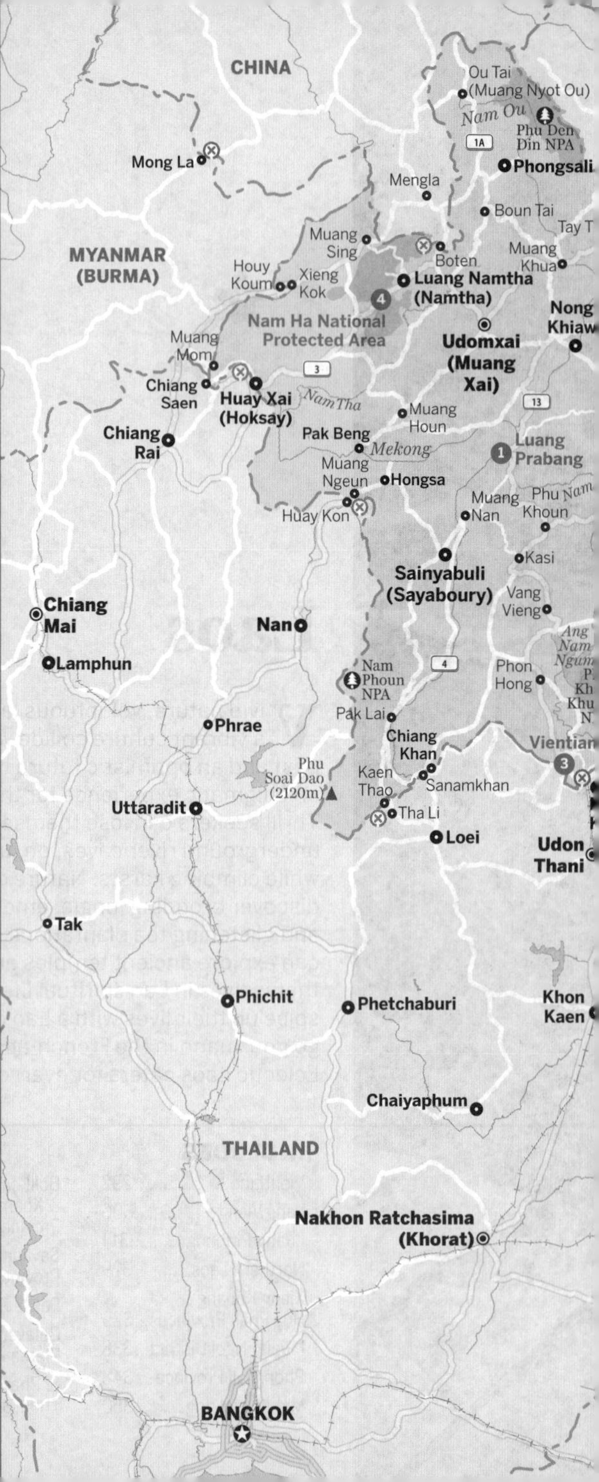

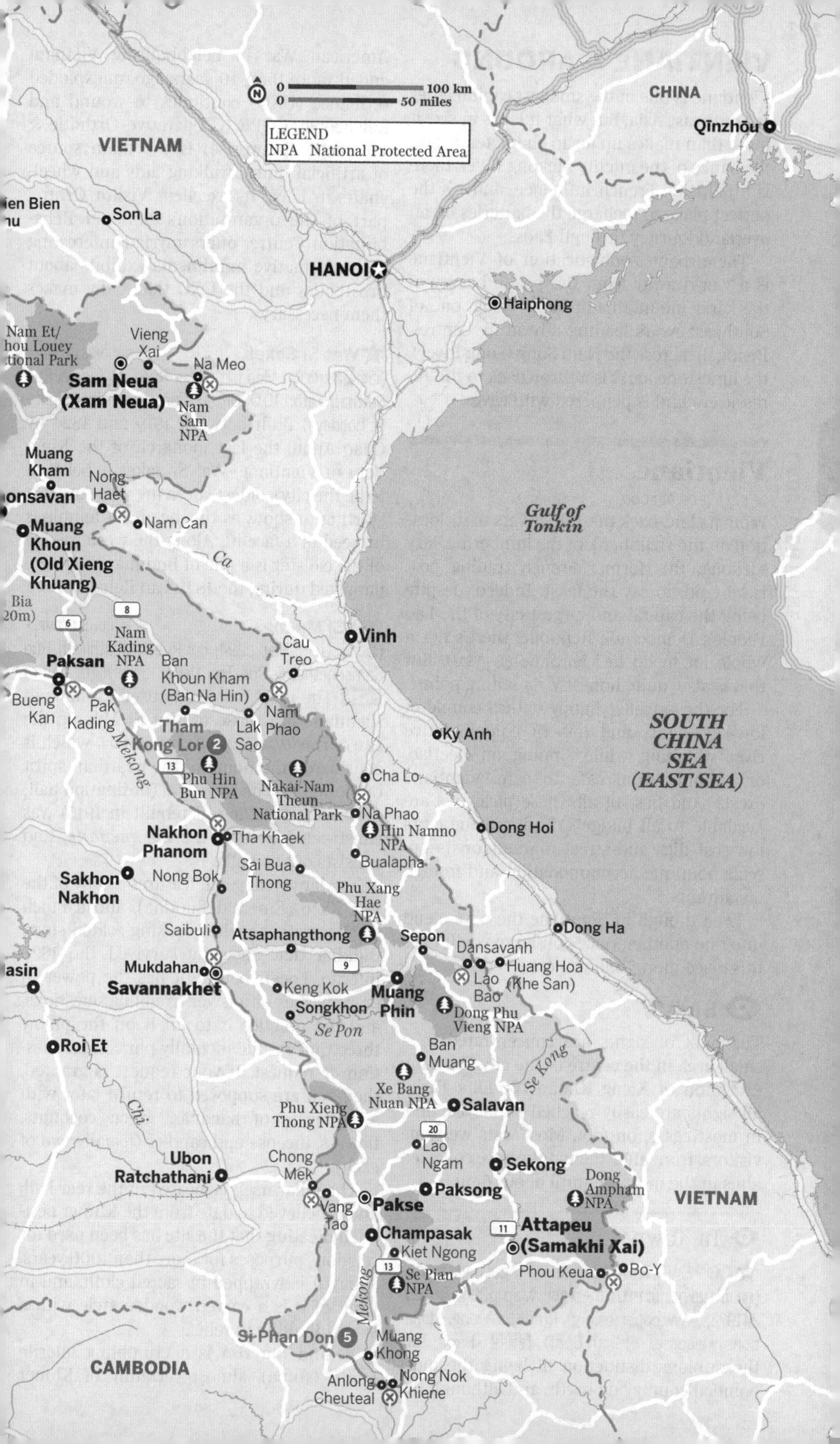

0 100 km
0 50 miles
LEGEND
NPA National Protected Area
CHINA
Qinzhou
VIETNAM
Son La
HANOI
Haiphong
Vieng Xai
Na Meo
Sam Neua (Xam Neua)
Nam Sam NPA
Muang Kham
Nong Haet
Nam Can
Muang Khoun (Old Xieng Khuang)
Ca
Gulf of Tonkin
Vinh
Cau Treo
Paksan
Nam Kading NPA
Ban Khoun Kham (Ban Na Hin)
Bueng Kan
Pak Kading
Nam Phao
Lak Sao
Tham Kong Lor 2
Ky Anh
SOUTH CHINA SEA (EAST SEA)
Mekong
Phu Hin Bun NPA
Nakai-Nam Theun National Park
Cha Lo
Na Phao
Hin Namno NPA
Nakhon Phanom
Tha Khaek
Dong Hoi
Sai Bua Thong
Bualapha
Sakhon Nakhon
Nong Bok
Phu Xang Hae NPA
Saibuli
Atsaphangthong
Sepon
Dong Ha
Dansavanh
Huang Hoa (Khe San)
Lao Bao
Mukdahan
Savannakhet
Keng Kok
Muang Phin
Songkhon
Dong Phu Vieng NPA
Se Pon
Roi Et
Ban Muang
Se Kong
Xe Bang Nuan NPA
Salavan
Phu Xieng Thong NPA
Chi
Lao Ngam
Chong Mek
Ubon Ratchathani
Sekong
Dong Ampham NPA
Paksong
Vang Tao
Pakse
VIETNAM
Champasak
Attapeu (Samakhi Xai)
Kiet Ngong
Se Pian NPA
Phou Keua
Bo-Y
Si Phan Don 5
Muang Khong
CAMBODIA
Anlong Cheuteal
Nong Nok Khiene

VIENTIANE & AROUND

Vientiane is one of the smallest capital cities in Southeast Asia, but what it lacks in size it more than makes up for in character. Set on the banks of the mighty Mekong River, there is a palpable French influence, and it's the perfect place to recharge the batteries on an overland journey through Laos.

The urbane sophistication of Vientiane is a world away from the poetic beauty of the karst mountains of Vang Vieng, one of Southeast Asia's leading adventure centres. Rising up across the Nam Song (Song River), the limestone karst is a throwback to the Jurassic era and is peppered with caves.

Vientiane

☎ 021 / POP 821,000

From its laid-back tuk-tuk drivers to its location on the right bank of the lumbering, lazy Mekong, this former French trading post is languid, to say the least. Indeed, despite being the capital and largest city of the Lao People's Democratic Republic, there's not a whole lot to do in Vientiane (ວຽງຈັນ). But that is also, quite honestly, its selling point.

For the traveller happy with a couple of low-key sights and lots of contemplative river watching while sipping on Beerlao, or hopping from cafe to cafe, Vientiane excels. And best of all, these pleasures are available to all budgets, be it via the city's low-cost digs and street markets or its upscale boutique accommodation and foreign restaurants.

Even though in Vientiane the days blend into one another, once you leave you'll miss this place more than you expected.

Sights

The bulk of sights are concentrated in a small area in the centre of the city. With the exception of Xieng Khuan (Buddha Park), all sights are easily reached by bicycle and, in most cases, on foot. Most wats welcome visitors, from after the monks have collected alms in the morning until about 6pm.

In Town

★ COPE Visitor Centre CULTURAL CENTRE

(ສູນຟື້ນຟູຄົນພິການແຫ່ງຊາດ; Map p294; ☎ 021-241972; www.copelaos.org; Rue Khu Vieng; donations welcome; ⏲ 9am-6pm) FREE Laos has the dubious distinction of being the most bombed country on earth, and although the American War in neighbouring Vietnam ended more than 40 years ago, unexploded ordnance (UXO) continues to wound and kill people. COPE (Cooperative Orthotic & Prosthetic Enterprise) is the main source of artificial limbs, walking aids and wheelchairs in Laos. Its excellent Visitor Centre, part of the organisation's National Rehabilitation Centre, offers myriad interesting and informative multimedia exhibits about prosthetics and the UXO that sadly makes them necessary.

★ Wat Si Saket BUDDHIST TEMPLE

(ວັດສີສະເກດ; Map p296; cnr Rue Lan Xang & Rue Setthathirath; 10,000K; ⏲ 8am-5pm, closed public holidays) Built between 1819 and 1824 by Chao Anou, the last monarch of the Kingdom of Vientiane, Wat Si Saket is believed to be the city's oldest surviving wat. And it is starting to show, as this beautiful temple is in need of a facelift. Along the western side of the cloister is a pile of Buddhas that were damaged during the 1828 Lao Rebellion.

Wat Si Muang BUDDHIST TEMPLE

(ວັດສີເມືອງ; Map p294; cnr Rue Setthathirath, Rue Samsenethai & Rue Tha Deua; ⏲ daylight hours) FREE The most frequently used grounds in Vientiane are those of Wat Si Muang, the site of the *lák méuang* (city pillar), which is considered the home of the guardian spirit of Vientiane. The large *sĭm* (ordination hall; destroyed in 1828 and rebuilt in 1915) was constructed around the *lák méuang,* and consists of two halls.

The large entry hall features a copy of the Pha Kaeo (Emerald Buddha), and a much smaller, rather melted-looking seated stone Buddha that allegedly survived the 1828 inferno. Locals believe it has the power to grant wishes or answer troubling questions, and the practice is to lift it off the pillow three times while mentally phrasing a question or request. If your request is granted, then you are supposed to return later with an offering of bananas, green coconuts, flowers, incense and candles (usually two of each).

The pillar itself is located in the rear hall, and is believed to date from the Khmer period, indicating that the site has been used for religious purposes for more than 1000 years. Today it is wrapped in sacred cloth, and in front of it is a carved wooden stele with a seated Buddha in relief.

Behind the *sĭm* is a crumbling laterite *jęhdii* (stupa), almost certainly of Khmer origin. In front of the *sĭm* is a little public park with a statue of King Sisavang Vong (r 1904–59).

Patuxai MONUMENT
(ປະຕູໄຊ, Victory Gate; Map p294; Rue Lan Xang; 3000K; ⌚8am-5pm) Vientiane's Arc de Triomphe replica is a slightly incongruous sight, dominating the commercial district around Rue Lan Xang. Officially called 'Victory Gate' and commemorating the Lao who died in prerevolutionary wars, it was built in the 1960s with cement donated by the USA intended for the construction of a new airport. Climb to the summit for panoramic views over Vientiane.

Around Town

★Xieng Khuan MUSEUM
(ຊຽງຄວນ, Suan Phut, Buddha Park; 5000K, camera 3000K, motorbike parking 5000K; ⌚8am-5pm) Located 25km southeast of central Vientiane, eccentric Xieng Khuan, aka Buddha Park, thrills with other-worldly Buddhist and Hindu sculptures, and was designed and built in 1958 by Luang Pu, a yogi-priest-shaman who merged Hindu and Buddhist philosophy, mythology and iconography into a cryptic whole. It's a bizarre, delightfully dilapidated compound that's great for a wander and a photo op.

Bus 14 (8000K, one hour) leaves Talat Sao Bus Station every 20 minutes for Xieng Khuan. Alternatively, charter a tuk-tuk (250,000K return).

★Pha That Luang BUDDHIST STUPA
(ພະທາດຫລວງ; Map p294; Rue 23 Singha; 10,000K, rental of long skirt to enter temple 5000K; ⌚8am-5pm) Golden Pha That Luang, located about 4km northeast of the city centre, is the most important national monument in Laos – a symbol of Buddhist religion and Lao sovereignty. Legend has it that Ashokan missionaries from India erected a *tâht* (stupa) here to enclose a piece of Buddha's breastbone as early as the 3rd century BC.

★Kaysone Phomvihane Memorial MUSEUM
(ພິພິດຕະພັນ ໄກສອນ ພິມວິຫານ; Km 6, Sivilay Village; 5000K; ⌚8am-noon & 1-4pm Tue-Sun) The former home of Kaysone Phomvihane, the first leader of an independent Laos, has been made into this quirky but worthwhile museum.

The house is inside the former USAID/CIA compound, known as 'Six Klicks City' because of its location 6km from central Vientiane. It once featured bars, restaurants, tennis courts, swimming pools, a commissary and assorted offices from where the Secret War was orchestrated. During the 1975 takeover of Vientiane, Pathet Lao forces ejected the Americans and occupied the compound. Kaysone lived here until his death in 1992.

LOCAL KNOWLEDGE

VIEWING PHA THAT LUANG

Each level of Pha That Luang has different architectural features in which Buddhist doctrine is encoded; visitors are supposed to contemplate the meaning of these features as they walk around. The first level is an approximately square base measuring 68m by 69m that supports 323 *sěe máh* (ordination stones). It represents the material world, and also features four arched *hŏr wái* (prayer halls), one on each side, with short stairways leading to them and beyond to the second level.

The second level is 48m by 48m and is surrounded by 120 lotus petals. There are 288 *sěe máh* on this level, as well as 30 small stupas symbolising the 30 Buddhist perfections *(báhlamée săhm-síp tat)*, beginning with alms-giving and ending with equanimity.

Arched gates again lead to the next level, a 30m by 30m square. The tall central stupa, which has a brick core that has been stuccoed over, is supported here by a bowl-shaped base reminiscent of India's first Buddhist stupa at Sanchi. At the top of this mound the superstructure, surrounded by lotus petals, begins.

The curvilinear, four-sided spire resembles an elongated lotus bud and is said to symbolise the growth of a lotus from a seed in a muddy lake bottom to a bloom over the lake's surface, a metaphor for human advancement from ignorance to enlightenment in Buddhism. The entire *tâht* (stupa) was regilded in 1995 to celebrate the 20th anniversary of the Lao People's Democratic Republic (Lao PDR), and is crowned by a stylised banana flower and parasol. From ground to pinnacle, Pha That Luang is 45m tall.

Vientiane

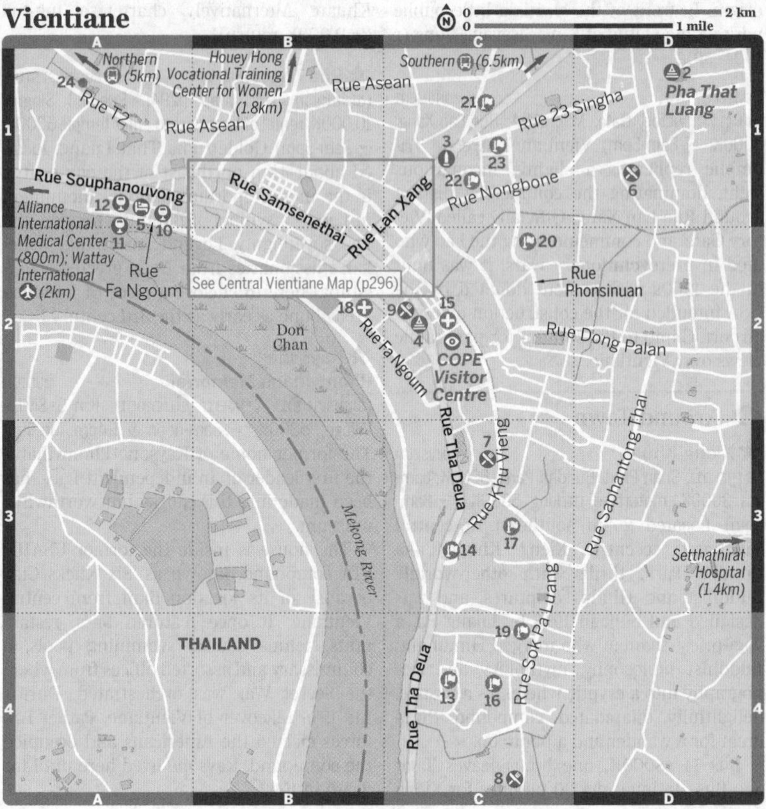

Today, the house includes Kaysone's half-empty bottles of scotch, tacky souvenirs from the Eastern bloc, running shoes, notepads and original Kelvinator air-conditioners. Even the winter coats he wore on visits to Moscow remain neatly hanging in the wardrobe. A Lao People's Revolutionary Party (LPRP) guide will show you through the house, making for a remarkably good-value experience.

Kaysone's house can be tricky to find, so it's easiest to backtrack from the nearby **Kaysone Phomvihane Museum** (ຫໍພິພິດທະພັນແລະອະນຸສາວລີໄກສອນພົມວິຫານ; Rte 13; 5000K; ⏲8am-noon & 1-4pm Tue-Sun). Head back towards the city centre and turn right at the first set of traffic lights, continuing about 1km until you see the sign on your right that says 'Mémorial du Président Kaysone Phomvihane'. Alternatively, a tuk-tuk will cost around 40,000K from the centre.

Activities

Backstreet Academy TOURS
(☎020-58199216; www.backstreetacademy.com) For some original local encounters, contact Backstreet Academy, a peer-to-peer travel website that specialises in connecting travellers to cultural experiences with local hosts. Choose from a *móoay láo* (kickboxing) class, a traditional dance lesson, a Lao cooking class in a private home, a clay art class, Zen meditation and a whole lot more.

Tuk Tuk Safari CULTURAL
(☎020-54333089; www.tuktuksafari.com; adult/child US$75/45) This community-conscious tour company gets under the skin of Vientiane in a tuk-tuk. Tour guide Ere has several different 'safaris' and can spirit you away to a Lao market, a rice farm, Vientiane's premier weaving houses or on food-centred expeditions.

Vientiane

Top Sights
1 COPE Visitor Centre C2
2 Pha That Luang D1

Sights
3 Patuxai C1
4 Wat Si Muang C2

Sleeping
5 Hotel Beau Rivage Mekong A1

Eating
6 Doi Ka Noi D1
7 Kuvieng Fried Chicken C3
8 Privet C4
9 PVO C2

Drinking & Nightlife
10 Laodi A1
11 Naga Boat A1
12 Spirit House A1

Information
13 Australian Embassy C4
14 Cambodian Embassy C3
15 Centre Médical de L'Ambassade de France C2
16 Chinese Embassy C4
17 German Embassy C3
18 International Clinic B2
19 Myanmar Embassy C4
20 Thai Consulate C2
21 Thai Embassy C1
22 UK Embassy C1
23 Vietnamese Embassy C1

Transport
24 Fuark Motorbike Service A1

Lao Bowling Centre BOWLING
(Map p296; 021-218661; Rue Khounboulom; per game with shoe hire from 11,000K; 9am-2am) Bright lights, Beerlao and boisterous bowlers are what you'll find here. While the equipment is in bad shape, it's still a fun place to come later in the evening for a Lao-style night out. It sometimes stays open into the wee hours. BYO socks.

Courses

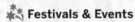

Houey Hong Vocational Training Centre for Women ARTS & CRAFTS
(021-560006; www.houeyhongvientiane.com; Ruelle 22, Rue Chao Anou; 8.30am-4.30pm Mon-Sat) You can learn how to dye textiles using natural pigments and then weave them on a traditional loom at this NGO centre, run by a Lao-Japanese woman. It was established north of Vientiane to train disadvantaged rural women in the dying art of natural dyeing and traditional silk-weaving practices.

Festivals & Events

You can rest assured that whatever the festival, celebrations in Vientiane will be as vigorous as they are anywhere in the country. Whatever you do, *don't* drive or ride about in the city during festivals; drunk driving is unfortunately the norm and accidents myriad.

Pi Mai CULTURAL
(Apr) Lao New Year is celebrated in mid-April with a mass water fight, and tourists are considered fair game. Be warned: drunk driving and theft go through the roof at these times so remain vigilant with your driver and wallet!

Bun Nam SPORTS
(Bun Suang Héua; Oct) A huge annual event at the end of *pansăh* (the Buddhist rains retreat) in October, during which boat races are held on the Mekong River. Rowing teams from all over the country, as well as from Thailand, China and Myanmar (Burma), compete; the river bank is lined with food stalls, temporary discos, carnival games and beer gardens for three days and nights.

Bun Pha That Luang CULTURAL
(That Luang Festival; Nov) Bun Pha That Luang, usually held in early November, is the largest temple fair in Laos. Festivities begin with a *wéean téean* (circumambulation) around Wat Si Muang, followed by a procession to Pha That Luang, which is illuminated all night for a week.

The festival climaxes on the morning of the full moon with the *đák bàht* ceremony, in which thousands of monks from across Laos receive alms. Fireworks cap off the evening and everyone makes merit or merry until dawn. Look out for devotees carrying *ƀạhsàht* (miniature temples made from banana stems and decorated with flowers and other offerings).

Sleeping

Vientiane is bursting with a wide range of accommodation, from cheap backpacker digs to beautiful boutique stays and huge monolithic corporate hotels. The cheaper end of the spectrum can be a bit dreary,

Central Vientiane

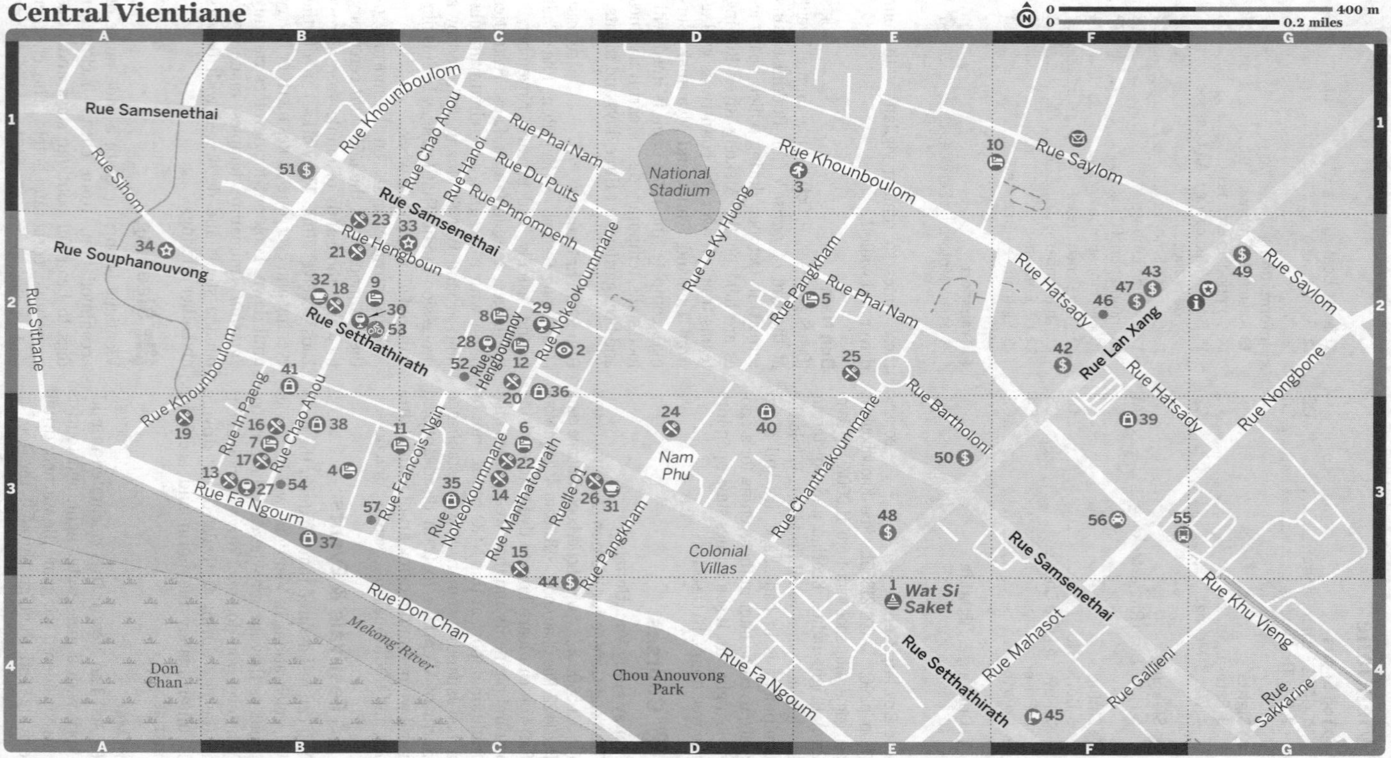
0 400 m
0 0.2 miles
Rue Samsenethai
Rue Sihom
Rue Souphanouvong
Rue Sithane
Rue Khounboulom
Rue Chao Anou
Rue Hanoi
Rue Phai Nam
Rue Du Puits
Rue Phnompenh
Rue Samsenethai
Rue Hengboun
Rue Setthathirath
Rue Nokeokoummane
Rue Hengbounnoy
National Stadium
Rue Le Ky Huong
Rue Khounboulom
Rue Pangkham
Rue Phai Nam
Rue Saylom
Rue Hatsady
Rue Lan Xang
Rue Saylom
Rue Nongbone
Rue Hatsady
Rue Bartholoni
Rue Chanthakoummane
Nam Phu
Rue In Paeng
Rue Chao Anou
Rue Francois Ngin
Rue Nokeokoummane
Rue Manthatourath
Ruelle 01
Rue Pangkham
Rue Fa Ngoum
Colonial Villas
Wat Si Saket
Rue Samsenethai
Rue Khu Vieng
Rue Mahasot
Rue Setthathirath
Rue Gallieni
Rue Sakkarine
Rue Don Chan
Mekong River
Don Chan
Chou Anouvong Park
Rue Fa Ngoum

Central Vientiane

◎ Top Sights
1 Wat Si Saket E4

◎ Sights
2 Lao National Culture Hall C2

Activities, Courses & Tours
3 Lao Bowling Centre E1

Sleeping
4 Ansara Hôtel B3
5 Day Inn Hotel E2
6 Hive Hostel C3
7 Lao Orchid Hotel B3
8 Lao Poet Hotel C2
9 My Box B2
10 Sailomyen Hostel F1
11 Souphaphone Guesthouse C3
12 Vayakorn Inn C2

Eating
13 Cabana B3
14 Café Vanille C3
15 Chokdee Cafe C3
16 Common Grounds B3
17 Han 3 Euey Nong B3
18 Ka-Tib-Khao B2
19 Khambang Lao Food Restaurant A3
20 Naked Espresso C2
21 Nemnueng Sihom B2
22 Pimentón C3
23 Rice Noodle – Lao Porridge B2
24 Scandinavian Bakery D3
25 Soukviman Cuisine Lao E2
26 Suzette C3

Drinking & Nightlife
27 Bor Pen Yang B3
28 Cocoon C2
29 Dresden C2
30 Earth B2
31 Le Trio D3
32 TitKafe B2

Entertainment
33 Anou Cabaret C2
34 Wind West A2

Shopping
35 Camacrafts C3
36 Carol Cassidy Lao Textiles C2
37 Night Market B3
38 Saoban B3
39 Talat Sao F3
40 The First D3
41 T'Shop Lai Gallery B2

Information
42 ANZ F2
43 Bank of Ayudhya F2
44 Banque pour le Commerce Extérieur Lao C4
45 French Embassy F4
46 Immigration Office F2
47 Joint Development Bank F2
48 Krung Thai Bank E3
49 Lao-Viet Bank G2
50 Siam Commercial Bank E3
51 Thai Military Bank B1

Transport
52 Avis-Budget C2
53 Lao Bike B2
54 Mixay Bike 2 .... B3
55 Talat Sao Bus Station F3
56 Taxi Stall F3
Thai–Lao International Bus .... (see 55)
57 TL Motor Bike B3

although there are a few gems. There are some exceptional midrangers in town, and a few of the upscale and boutique options are worth considering.

★ My Box HOSTEL **$**

(Map p296; ☎030-5671199; myboxhaysok@gmail.com; Rue Chao Anou; dm incl breakfast 80,000K; 🚭❄📶) The 12-bed dorms at this new hostel feel modern, clean and inviting – a stark contrast with most budget places in town. This vibe extends to the tidy, spacious common bathrooms and the lobby/cafe. And all this on a strip with a bit of a burgeoning nightlife buzz.

★ Sailomyen Hostel HOSTEL **$**

(Map p296; ☎020-78374941; www.facebook.com/sailomyenhostel; off Rue Saylom; incl breakfast dm 72,000K, r 170,000K; 🚭❄📶) Honestly (and astonishingly), there's little difference between the dorms and the new block of private rooms here. All are tidy and trendy, decked out in minimalist chic, with fluffy duvets and access to rain showers and the inviting cafe. A win-win situation.

Hive Hostel HOSTEL **$**

(Map p296; ☎020-98132074; www.facebook.com/hivelao; Rue Setthathirath; dm incl breakfast 60,000K; ❄📶) This hostel has a central location, a modern feel and three exceptionally cold air-con dorms with curtained-off bunks, lockers and sparklingly clean toilets. There's a funky little cafe on the ground floor where you'll eat your (simple) breakfast.

★ Vayakorn Inn HOTEL **$$**

(Map p296; ☎021-215348; www.vayakorn.biz; 19 Rue Hengbounnoy; r US$35; 🚭❄📶) On a quiet street just off increasingly hectic Rue Setthathirath, this tasteful, peaceful hotel is great value. Generously sized rooms are impeccably clean, with crisp linen, choice art, desks and modern bathrooms. The rooms on the upper floors have excellent city views.

★**Souphaphone Guesthouse** GUESTHOUSE **$$**
(Map p296; ☎021-261468; www.souphaphone.net; off Rue Francois Ngin; r incl breakfast US$27-38;) A very tidy and homey guesthouse with 25 spacious rooms, some with lots of sun, and all with fresh linen, cool tiled floors and pristine walls. If you don't need an in-house breakfast, you can chip a few dollars off the price.

Hotel Beau Rivage Mekong BOUTIQUE HOTEL **$$**
(Map p294; ☎021-243350; www.hbrm-laos.com; Rue Fa Ngoum; r incl breakfast US$52-69;) This pink boutique hotel still packs a punch, with 16 unique, spacious, sunny, loft-like rooms outfitted with pastel colours, terrazzo floors, waffled bedspreads and a pleasant garden out back. Large windows and balconies provide for maximum river views.

Day Inn Hotel HOTEL **$$**
(Map p296; ☎021-222985; dayinn@laopdr.com; 59/3 Rue Pangkham; r incl breakfast US$36-50;) From its inviting yellow exterior to its vintage terrazzo floors, this old-timer exudes charm. The 32 spotless rooms boast large beds, rattan furniture and a sunny, open vibe, and there's also free airport pick-up and laundry service.

Lao Poet Hotel HOTEL **$$**
(Map p296; ☎021-253537; www.laopoethotel.com; Rue Hengbounnoy; incl breakfast US$60-70, ste US$185-250;) The vibe at this new hotel – smooth concrete and lots of glass, potted plants, chunky carpets, patterned wallpaper, vintage and Lao touches – is tough to pin down, but somehow it just works. Opt for the slightly more expensive deluxe rooms, which have bathtubs and a bit more space.

★**Ansara Hôtel** BOUTIQUE HOTEL **$$$**
(Map p296; ☎021-213514; www.ansarahotel.com; off Rue Fa Ngoum; incl breakfast r US$140-160, ste US$190-360;) Achingly beautiful Ansara is housed in a compound of colonial-chic French villas with a heavy whiff of old Indochina. There are 28 rooms set across the property, including four suites, and all are lovely, offering wooden floor, balcony, flat-screen TV, bath and refined decorations. Its alfresco dining terrace is as refined as its Gallic cuisine.

★**Lao Orchid Hotel** HOTEL **$$$**
(Map p296; ☎021-264134; www.lao-orchid-hotel.com; Rue Chao Anou; r/ste incl breakfast US$75/145;) A classy, modern hotel with a swish lobby and chilled veranda cafe with a great view of the road. There are 33 welcoming rooms here with varnished wood floors, mint-fresh linen, desks, balconies, fridges and Indochinese-style furniture. Ask for a room at the front to take in the Mekong views.

Eating

For such a small capital city, Vientiane boasts a wide range of culinary options and is an exceptional spot for fine dining on a budget.

In Town

★**Nemnueng Sihom** VIETNAMESE **$**
(Map p296; ☎021-213990; Rue Hengboun; mains 10,000-40,000K; ⏲11am-10pm) Nemnueng Sihom is a long-standing, bustling restaurant that offers a fun eating experience. It specialises in *năem nĕuang* (Vietnamese barbecued pork meatballs) sold in 'sets' *(sut)* with *kòw Ƀûn* (white flour noodles with sweet-spicy sauce), fresh lettuce leaves, mint, basil, various sauces for dipping, sliced carambola (starfruit) and green banana – sort of a DIY spring roll.

★**PVO** VIETNAMESE **$**
(Map p294; ☎021-454663; Ruelle 2B; mains 10,000-35,000K; ⏲6.30am-4.30pm Mon-Sat, to 2pm Sun;) This fresh, no-frills eatery is one of the better places in town to grab lunch, and in addition to a variety of Vietnamese dishes, does some of the best *kòw jee* (Vietnamese-style baguette sandwiches) in town. Finish with the free, self-serve dessert bar.

Rice Noodle – Lao Porridge NOODLES **$**
(Map p296; ☎020-55414455; Rue Hengboun; mains 10,000-15,000K; ⏲4pm-1am) This is a good place to sample *kòw Ƀęeak sèn*, thick rice- and tapioca-flour noodles served in a slightly viscous broth with crispy deep-fried pork belly or chicken.

DON'T MISS

VIENTIANE'S CAFE SCENE

The French didn't leave much in the way of infrastructure in Laos, but they did leave a population addicted to caffeine. In central Vientiane, there's a cafe (or two) on every block, although the sleepy pace of the city doesn't exactly indicate this.

Tiny, French-run, old-school-feeling **Le Trio** (Map p296; ☎020-22553552; Rue Setthathirath; ⊙7am-5pm; 📶) is probably our favourite of the lot. The beans are roasted on-site (to a soundtrack of jazz), and a bag makes a clever souvenir. For something more modern, try **TitKafe** (Map p296; www.facebook.com/titkafe; Rue Setthathirath; ⊙7am-7pm Mon-Fri, 8am-7pm Sat & Sun; 📶), where drink options include nitro cold brew (and the music options, Top 40 pop). **Naked Espresso** (Map p296; ☎020-56222269; www.naked-espresso.com; Rue Nokeokoummane; mains 28,000-48,000K; ⊙7am-9pm Mon-Fri, 8am-9pm Sat & Sun; ❄📶🖉) probably isn't much different from your local back at home (although it might actually do better coffee), and if you're missing Western-style brunch, hit **Cabana** (Map p296; 15-16 Rue Fa Ngoum; mains 30,000-50,000K; ⊙7am-5pm; ❄📶🖉). **Common Grounds** (Map p296; ☎020-78727183; Rue Chao Anou; mains 35,000-43,000K; ⊙7am-8pm Mon-Sat; ❄📶🖉👪) has excellent coffee and a playground for kids, making it great for families, while the **Scandinavian Bakery** (Map p296; www.scandinavianbakerylaos.com; Nam Phu; mains 10,000-37,000K; ⊙6.30am-9pm; ❄📶), although it's seen better days, remains a godsend for Swedes missing their daily *fika* (coffee and a sweet treat).

Han 3 Euey Nong LAO $
(Map p296; Rue Chao Anou; mains 8000-25,000K; ⊙8am-8pm) Cheap and tidy, this busy family-run restaurant features tasty must-have dishes like *năem kòw* (crispy balls of deep-fried rice and sour pork sausage shredded into a salad-like dish) and the delicious *kòw Ƀûn nâm jąaou* (thin rice noodles served in a pork broth with pork, bamboo and herbs).

★Khambang Lao Food Restaurant LAO $$
(Map p296; ☎021-217198; 97/2 Rue Khounboulom; mains 20,000-90,000K; ⊙10.30am-3pm & 5-9pm; 📶) The slightly dreary, semi-open-air dining room couldn't be a bigger contrast with the tart, spicy, bold flavours served inside. This long-standing restaurant is the ideal introduction to Lao food via dishes such as *láhp* (spicy Lao-style salad of minced poultry or fish); roasted Mekong fish; stuffed frogs; *àw lám,* described on the menu as 'spicy beef stew'; and tasty Luang Prabang–style sausage.

★Suzette FRENCH $$
(Map p296; ☎020-58655511; www.facebook.com/suzette.vientiane; Rue Setthathirath; mains 35,000-58,000K; ⊙8am-9pm Tue-Sun; ❄🖉) This bright, contemporary-feeling place specialises in *galettes* (crêpes made with buckwheat flour). Pair yours with a dressed salad and a bottle of cider, and you have one of the tastiest, best-value French meals outside of the EU.

Ka-Tib-Khao LAO $$
(Map p296; www.facebook.com/pg/katibkhao; Rue Setthathirath; mains 40,000-100,000K; ⊙10am-2.30pm & 5-11pm; ❄) Ka-Tib-Khao (Rice Basket) has a reassuringly short and delicious menu of dishes, many from the country's north. Think sheets of deep-fried Mekong River weed served with a spicy dip, lemongrass-stuffed pork and Luang Prabang–style herbal sausages, all served in a setting that manages to feel both sophisticated and traditional.

Chokdee Cafe BELGIAN $$
(Map p296; ☎021-263847; Rue Fa Ngoum; mains 28,000-89,000K; ⊙10am-midnight; 📶) A Belgian restaurant and bar on the riverfront, Chokdee specialises in dishes from the homeland, including, of course, *moules* (mussels) and *frites* (French fries), as well as other hearty but delicious dishes for discerning gourmands. Consider the massive selection of imported Belgian beers, and you have one of the best places in town for non-Lao food.

Soukviman Cuisine Lao LAO $$
(Map p296; off Rue Chanthakoummane; mains 18,000-75,000K; ⊙10am-8pm; ❄📶) An upscale-ish place serving a hefty, but not too large, menu of Lao dishes. Choose from salads, soups, grilled dishes and more, including daily specials, although they're only listed in Lao. A decent jumping-off point for local cuisine.

The English-language sign simply says 'Cuisine Lao'.

Café Vanille BAKERY **$$**
(Map p296; ☎021-217321; Rue Nokeokoummane; breakfast from 40,000K; ⊙7am-6.30pm Mon-Sat, to 1pm Sun; ❄) Get here early before some of the city's best croissants run out. The simple interior makes for a nice place to read the paper over a tart, salad, panini or quiche, or you can sit outside on the small terrace.

★ **Pimentón** SPANISH **$$$**
(Map p296; ☎021-215506; www.pimentonrestaurant-vte.com; Rue Nokeokoummane; mains 60,000-200,000K; ⊙11am-2.30pm & 5-10pm Mon-Sat; ❄📶) Pimentón, with its open fire pit and beefy menu, is all about the meat. But to be honest, we didn't make it past the lengthy and appetising tapas menu. For a bit of everything, the set lunch (95,000K) is a wise strategy.

Around Town

Kuvieng Fried Chicken LAO **$**
(KFC; Map p294; Rue Khu Vieng; mains from 5000K; ⊙10am-8pm) This ramshackle restaurant draws locals for the combination of deep-fried chicken (the owner allegedly 'borrowed' the recipe from the other KFC), Lao-style papaya salad and, of course, French fries. Buy a Beerlao at the shop next door and you've got one of the most satisfying meals in town.

★ **Doi Ka Noi** LAO **$$**
(Map p294; ☎020-55898959; www.facebook.com/DoiKaNoi; off Rue Sisangvone; mains 40,000-60,000K; ⊙10am-2.30pm Tue-Thu, to 9pm Fri-Sun; ❄) It took one meal for Doi Ka Noi to become one of our favourite restaurants in Laos. With a menu that changes daily (check the restaurant's Facebook page at around 8.30am to see what's available), the dishes here range from Lao standards to regional specialities most of us have never heard of, with something to appeal to both newbies and grizzled foodies.

The dining room has a charming old-school vibe with handsome food-related photos adorning the walls.

Privet RUSSIAN **$$**
(Map p294; ☎020-78097784; https://russian-restaurant-privet.business.site; Rue Sithoong; mains 22,000-250,000K; ⊙11am-9pm Tue-Sun; ❄📶🖉) Dumplings, *zakuski* (small dishes eaten with vodka), pickled herring, blinis and caviar – peeps, Russian food is really tasty. And even if you don't agree or haven't tried it, this lively restaurant is worth a visit just for the kitsch factor (diners are encouraged to don fur hats and take selfies in front of a mural of Moscow's Red Square).

Drinking & Nightlife

Vientiane is no longer the illicit pleasure palace it once was. Beerlao has replaced opium as the drug of choice and brothels are strictly prohibited.

Most bars close by midnight, apart from a few late-night stragglers. Karaoke is popular, as are live-music performances.

★ **Laodi** BAR
(Map p294; www.facebook.com/rhumlaodi; Rue Fa Ngoum; ⊙5pm-2am) Refurbished shipping containers in front of a spooky abandoned building, riverside breezes, and local rum distilled by a Japanese resident. Laodi is hard to pin down but easy to enjoy. And best of all, the rum, made from Lao sugar cane grown near Vientiane, is delicious; try a tasting flight, which ranges in flavour from plain to passion fruit (we like the barrel-aged 'brown' and coffee).

★ **Earth** BAR
(Map p296; www.facebook.com/earthvientiane; Rue Chao Anou; ⊙5pm-midnight; 📶) At first glance, Earth looks as crunchy as a bowl of organic granola, but live music, cultural events, an eclectic soundtrack, craft beers, enthusiastic locals and fun staff mean that there's something here to appeal to just about everybody. Check the Facebook page to see what's on when you're in town.

★ **Spirit House** COCKTAIL BAR
(Map p294; ☎021-262530; Rue Fa Ngoum; cocktails 40,000-60,000K; ⊙7am-11pm; 📶) This traditional Lao house facing the Mekong has a well-stocked bar and a witty, helpful menu that doubles as a crash course in cocktails. A chilled soundtrack complements the dark woods and comfy couches of its stylish interior, or you can sit outside and gaze at the river. Hit the exceptionally fun happy hours weekdays from 4pm to 6pm.

Naga Boat BAR
(Map p294; www.facebook.com/pg/thenagaboat; Rue Fa Ngoum; ⊙5.30-11.30pm) Landlubbers rejoice: we've found the perfect cruise. This permanently beached vessel features stunning river views, some of Vientiane's better

cocktails, domestic and import draught beer and an implicit no-seasickness guarantee.

Dresden BAR
(Map p296; 139 Rue Nokeokoummane; ⏰5pm-midnight Mon-Sat) Just your typical German-themed bar as perceived through a Japanese lens and located in Laos. There's a good selection of booze (especially sake), unique insulated beer mugs, hand-chipped ice cubes and some fascinating bar snacks that bridge the culinary gap between Japan and Germany. Oddly enough, it works.

Cocoon COCKTAIL BAR
(Map p296; off Rue Hengbounnoy; ⏰6.30pm-2am Tue-Sun) Cocktail culture has arrived in Vientiane, and it takes the form of this dark, sleek, new bar concealed in a tiny side street. The signature drinks veer towards the fruity end of the spectrum; we'd suggest sticking to the classics.

Bor Pen Yang BAR
(Map p296; ☎020-27873965; Rue Fa Ngoum; ⏰10am-midnight; 📶) Overlooking mother Mekong, a cast of locals, expats, bar girls and travellers assembles at this tin-roofed, wood-raftered watering hole to gaze at the sunset over nearby Thailand. Western tunes, pool tables and a huge bar to drape yourself over, as well as international football and rugby on large flat-screen TVs.

Entertainment

Like everything else, Vientiane's entertainment scene is picking up as money and politics allow, but the range remains fairly limited. By law, entertainment venues must close by 11.30pm, though most push it to about midnight.

Lao Boxing SPECTATOR SPORT
(☎020-99999992; www.facebook.com/houayhongstadium; Houayhong Boxing Stadium, off Rue Chao Anou; ⏰7pm Sat) FREE Bouts of Lao boxing are held every Saturday at 7pm at Houayhong Boxing Stadium, located north-west of the city centre. It's free, and unlike the matches in Bangkok, you can get right up in the action.

Anou Cabaret LIVE MUSIC
(Map p296; ☎021-213630; Anou Paradise Hotel, cnr Rue Hengboun & Rue Chao Anou; ⏰9pm-1am) On the ground floor of the Anou Paradise Hotel, the cabaret has been swinging along here for years. It's a funny place, with old crooners and a palpable 1960s feel.

Wind West LIVE MUSIC
(Map p296; ☎021-265777; Rue Sihom; ⏰6pm-1am) A roadhouse-style bar and restaurant, Wind West has live Lao and Western rock music most nights. Depending on the night it can be heaving or completely dead, but the interior, hung with 10-gallon hats, antlers and wooden Native American statues, lends the place a folksy atmosphere.

Shopping

Just about anything made in Laos is available for purchase in Vientiane, including hill-tribe crafts, jewellery, traditional textiles and carvings. The main shopping area in town is along Rue Setthathirath and the streets radiating from it.

Downtown Vientiane is littered with stores selling textiles. Rue Nokeokoummane is the epicentre, but the city's main market, **Talat Sao** (Morning Market; Map p296; Rue Lan Xang; ⏰9am-5pm), is also a good place to buy fabrics. You'll find antiques as well as modern fabrics, plus utilitarian items such as shoulder bags), cushions and pillows.

Several shops along Rue Samsenethai, Rue Pangkham and Rue Setthathirath sell Lao and Tai tribal and hill-tribe crafts.

★ **T'Shop Lai Gallery** COSMETICS, HOMEWARES
(Map p296; ☎021-223178; www.laococo.com; off Rue In Paeng; ⏰8am-8pm Mon-Sat, 10am-6pm Sun) 🍃 Imagine a melange of aromas – aloe vera, coconut, honey, frangipani and magnolia – all of them emanating from body oils, soaps, sprays, perfumes, lip balms and more. These wonderful products are made with sustainable, locally sourced ingredients by disadvantaged women who make up the Les Artisans Lao cooperative.

There's also a fine gallery upstairs that rotates Lao and international artists' work.

★ **The First** GIFTS & SOUVENIRS
(Map p296; 168b Rue Samsenethai; ⏰8am-8pm) This bright-feeling shop has a broad but well-curated selection of items representing some of Laos' most reputable brands: beautiful textiles from Ock Pop Tok and Passa Paa, Lao jewellery from Serene's, soaps and other toiletries from Les Artisans Lao, rum from Laodi and chocolate from Marou.

Carol Cassidy Lao Textiles ARTS & CRAFTS
(Map p296; ☎021-212123; www.laotextiles.com; 108 Rue Nokeokoummane; ⏰8am-noon & 2-5pm Mon-Fri, to noon Sat, or by appointment) Lao Textiles sells contemporary, original-design

fabrics inspired by generations-old Lao weaving patterns, motifs and techniques. The American designer, Carol Cassidy, employs Lao weavers who work out the back of the attractive old French-Lao house. Internationally known, with high-end prices to match.

Camacrafts ARTS & CRAFTS
(Mulberries; Map p296; www.camacrafts.org; Rue Nokeokoummane; 10am-6pm Mon-Sat) Stocks silk clothes and weavings from Xieng Khuang Province, plus some bed and cushion covers in striking Hmong-inspired designs. All of the shop's Fairtrade products come from the artisan communities it supports in rural Laos.

Saoban ARTS & CRAFTS
(Map p296; 021-241835; www.saobancrafts.com; Rue Chao Anou; 9am-8pm) This small shop works with over 300 artisans in 14 communities across 10 provinces of Laos, selling everything from hand-woven silk textiles to bamboo baskets and silver jewellery. There are nice descriptions of where the products come from and who your purchase will support (mostly rural women from ethnic minorities). Prices tend to be cheaper than elsewhere in town.

Night Market MARKET
(Map p296; Rue Fa Ngoum; 6-10.30pm) Vientiane's night market lights up the riverfront with a selection of stalls hawking handicrafts and T-shirts. It doesn't quite have the atmosphere of Luang Prabang's, but it's nonetheless a decent place to browse and hone your haggling skills.

Information

DANGERS & ANNOYANCES

By international standards Vientiane has a very low crime rate, but there's a small risk of getting mugged.

- Be especially careful around the BCEL Bank on the riverfront, where bag snatchers, usually a two-person team with a motorbike, have been known to strike; common sense should be an adequate defence.
- Stay off the city's roads during festivals, particularly April's Pi Mai (p295), when drunk-driving-related accidents skyrocket.
- Call the **Tourist Police** (Map p296; 021-251128; Rue Lan Xang; 24hr) if you need to talk to an English-speaking police officer.

MEDICAL SERVICES

Vientiane's medical facilities can leave a lot to be desired, so for anything serious make a break for the border and the much more sophisticated hospitals in Thailand. Aek Udon International Hospital (www.aekudon.com) in Thailand can dispatch an ambulance to take you to Udon Thani. Less serious ailments can be dealt with in Vientiane.

Alliance International Medical Center (021-513095; www.aimclao.com; Rue Souphanouvong) This hospital treats basic ailments like broken bones and dispenses antibiotics.

Centre Médical de L'Ambassade de France (French Embassy Medical Center; Map p294; 021-214150; cnr Rue Khu Vieng & Rue Simeuang; 8.30am-noon & 1.30-7pm Mon, Tue, Thu & Fri, 8.30am-noon & 1.30-5pm Wed, Sat & Sun) Open to all, but visits outside regular hours by appointment only.

International Clinic (Map p294; 021-214024; Mahosot Hospital, Rue Fa Ngoum; 24hr) Part of the Mahasot Hospital; probably the best place for not-too-complex emergencies. Some English-speaking doctors. Take ID and cash.

Setthathirat Hospital (021-351156; Rue Khamphengmuang) This hospital northeast of the city is another option for minor ailments.

MONEY

There are plenty of banks, international ATMs and licensed money changers in the capital.

ANZ (Map p296; 021-222700; 33 Rue Lan Xang; 8.30am-3.30pm Mon-Fri) Main branch has ATMs; additional machines can be found on Rue Setthathirath and Rue Fa Ngoum.

Bank of Ayudhya (Krungsri; Map p296; 021-255522; 79/6 Rue Lan Xang; 8.30am-3.30pm Mon-Fri) Thai bank with ATM.

Banque pour le Commerce Extérieur Lao (BCEL; Map p296; cnr Rue Pangkham & Rue Fa Ngoum; 8.30am-7pm Mon-Fri, to 3.30pm Sat & Sun) Longest hours of any bank in town. Exchange booth on Rue Fa Ngoum and ATMs attached to the main building.

Joint Development Bank (Map p296; 75/1-5 Rue Lan Xang; 8.30am-4pm Mon-Fri, 9am-4pm Sat & Sun) Exchange and ATM.

Krung Thai Bank (Map p296; 021-213480; Rue Lan Xang; 8.30am-3.30pm Mon-Fri) With 24-hour ATM.

Lao-Viet Bank (Map p296; 021-251418; Rue Lan Xang; 8.30am-4pm Mon-Fri) ATM and money exchange.

Siam Commercial Bank (Map p296; 117 Rue Lan Xang; 8.30am-3.30pm Mon-Fri) Foreign exchange and ATM.

Thai Military Bank (Map p296; ☎ 021-216486; cnr Rue Samsenethai & Rue Khounboulom; ⏲ 8.30am-3.30pm Mon-Fri) Exchange and ATM.

TOURIST INFORMATION

Tourist Information Centre (MICT; Map p296; ☎ 021-212248; www.tourismlaos.org; Rue Lan Xang; ⏲ 8.30am-noon & 1.30-4pm) A worthwhile centre with easy-to-use descriptions of each province, helpful staff who speak some English, as well as brochures and regional maps.

VISAS

Immigration Office (Map p296; ☎ 021-212250; Rue Hatsady; ⏲ 8-11.30am & 1.30-4.30pm Mon-Fri) Getting an extension on a tourist visa is relatively easy. Go to the Immigration Office, in the Ministry of Public Security building opposite Talat Sao, fill out a form (5000K), supply your passport and a photo, pay a 25,000K administrative fee and then an additional 20,000K per day for the extra time you want. Return the next afternoon to collect your passport.

ℹ Getting There & Away

AIR

Departures from Vientiane's **Wattay International Airport** (VTE; ☎ 021-512165; www.vientianeairport.com; Rte 13), located around 4km northwest of the centre, are from the linked international and domestic terminals.

At research time, there were direct domestic flights between Vientiane and destinations in Laos including Luang Namtha (Namtha), Luang Prabang, Muang Khoun (Old Xieng Khuang), Pakse, Phongsali, Savannakhet, Sam Neua (Xam Neua) and Udomxai (Muang Xai); and direct international flights between Vientiane and points in China, Korea, Singapore, Thailand and Vietnam.

BUS

In Laos roads are poor and buses break down, so travel times can take longer than advertised. Buses use three different stations in Vientiane, all with some English-speaking staff, relatively clear timetables and fares, plus food and drink stands.

ℹ GETTING TO THAILAND: VIENTIANE TO NONG KHAI

Getting to the border At the Tha Na Leng (Laos)/Nong Khai (Thailand) border crossing (6am to 10pm), the Thai–Lao Friendship Bridge (Saphan Mittaphap Thai-Lao) spans the Mekong River. The Laos border is approximately 20km from Vientiane, and the easiest and cheapest way to the bridge is to cross on the Thai–Lao International Bus (p305). It conducts daily departures for the Thai cities of Bangkok, Khon Kaen, Nong Khai and Udon Thani. Alternative means of transport between Vientiane and the bridge include taxi (400B), tuk-tuk (50,000K/300B), jumbo (200B) or the number 14 Tha Deua bus from Talat Sao Bus Station (8000K) between 5.30am and 6pm.

To cross from Thailand, tuk-tuks are available from Nong Khai's train station (30B) and bus station (60B) to the Thai border post at the bridge. You can also hop on the Thai–Lao International Bus from Nong Khai bus station (55B, 1½ hours) or Udon Thani bus station (80B, two hours), both of which terminate at Vientiane's Talat Sao Bus Station. If flying into Udon Thani, a tuk-tuk from the airport to the city's bus station should cost about 120B.

It's also possible to cross the bridge by train, as tracks have been extended from Nong Khai's train station 3.5km into Laos, terminating at Dongphosy Station, about 13km from central Vientiane. From Nong Khai there are two daily departures (10am and 5.30pm, 30B, 15 minutes) and border formalities are taken care of at the respective train stations. But in reality, unless you are a trainspotter, it is much more convenient to use the international bus or other road transport.

At the border Travellers from most countries enjoy 30-day, visa-free access to Thailand. Lao visas (30 days) are available for US$20 to US$42, depending on your nationality. If you don't have a photo you'll be charged an extra US$1, and be aware that an additional US$1 'overtime fee' is charged from 6am to 8am and 4pm to 10pm on weekdays, as well as on weekends and holidays. Don't be tempted to use a tuk-tuk driver to get your Lao visa, no matter what they tell you, as it will take far longer than doing it yourself, and you'll have to pay for the 'service'. Insist they take you straight to the bridge.

Moving on Trains from Nong Khai to Bangkok leave at 7am, 6.30pm and 7.10pm and cost from 898B for a 2nd-class sleeper ticket (11 hours).

The **Northern Bus Station** (Rue Sithong), about 2km northwest of the airport, serves all points north. **Tong Li Bus Company** (☎021-242657; Northern Bus Station) runs a route to Kunming, China, from here. Minivans to Vang Vieng leave from here, though most people end up booking more expensive tourist buses from agencies in town.

BUSES FROM VIENTIANE

DESTINATION	STATION	COST (K)	DISTANCE (KM)	DURATION (HR)	DEPARTURES
Bangkok (Thailand)	Talat Sao	248,000	650	12-16	6pm
Ban Kong Lor	Southern	90,000	312	8-10	10am
Danang (Vietnam)	Southern	200,000	900	22	6pm
Don Khong	Southern	150,000	788	16-19	10.30am (fan)
Hanoi (Vietnam)	Southern	200,000	750	24	5.30pm, 6pm Mon, Wed, Fri, Sun
Huay Xai	Northern	200,000-220,000	869	24	8.30am, 5pm
Khon Kaen (Thailand)	Talat Sao	50,000	197	4	8.15am, 2.45pm
Luang Namtha	Northern	220,000	676	24	8.30am, 5pm
Luang Prabang	Northern	110,000-150,000	384	9-11	6.30am, 7am (van), 7.30am, 8am (VIP), 8.30am, 9am (van, VIP), 11am, 1.30pm, 4pm, 6pm, 7pm (van), 7.30pm (VIP), 8pm (VIP)
Nong Khai (Thailand)	Talat Sao	15,000	25	1½	7.30am, 9.30am, 12.40pm, 2.30pm, 3.30pm, 6pm
Pakse	Southern	110,000-170,000	677	8-18	frequent 10am-4pm (all fan); 5.15am, 6pm, 6.30pm, 7pm, 8pm, 8.30pm, 9pm (all VIP)
Phongsali	Northern	230,000-250,000	811	25-28	7.15am (fan), 6pm (sleeper)
Phonsavan	Northern	110,000-150,000	374	10-11	6.30am, 7.30am, 9.30am, 8pm (sleeper)
Sainyabuli	Northern	110,000-130,000	485	14-16	9am, 4pm, 6.30pm
Salavan	Southern	130,000-190,000	774	13-20	4.30pm (fan), 7.30pm, 8.30pm (VIP)
Sam Neua (Xam Neua)	Northern	190,000-210,000	612	22-24	9.30am, noon, 5pm (all VIP)
Savannakhet	Southern	75,000-120,000	457	8-11	frequent 5.30-9am or any bus to Pakse, 8.30pm (VIP)
Tha Khaek	Southern	60,000-80,000	332	5-6	4am, 5am, 6am, noon, or any bus to Savannakhet or Pakse; 1pm (VIP)
Udon Thani (Thailand)	Talat Sao	22,000	82	2½	8am, 9am, 10.30am, 11.30am, 2pm, 3pm, 4pm, 6pm
Vang Vieng	Northern	40,000-50,000	157	4	frequent 6am-5pm (van); 8.30am, 10am
Vinh (Vietnam)	Southern	150,000	460	16	8am, 6pm

The **Southern Bus Station** (Dong Dok Bus Station; Rte 13), also known as *khíw lot lák káo* (Km 9 Bus Station), is 9km out of town and serves everywhere to the south. **SDT** (☎020-2205352; Southern Bus Station, Rte 13) runs buses to various points in Vietnam from this station, including Danang, Hanoi and Vinh.

The final departure point is the **Talat Sao Bus Station** (Central Bus Station; Map p296; ☎021-216507; Rue Khu Vieng), from where desperately slow local buses run to destinations within Vientiane Province, and some more distant destinations, though for the latter you're better off going to the Northern or Southern Bus Stations. The **Thai–Lao International Bus** (Map p296; Talat Sao Bus Station, Rue Khu Vieng) also uses this station for its trips to Bangkok, Khon Kaen, Nong Khai and Udon Thani.

TRAIN

In 2009 tracks were extended from Nong Khai's train station across the Thai–Lao Friendship Bridge to Dongphosy in Laos, effectively forming Laos' first railway line. There are plans to extend the tracks 417km to the border with China at Boten by 2021, part of a US$7-billion plan (funded by the Chinese government) that will see the commencement of a national railway grid in the coming years. For now, however, Laos boasts a grand total of 3.5km of rolling track, making connections with Nong Khai in Thailand very inconvenient when compared with the Thai–Lao International Bus.

Getting Around

TO/FROM THE AIRPORT

Wattay International Airport From the airport, taxis to the centre cost US$7 (to Vang Vieng, US$90). Only official taxis can pick up at the airport. There is a shuttle bus linking the airport and Talat Sao Bus Station in the city centre, with departures every 40 minutes between 9.15am and 9.15pm (15,000K).

BICYCLE

Cycling is a cheap, easy and recommended way of getting around mostly flat Vientiane. Loads of guesthouses and several shops hire out bikes for 10,000K to 20,000K per day. Mountain bikes are available but are more expensive at 30,000K to 40,000K; try **Lao Bike** (Map p296; ☎020-54674345; Rue Setthathirath; ⊙8.30am-6pm) or **Mixay Bike 2** (Map p296; ☎020-77882510; Rue Chau Anou; scooter per 24hr 60,000-80,000K; ⊙8.30am-7.30pm).

CAR & MOTORCYCLE

There are several international car-hire companies with representation in Vientiane, including **Avis-Budget** (Map p296; ☎020-22861415; www.avis.la; Rue Setthathirath; ⊙8.30am-6pm Mon-Fri, to 1pm Sat & Sun) and **Sixt** (☎020-96590475; www.sixtlao.com; International Terminal, Wattay International Airport; ⊙8am-10.30pm). Keep in mind that while a basic sedan will get you around the city, you'll need a sturdy 4WD for trips further afield.

Scooters are a popular means of getting around Vientiane and can be hired throughout the centre of town, including from Mixay Bike 2. Other recommended hire places include the following:

TL Motor Bike (Map p296; ☎020-55528299; Rue Francois Ngin; scooters per day 70,000K; ⊙8am-8pm)

Fuark Motorbike Service (Map p294; ☎021-261970; fuarkmotorcross@yahoo.com; Rue T2; ⊙9am-6pm) A leading locally owned and operated motorbike-hire place that offers a range of well-maintained dirt bikes (from US$30 per day), with drop-offs at key cities around the country. Delivers the bikes to you.

TAXI

Car taxis of varying shapes, sizes and vintages can often be found stationed in front of the larger hotels, at the airport, or at the **stall** (Map p296; ☎021-454168; Rue Khu Vieng) across from Talat Sao. Bargaining is the general rule.

TUK-TUK

Drivers of jumbos and tuk-tuks will take passengers on journeys as short as 500m or as far as 20km. Understanding the various types of tuk-tuk is important if you don't want to be overcharged (and can save you arguments in addition to money). Tourist tuk-tuks are the most expensive, while share jumbos that run regular routes around town (eg Rue Luang Prabang to Rue Setthathirath or Rue Lan Xang to That Luang) are much cheaper, usually less than 10,000K per person.

Phu Khao Khuay National Protected Area (NPA)

Covering more than 2000 sq km of mountains and rivers, the underrated Phu Khao Khuay National Protected Area (NPA; ປ່າສະຫງວນແຫ່ງຊາດພູເຂົາຄວາຍ) is the most accessible protected area in Laos. Treks ranging in duration from a couple of hours to three days have been developed in partnership with Ban Na (ບ້ານນາ) and Ban Hat Khai (ບ້ານຫາດໄຂ), villages on the edge of the NPA.

Phu Khao Khuay (ພູເຂົາຄວາຍ; *poo cow kwai*) means 'Buffalo Horn Mountain', a name derived from local legend, and is home to three major rivers that flow off a sandstone mountain range. It boasts an extraordinary array of endangered wildlife, including wild elephants, gibbons, Asiatic black bears, clouded leopards, Siamese fireback pheasants and green peafowl. Depending on elevation, visitors may encounter dry evergreen dipterocarp (a Southeast Asian tree with two-winged fruit), mixed deciduous forest, conifer forest or grassy uplands. Several impressive waterfalls are accessible as day trips from Vientiane.

Sights & Activities

Detailed information on trekking, accommodation and getting to and from Phu Khao Khuay National Protected Area (NPA) can be found at the Tourist Information Centre (p303) in Vientiane. Trekking in Phu Khao Khuay costs 100,000K per person per day, and you must also purchase a permit to enter the NPA (40,000K) and contribute to the village fund (50,000K). If trekking from Ban Hat Khai you'll also have to pay for boat transport (100,000K per boat, up to two passengers).

Tat Leuk WATERFALL

(ຕາດເລີກ) FREE Tat Leuk is a small waterfall, but it's a beautiful place to camp for the night. You can swim above the falls if the water isn't too shallow, and the visitor centre has some information about the area, including a detailed guide to the 1.5km-long Huay Bon Nature Trail.

The visitor centre attendant can arrange local treks for between 60,000K and 160,000K, and rents quality four-person tents for 40,000K, plus hammocks, mattresses, mosquito nets and sleeping bags for 10,000K each. There's a very basic restaurant (best supplemented with food you bring from outside), a small library of wildlife books and a pair of binoculars.

From the junction to Ban Hat Khai village, turn left and continue another 6km until you see a rough 4km road on the left, which leads to Tat Leuk.

Tat Xai & Pha Xai WATERFALL

(ຕາດໄຊ ຜາໄຊ) FREE Tat Xai cascades down seven steps, and 800m downstream Pha Xai plunges over a 40m-high cataract. There's a pool that's good for swimming, though it can get dangerous during the wet season. Both waterfalls are accessed from Rte 13, just before Tha Bok. From the junction to Ban Hat Khai, it's 9km to Tat Xai and Pha Xai.

Sleeping & Eating

Homestay-style accommodation is available in both Ban Na and Ban Hat Khai for 40,000K per person per night, plus 30,000K per meal. The prices do not include transport from Vientiane and are not negotiable. All monies go to the village and NPA.

Even if you're not interested in a trek, a stay at Ban Na or Ban Hat Khai is a fascinating insight into Lao village life.

Ban Na offers 10 homestays in simple wooden houses (24-hour electricity and mosquito nets with bedding are provided). Vegetarian meals are possible. For bookings, contact Mr Bounathom/Mr Khampak (☎020-22208262), or find a Lao speaker to call ahead for you.

Ban Hat Khai is a pretty riverside village offering 11 homestays in traditional Lao houses, or in a guesthouse built especially for visitors; all include 24-hour electricity and mosquito nets. Vegetarian meals are available on request. To book a stay in Ban Hat Khai, contact Mr Khammoun (☎020-2224 0303) or find a Lao speaker to call ahead for you.

Homestays in Ban Na and Ban Hat Khai can provide wholesome meals for 30,000K. Vegetarians are catered for, although more complicated dietary requirements may be hard to deliver.

Getting There & Away

To get to Ban Na or Ban Hat Khai, hop on the Paksan-bound trucks that depart from Vientiane's Southern Bus Station (frequent from 7am to 3pm, three to four hours) or any bus headed south. For Wat Pha Baht Phonsan and Ban Na get off at Tha Pha Bat (25,000K) near the Km 81 stone; the shrine is right on Rte 13 and Ban Na is about 1.5km north and well signposted.

For Ban Hat Khai, keep on the bus until a turn-off left at Km 92, just before Tha Bok (30,000K). If you have your own transport, continue 8km along the smooth laterite road until you cross the new bridge. Turn right at the Y-intersection and it's 1km along a dirt road to Ban Hat Khai. Alternatively, villagers in Ban Hat Khai can arrange motorcyle (40,000K) or van (80,000K) pickup from Tha Bok, if you call ahead.

Vang Vieng

☎023 / POP 21,000

Like a rural scene from an old Asian silk painting, Vang Vieng (ວັງວຽງ) crouches low over the Nam Song (Song River) with a backdrop of serene cliffs and a tapestry of vivid green paddy fields. Thanks to the Lao government closing the river rave bars in 2012, the formerly toxic party scene has been driven to the fringes and the community is rebooting itself as an adrenaline-fuelled adventure destination. The town itself is no gem, as concrete hotels build ever higher in search of the quintessential view. But across the Nam Song lies a rural idyll; spend a few days here – hire a bike, zipline, climb a cliff, go tubing or trekking – and soak up one of the country's most stunningly picturesque spots.

Sights & Activities

Vang Vieng has recently evolved into Laos' number-one adventure destination, with tubing, kayaking, rafting, ziplining, mountain biking and world-class rock climbing all available. You can also explore the many caves that pepper the karst limestone peaks. Nowadays, the scene also includes noisy four-wheeled buggies.

Caves

Of the most accessible *tàm* (caves), most are signed in English as well as Lao, and an admission fee is collected at the entrance to each cave. The caves around Vang Vieng are spectacular, but caves come with certain hazards: they're dark, slippery and disorienting. A guide (often a young village boy) will lead you through a cave for a small fee; bring water and a torch (flashlight), and be *sure* your batteries aren't about to die. In fact, bearing in mind some of the 'lost in the darkness' horror stories that circulate, it's vital to have a spare torch.

For more extensive multicave tours, most guesthouses can arrange a guide. Trips including river tubing and cave tours cost around US$15/25 for a half-/full day.

Tham Nam CAVE
(ຖ້ຳນ້ຳ, Water Cave; 10,000K; ⏲8am-5pm) Tham Nam is the highlight of the cluster of caves north of Vang Vieng. The cave is about 500m long and a tributary of the Nam Song flows out of its low entrance. As with other caves in the area, there's a zipline and basic restaurant.

In the dry season you can wade into the cave, but when the water is higher you need to take a tube from the friendly woman near the entrance; the tube and headlamp are included in the entrance fee. Dragging yourself through the tunnel on the fixed rope is fun.

Tham Hoi CAVE
(ຖ້ຳຫອຍ; ⏲8am-5pm) FREE Located around 13km north of Vang Vieng, the entrance to Tham Hoi is guarded by a large Buddha figure; reportedly the cave continues about 3km into the limestone and an underground lake.

Tham Jang CAVE
(ຖ້ຳຈັງ; entry incl footbridge fee 15,000K; ⏲8am-5pm) The most famous of the caves around Vang Vieng, Tham Jang was used as a bunker to defend against marauding *jęen hór* (Yunnanese Chinese) in the early 19th century (*jąng* means 'steadfast'). Stairs lead up to the main cavern entrance.

Tham Loup CAVE
(ຖ້ຳຫຼູບ; ⏲8am-5pm) FREE Tham Loup, located a few kilometres north of Vang Vieng, is a large and delightfully untouched cavern with some impressive stalactites.

Tham Phu Kham & Blue Lagoon CAVE
(ຖ້ຳພູຄຳແລະໜອງນ້ຳສີຟ້າ; Ban Na Thong; 10,000K; ⏲7.30am-5.30pm) Located west of Vang Vieng, the vast Tham Phu Kham is considered sacred by Lao. The main cave chamber contains a Thai bronze reclining Buddha, and from here deeper galleries branch off into the mountain. It's hugely popular largely due to the lagoon in the cave, but overdevelopment, group tourists and noisy buggies have made it an unpleasant place to swim.

Tubing

Previously, just about every visitor to Vang Vieng went tubing down the Nam Song in an inflated tractor-tyre tube, although this was less about relaxing and more about getting blasted at loud riverside bars. These days, the bars are gone, and most visitors ride kayaks or longtail boats.

If you want to go old-school, the tubing drop-off point for the original yellow route is 3.5km north of town, and depending on the speed and level of the river it can be a soporific crawl beneath the jungle-vined karsts, or a speedy glide downstream back to Vang Vieng. There is also a newer red tubing route through private land 4km south of town.

The **yellow tubing operators** (⏲9am-8pm) and **red tubing operators** (☎020-99223339; ⏲9am-7pm) have similar hire fees and rules, though the yellow line requires a 20,000K refundable deposit (forfeited if you

Vang Vieng

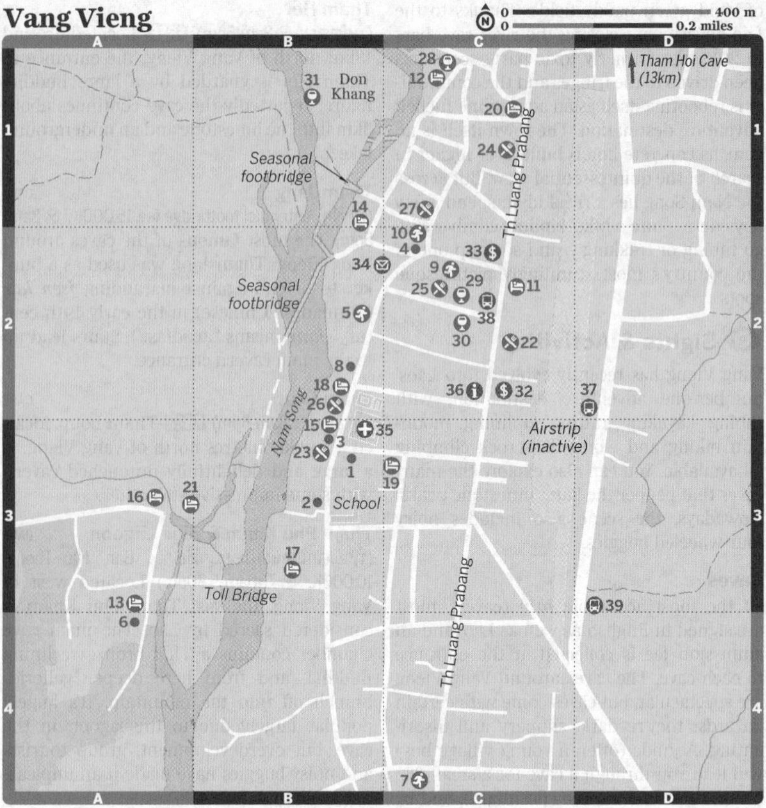

lose the tube). Life jackets are available and you can rent a dry bag. Tuk-tuk services can run you to the launch points.

Whether tubing or kayaking down the Nam Song, rivers can be dangerous, and in times of high water, rapids along the Nam Song can be quite daunting. Wear a life jacket when tubing, and it's worth asking how long the trip should take (durations vary depending on the time of year) so you can allow plenty of time to get back to Vang Vieng before dark, as it's pitch black by about 6pm in winter. Finally, don't forget that while tubing the Nam Song might be more fun when you're stoned, it's also more dangerous.

The other thing you should remember is to take something – a sarong, perhaps – to put on when you finish the trip and have to walk through town. The locals don't appreciate people walking around in bikinis or Speedos.

Kayaking

Kayaking has overtaken tubing as Vang Vieng's premier water sport, and trips are typically combined with other activities such as visits to caves and villages, optional climbing, cycling, and the traverse of a few rapids (the danger of which depends on the speed of the water). There are loads of operators and prices are about US$15 per person per day. Some of the best kayaking trips along the Nam Song are conducted by the excellent **Green Discovery** (☎023-511230; www.greendiscoverylaos.com; 1-day cycling tour per person US$28-56, half-/full-day rock climbing US$39/80; ⏲8am-9pm) and involve a lot of paddling. Another useful tour operator for kayaking is the well-established **VLT** (☎020-55208283; www.vangviengtour.com; ⏲8am-10.30pm).

Rock Climbing

The limestone walls around Vang Vieng have gained a reputation for some of the best climbing in Southeast Asia. More than

Vang Vieng

Activities, Courses & Tours

1 Adam's Rock Climbing School ... B3
2 AK Home Tours ... B3
3 Green Discovery ... B3
4 Namthip Tour ... C2
5 Red Tubing Operators ... B2
TCK ... (see 5)
Vang Vieng Challenge ... (see 3)
6 Vang Vieng Jeep Tour ... A4
7 Vang Vieng Sauna ... C4
8 VLT ... B2
9 Wonderful Tours ... C2
10 Yellow Tubing Operators ... C2
Yoga in Vang Vieng ... (see 18)

Sleeping

11 Central Backpackers Hostel ... C2
12 Champa Lao ... C1
13 Chez Mango ... A3
14 Grand View Guesthouse ... B1
15 Inthira ... B3
16 Maylyn Guest House ... A3
17 Riverside Boutique Resort ... B3
18 Silver Naga ... B2
19 Vang Vieng Plaza ... C3
20 Vang Vieng Rock Backpackers Hostel ... C1
21 Vieng Tara Villa ... A3

Eating

22 Breakfast Vendors ... C2
23 Cafe Eh Eh ... B3
24 Chantheo ... C1
25 Korean Restaurant ... C2
26 Sia Po ... B2
27 Tham Mada ... C1

Drinking & Nightlife

28 Earth ... C1
29 Gary's Irish Bar ... C2
30 Sakura Bar ... C2
31 Smile Beach Bar ... B1

Information

32 Agricultural Promotion Bank ... C2
33 BCEL ... C2
34 Post Office ... B2
35 Provincial Hospital ... B3
36 Tourist Information Center ... C2

Transport

37 Bus Stop ... D2
38 Malany Transport Co ... C2
39 VIP Bus Station ... D3

200 routes have been identified and most have been bolted. The routes are rated between 4a and 8b, with the majority being in or near a cave. The most popular climbing spots are near **Tham Non** (Sleeping Cave), with more than 20 routes, and the tougher **Sleeping Wall** nearby, where some routes have difficult overhangs.

The climbing season usually runs between October and May, with most routes too wet at other times. However, there are some rock-shaded overhangs on Phadeng Mountain that have been bolted down (23 routes), and can still be used in the wet season.

Adam's Rock Climbing School (☎020-56564499; www.vangviengclimbing.com; half-/full-day climbing 180,000/260,000K, 2-day course US$100, private half-day climbing guide from 320,000K; ⏲8am-9pm) offers fully outfitted courses ranging in skill from beginner to advanced. Adam himself is one of the most experienced climbers in the area; his multilingual guides get good reports and equipment rental is also available.

Green Discovery conducts climbing courses (half-/full day from US$30/39) and, when available, can provide a handy climbing guide to the area.

Ziplining

It's all about air and cable these days, with the jungles around Vang Vieng criss-crossed with adrenaline-inducing ziplines. The following tour outfits combine a trek, kayak, abseil or tubing session with zipping:

AK Home Tours (☎020-55033665; half-/full day 170,000/200,000K; ⏲8.30am-9.30pm)

Namthip Tour (☎020-55623536; ⏲7am-9pm)

TCK (☎023-511691; www.tckamazingtours.com; ⏲7am-9pm)

Vang Vieng Challenge (☎023-511230; www.greendiscoverylaos.com)

Wonderful Tours (☎023-511566; www.wonderfultourslaos.la; Th Khann Muang; ⏲7.30am-9.30pm)

Other Activities

★**Blue Lagoon 3** SWIMMING
(10,000K; ⏲8am-6pm) Forget the circus that is the original Blue Lagoon (Tham Phu Kham) and head 14km further west to the Blue Lagoon 3. The azure waters are fed by a natural spring that emerges from a nearby karst limestone peak and it is still relatively quiet compared with its more infamous namesake.

Tubes are available for hire, and there is a small zipline into the water, and a basic restaurant. It's usually quiet in the mornings, but can get busier in the afternoons as schoolkids come to cool off.

Vang Vieng Sauna
BATHHOUSE

(25,000K; ⊙2-9pm) A family-run, local-style herbal sauna. They provide tea, soap, bathing clothes and a towel; all you need to bring is yourself and a desire to sweat.

Yoga in Vang Vieng
YOGA

(Silver Naga; per session US$10, 2 sessions US$15; ⊙7.30-9am & 5-6.30pm) Daily yoga sessions are available at the Silver Naga hotel with an experienced international yoga instructor. The price is a bit high, but the instructors are some of the best we've had in Laos. You also get free entry to Silver Naga's pool after class!

🛏 Sleeping

Vang Vieng has a relatively broad but not entirely appealing spread of accommodation. In recent years, the cheap guesthouses have been knocked down and replaced by characterless, multistorey midrange places to accommodate package tourists, and there's been an uptick in boutiques along the riverside.

If Vang Vieng town isn't your scene, head out of town for a more serene location.

🛏 In Town

Vang Vieng Rock Backpackers Hostel
HOSTEL $

(☑020-52256686; www.facebook.com/Vangviengrockbackpackershostel; Th Luang Prabang; incl breakfast dm 40,000-60,000K; r 200,000K; ❋🛜) The thumping music and flashing disco lights set the tone when you enter this party hostel, which has an on-site bar with a pool table and table football. The clean and traveller-friendly rooms have between four and 14 beds (including a female-only dorm), all with private sockets and lights. Avoid the ground-floor dorms if you care about sleeping.

Grand View Guesthouse
GUESTHOUSE $

(☑020-55335599; r 130,000-300,000K; ❋❋🛜) This 22-room property is nestled on the riverbank overlooking Don Khang, although a new development means that the eponymous view is a bit of a misnomer. Nonetheless, rooms are spacious and tidy.

Central Backpackers Hostel
HOSTEL $

(☑020-56770677; www.vangviengbackpackers.com; Th Luang Prabang; r with fan/air-con 100,000/150,000K, tr 200,000K; ❋❋🛜) This hostel, with wedding-cake-style architecture, boasts private rooms with fan or air-con and private balcony and TV, and communal balconies to drink in the view of the cliffs. There's a huge lobby with a cafe and TV, and safety lockers too (BYO lock). Not much atmosphere but decent value.

★ Silver Naga
HOTEL $$

(☑023-511822; www.silvernaga.com; r incl breakfast US$65-180; ❋❋@🛜🏊) The handsome rooms here feature contemporary decoration and lots of nice touches like private balcony, flat-screen TV and rain shower. Staff are friendly and helpful, there is a 2nd-floor pool with a killer karst view that is open to nonguests for 50,000K, and a cafe was being added when we were in town.

Vang Vieng Plaza
HOTEL $$

(☑030-9260192; www.vangviengplazahotel.com; r incl breakfast US$40-100; ❋🛜🏊) This new-feeling hotel has one of the most imposing hotel lobbies in Vang Vieng. Like the lobby, the rooms are spacious and tidy, but don't have heaps of character. There's a pool that does a good job matching the aqua-blue tile design theme.

★ Riverside Boutique Resort
BOUTIQUE HOTEL $$$

(☑021-511726; www.riversidevangvieng.com; incl breakfast r US$110-169, ste US$305; ❋❋@🛜🏊) Sugar-white and uberstylish, this beautiful boutique belle offers generously spaced rooms wrapped around a citrus-green pool and a verdant garden looking out onto the karsts. Rooms themselves are gorgeous, with balconies, crisp white sheets, and chic decor straight from the pages of *Wallpaper*. It's located by the toll bridge.

★ Inthira
BOUTIQUE HOTEL $$$

(☑023-511070; www.inthirahotels.com; incl breakfast r US$98-128, ste US$220; ❋❋@🛜🏊) In new digs on the riverside, the Inthira is hands-down Vang Vieng's most sophisticated hotel. Dark steel, stained woods, terrazzo floors, vast flat-screen TVs and rain showers (and a Jacuzzi in the suites) leave the 38 rooms feeling effortlessly sleek and modern. But we suspect you'll remember the stunning views and the riverside deck and infinity pool.

LOCAL KNOWLEDGE

FROM PARTIES TO PARADISE

Back in 1999, Vang Vieng was a little-known affair where travellers came to float on tractor inner tubes down the river, cycle through its stunning karst country and maybe smoke the odd spliff between exploring its fantastical caves. Then the word got out – Vang Vieng was Southeast Asia's next hedonistic mecca – and backpackers were marking it on their party itinerary like a sort of Thailand's Ko Pha Ngan in the mountains, one with countless blasting rave platforms along the formerly bucolic tubing route.

But behind the revelry was a darker truth: by 2011 at least 25 Western visitors (mainly Aussies and Brits) had variously died from heart attacks, drownings and broken necks, having ridden the 'deathslide' (a hastily erected zipline over a seasonally perilously low river). In 2012, after more deaths and under pressure from the Australian government, the Lao government ordered the riverside bars to close.

Since then, with drugs generally off the menu (or at least out of sight), the town has been repositioning itself from party central to the rural village it once was. For the first time in years, mainstream tourists are heading to Vang Vieng, many en route to fabled Luang Prabang, stopping to kayak the Nam Song, go caving and climb the karsts. The new fear, it seems, is that the town may soon be overrun by package-tour groups that are, once again, reshaping its ephemeral identity.

Around Town

Chez Mango GUESTHOUSE **$**
(☎020-54435747; www.chezmango.com; bungalows 80,000-100,000K; 📶) Located over the bridge, Mango is friendly and scrupulously clean, and has seven basic but colourful bungalows (some with bathrooms) with private balconies in its flowery gardens. Shaded by trees, there's also a *sala* (open-sided shelter) to read in. Run by Noé, who also runs the excellent **Vang Vieng Jeep Tour** (☎020-54435747; noedouine@gmail.com; Chez Mango; minimum group of 4, per person 180,000K; ⏲9am-4pm) from here, this is a soporific and restful spot.

Maylyn Guest House GUESTHOUSE **$**
(☎020-55604095; www.facebook.com/maylynguesthouse; bungalows 60,000-120,000K, r 100,000-170,000K; 🚭❄📶) Over the bridge and run by gregarious Jo, this expansive, maze-like compound holds a mix of rather weathered but charming rooms and bungalows, both with and without air-con and en suite. The lush garden is a wonderland for kids and the overall vibe is relaxed and quiet.

★**Champa Lao** HOTEL **$$**
(☎020-55428518; www.facebook.com/champalaobungalows; r 80,000K, bungalows 200,000-600,000K; ❄📶) There's a variety of warm, cosy accommodation here, from basic fan rooms with shared bathrooms and mozzie nets in the main structure, to a string of bungalows and even the upper floor of a house. The communal garden, choked with plants, is a highlight and you can swing on a hammock while taking in the sunset and karst from its aerial balcony.

Bearlin Bungalow BUNGALOW **$$**
(☎020-58419000; bearlinbungalow@gmail.com; bungalows incl breakfast US$50-60; 🚭❄📶) A small resort set in a spotless garden on the road to the Blue Lagoon. One half of the ownership team is, unsurprisingly, German. There's meticulous attention to detail in the rooms (but no TV or refrigerator) and a menu that includes German dishes like currywurst and pork knuckle.

★**Vieng Tara Villa** BOUTIQUE HOTEL **$$$**
(☎030-5023102; www.viengtara.com; bungalows incl breakfast US$80-100; 🚭❄📶) This boutique resort takes full advantage of its location on the west-bank riverside to deliver some of the most stunning hotel views in Southeast Asia. Choose one of the villa paddy-view rooms, which are set on stilts in the middle of lush rice fields and accessible via a wooden walkway. And even if you're not staying here, stop by for a drink at the elevated cafe.

Eating

Vang Vieng's eating scene is, frankly, pretty dire. Although there are a couple of good local choices for breakfast, cookie-cutter Lao/backpacker places dominate, and your best options are, paradoxically, Chinese or Korean.

★**Tham Mada** LAO $
(mains 25,000-30,000K; ⏲7.30am-3pm & 5-9pm) The name here means 'normal', but there's lots that's unusual about this place. Chief among these is that the Korean owner is doing some of the better Thai-Lao food in town. Choose from a small menu that includes noodle soup, braised pork leg over rice, fried rice, and lighter dishes, all of which are prepared with care and are very tasty.

★**Breakfast Vendors** LAO $
(Th Luang Prabang; mains 10,000-15,000K; ⏲6-9am) A string of breakfast vendors sets up shop every morning serving basic but tasty Lao dishes, from noodles to rice porridge. One of relatively few places in town to get real Lao food.

Sia Po LAO $
(mains 15,000-40,000K; ⏲9am-10pm) To eat with the locals, head to this open-air Lao place. An English-language menu on the wall spans pounded salads, soups and grilled dishes, or you can simply point to whatever looks good on the grill. Don't forget the sticky rice. Located on the main strip across from Vang Vieng's hospital (no roman-script sign).

Chantheo LAO $
(Th Luang Prabang; mains 20,000-30,000K; ⏲1-9pm) In the evening, hit the strip of Th Luang Prabang where a vendor grills pork, chicken or duck, all of which are served with platters of fresh leaves and herbs. One of the few places in Vang Vieng where locals eat.

Cafe Eh Eh CAFE $
(☎030-5074369; breakfast 30,000-40,000K; ⏲6am-7pm; ❄📶✍) Cafe Eh Eh provides a chilled (we are talking air-con here) retreat from the downtown heat of Vang Vieng, offering a small selection of freshly made cakes and coffee. Breakfast is available, and a limited selection of sandwiches. The message board outside has helpful info on town happenings.

★**Korean Restaurant** KOREAN $$
(mains 50,000-150,000K; ⏲noon-10pm; ❄📶✍) Initially, we were drawn in by the Bee Gees soundtrack, and were pleased to discover that this place does some of the better foreign food in town. Let the friendly Korean owner guide you to a dish, which will inevitably be accompanied by *banchan,* an array of tart, spicy, salty and crunchy side dishes.

Drinking & Nightlife

Vang Vieng has ditched all-night parties in favour of a more chilled scene. However, there are still some late-night shenanigans at places such as Sakura Bar and the weekly 'Jungle' parties.

★**Smile Beach Bar** BAR
(⏲9am-10pm) This mega-chill riverside bar is a slice of the old Vang Vieng, before the buggies took over. Order a Beerlao (we don't recommend eating here) and swing in a hammock or dip your toes in the river; it's ideal for an afternoon or sunset drink and swim. Reach the bar by crossing the footbridge to Don Khang.

Smile is also the end point for yellow-route rafting trips along the Nam Song.

★**Earth** BAR
(www.facebook.com/earthvangvieng; ⏲2pm-midnight; 📶) Made from driftwood and clay, this artsy hillside bar-restaurant pipes out fine tunes to match the ambience, with live music nightly from 7pm. Check out the sumptuous view of the cliffs from the lamp-lit garden, while munching on potato wedges, burgers and salads (mains 30,000K to 90,000K). Located at the northern end of town; look for the glowing green sign.

Sakura Bar BAR
(☎020-78008555; ⏲7pm-midnight) At the time of writing, Sakura was one of the most popular bars in Vang Vieng, with the largest crowds and loudest music. Expect a raucous night with shot promotions (from 8pm to 9pm and after midnight) and lots of dancing.

Gary's Irish Bar IRISH PUB
(☎020-56115644; www.facebook.com/GarysIrishBar; ⏲9am-11.30pm; 📶) Still one of the best bars in town thanks to its friendly, unpretentious atmosphere, live music (Mondays, Wednesdays and Fridays from 9pm), free pool and cheap grub like homemade pies, burgers and Lao fare (mains 39,000K to 49,000K). The staff are extremely knowledgeable about the area.

Jungle Project CLUB
(www.facebook.com/jungleprojectvangvienglao; incl tuk-tuk from town 40,000K; ⏲11pm-late Fri) If you want to recapture the spirit of Va Va Vang Vieng before the clampdown on the town's formerly raucous party scene, the Jungle Project parties are the easiest way to get your flashback. Friday night is the big

all-nighter and it takes place at the decrepit Vang Vieng Mai Resort, about 2km north of town.

Information

DANGERS & ANNOYANCES

Most visitors leave Vang Vieng with nothing more serious than a hangover, but this tranquil setting is also the most dangerous place in Laos for travellers. Visitors die every year from river accidents and while caving. Theft can also be a problem, with fellow travellers often the culprits. Take the usual precautions and don't leave valuables outside caves.

Drugs have been a problem in the past here, but since a government-led crackdown in 2012, they are not so widespread. But dope is still around and local police are particularly adept at sniffing out spliffs, especially late at night. If you're caught with a stash of marijuana (or anything else), the normal practice is for police to take your passport and fine you 5 million kip or more than US$600. Don't expect a receipt, and don't bother calling your embassy.

MEDICAL SERVICES

Vang Vieng's modest **Provincial Hospital** (☎023-511019) has X-ray facilities and is fine for broken bones, cuts and malaria. However, if your ailment is more serious, you will need to get to Vientiane or Thailand.

MONEY

Agricultural Promotion Bank (Th Luang Prabang; ⌚8.30am-3.30pm) Exchanges cash, plus has an ATM.

BCEL (Th Khann Muang; ⌚8.30am-3.30pm) Exchanges cash and handles cash advances on Visa, Mastercard and JCB; also has ATMs around town.

TOURIST INFORMATION

Tourist Information Center (☎023-511707; Th Luang Prabang; ⌚8.30-11.30am & 2-4pm Mon-Fri) A useful port of call to pick up various leaflets on things to do in the area.

Getting There & Away

There are two bus stations in Vang Vieng, linking the town with a handful of large cities in Laos and destinations in Cambodia, Thailand and Vietnam.

NORTH BUS STATION

Buses, minibuses and *sŏrngtăaou* (passenger trucks) bound for Luang Prabang and Vientiane depart from the **North Bus Station** (Rte 13) about 2km north of town, although if you're coming in from Vientiane you'll most likely be dropped off at the **bus stop** (Rte 13) near the former runway, a short walk from the centre of town. Destination include the following:

Luang Prabang (minibus; 100,000K, six hours, twice daily)

Luang Prabang (bus; 90,000K, seven hours, daily)

Vientiane (fan; 40,000K, five hours, six daily)

Vientiane (minibus; 60,000K, three to four hours, daily)

Vientiane (bus; 50,000K, three to four hours, twice daily)

Vientiane (*sŏrngtăaou;* 40,000K, five hours, frequent departures)

VIP BUS STATION

Departures to destinations further abroad, both in Laos (including Vientiane) and in neighbouring countries, depart from the **VIP Bus Station** (Rte 13), located just east of the town centre. Tickets can be purchased in town at **Malany Transport Co** (☎023-511633; Th Luang Prabang; ⌚8am-8pm).

Note that, for distant destinations in Laos, there's a change of bus in Vientiane; buses to Bangkok and Chiang Mai also require a change at Nong Khai.

DESTINATION	COST (K)	DURATION (HR)	DEPARTURES
Bangkok (Thailand; bus)	270,000	17	9am & 1.30am
Chiang Mai (Thailand; bus)	350,000	17	9am & 10am
Danang (Vietnam; bus)	240,000	32	10am
Hanoi (Vietnam; bus)	220,000	28	10am
Hue (Vietnam; bus)	220,000	22	10am
Nong Khai (Thailand; bus)	90,000	5	9am
Pakse (bus)	180,000	16	1.30am
Phnom Penh (Cambodia; bus)	440,000	32	1.30am
Si Phan Don (Four Thousand Islands; bus)	240,000	20	1.30am
Siem Reap (Cambodia; bus)	440,000	36	1.30am

DESTINATION	COST (K)	DURATION (HR)	DEPARTURES
Tha Khaek (bus)	180,000	10	1.30am
Udon Thani (Thailand; bus)	90,000	7	9am
Vientiane (minibus)	40,000	4	10am & 1.30pm
Vientiane (bus)	40,000	4	9am & 1.30pm
Vinh (Vietnam; bus)	220,000	20	10am

Getting Around

'Downtown' Vang Vieng is easily negotiated on foot. Renting a bicycle (15,000K per day) or mountain bike (30,000K per day) is also popular; they're available almost everywhere. Most of the same places also rent motorcycles from about 50,000K per day (automatics cost 80,000K). For cave sites out of town you can charter *sŏrngtăaou* by the old market area near the footbridge to Don Khang; expect to pay around US$10 per trip up to 20km north or south of town.

LUANG PRABANG & AROUND

It's hard to imagine a more whimsical confection of delights than you find in lantern-strung Luang Prabang and its gorgeously green surrounding countryside. This is a region in which old-world colonial-era charm meets jungle adventure.

Beyond the evident history and heritage of the old French town are aquamarine waterfalls, meandering mountain-bike trails, top trekking opportunities, kayaking trips, river cruises and outstanding natural beauty, the whole ensemble encircled by hazy green mountains.

Luang Prabang

☎071 / POP 67,000

Luang Prabang (ຫລວງພະບາງ) slows your pulse and awakens your imagination with its combination of world-class comfort and spiritual nourishment. Sitting at the sacred confluence of the Mekong River and the Nam Khan (Khan River), nowhere else can lay claim to this Unesco-protected gem's romance of 33 gilded wats, saffron-clad monks, faded Indochinese villas and exquisite fusion cuisine.

Over the last 25 years Luang Prabang has seen a flood of investment, with French villas being revived as fabulous boutique hotels, and some of the best chefs in Southeast Asia moving in. The population has swollen, and yet still the peninsula remains as sleepy and friendly as a village, as if time has stood still here.

Sights

★**Phu Si** HILL

(ພູສີ; Map p316; 20,000K; ⊙6am-7pm) Dominating the old city centre and a favourite with sunset junkies, the 100m-tall Phu Si (prepare your legs for a steep 329-step ascent) is crowned by a 24m gilded stupa called **That Chomsi** (ທາດຈອມສີ; Map p316; admission incl with Phu Si). Viewed from a distance, especially when floodlit at night, the structure seems to float in the hazy air like a chandelier. From the summit, however, the main attraction is the city views.

Beside a flagpole on the same summit there's a small remnant anti-aircraft cannon left from the war years.

Ascending Phu Si from the northern side, stop at **Wat Pa Huak** (ວັດປ່າຮວກ; Map p316; admission by donation; ⊙daylight hours). The gilded, carved front doors are usually locked, but an attendant will open them for a tip. Inside, the original 19th-century murals show historic scenes along the Mekong River, including visits by Chinese diplomats and warriors arriving by river, and horse caravans.

Reaching That Chomsi is also possible from the southern and eastern sides. Two such paths climb through large **Wat Siphoutthabat Thippharam** (ວັດສີພຸດທະບາດ ທິບພາຣາມ; Map p316; ⊙daylight hours) FREE to a curious miniature shrine that protects a **Buddha Footprint** (ຮອຍພະບາດພະພຸດທະເຈົ້າ; Map p316). If this really is his rocky imprint, then the Buddha must have been the size of a brontosaurus. Directly southwest of here a series of gilded Buddhas are nestled into rocky clefts and niches around **Wat Thammothayalan** (ວັດທຳໂມໄທຍາລານ; Map p316; ⊙daylight hours); this monastery is free to visit if you don't climb beyond to That Chomsi.

Luang Prabang

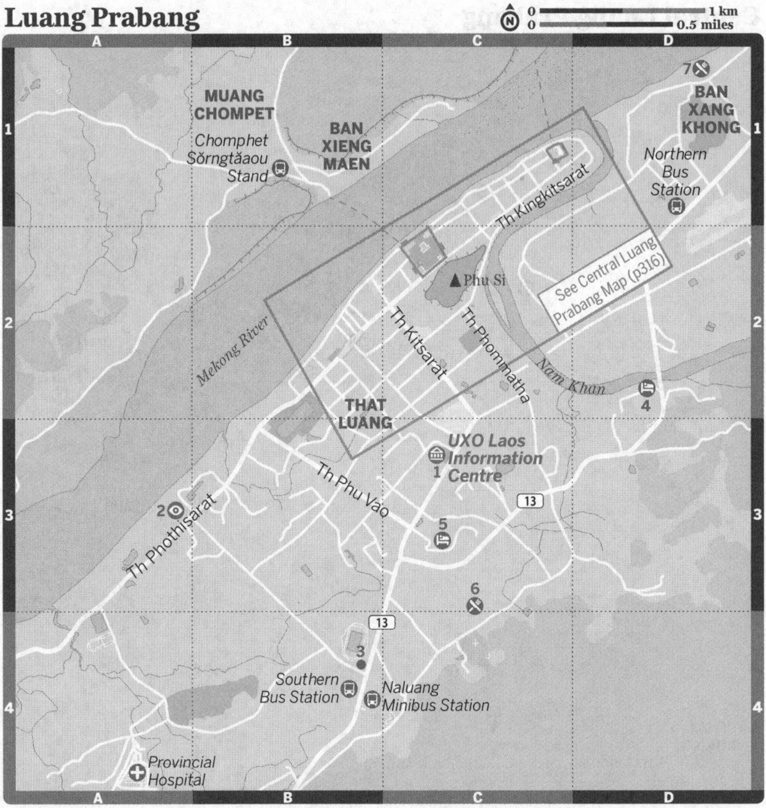

★**Wat Xieng Thong** BUDDHIST TEMPLE
(ວັດຊຽງທອງ; Map p316; off Th Sakkarin; 20,000K; 6am-6pm) Luang Prabang's best-known monastery is centred on a 1560 *sĭm* (ordination hall). Its roofs sweep low to the ground and there's a stunning 'tree of life' mosaic set on its western exterior wall. Close by are several stupas and three compact little chapel halls called *hŏr*. **Hŏr Đại**, shaped like a tall tomb, houses a standing Buddha. The **Hŏr Đại Pha Sai-nyàat**, dubbed La Chapelle Rouge – the Red Chapel – by the French, contains a rare reclining Buddha.

Fronted in lavish gilt work, the **Hóhng Kép Mîen** stores a ceremonial carriage, festooned with red-tongued *naga* (river serpents) designed to carry the golden funeral urns of Lao royalty.

★**UXO Lạos Information Centṛe** MUSEUM
(ສູນຂໍ້ມູນຂາວສານປະເທດລາວກຽວກັບການເກັບກູລະເບີດທີ່ບໍທັນແຕກ; Map p315; 020-22575123, 071-252073; www.uxolao.org; off Th

Luang Prabang

Top Sights

Sights

Activities, Courses & Tours

Sleeping

Eating

Entertainment

Central Luang Prabang

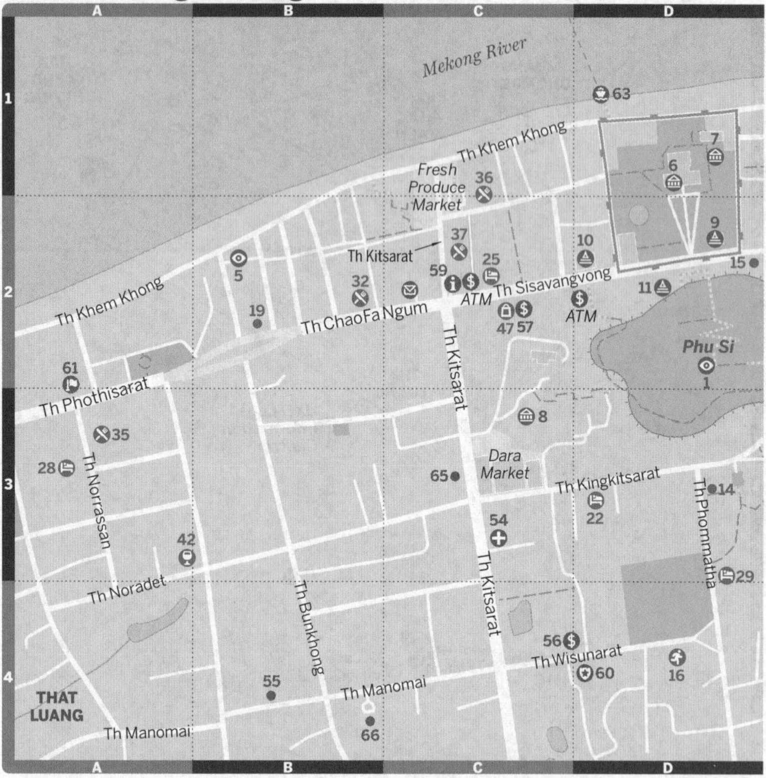

Central Luang Prabang

Top Sights
1 Phu Si....D2
2 Wat Xieng Thong....H1

Sights
3 Buddha Footprint....E2
4 Heuan Chan Heritage House....E1
5 Pha Tad Ke Botanical Garden....B2
6 Royal Palace....D1
7 Royal Palace Car Collection....D1
8 TAEC....C3
That Chomsi....(see 1)
9 Wat Ho Pha Bang....D2
10 Wat Mai Suwannaphumaham....D2
11 Wat Pa Huak....D2
12 Wat Siphoutthabat Thippharam....E2
13 Wat Thammothayalan....E2

Activities, Courses & Tours
14 Banana Boat Laos....D3
15 E-bike Adventures....D2
16 Lao Red Cross....D4
Luang Prabang Yoga....(see 45)
17 Luang Say Cruise....E2
18 Mandalao....E2
19 Motolao....B2
20 Shompoo Cruise....F1
Tamarind....(see 39)
21 White Elephant Adventures....E2

Sleeping
22 Aham Backpackers Hostel....D3
23 Apsara....G2
24 Cold River Guesthouse....E4
25 Indigo House....C2
26 Oui's Guesthouse....H2
27 Pack Luck Villa....F1
28 Satri House....A3
29 Villa Sayada....D3

Eating
30 Bouang Asian Eatery....E2
31 Dyen Sabai....F2
32 Joma Bakery Cafe....B2
33 Khaiphaen....E1

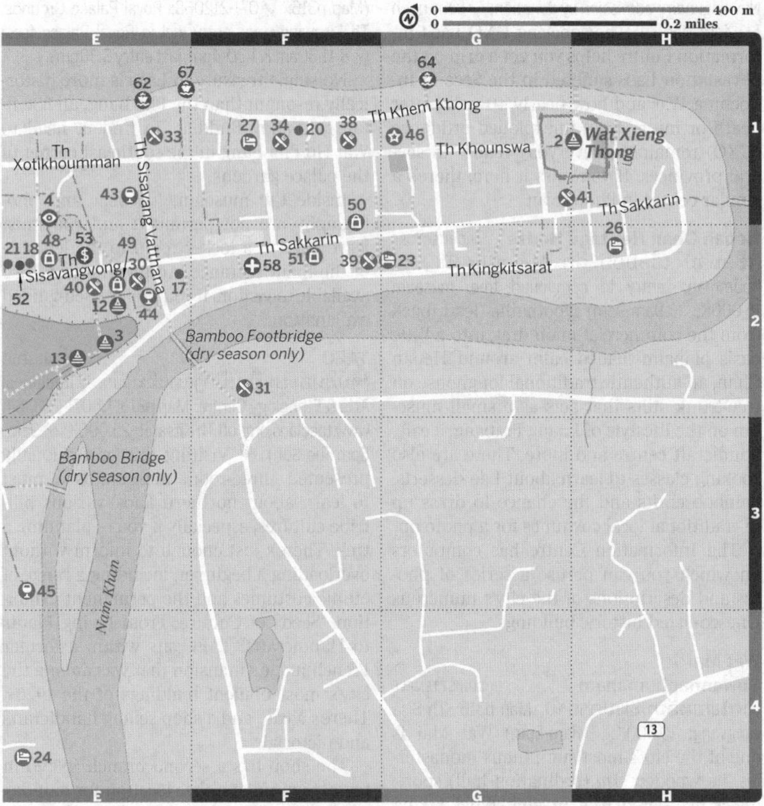

34	L'Elephant Restaurant	F1
35	Manda de Laos	A3
36	Morning Market	C1
37	Night Food Stalls	C2
	Paste	(see 23)
38	Popolo	F1
39	Tamarind	F2
40	Tangor	E2
41	Xieng Thong Noodle-Shop	G1

Drinking & Nightlife

42	Bar 525	A3
43	Chez Matt	E1
44	Icon Klub	E2
45	Utopia	E3

Entertainment

46	Garavek Storytelling	G1

Shopping

47	Handicraft Night Market	C2
48	Luang Prabang Artisans	E2
49	Naga Creations	E2
50	Ock Pop Tok Boutique	F1
51	TAEC Shop	F2

Information

52	All Lao Travel	E2
53	BCEL	E2
54	Chinese Hospital	C3
55	Immigration Office	B4
56	Lao Development Bank	C4
57	Minipost Booth	C2
58	Pharmacie	F2
59	Provincial Tourism Department	C2
60	Tourist Police	D4
61	Vietnamese Consulate	A2

Transport

62	Boats to Pak Ou Caves	E1
63	Cross-River Boats	D1
64	Galao Boat Pier	G1
65	KPTD	C3
66	Lao Airlines	B4
67	Longboat Office	E1

Naviengkham; admission by donation; ⏲8am-noon & 1-4pm Mon-Fri) The sobering UXO Laos Information Centre helps you get a grip on the devastation Laos suffered in the Second Indochina War and how nearly 40 years later death or injury from unexploded ordnance (UXO) remains an everyday reality in several provinces. If you miss it here, there's a similar centre in Phonsavan.

Heuan Chan Heritage House ARCHITECTURE
(ເຮືອນຈັນ ເຮືອນມໍລະດົກ; Map p316; Th Xotikhoumman; entry to compound free, museum 15,000K; ⏲9am-9pm) Footpaths lead back from the commercial main drag into a little oasis of palm-shaded calm around Heuan Chan, an authentic traditional longhouse on tree-trunk stilts that acts as a small museum on the lifestyle of Luang Prabang, a cafe, handicraft centre and more. There are also cooking classes to learn about Lao desserts, bamboo crafts and the chance to dress up in traditional local costumes for a photo op.

The Information Centre has computers on which you can peruse a series of photos and descriptions of the city's numerous Unesco-listed historic buildings.

Wat Mai Suwannaphumaham BUDDHIST TEMPLE
(ວັດໃຫມ່ສຸວັນນະພູມອາຮາມ; Map p316; Th Sisavangvong; 10,000K; ⏲8am-5pm) Wat Mai is one of the city's most sumptuous monasteries, its wooden *sĭm* (ordination hall) sporting a five-tiered roof in archetypal Luang Prabang style, while the unusually roofed front veranda features detailed golden reliefs depicting scenes from village life, the Ramayana and Buddha's penultimate birth. It was spared destruction in 1887 by the Haw gangs, who reportedly found it too beautiful to harm. Since 1894 it has been home to the Sangharat, the head of Lao Buddhism.

Royal Palace MUSEUM
(ພະຣາຊະວັງຊຽງແກ້ວ, Ho Kham; Map p316; ☎071-212068; Th Sisavangvong; 30,000K; ⏲8-11.30am & 1.30-4pm, last entry 3.30pm) Evoking traditional Lao and French beaux-arts styles, the former Royal Palace was built in 1904 and was home to King Sisavang Vong (r 1904–59), whose statue stands outside. Within are tasteful, decidedly sober residential quarters, with some rooms preserved much as they were when the king's son (and successor) was captured by the Pathet Lao in 1975. A separate outbuilding displays the five-piece **Royal Palace Car Collection** (Map p316; ☎071-212068; Royal Palace Grounds, Th Sisavangvong; entry incl in Royal Palace fees; ⏲8-11.30am & 1.30-4pm, last entry 3.30pm).

No single treasure in Laos is more historically resonant than the Pha Bang, an 83cm-tall gold-alloy Buddha. To find it, head to Wat Ho Pha Bang in the southeast corner of the palace gardens.

Inside the museum, footwear and photography are not permitted and you must leave bags in a locker room to the left side of the main entrance. An audio tour is also available to visitors if you prefer a self-guided explanation.

TAEC MUSEUM
(ສູນສິນລະປະພື້ນເມືອງແລະຊົນເຜົ່າ, Traditional Arts & Ethnology Centre; Map p316; ☎071-253364; www.taeclaos.org; off Th Kitsarat; 25,000K; ⏲9am-6pm Tue-Sun) Visiting this professionally presented three-room museum is a must to learn about northern Laos' various hill-tribe cultures, especially if you're planning a trek. There's just enough to inform without overloading a beginner, including a range of ethnic costumes and the permanent exhibition, 'Seeds of Culture: From Living Plants to Handicrafts'. TAEC sits within a former French judge's mansion that was among the city's most opulent buildings of the 1920s. There's a cafe and a shop selling handicrafts and pictorials.

The shop has a second branch (p325) in town. Sign up at either location for half-day workshops (from US$12) on Khmu bamboo weaving, Hmong embroidery or Katu back-strap weaving.

Ock Pop Tok Living Crafts Centre ARTS CENTRE
(ສູນຫັດຖະກຳຜ້າໄຫມອອກພົບຕົກ, OPT; Map p315; ☎071-212597; www.ockpoptok.com; 125/10 Ban Saylom; ⏲8am-6pm) FREE Set serenely close to the Mekong, this beautiful, traditionally styled workshop, where weavers, spinners and batik makers produce top-quality fabrics, offers free tours every half-hour. There's also a great riverside **Silk Road Cafe** serving drinks and excellent Lao food. Or try a cup of the surprisingly pleasant worm-poo tea, a unique infusion made from silk-worm droppings. Better still, why not try a bamboo-weaving **course** (Map p315; ☎071-212597; www.ockpoptok.com; 125/10 Ban Saylom; half-/full-day bamboo-weaving course US$26/42, Hmong Batik class US$52/69, 3-day natural dyeing & weaving course US$158; ⏲8.45am-4pm). There is also a beautiful

LOCAL KNOWLEDGE

TAK BAT: THE MONKS' CALL TO ALMS

Daily at dawn, saffron-clad monks pad barefoot through the streets while pious townsfolk place tiny balls of sticky rice in their begging bowls. It's a quiet, meditative ceremony through which monks demonstrate their vows of poverty and humility while lay Buddhists gain spiritual merit by the act of respectful giving.

Although such processions occur all over Laos, old Luang Prabang's peaceful atmosphere and extraordinary concentration of mist-shrouded temples mean that the morning's perambulations along Th Sakkarin create an especially romantic scene. Sadly, as a result, tourists are progressively coming to outnumber participants. Despite constant campaigns begging visitors not to poke cameras in the monks' faces, the amateur paparazzi seem incapable of keeping a decent distance. Sensitive, non-participating observers should follow these guidelines:

- Stand across the road from the procession or, better still, watch inconspicuously from the window of your hotel (where possible).
- Refrain from taking photos or at least do so from a considerable distance with a long zoom. Never use flash.
- Maintain the silence (arrive by bicycle or on foot; don't chatter).

boutique and a handful of elegant rooms available on-site.

Wat Ho Pha Bang BUDDHIST TEMPLE

(ວັດຫໍພະບາງ; Map p316; Royal Palace Grounds, Th Sisavangvong; entry incl in Royal Palace fees; 8-11.30am & 1.30-4pm, last entry 3.30pm) The sacred Pha Bang image, from which the city takes its name, is stored in this highly ornate pavilion that wasn't completed until 2011. The 83cm-tall, gold-alloy Buddha arrived in 1512, spiritually legitimising the Lan Xang royal dynasty as Buddhist rulers. It was cast around the 1st century AD in Sri Lanka and gifted to Laos by the kings of Angkor. It was twice carried off to Thailand (in 1779 and 1827) by the Siamese, but was finally restored to Laos in 1867.

Activities

Some of the most popular activities in Luang Prabang are based in the countryside beyond, including trekking, cycling, motocross, kayaking and rafting tours. Interactive options include getting down and dirty at Living Land (p320) or Laos Buffalo Dairy (p328). For an adrenaline rush, try Green Jungle Flight (p329) or Nahm Dong Park (p328), both offering lush gardens, waterfalls, natural pools, cafe and ziplines. In Luang Prabang itself, it's all about temple-hopping, cookery classes and cycling.

Luang Prabang Yoga YOGA

(Map p316; www.luangprabangyoga.org; classes 60/90min 40,000/60,000K; classes at 7.30am & 5pm) Slow down, unwind and sync your spirit to the city's relaxed vibe with yoga classes taught at serene locations, from lush riverside garden decks at daily Utopia (p324) to rooftop sunset views. The city's yoga cooperative keeps up-to-date information on classes and venues on its website. In our experience this is a well-run network of qualified teachers. All levels welcome.

Luang Prabang Yoga also runs relaxing three-day yoga retreats at the delicious Mandala Ou Resort (p339) in Nong Khiaw; see www.laosyogaretreats.com.

Lao Red Cross MASSAGE, SPA

(Map p316; 071-252856; Th Wisunarat; sauna 15,000K, traditional/aromatherapy massage per hour 50,000/80,000K; 1-8pm) This traditional blue Lao house was the original place to come for a sauna and massage before all the fancy spas arrived. It might be no frills, but well-trained staff give first-rate massages and there's a terrific sauna infused with medicinal plants that will clear your respiratory system like Vicks VapoRub!

Donations go directly to improving the lives of those living in the poorest villages in Laos.

Courses

★Tamarind COOKING

(Map p316; 020-77770484; www.tamarindlaos.com; Ban Wat Nong; full-day/evening course 285,000/215,000K) Join Tamarind at its lakeside pavilion for a day's tuition in the art of Lao cuisine, meeting in the morning at its restaurant before heading to the market for ingredients for classic dishes such as *mok phaa* (steamed fish in banana leaves). Evening classes don't include a market visit.

Backstreet Academy HANDICRAFTS
(www.backstreetacademy.com; US$22-33) Expanding across Southeast Asia, Backstreet Academy offers a range of immersive experiences with local craftspeople so visitors can learn a new skill. In Luang Prabang, they offer bow crafting and knife making for would-be jungle survivalists and woodcarving and weaving for something more sedate.

Tours

Luang Prabang has an abundance of travel agents vying for your patronage for half- to multiday tours. Tours to waterfalls and the Pak Ou Caves are particularly popular and prices are generally competitive (typically around 130,000K for the full day), but it still pays to shop around. The Pak Ou Caves and Tat Kuang Si are an odd combination, given that the sites are in opposite directions, but the advantage is that the vehicle to the Kuang Si waterfalls should be waiting when you return to the agency office from your boat trip. Note that tour prices don't include entry fees.

★ **Living Land** CULTURAL
(020-55199208; www.livinglandlao.org; Ban Phong Van; tours per person 344,000K; 8.30am-noon;) About 5km out of Luang Prabang, on the road to Tat Kuang Si, is this brilliant rice-farm cooperative, where you can spend half a day learning how to plant and grow sticky rice, the ubiquitous dish of Laos. This includes prepping the paddy with gregarious water-buffalo Rudolph – expect to be knee-deep in glorious mud! You'll never taste rice in the same way again. Kids love it.

Living Land helps educate children from disadvantaged families in the local community.

E-bike Adventures MOUNTAIN BIKING
(Map p316; 071-211152; www.ebike-laos.com; half-day US$59, full day with SUP/kayaking & lunch US$103) Enjoy a village and jungle romp on a state-of-the-art e-mountain bike in the beautiful countryside around Chateau Orientale, an opulent ecolodge located on the Nam Khan, with the option of an overnight stay. The ride takes in rice fields, local ethnic villages and a couple of river crossings, so prepare to get down and dirty if it rains (though it also offers professional protective gear).

Mountain-bike rides can be combined with kayaking on the river or stand-up paddleboarding. Overnight excursions and combination activities are also offered with camping or a stay at the lodge. There are some great family rooms that can be combined to offer villa living on the riverside.

White Elephant Adventures HIKING
(Map p316; 030-5789120; www.white-elephant-adventures-laos.com; 44/3 Th Sisavangvong; 8am-9.30pm) White Elephant is hailed for its relationships with remote Hmong and Khamu villages, allowing a deeper insight into their way of life on well-planned two- or three-day trekking experiences. Look out for the BMW motorbike and communist flag to find its office on the main drag.

Shompoo Cruise BOATING
(Map p316; 071-213189; www.shompoocruise.com; Th Khem Khong; cruise incl breakfast & 2 lunches US$130) An excellent way to see the Mekong in style from a comfortable longboat, and less expensive than other operators offering the same trip, Shompoo runs two-day cruises between Huay Xai and Luang Prabang. Departures are from the **Galao Boat Pier** (Map p316; Th Khem Khong). If leaving from Huay Xai, a guide will meet you at the Thai border.

Festivals & Events

Pi Mai CULTURAL
(Lao New Year; Apr) Large numbers of visitors converge on Luang Prabang for this 'water throwing' festival in April. Be careful of

ELEPHANT INTERACTIONS

There are lots of elephant camps located around Luang Prabang, but many of them promote elephant riding, which can be harmful to the animal. For the best elephant-interaction experience in Laos, make a short overnight side trip to the Elephant Conservation Center (p351) in Sainyabuli. **Mandalao** (Map p316; 030-5664014; www.mandalaotours.com; Th Sisavangvong; US$80-130; 8.30am-5.30pm;) offers responsible and recommended elephant interactions closer to Luang Prabang for those with limited time on their hands.

your camera getting soaked and prepare to be drenched! Advance bookings around this time are recommended.

Bun Awk Phansa CULTURAL
(End of the Rains Retreat; ☺ Sep/Oct) Bun Awk Phansa sees boat races on the Nam Khan in September or October. Buddhists send little boats made of banana leaves with lit candles inside downriver by night, chiefly to send the bad luck of last year away, and to also give thanks to Mother Mekong and the sentinel *naga* (river serpents) who dwell within her watery arms. Pure magic.

🛏 Sleeping

For sybarites looking to recapture the comforts of old Indochine, Luang Prabang has world-class hotels and stunning boutique belles, plus impressive ecolodges and resorts in the surrounding lush countryside. Mid-scale bargains can be found in clean, simple guesthouses, and loads of hostels and super-basic digs make for good budget options. In high season, prices rocket and availability is low. Old-town peninsular accommodation generally comes at a premium but is more peaceful.

🛏 In Town

★ Fan Dee GUESTHOUSE $
(Sa Sa Lao; Map p315; ☑ 020-55357317; fandee hotel@gmail.com; Ban Vieng Mai; dm US$5-9, r US$25-35; 🛜) 🏊 Like a luxury ecoresort for the budget crowd, this jungly oasis of thatch-roofed bungalows has an array of on-site activities, from cooking classes to mudbaths on decks overlooking the Nam Khan. Wood-built bunks hold some of the comfiest dorm beds in town, while many of the private rooms have bamboo walls that open to reveal stunning river views.

Perks include a self-wash laundry area, hammocks strewn about landscaped gardens, weekly bonfires and free shuttles to/from the city centre (otherwise a 2km walk).

Aham Backpackers Hostel HOSTEL $
(Map p316; ☑ 030-2136027; Th Kingkitsarat; dm incl breakfast 25,000-40,000K) A real budget crash pad, Aham offers fan-cooled dorm beds in compact rooms at rock-bottom prices. Somehow the rates include breakfast, which makes it an even better deal. Staff are friendly and helpful and it's close to some of the restaurants and bars on the south side of Mt Phu Si.

Villa Sayada HOTEL $
(Map p316; ☑ 071-254872; Th Phommatha; r 150,000-220,000K; ❄🛜) This nine-room minihotel offers generously sized cream and cloud-white rooms, with hung fabrics, handmade lamps and decent hot showers. There are small private balconies with pleasant views. Find it opposite Wat Wisunarat.

Oui's Guesthouse GUESTHOUSE $$
(Map p316; ☑ 071-252374, 020-54349589; Th King-kitsarat; r US$25-45; 🛜) In a peaceful setting at the end of the peninsula facing the Nam Khan, it's so quiet here you can almost hear the breeze. Downstairs rooms are simple wood-ceiling affairs with tile floors, ethnic curtains and swish bathrooms. For an extra 10 bucks you can get an upstairs room with veranda and riverine views.

Pack Luck Villa BOUTIQUE HOTEL $$
(Map p316; ☑ 071-253373; Th Thugnaithao; r US$40-70; ❄🛜) This impressive little boutique hotel has an eclectic feel of dark woods, paper lanterns, chrome fans and Persian rugs; by night, subtle lighting picks out flecks of gold leaf on its wine-red walls. Rooms are a little tight, but the three with upper balconies overlook the monks' morning meander. Downstairs is the popular Pack Luck Liquor wine bar.

Cold River Guesthouse GUESTHOUSE $$
(Map p316; ☑ 071-252810; www.coldriverluang prabang.com; Ban Meuana; r incl breakfast US$31-66; ❄🛜) Tucked away near the Nam Khan, this welcoming, family-run guesthouse is a home away from home in Luang Prabang. Rooms are beautifully decorated in tribal motifs from Passa Paa and include contemporary bathrooms, and the owners strive for zero use of disposable plastic. Substantial discounts are available for direct bookings.

Indigo House BOUTIQUE HOTEL $$
(Map p316; ☑ 071-212264; www.indigohouse. la; Th Sisavangvong; r incl breakfast US$60-70; ❄@🛜) A contemporary boutique property bookending the old-town peninsula, Indigo House has open-plan staircases leading to well-appointed rooms with a bold indigo colour scheme throughout. Breakfast is included at the excellent little Indigo Cafe downstairs, which is invitingly open to nonguests, plus there's a rooftop bar.

★ La Résidence Phou Vao LUXURY HOTEL $$$
(Map p315; ☑ 071-212530; www.belmond.com/la -residence-phou-vao-luang-prabang; r incl breakfast

US$160-460;) With its stunning hilltop grounds, seamless service and stylish wood rooms, Luang Prabang's first luxury hotel minted revivalist Indo-chic. The infinity pool reflects distant Phu Si and is flanked by a top-notch Franco-Lao restaurant. The Mekong Spa is spectacular and has won several global awards. No other hotel has such a sublime view of the city and mountains. Bliss!

Free use of bikes and free limo shuttle to the city, five minutes away.

★Satri House HISTORIC HOTEL **$$$**
(Map p316; 071-253491; www.satrihouse.com; off Th Phothisarat; r US$170-450;) This beautiful compound of villas (one is the former house of the Lao Red Prince) boasts stunning rooms with huge beds, fine furniture and a decorative flair unmatched by any other boutique in the city. Imagine pathways through lush gardens lit by statues of Indian gods, ornamental lily pools, a stunning jade swimming pool and a maze of Indo-chic corridors. The spa is terrific.

Apsara BOUTIQUE HOTEL **$$$**
(Map p316; 071-254670; www.theapsara.com; Th Kingkitsarat; r incl breakfast US$105-185;) Apsara commands fine views of the sleepy Nam Khan. Its Indochinese lobby is peppered with silk lanterns and the bar springs from an old classic film, while each of the open-plan rooms is individually designed. From its turquoise walls to its coloured glass Buddhas, everything about this place screams style. Rates plummet in low season.

Around Town

Hillside Resort RESORT **$$**
(030-5717342; www.hillsidelaos.com; r US$55-90;) Twelve kilometres south of Luang Prabang, Hillside Resort has eight bungalows and a family unit, plus plenty of activities on tap, including board games, *petang* (the Lao version of pétanque), volleyball and a swimming pool. Top set-up and exceptional value at these prices.

Lao Spirit Resort RESORT **$$**
(030-5140111; www.lao-spirit.com; r US$100-160) Lao Spirit is on the banks of the river 13km east of Luang Prabang and has a convivial collection of thatched cottages on sturdy brick stilts. Interiors have antique furniture and rosewood floors and the views are stunning. Trekking and kayaking available.

Eating

After the privations of the more remote areas in Laos your stomach will be turning cartwheels at the sheer choice and fine execution of what's on offer here. Aside from some very fine Lao restaurants, the gastro scene is largely French. Luang Prabang also has a terrific cafe culture, with bakeries at every turn.

Self-caterers should check out the **morning market** (Map p316; Ban Pakam; 5.30am-4pm Sat-Mon).

In Town

Xieng Thong Noodle-Shop LAO **$**
(Map p316; Th Sakkarin; noodle soup 15,000K; 7am-2pm) The best *kòw Ƅęeak sèn* (round rice noodles served in a broth with pieces of chicken or deep-fried crispy pork belly) in town is served from an entirely unexotic shopfront well up the peninsula. Popular with Chinese and Korean tourists, it usually runs out by 2pm.

Night Food Stalls LAO **$**
(Map p316; 6-10pm;) Food stalls emerge at dusk on a narrow street behind the tourist office with illuminated communal tables to sit at. There's no better place to taste a wide variety of cheap, well-cooked local food. There are plenty of vegetarian stalls offering a range of dishes for just 15,000K. Whole roast fish stuffed with lemongrass is a bargain at around 25,000K.

★Tamarind LAO **$$**
(Map p316; 071-213128; www.tamarindlaos.com; Th Kingkitsarat; mains 35,000-55,000K, set dinner 120,000-160,000K; 10am-10pm;) On the banks of the Nam Khan, mint-green Tamarind has created its very own strain of 'Mod Lao' cuisine. The à la carte menu features delicious sampling platters with bamboo dip, stuffed lemongrass and *meuang* (DIY parcels of noodles, herbs, fish and chilli pastes, and vegetables). There's also buffalo *láhp* and Luang Prabang sausage. Deservedly popular.

★Khaiphaen LAO **$$**
(Map p316; 030-5155221; www.tree-alliance.org/our-restaurants/khaiphaen.php; Th Sisavang Vatthana; mains 30,000-55,000K; 11am-10.30pm Mon-Sat, kitchen closes 9.30pm;) Khaiphaen is a popular training restaurant run by NGO Friends International that operates a network of inspired venues across

the region. The menu is Lao with a creative twist and includes buffalo carpaccio, five-spices pork belly and a pea and apple eggplant curry. The shakes are also creative. And do save space for the delicious desserts. Happy hour runs from 3pm to 6pm.

★Dyen Sabai LAO $$

(Map p316; 020-55104817; www.dyensabairestaurant.wordpress.com; Ban Phan Luang; mains 35,000-65,000K; 8am-11pm;) One of Luang Prabang's top destinations for fabulous Lao food. The eggplant dip and fried Mekong riverweed are as good as anywhere. Most seating is on recliner cushions in rustic open-sided pavilions. It's a short stroll across the Nam Khan bamboo bridge in the dry season or a free boat ride at other times. Two-for-one cocktails between noon and 7pm.

Bouang Asian Eatery FUSION $$

(Map p316; 020-55632600; Th Sisavangvong; mains 35,000-65,000K; 11.30am-9.30pm Mon-Sat;) This attractive eatery on the main drag puts a smile on your face with its colourful chairs, funky light fixtures and mural-covered wall. The hand-written menu of exceptional (and affordable) 'Lao revision' food includes intriguing fusions like gnocchi green curry and cinnamon-pork stew. The plating is as playful as the vibe.

Popolo INTERNATIONAL $$

(Map p316; 020-98996858; Th Khounswa; mains 35,000-85,000K; 11am-11pm;) Pitching itself as a 'cantina convivial', Popolo is the brainchild of the team from the ever-popular **Tangor** (Map p316; 071-260761; www.letangor.com; Th Sisavangvong; mains 35,000-135,000K; 11am-11pm;). Set in an old, exposed-brick building along quiet Th Khounswa, it still manages to draw a crowd to sample its creative cocktails and delicious Med-inspired menu that includes wood-fired pizzas, beef carpaccio and the Groovy Veggie, a vegan salad.

★Paste FUSION $$$

(Map p316; 071-254670; www.pastelaos.com; Apsara Hotel, Th Kingkitsarat; mains 120,000-280,000K; 11am-10pm;) Offering a Lao fusion menu inspired by the recipes of royal chef Phia Sing and sprinkled with some magic dust from Michelin-starred Thai chef Bongkoch 'Bee' Satongun, Paste brings fine dining to Luang Prabang. Try crunchy cured rice balls with sour sausage and clear curry with beef ribs, or the signature Bangkok Paste dish: yellow curry with blue swimmer crab.

There are several tasting menus for those wanting to embark on a gastronomic journey to discover the best in traditional Lao cuisine with a twist.

Manda de Laos LAO $$$

(Map p316; 071-253923; www.mandadelaos.com; 10 Th Norrassan; mains 80,000-180,000K; noon-10.30pm;) This stunning restaurant is set in a beautiful lantern-festooned garden flanking a lily pond that is pretty by day, but enchanting by night. The menu of classic Lao cuisine includes a fun DIY *lâhp* to make using a medley of herbs and spices, as well as delicious offerings such as slow-cooked duck, grilled river fish and chicken curry.

L'Elephant Restaurant FRENCH $$$

(Map p316; www.elephant-restau.com; Ban Wat Nong; mains 80,000-250,000K; 11.30am-10pm;) L'Elephant serves some of the most sophisticated cuisine in the city in a renovated villa with wooden floors, stucco pillars, stencilled ochre walls and bags of atmosphere. The Menu du Chasseur (265,000K) includes terrines, soups, duck breast and other Gallic specialities. The buffalo-steak tartare is amazing.

Around Town

Tea House TEAHOUSE $

(Map p315; 020-77773224; www.facebook.com/teahouse.luangprabang; Ban Xang Khong; mains 15,000-45,000K; 8am-5pm) Located in the weaving village of Ban Xang Khong, the Tea House specialises in organic herbal teas from all over Laos, including 400-year-old tea from Phongsaly Province and a host of health-inducing teas like rosella and turmeric. High-season tea-tasting sessions are available, as well as excellent-value Lao food with a smattering of international dishes.

Secret Pizza ITALIAN $$

(Map p315; 020-56528881; www.facebook.com/pizzasecret; Ban Nasaphanh; mains 50,000-60,000K; from 6.30pm Tue & Fri) All right, so the secret is out, but it's well worth sharing. Long the preserve of Luang Prabang residents, host Andrea prepares wood-fired pizzas, classic lasagne and homemade gnocchi in the garden of his lovely home. Profiteroles and a fine bottle of Italian wine round things off nicely. Signposted from the main road; it's at the end of Soi 3, off Rte 13.

Drinking & Nightlife

The main stretch of Th Sisavangvong northeast of the palace has plenty of drinking places, including some appealing wine bars. The main hub for drinkers is just south of Phu Si on Th Kingkitsarat. Legal closing time is 11.30pm and this is fairly strictly enforced, with the exception of a few out-of-town nightclubs and the notorious, late-night bowling – drunk bowlers, be warned not to drop the ball on your toes!

★Utopia BAR
(Map p316; www.utopialuangprabang.com; ⊙8am-11pm; 📶) Lush riverside bar with peaceful views of the Nam Khan, comfy recliner cushions, low-slung tables and leafy nooks. Chill over a fruit shake, burger or breakfast (mains 30,000K to 60,000K), play a board game or volleyball, or just lose yourself in a sea of candles come sunset. Brilliantly designed with faux Khmer ruins and creeper vines, this is surely the city's liveliest outdoor bar.

Luang Prabang Yoga (p319) runs regular classes here; check the website for the schedule.

★Icon Klub BAR
(Map p316; www.iconklub.com; Th Sisavang Vatthana; ⊙5.30-11.30pm; 📶) A beatnik boudoir more than a club, Icon pays homage to an older era and offers some of the best cocktails in town, including the devilish absinthe martini. A sculpted angel rises out of the wall and there are poetry slams, jam sessions and kick-ass tunes from Patti Smith to Tom Waits.

Chez Matt BAR
(Map p316; Th Sisavang Vatthana; ⊙7pm-late; 📶) Oxblood walls, low lights and a handsome bar glittering with polished crystal, this candlelit haunt is central and peaceful, adding a dash of upscale sophistication to the city's nocturnal landscape. With its cocktails, French and Italian wine cellar and chilled music, this makes for a good spot to dress up in your finest before going somewhere swish for dinner.

Bar 525 BAR
(Map p316; ☎071-212424; www.525cocktailsandtapas.com; Th Noradet; ⊙4.55-11.30pm; 📶) Parked down a quiet street, there's nothing retiring about this chic, urban bar. Sit outside stargazing on the terrace, inside at the long bar in low-lit style, or in the comfy lounge. Cocktails galore, glad rags, stunning photography on the walls and a sophisticated crowd. Snacks such as buffalo sliders and quesadillas are available. Prices match the ambience.

Entertainment

Garavek Storytelling THEATRE
(Map p316; ☎020-96777300; www.garavek.com; Th Khounswa; tickets 50,000K; ⊙6.30pm) *Garavek* means 'magical bird', and this enchanting hour-long show – comprising an old man dressed in tribal wear playing a haunting *khene* (Lao-style lyre) alongside an animated storyteller recalling local Lao folk tales and legends (in English) – takes your imagination on a flight of fancy. Held in an intimate 30-seat theatre. Book ahead in high season.

Moonlight Cinema CINEMA
(Map p315; www.ockpoptok.com/visit-us/whats-on; Ock Pop Tok Living Crafts Centre, 125/10 Ban Saylom; ticket incl return tuk-tuk & dinner adult/child 70,000/50,000K; ⊙6.15pm selected Fri; 📶) The latest films are shown at the Ock Pop Tok centre on selected Fridays at 7pm, screened after a 6.30pm dinner. Tuk-tuk transport is included; pickup is from in front of the **Joma Bakery Cafe** (Map p316; www.joma.biz; Th Chao Fa Ngum; mains 30,000-45,000K; ⊙7am-9pm; ❄📶) on Th Chao Fa Ngum at 6.15pm. Book via email.

Shopping

The best areas for shopping are Th Sisavangvong and the Mekong waterfront, where characterful boutiques selling local art, gilded Buddhas, handmade paper products and all manner of tempting souvenirs abound. Silver shops are attached to several houses in Ban Ho Xieng, the traditional royal silversmiths' district. And don't forget the night market, where you'll find a cornucopia of handicrafts.

★Handicraft Night Market MARKET
(Map p316; Th Sisavangvong; ⊙5.30-10pm) Every evening this tourist-oriented but highly appealing market assembles along Th Sisavangvong and is deservedly one of Luang Prabang's biggest tourist lures. Low-lit, quiet and devoid of hard selling, it has myriad traders hawking silk scarves and wall hangings, plus Hmong appliqué blankets, T-shirts, clothing, shoes, paper, silver, bags, ceramics, bamboo lamps and more.

Prices are remarkably fair but cheaper 'local' creations sometimes originate from China, Thailand or Vietnam – as a rule of thumb, if it's a scarf or bed runner, those with perfectly smooth edges are factory-made copies.

Ock Pop Tok Boutique CLOTHING, HANDICRAFTS
(Map p316; 071-254406; www.ockpoptok.com; Th Sakkarin; 8am-9pm) Ock Pop Tok works with a wide range of tribes to preserve their handicraft traditions. Fine silk and cotton scarves, chemises, dresses, wall hangings and cushion covers make perfect presents. Hop across Th Sakkarin to visit Ock Pop Tok's newer **Heritage Shop** for more classical textiles. Weaving courses (p318) are also available.

Luang Prabang Artisans ARTS & CRAFTS
(Map p316; 020-55571125; www.facebook.com/luangprabangartisanscafe; off Th Sisavangvong; 9am-6pm Mon-Sat, to 9pm Oct-Apr;) Located in a 100-year-old wooden home on a narrow lane running from the main street, this great little shop sells handicrafts like naturally dyed cushions, soft toys, and silk purses and scarves. There is a small on-site cafe for dropping after the shopping, with great juices and Lao food and a pretty shaded terrace where you can eat and relax.

Naga Creations JEWELLERY
(Map p316; 071-254400; Th Sisavangvong; 10am-10pm) One of the first jewellery shops to open in Luang Prabang, Naga Creations takes its inspiration from tribal motifs around Laos combined with an international eye for semi-precious stones from around the world. The result is some unique fusion pieces that will certainly catch the eye.

TAEC Shop ARTS & CRAFTS
(Map p316; www.taeclaos.org; Th Sakkarin; 9am-9pm) This shop sister to the TAEC (p318) museum is a safe way to buy the finest handicrafts made in Laos – be it clothes, bags or bed runners – in the knowledge they are not fakes and your purchase is directly benefiting local people. They make the perfect presents to take home.

Information

DANGERS & ANNOYANCES

Luang Prabang is an incredibly safe and intimate city, but of course there are always exceptions.

- Beware of buying drugs; you'll probably be offered them by tuk-tuk drivers, but given they may well be undercover cops and the fine is around US$500 if you get caught, it's not worth it.
- If you have a security box in your room, use it.
- Beware of leaving valuables out in hostels.

MEDICAL SERVICES

Chinese Hospital (Map p316; 071-254026; Ban Phu Mok; 24hr) Modern medical equipment and supplies, but sometimes short of trained personnel.

Pharmacie (Map p316; Th Sakkarin; 8.30am-8pm) Stocks basic medicines. On weekends, hours are variable.

Provincial Hospital (Map p315; 071-254027; Ban Phou Mock; doctor's consultation 200,000K, overnight stays 400,000K) This hospital is OK for minor problems, but for any serious illnesses consider flying to Bangkok or returning to Vientiane and neighbouring hospitals across the Thai border. Note that the hospital in Luang Prabang charges double for consultations at weekends or any time after 4pm. Doctors recommend that you arrive with a worker from your guesthouse who can help with translations.

MONEY

There are lots of ATMs in town. Several tour companies on Th Sisavangvong offer cash advances on Visa or Mastercard for around 3% commission. They'll also change money but rates tend to be poor.

BCEL (Map p316; Th Sisavangvong; 8.30am-3.30pm Mon-Fri) Changes major currencies in cash, has a 24-hour ATM and offers cash advances against Visa and Mastercard.

Lao Development Bank (Map p316; Th Wisunarat; 8.30am-3.30pm Mon-Fri) Has a 24-hour ATM.

Minipost Booth (Map p316; Th Sisavangvong; 8.30am-9pm) Changes most major currencies at fair rates and is open daily.

TOURIST INFORMATION

Provincial Tourism Department (Map p316; 071-212487; www.tourismluangprabang.org; Th Sisavangvong; 9-11.30am & 1.30-3.30pm Mon-Fri;) General information on festivals and ethnic groups. Also offers some maps and leaflets, plus information on buses or boats on a high-tech touchscreen computer. Great office run by helpful staff.

VISAS

Immigration office (Map p316; 071-212435; Th Pha Mahapatsaman; 8-11.20am & 2-4pm Mon-Fri) It's usually possible to extend a Lao visa for up to 30 extra days (20,000K per day) if you apply before it has expired. You'll need one passport-sized photo. Pickup is the following day at 3pm.

Getting There & Away

AIR

There has been a boom in international routes into the city ever since **Luang Prabang International Airport** (LPQ; ☎071-212173; www.luangprabangairport.com; 📶) got a smart new building and an expanded runway in 2013. Bangkok Airways (www.bangkokair.com) and Air Asia (www.airasia.com) both fly daily to Bangkok, while the latter also serves Kuala Lumpur. **Lao Airlines** (Map p316; ☎071-212172; www.laoairlines.com; Th Pha Mahapatsaman; ⏰8am-noon & 1-5pm Mon-Fri) serves Vientiane several times daily, as well as Pakse, Chiang Mai and Hanoi once daily. It also has frequent flights to Jinghong and Chengdu in China. Vietnam Airlines (www.vietnamairlines.com) flies to both Siem Reap (code-share with Lao Airlines) and Hanoi daily. Budget airline Scoot (www.flyscoot.com) now connects Luang Prabang to Singapore. It is easy to buy tickets through **All Lao Travel** (Map p316; ☎020-55571572, 071-253522; www.alllaoservice.com; Th Sisavangvong; ⏰8am-9pm).

BOAT

For slowboats to Pak Beng (130,000K, nine hours, 8.30am), it will likely be cheaper and easier to buy tickets from an agent in town than to take a tuk-tuk to the **navigation office** (⏰8-11am & 2-4pm) at the slowboat landing, located an inconvenient 10km north of the city in Ban Donemai. Through-tickets to Huay Xai (250,000K, two days) are also available, but you'll have to sleep in Pak Beng. This allows you to stay a little longer in Pak Beng should you like the place.

The more upscale **Luang Say Cruise** (Mekong Cruises; Map p316; ☎071-252553; www.luangsay.com; 50/4 Th Sakkarin; cruise US$303-506; ⏰8.30am-7pm) departs on two-day rides to Huay Xai from the Galao boat pier (p320) near Wat Xieng Thong. Rates include an overnight stay at the Luang Say Lodge in Pak Beng. A cheaper alternative is Shompoo Cruise (p320), a two-day cruise aboard a smart boutique boat; accommodation in Pak Beng is not included.

Fast, uncomfortable and seriously hazardous speedboats can shoot you up the Mekong to Pak Beng (190,000K, three hours) and Huay Xai (310,000K, seven hours). Boats depart when full with six or seven passengers, so your best bet is to arrive at the speedboat landing (next to the slowboat landing in Ban Donemai) at around 8am and form a group.

BUS

Predictably enough, the **Northern Bus Station** (Map p315; ☎071-252729; Rte 13) and **Southern Bus Station** (Bannaluang Bus Station; Map p315; ☎071-252066; Rte 13, Km 383) are at opposite ends of town. Several popular bus routes are duplicated by minibuses/minivans from the **Naluang minibus station** (Map p315; ☎071-212979; Rte 13), diagonally opposite the latter. Typical fares include Vientiane (150,000K, seven hours) with departures at 7.30am, 8.30am and 4pm; Vang Vieng (110,000K, five hours) at 8am, 9.30am, 10am, 2pm and 3pm; Luang Namtha (120,000K, eight hours) at 8.30am; and Nong Khiaw (55,000K, three hours) at 9.30am.

For less than double the bus fare, another option is to gather your own group and rent a comfortable six-seater minivan. Prices include photo stops and you'll get there quicker. Directly booked through the minibus station, prices are about 1,000,000K to Phonsavan or Vang Vieng and 800,000K to Nong Khiaw, including pickup from the guesthouse.

Vietnam

Head to the Naluang minibus station for buses to Dien Bien Phu (200,000K, 10 hours, leaves 6.30am) and Hanoi (350,000K, 24 hours, leaves 6pm) in Vietnam.

Getting Around

Compact Luang Prabang is easily walkable and best appreciated on foot. Bicycles come in handy for reaching some further-afield attractions, while tuk-tuks are needed for the airport, boat landings and bus stations.

TO/FROM THE AIRPORT

Taxi-vans at the airport charge 50,000K into the city centre (4km away) for one to two people. These will cost a bit more if three or four people share the ride. From town back to the airport you might pay marginally less.

BICYCLE

A satisfying way to get around is by bicycle. Numerous shops and some guesthouses have hire bikes for 15,000K to 30,000K per day.

Be careful to lock bicycles and motorbikes securely and don't leave them on the roadside overnight. Note that the peninsula's outer road is one-way anticlockwise: signs are easy to miss. Although you'll see locals flouting the rule, police will occasionally fine foreigners.

BOAT

Numerous boats to Pak Ou Caves depart between 8.30am and lunchtime; buy tickets at the easily missed little **longboat office** (Map p316; Th Khem Khong; ⏰8am-3pm). **Banana Boat Laos** (Map p316; ☎071-260654; www.bananaboatlaos.com; Ma Te Sai, Th Phommatha) offers better-organised boat trips for those who aren't worried about every last kip; boats leave from behind Wat Xieng Thong. There are also some handy **cross-river boats** (Map p316; 1-way

10,000K) connecting the old town with the rural west bank of the Mekong.

BUS

E-Bus is an electric zero-emission tuk-tuk (green and yellow) that used to circulate around the old town as a form of public transport, but now acts like a normal tuk-tuk. Prices are generally a fraction of what the old-school tuk-tuks charge, at about 10,000K for a short hop or 20,000K to the bus stations. Simply wave one down as it passes by.

The company also offers an **E-Bus Tour** (Map p315; ☎071-253899; www.laogreengroup.com; tour US$40, child under 10yr free; ⏲tours 8.30am-12.30pm & 1-4.30pm), which takes passengers around the city on a guided visit to local attractions.

CAR & MOTORCYCLE

Motorcycle rental typically costs 120,000K per day. **KPTD** (Map p316; ☎071-212077; Th Kitsarat; semi-automatic 100,000K, automatic 120,000K, 250cc dirt bikes per day US$70; ⏲8am-5pm) has a wide range of bikes available, including Honda Waves (semi-automatic), Honda Scoopy (automatic) and a thoroughly mean Honda CRF for motocross riders only. **Motolao** (Map p316; ☎020-54548449; www.motolao.com; Th Chao Fa Ngum; ⏲8.30am-5pm) rents Honda 250cc motorbikes.

SŎRNGTĂAOU

Located on the opposite side of the Mekong to Luang Prabang, about 400m up from the river, the **Chomphet sŏrngtăaou stand** (Map p315) serves local villages only.

TUK-TUK

Around town, locals often pay just 5000K for short tuk-tuk rides, but foreigners are charged a flat 20,000K per hop. To the slowboat landing or speedboat landing reckon on at least 50,000K for the vehicle.

Around Luang Prabang

North of Luang Prabang

Pak Ou Caves CAVE

(ຖ້ຳປາກອູ, Tham Ting; cave 20,000K, return boat tickets per person/boat 65,000/300,000K; ⏲boats depart 8.30-11am) Where the Nam Ou (Ou River) and Mekong River meet at Ban Pak Ou, two famous caves in the limestone cliff are crammed with myriad Buddha images. In the lower cave a photogenic group of Buddhas is silhouetted against the stunning riverine backdrop. The upper cave is a five-minute climb up steps (you'll need a torch), 50m into the rock face. Buy boat

BUSES FROM LUANG PRABANG

DESTINATION	STATION	COST (K)	DISTANCE (KM)	DURATION (HR)	DEPARTURES
Huay Xai	Northern	120,000	475	15	5.30pm
Huay Xai (VIP)	Northern	145,000	475	15	7pm
Luang Namtha	Northern	100,000	310	9	9am, 4pm
Luang Namtha (minibus)	Naluang	110,000	310	8	8.30am
Nong Khiaw	Northern	40,000	142	4	9am, 11am, 2pm
Nong Khiaw (minibus)	Naluang	55,000	142	3	9.30am
Phonsavan (minibus)	Naluang	110,000	262	8	9am
Phonsavan (ordinary/express)	Southern	95,000/105,000	262	10/9	8.30am
Sainyabuli	Southern	60,000	118	3	9am, 2pm
Sam Neua	Northern	150,000	390	17	8.30am, 5.30pm
Vang Vieng	Southern	95,000	185	7	9.30am
Vang Vieng (minibus)	Naluang	110,000	185	6	8.30am, 9.30am, 10am, 2pm, 3pm
Vieng Thong	Northern	120,000	275	10	8.30am, 5.30pm
Vientiane	Southern	110,000	384	9	10 daily btwn 6.30am & 7.30pm
Vientiane (sleeper)	Southern	150,000	384	9	8pm, 8.30pm
Vientiane (minibus)	Naluang	155,000	384	9	7am, 11am

tickets from the longboat office (p326) in Luang Prabang.

Most visitors en route to Pak Ou stop at the 'Lao Lao Village' Ban Xang Hay, famous for its whisky. The narrow footpath-streets behind the very attractive (if mostly new) wat are also full of weavers' looms, colourful fabric stalls and a few stills producing the wide range of liquors sold.

An alternative is to go by road to Ban Pak Ou (30km, around 150,000K return for a tuk-tuk), then take a motor-canoe across the river (20,000K return). Ban Pak Ou is 10km down a decent unpaved road that turns off Rte 13 near Km 405.

East of Luang Prabang

Tat Sae WATERFALL

(ຕາດແສ; 20,000K, child under 8yr free; 8am-5.30pm) The wide, multilevel cascade pools of this menthol-hued waterfall 15km southeast of Luang Prabang are a memorable sight from August to November. Unlike Tat Kuang Si, there's no single long-drop centrepiece and they dry up almost completely by February. But several year-round gimmicks keep visitors coming, notably a loop of 14 **ziplines** (020-54290848; per person 300,000K) that allows you to 'fly' around and across the falls.

Part of the attraction of a visit is getting here on a very pleasant seven-minute boat ride (20,000K per person return, 40,000K minimum) that starts from Ban Aen, a peaceful Lao village that's just 1km east of Rte 13 (turn east at Km 371.5). A 30-minute tuk-tuk from Luang Prabang costs up to 150,000K return, including a couple of hours' wait.

West of Luang Prabang

Nahm Dong Park PARK

(ສວນນ້ຳດົງ; 030-5609821; www.nahmdong.com; Nahm Dong Reservoir; entry 20,000K, 2/3 activities US$23/33, ziplining US$23;) This beautiful area of private park lies about 10km southwest of Luang Prabang in the rolling jungle-clad hills around town. Explore the forest, plunge into the waterfalls and pools here or dabble in some of the many activities on offer, including making mulberry paper, a Thai-Leu dreamcatcher or Hmong embroidery. For more of an adrenaline buzz, try the treetop walk and ziplines. There is also an excellent Lao restaurant and teahouse with a stunning valley view.

Overnight camping is also possible in the dry-season months of November to March if you want to release your inner Bear Grylls.

Kuang Si Butterfly Park NATURE RESERVE

(ສວນແມງກະເບື້ອກວາງຊີ; www.facebook.com/laos.kuang.si.butterflypark; adult/child 40,000/20,000K; 10.30am-4.30pm) Kuang Si Butterfly Park, 300m before the Kuang Si waterfall, was opened in 2014 as a breeding sanctuary for Laos' myriad butterflies. It's open to travellers, so you can wander the beautiful gardens on a tour, as well as having your feet nibbled by miniature fish at the foot spa. Great fun for kids. There's also a cafe here with special entry and cake combination tickets available.

★ **Tat Kuang Si** WATERFALL

(ຕາດກວາງຊີ; 20,000K; 8am-5.30pm) Thirty kilometres southwest of Luang Prabang, Tat Kuang Si is a many-tiered waterfall tumbling over limestone formations into a series of cool, swimmable turquoise pools; the term 'Edenic' doesn't do it justice. When you're not swinging off ropes into the water, there's a public park with shelters and picnic tables where you can eat lunch. Don't miss the free **Tat Kuang Si Bear Rescue Centre** (ສູນກູ້ໄພໝີຕາດກວາງຊີ; www.freethebears.org; Tat Kuang Si; admission incl with Tat Kuang Si ticket; 8.30am-4.30pm), where wild Asiatic moon bears, confiscated from poachers, are given a new lease of life.

Many cheap eateries line the entrance car park at the top end of the Khamu village of Ban Thapene, selling everything from local snacks to grilled chicken and fish.

Visiting Kuang Si by hired motorcycle is very pleasant now that the road here is decently paved and allows stops in villages along the way. By bicycle, be prepared for two long, steady hills to climb. A tuk-tuk from Luang Prabang costs 150,000K for one person, and 50,000K per person in a group of three, so it's best to get a group together. A private minivan will cost 350,000K.

Laos Buffalo Dairy FARM

(ຟາມນົມຄວາຍຢູ່ລາວ; 030-9690487; www.laosbuffalodairy.com; farm tours 50,000-100,000K; 9.30am-5.30pm) Set up by some Australian pioneers with no prior experience in farming, the Buffalo Dairy is now producing a range of delicious cheese and dairy products. Visitors can tour the working farm with English-speaking guides, learning how to milk a buffalo, help wash the pampered 'Ferdinand' and meet the resident rabbits. Ice cream and cakes are also on sale here, as well as a cheese platter. It is located 23km from Luang Prabang on the road to Kuang Si.

Even for visitors without children, it is a lot more interesting than you might anticipate, discovering how complicated it is to produce mozzarella from buffaloes, given the very limited amount of milk they produce. Nonvisitors can also stop at the ice-cream kiosk on the main road, which sells some mouthwatering local flavours such as lemongrass or ginger.

The buffaloes are mainly rented from local farmers who had never previously used their milk. Some of the income goes towards farmer and animal health benefits, as well as free English lessons for local students.

Green Jungle Park PARK

(ສວນປາດົງຊຽງ; ☎071-253899; www.laogreengroup.com; Ban Pakleuang; park entry US$3, ziplining & ropes courses US$30-65, trekking US$35, return boat transfer from Luang Prabang 10,000K; ⊙9am-4.30pm) Thirty-two kilometres west of the city, this slice of natural paradise reclaimed from a rubbish dump uses the forest and a stunning cascade as its backdrop for a spectacular cat's cradle of **ziplines** (900m), monkey bridges and rope courses. Also here are a cafe, flower gardens and natural swimming pools, an organic produce market and an elephant-viewing area where ex-logging jumbos can socialise.

To reach the park, you catch the comfy boat from behind the Royal Palace in Luang Prabang; you'll ride downriver for 30 minutes, then be taxied the rest of the way by road.

Pha Tad Ke Botanical Garden GARDENS

(ສວນພຶດສາຊາດຜາຕັດແກ; Map p316; ☎071-261000; www.pha-tad-ke.com; adult/child US$25/10; ⊙8am-6pm Thu-Tue) As relaxing as a trip to the spa, this botanical garden, opened in 2017 as the first in Laos, is a serene spot to read, take a stroll or perfect some yoga poses. The entry price, although steep, includes an orchid talk (11am or 3pm), a one-hour bamboo handicraft workshop (10am or 2pm) and free herbal-tea tastings in a cafe overlooking a lotus pond.

Boats depart from a dock in Ban Wat That (across from Pha Tad Ke's downtown reception office) between 9am and 4pm; it's a 15-minute ride down the Mekong to the park.

NORTHERN LAOS

Whether it's for trekking, cycling, kayaking, ziplining or a family homestay, a visit to northern Laos is for many the highlight of their trip. Dotted about are unfettered, dense forests home to big cats, gibbons and a cornucopia of animals, with a well-established ecotourism infrastructure to take you into their heart.

In the north you will also find a tapestry of vividly attired tribes unlike anywhere else in Laos.

Here the Land of a Million Elephants morphs into the land of a million hellish bends, and travel is not for the faint-hearted, as roads twist and turn through towering mountain ranges and serpentine river valleys.

Most northern towns are functional places, rebuilt after wholesale bombing during the 20th-century Indochina wars. But visitors aren't here for the towns; it's all about the rural life. River trips are a wonderful way to discover the bucolic scenery at a more languid pace.

Xieng Khuang & Hua Phan Provinces

Long and winding roads run in seemingly endless ribbons across these green, sparsely populated northeastern provinces towards the mysterious Plain of Jars and the fascinating Vieng Xai Caves. Both are truly intriguing places to visit if you're en route to or from Vietnam. Those with the time can add stops in Nong Khiaw and Vieng Thong. The latter is a gateway to the Nam Et/Phou Louey National Park and its 'tiger treks'. Almost anywhere else in either province is completely off the tourist radar.

The altitude, averaging more than 1000m, ensures a climate that's neither too hot in the hot season nor too cold in the cool season. In December and January, a sweater or jacket is appropriate at night and in the early morning, when seas of cloud fill the populated valleys and form other-worldly scenes for those looking down from passes or peaks.

Phonsavan

☎061 / POP 49,000

Phonsavan (ໂພນສະຫວັນ) is a popular base from which to explore the Plain of Jars. The town itself is very spread out, with its

Phonsavan

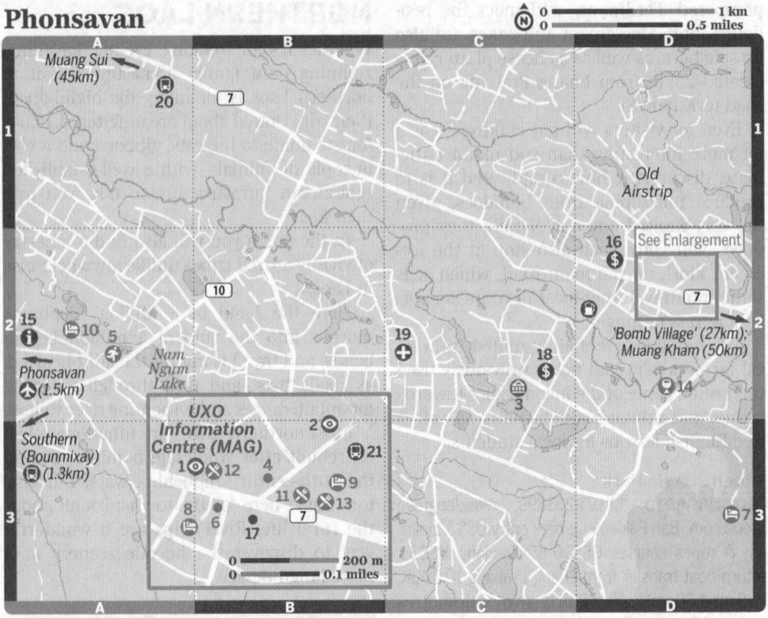

Phonsavan

Top Sights
1 UXO Information Centre (MAG) B3

Sights
2 Fresh Food Market B3
3 Xieng Khouang Provincial Museum C2
Xieng Khouang UXO-Survivors' Information Centre .... (see 1)

Activities, Courses & Tours
4 Lao Falang Travel Service B3
5 Lone Buffalo A2
6 Sousath Travel B3

Sleeping
7 Auberge Plaine des Jarres D3
8 Jennida Guesthouse II A3
9 Kong Keo Guesthouse B3
10 Pukyo Guesthouse A2

Eating
11 Bamboozle Restaurant & Bar B3
12 Cranky-T Café & Bar B3
Lao Falang Restaurant .... (see 4)
13 Nisha Restaurant B3

Drinking & Nightlife
14 Barview D2

Information
15 Xieng Khuang Tourist Office A2

Transport
16 BCEL D2
17 Lao Airlines B3
18 Lao Development Bank C2
19 Lao-Mongolian Friendship Hospital C2
20 Northern Bus Station A1
21 Phoukham Garden Minibus & Bus Station B3

two parallel main boulevards stretching for about 3km east–west. Fortunately, a very handy concentration of hotels, restaurants and tour agents is crammed into a short central 'strip'. More shops, markets and facilities can be found along Rte 7. But the town is best appreciated from the surrounding hills, several of which are pine-clad and topped with small resorts. Keep an eye out too for wooden powder-blue Hmong cottages on the mountain roads with firewood neatly stacked outside.

The region has long been a centre of Phuan language and culture (part of the Tai-Kadai family). There's also a strong Vietnamese presence.

Sights

About 1km apart at the southern edge of town are two hilltop **memorials** (open sunrise to sunset) to Pathet Lao and Vietnamese soldiers lost in the war.

★UXO Information Centre (MAG) CULTURAL CENTRE

(ສູນຂໍ້ມູນກຽວກັບລະເບີດທີ່ບໍ່ທັນແຕກ; ☎061-211010; www.maginternational.org/laos; donations encouraged; ⏱10am-8pm) FREE Decades after America's Secret War on Laos, unexploded bombs and mines remain a devastating problem throughout this region. Visit the thought-provoking UXO Information Centre, run by British organisation MAG (Mines Advisory Group), which has been helping to clear Laos' unexploded ordnance (UXO) since 1994. The centre's information displays underline the scale of the bomb drops, and there are also examples of (defused) UXO to ponder. Donations are encouraged: US$15 pays for the clearing of around 10 sq metres and a commemorative T-shirt.

Late-afternoon screenings show the powerful documentaries *Bomb Harvest* (4.30pm; www.redlampfilms.com/films-2/bomb-harvest-2), *Surviving the Peace* (5.50pm) and *Bombies* (6.30pm; www.bullfrogfilms.com/catalog/bombie.html). They are distressing but important, as they show the full scale of the trauma, from footage of US bombers in action to the ongoing casualties of their horrific legacy.

Xieng Khouang UXO-Survivors' Information Centre CULTURAL CENTRE

(ສູນຂໍ້ມູນກຽວກັບຜູ້ລອດໄພຈາກລະເບີດທີ່ບໍ່ທັນແຕກ ແຂວງຊຽງຂວາງ; www.laos.worlded.org; donations encouraged; ⏱8am-4pm Mon-Fri) FREE This UXO information centre and colourful, upbeat shop sells silk laptop bags, purses and handicrafts made by UXO survivors. Aside from displays including bomb parts and harrowing stories of recent victims, there's also a wealth of information on the Secret War and the different kinds of UXO that still present a danger in Laos today. Ask to see the video *Surviving Cluster Bombs*. Note that 90% of your donations go towards the treatment of UXO survivors.

Xieng Khouang Provincial Museum MUSEUM

(ຫໍພິພິດຕະພັນແຂວງຊຽງຂວາງ; 15,000K; ⏱9-11.30am & 1.30-4pm Tue-Sun) One of the most interesting provincial museums in Laos, Xieng Khouang Provincial Museum was funded with help from the German government. Downstairs are lots of detailed presentations about the Plain of Jars and the ancient history of the Xieng Khuang kingdom. Upstairs you'll find displays on more recent Lao history and the US bombing campaign that so devastated Xieng Khuang Province. Also includes some fascinating exhibits on the province's different ethnic communities.

Tours

Several agents on the main drag and virtually every guesthouse will be ready to slot you into a one-day Plain of Jars tour visiting the three main sites. The going rate is 150,000K including a noodle-soup lunch and entry fees. This price is contingent on there being at least seven fellow passengers.

Other advertised tours include trips to places such as Muang Khoun, Tham Piu or nearby hot springs, but these rarely garner enough customers for prices to be competitive. Try gathering your own group.

★Sousath Travel TOURS

(☎020-22967213; rasapet_lao@yahoo.com; Rte 7; ⏱8am-8pm) Sousath is the man who helped open the Plain of Jars to tourists, and the trips run by his son, Mr Nouds, are the most informative in town. Extremely knowledgeable about the region, Mr Nouds can also organise tours of the Ho Chi Minh Trail, homestays in Hmong villages and multi-day treks (including the Phakeo Trek).

For war obsessives he can plan trips to Long Tien, the clandestine runway in the Saisombun jungle created by the CIA during the Secret War. He also rents bikes (20,000K) and scooters (manual/automatic 80,000/100,000K).

Lao Falang Travel Service ADVENTURE

(☎020-23305614; Rte 7; 1-day all-inclusive trip US$150) Run by a dependable Italian guy, this outfit operates multiday and one-day motorbike tours, of which 70% to 85% are spent off-road (depending on your confidence). A one-day tour typically includes Jar Site 1, the Russian Tank and Muang Khoun. Dinner is included at the excellent **Lao Falang Italian restaurant** (mains 50,000-120,000K; ⏱7am-4pm & 5-10.30pm; 📶✍). Experienced guides ensure you don't go beyond your comfort zone.

Sleeping

Rooms in Phonsavan range from very basic guesthouse digs to midrange hotel rooms. Booking ahead is not usually necessary, nor is air-conditioning. There are also several smarter lodge-style hotels spread around town, including some imperiously perched atop pine-clad hills.

In Town

★Kong Keo Guesthouse GUESTHOUSE $
(020-285858; dm 50,000K, d in outside block 80,000K, bungalows 120,000K;) Run by the charming and extremely knowledgeable Kong, the seven-berth dorm is slightly cramped, but the outdoor block has large, clean rooms with mint-green walls and private bathrooms. More spacious are the six bungalows dotted about the garden. The UXO-decorated restaurant-bar has occasional barbecues, and Kong runs highly recommended tours to the Plain of Jars.

Jennida Guesthouse II GUESTHOUSE $
(020-28590001; d & tw 80,000K;) Don't be put off by the surreal sight of the Snow White and the Seven Dwarfs statues in the courtyard car park, as the spacious 42 rooms here are great value for money. The room decoration is tidy if simple and all rooms include a ceiling fan and attached bathroom. There is a handy minimart out front for essential supplies.

Around Town

Pukyo Guesthouse GUESTHOUSE $
(020-59556276; pukyoguesthouse@gmail.com; d & tw 100,000K;) Almost more a homestay than a guesthouse, this pad is run by a friendly Belgian-Lao couple. While the location is a little inconvenient for downtown, it's handy for the airport and the owners will run guests into town to explore the restaurants and bars. Super-clean and spacious rooms, plus a little cafe-bar in the main house.

Auberge Plaine des Jarres LODGE $$
(020-23533333; auberge_plainjars@yahoo.fr; d & tw incl breakfast US$40-50;) Perched on a pine-clad hilltop on the outskirts of town, this atmospheric lodge feels more alpine than Lao. Rooms are set in individual cabins and include simple touches like Lao textiles and a log fireplace in winter. The bar-restaurant is a welcome retreat on a cool winter night.

Eating & Drinking

Phonsavan has a sprinkling of quality Western restaurants. For a more local touch, regional specialities include *hét wâi* (wild matsutake mushrooms) or *nok qen dqwng* (fermented swallows); try the **fresh food market** (6am-5pm). In case you want to avoid a surprise, note that several Vietnamese restaurants serve *thit chó* (dog).

Nisha Restaurant INDIAN $
(020-98266023; Rte 7; meals 20,000-40,000K; 7am-10pm;) Cream-interiored Nisha is set in a simple shophouse, but the real colour is found in its excellent cuisine. The menu includes all the usual suspects like tikka masala and rogan josh, curries and a wide range of vegetarian options. However, it's the perfect application of spice and the freshness of the food that'll keep you coming back.

Cranky-T Café & Bar FUSION $$
(030-5388003; www.facebook.com/CrankyTLaos; Rte 7; mains 35,000-130,000K; 7am-10.30pm Mon-Sat, to 5pm Sun, happy hour 4-7pm;) Cranky-Ts has a stylish exposed-brick and red-wine-coloured interior, with the eponymous owner creating mouth-watering salads, sashimi, smoked-salmon crêpes and hearty fare like NZ sirloin with mash to fill you up after trekking the jar sites. Add to this cinnamon muffins, brownie cheesecake and a good selection of cocktails (35,000K), and you may spend much of the day here.

Bamboozle Restaurant & Bar INTERNATIONAL $$
(030-9523913; www.facebook.com/BamboozleRestaurantBar; Rte 7; meals 20,000-60,000K; 7-10.30am & 3.30-10.30pm, kitchen closes 9.30pm;) True to its name, with bamboo walls plus pretty lanterns strung from its ceiling, Bamboozle dishes up thin-crust pizza, salads, pasta dishes, good-sized cheeseburgers and flavoursome Lao cuisine. Add to this chilled beers and a rock-and-roll soundtrack and it's a winner. A percentage of the profits goes towards the **Lone Buffalo** (020-77159566; www.facebook.com/lonebuffalo; Hwy 1D), which supports the town's youth.

Barview BAR
(8am-11pm) Try this simple shack for sunset beers over the rice-paddy fields. Locals gather here to play guitars and munch on barbecued meat.

Information

DANGERS & ANNOYANCES

Don't underestimate the dangers of unexploded ordnance (UXO) in this most heavily bombed of provinces.

MEDICAL SERVICES

Lao-Mongolian Friendship Hospital (☎ 061-312166) May be able to assist with minor health concerns.

MONEY

Currency exchange is available at **Lao Development Bank** (☎ 061-312188; ⊙ 8.30am-3.30pm Mon-Fri), at **BCEL** (☎ 061-213297; Rte 7; ⊙ 8.30am-3.30pm Mon-Fri) and from several travel agents. There are three ATMs along Rte 7.

TOURIST INFORMATION

Xieng Khuang Tourist Office (☎ 061-312217; www.xiengkhouangtourism.com; ⊙ 8-11.30am & 1.30-4pm) Located in the middle of nowhere near the airport, this helpful office has English-speaking staff, a small exhibit and souvenirs recycled from war junk. Pick up free maps for Phonsavan and Xieng Khuang district, plus the brochure *Hidden Stories of Xieng Khoung* for alternative ideas on things to do aside from the jar sites.

Many tours include a stop here on the way to the jars to view the pile of war remnants stored behind the office.

Getting There & Away

Airline and bus timetables usually call Phonsavan 'Xieng Khuang', the name of the province, even though that was originally the name for nearby Muang Khoun.

AIR

Lao Airlines (☎ 020-22228658; www.laoairlines.com) (from US$75) and Lao Skyway (from 399,000K) both have daily connections between Phonsavan (Xieng Khuang) Airport and Vientiane. Lao Airlines operates a weekly flight to/from Luang Prabang in peak season. The airport is about 3km west of the town centre.

BUS

Longer-distance bus tickets pre-sold by travel agencies typically cost around 20,000K to 40,000K more than standard fares but include a transfer to the confusingly named **Northern Bus Station** (☎ 030-5170148), located 4km west of the centre, also sometimes known as the Provincial Bus Station. From here Vietnam-bound buses depart to Vinh (160,000K, 11 hours) at 6.30am on Tuesday, Thursday, Friday and Sunday, continuing seasonally on Mondays to Hanoi (320,000K). For Vientiane (110,000K, 11 hours) there are air-con buses at 7am, 8am, 10.30am, 4.30pm and 6.30pm, and a VIP bus (130,000K) at 8.30pm. These all pass through Vang Vieng, to where there's an additional 7.30am departure (95,000K). The sleeper here (150,000K) leaves at 8pm. For Luang Prabang (10 hours) both minivans (95,000K) and VIP buses (120,000K) depart at 8.30am and 6pm. There's an 8am bus to Sam Neua (80,000K, eight to 10 hours) and a 6pm sleeper (100,000K), plus two Vientiane–Sam Neua buses passing through.

The **Southern (Bounmixay) Bus Station** (Hwy 1D), 4km south of town, has a 6.45am bus every other day to Savannakhet (150,000K) that continues on to Pakse (170,000K).

Phoukham Garden Minibus and Bus Station (☎ 020-99947072; Th Xaysana; ⊙ 7am-8pm), in the east-central side of town (by the tourist strip), has minibuses leaving at 8.30am for Luang Prabang (110,000K), Vang Vieng (100,000K) and Nong Khiaw (150,000K), and 5am, 8am and 5pm minibuses for Vientiane (130,000K). There's also a VIP bus for Vientiane (130,000K) leaving from here at 7pm.

These are the three main terminals, though competing bus stations sprout like beanstalks in Phonsavan, so there may be alternative options for the destinations listed above.

Getting Around

Tuk-tuks cost from 15,000K for a short hop to about 30,000K to the airport. The best place to find them is around the Phoukham Garden Minibus & Bus Station. Lao Falang Travel Service (p331) rents 100cc and 150cc motorbikes (100,000K to 150,000K), ideal for reaching a selection of jar sites. Fill up at the petrol station in town.

Chauffeured six-seater vans or 4WDs can be chartered through the minibus station or most guesthouses; you're looking at US$200 to Sam Neua or Luang Prabang.

Plain of Jars

Mysterious giant stone jars of unknown ancient origin are scattered over hundreds of hilly square kilometres around Phonsavan, giving the area the misleading name of Plain of Jars (ທົ່ງໄຫຫິນ). Remarkably, little is known about the Austro-Asiatic civilisation that created them, although archaeologists estimate they date from the Southeast Asian iron age (500 BC to AD 200) and were likely used for elaborate burial rituals.

Smaller jars have long since been carted off by collectors, but around 2500 larger jars, jar fragments and 'lids' remain. As the region was carpet-bombed throughout the Indochina wars, it's miraculous that so many artefacts survived. Only nine of the 90 recorded jar sites have so far been cleared of UXO, and then only within relatively limited areas. These sites, and their access paths, are delineated by easily missed red-and-white marker stones: remain vigilant.

Sites 1, 2 and 3 form the bases of most tour loops.

Phonsavan is the closest base from which to take day trips here. For food, your best bet is to head back to Phonsavan.

Sights

Jar Site 1 ARCHAEOLOGICAL SITE

(Thong Hai Hin; 15,000K) The biggest and most accessible, Site 1 of the Plain of Jars features over 300 jars relatively close-packed on a pair of hilly slopes pocked with bomb craters. The biggest jar, **Hai Jeuam**, weighs around 25 tonnes, stands more than 2.5m high and is said to have been the mythical victory cup of Khun Jeuam. The bare, hilly landscape is appealing, although the views of Phonsavan airport seem discordant. There is a cafe, a gift shop and toilets near the entrance.

Pay your entrance fee at the small **Plain of Jars Visitor Centre**, which offers an informative museum-style display on the history of the jars and theories relating to their use.

Plain of Jars

Jar Site 2 ARCHAEOLOGICAL SITE

(Hai Hin Phu Salato; 10,000K) Site 2 of the Plain of Jars is a pair of hillocks divided by a shallow gully that forms the access lane. This rises 700m from the ticket desk in what becomes a muddy slither in wet conditions. To the left, in thin woodlands, look for a cracked stone urn through which a tree has managed to grow. To the right another set of jars sits on a grassy knoll with panoramas of layered hills, paddies and cow fields. Cold drinks are available at the ticket booth.

Jar Site 3 ARCHAEOLOGICAL SITE

(Hai Hin Lat Khai; 10,000K) The 150-jar Site 3 of the Plain of Jars sits on a hillside in pretty woodland near Ban Lat Khai village. The access road to Lat Khai leads east beside a motorbike-repair hut just before Ban Xiang Di (Ban Siang Dii). The ticket booth is beside a simple local restaurant that offers *fĕr* (rice noodles; 30,000K). The jars are accessed via a little wooden footbridge and an attractive 10-minute walk (or wade, depending on the season) through rice fields.

Getting There & Away

All three main jar sites can be visited by rented motorbike from Phonsavan in around five hours, while Site 1 is within bicycle range. Site 1 is just 8km southwest of central Phonsavan, 2.3km west of the Muang Khoun road (1D): turn at the signed junction in Ban Hay Hin. For Sites 2 and 3, turn west off the Muang Khoun road just past Km 8. Follow the paved road for 10km/14km to find the turnings for Sites 2/3, then follow muddy tracks for 0.5/1.8km, respectively.

Alternatively, sign up the night before to join one of several regular guided minibus tours. It really is worth the extra money to hear the war stories and get some context on both the jars and their creators. Most throw in a noodle-soup lunch at Site 2 or 3 and a quick stop to see the lumpy, rusting remnant of an armoured vehicle in a roadside copse at Ban Nakho: its nickname, the 'Russian Tank', exaggerates the appeal.

Vieng Thong

064 / POP 4000

The original name of Vieng Thong (ວຽງທອງ) was Muang Hiam, a Tai Daeng word meaning 'watch out', and this name still appears on most road markers. Back when tigers roamed the surrounding forests it was relevant, but these days only a handful may survive – or indeed none at all – in the enormous Nam Et/Phou Louey National Park (p336), on whose vast doorstep Vieng Thong

LOCAL KNOWLEDGE

A JARRING SITE

Lao folklore tells of a race of giants ruled by a powerful king named Khun Jeuam who ordered his people to make jars here to brew and store rice wine for celebrations of their victories on the battlefield. Modern archaeologists believe that the bone fragments, beads and burnt charcoal found in and around the jumbo-sized jars suggest that they were instead used as part of an elaborate funeral ceremony (for standard-sized people). French archaeologist Madeleine Colani was the first to float this theory, in the early 1930s, though it wasn't given too much credence until further archaeological research could begin anew in the 1990s once the region was finally safe to visit. Alternatively looted and carpet bombed over the years, very little remains today of the burial offerings that may have once been hidden in these rolling hills.

There are believed to be nearly 90 recorded jar sites in Xiangkhouang Province, each with as many as 300 stone ruins between 1m and 2.5m tall. Researchers think the sites may have been chosen for their magnetic properties, as the jars seem to attract lightning (while the local airport in Phonsavan appears to have an abysmal record of plane crashes!). Some 80% of the jars were carved from quarried sandstone, with the rest made of granite, limestone or conglomerate rock. Archaeologists have found smaller jar sights in Assam, India, southern China and Vietnam, suggesting that the Austro-Asiatic people who created these stone structures may have migrated along a trade route across Asia, reaching the height of their civilisation when they hit Laos.

The first jar sites didn't open to the public until 1992, following a bootstraps effort by locals to remove UXO. Six years later, Unesco initiated a decades-long project to safeguard the archaeological ruins, promote safe (and sustainable) tourism, and get the site on the World Heritage list, on which it was inscribed in 2019. Today, the Plain of Jars is the most popular attraction in the region.

sits. While the town is forgettable, the park is well worth a visit, which can be arranged through the park office at Vieng Thong Visitors' Center.

Vieng Thong has a clutch of guesthouses and food stalls, and a few restaurant stands at the bus station offer varied delicacies such as frog-on-a-stick to passing travellers. If you're travelling between Nong Khiaw and Sam Neua, stopping here for a night makes the 10-hour journey more palatable. The dazzling green rice fields around town are photogenic and short walks or bicycle rides can take you to pretty Tai Daeng, Hmong and Khamu villages.

★Nam Nern Night Safari SAFARI

(www.namet.org/namnern; night safaris per person in group of 2 & up 1,500,000K) Nam Nern Night Safari is a 24-hour, boat-based tour in the Nam Et/Phou Louey National Park. Highlights of the trip include a night-time boat ride 'spotlighting' for tigers, gaurs and white-cheeked gibbons. Seeing a tiger is very unlikely but there's hope of spotting sambar and barking deer. Sleeping is at an ecolodge overlooking the Nam Nern. The price includes a fireside dinner.

Book through the Nam Et/Phou Louey National Park office (p338) located in Vieng Thong.

The Nests WILDLIFE WATCHING

(www.namet.org/wp/en; 2-day trek per person in group of 2 & up 1,500,000K, 3-day trek per person in group of 2 & up 2,100,000K) The Nam Et/Phou Louey National Park office (p338) offers the chance to go on The Nests: two- and three-day treks with accommodation in cosy spherical baskets hanging from trees. This also involves wildlife-viewing from an observation tower at Poung Nied salt lick, which attracts animals such as the rare sambar deer.

Dorkkhounthong Guesthouse GUESTHOUSE $

(☎064-810017; d & tw 50,000-80,000K; ❄) The most appealing of Vieng Thong's limited options, this guesthouse is located right in the centre of the small town. Very clean, decent-sized rooms have hot showers, netted windows and comfortable beds. There's a pleasant 1st-floor sitting area and attractive views across riverside fields from the rear terrace.

DON'T MISS

NAM ET/PHOU LOUEY NATIONAL PROTECTED AREA

In the vast **Nam Et/Phou Louey National Park** (ປ່າສະຫງວນແຫ່ງຊາດນ້ຳແອດ-ພູເລີຍ), rare civets, Asian golden cats, river otters, white-cheeked crested gibbons and the utterly unique Laos warty newt *(Paramesotriton laoensis)* share 4200 sq km of relatively pristine forests. Approximately half of the park is an inaccessible core zone. The remaining area includes 98 ethnic-minority hamlets. Two-day wildlife-watching excursions have been pioneered to the park's remote Nam Nern field station, a roadless former village site where a campsite and surrounding walking trails have been professionally cleared of unexploded ordnance (UXO).

Trips are organised by the **Nam Et/Phou Louey National Park office** (☎064-810008; www.namet.org; ⏱8am-noon & 1-4.30pm Mon-Fri) in Vieng Thong, and contacting it well in advance is advisable since there's a limit of two departures per week. Night safaris cost 1,200,000K per person for a group of four, and include guides, cooks, food and camping equipment, with a significant proportion of your fee going into village development funds. The price also includes the 90-minute boat ride from Ban Sonkhua, around 50km east of Vieng Thong on Rte 1.

Dokchampa Guesthouse GUESTHOUSE $
(☎064-810005; d with/without bathroom 60,000/40,000K; 📶) This small guesthouse has basic rooms with hot-water showers, mosquito nets and squat toilets. The owners offer a few traveller-friendly services such as free wi-fi and bicycles for rent (30,000K per day).

Getting There & Away

Westbound buses arrive from Sam Neua around noon, continuing after lunch to Nong Khiaw (60,000K, five hours), Pak Mong and Luang Prabang (130,000K, nine hours). Eastbound, the best choice for Sam Neua is the 7am minibus (40,000K, six hours), as the two Sam Neua through-services (from Luang Prabang/Vientiane) both travel the road largely by night.

The bus station is 300m along Rte 6 from the market at the eastern edge of town.

Vieng Xai

☎064 / POP 4000

The thought-provoking 'bomb-shelter caves' of Vieng Xai (ວຽງໄຊ) are set amid dramatic karst outcrops and offer a truly inspirational opportunity to learn about northern Laos' painful 20th-century history. Imagine Vang Vieng, but with a compelling historical twist instead of happy tubing. Or think of it as Ho Chi Minh City's Cu Chi Tunnels cast in stone. The caves were shrouded in secrecy until they were opened to the world in 2007.

Many of Vieng Xai's cave sites still retain visible signs of their wartime roles, making the complex one of the world's most complete revolutionary bases to have survived from the Cold War period.

Sights

★ **Vieng Xai Caves** CAVE
(ຖ້ຳວຽງໄຊ; ☎064-315022; entry incl audio tour 60,000K, bicycle rental per tour/day 15,000/30,000K; ⏱9am-noon & 1-4pm) Joining a truly fascinating 18-point tour is the only way to see Vieng Xai's seven most important war-shelter cave complexes, set in beautiful gardens backed by fabulous karst scenery. A local guide unlocks each site while an audio guide gives a wealth of first-hand background information and historical context. The **Kaysone Phomvihane Cave** still has its air-circulation pump in working order and is the most memorable of the caves.

Tours leave from the cave office at 9am and 1pm. If you want a tour outside of these two times, you'll have to pay a 50,000K surcharge per group.

Tham Nọk Ann CAVE
(ຖ້ຳນົກແອ່ນ, Nok Ann Cave; 10,000K; ⏱8am-5pm) Tham Nok Ann is a soaring, well-lit cavern through which a river passes beneath awesome rock formations. It's dripping, creepy and very atmospheric, with a set of stairs leading up to an adjacent cave complex that once housed a Vietnamese military hospital. You could previously take a boat trip deeper into the cave, like a mini Tham Kong Lor experience with some huge jellyfish-like rock formations visible, but in recent years it has only been open for viewing on foot due to limited visitor numbers.

Look for a signpost on the main road about 5km before Vieng Xai and follow the small track around to the right until it dead-ends at an entrance booth and small suspension bridge.

Sleeping & Eating

There isn't a great selection of eating establishments in Vieng Xai and many have run out of food by 8pm. By 9pm the town is in hibernation. Several *fĕr* shops in the market serve rice and cheap noodle dishes until around 5pm.

Sabaidee Odisha (☎020-55577202; mains 15,000-45,000K; ⏰7am-9pm;) is a favourite for its fabulous Indian fare.

Sailomyen Guesthouse GUESTHOUSE **$**
(☎020-56596688; d 70,000K;) Built on stilts atop a serene artificial lake with a communal balcony that's perfect for daydreaming. The rooms may be small, with wonky carpeted floors, but there are hot showers, fans and mosquito nets. And did we mention the view? Picture jungle-clad hills with watercolour reflections.

Chitchareune Hotel HOTEL **$$**
(☎030-5150458; d & tw 120,000K, ste 250,000K;) This white monolith sits immediately south of Vieng Xai market and has clean air-con rooms with above-average furniture and stylish en suites. The parking lot doubles as the bus station for Vieng Xai so it is a convenient spot for arrival or departure.

Information

Vieng Xai Cave Tourist Office (☎064-315022; ⏰8-11.30am & 1-4pm) Around 1km south of the market, the cave office organises all cave visits, rents bicycles and has maps and a useful information board. There's even a display case full of old Lenin busts and assorted socialist iconograpy.

Getting There & Away

Getting to Vieng Xai requires a transfer in Sam Neua, where the **main bus station** (☎064-314270) is on a hilltop 1.2km south of the central monument, just off the Vieng Thong road. From here buses leave to Vientiane (190,000K, 20 hours) via Phonsavan (100,000K, 10 hours) at 10am, 1pm, 3pm and 5pm. An additional 7.30am Vientiane bus (190,000K) goes via Vieng Thong (60,000K, five hours), Nong Khiaw (140,000K, 12 hours) and Luang Prabang (150,000K, 17 hours). There are also daily minibuses to Luang

LOCAL KNOWLEDGE

UXO & WAR JUNK

During the Indochina wars, Laos earned the dubious distinction of becoming the most heavily bombed nation per capita in world history. Xieng Khuang Province was especially hard hit and even today, innumerable scraps of combat debris remain. Much of it is potentially deadly unexploded ordnance (UXO), including mortar shells, white phosphorous canisters (used to mark bomb targets) and assorted bombs. Some of the most problematic UXO comes from cluster bombs, 1.5m-long torpedo-shaped packages of evil whose outer metal casing was designed to split open lengthwise in mid-air, scattering 670 tennis-ball-sized bomblets ('bombies') over a 5000-sq-metre area. Once disturbed, a bombie would explode, projecting around 30 steel pellets like bullets, killing anyone within a 20m radius. Over 40 years after bombing ceased, almost one person a day is still injured or killed by UXO in Laos, 40% of them children. Tens of millions of bombies remain embedded in the land, causing an ever-present danger to builders, farmers and especially young children, who fatally mistake them for toys. And for impoverished villagers, the economic temptation to collect UXO to sell as scrap metal has caused numerous fatalities. Despite valiant ongoing clearance efforts, at current rates it would take an estimated 150 years to deal with the problem.

Cluster-bomb casings, which are not themselves explosive, have meanwhile found a wide range of more positive new uses. In some places you can see them reused as architectural features, feeding troughs, pots for growing spring onions or simply as ornaments around houses or hotels.

If you find any war debris, don't be tempted to touch it. Even if it appears to be an exhibit in a collection, beware that some hotels display war junk that's never been properly defused and might remain explosive. Even if it isn't live and dangerous, the Lao legal code makes it illegal to trade in war leftovers of any kind. Purchase, sale or theft of any old weaponry can result in a prison term of between six months and five years.

GETTING TO VIETNAM: NAM SOI TO NA MEO

Getting to the border If going to the Nam Soi (Vietnam)/Na Meo (Laos) border crossing (Km 175; 7am to 11.30am and 1.30pm to 5.30pm), the easiest transport option is to take the daily direct bus (sometimes minibus) between Sam Neua and Thanh Hoa (180,000K, 10 hours) that passes close to Vieng Xai but doesn't enter town. It departs twice daily at 8am and 10am. Prepurchase your ticket at the main bus station to avoid overcharging. 'Through tickets' to Hanoi still go via Thanh Hoa with a change of bus.

At the border Westbound, note that the Lao border post isn't a town. There are a few simple restaurant shacks but no accommodation and no waiting transport apart from the bus travelling from Thanh Hoa to Sam Neua, which passes by around 2pm.

Lao visas (p398) are available on arrival at this border but Vietnamese visas are not, so plan ahead if heading east.

Moving on Once in Thanh Hoa, there's a night train to Hanoi departing at 1.20am and arriving very early (around 5am). Alternatively, there is a morning train at 8.25am (arriving at 12.30pm). Tickets should cost US$14 but foreigners are often asked for significantly more.

Prabang (130,000K to 150,000K, 15 hours) at 7.30am and 4pm. Finally there is a Vieng Thong bus (50,000K) at 7.30am and 4pm.

Xam Neua's **Nathong bus station** is 1km beyond the airport on the Vieng Xai road at the easternmost edge of town (a tuk-tuk here costs 20,000K). There is now just one daily bus to Vieng Xai (20,000K, one hour), which leaves at 9.30am.

From Vieng Xai, there is just one daily bus to Sam Neua (20,000K, one hour), leaving at approximately 3pm from the bus station. Buses between Sam Neua and Thanh Hoa (one bus daily to each) can be flagged down on Rte 6. The bus for Thanh Hoa (180,000K) should pass by around 8.45am, while the bus for Sam Neua (20,000K) passes through around 4pm.

Visiting Vieng Xai by **rented taxi from Sam Neua** (☎020-5627510, 020-55982644; taxi rental to Vieng Xai Caves one-way/return 150,000/250,000K) costs around 250,000K per vehicle.

Muang Ngoi District

Tracts of green mountains are attractive wherever you go in northern Laos. But at Nong Khiaw and tiny Muang Ngoi Neua, the contours do something altogether more dramatic. At both places, vast karst peaks and towering cliffs rear dramatically out of the Nam Ou (Ou River), creating jaw-droppingly beautiful scenes. Both villages make convenient rural getaways from Luang Prabang and are accessible by riverboat from Muang Khua. Nong Khiaw also makes an excellent rural rest stop between Luang Prabang and Vieng Thong or Sam Neua.

Nong Khiaw

☎071 / POP 4000

Nong Khiaw (ໜອງຂຽວ) is a traveller's haven in the truest sense, offering pampering, good food, decent accommodation and bags of activities with established adventure-tour operators. Nestled on the west bank of the Nam Ou (the river almost currentless since the building of the dam upstream), spanned by a vertiginous bridge and bookended by towering limestone crags, it's surely one of the most photogenic spots in Laos. On the river's scenic east bank (officially called Ban Sop Houn) is the lion's share of guesthouses and restaurants.

Be aware that Nong Khiaw is alternatively known as Muang Ngoi (the name of the surrounding district), creating obvious confusion with Muang Ngoi Neua, a 75-minute boat ride further north.

Sights & Activities

At dusk a fabulous star show turns the indigo sky into a pointillist canvas subtly outlining the riverside massifs. Whether you're stationed at one of the town's two viewpoints, **Pha Daeng Peak** (ຈຸດຊົມວິວຜາແດງ; Pha Daeng Peak, Ban Sop Houn; 20,000K; ⏲5am-6pm) or **Sleeping Woman** (ຈຸດຊົມວິວນາງນອນ, Pha Nang None Mountain View; ☎020-55377400; Rte 1C, heading northwest from Nong Khiaw, roughly 1km out of town; 15,000K; ⏲7am-6pm), or just rubbernecking at these extraordinary karsts from ground level, you'll be manually shutting your jaw.

There are several ecotourism outfits in Nong Khiaw that offer trekking, cycling, paddleboarding and kayaking around the area.

★Nong Khiaw Jungle Fly ADVENTURE SPORTS
(☎020-22256151; http://nongkhiawjunglefly.com; Lao Outdoor Travel, Rte 1C; half/full-day tour US$37/49; ⏲8.30am-5pm) This highly recommended adventure park 10km out of town offers half-day and full-day tours that include canopy walks, 'Tarzan swings' and zipping through the jungle on 10 lines up to 400m long. There's also abseiling and trekking through the bamboo forest. Expect quality equipment and an emphasis on safety from the professional English-speaking guides.

Full-day trips run from 9am to 5pm, while half-day trips go from 8.30am to 1pm and 12.30pm to 5pm. You depart from (and return to) the Laos Outdoor Travel office by the bridge in Nong Khiaw.

Sleeping

In the low season, accommodation prices are definitely negotiable. Nong Khiaw offers mainly budget options, plus a few boutique beds.

Ou River House GUESTHOUSE $
(☎020-59945500; d 150,000-180,000K; 📶) Located in a floating barge on the Nam Ou, this place is definitely one of a kind in Nong Khiaw. It offers six simple fan-cooled rooms with attached bathrooms and a small terrace out front for soaking up the impressive views. There is a little cafe-restaurant on-site that's popular with Lao customers.

It is possible to swim in the river directly from the deck.

★Mandala Ou Resort BOUTIQUE HOTEL $$
(☎030-5377332; www.mandala-ou.com; d & tw US$43-68; 📶🏊) 🍃 This stunning boutique accommodation in cinnamon-coloured chalets – six facing the river – has imaginative features like inlaid glass bottles in the walls that allow more light, contemporary bathrooms and swallow-you-up beds. The owners are friendly and there's a terrific Thai and Western menu, the town's only pool and a yoga deck used by Luang Prabang Yoga (p319), which runs monthly retreats here.

There's also a herbal sauna, which is perfect for the cooler winter nights. Find it just a short stroll from the bus station.

★Nong Kiau Riverside GUESTHOUSE $$
(☎020-55705000; www.nongkiau.com; Ban Sop Houn; d & tw incl breakfast US$35-55; @📶) 🍃 Bungalows here are romantically finished with ambient lighting, wooden floors, woven bedspreads and mosquito nets. Each includes an attractive bathroom and balcony for blissful river views of the looming karsts. There's an excellent restaurant serving Lao food with a delicious breakfast buffet. It also has mountain bikes for hire. Discounts are available on room rates in the low season.

Eating

By night there are a few options to keep you awake, be it catching a film at **Delilah's Place** (Main St; mains 15,000-50,000K; ⏲7am-10pm; 📶), a sunset beer by the river, or a lively drink at **Q Bar** (☎020-99918831; Rte 1C, Ban Sop Houn; ⏲7am-11.30pm; 📶).

Vongmany Restaurant LAO $
(Ban Sop Houn; mains 20,000-50,000K; ⏲8.30am-10pm) This large, open rattan-and-wood restaurant serves very tasty locally sourced Lao food. The *láhp* here will put a bounce in your taste buds, while the buffalo steak is delicious, and the steamed fish and river shrimp are full of flavour.

★Coco Home Bar & Restaurant INTERNATIONAL $$
(☎020-23677818; Main St; mains 25,000-70,000K; ⏲8am-11pm; 📶) Run by Sebastien and Chok, this leafy riverside oasis has a great menu, with dishes like papaya salad, mango sticky rice, *mok phaa* (steamed fish in banana leaves) and duck in orange sauce. It's arguably the best place in town to delight your taste buds. Eat in the lush garden or upstairs on the terrace.

Information

MONEY

BCEL has two 24-hour ATMs: **one** (⏲24hr) at the end of the bridge on the Ban Sop Houn side, and **another** (⏲24hr) 100m after the bridge on the road heading to Pak Mong.

TOURIST INFORMATION

The **Tourist Information Office** (⏲8-11am & 2-4pm Mon-Fri), located above the boat landing, is rarely open. Much better is reliable Harp at **Delilah's Place** (☎020-54395686; www.delilahscafenongkhiaw.wordpress.com; Main St; dm/d 40,000/60,000K; 📶), a one-stop travel resource for bus and boat tickets and also decent budget digs.

Getting There & Away

BOAT

Riverboat rides are a highlight of visiting Nong Khiaw. However, since the Nam Ou was dammed, the trip to Luang Prabang is no longer possible. **Boats to Muang Ngoi Neua** (25,000K, 1¼ hours) leave at 11am and 2pm (in high season extra departures are possible), taking you through some of the most dramatic karst country in Laos.

BUS

The journey to Luang Prabang is possible in three hours but in reality usually takes at least four. Minivans or *sŏrngtăaou* (40,000K) run at 9am, 11am and 12.30pm, while air-con minibuses leave around 1.30pm (50,000K). Tickets are sold at the bus station, but the 11am service will wait for folks arriving off the boat(s) from Muang Ngoi. When a boat arrives from Muang Khua there'll usually be additional Luang Prabang minivans departing at around 3pm from either the bus station or **boat office** (8.30-11.30am & 1-3pm).

Getting Around

Bicycle rental makes sense for exploring local villages or reaching the Tham Pha Thok caves. Town bicycles cost 20,000K per day and mountain bikes cost 30,000K. Alternatively, hire a scooter (80,000/100,000K for a manual/automatic) from **Motorbike Rental Donkham Service** (030-9005476; Ban Sop Houn; 8am-7pm). Tuk-tuks to the nearby bus station cost 5000K.

Muang Ngoi Neua

071 / POP 1000

Muang Ngoi Neua (ເມືອງງອຍເໜືອ) is deliciously bucolic – a place to unwind and reset your soul. As the Nam Ou (Ou River) slides sedately beneath the shadow of sawtoothed karsts, cows wander the village's unpaved 500m-long road, while roosters strut past villagers mending fishing nets. Packed with cheap guesthouses and eateries, here there's enough competition to keep prices down. And while hammock-swinging on balconies is still de rigueur, there's plenty more to do if you have the energy, be it short, unaided hikes into timeless neighbouring villages, exploring caves, tubing and kayaking on the now pacified Nam Ou, or fishing and mountain biking.

Sights & Activities

Ensure you're by the river come sunset to enjoy one of the most photogenic views in Laos, as the sun falls like a mellow peach beyond the jagged black cliffs. A little after dawn it's also interesting to watch locals delivering alms to monks at the rebuilt monastery, **Wat Okadsayaram**.

Kayaking is a great way to appreciate the fabulous riverine scenery that stretches both ways along the Nam Ou. **Lao Youth Travel** (030-5140046; 7.30-10.30am & 1.30-6pm) is the most respected tour operator in town, has its own kayaks and is handily located where the boat-landing path passes by the two-storey Rainbow Guest House. The Ou now runs very gently after being dammed, making it safer for younger kids.

Numerous freelance guides offer a range of walks to Lao, Hmong and Khamu villages and regional waterfalls. Beware of those who claim to be recommended by us (they're not!). Prices are reasonable and some visits, such as to the That Mok falls, involve boat rides. Others are easy hikes that you could do perfectly well unguided. Take a photo with your phone of the map outside Lao Youth Travel for a rough guide to the area.

Phanoy Cave & Viewpoint CAVE

(ຖ້ຳພະນອຍ; 10,000K; 7am-5pm) Well signposted from the northern end of the main strip, the Phanoy Cave is a cool relief on a hot day. The cave lies about halfway up a steep track that leads to a striking viewpoint over the Nam Ou and Muang Ngoi Neua below. Definitely take a torch (flashlight) for the cave as a cluster of Buddha relics lies about a 10-minute walk through a pitch-black passageway.

It's best to allow about one to two hours to see both the cave and the viewpoint. Bring water from town as there is none available at the cave or viewpoint.

Sleeping

Uniquely for such a tiny place, budget accommodation abounds and English is widely spoken, so you get the experience of a remote village without the challenges. The only drawback is that the accommodation is showing its age compared with up-and-coming Nong Khiaw just down the river.

Lattanavongsa Guesthouse GUESTHOUSE $

(020-23863640; touymoy.laos@gmail.com; d & tw from 100,000K;) Lattanavongsa offers a choice of bungalows at two locations: above the boat landing, and on the main drag in a pretty garden. Powder-blue rooms have choice art, mozzie nets, fresh linen and gas-fired showers and all have balconies. Enjoy breakfast or dinner at its idyllically situated cafe above the boat landing, with unbroken cliff views. Book well ahead.

PDV Riverview Guesthouse GUESTHOUSE $
(☎020-22148777; pdvbungalows@gmail.com; dm/d/tr 30,000/100,000/100,000K, bungalows 50,000-120,000K; 📶) This place halfway down Main St offers fine riverside accommodation, with five fresh rooms and a six-berth dorm in a newer orange building with a sweeping Nam Ou panorama. The bungalows are nothing extraordinary but have great karst views and the usual balcony and hammock. Rates plummet in low season.

Ning Ning Guest House GUESTHOUSE $$
(☎030-5140863, 020-23880122; ningning_guesthouse@hotmail.com; bungalows 100,000K, d & tw 300,000K; 📶) Nestled around a peaceful garden, Ning Ning offers 10 wooden bungalows with mosquito nets, verandas, en suites, lily-white bed linen and walls draped in ethnic tapestries. There's also an impressive riverfront block with a terrace restaurant and rooms that have a decidedly more upscale look and sumptuous views, but no air-con.

Eating

Nightlife is limited in the village, but chilling over a sundowner Beerlao and watching the karsts from Riverside Restaurant is pure magic. Head to **Bee Tree** (mains 15,000-35,000K; ⏲11.30am-11.30pm; 📶) for a little more buzz.

★**Gecko Bar & Shop** LAO $
(☎020-58886295; muangngoihandmade@gmail.com; mains 15,000-40,000K; ⏲7am-9pm; 📶) Handmade woven gifts and tea are for sale at this delightful, memorable little cafe (two-thirds of the way down the main drag, on your left heading south). There's a nice terrace to sit and read on, the owners are charming and the food, spanning noodles to soups, and pancakes to curries, is among the most raved about in the village.

★**Riverside Restaurant** LAO $
(☎030-5329920; meals 25,000-60,000K; ⏲7am-11pm; 📶) Since being damaged by a storm, Riverside has come back better than ever. In the evening its Chinese lanterns sway in the breeze on the decked terrace, beneath the sentinel arms of an enormous light-festooned mango tree. Riverside has gorgeous cliff views, and its menu encompasses noodles, fried dishes, *láhp* and Indian fare.

Meem Restaurant LAO $
(Main St; mains 20,000-50,000K; ⏲7am-9.30pm; 📶) Halfway down Main St, welcoming Meem has wood floors and plenty of lounging cushions, and serves up flavoursome Lao and Indian fare, including delicious chicken masala, tomato curry, spring rolls and barbecued chicken and duck. By night, it has a magnetic attraction thanks to claypot candles and paper lanterns.

GUESTHOUSE VIEWS

Most of the basic guesthouses have inspiring views over the Nam Ou and its multilayered karst massifs. Savouring such views from your bungalow is one of Muang Ngoi's great attractions, so think twice before choosing an inland guesthouse just to save 10,000K.

Information

DANGERS & ANNOYANCES

Thefts from Muang Ngoi Neua's cheaper guesthouses tend to occur when over-relaxed guests leave flimsy doors and shutters unsecured or place valuables within easy reach of long-armed pincers – most windows here have no glass.

MONEY

There are no banks or ATMs here so bring plenty of cash from either Muang Khua (upriver) or Nong Khiaw (downriver). In an emergency you could exchange US dollars at a few of the guesthouses but rates are unsurprisingly poor.

Getting There & Away

Boats to Nong Khiaw (25,000K, one hour) leave around 9.30am, with tickets on sale from 8am at the **boat ticket office** (⏲8am-noon). At Nong Khiaw tuk-tuks wait above the boat landing for your arrival to take you to the bus station.

There is a boat from Muang Khua that runs if there is demand and it will pick up in Muang Ngoi Neua for Nong Khiaw around 1.30pm.

A new road running alongside the Nam Ou connecting Muang Ngoi Neua to Nong Khiaw has been created. However, it is still unsealed and passes through tributaries that have not yet been bridged; pretty useless for travellers unless you can hitch a lift with a boatman who happens to be there.

Northwestern Laos

Northern Udomxai and Luang Namtha provinces form a mountainous tapestry of rivers, forests and traditional villages that are home to almost 40 classified ethnicities. Luang Namtha is the most developed of several traveller-friendly towns ranged around the 2224-sq-km Nam Ha NPA, with hiking, biking, kayaking and boating adventures all easily organised at short notice.

Luang Namtha

☎086 / POP 29,000

Welcoming travellers like no other town in northern Laos, Luang Namtha (ຫລວງນ້ຳທາ) packs a powerful green hit with its selection of eco-minded tour companies catering for trekking to ethnically diverse villages, and cycling, kayaking and rafting in and around the stunning Nam Ha NPA.

Locally there's bags to do before you set out into the surrounding countryside, such as exploring the night market, or grabbing a rental bike and tootling around the gently undulating rice-bowl valleys to waterfalls and temples. In the golden glow of sunset distant mountain ridges form layered silhouettes, and while it's not the prettiest belle architecturally speaking, the friendly vibe of Luang Namtha will grow on you.

Sights

★**Nam Ha NPA** NATIONAL PARK

(ປ່າສະຫງວນແຫ່ງຊາດນ້ຳທາ; www.namha-npa.org) The 2224-sq-km Nam Ha NPA is one of Laos' most accessible natural preserves and home to clouded leopards. Both around and within the mountainous park, woodlands have to compete with pressure from villages of various ethnicities, including Lao Huay, Akha and Khamu. Since 1999, an ecotourism master plan has tried to ensure that tour operators and villagers work together to provide a genuine experience for trekkers while ensuring minimum impact on local communities and the environment.

Tours are limited to small groups, each agent has its own routes and, in principle, each village receives visitors no more than three times a week. Authorities don't dictate what villagers can and can't do, but by providing information on sustainable forestry and fishing practices it's hoped that forest protection will become a self-chosen priority for the communities.

Golden Stupa BUDDHIST TEMPLE

(ພະທາດຄຳ; 5000K; ⏲8am-5pm) By far Namtha's most striking landmark, this large golden stupa sits on a steep ridge directly northwest of town. It gleams majestically when viewed from afar. Up close, the effect is a bit more bling, but the views over town are impressive.

Ban Nam Di VILLAGE

(ບ້ານນ້ຳດີ, Nam Dy) Barely 3km out of Luang Namtha, this hamlet is populated by Lao Huay (Lenten) people; the women wear traditional indigo tunics with purple sash-belts and silver-hoop necklaces. They specialise in turning bamboo pulp into rustic paper, using cotton screens that you'll spot along the scenic riverbanks.

At the eastern edge of the village, a three-minute stroll leads from a small car park to a 6m-high **waterfall** (2000K). You'll find it's more of a picnic site than a scenic wonder but a visit helps put a little money into village coffers. Unless the water level is really high there's no need to struggle up and over the hillside steps so ignore that sign and walk along the pretty stream. Parking costs 1000/2000/3000K for a bicycle/motorcycle/car.

Tours

Luang Namtha is a major starting point for trekking, rafting, mountain biking and kayaking trips in the Nam Ha NPA. Many of the tours stop for at least a night in a traditional village, which offers a fascinating glimpse of local life and a chance to admire the colourful clothing of the Lao Huay and Akha peoples in particular.

Treks all follow carefully considered sustainability guidelines but they vary in duration and difficulty. Kayaking is a more popular alternative in the wet season, when land trails are muddy and leeches are a minor nuisance.

Namtha agents display boards listing their tour options and how many punters have already signed up, which is very helpful if you're trying to join a group to make things cheaper (maximum eight people). If you don't want others to join you, some agents will accept a 'private surcharge' of around US$50.

There are several things to keep in mind when choosing between the dozen or so agencies in town. Be sure to ask if you will spend more time in the villages or the jungle.

If it's the latter, will they take you through primary or secondary forest (and what percentage of the tour will be within the NPA)? How many hours of physical activity should you expect? If staying overnight, what will the sleeping conditions be like? Asking these basic questions will help you select the trip that's best for you.

There is a self-guided cycling tour around the Namtha Valley, which is a rewarding way to explore the region at your own pace. It is well-signposted around and beyond town and includes a mix of ethnic villages and cultural sites. Pick up a printed route map at the Provincial Tourism Office (p345) or download a copy here: http://luangnamtha tourism.org.

Hiker TREKKING
(☎020-59294245, 086-212343; www.thehikerlaos.com; Main St; ⊙8am-9pm) This outfit is garnering some glowing feedback. Cycling and kayaking trips are available but its main focus is trekking, with one- to seven-day options; the longest one is more hardcore (eight hours' trekking per day) and promises to take you into untouched areas deep in the Nam Ha jungle, while one-day treks are much easier.

Forest Retreat Laos ECOTOUR
(☎020-55680031, 020-55560007; www.forestretreatlaos.com; Main St; ⊙8am-9pm) Based at the Minority Restaurant (p344), this ecotourism outfit offers kayaking, trekking, homestays and mountain biking on one- to seven-day multi-activity adventures, and recruits staff and guides from ethnic-minority backgrounds where possible. It also runs a gruelling 60km one-day cycle trip to Muang Sing. Another option here is to take a cooking class.

Sleeping

Popular places fill up fast during the November–February high season. It's best to book ahead.

Most lodging in Luang Namtha is in the architecturally bland northern part of town around the traveller restaurants.

Many travellers opt for a homestay experience in northern Laos and Luang Namtha is one of the most popular destinations to arrange this. Homestays can be booked through the Provincial Tourism Office (p345) or one of the local tour operators. Homestays are available in the Lanten village of Ban Nam Dee, the Khamu village of Ban Nam Ha and the Tai Daeng village of Ban Pieng Ngam.

Luang Namtha

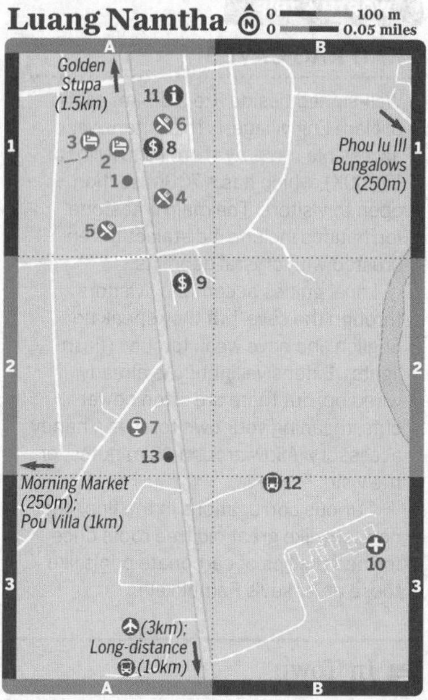

Luang Namtha

Activities, Courses & Tours
Forest Retreat Laos .... (see 5)
1 Hiker A1

Sleeping
2 Luang Namtha Inn A1
3 Zuela Guesthouse A1

Eating
4 Bamboo Lounge A1
5 Minority Restaurant A1
6 Night Market A1

Drinking & Nightlife
7 Classic A2

Information
8 BCEL A1
9 Lao Development Bank A2
10 Provincial Hospital B3
11 Provincial Tourism Office A1

Transport
Bike Shops .... (see 3)
12 District Bus Station B3
13 Lao Airlines A2

WORTH A TRIP

KAO RAO CAVES

Well-signed beside Rte 3, 1.5km east of Nam Eng village, is this extensive, accessible **cave system** (ຖ້ຳເກົາຫລາວ; 10,000K), which has a 700m section open to visitors. The main limestone formations include old stalactites encrusted with crystal deposits.

Local guides accompany visitors through the cave, but they speak no English and have weak torches (flashlights). Extensive lighting is already wired up, but there are often power cuts, meaning your own torch is a handy accessory. Allow around 45 minutes for the visit.

Curious corrugations in the floor that now look like great old tree roots once formed the lips of carbonate pools like those at Turkey's Pamukkale.

In Town

Luang Namtha Inn GUESTHOUSE $

(☎020-5536 3699; d & tw 100,000-120,000K; ❄📶) Under the same ownership as the long-running Adounsiri Guest House, this budget hotel on the main drag opened its doors in mid-2019. Included are tasteful bathrooms with hot-water showers, making it great value at current prices.

Zuela Guesthouse GUESTHOUSE $$

(☎020-22391966; www.zuela.asia; d old block with fan US$20, d & tw new block with air-con US$25-60; ❄📶) Located in a leafy courtyard, Zuela has an old block of spotless if slightly dark rooms with exposed-brick walls and en suites. The newer block has smarter rooms with glazed rattan ceilings, lemon-zest walls, desks and vivid local art. Besides its great restaurant, Zuela, it also offers mountain-bike and motorbike rental and tours.

Around Town

Phou Iu III Bungalows RESORT $$

(☎020-22390195; www.luangnamtha-oasis-resort.com; bungalows incl breakfast 250,000-450,000K; 📶🏊) This spacious resort sits in pretty, flowering gardens, although a swimming pool with waterslides and jungle gyms makes it slightly less serene for couples. Bungalows are spacious and nicely fitted out with lumber-wood beds, brick floors, fireplaces and inviting terraces. It's well signposted from the centre of town. Note that in December it's a little on the chilly side.

★**Pou Villa** BOUTIQUE HOTEL $$$

(☎086-212469; pouvillalnt@gmail.com; Khop Meaung Rd; bungalows from US$130; ❄@📶) Dramatically set on a hillside on the western edge of town, this is the most sophisticated accommodation in Luang Namtha. The small bungalows have big views and are appointed to an impressive four-star standard that is a revolution for Luang Namtha, including flat-screen TV, minibar and creature comforts like bathrobes and slippers.

Eating & Drinking

The lively **night market** (Rte 3A; ⏲7-11.30pm) is a good place for snack grazing. Find noodle stands galore in the **morning market** (noodles 10,000K; ⏲7am-5pm).

For tunes and drinks, the **Classic Bar & Restaurant** (☎020-59294245; www.facebook.com/theclassicview; ⏲3pm-midnight; 📶) and Bamboo Lounge, in particular, are reliable for a lively atmosphere.

Minority Restaurant LAO $

(mains 25,000-50,000K; ⏲7am-10.30pm; 📶) 🌿 This inviting, wood-beamed restaurant hidden down a little side alley offers the chance to sample dishes from the Khamu, Tai Dam and Akha tribes, as well as *láhp,* stir-fries, chicken curry and fried fish.

★**Bamboo Lounge** INTERNATIONAL $$

(☎020-29643190; www.bambooloungelaos.com; mains/pizzas 40,000/75,000K; ⏲7am-11.30pm, happy hour 5-7pm; 📶) 🌿 With its moss-green facade, this place is the favourite in town for travellers. It offers young people from remote villages employment and has donated more than 3000 books to local schools. It's alluring by night with its twinkling fairy lights, top tunes and outdoor terrace piping delicious aromas from its wood-fired oven. Myriad thin-crust pizza choices, plus regular specials like Mexican burritos.

And, unusually for Laos, it's completely nonsmoking.

Boat Landing Restaurant LAO $$

(☎086-312398; meals 35,000-160,000K; ⏲7am-8.30pm) The relaxing riverside setting complements some of the most authentic northern Lao cuisine on offer. From five-dish menus for two or three people to one-plate meals, the flavour combinations are divine. If you're baffled by the choice, try snacking on a selection of *jąaou* used as dipping sauces for balls of sticky rice. Located in the guesthouse of the same name.

Information

MEDICAL SERVICES

Provincial Hospital (Rte 3A; ⏲24hr) This hospital can do the basics like X-rays and dishing out antibiotics. Ask for English-speaking Dr Veokham.

MONEY

BCEL (⏲8.30am-3.30pm Mon-Fri) Changes major currencies (commission-free) and has 24-hour ATM.

Lao Development Bank (⏲8.30am-noon & 2-3.30pm Mon-Fri) Exchanges major currencies and has Western Union.

POST

Post Office (☎086-312007; ⏲8-11.30am & 1-4pm Mon-Fri)

TOURIST INFORMATION

Provincial Tourism Office (☎086-211534; http://luangnamthatourism.org; ⏲8-11.30am & 1.30-4pm Mon-Fri) Helpful resource for all things local, including trekking advice, plus an excellent website that is regularly updated.

Bamboo Lounge (www.bambooloungelaos.com) Produces an excellent guide to the area, which you can download online at www.luangnamthaguide.com.

RESPECTFUL TREKKING

When visiting tribal villages it is important to learn slightly different etiquette according to each local culture. The following notes focus particularly on the Akha, as Akha women's coin-encrusted indigo traditional clothing makes their villages popular trekking targets while their animist beliefs are also some of the most unexpected.

Shoes and feet Entering an ethnic Lao home it would be rude not to remove shoes, but in mud-floored dwellings of Hmong, Akha and some other tribal peoples, it is fine to keep them on. However, still avoid pointing your feet at anyone.

Toilets If there's a village toilet, use it. When in the forest be sure to dump waste away from watercourses. But in remote villages with no toilets at all, check with the guide as to the local custom: although trekking etiquette usually dictates burying faeces, in some villages the deposit will be gobbled up greedily by the local pigs, so it shouldn't be wasted! Nonetheless, carry out used toilet paper, tampons etc.

Photos While many hill-tribe boys are delighted to be photographed, most village women run from a camera. Asking permission to snap a passing stranger often results in refusal, which should be respected. However, if you're staying in a village homestay, your hosts may be happy for you to take a few snaps.

Gifts If you want to give gifts, consider fruit and vegetable seeds or saplings that continue to give after you've left. Always ask the guide first if it's appropriate to give anything and if so, only give directly to friends or to the village chief.

Beds In trekking villages it is common to sleep in the house of the village chief. In traditional Akha homes all the men sleep on one raised, curtained platform, most of the women on another (which it is taboo to visit). To make space for visitors, most men move out for the night to sleep in other houses, leaving the guide, trekkers and maybe a village elder or two to snuggle up in a line in the male section. Bringing a sleeping bag gives a greater semblance of privacy. Note that female trekkers count as 'honorary men'.

Spirits The spirit world is every bit as lively in hill-tribe cultures as it is in other Lao cultures and it would be exceedingly disrespectful for a visitor to touch a village totem (Tai Lü villages), a spirit gate (Akha) or any other taboo item. Ask the guide to explain, and don't even think of dangling yourself on an Akha swing (*hacheu*).

Women and babies Akha mothers believe that covering both breasts will attract harm to their newborn offspring. Eating stones while pregnant is another custom, while the Akha belief that twins are unlucky is common.

Getting There & Away

AIR

Both **Lao Airlines** (086-212072; www.laoairlines.com; 8am-noon & 1-5pm) (from US$85) and **Lao Skyway** (020-99990011; Luang Namtha Airport; 8am-noon & 1-5pm) (from US$50) fly to Vientiane daily.

BUS

There are two bus stations. The district bus station is walking distance from the traveller strip. The main long-distance bus station is 10km south of town. For buses at either station, prebooking a ticket doesn't guarantee a seat – arrive early and claim one in person.

Getting Around

Chartered tuk-tuks charge 20,000K per person between the long-distance bus station or airport and the town centre, more if you're travelling solo, plus they may try their luck and start much higher. Most agencies and guesthouses sell ticket packages for long-distance buses that include a transfer from the guesthouse and cost around 20,000K above the usual fare.

Cycling is the ideal way to explore the wats, waterfalls, villages and landscapes surrounding Luang Namtha. There are a couple of **bike shops** (per day bicycle 10,000-25,000K, motorcycle 30,000-60,000K; 9am-6.30pm) in front of the Zuela Guesthouse. Choose from a bicycle or motorcycle depending on how energetic you're feeling.

Vieng Phukha

086 / POP 4000

Sleepy Vieng Phukha (ວຽງພູຄາ; also spelt 'Phoukha') is an alternative trekking base for visiting the western limits of the Nam Ha National Protected Area, notably on three-day Akha trail hikes. Such trails see fewer visitors than many from Luang Namtha and the partly forested landscapes can be magnificent, though many hills in Vieng Phukha's direct vicinity have been completely deforested.

Sights & Activities

Just 15 minutes' stroll south of Rte 3 near Km 85 but utterly hidden in thick secondary woodlands is the almost invisible site of the 1530 temple **Wat Mahapot**. What little had survived the centuries was mostly pillaged for building materials around 1977, when all the residents moved back after the war, so now all you'll see is the odd scattering of bricks poking out from a tree-choked muddy rise. Getting there involves walking along a steep V-shaped gully that once protected the **Khúu Wíeng** (ramparts) of a short-lived 16th-century 'city'. Again there's nothing but muddy banks to see but a good guide (essential) can fill in sketchy historical details and explain the medicinal uses of plants you'll encounter on a 40-minute walking tour. There are no longer local tour guides operating here, but Mr Tong Mua at Tigerman Treks (p348) in Muang Sing can take you.

Nam Ha Hilltribe Ecotrek HIKING
(020-55086887; www.somhak1966.wixsite.com/ecotrek; 8am-noon & 1-6pm) Run by Somhack (an experienced Khamu hunter who hung up his gun to use his tracking skills as a guide), this great outfit has multiday treks (from moderately easy to challenging) from Vieng Phukha to explore the Nam Ha NPA.

Nam Ha Ecoguide Service Vieng Phoukha HIKING
(020-55985289; www.namha-npa.org; 8am-noon & 1.30-5pm) One- to five-day treks with homestays in Nam Ha NPA.

BUSES FROM LUANG NAMTHA

DESTINATION	COST (K)	DURATION (HR)	STATION	DEPARTURES
Dien Bien Phu (Vietnam)	130,000	10	long-distance	7.30am
Huay Xai ('Borkeo')	60,000	4	long-distance	9am, 12.30pm, 4pm
Luang Prabang	100,000	8	long-distance	9am, 7pm
Muang Sing	30,000	2	district	6 daily 8am-3.30pm
Nong Khiaw	100,000K	6	long-distance	9am
Vieng Phukha	30,000	1½	district	9.30am, 12.30pm
Vientiane	180,000-200,000	21-24	long-distance	8.30am, 2.30pm

Sleeping

Virtually all of Vieng Phukha's accommodation is in simple bungalows with cold showers. The tiny town centre consists of just three parallel streets, where you'll find a handful of guesthouses (and ecotourism outfits).

Thongmyxai Guesthouse GUESTHOUSE $
(☎020-22390351; d 50,000K) Just about the smartest accommodation in town, set in an attractive garden with bungalows.

Getting There & Away

Sŏrngtăaou for Luang Namtha (30,000K, 1½ hours) depart at around 9am and 12.30pm from the middle of town. Or you can wave down a Huay Xai–Namtha through-service (three daily).

Muang Sing

☎081 / POP 9000

Bordering Myanmar and within grasp of the green hills of China, Muang Sing (ເມືອງສິງ) is a rural outpost in the heart of the Golden Triangle. Formerly on the once infamous opium trail, it's a sleepy town of Tai Lü-style houses, where trekking has overtaken smuggling contraband as a means of livelihood. Hmong, Tai Lü, Akha and Tai Dam people in traditional dress attend the old market (arrive at dawn), giving the town a vaguely frontier feel.

Back in the late '90s, Muang Sing was one of the must-visit destinations in Laos, but with the end of fast boat services and the clampdown on the opium trade, it has dropped off the traveller radar. Recently, a growing Chinese population has settled here, replacing rice fields with banana and rubber plantations, the crops of which are destined for consumption on the other side of the border.

Sights & Activities

Sprinkled along the town's main street are a few classic Lao-French hybrid mansion-houses. These mostly 1920s structures have ground-floor walls of brick and stucco topped with a wooden upper storey featuring a wraparound roofed veranda. Classic examples house the tourist office and the Tribal Museum.

The **old market** (Main St), built in 1954, is all but abandoned these days. The bustling **new market** (⏲7am-10pm) is near the bus station and is very colourful first thing in the morning.

Muang Sing

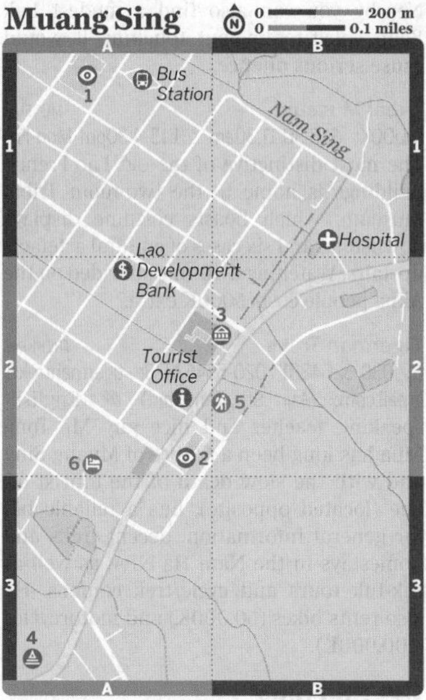

Muang Sing

Sights
1 Morning Market A1
2 Old Market A2
3 Tribal Museum B2
4 Wat Namkeo Luang A3

Activities, Courses & Tours
5 Tigerman Treks B2

Sleeping
6 Phou lu II Bungalows A2

Wat Namkeo Luang BUDDHIST TEMPLE
(ວັດນໍ້າແກ້ວຫລວງ) Wat Namkeo Luang is one of the most visually striking monastic buildings in Muang Sing. It features an entry porch with red-tongued golden *naga* (river serpent) and an unusually tall and ornate gilded stupa. Some villagers still draw water from shaduf-style lever wells in the slowly gentrifying *bâhn* (the general Lao word for house or village) opposite.

Nearby you can also find a modest Lak Bâan spirit-totem, but touching it would cause serious offence.

Tribal Museum MUSEUM
(5000K; ⏲8.30-11.30am & 1.15-4.30pm Mon-Fri) The most distinctive of the old Lao-French buildings is home to the two-room Tribal Museum, which boasts costume displays downstairs and six cases of cultural artefacts upstairs. Watching a 40-minute video on the Akha people costs 5000K extra.

Tigerman Treks TREKKING
(☎030-5264881, 020-55467833; tigermantrek@gmail.com; Main St; 7am-7pm) English-speaking teacher and nice guy Mr Tong Mua has long been a fixture of Muang Sing and with the slow death of the tourist office (located opposite), he's a reliable bet for general information, decent treks and homestays in the Nam Ha NPA, as well as tuk-tuk tours and cycle/trek combos. He also rents bikes (50,000K) and motorcycles (100,000K).

Sleeping

★Phou Iu II Bungalows GUESTHOUSE $$
(☎086-400012; www.muangsingtravel.com; bungalows small/medium/large 150,000/250,000/350,000K) Set around an expansive garden, the biggest bungalows have fun, outdoor, rock-clad shower spaces. All rooms have comfortable beds, mosquito nets, fans and small verandas, although the rooms are cold at night during the cool season. There's an on-site herbal sauna (10,000K) and massage (50,000K per hour), plus a small restaurant serving local Lao dishes.

Information

Lao Development Bank (⏲8am-noon & 2-3.30pm Mon-Fri) Exchanges key currencies like US dollars, Thai baht and Chinese yuan but the rates are poor.

Tourist Office (⏲8am-4pm Mon-Fri) Often understaffed so it may be closed, but there are some useful fact sheets on the walls.

Getting There & Around

From the **bus station** in the northwest corner of town, minibuses depart for Luang Namtha (30,000K, two hours) at 8am, 9.30am, 11am, 12.30pm, 2pm and 3.30pm.

Tour operators and guesthouses rent bicycles (30,000K per day).

Phongsali Province

No longer Laos, not yet China, Phongsali is a visual feast and is home to some of the nation's most traditional hill tribes. Trekkers might feel that they've walked onto the pages of *National Geographic*. For travellers, the province's most visited settlement is Muang Khua, a useful transit point linked by river to Nong Khiaw and by road to Dien Bien Phu in Vietnam. Further north the province is kept well off the standard tourist trail by arduous journeys on snaking roads that twist and turn endlessly. The only asphalt links Muang Khua to Udomxai and Phongsali and on to Mengla in China. Inconveniently, foreigners can't cross the Chinese border anywhere in the province. The road to Dien Bien Phu is now in great shape on the Lao side, but is not so great on the Vietnamese side.

Phongsali

POP 8500 / ☎088 / ELEV 1400M

As you approach Phongsali (ຜົ້ງສາລີ) via a sinuous mountain road, the town rears up suddenly on a ridgetop plateau. Often wrapped in mist, its atmospheric wooden Yunnanese shophouses and other buildings, spanning biscuit-brown to powder-blue, shelter below the peak of Phu Fa ('Sky Mountain'; 1625m), rising majestically in the background. The location gives the town panoramic views and a refreshing climate that can swing from pleasantly warm to downright cold in a matter of hours – expect icicles in the cold season and bring a jacket and waterproofs just in case, even in April.

The town's population is a mix of Phu Noi and Haw/Yunnanese, both long-term residents and more recent immigrants. That said, no one comes to Phongsali to experience the town; it's the trekking in the surrounding hill country that justifies the considerable effort to get here.

Sights & Activities

The town's modest but distinctive old-town area includes a three-block grid of rough, stone-flagged alleys and a winding street mostly lined with traditional **Yunnanese shophouses** FREE whose wooden frontages recall the architecture of old Kunming. Tiny, new and functional, the **Chinese Temple** overlooks a pond, behind which is **Wat Keo** (ວັດແກ້ວ), with its *petang*-playing monks.

Ban Komean VILLAGE

(ບ້ານກໍ່ມຽນ) Phongsali's famous tea village, Ban Komean, lies 14km out of town and commands stupendous valley views that sweep nearly 360 degrees when you stand on the promontory behind the school. The tea bushes are reputedly more than 400 years old and said to be the world's oldest. A fair percentage of the village's authentic Phu Noi homes are set on stone-pile platforms. Rent a tuk-tuk from Phongsali (250,000K return) or hire a bike from the tourist office for 50,000K per day.

If getting here by motorbike, take the Boun Neua road, turn left directly opposite the inspirationally named Km4 Nightclub (not the asphalt road just before), then curve steadily around on the main unpaved road, keeping left at most junctions but avoiding any turn that descends into the valley.

Phu Fa VIEWPOINT

(ພູຟ້າ, Sky Mountain; 5000K) For great views across town climb to the stupa-topped peak of Phu Fa (1625m); it's a punishing, tree-shaded climb of more than 400 stone steps. A ticket must be purchased on the last section of the ascent. An alternative descent returns to the Hat Sa road near a tea factory 2km east of town.

Museum of Tribes MUSEUM

(10,000K; 8-11.30am & 1.30-4.30pm Mon-Fri) This museum gives you a chance to deepen your understanding of the ethnic peoples of Phongsali Province. It contains a wealth of cultural information on animism and customs, with photos and historical background, as well as displays of the vividly coloured traditional clothing you're likely to see on your travels. If the door is locked, ask for the key from the post office across the road.

Amazing Phongsali Travel TREKKING

(088-210594, 020-55774354; www.explorephongsalylaos.com; Villa Amazing Maison Guesthouse; 8am-5pm or later) In order to encounter the 28 ethnicities in the province you need to penetrate deep jungle, and for this you'll require more than a guide who can take you to outlying villages along the road. Amazing Phongsali Travel is the main independent trekking operator in Phongsali, with a selection of treks that have brought rave reviews.

Sleeping & Eating

Something of a barren choice of digs awaits you in Phongsali, which doesn't acquit itself well in welcoming travellers. All places generally have hot water, a blessing in the cold winter, but electricity is sometimes limited to a few hours a day.

Flavoursome *kòw sóy* (noodle soup with minced pork and tomato) is available from **noodle stands** (noodles 15,000K; 6am-5pm) hidden away in the northwest corner of the **market** (6am-5pm), which is at its most interesting at dawn. The town's restaurant food is predominantly Chinese. *Đôm Ƀạh* (fondue-style fish soup) is a local speciality, notably served at simple places along the Hat Sa road (Km 2 and Km 4).

Sengsaly Guesthouse GUESTHOUSE $

(088-210165; d & tw 80,000-100,000K;) The best of three cheapies on the main drag, the Sengsaly has uber-basic 80,000K rooms with clean bedding, bare walls, tiled floors and private bathroom. Better rooms are in a newer, if overly colourful, block and come with a hot shower and veranda.

Laojhean Restaurant LAO $

(mains 25,000-50,000K; 7am-10.30pm) At this family-run noodle house the well-prepared food comes in decent-sized portions and is served with a smile. The menu's approximate English includes inscrutable offerings such as 'High-handed Pig's liver' and 'Palace Protects the Meat Cubelets'.

Information

BCEL (8.30am-3.30pm Mon-Fri) There is also a nearby ATM.

Lao Development Bank (8.30am-3.30pm Mon-Fri) Includes an ATM, represents Western Union and changes multiple currencies to kip.

Tourist Office (088-210098; www.phongsaly.net; 8-11.30am & 1.30-4pm Mon-Fri) Helpful maps and brochures are available online (and are free from most guesthouses). To book a tour out of hours, call 020-22572373 or one of the mobile numbers posted on the front door.

Getting There & Around

Phongsali's airport is actually at Boun Neua, but the only flights available are with Lao Skyway and are not listed on its website. It is necessary to book in person at its offices and the services are often cancelled due to bad weather or fog. It operates a desk at Phongsali Airport, but it inconveniently opens only two hours before flights depart.

Phongsali's main bus station is at Km 3, west of town. A *sŏrngtăaou* runs there from the market area (10,000K) at 6.30am but only very infrequently after that, so leave plenty of time. Route 1A has finally been sealed, allowing for safer, quicker and easier passage to and from Phongsali. The daily bus to Vientiane (230,000K, more than 20 hours) leaves at 8.30am and the VIP bus (250,000K) at 2pm, passing through Luang Prabang (140,000K). There's a 7.30am bus to Luang Namtha (60,000k), and a 7am bus to Dien Bien Phu (130,000K, five hours) on the Vietnamese side.

Amazing Phongsali Travel (p349) rents small motorbikes from 100,000K per day.

Middle Mekong

For many tourists the Middle Mekong region is seen merely in passing between Thailand and Luang Prabang – typically on the two-day slowboat route from Huay Xai via Pak Beng – but there's plenty to interest the more adventurous traveller. Bokeo, meaning 'Gem Mine', takes its name from the sapphire deposits in Huay Xai district, and the province harbours 34 ethnicities despite a particularly sparse population. Sainyabuli Province is synonymous with working elephants and the Elephant Conservation Center is just outside the eponymous capital. Other than in Huay Xai and Pak Beng you'll need a decent phrasebook wherever you go.

Western Sainyabuli remains particularly far off the traveller radar; places such as the dramatic Khop district are 'last frontiers' with a complex ethnic mix and reputedly high proportion of still-pristine forests.

Huay Xai

☎ 084 / POP 30,000

Separated from Thailand by the mother river that is the Mekong, Huay Xai (ຫວຍຊາຍ) is, for many, their first impression of Laos. While that used to be a bad thing, this oddly charming town has perked up in recent years. By night, roadside food vendors take to the streets, and there are some welcoming traveller guesthouses and cafes serving tasty food.

Huay Xai was allegedly home to a US heroin-processing plant during the Secret War, but these days the only things trafficked through here are travellers en route to Luang Prabang or the fabled Gibbon Experience, the most talked-about adventure in the country. Yet, with day trips to nearby ethnic villages and some worthwhile voluntourism opportunities, there are reasons to stick around for a day or so.

Sights & Activities

Huay Xai's modest tourist attractions include the Mekong views from several colourful wats.

★ **Gibbon Experience** ADVENTURE SPORTS
(☎ 084-212021, 030-5745866; www.gibbonexperience.org; 2-day Express US$180, 3-day Classic or Waterfall US$305; ⏲ 7am-5pm) At this long-running ecotourism project, a series of ziplines criss-cross the canopy in the Nam Kan NPA – home to clouded leopards, black bears and the black-crested gibbon – giving you the chance to soar across valleys and stay in 40m-high tree houses, claimed to be the world's tallest. There are three tour options (two-day Express, or three-day Classic and Waterfall), each involving a serious trek. Well-cooked meals are ziplined in by your guide.

The guides are helpful, though make sure you're personally vigilant with the knots in your harness. Wearing a helmet is optional, but we recommend asking for one given the speed you travel along the cable. Also check that your karabiner actually closes. Should it rain when you're ziplining, remember that you'll need more time to slow down with your brake (a humble bit of bike tyre). For all three tour options, we recommend being in good shape.

Prepayment online through PayPal works well but do be patient as communication isn't always immediate. One day before departure, check in at the Huay Xai **Gibbon Experience Office** (☎ 084-212021; www.gibbonexperience.org; Th Saykhong; ⏲ 8am-5pm) on Th Saykhong. Gloves (essential for using the ziplines) are provided. It's also advisable to bring a torch (flashlight), water bottle, toilet paper and earplugs to deflect the sound of a million crickets, but otherwise leave most of your baggage in the office storeroom. Everything you bring you must carry on your back over some steep hikes and on the ziplines. As there'll be no electricity, don't forget to precharge camera batteries.

Tragically, an accident here in March 2017 resulted in the death of one traveller and tours were temporarily suspended. Following investigations, the Gibbon Experience resumed services and began implementing a range of stricter safety protocols.

WORTH A TRIP

ELEPHANT CONSERVATION CENTER

The **Elephant Conservation Center** (ECC; ☎020-96590665; www.elephantconservationcenter.com; 2-day discovery US$210, 3-day exploration US$280, 7-day eco-volunteering US$470) offers one of the most inspiring experiences in Laos. Get to know the resident elephants as they bathe, feed and raise their young in a protected environment along the shores of Nam Tien lake. Visitors sleep and eat in their midst, learning about the plight of elephants in Laos from a team of experts and local guides.

Shorter two- and three-day trips include visits to the elephant nursery, socialisation area and hospital, while week-long volunteers also help with current projects. All tours include family-style Lao meals and basic accommodation in fan-cooled bungalows with shared bathrooms, as well as transport from/to Luang Prabang aboard the centre's own minibuses. Transport leaves Luang Prabang post office at 8am and departs from the ECC at around 2pm. There's also some smarter accommodation with private bathrooms in a lodge-style building; these rooms can be reserved for an additional US$100 per person.

Lao Red Cross MASSAGE
(☎084-211935; massage per hour from 50,000K, herbal sauna 20,000K; ⊙1.30-9pm Mon-Fri, from 10.30am Sat & Sun) Lao Red Cross offers Swedish-Lao massage and a traditional herbal sauna (from 4pm) in a stately old mansion beside the Mekong.

Sleeping & Eating

The central drag is packed with guesthouses and many more are dotted around the edge of town. Prices can be higher than elsewhere in Laos, even though the quality is lower.

BAP Guesthouse GUESTHOUSE $
(☎084-211083; Th Saykhong; d & tw with fan 60,000, d & tw with air-con 120,000K; ❄) Run by friendly English-speaking Mrs Changpeng, trusty BAP has 16 rooms, some with fan or air-con and private bathroom. There are four newer ones that merit a mention for their colourful quilts, wood accents, TVs and sunset views over the Mekong. The restaurant (mains 15,000K to 35,000K) is also popular for its fried-rice dishes, pasta and hearty breakfasts.

Little Hostel HOSTEL $
(☎030-5206329; https://littlehostel.wordpress.com; Th Saykhong; dm 40,000-70,000K; 📶) Colourful furnishings stand out against the concrete floors of this otherwise bare-bones hostel with a couple of four-berth dorms. The rooms are as clean as the showers and it's a friendly place to meet fellow travellers, with a large common area and a central location on the main drag. Rates vary widely from low to high season.

Riverside Houayxay Hotel HOTEL $$
(☎084-1211064;riverside_houayxay_laos@hotmail.com; d & tw 200,000-250,000K; ❄📶) Located just off the main strip and overlooking the mighty Mekong, this is the most upmarket hotel in the centre of town, although that's not saying much. Rooms are spacious, hot water is on tap, plus there's satellite TV and a minibar.

★**Daauw** LAO $
(http://daauwvillagelaos.com; mains 20,000-50,000K; ⊙6-10pm; 🖉) Probably the friendliest vibe in town; head here to soak up sunset views on its chill-out terrace decked in low cushions and an open-pit fire, and choose from freshly prepared organic Hmong food, wood-fired pizza, plenty of vegetarian options, or whole barbecued Mekong fish or chicken. If there's a crowd, linger for *laojitos:* mojitos made with *lòw-lów* (rice wine).

Daauw also runs a new daytime cafe by the stairs up to Wat Jom Khao Manilat. All of the income generated by both properties goes back into Project Kajsiab, an initiative to empower Hmong women.

Information

BCEL (Th Saykhong; ⊙8.30am-4.30pm Mon-Fri) Has a 24-hour ATM, exchange facility and Western Union.

Tourist Information Office (☎084-211162; Th Saykhong; ⊙8am-noon & 2-4.30pm Mon-Fri) Has free tourist maps of the town and some suggestions for excursions around the province.

Getting There & Away

For years, streams of Luang Prabang–bound travellers have piled into Huay Xai and jumped straight aboard a boat for the memorable descent of the Mekong. Today, improving roads mean an ever-increasing proportion opt instead for the overnight bus. But while slightly cheaper than the slowboat, the bus is far less social, less attractive and, at around 15 hours of travel, leaves most people exhausted on arrival.

BOAT

Slowboats currently depart from Huay Xai at 11.30am daily. Purchase tickets at the **slowboat ticket booth** (☎ 084-211659) for Pak Beng (100,000K, one day) or Luang Prabang (200,000K not including accommodation, two days). Sales start at 8am on the day of travel. Avoid buying a ticket from a travel company, as it will include an overpriced tuk-tuk transfer to the pier and then a long wait for the departure.

Most boats now offer comfortable minivan-style seats. If the boat operators try to cram on too many passengers (more than 70 or so), a tactic that really works is for later arrivals to simply refuse to get aboard until a second boat is provided.

The **speedboat landing** (☎ 084-211457; Rte 3, 200m beyond Km 202) is directly beneath Wat Thadsuvanna Phakham, 3km south of town. Six-passenger speedboats *(héua wái)* zip thrillingly but dangerously, and with great discomfort for those on board, to Pak Beng (180,000K, three hours) and Luang Prabang (350,000K, seven hours including lunch stop), typically departing around 10.30am.

Due to a section of the Nam Tha (Tha River) being dammed, it's no longer possible to catch a boat all the way up to Luang Namtha.

BUS

Note that Huay Xai–bound buses are usually marked 'Borkeo'. The bus station is 5km southeast of town. Buses to Luang Prabang (120,000K, 14 to 17 hours) depart at 10am and 4pm; for Luang Namtha (60,000K, four hours) they leave at 9am and 12.30pm; for Udomxai (90,000K, eight hours) there is one at 9.30am and 1pm. For Vientiane (230,000K, 25 hours) catch the 11.30am.

Travel-agency minibuses to Luang Namtha leave from central Huay Xai at around 9am (100,000K, four hours) but still arrive at Namtha's inconveniently out-of-town bus station.

Getting Around

Bicycles (30,000K per day) are available from Little Hostel (p351), while the Gibbon Experience Office (p350) rents electric motorbikes for 50,000K per day.

Tuk-tuks charge about 20,000K per person to the airport, bus station, or speedboat or slowboat landings.

Pak Beng

☎ 084 / POP 3500

A halfway riverine stop between Luang Prabang and Huay Xai (lunch for speedy longtails, overnight for slowboats), Pak Beng (ປາກແບງ) has some good places to stay and nice spots to eat, including bakeries and cafes.

The best time to enjoy this one-street town is late afternoon from on high at one of the restaurant balconies clinging to its vertiginous slope, watching the Mekong slide indolently by in a churn of gingery eddies,

GETTING TO THAILAND: HUAY XAI TO CHIANG KHONG

Getting to the border Since the completion of the Thai–Lao Friendship Bridge 4 at the Huay Xai/Chiang Khong border crossing in late 2013, the former ferry-boat crossing is for locals only.

Tuk-tuks cost about 30,000K per person to the immigration post. Alternatively, many agencies in Huay Xai sell tickets to Chiang Mai or Chiang Rai that include a tuk-tuk to the border, bus across the bridge and onward transport for about the same price as doing it yourself.

At the border Lao visas (p398) are available on arrival from US$30 to US$42 depending on nationality. A bus (25B) crosses the bridge to Thailand where a 30-day visa waiver is automatically granted to residents of most countries. There are ATMs and exchange counters at the heavily trafficked border post in Chiang Khong.

Moving on Most buses to Chiang Mai and Chiang Rai booked in Huay Xai will pick up at the border. Alternatively, buses for Chiang Rai (from 65B, 2½ hours) typically depart from Chiang Khong's bus station every hour from 6am to 5pm. **Greenbus** (☎ in Thailand 0066 53 241933; www.greenbusthailand.com) has a service to Chiang Mai at 9.45am. Several overnight buses for Bangkok (650B to 800B, 14 hours) leave at 3pm and 3.30pm.

LOCAL KNOWLEDGE

THE GOLDEN TRIANGLE REINVENTED

Around 5km north of Tonpheung, small Rte 3 abruptly undergoes an astonishing transformation. Suddenly you're gliding along a two-coloured paved avenue, lined with palm trees and immaculately swept by teams of cleaners. Golden domes and pseudo-classical charioteers rear beside you. No, you haven't ingested a happy pizza. This is the Golden Triangle's very own Laos Vegas, a casino and entertainment project that is still a work in progress but is planned to eventually cover almost 100 sq km. After 2.5km this surreal strip turns left and dead-ends after 600m at the Mekong beside another Disneyesque fantasy dome and a mini Big Ben. The huge casino here is open to all, but most of the games are aimed at Chinese or Thai gamblers and may not be familiar to other visitors. Electronic roulette tables are the most accessible of the games on offer.

This area of riverfront is part of the famous Golden Triangle, where Thailand and Laos face off, with Myanmar sticking a long-nosed sand bank between the two. Boat cruises potter past from the Thai side. On the Lao bank speedboats await but foreigners can't cross the border without prearranged authorisation.

dramatically framed by giant boulders and sharp jungle banks.

Sights & Activities

The tourist office offers treks to a Hmong village (400,000K per person in a group of four) or cooking classes (100,000K per person in a group of four), and can suggest a typical selection of local caves and waterfalls in the district to explore if you rent a motorbike. Ask at your guesthouse for a driver, as drivers around the market charge a steep 40,000K per hour.

A pleasant excursion is to cross the river by **motor canoe** (5000K) then walk for about 10 minutes diagonally right away from the river to a tiny, authentic Hmong hamlet.

Le Grand Pakbeng Resort also has a comprehensive tour program for those planning more than a one-night stop in this sleepy riverside town.

Sleeping

With almost 20 relatively similar options within five minutes' walk of the boat dock, it's worth shopping around. Guesthouse prices generally seem to drop the further up the hill you go. There are now several smarter places in town, mostly strung out along the hilltops to the west of town.

★Luang Say Lodge LODGE **$$**
(☎084-212296; www.luangsay.com; d & tw from US$73) Principally for the use of passengers aboard the **Luang Say Cruise** (☎071-252553, 020-55090718; www.luangsay.com; cruise US$379-542, single supplement from US$64; ⊙8-11.30am & 1.30-5pm Mon-Fri, 8-11.30am Sat & Sun), this traditional hardwood-and-rattan lodge has stylish bungalows in a pretty garden, overlooking a dramatic stretch of river, with fans and hot-water showers. A terrace restaurant for breakfast and dinner overlooks the Mekong. Be warned: it's a steep and sometimes slippery climb from the jetty to the hotel.

Le Grand Pakbeng Resort RESORT **$$$**
(☎081-214035; www.legrandpakbeng.com; d & tw US$130-300; ❄@📶🏊) Setting the standard for luxury accommodation in petite Pak Beng, Le Grand is a big resort located on a strategic hilltop just to the west of town. The rooms are spacious and sumptuously decorated with elegant touches, including twin sinks, a walk-in rain shower and a panoramic balcony.

There is an inviting infinity pool from which to take in the incredible views, an international restaurant and a walk-in wine cellar with the most extensive wine list this side of Luang Prabang. Impressive indeed.

Eating & Drinking

There's a string of eateries almost as long as the guesthouse strip. Most places have long menus and all charge around the same prices (mains 15,000K to 35,000K) for standard Lao, Thai and Western fare. By day, pick one with a good Mekong view. Most kitchens stop cooking around 9pm and by 10pm it might be a struggle just to find a beer.

The impressive bar-restaurant at the Luang Say Lodge is ideal for enjoying Mekong views with a sundowner such as a gin and tonic or a glass of wine. There are a couple of small bars in town for backpackers looking to party in Pak Beng, or at least have a drink or two.

DAMMING THE MEKONG FOR HYDROELECTRIC POWER

For millennia the Mekong River has been the lifeblood of Laos and the wider Mekong region. It's the region's primary artery, and about 60 million people depend on the rich fisheries and other resources provided by the river and its tributaries. The Mekong is the world's 12th-longest river and 10th largest in terms of volume. But unlike other major rivers, a series of rapids have prevented it from developing into a major transport and cargo thoroughfare, or as a base for large industrial cities.

When the Nam Theun 2 dam in Khammuan Province was approved by the World Bank in 2005, it was the equivalent of opening hydropower's Pandora's box. Since then hydropower has become an important contributor to Laos' economic growth. Six big dams are already in operation, seven are currently under construction, at least 12 more are planned, and development deals are ready to go on another 35.

The negative impacts associated with these dams have so far included forced displacement of local communities and the uprooting of their traditional riverine culture, flooding upstream areas, reduced sediment flows, and increased erosion downstream with resulting issues for fish stocks and those who work the rivers.

The most catastrophic consequence of dam building was the collapse of Saddle Dam D (p378) in Attapeu Province in 2018. This led to the outright destruction of villages, loss of human life and livestock, and displacement of thousands of villagers. While the government has attempted to deal with the fallout, there has been little questioning of the ongoing policy.

Less immediately visible, but with a potentially much greater influence in the long term, are the changes these dams will have on the Mekong's flood pulse, especially the Tonlé Sap Lake in Cambodia, which is critical to the fish spawning cycle, and thus the food source of millions of people.

More information can be found online, including through the Mekong River Commission (www.mrcmekong.org), which oversees the dam developments; Save the Mekong Coalition (https://savethemekong.net); and the WWF (www.panda.org).

Information

Guesthouses change money at unimpressive rates. Thai baht are also widely used here.

Lao Development Bank (24hr) Near the market, it has an ATM that has been known to run out of money at busy times.

Tourist Office (www.oudomxay.info; 7am-noon & 2-9pm) Free maps of town and can help arrange guides.

Getting There & Away

The downriver **slowboat** to Luang Prabang departs between 9am and 10am (110,000K, around eight hours) with request stops possible at Pak Tha and Tha Suang (for Hongsa). The slowboat for Huay Xai (110,000K, around nine hours) departs 8.30am.

Speedboats take around three hours to either Luang Prabang or Huay Xai, costing 200,000K per person assuming a crushed-full quota of six passengers (dangerous and highly uncomfortable, but cheaper than a 1,200,000K charter). Arriving by speedboat, local boys will generally offer to carry your bags for about 5000K (after some bargaining). If your bags are unwieldy this can prove money well spent, as when river levels are low you'll need to cross two planks and climb a steep sandbank to reach the road into town.

Get tickets at the boat ticket office.

CENTRAL LAOS

Ever since Tha Khaek opened its French-colonial shutters to travellers and the dramatic 7km-long underworld of Tham Kong Lor became a must-see fixture on itineraries, central Laos has been enticing visitors. Thanks to its honeycomb of caves and dragon-green jungle, activities on offer run from world-class rock climbing outside of Tha Khaek to trekking in the other-worldly karst forests of Hin Namno NPA.

This part of the country claims the most forest cover and the highest concentrations of wildlife, including some species that have disappeared elsewhere in Southeast Asia. With its rugged, intrepid travel, and stylish pockets of comfort in Savannakhet and Tha Khaek, central Laos makes for a great place to combine your inner Indiana Jones with a Bloody Mary.

Bolikhamsai & Khammuan Provinces

Bolikhamsai (ບໍລິຄຳໄຊ) and Khammuan (ຄຳມ່ວນ) straddle the narrow, central 'waist' of the country. Physically the land climbs steadily from the Mekong River valley towards the north and east, eventually reaching the Annamite Chain bordering Vietnam, via an area of moderately high but often spectacular mountains. Laid-back Tha Khaek is the logical base.

Lowland Lao dominate the population and, along with smaller groups of tribal Thais, are the people you'll mostly meet. In remoter areas the Mon-Khmer-speaking Makong people (commonly known as Bru) make up more than 10% of the population of Khammuan.

Much of the region is relatively sparsely populated and five large tracts of forest have been declared National Protected Areas (NPAs) and one a national park. These areas have become a major battleground between those wishing to exploit Laos' hydroelectricity capacity and those wishing to preserve the natural environment. They also represent an opportunity for visitors to witness some of the more pristine wilderness in mainland Southeast Asia.

Tha Khaek

051 / POP 38,000

This ex-Indochinese trading post is a delightful melange of crumbling French villas and the warped shopfronts of Chinese merchants, with an easy riverside charm that, despite the bridge over to nearby Thailand, shows few signs of change. It's from here that you begin 'The Loop', a three-day motorbike journey through shape-shifting landscapes, and you can also use Tha Khaek (ທ່າແຂກ) as a base from which to make organised day trips to Tham Kong Lor. There are more than a dozen other caves nearby, some with swimmable lagoons, that can be accessed by scooter or tuk-tuk.

Sights & Activities

Most of the activities take place in the karst countryside around Tha Khaek, including clambering the karst at Green Climbers Home (p357) or exploring the many caves that pepper the jagged mountains. A day trip to multiple caves with the Tourist Information Centre (p358) costs from 350,000K per person (for a group of six or more).

When it comes to Tha Khaek town, other than wandering the streets and soaking up the atmosphere, there's not a lot to keep you occupied.

Tham Pa Seuam CAVE

(ຖ້ຳປາເຊືອມ; entry 5000K, parking 3000K) A mini Tham Kong Lor, the river cave of Tham Pa Seuam runs for 3km, spanning some impressive stalactites and stalagmites. It's conveniently only 15km from Tha Khaek. A day trip to multiple caves, including Tham Pa Seuam, with the Tourist Information Centre (p358) costs from 350,000K per person (for a group of six or more) and includes a 400m boat ride into the main chamber.

WORTH A TRIP

THA KHAEK LOOP

This awe-inspiring three-day motorbike journey, known as the 'The Loop', has become the stuff of legend on the Southeast Asia backpacker circuit. If you're up to the challenge of navigating all 450km – and it is quite challenging – your reward is a highlights reel of rural Laos, with verdant jungles, raging rivers and soaring karst walls that hide subterranean wonderlands.

The trip starts and ends in Tha Khaek, where you can arrange for a sturdy motorbike and backpack storage with a number of respected rental companies. Most travellers then set off on The Loop counter-clockwise, taking in the swimming holes and minor caves east of town before zipping past the impregnable karst to overnight by the Nam Theun (Theun River) in Ban Tha Lang. Day two will have you biking past flooded valleys (and eerie dead forests) to the frontier town of **Lak Sao** before you cut south to the river cave of Tham Kong Lor (p359), the highlight of the entire trip. Though much of day three is spent on the highway returning to Tha Khaek, the road that leads you there is the most spectacular yet, zigzagging through the pristine jungle of Phu Hin Bun NPA (p358).

Tha Khaek

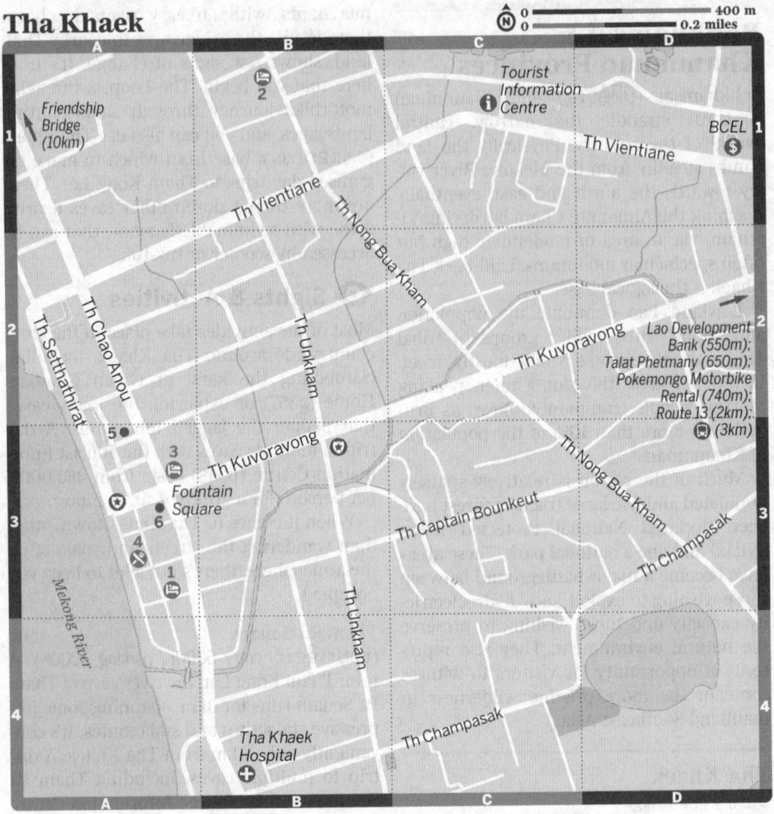

Tha Khaek

Activities, Courses & Tours

Green Discovery .... (see 3)

Sleeping

1 Bike & Bed Hostel A3
2 Dongsay Hotel B1
3 Inthira Hotel A3

Eating

4 Ping Kai Napong A3

Transport

Mad Monkey Motorbike .... (see 6)
5 Mixay Motor Rental A3
6 Wangwang Motor Rental A3

Tham Pha Chan CAVE

(ຖ້ຳພະໄມ້ຈັນຫອມ, Sandalwood Buddha Cave) FREE Tham Pha Chan has an entrance 60m high and about 100m wide. A stream runs about 600m through a limestone karst and in the dry season it's possible to walk to the far side. At its western end there is a sandalwood Buddha image about 15m above the ground, hence the cave's name.

Not far from Tham Pha Chan is the **Nam Don Resurgence** (ບໍ່ນ້ຳໂດນ), a cave where the Nam Don (Don River) emerges from the ground. It's quite a physical marvel to see the water coming up and out from the cave, and the lagoon that sits at the bottom of the tall limestone karst is a beautiful swimming spot.

Unfortunately, both are accessed via a rough road that runs 20km from the junction with Rte 13. Go by motorbike or tuk-tuk, or arrange an English-speaking guide through Tha Khaek's Tourist Information Centre (p358).

Tham Xieng Liap CAVE

(ຖ້ຳຊຽງລຽບ) FREE Turning off Rte 12 at Km 14 (before a bridge) you'll come across a sign pointing to this cave. Follow the dirt track south for about 400m near the village of Ban Songkhone (about 10.5km from Rte 13), to the stunning limestone cave Tham Xieng Liap, the entrance of which is at the base of a dramatic 300m-high cliff.

The cave is about 200m long and, in the dry season, you can walk/wade through and swim in the picturesque valley on the far side. *Paa faa* (soft-shelled turtles) live in the cave, while the cliffs outside are said to be home to the recently discovered *kan yoo* (Laotian rock rat). In the wet season you'll need to rent a boat (30,000K) from the Xieng Liap bridge.

Green Climbers Home CLIMBING
(☎020-56105622; www.greenclimbershome.com; Ban Kouanphavang; courses per person 140,000-700,000K; ⊙Oct-May) This efficiently run training school set in a valley in soaring karst country 18km from Tha Khaek is hugely popular, and often booked up thanks to its cosy cabanas, great food and excellent courses. It also boasts one of the easiest overhangs in the world to learn on and has beginner-, intermediate- and expert-level climbs, with more than 320 routes from class 4 to 8C.

To get here, a tuk-tuk by day costs 100,000K. For serious climbers, **accommodation** here includes dorms (55,000K) and bungalows (from 160,000K) with hot-water showers.

Green Discovery ADVENTURE SPORTS
(☎051-251390; www.greendiscoverylaos.com; Inthira Hotel, Th Chao Anou; ⊙8am-9.30pm) Green Discovery is the country's most experienced ecotourism outfit and runs a number of interesting trips around central Laos. A range of treks and kayaking excursions in the lush Phu Hin Bun NPA is available, including Tham Kong Lor (from US$70 for a day trip to US$155 for an overnight trip). Also arranges cycling and kayaking.

This branch of Green Discovery is also the logical place to organise a trip to Hin Namno NPA.

Sleeping & Eating

Tha Khaek has a decent spread of accommodation, including a couple of worthwhile midrange options, and a serviceable selection of eats; you don't need to stray too far from the riverfront strip to see what's available.

Bike & Bed Hostel HOSTEL $
(☎020-91710957; dm 55,000K; ❄📶) Housed in a handsome villa, the dorms here range from four to six beds. The beds themselves are pretty standard; the real reasons to stay are the homey vibe and the communal garden where you'll want to flop down with a cool drink and a book.

Dongsay Hotel HOTEL $$
(☎020-56785683; r incl breakfast 190,000-386,000K; ❄📶) Spacious, new-feeling rooms in a four-storey building. Perks such as friendly service, free bus station/border pickup and one of the only hotel lifts in Tha Khaek make this one of the better midrange options in town.

Inthira Hotel BOUTIQUE HOTEL $$
(☎051-251237; www.inthira.com; Th Chao Anou; incl breakfast r US$26-36, ste US$45; ⊖❄@📶) Set in an old French villa with a pretty facade, Inthira offers the most romantic, stylish digs in town. That said, some of the rooms have odd and sometimes inconvenient design features, and all could use a new coat of paint.

★**Ping Kai Napong** LAO $$
(Th Setthathirat; dishes 39,000-89,000K; ⊙10am-10pm) Ping Kai Napong specialises in grilled chicken, but the menu is a virtual tour of Lao cuisine, ranging from salads (the duck *láhp* is sublime) to soups. Easily the best of the riverside places.

Information

MEDICAL SERVICES

Tha Khaek Hospital (☎051-212084; cnr Th Chao Anou & Th Champasak; ⊙24hr)

MONEY

BCEL (Th Vientiane; ⊙8.30am-4.30pm Mon-Fri) Changes major currencies and offers cash advances on debit or credit card.

Lao Development Bank (Th Vientiane; ⊙8.30-11.30am & 1-4.30pm) Cash exchange only, plus an ATM.

POLICE STATIONS

Police (☎051-212083; cnr Th Kuvoravong & Th Unkham) Avoid passing by the station on motorbike if leaving town for the Loop, as the police here have been known to demand a fake tourist fee.

Tourist Police (☎051-213563; Fountain Sq) The police here know how to write insurance reports, if you can track down an officer.

TOURIST INFORMATION

Tourist Information Centre (☎020-55711797, 030-5300503; www.tourismkhammouane.org; Th Vientiane; ⏰8am-5pm) This excellent tourist office offers exciting one- and two-day treks in Phu Hin Boun NPA, including a homestay in a local village. There are also treks to the waterfall by Ban Khoun Kham and Tham Kong Lor (900,000K). Offers advice on journeying the Loop as well. Mr Somkiad speaks English well and is very helpful.

Getting There & Away

Tha Khaek's **bus station** (☎051-251519; Rte 13) is located about 3.5km from the town centre. Buses bound for Hanoi, Hue, Danang and Dong Hoi, in Vietnam, stop here, but the bus station staff weren't able to tell us any departure times or prices, and made clear that it's only possible to buy tickets on the bus.

Departures include the following:

Nakhon Phanom, Thailand (18,000K to 20,000K, 1½ hours, eight times daily)

Pakse (70,000K, six to seven hours, daily)

Savannakhet (30,000K, two to three hours, thrice daily)

Vientiane (60,000K to 80,000K, six hours, five times daily)

Vinh, Vietnam (200,000K, 12 to 15 hours, daily)

Talat Phetmany (Th Kuvoravong) is the departure point for *sŏrngtăaou* to Khammuan Province interior, including to Ban Kong Lor (75,000K, four hours, thrice daily).

Getting Around

It should cost about 30,000K to hire a jumbo (motorised three-wheeled taxi) to the bus terminal, though you'll need to negotiate. From the bus terminal, jumbos don't budge unless they're full or you're willing to fork out 50,000K or more to charter the entire vehicle. Rides around town cost around 15,000K per person.

A handful of places around town offer motorbike hire and most will store your luggage for free if you're doing the Loop (p355). Note that it's a common practice to hold passports until you return with the bike.

Mad Monkey (☎020-59939909; douangdavanh@yahoo.com; Fountain Sq; per day scooters 100,000K, 150-250cc dirt bikes 300,000K; ⏰8am-7pm) A great place to hire a tough, reliable motocross bike to tackle the Loop and other adventures. Mad Monkey has a couple of Honda 250cc dirt bikes and some perky 150cc Kawasaki Fox dirt bikes, plus the usual automatic and semi-automatic scooters. They're more expensive than elsewhere, but they're well maintained. The German-Lao owners are also a great source of information on the Loop.

Mixay Motor Rental (☎020-55124555; per day 70,000-120,000K; ⏰6.30am-6pm) Located in 'downtown' Tha Khaek.

Pokemongo (☎020-23431746; Thakhek Travel Lodge, Rte 13; per day 70,000-100,000K; ⏰7.30am-6pm) With reliable scooters for tackling the Loop, getting around town or exploring the closer caves.

Wangwang Motor Rental (☎020-56978535; Fountain Sq; per day 60,000-140,000K; ⏰7am-11pm) Offers a large range of motorbikes, including dirt bikes, scooters and more. If interested, you can return bikes rented here at Wangwang's sister shops in Pakse and Vientiane.

Phu Hin Bun NPA & Tham Kong Lor

Phu Hin Bun National Protected Area (ປ່າສະຫງວນແຫ່ງຊາດພູຫີນປູນ) is a huge (1580-sq-km) wilderness area of turquoise streams, monsoon forests and striking karst topography across central Khammuan. It was made a protected area in 1993 and it's no overstatement to say that this is some of

GETTING TO THAILAND: THA KHAEK TO NAKHON PHANOM

Getting to the border Crossing the Mekong at the Tha Khaek (Laos)/Nakhon Phanom (Thailand) border is now only possible for locals. Travellers can catch an international bus (18,000K/70B, around 1½ hours) to Nakhon Phanom via the Friendship Bridge from the main bus station in Tha Khaek. Buses run every hour or so from 8.15am to 5pm. If crossing the border after 4pm you'll have to pay an overtime fee.

At the border In Thailand, travellers from most countries are given visa-free, 30-day entry. In Tha Khaek, Lao immigration issues 30-day tourist visas on arrival and there's a BCEL money-exchange service and 24-hour ATM at the immigration office.

Moving on Once in Nakhon Phanom, buses depart regularly for Udon Thani and head to Bangkok at 7.30am and then regularly from 4.30pm to 7.30pm. Faster and almost as cheap are the budget flights to Bangkok offered by AirAsia and Nok Air, with several flights per day.

LOCAL KNOWLEDGE

DEADWOOD: ILLEGAL LOGGING IN LAOS

Laos has some of the largest remnant tracts of primary rainforest in mainland Southeast Asia. With China, Thailand and Vietnam having implemented stricter regulations to protect their own forests, Laos remains a vulnerable target for timber exploitation. The Environmental Investigation Agency (EIA) claims that the furniture industry in Vietnam has grown tenfold since 2000, with Laos facilitating the flow of its timber to enable this. An estimated 500,000 cu metres of logs find their way over the border every year. While an outwardly hard-line approach has been taken against mass logging by the government, it's the self-funded military and local officials in remote areas who can fall prey to bribes.

Forest cover fell from 70% in the 1940s to around 40% by 2010, with an annual rate of nearly 100,000 hectares disappearing every year. National Protected Areas (NPAs), which are supposed to be protected under Lao law, are prey to heavy illegal logging as they contain so much commercially valuable timber. While the valuable forest continues to disappear, the government is attempting a countrywide replantation program, but species being planted are usually commercial timbers and not rare rainforest hardwoods. In a promising development, Lao Prime Minister Thongloun Sisoulith announced a complete logging ban in Laos, effective from 1 June 2016. Yet in the two years since this ban, exports of finished wood products from Laos have, rather paradoxically, doubled, although the government claims that the raw material comes from plantation trees rather than natural forests.

the most breathtaking country in the region. Exploring the NPA on foot or by boat, it's hard not to feel awestruck by the very scale of the limestone cliffs that rise almost vertically for hundreds of metres into the sky. Arguably the highlight of the NPA is Tham Kong Lor, a 7.5km river passing through the cathedral-high limestone cave.

Ban Kong Lor (Kong Lor Village) is the most convenient base for visiting the cave and has numerous guesthouses and small resorts.

Sights & Activities

The Loop (p355), a circuit route best done on motorbike, is the best way to visit Phu Hin Bun NPA.

At Tham Kong Lor, the ticket office doubles as an informal information centre for the cave and the surrounding area. Beyond visiting the river cave, other activities include short treks in the scenic countryside around Ban Kong Lor or bicycle rides to soak up the scenery. The website http://konglor-natane-cave.com/en/ has details about outdoor pursuits in the area.

On the Ban Natane side of the cave, bikes can be hired from 20,000K for two hours to 40,000K for a full day, and there's a (relatively) well-marked route through the countryside that takes about 1½ hours to complete.

To the north of Phu Hin Bun NPA, ecotour operator Green Discovery (p357) was at the time of research constructing an ambitious zipline and canopy walk near the **Limestone Forest Viewpoint** (ຈຸດຊົມວິວປ່າຫີນປູນ; Rte 8); check in with its website or office in Tha Khaek for details.

Khammuan Province's Tourist Information Centre in Tha Khaek offers day trips to Tham Kong Lor (per person for a group of one/two/six 1,500,000/850,000/550,000K); speak to the ever-proficient Mr Somkiad. Green Discovery (p357) also runs one-day trips to Tham Kong Lor from US$70 per person and overnight trips from US$155 per person.

★ **Tham Kong Lor** CAVING, BOATING

(ຖ້ຳກອງລໍ; cave entrance & boat trip 65,000K, parking fee 10,000K; ⌚8am-4pm) A boat trip through the other-worldly Tham Kong Lor is an absolute must. The 7.5km river cave, situated in the wilderness of Phu Hin Bun NPA, runs through an immense limestone mountain. Your imagination will be in overdrive as the boat takes you further into the bat-black darkness and the fear dial will ratchet up as if you're on some natural Gothic ghost ride.

A section of Kong Lor has now been atmospherically lit, allowing you a greater glimpse of this epic spectacle; your longtail docks in a rocky inlet to allow you to explore a stalactite wood of haunting pillars and sprouting stalagmites that are like an abandoned *Star Trek* set.

WORTH A TRIP

PROTECTED AREAS IN CENTRAL LAOS

Central Laos is home to the majority of the country's protected areas – both National Protected Areas (NPAs) and national parks – and is possibly the best place to explore its wilderness. As these areas are also home to villages, visits are done via homestays, which means there's also the opportunity for a unique cultural experience.

The downside is that many of these areas truly are wild, and lack of infrastructure aside, you'll need help in securing the required permission to visit. In Bolikhamsai and Khammuan Provinces, Tha Khaek's Tourist Information Centre (p358) and Green Discovery (p357) control much of the action, while in Savannakhet, the excellent Marvelaos (p362) is the sole facilitator.

A rundown of the protected areas in central Laos:

Phu Hin Bun NPA (p358) This stunning protected area in Bolikhamsai and Khammuan Provinces includes Tham Kong Lor, so many visitors don't even realise that they've been there. It's really the only protected area in central Laos that visitors can approach independently, although there are guided tours that provide deeper access to the area.

Hin Namno NPA (ປ່າສະຫງວນຫີນໜາມໜໍ່) One of the most beautiful of the protected zones in southern Laos, this candidate for Unesco Natural World Heritage listing is also one of the most rugged and inaccessible, although this is starting to change. The homestay at **Ban Thongxam** (ບ້ານທອງຊຳ; 020-91301556; per person incl food 50,000K) allows a relatively accessible peek into remote village life and an excursion into some truly wild jungle and fascinating Ho Chi Minh Trail sites, while if you have the time and money, you can mount an expedition to the cave-bound river that is **Tham Lot Se Bang Fai** (ຖ້ຳລອດເຊບັ້ງໄຟ). Located in Khammuan Province.

Dong Phu Vieng NPA (ປ່າສະຫງວນແຫ່ງຊາດດົງພູວຽງ) The three-day trek offered here is a good balance of nature and culture, and spans hiking in varied jungle, stays at two Katang villages, and a boat ride along the beautiful Se Bang Hiang. In Savannakhet Province.

Nakai–Nam Theun National Park (ປ່າສະຫງວນແຫ່ງຊາດນາກາຍ-ນ້ຳເທີນ) Granted national-park status in 2019 and only recently opening its doors to tourism, this park – the country's largest protected area – is said to be a particularly good place to spot wildlife. In Bolikhamsai and Khammuan Provinces.

Phu Xang Hae NPA (ປ່າສະຫງວນແຫ່ງຊາດພູຊ້າງແຫ່) There's much potential in this protected area in Savannakhet Province, and at the time of writing, authorities were just starting to investigate ways to open it to tourism. Stay tuned.

Nam Kading NPA (ປ່າສະຫງວນແຫ່ງຊາດນ້ຳກະດິງ) In Bolikhamsai Province; unfortunately, at the time of writing, there was little or no infrastructure to accommodate those who want to visit this protected area.

Xe Bang Nuan NPA (ປ່າສະຫງວນເຊບັ້ງນວນ) Straddling Savannakhet and Salavan Provinces, this is the furthest off the beaten track of protected areas in central Laos.

Boat trips through Tham Kong Lor take up to an hour each way, and in dry season when the river is low, you'll have to get out while the boat operator and point person haul the wooden craft up rapids. At the other end of the cave, a brief five minutes upstream takes you to a refreshment stop. Catch your breath and then head back in for more adrenaline-fuelled excitement.

Life jackets are provided. Be sure to bring a torch (flashlight) as the ones for rent are inadequate, and wear rubber sandals: the gravel in the riverbed is sharp and it's often necessary to disembark and wade at several shallow points.

Tham Nam None CAVING

(ຖ້ຳນ້ຳນອນ; per person 120,000K) Only recently discovered, Tham Nam None has not yet been fully explored. At 15km, it is one of the longest river caves in Laos, and it's possible to trek into the cave in the dry season. Don't venture into this cave alone; contact Spring

River Resort to set up a trip, and take plenty of torches and batteries.

Sleeping & Eating

The restaurant scene in Ban Kong Lor is not the most sophisticated in central Laos, so many visitors end up eating at their guesthouse, though there is a handful of tourist-oriented restaurants. Ban Khoun Kham (Ban Na Hin) and Lak Sao have a spread of Lao restaurants and noodle shops.

Thongdam Guesthouse GUESTHOUSE $
(020-5570999; Ban Kong Lor; r 60,000K, bungalows 80,000K) This compound includes a strip of concrete rooms and a row of elevated wood bungalows. The latter have more space and natural light, and balconies that look over the rice fields and karst.

★**Spring River Resort** BUNGALOW $$
(020-59636111; www.springriverresort.com; Ban Tiou; bungalows US$20-45; closed Jun & Jul;) These stilted bungalows sit in an immaculately landscaped, jungle-like garden at the edge of Nam Hin Bun. The more expensive rooms have en suite bathrooms, considerably more space and private balconies to enjoy the lush river view. Easily the most charming place to stay in the region. The attached riverside restaurant (mains 35,000K to 50,000K) has a memorable setting and tasty food.

There's a clear-water creek nearby to cool off in, and you can hire kayaks.

Getting There & Away

The larger towns and villages in this region are connected by good-quality roads, and there are links with Vietnam, though some of the more rural roads are very poor and impassable during the rainy season.

If you're headed directly to Tham Kong Lor, from Talat Phetnamy in Tha Khaek, very slow *sŏrngtăaou* depart for Ban Kong Lor at 7am, 2.30pm and 3.30pm (75,000K, four hours). There's also now a direct daily bus between Vientiane and Ban Kong Lor (70,000K, seven hours), which departs at 9am or from the Southern Bus Station in the capital at 10am.

The 40km road from Ban Khoun Kham (Ban Na Hin) to Ban Kong Lor runs a largely straight path through a beautiful valley of rice fields hemmed in on either side by towering karst cliffs. It's an easy one-hour motorbike or *sŏrngtăaou* ride. From Ban Kong Lor, *sŏrngtăaou* to Ban Khoun Kham (25,000K) depart at 10am, 1pm and 3pm.

Savannakhet Province

Savannakhet is the country's most populous province and is home to about 15% of all Lao citizens. The population of around one million includes Lowland Lao, Tai Dam, several small Mon-Khmer groups and communities of Vietnamese and Chinese.

Stretching between the Mekong and Thailand in the west and the Annamite Mountains and Vietnam in the east, it has become an important trade corridor between these two bigger neighbours.

The eponymous provincial capital is one of the more charming cities in Laos, not to mention a natural jumping-off point for the province's protected wildernesses.

There are three NPAs here: Dong Phu Vieng to the south of Rte 9; remote Phu Xang Hae to the north; and Xe Bang Nuan, straddling the border with Salavan Province. Eastern Savannakhet is a good place to see remnants of the Ho Chi Minh Trail, the primary supply route to South Vietnam for the North Vietnamese Army during the Second Indochina War.

Savannakhet

041 / POP 91,000

Languid, time-trapped and somnolent during the sweltering days that batter the old city's plasterwork, Savannakhet (ສະຫວັນນະເຂດ) is a charming blend of past and present Laos. The highlight is the historic quarter with its impressive display of decaying early-20th-century architecture. There's little to do in town but wander the riverfront and cool off in one of a clutch of stylish restaurants and bijou cafes that are steadily growing in number.

That said, there's plenty to do outside of town and outfits such as Marvelaos (p362) can help you plan intrepid trips into the nearby countryside and NPAs.

Sights & Activities

Much of the charm of Savannakhet is in simply wandering through the quiet streets in the town centre, between the old and new buildings, the laughing children and the slow-moving, *petang*-playing old men. The Tourist Information Centre (p364) produces *Savannakhet Downtown,* a brochure featuring a self-guided tour of the city's most interesting buildings.

Savannakhet

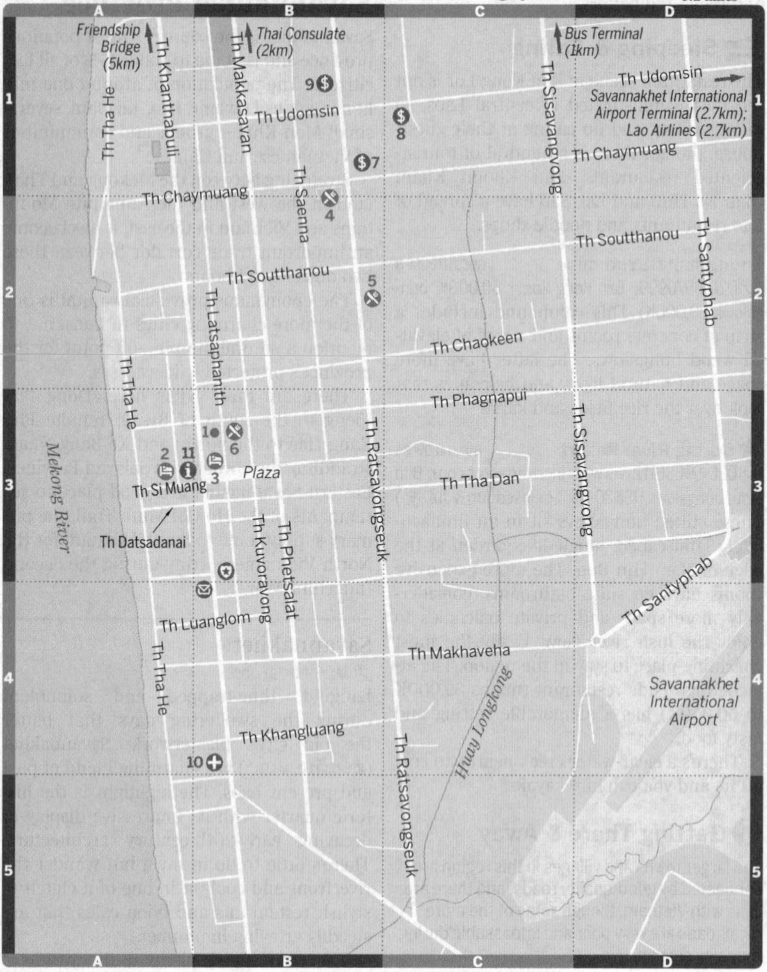

Dong Natad WILDLIFE RESERVE

(ດົງນາຕາດ) Dong Natad is a sacred, semi-evergreen forest within a provincial protected area 15km east of Savannakhet. It's home to two villages that have been coexisting with the forest for about 400 years, with villagers gathering forest products such as mushrooms, honey, fruit, oils, resins and insects. It's possible to visit Dong Natad by bicycle, motorbike or tuk-tuk from Savannakhet.

Marvelaos and Savannakhet's Tourist Information Centre (p364) offer various programs, ranging from multi-day homestays to one-day cycling trips. These community-based trips have had plenty of positive feedback and the combination of English-speaking guide and village guide is a great source of information about how the local people live. If you visit, there's a good chance you'll encounter villagers collecting red ants, cicadas or some other critter, depending on the season; all are important parts of their diet and economy. Make arrangements at least a day ahead.

★ **Marvelaos** TOURS

(☎030-5873604, 020-55552927; www.marvelaos.com; 283 Th Latsapanith; ⊙8.30am-6pm Mon-Sat) Enthusiastic and reliable Alex and Tek

Savannakhet

Activities, Courses & Tours
1 Marvelaos B3

Sleeping
2 Hostel Savan Cafe A3
3 Vivanouk Homestay B3

Eating
4 Café Chez Boune B2
5 Khao Piak Mae Tik B2
6 No Name Grill Place B3

Information
7 BCEL B1
8 Lao Development Bank C1
9 Phongsavanh Bank B1
10 Provincial Hospital B4
11 Tourist Information Centre A3

offer tours of Savannakhet, including guided homestays (for two people, all-inclusive, US$160) and cycling trips (US$175) to Dong Natad and destinations further abroad, including overnight treks in Dong Phu Vieng NPA (US$360) and, by the time you read this, possibly Phu Xang Hae NPA. Highly recommended.

Marvelaos can also help arrange transport, and hires out bicycles (per day 30,000K) and motorcycles (per day 100,000K).

Sleeping

Savannakhet has decent budget and midrange options but little to excite if you're looking for luxury. Most accommodation is located within walking distance of the attractive old town.

★**Hostel Savan Cafe** HOSTEL $
(☎020-91243402; Th Si Muang; dm 70,000K, r 200,000K; ❄📶) This swanky hostel will make you feel like a million bucks on just a few thousand kip. Located right in the heart of 'downtown' Savannakhet, the handsome two- to six-bed dorms (and a couple of private rooms) provide access to a trendy floor-level cafe, leafy lounge zones and a tiled rooftop patio with sweeping sunset views of the Mekong.

★**Vivanouk Homestay** HOMESTAY $$
(☎020-91606030; www.vivanouk.com; Th Latsaphanith; r without bathroom US$20-40; 🚭❄📶) This funky little place is akin to a boutique homestay. There are just three rooms sharing two bathrooms – one with an outdoor shower – and delightfully decorated in a contemporary-colonial fusion style. Breakfast is available downstairs in an artsy venue that doubles as a bar by night.

Eating

Savan has one of the liveliest food scenes in the country. In particular, it's a great place for Lao-style breakfast and lunch, and it's possible to find Western food for dinner.

★**No Name Grill Place** LAO $
(Th Phagnapui; mains from 10,000K; ⏲9am-1pm) Keep your eyes peeled for smoke from the grill and uniformed officials – two signs of a good place to eat in Laos. This tin-roofed, dirt-floored place excels at anything grilled – simply point to what looks good – especially when coupled with sides of spicy papaya salad, hearty bamboo soup and sticky rice.

Khao Piak Mae Tik LAO $
(☎020-77744248; Th Ratsavongseuk; mains 10,000K; ⏲24hr) Mae Tik sells a delicious *kòw ƀęeak sèn*. Look for the tiny roadside shack with the wooden sign.

Café Chez Boune INTERNATIONAL $$
(www.cafechezboune.com; Th Chaymuang; mains 60,000-160,000K; ⏲7am-10pm; ❄📶) Chez Boune has a French-speaking owner and a wood-decked dining room. It's one of the better places in the area for Western food. If you want to keep it semi-local, opt for the delicious beef ragout (known in Lao as *lagoo*), one of few examples of French-Lao fusion.

Information

MEDICAL SERVICES

Provincial Hospital (☎041-212717; Th Khanthabuli; ⏲24hr)

MONEY

BCEL (Th Ratsavongseuk; ⏲8.30am-4.30pm) and **Lao Development Bank** (Th Udomsin; ⏲8.30-11.30am & 1-4.30pm) both have cash exchange, credit-card advances and an ATM.

Phongsavanh Bank (☎041-300888; Th Ratsavongseuk; ⏲8.30am-4pm Mon-Fri, to 11.30am Sat) has cash exchange, Western Union and an ATM.

POLICE STATIONS

Police Station (☎041-260173; Th Khanthabuli; ⏲24hr)

TOURIST INFORMATION

Marvelaos (p362) The best resource for local information.

Tourist Information Centre (☎041-212755; Th Si Muang; ⊙8-11.30am & 1.30-4pm Mon-Fri) Has a selection of aged but well-produced brochures on Savannakhet and its surrounds, but not much else.

Getting There & Away

AIR

Savannakhet's **airport** (☎041-212140; Th Kaysone Phomvihane) is served solely by Lao Airlines, with connections to Vientiane (from 400,000K, 55 minutes, four weekly), Pakse (from 190,000K, 30 minutes, four weekly) and Bangkok (from US$86, 80 minutes, four weekly). Tickets can be purchased at the **Lao Airlines office** (☎041-212140; www.laoairlines.com; Savannakhet Airport; ⊙8.30am-4pm Sun, Mon, Wed & Fri) at the airport, online or with travel agents in town.

An alternative option for those wanting to save money on the Bangkok route is to cross the Friendship Bridge and connect with the fly-drive services offered with AirAsia or Nok Air via Nakhon Phanom Airport; tickets are available from less than 1000B.

BUS

Savannakhet's relatively orderly **bus terminal** (Th Makkasavan), usually called the *khíw lot,* is at the northern edge of town. If you're headed north or south, in addition to the services listed, it's also usually possible to hop on one of the regular buses passing through to/from Vientiane.

Destinations include the following:

Danang, Vietnam (150,000K, 12 hours, three times weekly)

Hanoi, Vietnam (250,000K, 24 hours, four times weekly, all sleeper)

Hue, Vietnam (110,000K, 10 hours, daily)

Mukdahan, Thailand (13,000K, 45 minutes, hourly 8.15am to 7pm)

Pakse (40,000K, five to six hours, twice daily)

Tha Khaek (30,000K, 2½ to four hours, frequent departures 7am to 1pm)

Vientiane (75,000K to 120,000K, eight to 11 hours, frequent departures 6am to 1.30pm, plus 8.30pm sleeper)

Getting Around

Savannakhet is just big enough that you might occasionally need a jumbo. A charter around town costs about 15,000K and more like 20,000K to the bus station. Jumbos make the trip from the airport for 30,000K, although rates may start higher for new arrivals fresh off the plane.

Marvelaos (p362) hires out bicycles (per day 30,000K) and motorcycles (per day 100,000K).

GETTING TO THAILAND: SAVANNAKHET TO MUKDAHAN

Since the construction of the second Thai–Lao Friendship Bridge back in 2006, non-Thai and non-Lao citizens are not allowed to cross between Mukdahan and Savannakhet by boat.

Getting to the border The Thai–Lao International Bus crosses the Savannakhet (Laos)/Mukdahan (Thailand) border crossing (6am to 10pm) in both directions. From Savannakhet's bus terminal, the Thai–Lao International Bus (13,000K, 45 minutes) departs approximately every hour from 8.15am to 7pm. It leaves Mukdahan's bus station (50B, 45 minutes) roughly every hour from 7.30am to 7pm and also stops at the border crossing to pick up passengers.

At the border Be sure not to board the Savan Vegas Casino staff bus at the border, as this also stops at the international bus stop but heads out of town to the eponymous casino resort.

The Lao border offers 30-day tourist visas on arrival. If you don't have a photo you'll be charged the equivalent of US$1. An additional US$1 'overtime fee' is charged from 6am to 8am and 6pm to 10pm on weekdays, as well as on weekends and holidays. Most nationalities do not require a visa to cross into Thailand; check with the Thai consulate (p396) in Savannakhet.

Moving on Onward from Mukdahan, there are at least five daily buses bound for Bangkok. Alternatively, to save time, consider a fly-drive option with AirAsia or Nok Air, including an express minivan to Nakhon Phanom Airport and a budget flight to Bangkok.

GETTING TO VIETNAM: SAVANNAKHET TO DONG HA

Getting to the border Crossing the Dansavanh (Laos)/Lao Bao (Vietnam) border (7am to 7.30pm) is a relative pleasure. From Savannakhet's bus terminal, buses leave for Dansavanh (40,000K, five to six hours) at 7am and noon. Alternatively, consider breaking the journey for a night in Sepon, which you can use as a base for seeing the Ho Chi Minh Trail; there are relatively frequent *sŏrngtăaou* to Dansavanh between 7am and 3pm (20,000K, one hour).

The bus station in Dansavanh is about 1km short of the border; Vietnamese teenagers on motorbikes are more than happy to take you the rest of the way for about 10,000K.

At the border The Lao border offers 30-day tourist visas on arrival and has an exchange booth. Some nationalities require a Vietnam visa in advance, so check with the Vietnamese embassy (p396) in Savannakhet. Most regional visitors, Scandinavian visitors, and British, French, German, Italian and Spanish visitors do not need a visa for short stays.

Moving on Once through, take a motorbike (40,000d or US$2) 2km to the Lao Bao bus terminal and transport to Dong Ha (50,000d, two hours) on Vietnam's main north–south highway and railway. Entering Laos, there are buses to Savannakhet (40,000K, five to six hours) at 7am and 9am, as well as regular *sŏrngtăaou* to Sepon (30,000K, one hour) from 7am to 5pm. Simple accommodation is available on both sides of the border.

If you're in a hurry, an alternative is to take one of the various direct buses from Savannakhet bound for the Vietnamese cities of Hanoi, Hue and Danang.

SOUTHERN LAOS

Southern Laos is dominated by the Bolaven Plateau, a fertile highland that spreads over four of the region's provinces. It is the site of Laos' thriving coffee plantations and also many of the region's beautiful waterfalls.

Pakse is the 'big smoke', a mid-sized town tuned in to travellers' needs with accommodation and restaurants. It's the base for tours into the Bolaven Plateau and other destinations, and is well endowed with tour and bike-hire companies. Wat Phu Champasak, a striking remnant of the once-mighty Khmer empire, can be reached from here, or from the small town of Champasak.

The mighty Mekong plunges and spills to its widest point in Si Phan Don, which has established itself as a backpacker place-to-be, but also has some exquisite boutique hotel accommodation. Here are opportunities to take relaxing bicycle rides through the local villages, go kayaking or ziplining, or view the increasingly rare Irrawaddy dolphins.

Pakse Region

While most visitors to the south base themselves in Pakse city, the region's real gems lie in the surrounding countryside. Wat Phu Champasak is a must-see, and the Se Pian NPA is good for nature lovers, while the islands of Don Kho and Don Daeng provide easy insight into Lao culture.

Once part of the Cambodian Angkor empire, Champasak Province was later absorbed into the Lan Xang kingdom and eventually became an independent kingdom from the early 18th century to the beginning of the 19th century. Today it has a population of more than 700,000, including lowland Lao (many of them Phu Thai), Khmers and a host of small upland Mon-Khmer groups, most of whom inhabit the Bolaven Plateau region.

Pakse

☎031 / POP 68,330

Pakse (ປາກເຊ), the capital of Champasak Province and the gateway to southern Laos, sits at the confluence of the Mekong and the Se Don (Don River). It's a relatively lively town with lots of accommodation and eating options, as well as transport connections, and many travellers base themselves here for forays to surrounding attractions such as the Bolaven Plateau (p376) and Wat Phu Champasak (p373). The many good restaurants, stylish hotels and clued-in tour companies make it a comfortable and convenient home base.

Pakse

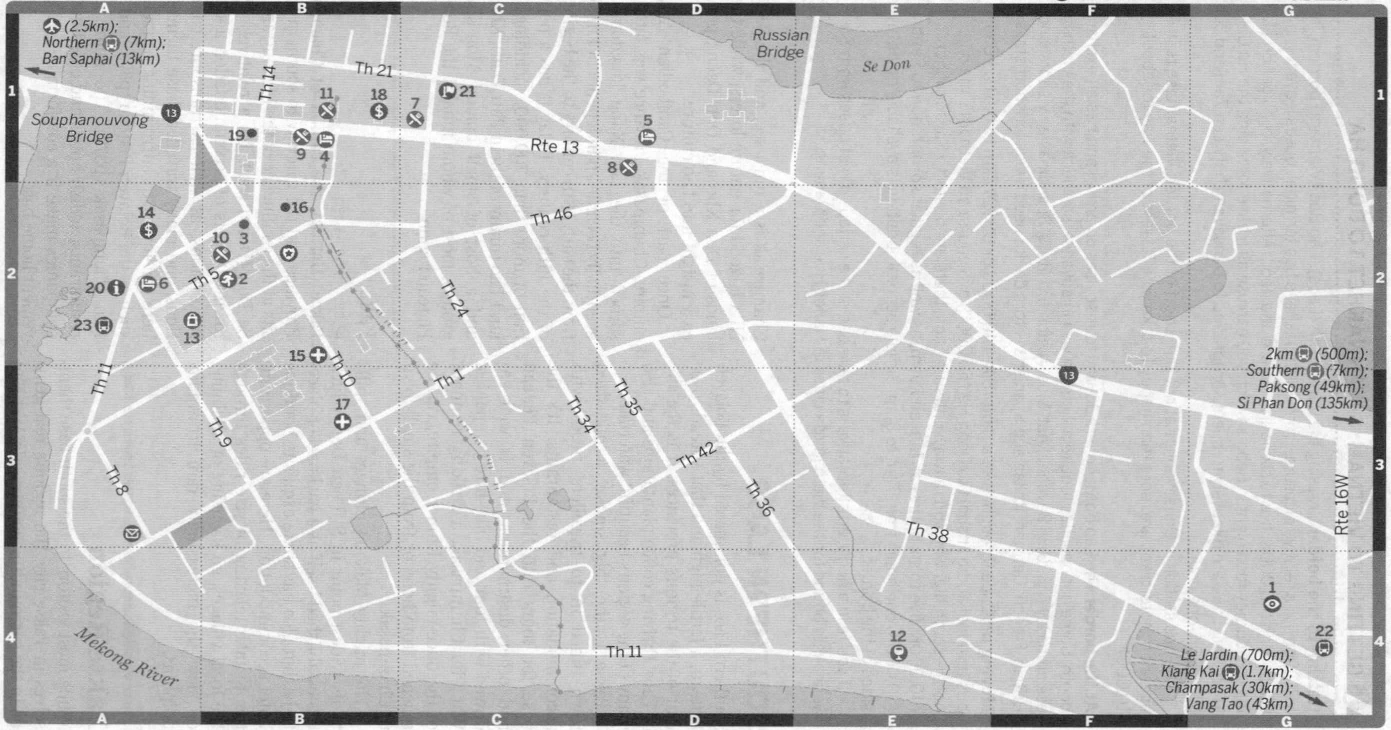
(2.5km);
Northern (7km);
Ban Saphai (13km)
Souphanouvong Bridge
Russian Bridge
Se Don
Th 21
Th 14
Rte 13
Th 46
Th 5
Th 11
Th 10
Th 1
Th 9
Th 8
Th 24
Th 34
Th 35
Th 42
Th 36
Th 38
Rte 16W
Mekong River
2km (500m);
Southern (7km);
Paksong (49km);
Si Phan Don (135km)
Le Jardin (700m);
Kiang Kai (1.7km);
Champasak (30km);
Vang Tao (43km)

Pakse

Sights & Activities

Pakse is much more a home base than a place to take in the sights. **Wat Phou Salao** (ວັດພູສະເຫຼົ້າ; Rte 16) is a worthwhile trip (by tuk-tuk, or on foot if you're fit) for its views, especially at sunset.

Talat Dao Heuang MARKET
(ຕະຫຼາດດາວເຮືອງ; ⊙5am-6pm) This vast market near the Lao–Japanese Bridge is one of the biggest in the country. It's at its most chaotic in the food zones, but just about anything a person might need – from medicinal herbs to mobile phones – is sold here. It's well worth a visit.

Champasak Historical Heritage Museum MUSEUM
(ພິພິດທະພັນມໍລະດົກປະຫວັດສາດຈຳປາສັກ; Rte 13; 10,000K; ⊙8.30-11.30am & 2-4pm Mon-Fri) Highlights here include ancient bronze drums, stone carvings unearthed up on the Bolaven Plateau, stelae with Tham script dating from the 15th to 18th centuries, Khmer stone carvings, and musical instruments. Also of interest is the textile and jewellery collection from ethnic minorities such as the Nyaheun, Suay and Laven, with large iron ankle bracelets and ivory earplugs.

At the time of research, this museum had just moved to a new location. It's not clear if this is a permanent move, but in any case you may find tuk-tuk drivers unaware of its location. It's near the old swimming pool (*sá wài nâm*) about 7km out of town on Rte 13.

Dok Champa Massage MASSAGE
(☎020-54188778; Th 5; massages 60,000-100,000K; ⊙9am-10pm) Dok Champa delivers Lao massage, foot massage, herbal remedies and more. Staff are friendly and professional, and there is a resident *ajahn* (teacher) on hand supervising the staff.

Tours

Most people organise their southern Laos tours and treks in Pakse. Pretty much all hotels and travel agencies sell a standard selection of day trips to the Bolaven Plateau, Wat Phu Champasak and Kiet Ngong. Miss Noy (p369) is probably the best place in town to get tour and travel information.

The cheapest tours are simply transportation; admission fees and meals are not included and there is no guide. For many people this is fine, but for others it's a disappointing surprise. Be sure you know what you are getting before you agree to go.

★**Green Discovery** ADVENTURE
(☎031-252908; www.greendiscoverylaos.com; Th 10; 2-day Tree Top Explorer tour 2-/4-person group per person US$399/329; ⊙8am-8.30pm) Green Discovery is one of the foremost eco- and adventure-tour companies in Laos. Its signature trip is the Tree Top Explorer adventure in **Dong Hua Sao NPA** (ປ່າສະຫງວນແຫ່ງຊາດດົງຫົວສາວ) near Paksong, consisting of two or three days' ziplining, canopy walking and jungle trekking around waterfalls beyond any roads.

Accommodation is in ecofriendly huts set high up above the forest floor.

Green Discovery also runs tours to many other destinations, such as the Phu Xieng Thong and Se Pian NPAs.

Vat Phou Cruises CRUISE
(031-251446; www.vatphou.com; just off Th 11; office 8am-5pm Mon-Sat, no cruises in Jun) Operates three-day luxury Mekong cruises between Pakse and Si Phan Don, including visits to Wat Phu Champasak (p373) and Khon Phapheng Falls (p383).

Sleeping

The tourist centre is on Rte 13 between the Souphanouvong Bridge (formerly the French Bridge) and Th 24. Stay here if you want easy access to travel agencies, motorbike rentals, money changers and touristy restaurants. Around the corner you'll find more hotels and restaurants in the commercial district, which is centred on the **Doungdy Plaza** (Th 5; 8am-7pm). If you're staying anywhere else, rent a motorbike or bicycle to get around.

Alisa Guesthouse GUESTHOUSE $
(031-251555; www.alisa-guesthouse.com; Rte 13; r 130,000-160,000K, f 210,000K;) Perhaps the best-value lodging in Pakse, Alisa has sparkling rooms, tiled floors, solid wood beds, armoires, working satellite TV and a fridge. Service is good, too. The only significant knock is that some rooms barely catch a wi-fi signal. No surprise, it's often full.

★**Residence Sisouk** BOUTIQUE HOTEL $$
(031-214716; www.residence-sisouk.com; cnr Th 9 & Th 11; r incl breakfast US$60-80;) This exquisite boutique hotel occupies a lovely old house and evokes a bit of old France. The rooms enjoy polished hardwood floors, flat-screen TVs, verandas, Hmong bed runners, stunning photography and fresh flowers everywhere. Breakfast is in the penthouse cafe with great views. Paying extra gets you a bigger, brighter room with a balcony in front. Rates drop 30% in low season.

Le Jardin BOUTIQUE HOTEL $$
(030-9463324; www.lejardindepakse.com; r US$70;) One of the nicest places to stay in Pakse, Le Jardin oozes old colonial charm, with yellow-ochre-and-white-trim walls and floral tiling throughout. The garden adds to the atmosphere, and the rooms are decorated with artworks and stylish touches. It's a bit out of town, just behind Dao Heuang market, but there's a free shuttle into the main restaurant hub every evening at 7pm.

Note that in Lao it's pronounced *'ler jardaeng'*.

★**Athena Hotel** HOTEL $$$
(031-214888; www.athenahotelpakse.com; Rte 13; r incl breakfast US$60-90;) Athena's subdued style features tasteful timber finishes and a classy ambience. The beds are marshmallowy delights, and dimming inlaid ceiling lights let you illuminate them in many ways. The cosy pool is most welcome after a day out on dusty roads and there's an upmarket thatch-roofed *sala* for relaxing (or photo ops). It's about a 10-minute walk from the tourist centre.

Eating & Drinking

Two good morning spots for delicious *fěr* are the **Noodle Shop Mengky** (Rte 13; noodles 20,000K; 6am-1pm) and the more tourist-friendly **Lankham Noodle Shop** (Rte 13; noodles 20,000-50,000K; 6am-2pm;) across the road.

The Pon Sai area at the junction of Th 34 and Th 46 bustles with small shops and street vendors selling *fěr,* baguettes, *kòw něeo bîng* (grilled, egg-dipped sticky rice patties) and many doughy delights. It's best in the morning, but some shops stay open through the day and into the night.

Le Panorama is a required stop for a sunset Beerlao or two. For a more local touch, there are a few floating restaurants along the rivers that catch some of the twilight. For the best sunset, cross the Souphanouvong Bridge and walk left to the mouth of the Se Don, or continue to one of the bars on the Mekong River just past it.

★**Delta Coffee** CAFE $
(Rte 13; mains 25,000-50,000K; 7am-9pm;) Delta offers a lot more than the name suggests. Owners Alan and Siriporn serve coffee from their plantation near Paksong, but also have a menu that includes pizza, spinach lasagne and a full range of Lao and Thai dishes. Recommended.

Daolin Restaurant LAO, INTERNATIONAL $
(Rte 13; mains 15,000-50,000K; 7am-10pm;) Overlook the traffic noise – this popular restaurant has great food and service. It has some of the best Thai food in town and is a great introduction to Lao food, with set

meals of sticky rice, steamed veggies, chilli sauce and fried fish/chicken/pork. Vegetarians can try Lao food that is usually meat-based, such as pumpkin soup *(om mahk éu)* and mushroom *gôy.*

★Le Panorama LAO, INTERNATIONAL $$
(Th 5; mains 35,000-85,000K; ⌚4.30-10pm; 📶✍) The rooftop restaurant of the Pakse Hotel serves up delicious Franco-Asian cuisine and unbeatable 360-degree city views. The menu includes duck breast, pizza and a succulent *ƃah neung het hŏrm* (stuffed fish steamed in banana leaves).

Champahom BAR
(Th 11) A chill place to drink and snack, this Thai-owned bar has live music (usually Carabao-style Thai country music) most nights except Sunday from about 7.30pm to 9pm.

ℹ Information

EMBASSIES & CONSULATES

The Vietnamese Consulate (p396) issues visas for US$50 in two working days, express visas for US$60.

MEDICAL SERVICES

International Hitech Polyclinic (VIP Clinic; ☎031-214712; ihpc_lao@yahoo.com; cnr Th 1 & Th 10; ⌚24hr) Adjacent to the **public hospital** (☎030-5785709; Th 10; ⌚24hr), it has English-speaking staff and much higher standards of care, service and facilities, plus a pharmacy.

MONEY

Banks, such as the conveniently located **BCEL** (Th 11; ⌚8.30am-3.30pm Mon-Fri) and **Lao Development Bank** (Rte 13; ⌚8.30am-3.30pm Mon-Fri), have the best currency-exchange rates, though the exchange counter at the **Lankham Hotel** (⌚7am-7pm) is good too. All three give cash advances (3% commission) on credit cards. LDB also has Western Union and can exchange US-dollar travellers cheques (1%). ATMs are plentiful in the city centre.

POLICE STATIONS

Main Police Station (☎031-252127)

TOURIST INFORMATION

Provincial Tourism Office (☎020-9204994; Th 11; ⌚8am-4pm Mon-Fri) Mostly exists to hand out maps and brochures, but some staff can answer questions or help you make bookings for homestays and activities at Kiet Ngong, Don Kho and Don Daeng. Note: at the time of research, the office was planning to move, so it may have relocated by the time you read this; enquire locally for the latest.

Miss Noy (☎020-22272278; noy7days@hotmail.com; Rte 13; per day bicycles 10,000K, motorbikes 60,000K; ⌚8am-8pm) The gang here is seriously clued in to the region, especially the Bolaven Plateau.

VISAS

Pakse's **immigration bureau** (Th 10; ⌚8-11am & 2-4pm Mon-Fri) is next to the Foreigner Control Area of the main police station in a low-lying mint-green building. To extend your stay, bring a photocopy of your passport name page and visa, two photos, and 50,000K plus 20,000K per day. An extension for a minimum of three days and a maximum of 30 should be ready the next afternoon.

ℹ Getting There & Away

AIR

The **Pakse International Airport** (Rte 13) is 2.5km northwest of the Souphanouvong Bridge. A tuk-tuk to/from the airport will cost about 40,000K.

Lao Airlines (☎031-212252; www.laoairlines.com; Pakse International Airport; ⌚8am-5pm) has direct flights to the following cities in Asia:

Bangkok US$115, four weekly
Ho Chi Minh City US$105, three weekly
Luang Prabang 1,010,000K, three weekly
Savannakhet 375,000K, four weekly
Siem Reap US$100, five weekly
Vientiane 770,000K, three daily

A better way to fly to Bangkok is to travel overland to Ubon Ratchathani and catch a budget flight from there, which is considerably cheaper.

BOAT

A tourist boat motors from Pakse to Champasak (one way per person 70,000K) at 8.30am, provided there are enough punters – in the low season there usually aren't. It's two hours downstream to Champasak, and a bit longer on the return. Book through Miss Noy or call **Mr Khamlao** (☎020-22705955; per boat US$70), who runs his own separate boat.

BUS

Pakse, frustratingly, has many bus and *sŏrngtăaou* (passenger truck) stations. The vast majority of tourists simply book bus journeys through their guesthouse or a travel agency, and since these are either special tourist buses that pick you up in the centre or include a free transfer to the relevant departure point, the prices are usually reasonable.

Note that on long-distance routes to Cambodia and Vietnam you'll want to be careful which company you use: choosing the wrong one could cost you several hours and cause a lot of pain. Buy your ticket from a travel agency that actually knows the details of the route, rather than a guesthouse, which probably does not.

There are six main stations:

Southern Bus Terminal (Rte 13) Pakse's main bus station, with departures to most places. Also known as *kîw lot lák Þaat* (8km bus terminal) because it's 8km east of town on Rte 13.

Northern Bus Terminal (Rte 13) This is the most orderly of the stations and is usually called *kîw lot lák jét* (7km bus terminal); it's – you guessed it – 7km north of town. Only for northern destinations. The English-language signs on departures are frequently wrong.

Talat Dao Heuang Vans and *sŏrngtăaou* to nearby destinations, such as the Thai border, depart from a very chaotic lot in the southeast corner of the market and also from Th 38 in front of the market.

2km Bus Station (Sengchalern Bus Station; ☎031-212428; Rte 13) Also known as Sengchalern station, after the company that owns it; the office is in the lobby of SL Guest House, which is in front of Friendship Mall.

VIP Bus Station (Th 11) Also called Thasalakham station, it only serves VIP night buses to Vientiane and towns along the way. There are a number of companies here, all offering the same tickets at the same price.

Kiang Kai Bus Station (off Th 38) This small, hard-to-find station, in a red-and-yellow building set back well off Th 38, is 1.5km past the Japanese bridge. It's used by buses to/from Thailand, though these also use the Southern Bus Terminal, as well as buses to Vientiane.

Champasak & Si Phan Don (Four Thousand Islands)

Regular *sŏrngtăaou* leave Talat Dao Heuang for Champasak (20,000K, one hour) until noon or so – sometimes even as late as 2pm. There's also a morning tourist bus-boat combo to Champasak (65,000K, 1½ hours) offered by most travel agencies. Be sure your ticket includes the boat crossing from Ban Muang. The regular price for the boat is 10,000K per person or 30,000K if you're alone.

For Si Phan Don, tourist buses and minivans – including pickups in town and boat transfer to Don Khong (60,000K, 2½ hours), Don Det (75,000K, three hours) and Don Khon (80,000K, 3¼ hours) – are most comfortable and convenient. Book these through any guesthouse or travel agent. All departures are in the morning around 8am.

If you want to leave later in the day, take a *sŏrngtăaou* from the Southern Bus Terminal to Ban Nakasang (for Don Det and Don Khon; 40,000K, 3½ hours). These depart hourly until 5pm and go via Hat Xai Khun (for Don Khong).

One *sŏrngtăaou* services Kiet Ngong (30,000K, two hours), leaving at 1pm.

Vientiane & Points North

Most travellers prefer the comfortable 'VIP' night sleeper buses to Vientiane (170,000K, 10 hours). You can book these through your guesthouse or head to the conveniently located VIP Bus Station, from where there are several nightly departures, all leaving at 8.30pm; or the 2km Bus Station, with one departure at 8pm. It's possible to take these buses to Tha Khaek (130,000K, 4½ hours) and Seno (for Savannakhet; 100,000K, three hours).

If you prefer day travel, slower-moving, ordinary air-con buses (110,000K, 12 to 14 hours) depart throughout the day from the Southern Bus Terminal, stopping occasionally to pick up more passengers at the Northern Bus Terminal. These buses also go to Tha Khaek (60,000K, five hours) and Seno (65,000K, seven hours).

Neighbouring Countries

Travelling to Cambodia (p388) is a guaranteed hassle, while entering Thailand is a breeze. Travelling to Vietnam falls in between.

The most comfortable way to Hue (200,000K, 12 hours) and Danang (230,000K, 14 hours) in Vietnam is to catch one of the morning sleeper buses from the Southern Bus Terminal, which for legal reasons use the long route through the Lao Bao border east of Savannakhet. Note that these do not go every day – sometimes a regular bus goes instead and sometimes there is simply no bus. Up to three hours faster for the same price are the modern, comfortable minibuses that go via Salavan and use the Lalay border (p379), though the drivers tend to be reckless. Then there are the slower and truly crappy cargo buses that only save a few of their seats for passengers. These make for a very uncomfortable and much longer journey. If there is no large bus, some unscrupulous travel agencies will book passengers on these buses without telling them, so be sure you know what vehicle your ticket is really for. For Kom Tun or Ho Chi Minh City you travel via the Bo Y border. Some travel agencies sell tickets for direct buses to Ho Chi Minh City (450,000K, 15 hours), but these go via the southern route, so you need to buy a Cambodian visa. It takes several hours longer, but is actually much cheaper to travel to Kom Tum and take a connecting bus (240,000d) from there.

ℹ Getting Around

Local transport in Pakse is expensive by regional standards. Figure on 10,000K to 20,000K for a short tuk-tuk ride. A ride to the Northern or Southern Bus Terminals costs 15,000K per person shared and 50,000K for a whole tuk-tuk.

GETTING TO THAILAND: VANG TAO TO CHONG MEK

Getting to the border Other than finding the right counters to use at immigration, crossing at the Vang Tao (Laos)/Chong Mek (Thailand) border (open 6am to 8pm) is straightforward.

The easiest way to get there is on the Thai–Lao International Bus (60,000K, 2½ to three hours, 8.30am and 3pm) between Pakse's Southern Bus Terminal and Ubon Ratchathani's bus station. It picks up more passengers at the little Kiang Kai Bus Station on the way. If you're travelling *to* Pakse (departures from Ubon at 9.30am and 1.30pm, 200B) note that this bus does wait long enough for people to get Lao visas.

There are also frequent minivans from Pakse to Vang Tao (20,000K, 45 minutes) departing from the street in front of Talat Dao Heuang and also *sŏrngtăaou* (passenger trucks) leaving from inside the market until about 4pm. Vans to Vang Tao also depart hourly from the Southern Bus Terminal. You'll be dropped off in a dusty/muddy parking area about 500m from the Lao immigration office.

If you're headed to Bangkok (225,000K, 13 hours), a direct service (that sometimes involves changing buses at Ubon) departs the Southern Bus Terminal daily at 4pm. Pakse travel agents also offer a combination bus/sleeper train ticket to the Thai capital, with prices starting at 310,000K for 2nd-class fan carriages and going much higher for better service.

At the border Laos issues visas on arrival (around US$35, or 1500B, depending on which passport you hold), while on the Thai side most nationalities are issued 30-day visa waivers free of charge. You walk between the two countries using a pointless underground tunnel for part of the way.

Although it seems like a scam, there is a legitimate overtime fee on the Laos side after 4pm weekdays and all day on weekends and holidays. The real scam is that the officials are likely to demand 100B even though the actual price is 10,000K. Just tell them you want a receipt and you'll pay the correct price.

Moving on Minivans head to Ubon (100B, 1¼ hours, every 30 minutes) from Chong Mek's bus terminal, which is 600m (20B by motorcycle taxi) up the main road. Alternatively, informal taxi drivers hang around immigration and charge 1000B to anywhere in Ubon Ratchathani city.

BICYCLE

Cycling around to the city's few sites can make for a pleasant few hours. Miss Noy (p369) hires bikes.

CAR & MOTORCYCLE

Several shops and guesthouses in the tourist belt along Rte 13 rent motorbikes from 50,000K per day for 100cc bikes, rising to 100,000K for an automatic Honda Scoopy. Safe bets are Miss Noy (p369), which has a nightly planning meeting for those heading to the Bolaven Plateau, and **Pakse Travel** (☎020-22277277; Rte 13; ⏰7.30am-8.30pm).

Talk to any travel agency or hotel about hiring a car with driver, which should cost about US$100 (plus fuel) depending on where you want to go. **Avis** (☎031-214946; www.avis.la; Th 10; per day from US$75; ⏰8.30am-6pm Mon-Fri, 9am-1pm Sat & Sun) rents out pickups and SUVs with or without drivers and can provide paperwork to allow the cars to go to Thailand and Vietnam (but not Cambodia).

Don Kho & Ban Saphai

The Mekong-hugging Ban Saphai (Saphai Village; ບ້ານສະພາຍ) and adjacent island of Don Kho (ດອນໂຄ) just north of Pakse are famous for their weaving. Women work on large looms underneath their homes producing silk and cotton dresses and other products, and are happy to show you how. While this is a well-known destination, it's not overrun. The rarely visited Ban Don Khoh (Don Khoh Village; ບ້ານດອນເຂາະ), not far away, does impressive stone carving. These three destinations combine for a good half-day trip out of Pakse and cultural explorers can dig deeper with a night at Don Kho's homestay.

Ban Saphai Handicraft Centre CULTURAL CENTRE
(ສູນຫັດຖະກຳບ້ານສະພາຍ; ⏰6am-7pm) Next to the boat pier, several weavers have their

looms here and locally woven textiles and other crafts are on sale. Some people here can speak a little English. They will call to arrange your homestay and/or activities on Don Kho.

Don Kho Homestay HOMESTAY $
(per person 30,000K, per meal 20,000K) Don Kho is a great place to experience a village homestay. Just turn up on the island and say 'homestay' and the villagers will sort you out. Meals are taken with the host family and, in our experience, the food is delicious. The Provincial Tourism Office (p369) in Pakse can arrange things in advance.

Getting There & Away

Ban Saphai is 16km north of Pakse's Souphanouvong Bridge and the turn-off is clearly signed. *Sŏrngtăaou* from Pakse to Ban Saphai (20,000K, 45 minutes) leave fairly regularly from the street in front of the Talat Dao Heung (p370).

From Ban Saphai to Don Kho, longtail boats cost 40,000K round trip and can hold up to five people. Set a time for pickup, or take the boatman's phone number and call when you want to return.

Ban Don Khoh is between Pakse and Ban Saphai, 9km from the Souphanouvong Bridge. The turn is unmarked, but it's the paved road going west just before the bus station.

Champasak

031 / POP 15,440

It's hard to imagine Champasak (ຈຳປາສັກ) as a seat of royalty, but from 1713 until 1946 it was just that. These days the town is a somnolent place, the fountain circle (that no longer hosts a fountain) in the middle of the main street alluding to a grandeur long since departed, along with the former royal family. Scattered French colonial–era buildings share space with traditional Lao wooden stilt houses, and the few vehicles that venture down the narrow main street (which pretty well comprises most of the town) share it with chickens and cows.

With a surprisingly good range of accommodation and several attractions in the vicinity – most notably the Angkor-period ruins of Wat Phu Champasak – it's easy to see why many visitors to the region prefer staying in Champasak over bustling Pakse.

Just about everything in Champasak is spread along the riverside road on both sides of the fountain circle.

Sights & Activities

Champasak has a few mildly interesting temples, and soaking up the Mekong scenery and seeing local life along the riverfront road can make for a wonderful day.

Wat Muang Kang BUDDHIST TEMPLE
(ວັດເມືອງກາງ, Wat Phuthawanaram) About 5km south of town along the Mekong stands the oldest active temple in Champasak, and one of the most interesting in southern Laos. The soaring Thai-style *ubosot* (ordination hall), with its red-tiled roof (under reconstruction during our visit) and ring of pillars, is impressive, but the *hŏr tại* (Tripitaka library), with its elements of Lao, Chinese, Vietnamese and French-colonial architecture, is striking.

Champasak Spa SPA
(020-56499739; www.champasak-spa.com; massage 80,000-160,000K; 10am-noon & 1-7pm, closed Mon May-Oct, all of Jun) Run by Nathalie, this is a fragrant oasis of free tea and sensitively executed treatments using locally grown and sourced organic bio products. And it creates jobs for local residents. A full-day spa package (reservations required) comprising facial, body scrub, hair spa, massage and lunch costs 550,000K.

Sleeping & Eating

Finding a room in Champasak is straightforward enough except during the **Wat Phu Champasak Festival** (usually in February), when you can camp on the grounds of Wat Phu Champasak. Luxury and homestay accommodation is also available on nearby Don Daeng.

★ **Nakorn Cafe Guest House** GUESTHOUSE $$
(020-98177964; r US$38-45;) This Lao-Belgian-owned spot on the river a tad south of the main drag has the cleanest rooms in town, with private balconies, beautifully tiled interiors and luxurious rain showers. There's a second unit of rooms overlooking the Mekong a few doors down, with a two-level family room (US$70). Optional breakfast at the Nakorn Cafe is US$7 extra.

★ **Residence Bassac Hotel** BOUTIQUE HOTEL $$$
(030-5407587; www.residencebassac.com; r incl breakfast US$86-110;) The belle of the river, the Residence has rooms that are a mix of old and new, but all ooze charm and

induce relaxation. And all have little touches of luxury – ambient lighting, flat-screen TVs, safes and rain showers – that set them apart from the in-town competition.

★**Nakorn Cafe Restaurant** LAO, INTERNATIONAL $
(mains 20,000-53,000K; ⊙7.30am-9.30pm;) A pleasant melange of classy and casual, this riverside restaurant has a small mixed menu that covers duck *láhp* to chicken green curry to tuna sandwiches. There are some Belgian beers on the menu, and also plenty of local advice available from the affable owners.

☆ Entertainment

Shadow Puppet Theatre & Cinema Tuktuk CINEMA, PUPPETRY
(020-55081109; 50,000K; ⊙Nov-Apr) Run by Frenchman Yves Bernard, this magical theatre next to the tourist office tells a story from the *Ramayana* with traditional shadow puppets, while on Wednesday and Saturday nights it screens the Academy Award–nominated silent film *Chang* (1927). What makes it so great is the live musicians providing the soundtrack.

Chang was filmed over 18 months in the jungles of northeast Thailand by the writer and director of Hollywood's original *King Kong*.

ℹ Information

Champasak District Visitor Information Centre (030-9239673; ⊙8am-4.30pm Mon-Fri, also open weekends Sep-Apr) The staff here are friendly and can give information and also arrange boats to, and accommodation on, Don Daeng. Local guides, some of whom speak English, lead day walks around Wat Phu and can accompany you to Uo Moung. You can also arrange boats to Uo Moung here (350,000K), taking in Don Daeng and Wat Muang Kang.

Lao Development Bank (⊙8.30am-3.30pm Mon-Fri) Has an ATM, changes cash and does Western Union.

ℹ Getting There & Away

Champasak is 30km from Pakse along a beautiful, almost empty sealed road running along the west bank of the Mekong. *Sŏrngtăaou* to Pakse (20,000K, one hour) depart only in the morning, up to around 8am. There are also tourist buses and boats direct to/from Pakse, but they don't run often due to lack of demand.

The regular morning tourist buses from Pakse to Champasak (55,000, 1½ hours) are actually the buses heading to Si Phan Don. These drop you at Ban Muang on the eastern bank of the Mekong, where a small ferry (20,000K per person, 30,000K for motorbikes) crosses to the village of Ban Phaphin just north of Champasak. Be sure you know whether your ticket includes the ferry or not. (The ferry operators won't rip you off over this, but some of the ticket agents in Pakse have been known to.) None of the tickets include the final 2km into Champasak, so you'll probably need to walk it.

To reach Si Phan Don you can also use the Ban Muang ferry route or travel by boat (US$240 private; the Champasak District Visitor Information Centre will know if others are interested in sharing the cost).

ℹ Getting Around

All guesthouses rent bicycles (10,000K to 20,000K per day) and a few, including **Anouxa** (020-55339008; r with fan 60,000K, with air-con 100,000-200,000K;), also have motorbikes (from 70,000K per day). Anouxa also has mountain bikes, a rarity in Champasak.

Wat Phu World Heritage Area

A visit to the ancient Khmer religious complex of Wat Phu (ວັດພູຈຳປາສັກ) is one of the highlights of southern Laos. Stretching 1400m up the slopes of Phu Pasak (also known more colloquially as Phu Khuai or Mt Penis), Wat Phu is small compared with the monumental Angkor-era sites near Siem Reap in Cambodia. However, you know the old adage about location, location, location! The tumbledown pavilions, ornate Shiva-lingam sanctuary, enigmatic crocodile stone and tall trees that shroud much of the upper walkway in soothing shade give Wat Phu an almost mystical atmosphere. These, and a layout that is unique in Khmer architecture, led to Unesco declaring the Wat Phu complex a World Heritage Site in 2001.

An electric cart shuttles guests from the ticket-office area past the *baray* (ceremonial pond; *năwng sá* in Lao). After that, you must walk.

It is possible to sleep at a guesthouse near the entrance to Wat Phu, but spending the night next to the Mekong in Champasak town is far superior.

◉ Sights

★**Wat Phu Champasak** RUINS
(50,000K, motorbike parking 5000K; ⊙site 8am-6pm, museum to 4.30pm) Bucolic Wat Phu sits in graceful decrepitude, and while it lacks the arresting enormity of Angkor in

Cambodia, given its few visitors and more dramatic natural setting, these small Khmer ruins evoke a more soulful response. While some buildings are more than 1000 years old, most date from the 11th to 13th centuries. The site is divided into six terraces on three levels joined by a frangipani-bordered stairway ascending the mountain to the main shrine at the top.

Visit in the early morning for cooler temperatures (it gets really hot during the day, and on the lower levels there isn't any shade) and to capture the ruins in the best light. Make sure to grab a map at the entrance as there is little to no signage here.

➡ Lower Level

The electric cart takes you past the great *baray* (ceremonial pond; *nŏrng sá* in Lao) and delivers you to the large sandstone base of the ancient main entrance to Wat Phu. Here begins a causeway-style ceremonial promenade lined by stone lotus buds and flanked by two much smaller *baray* that still fill with water, lotus flowers and the odd buffalo during the wet season.

➡ Middle Level

Wat Pu's middle section features two exquisitely carved **quadrangular pavilions** built of sandstone and laterite that are believed to date from the mid-10th or early 11th century. The buildings consist of four galleries and a central open courtyard. Wat Phu was converted into a Buddhist site in later centuries but much of the original Hindu sculpture remains in the lintels, which feature various forms of Vishnu and Shiva.

A good example is the eastern pediment of the north pavilion, which is a relief of Shiva and Parvati sitting on Nandi, Shiva's bull mount.

Next to the southern pavilion stands the much smaller **Nandi Hall** (dedicated to Shiva's mount). It was from here that an ancient royal road once led over 200km to Angkor Wat in Cambodia. In front is a smaller version of the initial causeway, this one flanked by two collapsed galleries, leading to a pair of steep staircases.

At the base of a second stairway is an impressive and now very holy **dvarapala** (sentinel figure) standing ramrod straight with sword held at the ready. Most Thai and Lao visitors make an offering to his spirit before continuing up the mountain. If you step down off the walkway and onto the grassy area just north of here you'll come to the remains of a yoni pedestal, the cosmic vagina-womb symbol associated with Shaivism, and two unusually large, headless and armless **dvarapala statues** half-buried in the grass. These are the largest *dvarapala* found anywhere in the former Angkorian kingdom.

After the *dvarapala* a rough sandstone path ascends quickly to another steep stairway, atop which is a small terrace holding six ruined brick shrines – only one retains some of its original form. From here two final staircases, the second marked by crouching guardians also sans heads and arms, take you to the top, passing through the large terraces you saw clearly from the bottom of the mountain.

Shade is provided along much of this entire middle-level route from *dork jąmpąh* (plumeria or frangipani), the Lao national tree.

➡ Upper Level

On the uppermost level of Wat Phu is the **sanctuary** itself. It has many carvings, notably two guardians and two *apsara* (celestial dancers), and it once enclosed a Shiva lingam that was bathed, via a system of sandstone pipes, with waters from the **sacred spring** that still flows behind the complex. The sanctuary now contains a set of very old, distinctive Buddha images on an altar. The brick rear section, which might have been built in the 9th century, is a *cella* (cell), where the holy lingam was kept.

Sculpted into a large boulder behind the sanctuary is a Khmer-style **Trimurti**, the Hindu holy trinity of Shiva, Vishnu and Brahma. Further back, beyond some terracing to the south of the Trimurti, is the cave from which the holy spring flowed into the sanctuary. Up a rough path to the north of the Trimurti, a **Buddha footprint** and an elephant are carved into a rock wall.

Just north of the Shiva lingam sanctuary, amid a mess of rocks and rubble, look around for two unique stone carvings known as the **elephant stone** and the **crocodile stone**. Crocodiles were semi-divine figures in Khmer culture, but despite much speculation that the stone was used for human sacrifices, its function – if there was one – remains unknown. The crocodile is believed to date from the Angkor period, while the elephant is thought to date from the 16th century. Also look out for an interesting chunk of staircase framed by two snakes and some small caves that were probably used for meditation in ancient days.

When you've seen everything here, just sitting and soaking up the wide-angle view of the *baray*, the plains and the Mekong is fantastic. A small shop sells snacks and drinks.

Getting There & Away

Wat Phu Champasak is 43km from Pakse and 10km from Champasak. It's a flat, easy bike ride from Champasak, though there's not a lot of shade. A tuk-tuk from Champasak will cost around 100,000K return.

Kiet Ngong

030

Sitting on the edge of a bird-rich wetland about 9km from Rte 13, the Lao Loum village of Kiet Ngong (ບ້ານກຽດໂງ້ງ) is the best way to explore the Se Pian National Protected Area. As well as birds and an unusually large herd of buffalo, the wetland is also home to elephants (which are almost exclusively used for tourist treks).

Note that elephant interactions such as rides are harmful for the animals. Contrary to popular belief, elephants' backs are not very strong, and there is increasing evidence that riding damages their health.

Visitors heading to Kiet Ngong are expected to pay a 25,000K entry fee for Se Pian NPA at the little white building 2km east of Rte 13 that you pass on your way there, though attendance here can be intermittent.

Sights & Activities

The community-run **Visitor Information Centre** (030-9552120; 8am-4pm) organises homestays, trekking, birdwatching and other activities. It's best to contact it in advance, although you can usually just show up and arrange things on the spot.

Forest walks and traditional canoe rides (July to March only) in the swamp are the real highlights here. Trips into the jungle of the Se Pian NPA can range from half-day nature walks to extended overnight treks. Camping gear is available for hire. The wetland, **Bueng Kiet Ngong** (ບຶງກຽດໂງ້ງ), covers 13.8 sq km and was designated a Ramsar Site (a wetland of international importance) in 2010. It's emerging as a birdwatching destination, with the rare white-winged duck a possible tick.

Guides cost 100,000K per day, with additional costs depending on the particular activity. Things can be arranged either at the Visitor Information Centre or Kingfisher Ecolodge, although mountain biking (per person 430,000K with two people) is only available from the lodge.

Se Pian NPA NATIONAL PARK

(ປ່າສະຫງວນແຫ່ງຊາດເຊປຽນ; www.xepian.org)

Se Pian NPA is one of the most important protected areas in Laos. The 2400-sq-km park boasts small populations of Asiatic black bears, yellow-cheeked crested gibbons and Siamese crocodiles, and is home to many birds, including the rare sarus crane, vultures and hornbills. Banteng, gaurs and tigers once roamed here, but sightings of these creatures have been rare to nonexistent in recent years.

Stretching from Rte 13 in the west into Attapeu Province in the east, and to the Cambodian border in the south, it is fed by three major rivers: the Se Pian, Se Khampho and Se Kong.

It's almost impossible to visit the park under your own steam, but you can get into the park for either tough multiday jungle treks or short nature walks, bike trips and boat rides through Kiet Ngong village or Green Discovery tour company (p367) in Pakse. If you're feeling really frisky and adventurous, you could try to charter a boat down the Sekong from Sanamsay, on Rte 18A about 35km west of Attapeu. This trip towards the Cambodian border would get you deep into a scenic section of Se Pian NPA.

Sleeping & Eating

In addition to the excellent Kingfisher Ecolodge, the Kiet Ngong community offers two types of accommodation, both booked through the Visitor Information Centre. Choose from a homestay with a local family or the community guesthouse with dorm-style sleeping in bungalows in a great spot overlooking the wetland. Some, but not all, homestay homes have hot-water showers. Both options cost 40,000K per person, plus 30,000K for meals.

★**Kingfisher Ecolodge** LODGE $$

(020-55726315; www.kingfisherecolodge.com; bungalows 800,000K; closed May & Jun;)

Run by a Lao-Italian family, the Kingfisher Ecolodge is set on 7 hectares at the edge of the wetland, about 700m past Kiet Ngong village. It's a beautiful spot. Sitting on your balcony at dawn and watching birds flit across the wetland is a memorable experience and the two-tiered restaurant-bar could easily be in an East African safari lodge.

The seven comfortable bungalows have a great safari feel, with natural timbers and thatched grass, and huge wooden countertops in the bathrooms, polished hardwood pillars and floors, lovely beds and – the pièce de résistance – large balconies with hammocks. The economy rooms have more modest balconies and share a spotless bathroom. Air-con rooms and a swimming pool were being planned at the time of research.

Most activities offered by the Visitor Information Centre are also offered here, with the addition of full-day guided mountain-bike tours (per person 430,000K with two people) into Se Pian NPA. And it lives up to the 'eco' in its name by supporting the local school, using solar power and promoting conservation within Se Pian NPA.

Wi-fi is available only in the restaurant.

Getting There & Away

Kiet Ngong is 56km from central Pakse. Most visitors come here as part of a tour, but travelling independently is fairly easy. One van or *sǒrngtǎaou* (30,000K, two to 2½ hours) leaves Kiet Ngong for Lak 8 bus station in Pakse at about 8am and heads back at 11am. Kiet Ngong is often mispronounced so ask instead for 'Phu Asa'. Alternatively, board anything going south on Rte 13, get off at Ban Thang Beng and call the Visitor Information Centre for a pickup by motorcycle (25,000K per person) for the last 9km to the village.

Bolaven Plateau Region

Spreading across parts of all four southern provinces, the fertile Bolaven Plateau (ພູພຽງບໍລະເວນ; known in Lao as Phu Phieng Bolaven) is famous for its cool climate, dramatic waterfalls and high-grade coffee.

The French started planting coffee, rubber and bananas in the early 20th century, but many left following independence in the 1950s and the rest followed when US bombardment began in the late '60s. Controlling the Bolaven Plateau was considered strategically vital to both the Americans and the North Vietnamese, as evidenced by the staggering amount of unexploded ordnance (UXO) still lying around. But where it has been cleared, both local farmers and large companies are busy cultivating coffee. Other local products include fruit, cardamom, rattan and, more recently, avocados.

The largest ethnic group on the plateau is the Laven (Bolaven means 'Home of the Laven'). Several other Mon-Khmer ethnic groups, including the Alak, Katu, Tahoy and Suay, also live on the plateau and its escarpment.

Tat Lo

☎030

Tat Lo (ຕາດເລາະ; pronounced *dàht ló*) has taken a place on the backpacker trail thanks to an attractive setting, cheap accommodation and some beautiful waterfalls. It eschews the party scene of Don Det and Vang Vieng, and locals are set on it staying this way. The result is a serenity that sees many visitors stay longer than they planned.

The availability of day treks makes Tat Lo by far the best base for getting to know the Bolaven Plateau, even though it actually sits against the foot of it, rather than up on top of it. The real name of Tat Lo village is Ban Saen Vang, but these days everybody just calls it Tat Lo.

Sights & Activities

There are three waterfalls on this stretch of river: Tat Lo, Tat Hang and Tat Soung. Tat Lo, ironically, is the least impressive. In fact, all three are much less beautiful than they once were due to the building of a new dam.

Note that dam authorities upstream release water in the evening and being in its path could be fatal. Check with locals about the release time before you visit the falls.

The Tat Lo Guides Association, operated out of the Tat Lo Tourism Information Centre (p378), offers highly recommended walks (half-/full day 80,000/160,000K per person) combining all three waterfalls – Tat Hang, Tat Lo and Tat Soung – with visits to Katu, Tahoy and/or Suay ethnic-minority villages.

For something more adventurous they can also lead you to some more distant waterfalls and cultural stops, such as a cave with ancient stone caskets. Or consider the two-day excursion to **Phou Tak Khao** (ພູຕາກຂາວ) mountain, with an overnight stay in a Suay village. This costs US$100/60 per person for a group of two/four people with local guides; English-speaking guides cost extra.

★Tat Soung WATERFALL

(ຕາດສູງ; parking 5000K) Tat Soung is a 50m drop over the edge of the Bolaven Plateau,

LOCAL KNOWLEDGE

LAO COFFEE

The high, flat ground, fertile, mineral-rich volcanic soils and heavy rainfall of the Bolaven Plateau are ideal for growing coffee, and the region produces some of the best and most expensive beans on earth: arabica, arabica typica and robusta are all grown here. The 'coffee town' of **Paksong** is at the centre of it all.

The French introduced coffee to the Bolaven Plateau in the early 1900s and the arabica typica shipped home became known as the 'champagne of coffee'. The carpet bombing of the '60s and '70s put the brakes on the business, but things began to pick up in the 1990s and now nearly 30,000 tonnes of green coffee beans – 90% of all coffee produced in Laos – are grown in Paksong and the adjacent Tha Taeng districts.

Though the money provided by growing coffee has benefited thousands of people in the area, particularly women, water pollution and deforestation are serious downsides to the coffee boom.

The largest producer is Pakse-based Dao Heung. You'll see the factory on the drive up to Paksong, as well as the owner's ostentatious mansion in Pakse, next to the Japanese bridge.

Two very different coffee shops in Paksong, **Won Coffee** (Rte 16, Paksong; ⌚7am-5.30pm; 📶) and **Jhai Coffee House** (www.jhaicoffeehouse.com; Rte 16, Paksong; ⌚8am-5.30pm; 📶) – just 200m from each other, on the south side of the road in the centre of town near the hospital – offer top-shelf brews, and Won Coffee offers educational coffee tours. These **tours** (☎020-22760439; www.paksong.info; per person coffee tour 50,000K, tour incl roasting workshop 180,000K) should be booked in advance, but you can try your luck just showing up.

and though the dam has affected these falls more than the others – slowing them to a trickle for most of the year – you can walk around the rocky top of the falls from where the views are fantastic. During heavy rains from August to October, when they reach their full width, the falls themselves are quite spectacular too.

Tat Soung is 8km south of Tat Lo town, uphill almost the entire way. Along the way, 3.5km out of Tat Lo, you'll pass a sign for the bottom of the falls at Ban Kiang Tat Soung (Kiang Tat Soung Village). (Note that the sign inside the village saying 'top' is a mistake.) It's a fun walk and a beautiful destination, and young guides will offer to walk you there for a small tip. It's a round trip of about 1.5km. Definitely don't leave anything in your motorcycle basket; chances are it won't be there when you get back.

Tat Lo WATERFALL

(ຕາດເລາະ) FREE Tat Lo, about 500m upriver from Tat Hang, is a little bigger than its neighbour, but probably won't knock your socks off. To get here, walk past Saise Resort's bungalows and follow the road to the end, then you need to scramble over some rocks. To reach the top of the falls, it's 1km up the eastern road from the village's junction to the signed turn-off.

Sleeping & Eating

If you book a room in advance, ask your guesthouse about free transfers from the highway (Rte 20). The Tat Lo Tourism Information Centre (p378) can arrange homestays for 25,000K per person.

Generally, people just eat at their guesthouses, though there are several small non-affiliated restaurants around.

★ Mr Vieng Coffee & Homestay HOMESTAY $

(☎020-99837206; Ban Houay Houn; per person 20,000K, per meal 15,000K) This fun, friendly homestay on a coffee plantation in **Ban Houay Houn** (ບ້ານຫ້ວຍຫຸນ) sits just in from Rte 20, 19km southwest of Tat Lo. Rooms are simple, but quite good for the price, and the Katu couple who run it give plantation tours (15,000K per person), and make and sell weavings. A grass-roofed pavilion to showcase weaving and other products was under construction at the time of research.

Saise Resort LAO, THAI $

(mains 20,000-60,000K; ⌚7am-9pm; 📶) Saise Resort has good food (mostly Thai) served

LOCAL KNOWLEDGE

ATTAPEU DAM COLLAPSE

On 23 July 2018 at around 8pm the Saddle Dam D portion of a large hydroelectric project in southern Laos, under pressure from more intense than usual seasonal rainfall in the form of tropical storm Son-Tinh, collapsed, causing a flash flood of billions of litres of water to wash into Attapeu's Sanamsai district. The result was a virtual tsunami, a wall of water, mud, trees and rocks (some as big as trucks) that smashed into and over a number of villages, including Hinlat, Ban Mai, Tha Hin and Samong, which were destroyed.

While officials had been aware of the imminence of the collapse and made efforts to warn people, some of the villagers only became aware of the event when they saw the mass of destruction racing towards them. They attempted to flee in whatever way possible, clambering up trees with children in their arms or seeking high roofs (not all of which were safe: the schoolhouse in Ban Mai ended up with a massive 20m-long tree trunk atop its smashed roof). An estimated 120 people died or went missing as a result of the tragedy, and thousands were displaced.

on a great deck with an awesome view of Tat Hang. It's worth making one trip out here during your stay for the views alone.

Information

The only financial resource in this area is an ATM up at the highway, though guesthouses change money at terrible rates; you're better off changing money before you arrive.

The helpful **Tat Lo Tourism Information Centre** (☎020-54455907; kouka222@hotmail.com; ⊙8-11.30am & 1.30-4.30pm Mon-Fri, daily Nov-Feb) runs the Tat Lo Guides Association (p376). It should be your first stop if you need a guide or info on local excursions, or plan to venture deeper into Salavan Province and beyond. It can also help you with public-transport options around the Bolaven Plateau. Maps and brochures on the region are available. Kouka speaks English and is worth contacting in advance to book as a guide.

Getting There & Around

Just say 'Tat Lo' at Pakse's Southern Bus Terminal (p370) and you'll be pointed to one of the nine daily buses to Salavan that stop on Rte 20 at Ban Khoua Set (30,000K, two hours), from where it's a 1.5km walk or moto-taxi ride (10,000K) to Tat Lo.

The Tat Lo Tourism Information Centre can call to have buses to Vietnam stop and pick you up at Ban Khoua Set.

Salavan

☎034 / POP 12,700

Salavan (ສາລະວັນ; spelt various ways, including Saravan and Saravane) is just 30km from popular Tat Lo, but is not heavily visited. The town is rather pleasant, but the best thing visitors can do here is get out and explore the ethnic diversity of the countryside.

While more than half of the population of Salavan Province is ethnically Lao (Loum and Soung), few are native to this area. The remainder of the 350,000 inhabitants belong to various Mon-Khmer groups, including the Tahoy, Lavai, Alak, Laven, Ngai, Tong, Pako, Kanay, Katu, Kado and Katang, the last being expert weavers.

Sleeping & Eating

Most lodging is on Rte 15 west of the centre and there are some more choices on the way into town from the south.

Despite its size, Salavan is one of Laos' most culinarily challenged towns. That said, **Sabaidee Salavan** (mains 15,000-50,000K; ⊙7am-8.30pm) is pretty good and has an English menu. It has all the standard Lao and Thai dishes, and also offers sukiyaki.

Phonexay Hotel HOTEL $
(☎020-91999655; Rte 15; r with fan 780,000K, r with air-con 120,000-200,000K; ❄📶) As the main building is fairly newish and the rooms have wi-fi, this mostly clean place 1.5km west of the market is the best lodging choice in town. Rooms in the newer building are large, spotless and well appointed, although wi-fi was patchy when we visited.

Information

DANGERS & ANNOYANCES

UXO remains a serious problem in rural areas, so exercise caution if you go out exploring the province beyond main roads: stick to established tracks and trails.

MONEY

There are several banks and ATMs in town, including some around the market.

TOURIST INFORMATION

Salavan Tourism Centre (☎034-211528; ⏲8am-4pm Mon-Fri) Staff are eager to help and some are knowledgeable about tourism in the area. It's south of the market, next to the large, glass-fronted Phongsavanh Bank building.

Getting There & Away

Salavan's bus terminal is 2km west of the town centre, where Rte 20 meets Rte 15. There are nine daily buses to Pakse (30,000K, three hours), with three (8.30am, 4pm, 4.30pm) continuing on to Vientiane (regular/sleeper 130,000/190,000K, 12 to 14 hours), and one bus to Attapeu (50,000K, 4½ hours).

No buses to Vietnam originate here, but you can hope that one passing through from Pakse has empty seats.

Sekong

☎038 / POP 20,000

Built from scratch on its namesake river in 1984 (the year Sekong Province was created), Sekong makes a good base from which to explore some interesting waterfalls nearby. It's not a destination as such, so tourist infrastructure is minimal, but a new bridge across the Sekong shortens the route from Ubon Ratchathani in Thailand, to the Vietnamese port of Danang. A border crossing should also be part of the equation, though it is still a work in progress.

By population, Sekong (ເຊກອງ) is the smallest of Laos' provinces and also the most ethnically diverse: almost all of its 90,000 inhabitants are from one of 14 different Mon-Khmer tribal groups, with the Alak, Katu, Talieng, Yai and Nge the largest. The belief systems of these diverse groups mix animism and ancestor worship, so you won't see any temples here.

Sights

South of Sekong, Rte 16 morphs into Rte 11 and the waterfalls along this road have more appeal than anything actually in the town.

For a bit of easy adventure, take a relaxed ride on the highway to Dak Cheung. It's a beautiful and still relatively remote region, especially once you hit the mountains.

Tat Hua Khon WATERFALL

(ຕາດຫົວຄົນ) FREE Three kilometres south of the Tat Faek turn-off from Rte 11 (just past the market), this waterfall is an impressive 100m wide. The P&S Garden (p380) resort, which runs this place, has done an excellent job of setting up rustic facilities, including good trails and boardwalks through the forest, and a restaurant.

The name means 'Head Falls', referring to certain rock formations in the face of the falls that resemble human heads. The 2018 dam collapse in Attapeu had a significant impact on the place, with a planned natural herbal garden, as well as the resort's kayaks, washed away in the deluge.

Tat Faek WATERFALL

(ຕາດແຟກ) FREE Sixteen kilometres south of Sekong, and well-signed off Rte 11, is this wide, beautiful 5m-high waterfall where you

GETTING TO VIETNAM: LA LAY TO LALAY

Getting to the border Most people travelling from Pakse to Hue and Danang use sleeper buses, which go through the Lao Bao border crossing east of Savannakhet. The faster minibuses, on the other hand, go via Salavan and cross at La Lay (Laos)/Lalay (Vietnam). If you're in Salavan, you don't need to backtrack to Pakse. There are usually seats available when the buses from Pakse pass through. There isn't much traffic on this route, so doing the trip in stages is not recommended, but if you're set on it, start with the 7.30am minibus to Samouy (35,000K, 3½ hours), which is very near the border.

At the border The border is open from 6am to 7pm and though it's little more than a shack you will probably not have any hassles (other than the usual Lao overtime fee), assuming you have your Vietnamese visa already, or don't need one. In the reverse, you can get a Lao visa at the border.

Moving on For those going in stages, most of the traffic here is trucks, so you should be able to buy an onward ride, though be sure you know whether the driver will be taking a right at the junction to Hue and Danang or turning left to Đông Hà.

can swim in the pool atop the falls. At the time of our visit, the concession that had run the place for many years, including shacks to stay in at the top of the falls, had had its licence revoked, and there was no one there to collect entry fees. It is still a nice place to wander around, though.

If and when new management takes over, the picture (including entry fees) will certainly change.

Sleeping & Eating

Sekong has several basic guesthouses and hotels, though staying at P&S Garden at Tat Hua Khon is perhaps a better option. Sekong is not particularly well endowed with restaurants.

P&S Garden RESORT $
(020-55557585; Rte 11; 1-/2-person tents 40,000/60,000K;) This lovely resort at Tat Hua Khon (p379) is a welcome surprise. For accommodation there are tents, which are pitched on a stilted and thatched-roof platform and scattered throughout the neat and picturesque grounds. Damage from the 2018 Attapeu dam collapse (p378) had a big effect on the site, and plans for guest rooms were on hold at the time of our visit.

The restaurant serves coffee, herbal teas and juice and a small menu (mains 20,000K to 80,000K) of Lao food, including 'bugs' (roasted crickets) in season and spicy papaya salad.

Information

Banks and ATMs are spread around town. The **Lao Development Bank** (8am-3.30pm Mon-Fri), 200m southwest of the market on the central road, changes Thai baht, euros, US dollars and more, and has a Western Union branch.

The **Sekong Provincial Tourism Office** (038-211361; 2nd fl; 8-11.30am &1-4.30pm Mon-Fri) is 700m west of the market on the central road. Don't expect much help here. They do say they can arrange guides from among their staff, but the cost is prohibitive.

Getting There & Away

Sekong's dusty bus station is 1.5km out of town to the north off Rte 16. Hourly services to Pakse (35,000K, 3½ hours) pass through Paksong (20,000K, 1½ hours). There are also five daily buses to Attapeu (20,000K, two hours) and one departing in the early morning to Salavan (30,000K, 2½ hours).

Si Phan Don (Four Thousand Islands)

031

Si Phan Don (ສີ່ພັນດອນ) is where Laos becomes the land of the lotus-eaters, an archipelago of islands where the pendulum of time swings slowly and postcard-worthy views are the rule rather than the exception. Many a traveller has washed ashore here, succumbed to its charms and stayed longer than expected.

Down here the Mekong bulges to a breadth of 14km – the river's widest reach along its 4350km journey from the Tibetan Plateau to the South China Sea – and if you count every islet and sandbar that emerges in the dry months the name, which literally means 'Four Thousand Islands', isn't that much of an exaggeration.

Don Khong

031 / POP 55,000

Life moves slowly on Don Khong (ດອນໂຂງ; Khong Island), like a boat being paddled against the flow on the Mekong. It's a pleasant place to spend a day or two, wandering past fishing nets drying in the sun, taking a sunset boat ride, pedalling about on a bicycle or just chilling and reading by the river. Some of the accommodation options here make a stay worthwhile in their own right.

Don Khong measures 18km long by 8km at its widest point. Most of the islanders live on the perimeter and there are only two proper towns: lethargic Muang Khong on the eastern shore and the charmless market town of Muang Saen on the west; an 8km road links the two.

Khamtay Siphandone, the postman who went on to serve as president of Laos from 1998 to 2006, was born in Ban Hua Khong at the north end of Don Khong in 1924.

Sights

Don Khong is a pretty island with rice fields and low hills in the centre and simple-life villages around the perimeter, and a bike trip around the island makes for a fantastic day for cultural travellers. The road around the island is paved, though heavily potholed, the whole way. The temples in Ban Hin Siew (Hin Siew Village) and Ban Hang Khong (Hang Khong Village) at the southern end of the island have old buildings that are worth a quick peek if you happen to be passing by.

A bridge in Ban Hua Khong Lem makes it easy to extend your exploration from Don Khong to sparsely populated and rarely visited Don San. A frequently rough dirt track follows the east side 6km to the very tip of the island where, when the river is low, a beach emerges. This is Si Phan Don's northernmost point.

Ban Hin Siew Tai Palm Sugar Trees FARM
(ຕົ້ນຕານບ້ານຫີນສຽວໃຕ້) Although sugar palms can be seen across the island, Ban Hin Siew Tai is southern Laos' sugar capital. Many farmers here climb the trees twice a day to collect the juice and then boil it down to sugar, and if you see them working you are welcome to pop in for a visit. The sugar season is from November to February and early morning is the best time to go.

Don Khong History Museum MUSEUM
(ພິພິດທະພັນປະຫວັດສາດດອນໂຂງ; Muang Khong; 5000K; ⌚8.30-11.30am & 1-4pm Mon-Fri) When the local governor built this two-storey French colonial–style home in 1935, he was so proud of himself that he christened it Sathanavoudthi, which means 'Garden of Eden' in an old Lao dialect. Level-headed locals just called it 'The Brick House'. In 2010 it was restored and now houses one of Laos' smallest museums. But the musical instruments, animal traps and photos of the Don Khon railway are worth a few minutes of your time.

It is usually kept shut, but go around the back and someone will open it for you.

Muang Khong Market MARKET
(ຕະຫຼາດເມືອງໂຂງ; Muang Khong; ⌚5.30-8am) This little morning market, full of both farmed and foraged foods, is a vibrant slice of island life.

Festivals & Events

Bun Suang Heua BOAT RACING
(Bun Nam; ⌚Nov/Dec) A boat-racing festival is held on Don Khong in early December or late November around National Day. Four days of carnival-like activity include longboat races opposite Muang Khong, much closer to the shore than in larger towns.

Sleeping & Eating

The island has some of the best accommodation in Si Phan Don, though if you're looking for waterfront bungalows, or a party scene, you're better off heading further south to Don Det and Don Khon.

There are few restaurants in Muang Khong other than those attached to accommodation (which all do about the same menu and to a similar standard). But it's still easy to eat local, as there are some simple joints along the big road behind the guesthouses. For an early breakfast, cooked food is available at the market.

★Don Som Riverside Guesthouse GUESTHOUSE $
(☎030-9434108; Don Som; r with/without bathroom 85,000/58,000K) This guesthouse, run by a friendly Dutch-Lao couple, is deservedly popular because of its stunning location on Don Som, which is a short ferry ride from Don Khong. There is no wi-fi, so the emphasis is on simple living. Rooms are in rustic but attractive and neat wooden bungalows, one of which has a shared bathroom.

There is a restaurant, and Lao cooking courses are also available.

★Pon Arena Hotel BOUTIQUE HOTEL $$
(☎031-515018, 020-22270037; www.ponarenahotel.com; Muang Khong; r incl breakfast US$50-85; [air-con, wi-fi, pool]) This upscale hotel has a great location right on the river and beautifully designed rooms with soft beds, neat wood trim and flat-screen TVs, plus two swimming pools, one of which is so close to the river it actually sticks out over it. There are a number of buildings, and at the time of our visit the hotel was expanding.

ℹ Information

Agricultural Promotion Bank (Muang Khong; ⌚8am-3.30pm Mon-Fri) Exchanges major currencies and has an ATM out front.

BCEL ATM (Muang Khong) Below the Lao Telecom tower.

Don Khong Tourist Information Centre (☎030-9682036, 020-29250303; bkouam1960@yahoo.com; Muang Khong; ⌚8am-4pm Mon-Fri) Near the boat landing, this office is run by helpful Mr Phan and Mr Boun. There's information for the whole Si Phan Don region and they can set you up with a local guide for 80,000K per day.

Muang Khong Hospital (⌚24hr) At the far southern edge of town. There are some English-speaking staff.

Police Station A block back from the river in Muang Khong.

Si Phan Don

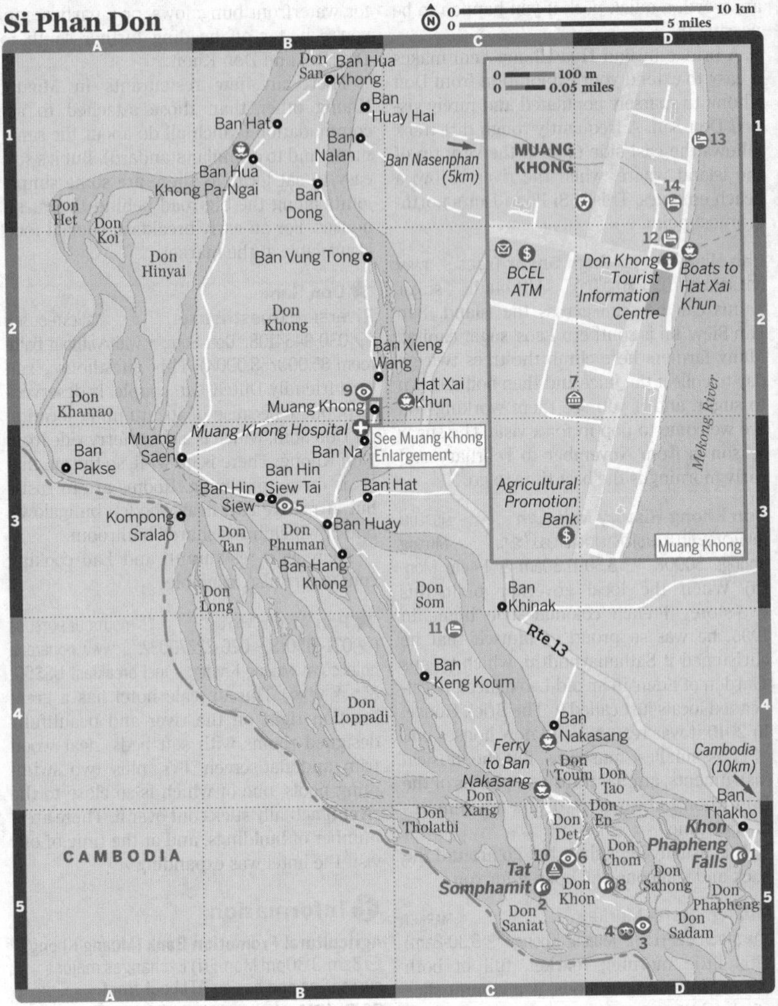

Getting There & Away

BOAT

The Don Khong boat operators' association runs a boat most days to Don Det and Don Khon (one way/return per person 40,000/60,000K) at 8.30am and departing Don Det at 3pm. It's 1½ hours downstream and two hours back. The rate rises if there are fewer than six people as there is a fixed price per boat of 250,000K. You can book this trip through any guesthouse. The boat landing is easy to spot, right opposite the tourist information centre.

BUS

The vast majority of travellers ride the tourist bus, which always includes getting dropped off on Rte 13 with a connecting leg to the island. Sometimes you will get dropped off at the road to the bridge and head to Muang Khong by tuk-tuk. Other times you will be dropped off at Hat Xai Khun on the mainland (1km from the highway) and then squeezed into a small **ferry**. If you need the **boat** or tuk-tuk on your own, the price is 15,000K per head, with a 30,000K minimum.

For leaving the island, tourist transport heading south to Don Det (70,000K) and Don Khon

Si Phan Don

(80,000K including boat transfers, two hours) passes by Hat Xai Khun about 10am, while pickup for going north to Pakse (70,000K, two hours) is about noon.

There are also non-air-conditioned buses (50,000K, three hours) from Muang Khong to Pakse's Southern Bus Terminal (p370) leaving between 6am and 9.30am. They pick up passengers in Muang Khong on the way. At other times, you can go to Rte 13 and wait for the hourly Pakse–Nakasang *sŏrngtăaou*.

Getting Around

If you're up for some adventure, you can walk, cycle or motorbike 15km across Don Som down to Don Det with a **ferry ride** (10,000K per person) at each end. In the rainy season this trip ranges from tough to impossible due to mud. People in Muang Khong will have only a rough idea what the conditions are at any particular time, but the ferryman will know everything for certain.

Motorbikes (from 60,000K to 80,000K per day) that are real clunkers and newish bicycles (10,000K per day) can be hired at several places on the tourist strip in Muang Khong.

Don Det & Don Khon

The vast majority of travellers to Si Phan Don end up on these twin islands. Don Det (ດອນເດດ) is defined by its hippyesque party scene, though it's really quite mild and there's nothing stronger than grass in the 'happy' snacks sold openly at some bars.

Of course there's much more to these two islands. Heading south from Ban Hua Det (Hua Det Village), the guesthouses thin out and the icons of rural island life – fishers, rice farmers, weavers, buffalo, sugar palms – are on full display. Chill in a hammock, wander aimlessly around the islands or languidly drift downstream in an inner tube in the turquoise arms of the Mekong.

The serenity continues across the French bridge on Don Khon (ດອນຄອນ), but down here there are also some gorgeous waterfalls to visit, sandy beaches to lounge on, dolphins to spot and even a little patch of wilderness to explore.

Sights

These twin islands are famous as places for soaking up low-key village life rather than ticking off a list of attractions. Don Det in particular doesn't have any sights to speak of, but the dolphins and waterfalls on Don Khon are genuinely wonderful.

★Khon Phapheng Falls WATERFALL
(ຕາດຄອນພະເພັງ; 55,000K; ⏲8am-5pm) More a glorified set of rapids than a waterfall, but oh, how glorious it is. The largest and by far the most awesome waterfall anywhere along the Mekong, Khon Phapheng is pure, unrestrained aggression, as millions of litres of water crash over the rocks. While pricier than the similar Tat Somphamit (p384), this place, with its gardens and walking paths, is more attractive. You can also get down closer to the rapids.

There are several viewpoints in resort-like grounds, plus many restaurants and snack shops. With luck you can catch some rainbows in the early-morning mist. And like all the waterfalls in this area, there's a shaky network of bamboo scaffolds on the rocks next to the falls used by daring fishers. A free shuttle runs continuously between both ends of the park – a 500m trip.

Be sure to check out the pavilion for the legendary Manikhote tree (p384), which is 150m or so in from the entrance. You can't miss it, actually.

Khon Phapheng is on the eastern shore of the Mekong near Ban Thakho. From Ban Nakasang it's 3km out to Rte 13, then 8.5km

LOCAL KNOWLEDGE

THE WEIRD & WONDERFUL MANIKHOTE TREE

As you enter the manicured grounds of the Khon Phapheng Falls (p383), the path eventually leads you to a lavish, spired Lao-style pavilion. This is the shrine to the legendary Manikhote tree, which once stood, solitary, mysterious and unreachable, on a rocky rise in the centre of the raging torrent of Khon Phapheng.

The tree's unusual appearance gave rise to much folklore. It was said that the tree was the sole member of its species, and that its roots reached skyward while its branches were rooted on the rock (indeed, it did look that way). Furthermore, it was said that when it fruited, it delivered three different kinds of fruit, depending on the branch the fruit appeared on. Some of the fruits would give the eater eternal life, others would turn you into a monkey. Of course, no one ever ate any of the fruits because the tree was inaccessible.

The tree had stood at its location for as long as anyone could remember, and had been the subject of legend for many generations. Some said that it was mentioned in the ancient Indian epic, the *Ramayana*. But on 19 March 2012, Manikhote toppled and died. Efforts were made to retrieve it. The first attempt was unsuccessful, but did manage to secure the tree to the rock so that it wouldn't wash away. It was finally 'rescued' by helicopter and an army team on 13 January 2013. Apparently the tree was only able to be moved once a shaman had made a promise to it that they would not be taking it away from the falls, and even then only after seven days and nights of chanting.

Not all of the tree could be salvaged. What remains of it now lies in a Perspex 'coffin', the central part of the shrine, an object of devotion and offerings from Lao people from all corners of the country.

southeast to the turn-off and another 1.5km to the falls. A tuk-tuk from Nakasang costs about 50,000K return with an hour's wait time. You can also easily motorcycle down from Don Khong. The falls are included in kayak tours out of Don Det and Don Khon. Since amateurs can't kayak anywhere near these falls, you'll be taken there by vehicle as your kayaks are driven up to Ban Nakasang.

★Tat Somphamit WATERFALL
(ຕາດສົມພາມິດ, Li Phi Falls; Don Khon; 35,000K; ⏲ticket booth 8am-5pm) Now billing itself as the Don Khone Somphamit Waterfalls Park, vast Tat Somphamit (also called Li Phi) is a gorgeous set of raging rapids. Recent developments include clear walking paths and the Mekong Fly zipline. While local fishers risk their skin edging out onto rocks, don't try this yourself – the rapids are extremely dangerous, and there have been deaths.

Khon Pa Soi Falls WATERFALL
(ຕາດຄອນປາສ້ອຍ; Don Khon) FREE Although it's not the largest waterfall on the islands, Khon Pa Soi Falls is still pretty impressive, and it never gets crowded due to its isolated location. From the little **restaurant** (sometimes only serving cold drinks) cross the big, fun (or scary, depending on the person) wooden suspension bridge to Don Pa Soi island and follow the roar 200m to the main waterfall.

Activities

Dolphin Watching

A small and diminishing pod of severely endangered Irrawaddy dolphins (p386) lives along the southern shore of Don Khon and spotting these rare creatures in the wild is a highlight of any trip to southern Laos. The population has dropped to just three, as some have died and others have gone south. Though nothing in nature is guaranteed, sightings here are virtually certain.

Boats are chartered (70,000K, maximum four people) from the old French landing pier in Ban Hang Khon. The pier itself is worth a trip just for the spectacular views of the Mekong, which spreads wide on either side of you, with vistas out over to Cambodia. Where you go depends on where the dolphins are. In the hot season they stay close to the village, but when the river runs high they can travel further away. You may be able to see them from your boat, or you may need to disembark in Cambodia and walk to a spot that overlooks the conservation zone. This may require a 20,000K payment to the officials there. Try to go in the early morning or early evening to avoid the heat.

The boat trips from Bang Hang Khon can combine dolphin-watching with Khon Phapheng Falls (p383; 250,000K) or little **Nook Xume waterfall** (100,000K).

Active Pursuits

For an exhilarating soar over the raging rapids of Tat Somphamit, **Mekong Fly** (☎030-4999989; Don Khon; 250,000K; ⊙8am-5pm) can't be beat. The zipline has seven platforms and includes some walking and bridge-crossing as well.

Kayaking around the islands is very popular, and for good reason considering the sublime beauty of the Mekong in these parts. Full-day trips (180,000K per person) paddle to Khon Pa Soi Falls and then down to the dolphin pool – unlike the regular dolphin-watching trips, seeing them while on a kayak tour is hit or miss – before you visit Khon Phapheng Falls (p383) by vehicle. Prices are sometimes negotiable – mostly in the low season – or, in lieu of a discount, some guesthouses will give you free breakfast the morning of the tour if you book it through them.

Due to the potential dangers, most businesses are unwilling to just rent out kayaks. **Tubing** (10,000K), however, is a big thing here. But don't float past the French bridge or you'll hit the fast currents that feed into the lethal falls. You could also have a boat take you upstream so that you'll float back to Don Det. December to July is the best season, but you can go any time.

A relaxing alternative to the kayak tours are the afternoon **BBQ boat tours** (55,000K per person or 40,000K just for transport), such as that offered by **Souksan Guesthouse** (☎020-91808944; Don Khon; r with fan 50,000-60,000K; 📶). All guesthouses can also arrange other sorts of boat tours: sunset cruises, full-day island hops, morning bird-watching trips, fishing – you name it.

Sleeping

The common wisdom is to stay on Don Det to party, and Don Khon to get away from it

WORTH A TRIP

EXPLORING DON KHON VIA BICYCLE

A bike trip around Don Khon is a pure delight. Begin in Ban Khon (Khon Village) and take the paved path to Ban Don Khon Neua temple, then follow the twisting little paths through the rice paddies until you reach the riverbank.

Head south and you'll soon see large portions of the concrete **diversion walls** the French built to direct logs. Usually sent down from forests in Sainyabuli Province, west of Vientiane, the logs were lashed together into rafts of three. To prevent them going off course, a Lao 'pilot' would board the raft and steer it through the maze of islands. When they reached the critical area at the north end of Don Khon, the pilots were required to guide the raft onto a reinforced-concrete wedge, thus splitting the binds and sending the logs into the correct channel. The pilot would jump for his life moments before impact.

Turn at the sign for Khon Pa Soi Falls, which is reached by a big wooden suspension bridge that would be worth a visit even if there was no waterfall here. The path used to continue on to the south of the island, but the bridges have been washed out. For now you will have to backtrack until you see a road diverging left, which will take you to the old railbed road. This will take you down to the southern point, Ban Hang Khon, where there is the ruin of an old **French port** and a spectacular view of the Mekong at the southern tip of the island. Dolphin-watching tours are offered from here.

The village also has a hilltop **viewpoint** (ຈຸດຊົມວິວບ້ານຫາງຄອນ; Ban Hang Khon, Don Khon), a decrepit old French colonial–era **steam locomotive** (ຫົວລົດໄຟຈັກອາຍນ້ຳບ້ານຫາງຄອນ; Don Khon), several restaurants and a real village homestay (p386).

Head back north along the old railbed 5km across the island to Ban Khon Tai. Next to the photogenic **French Bridge** sits another, better-preserved French **steam locomotive** (ຫົວລົດໄຟຈັກອາຍນ້ຳບ້ານຄອນ; Don Khon). From here, head southwest, taking either the road around or through historic **Wat Khon Tai** (ວັດຄອນໃຕ້; Don Khon) to finish your trip at the impressive waterfall Tat Somphamit.

Be sure to ask about the conditions before setting off in the rainy season as the dusty roads often turn into chocolate pudding.

LOCAL KNOWLEDGE

DOLPHINS ENDANGERED

The Irrawaddy dolphin (*Orcaella brevirostris*, called *pąa khaa* in Lao) is one of the Mekong River's most fascinating creatures, and one of its most endangered. The dark-blue to grey cetaceans grow to 2.75m long and are recognisable by their bulging foreheads, perpetual grins and small dorsal fins. They are unusually adaptable and can live in fresh water, brackish-water estuaries or semi-enclosed saltwater bodies such as bays.

Among the Lao and Khmer, Irrawaddy dolphins are traditionally considered reincarnated humans and there are many stories of dolphins having saved the lives of fishers or villagers who have fallen into the river or been attacked by crocodiles. These cultural beliefs mean that neither the Lao nor the Khmer intentionally capture dolphins for food or sport.

But gill netting and years of destructive fishing practices such as dynamite fishing in Cambodia have inevitably taken their toll on the dolphins. Education and conservation programs to save the dolphins continue, particularly in Cambodia, but gill netting remains a constant threat – dolphins need to surface and breathe every two to three minutes, and will usually drown before fishers even know they are in the nets.

In Laos, dolphins used to travel up the Se Kong (Kong River), but these days they are largely confined to a 600m-wide, 50m-deep (in the wet season) pool on the Cambodian border known in Lao as Boong Pa Gooang and in Cambodian as Anlong Cheuteal. Only three dolphins survive in this pool.

all. But in fact the party is confined to the northern tip of Don Det, and the quietest and most isolated guesthouses in all of Si Phan Don are actually on the southern portion of Don Det.

Many places offer low-season discounts; sometimes it's automatic and sometimes you need to ask.

Don Det

Don Det's best accommodation options – and its highest prices – are on the sunrise side, though there are still plenty of good budget beds here too. Flimsy bamboo bungalows predominate on the sunset side, with some pleasant exceptions. The drawback here is that late in the day rooms become furnace-like after baking in the afternoon sun. On the other hand, there's less boat traffic (ie noise) here.

On both sides of the island, walk far enough (on the sunrise side this means going past the old French port in Don Det village) and the modest party scene of Ban Hua Det feels light years away. The sunset side gets downright rural after a kilometre or so.

River Garden Bungalows BUNGALOW **$**
(☎ 020-59575055; sunrise side, Don Det; r 60,000-100,000K) These atmospheric timber bungalows close to the bridge to Don Khon are good value. Rooms have river views and bathrooms but no air-con (they have fans). The attached restaurant serves Lao, Thai and Western food (dishes 15,000K to 40,000K).

★ **Baba Guesthouse** GUESTHOUSE **$$**
(☎ 020-98893943; www.dondet.net; sunrise side, Ban Hua Det, Don Det; r 350,000K; ❄ 📶) This solid guesthouse looks out at the Mekong on one side, and emerald paddy fields on the other. The price is a bit above average for this area, but you get more for your money here. Rooms are sleekly white and almost luxurious, with private balcony, tasteful decor, mosquito net and spotless bathroom. There's also an attached restaurant (open 7am to noon).

The terraced restaurant over the river is as classy as the guesthouse and is a great breakfast spot. The owners are the perfect hosts. They offer steep discounts in low season.

Don Khon

There's a good mix of both budget and better places here. Except for the village **homestay** (☎ 020-98893204; Ban Hang Khon, Don Khon; per person 36,000K, per meal 30,000K) and Pomelo Guesthouse in Ban Hang Khon, all Don Khon accommodation is in Ban Khon village facing Don Det. It's a pretty peaceful town (no partying here) but it's not exactly oozing an island vibe.

Pa Kha Guesthouse GUESTHOUSE $
(☎020-55841522; Don Khon; r with fan/air-con 80,000/120,000K; ❄📶) Great-value digs with welcoming, clean rooms, good service and a quiet location. The cheapest rooms are on the river; the newer air-con rooms are across the road, as is the restaurant.

★**Pomelo Guesthouse** GUESTHOUSE $$
(☎020-97925893; Ban Hang Khon, Don Khon; r US$25; 📶) Run by a Thai-Swiss couple, this rustic and tasteful guesthouse has a stunning location over the river in Ban Hang Khon. There are two spacious rooms in a traditional stilt home with rain showers and sweeping views, as well as two bungalows. There's a private swimming platform and a kayak free for guests.

★**Sala Done Khone** BOUTIQUE HOTEL $$
(☎031-515050; www.salalaoboutique.com; Don Khon; r incl breakfast US$60-80; ❄📶) Five hotels in one, Sala Done Khone has both the classiest and the most original rooms in Si Phan Don. Its signature unit, the French Residence, is a renovated 1896 trading headquarters with timbered interiors, beautiful original tiled floors and louvred blinds, while out on the river the Sala Phae wing features floating cottages with bio-safe toilets and private decks.

The newest Ban Din rooms are built of clay and other eco-friendly materials, and are just as lovely and comfortable as the others.

Eating & Drinking

Most guesthouses serve a range of breakfast standards, plus Lao, Thai and Western favourites from virtually identical menus. Stand-alone restaurants are usually a step above the guesthouses and the extra 5000K to 10,000K per dish that they charge is worth it. Generally the best dining is on Don Khon and the sunrise side of Don Det just south of Ban Hua Det.

Ban Hua Det is where the action is. There's a semi-solid midnight curfew when the bars wind down and the action moves to the 'beach' (under water in the rainy season), where bonfires and midnight dips are not unheard of.

★**Chez Fred et Lea** INTERNATIONAL, LAO $
(☎020-22128882; Ban Khon, Don Khon; mains 20,000-50,000K; ⏰7am-10pm; 📶) This cafe and *salon de thé* serves organic coffees and teas, as well as top-quality Lao and Western cuisine that you won't find elsewhere on the island. There are no river views, but the Lao-French couple who run the place make up for it with inviting tunes and the freshest of ingredients. Try a Lao or French set menu for 80,000K.

★**Little Eden Restaurant** LAO, INTERNATIONAL $$
(sunset side, Ban Hua Det, Don Det; mains 35,000-140,000K; 📶) Catching the breeze from the tip of the island, Little Eden's perfectly placed waterfront restaurant is one of the best spots to eat upmarket Lao and Western cuisine with tender *duck à l'orange*, spaghetti bolognese and fish *lâhp* using Mekong catfish.

4000 Island Bar BAR
(☎020-96476088; sunrise side, Ban Hua Det, Don Det; ⏰7am-11pm; 📶) Good Western and Indian food, cold drinks, friendly service and a soothing vibe combine to make this a perennial favourite among travellers. You can make new friends around the pool table, throw some darts, play your favourite tunes or just kick back with a coffee shake or a cocktail, relax and enjoy the view.

Information

MEDICAL SERVICES

Don Khon has a simple **health clinic** (Ban Khon, Don Khon), while Don Det has just a small **pharmacy** (sunset side, Ban Hua Det, Don Det). These services can also be found in Ban Nakasang on the mainland. The nearest proper health facility is on Don Khong, but for anything serious you should head straight to Pakse.

MONEY

There are no banks on the islands, though an increasing number of businesses accept plastic. Cash can be exchanged, at generally poor rates, at most guesthouses and some, including Baba on Don Det, do cash advances on credit cards for a 6% commission. There's an Agricultural Promotion Bank and a BCEL with ATMs on the main drag in Ban Nakasang. Kayaking tours budget enough time at the end of the trip for people to make an ATM stop.

TOURIST INFORMATION

There is no tourism office on these islands, so you're left with guesthouses and travel agencies, which in fact do a lot more than most tourist offices. The Baba Guesthouse website (www.dondet.net) has lots of helpful information.

Getting There & Away

Boat prices between Ban Nakasang and the islands are fixed by a local boat association, and there are very few running each day on a shared basis. Expect to pay 15,000K per person (or 30,000K if travelling on your own) to Don Det, and 20,000K per person (or 60,000K if travelling alone) to Don Khon.

For Pakse, most travellers book tickets on the island, which includes the local boat and a noon bus or minibus (60,000K, three hours). If you want to leave at another time there are *sŏrngtăaou* from Ban Nakasang to the Southern Bus Terminal (p370) in Pakse (40,000K, 3½ hours) every hour until noon. One shared boat always leaves the islands in time for the 8am *sŏrngtăaou*. These all stop in Hat Xai Khun (for Don Khong).

Even in the best of circumstances, travel to Cambodia from the islands by public transport is a hassle. **Green Paradise Travel** (☎ 020-99533939, 020-55494928; greenparadisetours99@gmail.com; sunrise side, Ban Hua Det, Don Det; ⏰7am-9.30pm) has a decent service

GETTING TO CAMBODIA: NONG NOK KHIENE TO TRAPAENG KRIEL

Getting to the border The Nong Nok Khiene (Laos)/Trapaeng Kriel (Cambodia) border (open 6am to 6pm) is a popular route for backpackers on the Indochina overland circuit, and it is always a real hassle.

The Cambodian company Sorya Transport runs the Pakse–Phnom Penh route from Pakse's Southern Bus Terminal (p370) (7.30am, 220,000K) and is the best choice. Sengchalern bus company provides daily service from Pakse to Phnom Penh (230,000K, 12 to 14 hours) via Stung Treng (120,000K, six hours) and Kratie (160,000K, nine hours), but the method of travel varies. Sometimes it sends a big bus that goes direct the whole way, other times it sends you to the border in a minibus and you change vehicles there, and you might even have to change a third time at Stung Treng. These vehicle changes often lead to long delays. Regardless of which vehicle, departures are at 7am from the 2km Bus Station (p370), with a stop to pick up more passengers at the Southern Bus Terminal. Tickets for this route sold from the islands in Si Phan Don will include the ferry from the island and, if needed, a minivan to take you to the connecting point.

Sengchalern at the 2km Bus Station also sells tickets to Siem Reap (280,000K), but this extra long trip is not recommended. It's better to use reliable **Asia Van Transfer** (AVT; www.asiavantransfer.com), which departs from the border at 11.30am and takes the northern route to Siem Reap (US$20), arriving at about 7pm. The price includes a tuk-tuk ride to your hotel. It takes internet bookings, but this means you have to get yourself to the border. In Don Det, Green Paradise Travel (p388) and a few guesthouses sell combo tickets for AVT (270,000K) that include the boat to Nakasang and a minivan to the border. A similar ticket from a travel agency in Pakse costs 260,000K. **Wonderful Tours** (☎ 020-55705173; Ban Hua Det, Don Det; ⏰7am-9.30pm) in Don Det also specialises in tickets to Cambodia, but it uses Cambodian local transport.

At the border Both Lao and Cambodian visas are available on arrival, while bribes, scams and rudeness seem to be a mandatory part of the process. In Laos, you'll pay a US$2 (or the equivalent in kip or baht) 'overtime' or 'processing' fee, depending on when you cross, upon both entry and exit. In Cambodia, the price of a visa is increased to US$35 from the actual US$30. In addition, US$1 is charged for a cursory medical inspection upon arrival in the country, and a US$2 processing fee is levied upon exit. All of these fees can be avoided if you are willing to wait it out, but this will probably take so long that your bus may leave without you. The bus companies charge an extra US$5 or more to handle your paperwork with the border guards, even if you already have a visa. Technically this isn't a scam, since you are getting a service in return for your money, but they will not tell you that this service is optional. To avoid this fee, insist on doing your own paperwork and walk through immigration on your own; it's not hard.

Moving on Aside from the buses mentioned above, there's virtually zero traffic here. If you're dropped at the border, expect to pay about US$45 for a private taxi heading south to Stung Treng, or 150,000/60,000K for a taxi/*săhm-lór* (three-wheeled pedicab) heading north to Ban Nakasang.

that includes boat and vehicle transfers to the border.

River travel to Don Khong (500,000K) and Champasak (US$200) is only available by chartered boat, but very often there are other people willing to join together to share the cost. For Don Khong you could also call **Done Khong Guesthouse** (☎ 020-52535999; donekhong.gh@gmail.com; Muang Khong; r with fan/air-con 70,000/100,000K; ❄ 📶) or **Pon's Riverside Guesthouse** (☎ 020-55406798; Muang Khong; r 100,000K; ❄ 📶) on that island to see if a boat is coming from there in the morning. If so, you can probably buy a seat (50,000K) for the return journey.

UNDERSTAND LAOS

History

Throughout its long history, the inhabitants of modern-day Laos have been subject to the politics and aspirations of more powerful neighbours in Cambodia, Vietnam, Thailand and China. Even its first taste of nationhood, with the rise of the Lan Xang kingdom, was achieved thanks to Khmer military muscle.

Kingdom of Lan Xiang

Before the French, British, Chinese and Siamese drew a line around it, Laos was a collection of disparate principalities subject to an ever-revolving cycle of war, invasion, prosperity and decay. Laos' earliest brush with nationhood was in the 14th century, when Khmer-backed Lao warlord Fa Ngum conquered Wieng Chan (Vientiane). It was Fa Ngum who gave his kingdom the title still favoured by travel romantics and businesses – Lan Xang, or (Land of a) Million Elephants. He also made Theravada Buddhism the state religion and adopted the symbol of Lao sovereignty that remains in use today, the Pha Bang Buddha image, after which Luang Prabang is named. Lan Xang reached its peak in the 17th century, when it was the dominant force in Southeast Asia.

The French

After taking over Annam and Tonkin (modern-day Vietnam) in 1883, the French negotiated with Siam to relinquish its territory east of the Mekong; thus, Laos was born and absorbed into French Indochina.

The country's diverse ethnic make-up and short history as a nation state meant nationalism was slow to form. The first nationalist movement, the Lao Issara (Free Lao), was created to prevent the country's return to French rule after the invading Japanese left at the end of WWII. In 1953 sovereignty was granted to Laos by the French. Internecine struggles followed, with the Pathet Lao (Country of the Lao) army forming an alliance with the Vietnamese Viet Minh, which had also been opposing French rule in its own country. Laos was set to become a stage on which the clash of communist ambition and US anxiety over the perceived Southeast Asian 'domino effect' played itself out.

The Secret War

In 1954 at the Geneva Conference, Laos was declared a neutral nation – as such neither Vietnamese nor US forces could cross its borders. Thus began a game of cat and mouse as a multitude of CIA operatives secretly entered the country to train anticommunist Hmong fighters in the jungle. From 1964 to 1973, the US, in response to the Viet Minh funnelling massive amounts of war munitions down the Ho Chi Minh Trail, devastated eastern and northeastern Laos with nonstop carpet-bombing (reportedly a plane load of ordnance was dropped every eight minutes). The intensive campaign exacerbated the war between the Pathet Lao and the US-backed Royal Lao Army and, if anything, increased domestic support for the communists.

The US withdrawal in 1973 saw Laos divided up between Pathet Lao and non-Pathet Lao, but within two years the communists had taken over completely and the Lao People's Democratic Republic (PDR) was created, under the leadership of Kaysone Phomvihane. Around 10% of Laos' population fled, mostly to Thailand. The remaining opponents of the government – notably tribes of Hmong who fought with and were funded by the CIA – were suppressed or sent to re-education camps for indeterminate periods. It's alleged that two of these camps still endure in the far north, though this is hotly denied.

Modern Laos

Kaysone Phomvihane died in 1992. He had been the leading figure in Lao communism for more than a quarter of a century. General Khamtay Siphandone became both president of the Lao People's Revolutionary Party (LPRP) and prime minister. His rise signalled control of the party by the revolutionary generation of military leaders. When Khamtay stepped down in 2006, he was succeeded by his close comrade, General Chummaly Sayasone.

The economic prosperity of the mid-1990s rested on increased investment and foreign aid, on which Laos remained very dependent. The Lao PDR enjoyed friendly relations with all its neighbours. In 1997 Laos joined the Association of Southeast Asian Nations (ASEAN).

In the decade to 2010, China greatly increased investment in Laos to equal that of Thailand. Japan remained the largest aid donor. However, Chinese companies invested in major projects in mining, hydropower and plantation agriculture and timber. Meanwhile, cross-border trade grew apace. Increased economic power brought political influence at the expense of Vietnam, though Lao–Vietnamese relations remained close and warm. Senior Lao Party cadres still take courses in Marxism–Leninism in Vietnam, although their economic inspiration more likely comes from the mighty northern neighbour, China.

In April 2016 vice president Bounnhang Vorachith became president of the Lao PDR, establishing himself as a force against corruption. Calling for a halt on logging, making a pledge to reforest 70% of Laos by 2020 and (allegedly) sacking many of his ministers and replacing them with people he could trust, he set the stage for the August gathering of ASEAN, held in Laos and attended by US President Barack Obama. This followed high-profile visits from John Kerry earlier in the year and Hillary Clinton in 2012. America seemed keen to signal to China it intended to take an interest in Laos' future; the Asian superpower continues funding dams and high-speed rail lines into Laos, placing the diminutive country ever more in its debt, as a key conduit to Southeast Asia in its 'new Silk Road' trade strategy. The 2018 dam collapse in Attapeu was a grim reminder of the costs this kind of progress can have, and the challenges that face the Lao government.

People & Culture

People & Population

As many as 132 ethnic groups make up the people of Laos. Sixty per cent of these people are Lao Loum (lowland Lao); they have the most in common with their Thai neighbours, and it's their cultural beliefs and way of life that are largely known as 'Lao culture'. The remainder are labelled according to the altitude their groups live at: Lao Thai (living in valleys up to an altitude of 400m, composed of Black Thai and White Thai); Lao Thoeng (living on mid-level mountain slopes, including Khamu, Lamet and Alak); and Lao Soung (living 1000m or more above sea level, including the Hmong, Mien and Akha).

Trying to homogenise the people and psyche of Laos is precarious, as the country is really a patchwork of different beliefs, ranging from animism to the prevailing presence of Theravada Buddhism; often both combined. But certainly there's a commonality in the laid-back attitude you'll encounter. Some of this can be ascribed to Buddhism, with its emphasis on controlling extreme emotions by keeping *jai yen* (cool heart) and making merit – doing good in order to receive good. You'll rarely hear a heated argument, and can expect a level of kindness unpractised to such a national degree in neighbouring countries.

The Lao are very good at enjoying the 'now', and they do this with a mixture of the *bor ɓen nyǎng* (no problem) mentality and a devotion to *móoan* (fun). If a job is *bor móoan* (no fun), it is swiftly abandoned in pursuit of another, even if it means less income.

Government spending on education amounts to 11.7% of total public spending. Education has improved in recent years, with school enrolment rates at 85%, though many drop out by the time they reach secondary education – the planting and harvesting of crops, especially among the highlands, is seen as more important than education, as the whole family is involved.

Arts & Architecture

The true expression of Lao art is found in its religious sculpture, temples and handicrafts. Distinctively Lao is the Calling for Rain Buddha, a standing image with hands held rigidly at his sides. Similarly widespread is the Contemplating the Bodhi Tree Buddha, with crossed hands at the front.

Wats in Luang Prabang feature *sĭm* (chapels), with steep, low roofs. The typical Lao *thâat* (stupa) is a four-sided, curvilinear, spire-like structure. There are also hints of classical architectural motifs entering modern architecture, as with Vientiane's Wattay International Airport.

Many of the beautiful villas from the days of Indochina were torn down by the new regime in favour of harsh Soviet designs, though fortunately there are plenty of villas left, with their distinctive shuttered windows and classic French-provincial style.

Traditional Lao art has a more limited range than that of its Southeast Asian neighbours, partly because Laos has a more modest history as a nation state and partly because its neighbours have stolen or burnt what art did exist. Upland crafts include gold- and silversmithing among the Hmong and Mien tribes, and tribal Thai weaving (especially among the Thai Dam and Thai Lü). Classical music and dance have all but evaporated, partly due to the vapid tentacles of Thai pop and the itinerant nature of Laos' young workforce.

Religion

Most lowland Lao are Theravada Buddhists and many Lao males choose to be ordained temporarily as monks, typically spending anywhere from a month to three years at a wat. Indeed, a young man is not considered 'ripe' until he has completed his spiritual term. After the 1975 communist victory, Buddhism was suppressed, but it soon became clear that its religious omnipresence was too strong and by 1992 the government relented. However, monks are still forbidden to promote *pěe* (spirit) worship, which has been officially banned in Laos along with *săiyasàht* (folk magic).

SPIRIT CULTS

No matter where you are in Laos the practice of *pěe* (spirit) worship, sometimes called animism, won't be far away. *Pěe* worship predates Buddhism and despite being officially banned it remains the dominant non-Buddhist belief system. But for most Lao it is not a matter of Buddhism *or* spirit worship. Instead, established Buddhist beliefs coexist peacefully with respect for the *pěe* that are believed to inhabit natural objects.

An obvious example of this coexistence is the 'spirit houses', which are found in or outside almost every home. Spirit houses are often ornately decorated miniature temples, built as a home for the local spirit. Residents must share their space with the spirit and go to great lengths to keep it happy, offering enough incense and food that the spirit won't make trouble for them.

In Vientiane, Buddhism and spirit worship flourish side by side at Wat Si Muang. The central image at the temple is not a Buddha figure but the *lák méuang* (city pillar from the time of the Khmer empire), in which the guardian spirit for the city is believed to reside. Many local residents make daily offerings before the pillar, while at the same time praying to a Buddha figure. A form of *pěe* worship visitors can partake in is the *bąasĭi* ceremony.

Outside the Mekong River valley, the *pěe* cult is particularly strong among the tribal Tai, especially the Tai Dam, who pay special attention to a class of *pěe* called *ten*. The *ten* are earth spirits that preside not only over the plants and soil, but over entire districts as well. The Tai Dam also believe in the 32 *kwăn* (guardian spirits). *Mŏr* (master/shaman), who are specially trained in the propitiation and exorcism of spirits, preside at important Tai Dam festivals and ceremonies. It is possible to see some of the spiritual beliefs and taboos in action by staying in a Katang village during a trek into the forests of Dong Phu Vieng NPA.

The Hmong–Mien tribes also practise animism, plus ancestral worship. Some Hmong groups recognise a pre-eminent spirit that presides over all earth spirits; others do not. The Akha, Lisu and other Tibeto-Burman groups mix animism and ancestor cults.

THE LAO PSYCHE

To a large degree 'Lao-ness' is defined by Buddhism, specifically Theravada Buddhism, which emphasises the cooling of human passions. Thus strong emotions are taboo in Lao society. *Kamma* (karma; intentional action), more than devotion, prayer or hard work, is believed to determine one's lot in life, so the Lao tend not to get too worked up over the future. It's a trait often perceived by outsiders as a lack of ambition.

Lao commonly express the notion that 'too much work is bad for your brain' and they often say they feel sorry for people who 'think too much'. Education in general isn't highly valued, although this attitude is changing with modernisation and greater access to opportunities beyond the country's borders. Avoiding any undue psychological stress, however, remains a cultural norm. From the typical Lao perspective, unless an activity – whether work or play – contains an element of *móoan* (fun), it will probably lead to stress.

The contrast between the Lao and the Vietnamese is an example of how the Annamite Chain has served as a cultural fault line dividing Indo-Asia and Sino-Asia, as well as a geographic divide. The French summed it up as: 'The Vietnamese plant the rice, the Cambodians tend the rice and the Lao listen to it grow.' And while this saying wasn't meant as a compliment, a good number of French colonialists found the Lao way too seductive to resist, and stayed on.

The Lao have always been quite receptive to outside assistance and foreign investment, since it promotes a certain degree of economic development without demanding a corresponding increase in productivity. The Lao government wants all the trappings of modern technology – the skyscrapers seen on socialist propaganda billboards – without having to give up Lao traditions, including the *móoan* philosophy. The challenge for Laos is to find a balance between cultural preservation and the development of new attitudes that will lead the country towards a measure of self-sufficiency.

Food & Drink

Food

Lao cuisine lacks the variety of Thai food, but there are some distinctive dishes to try. The standard Lao breakfast is *fĕr* (rice noodles), usually served floating in a broth with vegetables and a meat of your choice. The trick is in the seasoning, and Lao people will stir in some fish sauce, lime juice, dried chillies, mint leaves, basil, or one of the wonderful speciality hot chilli sauces that many noodle shops make, testing it along the way.

Láhp is the most distinctively Lao dish, a delicious spicy salad made from minced beef, pork, duck, fish or chicken, mixed with fish sauce, small shallots, mint leaves, lime juice, roasted ground rice and lots and lots of chillies. Another famous Lao speciality is *đạm màhk hung* (known as *som tam* in Thailand), a salad of shredded green papaya mixed with garlic, lime juice, fish sauce, sometimes tomatoes, palm sugar, land crab or dried shrimp and, of course, chillies by the handful.

In lowland Lao areas almost every dish is eaten with *kòw nĕeo* (sticky rice), which is served in a small basket. Take a small amount of rice and, using one hand, work it into a walnut-sized ball before dipping it into the food.

In main centres, delicious French baguettes are a popular breakfast food. Sometimes they're eaten with condensed milk, or with *kai* (eggs) in a sandwich that also contains Lao-style pâté and vegetables.

Drink

ALCOHOLIC DRINKS

Beerlao remains a firm favourite with 90% of the nation, while officially illegal *lòw-lów* (Lao liquor, or rice whisky) is a popular drink among lowland Lao. It's usually taken neat and offered in villages as a welcoming gesture.

NONALCOHOLIC DRINKS

Water purified for drinking purposes is simply called *nâam deum* (drinking water), whether it's boiled or filtered. All water offered to customers in restaurants or hotels will be purified, and purified water is sold everywhere. Having said that, do be careful of the water you drink and check that the ice in your drink originated from a bottle.

Juice bars proliferate around Vientiane and Luang Prabang, and smoothies are usually on the menu in most Western-leaning cafes. Lao coffee is usually served strong and sweet. Lattes and cappuccinos are springing up across the country, with pasteurised milk coming from Thailand.

Chinese-style green tea is the usual ingredient in *nâm sáh* or *sáh lôw* – the weak, refreshing tea traditionally served free in restaurants. If you want Lipton-style tea, ask for *sáa hâwn* (hot tea).

Environment

Deforestation

In 2016 the new president of Laos banned the export of timber and logs, throwing long-established illegal smuggling operations into panic. Since the ban, truckloads of hardwood have been seized from forest hideouts and sawmills across the country. In 2015 Radio Free Asia exposed a Lao politburo member's son as a smuggling kingpin of hardwood trees across the border into China via Mohan, and it's widely alleged that illegal logging has been clandestinely run by elements of the Lao Army, such as in Khammuan Province and remote areas of the country's far south.

The national electricity-generating company also profits from the timber sales each time it links a Lao town or village with the national power grid, as it clear-cuts along Lao highways. Large-scale plantations and mining, as well as swidden (slash-and-burn) methods of cultivation, are also leading to habitat loss. This can have a knock-on effect in rural communities: in some rural areas 70% of non-rice foods come from the forest.

The current president has pledged to recover forest levels to 70% by 2025. It remains to be seen how successful the government will be in carrying out this pledge.

Wildlife

The mountains, forests and river networks of Laos are home to a range of animals both endemic to the country and shared with its Southeast Asian neighbours. Nearly half of the animal species native to Thailand are shared by Laos, with the higher forest cover and fewer hunters meaning that numbers are often greater in Laos. Almost all wild animals, however, are threatened to some extent by hunting and habitat loss.

In spite of this Laos has seen several new species discovered in recent years, such as the bent-toed gecko and long-toothed pipistrelle bat, while others thought to be extinct have turned up in remote forests. Given their rarity, these newly discovered species are on the endangered list.

ECOTOURISM IN LAOS

With forests covering about half of the country, two national parks, 18 National Protected Areas (NPAs), 49 ethnic groups, over 650 bird species and hundreds of mammals, Laos has some of Southeast Asia's healthiest ecosystems.

Following the success of the Nam Ha Ecotourism Project in Luang Namtha Province, which began in 1999, the ecotourism industry has grown using a sustainable, internationally developed blueprint that seeks to protect and preserve the interests of ethnic people, wildlife and forests.

Many tour companies in Laos have endured since the inception of ecotourism because they have honoured their pledges to local tribes and conservation. Before splashing out on a trek, ask the following questions:

- Are you in a small group that will not disturb village life?
- Will you be led by a local guide?
- Will your trip directly benefit local people whose forests/village you are passing through?
- Does the company channel some of its profits into conservation or local education charities, or is it directly affiliated with organisations such as the WWF and WCS?

See www.ecotourismlaos.com for further information on environmentally sustainable tourism in Laos.

As in Cambodia, Vietnam, Myanmar and much of Thailand, most of the fauna in Laos belongs to the Indochinese zoogeographic realm (as opposed to the Sundaic domain found south of the Isthmus of Kra in southern Thailand or the Palaearctic to the north in China).

Notable mammals endemic to Laos include the lesser panda, raccoon dog, Lao marmoset rat, Owston's civet and the pygmy slow loris. Other important exotic species found elsewhere in the region include the Malayan and Chinese pangolins, 10 species of civet, the Javan and crab-eating mongoose, the serow (sometimes called Asian mountain goat) and goral (another type of goat-antelope), and cat species including the marbled cat, leopard cat and Asian golden cat.

Among the most significant of Laos' wildlife are the primates. Several smaller species are known, including Phayre's leaf monkey, François' langur, the Douc langur and several macaques. Two other primates that are endemic to Laos are the concolour gibbon and snub-nosed langur. It's the five species of gibbon that attract most attention. Sadly, the black-crested gibbon is endangered, being hunted both for its meat and to be sold as pets in Thailand. Several projects are underway to educate local communities to set aside safe areas for the gibbons.

Endangered Species

ASIAN TIGER

Historically, hundreds of thousands of tigers populated Asia, yet today there may be as few as 3000 left in the entire world, occupying a mere 7% of their original range. No tigers have been sighted in the wild in Laos in the last several years.

MEKONG CATFISH

Growing up to 3m in length and weighing in at 300kg, the world's largest freshwater fish is unique to the Mekong River. Over the past 10 years or so their numbers have dropped an astonishing 90% due to overfishing and, more pointedly, the building of hydroelectric dams that block their migratory paths. There may only be a few hundred left.

IRRAWADDY DOLPHIN

Beak-nosed and less extroverted than their bottlenose counterparts, these shy and critically endangered mammals inhabit a 190km stretch of the Mekong River between Cambodia and Laos. Recent estimates suggest that between 64 and 76 members survive. The best place to see them in Laos is off the southern tip of Don Khon, where a small pod congregates in a deepwater pool. Gillnet fishing and pollution have nearly wiped them out. During their reign in the late 1970s, the Khmer Rouge used to dynamite them indiscriminately.

BLACK-CRESTED GIBBON

The gibbon is the jungle's answer to Usain Bolt. These heavily poached, soulful animals sing with beautiful voices – usually at dawn – which echo hauntingly around the forest, and they majestically race through the canopy quicker than any other ape. Males are black and females golden, and, in Laos, they only exist in Bokeo Province. The black-crested gibbon is one of the world's rarest, most endangered species of gibbon.

SURVIVAL GUIDE

Directory A–Z

ACCOMMODATION

Since the country opened to foreigners in the early 1990s, guesthouses have been steadily multiplying, and most villages that merit a visit will have some form of accommodation. In cities such as Vientiane and Luang Prabang, prices vary wildly, with some truly exceptional boutique hotels that could excite even the most jaded *New York Times* or *Hip Hotels* editor. At the other end of the scale, budget digs – usually a room with a fan and sometimes an en suite – are getting better every year. Even though guesthouse prices are rising, they're still unbeatable value when compared with the West; at less than 80,000K (about US$10) a night, who can argue? The cheapest accommodation is in the far north and deepest south.

Prices of low- and high-season accommodation in Laos differ considerably. High season falls between December and February (the cooler months), and is more expensive. All prices listed in this book are for this period, so should you be travelling at another time of year make sure you ask for a discount.

Types of Accommodation in Laos

It's worth booking in advance in popular destinations like Luang Prabang and Vientiane during the peak-season months of November to February and around Lao New Year in April.

Guesthouses There is a wide range of guesthouses around the country from the budget to the boutique.

Homestays There is an increasing number of homestay options all over the country, particularly in or near National Protected Areas (NPAs).

Hostels There aren't many hostels in upcountry Laos, but there are plenty in popular tourist locations.

Hotels Laos has a good selection of hotels, from cheap business pads to luxury heritage hotels.

Price Ranges

The following price ranges refer to a high-season double room with attached bathroom, unless otherwise stated.

$ less than US$25 (200,000K)

$$ US$25–75 (200,000–600,000K)

$$$ more than US$75 (600,000K)

ACTIVITIES

Boat Trips, Kayaking & Tubing

With the Mekong cutting a swath through the heart of the country, it's hardly surprising to find that boat trips are a major drawcard here. There are also opportunities to explore small jungled tributaries leading to remote minority villages.

Kayaking has exploded in popularity in Laos in the past few years, particularly around Luang Prabang, Nong Khiaw, Vang Vieng and Si Phan Don. Kayaking trips start from around US$25 per person and are often combined with cycling.

Tubing down the river has long been a popular activity in Vang Vieng and is now a more sedate affair with the clampdown on riverside bars, rope swings and aerial runways.

Cycling

Laos is slowly but steadily establishing itself as a cycling destination. For hard-core cyclists, the mountains of northern Laos are the ultimate destination. For those who like a gentler workout, meandering along Mekong villages is memorable, particularly in southern Laos around Si Phan Don.

In most places that see a decent number of tourists, simple single-speed bicycles can be hired for around 10,000K per day. Better mountain bikes will cost from 40,000K to 80,000K per day or US$5 to US$10. Serious tourers should bring their own bicycle. The choice in Laos is fairly limited compared with neighbouring Thailand or Cambodia.

Several tour agencies and guesthouses offer mountain-biking tours, ranging in duration from a few hours to several weeks.

Motorbiking

For those with a thirst for adventure, motorbike trips into remote areas of Laos are unforgettable. The mobility of two wheels is unrivalled. Motorbikes can traverse trails that even the hardiest 4WD cannot follow. It puts you closer to the countryside – its smells, people and scenery – compared with getting around by car or bus. Just remember to watch the road when the scenery is sublime. Motorbiking is still the mode of transport for many Lao residents, so you'll find repair shops everywhere. If you're not confident riding a motorbike, it's comparatively cheap to hire someone to ride it for you. For those seeking true adventure there is no better way to go.

In addition, public transport is fairly undeveloped in some regions, with your only choices being to go by motorbike or hire a car or tuk-tuk.

Rock Climbing & Caving

Vang Vieng and Tha Khaek have some of the best organised climbing in Southeast Asia, along with excellent instructors and safe equipment. Climbing costs from about US$25 per person in a group of four and rises for more specialised climbs or for instruction.

Real caving of the spelunker variety is not really on offer unless you're undertaking a professional expedition. However, there are many extensive cave systems that are open to visitors.

Trekking

Trekking in Laos is all about exploring the National Protected Areas (NPAs) and visiting the colourful ethnic-minority villages, many of which host overnight trekking groups. Anything is possible, from half-day hikes to week-long expeditions that include cycling and kayaking. Most treks have both a cultural and an environmental focus, with trekkers sleeping in village homestays and money going directly to some of the poorest communities in the country. There are now a dozen or more areas you can choose from. Less strenuous walks include jungle hikes to pristine waterfalls and village walks in remote areas. The scenery is often breathtaking, featuring plunging highland valleys, tiers of rice paddies and soaring limestone mountains.

Treks are mostly run by small local tour operators and have English-speaking guides. Prices, including all food, guides, transport, accommodation and park fees, start at about US$25 per person per day for larger groups. For more specialised long treks into remote areas, prices can run into several hundred dollars. In most cases you can trek with as few as two people, with per-person costs falling with larger groups.

BOOKS

The Coroner's Lunch (Colin Cotterill; 2004) Delve into the delightful world of Dr Siri, full-time national coroner in the 1970s and part-time supersleuth.

Ant Egg Soup (Natacha Du Pont de Bie; 2004) Subtitled *The Adventures of a Food Tourist in Laos;* the author samples some local delicacies.

One Foot in Laos (Dervla Murphy; 1999) Renowned Irish travel writer explores Laos back in the early 1990s.

A Great Place to Have a War (Joshua Kurlantzick; 2017) A look at America's Secret War in Laos, including its effects on the nation and the CIA.

CUSTOMS REGULATIONS

Customs inspections at ports of entry are lax, as long as you're not bringing in more than a moderate amount of luggage. You're not supposed to enter the country with more than 500 cigarettes or 1L of distilled spirits. All the usual prohibitions on drugs, weapons and pornography apply.

EMBASSIES & CONSULATES

There are about 25 embassies and consulates in Vientiane. Many nationalities are served by their embassies in Bangkok (eg New Zealand and the Netherlands), Hanoi (eg Ireland) or Beijing.

Australian Embassy (Map p294; ☎021-353800; www.laos.embassy.gov.au; Km 4, Rue Tha Deua, Vientiane; ⏰8.30am-5pm Mon-Fri) Also represents nationals of Canada.

Cambodian Embassy (Map p294; ☎021-314952; www.cambodianembassy-laos.com; Km 3, Rue Tha Deua, Vientiane; ⏰8am-noon & 2-5pm Mon-Fri) Issues visas for US$30.

Chinese Embassy (Map p294; ☎021-315100; http://la.china-embassy.org/eng; Rue Wat Nak Nyai, Vientiane; ⏰8-11.30am Mon-Fri) Issues visas in four working days (less for a fee). Some travellers report sudden and unannounced 'changes in policy' preventing them from applying for visas.

French Embassy (Map p296; ☎021-267400; www.ambafrance-laos.org; Rue Setthathirath, Vientiane; ⏰9am-12.30pm & 2-5.30pm Mon-Fri)

German Embassy (Map p294; ☎021-312110; www.vientiane.diplo.de; Rue Sok Pa Luang, Vientiane; ⏰9am-noon Mon-Thu)

Myanmar Embassy (Map p294; ☎021-314910; Rue Sok Pa Luang, Vientiane; ⏰8.30am-noon Mon-Fri) Issues tourist visas in three working days for US$40, but can turn a visa around the same day on request if you already have a ticket to travel.

Thai Embassy (Map p294; ☎021-214581; http://vientiane.thaiembassy.org/en/; Rue Kaysone Phomvihane, Vientiane; ⏰8.30am-noon & 1-4.30pm Mon-Fri) For visa renewals and extensions, head to the consulates in **Vientiane** (Map p294; ☎021-415335; http://vientiane.thaiembassy.org/en/; 15 Rue Bourichane, Vientiane; ⏰8.30-noon & 1-3pm Mon-Fri) or **Savannakhet** (☎041-212373; Rte 9; ⏰8.30am-4.30pm Mon-Fri), which issue tourist and nonimmigrant visas (1000B).

UK Embassy (Map p294; ☎030-7700000; www.gov.uk/world/organisations/british-embassy-vientiane; Rue Yokkabat, Vientiane; ⏰8.30-11.30am Mon-Fri)

US Embassy (☎021-487000; https://la.usembassy.gov; Km 9, Rue Tha Deua, Vientiane; ⏰7.30am-4pm Mon-Fri) Based to the south of the city.

Vietnamese Embassy (Map p294; ☎021-451990; www.mofa.gov.vn/vnemb.la; 85 Rue 23 Singha, Vientiane; ⏰8.30-11.30am & 1.30-5pm Mon-Fri) Issues tourist visas in three working days for US$55, or in one day for US$65. The **Luang Prabang consulate** (Map p316; www.vietnamconsulate-luangprabang.org; Th Phothisarat; ⏰8-11.30am & 1.30-5pm Mon-Fri) issues tourist visas for US$50 in 24 hours or US$40 if you wait three days. At the consulate in **Pakse** (☎020-99691666; https://vnconsulate-pakse.mofa.gov.vn; Th 21; ⏰8.30-11.30am & 2.30-4.30pm Mon-Fri), visas cost US$60.

FOOD

Virtually all restaurants in Laos are inexpensive by international standards. The following price ranges refer to a main course.

$ less than US$5 (40,000K)

$$ US$5–15 (40,000–120,000K)

$$$ more than US$15 (120,000K)

INTERNET ACCESS

Free wi-fi is pretty standard these days and available in most guesthouses, hotels and cafes in the main tourist destinations around Laos. Internet cafes are still around in Vientiane but are increasingly rare elsewhere. If you can find one, it's generally possible to get online from 5000K to 10,000K per hour.

LEGAL MATTERS

Although Laos guarantees certain rights, the reality is that you can be fined, detained or deported for any reason, as has been demonstrated repeatedly in cases involving foreigners.

If you stay away from anything you know to be illegal, you should be fine. If not, things might get messy and expensive. Drug possession and using prostitutes are the most common crimes for which travellers are caught, often with the dealer or consort being the one to inform the authorities. Sexual relationships between foreigners and Lao citizens who are not married are illegal; penalties for failing to register a relationship range from fines of US$500 to US$5000, and possibly imprisonment or deportation.

If you are detained, ask to call your embassy or consulate in Laos, if there is one. A meeting or phone call between Lao officers and someone from your embassy/consulate may result in quicker adjudication and release.

Police sometimes ask for bribes for traffic violations and other petty offences.

LGBTIQ+ TRAVELLERS

For the most part Lao culture is pretty tolerant of homosexuality, although lesbianism is often either denied completely or misunderstood. In any case, public displays of affection, whether heterosexual or homosexual, are frowned upon.

While there are no laws criminalising homosexuality, the gay and lesbian scene is certainly more hidden these days and not nearly as prominent as in neighbouring Thailand. Authorities sometimes shut down drag shows in Vientiane and have banned gay-friendly establishments from marketing themselves as such with rainbow flags. That doesn't mean they've disappeared!

Check out **Utopia** (www.utopia-asia.com) for gay travel information and contacts in Laos, including some local gay terminology.

MAPS

The best all-purpose country map that's generally available is GT-Rider.com's *Laos,* which has a scale of 1:1,650,000. It's available at bookshops in Thailand and at many guesthouses in Laos, as well as online at www.gt-rider.com.

Chiang Mai–based Hobo Maps has produced a series of good maps of Vientiane, Luang Prabang and Vang Vieng. The Lao Ministry of Information, Culture and Tourism (MICT) has also created a few city maps; pick one up at the tourist information centre (p303) in Vientiane.

MONEY

The official national currency is the Lao kip (K), but Thai baht (B) and US dollars (US$) are also commonly accepted.

ATMs

ATMs are now found all over Laos. But before you get too excited, ATMs dispense a maximum of 700,000K to 2,000,000K (about US$85 to US$250) per transaction, depending on the bank, not to mention a variable withdrawal fee. If you also have to pay extortionate charges to your home bank on each overseas withdrawal, this can quickly add up.

Bargaining

Bargaining in most places in Laos is not nearly as tough as in other parts of Southeast Asia. Lao-style bargaining is generally a friendly transaction where two people try to agree on a price that is fair to both of them. Good bargaining, which takes practice, is one way to cut costs.

Cash

Laos relies heavily on the Thai baht and the US dollar for the domestic cash economy. An estimated one-third of all cash circulating in Vientiane, in fact, bears the portrait of the Thai king, while another third celebrates US presidents. Kip is usually preferred for small purchases, while more expensive items and services may be quoted in kip, baht or US dollars. Anything costing the equivalent of US$100 or more is likely to be quoted in US dollars.

The majority of transactions will be carried out in kip, however, so it's always worth having a wad in your pocket. Notes come in denominations of 500, 1000, 2000, 5000, 10,000, 20,000, 50,000 and 100,000 kip. Small vendors, especially in rural areas, will struggle to change 100,000K notes.

Credit Cards

A growing number of hotels, upmarket restaurants and gift shops in Vientiane and Luang Prabang accept Visa and MasterCard, and, to a much lesser extent, Amex and JCB. However, many places will also pass on the transaction fee to the customer, usually around 3%. Outside of the main towns, credit cards are virtually useless.

Banque pour le Commerce Extérieur Lao (BCEL) branches in most major towns offer cash advances/withdrawals on MasterCard and Visa credit/debit cards for a 3% transaction fee. Other banks may have slightly different charges, so it might be worth shopping around in Vientiane.

Money Changers

After years of volatility the kip has in recent times remained fairly stable at about 8500K to the US dollar. Don't, however, count on this remaining the same.

Generally, exchange rates are virtually the same whether you're changing at a bank or a money changer. Both are also likely to offer a marginally better rate for larger bills (US$50 and US$100) than smaller bills (US$20 and less). Banks in Vientiane and Luang Prabang can generally change UK pounds, euros, Canadian, US and Australian dollars, Thai baht and Japanese yen. Elsewhere most provincial banks usually change only US dollars or baht.

Licensed money changers maintain booths around Vientiane (including at Talat Sao) and at some border crossings. Their rates are similar to the banks, but they stay open longer.

There's no real black market in Laos and unless there's an economic crash, that's unlikely to change.

Travellers Cheques

Travellers cheques can be cashed at most banks in Laos, but normally only in exchange for kip. Cheques in US dollars are the most readily acceptable. Very few merchants accept travellers cheques.

OPENING HOURS

Bars and clubs 5–11.30pm (later in Vientiane)
Government offices 8am–noon and 1– 5pm Monday to Friday
Noodle shops 7am–1pm
Restaurants 10am–10pm
Shops 9am–6pm

POST

Sending post from Laos is not all that expensive and is fairly reliable, but people still tend to wait until they get to Thailand to send parcels. If heading to Cambodia, it's probably smarter to post your parcels from Laos.

Leave packages open for inspection by a postal officer. Incoming parcels might also need to be inspected and there may be a small charge for this mandatory 'service'.

The main post office in **Vientiane** (Map p296; ☎021-216425; Rue Saylom; ⏰8am-5pm Mon-Fri) has a poste restante service.

PUBLIC HOLIDAYS

Schools and government offices are closed on the following official holidays, and the organs of state move pretty slowly, if at all, during festivals.

International New Year 1 January
Army Day 20 January
International Women's Day 8 March
Lao New Year 14–16 April
International Labour Day 1 May
International Children's Day 1 June
Lao National Day 2 December

SAFE TRAVEL

Over the last couple of decades Laos has earned a reputation among visitors as a remarkably safe place to travel, with little crime reported and few of the scams often found in more touristed places such as Vietnam, Thailand and Cambodia. However, in more recent years, there has been a small rise in petty crimes, such as theft and low-level scams, which are more annoying than dangerous.

Large areas of eastern and southern Laos are contaminated by unexploded ordnance (UXO). According to surveys by the Lao National UXO Programme (UXO Lao) and other non-government UXO clearance organisations, the provinces of Salavan, Savannakhet and Xieng Khuang are the most severely affected, followed by Champasak, Hua Phan, Khammuan, Luang Prabang, Attapeu and Sekong.

Statistically, the UXO risk for foreign visitors is low, but travellers should exercise caution when considering off-road wilderness travel in the aforementioned provinces. Stick only to marked paths. And never touch an object that may be UXO, no matter how old and defunct it may appear.

TELEPHONE

With a local SIM card and a 3G/4G or wi-fi connection, the cheapest option is to use internet-based messaging and call apps. Topping up a phone for as little as 50,000K can give you enough data to last a month.

International calls can be made from Lao Telecom offices or the local post office in most provincial capitals and are charged on a per-minute basis, with a minimum charge of three minutes. Calls to most countries cost about 2000K to 4000K per minute. Office hours typically run from about 7.30am to 9.30pm.

Mobile Phones

Roaming is possible in Laos but is generally expensive. Local SIM cards and unlocked mobile phones are readily available.

TOURIST INFORMATION

The Department of Tourism Marketing, part of the Ministry of Information, Culture and Tourism (MICT), has tourist offices all over Laos, with the ones in Vientiane and Luang Prabang particularly helpful.

Many offices are well stocked with brochures and maps, and have easily understood displays of their provincial attractions and English-speaking staff to answer your questions. Offices in Tha Khaek, Savannakhet, Pakse, Luang Namtha, Sainyabuli, Phongsali and Sam Neua are all pretty good, with staff trained to promote treks and other activities in the area and able to hand out brochures and first-hand knowledge. They should also be able to help with local transport options and bookings. Alternatively, you can usually get up-to-date information from a popular guesthouse.

The MICT also runs three very good websites that offer valuable predeparture information:

Central Laos Trekking (www.trekkingcentrallaos.com)
Ecotourism Laos (www.ecotourismlaos.com)
Ministry of Information, Culture and Tourism (www.tourismlaos.org)

VISAS

The Lao government issues 30-day tourist visas on arrival at all international airports and most international border crossings.

The whole process is very straightforward. You need between US$30 and US$42 in cash, one passport-sized photo and the name of a hotel or guesthouse. Those without a photo, or who are arriving on a weekend, holiday or after office hours, will have to pay an additional one or two dollars.

The visa fee varies depending on the passport of origin, with Canadians having to fork out the most (US$42) and most other nationalities paying between US$30 and US$35. It's cheaper to pay in US dollars, as a flat rate of 1500B (around US$45) is applicable in Thai baht. No other foreign currencies are accepted.

Visa Extensions

The 30-day tourist visa can be extended for an additional 90 days at a cost of 20,000K per day, but only in major cities such as Vientiane, Luang Prabang, Pakse and Savannakhet.

VOLUNTEERING

Volunteers have been working in Laos for years, usually on one- or two-year contracts that include a minimal monthly allowance. Volunteers are often placed with a government agency and attempt to help advance development in the country. These sorts of jobs can lead to nonvolunteer work within the nongovernment organisation (NGO) community.

The alternative approach to volunteering, where you actually pay to be placed in a 'volunteer' role for a few weeks or months, has yet to arrive in Laos in any great capacity. A couple of groups in Luang Prabang need volunteers occasionally, and there are also local projects in places as diverse as Huay Xai, Muang Khua and Sainyabuli.

Australian Volunteers International (www.australianvolunteers.com) Places qualified Australian residents on one- to two-year contracts.

Voluntary Service Overseas (VSO; www.vsointernational.org) Places qualified and experienced volunteers for up to two years.

WOMEN TRAVELLERS

Laos is generally an easy country for women to travel around, although it is necessary to be more culturally sensitive when compared with Southeast Asia's more developed destinations, as much of rural Laos is still very traditional. Violence against women travellers is extremely rare, but if travelling solo, it may be useful to team up with other travellers on long overland journeys into remote areas of the country.

It's highly unusual for Lao women to wear tank tops, short skirts or shorts. It may be common to see foreign visitors dressed like this in places like Vang Vieng for river tubing or at the Kuang Si Falls, but in most rural areas it is best to dress more conservatively. If you're planning on bathing in a village or river, a sarong is essential.

Traditionally women didn't sit on the roofs of riverboats, because this was believed to bring bad luck. These days most captains aren't so concerned, but if you are asked to get off the roof while men are not, this is why.

WORK

With a large number of aid organisations and a fast-growing international business community, especially in energy and mining, the number of jobs available to foreigners is increasing, but it's still relatively small. The greatest number of positions are in Vientiane.

Possibilities include teaching English privately or at one of the handful of language centres in Vientiane. Certificates or degrees in English teaching aren't absolutely necessary, but they do help attract a better rate of pay.

If you have technical expertise or international volunteer experience, you might be able to find work with a UN-related program or an NGO providing foreign aid or technical assistance to Laos. These jobs are difficult to find; your best bet is to visit the Vientiane offices of each organisation and enquire about personnel needs and vacancies. For a list of NGOs operating in Laos, see the excellent www.directoryofngos.org.

Getting There & Away

Many travellers enter or exit Laos via the country's numerous land and river borders. Flying into Laos is a relatively easy option as there is only a small number of airlines serving Laos and prices don't vary much. Flights and tours can be booked online at www.lonelyplanet.com/bookings.

ENTERING LAOS

Thirty-day tourist visas are readily available on arrival at international airports and most land borders.

Air

Laos has air connections with regional countries including Thailand, Vietnam, Cambodia, Malaysia, Singapore, China and South Korea. The most convenient international gateway to Laos is Bangkok and there are plenty of flights to the Thai capital. If heading to Laos for a shorter holiday, it is cheaper to take an indirect flight to Bangkok with a stop on the way. Once in Bangkok, there are planes, trains and buses heading to Laos.

Land

Laos shares land and/or river borders with Thailand, Myanmar (Burma), Cambodia, China and Vietnam. Border-crossing details change regularly, so ask around and check Thorn Tree (lonelyplanet.com/thorntree) before setting off.

It's possible to bring a car or motorcycle into Laos from Cambodia and Thailand with the right paperwork, but not from Vietnam, China or

Myanmar. Lao customs does not object to visitors bringing bicycles into the country.

Getting Around

AIR

Lao Airlines (www.laoairlines.com) The main airline in Laos handling domestic flights, including between Vientiane and Luang Prabang, Luang Nam Tha, Pakse, Phonsavan, Savannakhet and Udomxai.

Lao Skyway (www.laoskyway.com) A newer domestic airline with flights from Vientiane to Udomxai, Luang Prabang, Huay Xai, Phonsavan, Luang Namtha, Phongsali and Sam Neua. Note that some services such as flights to Phongsali and Sam Neua do not appear on the airline website and can only be booked via the Lao Skyway offices.

With the exception of Lao Airlines offices in major cities, where credit cards are accepted for both international and domestic tickets, it is necessary to pay cash in US dollars if not booking online.

BICYCLE

The stunningly beautiful roads and light, relatively slow traffic in most towns and on most highways make Laos arguably the best country for cycling in Southeast Asia.

Simple single-speed bicycles can be hired in most places that see a decent number of tourists, usually costing about 20,000K per day. Better mountain bikes will cost from 30,000K to 80,000K per day.

BOAT

More than 4600km of navigable rivers are the highways and byways of traditional Laos, the main thoroughfares being the Mekong, Nam Ou, Nam Khan, Nam Tha, Nam Ngum and Se Kong. The Mekong is the longest and most important route and is navigable year-round between Huay Xai in the north and Savannakhet in the south, though new dams make this increasingly difficult without changing boats. Smaller rivers accommodate a range of smaller boats, from dugout canoes to 'bomb boats' made from war detritus.

MOTORCYCLE TIPS

There are few more liberating travel experiences than renting a motorbike and setting off: stopping where you want, when you want. The lack of traffic and stunningly beautiful roads make Laos one of the best places in the region to do it. There are, however, a few things worth knowing before you hand over your passport as collateral to rent a bike.

The bike Price and availability mean that the vast majority of travellers rent Chinese 110cc bikes. No 110cc bike was designed to be used like a dirt bike, however – Japanese bikes deal with the roads better and are worth the extra few dollars a day.

The odometer Given that many roads have no kilometre stones and turn-offs are often unmarked, it's worth getting a bike with a working odometer. Most bike shops can fix an odometer in about 10 minutes for a few dollars. Money well spent, as long as you remember to note the distance when you start.

The gear Don't leave home without sunscreen, a hat, a plastic raincoat or poncho, a bandanna and sunglasses. Even the sealed roads in Laos get annoyingly dusty, so these last two are vital. A helmet is essential (ask for one if it isn't offered), as is wearing trousers and shoes, lest you wind up with the ubiquitous leg burn from the exhaust.

The problems Unless you're very lucky, something *will* go wrong. Budget some time for it.

The responsibility In general, you can ride a motorbike in Laos without a licence, a helmet or any safety gear whatsoever, but for all this freedom you must take all the responsibility. If you have a crash, there won't be an ambulance to pick you up, and when you get to the hospital, facilities will be basic. Carrying a basic medical kit and phone numbers for hospitals in Thailand and your travel-insurance provider is a good idea. The same goes for the bike. If it really dies you can't just call the company and get a replacement. You'll need to load it onto the next pickup or *sŏrngtăaou* and take it somewhere they can fix it. Don't abandon it by the road, or you'll have to pay for another one.

Whether it's on a tourist boat from Huay Xai to Luang Prabang or on a local boat you've rustled up in some remote village, it's still worth doing at least one river excursion while in Laos.

BUS

Long-distance public transport in Laos is either by bus or *sŏrngtăaou* (literally 'two rows'), which are converted pickups or trucks with benches down either side. Private operators have established VIP buses on some busier routes, offering faster and more luxurious air-con services that cost a little more than normal buses. Many guesthouses can book tickets for a small fee.

Sŏrngtăaou usually service shorter routes within a given province, though these vehicles are slowly being phased out across Laos and replaced by minivans. Many decent-sized villages still have at least one *sŏrngtăaou,* which will run to the provincial capital and back most days.

CAR & MOTORCYCLE

Chinese- and Japanese-made 100cc and 110cc step-through motorbikes can be hired for approximately 40,000K to 120,000K per day in most large centres and some smaller towns, although the state of the bikes can vary greatly. No licence is required, though you will have to leave your passport as collateral. Try to get a Japanese bike if travelling any distance out of town. In Vientiane, Luang Prabang, Vang Vieng, Tha Khaek and Pakse, 250cc dirt bikes are available from around US$25 to US$50 per day.

It's possible to hire a self-drive vehicle, but when you consider that a driver usually costs little more, takes responsibility for damage and knows where they're going, it seems less appealing. Costs run from US$40 to US$100 per day, depending on the route.

Vientiane-based Avis-Budget (p305) is a reliable option for car hire.

When it comes to motorbikes, try **Driven By Adventure** (☎020-58656994; www.hochiminhtrail.org; rental per day US$38-95, tours per day from US$190) or Fuark Motorbike Service (p305) in Vientiane.

AT A GLANCE

POPULATION
Thailand: 69.8 million

CAPITAL CITY
Bangkok

BEST MASSAMAN CURRY
Ginger & Kafe @ The House (p472)

BEST BIRDWATCHING
Doi Chiang Dao Wildlife Sanctuary (p476)

BEST CRAFT BEER SELECTION
Tasting Room by Mikkeller (p431)

WHEN TO GO

Nov–Feb Thailand's 'winter' is the best time to visit.

Mar–Jun The least desirable time to visit is during Thailand's hot season.

Late Jun–Oct Expect monsoon rains; storms are usually confined to an hour's downpour.

Sukhothai Historical Park (p481)

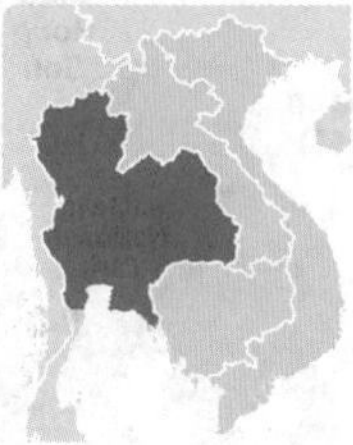

Northern Thailand

We suspect that the secret of Thailand's popularity, in particular that of its northern half, is that it packs a bit of everything. Bangkok is one of the most vibrant cities in Southeast Asia, yet if contemporary Thai living is not your thing, you can delve into the country's past at historical parks such as those at Sukhothai or Phanom Rung. Similarly, fresh-air fiends will be satiated by upcountry expeditions ranging from a rafting trip in Nan to the cliff-top views from Ubon Ratchathani's Pha Taem National Park. And culture junkies can get their fix at a homestay in the country's northeast or via a trek in northern Thailand. What's not to love?

INCLUDES

Northern Thailand Highlights

1 Chiang Mai Markets (p466) Picking up some bargains at the Night Bazaar, Saturday Walking Street and Sunday Walking Street.

2 Pha Taem National Park (p463) Feeling awestruck by the scenery.

3 Sukhothai (p481) Cycling around the awesome ruins of Thailand's 'golden age'.

4 Pai (p478) Enjoying outdoor adventures by day and bar-hopping by night in northern Thailand's most popular backpacker destination.

5 Ko Chang (p444) Beachcombing and jungle trekking.

6 Bangkok (p406) Recovering from the hardships of the upcountry in Thailand's modern and decadent capital.

7 Mae Hong Son (p494) Kicking back in this laid-back town with a palpable Myanmar influence.

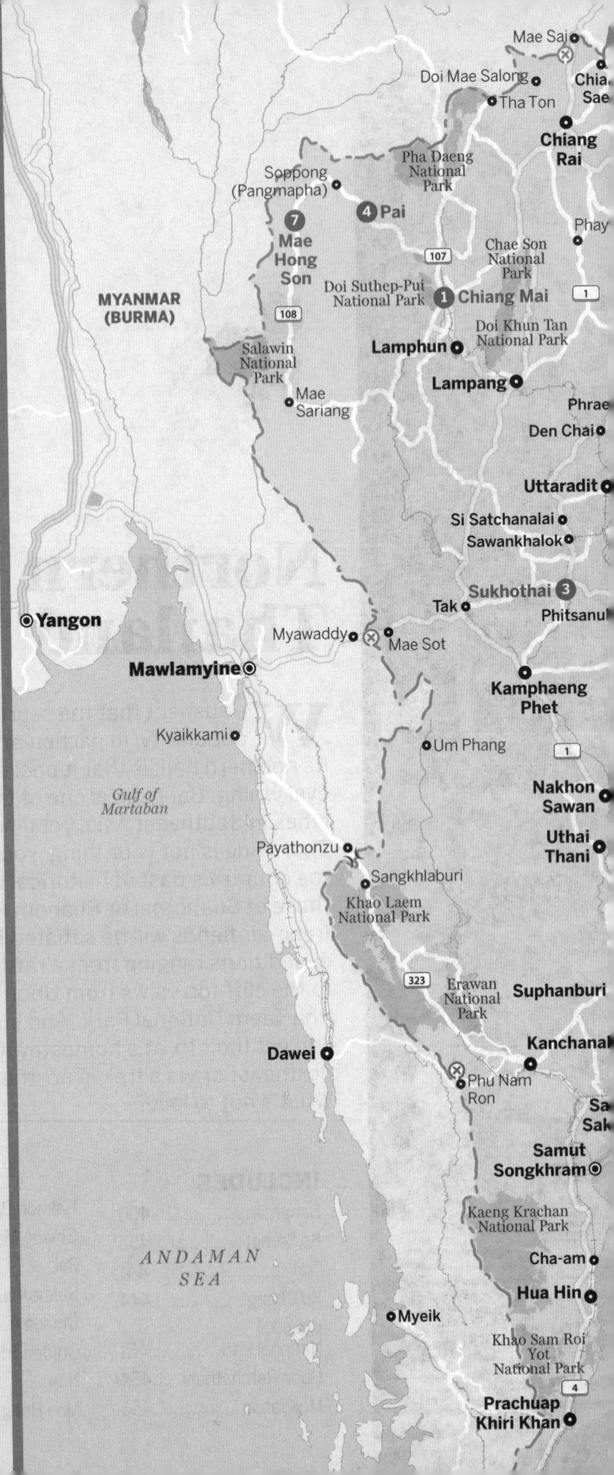

Huay Xai (Hoksay)
Chiang Khong
0 200 km
0 100 miles
Luang Prabang
Muang Ngeun
Huay Kon
VIETNAM
101
LAOS
Vang Vieng
Nan
Paksan
Bueng Kan
Pak Kading
Ban Kham Pia
VIENTIANE
Mekong
Chiang Khan
Nong Khai
222
Kaen Thao
Tha Li
Ban Phue
Udon Thani
Loei
Nakhon Phanom
Tha Khaek
210
Dan Sai
Nong Bua Lamphu
Sakhon Nakhon
Phu Hin Rong Kla National Park
21
That Phanom
Lom Sak
227
213
Thung Salaeng Luang National Park
Nam Nao National Park
Phu Wiang National Park
Savannakhet
Mukdahan
Phetchaburi
12
Khon Kaen
208
Mahasarakham
Roi Et
212
21
2
219
Amnat Charoen
225
Chaiyaphum
Yasothon
23
Pha Taem National Park
2
Ubon Ratchathani
Pakse
Phimai
Chong Mek
Vang Tao
Si Saket
Nakhon Ratchasima (Khorat)
Surin
Lopburi
2
24
Pak Chong
Nang Rong
Chong Chom
Choam Sa-Ngam
Phu Chong Nayoi National Park
Ayuthaya
Khao Yai National Park
O Smach
Choam
Anlong Veng
Prachinburi
Nong Nok Khiene
Bangkok
CAMBODIA
Aranyaprathet
Poipet
Chonburi
Siem Reap
Tonlé Sap
Psar Pruhm
Pong Nam Ron
Rayong
Ban Phe
Chanthaburi
Ko Samet
3
Trat
Laem Ngop
5
Ko Chang
Ko Kut
GULF OF THAILAND

BANGKOK

02 / POP 9,600,000

Same same, but different. This T-shirt line epitomises Bangkok (กรุงเทพฯ), where the familiar and exotic come together like the robust flavours on a plate of *pàt tai*.

Sights

Ko Ratanakosin & Thonburi

★Wat Phra Kaew BUDDHIST TEMPLE

(วัดพระแก้ว; Map p412; Th Na Phra Lan; 500B; 8.30am-3.30pm; Chang Pier, Maharaj Pier) Architecturally fantastic, this temple complex is also the spiritual core of Thai Buddhism and the monarchy, symbolically united in what is the country's most holy image, the Emerald Buddha. Attached to the temple complex is the Grand Palace (p414), the former royal residence, once a sealed city of intricate ritual and social stratification. The ground was consecrated in 1782, the first year of Bangkok rule, and is today Bangkok's biggest tourist attraction and a pilgrimage destination for devout Buddhists.

➡ Emerald Buddha

Upon entering Wat Phra Kaew you'll meet the *yaksha*, brawny guardian giants from the *Ramakian* (the Thai version of the Indian epic, *Ramayana*). Beyond them is a courtyard where the central *bòht* (ordination hall) houses the Emerald Buddha. The spectacular ornamentation inside and out does an excellent job of distracting first-time visitors from paying their respects to the image. Here's why: the Emerald Buddha is only 66cm tall and sits so high above worshippers in the main temple building that the gilded shrine is more striking than the small figure it cradles. No one knows exactly where it comes from or who sculpted it, but it first appeared on record in 15th-century Chiang Rai in northern Thailand. Stylistically it seems to belong to Thai artistic periods of the 13th to 14th centuries.

Because of its royal status, the Emerald Buddha is ceremoniously draped in monastic robes. There are now three royal robes: for the hot, rainy and cool seasons. The three robes are still solemnly changed by the king at the beginning of each season.

➡ Ramakian Murals

Outside the main *bòht* is a stone statue of the Chinese goddess of mercy, Kuan Im, and nearby are two cow figures, representing the year of Rama I's birth. In the 2km-long cloister that defines the perimeter of the complex are 178 murals depicting the *Ramakian* in its entirety, beginning at the north gate and moving clockwise around the compound.

The story begins with the hero, Rama (the green-faced character), and his bride, Sita (the beautiful topless maiden). The young couple is banished to the forest, along with Rama's brother. In this pastoral setting, the evil king Ravana (the character with many arms and faces) disguises himself as a hermit in order to kidnap Sita.

Rama joins forces with Hanuman, the monkey king (depicted as the white monkey), to attack Ravana and rescue Sita. Although Rama has the pedigree, Hanuman is the unsung hero. He is loyal, fierce and clever. En route to the final fairy-tale ending, great battles and schemes of trickery ensue until Ravana is finally killed. After withstanding a loyalty test of fire, Sita and Rama are triumphantly reunited.

If the temple grounds seem overrun by tourists, the mural area is usually mercifully quiet and shady. Admission to the temple is included in the ticket for the Grand Palace.

★Wat Pho BUDDHIST TEMPLE

(วัดโพธิ์/วัดพระเชตุพน, Wat Phra Chetuphon; Map p412; www.watpho.com; Th Sanam Chai; 200B; 8.30am-6.30pm; Tien Pier) You'll find (slightly) fewer tourists here than at neighbouring Wat Phra Kaew, but Wat Pho is our absolute favourite among Bangkok's biggest sights. In fact, the compound incorporates a host of superlatives: the city's largest reclining Buddha, the largest collection of Buddha images in Thailand and the country's earliest centre for public education. Almost too big for its shelter is Wat Pho's highlight, the genuinely impressive **Reclining Buddha**, housed in a pavilion on the western edge of the temple complex.

The rambling grounds of Wat Pho cover 8 hectares, with the major tourist sites occupying the northern side of Th Chetuphon and the monastic facilities found on the southern side. The temple compound is also the national headquarters for the teaching and preservation of traditional Thai medicine, including Thai massage, a mandate legislated by Rama III when the tradition was in danger of extinction. The famous massage school has two **massage pavilions** (Map p412; Th Sanam Chai, Wat Pho; Thai massage per hour from 540B; 9am-4pm; Tien Pier) located within the temple area and additional rooms within the **training facility** (Map p412; 02 622 3551;

Greater Bangkok

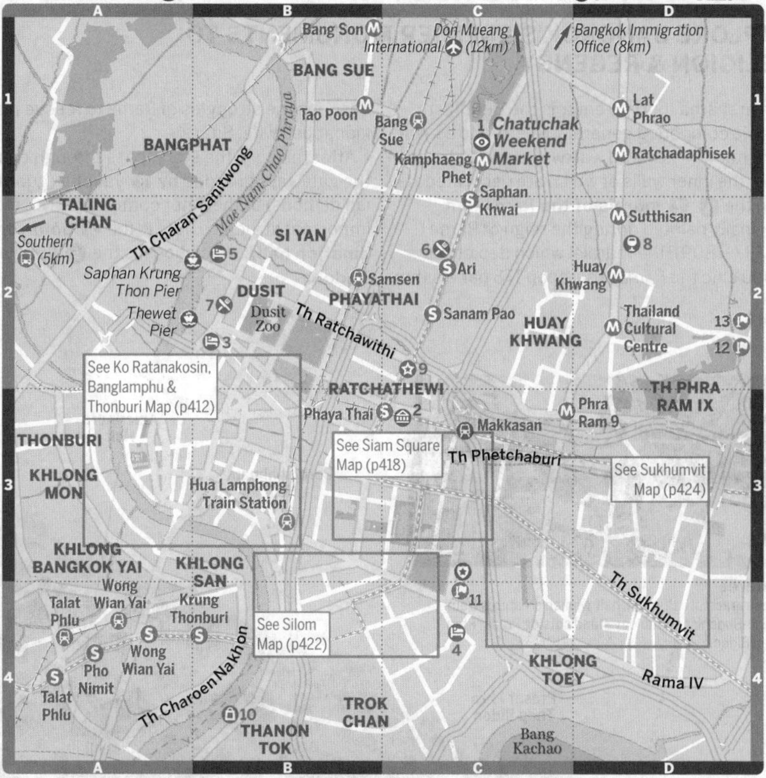

Greater Bangkok

Top Sights
1 Chatuchak Weekend Market C1

Sights
Clock Tower .... (see 1)
2 Suan Pakkad Palace Museum C3

Sleeping
3 Phra-Nakorn Norn-Len B2
4 S1 Hostel C4
5 Siam B2

Eating
6 Baan Pueng Chom C2
7 Krua Apsorn B2

Drinking & Nightlife
8 Fake Club The Next Gen D2

Entertainment
9 Saxophone Pub & Restaurant C2

Shopping
10 Asiatique B4

Information
11 Australian Embassy C4
12 Cambodian Embassy D2
Chatuchak Park Office .... (see 1)
13 Laotian Embassy D2

www.watpomassage.com; 392/32-33 Soi Phen Phat; lessons from 2500B, Thai massage per hour from 540B; ⏲lessons 9am-4pm, massage 9am-8pm; Tien Pier) outside the temple.

A common public ritual at the temple of the Reclining Buddha is to donate coins (representing alms) in a series of metal

(Continued on page 414)

Wat Phra Kaew & Grand Palace

EXPLORE BANGKOK'S PREMIER MONUMENTS TO RELIGION & REGENCY

The first area tourists enter is the Buddhist temple compound generally referred to as Wat Phra Kaew. A covered walkway surrounds the area, the inner walls of which are decorated with the ❶ ❷ **murals of the Ramakian**. Originally painted during the reign of Rama I (r 1782–1809), the murals, which depict the Hindu epic the *Ramayana*, span 178 panels that describe the struggles of Rama to rescue his kidnapped wife, Sita.

After taking in the story, pass through one of the gateways guarded by ❸ **yaksha** (guardian demons) to the inner compound. The most important structure here is the ❹ **bòht (ordination hall)**, which houses the ❺ **Emerald Buddha**.

Kinaree
These graceful half-swan, half-women creatures from Hindu-Buddhist mythology stand outside Prasat Phra Thep Bidon.

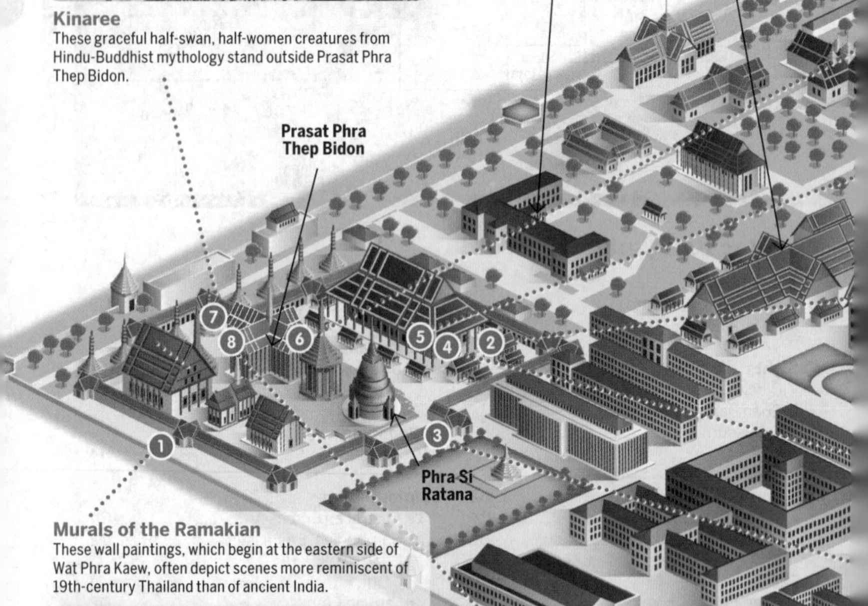

Murals of the Ramakian
These wall paintings, which begin at the eastern side of Wat Phra Kaew, often depict scenes more reminiscent of 19th-century Thailand than of ancient India.

Hanuman
Rows of these mischievous monkey deities from Hindu mythology appear to support the lower levels of two small *chedi* near Prasat Phra Thep Bidon.

Head east to the so-called Upper Terrace, an elevated area home to the 6 **spires of the three primary chedi**. The middle structure, Phra Mondop, is used to house Buddhist manuscripts. This area is also home to several of Wat Phra Kaew's noteworthy mythical beings, including beckoning 7 **kinaree** and several grimacing 8 **Hanuman**.

Proceed through the western gate to the compound known as the Grand Palace. Few of the buildings here are open to the public. The most noteworthy structure is 9 **Chakri Mahaprasat**. Built in 1882, the exterior of the hall is a unique blend of Western and traditional Thai architecture.

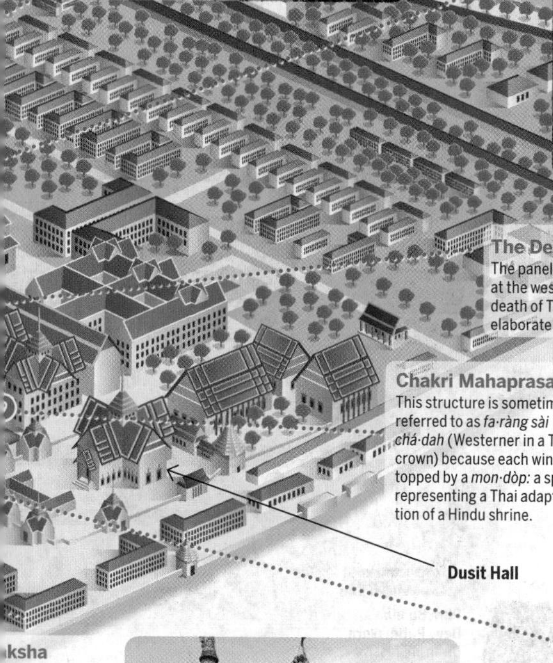

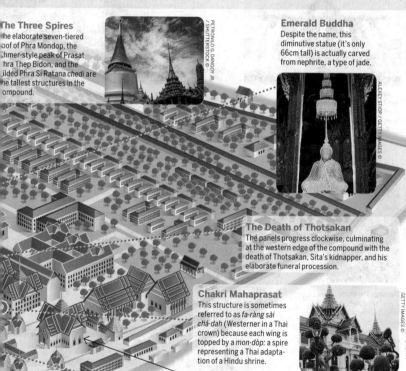

The Three Spires
he elaborate seven-tiered oof of Phra Mondop, the Khmer-style peak of Prasat hra Thep Bidon, and the ilded Phra Si Ratana *chedi* are he tallest structures in the ompound.

PETRONILO G. DANGOY JR. / SHUTTERSTOCK ©

Emerald Buddha
Despite the name, this diminutive statue (it's only 66cm tall) is actually carved from nephrite, a type of jade.

ALEXEY STIOP / GETTY IMAGES ©

The Death of Thotsakan
The panels progress clockwise, culminating at the western edge of the compound with the death of Thotsakan, Sita's kidnapper, and his elaborate funeral procession.

Chakri Mahaprasat
This structure is sometimes referred to as *fa·ràng sài chá·dah* (Westerner in a Thai crown) because each wing is topped by a *mon·dòp:* a spire representing a Thai adaptation of a Hindu shrine.

DESIGN PICS / BLAKE KENT / GETTY IMAGES ©

Bòht (Ordination Hall)
This structure is an early example of the Ratanakosin school of architecture, which combines traditional stylistic holdovers from Ayuthaya along with more modern touches from China and the West.

ksha
ch entrance the Wat Phra ew compound is tched over by a r of vigilant and ormous *yaksha*, es or giants from du mythology.

ZZVET / GETTY IMAGES ©

Wat Pho

A WALK THROUGH THE BIG BUDDHAS OF WAT PHO

The logical starting place is the main *wí·hăhn* (sanctuary), home to Wat Pho's centrepiece, the immense ❶ **Reclining Buddha**. In addition to its enormous size, note the ❷ **mother-of-pearl inlay** on the soles of the statue's feet. The interior walls of the *wí·hăhn* are covered with murals that depict previous lives of the Buddha, and along the south side of the structure there are 108 bronze monk bowls; for 20B you can buy 108 coins, each of which is dropped in a bowl for good luck.

Exit the *wí·hăhn* and head east via the two ❸ **stone giants** who guard the gateway to the rest of the compound. Directly south of these are the four towering ❹ **royal chedi**.

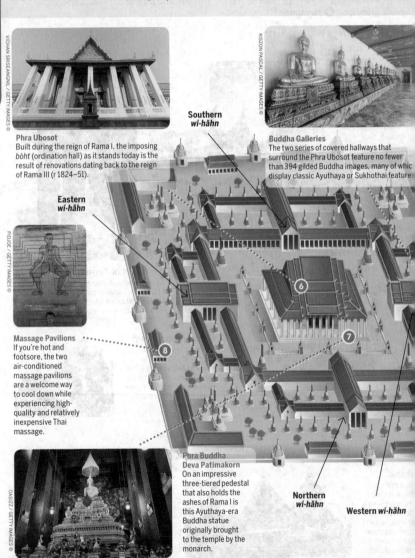

VICHAN SRISEANGNIL / GETTY IMAGES ©

Phra Ubosot
Built during the reign of Rama I, the imposing *bòht* (ordination hall) as it stands today is the result of renovations dating back to the reign of Rama III (r 1824–51).

KISZON PASCAL / GETTY IMAGES ©

Buddha Galleries
The two series of covered hallways that surround the Phra Ubosot feature no fewer than 394 gilded Buddha images, many of whic display classic Ayuthaya or Sukhothai feature

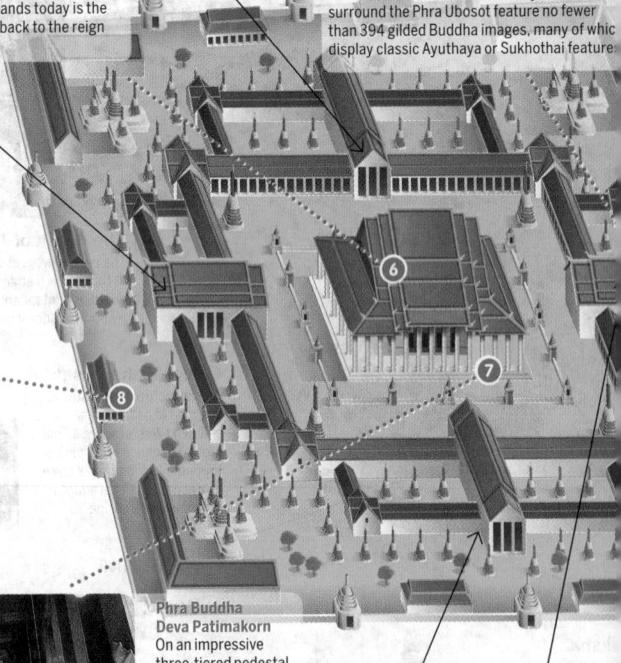

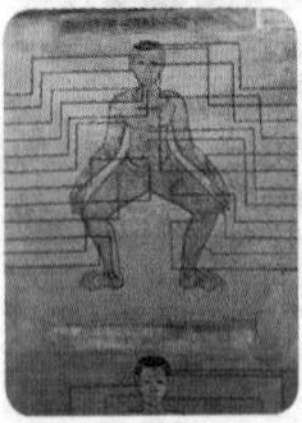

PIDJOE / GETTY IMAGES ©

Massage Pavilions
If you're hot and footsore, the two air-conditioned massage pavilions are a welcome way to cool down while experiencing high-quality and relatively inexpensive Thai massage.

OASIZZ / GETTY IMAGES ©

Phra Buddha Deva Patimakorn
On an impressive three-tiered pedestal that also holds the ashes of Rama I is this Ayuthaya-era Buddha statue originally brought to the temple by the monarch.

Continue east, passing through two consecutive ❺ **galleries of Buddha statues** linking four *wí·hăhn*, two of which contain notable Sukhothai-era Buddha statues; these comprise the exterior of ❻ **Phra Ubosot**, the immense ordination hall that is Wat Pho's second-most noteworthy structure. The base of the building is surrounded by bas-relief inscriptions, and inside is the notable Buddha statue, ❼ **Phra Buddha Deva Patimakorn**.

Wat Pho is often referred to as Thailand's first university, a tradition that continues today in an associated traditional Thai medicine school and, at the compound's eastern extent, two ❽ **massage pavilions**.

Interspersed throughout the eastern half of the compound are several additional minor *chedi* and rock gardens.

TAKEPICSFORFUN / GETTY IMAGES ©

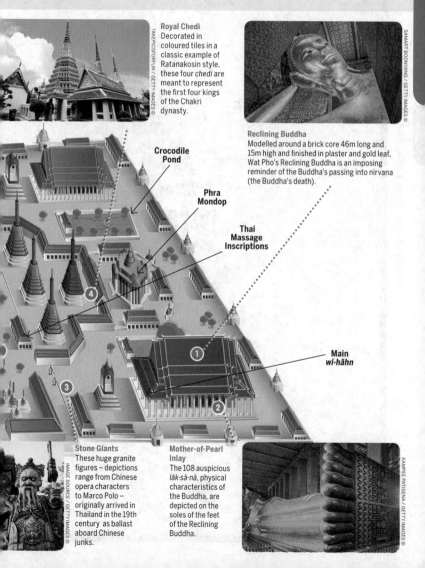

Royal Chedi
Decorated in coloured tiles in a classic example of Ratanakosin style, these four *chedi* are meant to represent the first four kings of the Chakri dynasty.

SAMART BOONYANG / GETTY IMAGES ©

Reclining Buddha
Modelled around a brick core 46m long and 15m high and finished in plaster and gold leaf, Wat Pho's Reclining Buddha is an imposing reminder of the Buddha's passing into nirvana (the Buddha's death).

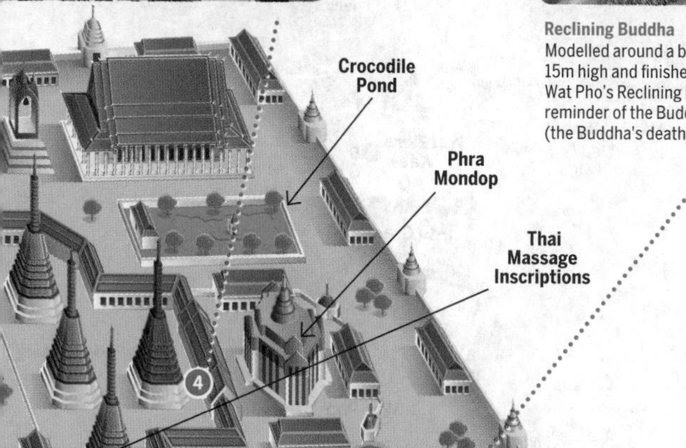

IMAGE SOURCE / GETTY IMAGES ©

Stone Giants
These huge granite figures – depictions range from Chinese opera characters to Marco Polo – originally arrived in Thailand in the 19th century as ballast aboard Chinese junks.

Mother-of-Pearl Inlay
The 108 auspicious *lák·sà·nà*, physical characteristics of the Buddha, are depicted on the soles of the feet of the Reclining Buddha.

KAMPEE PATISENA / GETTY IMAGES ©

Ko Ratanakosin, Banglamphu & Thonburi

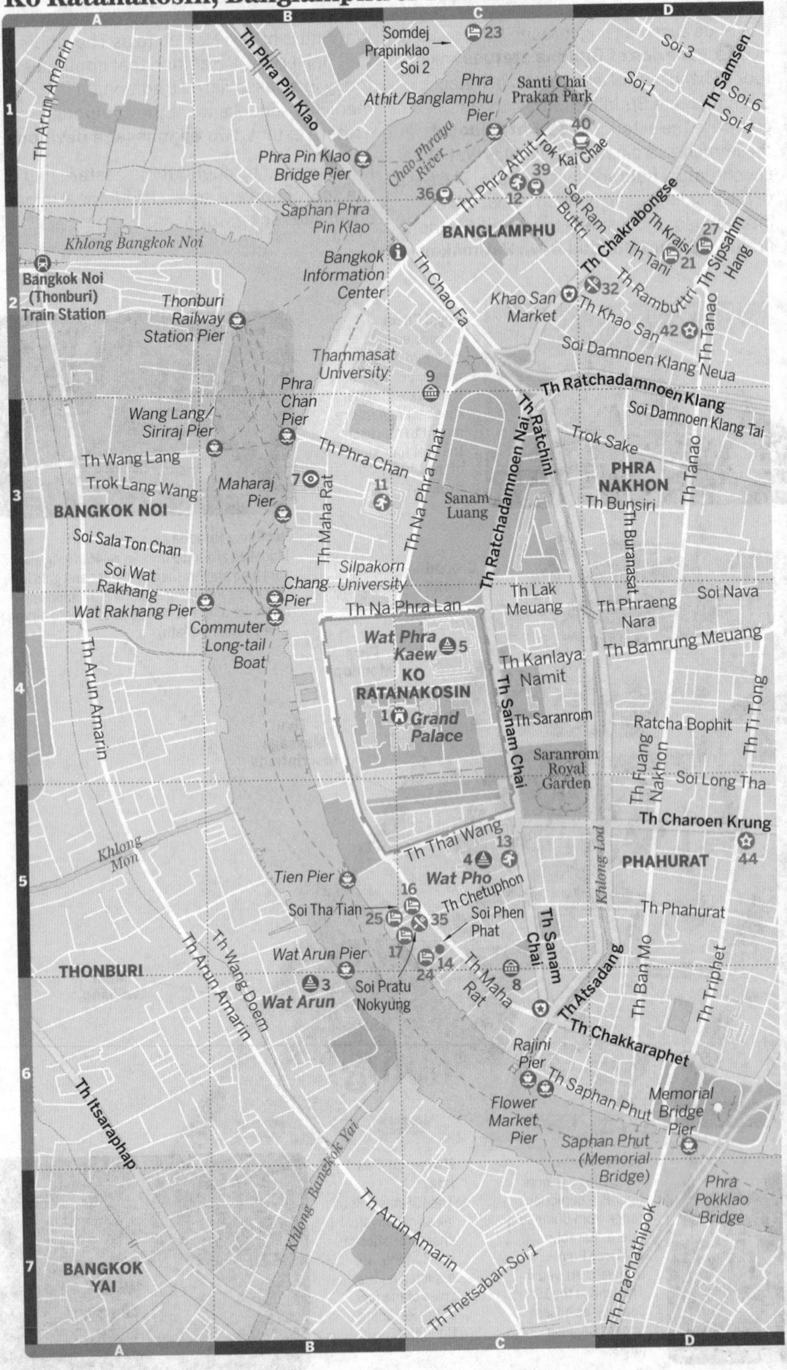

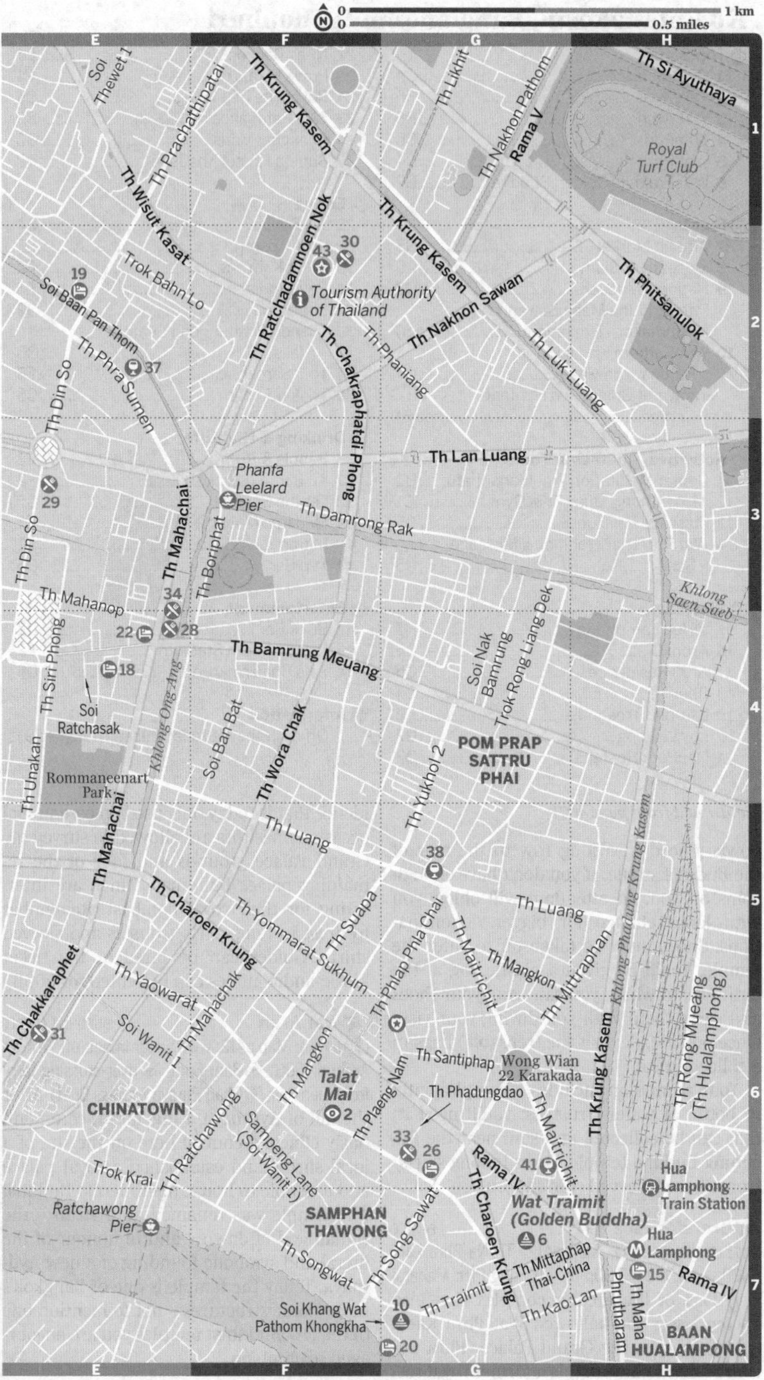
0 1 km
0 0.5 miles
Th Si Ayuthaya
Royal Turf Club
Th Krung Kasem
Th Prachathipatai
Soi Thewet 1
Th Likhit
Th Nakhon Pathom
Rama V
Th Wisut Kasat
Th Ratchadamnoen Nok
Trok Bahn Lo
Soi Baan Pan Thom
Tourism Authority of Thailand
Th Nakhon Sawan
Th Phitsanulok
Th Phra Sumen
Th Chakraphatdi Phong
Th Phaniang
Th Luk Luang
Th Din So
Th Lan Luang
Phanfa Leelard Pier
Th Damrong Rak
Th Mahachai
Th Boriphat
Khlong Saen Saeb
Th Mahanop
Th Bamrung Meuang
Soi Nak Bamrung
Trok Rong Liang Dek
Th Siri Phong
Soi Ratchasak
Khlong Ong Ang
Soi Ban Bat
Th Wora Chak
POM PRAP SATTRU PHAI
Th Unakan
Rommaneenart Park
Th Yukhol 2
Th Luang
Khlong Phadung Krung Kasem
Th Charoen Krung
Th Yommarat Sukhum
Th Suapa
Th Phlap Phla Chai
Th Maitrichit
Th Mangkon
Th Mittraphan
Th Chakkaraphet
Th Yaowarat
Th Mahachak
Soi Wanit 1
Th Santiphap
Wong Wian 22 Karakada
Th Rong Mueang (Th Hualamphong)
Talat Mai
Th Plaeng Nam
Th Phadungdao
CHINATOWN
Th Ratchawong
Sampeng Lane (Soi Wanit 1)
Rama IV
Trok Krai
Hua Lamphong Train Station
Ratchawong Pier
SAMPHAN THAWONG
Th Song Sawat
Wat Traimit (Golden Buddha)
Hua Lamphong
Th Songwat
Th Mittaphap Thai-China
Th Traimit
Th Kao Lan
Phrutharam
Th Maha
Soi Khang Wat Pathom Khongkha
BAAN HUALAMPONG

Ko Ratanakosin, Banglamphu & Thonburi

Top Sights
1 Grand Palace ... C4
2 Talat Mai ... F6
3 Wat Arun ... B6
4 Wat Pho ... C5
5 Wat Phra Kaew ... C4
6 Wat Traimit (Golden Buddha) ... G7

Sights
7 Amulet Market ... B3
8 Museum of Siam ... C5
9 National Museum ... C3
Phra Buddha Maha Suwanna Patimakorn Exhibition ... (see 6)
10 Wat Pathum Khongka Ratchaworawihan ... G7
Yaowarat Chinatown Heritage Center ... (see 6)

Activities, Courses & Tours
11 Center Meditation Wat Mahadhatu ... B3
12 Jaroenthong Muay Thai Gym ... C1
13 Massage Pavilions ... C5
14 Wat Pho Thai Traditional Massage School ... C5

Sleeping
15 @Hua Lamphong ... H7
16 Arom D ... C5
17 Arun Residence ... C5
18 Chern ... E4
19 Lamphu Treehouse ... E2
20 Loy La Long ... G7
21 NapPark Hostel ... D2
22 Niras Bankoc ... E4
23 Praya Palazzo ... C1
24 Royal ThaTien Village ... C5
25 Sala Ratanakosin ... B5
26 Shanghai Mansion ... G6
27 Suneta Hostel Khaosan ... D2

Eating
28 Jay Fai ... E4
29 Krua Apsorn ... E3
30 Likhit Kai Yang ... F2
31 Royal India ... E6
32 Shoshana ... D2
33 Thanon Phadungdao Seafood Stalls ... G6
34 Thip Samai ... E3
35 Tonkin Annam ... C5

Drinking & Nightlife
36 Babble & Rum ... C1
37 Ku Bar ... E2
38 Let the Boy Die ... G5
39 Madame Musur ... C1
40 Mitramit ... D1
41 Tep Bar ... G6

Entertainment
42 Brick Bar ... D2
43 Rajadamnern Stadium ... F2
44 Sala Chalermkrung ... D5

Information
Office of the National Museum ... (see 9)

(Continued from page 407)

bowls placed in a long row to the rear of the Buddha statue. If you don't have enough coins on you, an attendant will oblige you with loose change for bigger denominations. Shoes must be taken off to enter the temple. You'll be given a plastic bag at the entrance, in which you can wrap your shoes and carry them with you during your visit. Once outside, deposit the (reusable) bags in a collection vat.

Your admission includes a complimentary bottle of water (trust us: you'll need it) that can be collected at a stall near the Reclining Buddha temple. Dress in long skirts/trousers and sleeved shirts when you visit.

★Grand Palace PALACE

(พระบรมมหาราชวัง; Map p412; Th Na Phra Lan; 500B; 8.30am-3.30pm; Chang Pier, Maharaj Pier) Part of the greater complex that also encompasses the hallowed Wat Phra Kaew (p406) temple, the Grand Palace (Phra Borom Maharatchawang) is a former royal residence that is today only used on ceremonial occasions. Visitors are allowed to survey the Grand Palace grounds and four of the remaining palace buildings, which are interesting for their royal bombast. Remember to dress in long skirts/trousers and sleeved shirts. Guides can be hired at the ticket kiosk; audio guides can be rented for 200B.

★Wat Arun BUDDHIST TEMPLE

(วัดอรุณฯ; Map p412; www.watarun.net; off Th Arun Amarin; 50B; 8am-6pm; river-crossing ferry from Tien Pier, Chao Phraya Express Boat) After the fall of Ayuthaya, King Taksin ceremoniously clinched control here on the site of a local shrine and established a royal palace and a temple to house the Emerald Buddha. The temple was renamed after Arun – the Indian god of dawn – and in honour of the literal and symbolic founding of a new Ayuthaya. Today the temple is one of Bangkok's most iconic structures – not to mention one of the few Buddhist temples you are encouraged to climb on.

National Museum MUSEUM

(พิพิธภัณฑสถานแห่งชาติ; Map p412; 4 Th Na Phra That; 200B; ⏲9am-4pm Wed-Sun; ⛴Chang Pier, Maharaj Pier) Thailand's National Museum is home to an impressive collection of items dating from throughout the country's glittering past. Most of the museum's structures were built in 1782 as the palace of Rama I's viceroy, Prince Wang Na. Rama V turned it into a museum in 1874, and today there are three permanent exhibitions spread out over several buildings. The principal exhibition, **Gallery of Thai History**, is home to some of the country's most beautiful Buddha images and sculptures of Hindu gods.

Museum of Siam MUSEUM

(สถาบันพิพิธภัณฑ์การเรียนรู้แห่งชาติ; Map p412; Th Maha Rat; 200B; ⏲10am-6pm Tue-Sun; 👪; ⛴Tien Pier) This fun museum's collection employs a variety of media to explore the origins of the Thai people and their culture. Housed in a European-style 19th-century building that was once the Ministry of Commerce, the exhibits are presented in a contemporary, engaging and interactive fashion not typically found in Thailand's museums. They are also refreshingly balanced and entertaining, with galleries dealing with a range of questions about the origins of the nation and its people.

Amulet Market MARKET

(ตลาดพระเครื่องวัดมหาธาตุ; Map p412; Th Maha Rat; ⏲7am-5pm; ⛴Chang Pier, Maharaj Pier) This arcane and fascinating market claims both the footpaths along Th Maha Rat and Th Phra Chan, as well as a dense network of covered market stalls that runs south from Phra Chan Pier. The easiest entry point is clearly marked 'Trok Maha That'. The trade is based around small talismans highly prized by collectors, monks, taxi drivers and people in dangerous professions.

Chinatown

★Wat Traimit (Golden Buddha) BUDDHIST TEMPLE

(วัดไตรมิตร, Temple of the Golden Buddha; Map p412; Th Mittaphap Thai-China; 40B; ⏲8am-5pm; ⛴Marine Department Pier, Ⓜ Hua Lamphong exit 1) The attraction at Wat Traimit is undoubtedly the impressive 3m-tall, 5.5-tonne, **solid-gold Buddha image**, which gleams like, well, gold. Sculpted in the graceful Sukhothai style, the image was 'discovered' some 65 years ago beneath a stucco/plaster exterior, when it fell from a crane while being moved within the temple compound. It's speculated that the covering was added to protect it from marauding Burmese invaders, during a siege either in the late Sukhothai period or the Ayuthaya period.

The temple itself is said to date from the early 13th century. Donations and a constant flow of tourists have proven profitable, and the statue is now housed in an imposing four-storey marble structure called Phra Maha Mandop. The 2nd floor of the building is home to the **Yaowarat Chinatown Heritage Center** (ศูนย์ประวัติศาสตร์เยาวราช; Map p412; Th Mittaphap Thai-China, Wat Traimit/Golden Buddha; 100B; ⏲8am-5pm Tue-Sun; ⛴Marine Department Pier, Ⓜ Hua Lamphong exit 1), a small but engaging museum with multimedia exhibits on the history of Bangkok's Chinatown and its residents, while the 3rd floor is home to the **Phra Buddha Maha Suwanna Patimakorn Exhibition** (นิทรรศการพระพุทธมหาสุวรรณปฏิมากร; Map p412; Th Mittaphap Thai-China, Wat Traimit/Golden Buddha; 100B; ⏲8am-5pm Tue-Sun; ⛴Marine Department Pier, Ⓜ Hua Lamphong exit 1), which has exhibits on how the statue was made.

★Talat Mai MARKET

(ตลาดใหม่, New Market; Map p412; Soi Yaowarat 6/Charoen Krung 16; ⏲6am-6pm; ⛴Ratchawong Pier, Ⓜ Hua Lamphong exit 1 & taxi) With some two centuries of commerce under its belt, New Market is no longer an entirely accurate name for this strip of commerce. Regardless, this is Bangkok's quintessential Chinese market, and the dried goods, seasonings, spices and sauces will be familiar to anyone who's ever spent time in China. Even if you're not interested in food, the hectic atmosphere (watch out for motorcycles squeezing between shoppers) and exotic sights and smells create a somewhat surreal sensory experience for curious wanderers.

★Talat Noi AREA

(ตลาดน้อย; Map p422; off Th Charoen Krung; ⏲7am-7pm; ⛴Marine Department Pier) This microcosm of soi (lane) life is named after a small *(nói)* market *(đà·làht)* that sets up between Soi 22 and Soi 20, along the atmospheric Soi Wanit 2 that runs parallel to Th Charoen Krung. Wandering here you'll find maze-like tentacular soi turning in on themselves, weaving through innumerable grease-stained machinery shops, grocery outlets, warehouses and people's living rooms. The crumbling buildings, vivid wall art and tree-boughed alleyways make it a fantastic area for casual ambling and candid street photography.

Siam Square, Pratunam, Phloen Chit & Ratchathewi

★Jim Thompson House HISTORIC BUILDING
(เรือนไทยจิมทอมป์สัน; Map p418; ☎02 218 7368; www.jimthompsonhouse.com; 6 Soi Kasem San 2; adult/student 200/100B; ⊙9am-6pm, compulsory tours every 30min; klorng boat Sapan Hua Chang Pier, S National Stadium exit 1) This jungly compound is the former home of the eponymous American silk entrepreneur and art collector. Born in Delaware in 1906, Thompson briefly served in the Office of Strategic Services (the forerunner of the CIA) in Thailand during WWII. He settled in Bangkok after the war, when his neighbours' handmade silk caught his eye and piqued his business sense. He sent samples to fashion houses in Milan, London and Paris, gradually building a steady worldwide clientele.

★Suan Pakkad Palace Museum MUSEUM
(วังสวนผักกาด; Map p407; www.suanpakkad.com; Th Si Ayuthaya; 100B; ⊙9am-4pm; S Phaya Thai exit 4) An overlooked treasure, Suan Pakkad (literally 'lettuce farm') is a collection of eight traditional wooden Thai houses that was once the residence of Princess Chumbon of Nakhon Sawan and before that a lettuce farm. Within the stilt buildings are displays of art, antiques and furnishings, and the landscaped grounds are a peaceful oasis complete with ducks, swans and a semi-enclosed garden.

Riverside, Silom & Lumphini

★Lumphini Park PARK
(สวนลุมพินี; Map p422; bounded by Th Sarasin, Rama IV, Th Witthayu/Wireless Rd & Th Ratchadamri; ⊙4.30am-9pm; ; M Lumphini exit 3, Si Lom exit 1, S Sala Daeng exit 3/4, Ratchadamri exit 2) Named after the Buddha's birthplace in Nepal (Lumbini), Lumphini Park is central Bangkok's largest and most popular park. Its 58 hectares are home to an artificial lake surrounded by broad, well-tended lawns, wooded areas, walking paths and startlingly large resident monitor lizards to complement the shuffling citizens. It's the best outdoor escape from Bangkok without actually leaving town. The park was originally a royal reserve, but in 1925 Rama VI (King Vajiravudh; r 1910–25) declared it a public space.

★SkyWalk at King Power Mahanakhon VIEWPOINT
(Map p422; ☎02 677 8721; www.kingpowermahanakhon.co.th/skywalk; 114 Th Naradhiwas Rajanagarindra; observatory/rooftop 850/1050B; ⊙10am-midnight; S Chong Nonsi exit 3) Offering an unparalleled 360-degree view of Bangkok's cityscape, this two-tiered viewpoint is perched atop King Power Mahanakhon, currently Thailand's tallest building. Stepping onto the dizzying SkyWalk – a glass-floored balcony dangling 78 floors above the earth at 310m – is a spine-chilling experience, but you can soothe your nerves afterwards with a stiff sundowner at the open-air bar one flight up on the skyscraper's pinnacle at 314m. An indoor 74th-floor observatory offers a less adrenalised experience, and comes 200B cheaper.

Thanon Sukhumvit

★Siam Society & Kamthieng House MUSEUM
(สยามสมาคม & บ้านคำเที่ยง; Map p424; www.siam-society.org; 131 Soi 21/Asoke, Th Sukhumvit; adult/child 100B/free; ⊙9am-5pm Tue-Sat; M Sukhumvit exit 1, S Asok exit 3 or 6) Kamthieng House transports visitors to a northern Thai village complete with informative displays on daily rituals, folk beliefs and everyday household chores, all within the setting of a traditional wooden house. This museum is operated by – and shares space with – the Siam Society, publisher of the renowned *Journal of the Siam Society* and a valiant preserver of traditional Thai culture.

Northern Bangkok

★Chatuchak Weekend Market MARKET
(ตลาดนัดจตุจักร, Talat Nat Jatujak; Map p407; www.chatuchakmarket.org; 587/10 Th Phahonyothin; ⊙9am-6pm Sat & Sun, plants 7am-6pm Wed & Thu, wholesale 6pm-midnight Fri; M Chatuchak Park exit 1, Kamphaeng Phet exits 1 & 2, S Mo Chit exit 1) Among the largest open-air markets in the world, Chatuchak (also referred to as 'Jatujak' or simply 'JJ Market') seems to unite everything buyable, from used vintage sneakers to baby squirrels. Plan to spend a full day here, as there's plenty to see, do and buy. But come early, ideally around 10am, to beat the crowds and the heat. There is an information centre and bank with ATMs and foreign-exchange booths at the **Chatuchak Park Office** (Map p407; Chatuchak Weekend Market, Th Phahonyothin; ⊙9am-6pm Sat & Sun;

Ⓜ Kamphaeng Phet exits 1 & 2, Chatuchak Park exit 1, Ⓢ Mo Chit exit 1), near the northern end of the market's Soi 1, Soi 2 and Soi 3.

Schematic maps and toilets are located throughout the market; use the clock tower as a handy landmark.

Activities

★Supanniga Cruise CRUISE

(Map p422; ☎02 714 7608; www.supannigacruise.com; River City; cocktail/dinner cruises 1250/3250B; ⏲cruises 4.45-5.45pm & 6.15-8.30pm; ⛴Si Phraya/River City Pier) Breathing life into the somewhat tired Bangkok dinner-cruise genre is this outfit, linked with the Thai restaurant of the same name (p428). Options include a sunset cocktail cruise or a dinner cruise, the latter revolving around the same regional Thai dishes that have made the restaurant a city favourite.

★Oriental Spa SPA

(Map p422; ☎02 659 9000; www.mandarinoriental.com; Mandarin Oriental; massage & spa packages from 2900B; ⏲9am-10pm; ⛴Oriental Pier & hotel shuttle boat) Regarded as among the premier spas in the world, the Oriental Spa is located in a charming villa on the western bank of the Chao Phraya River, and pretty much sets the standard for Asian-style spa treatment among its peers. Depending on where you flew in from, the jet-lag massage might be a good option. All treatments require advance booking.

Asia Herb Association MASSAGE

(Map p424; ☎02 392 3631; www.asiaherbassociation.com; 58/19-25 Soi 55/Thong Lor, Th Sukhumvit; Thai massage from 500B, with herbal compress 1½hr 1100B; ⏲9am-midnight; Ⓢ Thong Lo exit 3) With multiple branches along Th Sukhumvit, this Japanese-owned chain specialises in massage using *prà·kóp* (traditional Thai herbal compresses) filled with 18 different herbs.

Health Land MASSAGE

(Map p422; ☎02 637 8883; www.healthlandspa.com; 120 Th Sathon Neua/North; massage from 600B; ⏲9am-11pm; Ⓢ Surasak exit 1/3) This main branch of a long-standing Thai massage mini-empire is located in Sathorn, and offers a range of great-value massage and spa treatments in a tidy environment. The staff are excellently trained, and it's so popular with locals and tourists that you must call and book in advance, especially if you're planning a weekend visit.

★Cooking with Poo & Friends COOKING

(☎080 434 8686; www.cookingwithpoo.com; classes 1500B; ⏲8.30am-1pm; 👪) This popular cooking course was started by a native of Khlong Toey's slums and is held in her neighbourhood. Courses, which must be booked in advance, span three dishes and include a visit to **Khlong Toey Market** (ตลาดคลองเตย; Map p424; cnr Th Ratchadaphisek & Rama IV; ⏲5-10am; Ⓜ Khlong Toei exit 1) and transport to and from Emporium Shopping Centre.

Jaroenthong Muay Thai Gym MARTIAL ARTS

(Map p412; ☎02 629 2313; www.jaroenthongmuaythaikhaosan.com; Th Phra Athit; lessons from 600B; ⏲drop-in hours 10-11.30am & 2-8pm; ⛴Phra Athit/Banglamphu Pier) With branches around the country, this lauded martial-arts gym has a training centre a short walk from Th Khao San. Beginners can drop in and train in air-conditioned comfort, while the more experienced can opt for longer training regimens.

Center Meditation Wat Mahadhatu MEDITATION

(Map p412; ☎02 222 6011; Section 5, Th Maha Rat, Wat Mahathat; donations accepted; ⏲classes 1pm & 6pm; ⛴Chang Pier, Maharaj Pier) Located within Wat Mahathat, this small centre offers informal daily meditation classes. Taught by English-speaking teachers, classes last between two and three hours. Longer periods of study, which include accommodation and food, can be arranged, but students are expected to follow a strict regimen of conduct.

Festivals & Events

Chinese New Year CULTURAL

(⏲Jan or Feb) Thai-Chinese celebrate the Lunar New Year with a week of house cleaning, lion dances and fireworks. Most festivities centre on Chinatown. Dates vary.

Songkran CULTURAL

(⏲mid-Apr) The celebration of the Thai New Year has morphed into a water war with high-powered water guns and water balloons being launched at suspecting and unsuspecting participants. The most intense water battles take place on Th Silom and Th Khao San, and festivities continue for three days.

Vegetarian Festival FOOD & DRINK

(⏲Sep or Oct) Running for nine days, this Chinese-Buddhist festival wheels out yellow-bannered streetside vendors serving meatless meals. The greatest concentration of vendors is found in Chinatown. Dates vary.

Siam Square

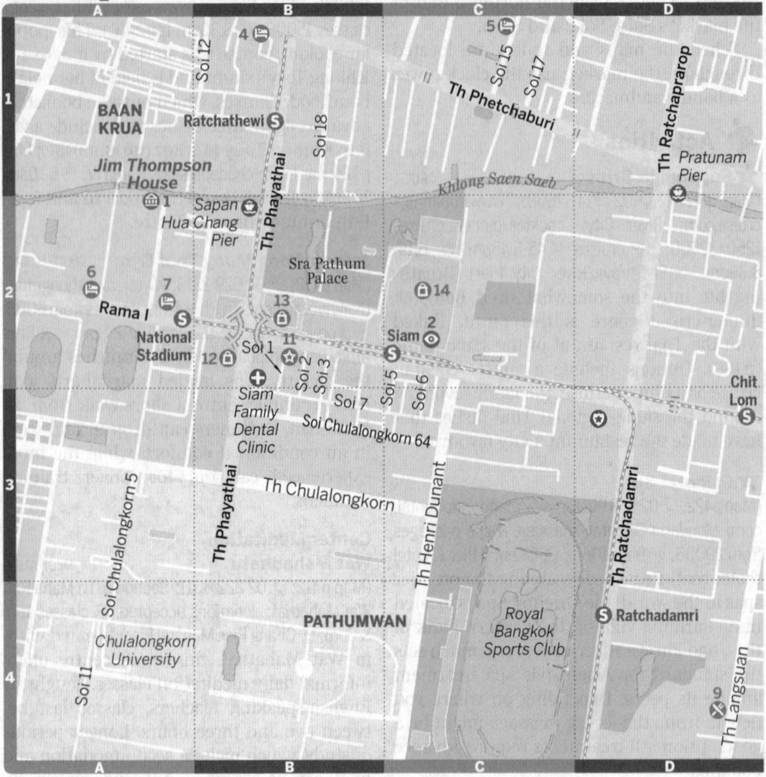

Loi Krathong CULTURAL

(Nov) A beautiful festival where, on the night of the full moon, small lotus-shaped boats made of banana leaf and containing a lit candle are set adrift on the Chao Phraya River. One of the best locations for watching the festivities is from the promenade at Asiatique (p433). The lake within Lumphini Park (p416) is an alternative venue for the ritual.

Sleeping

If your idea of the typical Bangkok hotel was influenced by *The Hangover Part II*, you'll be relieved to learn that the city is home to a variety of modern hostels, guesthouses and hotels. Much of Bangkok's accommodation offers excellent value, and competition is so intense that discounts are almost always available. Thanks to the abundance of options, booking ahead isn't generally required apart from at some of the smaller boutique places.

Banglamphu

Suneta Hostel Khaosan HOSTEL $

(Map p412; 02 629 0150; www.sunetahostel.com; 209-211 Th Kraisi; dm/r incl breakfast from 470/1200B; ; Phra Athit/Banglamphu Pier) A pleasant, low-key atmosphere, a unique, retro-themed design (some of the dorm rooms resemble sleeping-car carriages), a location just off the main drag and friendly service are what make Suneta stand out among the tight competition.

★Lamphu Treehouse HOTEL $$

(Map p412; 02 282 0991; www.lamphutreehotel.com; 155 Wanchat Bridge, off Th Prachathipatai; d incl breakfast from 1650B; ; klorng boat Phanfa Leelard Pier) Despite the name, this attractive midranger has its feet firmly on land, and as such represents brilliant value. The wood-panelled rooms are attractive, inviting and well maintained, and the rooftop sun lounge, pool, internet cafe, restaurant

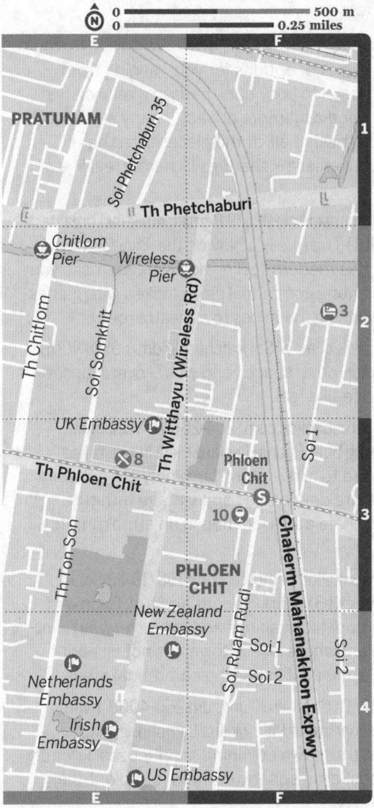

Siam Square

Top Sights
1 Jim Thompson House A2

Sights
2 Sea Life Ocean World C2

Sleeping
3 AriyasomVilla F2
4 Bed Station Hostel B1
5 Boxpackers Hostel C1
6 Chao Hostel A2
7 Lub d A2
Siam@Siam .... (see 6)

Eating
8 Eathai E3
9 Gaa D4
Gourmet Paradise .... (see 14)

Drinking & Nightlife
10 Hair of the Dog F3

Entertainment
11 Apex Scala B2
Major Cineplex .... (see 14)

Shopping
12 MBK Center B2
13 Siam Discovery B2
14 Siam Paragon C2

and quiet canalside location ensure you may never feel the need to leave. A nearby annexe increases the odds of snagging an elusive reservation.

★ **Praya Palazzo** HOTEL $$$
(Map p412; 02 883 2998; www.prayapalazzo.com; 757/1 Somdej Prapinklao Soi 2; d incl breakfast from 3600B; hotel shuttle boat from Phra Athit/Banglamphu Pier) After lying dormant for over 30 years, this elegant 19th-century mansion in Thonburi was reborn as an attractive riverside boutique hotel in 2011. The 17 rooms can seem rather tight, and river views can be elusive, but the meticulous renovation, handsome antique furnishings and bucolic atmosphere deliver a boutique hotel with authentic old-world charm. The fact that the hotel is located on a canal-bound islet and can only be accessed by the riverway makes it an unwise choice for night owls, but an excellent hideaway for solitude seekers.

Ko Ratanakosin & Thonburi

Arom D HOSTEL $$
(Map p412; 02 622 1055; www.aromdhostel.com; 336 Th Maha Rat; dm/r incl breakfast 800/2250B; Tien Pier) The rooms here are united by a cutesy design theme and a host of inviting communal areas, including a rooftop deck, computers and a ground-floor cafe. They don't have much space and could use a bit of TLC, but they do have style. Also, you're right in the heart of the hipster Tien village area.

Royal ThaTien Village HOTEL $$
(Map p412; 095 151 5545; www.theroyalthatien.com; 392/29 Soi Phen Phat; s & d from 900B; Tien Pier) These 12 rooms spread over two converted shophouses are relatively unassuming, but TV, fridge, air-con, lots of space and shiny wood floors, not to mention a cosy homestay atmosphere, edge this place into the recommendable category. It's popular, so be sure to book ahead.

★ **Arun Residence** HOTEL $$$
(Map p412; 02 221 9158; www.arunresidence.com; 36-38 Soi Pratu Nokyung; d incl breakfast from

BUDGET BANGKOK DIGS

If you're on a shoestring budget, Bangkok has plenty of options for you, ranging from high-tech, pod-like dorm beds in a brand-new hostel to cosy bunk beds in a refurbished Chinatown shophouse. (If you decide that you need a bit more privacy, nearly all of Bangkok's hostels also offer private rooms.) And best of all, at the places listed here, you can count on bathrooms to be clean and convenient – sharing will hardly feel like a compromise. Some of our picks:

Lub*d (Map p418; ☑ 02 612 4999; www.lubd.com/siamsquare; 925/9 Rama I; dm/r incl breakfast from 900/1400B; ❀ @ 🛜 ; ⑤ National Stadium exit 1) The title is a play on the Thai *làp dee*, meaning 'sleep well', but the fun atmosphere at this modern-feeling hostel might make you want to stay up all night. Diversions include an inviting communal area stocked with games and a bar, and thoughtful facilities range from washing machines to a theatre room.

Chern (Map p412; ☑ 02 621 1133; www.chernbangkok.com; 17 Soi Ratchasak; dm/r 350/900B; ❀ @ 🛜 ; 🚤 klorng boat Phanfa Leelard Pier) The vast, open spaces and white, overexposed tones of this hostel converge in an almost afterlife-like feel.

Niras Bankoc (Map p412; ☑ 02 221 4442; www.nirasbankoc.com; 204-206 Th Mahachai; dm/d incl breakfast from 400/1300B; ❀ 🛜 ; 🚤 klorng boat Phanfa Leelard Pier) Niras takes advantage of its location in an antique shophouse to arrive at a charmingly old-school feel. Both the four- and six-bed dorms here feature dark woods and vintage furniture, with access to friendly staff, a cosy ground-floor cafe and a location in an atmospheric corner of the city.

Silom Art Hostel (Map p422; ☑ 02 635 8070; www.silomarthostel.com; 198/19-22 Soi 14, Th Silom; dm/r 450/950B; ❀ @ 🛜 ; ⑤ Chong Nonsi exit 3) Quirky, bright and fun, Silom Art Hostel combines recycled materials, unconventional furnishings and colourful wall paintings to culminate in a hostel that's quite unlike anywhere else in town. It's not all about style, though: beds are comfortable, and there are lots of appealing communal areas.

Loftel 22 (Map p422; ☑ 086 807 1144; 952 Soi 22, Th Charoen Krung; dm 250-400B; r with shared bathroom 700-1300B; ❀ @ 🛜 ; 🚤 Marine Department Pier, Ⓜ Hua Lamphong exit 1) Stylish, inviting dorms have been coaxed out of these two adjoining shophouses. Friendly service and a location in one of Chinatown's most atmospheric corners round out the package.

NapPark Hostel (Map p412; ☑ 02 282 2324; www.nappark.com; 5 Th Tani; dm 440-550B; ❀ @ 🛜 ; 🚤 Phra Athit/Banglamphu Pier) This popular hostel features dorm rooms of various sizes, the smallest and most expensive of which boasts six pod-like beds outfitted with power points, mini-TV, reading lamp and wi-fi.

Chao Hostel (Map p418; ☑ 02 217 3083; www.chaohostel.com; 8th fl, 865 Rama I, Siam@Siam Bldg; dm/r 550/1400B; ❀ @ 🛜 ; ⑤ National Stadium exit 1) Blending modern minimalist and Thai design elements, not to mention tonnes of open space, Chao is one of the most sophisticated hostels in Bangkok.

Oneday Hostel (Map p424; ☑ 02 108 8855; www.onedaybkk.com; 51 Soi 26/Soi Ari, Th Sukhumvit; dm/d incl breakfast from 350/1000B; ❀ @ 🛜 ; ⑤ Phrom Phong exit 4) Attached to a cafe and coworking space is this modern, open-feeling hostel. Dorms span four to eight beds and are united by a handsome industrial-design theme and inviting, sun-soaked communal areas.

S1 Hostel (Map p407; ☑ 02 679 7777; 35/1-4 Soi Ngam Du Phli; dm/r from 330/900B; ❀ @ 🛜 ; Ⓜ Lumphini exit 1) A huge hostel with dorm beds decked out in a simple yet attractive primary-colour scheme. A host of facilities (laundry, kitchen, rooftop garden) and a convenient location within walking distance of the MRT make it great value.

Bed Station Hostel (Map p418; ☑ 02 019 5477; www.bedstationhostel.com; 486/149-150 Soi 16, Th Phetchaburi; dm/d from 490/1350B; ❀ @ 🛜 ; ⑤ Ratchathewi exit 3) An industrial-chic theme unites the dorms at this modern-feeling hostel. They range from four to eight beds and include access to tidy toilet facilities and a laundry room.

4200B; ❄@📶; ⛴Tien Pier) Although strategically located on the river directly across from Wat Arun (p414), this multilevel wooden house has much more than just great views. The seven rooms here manage to feel both homey and stylish (the best are the top-floor, balcony-equipped suites). There are also inviting communal areas, including a library, rooftop bar and restaurant. Advance reservations absolutely essential.

Sala Ratanakosin HOTEL $$$
(Map p412; ☎02 622 1388; www.salaresorts.com/rattanakosin; Soi Tha Tian; d incl breakfast from 4000B; ❄@📶; ⛴Tien Pier) Sala has a sleek, modernist feel – a somewhat jarring contrast with the former warehouse in which it's located. The 15 rooms are decked out in black and white, and have open-plan bathrooms and big windows looking out on the river and Wat Arun. They can't be described as vast, but will satisfy the fashion-conscious.

Chinatown

@Hua Lamphong HOSTEL $
(Map p412; ☎02 639 1925; www.hualamphonghostel.com; 326/1 Rama IV; dm 350B, r 900-1100B; ❄@📶; M Hua Lamphong exit 1) Not only does this hostel provide the most handy access to Bangkok's main train terminal, it's also clean and very well run. The private rooms, some of which are huge and feature balconies, are particularly good value. Factoring in convenience, comfort and amenities in equal measures, this place easily features among the city's best hostels.

★ **Shanghai Mansion** HOTEL $$
(Map p412; ☎02 221 2121; www.shanghaimansion.com; 479-481 Th Yaowarat; r/ste incl breakfast from 2100/3500B; ❄@📶; ⛴Ratchawong Pier, M Hua Lamphong exit 1 & taxi) Easily the most consciously stylish place to stay in Chinatown, this award-winning boutique hotel screams Shanghai c 1935 with stained glass, an abundance of lamps, bold colours and cheeky kitsch. If you're willing to splurge, ask for one of the bigger streetside rooms with tall windows that allow more light. It's located smack in Chinatown's atmospheric centre.

★ **Loy La Long** HOTEL $$$
(Map p412; ☎02 639 1390; www.loylalong.com; 1620/2 Th Songwat, Wat Pathum Khongka Ratchaworawihan; s/d incl breakfast 2700/4900B; ❄📶; ⛴Ratchawong Pier, M Hua Lamphong exit 1 & taxi) Rustic, retro, charming: the six rooms in this teak house lay claim to more than their share of personality. Occupying a prestigious location stilted over the Chao Phraya's waters, it also has a hidden, almost secret, feel. The only hitch is in finding it; proceed to Th Songwat and cut through **Wat Pathum Khongka Ratchaworawihan** (วัดปทุมคงคาราชวรวิหาร; Map p412; off Th Songwat; ⏲daylight hours; ⛴Marine Department Pier, M Hua Lamphong exit 1 & taxi) to the riverside.

Siam Square, Pratunam, Phloen Chit & Ratchathewi

Boxpackers Hostel HOSTEL $
(Map p418; ☎02 656 2828; www.boxpackershostel.com; 39/3 Soi 15, Th Phetchaburi; dm/q from 420/1800B; ❄📶; S Ratchathewi exit 1 & taxi) A contemporary, sparse hostel with dorms ranging in size from four to 12 double-decker pods – some of which are double beds. Communal areas are inviting, and include a ground-floor cafe and a lounge with pool table. A linked hotel also offers 14 small but similarly attractive private rooms.

★ **Siam@Siam** HOTEL $$$
(Map p418; ☎02 217 3000; www.siamatsiam.com; 865 Rama I; d incl breakfast from 3300B; ❄@📶🏊; S National Stadium exit 1) A seemingly random mishmash of colours and industrial/recycled materials here result in a style one could describe as 'junkyard chic' – in a good way. The rooms are found between the 14th and 24th floors, and offer terrific city views. There's a rooftop restaurant and an excellently maintained 11th-floor pool.

Riverside, Silom & Lumphini

★ **Warm Window** HOSTEL $
(Map p422; ☎02 235 8759; www.warmwindowsilom.com; 50/18-19 Th Pan; dm/d incl breakfast from 360/1200B; ❄@📶; S Surasak exit 1/3) A 2019 addition to Silom's ever-evolving hostel scene, this sleek address has two fantastic 10-bed dorms, both of which feature comfy, curtain-lined bunk beds fitted with elegant wood panelling. The private rooms are an absolute steal for the price, and the downstairs cafe is a superb place to lounge in if you feel like some me-time amid your city-wide explorations.

★ **kokotel** HOTEL $$
(Map p422; ☎02 235 7555, 02 026 3218; www.kokotel.com; 181/1-5 Th Surawong; s/d incl breakfast 1600/2600B; ❄@📶; S Chong Nonsi exit 3) Quite possibly one of Bangkok's most

Silom

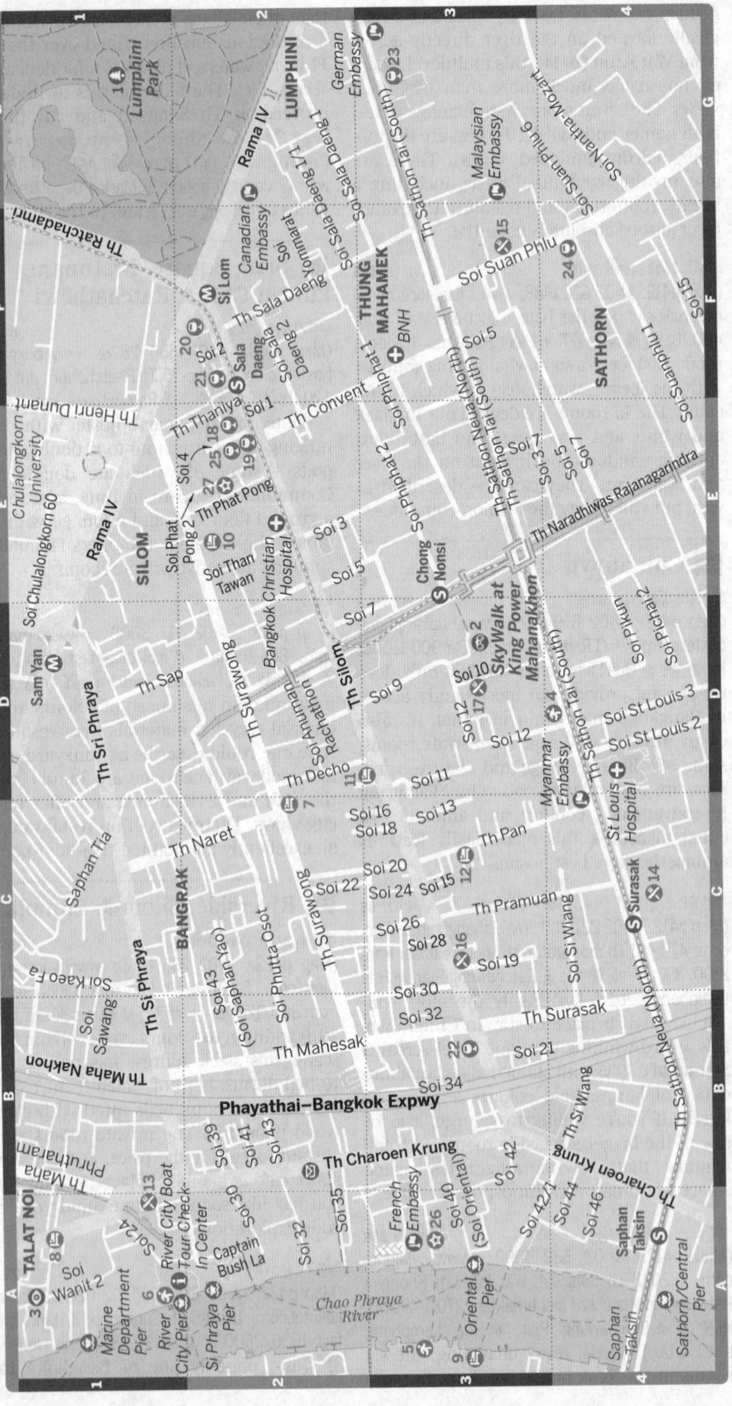

Lumphini Park
LUMPHINI
Rama IV
Th Ratchadamri
German Embassy
Canadian Embassy
Malaysian Embassy
Th Sathon Tai (South)
Soi Nantha-Mozart
Soi Suan Phlu 6
Soi Suan Phlu
Soi Yommarat
Soi Sala Daeng 1
Soi Sala Daeng 1/1
Th Sala Daeng
Si Lom
Sala Daeng
Soi Sala Daeng 2
THUNG MAHAMEK
BNH
SATHORN
Soi 15
Soi Suanplu 1
Soi 5
Soi Phiphat 1
Th Sathon Neua (North)
Soi 2
Soi 1
Th Henri Dunant
Th Thaniya
Th Convent
Chulalongkorn University
Soi 4
Th Phat Pong
Soi Phat Pong 2
Soi Chulalongkorn 60
Rama IV
SILOM
Soi Than Tawan
Bangkok Christian Hospital
Soi 3
Soi Phiphat 2
Chong Nonsi
Th Naradhiwas Rajanagarindra
Soi 7
Soi 3
Sam Yan
Th Sap
Th Surawong
Th Silom
SkyWalk at King Power Mahanakhon
Soi Pikun
Soi Pichai 2
Th Sri Phraya
Soi 9
Soi 10
Soi 12
Soi Anuman Rachathon
Th Sathon Tai (South)
Soi St Louis 3
Soi St Louis 2
Th Decho
Soi 11
Myanmar Embassy
St Louis Hospital
Soi 16
Soi 18
Soi 13
Th Naret
Saphan Tia
Th Pan
Soi 20
Soi 22
Soi 24
Soi 15
BANGRAK
Th Pramuan
Surasak
Soi 26
Soi 28
Soi Si Wiang
Soi 19
Th Si Phraya
Soi Kaeo Fa
Soi 43
(Soi Saphan Yao)
Soi Phutta Osot
Soi 30
Soi 32
Th Surasak
Soi Sawang
Th Mahesak
Soi 21
Th Maha Nakhon
Soi 34
Phayathai–Bangkok Expwy
Th Si Wiang
Th Sathon Neua (North)
Soi 39
Soi 41
Soi 43
Th Charoen Krung
Soi 42
Th Charoen Krung
Th Maha Phruttharam
Soi 24
River City Boat Tour Check-In Center
Soi 30
Soi 35
French Embassy
Soi 40 (Soi Oriental)
Soi 42/1
Soi 44
Soi 46
TALAT NOI
Soi Wanit 2
Captain Bush La
Saphan Taksin
Chao Phraya River
Oriental Pier
Marine Department Pier
River City Pier
Si Phraya Pier
Sathorn/Central Pier
500 m
0.25 miles

Silom

Top Sights
1 Lumphini Park G1
2 SkyWalk at King Power Mahanakhon D3

Sights
3 Talat Noi A1

Activities, Courses & Tours
4 Health Land D4
5 Oriental Spa A3
6 Supanniga Cruise A1

Sleeping
7 kokotel C2
8 Loftel 22 .... A1
9 Peninsula Hotel A3
10 Siam Heritage E2
11 Silom Art Hostel D3
12 Warm Window C3

Eating
13 80/20 .... A1
14 Chef Man C4
15 Saawaan F3
16 Saravana Bhavan C3
17 Supanniga Eating Room D3

Drinking & Nightlife
18 Balcony E2
19 Banana Bar on 4 .... E2
20 DJ Station F2
21 G Bangkok F2
22 Maggie Choo's B3
23 Moon Bar G3
24 Smalls F4
25 The Stranger E2

Entertainment
26 Bamboo Bar A3
27 Patpong E2

family-friendly accommodations, kokotel unites big, sun-filled rooms with puffy beds, an expansive children's play area and a downstairs cafe (with, appropriately, a slide). Friendly rates – including super sales conducted from time to time – also make it great value, especially considering its central location.

Siam Heritage BOUTIQUE HOTEL **$$**
(Map p422; ☎02 353 6166; www.thesiamheritage.com; 115/1 Th Surawong; d incl breakfast from 1800B; ❄@📶🏊; M Si Lom exit 2, S Sala Daeng exit 1) Tucked off busy Th Surawong, this hotel overflows with homey Thai charm – and is a total steal at its competitive midrange price point. The 73 rooms are decked out in silk and dark woods with classy design touches and thoughtful amenities. There's an inviting rooftop garden/pool/spa, and it's all cared for by a team of professional, accommodating staff. Highly recommended.

★ **Peninsula Hotel** HOTEL **$$$**
(Map p422; ☎02 020 2888; www.peninsula.com; 333 Th Charoen Nakhon; d incl breakfast from 8800B; ❄@📶🏊; ⛴hotel shuttle boat from Sathorn/Central Pier) The matchless and ageless Pen has it all: the location (towering over the river); the reputation (it's consistently among the world's top-ranking luxury hotels); and one of the highest levels of service in town. Its stately rooms are an absolute delight to stay in, and a lavish breakfast at the riverside open-air restaurant provides the perfect start to your day.

Thanon Sukhumvit

FU House Hostel HOSTEL **$**
(Map p424; ☎062 919 8202; 77 Soi 8, Th Sukhumvit; dm/r 350/1350B; ❄📶; S Nana exit 4) Great for a quiet, low-key stay is this two-storey wooden villa on a residential street. Choose between attractive bunk beds in one of two spacious, private-feeling dorms, or rooms with en suite bathrooms.

★ **Mövenpick** HOTEL **$$**
(Map p424; ☎02 119 3100; www.movenpick.com/en/asia/thailand/bangkok/bangkok; 47 Soi 15, Th Sukhumvit; d incl breakfast from 3000B; ❄@📶🏊; S Nana exit 3) A pleasant surprise awaits you at this fantastic hotel, which amazingly manages to offer top-end luxuries and amenities at prices that just about skirt the top of the midrange bracket. Rooms are thoughtfully appointed and have plenty of light, and the rooftop pool (though somewhat smallish) is a great place for a relaxing swim.

Tints of Blue HOTEL **$$**
(Map p424; ☎099 289 7744; www.tintsofblue.com; 47 Soi 27, Th Sukhumvit; d incl breakfast 2000-2200B; ❄📶🏊; M Sukhumvit exit 2, S Asok exit 6) The location in a leafy, quiet street is reflected in the rooms here, which manage to feel secluded, homey and warm. Equipped with kitchenettes, lots of space and natural light, and balconies, they're also great value for this price. There's a pleasantly stretched out – if tiny – swimming pool on the terrace, and a mini gym for a quick cardio session.

Sukhumvit

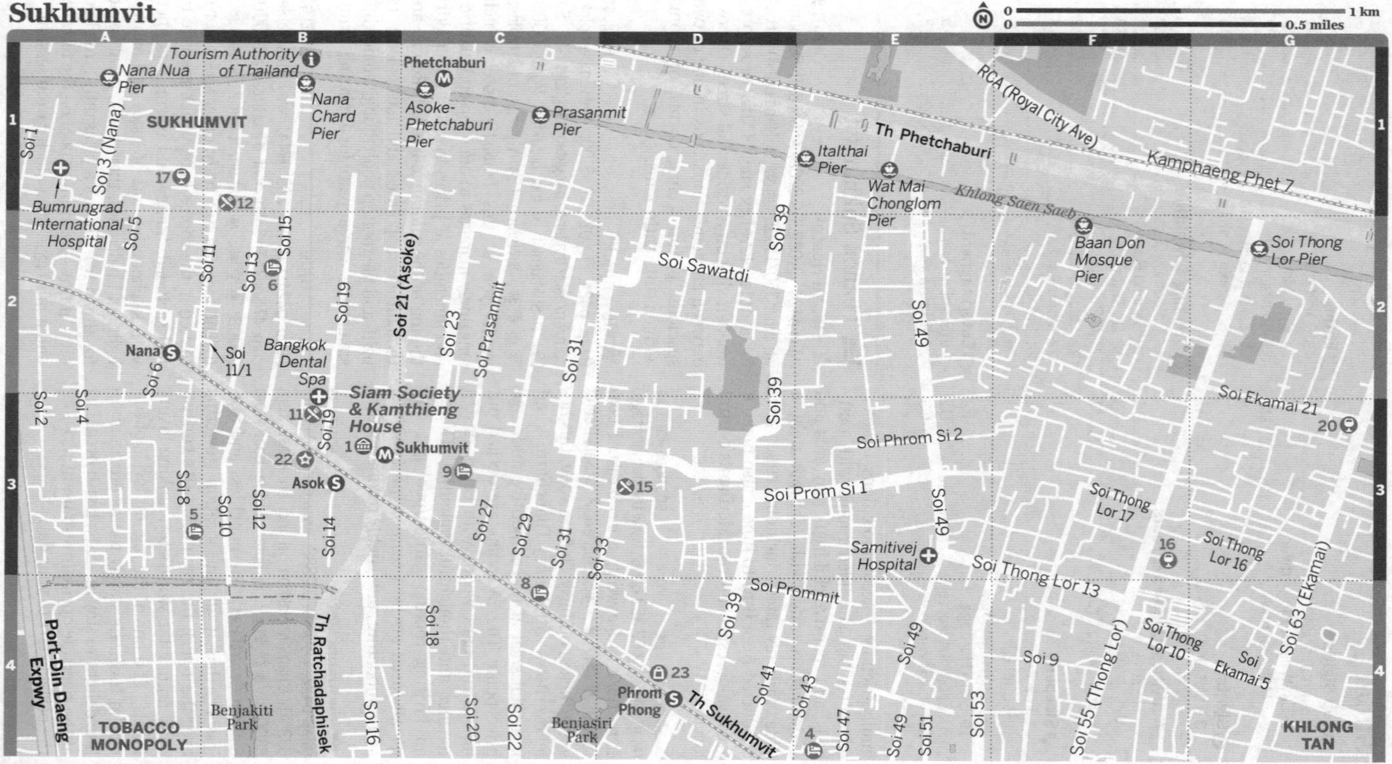
0 — 1 km
0 — 0.5 miles
A B C D E F G
1 2 3 4
Tourism Authority of Thailand
Nana Nua Pier
Nana Chard Pier
Phetchaburi
Asoke-Phetchaburi Pier
Prasanmit Pier
SUKHUMVIT
Soi 1
Soi 3 (Nana)
Bumrungrad International Hospital
Soi 5
Soi 11
Soi 13
Soi 15
Soi 19
Soi 21 (Asoke)
Soi 23
Soi Prasanmit
Soi 31
Soi Sawatdi
Soi 39
Th Phetchaburi
Italthai Pier
Wat Mai Chonglom Pier
Khlong Saen Saeb
RCA (Royal City Ave)
Kamphaeng Phet 7
Baan Don Mosque Pier
Soi Thong Lor Pier
Soi 49
Soi Ekamai 21
Soi Phrom Si 2
Soi Prom Si 1
Nana
Soi 11/1
Bangkok Dental Spa
Siam Society & Kamthieng House
Sukhumvit
Asok
Soi 2
Soi 4
Soi 6
Soi 8
Soi 10
Soi 12
Soi 14
Soi 16
Soi 18
Soi 20
Soi 22
Soi 27
Soi 29
Soi 33
Soi 41
Soi 43
Soi 47
Soi 51
Soi 53
Soi Prommit
Samitivej Hospital
Soi Thong Lor 13
Soi Thong Lor 17
Soi Thong Lor 16
Soi Thong Lor 10
Soi Ekamai 5
Soi 9
Soi 55 (Thong Lor)
Soi 63 (Ekamai)
Th Ratchadaphisek
Port-Din Daeng Expwy
TOBACCO MONOPOLY
Benjakiti Park
Benjasiri Park
Phrom Phong
Th Sukhumvit
KHLONG TAN
1 4 5 6 8 9 11 12 15 16 17 20 22 23

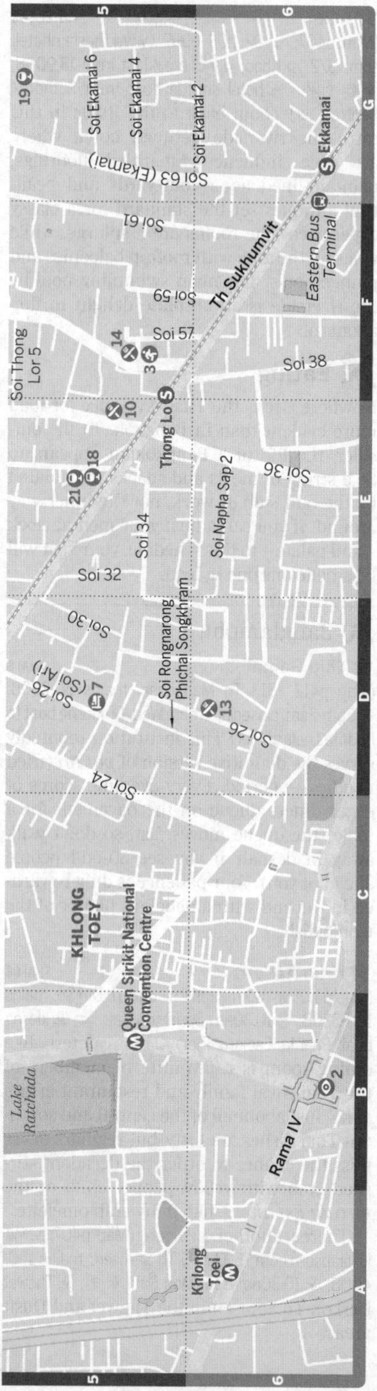

Sukhumvit

Top Sights
1 Siam Society & Kamthieng House B3

Sights
2 Khlong Toey Market B6

Activities, Courses & Tours
3 Asia Herb Association F5

Sleeping
4 Cabochon Hotel E4
5 FU House Hostel A3
6 Mövenpick B2
7 Oneday Hostel D5
8 S31 .... C4
9 Tints of Blue C3

Eating
10 Bo.lan E5
11 Charley Browns Mexicana B3
12 Daniel Thaiger B1
13 Indus D6
14 Soul Food Mahanakorn F5
15 Sri Trat D3

Drinking & Nightlife
16 Beam F3
17 Havana Social Club A1
18 Studio Lam E5
19 Tasting Room by Mikkeller G5
20 Tuba G3
21 WTF E5

Entertainment
22 The Living Room B3

Shopping
23 Emquartier D4

S31 HOTEL $$
(Map p424; ☎02 260 1111; www.s31hotel.com; 545 Soi 31, Th Sukhumvit; d incl breakfast from 3500B; ; S Phrom Phong exit 5) The bold patterns and graphics of its interior and exterior make the S31 a fun, youthful choice. Thoughtful touches like kitchenettes with large fridge, super-huge beds, and courses (Thai boxing and yoga) prove that the style also has substance. Significant discounts can be found online, and additional branches are located on Soi 15 and Soi 33.

★**AriyasomVilla** HOTEL $$$
(Map p418; ☎02 254 8880; www.ariyasom.com; 65 Soi 1, Th Sukhumvit; d incl breakfast from 6400B; ; S Phloen Chit exit 3) Located at the end of Soi 1 behind a wall of tropical greenery, this beautifully renovated 1940s-era villa is one of the worst-kept accommodation

BANGKOK TREE HOUSE

Located in the lush green zone known as the Phrapradaeng Peninsula, **Bangkok Tree House** (☎082 995 1150; www.bangkoktreehouse.com; near Wat Bang Na Nork, Phrapradaeng, Samut Prakan; bungalows incl breakfast 3600-5300B; ❄@🛜🏊; Ⓢ Bang Na exit 2 & taxi) has 12 multilevel bungalows stylishly sculpted from sustainable and recycled materials, giving it the feel of a sophisticated, ecofriendly summer camp. Thoughtful amenities include private computers equipped with movies, free mobile-phone and bicycle use and free ice cream. Significant online discounts are available.

secrets in Bangkok. The 24 rooms are spacious and meticulously outfitted with thoughtful Thai design touches and sumptuous, beautiful antique furniture. There's also a spa and an inviting tropical pool. Book well in advance.

Cabochon Hotel BOUTIQUE HOTEL $$$
(Map p424; ☎02 259 2871; www.cabochonhotel.com; 14/29 Soi 45, Th Sukhumvit; d incl breakfast from 5800B; 🚭❄🛜🏊; Ⓢ Phrom Phong exit 3) The Cabochon, which means polished gem, is indeed a diamond in rowdy Bangkok. Rooms are light-filled and unfussy, and packed with thoughtful curiosities such as antique telephones, typewriters, tortoise shells, model aeroplanes and vintage tea sets. Venture to the rooftop pool or nosh street-food-style on mouth-watering Thai and Laotian dishes at the cosy Thai Lao Yeh Restaurant.

Thewet & Dusit

★**Phra-Nakorn Norn-Len** HOTEL $$
(Map p407; ☎02 628 8188; www.phranakorn-nornlen.com; 46 Soi Thewet 1; d incl breakfast 2200-4200B; ❄@🛜; ⛴Thewet Pier) Set in an enclosed garden compound decorated like a Bangkok neighbourhood of yesteryear, this bright and cheery hotel is fun and atmospheric, and stupendous value. Although the 31 rooms are attractively furnished with antiques and paintings, it's worth noting that they don't include TV, a fact made up for by daily activities, massage and endless opportunities for peaceful relaxing.

★**Siam** HOTEL $$$
(Map p407; ☎02 206 6999; www.thesiamhotel.com; 3/2 Th Khao; d incl breakfast from 18,900B; ❄@🛜🏊; ⛴hotel shuttle boat from Sathorn/Central Pier) Zoom back to the 1930s in this retro-chic riverside heritage hotel, where art deco influences, marbled floorings, plantain-lined aqua courtyards and beautiful antiques set the standard for a classy experience. The rooms are a splurge, while villas up the ante with rooftop balconies and plunge pools. The main swimming pool by the riverside is an absolute delight to flop about in.

Eating

Nowhere else is the Thai reverence for food more evident than in Bangkok. To the outsider, the life of a Bangkokian appears to be a string of meals and snacks punctuated by the odd stab at work, not the other way around. If you can adjust your mental clock – and palate – to this schedule, your visit will be a delicious one indeed.

Banglamphu

★**Thip Samai** THAI $
(Map p412; 313 Th Mahachai; mains 50-250B; ⏲5pm-2am, closed alternate Wed; ⛴klorng boat to Phanfa Leelard Pier) This institution reputedly serves the definitive version of *pàt tai* (fried noodles) – period. Every evening, scores of eager diners queue on the pavement for a table (the queue moves fast, so don't walk away in despair if you see 50-odd people ahead of you). Your patience is duly rewarded in the end with a delicious platter of the iconic dish.

★**Krua Apsorn** THAI $$
(Map p412; www.kruaapsorn.com; Th Din So; mains 100-350B; ⏲10.30am-8pm Mon-Sat; ❄; ⛴klorng boat Phanfa Leelard Pier) This cafeteria-like dining room is a favourite of members of the Thai royal family and restaurant critics alike. Just about all of the central and southern Thai dishes are tasty, but regulars never miss the chance to order the decadent stir-fried crab with yellow-pepper chilli or the *tortilla Española*-like fluffy crab omelette.

There's another **branch** (Map p407; www.kruaapsorn.com; 503-505 Th Samsen; mains 150-400B; ⏲10.30am-8pm Mon-Sat; ❄🛜; ⛴Thewet Pier) on Th Samsen in the Thewet and Dusit area.

Shoshana ISRAELI **$$**
(Map p412; 88 Th Chakrabongse; mains 80-300B; ⌚10am-11.30pm; ❄ ✍; ⛴ Phra Athit/Banglamphu Pier) One of Khao San's longest-running Israeli restaurants, Shoshana might resemble your grandparents' living room right down to the tacky wall art and plastic placemats. Feel safe ordering anything deep-fried – the kitchen staff do an excellent job of it – and don't miss the deliciously garlicky eggplant dip.

★ **Jay Fai** THAI **$$$**
(Raan Jay Fai; Map p412; 327 Th Mahachai; mains 200-1000B; ⌚2pm-2am Tue-Sat; ⛴ klorng boat Phanfa Leelard Pier) Wearing ski goggles and furiously cooking over a charcoal fire, septuagenarian Jay Fai is renowned for serving Bangkok's tastiest (and priciest) crab omelettes and *pàt kêe mow* (wide rice noodles fried with seafood and Thai herbs). The price, however, is justified by copious fresh seafood, plus a distinct frying style resulting in an almost oil-free finished dish.

The restaurant is located in a virtually unmarked shophouse, but walking down the road, it's quite impossible to miss the sight of the one-Michelin-star chef cooking away with superhero fervour in the open kitchen.

Ko Ratanakosin & Thonburi

★ **Tonkin Annam** VIETNAMESE **$$**
(Map p412; ☎093 469 2969; 69 Soi Tha Tien; mains 150-300B; ⌚11am-10pm Wed-Mon; ❄; ⛴ Tien Pier) The retro-minimalist interior here might be a red flag for hipster ethnic cuisine, but Tonkin Annam serves some of the best Vietnamese food in Bangkok. Come for the *phó* (noodle soup), deliciously tart and peppery banana blossom salad, or dishes you won't find elsewhere, such as *bánh bèo* (steamed cups of rice flour topped with pork), a speciality of Hue.

Chinatown

80/20 INTERNATIONAL **$$**
(Map p422; ☎099 118 2200; 1052-1054 Th Charoen Krung; mains 250-450B; ⌚6-11pm Tue-Sun; ❄ 📶; ⛴ Si Phraya/River City Pier, Ⓜ Hua Lamphong exit 1) Renovated in 2019, 80/20 continues to excel at what it has always done with perfection – blending Thai and Western ingredients and dishes to arrive at something altogether unique. The often savoury-leaning desserts are especially worth the trip. It's a progressive breath of air in an otherwise conservative Chinatown dining scene.

Thanon Phadungdao Seafood Stalls STREET FOOD **$$**
(Map p412; cnr Th Phadungdao & Th Yaowarat; mains 100-400B; ⌚4pm-midnight Tue-Sun; ⛴ Ratchawong Pier, Ⓜ Hua Lamphong exit 1) After sunset, this line of open-air restaurants – each claiming to be better than its neighbour – becomes a culinary supernova of outdoor barbecues, screaming staff, iced seafood trays and messy pavement seating. True, the vast majority of diners are foreign tourists, but this has little impact on the cheerful setting, the fun experience and the cheap bills.

Royal India INDIAN **$$**
(Map p412; 392/1 Th Chakkaraphet; mains 150-300B; ⌚10am-10pm; ❄ ✍; ⛴ Memorial Bridge Pier) This hole-in-the-wall restaurant has long been the most reliable place to eat in Bangkok's Indian neighbourhood. The kebabs and naans (oven-baked flatbreads) here give stiff competition to Delhi's *dhabas* (local eateries). Vegetarians will love the creamy *palak paneer* (cottage-cheese cubes in spinach sauce) to go with their bread of choice.

Siam Square, Pratunam, Phloen Chit & Ratchathewi

★ **Eathai** THAI **$**
(Map p418; 1031 Th Phloen Chit, basement, Central Embassy; mains 60-350B; ⌚10am-10pm; ❄ ✍; Ⓢ Phloen Chit exit 5) This expansive food court spans Thai dishes from just about every corner of the country, including those from several famous Bangkok restaurants and street stalls. It's one of the best places to sample the whole gamut of flavours, tastes and textures of Thai cuisine without venturing out of the comfortable environs of a luxury shopping mall.

★ **Gaa** INTERNATIONAL **$$$**
(Map p418; ☎091 419 2424; www.gaabkk.com; 68/4 Soi Langsuan; set menu 3200B; ⌚6-9.30pm Wed-Mon; ❄ ✍; Ⓢ Ratchadamri exit 2) This acclaimed restaurant is run by Michelin-starred chef Garima Arora (a protégé of former Bangkok chef Gaggan Anand) who also honed her craft at Copenhagen's famed Noma. Classic Indian and Thai dishes are the specialities here, upgraded with modern

cooking techniques and presented in artful 10- to 12-course tasting menus. Wine pairing (if opted for) doubles the bill. Reservations absolutely essential.

Riverside, Silom & Lumphini

Saravana Bhavan SOUTH INDIAN $
(Map p422; 02 635 4556; 663 Th Silom; mains 100-250B; 9.30am-10.30pm; ; Surasak exit 1) This well-reputed overseas branch of a legendary Indian eating house makes a fabulous range of southern Indian vegetarian dishes. We love the *dosai* (crispy rice-flour crepes), *ghee pongal* (savoury pudding made from stone-ground rice and lentils) and *vada* (deep-fried savoury doughnuts made of lentil batter). Highly recommended for vegetarians with a palate for subcontinental flavours.

Though the restaurant technically looks onto Th Silom, the entrance and staircase leading up to the 1st-floor dining area is on the building's western side, on Soi 19.

★**Supanniga Eating Room** THAI $$
(Map p422; www.supannigaeatingroom.com; 28 Soi 10, Th Sathon Neua/North; mains 150-350B; 11.30am-2.30pm & 5.30-11.30pm; ; Chong Nonsi exit 1/5) Supanniga has three outlets across Bangkok (plus a superpopular dinner cruise), but this branch in Sathorn is a favourite in terms of ambience and service. A brilliant selection of northern Thai dishes is on offer, with specials such as grilled Isan sausages, stir-fried sun-dried beef jerky, and baby squid stuffed with ground pork. Ask for an upstairs (quieter) table. Reservations are essential, especially on weekends.

Chef Man CHINESE $$
(Map p422; 02 212 3789; 33/1 Th Sathon Tai/South, Hotel Eastin Grand Sathon; mains 150-350B; 11am-2.30pm & 6-10pm; ; Surasak exit 4) If you're a dumpling fan, drop into this elegant restaurant during lunchtime, when its open kitchen serves some of the nicest dim sum and *siu mai* (open-face Chinese dumplings) you can bite into. Other Sichuan-style dishes, including delicious duck, fish and vegetarian preparations, are also on offer. Dinner is largely the preserve of local patrons, who converge with their families.

★**Saawaan** THAI $$$
(Map p422; 02 679 3775; www.saawaan.com; 39/19 Soi Suan Phlu; set menu 2450B; 6pm-midnight; ; Chong Nonsi exit 5) Two exceptionally talented chefs run what can easily be called one of the finest Thai restaurants in the world. Its name meaning 'heaven', this chic address has a seven-course tasting menu themed on cooking methods, featuring dishes that are inherently Thai but are executed with the fanciness, finesse and flair worthy of a Michelin-starred restaurant (which it is).

Expect dishes conjured from sea urchins, wild betel leaves or rice-paddy crabs, and wacky desserts (such as bitter chocolate with a hint of the stinky durian fruit). Advance bookings – and smart attire – essential.

Thanon Sukhumvit

★**Indus** INDIAN $$
(Map p424; 086 339 8582; www.indusbangkok.com; 71 Soi 26/Soi Ari, Th Sukhumvit; mains 150-400B; 11.30am-2.30pm & 6-10.30pm; ; Phrom Phong exit 4) Unless someone conclusively proves otherwise, Indus will reign as Bangkok's finest traditional Indian restaurant. Its North Indian staples such as *biryani,* kebab, dhal (spicy lentil soup) and myriad vegetarian dishes in tomato- or yoghurt-based curries are as good as those served at the best New Delhi restaurants. To make the most of it, go for the 990B all-you-can-eat buffet.

Sri Trat THAI $$
(Map p424; 02 088 0968; www.facebook.com/sritrat; 90 Soi 33, Th Sukhumvit; mains 200-450B; noon-11pm Wed-Mon; ; Phrom Phong exit 5) This fabulous restaurant specialises in the unique fare of Thailand's eastern provinces, Trat and Chanthaburi. What this means is lots of rich, slightly sweet, herbal flavours, fresh seafood and dishes you won't find anywhere else in town. That's also because it's a family operation, and most of the recipes originate in the family kitchen.

Soul Food Mahanakorn THAI $$
(Map p424; 02 714 7708; www.soulfoodmahanakorn.com; 56/10 Soi 55/Thong Lor, Th Sukhumvit; mains 150-350B; 5.30pm-midnight; ; Thong Lo exit 1/3) This contemporary Thai diner is a favourite go-to place for an old-school comfort meal. The menu – incorporating tasty interpretations of rustic Thai dishes – has not changed over several years, but the top quality of the food hasn't wavered either. The bar serves deliciously boozy, Thai-influenced drinks, as well as cocktails and a few craft beers. Reservations recommended.

Charley Browns Mexicana MEXICAN $$
(Map p424; 02 244 2553; www.facebook.com/charleybrownsmexicana; 19/9 Soi 19, Th Sukhumvit; mains 150-350B; noon-11pm; ; Asok exit 1) Chef Primo's flair for living it large reflects in the menu at this fun and irreverent restaurant serving authentic provincial Mexican dishes. Go beyond the usual taco-burrito drill and try the *albondigas* (meatballs) or the *pescadilla* – deep-fried corn tortilla stuffed with sea bass. Brave drinkers can try pairing their meal with a jalapeño margarita. Dancing sessions held on select days.

Daniel Thaiger AMERICAN $$
(Map p424; 084 549 0995; www.facebook.com/danielthaiger; Soi 11, Th Sukhumvit; burgers from 260B; 11am-8pm; ; Nana exit 3) Bangkok's most-loved burgers – read ultrajuicy beef or lamb patties served in a brioche bun – are served from this American-run, food-truck-turned-restaurant that now operates out of a tiny shophouse on Soi 11. Sides include crunchy fries and the insanely crispy (and popular) onion rings. There's an exhaustive list of imported beers to go with your choice of food.

★ **Bo.lan** THAI $$$
(Map p424; 02 260 2962; www.bolan.co.th; 24 Soi 53, Th Sukhumvit; set meals 3280-3680B; 6-10.30pm Tue-Fri, noon-2.30pm & 6-10.30pm Sat & Sun; ; Thong Lo exit 1) Upscale Thai is often more garnish than flavour, but Bo.lan has proved to be the exception. Bo and Dylan (Bo.lan is a play on words that means 'ancient') take a scholarly approach to Thai cuisine, and generous set meals featuring full-flavoured Thai dishes are the results of this tuition (à la carte is not available; meat-free meals are). Reservations recommended.

Thewet & Dusit

★ **Likhit Kai Yang** THAI $
(Map p412; off Th Ratchadamnoen Nok; mains 50-200B; 10am-8.30pm; ; Thewet Pier, Phaya Thai exit 3 & taxi) Located just behind Rajadamnern Stadium, this decades-old restaurant is where locals come for a north-eastern-style meal before a Thai boxing match. The friendly English-speaking owner will steer you through the ordering, but don't miss the deliciously herbal, eponymous 'charcoal roasted chicken'. There's no English-language sign; look for the bright pink shopfront and an overwhelming grilled-garlic smell emanating from inside.

Northern Bangkok

Baan Pueng Chom THAI $$
(Map p407; 02 279 4204; Soi Chua Chit, off Soi 7/Ari, Th Phahonyothin; mains 150-350B; 11am-2pm & 4-10pm Mon-Sat; ; Ari exit 1) These days, it takes venturing to Bangkok's northern 'burbs to find an old-school Thai restaurant like this. Ensconced in a watery jungle of a garden, Baan Pueng Chom has a fat, illustrated menu of typically full-flavoured, fragrant Thai dishes you're unlikely to find elsewhere. Call ahead if you wish to sit indoors.

Drinking & Nightlife

Shame on you if you think Bangkok's only nightlife options include the word 'go-go'. As in any big international metropolis, the drinking and partying scene in Bangkok ranges from trashy to classy and touches on just about everything in between.

Banglamphu

★ **Mitramit** TEAHOUSE
(Map p412; 32 Th Phra Sumen; 2-11pm Sat-Thu; Phra Athit/Banglamphu Pier) A superb modern interpretation of a classic Bangkok teahouse, this tiny, atmospheric shophouse serves delectable blends of premium tea sourced from China and other regional tea-growing centres. Sit at one of its jade-green marble-topped tables and order a flask of your preferred brew, which comes with a complimentary serving of desserts. The owner is a trove of Thai cultural information.

★ **Ku Bar** BAR
(Map p412; www.facebook.com/ku.bangkok; 3rd fl, 469 Th Phra Sumen; 7pm-midnight Wed-Mon; klorng boat Phanfa Leelard Pier) Tired of buckets and cocktails that revolve around Red Bull? Head to Ku Bar, the polar opposite of the Khao San party scene. Climb three floors of stairs (look for the tiny sign) to emerge at an almost comically minimalist interior where sophisticated fruit- and food-heavy cocktails (sample names: Lychee, Tomato, Pineapple/Red Pepper) and obscure music augment the underground vibe.

Madame Musur BAR
(Map p412; www.facebook.com/madamemusur; 41 Soi Ram Buttri; 8am-midnight; Phra Athit/Banglamphu Pier) Madame Musur pulls

off that elusive combination of northern Thailand meets *The Beach* meets Th Khao San. It's a fun place to chat, drink and people-watch, and it's also not a bad place to eat, with a short menu of northern Thai dishes priced from 100B to 250B.

Babble & Rum BAR
(Map p412; www.nexthotels.com; 23 Th Phra Athit, Riva Surya hotel; 5-10pm; Phra Athit/Banglamphu Pier) This is one of the few riverside bars along this stretch of the Chao Phraya River. Come for the sunset views and breezes – or for the generous happy-hour drinks.

Chinatown

★Let the Boy Die MICROBREWERY
(Map p412; 425 Th Luang; 5pm-midnight; M Hua Lamphong exit 1) Quirky name aside, this watering hole originally opened in 2015 as Bangkok's first craft-beer bar. Given Thailand's liquor laws (heavily tilted against craft brewing at the time), it subsequently went on a two-year hiatus, but then came back as a microbrewery with 12 locally brewed beers on tap. Try the nutty stout or the American-style IPA, and mingle with fellow hopheads.

★Tep Bar BAR
(Map p412; 69-71 Soi Nana; 7pm-midnight Tue-Sun; M Hua Lamphong exit 1) No one ever expects to find a bar this sophisticated – yet this fun – in Chinatown. Tep hits the spot with Thai-tinged, contemporary interiors and boozy signature cocktails; it also stocks a few delicious local rice-based brews. There are tasty drinking snacks on the side, and raucous live folk-music performances from Thursday to Sunday.

Siam Square, Pratunam, Phloen Chit & Ratchathewi

Hair of the Dog CRAFT BEER
(Map p418; www.hairofthedogbkk.com; 888/26 Th Phloen Chit, 1st fl, Mahathun Plaza; 5pm-midnight Mon-Sat; S Phloen Chit exit 2) The craft-beer craze that has swept Bangkok over the last few years is epitomised at this semiconcealed bar. With a morgue theme, dozens of bottles and 13 rotating taps, it's a great place for a hoppy night out. There's usually a unique 'tap of the month' selection, served and consumed with great vigour.

Riverside, Silom & Lumphini

★Smalls BAR
(Map p422; www.facebook.com/smallsbkk; 186/3 Soi Suan Phlu; 7pm-2am; S Chong Nonsi exit 5) Smalls aptly resembles a quintessential New York jazz bar. Fixtures include a revolving main door, a cheekily decadent interior, an inviting rooftop, food-themed nights (check the Facebook page) and live jazz on Wednesdays and Fridays. The eclectic cocktails are strong, and the absinthe servings are both generous and recommended.

★Moon Bar BAR
(Vertigo; Map p422; www.banyantree.com; 21/100 Th Sathon Tai/South, 61st fl, Banyan Tree Hotel; 5pm-1am; M Lumphini exit 2) An alarmingly short barrier at this rooftop bar is all that separates patrons from the street, 61 floors down. Moon Bar claims to be among the highest alfresco bars in the world. It's a great place to meet, greet and generally hang out with friends old and new. The hoppy house beer, called Banyan Tree IPA, is a must-try. Dress to impress.

DJ Station GAY
(Map p422; www.dj-station.com; Soi 2, Th Silom; admission from 150B; 9pm-2am; M Si Lom exit 2, S Sala Daeng exit 3) One of Bangkok's – and indeed Asia's – most legendary gay dance clubs. The crowd here is a mix of Thai guppies (gay professionals) and a few Westerners. If it has already filled up by the time you get here, try any of the other similar clubs on and around the street.

Thanon Sukhumvit

★WTF BAR
(Map p424; www.wtfbangkok.com; 7 Soi 51, Th Sukhumvit; 6pm-1am Tue-Sun; ; S Thong Lo exit 3) This cool and friendly neighbourhood bar also packs in a gallery space. Arty locals and resident foreigners come for the old-school cocktails, live music, DJ events, poetry readings, art exhibitions and tasty bar snacks. And we, like them, give WTF our top rating. The negroni here comes with a dash of spice, and is easily the best in Bangkok.

★Studio Lam BAR, CLUB
(Map p424; www.facebook.com/studiolambangkok; 3/1 Soi 51, Th Sukhumvit; 6pm-1am Tue-Sun; S Thong Lo exit 3) Studio Lam is an extension of uberhip record label ZudRangMa, and has

LGBTIQ+ BANGKOK

Bangkok has a notable LGBTIQ-friendly vibe to it. From kinky underwear shops and drag events to gay bars and lesbian-only get-togethers – you could eat, shop and play here for days without ever leaving the comfort of welcoming venues. Unlike elsewhere in Southeast Asia, homosexuality is not criminalised in Thailand and the general attitude remains extremely laissez-faire.

Best Bars

The Stranger (Map p422; www.facebook.com/thestrangerbar; Soi 4, Th Silom; ⏲6pm-1am; Ⓜ Si Lom exit 2, Ⓢ Sala Daeng exit 1) Probably the most low-key, sophisticated venue on Soi 4.

Balcony (Map p422; www.balconypub.com; Soi 4, Th Silom; ⏲5.30pm-2am; 📶; Ⓜ Si Lom exit 2, Ⓢ Sala Daeng exit 1) Streetside watering hole for local and visiting LGBTIQ folk.

Maggie Choo's (Map p422; www.maggiechoos.com; Fenix Silom, basement, Novotel Bangkok, 320 Th Silom; ⏲7.30pm-2am; Ⓢ Surasak exit 1) Weekends feature pulsating parties and flashy drag shows at this popular boozer.

Best Dance Clubs

G Bangkok (Map p422; Soi 2/1 Th Silom; admission from 300B; ⏲8pm-2am; Ⓜ Si Lom exit 2, Ⓢ Sala Daeng exit 3) Where to go after all the other Silom bars have closed.

Fake Club The Next Gen (Map p407; www.facebook.com/fakeclubthenextgen; 222/32 Th Ratchadaphisek; ⏲8pm-2am; Ⓜ Sutthisan exit 3) Suburban megaclub in handsome digs.

Banana Bar on 4 (Map p422; Soi 4, Th Silom; ⏲7pm-2am; Ⓜ Si Lom exit 2, Ⓢ Sala Daeng exit 1) Chill dance club on the city's gayest street.

a Jamaican-style sound system custom-built for world and retro-Thai DJ sets and the occasional live show. The bar stocks some fabulous house-made infusions (ginger and rhubarb, to name a couple) that lend inimitable flavours to its signature cocktails. It's packed to the gills on weekends.

Tuba BAR
(Map p424; www.facebook.com/tubabkk; 34 Room 11-12 A, Soi Thong Lor 20/Soi Ekamai 21; ⏲11am-2am; Ⓢ Ekkamai exit 1/3 & taxi) Part storage room for over-the-top vintage furniture, part restaurant and part friendly local boozer, this quirky bar certainly doesn't lack diversity – nor fun. Indulge in a whole bottle (they'll hold onto it for your next visit if you don't finish it) and don't miss the chicken wings or the delicious deep-fried *lâhp* (spicy, herbal mincemeat salad).

Tasting Room by Mikkeller MICROBREWERY
(Map p424; www.tastingroombkk.com; 26 Yaek 2, Soi Ekamai 10; ⏲5pm-midnight; Ⓢ Ekkamai exit 1/3 & taxi) These buzz-generating Danish 'gypsy' brewers have set up shop in Bangkok, granting us more than 30 beers on tap. Expect brews ranging from the local (Sukhumvit Brown Ale) to the insane (Beer Geek, a 13%-alcohol oatmeal stout), as well as an inviting atmosphere and good bar snacks.

Havana Social Club CLUB
(Map p424; www.facebook.com/pg/havanasocialbkk; Soi 11, Th Sukhumvit; ⏲6pm-2am) Locate the phone booth, dial the secret code (the doorman will help you out here) and cross the threshold to pre-revolution Havana. Part bar, part dance club, Havana combines live music, great drinks and an expat-heavy crowd who all seem to know the right dance steps. No shorts, sandals, flip-flops or backpacks – in other words, look sharp to enter.

Beam CLUB
(Map p424; www.beamclub.com; 72 Courtyard, 72 Soi 55/Thong Lor, Th Sukhumvit; ⏲8pm-2am Wed-Sat; Ⓢ Thong Lo exit 1/3 & taxi) High-profile guest DJs spinning deep house and techno, a diverse crowd and a dance floor that literally vibrates have combined to make Beam Bangkok's club of the moment. Check the website for special events.

☆ Entertainment

Although Bangkok often seems to cater to the inner philistine in all of us, the city is home to a diverse but low-key art scene. Add to this dance performances, live music and, yes, the infamous go-go bars, and you have a city whose entertainment scene spans from – in local parlance – *lo-so* (low society) to *hi-so* (high society).

★Brick Bar LIVE MUSIC

(Map p412; www.brickbarkhaosan.com; basement, Buddy Lodge, 265 Th Khao San; admission Sat & Sun 150B; ⊙8pm-2am; Phra Athit/Banglamphu Pier) This basement pub, a favourite destination in Bangkok for live music, hosts a nightly revolving cast of bands for an almost exclusively Thai crowd – many of whom will end the night dancing on the tables. Brick Bar can get infamously packed, so be sure to arrive there early.

★Bamboo Bar LIVE MUSIC

(Map p422; 02 659 9000; www.mandarinoriental.com; 48 Soi 40/Oriental, Mandarin Oriental; ⊙5pm-12.30am Sun-Thu, to 1.30am Fri & Sat; Oriental Pier) After more than 65 years of service, the Mandarin Oriental's Bamboo Bar remains one of the city's premier locales for live jazz. Guest vocalists are flown in from across the globe – check the website to see who's in town – and the music starts at 9pm nightly.

★The Living Room LIVE MUSIC

(Map p424; 02 649 8888; www.thelivingroomatbangkok.com; 250 Th Sukhumvit, level 1, Sheraton Grande Sukhumvit; ⊙6pm-midnight; M Sukhumvit exit 3, S Asok exit 2) Don't let looks deceive you: every night this bland hotel lounge transforms into the city's best venue for live jazz. True to the name, there's comfy, sofa-based seating, all of it within earshot of the music. Enquire ahead of time to see which sax master or hide-hitter is in town. An entry fee of 300B is charged after 8.30pm.

★Rajadamnern Stadium SPECTATOR SPORT

(สนามมวยราชดำเนิน; Map p412; www.rajadamnern.com; off Th Ratchadamnoen Nok; tickets 3rd class/2nd class/club class/ringside 1000/1500/1800/2000B; ⊙matches 6.30pm Mon, Wed & Thu, 3pm & 6.30pm Sun; Thewet Pier, S Phaya Thai exit 3 & taxi) Rajadamnern Stadium is Bangkok's oldest and most venerable venue for *moo·ay tai* (Thai boxing; also spelt *muay Thai*). Be sure to buy tickets from the official ticket counter or online, not from touts and scalpers who hang around outside the entrance.

Saxophone Pub & Restaurant LIVE MUSIC

(Map p407; 02 246 5472; www.saxophonepub.com; 3/8 Th Phayathai; ⊙6pm-2am; S Victory Monument exit 2) After 30 years, Saxophone remains Bangkok's premier live-music venue – a dark, intimate space where you can pull up a chair just a few metres away from the band and see their every bead of sweat. If you prefer some mystique surrounding your musicians, watch the blues, jazz, reggae or rock from the balcony.

Apex Scala CINEMA

(Map p418; 02 251 2861; Soi 1, Siam Sq; S Siam exit 2) A flagrantly 1960s-era cinema in central Bangkok, the Scala's one screen shows a mix of contemporary Hollywood and films from the past.

Parking Toys LIVE MUSIC

(02 907 2228; 17/22 Soi Mayalap, off Kaset-Navamin Hwy; ⊙7pm-2am; M Chatuchak Park exit 2 & taxi, S Mo Chit exit 3 & taxi) One of northern Bangkok's best venues for live music, Parking Toys hosts an eclectic revolving cast of bands ranging in genre from rockabilly to electro-funk jam acts. Take a taxi north from BTS Mo Chit (or MRT Chatuchak Park) and go to Kaset intersection, then turn right on Th Kaset-Navamin. Parking Toys is past the second traffic light.

Sala Chalermkrung THEATRE

(Map p412; 02 224 4499; www.salachalermkrung.com; 66 Th Charoen Krung; tickets 800-1200B; ⊙shows 7.30pm Fri; Memorial Bridge Pier, M Hua Lamphong exit 1 & taxi) This art-deco Bangkok landmark, a former cinema dating to 1933, is one of the few remaining places *kŏhn* (masked dance-drama based on stories from the *Ramakian*, the Thai version of the Indian epic *Ramayana*) can be witnessed. The weekly traditional dance-drama is enhanced here by laser graphics, high-tech audio and English subtitles. Concerts and other events are also held; check the website for details.

Patpong RED-LIGHT DISTRICT

(Map p422; Th Phat Phong & Soi Phat Phong 2; ⊙6pm-2am; M Si Lom exit 2, S Sala Daeng exit 1) Once billed as the world's most notorious red-light district, Patpong is now a much watered-down version of its former self. These days, a flea market frequented by curious tourists coexists with a bunch of dodgy go-go bars that advertise pole dances and the infamous upstairs 'ping-pong shows'. Sex work is illegal in Thailand, but many bars nonetheless double as pickup joints.

Shopping

Prime your credit card and shine your baht – shopping is serious business in Bangkok. Hardly a street corner in this city is free from a vendor, hawker or impromptu stall, and it doesn't stop there: Bangkok is also home to one of the world's largest outdoor markets, not to mention some of Southeast Asia's largest malls.

Siam Square, Pratunam, Phloen Chit & Ratchathewi

★ MBK Center SHOPPING CENTRE

(Map p418; cnr Rama I & Th Phayathai; 10am-10pm; S National Stadium exit 4) This eight-storey market in a mall has emerged as one of Bangkok's top attractions. On any given weekend half of Bangkok's residents (and most of its tourists) can be found here combing through a seemingly inexhaustible range of small stalls, shops and merchandise.

MBK is Bangkok's cheapest place to buy mobile phones and accessories (4th floor). It's also one of the better places to stock up on camera gear (ground floor and 5th floor), and the expansive food court (6th floor) is one of the best in town.

★ Siam Discovery SHOPPING CENTRE

(Map p418; www.siamdiscovery.co.th; cnr Rama I & Th Phayathai; 10am-10pm; S Siam exit 1) With an open, almost market-like feel and an impressive variety of unique goods ranging from housewares to clothing (including lots of items by Thai designers), the fashionable Siam Discovery is hands down the most design-conscious mall in town. Alongside established stores, don't forget to check out the kiosks, which often display some excellent locally designed merchandise.

Siam Paragon SHOPPING CENTRE

(Map p418; www.siamparagon.co.th; 991/1 Rama I; 10am-10pm; S Siam exit 3/5) As much an air-conditioned urban park as it is a shopping centre, Siam Paragon is home to **Sea Life Ocean World** (www.sealifebangkok.com; adult/child from 1090/890B; 10am-9pm), **Major Cineplex** (02 129 4635; www.majorcineplex.com; 5th fl, Siam Paragon), and **Gourmet Paradise** (mains 50-200B; 10am-10pm;), a huge basement-level food court with dozens of dining options. Then there are stores and more stores, selling clothes, souvenirs, accessories, electronics, and even Rolls-Royce and McLaren cars! On the 3rd floor is **Kino-kuniya**, Thailand's largest English-language bookshop.

Riverside, Silom & Lumphini

★ Asiatique MARKET

(Map p407; Soi 72-76, Th Charoen Krung; 4pm-midnight; Sathorn/Central Pier & mall shuttle boat) Considered one of Bangkok's most popular night markets, Asiatique is housed within restored warehouses next to the Chao Phraya River. Expect clothing, handicrafts, souvenirs, several dining and drinking venues, and a 60m-high Ferris wheel. To get here, take one of the frequent, free shuttle boats from Sathorn (Central) Pier that run from 4pm to 11.30pm.

Thanon Sukhumvit

Emquartier SHOPPING CENTRE

(Map p424; www.theemdistrict.com; 693-695 Th Sukhumvit; 10am-10pm; S Phrom Phong exit 1) Arguably one of Bangkok's flashiest malls. Come for brands you're not likely to find elsewhere, or get lost in the Helix, a seemingly never-ending spiral of innumerable restaurants and stores.

Information

DANGERS & ANNOYANCES

Generally, Bangkok is a safe city, but it's good to keep the following in mind to avoid joining the list of tourists sucked in by Bangkok's numerous scam artists:

Gem scam We're literally begging you – if you aren't a gem trader do not buy unset stones in Thailand. Period.

Closed today Ignore any 'friendly' local who tells you that an attraction is closed for a Buddhist holiday or for cleaning.

Túk-túk rides for 20B These alleged 'tours' bypass the sights and instead cruise to all the fly-by-night gem and tailor shops that pay commissions.

Flat-fare taxi ride Flatly refuse any driver who quotes a flat fare, which will usually be three times more expensive than the reasonable meter rate.

Friendly strangers Be wary of smartly dressed men who approach you asking where you're from and where you're going.

MEDICAL SERVICES

The following hospitals have English-speaking doctors and staff, and world-class facilities:

Bangkok Christian Hospital (Map p422; 02 625 9000; 124 Th Silom; M Si Lom exit 2, S Sala Daeng exit 1) Modern, central hospital.

BNH (Map p422; ☎02 022 0700; www.bnhhospital.com; 9/1 Soi Convent; Ⓜ Si Lom exit 2, Ⓢ Sala Daeng exit 2/4) Modern, centrally located hospital.

Bumrungrad International Hospital (Map p424; ☎02 066 8888; www.bumrungrad.com; 33 Soi 3, Th Sukhumvit; ⏲24hr; Ⓢ Nana exit 1) An internationally accredited hospital.

Samitivej Hospital (Map p424; ☎02 022 2222; www.samitivejhospitals.com; 133 Soi 49, Th Sukhumvit; ⏲24hr; Ⓢ Phrom Phong exit 3 & taxi) Acclaimed modern hospital.

St Louis Hospital (Map p422; ☎02 838 5555; www.saintlouis.or.th; 215 Th Sathon Tai/South; Ⓢ Surasak exit 4) Modern hospital preferred by locals.

Dentists

Business is good in the teeth game, partly because so many *fa·ràng* (Westerners) are combining their holiday with a spot of cheap root-canal work or some 'personal outlook' care – a teeth-whitening treatment by any other name. Prices are a bargain compared with those in Western countries and the quality of dentistry is generally high.

Bangkok Dental Spa (Map p424; ☎088 919 2995; www.bangkokdentalspa.com; 2nd fl, Methawattana Bldg, 27 Soi 19, Th Sukhumvit; ⏲by appointment only; Ⓜ Sukhumvit exit 3, Ⓢ Asok exit 1) Dental-care centre with a spa-like environment.

Dental Hospital (☎02 092 2000; www.dentalhospitalbangkok.com; Soi 77, Th Sukhumvit; ⏲9am-8pm Mon-Sat, to 4.30pm Sun; Ⓢ On Nut exit 1) A private dental clinic with dentists who speak fluent English.

Siam Family Dental Clinic (Map p418; ☎081 987 7700; www.siamfamilydental.com; 209 Th Phayathai; ⏲11am-8pm Mon-Fri, 10am-7pm Sat & Sun; Ⓢ Siam exit 2) Private dental clinic in central Bangkok.

TOURIST INFORMATION

Tourist Police (call centre 1155; www.touristpolice.go.th) The best way to deal with most problems requiring police assistance or intervention (usually a rip-off or theft) is to contact the tourist police, who are used to dealing with foreigners and can be very helpful in the event you are arrested.

Bangkok Information Center (Map p412; ☎02 225 7612-4; 17/1 Th Phra Athit; ⏲8am-7pm Mon-Fri, 9am-5pm Sat & Sun; ⛴ Phra Athit Pier) Handles city-specific tourism information.

Tourism Authority of Thailand (TAT; ☎02 134 0040, call centre 1672; www.tourismthailand.org; 2nd fl, btwn Gates 2 & 5, Suvarnabhumi International Airport; ⏲24hr) TAT runs a counter at Suvarnabhumi International Airport.

Tourism Authority of Thailand (TAT; Map p412; ☎02 283 1500, nationwide 1672; www.tourismthailand.org; cnr Th Ratchadamnoen Nok & Th Chakraphatdi Phong; ⏲8.30am-4.30pm; ⛴ klorng boat Phanfa Leelard Pier) Banglamphu branch.

VISAS

Bangkok Immigration Office (☎02 141 9889; www.bangkok.immigration.go.th; Bldg B, Government Centre, Soi 7, Th Chaeng Watthana; ⏲8.30am-noon & 1-4.30pm Mon-Fri; Ⓜ Chatuchak Park exit 2 & taxi, Ⓢ Mo Chit exit 3 & taxi) Visa extensions are filed at this office.

ℹ Getting There & Away

AIR

Bangkok has two airports. Located 30km east of central Bangkok, **Suvarnabhumi International Airport** (☎02 132 1888; www.airportthai.co.th; Samut Prakan) began commercial international and domestic service in 2006. The airport's name is pronounced *sù·wan·ná·poom*.

Bangkok's other airport, **Don Mueang International Airport** (☎02 535 1192; www.airportthai.co.th; Don Mueang), 25km north of central Bangkok, was retired from service in 2006 only to reopen later as the city's de facto budget hub. Terminal 1 handles international flights, while Terminal 2 is for domestic destinations.

BUS & MINIVAN

Buses and minivans using government bus stations are far more reliable and less prone to incidents of theft than private connections departing from Th Khao San or other tourist centres.

Privately run minivans, called *rót đôo*, are a fast and relatively comfortable way to get between Bangkok and its neighbouring provinces. The various routes depart from their respective bus stations (for example, minivans to Ayuthaya depart from the Northern & Northeastern Bus Terminal, those to Ban Phe from the Eastern Bus Terminal).

Eastern Bus Terminal

The **Eastern Bus Terminal** (Map p424; ☎02 391 2504; Soi 40, Th Sukhumvit; Ⓢ Ekkamai exit 2) is the departure point for buses to Pattaya, Rayong, Chanthaburi and other points east, except for the border crossing at Aranya Prathet. Most people call it *sà·tăh·nee èk·gà·mai* (Ekamai station). It's near the Ekkamai BTS station.

Northern & Northeastern Bus Terminal

The **Northern & Northeastern Bus Terminal** (Mo Chit; ☎northeastern routes 02 936 2852, ext 602/605, northern routes 02 936 2841, ext 325/614; Th Kamphaeng Phet; Ⓜ Kamphaeng Phet exit 1 & taxi, Ⓢ Mo Chit exit 3 & taxi) is located just north of Chatuchak Park. This hectic bus station is also commonly called *kŏn sòng mŏr chít* (Mo Chit station) – not to be confused with Mo Chit BTS station. Buses depart

GETTING TO CAMBODIA: ARANYA PRATHET TO POIPET

The town of Aranya Prathet (aka Aran), 6km short of the principal Thailand–Cambodia border crossing, is known to Thais mostly for smuggling and gambling. (The casinos are over the border in Poipet.) For travellers, it's the busiest border crossing for trips to Angkor Wat and few actually stop here longer than needed to get their passport stamped. As border towns go, it's not that bad. If you do spend a little time, **Talat Rong Kluea**, near the frontier itself, is worth exploring. The market is mainly thrift-store tat and cheaply made junk, but the Rong Kluea experience isn't about what's being sold – it's about seeing the caravans of Cambodian traders pushing huge handcarts through a market so vast that many of the Thai shoppers rent bikes (20B per day) and motorcycles (100B per three hours) to get about.

Getting to the border There are expensive but convenient direct bus services from Bangkok to Siem Reap (eight to 10 hours). Nattakan (www.bookmebus.com; US$28) and Giant Ibis (www.giantibis.com; US$32) are relatively reliable operators.

Buses from Bangkok's Mo Chit (240B, 4½ hours, hourly), Ekamai (240B, four hours, five daily) and Suvarnabhumi Airport (205B, 3½ hours, two daily) bus stations head to Aran's bus station, 6km short of the frontier itself. Some go to the border itself: these have 'Rong Klua market' as a destination.

Minivans from Bangkok's Victory Monument (230B, four hours, every 30 minutes) go to a point just short of the border itself.

Other bus and minibus services sold on Khao San Rd in Bangkok and elsewhere in Thailand may seem cheap and convenient, but they haven't been nicknamed 'scam buses' for nothing: by using them you'll subject yourself to being hassled and ripped off.

All bus services may offer you 'VIP processing' of Cambodian visas before you reach the border: don't do it. Wait and get your visa at the border.

Two daily trains (5.55am and 1.05pm) also make the run from Bangkok's Hua Lamphong Station (3rd class 48B, six hours) to the city, returning at 6.40am and 1.55pm.

From Aran bus terminal or train station, you'll need to take either a *sŏrng·tăa·ou* (passenger pickup trucks; 15B), a motorcycle taxi (60B) or a túk-túk (motorised vehicle, pronounced *đúk đúk;* 80B) the final 6km to the border.

Aran also has buses from the bus terminal to Chanthaburi (160B, four hours, hourly), Khorat (200B, four hours, six daily) and Surin (150B to 200B, six hours, three daily).

At the border The border is open from 7am to 8pm daily. There are many persistent scammers on the Thai side trying to get you to buy your Cambodia visa through them, but no matter what they might tell you, there's absolutely no good reason to get visas anywhere except the border. Buying them elsewhere costs more and takes longer. Don't even show your passport to anyone before you reach Thai immigration and don't change money.

After getting stamped out of Thailand – a straightforward process – follow the throng to Cambodian Immigration and find the 'Visa on Arrival' sign if you don't already have a visa. You'll need US$30 and a passport photo. Weekday mornings you might finish everything in 10 to 20 minutes, but if you arrive after noon it could take an hour or more. Weekends and holidays, when many Thais arrive to gamble and foreign workers do visa runs, are also busy. You will probably be offered the opportunity to pay a 'special VIP fee' of 200B to jump to the front of the queue. You will almost certainly be asked to pay another small 'fee', which will be called a 'stamping' or 'overtime' fee. You should refuse, though doing so might mean you have to wait a few extra minutes.

Moving on There are frequent buses and share taxis from Poipet to Siem Reap along a good sealed road from the main bus station, which is about 1km away (2000r by motorcycle taxi) around the main market, one block north of Canadia Bank on NH5. Poipet also has a second 'international' bus station 9km east of town: prices are double here, and the station is only used by uninformed or gullible foreigners who get swept into the free shuttle that takes travellers out to it.

from here for all northern and northeastern destinations, as well as regional international destinations including Pakse (Laos), Phnom Penh (Cambodia), Siem Reap (Cambodia) and Vientiane (Laos). To reach the bus station, take BTS (Skytrain) to Mo Chit or MRT (Metro) to Kamphaeng Phet and transfer onto city bus 3, 77 or 509, or hop on a taxi or motorcycle taxi.

Southern Bus Terminal

The **Southern Bus Terminal** (Sai Tai Mai; ☎02 422 4444, call centre 1490; Th Boromaratchachonanee), commonly called *săi đâi mài*, lies a long way west of the centre of Bangkok. Besides serving as the departure point for all buses to destinations south of Bangkok, transport to Kanchanaburi and western Thailand also departs from here. The easiest way to reach the station is by taxi, or you can take bus 79, 159, 201 or 516 from Th Ratchadamnoen Klang.

TRAIN

Also known as Thonburi, **Bangkok Noi** (☎call centre 1690; www.railway.co.th/main/index_en.html; off Th Itsaraphap; ⛴Thonburi Railway Station) is a minuscule train station with departures for Kanchanaburi, Nakhon Pathom and Nam Tok.

The city's main train terminus is known as **Hua Lamphong** (☎call centre 1690; www.railway.co.th; off Rama IV; Ⓜ Hua Lamphong exit 2). Ignore all touts here and avoid the travel agencies. To check timetables, destinations and fares, visit the official website of the State Railway of Thailand (www.railway.co.th/main/index_en.html).

Wongwian Yai (☎02 465 2017, call centre 1690; www.railway.co.th/main/index_en.html; off Th Phra Jao Taksin; Ⓢ Wongwian Yai exit 4 & taxi) is a tiny station and the jumping-off point for the commuter line to Samut Sakhon (also known as Mahachai).

Getting Around

TO/FROM SUVARNABHUMI INTERNATIONAL AIRPORT

Bus & Minivan

- There is a public-transport centre 3km from the airport that includes a bus terminal with buses to a handful of provinces and inner-city-bound buses and minivans. A free airport shuttle connects the transport centre with the passenger terminals.
- Bus lines that city-bound tourists are likely to use include line 551 to BTS Victory Monument station (40B, frequent from 5am to 10pm) and 552 to BTS On Nut (20B, frequent from 5am to 10pm). From these points, you can continue by public transport or taxi to your hotel.

Taxi

- Metered taxis are available kerbside at Floor 1 – ignore the 'official airport taxi' touts who approach you inside the terminal. Punch a slip at the gate, which will give you a parking-bay number corresponding to an available taxi.
- Typical metered fares from Suvarnabhumi include 250B to 300B to Th Sukhumvit, 250B to 350B to Th Khao San or Silom, and about 400B to Mo Chit. Toll charges (paid by passengers) vary between 20B and 70B, depending on how much of the highway you wish to use. Note that there's a 50B surcharge added to all fares departing from the airport, payable directly to the driver.

Train

The **Airport Rail Link** (☎call centre 1690; www.srtet.co.th) connects Suvarnabhumi International Airport with the BTS stop at Phaya Thai (45B, 30 minutes, from 6am to midnight) and the MRT stop at Phetchaburi (45B, 25 minutes, from 6am to midnight). Trains depart roughly every 15 minutes.

TO/FROM DON MUEANG INTERNATIONAL AIRPORT

Bus

- From outside the arrival hall, there are four bus lines: bus A1 stops at BTS Mo Chit (50B, frequent from 7.30am to 11.30pm); A2 stops at BTS Mo Chit and BTS Victory Monument (50B, every 30 minutes from 7.30am to 11.30pm); A3 stops at Pratunam and Lumphini Park (50B, every 30 minutes from 7.30am to 11.30pm); and A4 stops at Th Khao San and Sanam Luang (50B, every 30 minutes from 7.30am to 11.30pm).
- Public buses stop on the highway in front of the airport. Useful lines include 29, with a

INTERNATIONAL BUSES

A handful of buses bound for international destinations depart from Bangkok's Northern & Northeastern Bus Terminal.

DESTINATION	COST (B)	DURATION (HR)	DEPARTURE
Pakse (Laos)	900	12	8.30pm
Phnom Penh (Cambodia)	750	11	1.30am
Siem Reap (Cambodia)	750	7	9am
Vientiane (Laos)	900	10	8pm

stop at Victory Monument BTS station before it terminates at Hua Lamphong Train Station (24 hours); line 59, with a stop near Th Khao San (24 hours); and line 538, stopping at Victory Monument BTS station (4am to 10pm). Fares are approximately 20B.

Taxi

As at Suvarnabhumi, public taxis leave from outside both arrival halls – you'll have to collect a slip from the taxi booth before exiting the arrival hall. There is a 50B airport charge added to the meter fare.

Train

The walkway that crosses from the airport to the Amari Airport Hotel also provides access to Don Mueang Train Station, which has trains to Hua Lamphong Train Station every one to 1½ hours from 4am to 11.30am and then roughly hourly from 2pm to 9.30pm (from 5B to 10B).

BOAT

Two fleets of boats, one that runs along the Chao Phraya River and the other along canals, serve Bangkok's commuters.

Klorng Boats

Canal taxi boats run along Khlong Saen Saep (Banglamphu to Ramkhamhaeng) and are an easy way to get between Banglamphu and Jim Thompson House, the Siam Sq shopping centres (get off at Sapan Hua Chang Pier for both) and other points further east along Th Sukhumvit – after a mandatory change of boat at Pratunam Pier.

➡ These boats are mostly used by daily commuters and pull into the piers for just a few seconds – jump straight on or you'll be left behind.

➡ Fares range from 12B to 15B and boats run from 5.30am to 7.15pm from Monday to Friday, from 6am to 6.30pm on Saturday and from 6am to 6pm on Sunday.

River Ferries

The **Chao Phraya Express Boat** (☎ 02 445 8888; www.chaophrayaexpressboat.com) operates the main ferry service along the Chao Phraya River. The central pier is known as Sathorn/Central Pier or Saphan Taksin, and connects to the BTS at Saphan Taksin station.

➡ Boats run from 6am to 7pm. Hold on to your ticket as proof of purchase (an occasional formality).

➡ The most common boats are the orange-flag vessels. These run from Wat Rajsingkorn in the south to Nonthaburi in the north, stopping at all major piers. Fares are a flat 15B, and boats run frequently from 6am to 7pm.

➡ Green-flag and yellow-flag boats skip a few piers along the way and are thus slightly quicker than the orange-flag vessels. They are fewer in number, though.

➡ A blue-flagged tourist boat (60B, every 30 minutes from 9.30am to 5.30pm) runs from Sathorn/Central Pier to Phra Athit/Banglamphu Pier, with stops at major sightseeing piers. A 200B all-day pass is also available, but unless you plan on doing a lot of boat travel, it's not great value.

➡ There are also dozens of cross-river ferries, which charge 3B and run every few minutes until late at night.

➡ Private long-tail boats can be hired for sightseeing trips at Phra Athit/Banglamphu Pier, Chang Pier, Tien Pier and Oriental Pier.

BTS & MRT

The elevated **BTS** (Skytrain; ☎ call centre 02 617 6000, tourist information 02 617 7341; www.bts.co.th), also known as the Skytrain *(rót fai fáa)*, whisks you through 'new' Bangkok (Silom, Sukhumvit and Siam Sq). The interchange between the two lines is at Siam station and trains run frequently from 6am to midnight. Fares range from 16B to 52B or 140B for a one-day pass. Most ticket machines only accept coins, but change is available at the information booths.

Bangkok's Metro, the **MRT** (☎ 02 354 2000; www.transitbangkok.com), is most helpful for people staying in the Sukhumvit or Silom area to reach the train station at Hua Lamphong. Fares cost from 16B to 42B. The trains run frequently from 6am to midnight.

At the time of research, both networks were being extended in several directions to meet increasing commuter traffic, with completion deadlines staggered over a number of years.

BUS

Bangkok's public buses are run by the **Bangkok Mass Transit Authority** (☎ 02 246 0973, call centre 1348; www.bmta.co.th).

➡ As the routes are not always clear, and with Bangkok taxis being such a good deal, you'd really have to be pinching pennies to rely on buses as a way to get around Bangkok.

➡ Air-con bus fares range from 12B to 25B; fares for fan-cooled buses start at 10B.

➡ Most of the bus lines run between 5am and 10pm or 11pm, except for the 'all-night' buses, which run from 3am or 4am to midmorning.

CAR & MOTORCYCLE

There are numerous car (and motorcycle) hire agencies in Bangkok, but it's a vast, intimidating, confusing, dangerous place in which to drive (and park) and is probably best left to the experts. If you need private transport, consider hiring a car and driver through your hotel or hire a taxi driver that you find trustworthy.

MOTORCYCLE TAXIS

➡ Motorcycle taxis (known as *motorsai*) serve two purposes in traffic-congested Bangkok. Most commonly and popularly, they form an integral part of the public-transport network, running from the corner of a main thoroughfare, such as Th Sukhumvit, to the far ends of soi (streets) that run off that thoroughfare. Riders wear coloured, numbered vests and gather at either end of their soi, usually charging 10B to 20B for the trip. Helmets are available for pillion riders, but their hygiene is questionable.

➡ The other obvious purpose of *motorsai* is to beat the traffic, given their ability to slide through piled-up traffic. Just tell your rider where you want to go, negotiate a price (from 20B for a short trip up to about 150B going across town), strap on the helmet and say a prayer to any god you're into.

TAXI

➡ Although many first-time visitors are hesitant to use them, Bangkok's taxis are – in general – new and comfortable and the drivers are courteous and helpful, making them an excellent way to get around.

➡ All taxis are required to use their meters, which start at 35B, and fares to most places within central Bangkok cost 60B to 100B. Freeway tolls – 25B to 120B depending on where you start or end – must be paid by the passenger.

➡ App-based yellow-green taxis through Grab are available for 20B above the metered fare.

➡ If you leave something in a taxi your best chance of getting it back (still pretty slim) is to call 1644.

TÚK-TÚK

➡ Bangkok's iconic túk-túk (pronounced *đúk đúk;* motorised three-wheel taxis) are used by Thais for short hops. For foreigners, however, these emphysema-inducing machines are part of the Bangkok experience, so despite the fact that they overcharge outrageously and you can't see anything due to the low roof, pretty much everyone takes a túk-túk at least once.

➡ Túk-túk are notorious for taking little 'detours' to commission-paying gem and silk shops and massage parlours. En route to 'free' temples, you'll meet 'helpful' locals who will steer you to even more rip-off opportunities. Ignore anyone offering too-good-to-be-true 20B trips on 'special days'.

➡ The vast majority of túk-túk drivers ask too much from tourists (expat *fa·ràng* never use them). Expect to be quoted a 100B fare, if not more, for even the shortest trip. Try bargaining them down to about 50B for a short trip, preferably at night when the pollution (hopefully) won't be quite so bad. Once you've done it, you'll find that taxis are cheaper, cleaner, cooler and quieter.

ⓘ GRAB A RIDE

App-based taxi service Grab is by far the most popular way to get around town for Bangkokians, not least because it saves them from negotiating and dealing with the infamously pesky drivers of Bangkok's conventional taxis. The Grab app is easy to download and use to request a ride. Pin your location and destination and the JustGrab service will find the nearest vehicle for your journey. If you have a preference for a taxi, select GrabTaxi, while GrabCar is solely for private vehicles.

THAILAND'S EASTERN SEABOARD

Ko Samet

Tiny Ko Samet (เกาะเสม็ด) has been attracting backpackers making the relatively short hop from Bangkok for years, but these days you'll find just as many Thais and Chinese tour groups. The sandy shores, cosy coves and aquamarine waters attract ferry-loads of Bangkokians looking to party each weekend, while tour groups pack out the main beach and many resorts. Fire-juggling shows and beach barbecues are nightly events on the northern beaches, but the southern parts of the island are far more secluded and sedate.

Despite being the closest major island to Bangkok, Ko Samet remains surprisingly underdeveloped, with a thick jungle interior crouching beside the low-rise hotels. Most of the southern coves have only one or two resorts.

Sights & Activities

On some islands you beach-hop, but on Ko Samet you cove-hop. The coastal footpath traverses rocky headlands, cicada-serenaded forests and one stunning bay after another, where the mood becomes successively more mellow the further south you go.

Sleeping

Though resorts are replacing bungalows, much of Ko Samet's accommodation is simple and old-fashioned. There are a few fan rooms for less than 700B and air-con bungalows with sea views can go for 1000B to 1500B. Beaches south of Hat Sai Kaew have only a handful of places. Look for discounts during low season and on weekdays.

A word on noise: popular beaches Hat Sai Kaew, Ao Hin Khok, Ao Phai and Ao Wong Deuan host well-amplified night-time parties.

Apaché BUNGALOW $

(☎081 452 9472; Ao Thian; d 800-1500B; ❄📶) Eclectic, quirky decorations and a cheerfully random colour scheme add character to this superchilled spot at the southern end of a tranquil strip. Bungalows are basic but adequate. The on-site restaurant on stilts is well worthwhile.

★ **Ao Nuan Bungalows** BUNGALOW $$

(☎038 644334, 081 781 4875; Ao Nuan; bungalows with fan 900-1200B, with air-con 1500-3000B; ❄📶) Samet's one remaining bohemian bay is tucked off the main road down a dirt track. Running down a jungle hillside to the sea, these cute wooden bungalows range from simple fan-cooled affairs with shared cold-water bathroom to romantic air-conditioned retreats with elegant deck furniture. There's a bar and simple restaurant; if you need more action, Ao Phutsa is a few minutes' stroll away. You can make reservations by SMS.

★ **Viking Holidays Resort** BUNGALOW $$

(☎038 651126; www.vikingholidaysresort.com; 101/4 Moo 3, Ao Thian; d incl breakfast 1500-1800B; ❄📶) One of a line of casual bungalow complexes on this tranquil beach, Viking is well run and has pretty, compact, carpeted rooms decorated with strings of seashells. Staff are particularly helpful and friendly, and speak good English. Unlike with many Ko Samet bungalows, you can book online (and pick your bungalow location).

Tubtim Resort RESORT $$

(☎038 644025; www.samedtubtim.com; 13/15 Moo 4, Ao Phutsa; d incl breakfast with fan 630-1050B, with air-con 2100-4500B; ❄📶) This long-running resort on Ao Phutsa (Ao Tub Tim) occupies a secluded stretch of sand and offers a wide range of timber cottages, from budget fan rooms to spacious air-con bungalows. It's a sociable place with nightly barbecues, and has a good beach bar and restaurant. The best cottages are right by the sand, giving a great outlook from bed, desk and deck.

Paradee Resort RESORT $$$

(☎038 644284; www.samedresorts.com/paradee; 76 Moo 4, Ao Kiu; villas incl breakfast 15,000-35,000B, ste from 70,000B; ❄📶🏊) Exclusive and offering the ultimate in privacy, this sleek resort near Ko Samet's southern end is one of the island's most luxurious. Golf carts hum about among discreetly screened thatched villas, most of which have their own Jacuzzi. The lovely beach is effectively private and, across the road, a bar deck lets you appreciate the sunset views from the island's western shore.

Eating & Drinking

Food in Ko Samet is adequate rather than spectacular and you certainly won't be blown away by the service. Beaches are strung with restaurants and bars that are good for anything from slap-up Thai meals to cold beer. Many hotels and guesthouses have restaurants doing beach barbecues with all manner of seafood at night.

On weekends Ko Samet is a boisterous night owl, with tour groups crooning away on karaoke machines and the young ones slurping down beer and buckets to a techno beat. There is usually a crowd on Hat Sai Kaew, Ao Hin Khok, Ao Phai and Ao Wong Deuan.

Jep's Restaurant INTERNATIONAL $$

(☎038 644112; Ao Phai; mains 150-450B; ⊙7am-11pm) Canopied by arching tree branches decorated with pendant lights, this pretty place right on the sand does a wide range of international food, from Mexican to Italian to crepes, along with the obligatory Thai dishes.

Funky Monkey INTERNATIONAL $$

(Na Dan; mains 70-450B; ⊙8.30am-11pm; 📶) At the end of the street near the national-park post, Funky Monkey is regarded by many as making Ko Samet's best pizza. It certainly does a satisfying line in international comfort food such as English breakfast and burgers, along with staple Thai dishes. It's a good place to meet travellers over a cold beer.

Breeze BAR

(☎038 644100; www.samedresorts.com; Ao Prao Resort, Ao Prao; ⊙7am-10.30pm; 📶) On the sunset side of the island, this is a lovely sea-view restaurant perfect for a sundowner. You will need private transport to reach it, or it's a 2.5km walk from Hat Sai Kaew.

Ko Samet

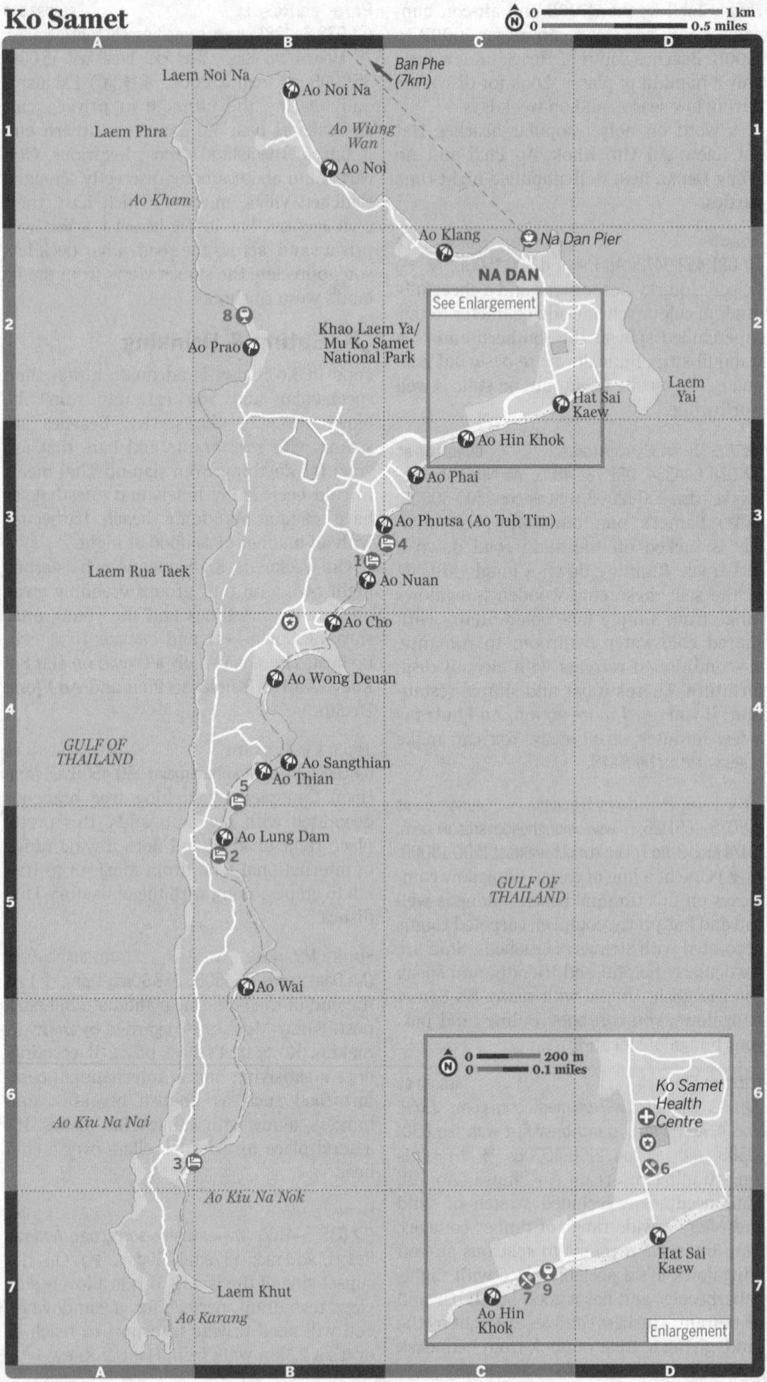
0 1 km
0 0.5 miles
A
B
C
D
1
2
3
4
5
6
7
Ban Phe (7km)
Laem Noi Na
Ao Noi Na
Laem Phra
Ao Wiang Wan
Ao Noi
Ao Kham
Ao Klang
Na Dan Pier
NA DAN
See Enlargement
8
Ao Prao
Khao Laem Ya/ Mu Ko Samet National Park
Laem Yai
Hat Sai Kaew
Ao Hin Khok
Ao Phai
Ao Phutsa (Ao Tub Tim)
4
1
Laem Rua Taek
Ao Nuan
Ao Cho
Ao Wong Deuan
GULF OF THAILAND
Ao Sangthian
Ao Thian
5
Ao Lung Dam
2
GULF OF THAILAND
Ao Wai
0 200 m
0 0.1 miles
Ko Samet Health Centre
6
Ao Kiu Na Nai
3
Ao Kiu Na Nok
Hat Sai Kaew
7
9
Ao Hin Khok
Laem Khut
Ao Karang
Enlargement

Ko Samet

Sleeping

1 Ao Nuan Bungalows B3
2 Apaché B5
3 Paradee Resort A6
4 Tubtim Resort C3
5 Viking Holidays Resort B4

Eating

6 Funky Monkey D6
7 Jep's Restaurant C7

Drinking & Nightlife

8 Breeze B2
9 Naga Bar C7

Naga Bar BAR
(Ao Hin Khok; 3pm-late) This busy beachfront bar covered in Day-Glo art is run by a friendly bunch of locals offering good music, lots of whisky and vodka/Red Bull buckets. The 80B happy-hour cocktails (from 2pm to 9pm) seem like a good deal but they're noticeably watered down. Things get lively later on, with dance-floor action and free body painting.

Information

The island has plenty of ATMs, including some near the Na Dan pier, outside the 7-Eleven behind Hat Sai Kaew, and at Ao Wong Deuan, Ao Thian and Ao Phutsa, as well as at several resorts.

Ko Samet Health Centre (081 861 7922, 038 644123; emergency 24hr) On the main road between Na Dan and Hat Sai Kaew.

Tourist Police (24hr 1155) On the main road between Na Dan and Hat Sai Kaew. There's a substation (24hr 1155) at Ao Wong Deuan.

Getting There & Away

Ko Samet is accessed via the mainland piers in Ban Phe. All ferry companies charge the same fares (one way/return from mainland 70/100B, one way from island 50B, 40 minutes, hourly, 8am to 5pm) and dock at **Na Dan** (usage fee 20B), Ko Samet's main pier. The last boat back to the mainland leaves at 6pm.

If you are staying at Ao Wong Deuan or further south, you can catch a ferry or speedboat from the mainland directly to the beach (ferry/speedboat 90/300B, two to three daily departures).

Speedboats (one way 200B to 500B) drop you at the beach of your choice, but usually only leave when they have enough passengers. Otherwise, you can charter one for around 1500B.

Trat

039 / POP 22,000

Trat (ตราด) is a major transit point for Ko Chang and coastal Cambodia, and worth a stop anyway for its underappreciated old-world charm. The guesthouse neighbourhood occupies an atmospheric wooden shophouse district, backing on to the riverfront and bisected by winding sois. It's filled with typical Thai street life: children riding bikes, homemakers running errands and small businesses selling trinkets and necessities.

Sights

Walk down Th Lak Meuang and you will see that the top floors of shophouses have been converted into nesting sites for birds that produce the edible nests considered a Chinese delicacy. Swiflets' nests were quite rare (and expensive) in the past because they were only harvested from precipitous sea caves by trained, daring climbers. In the 1990s entrepreneurs figured out how to replicate the cave atmosphere in multistorey shophouses and the business has since become a key operation in Trat.

Trat Province

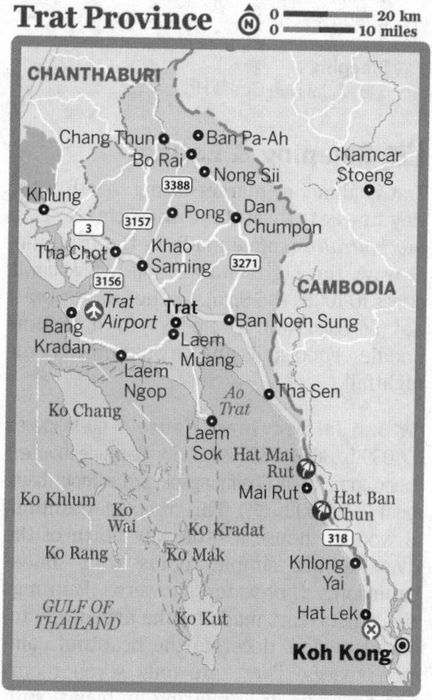

Trat

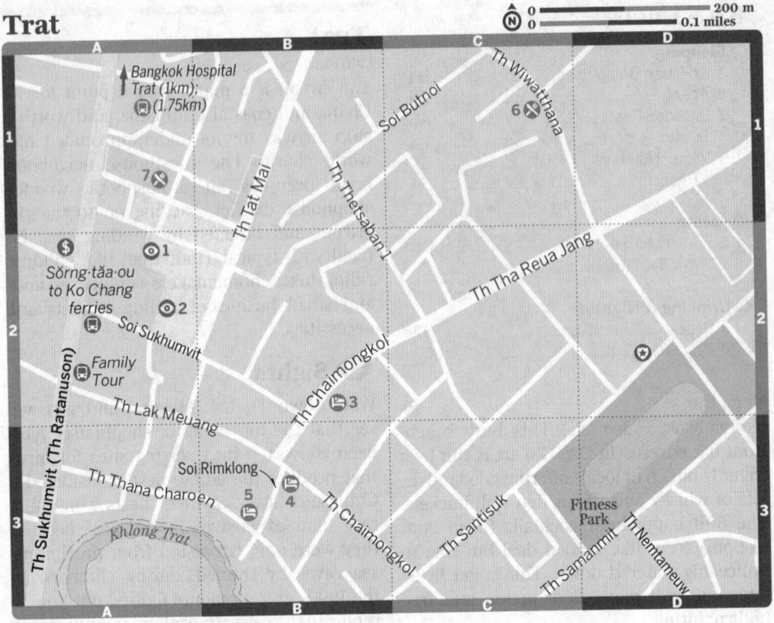

Trat

Sights

1 Day Market A2
2 Indoor Market A2

Sleeping

3 Ban Jai Dee Guest House B2
4 Rimklong Boutique Hotel B3
5 Yotin Guest House B3

Eating

6 Namchok C1
7 Night Market A1

Sleeping & Eating

Trat is all about market eating: head to the **day market** (Th Tat Mai; 6am-5pm) for *gah·faa bohrahn* (coffee made in the traditional way), the **night market** (off Th Sukhumvit; dishes 10-100B; 5-9pm), or the **indoor market** (Soi Sukhumvit; 6am-5pm) for lunchtime noodles. Food stalls line Th Sukhumvit come nightfall.

★Ban Jai Dee Guest House GUESTHOUSE $

(039 520678, 083 589 0839; banjaideehouse@yahoo.com; 6 Th Chaimongkol; s/d without bathroom 250/300B;) This relaxed traditional wooden house a little way north of the riverside has simple rooms with shared bathrooms (hot-water showers). Paintings and objets d'art made by the artistically inclined owners decorate the beautiful common spaces. There are only seven rooms and an addictively relaxing ambience so it can fill fast. The owners are full of helpful information.

Yotin Guest House GUESTHOUSE $

(089 224 7817; Th Thana Charoen; d 300-450B;) Backing a typically venerable building in Trat's lovely old quarter, these are pretty, inviting refurbished rooms with colourful linen and comfortable mattresses. Cheaper rooms are compact and either share a bathroom or have a very tight en suite. The couple who run the place are thoughtful and helpful: it's a very sound base. You can hire bikes here.

★Rimklong Boutique Hotel BOUTIQUE HOTEL $$

(039 523388, 081 861 7181; 194 Th Lak Meuang; d 950-1180B;) Run by refined and helpful Mr Tuu, this hotel offers five compact, sparkling rooms in the heart of the old part of town. Prices are reasonable for the

quality. Additional rooms are in an annexe a few paces down the soi. The cafe at the front does real espresso and cocktails.

★**Namchok** THAI $$

(Th Wiwatthana; mains 80-250B; ⌚10am-10pm) This simple open-sided restaurant north of the centre is deservedly a local favourite, with some excellent seafood dishes and well-meaning service from an army of young helpers. There's a helpful English menu, with such intriguing dishes as stir-fried ostrich with black pepper, and fried softshell crab. It's only signposted in Thai: look for the Coke logos and concrete bench seating.

ℹ Information

You'll find the bulk of banks and ATMs on Th Sukhumvit (often called Th Ratanuson), including **Krung Thai Bank** (Th Sukhumvit; ⌚8.30am-4.30pm Mon-Fri).

Bangkok Hospital Trat (☎039 522555; www.bangkoktrathospital.com; 376 Mu 2, Th Sukhumvit; ⌚24hr) Located 400m north of the town centre, this hospital offers the best health care in the region.

Police Station (☎24hr 1155; cnr Th Santisuk & Th Wiwatthana) A short walk from Trat's centre.

ℹ Getting There & Away

AIR

Bangkok Airways (☎039 525767; www.bangkokair.com; Trat Airport; ⌚8.30am-6.30pm) operates three daily flights to/from Bangkok Suvarnabhumi International Airport (one hour) to Trat Airport, 35km northwest of the city. A shared taxi or minibus from the airport into town costs 500B; to the Ko Chang ferry pier it's 300B.

BOAT

The piers that handle boat traffic to/from Ko Chang are located west of Laem Ngop, about 30km southwest of Trat. There are three piers, each used by different boat companies, but the most convenient services are through Koh Chang Ferry (p448), from Tha Thammachat, and Centrepoint Ferry (p448), from Tha Centrepoint.

Sŏrng·tăa·ou (Th Sukhumvit) to Laem Ngop and the piers (50B to 80B per person, 300B for the whole vehicle, 40 minutes) leave from Th Sukhumvit, just past the market. These will pick up from guesthouses in the morning. It should be the same charter price if you want to go directly from Trat's bus station to the pier.

You can catch a bus from Bangkok's Eastern (Ekamai) station all the way to Tha Centrepoint (250B, five hours, three morning departures).

TRANSPORT FROM TRAT

Trat's bus station is 2km out of town, and serves the following destinations:

DESTINATION	FARE (B)	DURATION (HR)	FREQUENCY
Bangkok Eastern (Ekamai) Bus Terminal	230	4½	hourly 7am-11.30pm
Bangkok Northern & Northeastern (Mo Chit) Bus Terminal	240	5½	2 daily
Bangkok Suvarnabhumi International Airport	240	4-4½	3 daily
Chanthaburi	58	1	6 daily

Minivans run to the following destinations:

DESTINATION	FARE (B)	DURATION (HR)	FREQUENCY
Bangkok Eastern (Ekamai) Bus Terminal	280	4	every 2hr 8.30am-4.30pm
Bangkok Northern & Northeastern (Mo Chit) Bus Terminal	270	4	every 2hr 8.30am-4.30pm
Chanthaburi	70	50min	frequent 6am-6pm
Hat Lek (for the border with Cambodia)	120	1½	hourly 5am-6pm
Pattaya	300	3½	every 2hr 8am-6pm
Rayong/Ban Phe (for Ko Samet)	200	3½	every 2hr 8am-6pm

A useful minivan operator is **Family Tour** (☎081 940 7380; Th Sukhumvit), with services to Bangkok, as well as to Phnom Penh and Siem Reap.

GETTING TO CAMBODIA: HAT LEK TO CHAM YEAM

Getting to the border The closest Thailand–Cambodia crossing from Trat is Hat Lek to the Cambodian town of Cham Yeam, and then on to Ko Kong. Minivans run to Hat Lek (120B, 1½ hours, hourly 5am to 6pm) from Trat's bus station. Agents in Trat sell through-tickets to Sihanoukville, Phnom Penh and Siem Reap by minivan for 600B, but these involve a change of transport at the border.

At the border Attempts to overcharge for the Cambodian visa (officially US$30) at this border are common; officials may quote the e-visa rate (US$37) or demand payment in Thai baht (1200B) at an unfavourable exchange rate. You will need a passport photo. To avoid the hassle, you may decide that getting an e-visa beforehand is worthwhile. Avoid anyone who says you require a 'medical certificate' or other paperwork. The border opens at 7am and closes at 8pm.

Thai visas can be renewed at this border, but note that visas at land borders are now limited to two per year. They'll give you 30 days.

Moving on Take a taxi (US$10), túk-túk (US$5) or *moto* (motorcycle taxi; US$3) to Ko Kong, where you can catch onward transport to Sihanoukville (four hours, one or two departures per day) and Phnom Penh (five hours, two or three departures until 11.30am).

This route includes a stop at Suvarnabhumi (airport) bus station as well as Trat's bus station. In the reverse direction, buses have two afternoon departures from Laem Ngop.

Ko Chang

039 / POP 10,000

With steep, jungle-covered peaks, picturesque Ko Chang (Elephant Island; เกาะช้าง) retains its remote and rugged spirit – despite the transformation of parts of it into a package-tour destination. Sweeping bays are sprinkled along the west coast; some have superfine sand, others have pebbles. What the island lacks in sand it makes up for in an unlikely combination: accessible wilderness with a thriving party scene.

Because of its relative remoteness, Ko Chang has been slower to register on the tourist radar than the Gulf and Andaman Coast islands. Today, it's still a slog to get here, but its resorts are busy with package tourists, Cambodia-bound backpackers and island-hopping couples funnelling through to more remote islands in the marine park. Along the populous west coast are sprawling minitowns that have outpaced the island's infrastructure. For a taste of old-school Chang, head to the southeastern villages and mangrove forests of Ban Salak Phet and Ban Salak Kok.

Sights & Activities

Although Thailand's second-largest island has accelerated into the modern world with some understandable growing pains, Ko Chang retains its tropically hued seas, critter-filled jungles and a variety of water sports for athletic beach bums.

Ko Chang's mountainous interior is predominately protected as a **national marine park** (อุทยานแห่งชาติหมู่เกาะช้าง; 039 510927; www.dnp.go.th; daily entrance adult/child 200/100B). The forest is lush and alive with wildlife and threaded by silver-hued waterfalls and trekking routes.

The west coast is by far the most developed part of Ko Chang, thanks to its beaches and bays. Public *sŏrng·tăa·ou* make beach-hopping easy and affordable. Some beaches are rocky, so it's worth bringing swim booties for the kids. Most of the time the seas are shallow and gentle but be wary of rips during storms and the wet season (May to October). Head down to Bang Bao pier for dive shops, island-hopping trips, inter-island transport, and some decent shopping and seafood restaurants.

Diving

The dive sites near Ko Chang offer a variety of coral, fish and beginner-friendly shallow waters. By far the most pristine diving in the area is around **Ko Rang**, an uninhabited island protected from fishing by its marine-park status.

Ko Yak, **Ko Tong Lang** and **Ko Laun** are shallow dives perfect for both beginners and advanced divers. There are lots of coral, schooling fish, pufferfish, morays, barracuda, rays and the occasional turtle.

One-day diving trips typically start at 3000B. Think 15,000B per person for PADI or other certification. Many dive shops remain open during the rainy season (May to October) but visibility and sea conditions are generally poor.

BB Divers DIVING
(086 129 2305; www.bbdivers-koh-chang.com; Bang Bao; 2 boat dives 3000B) Based at Bang Bao, this well-run diving outfit has branches in Lonely Beach and Hat Sai Khao, as well as outposts on Ko Kut and Ko Mak (high season only).

Scuba Academy DIVING
(039 611485; www.scubaacademykohchang.com; Bang Bao; snorkelling 800B, 2 tank dives 2500B) The newest dive outfit on Ko Chang has an experienced team of instructors and divemasters and is competitively priced.

Kayaking

Ko Chang cuts an impressive and heroic profile when viewed from the sea aboard a kayak. The water is generally calm and a few offshore islands provide a paddling destination that is closer than the horizon. Many hotels rent open-top kayaks (from 300B per day) that are convenient for near-shore outings and noncommittal kayakers; some provide them for free. Contact **SEA Kayaking** (092 475 0444; https://southeastasiakayaking.com; Emerald Cove Resort, Khlong Prao; 1-day expedition 4000B) for more serious apparatus.

Hiking

Ko Chang has a well-developed trekking scene, with inland routes that lead to lush forests filled with birds, monkeys and flora. A handful of English-speaking guides grew up near the jungle and are happy to share their secrets. Try Tan at **Tan Trekking** (089 645 2019; www.thailandadventureguide.com; hikes 600-1100B) or **Mr Raht** (086 155 5693; kohchang_trekking@yahoo.com).

Courses

Ka-Ti Culinary Cooking School COOKING
(Khlong Prao; 1500B; 11am-3.30pm Mon-Sat) Recommended hands-on cooking (and eating) classes complete with recipe book. If you want to know what the food is like in advance, visit the excellent **restaurant** (www.facebook.com/katikhruathai; Khlong Prao; mains 120-580B; 11am-10pm Mon-Sat, 5-10pm Sun;).

Sleeping

The northern and eastern parts of the island are less developed than the west coast and more isolated. You will likely need your own transport to not feel lonely out here, but you'll be rewarded with a quieter, calmer experience.

On the west coast, Lonely Beach is still the best budget option; Hat Kaibae is the best-value option; and White Sand Beach (Hat Sai Khao) is the most overpriced.

★ **Pajamas Hostel** HOSTEL $
(039 510789; www.pajamaskohchang.com; Khlong Prao; dm 480-630B, d/f 2430/4410B;) A couple of kilometres north of the main Khlong Prao strip and a short walk from the beach, this superb hostel oozes relaxation, with an open-plan lounge and bar overlooking the swimming pool. Modern air-con dorms are upstairs. Private rooms have platform beds, a cool, light feel and your own terrace/balcony. Spotless, and exceedingly well run.

★ **Paradise Cottage** BUNGALOW $
(081 773 9337; www.paradisecottageresort.com; 104/1 Mu 1, Lonely Beach; d with fan 400-1400B, with air-con 1200-2500B;) Hammock-clad pavilions face the sea or pool, and compact, handsome rooms are scattered around the garden at this well-run and gloriously relaxing retreat. The sea-view

LOCAL KNOWLEDGE

DON'T FEED THE WILDLIFE

On many of the around-the-island boat tours, operators amaze their guests with a stop at a rocky cliff to feed the wild monkeys. It seems innocent enough, even entertaining, but there's an unfortunate consequence: the animals become dependent on this food source and when the boats don't come as often during the low season the young and vulnerable ones are ill-equipped to forage in the forest.

The same goes for the dive or boat trips that feed the fish leftover lunches, or bread bought on the pier specifically for this purpose. It might be a fantastic way to see a school of brilliantly coloured fish, but the creatures then forsake the coral reefs for an easier meal, and without the daily grooming efforts of the fish the coral is soon overgrown with algae and will eventually suffocate.

Ko Chang

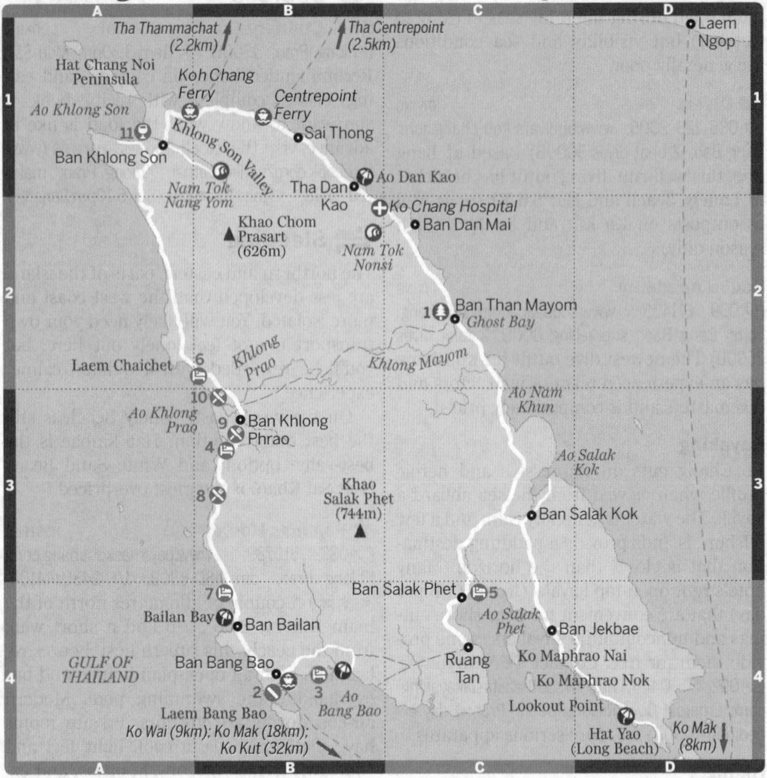

Ko Chang

Sights
1 Mu Ko Chang National Marine Park C2

Activities, Courses & Tours
2 BB Divers B4
Ka-Ti Culinary Cooking School ..... (see 9)
Scuba Academy ..... (see 2)
SEA Kayaking ..... (see 4)

Sleeping
3 Bang Bao Beach Resort B4
4 Dewa B3
5 Mangrove Hideaway C4
6 Pajamas Hostel B2
7 Paradise Cottage B4

Eating
8 Barrio Bonito B3
9 Ka-Ti Culinary B3
10 Phu-Talay B3

Drinking & Nightlife
11 Shambhala A1

rooms have air-con and a marvellous outlook, while the cheapest ones have fans. At low tide a sandbank just beyond the rocks can be reached. It's far enough away from the noisy clubs to ensure sleep.

★ **Bang Bao Beach Resort** BUNGALOW $$
(☎093 327 2788; www.bangbaobeachresort.com; Hat Khlong Koi; d 1500-2300B; ❄) Set along green lawn right on Khlong Koi beach, just east of Bang Bao, this is a marvellous spot. Old and new bungalows are available; both are attractively wooden and air-conditioned. It's a very efficiently run spot with easy access to beach bars and restaurants alongside. Walk along the beach from the canal bridge or drive the long way round.

★Mangrove Hideaway GUESTHOUSE $$
(☎080 133 6600; www.themangrovehideaway.com; Ban Salak Phet; d 1930-3640B; ⊙closed Jun & Sep; ❄📶) 🍃 Facing the mangrove forest, this environmentally friendly guesthouse is a fabulous spot. Crisp, attractive rooms face the verdant front garden, while the sumptuous superior suites have gorgeous wooden floors and overlook the dining area and mangroved river estuary. There's an open-air Jacuzzi and massage area upstairs; the resort was made using locally sourced wood and employs residents of nearby villages.

Dewa RESORT $$$
(☎039 557341; www.thedewakohchang.com; Khlong Prao; d incl breakfast 5800-15,200B; ❄@📶≋) One of the top luxury pads in these parts, everything about Dewa is chic, from the dark-tiled 700-sq-metre pool to the contemporary Thai-style rooms that are a design dream. Naturally there's a secluded bit of beach, a couple of outstanding restaurants and a full-service spa. Expect big discounts in low season.

Eating & Drinking

★Barrio Bonito MEXICAN $$
(☎080 092 8208; Hat Kaibae; mains 250-320B; ⊙5-10pm Jul-late May; 📶✍) Fab fajitas, burritos, tacos and cocktails are served by a charming French-Mexican couple at this roadside spot in the middle of Kaibae. Offering authentic, delicious, beautifully presented food and stylish surroundings, this is one of the island's finest places for a night out.

Phu-Talay SEAFOOD $$
(☎039 551300; 4/2 Mu 4, Khlong Prao; mains 90-300B; ⊙10am-10pm) A beautiful place right on the canal, Phu-Talay has wooden floors, blue-and-white decor, a picturesque deck and its own boat (for pickup from nearby accommodation). It specialises in seafood, with standout softshell crab, prawns and other fish dishes, and is far more reasonably priced than many other seafood places.

★Shambhala BAR
(☎098 579 4381; Siam Royal View, Ao Khlong Son; ⊙11am-10pm or later Thu-Tue) Perched at the north end of the island, past the flash marina, this poolside bar has a magnificent outlook across green lawn to a secluded golden sweep of beach. It's the perfect spot for a sundowner cocktail; it also turns out quality Thai and international dishes. Enter via the southernmost 'Marina' entrance to the Siam Royal View complex.

Information

There are banks with ATMs and exchange facilities along all the west-coast beaches.

WORTH A TRIP

ISLANDS CLOSE TO KO CHANG

Ko Kut (เกาะกูด), also widely called Ko Kood, is often feted as the perfect Thai island, and it is hard to argue with such an accolade. The supersoft sands are like talcum powder; the water lapping the bays is clear; and there are more coconut palms than people.

Unlike its larger neighbour Ko Chang, here you can escape from any serious nightlife or noise – though there's an infectious little live-music scene in season. Unlike Ko Wai and Ko Mak, it feels large enough that you can explore and enjoy time away from the beach. Kayaking, snorkelling and visits to waterfalls are the main activities.

Ko Kut has long been the domain of package-tour resorts and a seclusion-seeking elite. But the island is becoming more egalitarian, and independent travellers, families, couples and backpackers will find a base here.

Sweet little **Ko Mak** (เกาะหมาก) measures just 16 sq km and doesn't have any speeding traffic, wall-to-wall development, noisy beer bars or crowded beaches. Its palm-fringed bays are bathed by gently lapping water, and the interior is a peaceful landscape of coconut and rubber plantations.

Ko Mak has budget guesthouses, a couple of dive outfits and a decent restaurant and bar scene back from Ao Khao. Visiting the island is easier in high season (December to March); during low season (May to September) many boats stop running.

Stunning, tiny **Ko Wai** (เกาะหวาย) is barely developed but endowed with clear waters, intact glowing coral reefs for snorkelling off the beach and a handsome view across to Ko Chang. Expect to share the bulk of your afternoons with day trippers, but if you stay at one of the five simple bungalow resorts, the remainder of your time will be peaceful.

Ko Chang Hospital (☎039 586131; Ban Dan Mai) Public hospital with a good reputation and affordably priced care; south of the ferry terminal.

Tourist Police Office (☎1155; Khlong Prao) Next to the temple in Khlong Prao. Also has smaller police boxes at White Sand Beach (Hat Sai Khao) and Hat Kaibae.

DANGERS & ANNOYANCES

- Take extreme care when driving from Ban Khlong Son south to White Sand Beach (Hat Sai Khao), as the road is steep and treacherous, with several hairpin turns. There are mudslides and poor conditions during storms. If you rent a motorbike, ride carefully between Hat Kaibae and Lonely Beach, especially in the wet season. Wear protective clothing and a helmet when riding on a motorcycle.
- The police conduct regular drug raids on the island's accommodation. If you get caught with narcotics, you could face heavy fines or imprisonment.
- Be aware of the cheap minibus tickets from Siem Reap to Ko Chang; these usually involve some sort of time- and money-wasting commission scam.
- Ko Chang is considered a low-risk malarial zone, meaning that liberal use of mosquito repellent is probably an adequate precaution.

Getting There & Away

Whether starting from Bangkok or Cambodia, it is an all-day haul to reach Ko Chang overland. Overnighting in Trat is a pleasant way to break the journey.

Ferries from the mainland (Laem Ngop) leave from either Tha Thammachat, operated by **Koh Chang Ferry** (☎039 555188; https://kohchangferries.com; adult/child/car 1 way 80/30/120B; ⏰6.30am-7pm), or Tha Centrepoint with **Centrepoint Ferry** (☎039 538196; https://kohchangferries.com; Tha Centrepoint; adult 1 way/return 80/150B, child 1 way/return 40/70B, car 1 way/return 100/180B; ⏰hourly 6am-7.30pm, to 7pm May-Oct). Boats from Tha Thammachat arrive at Tha Sapparot, Centrepoint ferries at a pier 3km further south. Koh Chang ferries are faster and a little better.

Travel agents in Ko Chang sell through-tickets including boat and minivan to Siem Reap (650B) and Phnom Penh (900B) in Cambodia, though these require a change of bus at the border.

It is possible to go to and from Ko Chang from Bangkok's Eastern (Ekamai) bus terminal via Chanthaburi and Trat; there are also direct bus and minibus **services** (☎083 794 2122; www.bussuvarnabhumikohchang.com) from Bangkok's Suvarnabhumi International Airport.

The closest airport is in Trat. **Ko Chang Minibus** (☎087 785 7695; www.kohchangminibus.com) offers a variety of transfer packages from airport to beach.

Bang Bao Boat (☎039 558046; www.kohchangbangbaoboat.com; Ban Bang Bao; ⏰Nov-Apr) runs an interisland ferry that connects Ko Chang with Ko Mak and Ko Wai (with a speedboat connection from there to Ko Kut) during the high season. Boats leave from Bang Bao in the southwest of the island.

Speedboats travel between the islands during high season from both Bang Bao and Hat Kaibae.

KO CHANG TRANSPORT CONNECTIONS

ORIGIN	DESTINATION	BOAT	BUS
Bangkok's Eastern Bus Terminal (Ekamai)	Tha Thammachat (Laem Ngop)		280B, 6hr, 2 daily
Ko Chang	Bangkok's Suvarnabhumi International Airport		1-way/return 600/900B, 6-7hr, 2-3 daily
Ko Chang	Ko Kut	speedboat 900B, 2½hr, 3 daily; wooden boat plus speedboat 700B, 5hr, 1 daily	
Ko Chang	Ko Mak	speedboat 600B, 1hr, 3 daily; wooden boat 400B, 2hr, 1 daily	
Ko Chang	Ko Wai	speedboat 400B, 30min, 3 daily; wooden boat 300B, 1hr, 1 daily	
Tha Centrepoint (Laem Ngop)	Ko Chang	80B, 40min, hourly 6am-7.30pm	
Tha Thammachat (Laem Ngop)	Ko Chang	80B, 30min, every 45min 6.30am-7pm	

GETTING TO CAMBODIA: BAN PAKARD TO PAILIN

Getting to the border Minivans (092 037 6266) depart Chanthaburi at a stop across the river from the River Guest House (090 936 7499; www.facebook.com/theriverguesthouse; 3/5-8 Th Si Chan; d 450-700B, tr/f 850/950B;), where you can book your spot, to Ban Pakard (200B, 1½ hours, 10am and noon). There are also *sŏrng·tăa·ou* from the bus station (100B, two hours) that tend to leave early.

At the border This is a far less busy and more pleasant crossing than Poipet further north. You need a passport photo and US$30 for the visa fee. Cambodian e-visas aren't officially accepted here, though some travellers have reported getting through. Demanding US$35 for the visa is standard practice here.

Moving on Hop on a motorbike taxi to Pailin in Cambodia. From there, you can catch frequent shared taxis (US$5 per person, 1½ hours) to scenic Battambang. After that, you can move on to Siem Reap by boat, or Phnom Penh by bus.

NORTHEASTERN THAILAND

The northeast is Thailand's forgotten backyard. Isan (อีสาน), as it's usually called, offers a glimpse of the Thailand of old: rice fields along the horizon, water buffalo wade in muddy ponds, silk weavers work looms under their homes, and pedal-rickshaw riders pull passengers down city streets.

Spend a little time in the region and you'll discover as many differences as similarities to the rest of Thailand. The language, food and culture are more Lao than Thai, with hearty helpings of Khmer and Vietnamese thrown in. And spend time here you should, because it's home to some of Thailand's best historic sites, national parks and festivals. Thailand's tourist trail is at its bumpiest here (English is rarely spoken), but the fantastic attractions and daily interactions could end up being highlights of your trip.

Nakhon Ratchasima (Khorat)

044 / POP 166,000

Nakhon Ratchasima (นครราชสีมา; often known as Khorat) is a big, busy city with little in the way of sights, but one that for many travellers serves as the gateway to Isan. Khorat (โคราช) is at its best in its quieter nooks, such as inside the eastern side of the historic moat, where local life goes on in a fairly traditional way and you are more likely to run into a metre-long monitor lizard than another traveller.

Sleeping & Eating

Sansabai House HOTEL $

(044 255144; www.sansabai-korat.com; Th Suranaree; d with fan 300B, with air-con 450-1000B;) Long the best budget sleep in Khorat, this clean, quiet and friendly place has spacious rooms with good mattresses, mini-fridges and little balconies. If you can live without air-con, the fan-cooled rooms are particularly good value. It has a small restaurant-cafe (7am to 8pm) out back.

Rom Yen Garden Place HOTEL $$

(044 260116; www.romyenhotel.com; Th Jomsurangyat; d from 990B;) With a very modern, welcoming feel, this stylish hotel is a great addition to Khorat's accommodation roster. The comfy, attractive rooms are good value and there's a pool, a fitness centre and a large deck in front. It's set back off the road, so noise isn't much of an issue. Add 200B per person for the with-breakfast rate.

Wat Boon Night Bazaar MARKET $

(Th Chomphon; 5-9.30pm) This is the largest night market inside the old town. All the usual Thai and Isan dishes are available for takeaway.

★**Daya's Cafe** THAI $$

(256/17 Yommarat Rd; coffee 35-50B, mains 80-300B, burgers 110-300B; 8am-7pm Fri-Wed;) One of a number of funky little cafes on this stretch of Th Yommarat, Daya's is a friendly place that serves good strong coffee, but it's the delicious handmade burgers and exquisitely presented contemporary Thai dishes that really make this place stand out.

Nakhon Ratchasima (Khorat)

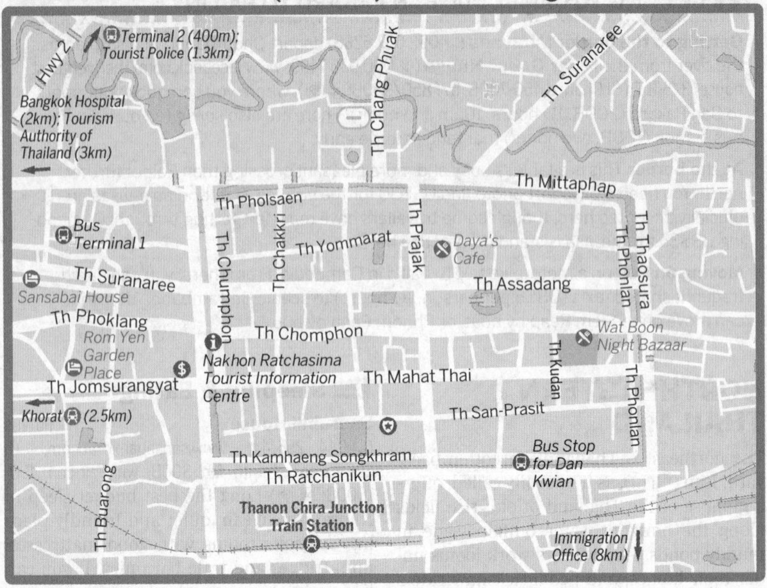

Information

Bangkok Hospital (☎044 429999; www.bangkokhospital.com; Th Mittaphap) has a 24-hour casualty department and many English-speaking doctors. **Bangkok Bank** (Th Jomsurangyat; ⏰10.30am-7pm) in Klang Plaza mall is the only city-centre bank open evenings and weekends.

Tourism Authority of Thailand (TAT; ☎044 213666; tatsima@tat.or.th; 2102-2104 Th Mittaphap; ⏰8.30am-4.30pm) Khorat's branch of TAT is inconveniently located 3km or 4km west of the centre, next to the Sima Thani Hotel. Staff speak very little English.

Getting There & Away

Khorat has two bus terminals. Terminal 1 in the city centre serves Bangkok (191B, 3½ to four hours, frequent) and most towns within the province, including Pak Chong (56B to 72B, 1½ to two hours, frequent 5.30am to 6.30pm) and Pak Thong Chai (21B, one hour, frequent). Minivans to Pak Chong (66B, 1½ hours, frequent 6.30am to 8pm) also leave from this terminal. Buses to most other destinations, plus more Bangkok buses and minivans, use the much larger Terminal 2, north of the centre.

Many trains pass through Khorat train station. Destinations include Bangkok via Ayuthaya (50B to 425B, four to six hours, 10 trains) and Ubon Ratchathani (58B to 453B, five to six hours, 11 trains). Khorat's smaller Thanon Chira Junction train station is closer to the old city, so it may be more convenient to get off there.

Getting Around

There are fixed *sŏrng·tăa·ou* (8B) routes through the city.

Túk-túk cost between 50B and 80B to most places in town. Motorcycle taxis and *săhm·lór* (pedicabs), both of which are common, always cost less.

Around Nakhon Ratchasima

Phimai

The unassuming little town of Phimai (พิมาย) is home to one of Thailand's finest surviving Khmer temple complexes – Prasat Phimai was the architectural inspiration for Cambodia's Angkor Wat, It's an easy day trip out of Nakhon Ratchasima (Khorat), but if you prefer the quiet life, you could always make Khorat a day trip out of Phimai instead.

★**Phimai Historical Park** HISTORIC SITE
(อุทยานประวัติศาสตร์พิมาย; ☎044 471568; Th Ananthajinda; 100B; ⏰7am-6pm, visitors centre 8.30am-4.30pm) Prasat Phimai is one of the most impressive Khmer ruins in Thailand,

both in its grand scale and its intricate details. Though built as a Mahayana Buddhist temple, its carvings feature many Hindu deities, and many design elements – most notably the main shrine's distinctive *prang* tower – were later used at Angkor Wat. There has been a temple at this naturally fortified site since at least the 8th century, though most of the existing buildings were erected in the late 11th century by Khmer King Jayavarman VI.

Phimai National Museum MUSEUM
(พิพิธภัณฑสถานแห่งชาติพิมาย; ☎044 471167; Th Tha Songkran; 100B; ⊙9am-4pm) One of the biggest and best museums in Isan, the Phimai National Museum is well worth a visit. Situated on the banks of Sa Kwan, a 12th-century Khmer reservoir, the museum consists of two spacious buildings housing a fine collection of Khmer sculptures from not just Phimai but also many other ruins from around Isan. Though the focus is on the Khmer era, there are also artefacts from Muang Sema, distinctive trumpet-mouthed and black Phimai pottery from Ban Prasat and Buddha images from various periods.

Getting There & Away

Buses (50B, one hour) and minivans (50B, one hour) to Phimai leave Nakhon Ratchasima's Bus Terminal 2 about every 30 minutes throughout the day.

Khao Yai National Park

Up there on the podium with some of the world's greatest parks, **Khao Yai** (อุทยานแห่งชาติเขาใหญ่; ☎086 092 6529; 400B, car/motorcycle 50/30B; ⊙entrance 6am-6pm) is Thailand's oldest and most visited national park.

BUSES & MINIVANS FROM NAKHON RATCHASIMA (KHORAT) TERMINAL 2

DESTINATION	FARE (B)	DURATION (HR)	FREQUENCY
Aranya Prathet (border with Cambodia)	157	4	5.30am, 9am, noon, 3pm, 4pm
Ayuthaya (minivan)	132	3½-4	6am, 7am, 8am, 5pm, 6pm
Bangkok	148-508	4	frequent
Bangkok (minivan)	171	4	frequent 6.30am-7.30pm
Chiang Mai	526-613	13	7 departures 3am-8.30pm
Khon Kaen	146-220	3½-4	frequent
Khon Kaen (minivan)	126	3-3½	every 40min 6.40am-6.30pm
Krabi	924	16	4.50pm
Loei	252-342	7	hourly 5am-midnight
Lopburi	164	4-4½	6am, 8am, 10.45am, 1.30pm
Lopburi (minivan)	148	3½-4	every 40min 4.50am-6.30pm
Nang Rong	119	2	half-hourly 4.50am-8.10pm
Nang Rong (minivan)	64	2	every 30min 4.30am-8.10pm
Nong Khai	257-409	6	11 departures, mostly in the afternoon
Mukdahan	297	7-8	6.15am, 8.30am, 12.30pm, 2.30pm, 6.30pm
Phimai	50	1	every 30min 5am-10pm
Phimai (minivan)	50	1	hourly 10am-5.30pm
Surin	115-218	4	every 30min
Trat	324	8-9	1am, 3am, 8.30am, 10.30am, 11.45am, 9pm
Ubon Ratchathani	248-386	7-8	hourly
Udon Thani	178-300	5½	frequent
Vientiane (must have Lao visa)	900	6	noon

Covering 2168 sq km, Khao Yai incorporates one of the largest intact monsoon forests remaining in mainland Asia, which is why it was named a Unesco World Heritage site (as part of the Dong Phayayen–Khao Yai Forest Complex). But despite its size, it's one of the easiest national parks in Thailand for independent travellers to visit.

Activities

There are five hiking trails through the forest that visitors can walk on their own. All other forest hiking requires a guide. Park rangers can be hired as guides (500B to 1000B per group depending on the time) through the visitors centre. They can also lead you on longer off-trail treks, but only if they speak English or you speak Thai, so deep forest exploration is best done with a private guide arranged through local tour companies or hotels.

No matter where you hike, you should wear boots and long trousers. During the rainy season leeches are a problem. Mosquito repellent helps keep them away, but the leech socks sold in the visitors centre work much better.

Both the size and variety of habitats make Khao Yai one of the best wildlife-watching spots in Thailand. Around 200 elephants tramp the park's boundaries. Other mammals include tigers, leopards, bears, gaur, barking deer, otters, various gibbons and macaques and some rather large pythons. Khao Yai's bird list boasts 392 species, and one of Thailand's largest populations of hornbills lives here, including the great hornbill (*nók gòk* or *nók gah·hang*).

Sleeping & Eating

There are dozens of places to stay on and near Th Thanarat and in the gateway town of Pak Chong. Within the park, there are campsites and a variety of rooms and bungalows. You must book accommodation inside the park via the national-park website (http://nps.dnp.go.th/reservation.php) or in person at the park.

The park has restaurants at all busy locations, including the visitors centre, campgrounds and some waterfalls. Outside the park there are many restaurants along Th Thanarat.

At Home Hostel HOSTEL $

(☎081 490 6601; Pak Chong; dm 280-300B, d 600-750B; ❄📶) This friendly hostel is run by helpful staff who speak excellent English, and is the best of a handful of hostels in Pak Chong. It rents motorbikes (per day 300B), but it's a rather long slog to the park from here. The hostel is down the lane diagonally opposite the 7-Eleven near from where the *sŏrng·tăa·ou* leave to get to the park.

San Khao Yai Guesthouse BUNGALOW $$

(☎086 245 7882; www.sankhaoyaitour.com; Th Thanarat; bungalows 800B; ❄📶) These colourful cottages just 100m from the park entrance are basic but very clean and a step up from most other budget lodging in the area. There's no better place to be if you want to stay outside the park but get an early start on your wildlife-watching. It also rents out motorcycles (per day 500B; deposit 20,000B or passport), arranges tours and serves food and beer.

★**Hotel des Artists** HOTEL $$$

(☎044 297444; hoteldesartists@gmail.com; Km 22, Th Thanarat; d incl breakfast from 2800B; ❄@📶🏊) This tasteful hotel goes for French-colonial chic rather than the typical nature theme, though with its mountain views out the back you won't forget where you are. The rooms are gorgeous, though small, and open out beside an unusual, slimline swimming pool.

Getting There & Away

Sŏrng·tăa·ou travel the 30km from Pak Chong down Th Thanarat to the park's northern gate (40B, one hour) every 30 minutes from 6am to 5pm. It's another 14km to the visitors centre, but park guards are used to talking drivers into hauling people up there if there's a big group. The last *sŏrng·tăa·ou* from the park gate back to Pak Chong departs around 3pm.

Buses and minivans from Pak Chong depart from the centre of town along the main road. Frequent minivans (66B, 1½ hours) and occasional 2nd-class buses (56B, two hours) to Khorat use a bus stop about 500m northeast of the deer statue between 5am and 6pm. Minivans to Bangkok (160B, three hours, every 30 minutes) depart from both sides of the road near the deer statue. First-class buses to both Bangkok (133B, three hours) and Khorat (72B, 1½ hours) stop at Ratchasima Tour across the highway from the deer statue.

You can also get to Pak Chong easily by train from Bangkok (86B to 292B, four to 4½ hours, every two hours) and Khorat (18B to 251B, 1½ hours, every two hours).

Phanom Rung Historical Park

The most spectacular Khmer monument in Thailand, Prasat Phanom Rung or 'Big Mountain Temple' sits on the summit of a spent volcano 200m above the paddy fields. About 8km down below is the wonderful but often overlooked Prasat Muang Tam or 'Lower City Temple'.

★**Prasat Phanom Rung** RUINS

(ปราสาทเขาพนมรุ้ง; ☎044 666251; 100B, combined ticket with Prasat Muang Tam 150B; ⏲6am-6pm) Prasat Phanom Rung has a knock-you-dead location. Crowning the summit of a spent volcano, this sanctuary sits 200m above the paddy fields below. To the southeast you can see Cambodia's Dongrek Mountains, and it's in this direction that the capital of the Angkor empire once lay. The temple was erected as a Hindu monument to Shiva between the 10th and 13th centuries, the bulk of it during the reign of King Suriyavarman II (r CE 1113–50).

Prasat Muang Tam RUINS

(ปราสาทเมืองต่ำ; ☎044 666251; 100B, combined ticket with Prasat Phanom Rung 150B; ⏲6am-6pm) In the little village of Khok Meuang, the restored Khmer temple of Prasat Muang Tam is an ideal bolt-on to any visit to Phanom Rung, which is only 8km to the northwest. Dating back to the late 10th or early 11th century, this is generally considered Isan's third most interesting temple complex in terms of size, atmosphere and the quality of restoration work, but because so few people visit it is some people's favourite.

★**Baan Bong Pha Om** GUESTHOUSE $

(☎084 236 5060, 095 620 5932; Ban Ta Pek; d incl breakfast 490-1000B; ❄📶) Bringing artistic flair and fantastic value to the rice fields of rural Buriram, this family-run place is fun, attractive and utterly relaxing. Many of the 14 creative rooms are up on stilts, with balconies and open-air showers. Some are in converted shipping containers, while the best – the House rooms (690B) and the Big Room (1000B) – are borderline luxurious and worth the extra baht.

ℹ Getting There & Away

There's no public transport to Phanom Rung or Muang Tam. The best budget option is hiring a motorcycle (per day 250B) from Baan Bong Pha Om (p453). Motorcycle taxis charge 600B return from Nang Rong. A car with driver will cost 1000B. It costs 100/200B for the motorcycle/car to add Muang Tam.

ℹ GETTING TO CAMBODIA

Chong Sa-Ngam to Choam

Getting to the border This border crossing in Si Saket Province sees very little traffic, despite the road to Siem Reap being in excellent shape, because the route isn't serviced by public transport. Lots of private minivans shuttle gamblers from Si Saket and Ubon Ratchathani cities, so you could check with a travel agent about joining one.

At the border The border is open 7am to 8pm and there's the usual 5B overtime fee outside business hours and on weekends. Cambodian visas are available on arrival.

Moving on Private vehicles (called 'taxis') park right at the border and charge 3000B for the drive to Siem Reap. You can try to join others for the trip, but it can be a long wait.

Chong Chom to O Smach

Getting to the border Because of the casino, there are plenty of public mini-buses (45B, 1½ hours, frequent from 5.30am to 6.30pm) from Surin's bus terminal to the border at Chong Chom.

At the border The Cambodian border is open from 7am to 10pm and visas are available on the spot. There's a 5B fee at Thai immigration on weekends and early mornings/late afternoons.

Moving on There are two buses from O Smach to the City Angkor Hotel in Siem Reap (350B, three hours, 8am and 5pm). Chartering a 'taxi' (drivers wait at the border looking for passengers) for the drive to Siem Reap should cost 2000B or less, and you can wait for others to share the costs, though this is generally only possible in the morning.

Alternatively, you can take a bus from Nang Rong (or any Khorat–Surin bus) to the busy Ban Tako (20B to 30B, 20 minutes, every 30 minutes) junction 14km east of Nang Rong, where motorcycle taxis usually charge 300B to Phanom Rung, including waiting time.

Ubon Ratchathani

045 / POP 86,800

Few cities in Isan reward aimless wandering as richly as Ubon Ratchathani (อุบลราชธานี). Racked up against Mae Nam Mun, Thailand's second-longest river, there are many interesting temples beckoning culture-loving travellers.

Ubon is a financial, educational and agricultural centre. It's not a busy tourist destination, but the nearby Thai–Lao border crossing at Chong Mek generates a small but steady stream of travellers.

Sights

Ubon Ratchathani National Museum MUSEUM

(พิพิธภัณฑสถานแห่งชาติอุบลราชธานี; Th Kheuan Thani; 100B; 9am-4pm Wed-Sun) Occupying the former city hall (built in 1918), this is a very informative museum with plenty on show, from Dvaravati-era Buddhas and 2000-year-old Dong Son bronze drums to Ubon textiles and clever little animal traps. The museum's most prized possession is a 9th-century Khmer Ardhanarisvara, a composite statue combining Shiva and his consort Uma into one being. It's one of just two ever found in Thailand.

Sleeping & Eating

28 Rachabutr Hostel HOSTEL $

(089 144 3789; 28 Th Ratchabut; dm 180-230B, r with fan 280-380B, with air-con 430B;) Friendly and welcoming, with a great location, this home-turned-hostel, run by a charming elderly woman, is very backpacker-friendly. Rooms are simple (the dorms have just thin mattresses on the floor), and it's shared bathrooms only, but the whole place has character, with bric-a-brac furniture and creaky wooden floorboards. Some rooms have partial river views. Also rents motorbikes (200B).

★**Outside Inn** GUESTHOUSE $$

(088 581 2069; www.theoutsideinnubon.com; 11 Th Suriyat; d incl breakfast 650-799B;) A nice little garden lounge area sets the relaxed, communal vibe here. The rooms are large, comfy and fitted with tastefully designed reclaimed-timber furnishings. Owners Brent and Tun are great hosts, cook some good **food** (mains 50-225B; 11am-2.30pm & 5-9pm;), and have lots of advice on what to see and do in the area.

It's a long walk to the town's main attractions, but there are bikes (free for guests) and motorcycles (per day 250B), and *sŏrng·tăa·ou* 10 can deliver you from the bus station.

★**Rung Roj** THAI $

(Th Nakhonban; mains 60-140B; 10am-8.30pm Mon-Sat) An Ubon institution serving excellent food, using family recipes and only fresh ingredients. From the outside it looks more like a well-to-do house than a restau-

GETTING TO LAOS: UBON RATCHATHANI TO PAKSE

Getting to the border Almost every traveller uses the direct Ubon Ratchathani–Pakse buses (200B, three hours, 9.30am and 2.30pm), which wait long enough for you to buy Lao visas at the border. Otherwise, Chong Mek's little bus terminal serves minivans to/from Ubon Ratchathani (120B, two hours, every 30 minutes) via Khong Jiam and Phibun Mangsahan, and buses for Bangkok (484B to 638B, 12 hours, five daily). It's 600m from the bus station to the border; motorcycle taxis charge 20B.

At the border The border is open from 6am to 8pm and the crossing, involving walking though an underground tunnel, is largely hassle-free. Although it seems like a scam, there is a legitimate overtime fee on the Laos side after 4pm weekdays and all day on weekends and holidays. The real scam is that the officials ask for 100B even though the actual price is 10,000 Lao kip (about 40B). Just tell them you want a receipt and you'll pay the correct price. They sometimes ask for this at other times, but they're usually not too insistent.

Moving on Pakse is about an hour away in one of the frequent minivans (20,000K, 45 minutes) or *sŏrng·tăa·ou* that park in a dusty/muddy parking area about 500m from the Lao immigration office.

Ubon Ratchathani

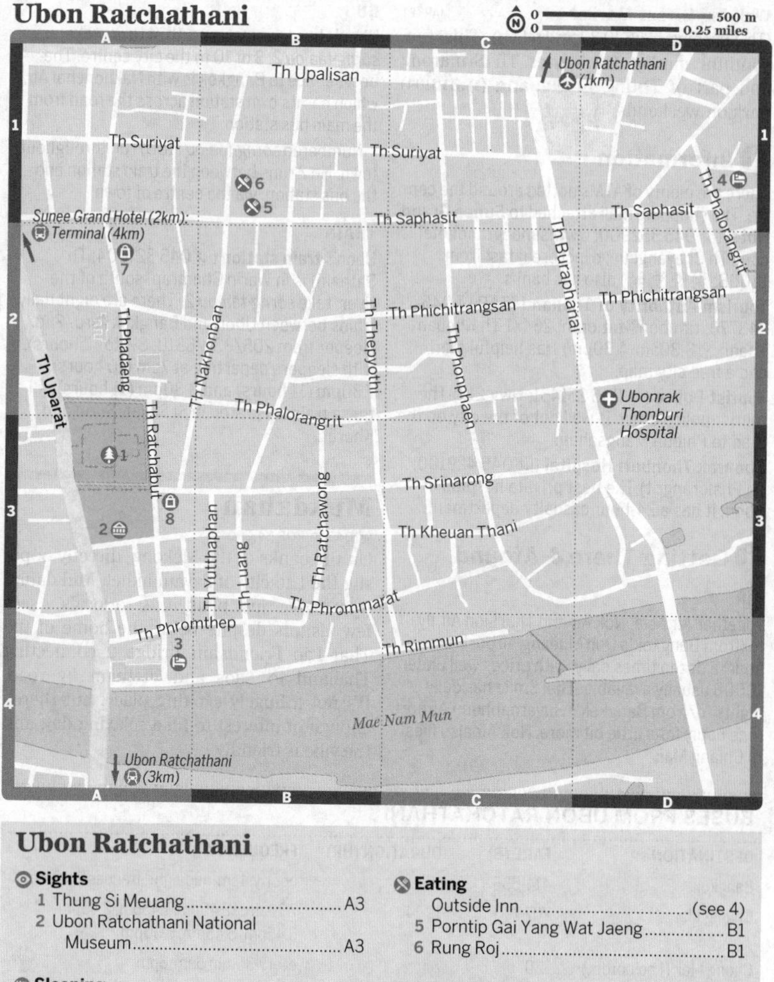

Ubon Ratchathani

Sights
1 Thung Si Meuang.......A3
2 Ubon Ratchathani National Museum.......A3

Sleeping
3 28 Rachabutr Hostel.......A4
4 Outside Inn.......D1

Eating
Outside Inn.......(see 4)
5 Porntip Gai Yang Wat Jaeng.......B1
6 Rung Roj.......B1

Shopping
7 Punchard.......A2
8 Walking Street Market.......A3

rant, and inside it has 1950s and '60s classic rock-and-roll music and decor to match.

Porntip Gai Yang Wat Jaeng THAI $
(Th Saphasit; mains 40-130B; 8am-6pm) It looks like a tornado has whipped through this no-frills spot, but the chefs cook up a storm of their own. This is considered by many to be Ubon's premier purveyor of *gài yâhng* (grilled chicken), *sôm·đam* (spicy green-papaya salad), sausages and other classic Isan foods. Eat in the fan-cooled shack out front, or with air-con out back.

Shopping

Isan may be silk country, but Ubon is a cotton town and there are several good shops selling handwoven fabric, clothing, bags etc, many of them coloured with natural dyes.

Punchard ARTS & CRAFTS
(089 719 9570; www.punchard.net; Th Phadaeng; 9am-6.30pm Thu-Tue) Though pricey, this is the best all-round handicrafts shop in Ubon. It specialises in silks and homewares; many of its products merge old methods and modern designs.

Walking Street Market MARKET
(Th Srinarong; ⌚6-10.30pm Fri-Sun) This fun, youthful market takes over Th Srinarong and part of **Thung Si Meuang** (ทุ่งศรีเมือง) park on weekends.

Information

There are plenty of ATMs dotted around the centre. The shopping mall attached to **Sunee Grand Hotel** (☎045 352900; www.suneegrandhotel.com; Th Chayangkun; d incl breakfast from 1800B; ❄@📶🏊) also has banks.

Tourism Authority of Thailand (TAT; ☎045 243770; tatubon@tat.or.th; 264/1 Th Kheuan Thani; ⌚8.30am-4.30pm) Has helpful staff and a free city map.

Tourist Police (☎045 251451; Hwy 217) The tourist-police office is well out of the city on the road to Phibun Mangsahan.

Ubonrak Thonburi Hospital (☎045 429100; Th Phalorangrit) The best private hospital in Ubon, it has a 24-hour casualty department.

Getting There & Around

AIR

Together Air Asia, Nok Air and Thai Lion Air fly to/from Bangkok's Don Mueang Airport (one hour) a dozen times daily, with prices well under 1000B usually available. Thai Smile has daily flights to/from Bangkok's Suvarnabhumi Airport (one hour) for a little bit more. Nok Air also flies to Chiang Mai.

BUS

Ubon's bus terminal is north of town; take *sŏrng·tăa·ou* 2, 3 or 10 to the city centre. The best service to Bangkok is with Nakhonchai Air, which has its own station across the road from the main bus station.

Numbered *sŏrng·tăa·ou* (10B) run throughout town. No 2 runs between the train station and the bus station, via the centre of town.

TRAIN

Ubon's **train station** (☎045 321004; Th Sathani) is in Warin Chamrap, south of the river; take *sŏrng·tăa·ou* 2. There are eight daily trains between Ubon and Bangkok (3rd/2nd/sleeper from 205/331/631B, 8½ to 12 hours), with sleepers departing at 7pm (10 hours), 7.30pm (11 hours) and 8.30pm (11 hours). All these trains also stop in Si Saket, Surin and Khorat.

Mukdahan

☎042 / POP 34,290

On the banks of the Mekong, directly opposite the Lao city of Savannakhet, Mukdahan (มุกดาหาร) – just plain *múk* to locals – sees few visitors despite being the home of the Thai–Lao Friendship Bridge 2 connecting Thailand to Laos and Vietnam by road. It's not a hugely exciting place, but there's enough of interest to fill a relaxing day, and the vibe is friendly.

BUSES FROM UBON RATCHATHANI

DESTINATION	FARE (B)	DURATION (HR)	FREQUENCY
Bangkok	414-556	10	hourly 4am-midnight, frequent 4-8pm
Chiang Mai	707-790	12-14	7.30am, 12.45pm, 1.45pm, 2.45pm, 3.45pm, 5.45pm, 6.30pm
Chong Mek (Lao border)	120	2	every 30min 5am-6pm
Khon Kaen	176-244	4½-5	every 30min 5.30am-5.40pm
Khong Jiam	40	1½	every 30min 5am-6pm
Mukdahan	130	2½	5.45am, 7.30am, 8.40am, 11.30am, 1pm
Mukdahan (minivan)	111	2½	every 30min 6am-5.30pm
Nakhon Ratchasima (Khorat)	248-386	7-8	hourly 5am-8pm
Nang Rong	144-265	5-6	hourly 5am-8pm
Pakse (Laos)	200	3	9.30am & 2.30pm
Rayong	515-801	13	7am, 7.15am, 5pm, 6pm, 7.30pm, 7.45pm, 8pm, 8.15pm
Surin	130-202	3½	hourly 5am-8pm
Udon Thani	284-332	7	every 30min 5.30am-5.40pm
Yasothon	66-99	2	hourly 5.30am-5.30pm
Yasothon (minivan)	80	2	hourly 5.30am-5.30pm

Sights

Hor Kaew Mukdahan MUSEUM

(หอแก้วมุกดาหาร; Th Samut Sakdarak; 50B; ⊙8am-6pm) This eye-catching 65m-tall tower was built for the 50th anniversary of King Rama IX's ascension to the throne. The nine-sided base has a good museum with displays (labelled in English) on the eight ethnic groups of the province. There are great views and a few more historical displays in 'The 360° of Pleasure in Mukdahan by the Mekong' room, up at the 50m level. The ball on the top holds a locally revered Buddha image believed to be made of solid silver.

Indochina Market MARKET

(ตลาดอินโดจีน, Talat Indojin; Th Samran Chaikhongtai; ⊙8am-5pm) Among Thais, Mukdahan is most famous for this riverside market, which stretches along and under the promenade. Most Thai tour groups on their way to Laos and Vietnam make a shopping stop for cheap food, clothing and assorted trinkets – much of it from China and Vietnam – plus silk and cotton fabrics made in Isan. A massive renovation project, with little sign of completion, has meant the market has had to trade from temporary street-side stalls for more than two years.

Sleeping & Eating

Ban Rim Suan HOTEL $

(☎042 632980; www.banrimsuan.weebly.com; Th Samut Sakdarak; d old/new wing 350/450B; ❄📶) This place offers a good budget deal whether you take the plain older rooms or the better newer ones, which is why it's often full. It's a tad south of the centre, but that makes it convenient for dinner and drinks along the river. No English spoken.

Riverfront Hotel HOTEL $$

(☎042 633348; www.riverfrontmukdahan.com; Th Samran Chaikhongtai; d & tw incl breakfast from 850B, with river view from 1250B; ❄@📶) Managed by a charming elderly woman who speaks good English, this place near the market is tastefully decorated, with plenty of timber finishings and furnishings and cool-tile flooring. Most of the cheapest rooms have partial river views from small balconies, but other rooms really make the most of the riverfront location.

★**Bao Pradit** THAI $

(Th Samran Chaikhongtai; mains 30-300B; ⊙11am-10pm; 📶) It's a bit of a trek south of the centre, but this is a real Isan restaurant with dishes such as *gôry kài mót daang* (raw meat 'salad' with red-ant eggs) and *gang wăi* (rattan curry). Though the English menu is mysterious (Bao Pradit doesn't really serve python), it's rare that a restaurant of this sort has any English.

Mukdahan Night Market MARKET $

(Th Song Nang Sathit; ⊙4-9pm) Mukdahan's night market is the most buzzing place in town for evening food. It has all the Thai and Isan classics, but it's the Vietnamese vendors that set it apart. A few sell *băhn dah* (they'll tell you it's 'Vietnamese pizza'), which combines soft noodles, pork, spring onions and an optional egg served on a crispy cracker.

GETTING TO LAOS: MUKDAHAN TO SAVANNAKHET

Getting to the border Thai and Lao citizens can use the boats that cross the Mekong from Mukdahan's city centre, while everyone else must use the bridge. The easiest way to cross is with the direct buses to Savannakhet (45B to 50B, hourly 7.30am to 7pm) from Mukdahan's bus station. There's a 5B fee during weekends, holidays and non-business hours.

At the border The border is open from 6am to 10pm. The crossing to Savannakhet can take from one to two hours, depending on the length of the immigration queues. There's time enough at the border to get a Lao visa.

Moving on From Savannakhet there are buses to various points in Laos, as well as Vietnam.

Getting There & Around

Mukdahan does not have an airport, but Air Asia and Nok Air have daily fly-and-ride services using both Nakhon Phanom and Ubon Ratchathani airports.

Mukdahan's bus terminal is on Rte 212, 2km west of town. Yellow *sŏrng·tăa·ou* (10B, 6.30am to 5pm) run to the station from the centre of town. Túk-túk from the bus station cost 50B to the city centre.

Minivan destinations include Khon Kaen, Nakhon Phanom, That Phanom, Ubon Ratchathani and Udon Thani. Most buses to Bangkok (477B to 778B, 10 to 11 hours) depart between 5pm and 8pm.

Nakhon Phanom

042 / POP 22,710

Nakhon Phanom (นครพนม) means 'City of Mountains', but the undulating sugarloaf peaks all lie across the river in Laos, so you'll be admiring rather than climbing them. The views are fantastic, though, especially during a hazy sunrise.

Sights

Ho Chi Minh House MUSEUM
(บ้านโฮจิมินห์; 042 522430; Ban Na Chok; donations appreciated; daylight hours) FREE The best of the three Ho Chi Minh–related attractions in **Ban Na Chok village**, this is a replica of the simple wooden house where 'Uncle Ho' sometimes stayed in 1928 and 1929 while planning his resistance movement in Vietnam. A few of the furnishings are believed to be originals. It's a private affair located within a lush, flower- and fruit-tree-filled garden in the back of a family home, and they're very proud of it.

Former Governor's Residence Museum MUSEUM
(จวนผู้ว่าราชการจังหวัดนครพนม (หลังเก่า); Th Sunthon Wijit; adult/child 50/20B; 9am-5pm Wed-Sun) Museum Juan, as it's also known, is on the riverfront and fills a beautiful restored 1925 mansion with photos of old Nakhon Phanom, many labelled in English. Out the back are detailed displays on the illuminated boat procession **Lai Reua Fai** (late Oct/early Nov), and cooking utensils in the old kitchen. Bai-Tong, the gift shop's owner and artist, speaks excellent English and is a great source of local advice.

GETTING TO LAOS: NAKHON PHANOM TO THA KHAEK

Getting to the border Passenger ferries cross the Mekong to Tha Khaek in Laos, but they're for Thai and Lao travellers only. All other travellers must use the Third Thai–Lao Friendship Bridge, north of the city. The easiest way to cross is to take the bus directly to Tha Khaek from Nakhon Phanom's bus station (70/75B weekdays/weekends, eight departures from 8am to 5pm).

At the border The Thai border is open from 6am to 10pm. All immigration formalities, including getting Lao visas, are handled at the bridge. Things get pretty chaotic when droves of Vietnamese workers are passing through.

Moving on The bus tends to wait a long time at the bridge, so total travel time to Tha Khaek can be more than two hours.

Sleeping & Eating

Landmark Nakhon Phanom Hotel HOTEL $$
(042 530890; Th Nittayo; d & tw incl breakfast 950-1250B, ste 2800B;) Brand new in 2019, this stylish little hotel has a great location (reflected in the prices) and elegant, well-furnished rooms. The back rooms (950B) have no natural light, though, so upgrade to one of the front rooms with a balcony (1250B) or, if you can afford it, one of the fabulous river-view suites.

777 Hometel HOTEL $$
(Tong Jed Hometel; 042 514777; Th Tamrongprasit; d incl breakfast 600-800B;) Don't let the boxy exterior put you off – inside are some fairly stylish rooms. It's well managed, priced right and has some of the friendliest staff in town. Bike rental available too.

Aunt Kaew's Noodles NOODLES $
(ก๋วยเตี๋ยวป้าแก้ว; Th Ratsadonutis; noodles 50B; 8am-3pm Mon-Sat) The auntie who rules this simple, open-fronted noodle house – wildly popular with the locals – knocks up delicious bowls of glass noodles mixed with thick slices of beef and crunchy bean sprouts. There's a complimentary cup of iced tea and a warm welcome.

Night Market THAI $
(Th Fuang Nakhon; 4-10pm) Nakhon Phanom's night market is large and diverse (Thai, Isan, Vietnamese, international) but has few places to sit.

Getting There & Around

Nakhon Phanom's airport is located 20km west of town. Air Asia and Nok Air fly several times daily to/from Bangkok's Don Mueang Airport. A taxi from the airport into town costs 150B to 200B.

Nakhon Phanom's bus terminal is a short walk west of the town centre. From here buses head to Nong Khai (200B, seven to eight hours, 11am), Udon Thani (147B to 200B, four hours, every 45 minutes from 7.15am to 5pm), Khon Kaen (212B, five hours, 13 daily from 5.50am to 9.30pm) and Ubon Ratchathani (155B to 200B, 4½ hours, 7am, 8.30am and 2pm).

Most people use minivans for Ubon Ratchathani (182B, four hours, hourly from 5.45am to 4pm) and Mukdahan (80B, 2½ hours, frequent from 5.30am to 6pm), all of which stop in That Phanom (40B, one hour). There are frequent buses to Bangkok (554B to 862B, 11 to 12 hours) between 4.30pm and 7.30pm, plus two in the morning (7.30am and 7.45am), and three to Chiang Mai (737B, 14 to 15 hours, 9am, 3pm and 5pm).

Sŏrng·tăa·ou to That Phanom (50B, 1½ hours, frequent 7am to 5pm) park next to Kasikornbank in the town centre.

Nong Khai

☎042 / POP 47,600

Sitting on the banks of the Mekong, just across from Vientiane in Laos, Nong Khai (หนองคาย) has been a hit with travellers for years. Its popularity is about more than just its proximity to Vientiane and its bounty of banana pancakes, though. Seduced by its dreamy pink sunsets and sluggish pace of life, many visitors who mean to stay one night end up bedding down for many more.

Sights

★Sala Kaew Ku SCULPTURE

(ศาลาแก้วกู่, Wat Khaek; 40B; 7am-6pm) One of Thailand's most enigmatic attractions, Sala Kaew Ku can't fail to impress. Built over 20 years by Luang Pu Boun Leua Sourirat, a mystic who died in 1996, the park features a wonderful smorgasbord of bizarre cement statues of Buddha, Shiva, Vishnu and other deities. The main shrine building is packed with hundreds of smaller sculptures of various description and provenance, photos of Luang Pu at various stages throughout his life, and his corpse under a glass dome ringed by flashing lights.

Wat Pho Chai BUDDHIST TEMPLE

(วัดโพธิ์ชัย; Th Phochai; daylight hours, ubosot 6am-6.30pm) FREE Luang Po Phra Sai, a large Lan Xang–era Buddha image awash with gold, bronze and precious stones, sits at the hub of Nong Khai's holiest temple. The head of the image is pure gold, the body is bronze and the *ùt·sà·nít* (flame-shaped head ornament) is set with rubies. Due to the great number of miracles attributed to it, this royal temple is a mandatory stop for most visiting Thais.

Tha Sadet Market MARKET

(ตลาดท่าเสด็จ; Th Rimkhong; 8.30am-6pm) This is the most popular destination in town. Almost everyone loves a stroll through this covered market despite it being a giant tourist trap. It offers the usual mix of clothes, electronic equipment, food and assorted bric-a-brac, most of it imported from Laos and China, but there are also a few shops selling quirky and quality stuff.

Sleeping & Eating

Catering to the steady flow of backpackers, Nong Khai's budget lodging selection is the best in Isan, and there are many good midrangers too.

★Mut Mee Garden Guesthouse GUESTHOUSE $

(☎042 460717; www.mutmee.com; Soi Mutmee; d 220-1200B;) Nong Khai's budget classic has a riverfront garden so relaxing it's intoxicating, and most nights it's packed with travellers. Mut Mee caters to many budgets, with a huge variety of rooms (the cheapest with shared bathroom, the most expensive with an awesome balcony) clustered around the thatched-roof garden lounge, where owner Julian freely shares his wealth of knowledge about the area.

E-San Guesthouse GUESTHOUSE $

(☎086 242 1860; 538 Soi Srikhunmuang; d with fan & shared bathroom 300B, with air-con 500B;) Just off the river in a small, beautifully restored wooden house ringed by a long veranda, this is an atmospheric place for backpackers to stay. The air-con rooms in a new building are fine, though they lack the character of the original house. Bikes are free. There are two other wooden guesthouses on the same street.

Mae Ut VIETNAMESE $

(637 Th Meechai; mains 50-100B; 9.30am-4pm) This little place, serving just four items, including fried spring rolls, *khâo gee·ab bahk mŏr* (fresh noodles with pork), and a Vietnamese take on a pancake-pizza, is essentially grandma's kitchen, and it's fascinating to watch the food being made to order on large banana leaves. No English sign, and English is limited, but the welcome is friendly.

Dee Dee Pohchanah THAI $

(1155/9 Th Prajak; mains 50-150B; 11am-1am;) How good is Dee Dee? Just look at the dinner-time crowds. But don't be put off by them: despite having a full house every night, this open-air place is a well-oiled machine and you won't be waiting long.

Central Nong Khai

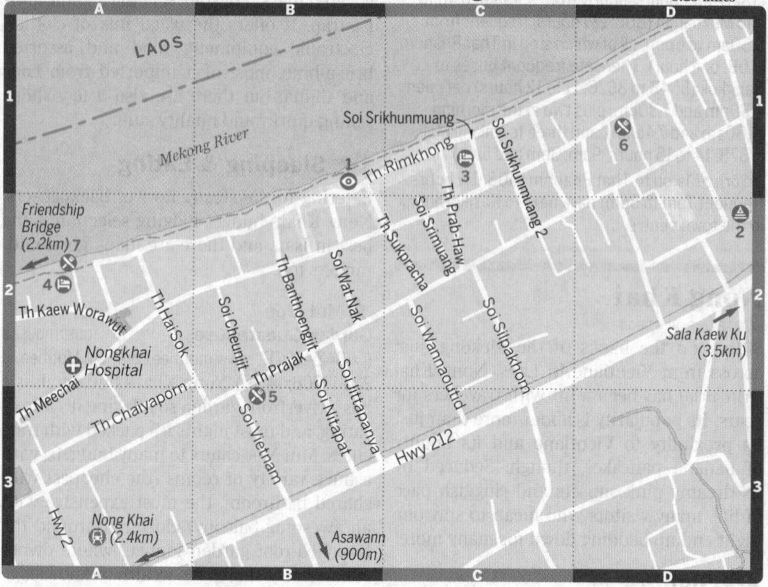

Central Nong Khai

Sights
1 Tha Sadet Market B1
2 Wat Pho Chai D2

Sleeping
3 E-San Guesthouse C1
4 Mut Mee Garden Guesthouse A2

Eating
5 Dee Dee Pohchanah B3
6 Mae Ut D1
7 Nagarina A2

Nagarina THAI $$
(☎081 975 0516; Th Rimkhong; mains 50-480B; ⏰10am-9pm) Docked down below Mut Mee Garden Guesthouse (p459), this floating restaurant specialises in Thai and Isan fish dishes, and though the prices are a bit high, the quality is good. There's a one-hour sunset cruise most nights (80B; at least 10 guests needed before the cruise will go ahead) around 5pm or 5.30pm; order food at least 30 minutes before departure.

Information

There are banks with extended opening hours at Asawann shopping centre.

Immigration (☎042 990935; Hwy 2; ⏰8.30am-noon & 1-4.30pm Mon-Fri) One kilometre south of the Friendship Bridge. Offers Thai visa extensions.

Nongkhai Hospital (☎042 413456; Th Meechai; ⏰24hr) Has a 24-hour casualty department.

Getting There & Away

AIR

The nearest airport is 55km south in Udon Thani. **Udon Kaew Tour** travel agency runs minivans (200B per person) to/from the airport. Coming into town it will drop you at your hotel or the bridge; going back you need to get yourself to its office. It's best to buy tickets in advance.

BUS

Nong Khai bus terminal is located just off Th Prajak, about 1.5km from the main pack of riverside guesthouses.

Destinations include the following:

Bangkok (329B to 714B, 10 to 11 hours, frequent departures)

Bangkok Suvarnabhumi International Airport (464B, 10 hours, daily)

Bueng Kan (van; 150B, 2½ hours, frequent departures)

Chiang Mai (750B to 820B, 12 hours, daily)

Kanchanaburi (495B, 12 hours, daily)

Khon Kaen (120B to 155B, 3½ to four hours, hourly 7am to 6pm)

Loei (140B, seven to eight hours, daily)

Nakhon Phanom (200B, seven to eight hours, daily)

Nakhon Ratchasima (257B to 409B, six hours, hourly 6am to 8.45pm)

Sangkhom (60B, 2½ hours, twice daily)

Udon Thani (van; 50B, one hour, frequent departures)

TRAIN

For Bangkok, one daytime express train (2nd-/3rd-class seat 498/253B, 9½ hours, 7.45am) and three evening express trains (10 hours, 11 hours and 11½ hours respectively, 6.30pm, 6.50pm and 7.40pm) leave from Nong Khai train station, which is 2km west of the city centre. Only the latest of the evening trains has sleeper accommodation (1st-/2nd-class sleeper from 1357/898B).

Getting Around

Nong Khai is a great place for cycling due to the limited traffic and the nearby countryside. Many guesthouses let you use their bikes for free. If you need to hire one, **Khun Noui**, who sets up on the roadside across from the entrance to Mut Mee, has reliable bikes (50B per day) and motorcycles (200B).

You can find metered taxis at the bus station and the bridge. Generally, people agree on a price rather than use the meter. A túk-túk between the Mut Mee area and the bus station or the bridge will cost about 60B and 100B respectively for two people.

Chiang Khan

What was once a sleepy, little-known Mekong-side town full of traditional timber shophouses became a trendy destination for Thais and is now full of cute cafes, gift shops and places for taking selfies. That said, Chiang Khan (เชียงคาน) is far from spoiled and is still a charming place to visit. The photogenic views of the river and the Lao mountains beyond are still there, as are the old buildings, and things remain peaceful in the daytime before the evening shopping stampede begins. Every evening Th Chai Khong turns into a busy Walking Street market with buskers, artists and street-food vendors. Chiang Khan is less busy in the hot and rainy seasons (April to September).

Garage BOUTIQUE HOTEL **$**
(☎081 565 4330; Th Srichiang Khan; s/d/tr/q 500/600/700/800B; ❄📶) A quirky guesthouse for the hipster tourist, this funky little place has a gritty, urban-warehouse vibe, a car-garage theme and five individualised rooms, including one with a double bed inside a converted VW camper van! Owner Jo speaks English, and runs a home-brew bar around the corner.

Old Chiangkhan Boutique Hotel BOUTIQUE HOTEL **$$$**
(☎088 340 3999; Soi 20, Th Chai Khong; d incl breakfast 1600-1800B; ❄📶) This stately old Thai-style home, built in 1852, has been

GETTING TO LAOS: NONG KHAI TO VIENTIANE

Getting to the border If you already have your Lao visa, the easiest way to Vientiane is the direct bus from Nong Khai's bus terminal (55B, 1½ hours, six daily 7.30am to 6pm). There's also a bus to Vang Vieng (270B, six hours, 9.40am). There's a 5B surcharge for tickets to Laos on weekends, holidays and the 7.30am and 6pm weekday services.

If you plan to get your visa at the border (6am to 10pm), take a túk-túk there – expect to pay 100B from the bus station or 60B from the town centre. Unless you're travelling in a large group, there's no good reason to use a visa service agency, so don't let a driver take you to one.

You can also go to Laos by train (there are immigration booths at both stations), though it doesn't go through to Vientiane, so this is not recommended. The 15-minute ride (20B to 30B, 7.30am and 2.45pm) drops you in Thanaleng (aka Dongphasay) station just over the bridge, leaving you at the mercy of túk-túk drivers who charge extortionate prices.

At the border After getting stamped out of Thailand, you can take the buses (15B to 20B) that carry passengers across the bridge to the hassle-free, but sometimes busy, Lao immigration checkpoint, where 30-day visas are available.

Moving on It's about 20km to Vientiane. Plenty of buses, túk-túk and taxis will be waiting for you, and it's easy to find fellow travellers to share the costs.

OFF THE BEATEN TRACK

BUENG KAN

Most travellers pass through little Bueng Kan (บึงกาฬ) on their way to wonderful Wat Phu Thok. You can also cross the Mekong to Laos from here.

Sights

Wat Phu Thok (วัดภูทอก; ⊙6am-5pm, closed 10-16 Apr) With its network of rickety staircases and walkways built in, on and around a giant sandstone outcrop, Wat Phu Thok is one of the region's wonders. The precarious paths lead past shrines and *gù·đì* (monk's huts) that are scattered around the mountain on cliffs and in caves and provide fabulous views over the surrounding countryside. A final scramble up roots and rocks takes you to the forest on the summit, which is considered the 7th level.

Phu Wua Wildlife Sanctuary (เขตรักษาพันธุ์สัตว์ป่าภูวัว; ☎081 260 1845; 100B) One of the most important wildlife reserves in Isan, Phu Wua is home to more than 40 elephants. It's a ruggedly beautiful area with lots of exposed bedrock and several large waterfalls. If you have your own vehicle you can visit the waterfalls independently, and trekking trips inside the park can be arranged through **Bunloed's Huts** (☎087 861 0601; www.bunloedhuts.jimdo.com; Ban Kham Pia; s in bungalow 260-300B, d in bungalow 320-360B, s/d with shared bathroom 200/260B, s/d in tent 80/100B, meals 60-100B; 📶), an excellent homestay on the eastern edge of the reserve.

Thai-Lao Market (ตลาดไทย-ลาว; Soi Buengkan; ⊙4am-1pm Tue & Fri) This market is filled with sellers from both sides of the river and it can get pretty lively. It's mostly the same goods found in regular Thai markets, but some Lao vendors bring forest products such as mushrooms and herbal remedies.

Sleeping

Rachawadee Hotel (☎042 492119; www.rachavadeehotel.com; Th Bungkan; d 450B; ❄📶) Basic but clean and good for the price, this L-shaped hotel has the best budget rooms in town. It's two blocks back from the riverfront promenade, at the north-western end of town (to your left as you face the river), so it's quiet but convenient. There are some wonky old bikes available free for guests. No English sign.

Getting There & Away

Bueng Kan's oversized bus station is out on the highway east of town. There are frequent buses and minivans to Nong Khai and Udon Thani, as well as 12 daily buses to Bangkok (511B to 874B, 13 hours).

Border Crossing to Paksan (Laos)

Although it's very rarely done by travellers, you can cross the Mekong from Bueng Kan to Paksan, but only if you already have your Lao visa.

Getting to the border The pier is 2.5km northwest of town and immigration formalities are done there. A túk-túk from the city centre costs 60B to 70B.

At the border Boats (per person 60B) cross the river frequently between 8.30am and 4pm on weekdays and infrequently on weekends, leaving when they have about 20 passengers. You can go any time you want if you pay the full 1200B.

Moving on Túk-túk wait on the Lao shore, though the highway and a few hotels are an easy walk from the landing.

modified and converted into a hotel. It has tastefully decorated rooms, all with double beds, around a courtyard. The more expensive rooms have Mekong views.

★**Ting Song Tam** THAI $
(☎088 029 8251; Soi 21, Th Srichiang Khan; mains 30-100B; ⊙8.30am-6pm) One of our favourite restaurants in Loei Province. There's a full

Isan menu but its speciality is *đôrng dêng* noodles (a super-thick version of *kà·nŏm jeen*), which are made fresh when you order. Add them to your *sôm·đam* (50B) or eat with chilli sauce and vegetables, a Chiang Khan speciality called *kôw bûn rórn* that pairs well with *gài yâhng* (grilled chicken).

Getting There & Away

Sŏrng·tăa·ou to Loei (35B, 1½ hours) depart about every 30 minutes from a stop on Th Srichiang Khan (at Soi 26). Buses to Loei (34B, one hour, hourly 6.30am to 3.30pm) leave from the Nakhonchai Transport terminal. They continue to Khorat (283B, seven hours).

Four companies, with buses departing from their own offices, make the run to Bangkok (10 to 11 hours) in the morning and early evening: Air Muang Loei, 999 VIP, Phu Kradung Tours and Sun Bus. Tickets range from 419B to 652B; 999 and Sun Bus have the best VIP service.

NORTHERN PROVINCES

Northern Thailand's beautiful, rugged geography is the region's great temptation, and the country's most iconic waterfalls and caves, as well as white-water rapids and jungle trails, can be found here. As much of a draw are the diverse minorities who populate the villages, while Northern Thailand's proximity to Laos and Myanmar gives the region a unique multicultural feel.

Conversely, the south of the region is regarded as the birthplace of much of Thai culture. History buffs can go back in time at Sukhothai Historical Park and Kamphaeng Phet Historical Park.

Getting There & Away

For those in a hurry, Northern Thailand's air links are surprisingly good. Nok Air, Air Asia, Thai Lion Air, Bangkok Airways and Thai Smile connect several provincial capitals in the region with Bangkok or Chiang Mai.

Just about everywhere in the region is accessible by bus and, increasingly, minivan, except among the communities along the Myanmar border, where the *sŏrng·tăa·ou* is the transport of choice.

Chiang Mai

053 / POP 201,000

The former seat of the Lanna kingdom, Chiang Mai (เชียงใหม่) is a blissfully calm and laid-back place to relax and recharge your batteries. Participate in a vast array of activities on offer, or just stroll around the backstreets and discover a city that is still firmly Thai in its atmosphere and attitude.

Sights

★Talat Warorot MARKET

(ตลาดวโรรส; cnr Th Chang Moi & Th Praisani; 6am-5pm) Chiang Mai's oldest public market, Warorot (also spelt Waroros) is a great

OFF THE BEATEN TRACK

PHA TAEM NATIONAL PARK

A long cliff named Pha Taem is the centrepiece of the awesome but unheralded **Pha Taem National Park** (อุทยานแห่งชาติผาแต้ม; 045 252581; 400B, car/motorcycle 30/20B), which covers 340 sq km along the Mekong River. From the top you get a bird's-eye view across the Mekong into Laos, and down below a fabulous tree-shaded walking trail passes prehistoric rock paintings.

The wilderness north of the cliff holds more ancient art, some magnificent waterfalls (all flowing June to December) and scattered rock fields known as Sao Chaliang, which are oddly eroded mushroom-shaped stone formations.

Many Thais come here for the sunrises. Pha Cha Na Dai cliff, which requires a high-clearance vehicle to reach, serves Thailand's first sunrise view of each day. But Pha Taem cliff is only about one minute behind.

Pha Taem has campsites and bungalows to stay in. There's also a collection of uninspiring 'resorts' on the road to the park and along the Mekong below the park.

Pha Taem is 18km from Khong Jiam along Rte 2112. There's no public transport, but you could come on a rented motorbike or car from Khong Jiam. Túk-túk ask for 600B for the return trip. Return boat trips here from Khong Jiam cost 2000B, but they don't allow you to get off the boat and explore the park.

Central Chiang Mai

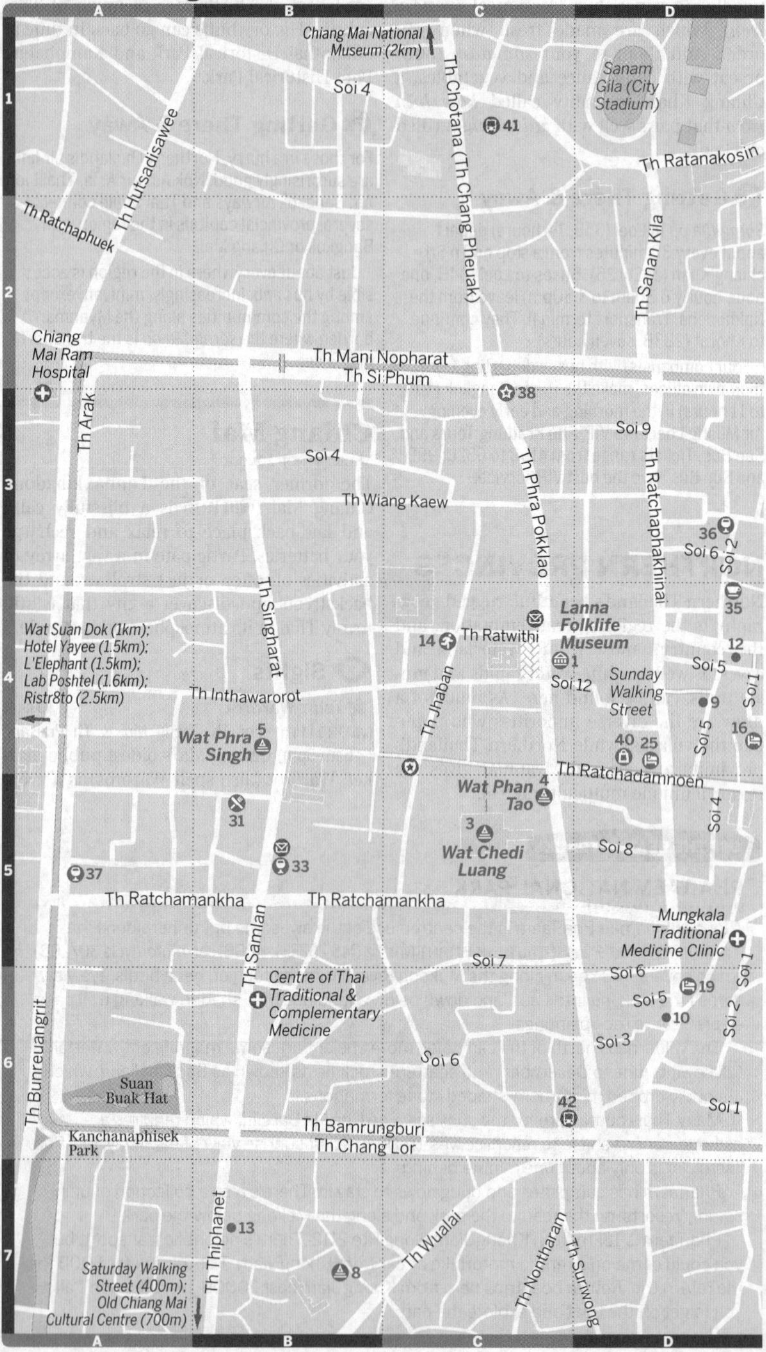

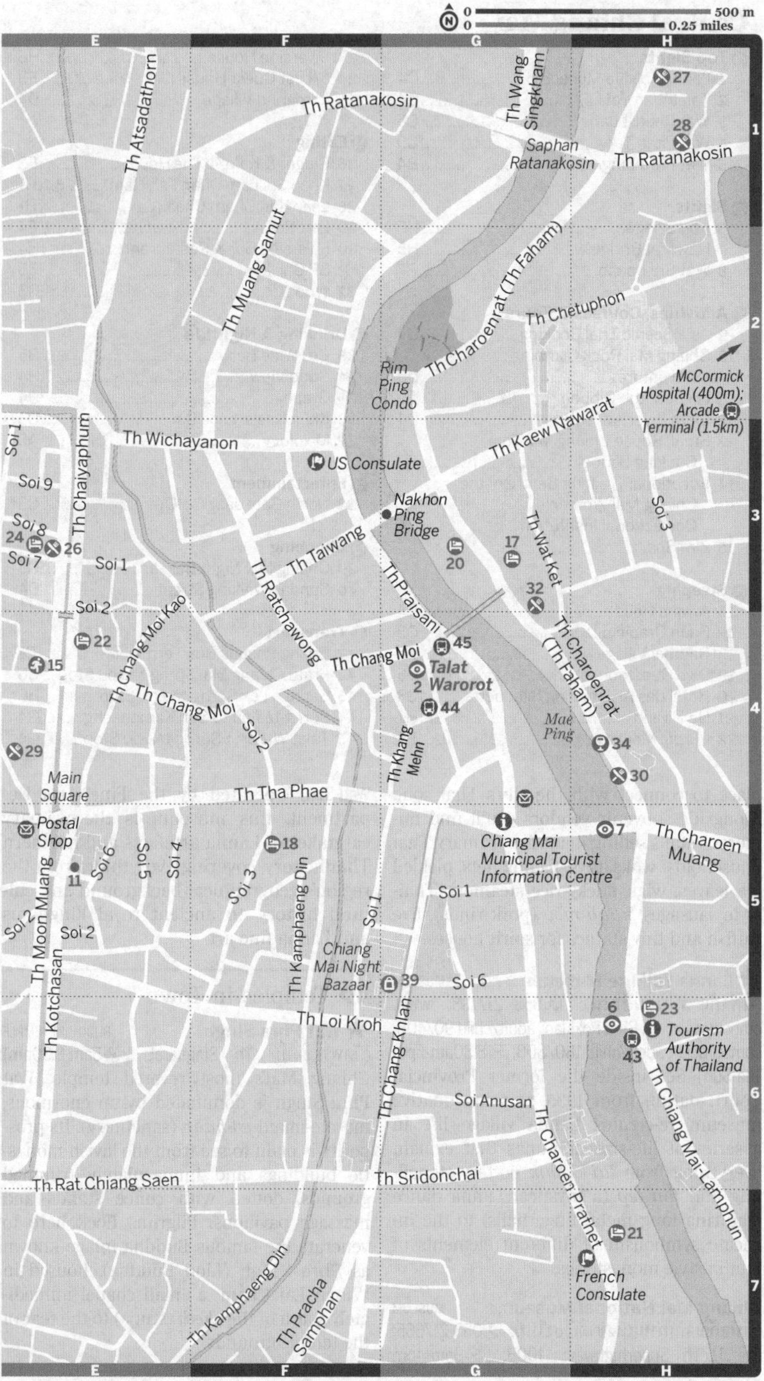
0 500 m
0 0.25 miles
E
F
G
H
1
2
3
4
5
6
7
Th Ratanakosin
Th Atsadathorn
Th Wang Singkham
Saphan Ratanakosin
Th Ratanakosin
27
28
Th Muang Samut
Th Charoenrat (Th Faham)
Th Chetuphon
Rim Ping Condo
McCormick Hospital (400m); Arcade Terminal (1.5km)
Th Kaew Nawarat
Soi 1
Th Chaiyaphum
Th Wichayanon
US Consulate
Soi 9
Soi 8
24
26
Soi 7
Soi 1
Nakhon Ping Bridge
Th Taiwang
Soi 3
Th Ratchawong
20
17
Th Wat Ket
32
Th Praisani
Soi 2
22
Th Chang Moi Kao
45
Th Chang Moi
Talat Warorot
2
15
Th Chang Moi
44
Th Charoenrat (Th Faham)
Soi 2
Mae Ping
34
29
Th Khang Mehn
30
Main Square
Th Tha Phae
Postal Shop
7
Th Charoen Muang
18
Chiang Mai Municipal Tourist Information Centre
11
Soi 6
Soi 5
Soi 4
Soi 3
Soi 1
Th Moon Muang
Soi 2
Soi 2
Th Kamphaeng Din
Soi 1
Chiang Mai Night Bazaar
39
Soi 6
Th Kotchasan
6
23
Th Loi Kroh
Tourism Authority of Thailand
43
Th Chang Khlan
Soi Anusan
Th Chiang Mai-Lamphun
Th Charoen Prathet
Th Rat Chiang Saen
Th Sridonchai
21
French Consulate
Th Kamphaeng Din
Th Pracha Samphan

Central Chiang Mai

Top Sights
1 Lanna Folklife Museum C4
2 Talat Warorot G4
3 Wat Chedi Luang C5
4 Wat Phan Tao C5
5 Wat Phra Singh B4

Sights
6 Iron Bridge H6
7 Nawarat Bridge H5
8 Wat Srisuphan B7

Activities, Courses & Tours
9 Asia Scenic Thai Cooking D4
10 Chiang Mai Rock Climbing Adventures D6
11 Flight of the Gibbon E5
12 Siam River Adventures D4
13 Small House Chiang Mai Thai Cooking School B7
14 Vocational Training Centre of the Chiang Mai Women's Correctional Institution C4
15 Zira Spa E4

Sleeping
16 Awana House D4
17 Baan Orapin G3
18 Banthai Village F5
19 Diva Guesthouse D6
20 Hotel des Artists Ping Silhouette G3
21 Na Nirand H7
22 Purple Monkey E4
23 Riverside House H6
24 Sri Pat Guest House E3
25 Tamarind Village D4

Eating
26 Ginger & Kafe @ The House E3
27 Khao Soi Lam Duan Fah Ham H1
28 Laap Kao Cham Chaa H1
29 Lert Ros E4
30 Riverside Bar & Restaurant H4
31 SP Chicken B5
32 Woo G3

Drinking & Nightlife
33 Cru Wine Bar B5
34 Good View H4
35 Graph D4
36 Khun Kae's Juice Bar D3
37 Mixology A5

Entertainment
38 North Gate Jazz Co-Op C3

Shopping
39 Chiang Mai Night Bazaar G5
40 Sunday Walking Street D4

Transport
41 Chang Pheuak Bus Terminal C1
42 Pratu Chiang Mai Sŏrng·tăa·ou Stop ... C6
43 Saphan Lek Sŏrng·tăa·ou Stop H6
44 Sŏrng·tăa·ou to San Kamphaeng G4
45 Talat Warorot Sŏrng·tăa·ou Stop G4

place to connect with the city's Thai soul. Alongside souvenir vendors you'll find numerous stalls selling items for ordinary Thai households: woks, toys, fishing nets, pickled tea leaves, wigs, sticky-rice steamers, Thai-style sausages, *kâab mŏo* (pork rinds), live catfish and tiny statues for spirit houses.

★Lanna Folklife Museum MUSEUM
(พิพิธภัณฑ์พื้นถิ่นล้านนา; ☎053 217793; www.cmocity.com; Th Phra Pokklao; adult/child 90/40B, combo ticket adult/child 180/80B; ⊗8.30am-5pm Tue-Sun) Set inside the former Provincial Court, dating from 1935, this imaginative museum re-creates Lanna village life in a series of life-size dioramas that explain everything from *lai·krahm* pottery stencilling and *fon lep* (a mystical Lanna dance featuring long metal fingernails) to the intricate symbolism of different elements of Lanna-style monasteries.

Chiang Mai National Museum MUSEUM
(พิพิธภัณฑสถานแห่งชาติเชียงใหม่; ☎053 217665; Rte 11/Th Superhighway; 100B; ⊗9am-4pm Wed-Sun) Operated by the Fine Arts Department, this museum is the primary caretaker of Lanna artefacts and northern Thai history, covering everything from the region's geographical background and cultural history, to ancient royal kingdoms and Lanna fine art.

Temples in Town

★Wat Phra Singh BUDDHIST TEMPLE
(วัดพระสิงห์; Th Singharat; ⊗5am-8.30pm) Chiang Mai's most revered temple, Wat Phra Singh is dominated by an enormous, mosaic-inlaid *wí·hăhn* (sanctuary). Its prosperity is plain to see from the lavish monastic buildings and immaculately trimmed grounds, dotted with coffee stands and massage pavilions. Pilgrims flock here to venerate the famous Buddha image known as **Phra Singh** (Lion Buddha), housed in Wihan Lai Kham, a small chapel immediately south of the *chedi* (stupa) to the rear of the temple grounds.

★**Wat Phan Tao** BUDDHIST TEMPLE
(วัดพันเถา; Th Phra Pokklao; donations appreciated; ⏲daylight hours) Without doubt the most atmospheric wát in the old city, this teak marvel sits in the shadow of Wat Chedi Luang. Set in a compound full of fluttering orange flags, the monastery is a monument to the teak trade, with an enormous prayer hall supported by 28 gargantuan teak pillars and lined with dark teak panels, enshrining a particularly graceful gold Buddha image.

★**Wat Chedi Luang** BUDDHIST TEMPLE
(วัดเจดีย์หลวง; Th Phra Pokklao; adult/child 40/20B; ⏲5am-10.30pm) Wat Chedi Luang isn't as grand as Wat Phra Singh, but its towering, ruined Lanna-style *chedi* (built in 1441) is much taller and the sprawling compound around the stupa is powerfully atmospheric. The famed Phra Kaew (Emerald Buddha), now held in Bangkok's Wat Phra Kaew, resided in the eastern niche until 1475; today, you can view a jade replica.

Temples Outside Town

★**Wat Phra That Doi Suthep** BUDDHIST TEMPLE
(วัดพระธาตุดอยสุเทพ; Th Huay Kaew, Doi Suthep; 30B; ⏲5am-9pm) Overlooking the city from its mountain throne, Wat Phra That Doi Suthep is one of northern Thailand's most sacred temples, and its founding legend is learned by every schoolkid in Chiang Mai. The wát is a beautiful example of northern Thai architecture, reached via a 306-step staircase flanked by *naga* (mythical sea serpents). The climb is intended to help devotees accrue Buddhist merit.

★**Wat Pha Lat** BUDDHIST TEMPLE
(วัดผาลาด) A hidden jungle temple tucked into the mountain along the way to Wat Phra That Doi Suthep. Old stone structures, intricate carvings, *naga*-flanked stairways and Buddhist statues dot the serene grounds, and a walkway over a sheetrock waterfall affords postcard-pretty views of Chiang Mai. The temple was seldom visited before 2018, but word of its beauty spread among travellers and expats, and the Monk's Trail (a jungle path from the city to the temple) is now an open secret.

Wat Umong Suan Phutthatham BUDDHIST TEMPLE
(วัดอุโมงค์; Soi Wat Umong, Th Khlong Chonprathan; 20B; ⏲daylight hours) Not to be confused with the small Wat Umong in the old city, this historic forest wát is famed for its sylvan setting and its ancient *chedi*, above a brick platform wormholed with passageways, built around 1380 for the 'mad' monk Therachan. Keep an eye out for the Sri Lankan–style stupa, and as you wander the arched tunnels, look for traces of the original murals and several venerated Buddha images.

Activities

★**Monk's Trail** HIKING
This dreamy, increasingly popular jungle hike to Wat Pha Lat takes about 45 minutes, starting from behind Chiang Mai University and snaking up through the forest before reaching the temple. Monks are regularly seen hiking in sandals, but close-toed shoes are a better choice for the loose rocks and steep parts. Bring mosquito repellent and dress appropriately for visiting the temple.

MONK CHATS

If you're curious about Buddhism, many Chiang Mai temples offer popular Monk Chat sessions, where novice monks get to practise their English and tourists get to find out about the inner workings of monastery life. It's a fascinating opportunity to discover a little more about the rituals and customs that most Thai men undertake for at least a small portion of their lives. Remember to dress modestly as a sign of respect: cover your shoulders and knees. Because of ritual taboos, women should take care not to touch the monks or their belongings, or to pass anything directly to them.

Wat Suan Dok (วัดสวนดอก; Th Suthep; donations accepted, hall admission 20B; ⏲daylight hours) Has a dedicated room for Monk Chats from 4pm to 7pm Monday to Friday.

Wat Srisuphan (วัดศรีสุพรรณ; Soi 2, Th Wualai; ⏲6am-6pm) Holds chats from 5.30pm to 7.15pm on Tuesday, Thursday and Saturday, with meditation sessions following.

Wat Chedi Luan Has a table under a shady tree where monks chat from 8am to 5pm daily.

Siam River Adventures RAFTING
(☎089 515 1917; www.siamrivers.com; 17 Th Ratwithi; per day from 1800B; ⏲8.30am-8pm) In operation since 2000, this outfit running white-water rafting and kayaking trips has a good reputation for safety and professionalism. The guides have specialist rescue training and additional staff are located at dangerous parts of the river with throw ropes. Trips can be combined with elephant encounters and overnight village stays.

Flight of the Gibbon ZIPLINING
(☎053 010660; www.flightofthegibbon.com; 29/4-5 Th Kotchasan; day tours 4199B; ⏲8am-5.30pm) This adventure outfit started the zipline craze, with nearly 5km of wire strung up like spiderwebs in the gibbon-populated forest canopy near Ban Mae Kampong, an hour's drive east from Chiang Mai. The day tour includes an optional village visit, waterfall walk and lunch cooked by the community. There are also multiday, multiactivity tours that can include a night at a village homestay.

Thai Elephant Care Center ELEPHANT INTERACTION
(☎053 206247; www.thaielephantcarecenter.com; Mae Sa; entrance 250B, half-/full-day program 2000/3000B) This small centre at Mae Sa, about 25km northwest of Chiang Mai, was set up to provide care for elderly elephants retired from logging camps and elephant shows. There are no rides, and visitors feed the old-timers with ground grass, herb balls and bananas, help out at bath time, and visit the cemetery for elephants who have died of old age.

★ **Zira Spa** SPA
(☎053 222288; www.ziraspa.com; 8/1 Th Ratwithi; treatments 700-6200B; ⏲10am-10pm) In the centre of Chiang Mai, Zira Spa offers some of the best spa treatments and massages in the region, all for a decent price. You need to book in advance for the larger spa packages, but same-day service is available for one or two of the 30-, 60- or 90-minute treatments.

Vocational Training Centre of the Chiang Mai Women's Correctional Institution MASSAGE
(☎053 122340; 100 Th Ratwithi; foot or traditional massage from 200B; ⏲8am-4.30pm, from 9am Sat & Sun) Offers fantastic massages performed by female inmates participating in the prison's job-training rehabilitation program. The cafe next door is a nice spot for a post-massage brew.

TREKKING IN CHIANG MAI

Thousands of visitors trek into the hills of northern Thailand each year hoping to see fantastic mountain scenery, interact with traditional hill-tribe communities and meet elephants. A huge industry has grown up to cater to this demand, but the experience is very commercial and may not live up to everyone's notion of adventure.

The standard package involves a one-hour minibus ride to Mae Taeng or Mae Wang, a brief hike to an elephant camp, bamboo rafting and, for multiday tours, an overnight stay in or near a hill-tribe village. Many budget guesthouses pressure their guests to take these trips because of the commissions paid, and may ask guests to stay elsewhere if they decline. Note that they also arrange elephant rides, though these are not recommended as rides can be detrimental to the health of the animals.

While these packages are undeniably popular, they may visit elephant camps that have a questionable record on elephant welfare. Hill-tribe trips can also disappoint, as many of the villages now house a mix of tribal people and Chinese and Burmese migrants and have abandoned many aspects of the traditional way of life. Rafting can also be a tame drift on a creek rather than an adrenalin-charged rush over white water.

If you crave real adventure, you'll have to be a bit more hands-on about organising things yourself. To get deep into the jungle, rent a motorcycle and explore the national parks north and south of Chiang Mai; Chiang Dao is an excellent place to base yourself for jungle exploration. To see elephants in natural conditions, spend a day at Thai Elephant Care Center, then raft real white water with Siam River Adventures. To encounter traditional hill-tribe culture, you'll need to travel to more remote areas than you can reach on a day trip from Chiang Mai; your best bet is to travel to Tha Ton and book a multiday trek from there.

WORTH A TRIP

CHANGCHILL

After working with World Animal Protection for nearly two years, **ChangChill** (064 340 6776; http://changchill.com; 45/2 Mu 19, Baan Pratumuang; full day adult/child 2500/1800B; 10am-3pm) became the only elephant reserve in northern Thailand to be designated elephant-friendly by the animal-welfare organisation, and opened its doors to visitors in April 2019. There are no rides here, no assistance with baths, no human interaction whatsoever. Instead, guests spend the day watching the elephants from an observation deck, learning about their behaviour, gathering food for them and chatting with mahouts.

While it may not get your adrenalin pumping, watching elephants behave naturally has its rewards. Not only does the experience feel highly authentic and educational, but it also supports an ethical approach to wildlife tourism, promoting the safety and happiness of both the elephants and their handlers.

The sanctuary is located 1½ hours southwest of Chiang Mai, and offers transport to and from the city.

Courses

Chiang Mai Rock Climbing Adventures ADVENTURE
(CMRCA; 053 207102; www.thailandclimbing.com; 55/3 Th Ratchaphakhinai; climbing course from 3995B, climbing gym day pass 250B; 8am-8pm) With a very experienced and passionate owner, CMRCA developed and maintains all of the climbs at the limestone crag Crazy Horse Buttress, with bolted sport routes in the French 5a to 8b+ range. As well as climbing and caving courses for all levels, it runs a shuttle bus to the crag daily at 8am (395B return; book one day before).

You can rent all the gear you need here, either piece by piece, or as a 'full set' for two climbers (1875B)

★**Small House Chiang Mai Thai Cooking School** COOKING
(095 674 4550; www.chiangmaithaicooking.com; 19/14 Th Thiphanet; group classes per person 1500B, day-long private classes from 3500B) Arm offers delightful and intimate Thai cooking classes in a dwelling outside Chiang Mai. Courses include transport and a visit to a local market, and they span northern Thai dishes. The small two- to four-person classes feel more local than touristy.

Asia Scenic Thai Cooking COOKING
(053 418657; www.asiascenic.com; 31 Soi 5, Th Ratchadamnoen; half-day courses 800-1000B, full-day courses 1000-1200B; half-day courses 9am-2pm & 5-9pm, full-day courses 9am-3pm) On Khun Gayray's cooking courses you can study in town or at a peaceful out-of-town farm. Courses cover soups, curries, stir-fries, salads and desserts, so you'll be able to make a three-course meal after a single day.

Thai Massage School of Chiang Mai HEALTH & WELLBEING
(TMC; 053 854330; www.tmcschool.com; 203/6 Th Chiang Mai-Mae Jo; basic courses from 8500B) Northeast of town, this well-known school offers a government-licensed massage curriculum. There are three foundation levels and an intensive teacher-training program.

Doi Suthep Vipassana Meditation Center HEALTH & WELLBEING
(053 295012; www.fivethousandyears.org; Wat Phra That Doi Suthep, Th Huay Kaew; by donation) Set within the grounds of Wat Phra That Doi Suthep (p467), this centre offers meditation training retreats for all levels, lasting from four to 21 days.

Tours

★**Green Trails** ADVENTURE
(053 141356; www.green-trails.com; 111/70 Th Mahidol; treks for 2 people from 2900B) A very reliable, eco and socially responsible outfit that can arrange trekking trips to Doi Inthanon, overnight trips to Ban Mae Kampong, responsible elephant encounters and much more. Overnight trips to Akha, Lisu and Palong villages in Chiang Dao and to Hmong villages in Mae Rim are particularly rewarding.

★**Chiang Mai on Three Wheels** TOURS
(053 141356; www.chiangmaionthreewheels.com; 111/70 Th Mahidol; 4hr tours for 2 people 1700B) There are few better ways to tour Chiang Mai than by slow, quiet, culturally immersive săhm·lór (three-wheel pedicabs; also spelt săamláw). This organisation helps promote this dying industry by connecting tourists with the often non-English-speaking

drivers and pairs you with an English-speaking guide. Profits go entirely to the drivers and to support their industry.

Festivals & Events

Flower Festival CULTURAL
(early Feb) A riot of blooms, held over a three-day period. There are flower displays, cultural performances and beauty pageants, plus a floral parade from Saphan Nawarat to Suan Buak Hat.

Songkran NEW YEAR
(mid-Apr) The traditional Thai New Year (13 to 15 April) is celebrated in Chiang Mai with an infectious enthusiasm that's made it one of the best places in the country to be for the occasion. Thousands of revellers line all sides of the moat to throw water on passers-by and each other, while more restrained Songkran rituals are held at Wat Phra Singh.

Loi Krathong RELIGIOUS
(Oct/Nov) Also known as Yi Peng, this lunar holiday is celebrated along Mae Ping with the launching of small lotus-shaped boats honouring the spirit of the river, and the release of thousands of illuminated lanterns into the night sky.

Sleeping

Accommodation prices in the city are slowly creeping up, but you can still find a respectable air-con room from 650B. Make reservations far in advance if visiting during Chinese New Year, Songkran or other holiday periods.

In Town

★Purple Monkey HOSTEL $
(099 150 5534; https://purple-monkey-chiang-mai.business.site; 56/6 Th Chaiyaphum; incl breakfast dm 150B, d with fan/air-con 400/480B;) This sister hostel to the wildly popular namesake in Pai opened just outside the eastern edge of Chiang Mai's old city in 2019. Rooms in the five-storey hostel are adequate and clean, but the social atmosphere and events (including pub crawls and rooftop parties) are the real draw for backpackers. Great location near markets and bars.

Lab Poshtel HOSTEL $
(063 361 4426; https://thelabposhtel.com; 64 Th Sirimungklajarn; dm 490B, d incl breakfast 1090B;) A laboratory-themed boutique hostel that takes this theme very seriously. The bright, stylish common space is somewhat creepily decorated with things like beakers, lab coats, mounted insects and anatomy charts. But the vibe is otherwise cosy, and the attached cafe, lifestyle shop and quaint outdoor bar are all fabulous.

Diva Guesthouse GUESTHOUSE $
(053 273851; www.divaguesthouse.com; 84/13 Th Ratchaphakhinai; dm 130-190B, s/d from 330/380B;) An energetic, vaguely bohemian spot on busy Th Ratchaphakhinai, Diva offers the full backpacker deal – dorm beds, budget boxrooms, adventure tours, net access, ambient tunes, and fried rice and *sà·dé* (grilled meat with peanut sauce) in the downstairs cafe. Accommodation ranges from dorms to family rooms and comes with either fan or air-con.

★Sri Pat Guest House HOTEL $$
(053 218716; http://sri-pat-guest-house.hotelschiangmai.net; 16 Soi 7, Th Moon Muang; d from 1500B;) A standout flashpacker guesthouse with all the trimmings: wi-fi, pool, wood-decked communal areas, scattered Buddha carvings and smart tiled rooms with flat-screen TVs and little Thai details. You get plenty of personality for your baht and staff members are cheerful and friendly.

Awana House HOTEL $$
(053 419005; www.awanahouse.com; 7 Soi 1, Th Ratchadamnoen; d with fan 495B, with air-con 700-1000B;) The pick of the guesthouses around the medieval city gate of Pratu Tha Phae has rooms for every budget – all kept spotless – and a mini swimming pool under cover on the ground-floor terrace. Rooms get more comfortable and better decorated as you move up the price scale and there's a rooftop chill-out area with views across old Chiang Mai.

★Tamarind Village HOTEL $$$
(053 418 8969; www.tamarindvillage.com; 50/1 Th Ratchadamnoen; d incl breakfast from 5200B, ste 8200-10,700B;) This refined, atmospheric Lanna-style property sprawls across the grounds of an old tamarind orchard in a prime location off Th Ratchadamnoen. Walkways covered by tiled pavilions lead to secluded and beautiful spaces, and tall mature trees cast gentle shade around the huge pool and gardens. Design-magazine-worthy rooms are full of gorgeous tribal fabrics and artefacts.

★**Hotel des Artists Ping Silhouette** BOUTIQUE HOTEL $$$
(☎053 249999; www.hotelartists.com; 181 Th Charoenrat/Th Faham; d incl breakfast from 3720B; ❄📶🏊) An elegant, minimalist boutique hotel channeling the Chinese and European roots of its neighbourhood with chinoiserie details throughout, including two Tang Dynasty–style horse statues perched beside a rectangular koi pond. The on-site cafe mimics a Chinese merchant shophouse, while the accommodation is plush and modern with high ceilings and relaxing terraces. The saltwater pool is divine.

Outside Town Centre

Riverside House GUESTHOUSE $$
(☎053 241860; www.riversidehouse-chiangmai.com; 101 Th Chiang Mai-Lamphun; d incl breakfast 1000-1300B; ❄@📶🏊) Plain yet spotless and rather large rooms are spread across three blocks; you pay top baht for the central block, by the pool and away from the traffic noise, but all the rooms are good for the money. It's great value and a fine choice for families. Note that, despite the name and location, only a few rooms offer river views.

Chai Lai Orchid RESORT $$
(☎086 923 0867; www.chailaiorchid.com; 202 Mu 9, Tambon Mae Win, Mae Wang; d 1500-1800B; ❄📶) If you've ever wanted to be woken up by an elephant at your window, here's your chance. This collection of comfortable jungle huts is planted in the middle of the forest, just beside an elephant camp, and is reached via a suspended footbridge across Mae Wang. Well-run by an NGO, the resort provides educational and professional development for at-risk women.

The property is 44km southwest of Chiang Mai.

★**Banthai Village** HOTEL $$$
(☎053 252789; www.banthaivillage.com; 19 Soi 3, Th Tha Phae; d incl breakfast 3600-4800B, ste 5600-7800B; ❄@📶🏊) True to its name, Banthai does indeed resemble a country village transported to the modern city. The hotel sprawls over a series of wooden buildings with broad balconies, surrounding an idyllic pool and gardens overflowing with birds-of-paradise flowers. Rooms do the heritage thing, but subtly, with low wooden beds, dark-wood furniture, and scattered cushions and triangular Thai pillows.

★**Dhara Dhevi** RESORT $$$
(☎053 888888; www.dharadhevi.com; 51/4 Th Chiang Mai–San Kamphaeng, off Rte 1006; d from 12,500B; ❄@📶🏊) At first sight it's hard to tell if Dhara Dhevi is a resort or an ancient temple complex. In fact the structures were built in the 2000s, yet they're jaw-droppingly opulent with amazing attention to detail. The re-created traditional Lanna village sprawls over grounds full of whitewashed colonnades, teak pavilions, antiques and landscaped ponds and rice terraces.

Baan Orapin B&B $$$
(☎053 243677; www.baanorapin.com; 150 Th Charoenrat/Th Faham; d incl breakfast 1800-4000B; ❄📶🏊) Set within the historic Wat Ket district, Baan Orapin has been a family affair since the owner's relatives first occupied the stately teak house and surrounding gardens in 1914. Today, two elegant villas situated in the front and rear of the property contain 15 guest rooms full of graceful furniture and fabrics.

Na Nirand BOUTIQUE HOTEL $$$
(☎053 280988; www.nanirand.com; 1/1 Soi 9, Th Charoen Prathet; d from 7500B; ❄📶🏊) A magnificent, giant, century-old rain tree anchors this romantic boutique property perched at the edge of Mae Ping. A restored teak house contains the spa and a small library, while posh villas flank a relaxing swimming pool and are defined by ornate woodcarvings, Lanna textiles and rattan furnishings made by local artisans. Bathrooms are huge, with freestanding tubs and rain showers.

Eating

The city's fabulous night markets, which sprawl around the main city gates and several other locations, offer the best food.

★**Laap Kao Cham Chaa** THAI $
(Th Ratanakosin; mains 50-200B; ⏲noon-9pm Mon-Sat) Popularised by the late, great Anthony Bourdain, this low-key street stall beneath a rain tree (after which it is named) is now a staple for authentic northern Thai food. Plop down in a plastic chair, grab a Singha and feast on heaping plates of pounded-pomelo salad, Thai-style beef or pork *lâhp* (raw or cooked) and crab paste.

★**SP Chicken** THAI $
(9/1 Soi 1, Th Samlan; mains 40-170B; ⏲10am-5pm) Chiang Mai's best chicken emerges daily from the grills at this tiny cafe near Wat

Phra Singh. The menu runs to salads and soups, but most people just pick a half (90B) or whole (170B) chicken, and dip the moist meat into the spicy, tangy sauces provided.

Lert Ros THAI $
(Soi 1, Th Ratchadamnoen; mains 30-160B; ⊙noon-9pm) As you enter this local hole in the wall, you'll pass the main course: delicious whole tilapia fish, grilled on coals and served with a fiery Isan-style dipping sauce. Eaten with sticky rice, this is one of the great meals of Chiang Mai. The menu also includes fermented pork grilled in banana leaves, curries and *sôm·đam*.

Khao Soi Lam Duan Fah Ham THAI $
(352/22 Th Charoenrat/Th Faham; mains from 40B; ⊙9am-4pm) North of the Th Ratanakosin bridge on the east bank, Th Faham is known as Chiang Mai's *kôw soy* (wheat-and-egg noodles in curry broth) ghetto. Khao Soi Lam Duan Fah Ham is the pick of the bunch, serving delicious bowls of *kôw soy* to eager crowds of punters.

★Woo CAFE $$
(☎052 003717; www.woochiangmai.com; 80 Th Charoenrat/Th Faham; mains 150-500B; ⊙10am-10pm; 📶) A riverside, three-in-one stop for delicious meals, contemporary art and perhaps a bit of shopping. The stylish, modern cafe specialises in Thai food, salads and freshly baked goods, but the menu is enormous and also includes every imaginable beverage. Edgy art adorns the walls, and regular exhibitions feature a rotating crop of Thai artists.

★Ginger & Kafe @ The House THAI $$
(☎053 287681; www.thehousebygingercm.com; 199 Th Moon Muang; mains 160-390B; ⊙10am-11pm) Dining at the restaurant in The House boutique feels like eating in a posh Thai mansion, with antique furniture, comfy sofas and fine china. The Thai food is delicious and lavishly presented, with wonderful dishes including items like Massaman curry with slow-cooked beef in lime-coconut cream. There's also a lovely fashion shop and a swanky cocktail lounge under the same ownership next door.

Riverside Bar & Restaurant INTERNATIONAL $$
(☎053 243239; www.theriversidechiangmai.com; Th Charoenrat/Th Faham; mains 100-370B, dinner cruise adult/child 180/90B; ⊙10am-1am) Almost everyone ends up at Riverside at some point in their Chiang Mai stay. Set in an old teak house, it feels like a countryside reimagining of a Hard Rock Cafe, and bands play nightly until late. Stake out a claim on the riverside terrace or the upstairs balcony to catch the evening breeze on Mae Ping.

L'Elephant FRENCH $$$
(☎097 970 8947; http://lelephantchiangmai.com; 7 Soi 11, Th Sirimungklajarn; set lunch/dinner from 550/670B; ⊙11.30am-4pm & 5.30-10pm Tue-Sun) When you simply can't stomach any more Thai street food, saunter into this elegant oasis and feast on melt-in-your-mouth beef carpaccio, hearty ox tongue stew and tender (and crunchy!) duck confit. Service is friendly and on the ball, and the charming rooms, corridors and garden are tastefully adorned in fine art and antiques. The tasting menus offer superb value.

Drinking & Nightlife

Chiang Mai has three primary areas for watering holes: the old city, the riverside and Th Nimmanhaemin.

★Graph COFFEE
(☎086 567 3330; www.graphdream.com; 25/1 Soi 1, Th Ratwithi; coffee 80-220B; ⊙9am-5pm; 📶) A tiny cafe with enormously good coffee. Only about 10 people fit inside, and the line often snakes down the old city block. Favourites include the Nitro cold-brew coffee with orange and lime, and the 'boy with girlfriend', which comes with lime, raw sugar, soda and espresso.

★Ristr8to COFFEE
(☎053 215278; www.ristr8to.com; Th Nimmanhaemin; espresso drinks from 88B; ⊙7am-6pm) Inspired by Australian coffee culture and using roasting skills learned in the US, this place takes your cup of joe to the highest heights, from flat whites and marocchinos to the hyper-caffeinated doppio ristretto that uses 18g of ground coffee and award-winning latte art. The small brick-walled cafe is well loved and often packed. There's also a Ristr8to Lab near Soi 3.

★Good View BAR
(www.goodview.co.th; 13 Th Charoenrat/Th Faham; ⊙10am-1am) Good View attracts plenty of locals, with a big menu of Thai standards, Japanese dishes and Western options (mains 100B to 400B), and a nightly program of house bands with rotating line-ups (meaning the drummer starts playing guitar and the bass player moves behind the piano).

Cru Wine Bar WINE BAR
(☎089 552 2822; www.facebook.com/CRUwinebarcm; 2nd fl, 8-10 Th Samlan; glasses 150-300B; ⏲6pm-midnight Tue-Sun) Chiang Mai's only wine bar is up a hidden stairway with just a tiny sign pointing the way, but those who uncover it are in for a treat. The cosy space is adorned in dark wood and fairy lights, and the well-chosen, rotating international wine offerings pair well with a small menu of delicious tapas.

Hotel Yayee ROOFTOP BAR
(☎099 269 5885; 17/5 Soi Sai Naam Peung; ⏲5-11.30pm) Overlooking Doi Suthep and the Nimmanhaemin neighbourhood, Hotel Yayee's 5th-floor rooftop bar is a delightful spot to take in the sunset as you sip a speciality cocktail. Owned by a popular Thai actor, the fern-filled bar is one of Chiang Mai's best rooftop options.

Mixology BAR
(61/6 Th Arak; ⏲5pm-midnight Tue-Sun) A tiny, eclectic bar with a huge selection of microbrews, a thick menu of fruity house drinks, burgers and northern Thai eats, and a lounging dog. Even if you drink too many chilli-infused 'pick me ups', you probably won't regret it the next day.

Khun Kae's Juice Bar JUICE BAR
(☎081 022 9292; Soi 7, Th Moon Muang; drinks from 40B; ⏲9am-7.30pm) Our vote for Chiang Mai's best juice shack. Tonnes of fresh fruit, heaps of delicious combinations, generous serves and all this for prices that are almost comically low.

☆ Entertainment

★**Old Chiang Mai Cultural Centre** DANCE
(ศูนย์วัฒนธรรมเชียงใหม่; ☎053 202993; https://oldchiangmai.com; 185/3 Th Wualai; per person from 570B; ⏲7-10pm) For an interactive immersion in all things Lanna, this first-of-its-kind Khantoke dinner-theatre experience remains unparalleled in Thailand. Guests stretch out on floor mats to feast on northern Thai dishes served family-style on rattan trays, while musicians strum, blow and beat traditional instruments as costumed performers dance, chant and twirl the occasional sword.

★**North Gate Jazz Co-Op** LIVE MUSIC
(www.facebook.com/northgate.jazzcoop; 95/1-2 Th Si Phum; ⏲7pm-midnight) This compact jazz club tends to pack in as many musicians as it does patrons, with local and visiting instrumentalists offering nightly sets and experimental jam sessions that tend to go long. The performances are so inspired that a crowd regularly gathers at tables set up on the sidewalk; arrive early to get a good spot.

Shopping

★**Sunday Walking Street** MARKET
(ถนนเดินวันอาทิตย์; Th Ratchadamnoen; ⏲6-11pm Sun) On Sunday afternoon Th Ratchadamnoen is taken over by the boisterous Sunday Walking Street, which feels even more animated than Th Wualai's **Saturday Walking Street** (ถนนเดินวันเสาร์; Th Wualai; ⏲4-11pm Sat) because of the energetic food markets that open up in wát courtyards along the route, in addition to the usual selection of handmade items and northern Thai-themed souvenirs.

Baan Kang Wat ARTS & CRAFTS
(www.facebook.com/Baankangwat; 123/1 Mu 5 Muang, Th Baan Ram Poeng, Suthep; ⏲10am-6pm Tue-Sat, from 7am Sun) Though a little out of the way, Baan Kang Wat is worth the trip simply to coo over the cute architecture and picturesque ambience. The open-air artists enclave is home to several small art and handicraft shops and studios, intimate cafes, a community garden and plenty of potted succulents.

Chiang Mai Night Bazaar MARKET
(Th Chang Khlan; ⏲6pm-midnight) Chiang Mai Night Bazaar is one of the city's main night-time attractions, especially for families, and is the legacy of the original Yunnanese trading caravans that stopped here along the ancient route between Simao (China) and Mawlamyaing (on Myanmar's Gulf of Martaban). Today the night bazaar sells the usual tourist souvenirs, similar to what you'll find at Bangkok's street markets.

ℹ Information

Chiang Mai Immigration Office (☎053 201755; www.chiangmaiimm.com; 71 Th Sanambin; ⏲8.30am-4.30pm Mon-Fri) Chiang Mai's foreign-services office, where visa extensions and other such things are handled.

Chiang Mai Ram Hospital (☎053 920300; www.chiangmairam.com; 8 Th Bunreuangrit) The most modern hospital in town.

Main Post Office (☎053 241070; Mae Khao Mu Soi 4; ⏲8.30am-4.30pm Mon-Fri, 9am-noon Sat & Sun) Other convenient branches on Th Samlan (⏲8.30am-4.30pm Mon-Fri, 9am-noon Sat), Th Praisani (⏲8.30am-5pm

Mon-Fri, 9am-4pm Sat), Th Phra Pokklao (⌚9am-4pm Mon-Sat), and at the airport and university.

Tourism Authority of Thailand (TAT; ☎053 248604; www.tourismthailand.org; Th Chiang Mai-Lamphun; ⌚8am-5pm) English-speaking staff provide maps and advice on travel across Thailand.

Tourist Police (☎053 212147, 24hr emergency 1155; 196 Soi Sriwichai; ⌚6am-midnight) Volunteer staff speak a variety of languages.

DANGERS & ANNOYANCES

Compared to Bangkok, Chiang Mai is a safe haven for tourists. But keep in mind:

- During rush hour, traffic can snarl. Take care when crossing busy roads, as motorcyclists and *rót daang* ('red trucks', operating as shared taxis) drivers rarely give way.
- In March and April, smoky, dusty haze becomes a massive problem because of farmers burning off their fields. Don't go at this time.
- Outbreaks of dengue fever are common in the monsoon; protect yourself from mosquitoes, especially in the daytime.
- In 2019, a tourist died on the zipline at Flight of the Gibbon, and a number have drowned after cliff-jumping at Grand Canyon Water Park.

Getting There & Away

AIR

Domestic and international flights arrive and depart from Chiang Mai International Airport, 3km southwest of the old city.

Air Asia, Bangkok Airways, Nok Air and Thai Smile handle most domestic routes. Tickets to Bangkok start at around 540B. Heading south, expect to pay from 2160B to Phuket and 1080B to Surat Thani.

There are regular flights to Kuala Lumpur (Malaysia), Yangon (Myanmar), Hanoi (Vietnam) and destinations around China. Lao Airlines has direct flights to Luang Prabang, and there are less frequent services to Ho Chi Minh City (Vietnam). To reach Cambodia, you'll have to go via Bangkok.

The airport has luggage storage (7am to 9pm, 200B per day), a post-office branch (8.30am to 8pm), banks and a tourist-assistance centre.

BUS SERVICES FROM CHIANG MAI'S ARCADE TERMINAL

DESTINATION	FARE (B)	DURATION (HR)	FREQUENCY
Bangkok	488-759	10	frequent
Chiang Khong	202-451	6½	1 daily
Chiang Rai	166-288	4	frequent
Khon Kaen	535	12	5 daily
Khorat (Nakhon Ratchasima)	540-662	12	11 daily
Lampang	66-143	1½	hourly
Lampang (minivan)	83	1	hourly
Lamphun	30	1	hourly
Luang Prabang (Laos)	1200	20	9am (Mon, Wed, Fri, Sat, Sun)
Mae Hong Son (minivan)	250	5	3 daily
Mae Sai	205-234	5	7 daily
Mae Sariang	104-187	4-5	6 daily
Mae Sot	290	6	3 daily
Nan	197-254	6	6 daily
Nong Khai	890	12	1 daily
Pai (minivan)	150	3	hourly
Phayao	142-249	3	hourly
Phitsanulok	210-320	5-6	frequent
Phrae	133-266	4	4 daily
Phuket	1646	22	1 daily
Sukhothai	225-290	5-6	hourly
Ubon Ratchathani	802	15	5 daily
Udon Thani	594-832	11	4 daily
Vientiane (Laos)	890	10	1 daily

BUS

Chiang Mai has two bus stations, and *sŏrng·tăa·ou* run from fixed stops to towns close to Chiang Mai.

Arcade Bus Terminal

About 3km northeast of the city centre, near the junction of Th Kaew Nawarat and Rte 11, Chiang Mai's main long-distance station handles all services, except for buses to northern Chiang Mai Province. This is the place to come to travel on to Bangkok or any other major city in Thailand.

A chartered *rót daang* ('red truck', operating as a shared taxi) from the centre to the bus stand will cost about 60B; a túk-túk will cost 80B to 100B. There are also two bus routes between the bus terminals and town: B1 makes stops at Chiang Mai's train station and Tha Phae Gate (15B, hourly 6am to 6pm), and B2 makes stops at Tha Phae Gate and Chiang Mai International Airport (15B, hourly 6am to 6pm).

There are two terminal buildings. Nominally, Building 2 is for towns north of Chiang Mai and Building 3 is for towns south of Chiang Mai, but in practice buses leave from both terminals to most destinations. A third depot behind Building 2 is used by Nakornchai Air, which has luxury buses to Bangkok and almost everywhere else in Thailand.

There is a regular international bus service linking Chiang Mai to Luang Prabang, via Bokeo, Luang Namtha and Udom Xai. You can also travel by bus across to Nong Khai and on to Vientiane.

Chang Pheuak Bus Terminal

Just north of the old city on Th Chotana (Th Chang Pheuak), the Chang Pheuak Bus Terminal is the main departure point for journeys to the north of Chiang Mai Province. Government buses leave regularly to the following destinations:

Chiang Dao 40B, 1½ hours, every 30 minutes
Hot 50B, two hours, every 20 minutes
Samoeng 90B, two hours, six daily
Tha Ton 92B, four hours, seven daily

Local blue *sŏrng·tăa·ou* run to Lamphun (30B, 1½ hours, frequent) and yellow ones head for Mae Rim (30B, 30 minutes, frequent). Air-con minibuses to Chiang Dao (150B, two hours, hourly) leave from Soi Sanam Gila, behind the bus terminal.

TRAIN

Chiang Mai Train Station is about 2.5km east of the old city. Trains run five times daily on the main line between Bangkok and Chiang Mai. The train station has an ATM, a left-luggage room (6am to 6pm, 50B per item) and an advance-booking counter (you'll need your passport to book a ticket).

Between Chiang Mai and Bangkok's Hualamphong station, the most comfortable trains are the overnight special express services leaving Chiang Mai at 5pm and 6pm, and arriving in Bangkok at 6.15am and 6.50am. In the opposite direction, trains leave Hualamphong at 6.10pm and 7.35pm. See the State Railway of Thailand website (www.thairailways.com) for the latest information.

Around Chiang Mai

North of Chiang Mai, the land rucks up into forested mountains on either side of Mae Nam Ping as northern Thailand merges into southeastern Myanmar. With a chartered *rót daang* or rented motorcycle (with sufficient horsepower) you can roam high into the hills, visiting national parks, spectacular viewpoints, Royal Project farms and minority villages.

Mae Sa Valley & Samoeng

You don't have to roam far from the city limits to get into the jungle. Branching west off Rte 107 at Mae Rim, Rte 1096 winds past a string of tacky day-trip attractions – crocodile and monkey shows, elephant camps, orchid farms, shooting ranges, all-terrain-vehicle hire companies, even a cobra farm – before climbing steadily into the forested Mae Sa Valley (หุบเขาแม่สา). The road continues in a winding loop past charging waterfalls and a series of Royal Project farms and then morphs into Rte 1269 at the turn-off to the sleepy country village of Samoeng (สะเมิง), making for a thoroughly enjoyable 100km round-trip from Chiang Mai.

Mon Cham VIEWPOINT

(ม่อนแจ่ม; Nong Hoi Mai) FREE An agricultural wonderland at 1400m, Mon Cham draws mostly domestic tourists for its crisp air, camping opportunities and jaw-dropping views of multicolored crop terraces. The area has become a destination thanks to the Nong Hoi Royal Project, which promotes the growth of sustainable, high-income crops, including strawberries, cabbage, herbs and lavender, by local Hmong people.

Nam Tok Mae Sa WATERFALL

(น้ำตกแม่สา; adult/child 100/50B, car 30B; 8.30am-4.30pm) Off Rte 1096, only 6km from the Mae Rim turn-off, Nam Tok Mae Sa is part of Doi Suthep-Pui National Park. The cascade is a picturesque spot to picnic or tramp around in the woods for a bit and it's a favourite weekend getaway for locals.

Queen Sirikit Botanic Gardens GARDENS (สวนพฤกษศาสตร์สมเด็จพระนางเจ้าสิริกิติ์; www.qsbg.org; Rte 1096; adult/child 100/50B, car/motorcycle 100/30B; ⏲8.30am-4.30pm) At Queen Sirikit Botanic Gardens, 227 hectares have been set aside for plantations, nature trails and vast greenhouses full of exotic and local flora. Near the administration building is the orchid collection, containing over 400 species, the country's largest public display. The Rainforest House recreates a southern Thai forest, with ferns, palms, ginger and other tropical species.

★**Proud Phu Fah** BOUTIQUE HOTEL $$$ (☎053 879389; www.proudphufah.com; Rte 1096, Km 17; d incl breakfast 5500-15,000B; ❄@📶🏊) Sitting in the western wedge of the Mae Sa Valley, this stylish boutique hotel has comfortable designer villas strung along a trickling brook, designed to give the illusion of sleeping amid the great outdoors. The open-air **restaurant** (dishes 110B to 400B) serves healthy Thai food, with lovely views over the lawns and mountains.

Getting There & Around

To take advantage of what this area has to offer, you're best off hiring a motorcycle or car. *Sŏrng·tăa·ou* go to Samoeng (90B, two hours, six daily) from the Chang Pheuak Bus Terminal in Chiang Mai. In Samoeng, the vehicles stop near the market, across from Samoeng Hospital.

Chiang Dao

In a lush jungle setting in the shadow of a mighty limestone mountain, Chiang Dao (เชียงดาว) is where expats and domestic travellers come to escape the heat of the plains. It gets cooler still as you leave the village and climb towards the summit of Doi Chiang Dao (2175m). The forest is a popular stop for birdwatchers and trekkers, and at the base of the mountain is a highly venerated wát marking the entrance to one of Thailand's deepest limestone caverns.

Sights

Doi Chiang Dao Wildlife Sanctuary NATURE RESERVE (ดอยเชียงดาว, Doi Luang; 200B; ⏲Nov-Mar) Doi Chiang Dao rises dramatically above the plain, wrapped in a thick coat of tropical forest. This jungle wonderland is one of Thailand's top spots for birdwatching, with more than 300 resident bird species, and is one of the best places in the world to see giant nuthatches and Hume's pheasants. It's a steep full-day hike to the summit, which offers spectacular views over the massifs. Guides typically charge between 1000B and 2000B per person; an overnight stay costs 500B.

Wat Tham Chiang Dao CAVE (ถ้ำเชียงดาว, Chiang Dao Cave; 40B; ⏲7am-5pm) Set in pretty grounds that teem with jungle butterflies, this forest wát sits at the entrance to Chiang Dao Cave, a chilly warren of passageways that extend more than 10km beneath the limestone massif of Doi Chiang Dao. For Buddhists, the cave is a meditation retreat, a sort of extension of the wát itself, and the twisting tunnels overflow with stalactites and stalagmites.

Sleeping & Eating

Chiang Dao Hut GUESTHOUSE $ (☎053 456625; http://chiangdaohut.com; 303 Moo 5; bungalows from 315B; 📶) This cute collection of rooms and bungalows is set in a glade that drops down to a stream. Cheaper accommodation has shared bathrooms with hot water, and the atmosphere is appropriately laid-back and unhurried. Tasty meals are on offer in the open-air restaurant, **Hut Kitchen**, across the street.

Chiang Dao Nest GUESTHOUSE $$ (☎053 456242; www.chiangdaonest.com; bungalows 995-3500B; @📶🏊) The guesthouse that put Chiang Dao on the map is a charming country retreat, with comfortable, bamboo-weave bungalows scattered around a gorgeous tropical garden with plenty of shady gazebos where you can kick back with a book. There's a lovely, forest-flanked swimming pool with mountain views, and a pavilion with a ping-pong table.

★**Chiang Dao Nest** INTERNATIONAL $$ (☎053 456242; www.chiangdaonest.com; mains 315-695B; ⏲8am-3.30pm & 6-9.30pm; 🍷) The undisputed culinary highlight of the area, Chiang Dao Nest is worth the trip from Chiang Mai all by itself. Discover imported ales, fine wines and sophisticated modern European dishes you wouldn't expect to find in the jungle, such as salmon fillet wrapped in filo pastry with green tapenade. For equally outrageous Thai fare, head to **Nest 2** (☎089 545 9302; www.chiangdaonest.com; Ban Tham; bungalows 995-3500B; ❄📶) down the road.

Getting There & Around

Chiang Dao is 72km north of Chiang Mai along Rte 107. Buses travel to Chiang Mai (40B, 1½ hours, every 30 minutes) and Tha Ton (63B, 2½ hours, five daily). There are also air-conditioned minivans to Chiang Mai (150B, two hours, hourly).

Some of the lodges rent out mountain bikes (from 150B per day) and motorbikes (from 350B).

Tha Ton

The northernmost town in Chiang Mai Province feels a long way from the provincial capital. Modern Tha Ton (บ้านท่าตอน) is a quiet backwater that sees just a trickle of tourists headed downriver towards Chiang Rai.

Interesting detours in the area include boat trips up to the Myanmar border and road trips to Mae Salong or the hot springs at Doi Pha Hompok National Park.

Watch out for aggressive packs of dogs as you wander around.

Sights & Activities

Resorts in Tha Ton can arrange **treks** and **bamboo rafting trips** to a string of hill-tribe villages inhabited by Palaung, Black Lahu, Akha, Karen and Yunnanese people. These are more traditional than the tribal villages close to Chiang Mai. Expect to pay around 1000B per person for a day trek, and from 3000B for a two-day rafting tour.

Wat Tha Ton BUDDHIST TEMPLE
(วัดท่าตอน; Rte 107; donations appreciated; ⏲ daylight hours) Just south of the bridge, this intriguing and popular monastery complex sprawls west from Tha Ton over a series of forested hills. The wát buildings are spread over nine levels and each comes with its own collection of supersize statues and stunning views north towards Myanmar or east across the Tha Ton plain.

Chiang Rai Boat Trip BOATING
(☎053 053727; per person 400B; ⏲ departs 12.30pm) During the rainy season and for as long as water levels stay high (July to December), long-tail boats make the journey between Chiang Rai and Tha Ton daily. It's a scenic trip, passing tracts of virgin forest, riverside monasteries, and villages of thatched huts with fishers casting nets in the shallows.

Sleeping & Eating

Tha Ton's guesthouses are strung out along both sides of the river by the bridge, and most can arrange treks, boat trips, and motorcycle and bicycle hire. Note that some resorts close during the quiet season (January to June), when the river is too low for boat trips.

Garden Home Nature Resort RESORT $
(☎053 373015; gardenhome14@hotmail.com; d with fan from 300B, with air-con 500-1500B; ❄📶) Neat thatch-roofed bungalows are dotted around a calm, green compound full of lychee trees and bougainvillea at this tranquil riverside spot. There are also a few stone bungalows, and three larger, more luxurious bungalows on the river with TVs, fridges and lovely verandas.

★ **Old Tree's House** RESORT $$
(☎085 722 9002; www.facebook.com/Theoldtreeshouse; Rte 107; bungalows incl breakfast 1300-3300B; ❄📶🏊) After an uninspiring approach beside a cement works, you'll struggle to suppress the oohs and aahs as you reach the tropical garden at this French-Thai operation on the hillside. From the restaurant overlooking the valley to the immaculate bamboo-weave bungalows and postcard-pretty palm-fringed pool, Old Tree's doesn't put a foot wrong. Look for the turn-off 400m past Tha Ton.

Laap Lung Pan THAI $
(Rte 107; mains 30-60B; ⏲ 7am-8pm) The go-to place in Tha Ton for northern Thai–style eats. There's no English-language menu; simply point to whatever pot or item on the grill looks tasty. There's no English-language sign either; look for the Coke ad roughly across from the entrance to Wat Tha Ton.

Sunshine Cafe CAFE $
(mains 60-170B; ⏲ 8am-10pm) This is the place to come for freshly brewed coffee in the morning. The spicy salads are excellent, and there's also a wide selection of Western breakfasts, including muesli, fresh fruit and yogurt. It's located on the main road, just before the bridge.

Getting There & Around

The main bus stand in Tha Ton is a long hike south along the highway, but buses also swing by the parking lot just north of the bridge. Services include the following:

Bangkok 500B to 800B, 12 hours, daily (6pm)
Chiang Dao 63B, 2½ hours, five daily
Chiang Mai 92B, four hours, seven daily

To reach Chiang Rai by road, take a *sŏrng·tăa·ou* to Mae Salong (60B, 1½ hours, three daily).

With your own car or motorcycle, you can continue to Mae Salong along Rte 107, turning off onto Rte 1089, following a fully paved but sometimes treacherous mountain road and passing scattered Lisu and Akha villages.

Pai

053 / POP 3000

First-time visitors to Pai (ปาย) might wonder if they've strayed into a northern version of a Thai island getaway, only without the beaches. But Pai's popularity has yet to diminish its nearly picture-perfect setting in a mountain valley that offers natural adventures aplenty. And the town's temples and fun afternoon market are a reminder that Pai has not forgotten its transnational status as a town with roots in Myanmar's Shan State, or that it is a crossroads for the ethnic minorities who live in the nearby hills. There's heaps of quiet accommodation tucked away and a relaxed vibe that prevents some people from ever leaving.

Sights & Activities

Most of Pai's sights are found outside the city centre, making hiring a motorcycle a necessity.

Nam Tok Mo Paeng WATERFALL
(น้ำตกหมอแปง) The most popular waterfall in the vicinity of Pai, Nam Tok Mo Paeng has a couple of pools that are suitable for swimming. The waterfall is about 8km from Pai along the road that also leads to **Wat Nam Hoo** (วัดน้ำฮู; Ban Nam Hoo; daylight hours) FREE – it's a long walk, but it's an OK bike ride or short motorcycle trip.

Pai Canyon NATURE RESERVE
(กองแลนปาย; Rte 1095; daylight hours) Pai Canyon is located 8km from Pai along the road to Chiang Mai. A paved stairway here culminates in an elevated lookout over high rock cliffs and the Pai valley. It is best climbed in the early morning when it's not too hot, or at sunset for the views.

Tha Pai Hot Springs HOT SPRINGS
(บ่อน้ำร้อนท่าปาย; adult/child 300/150B; 7am-6pm) Across Mae Nam Pai and 7km southeast of town via a paved road is this well-kept local park. Through it flows a scenic stream, which mixes with the hot springs in places to make pleasant bathing areas. The water is also diverted to a couple of nearby spas.

Pai Adventures RAFTING
(062 293 5978, 053 699326; www.paiadventures.com; 138 Th Chaisongkhram; 10.30am-10pm) The one- or two-day white-water rafting trips (from June to October) offered by this recommended outfit can be combined with hiking and other activities. They video your descent down the rapids and will send the results to you for free. There's also a jungle-survival course (available upon request).

Duang Trekking TREKKING
(084 741 8648, 065 421 1418; lungteng1@gmail.com; Th Chaisongkhram; 7am-9pm) A long-established local agency for trekking, white-water and bamboo rafting, kayaking and day tours. Treks start at 1000B per day per person (minimum group of two people), while kayaking and white-water rafting trips begin at 1800B per day per person (also with a minimum of two people).

Courses

The curriculum of courses available in Pai ranges from circus arts and drumming to yoga in all its forms. Keep an eye on the flyers in every cafe, or check the *Pai Events Planner* (PEP) or the *Pai Explorer* (www.facebook.com/PaiExplorer) to see what's on when you're in town.

Pai Cookery School COOKING
(081 706 3799; www.facebook.com/paicookeryschool; Th Wanchalerm; 600-750B; 11am-1.30pm & 2-6.30pm) With more than 20 years of experience, this outfit offers a variety of daily cooking courses covering three to five dishes. The afternoon course involves a trip to the market for ingredients. Contact them a day in advance. Note they may be moving location; call or check the Facebook page.

Pai Traditional Thai Massage HEALTH & WELLBEING
(PTTM; 083 577 0498; 68/3 Soi 1, Th Wiang Tai; massage per 1/1½/2hr 200/300/400B, sauna per visit 100B, 3-day massage course 3500B; 9am-9pm) This long-standing, locally owned outfit offers very good northern Thai massage, as well as a sauna (November to February only) where you can steam yourself in medicinal herbs. Three-day massage courses begin every Monday and Friday and run three hours per day.

Pai

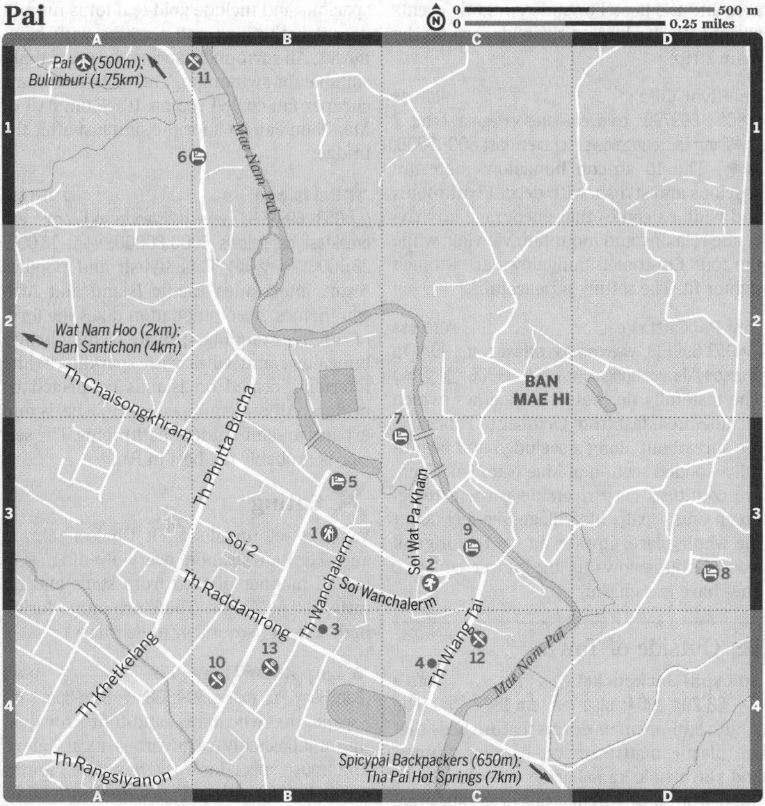

Pai

Activities, Courses & Tours

1 Duang Trekking ... B3
2 Pai Adventures ... C3
3 Pai Cookery School ... B4
4 Pai Traditional Thai Massage ... C4

Sleeping

5 Common Grounds Pai ... B3
6 Pai Island ... B1
7 Pai River Villa ... C3
8 Pairadise ... D3
9 Rim Pai Cottage ... C3

Eating

10 Chew Xin Jai ... B4
11 Larp Khom Huay Poo ... B1
12 Maya Burger Queen ... C4
13 Om Garden Cafe ... B4

Sleeping

Pai is reportedly home to more than 500 hotels, hostels, guesthouses and resorts. Despite the hotel glut, accommodation in Pai can be nearly impossible to come by during the height of the Thai tourist season (December and January); book ahead. Conversely, during the low season (June to September) nearly all the midrange and top-end places, and some budget ones, cut their rates, sometimes by as much as 60%.

In Town

★Common Grounds Pai HOSTEL $
(☎062 034 8509; www.commongroundspai.com; off Th Chaisongkhram; dm/r 295/895B; ❄📶) The best and most social hostel in Pai, Common Grounds offers well-maintained, comfy, six-bed dorms with lockers and their own bathrooms. The split-level private rooms come with decent beds, big windows and smooth cement walls. There's a large communal bar

area and the hostel organises nightly events around Pai. It's located riverside, just off the main strip.

Pai River Villa   HOTEL **$$**
(☑053 699796; pairivervillaresort@gmail.com; 7 Th Wiang Tai; bungalows incl breakfast 800-1500B; ✳🛜) The 10 air-con bungalows here are spacious and stylish, with decent bathrooms and wide balconies that encourage lazy riverside relaxing and mountain viewing, while the four fan-cooled bungalows are a much tighter fit. The setting is peaceful.

Rim Pai Cottage   HOTEL **$$$**
(☑053 699133; www.rimpaicottage.com; 99/1 Th Chaisongkhram; bungalows 2200-3300B; ✳🛜🏊) The tastefully decorated bungalows (which include breakfast from October to February) are spread out along a secluded and beautifully wooded section of Mae Nam Pai. There are countless cosy riverside corners to relax in and a palpable village-like feel about the whole place. Opt for one of the original wooden bungalows as the newer concrete ones have less charm.

🛏 Outside of Town

Spicypai Backpackers   HOTEL **$**
(☑088 294 2004; Mae Yen; dm 180B; 🛜) The large, semi-open-air dorms feature beds that are plastic mattresses on bamboo frames, and the whole ramshackle place could be lifted from a *Survivor* episode. Communal areas include hammocks slung under shade and a firepit, continuing the rustic theme, as does the location down a dirt track surrounded by rice fields. It's 750m east of Mae Nam Pai, just off the road to Tha Pai Hot Springs.

★Bulunburi   HOTEL **$$**
(☑053 698302; Ban Pong; bungalows incl breakfast 750-3000B; ✳🛜🏊) Set in a tiny, secluded valley of rice fields and streams, the seductively bucolic location of this place is as much a reason to stay as the attractive accommodation. The 11 bungalows, which range from tight fan-cooled rooms to huge two-bedroom houses, aren't flash but they're well equipped and comfortable. Book ahead; some people stay here for months.

Pairadise   HOTEL **$$**
(☑053 698065; www.pairadise.com; Ban Mae Hi; r & bungalows 600-1500B; ✳🛜🏊) This neat resort looks over the Pai Valley from atop a ridge just outside town. The bungalows are spacious and include gold-leaf lotus murals, decent bathrooms and terraces with hammocks. All surround a spring-fed pond that's suitable for swimming. There are also some cheaper fan-cooled rooms. It's 750m east of Mae Nam Pai; look for the sign just after the bridge.

★Pai Island   RESORT **$$$**
(☑053 699999; www.paiislandresort.com; incl breakfast bungalows 6000-8000B; villas 18,000-28,000B; ✳🛜🏊) This stylish and popular resort intertwines Pacific Island and African themes. Accommodation takes the form of 10 free-standing, private-feeling luxury bungalows and villas with sparkling white interiors, located on islands connected by bridges. All are equipped with jacuzzis and expansive semi-outdoor bathrooms. The service is probably the best in Pai.

🍴 Eating

Vendors set up along Th Chaisongkhram and Th Rangsiyanon every evening, selling all manner of food from stalls and refurbished VW vans. There are more during high season (November to February).

★Larp Khom Huay Poo   THAI **$**
(Ban Huay Pu; mains 50-100B; ⏱8am-8pm; 🛜) Escape the wheatgrass-and-tofu crowd at this unabashedly carnivorous local eatery. The house special is *'larp moo kua'*, northern-style *lâhp* (minced pork fried with herbs and spices). Accompanied by sticky rice, bitter herbs and an ice-cold beer, it's one of the best meals in Pai. The soups and bamboo worms are fine, too. Located 1km north of town, on the road to Mae Hong Son.

★Om Garden Cafe   INTERNATIONAL **$**
(off Th Raddamrong; mains 60-140B; ⏱8.30am-5pm Wed-Mon; 🛜🍴) Meat-free takes on international dishes, fresh-pressed juices, a pleasant shaded garden, a noticeboard advertising yoga classes, the odd hippy: basically everything you'd expect at a place called Om Garden, except that the food is actually good. It's not exclusively veggie: dishes range from Middle Eastern meze to breakfast burritos, salads and pasta. There are also pastries and fine coffee.

Maya Burger Queen   AMERICAN **$**
(www.facebook.com/MayaBurgerQueen; Th Wiang Tai; mains 80-165B; ⏱1-10pm; 🛜🍴) Burgers are a big deal in Pai and our arduous research has concluded that Maya does the

best job. Everything is homemade, from the soft, slightly sweet buns to the rich garlic mayo that accompanies the thick-cut fries. There are no less than six veggie-burger options, too.

Chew Xin Jai VEGAN $
(off Th Rangsiyanon; mains 49-139B; ⌚8am-7pm; 📶✍) Chew Xin Jai stands out from Pai's ever-increasing number of vegan/veggie eating spots by virtue of its Chinese take on vegetarian cuisine, with Taiwanese fried rice, dumplings, spring rolls and a faux duck soup. There's no Roman-script sign; look for the Chinese-style building adorned with three Chinese characters.

Getting There & Away

Pai's minivan station handles all public transport to and from town. It is wise to book tickets a day in advance.

Destinations include the following:

Chiang Mai (150B, three to four hours, hourly 7am to 5pm)
Mae Hong Son (150B, three to four hours, daily)
Soppong (Pangmapha; 100B, 1½ hours, daily)

Aya Service also runs air-con minivan buses to Chiang Mai (150B, three hours, hourly 7am to 5.30pm).

Getting Around

Most of Pai is accessible on foot. Motorcycle taxis wait at the stand next to the minivan station. It costs 50B to Ban Santichon village and 100B to Nam Tok Mo Paeng waterfall.

There are many places around town that rent out motorbikes (from 100B per day) and bicycles (from 50B per day).

Sukhothai

☎055 / POP 37,000

Most people are drawn to Sukhothai Province (จังหวัดสุโขทัย) by the ruins of the eponymous former kingdom, one of Thailand's most historically significant and impressive destinations.

The Sukhothai (Rising of Happiness) Kingdom flourished from the mid-13th century to the late 14th century. This period is often viewed as the golden age of Thai civilisation, and the religious art and architecture of the era are considered to be the most classic of Thai styles.

The market town of Sukhothai (สุโขทัย; often known as New Sukhothai) is located 12km east of the Sukhothai Historical Park on the Mae Nam Yom. While not particularly interesting, its relaxed atmosphere, good transport links and excellent-value accommodation make it a pleasant base from which to explore the old-city ruins.

Sights

★Sukhothai Historical Park HISTORIC SITE
(อุทยานประวัติศาสตร์สุโขทัย; ☎055 697527; central, northern & western zones 100B, plus bicycle 10B; ⌚central zone 6.30am-7.30pm, to 9pm Sat, northern & western zones 6.30am-7.30pm) The Sukhothai Historical Park ruins are one of Thailand's most impressive World Heritage sites. The park includes the remains of 21 historical sites and four large ponds within the old walls, with an additional 70 sites within a 5km radius. The ruins are divided into five zones; the central, northern and western zones each have a separate 100B admission fee. Note that motorbikes and cars are no longer allowed inside the park.

➡ Central Zone
(อุทยานประวัติศาสตร์สุโขทัย โซนกลาง; 100B, plus bicycle 10B; ⌚6.30am-7.30pm Sun-Fri, to 9pm Sat) This is the historical park's main zone and home to what are arguably some of the park's most impressive ruins. On Saturday night much of the central zone is illuminated and remains open until 9pm.

➡ Western Zone
(อุทยานประวัติศาสตร์สุโขทัย โซนตะวันตก; 100B, plus bicycle 10B; ⌚6.30am-7.30pm) The western zone of Sukhothai Historical Park, at its furthest extent 2km west of the old city walls, is the most expansive. In addition to **Wat Saphan Hin** (วัดสะพานหิน; western zone, Sukthothai Historical Park; 100B, plus bicycle 10B; ⌚6.30am-7.30pm), several mostly featureless ruins can be found. A bicycle or motorcycle is necessary to explore this zone.

➡ Northern Zone
(อุทยานประวัติศาสตร์สุโขทัย โซนเหนือ; 100B, plus bicycle 10B; ⌚6.30am-7.30pm) The northern zone of Sukhothai Historical Park, 500m north of the old city walls, is easily reached by bicycle.

Ramkhamhaeng National Museum MUSEUM
(พิพิธภัณฑสถานแห่งชาติรามคำแหง; Sukhothai Historical Park; 150B; ⌚9am-4pm) Near the entrance to the central zone, this museum

is a decent starting point for exploring the historical-park ruins. A replica of the famous Ramkhamhaeng inscription, said to be the earliest example of Thai writing, is kept here among an impressive collection of Sukhothai artefacts. Admission to the museum is not included in the ticket to the central zone.

Tours

Cycling Sukhothai CYCLING
(055 612519, 085 083 1864; www.cycling-sukhothai.com; off Th Jarodvithithong; half-/full day 800/990B, sunset tour 450B;) A resident of Sukhothai for 20-odd years, Belgian cycling enthusiast Ronny Hanquart offers themed bike tours, such as the Historical Park Tour, which also includes stops at lesser-seen wát and villages. The office is about 1.2km west of the Mae Nam Yom, off Th Jarodvithithong in New Sukhothai; free transport can be arranged. There are trailers and special seats for kids.

Sleeping

New Sukhothai

New Sukhothai has some of the best-value budget accommodation in northern Thailand. Clean, cheerful hotels and guesthouses abound, with many places offering attractive bungalows, free pickup from the bus station and free use of bicycles.

Ban Thai GUESTHOUSE $
(055 610163; banthai_guesthouse@yahoo.com; 38 Th Prawet Nakhon; r & bungalows 350-800B;) New Sukhothai's longest-running guesthouse, Ban Thai is a relaxed, friendly spot. The cheapest rooms are plain and fan-only but the cute and compact bungalows set around an attractive garden are a decent deal.

Foresto HOTEL $$
(095 125 9689; www.forestosukhothai.com; 16/1-3 Th Prawet Nakhon; r 1250-1600B;) Wind through a semisecluded garden to find 15 spacious and stylish rooms, all with decent bathrooms. Choose from the vast rooms in the main structure or the newer rooms that resemble glass cubes and come with big windows. The pool is a bonus.

Sabaidee House HOTEL $$
(055 616303; www.sabaideehouse.com; 81/7 Th Jarodvithithong; r incl breakfast 500-800B;) This cheery guesthouse in a semi-rural setting has seven attractive bungalows set in a shady garden, and four less-impressive rooms that share bathrooms in the main structure. There's also a pool and a restaurant. It's tucked down a quiet lane off Th Jarodvithithong, about 200m before the intersection with Rte 101; look for the sign.

Sukhothai Historical Park

There's an increasing number of options near the park, many of them upscale. Prices tend to go up during the Loi Krathong festival.

★Thai Thai Sukhothai Guesthouse HOTEL $$
(055 697022; www.thaithaisukhothai.com; off Rte 1272; incl breakfast r 1000-1250B, bungalows 1400B;) This place isn't a guesthouse but is instead a very comfortable hotel that gets rave reviews. The bungalows with their big balconies are especially enticing, but all the rooms are tastefully decorated, spacious and up to date. The service is as good as it gets in Sukhothai and there's a decent-sized pool.

★Orchid Hibiscus Guest House HOTEL $$
(055 633284; www.orchidhibiscus-guesthouse.com; 407/2 Rte 1272; r/bungalows incl breakfast 900/1500B;) This collection of rooms and bungalows is spread across two compounds; both have pools and are surrounded by a relaxing, manicured garden packed with plants and flowers. Rooms are spacious, spotless and fun, featuring colourful design details and accents, plus four-poster beds. It's on Rte 1272, about 500m off Rte 12 the turn-off is between the Km 48 and Km 49 markers.

★Ruean Thai Hotel HOTEL $$$
(055 612444; www.rueanthaihotel.com; 181/20 Soi Pracha Ruammit; r incl breakfast 1480-2180B, ste 4000-4600B;) At first glance you might mistake this eye-catching complex for a Buddhist temple or a traditional Thai house. The upper-level rooms follow a distinct Thai theme, while the poolside rooms are slightly more modern; there's a concrete building with simple air-con rooms out the back. Service is both friendly and flawless, and the whole place boasts a resort-like feel.

Eating & Drinking

A string of food stalls and simple tourist-oriented restaurants can be found along the road to the historical park, while there's also a spread of eating options in Sukhothai itself.

★ Jayhae THAI $

(off Th Jarodvithithong; dishes 40-120B; ⌚7am-4pm;) You haven't been to Sukhothai if you haven't tried the noodles at Jayhae, an extremely popular restaurant that serves Sukhothai-style noodles, *pàt tai* and tasty coffee drinks. It's located about 1.3km west of Mae Nam Yom.

Poo Restaurant MULTICUISINE $

(24/3 Th Jarodvithithong; mains 50-250B; ⌚9am-11pm;) Named after its original owner (if you were wondering), Poo is a traveller-friendly spot that serves everything from tasty Sukhothai noodles to Thai and Western classics. Portions are big. It's also fine for an evening drink: it does cocktails and has a small selection of Belgian beers.

Chopper Bar BAR

(Th Prawet Nakhon; ⌚5pm-midnight;) Travellers and locals congregate at this 2nd-floor bar with a vague cowboy theme for drinks, food (the menu is thoughtfully divided into spicy and nonspicy sections) and live music. Take advantage of Sukhothai's cool evenings on the rooftop terrace. The bar is owned by Sukhothai's finest locksmith, just in case you get locked out.

Information

Sukhothai Hospital (☎055 610280; Th Jarodvithithong) Located just west of New Sukhothai.

Tourism Authority of Thailand (TAT; ☎055 616228, nationwide 1672; www.tourismthaiand.org; Th Jarodvithithong; ⌚8.30am-4.30pm) About 750m west of the bridge in New Sukhothai, this office has a pretty good selection of maps and brochures and a few English-speaking staff.

Tourist Police (☎1155; Rte 12; ⌚24hr) A tourist-police outpost close to the Sukhothai Historical Park.

Getting There & Away

Sukhothai Airport is located 27km north of town. Bangkok Airways has two daily flights to/from Bangkok's Suvarnabhumi International Airport (from 1690B, 1¼ hours). Eddy Rent A Car operates a minivan service between the airport and New Sukhothai or Sukhothai Historical Park. Alternatively, AirAsia and Nok Air offer minivan transfers to/from both old and New Sukhothai via the airport in Phitsanulok, less than an hour away.

Sukhothai's bus station is almost 1km northwest of the centre of New Sukhothai; a motorcycle taxi between here and central New Sukhothai should cost around 50B, or you can hop on any *sŏrng·tăa·ou* bound for Sukhothai Historical Park – they stop at the bus station on their way out of town (30B, 10 minutes, frequent from 6am to 5.30pm).

Destinations include the following:

Bangkok (255B to 382B, six to seven hours, frequent departures)

Chiang Mai (211B to 390B, five to six hours, frequent departures)

Chiang Rai (256B, nine hours, twice daily)

Kamphaeng Phet (74B, 1½ hours, frequent departures)

Khon Kaen (310B to 410B, seven hours, seven daily)

Lampang (220B, three hours, frequent departures)

Mae Sot (153B to 191B, three hours, twice daily)

Mukdahan (550B, 10 hours, twice daily)

Phitsanulok (52B, one hour, frequent departures)

Sawankhalok (28B, one hour, hourly 6.40am to 5pm)

Si Satchanalai (49B, 1½ hours, hourly 6.40am to 5pm)

Alternatively, if you're staying near the historical park, Win Tour has an office where you can board buses to Bangkok (338B to 395B, six hours, 8.20am, 12.20pm and 9.50pm) and Chiang Mai (225B to 290B, five hours, 6.40am, 9.50am, 12.10pm and 2pm).

Getting Around

A *săhm·lór* ride within New Sukhothai should cost no more than 40B to 50B.

Relatively frequent *sŏrng·tăa·ou* run between New Sukhothai and Sukhothai Historical Park (30B, 30 minutes, 6am to 5.30pm), leaving from a stop on Th Jarodvithithong. Motorcycle taxis run between the town or bus station and the historical park for 120B.

The best way to get around the historical park is by bicycle; bikes can be hired at shops outside the park entrance for 30B for five hours (6am to 6pm).

Motorbikes (from 200B for 24 hours) can be hired at many guesthouses in New Sukhothai.

Chiang Rai

053 / POP 77,000

This small, amiable city is worth getting to know, with its relaxed atmosphere, fine local food and good-value accommodation. This is despite the fact that Chiang Rai Province has such a diversity of attractions that its capital is often overlooked. It's also the logical base from which to plan excursions to the more remote corners of the province.

Founded by Phaya Mengrai in 1262 as part of the Lao–Thai Lanna kingdom, Chiang Rai (เชียงราย) didn't become a Siamese territory until 1786.

Sights

★Mae Fah Luang Art & Culture Park — MUSEUM

(ไร่แม่ฟ้าหลวง; www.maefahluang.org; 313 Mu 7, Ban Pa Ngiw; adult/child 200B/free; 8.30am-5.30pm Tue-Sun) In addition to a museum that houses one of Thailand's biggest collections of Lanna artefacts, this vast, meticulously landscaped compound includes antique and contemporary art, Buddhist temples and other structures. It's located about 4km west of the centre of Chiang Rai; a túk-túk or taxi here will run to around 100B.

★Hilltribe Museum & Education Center — MUSEUM

(พิพิธภัณฑ์และศูนย์การศึกษาชาวเขา; www.pdacr.org; 3rd fl, 620/25 Th Thanalai; 50B; 9am-6pm Mon-Fri, 10am-6pm Sat & Sun) This museum and cultural centre is a good place to visit before undertaking any hill-tribe trek. Run by the nonprofit Population & Community Development Association (PDA), the venue has displays that are underwhelming in their visual presentation but contain a wealth of information on Thailand's various tribes and the issues that surround them.

A visit begins with a 20-minute slide show on Thailand's hill tribes, followed by a self-guided exploration among exhibits that include the typical clothing of six major tribes, folk implements and other anthropological objects. The curator is passionate about his museum and, if present, will talk about the different hill tribes, their histories, recent trends and the community projects that the museum helps fund.

Oub Kham Museum — MUSEUM

(พิพิธภัณฑ์อูบคำ; www.oubkhammuseum.com; Th Nakhai; adult/child incl tour 300/200B; 8am-5pm) This slightly zany private museum houses an impressive collection of paraphernalia from virtually every corner of the former Lanna kingdom. The items, some of which truly are one of a kind, range from a monkey-bone food taster used by Lanna royalty to an impressive carved throne from Chiang Tung, Myanmar. Guided tours are obligatory and include a walk through a gilded artificial cave holding several Buddha statues, complete with disco lights and fake torches! The museum is located 2km west of the town centre and can be a bit tricky to find; túk-túk will go here for about 60B.

Tours

Nearly every guesthouse, hotel and travel agency in Chiang Rai offers hiking excursions in hill country, some of which have a grassroots, sustainable or nonprofit emphasis.

Trek pricing depends on the types of activities and the number of days and participants. A one-day trek for four people should start at around 1300B per person. For a three-night trek for four people, rates start at around 3500B per person. Everything from accommodation to transport and food is normally included in the price.

★Rai Pian Karuna — TREKKING

(062 246 1897; www.facebook.com/raipiankaruna; treks 2000-5000B) This community-based social enterprise conducts one-day and multiday treks and homestays at Akha, Lahu and Lua villages in Mae Chan, north of Chiang Rai. Other activities, from week-long volunteering stints to cooking courses, are also on offer.

PDA Tours & Travel — TREKKING

(053 740088; Hilltribe Museum & Education Center, 3rd fl, 620/25 Th Thanalai; treks 1200-3900B; 9am-6pm Mon-Fri, 10am-6pm Sat & Sun) One- to three-day treks are available through this NGO. Profits go back into community projects that include HIV/AIDS education, mobile health clinics, education scholarships and the establishment of village-owned banks.

Mirror Foundation — TREKKING

(053 719554; www.thailandecotour.org; 1-/2-/3-day treks from 2800/4300/5650B) Although its rates are higher than other outfits, trekking with this nonprofit NGO helps support the training of its local guides. Treks range from one to three days and traverse the Akha, Karen and Lahu villages of Mae Yao District, north of Chiang Rai.

Chiang Rai

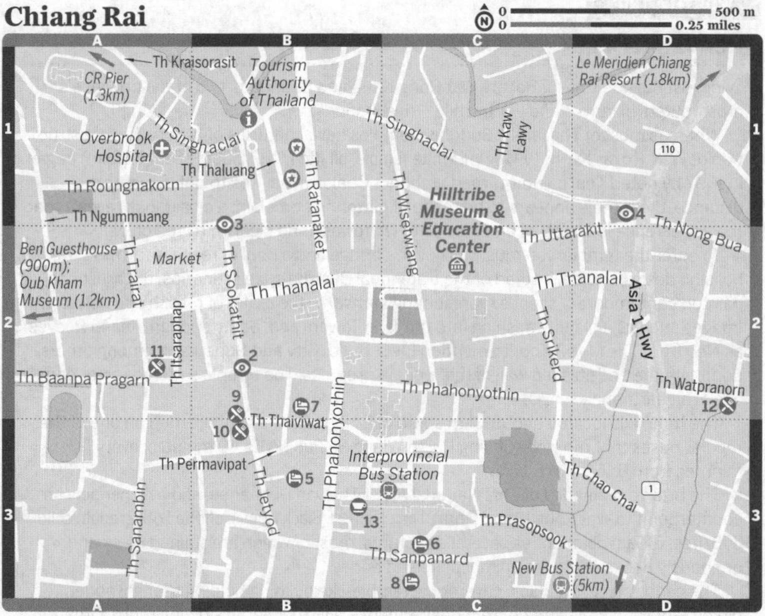

Chiang Rai

Top Sights
1 Hilltribe Museum & Education Center C2

Sights
2 Clock Tower B2
3 Clock Tower B1
4 King Mengrai Monument D1

Activities, Courses & Tours
PDA Tours & Travel .... (see 1)

Sleeping
5 Baan Bua Guest House B3
6 Baan Warabordee C3
7 Bed & Bike Poshtel B2
8 Na-Rak-O Resort C3

Eating
9 Heaven Burger B2
10 Khao Soi Phor Jai B3
11 Kunda Vegan Vegetarian A2
12 Lung Eed D2

Drinking & Nightlife
13 BaanChivitMai Bakery B3

Sleeping

In Town

Bed & Bike Poshtel HOSTEL $
(☎064 848 6566; bedandbikechiangrai@gmail.com; 869/53-54 Th Thaiviwat; 4-/8-bed dm 240/220B, r incl breakfast 500-700B; ❄📶) There's an industrial theme – metal, wood and stone floors – to the design at this well-kept place. Dorms are windowless but comfortable, with curtains, reading lights and lockers. The private rooms share clean bathrooms. The downstairs cafe-bar features a pool table, and bikes can be hired.

Baan Bua Guest House GUESTHOUSE $
(☎053 718880; baanbua@yahoo.com; 879/2 Th Jetyod; r 350-600B; ❄📶) Set around a peaceful garden, this quiet, friendly guesthouse is a decent budget option. The 17 rooms, the cheapest of which are fan-only, are a little dated (no TVs) but are clean and have small porches. There's also a wood-floored traditional house with four bedrooms for rent (2100B).

Baan Warabordee HOTEL $$
(☎053 754488; warabordee59@hotmail.com; 59/1 Th Sanpanard; r incl breakfast 800-1100B; ❄📶) A quiet, good-value hotel has been created

WORTH A TRIP

HEAVEN & HELL

Lying just outside Chiang Rai are Wat Rong Khun and Baandam, two of the province's most touted, bizarre – and worthwhile – destinations.

Whereas most of Thailand's Buddhist temples have centuries of history, the construction of **Wat Rong Khun** (วัดร่องขุ่น; White Temple; off Rte 1/AH2; 50B; ⌚8am-5.30pm) began in 1997 by noted Thai painter turned architect Chalermchai Kositpipat. Seen from a distance, the temple appears to be made of glittering porcelain; a closer look reveals that the appearance is due to a combination of whitewash and clear-mirrored chips.

To enter the temple, you must walk over a bridge and a pool of reaching arms (symbolising desire). Inside, instead of the traditional Buddha's-life scenarios, the artist has painted contemporary scenes representing *samsara* (the realm of rebirth and delusion). Images such as a plane smashing into the Twin Towers and, oddly enough, Keanu Reeves as Neo from *The Matrix* (not to mention Elvis, Hello Kitty and Superman, among others), dominate the one finished wall of this work in progress. The temple suffered minor damage in an earthquake in 2014.

The temple is located about 13km south of Chiang Rai. To get here, hop on one of the regular buses that run from Chiang Rai to Wiang Pa Pao (20B, 40 minutes, every 30 minutes from 6.15am to 6.10pm).

The bizarre brainchild of Thai National Artist Thawan Duchanee, and a rather sinister counterpoint to Wat Rong Khun, **Baandam** (บ้านดำ, Black House; off Rte 1/AH2; adult/child 80B/free; ⌚9am-5pm) unites several structures, most of which are stained black and ominously decked out with animal pelts and bones.

The centrepiece is a black, cavernous, temple-like building holding a long wooden dining table and chairs made from deer antlers – a virtual Satan's dining room. Other buildings include white, breast-shaped bedrooms, dark phallus-decked bathrooms and a bone- and fur-lined 'chapel'. The structures have undeniable northern Thai influences, but the dark tones, flagrant flourishes and all those dead animals coalesce in a way that is more fantasy than reality.

Baandam is located 13km north of Chiang Rai in Nang Lae, a 30-minute journey on any Mae Sai–bound bus (20B).

from this three-storey Thai villa. Rooms are decked out in dark woods and light fabrics and there's an inviting garden. Expect a 30% discount in the low season (May to October).

Na-Rak-O Resort HOTEL **$$**
(☎081 951 7801; www.facebook.com/narakoresort; off Th Sanpanard; r incl breakfast 900-1300B; ❄📶) *Nâh·rák* is Thai for 'cute', a spot-on description of this tucked-away hotel that has bright rooms decked out in pastel colours and strewn with beanbags. Beds are raised off the floor Chinese-style, the bathrooms are big and the staff smiley.

Outside Town Centre

★Bamboo Nest de Chiang Rai GUESTHOUSE **$$**
(☎089 953 2330, 095 686 4755; www.bamboonest-chiangrai.com; bungalows incl breakfast & dinner 1100-1400B) The Lahu village that's home to this unique place is only an hour's drive from Chiang Rai but feels very remote. Accommodation consists of simple but spacious bamboo huts perched on a steep hill overlooking tiered rice fields. Electricity is provided by solar panels, so give your devices a rest and instead take part in activities ranging from birdwatching to hiking.

Bamboo Nest is about 2km from the headquarters of Lamnamkok National Park; free transport to/from Chiang Rai is available for those staying for two nights or more.

Ben Guesthouse GUESTHOUSE **$$**
(☎053 716775; www.benguesthousechiangrai.com; 351/10 Soi 4, Th Sankhongnoi; r 400-600B, ste 1200B; ❄📶🏊) This spotless compound has a bit of everything, from fan-cooled cheap rooms to immense suites, not to mention a pool. Rooms are plain and simple but reasonably sized and share long balconies.

It's 1.2km from the town centre, at the end of Soi 4 on Th Sankhongnoi (the street is called Th Sathanpayabarn where it intersects with Th Phahonyothin).

★Le Meridien Chiang Rai Resort HOTEL $$$
(☎053 603333; www.lemeridien.com; 221/2 Th Kwaewai; incl breakfast r 7000-9000B, ste 20,000B; ❄📶🏊) Chiang Rai's grandest upscale resort is about 2km outside the city centre on a beautiful stretch of the Mae Nam Kok. Rooms are immense and decked out in greys, whites and blacks, and are as comfortable as the prices suggest. The compound includes two restaurants, an infinity pool and a gym and spa.

Eating & Drinking

Come dinner time, you'll inevitably be pointed in the direction of Chiang Rai's night bazaar, but the food there is generally average – you've been warned. Instead, if you're in town on a weekend, hit the vendors at Chiang Rai's open-air markets, Thanon Khon Muan and the Walking Street, which feature a good selection of local dishes.

Th Jetyod is Chiang Rai's rather tacky drinking strip. The streets close to Th Jetyod are also home to a growing number of Thai-style bars, a few with live music.

★Lung Eed THAI $
(Th Watpranorn; mains 40-60B; ⏲11am-9pm Mon-Sat) One of Chiang Rai's most delicious dishes is available at this simple, friendly shophouse restaurant. There's an English-language menu on the wall, but don't miss the sublime *lâhp gài* (minced chicken fried with local spices and topped with crispy deep-fried chicken skin, shallots and garlic). The restaurant is about 150m east of Rte 1/AH2.

★Heaven Burger BURGERS $
(1025/5 Th Jetyod; mains 99-129B; ⏲8am-9pm; 🖉) Owned and run by the whip-smart Jane, a member of the Akha minority, this place has a rustic setting with random garden furniture and sawn-off doors as tables. The food is great – all-day breakfasts and, above all, superb burgers, including a fine veggie option; all burgers come with home-made buns and gratinéed potato-skin fries.

Khao Soi Phor Jai THAI $
(Th Jetyod; mains 40-50B; ⏲8am-4pm) Phor Jai serves mild but delicious bowls of the eponymous curry noodle dish, as well as a few other northern Thai staples. There's no Roman-script sign, but look for the open-air shophouse with the white-and-blue interior.

★Kunda Vegan Vegetarian VEGETARIAN $$
(www.kundacafe.com; 372 Trairat Rd; mains 150-360B; ⏲9am-5pm; 🖉) There's no tofu, no wi-fi and no reservations at this delightful addition to the Chiang Rai dining scene set over two floors of a former shophouse. Lounge on cushions and enjoy the old-school wood-panelled decor while tucking into vegan or veggie breakfasts, crêpes, salads and super smoothies. Everything – the bread, pesto, yoghurt and hummus – is made fresh daily.

★BaanChivitMai Bakery CAFE
(www.bcmthai.com; Th Prasopsook; ⏲8am-6pm Mon-Fri, to 5pm Sat & Sun; 📶) In addition to a proper cup of joe made from local beans, there are surprisingly authentic Swedish-style sweets and Western-style meals and sandwiches at this popular bakery. Profits go to BaanChivitMai, an organisation that runs homes and education projects for vulnerable, orphaned or AIDS-affected children.

Information

Overbrook Hospital (☎053 711366; www.overbrook-hospital.com; Th Singhaclai) English is spoken at this modern hospital.

Tourism Authority of Thailand (TAT; ☎053 717433, nationwide 1672; tatchrai@tat.or.th; Th Singhaclai; ⏲8.30am-4.30pm) English is limited, but staff here do their best to give advice and can provide a small selection of maps and brochures.

Tourist Police (☎053 740249, nationwide 1155; Th Uttarakit; ⏲24hr) English is spoken and police are on standby around the clock.

Getting There & Away

AIR

Chiang Rai International Airport is approximately 8km north of the city. A new bus connects the airport with Chiang Rai's two bus stations (6am to 6pm, every 40 minutes, 20B). Taxis run into town from the airport for 160B. From town, a metered trip with Chiang Rai Taxi will cost around 130B.

There are 15 daily flights to Bangkok's Don Mueang International Airport and 14 to Bangkok's Suvarnabhumi International Airport.

BOAT

Passenger boats ply Mae Nam Kok between Chiang Rai and Tha Ton in Chiang Mai (400B, three hours), stopping at Ban Ruam Mit (100B, one hour) along the way. Boats depart from the CR Pier, 2km northwest of town, at 10.30am daily. A túk-túk to the pier should cost about 80B.

BUS & MINIVAN

Buses bound for destinations within Chiang Rai Province, as well as some minivans and mostly slow, fan-cooled buses bound for a handful of northern Thailand destinations, depart from the interprovincial bus station in the centre of town. If you're heading beyond Chiang Rai, you'll have to go to the new bus station, 5km south of town.

Frequent *sŏrng·tăa·ou* linking the new bus station and the interprovincial station run from 6am to 5.30pm (20B, 15 minutes). Or you can catch the purple-coloured bus that links the airport to the bus stations (6am to 6pm, every 40 minutes, 20B).

There's a direct international bus from Chiang Rai to Luang Prabang (Laos). There are also buses to Bokeo and Huay Xai (both in Laos), where it's possible to connect to Kunming (China), Luang Nam Tha (Laos) and Vientiane (Laos).

Getting Around

Central Chiang Rai is easy enough to tackle on foot or by bicycle. Bicycles (from 50B per day) and motorbikes (from 200B per day) can be hired from your accommodation or at travel agencies and shops around town. Otherwise, túk-túk congregate around the interprovincial bus station and charge approximately 30B to 50B per person for destinations in town.

Golden Triangle

The tri-country border of Thailand, Myanmar and Laos is often known as the Golden Triangle.

Sop Ruak

The borders of Myanmar, Thailand and Laos meet at Sop Ruak (สบรวก), at the confluence of Nam Ruak and the Mekong River. The town's two opium-related museums are both worth a visit, and a boat trip is an enjoyable way to pass an hour. But the only reason to overnight here is if you've already booked a room in one of the area's outstanding luxury hotels.

★Hall of Opium MUSEUM

(หอฝิ่น; Rte 1290; adult/child 200B/free; ⏲8.30am-4pm Tue-Sun) One kilometre north of Sop Ruak on a 40-hectare plot opposite the Anantara Golden Triangle Resort & Spa, the Mae Fah Luang Foundation has established the 5600-sq-metre Hall of Opium. The multimedia exhibitions include a fascinating history of opium, as well as engaging and informative displays on the effects

BUSES FROM CHIANG RAI

DESTINATION	FARE (B)	DURATION (HR)	FREQUENCY
Bangkok	544-890	11-12	frequent 8.30am-7.50pm (new bus station)
Bokeo (Laos)	220	3	10am & 4.30pm (new bus station)
Chiang Khong	65	2	frequent 6am-5pm (interprovincial bus station)
Chiang Mai	129-258	3-7	frequent 6.15am-7.30pm (interprovincial bus station)
Chiang Saen	37	1½	frequent 6am-5pm (interprovincial bus station)
Huay Xai (Laos)	220	3	10am (new bus station)
Lampang	137-274	4-5	8.40am, 10am, 1.20pm (interprovincial bus station)
Luang Prabang (Laos)	950	18	12.30pm Mon, Wed, Fri, Sun (new bus station)
Mae Chan (for Mae Salong/Santikhiri)	25	45min	frequent 6am-5pm (interprovincial bus station)
Mae Sai	39	1½	frequent 6am-5pm (interprovincial bus station)
Mae Sot	416	12	8.40am (new bus station)
Nakhon Ratchasima	569-664	12-13	4 departures 6.30am-7.20pm (new bus station)
Phayao	60-120	1½-2	8.40am, 10am, 1.20pm (interprovincial bus station)
Phitsanulok	304-355	6-7	hourly 6.30am-7.30pm (new bus station)
Phrae	185-216	4	frequent 6am-6pm (new bus station)
Sukhothai	231	8	hourly 7.30-10.30am (new bus station)
Ubon Ratchathani	884	12	2pm (new bus station)

of opium abuse on individuals and society. Well balanced and worth investigating.

Wat Prathat Pukhao BUDDHIST TEMPLE
(วัดพระธาตุภูเข้า; Rte 1290; ⊙daylight hours) FREE Wat Prathat Pukhao provides the best viewpoint of the Mekong junction of Thailand, Laos and Myanmar. There are steps up to the temple next to the House of Opium.

House of Opium MUSEUM
(บ้านฝิ่น; Rte 1290; 50B; ⊙7am-7pm) This small but informative museum features historical displays pertaining to opium culture. Exhibits include the various implements used in the planting, harvesting, use and trade of the *Papaver somniferum* resin, including pipes, weights and scales. The museum is at the southeastern end of Sop Ruak, roughly across from the huge Buddha statue at Phra Chiang Saen Si Phaendin.

Getting There & Away

There are frequent *sŏrng·tăa·ou* to Chiang Saen (20B, 15 minutes, 7am to noon) and Mae Sai (40B, 30 minutes, every 40 minutes from 8am to 1pm), both of which can be flagged down along the main strip. It's a flat and easy 9km bicycle ride from Chiang Saen to Sop Ruak.

Doi Mae Salong (Santikhiri)

☎053 / POP 20,000

Doi Mae Salong (ดอยแม่สลอง) was originally settled by Chinese soldiers from Yunnan Province who fled communist rule in 1949. Generations later, the language, culture and cuisine of this unique community persists. The Chinese vibe, mountain setting and abundance of hill peoples and tea plantations converge in a destination quite unlike anywhere else in Thailand. It's a great place to kick back in for a couple of days, and the surrounding area is exceptional for self-guided exploration.

Sights & Activities

Shin Sane Guest House and Little Home Guesthouse have free maps showing approximate trekking routes to Akha, Lisu, Mien, Lahu and Shan villages in the area.

The best hikes are north of Mae Salong between Ban Thoet Thai and the Myanmar border. Check local travel conditions before heading off in this direction.

Shin Sane Guest House also leads pony treks to four nearby villages for 600B for about three or four hours, although the ponies won't carry anyone over 60kg.

Morning Market MARKET
(ตลาดเช้าดอยแม่สลอง; off Rte 1130; ⊙6-8am) A tiny but busy and vibrant morning market convenes at the T-intersection near Shin Sane Guest House. The market attracts town residents and hill peoples from the surrounding districts and is worth waking up early for.

Wat Santikhiri VIEWPOINT
(วัดสันติคีรี) To soak up the great views from Wat Santikhiri, go past the market and ascend 718 steps (or take the road if you have a motorbike or car). The wát is of the Mahayana tradition and Chinese in style.

Sleeping & Eating

★Baan Hom Muen Li HOTEL $$
(Osmanthus; ☎053 765455; osmanhouse@hotmail.com; Rte 1130; r incl breakfast 1200-1500B; ❄📶) Slap in the middle of town, this stylish place consists of 22 rooms artfully decked out in modern and classical Chinese themes. Go for the more expensive upstairs rooms, which have big balconies offering fine views over the surrounding tea plantations. There's no Roman-script sign.

Little Home Guesthouse GUESTHOUSE $$
(☎053 765389; www.maesalonglittlehome.com; Rte 1130; r & bungalows 800-1000B; ❄📶) Located near the morning-market intersection is this large yellow building backed by a

LOCAL KNOWLEDGE

MAE SALONG CUISINE

The very Chinese breakfast of *bah·tôrng·gŏh* (deep-fried dough sticks) and hot soybean milk at the morning market is a great way to start the day. In fact, many Thai tourists come to Doi Mae Salong simply to eat Yunnanese dishes such as *màn·tŏh* (steamed Chinese buns) served with braised pork belly and pickled vegetables, or black chicken braised with Chinese-style herbs. Homemade wheat and egg noodles are another speciality of Doi Mae Salong, and are served with a local broth that combines pork and a spicy chilli paste. They're available at several places in town.

handful of attractive bungalows. Rooms are a reasonable size – the more expensive ones come with air-con – and are tidy and sunny, while the good-value bungalows have balconies. The owners are friendly and helpful.

★ **Phu Chaisai Resort & Spa** RESORT $$$
(☎053 910500; www.phu-chaisai.com; off Rte 1130; bungalows incl breakfast 4200-11,200B;) On a remote bamboo-covered hilltop, this resort is the most unique place to stay in the Mae Salong area. The more you pay, the bigger your bungalow and the better the views, but all the bungalows feature bamboo furniture, comfy beds and balconies. It's a lovely setting and the spa gets rave reviews. Your stay includes access to a host of activities (spa treatments, massage, yoga, day hikes, rafting, swimming) to keep you occupied. Transport from Chiang Rai is available for 824B.

★ **Salima Restaurant** CHINESE $$
(Rte 1130; mains 50-250B; 9am-8pm) One of the friendliest restaurants in town also happens to be the one serving the tastiest food. Salima does tasty Muslim-Chinese dishes, including a rich Yunnan-style beef curry and a deliciously tart, spicy tuna and tea-leaf salad. The noodle dishes are equally worthwhile and include a beef *kôw soy*. No alcohol is served.

Salima is located five minutes' walk south of the 7-Eleven.

Information

There are a couple of ATMs that accept foreign cards on the main road through Mae Salong.

Getting There & Around

The easiest way to get to Doi Mae Salong from Chiang Rai is to take a bus to Mae Chan, from where *sŏrng·tăa·ou* run to Doi Mae Salong from the market area when full (50B, one hour). It's best to get to Mae Chan in the morning as transport dries up later in the day. You can also charter your own *sŏrng·tăa·ou* for 500B. In the reverse direction, you can flag down *sŏrng·tăa·ou* near Doi Mae Salong's 7-Eleven.

You can also reach Doi Mae Salong by road from Tha Ton in Chiang Mai. Yellow *sŏrng·tăa·ou* bound for Tha Ton stop near Little Home Guesthouse four times daily (60B, one hour).

Much of Doi Mae Salong is approachable on foot. If you want to go further (or are struggling with the hills), motorcycle taxis congregate by the 7-Eleven. A few places rent motorbikes (200B per day).

Chiang Khong

☎053 / POP 14,500

Chiang Khong (เชียงของ) was historically an important market town for local communities and for trade with northern Laos. In 2013, a bridge over the Mekong River connecting Chiang Khong with Huay Xai in Laos was opened. From Huay Xai, it's a two-day slow boat or a 14-hour bus trip to Luang Prabang. It's also possible to travel quickly and easily to Yunnan Province in China from Huay Xai.

Sleeping & Eating

Namkhong Resort HOTEL $
(☎053 791055; tigerkriang911@hotmail.com; 94/2 Th Sai Klang; r incl breakfast 200-800B;) Just off the main drag is this semi-secluded compound of tropical plants and handsome wooden structures. It's a popular spot: even the fan-cooled, shared-bathroom cheapies go quickly. The most expensive rooms come with air-con and private bathrooms. There's an attached restaurant and the swimming pool is a bonus.

★ **Sleeping Well Hostel** HOSTEL $$
(☎097 280 4040; info.sleepingwell@gmail.com; 10/8 Th Sai Klang; dm 190B, r 490-1090B;) Housed in a stylish four-storey building connected by a winding staircase, the eight-bed dorm and rooms here are spotless and fresh, with white and wood finishes. A variety of rooms are available: the cheapest with shared bathrooms, the most expensive rooftop options with private terraces. There are communal spaces throughout and a downstairs cafe-restaurant.

★ **Khao Soi Pa Orn** THAI $
(Soi 6, Th Sai Klang; mains 30-60B; 8am-4pm) The Chiang Khong version of *kôw soy* – the famous northern curry noodle soup – forgoes the curry broth and replaces it with clear soup topped with a rich, spicy minced-pork mixture. It's still delicious, and this place is a compulsory stop for Thai tourists passing through town. A few rice dishes are also available. There's no Roman-script sign, but it's located next to the giant highway-distance marker.

Bamboo Mexican House INTERNATIONAL $$
(Th Sai Klang; mains 160-280B; 8am-8.30pm;) Run by a guitar-playing hippy with a love of Mexican dishes, this chilled, long-standing spot offers burritos, enchiladas and tacos, as well as pasta and a few

Thai dishes. Fine coffee and tasty homemade breads and cakes are also on offer. It opens early and can provide boxed lunches for the boat ride to Luang Prabang.

Getting There & Away

Chiang Khong has a bus station located 3km south of town, which is exclusively for buses to Bangkok. But buses departing from there also stop in town, close to the market or at the **Sombat Tour** office, both south of the centre of town. Buses for other destinations also pick up and drop off passengers at various points near the markets.

Destinations include the following:

Bangkok (592B to 921B, 13 hours, 7.25am and frequent departures 3pm to 4.30pm)
Chiang Mai 202B to 395B, six to seven hours, thrice daily)
Chiang Rai (65B, 2½ hours, frequent departures)
Phayao (108B to 139B, three hours, twice daily)

There are daily minivans to Chiang Mai (350B, five to six hours, 10am and 5pm), which will pick you up at your guesthouse. If you're bound for Chiang Saen, you'll first need to take a *sŏrng·tăa·ou* to Hat Bai from a stall on Th Sai Klang (50B, one hour, around 8am), where you'll need to transfer to another Chiang Saen–bound *sŏrng·tăa·ou*.

Nan

Nan (น่าน) is not the kind of destination most travellers are going to stumble upon, as it's remote by Thai standards. But if you take the time to get here, you'll be rewarded with a relaxed city rich in both culture and history.

Many of Nan's residents are Tai Lü, the ancestors of immigrants from Xishuangbanna in southwestern China's Yunnan Province. Their cultural legacy can be seen in the city's art and architecture, particularly in its exquisite temples. But there's also a strong Lanna influence here, as revealed in the remains of the old city wall and several early wát.

Sights & Activities

Nan has nothing like the organised trekking industry found in Chiang Rai and Chiang Mai, and many visitors, particularly Thais, opt to float rather than walk. White-water rafting along Mae Nam Wa, in northern Nan, is only possible when the water level is high (from September to December), and is said to be best during the early part of the

GETTING TO LAOS: CHIANG KHONG TO HUAY XAI

Getting to the border The jumping-off point is the Friendship Bridge, around 10km south of Chiang Khong, via a 140B chartered săhm·lór ride or a 50B white-passenger-truck ride running the route from downtown or the bus-stop market area.

At the border After completing border formalities at the Thai immigration office, you'll board a shuttle bus (from 20B, 8am to 6pm) across the 630m span. On the Lao side, foreigners can purchase a 30-day visa for Laos upon arrival in Huay Xai for US$30 to US$42, depending on nationality. On your return to Thailand, unless you've already received a Thai visa, immigration will grant you permission to stay in the country for 30 days if you hold a passport from one of the 64 countries that has a visa-exemption arrangement with Thailand (or 15 days if you don't).

Moving on From the Lao side of the bridge, it's an exorbitant 100B/30,000K per person săhm·lór ride to the boat pier or Huay Xai's bus terminal. Bus destinations from Huay Xai include Luang Nam Tha (60,000K, four hours, 9am and 12.30pm), Luang Prabang (120,000K, 14 hours, 10am and 4pm), Udomxai (90,000K, eight hours, 9.30am and 1pm) and Vientiane (230,000K, 25 hours, 11.30am).

If time is on your side, the daily slowboat (200,000K, 11.30am) to Luang Prabang takes two days, including a night in the village of Pak Beng. Note that the ticket price does not include accommodation in Pak Beng. Avoid the noisy fast boats (350,000K, six hours, from 9am to 11am) as they are both dangerous and uncomfortable. Booking tickets through a Chiang Khong–based agent such as Easy Trip costs slightly more, but they arrange tickets for you and provide transport and a boxed lunch for the boat ride.

If you already hold a Chinese visa, it's also possible to head to China from Huay Xai. Catch the bus to Luang Nam Tha, where there are daily buses bound for Jinghong (100,000K, six hours, 8am) in Yunnan Province.

GETTING TO LAOS: BAN HUAY KON TO MUANG NGEUN

Located 140km north of Nan, Ban Huay Kon is a sleepy village in the mountains near the Lao border. There's a border market on Saturday morning, but most people come here because of the town's status as an international border crossing into Laos.

Getting to the border To Ban Huay Kon, there are five daily minivans originating in Phrae and stopping in Nan between 5am and noon (95B, three hours). In the opposite direction, minivans bound for Nan (95B, three hours), Phrae (172B, five hours) and Den Chai (for the train; 200B) leave Ban Huay Kon at 9.15am, 10am, 11am, noon and 3pm.

At the border After passing the Thai immigration booth, foreigners can purchase a 30-day visa for Laos for US$30 to US$42, depending on nationality. There is an extra US$1 or 50B charge after 4pm and on weekends.

Moving on You can then proceed 2.5km to the Lao village of Muang Ngeun, where you could stay at the Phouxay Guesthouse or, if you're heading onward, go to the tiny Passenger Car Station beside the market, from where *sŏrng·tăa·ou* leave for Hongsa (40,000K, 1½ hours) between 2pm and 4pm.

rainy season. The rapids span Classes I to IV and pass through intact jungle and remote villages.

★Wat Phumin BUDDHIST TEMPLE
(วัดภูมินทร; cnr Th Suriyaphong & Th Pha Kong; donations appreciated; ⏲daylight hours) Nan's most famous Buddhist temple is celebrated for its exquisite murals, executed during the late 19th century by a Thai Lü artist named Thit Buaphan. The exterior of the temple takes the form of a cruciform *bòht* that was constructed in 1596 and restored during the reign of Chao Anantavorapitthidet (1867–74). The ornate altar in the centre of the *bòht* has four sides, with four Sukhothai-style sitting Buddhas facing in each direction.

★Nan National Museum MUSEUM
(พิพิธภัณฑสถานแห่งชาติน่าน; Th Pha Kong; ⏲9am-4pm Wed-Sun) FREE Housed in the 1903 vintage palace of Nan's last two feudal lords, this museum first opened its doors in 1973. It's one of the country's better provincial museums, featuring exhibits on Nan's ethnic minorities, local history and architecture, archaeology, royal regalia, weapons, ceramics, Buddhism and religious art, and there are English labels for most items. Also on display is a rare 'black' elephant tusk said to have been presented to a Nan lord more than 300 years ago by the Khün ruler of Chiang Tung (Kyaingtong).

Fhu Travel TREKKING
(☎054 710636, 081 287 7209; www.facebook.com/fhutravel; 453/4 Th Sumon Thevarat; trekking per person 1800B; ⏲9am-5pm) This long-standing outfit offers one-day treks around Nan. It can also organise kayaking (from 1500B) and rafting (from 2500B).

Sleeping & Eating

Ban Himwat Hostel HOSTEL $
(☎091 858 6516; www.facebook.com/BanHimwatHostel; 31 Soi 1, Th Pha Kong; dm 400B; 📶) Everything is spotless at this newish hostel that mostly sees Thai travellers. The six- and 10-bed dorms come with decent mattresses and their own bathrooms. The hostel is in a peaceful location with a shaded outside area and there are free bicycles for guests to use.

Yindee Traveller's Lodge HOSTEL $
(☎081 806 0347; www.yindeetravellerslodge.com; 200/17 Th Mano; dm 350B, r 900-1000B; ❄📶) Right by the river, and with a roof terrace for sunset views and beers, this new place has dorms that are well set up with lockers, private lights, curtains and OK mattresses. There are two compact private rooms and free bicycles to use.

Crazy Noodle THAI $
(Th Kha Luang; mains 30-60B; ⏲8.30am-8.30pm; 📶) The locals think the owner here is *ting-tong* (crazy), so his shop is named accordingly. But he's friendly and seems sane to us. His noodles are fine as well, topped with tender pork and served with a spicy broth.

★Gin INTERNATIONAL $$
(www.facebook.com/ginrestaurant; 83/3 Th Sumon Thevarat; dishes 100-250B; ⏲11am-10pm) This cosy place doesn't look like much, but its menu mixes Thai and international cuisine to impressive effect. There are tart, colourful Thai salads and imaginative mains, such as

soft-shell crab with mango, and white snapper with tomato puree and pepper garnish. It also serves pasta and the best steaks in Nan.

Shopping

Nan is one of the best places in northern Thailand to pick up souvenirs. Good buys include local textiles, especially the Tai Lü weaving styles, which typically feature red-and-black thread on white cotton in floral, geometric and animal designs. Local Hmong appliqué and Mien embroidery are of excellent quality. Htin grass-and-bamboo baskets and mats are worth a look, too.

Walking Street MARKET
(Th Pha Kong; 5-10pm Fri-Sun) Every Friday, Saturday and Sunday evening, the stretch of Th Pha Kong in front of Wat Phumin is closed and vendors set up shop to sell food, textiles, clothing and local handicrafts.

Information

Tourist Centre (054 751169; Th Pha Kong; 8.30am-noon & 1-4.30pm) This helpful information centre is opposite Wat Phumin and hidden behind vendors and coffee shops.

Getting There & Around

Nan Nakhon Airport is located about 3km north of town. Air Asia has three daily flights to/from Bangkok's Don Mueang International Airport (from 1000B, 1½ hours). Klay Airport Taxi offers airport transfers for 100B per person.

From Nan, all buses, minivans and *sŏrng·tăa·ou* leave from the bus station at the southwestern edge of town. A motorcycle taxi between the station and the centre of town costs 30B.

If you're connecting to the train station at Den Chai in Phrae, you can hop on any bus bound for Chiang Mai or Bangkok.

Doi Phu Kha National Park

This large **national park** (อุทยานแห่งชาติดอยภูคา; 082 194 1349, accommodation 02 562 0760; www.dnp.go.th; 200B) is centred on 2000m-high Doi Phu Kha, Nan Province's highest peak, in Amphoe Pua and Amphoe Bo Kleua, about 75km northeast of Nan. There are several Htin, Mien and Thai Lü villages in the park and vicinity, as well as a couple of caves and waterfalls, and endless opportunities for forest walks. The park is often cold in the cool season and especially wet in the wet season.

Park HQ has a basic map, and staff can arrange a guide for walks or more extended excursions around the area, plus rafting on Nam Wa.

The park offers a variety of bungalows (two to 10 people; 300B to 3200B), and there is a nearby restaurant and shop. The cheapest bungalows are very basic, while the more expensive ones are reasonably comfortable and come with hot water and wi-fi. Two-person tents are also available for hire for 400B per night.

To reach the national park by public transport you must first take a bus or *sŏrng·tăa·ou* to Pua (50B, two hours, hourly 6am to 5pm). Get off at the 7-Eleven, then cross the highway to board one of the two daily *sŏrng·tăa·ou* (50B, 30 minutes) that depart at 8.30am and 9.30am.

BUSES FROM NAN

In addition to buses, there are also daily minivans to Ban Huay Kon (on the border with Laos; 95B, three hours, five departures from 5am to noon) and Phrae (83B, two hours, every 40 minutes from 5.30am to 6pm).

DESTINATION	FARE (B)	DURATION (HR)	FREQUENCY
Bangkok	464-790	10-11	frequent 8-10am & 6.15-7.45pm
Chiang Mai	197-395	6	frequent 7.30am-5pm & 10.30pm
Chiang Rai	181	6	9am
Lampang	203	4	frequent 8.30am-10.30pm
Luang Prabang (Laos)	660	9	8am Tue & Fri
Phayao	190	4	7.30am & 1.30pm
Phitsanulok	181	4	5 departures 7.45am-5.15pm
Phrae	110	2½	8 departures 8.30am-10.30pm
Pua (for Doi Phu Kha National Park)	50	2	hourly 6am-5pm

Mae Hong Son

053 / POP 7000

Surrounded by forested mountains and with a remote and pretty setting by a tranquil lake, Mae Hong Son (แม่ฮ่องสอน) fits many travellers' preconceived notions of how a northern Thai town should look. A palpable influence from Myanmar and, best of all, there's hardly a túk-túk or tout to be seen. This doesn't mean Mae Hong Son is uncharted territory – tour groups have been coming here for years – but the city is far more laid-back than Pai, while its potential as a base for activities, from boat trips to trekking, ensures that your visit can be quite unlike anyone else's..

Sights & Activities

★ Wat Phra That Doi Kong Mu BUDDHIST TEMPLE
(วัดพระธาตุดอยกองมู; daylight hours) Climb the hill west of town, Doi Kong Mu (1500m), to visit this temple compound, also known as Wat Plai Doi. Two Shan *chedi,* erected in 1860 and 1874, enshrine the ashes of monks from Myanmar's Shan State. Around the back of the wát you can see a tall, slender, standing Buddha and catch views west of the ridge. There's also a cafe and a small tourist market.

Wat Jong Klang BUDDHIST TEMPLE
(วัดจองกลาง; Th Chamnansatit; daylight hours) Wat Jong Klang houses century-old glass *Jataka* paintings and a **museum** (พิพิธภัณฑ์วัดจองกลาง; Wat Jong Klang, Th Chamnansatit; entry by donation; 8am-6pm) with 150-year-old wooden dolls from Myanmar that depict some of the agonies of the wheel of life. The temple is lit at night and is reflected in Nong Jong Kham – a popular photo op for visitors. Wat Jong Klang has several areas that women are forbidden to enter – not unusual for Burmese-Shan Buddhist temples.

★ Nature Walks TREKKING
(089 552 6899; www.naturewalksthai-myanmar.com) Treks with Nature Walks might cost more than elsewhere, but Chan, a Mae Hong Son native, is probably the best guide in town. Hikes range from day-long nature walks to multiday journeys across the province. Chan can also arrange custom nature-based tours, such as the orchid-viewing tours he conducts from March to May.

★ Nam Rin Tour HIKING
(053 614454; rutsiri506@gmail.com; Th Khunlumprapas; 8am-9pm) The sardonic Mr Dam advertises 'bad sleep, bad jokes', but his treks get good feedback. They start at 1500B per day per person (minimum two people). Mr Dam has an admirable policy of refusing to take people to the long-necked Kayan villages, or on any elephant-themed tours. As he rightly says, the elephants don't want to hang out with humans.

Sleeping & Eating

There's a fair range of accommodation here, although Mae Hong Son lacks genuine hostels. Outside of the high season (November to February), prices are normally discounted by up to a third.

Friend House GUESTHOUSE $
(053 620119; 20 Th Pradit Jong Kham; r 150-500B;) A long-standing budget option, Friend House has simple but spotless fan-cooled, mattress-on-the-floor rooms. The more expensive ones are larger and come with private bathrooms. The riverside location is a bonus; the small garden has views across to Wat Jong Klang.

★ Sang Tong Huts HOTEL $$
(053 611680; www.sangtonghuts.org; off Th Maka Santi; bungalows 1200-1600B, f 2400B;) This clutch of ecofriendly, fan-cooled, TV-free, bamboo and wood bungalows is set in an expansive forested garden just outside town and has loads of character. All the huts are individually designed and decorated – some come with stairs to the bathrooms – and they're spaced out from each other for privacy. It's a mellow and popular spot, so book ahead.

★ Fern Resort RESORT $$$
(053 686110; www.fernresort.info; off Rte 108; bungalows incl breakfast 2000-2500B;) This veteran resort is one of the more pleasant places to stay in northern Thailand. The 37 wooden bungalows are spaced out for privacy among tiered rice paddies and streams and are simple but comfortable. There are no TVs, but two swimming pools, a pétanque court and the nearby nature trails at the adjacent Mae Surin National Park will keep you busy.

★ Little Good Things MULTICUISINE $
(www.facebook.com/littlegoodthings; off Th Khunlumprapas; mains 40-100B; 9am-3pm Wed-Sun;

(wifi, vegetarian) This small and tempting vegan cafe-restaurant offers breakfast options and light, Thai-influenced meals, all of which are meat-free, made with love, wholesome, embarrassingly cheap and, most importantly, delicious. It sometimes shuts down for a month in the rainy season (June to September).

★Morning Market THAI $
(off Th Phanich Wattana; mains 20-50B; ⏲6am-9am) Mae Hong Son's morning market is a fun place to have breakfast. Several vendors at the northern end of the market sell unusual fare such as *tòo·a poo ùn,* a noodle dish from Myanmar supplemented with thick split-pea porridge and deep-fried 'Burmese tofu'.

Salween River Restaurant & Bar INTERNATIONAL $
(23 Th Pradit Jong Kham; mains 70-280B; ⏲8am-10pm; wifi, vegetarian) Salween is an old-school traveller's hang-out, with a menu ranging from burgers to Burmese, beers and cocktails and a few shelves of paperbacks. But unlike most similar places, Salween offers tasty food and as a consequence is enduringly popular: you can tell how busy Mae Hong Son is by whether Salween's dining room is full.

ℹ Getting There & Away

Mae Hong Son's tiny airport has two daily flights to Chiang Mai.

ℹ Getting Around

Most of Mae Hong Son's attractions are outside town, so renting a motorcycle or bicycle is a wise move. There are a number of places around town, such as Titan, offering bicycle hire. Other places, including Friend Tour and JD, have motorbike hire.

UNDERSTAND THAILAND

History

Rise of Thai Kingdoms

It is believed that the first Thais migrated southwest from modern-day Yunnan and Guangxi, China, to what is today known as Thailand. They settled along river valleys and formed small farming communities that eventually fell under the dominion of the expansionist Khmer empire of present-day Cambodia. What is now southern Thailand, along the Malay peninsula, was under the sway of the Srivijaya empire based in Sumatra. By the 13th and 14th centuries, what is considered to be the first Thai kingdom – Sukhothai (meaning 'Rising Happiness') – emerged and began to chip away at the crumbling Khmer empire. The Sukhothai kingdom is regarded as the cultural and artistic kernel of the modern Thai state.

Sukhothai was soon eclipsed by another Thai power, Ayuthaya, established by King U Thong in 1350. This new centre developed into a cosmopolitan port on the Asian trade route, courted by various European nations. The small nation managed to thwart foreign takeovers, including one orchestrated by a Thai court official – a Greek man named Constantine Phaulkon – to advance French interests. For 400 years and 34 successive reigns, Ayuthaya dominated Thailand, until the Burmese led a successful invasion in 1765, ousting the monarch and destroying the capital.

The Thais eventually rebuilt their capital in present-day Bangkok, established by the Chakri dynasty, which continues to occupy

BUSES & MINIVANS FROM MAE HONG SON

Mae Hong Son's bus and minivan terminal is 1km south of the city; a túk-túk or motorcycle ride to/from here costs 60B.

DESTINATION	FARE (B)	DURATION (HR)	FREQUENCY
Bangkok (bus)	851-1134	15	4pm & 4.30pm
Chiang Mai (bus)	350	8-9	8pm & 9pm
Chiang Mai (minivan)	250	6	hourly 7am-5pm
Khun Yuam (minivan)	100	1½	8am & 2pm
Mae Sariang (minivan)	200	3½	8am & 2pm
Pai (minivan)	150	2½	hourly 7am-5pm
Soppong (minivan)	100	1½	hourly 7am-5pm

the throne today. As Western imperialism marched across the region, King Mongkut (Rama IV, r 1851–68) and his son and successor, King Chulalongkorn (Rama V, r 1868–1910), successfully steered the country into the modern age without becoming a colonial vassal. In return for the country's continued independence, King Chulalongkorn ceded huge tracts of Laos and Cambodia to French-controlled Indochina – an unprecedented territorial loss in Thai history.

A Struggling Democracy

In 1932 a peaceful coup converted the country into a constitutional monarchy, loosely based on the British model. What followed has been a near-continuous cycle of power struggles among three factions – the elected government, military leaders and the monarchy backed by the aristocrats. These groups occasionally form tenuous allegiances based on mutual dislike for the opposition, and the resulting power grab is often a peaceful military takeover sometimes dubbed the 'smooth as silk' coup.

During the mid-20th century the military dominated the political sphere with an anticommunist position widely regarded as being ineffectual, except in the suppression of democratic representation and civil rights. In 1973 student activists staged demonstrations calling for a real constitution and the release of political dissidents. A brief respite came, with reinstated voting rights and relaxed censorship. But in October 1976 a demonstration on the campus of Thammasat University in Bangkok was brutally quashed, resulting in hundreds of casualties and the reinstatement of authoritarian rule. Many activists went underground to join armed communist insurgency groups hiding in the northeast.

In the 1980s, as the regional threat of communism subsided, the military-backed prime minister Prem Tinsulanonda stabilised the country and moved towards a representative democracy. The military reemerged in 1991 to overthrow the democratically elected government; this was the country's 10th successful coup since 1932. In May 1992 huge demonstrations led by Bangkok's charismatic governor Chamlong Srimuang erupted throughout the city and the larger provincial capitals. The bloodiest confrontation occurred at Bangkok's Democracy Monument, resulting in nearly 50 deaths, but it eventually led to the reinstatement of a civilian government.

Same Same but Different

Straddling the new millennium, Thailand seemed to have entered an age of democracy. Elected governments oversaw the 1997 enactment of Thailand's 16th constitution, the first charter in the nation's history not written under military order. The country pulled through the 1997 Asian currency crisis and entered a stable period of prosperity in the early 2000s. Telecommunications tycoon Thaksin Shinawatra and his populist Thai Rak Thai party were elected in 2001 and, with little political opposition, Thaksin consolidated his power over the next five years in all ranks of government, stifling press criticism and scrutiny of his administration.

In 2006 Thaksin was accused of conflicts of interest in relation to his family's sale of their Shin Corporation to the Singaporean government for 73 billion baht (US$1.88 billion), a tax-free gain thanks to legislation that he helped craft. Meanwhile Thaksin's working-class and rural base rallied behind him, spotlighting long-standing class divides within Thai society.

Behind the scenes the military and the aristocrats forged an allegiance that resulted in the 2006 coup of the Thaksin government. The military banned Thaksin's political party (Thai Rak Thai), only to have the regenerated party, now named Pheu Thai, win the 2007 elections. In response, the aristocrats staged massive protests in Bangkok that took over the parliament building and closed down the city's two airports for a week in November 2008.

The Constitutional Court sided with the elites and dissolved Pheu Thai due to a technicality. This decision by the courts was viewed by pro-Thaksin factions as a silent coup. A new coalition was formed in December 2008, led by Oxford-educated Abhisit Vejjajiva, leader of the Democrat party and Thailand's fourth prime minister for the year.

The pro-Thaksin faction (known as 'Red Shirts') retaliated with a crippling, two-month demonstration in Bangkok's central shopping district that was ended in May 2010 through military force. The crackdown resulted in 91 deaths and US$1.5 billion in arson damage.

A NEW KING

The May 2019 coronation of King Maha Vajiralongkorn marked the end of an era for Thailand. King Vajiralongkorn, also known as Rama X, was crowned in an elaborate three-day ceremony in Bangkok that took place over two and a half years after the death of his father, Rama IX, in October 2016.

The 67-year-old King Vajiralongkorn is a more unknown quantity than his beloved father, who ruled for 70 years and was the only monarch most Thais had ever known. King Vajiralongkorn was educated in the UK and Australia and has spent much of his adult life serving in the Thai armed forces. His first royal command saw him promise to reign with righteousness, as his father did at his coronation. But Rama X also surprised the country by embarking on his fourth marriage just three days before the coronation ceremony.

What kind of monarch Rama X will be remains unclear, but there are indications that he will be assertive. In 2018, he ordered that the estimated US$30 billion in assets held by the Crown Property Bureau be transferred to his name. During the 2019 election campaign, Rama X intervened to prevent his eldest sister from running as a candidate for prime minister.

It seems certain that King Vajiralongkorn will maintain the close relationship between the royal palace and the military. Most Thais hope that he will rule with stability and decorum but, due to some of the strictest *lèse-majesté* laws in the world, the Thai public does not generally express candid sentiments about the monarchy.

Elections were held again in 2011 and Pheu Thai won a clear majority. Thaksin's sister, Yingluck Shinawatra, became Thailand's first female prime minister. She raised the minimum wage to 300B per day and introduced a populist rice-pledging scheme intended to boost farmers' incomes, only to see it become an expensive flop. But it was her government's attempt to introduce an amnesty bill that would have allowed Thaksin's return that led to her becoming the second member of the Shinawatra clan to be overthrown in a coup. On 7 May 2014 Yingluck stepped down and on 22 May the military, under General Prayuth Chan-o-cha, took over.

Prayuth's government, known as the National Council for Peace and Order (NCPO), aggressively silenced critics of military rule and amended the constitution to give the military more powers. But it failed to address Thailand's slumping economy. Foreign investment, exports and GDP all contracted and by 2019 economic growth was at its lowest point since the coup.

A much-delayed 2019 election saw Prayuth's new Palang Pracharath party fail to win a parliamentary majority, as the Shinawatra-backed Pheu Thai party captured the most seats. Under the latest constitution, though, the unelected, 250-member senate (the upper house of parliament) also votes on the appointment of the prime minister, and Prayuth was duly chosen to head a coalition government in June 2019.

People & Culture

Thailand's cohesive national identity provides a unifying patina for ethnic and regional differences that evolved through historical migrations and geographic kinships with ethnically diverse neighbours.

The National Psyche

Paramount to the Thai philosophy of life is *sà·nùk* (fun) – each day is celebrated with food and conversation, foreign festivals are readily adopted as an excuse for a party and every task is measured on the *sà·nùk* meter.

The social dynamics of Thai culture can be perplexing. The ideals of the culture are based on Buddhist principles and include humility, gratitude and filial piety. These golden rules are translated into such social conventions as saving face *(nâa),* in which confrontation is avoided and people endeavour not to embarrass themselves or other people.

An important component of saving face is knowing one's place in society: all relationships in Thai society are governed by conventions of social rank defined by age, wealth, status, and personal and political power. Thais 'size up' a Westerner's social status with a list of common questions: Where are you from? How old are you? Are you married? To a Thai these questions are

THAILAND'S HILL PEOPLES

Thailand's hill-people communities (referred to in Thai as *chao khao*, literally 'mountain people') are ethnic minorities who have traditionally lived in the country's mountainous frontier. Most migrated from Tibet and parts of China some 200 years ago and settled along Southeast Asia's mountain belt from Myanmar to Vietnam. The Tribal Research Institute in Chiang Mai recognises 10 different hill-people groups, but there may be up to 20 in Thailand. Increasing urban migration has significantly altered the hill peoples' cultural independence.

Hill-People Groups

The **Karen** are the largest hill-people community in Thailand and number about 47% of the total hill-people population. They tend to live in lowland valleys and practise crop rotation rather than swidden (slash and burn) agriculture. Their numbers and proximity to mainstream society have made them the most integrated and financially successful of the hill-people groups. Thickly woven V-neck tunics of various colours are their traditional dress.

The **Hmong** are Thailand's second-largest hill-people group and are especially numerous in Chiang Mai Province. They usually live on mountain peaks or plateaus above 1000m. Traditional dress is a simple black jacket and indigo or black baggy trousers. Sashes may be worn around the waist, and embroidered aprons draped front and back.

The **Akha** are among the poorest of Thailand's ethnic minorities and live mainly in Chiang Mai and Chiang Rai Provinces, along mountain ridges or steep slopes 1000m to 1400m in altitude. They are regarded as skilled farmers but are often displaced from arable land by government intervention. Their traditional garb includes a headdress of beads, feathers and dangling silver ornaments.

Other minority groups include the Lisu, Lahu and Mien.

Village Etiquette

If you're planning on visiting hill-people villages, talk to your guide about dos and don'ts. Here are some general guidelines.

- Always ask permission before taking photos, especially at private moments inside dwellings. Many traditional belief systems view photography with suspicion. Some minorities will ask for money in exchange for a photo; honour their request.
- Show respect for religious symbols and rituals. Don't touch totems at village entrances or sacred items. Don't participate in ceremonies unless invited to join in.
- Avoid cultivating a tradition of begging, especially among children. Instead talk to your guide about donating to a local school.
- Avoid public nudity and be careful not to undress near an open window where village children might be able to peep in.
- Don't flirt with members of the opposite sex unless you plan to marry them. Don't drink or do drugs with the villagers; altered states sometimes lead to culture clashes.
- Smile at villagers even if they stare at you; ask your guide how to say 'hello' in the local language.
- Avoid public displays of affection, which in some traditional systems are viewed as offensive to the spirit world.
- Don't interact with the villagers' livestock; these creatures are valuable possessions, not entertainment.

matters of public record and aren't considered impolite.

Religion and the monarchy, which is still regarded by many as divine, are the culture's sacred cows. Whatever you do, don't insult the king or disrespect his image, especially in the current era of ultra-sensitivity towards the institution of the monarchy.

Lifestyle

Thailand straddles the divide between the highly Westernised urban life in major cities and the traditional rhythms of rural, agricultural life. But several persisting customs offer a rough snapshot of daily life. Thais wake up early, thanks in part to the roosters that start crowing some time after sunrise. In the grey stillness of early morning, barefoot monks carrying large round bowls travel through the town to collect their daily meals from the faithful. Homemakers are already awake, steaming rice and sweeping their front porches with stiff-bristled brooms. Soon business is in full swing: the vendors have arrived at their favourite corner to feed the uniformed masses, be they khaki-clad civil servants or white-and-black-wearing university students.

Eating appears to make up the rest of the day. Notice the shop staff, ticket vendors or even the office workers: they can be found in a tight circle swapping gossip and snacking (or *gin lên*, literally 'eat for fun'). Then there is dinner and after-dinner and then the whole seemingly chaotic, yet highly ordered, affair starts all over again.

Population

About 75% of citizens are ethnic Thais, further divided by geography (north, central, south and northeast). Each group speaks its own Thai dialect and to a certain extent practises customs unique to its region or influenced by neighbouring countries. Politically and economically, the central Thais are the dominant group. People of Chinese ancestry, many of whom have been in Thailand for generations, make up roughly 14% of the population. Other large minority groups include the Malays in the far south, the Khmers in the northeast and the Lao, spread throughout the north and east. Smaller non-Thai-speaking groups include the hill peoples living in the northern mountains. An increasing community of economic migrants, predominately from Myanmar, is changing the racial and cultural demographics of Thailand.

Religion

Alongside the Thai national flag flies the yellow flag of Buddhism – Theravada Buddhism (as opposed to the Mahayana schools found in East Asia and the Himalayas). Country, family and daily life are all married to religion. Every Thai male is expected to become a monk for a short period in his life, since a family earns great merit when a son 'takes robe and bowl'.

More evident than the philosophical aspects of Buddhism is the everyday fusion with animist rituals. Monks are consulted to determine an auspicious date for a wedding or the likelihood of success for a business.

THAI ETIQUETTE

Thais are generally very understanding and hospitable, but there are some important taboos and social conventions.

Monarchy It is a criminal offence to disrespect the royal family; treat objects depicting the king (like money) with respect.

Temples Wear clothing that covers to your knees and elbows. Remove all footwear before entering. Sit with your feet tucked behind you, so they are not facing the Buddha image. Women should never touch a monk or a monk's belongings; step out of the way on footpaths and don't sit next to them on public transport.

Modesty At the beach, avoid public nudity or topless sunbathing. Cover up going to and from the beach.

Body language Avoid touching anyone on the head and be careful where you point your feet; they're the lowest part of the body literally and metaphorically.

Keep your cool Thailand is a non-confrontational culture. Don't get angry; smile and things will work out.

Saving face Thais believe strongly in the concept of saving face, ie avoiding confrontation and endeavouring not to embarrass themselves or other people. The ideal face-saver doesn't bring up negative topics in conversation, doesn't express firm convictions or opinions and doesn't claim to have any expertise.

Spirit houses *(phrá phuum)* are constructed outside buildings and homes to encourage the spirits to live independently from the family, but to remain comfortable so as to bring good fortune to the site.

Roughly 95% of the population practises Buddhism, but in southern Thailand there is a significant Muslim community.

Arts

Sculpture & Architecture

Thailand's most famous sculptural output has been its bronze Buddha images, coveted the world over for their originality and grace. Traditional architecture is more visible as it is applied to simple homes and famous temples. Ancient Thai homes consisted of a single-room teak structure raised on stilts, since most Thais once lived along river banks or canals. The space underneath also served as the living room, kitchen, garage and barn. Rooflines in Thailand are steeply pitched and often decorated at the corners or along the gables with motifs related to the *naga* (mythical sea serpent), long believed to be a spiritual protector. Temple buildings demonstrate more formal aspects of traditional architecture and artistic styles.

TEMPLE ARCHITECTURE

Planning to conquer Thailand's temples and ruins? With this handy guide, you'll be able to sort out your wát (Thai temple complex) from your what's that.

Chedi Large bell-shaped tower usually containing five structural elements symbolising (from bottom to top) earth, water, fire, wind and void; relics of Buddha or a Thai king are housed inside the *chedi*; also known as a stupa.

Prang Towering phallic spire of Khmer origin serving the same religious purpose as a *chedi*.

Wí·hăhn Main sanctuary for the temple's Buddha sculpture and where laypeople come to make offerings; sometimes it is translated as the 'assembly hall'. Typically the building has a three-tiered roofline representing the triple gems (Buddha, the teacher; Dharma, the teaching; and Sangha, the followers).

Music

Classical Thai music was developed for the royal court as an accompaniment to classical dance-drama and other forms of theatre. Traditional instruments have more pedestrian applications and can often be heard at temple fairs or provincial festivals. Whether used in the high or low arts, traditional Thai music has an incredible range of textures and subtleties, hair-raising tempos and pastoral melodies.

In the north and northeast there are several popular wind instruments with multiple reed pipes, which function like a mouth organ. Chief among these is the *kaan,* which originated in Laos; when played by an adept musician it sounds like a calliope organ. It is used chiefly in *mŏr lam* music, a rural folk tradition often likened to the American blues. A near cousin to *mŏr lam* is *lôok tûng* (literally 'children of the fields'), which enjoys a working-class fan base much as country music does in the US.

Popular Thai music has borrowed rock-and-roll's instruments to create perky teeny-bop hits, hippie protest ballads, garage rock and urban indie anthems. It is an easy courtship with Thai classic rock, like the decades-old group Carabao and the folk style known as *pleng pêu·a chee·wít* (songs for life). These days, guitar-based rock bands have been joined by many hip-hop acts and electronic-music outfits.

Theatre & Dance

Traditional Thai theatre consists of six dramatic forms, including *kŏhn,* a formal masked dance-drama depicting scenes from the Ramakian (the *Thakŏhi* version of India's *Ramayana*), that were originally performed only for the royal court. Popular in rural villages, *lí·gair* is a partly improvised, often bawdy folk play featuring dancing, comedy, melodrama and music. The southern Thai equivalent is *má·noh·rah,* which is based on a 2000-year-old Indian story. Shadow-puppet plays *(năng)* found in southern Thailand demonstrate that region's shared cultural heritage with Malaysia and Indonesia.

Food & Drink

Food

Thai food is a complex balance of spicy, salty, sweet and sour. The ingredients are fresh and zesty, with lots of lemongrass, basil, coriander and mint. Chilli peppers pack a nose-running, tongue-searing burn. And pungent *nám Ƀlah* (fish sauce; generally made from anchovies) adds a touch of the sea. Throw in a little lime and a pinch of sugar and you've got the true taste of Thailand.

Day and night markets, pushcart vendors, makeshift stalls, open-air restaurants – Thais eat most of their meals outside of the home as prices are relatively low and local cooks are famous for a particular dish. No self-respecting shoestringer would shy away from the pushcarts in Thailand for fear of stomach troubles.

For breakfast and late-night snacks, Thais nosh on *gŏo·ay đĕe·o*, a noodle soup with chicken or pork and vegetables. There are two major types of noodles: *sên lék* (thin) and *sên yài* (wide and flat). Before you dig into your steaming bowl, first use the chopsticks and a rounded soup spoon to cut the noodles into smaller segments so they are easier to pick up. Then add to taste a few teaspoonfuls of the provided accompaniments: dried red chilli, sugar, fish sauce and vinegar. It's a combination that is pure Thai.

Thais are social eaters: meals are rarely taken alone and dishes are meant to be shared. Usually a small army of plates will be placed in the centre of the table, with individual servings of rice for each diner. The protocol goes like this: ladle a spoonful of food at a time on to your plate of rice. Dishes aren't passed in Thailand; instead you reach across the table to the different items. When you are full, leave a little rice on your plate (an empty plate is a silent request for more rice) and place your fork so that it is cradled by the spoon in the centre of the plate.

Even when eating with *fa·ràng*, it is wise to order 'family style', as dishes are rarely synchronised. Ordering individually will leave one person staring politely at a hot plate and another staring wistfully at the kitchen.

Remember: in Thailand, chopsticks are used for noodle dishes and a spoon and fork for rice dishes. Many curries and soups are served in bowls but should be ladled onto a bed of rice rather than eaten directly from the bowl.

NORTHERN THAI CUISINE

Probably the least spicy of all Thailand's regional cuisines, the food of northern Thailand is more reliant on bitter flavours and dried spices. Northern Thai food is also very seasonal, reflecting the locals' love of vegetables. Pork is the most commonly used meat, although chicken is widely available, and *kôw nĕe·o* (sticky rice) is the traditional accompaniment.

Dishes you are likely to come across in northern Thailand include the following:

Gaang hang·lair An import from Myanmar, this rich pork curry is frequently served at festivals and ceremonies

Kà·nŏm jeen nám ngée·o A dish of rice noodles served with a tart pork- and tomato-based broth.

Kôw soy A popular curry-based noodle dish that likely originated in Myanmar.

Lâhp kôo·a Literally 'fried *lâhp*', this dish is a northern take on the famous Thai minced-meat 'salad', with the meat fried with a mixture of dried spices.

Drink

Water purified for drinking is simply called *náam dèum* (drinking water), whether boiled or filtered. All water offered in restaurants, offices or homes will be purified. Ice is generally safe in Thailand. *Châa* (tea) and *gah·faa* (coffee) are prepared strong, milky and sweet – an instant morning buzz.

Thanks to the tropical bounty, fruit juices are sold on every corner. Thais prefer a little salt to cut the sweetness of the juice; the salt also has some mystical power to make a hot day tolerable.

Cheap beer goes hand in hand with backpacker ghettos. Beer Chang, Beer Singha (pronounced 'sing', not 'sing-ha') and Beer Leo are a few local brands. Thais have created yet another innovative method for beating the heat: they drink their beer with ice to keep the beverage cool and crisp.

More a ritual than a beverage, Thai whisky usually runs with a distinct crowd: soda water, Coke and ice. Fill the short glass with ice cubes, two-thirds whisky, one-third soda and a splash of Coke. Thai tradition dictates that the youngest in the crowd is responsible for filling the other drinkers' glasses. Many travellers prefer to go straight to the ice bucket with shared straws, not forgetting a dash of Red Bull in cocktails to keep them going.

Environment

Thailand spans a distance of 1650km from its northern tip to its southern tail, a distance that encompasses 16 latitudinal degrees and a variety of ecological zones, making it one of the most environmentally diverse countries in Southeast Asia.

The Land

Thailand's odd shape is often likened to the head of an elephant, with the trunk being the Malay peninsula and the head being the northern mountains. Starting at the crown of the country, northern Thailand is dominated by the Dawna-Tenasserim mountain range. Dropping into the central region, the topography mellows into rice-producing plains fed by rivers that are as revered as the national monarchy. Thailand's most exalted river is Chao Phraya.

Tracing the contours of Thailand's northern and northeastern border is another imposing watercourse: the Mekong, which both physically separates and culturally fuses Thailand with its neighbours. The landscape of Thailand's northeastern border is occupied by the arid Khorat Plateau, rising some 300m above the central plain.

The kingdom's eastern rivers dump their waters into the Gulf of Thailand. Sliding further south is the Malay peninsula, a long trunk-like land mass. On the western side extends the Andaman Sea, a splendid tropical setting of stunning blue waters and dramatic limestone islands.

Wildlife

In the northern half of Thailand most indigenous species are classified zoologically as Indo-Chinese, referring to fauna originating from mainland Asia.

Thailand is particularly rich in bird life: more than 1000 resident and migrating species have been recorded and approximately 10% of all world bird species dwell here.

Thailand's most revered indigenous mammal, the elephant, once roamed wild in the country's dense virgin forests. Integral to Thai culture, the elephant symbolises wisdom, strength and good fortune. White elephants are even more auspicious and by tradition are donated to the king. Sadly, elephants are now endangered, having lost their traditional role in society and much of their habitat, as have the dwindling numbers of tigers.

The animals visitors are most likely to see or encounter are the 12 species of monkeys and gibbons indigenous to Thailand.

Environmental Issues

As in all countries with a high population density, Thailand's ecosystems are under enormous pressure: natural forest cover in 1961 was 53.5%; by 2016 it had declined to about 31.6% of land area, according to the World Bank.

ENDANGERED SPECIES

Thailand's most famous animals are also its most endangered. The Asian elephant, a smaller cousin to the African elephant, once roamed the forests of Indochina in great herds. But the wild elephant faces extinction due to habitat loss and poaching. The population of wild elephants in Thailand is now estimated between 2000 to 3000, according to statistics from the Thai Elephant Conservation Center, with another 2,700 so-called domesticated elephants in the country.

Reclusive wild Indochinese tigers stalk parts of Thailand, especially the hinterlands between Thailand and Myanmar, but in ever-decreasing numbers. It is notoriously difficult to obtain an accurate count, but experts estimate that between 150 and 200 wild tigers remain in Thailand. Although tiger hunting and trapping is illegal, poachers continue to kill the cats for the overseas wildlife trade. Thailand, though, has stepped up its tiger conservation efforts and tiger cubs were spotted for the first time in Khao Yai National Park in 2017.

In response to environmental degradation, the Thai government created protected natural areas and outlawed logging. Thailand designated its first national park (Khao Yai) in the 1960s and has added over 100 parks, including marine environments, to the list since. Together these cover 15% of the country's land and sea area, one of the highest ratios of protected to unprotected areas of any nation in the world. Since the turn of the millennium, forest loss has slowed to about 0.6% per year (according to the World Bank).

Though the conservation efforts are laudable, Thailand's national parks are poorly funded and poorly protected from commercial development, illegal hunting and logging, and swidden agriculture. The passing of the 1992 Environmental Act was an encouraging move by the government, but standards still lag behind those of Western nations. Thailand is a signatory to the UN Convention on International Trade in Endangered Species (CITES), but the country remains an important transport link and marketplace for the global wildlife trade.

SURVIVAL GUIDE

Directory A–Z

ACCESSIBLE TRAVEL

Thailand presents one large, ongoing obstacle course for the mobility-impaired.

The following tour operators specialise in accessible tours to and accommodation in Thailand, and have their own adapted vehicle(s):

Gehandicapten (+31 36 537 6677; http://gehandicapten.com)

Wheelchair Holidays Thailand (+66 8 1375-0792; www.wheelchairtours.com)

Wheelchair Thailand Tours (http://wheelchair-thailand-tours.weebly.com)

ACCOMMODATION

Finding a place to stay in Thailand is easy. For peace of mind, book a room for your arrival night; after that, you can wing it. Bear in mind, however, that vacancies can become scarce during certain holidays and peak travel periods.

Guesthouses Family-run options are the best. Rooms run from basic (bed and fan) to plush (private bathroom and air-con).

Hotels From boutique to business, hotels offer mostly modern rooms and sometimes a swimming pool.

Hostels Just as the standard of guesthouses has improved, hostels have become more modern and stylish.

Price Ranges

In big cities and resorts, the following price ranges refer to a double room and are the high-season walk-in rates.

$ less than 1000B
$$ 1000B–4000B
$$$ more than 4000B

In small towns, the following price ranges are used:

$ less than 600B
$$ 600B–1500B
$$$ more than 1500B

CUSTOMS REGULATIONS

Thailand allows the following items to be brought in duty free:

- reasonable amount of personal effects (clothing and toiletries)
- professional instruments
- 200 cigarettes
- 1L of wine or spirits

Thailand prohibits the import of the following items:

- firearms and ammunition (unless registered in advance with the police department)
- illegal drugs
- pornographic material

An export licence is required for any antique reproductions or newly cast Buddha images.

ELECTRICITY

Thailand uses 220V AC electricity. Power outlets most commonly feature two-prong round or flat sockets.

EMBASSIES & CONSULATES

Foreign embassies are located in Bangkok; some nations also have consulates in Chiang Mai, Pattaya, Phuket and Songkhla.

Australian Embassy (Map p407; 02 344 6300; www.thailand.embassy.gov.au; 181 Th Witthayu/Wireless Rd, Bangkok; 8.30am-4.30pm Mon-Fri; M Lumphini exit 3) Consulates in Chiang Mai, Ko Samui and Phuket.

Cambodian Embassy (Map p407; 02 957 5851; 518/4 Soi Ramkhamhaeng 39, Th Pracha Uthit, Bangkok; 8.30am-noon & 2-5pm Mon-Fri; M Phra Ram 9 exit 3 & taxi) Consulate in Sa Kaew.

Canadian Embassy (Map p422; 02 646 4300; www.thailand.gc.ca; 15th fl, Abdulrahim Pl, 990 Rama IV, Bangkok; 9am-noon Mon-Fri; M Si Lom exit 2, S Sala Daeng exit 4) Consulate in Chiang Mai (053 850147; 151 Superhighway, Tambon Tahsala; 9am-noon Mon-Fri).

French Embassy (Map p422; 02 657 5100; www.ambafrance-th.org; 35 Soi 36/Rue de Brest, Th Charoen Krung, Bangkok; 8.30am-noon Mon-Fri; Oriental Pier) Consulates in Chiang Mai (053 281466; 138 Th Charoen Prathet; 10am-noon Mon & Wed-Fri), Chiang Rai and Pattaya.

German Embassy (Map p422; 02 287 9000; www.bangkok.diplo.de; 9 Th Sathon Tai/South, Bangkok; 8.30-11.30am Mon-Fri; M Lumphini exit 2)

Irish Embassy (Map p418; 02 016 1360; www.dfa.ie/irish-embassy/thailand; 12th fl, 208 Th Witthayu/Wireless Rd; 9.30am-12.30pm & 2.30-3.30pm Mon-Thu, 9.30am-noon Fri; S Phloen Chit exit 1)

Laotian Embassy (Map p407; 02 539 6667; 502/1-3 Soi Sahakarnpramoon, Th Pracha Uthit/Soi Ramkhamhaeng 39, Bangkok; 8am-noon & 1-4pm Mon-Fri; M Phra Ram 9 exit 3 & taxi)

Malaysian Embassy (Map p422; 02 629 6800; www.kln.gov.my/web/tha_bangkok/home; 33-35 Th Sathon Tai/South, Bangkok; 8am-4pm Mon-Fri; M Lumphini exit 2) Consulate in Songkhla.

Myanmar Embassy (Map p422; 02 233 7250; www.mfa.go.th; 132 Th Sathon Neua/North, Bangkok; 9am-noon & 1-3pm Mon-Fri; S Surasak exit 1/3)

Netherlands Embassy (Map p418; 02 309 5200; www.netherlandsworldwide.nl/countries/thailand; 15 Soi Ton Son; 8.30am-noon & 1.30-4.30pm Mon-Thu, 8.30-11.30am Fri; S Chit Lom exit 4)

New Zealand Embassy (Map p418; 02 254 2530; www.nzembassy.com/thailand; 87 Th Witthayu/Wireless Rd, 14th fl, M Thai Tower, All Seasons Pl; 8am-noon & 1-2.30pm Mon-Fri; S Phloen Chit exit 5)

UK Embassy (Map p418; 02 305 8333; www.gov.uk/government/world/organisations/british-embassy-bangkok; 14 Th Witthayu/Wireless Rd; 8am-4.30pm Mon-Thu, to 1pm Fri; S Phloen Chit exit 5)

US Embassy (Map p418; 02 205 4000; https://th.usembassy.gov; 95 Th Witthayu/Wireless Rd; 8am-4pm Mon-Fri; S Phloen Chit exit 5) Consulate in Chiang Mai (053 107700; https://th.usembassy.gov; 387 Th Wichayanon; 7.30am-4.30pm Mon-Fri).

FESTIVALS & EVENTS

Many Thai festivals are linked to Buddhist holy days and follow the lunar calendar. Thus they fall on different dates each year. Businesses typically close and transport becomes difficult preceding any public holiday or national festival. The following are popular national festivals:

Songkran Festival From 12 to 14 April, Buddha images are 'bathed', monks and elders have their hands respectfully sprinkled with water and a lot of water is wildly tossed about on everyone else. Bangkok and Chiang Mai are major battlegrounds.

Loi Krathong On the night of the full moon in November, small lotus-shaped boats made of banana leaves and decorated with flowers and candles are floated on waterways in honour of the river goddess.

FOOD

The following price ranges refer to a main dish.

$ less than 150B

$$ 150B–350B

$$$ more than 350B

INSURANCE

A travel-insurance policy to cover theft, loss and medical problems is an excellent idea. Be sure that your policy covers ambulances or an emergency flight home. Some policies specifically exclude 'dangerous activities', which can include scuba diving, motorcycling and even trekking. A locally acquired motorcycle licence is not valid under some policies.

Worldwide travel insurance is available at www.lonelyplanet.com/travel-insurance. You can buy, extend and claim online any time – even if you're already on the road.

INTERNET ACCESS

Wi-fi is almost standard in hotels, guesthouses and cafes. Signal strength can deteriorate in the upper floors of a multistorey building; request a room near a router if wi-fi is essential. Cellular data networks continue to expand and increase in capability.

LEGAL MATTERS

In general, Thai police don't hassle foreigners, especially tourists. One major exception is drugs – there are strict laws in relation to the possession and trafficking of narcotics.

If you are arrested for any offence, the police will allow you the opportunity to make a phone call, either to your embassy or consulate in Thailand if you have one, or to a friend or relative if not. Thai law does not presume an indicted detainee to be either guilty or innocent but rather a 'suspect', whose guilt or innocence will be decided in court. Trials are usually speedy.

LGBTIQ+ TRAVELLERS

Thai culture is relatively tolerant of both male and female homosexuality. There is a fairly prominent LGBTIQ+ scene in Bangkok, Pattaya and Phuket. With regard to dress or mannerism, the LGBTIQ+ community is generally accepted without comment. However, public displays of affection – whether heterosexual or homosexual – are frowned upon.

Utopia (www.utopia-asia.com) posts lots of Thailand information for LGBTIQ+ travellers and publishes a gay guidebook to the kingdom.

MONEY

Most places in Thailand deal only with cash. Some foreign credit cards are accepted in high-end hotels, restaurants and shops and by travel agents. ATMs are everywhere, but charge a 220B withdrawal fee for transactions with foreign cards.

Banks or private money changers offer the best foreign-exchange rates. When buying baht, US dollars is the most accepted currency, followed by British pounds, euros and Chinese yuan.

Coins come in 1B, 2B (gold-coloured), 5B and 10B denominations. There are 100 satang to 1B and occasionally you'll see 25 and 50 satang coins.

Notes are denominations of 20B, 50B, 100B, 500B and 1000B.

OPENING HOURS

Banks and government offices close for national holidays. Some bars and clubs close during elections and certain religious holidays when alcohol sales are banned. Shopping centres have banks that open late.

Banks 8.30am to 4.30pm; 24-hour ATMs
Bars 6pm to midnight or 1am
Clubs 8pm to 2am
Government offices 8.30am to 4.30pm Monday to Friday; some close for lunch
Restaurants 8am to 10pm
Shops 10am to 7pm

POST

Thailand has a very efficient postal service and local postage is inexpensive. Don't send cash or other valuables through the mail.

PUBLIC HOLIDAYS

Government offices and banks close their doors on the following public holidays.

1 January New Year's Day
February (date varies) Makha Bucha Day, Buddhist holy day
6 April Chakri Day, commemorating the founder of the Chakri dynasty, Rama I
13–15 April Songkran Festival
1 May Labour Day
5 May Coronation Day
May/June (date varies) Visakha Bucha, Buddhist holy day
July 28 King Maha Vajiralongkorn's Birthday
July/August (date varies) Asanha Bucha, Buddhist holy day
12 August Queen Sirikit's Birthday/Mother's Day
23 October Chulalongkorn Day
5 December Commemoration of Late King Bhumiphol/Father's Day
10 December Constitution Day
31 December New Year's Eve

SAFE TRAVEL

Thailand is generally a safe country to visit, but it's smart to exercise caution, especially when it comes to dealing with strangers (both Thai and foreigners) and travelling alone.

➡ Assault of travellers is relatively rare in Thailand, but it does happen.
➡ Possession of drugs can result in a year or more of prison time. Drug smuggling carries considerably higher penalties, including execution.
➡ Disregard all offers of free shopping or sightseeing help from strangers. These are scams that invariably take a commission from your purchases.

The **tourist police** (☎1155) are a useful point of call if you are in trouble.

Ongoing violence in the deep south has made the crossing at Sungai Kolok into Malaysia potentially dangerous, and most Muslim-majority provinces (Yala, Pattani, Narathiwat and Songkhla) should be avoided by casual visitors.

TELEPHONE

The telephone country code for Thailand is 66 and is used when calling the country from abroad. All Thai telephone numbers are preceded by a '0' if you're dialling domestically (the '0' is omitted when calling from overseas). After the initial '0', the next three numbers represent the provincial area code, which is now integral to the telephone number. If the initial '0' is followed by a '6', an '8' or a '9' then you're dialling a mobile phone.

International Calls

If you want to call an international number from a telephone in Thailand, you must first dial an international access code plus the country code followed by the subscriber number.

In Thailand there are various international access codes charging different rates per minute. The standard direct-dial prefix is 001; it is operated by CAT and is considered to have the best sound quality. It connects to the largest number of countries, but it is also the most expensive. The next best is 007, a prefix operated by TOT, with reliable quality and slightly cheaper rates. Economy rates are available through different carriers – do an internet search to determine promotional codes.

Mobile Phones

The easiest option for making calls in Thailand is to buy a local SIM card. Make sure that your mobile phone is unlocked before travelling.

Local SIM cards can be bought at any 7-Eleven or any of the mobile-phone providers' stores. Tourist SIM cards cost as little as 49B. Various talk-and-data packages are available and SIM cards can be topped up with additional funds. Bring your passport when you buy a SIM card, so the card can be registered to your name.

Thailand is on the GSM network. The main mobile-phone providers include AIS (www.ais.co.th), DTAC (www.dtac.co.th) and True Move (http://truemoveh.truecorp.co.th), all of which operate on a 4G network. Coverage and quality of the different carriers varies from year to year based on network upgrades and capacity. Carriers usually sell talk-data packages based on usage amounts.

TIME

Thailand is seven hours ahead of GMT/UTC. Times are often expressed according to the 24-hour clock.

TOILETS

Increasingly, the Asian-style squat toilet is less of the norm in Thailand. There are still specimens in rural places, provincial bus stations, older homes and modest restaurants, but the Western-style toilet is becoming more prevalent and appears wherever foreign tourists can be found. Some toilets also come with a small spray hose – Thailand's version of the bidet.

TOURIST INFORMATION

The Tourism Authority of Thailand (TAT) has offices throughout the country that distribute maps and sightseeing advice. TAT offices do not book accommodation, transport or tours.

> **THAILAND'S IMMIGRATION OFFICES**
>
> Visa extensions and other formalities can be addressed at the immigration offices in Bangkok (p434) and Chiang Mai (p474).
>
> Remember to dress in your Sunday best when doing official business in Thailand and do all visa business yourself (avoid hiring a third party). For all types of visa extensions, take two passport-sized photos and one copy each of the photo and visa pages of your passport.

VISAS

Thailand has visa-exemption and visa-on-arrival agreements with 64 countries (including European countries, Australia, New Zealand and the USA). Depending on nationality, these citizens are issued a 14- to 90-day visa exemption. Note that for some nationalities, less time (15 days rather than 30 days) is given if arriving by land rather than air. Check the Ministry of Foreign Affairs (www.mfa.go.th) website for more details.

Without proof of an onward ticket and sufficient funds for your projected stay, you can be denied entry, but in practice this is a formality that is rarely checked.

If you plan to stay in Thailand longer than 30 days, you should apply for the 60-day tourist visa from a Thai consulate or embassy before your trip. Recent changes to this visa now allow multiple entries within a six-month period.

Visa Extensions

You can extend your visa by applying at any immigration office in Thailand. The usual fee for a visa extension is 1900B. Those issued with a standard stay of 15 or 30 days can extend their stay for 30 days if the extension is handled before the visa expires. The 60-day tourist visa can be extended by up to 30 days at the discretion of Thai immigration authorities.

Another visa-renewal option is to cross a land border. A new 15- or 30-day visa exemption, depending on the nationality, will be issued upon your return.

If you overstay your visa, the usual penalty is a fine of 500B per day, with a 20,000B limit. Fines can be paid at the airport, or in advance at an immigration office. If you've overstayed only one day, you don't have to pay.

VOLUNTEERING

There are many wonderful volunteering organisations in Thailand that provide meaningful work and cultural engagement. Volunteer Work Thailand (www.volunteerworkthailand.org) maintains a database of opportunities.

WORK

Thailand is a huge destination for temporary work stints, especially those involving English teaching. To work legally in the country, you need a non-immigrant visa and a work permit – which legitimate institutions should be able to provide. An excellent resource for background on teaching in Thailand, as well as a resource for jobs, is Ajarn (www.ajarn.com).

Getting There & Away

AIR

Bangkok has one primary international airport (Suvarnabhumi International Airport) plus a budget carrier airport (Don Mueang Airport) with international connections mainly to Asian countries. Chiang Mai, Chiang Rai, Hat Yai, Krabi, Samui, Pattaya and Phuket also have some international flights from nearby countries, especially China.

LAND

Thailand shares land borders with Cambodia, Laos, Malaysia and Myanmar (Burma). Visas on arrival are available for land crossings into Cambodia, Laos and Malaysia. Pre-arranged visas are required for land entry into Myanmar. Improved highways and bridges have made it easier to travel overland to/from China via Laos.

Getting Around

AIR

Hopping around the country by air continues to be affordable. Most routes originate from Bangkok (both Don Mueang and Suvarnabhumi International Airports), but Chiang Mai, Hat Yai, Ko Samui, Phuket and Udon Thani all have a few routes to other Thai towns.

BICYCLE

Bicycles are a great way to explore the more rural, less-trafficked corners of Thailand. They can usually be hired from guesthouses for as little as 50B per day, though they aren't always high quality. A good resource for cycling in the country is Bicycle Thailand (www.bicyclethailand.com).

BOAT

Long-tail boats are a staple of transport on rivers and canals in Bangkok and neighbouring provinces, and between islands.

Between the mainland and small, less-touristed islands, the standard craft is a wooden boat, 8m to 10m long, with an inboard engine, a wheelhouse and a simple roof to shelter passengers and cargo. To more popular destinations, faster hovercraft (jetfoils) and speedboats are the norm.

BUS & MINIVAN

The Thai bus service is widespread, convenient and fast. Reputable companies operate out of the government bus stations, not the tourist centres such as Bangkok's Th Khao San. Starting at the top, VIP buses are the closest you will come to a rock star's tour bus. The seats recline, the air-con is frosty and an 'air hostess' dispenses refreshments. Various diminishing classes of air-con buses strip away the extras until you're left with a fairly beat-up bus with an asthmatic cooling system.

Minivans are increasingly superseding buses in parts of northern Thailand. They make a convenient option for trips to nearby cities. Sometimes, they will pick you up and drop you off at your accommodation, but they often depart from and arrive at bus stations, too.

For long-distance trips, or busy routes, purchase tickets the day before.

ROAD SAFETY

Thailand's roads are dangerous. In 2018, they were the deadliest in Southeast Asia and the seventh-deadliest in the world, according to the World Health Organization.

Fatal bus crashes make headlines, but nearly 75% of vehicle accidents in Thailand involve motorcycles. Many tourists are injured riding motorcycles because they don't know how to handle the vehicles and are unfamiliar with local driving conventions.

If you are a novice motorcyclist, familiarise yourself with the vehicle in an uncongested area of town and stick to the smaller 100cc automatic bikes. Drive slowly, especially when roads are slick or when there is loose gravel or sand. Remember to distribute weight as evenly as possible across the frame of the bike to improve handling. And don't expect other vehicles to look out for you. Always wear a helmet.

CAR & MOTORCYCLE

Cars and motorcycles can be rented in most tourist towns. Inspect the vehicle before committing. Document any existing damage to avoid being charged for it. Always verify that the vehicle is insured for liability before signing a rental contract, and ask to see the dated insurance documents.

Motorcycle travel is a popular way to do local sightseeing. Motorcycle rental usually requires that you leave your passport as a deposit.

Thais drive on the left-hand side of the road – most of the time. Every two-lane road has an invisible third lane in the middle that all drivers use as a passing lane. The main rule to be aware of is that 'might makes right' and smaller vehicles always yield to bigger ones. Drivers usually use their horns to indicate that they are passing.

An International Driving Permit is necessary to drive vehicles in Thailand, but this is rarely enforced for motorcycle hire.

HITCHING

It is uncommon to see people hitching, since bus travel is inexpensive and reliable. Hitching becomes an option where public transport isn't available. In this case you can usually catch a ride, but remember to use the Asian style of beckoning: hold your arm out towards the road, palm-side down and wave towards the ground.

Hitching is never entirely safe, and travellers who do so should understand that they are taking a small but potentially serious risk.

LOCAL TRANSPORT

Motorcycle Taxi

Many cities in Thailand have *mor·đeu·sai ráp jâhng*, motorcycle taxis that can be hired for short distances. If you're empty-handed or travelling with a small bag, they can't be beaten for transport in a pinch.

In most cities, you'll find motorcycle taxis clustered near street intersections, as well as at bus and train stations. Usually, the drivers wear numbered orange, yellow or green vests. You'll need to establish the price beforehand.

Săhm·lór & Túk-Túk

Săhm·lór (also spelt '*săamláw*'), meaning 'three wheels', are pedal rickshaws found mainly in small towns for short hops. Their modern replacements are the motorised túk-túk, named for the throaty cough of their two-stroke engines. In Bangkok and other tourist centres, túk-túk drivers often grossly overcharge foreigners.

You must bargain and agree on a fare before accepting a ride.

Sŏrng·tăa·ou

Sŏrng·tăa·ou (literally, 'two benches') are small pickup trucks with a row of seats down each side. In some towns, *sŏrng·tăa·ou* serve as public buses running regular, fixed-fare routes. But in tourist towns, they act as shared taxis or private charters; in this case agree on a fare beforehand.

TRAIN

The State Railway of Thailand operates comfortable and moderately priced, but rather slow, services. All rail travel originates in Bangkok and radiates north, south and northeast. Trains are especially convenient for overnight travel between Bangkok and Chiang Mai.

The SRT operates passenger trains in three classes – 1st, 2nd and 3rd – but each class varies depending on the train type (ordinary, rapid or express). Rapid and express trains make fewer stops than ordinary trains.

Fares are calculated from a base price with surcharges added for distance, class and train type. Extra charges are added for air-con and for sleeping berths (either upper or lower).

Advance bookings can be made from one to 60 days before your intended date of departure. You can make bookings in person at any train station. Train tickets can also be purchased at travel agencies, which usually add a service charge to the ticket price. If you are making an advance reservation from outside the country, contact a licensed travel agent: the SRT no longer operates its own online ticket service.

Understand the Mekong Region

History

This vibrant region has a history as long and dramatic as the Mekong River that cuts through its heart. The Mekong played host to some of the most brutal wars of the 20th century and the bloodiest revolutions. However, calmer waters lie ahead, as the region has been relatively peaceful and stable for the first time in generations.

The Mekong Valley and Khorat Plateau were inhabited as far back as 10,000 years ago, and rice was grown in northeastern Thailand as early as 4000 BCE. China, by contrast, was still growing millet at the time.

Early Empire

The history of this great region is also the history of two great civilisations colliding. China and India may be making headlines today as the emerging giants of the 21st century, but that's old news. They have long been great powers and have historically influenced the Mekong region, from art and architecture to language and religion.

Indian culture was disseminated through much of the Mekong region via contact with seafaring Indian merchants calling at trading settlements along the coast of present-day Thailand, Cambodia and Vietnam. Some of these settlements were part of nascent kingdoms, the largest of which was known as Funan to the Chinese, and occupied much of what is southeastern Cambodia today.

The Funanese constructed an elaborate system of canals for the transportation and irrigation of rice. The principal port city of Funan was Oc-Eo in the Mekong Delta. Funan was famous for its refined art and architecture, and its kings embraced the worship of Hindu deities Shiva and Vishnu and, concurrently, Buddhism.

Vietnam Under Occupation

The Chinese ruled Vietnam for 1000 years, introducing Confucianism, Taoism and Mahayana Buddhism to Vietnam, as well as a written character system. Meanwhile, the Indians brought Theravada Buddhism. Monks carried with them the scientific and medical knowledge of these two great civilisations, and Vietnam was soon producing its own great doctors, botanists and scholars.

In the early 10th century, the Tang dynasty in China collapsed. The Vietnamese seized the initiative and launched a revolt against Chinese

TIMELINE

4200 BCE

Cave dwellers capable of making pots inhabit caves around Laang Spean; archaeological evidence suggests the vessels these people were making are similar to those made in Cambodia today.

c 2000 BCE

The Bronze Age Dong Son culture emerges in the Red River Delta around Hanoi. It's renowned for its rice cultivation and the production of bronzeware, including drums and gongs.

c 100 CE

The process of Indianisation begins in the Mekong region: the religions, language, sculpture and culture of India take root through maritime contact with Cambodia.

rule in Vietnam. In 938, popular patriot Ngo Quyen finally vanquished the Chinese armies at a battle on the Bach Dang River, luring the Chinese ships onto sharpened stakes and ending a millennium of Chinese rule. However, it wasn't the last time the Vietnamese would tussle with their mighty northern neighbour.

From the 11th to 13th centuries, Vietnamese independence was consolidated under the enlightened emperors of the Ly dynasty. During the Ly dynasty many enemies, including the Chinese, the Khmer and the Cham – based out of the Champa kingdom in what is today southeastern Vietnam – launched attacks on Vietnam, but all were repelled.

The Rise of Chenla

From the 6th century the Funan kingdom's importance as a port of call declined, and Cambodia's population gradually settled along the Mekong and Tonlé Sap Rivers, where the majority remains today.

Chinese records refer to the rise of the Chenla empire, divided into 'water Chenla' (lower) and 'land Chenla' (upper). Water Chenla was located around Angkor Borei and the temple mount of Phnom Da near present-day Takeo; land Chenla was in the upper reaches of the Mekong River and east of Tonlé Sap lake, around Sambor Prei Kuk, one of the first great temple cities of the Mekong region.

What is certain is that the people of the lower Mekong were well known to the Chinese, and the region was becoming gradually more cohesive. Before long the fractured kingdoms of Chenla would merge to become the greatest empire in Southeast Asia.

The Khmer Empire

A popular place of pilgrimage for Khmers today is the sacred mountain of Phnom Kulen, to the northeast of Angkor, home to an inscription that tells us that in 802 Jayavarman II proclaimed himself a 'universal monarch', or a *devaraja* (god king). Jayavarman set out to bring the region under his control through alliances and conquests. He was the first monarch to rule all of what we call Cambodia today, and the first of a long succession of kings who presided over the Southeast Asian empire that was to leave the stunning legacy of Angkor.

There are few surviving contemporary accounts of Angkor, but Chinese emissary Chou Ta Kuan lived there in 1296 and his observations have been republished as *The Customs of Cambodia*, a fascinating insight into that period.

The Romans of Asia

The Khmers built massive irrigation systems and a sophisticated network of highways to connect the outposts of their empire, much like the Romans did. Roads fanned out from Angkor, connecting the capital with satellite cities such as Ayuthaya and Phimai in Thailand and as far away as Wat Phu in southern Laos.

600

The first inscriptions are committed to stone in Cambodia in ancient Khmer, offering historians the first contemporary accounts of the pre-Angkorian period other than from Chinese sources.

802

Jayavarman II proclaims independence from Java, marking the start of the Khmer empire of Angkor, which controls much of the Mekong region from the 10th to 13th centuries.

1049

Suryavarman I annexes the Dravati kingdom of Lopburi in Thailand and widens his control of Cambodia, stretching the empire to perhaps its greatest extent.

1238

Sukhothai (Land of Rising Happiness) is born, considered the first Thai kingdom in what is contemporary Thailand. It begins to exert pressure on the ailing Khmer empire.

From 1113, King Suryavarman II embarked on another phase of expansion, waging wars against Champa and Vietnam and constructing Angkor Wat, the mother of all temples and the world's largest religious building. It was dedicated to the Hindu deity Vishnu and designed as Suryavarman II's funerary temple.

Enter Sandstone Man

Suryavarman II had brought Champa to heel and reduced it to vassal status. In 1177, the Chams struck back with a naval expedition up the Mekong and into Tonlé Sap lake. They took the city of Angkor by surprise and put King Dharanindravarman II to death. A year later a cousin of Suryavarman II gathered forces and defeated the Chams in another naval battle. The new leader was crowned Jayavarman VII in 1181.

A devout follower of Mahayana Buddhism, Jayavarman VII built the city of Angkor Thom and many other massive monuments visited by tourists around Angkor today. Immortalised in sandstone and on T-shirts, Jayavarman is deified by many Cambodians as their greatest leader, a populist who promoted equality, and a socially conscious leader who built schools and hospitals for his people.

Southeast Asian kingdoms were not states in the modern sense, with fixed frontiers, but varied in their extent. Outlying *meuang* (principalities or city-states) transferred their allegiance elsewhere when the centre was weak. This is why scholars prefer the term 'mandala', meaning 'circle of power'.

The Fall

Following the reign of Jayavarman VII, temple construction effectively ground to a halt, largely because public works quarried local sandstone into oblivion and the population was left exhausted. Meanwhile, the overworked irrigation network was silting up due to massive deforestation in the heavily populated areas to the north and east of Angkor. The state religion reverted to Hinduism for a century or more and outbreaks of iconoclasm saw Buddhist sculpture vandalised or altered.

The ascendent Thai kingdom of Sukhothai grew in strength and made repeated incursions into Angkor, finally sacking the city in 1431. During this period, perhaps drawn by the opportunities for sea trade with China and fearful of the increasingly bellicose Thais, the Khmer elite began to migrate to the Phnom Penh area. Angkor was abandoned to pilgrims, holy men and the elements.

The Golden Age of Siam

Several Thai principalities in the Mekong valley united in the 13th and 14th centuries to create Sukhothai (Land of Rising Happiness). Thai princes wrested control of the territory from the Khmers, whose all-powerful empire at Angkor was slowly disintegrating. Sukhothai is considered by the Thais to be the first true Thai kingdom. It was annexed by Ayuthaya in 1376, by which time a national identity of sorts had been forged.

1431

The expansionist Thais sack Angkor definitively, carting off most of the royal court, including nobles, priests, dancers and artisans, to Ayuthaya. It's an irrevocable spiritual and cultural loss for Cambodia.

1516

Portuguese traders land at Danang, sparking the start of European interest in Vietnam. They set up a trading post in Faifo (present-day Hoi An) and introduce Catholicism to the Vietnamese.

1560

King Setthathirat moves the capital of Lan Xang (modern-day Laos) from Luang Prabang to Viang Chan, today known as Vientiane.

1767

Following several centuries of military rivalry, the Burmese sack the Thai capital of Ayuthaya, forcing its relocation to Thonburi, then to the present-day location of Bangkok.

THE MONGOLS IN THE MEKONG

The marauding Mongols left an indelible mark on the peoples of the Mekong as they initiated a major shift in the region's balance of power.

In 1253, Kublai Khan, grandson of Genghis, attacked the Thai state of Nan Chao, which was located in Xishuangbanna in the south of Yunnan. Thais had already been migrating south for several centuries, and settling in parts of Laos and northern Thailand. However, the sacking of their capital provoked a mass exodus and brought the Thais into conflict with the waning Khmer empire. The Mongol empire evaporated into the dust of history, but with the sacking of the Thai capital, the die was cast: it was the Thais versus the Khmers, a conflict that has persisted through the centuries to the present day.

In 1288, Kublai Khan planned to attack Champa and demanded the right to cross Vietnamese territory. The Vietnamese refused, but the Mongol hordes – all half a million of them – pushed ahead, seemingly invulnerable. However, they met their match in the legendary general Tran Hung Dao. He defeated them in the battle of Bach Dang River, one of the most celebrated victories among many the Vietnamese have won.

The Thai kings of Ayuthaya grew very powerful in the 14th and 15th centuries, taking over the former Khmer strongholds in present-day central Thailand. Although the Khmers had been their adversaries in battle, the Thai kings of Ayuthaya adopted many facets of Khmer culture, including court customs, language and culture. The cultural haemorrhage that took place with the 1431 sacking of Angkor continues to strain relations between the two neighbours. Some Thais claim Angkor as their own, while the Khmers bemoan the loss of Khmer kickboxing, classical Khmer dance and Khmer silk to the all-powerful Thai brand.

Angkor's loss was Ayuthaya's gain and it went on to become one of the greatest cities in Asia. It's been said that London, at the time, was a village in comparison. The kingdom sustained an unbroken monarchical succession through 34 reigns from King U Thong (r 1350–69) to King Ekathat (r 1758–67).

> 'Among the Asian nations, the Kingdom of Siam is the greatest. The magnificence of the Ayuthaya court is incomparable.' Engelbert Kaempfer (German explorer), 1690

Lan Xang, the Birth of Laos

As the power of Sukhothai grew, the Cambodian court looked around for an ally, and found one in Fa Ngum, an exiled Lao prince who was being educated at Angkor.

King Jayavarman VIII married Fa Ngum to a Khmer princess and offered him an army of more than 10,000 troops. He pushed north to wrest the middle Mekong from the control of Sukhothai and its allied Lanna kingdom. By 1353 he declared himself king of Lan Xang Hom Khao, meaning 'Land of a Million Elephants and the White Parasol'. This was

1772

Cambodia is caught between the powerful Vietnamese and Siamese; the latter burn Phnom Penh to the ground, another chapter in the story of inflamed tensions that persist today.

1802

Emperor Gia Long takes the throne to reign over a united Vietnam for the first time in decades, and the Nguyen dynasty is born, ruling until 1945.

1834

The Vietnamese take control of much of Cambodia during the reign of Emperor Minh Mang and begin a slow revolution to 'teach the barbarians their customs'.

1864

The French force Cambodia into the Treaty of Protectorate, which ironically does prevent the small kingdom from being wiped off the map by its more powerful neighbours, Thailand and Vietnam.

really the last hurrah of the declining Khmer empire and quite probably served only to weaken Angkor and antagonise the Thais.

Within 20 years of its birth, Lan Xang had expanded eastward to pick off parts of a disintegrating Champa and along the Annamite Mountains in Vietnam. Fa Ngum earned the sobriquet 'the Conqueror' because of his constant preoccupation with warfare. Theravada Buddhism became the state religion in Lan Xang when King Visounarat accepted the Pha Bang, a gold Buddha image, from his Khmer sponsors.

By naming his kingdom Lan Xang Hom Khao, Fa Ngum was making a statement. Elephants were the battle tanks of Southeast Asian warfare, so claiming to be 'Kingdom of a Million Elephants' was essentially a warning to surrounding kingdoms: 'Don't mess with the Lao!'

Vietnamese Expansion

The Chinese seized control of Vietnam once more in the early 15th century, carrying the national archives and some of the country's intellectuals off to China – an irreparable loss to Vietnamese civilisation. The poet Nguyen Trai (1380–1442) wrote of this period: 'Were the water of the Eastern Sea to be exhausted, the stain of their ignominy could not be washed away; all the bamboo of the Southern Mountains would not suffice to provide the paper for recording all their crimes.'

In 1418, wealthy philanthropist Le Loi rallied the people against the Chinese. Upon victory in 1428, Le Loi declared himself Emperor Le Thai To, the first in the long line of the Le dynasty. To this day, Le Loi is highly revered as one of the country's all-time national heroes. Le Loi and his successors launched a campaign to take over Cham lands to the south and wiped the kingdom of Champa from the map; parts of eastern Laos were forced to kowtow to the might of the Vietnamese.

The Dark Ages

The glorious years of the Khmer empire and the golden age of Ayuthaya were no guarantee of future success and the 18th century proved a time of turmoil. This was the dark ages – when the countries of the Mekong were convulsed by external threats and internal intrigue.

The Continuing Decline of Cambodia

From 1600 until the arrival of the French in 1863, Cambodia was ruled by a series of weak kings who were forced to seek the protection – at a price – of either Thailand or Vietnam. In the 17th century, assistance from the Nguyen lords of southern Vietnam was given on the condition that Vietnamese be allowed to settle in what is now the Mekong Delta region of Vietnam, at that time part of Cambodia and today still referred to by the Khmers as Kampuchea Krom (Lower Cambodia).

In the west, the Thais controlled the provinces of Battambang and Siem Reap from 1794; by the late 18th century they had firm control of the Cambodian royal family.

1883

The French impose the Treaty of Protectorate on the Vietnamese, bringing together Tonkin in the north, Annam in the centre and Cochinchina in the south, marking the start of 70 years of colonial control.

1893

France gains sovereignty over all Lao territories east of the Mekong, thus consolidating its control over the Mekong region as part of its colony of Indochina.

1907

French authorities negotiate the return of Siem Reap, Battambang and Preah Vihear to Cambodia, under Siamese control since 1794; Laos loses out as territory to the west of the Mekong is conceded in the deal.

1930

Ho Chi Minh establishes the Indochinese Communist Party; it splits into three national communist forces: the Viet Minh in Vietnam, the Khmer Rouge in Cambodia and the Pathet Lao in Laos.

The Threat of Burma

Meanwhile, the so-called golden age of Ayuthaya was starting to lose its shine. In 1765, the Burmese laid siege to the capital for two years and the city fell. Everything sacred to the Thais was destroyed, including temples, manuscripts and religious sculpture. The Thais vented their frustrations on their Lao neighbours. The 17th century had been Lan Xang's very own golden age, but the first Lao unified kingdom began to unravel by the end of the century. The country split into the three kingdoms of Luang Prabang, Viang Chan (Vientiane) and Champasak.

Civil War in Vietnam

In a dress rehearsal for the tumultuous events of the 20th century, Vietnam found itself divided in half through much of the 17th and 18th centuries. It wasn't until the dawn of a new century, in 1802, that Nguyen Anh proclaimed himself Emperor Gia Long, thus beginning the Nguyen dynasty. For the first time in two centuries, Vietnam was united, with Hue as its new capital city.

Between 1944 and 1945, the Viet Minh received funding and arms from the US Office of Strategic Services (OSS; today the CIA). When Ho Chi Minh declared independence in 1945, he had OSS agents at his side and borrowed liberally from the American Declaration of Independence.

The French Protectorate

Marco Polo was the first European to cross the Mekong and penetrate the east. In the following centuries many more Europeans followed in his wake, trading in ports as diverse as Ayuthaya and Faifo (Hoi An). However, it was France that was to ultimately lay claim to much of the region.

The concept of 'protectorate' was often employed as a smokescreen by European colonial powers in order to hide their exploitative agenda. However, for the weak and divided kingdoms of Cambodia and Laos, French intervention came not a moment too soon. Both were starting to feel the squeeze as expansionist Thailand and Vietnam carved up their territory. Were it not for the French, it is quite plausible that Cambodia and Laos would have gone the way of Champa, a mere footnote in history, a people without a homeland.

Indochina is Born

France's military activity in Vietnam began in 1847, when the French Navy attacked Danang harbour in response to Emperor Thieu Tri's suppression of Catholic missionaries. Saigon was seized in early 1859 and, in 1862, Emperor Tu Duc signed a treaty that gave the French the three eastern provinces around Saigon.

Cambodia succumbed to French military might in 1864, when French gunboats intimidated King Norodom I (r 1860–1904) into signing the Treaty of Protectorate. In Laos, the same technique was employed with much success. In 1893 a French warship forced its way up the Chao Phraya River to Bangkok and trained its guns on the palace. Under

1939

Following a nationalist coup by a pro-fascist military leadership, Siam changes its name to Thailand in an effort to cement control of the Thai peoples in the Mekong region; the government chooses to side with Japan in WWII.

1941

Japan sweeps through mainland Southeast Asia during WWII, occupying French Indochina in cooperation with pro–Vichy France colonial authorities and winning Thailand's support in return for the promise of territory.

1945

Ho Chi Minh proclaims Vietnamese independence on 2 September in Ba Dinh Sq in Hanoi, but the French have other ideas, sparking 30 years of Vietnamese warfare – first against the French and then the Americans.

1953

Cambodia and Laos go it alone with independence from France, almost insignificant sacrifices as the colonial power attempts to cling to control in Vietnam.

duress, the Siamese agreed to transfer all territory east of the Mekong to France, and Laos became part of Indochina.

In 1883 the French attacked Hue and imposed the Treaty of Protectorate on the imperial court of Vietnam. The Indochinese Union proclaimed by the French in 1887 may have ended the existence of an independent Vietnamese state, but active resistance continued in various parts of the country for the duration of French rule.

The Thais Hold Out

The Thais are proud of their independent history and that they were never colonised. Successive Thai kings courted the Europeans while maintaining their neutrality. It was an ambiguous relationship, best summed up by King Mongkut: 'Whatever they have invented or done, we should know of and do, we can imitate and learn from them, but do not wholeheartedly believe in them.'

The French were able to exert some influence over the Siamese, convincing Siam to return the northwest provinces of Battambang, Siem Reap and Sisophon to Cambodia in 1907 in return for concessions of Lao territory. This returned Angkor to Cambodian control for the first time in more than a century.

In the end, it was less the Thai manoeuvring that kept the country independent, but the realisation by the British in Burma (present-day Myanmar) and the French in Indochina that a buffer zone would prevent open warfare.

As WWII drew to a close, Japanese rice requisitions, in combination with floods and breaches in the dikes, caused a horrific famine – two million of northern Vietnam's 10 million people starved to death.

Communism & WWII

The first Marxist grouping in Indochina was the Vietnam Revolutionary Youth League, founded by Ho Chi Minh in Canton, China, in 1925. This was succeeded in February 1930 by the Vietnamese Communist Party, part of the Indochinese Communist Party (ICP). As the desire for independence grew in Vietnam, the communists proved adept at tuning into the frustrations and aspirations of the population, and effectively channelling their demands for fairer land distribution.

War Gamesmanship

In WWII Japanese forces occupied much of Asia, and Indochina was no exception. With many in France collaborating with the occupying Germans, the French in Indochina ended up on the side of the Japanese.

In 1941, Ho formed the League for the Independence of Vietnam, much better known as the Viet Minh. Receiving assistance from the US government, Ho resisted the Japanese-French alliance and carried out extensive political activities throughout the war. Ho was pragmatic, patriotic and populist, and understood the need for national unity.

1955

Cambodia's King Norodom Sihanouk abdicates to enter a career in politics; he founds the Sangkum Reastr Niyum (People's Socialist Community) and wins the election with ease.

1956

Vietnam remains divided at the 17th Parallel into communist North Vietnam, under the leadership of Ho Chi Minh, and 'free' South Vietnam, under the rule of President Ngo Dinh Diem.

1959

The Ho Chi Minh Trail, which had been in existence for several years during the war against the French, reopens for business and becomes the main supply route to the South for the next 16 years.

1962

The International Court rules in favour of Cambodia in the long-running dispute with Thailand over Preah Vihear, perched on the Dangkrek Mountains; it continues to create friction between the neighbours today.

A False Dawn

As events unfolded in Europe, the French and Japanese fell out and the Viet Minh saw its opportunity. By the spring of 1945, the Viet Minh controlled large parts of Vietnam, particularly in the north. On 2 September 1945 Ho Chi Minh declared independence. Throughout this period, Ho wrote no fewer than eight letters to President Harry Truman and the US State Department asking for American aid, but received no replies.

Having prevailed in Europe, the French wasted no time returning to Indochina, making the countries 'autonomous states within the French Union', but retaining de facto control. French general Jacques Philippe Leclerc pompously declared: 'We have come to reclaim our inheritance.'

In the north, Chinese Kuomintang troops were fleeing the Chinese communists and pillaging their way southward towards Hanoi. Ho tried to placate the Chinese, but as the months of Chinese occupation dragged on, he concluded 'better the devil you know' and accepted a temporary return of the French.

War with the French

In the face of determined Vietnamese nationalism, the French proved unable to regain control. Despite massive US aid and significant indigenous anticommunist elements, it was an unwinnable war. As Ho said to the French at the time, 'You can kill 10 of my men for every one I kill of yours, but even at those odds you will lose and I will win.'

The whole complexion of the First Indochina War changed with the 1949 victory of communism in China. As Chinese weapons flowed to the Viet Minh, the French were forced onto the defensive. After eight years of fighting, the Viet Minh controlled much of Vietnam and neighbouring Laos. On 7 May 1954, after a 57-day siege, more than 10,000 starving French troops surrendered to the Viet Minh at Dien Bien Phu.

This was a catastrophic defeat that brought an end to the French colonial adventure in Indochina. The next day, the Geneva Conference opened to negotiate an end to the conflict, with the French suddenly lacking any cards left to bring to the table. By the conference's end, France's colonial period in Indochina would be over and Vietnam, Cambodia and Laos would be internationally recognised as independent states.

For a full Cambodian history, from humble beginnings in the prehistoric period through the glories of Angkor and through the Khmer Rouge period, seek out a copy of *A History of Cambodia* (4th Edition; 2007) by David Chandler.

Independence for Vietnam, Cambodia & Laos

The Geneva Accords resulted in two Vietnams. Ho Chi Minh led the communist northern zone, while the South was ruled by Ngo Dinh Diem, a fiercely anticommunist Catholic. Nationwide elections scheduled for

1965

The first US marines wade ashore at Danang as the war in Vietnam heats up, and the Americans commit ground troops to avoid the very real possibility of a communist victory.

1968

The Viet Cong launches the Tet Offensive, a synchronised attack throughout the South that catches the Americans unaware. Iconic images of this are beamed into households all over the USA.

1969

US President Richard Nixon authorises the secret bombing of Cambodia as an extension of the war in Vietnam; the campaign continues until 1973, killing up to 250,000 Cambodians.

1970

Cambodia leader Norodom Sihanouk is overthrown in a coup engineered by his general Lon Nol and cousin Prince Sirik Matak, thus beginning Cambodia's bloody descent into civil war and genocide.

1956 were never held, as the Americans and the South rightly feared that Ho Chi Minh would win easily.

In Laos, the convention set aside two northeastern provinces (Hua Phan and Phongsali) as regroupment areas for Pathet Lao ('Land of the Lao', or communist) forces. The tragedy for Laos was that when, after two centuries, the independent Lao state was reborn, it was conceived in the nationalism of WWII, nourished during the agony of the First Indochina War and born into the Cold War. Thus, from its inception, it was torn by ideological division, which the Lao tried mightily to overcome, but which was surreptitiously stoked by outside interference.

Cambodia's sudden independence was a huge victory for its young king, Prince Norodom Sihanouk, who had been placed on the throne in 1941 by French Admiral Jean Decoux. The assumption was that he would be naive and pliable. As he grew in stature, this proved to be a major miscalculation. In 1953 King Sihanouk embarked on his 'royal crusade': his travelling campaign to drum up international support for independence, which was proclaimed on 9 November 1953 and recognised shortly after in Geneva. In 1955 Sihanouk abdicated, afraid of being marginalised amid the pomp of royal ceremony. The 'royal crusader' became 'citizen Sihanouk' and vowed never again to return to the throne.

The War in Vietnam

During the first few years of his rule, Diem consolidated power effectively. During Diem's 1957 official visit to the US, President Eisenhower called him the 'miracle man' of Asia. As time went on Diem became increasingly tyrannical in dealing with dissent.

In the early 1960s, the South was rocked by anti-Diem unrest led by university students and Buddhist clergy. The US decided Diem was a liability and threw its support behind a military coup. A group of young generals led the operation in November 1963. Diem was to go into exile, but the generals got overexcited and both Diem and his brother were killed. He was followed by a succession of military rulers who continued his erratic policies and dragged the country deeper into war.

For a human perspective on the North Vietnamese experience during the war, read *The Sorrow of War* by Bao Ninh (1990), a poignant tale of love and loss that shows the soldiers from the North had the same fears and desires as most American GIs.

War Breaks Out

The North's campaign to 'liberate' the South began in the late 1950s with the creation of the National Liberation Front (NLF), nicknamed the Viet Cong (VC) by the Americans. By early 1965, Hanoi was sending regular North Vietnamese Army (NVA) units down the Ho Chi Minh Trail and the Saigon government was on its last legs. To the Americans, Vietnam was the next domino and could not topple. It was clearly time for the Americans to 'clean up the mess', as one of Lyndon Johnson's leading officials put it.

1973

All sides in the Vietnam conflict sign the Paris Peace Accords on 27 January 1973, supposedly bringing an end to the war in Vietnam, but it's actually a face-saving deal for the US to 'withdraw with honour'.

1975

The Khmer Rouge enters Phnom Penh on 17 April, implementing one of the bloodiest revolutions in history; North Vietnamese forces take Saigon on 30 April, renaming it Ho Chi Minh City; Vietnam is reunified.

1978

Vietnam invades Cambodia on Christmas Day in response to border attacks; the Khmer Rouge is overthrown weeks later; a decade-long war between communist 'brothers' begins.

1986

Doi moi (economic reform), Vietnam's answer to perestroika and the first step towards re-engaging with the West, is launched with a rash of economic reforms.

For the first years of the conflict, the American military was boldly proclaiming victory upon victory, as the communist body count mounted. However, the Tet Offensive of 1968 brought an alternative reality into the homes of the average American. On the evening of 31 January, as Vietnam celebrated the Lunar New Year, the VC launched a series of strikes in more than 100 cities and towns, including Saigon. As the TV cameras rolled, a VC commando team took over the courtyard of the US embassy in central Saigon. The Tet Offensive killed about 1000 US soldiers and 2000 Army of the Republic of Vietnam (ARVN) troops, but VC losses were more than 10 times higher, at around 32,000 deaths. For the VC the Tet Offensive ultimately proved a success: it made the cost of fighting the war unbearable for the Americans.

Simultaneously, stories began leaking out of Vietnam about atrocities and massacres carried out by US forces against unarmed Vietnamese civilians, including the infamous My Lai Massacre. This helped turn the tide against the war, and antiwar demonstrations rocked American university campuses and spilled onto the streets.

During the US bombing of 1964–73, some 13 million tonnes of bombs – equivalent to 450 times the energy of the atomic bomb used on Hiroshima – were dropped on the Indochina region. This equates to 265kg for every man, woman and child in Vietnam, Cambodia and Laos.

Tricky Dick's Exit Strategy

Richard Nixon was elected president in 1968 in part because of a promise that he had a 'secret plan' to end the war. Nixon's strategy called for 'Vietnamisation', which meant making the South Vietnamese fight the war without US troops.

The 'Christmas bombing' of Haiphong and Hanoi at the end of 1972 was meant to wrest concessions from North Vietnam at the negotiating table. Eventually, the Paris Peace Accords were signed by the US, North Vietnam, South Vietnam and the VC on 27 January 1973, which provided for a ceasefire, the total withdrawal of US combat forces and the release of 590 US prisoners of war (POWs).

The End is Nigh

In January 1975 the North Vietnamese launched a massive ground attack across the 17th Parallel using tanks and heavy artillery. Whole brigades of ARVN soldiers disintegrated and fled southward, joining hundreds of thousands of civilians clogging Hwy 1. The North Vietnamese pushed on to Saigon and on the morning of 30 April 1975 their tanks smashed through the gates of Saigon's Independence Palace (now called Reunification Palace). The long war was over, Vietnam was reunited and Saigon was renamed Ho Chi Minh City.

The Reunification of Vietnam

Vietnam may have been united, but it would take a long time to heal the scars of war. Damage from the fighting extended from unmarked

1991

The Paris Peace Agreements are signed, in which all Cambodian parties (including, controversially, the Khmer Rouge) agree to participate in free and fair elections supervised by the UN, held in 1993.

1997

Asian financial crisis grips the Mekong region; Cambodia is convulsed by a coup and becomes a pariah once more; Laos and Myanmar (Burma) join the Association of Southeast Asian Nations (Asean).

1998

Following a government push on the Khmer Rouge's last stronghold at Anlong Veng, Pol Pot dies on 15 April; rumours about the circumstances of his death swirl around Phnom Penh.

1999

Cambodia finally joins Asean after a two-year delay; the other Southeast Asian nations welcome the country back to the world stage.

THE SECRET WAR IN LAOS

Before his assassination in 1963, President John F Kennedy gave the order to recruit a force of 11,000 Hmong under the command of Vang Pao. They were trained by several hundred US and Thai Special Forces advisers and supplied by Air America, all under the supervision of the CIA. The secret war had begun.

Over the next 12 years the Hmong 'secret army' fought a continuous guerrilla campaign against heavily armed North Vietnamese regular army troops occupying the Plain of Jars. They were supported throughout by the US.

In 1964 the US began its air war over Laos, with strafing and bombing of communist positions on the Plain of Jars. As North Vietnamese infiltration picked up along the Ho Chi Minh Trail, bombing was extended across all of Laos. According to official figures, the US dropped 2,093,100 tonnes of bombs in 580,944 sorties. The total cost was US$7.2 billion, or US$2 million a day for nine years. No one knows how many people died, but one-third of the population of 2.1 million became internal refugees.

minefields to war-focused, dysfunctional economies; from a chemically poisoned countryside to a population that had been physically or mentally battered.

The party decided on a rapid transition to socialism in the south, but this proved disastrous for the economy. Reunification was accompanied by widespread political repression. Despite repeated promises to the contrary, hundreds of thousands of people who had ties to the previous regime had their property confiscated and were rounded up and imprisoned without trial in forced-labour camps, euphemistically known as re-education camps.

Australian author and documentary film-maker John Pilger was one of the original rabble-rousing left-wing journalists and documentary film-makers. Get to grips with his hard-hitting views on the war in Vietnam at www.johnpilger.com.

Sideshow: the Civil War in Cambodia

The 1950s were seen as Cambodia's golden years and Sihanouk successfully maintained Cambodia's neutrality into the 1960s. However, with the war in Vietnam raging across the border, Cambodia was being sucked slowly into the vortex.

By 1969 the conflict between the Cambodian army and leftist rebels had become more serious, as the Vietnamese sought sanctuary deeper in Cambodia. In March 1970, while Sihanouk was on a trip to France, he was overthrown in a coup by General Lon Nol, his army commander. Sihanouk took up residence in Beijing and formed an alliance with the Cambodian communists, nicknamed the Khmer Rouge (Red Khmer), who exploited this partnership to gain new recruits.

On 30 April 1970, US and South Vietnamese forces invaded Cambodia in an effort to flush out thousands of Viet Cong and North Vietnamese troops. The Vietnamese communists withdrew deeper into Cambodia.

2001

Telecommunications tycoon Thaksin Shinawatra is elected prime minister of Thailand, setting the country on a divisive course.

2004

King Sihanouk abdicates in Cambodia, closing the chapter on 63 years as monarch, politician and statesman, and is succeeded by his son King Sihamoni.

2004

The first US commercial flight since the end of the Vietnam War touches down in Ho Chi Minh City, as US–Vietnamese business and tourism links mushroom.

2004

The 26 December Indian Ocean tsunami kills over 5000 people in Thailand and damages tourism and fishing industries.

The Secret Bombing

In 1969, the US began a secret program of bombing suspected communist base camps in Cambodia. For the next four years, until bombing was halted by the US Congress in August 1973, huge areas of the eastern half of the country were carpet-bombed by US B-52s, killing thousands of civilians and turning hundreds of thousands more into refugees.

Despite massive US military and economic aid, Lon Nol never succeeded in gaining the initiative against the Khmer Rouge. Large parts of the countryside fell to the rebels and many provincial capitals were cut off from Phnom Penh. On 17 April 1975, Phnom Penh surrendered to the Khmer Rouge.

Hitch a ride with Michael Herr and his seminal work *Dispatches* (1977). A correspondent for *Esquire* magazine, Herr tells it how it is, as some of the darkest events of the war in Vietnam unfold around him, including the siege of Khe Sanh.

The Land of a Million Irrelevants

War correspondents covering the conflict in Indochina soon renamed Lan Xang (ie Laos) 'the Land of a Million Irrelevants'. However, the ongoing conflict was very relevant to the Cold War and the great powers were playing out their power struggles on this most obscure of stages. Successive governments came and went so fast they needed a revolving door in the national assembly.

Upcountry, large areas fell under the control of communist forces. The US sent troops to Thailand, in case communist forces attempted to cross the Mekong, and it looked for a time as if the major commitment of US troops in Southeast Asia would be to Laos rather than Vietnam. Both the North Vietnamese and the Americans were jockeying for strategic advantage, and neither was going to let Lao neutrality get in the way.

By mid-1972, when serious peace moves got under way, some four-fifths of Laos was under communist control. Unlike Cambodia and Vietnam, the communists were eventually able to take power without a fight. City after city was occupied by the Pathet Lao (communist forces) and in August 1975 they marched into Vientiane unopposed.

For the full story on how Cambodia was sucked into hell, read *Sideshow: Kissinger, Nixon and the Destruction of Cambodia* (1979) by William Shawcross.

The Khmer Rouge & Year Zero

Upon taking Phnom Penh, the Khmer Rouge implemented one of the most radical and brutal restructurings of a society ever attempted; its goal was to transform Cambodia into a Maoist, peasant-dominated agrarian cooperative. Within days of the Khmer Rouge coming to power the entire population of the capital, including the sick, elderly and infirm, was forced to march out to the countryside. Disobedience of any sort often brought immediate execution. The advent of Khmer Rouge rule was proclaimed Year Zero. Currency was abolished and postal services were halted. The country was cut off from the outside world.

2006
Thaksin government is overthrown in a coup and the Thai prime minister forced into exile.

2010
Comrade Duch, aka Kaing Guek Eav, former commandant of the notorious S-21 prison in Phnom Penh, becomes first Khmer Rouge leader convicted of crimes against humanity.

2010
Pro-Thaksin 'Red Shirt' activists occupy central Bangkok for two months; military crackdown results in 91 deaths.

2011
Cambodia and Thailand trade blows over the ancient border temple of Prasat Preah Vihear on the Dangkrek Mountains; Asean attempts to broker a lasting settlement.

Counting the Cost of Genocide

Pol Pot's initial fury upon seizing power was directed against the former regime. All of the senior government and military figures who had been associated with Lon Nol were executed within days of the takeover. Then the centre shifted its attention to the outer regions, a process that saw thousands perish.

It is still not known exactly how many Cambodians died at the hands of the Khmer Rouge during the three years, eight months and 20 days of its rule. The Vietnamese claimed three million deaths, while foreign experts long considered the number closer to one million. Yale University researchers undertaking ongoing investigations estimated that the figure was close to two million.

Hundreds of thousands of people were executed by the Khmer Rouge leadership, while hundreds of thousands more died of famine and disease. Meals consisted of little more than watery rice porridge twice a day, but were meant to sustain men, women and children through a back-breaking day in the fields. Disease stalked the work camps, with malaria and dysentery striking down whole families; death was a relief for many from the horrors of life. Some zones were better than others, some leaders fairer than others, but life for the majority was one of unending misery and suffering in this 'prison without walls'.

François Bizot was kidnapped by the Khmer Rouge, interrogated by Comrade Duch and is believed to be the only foreigner to have been released. Later he was holed up in the French embassy in April 1975. Read his harrowing story in *The Gate* (2003).

As the centre eliminated more and more moderates, Angkar (the organisation) became the only family people needed and those who did not agree were sought out and crushed. The Khmer Rouge detached the Cambodian people from all they held dear: their families, their food, their fields and their faith. Even the peasants who had supported the revolution could no longer blindly follow such insanity. Nobody cared for the Khmer Rouge by 1978, but nobody had an ounce of strength to do anything about it...except the Vietnamese.

The Vietnamese Move In

From 1976 to 1978, the Khmer Rouge instigated a series of border clashes with Vietnam, and claimed the Mekong Delta, once part of the Khmer empire. On 25 December 1978 Vietnam launched a full-scale invasion of Cambodia, toppling the Pol Pot government two weeks later, and installing a new government led by several former Khmer Rouge officers, including current Prime Minister Hun Sen, who had defected to Vietnam in 1977.

The Khmer Rouge's patrons, the Chinese communists, launched a massive reprisal raid across Vietnam's northernmost border in early 1979 in an attempt to buy their allies time. It failed. After 17 days the Chinese withdrew, their fingers badly burnt by their Vietnamese enemies. The

2011

Red Shirts back in power as Yingluck Shinawatra becomes Thailand's first female prime minister.

2012

Cambodia's former king Norodom Sihanouk dies a national hero.

2013

Vietnam War hero General Giap, seen as an antidote to the country's corrupt modern-day leadership, dies. Millions pay their respects.

2013

Cambodia's opposition party surprisingly wins 45% of vote in Cambodia's elections, but cries foul and protesters take to the streets.

Vietnamese then staged a show trial in Cambodia in which Pol Pot and Ieng Sary were condemned to death in absentia for their genocidal acts.

In 1984, the Vietnamese overran all the major rebel camps inside Cambodia, forcing the Khmer Rouge and its allies to retreat into Thailand. From this time the Khmer Rouge and its allies engaged in guerrilla warfare aimed at demoralising its opponents. Tactics used included shelling government-controlled garrison towns, planting thousands of mines in rural areas, attacking road transport, blowing up bridges, kidnapping village chiefs and targeting civilians. The Khmer Rouge also forced thousands of men, women and children living in the refugee camps it controlled to work as porters, ferrying ammunition and other supplies into Cambodia across heavily mined sections of the border.

The Vietnamese, for their part, laid the world's longest minefield, known as K-5 and stretching from the Gulf of Thailand to the Lao border, in an attempt to seal out the guerrillas. They also sent Cambodians into the forests to cut down trees on remote sections of road to prevent ambushes. Thousands died of disease and from injuries sustained from land mines. The Khmer Rouge was no longer in power, but for many the 1980s were almost as tough as the 1970s – one long struggle to survive.

Several of the current crop of Cambodian leaders were previously members of the Khmer Rouge, including Prime Minister Hun Sen and Head of the National Assembly Heng Samrin, although there is no evidence to implicate them in mass killings.

Reversal of Fortune

The communist cooperatives in Indochina were a miserable failure and caused almost as much suffering as the wars that had preceded them. Pragmatic Laos was the first to liberalise in response to the economic stagnation, and private farming and enterprise were allowed as early as 1979. However, the changes came too late for the Lao royal family and the last king and queen are believed to have died of malnutrition and disease in a prison camp sometime in the late 1970s.

Vietnam was slower to evolve, but the arrival of President Mikhail Gorbachev in the Soviet Union meant glasnost (openness) and perestroika (restructuring) were in, and radical revolution was out. *Doi moi* (economic reforms) were experimented with in Cambodia and introduced to Vietnam. As the USSR scaled back its commitments to the communist world, the outposts were the first to feel the pinch. The Vietnamese decided to unilaterally withdraw from Cambodia in 1989, as they could no longer afford the occupation. The party in Vietnam was on its own and needed to reform to survive. Cambodia and Laos would follow its lead.

A New Beginning

You may be wondering what happened to Thailand in all of this? Well, compared with the earth-shattering events unfolding in Indochina, things were rather dull. Thailand profited as its neighbours suffered, providing air bases and logistical support to the Americans during the war

2014
The Thai military under General Prayuth Chan-o-cha overthrows Yingluck Shinawatra's Puea Thai Party government.

2016
Asean common market goes into effect, tying the Mekong countries closer together.

2016
Vice President of Laos Bounnhang Vorachith becomes Laos' new supreme leader.

2016
Revered King Bhumibol Adulyadej (Rama IX) dies at 88, setting off a year of mourning in Thailand.

in Vietnam. As the war and revolution consumed a generation in Cambodia, Laos and Vietnam, Thailand's economy prospered and democracy slowly took root, although coups remain common currency right up to the present day – largely because of the divisiveness of billionaire tycoon Thaksin Shinawatra, who served as prime minister from 2001 to 2006 before being ousted by the military and forced into exile. The power struggle between Thaksin's 'Red Shirt' supporters and their 'Yellow Shirt' opponents has dominated the headlines in Thailand for more than a decade. Meanwhile, southern Thailand continues to be gripped by an Islamic insurgency that has claimed hundreds of lives.

Jon Swain's *River of Time* (1995) takes the reader back to an old Indochina, partly lost to the madness of war, and includes first-hand accounts of the French embassy stand-off in the first days of the Khmer Rouge takeover.

Cambodia was welcomed back to the world stage in 1991 with the signing of the Paris Peace Agreements, which set out a UN road map to free and fair elections. There have been many hiccups along the way, including coups and a culture of impunity, but Cambodia has come a long way from the dark days of the Khmer Rouge. Democracy is hardly flourishing – corruption most certainly is – but life is better for many than it has been for a long time. Attempts to bring the surviving Khmer Rouge leadership to trial continue to stumble along.

Vietnam has followed the Chinese road to riches, taking the brakes off the economy while keeping a firm hand on the political steering wheel. With only two million paid-up members of the Communist Party and around 90 million Vietnamese, it is a road they must follow carefully. However, the economy has been booming since the country joined the World Trade Organisation in 2006. Industry and manufacturing have led the way, along with tourism – the country welcomed a record 18 million visitors in 2019, up from 10 million in 2016.

In Laos, hydroelectric power is a big industry and looks set to subsidise the economy in the future, with up to 140 dam projects in the works. But the dams are taking a terrible toll on fish stocks and there are safety concerns after the tragic collapse of a dam in Attapeu Province in 2018. Meanwhile, illegal logging remains a major problem (as it is in Cambodia), with demand for timber in China, Thailand and Vietnam driving the destruction. Tourism has good prospects and Laos is carving a niche for itself as the ecotourism darling of Southeast Asia.

On a global scale, the Mekong region has been very lightly affected by the Covid-19 panademic, despite the proximity of China and densely-populated cities. Border closures, quarantining in designated facilities and highly effective contact tracing have kept cases and deaths low. However, vaccination programmes have been slow off the mark and fully restarting the tourist economy will present a real challenge.

Like the river that binds them, the countries of the Mekong region have a turbulent past and an uncertain future.

2017

Cambodia's Supreme Court dissolves the opposition CNRP, paving the way for the ruling CPP party of Prime Minister Hun Sen to win all 125 seats in the National Assembly the following year.

2018

Scores die after the Saddle D dam in Laos' southern Attapeu Province collapses, raising more concerns about the country's plans to build some 140 dams.

2019

King Vajiralongkorn, Rama X, is formally crowned in an elaborate three-day ceremony in Bangkok.

2020–21

The Mekong region is largely successful in containing Covid-19 cases with border closures and contact tracing. Protests against the Thai monarchy erupt in Bangkok.

People & Culture

The Mekong region is not known as Indochina for nothing – geographically it's the land in between China and India. China has shaped the destiny of Vietnam and continues to cast a shadow over the Mekong region; India exported its great religions, language, culture and sculpture to Cambodia, Laos and Thailand. With a millennium of influence from two of the world's great civilisations, it is hardly surprising that there is such a dynamic variety of culture in the Mekong region today.

Lifestyle

Traditionally, life in the Mekong region has revolved around family, fields and faith, the rhythm of rural existence continuing for centuries. For the majority of the population still living in the countryside, these constants have remained unchanged, with several generations sharing the same roof, the same rice and the same religion.

Above Karen women (p531), Chiang Mai, Thailand

But in recent decades these rhythms have been jarred by war and ideology, as peasants were dragged from all they held dear to fight in civil wars, or were herded into cooperatives as communism tried to assert itself as the moral and social beacon in the lives of the people. But Buddhism is back, and for many older Mekong residents the temple or pagoda remains an important pillar in their lives.

A typical day in the Mekong region starts early. Country folk tend to rise before dawn, woken by the cry of cockerels and keen to get the most out of the day before the temperature heats up. This habit has spilled over into the towns and cities and many urban dwellers rise at the crack of dawn for a quick jog, a game of badminton or some t'ai chi moves.

The famous Hindu epic the *Ramayana* is known as the *Ramakian* in Thailand, the *Reamker* in Cambodia and *Pha Lak Pha Lam* in Laos.

Food is almost as important as family in this part of the world – and that is saying something. Breakfast comes in many flavours, but Chinese congee (rice soup) and noodle soups are universally popular. Long lunch breaks are common (and common sense, as they avoid the hottest part of the day). The working day winds down for some around 5pm and the family will try to come together for dinner and trade tales about their day.

People

As empires came and went, so too did the populations, and many of the countries in the Mekong region are far less ethnically homogenous than their governments would have us believe. It wasn't only local empire building that had an impact: colonial meddling left a number of people stranded beyond their borders. There are Lao and Khmer in Thailand, Khmer in Vietnam, Thai (Dai) in Vietnam and Chinese everywhere. No self-respecting Mekong town would be complete without a Chinatown.

The mountains of the Mekong region provide a home for a mosaic of minority groups, often referred to as 'hill tribes'. Many of these groups migrated from China and Tibet and have settled in areas that lowlanders considered too challenging to cultivate. Colourful costumes and unique traditions draw increasing numbers of visitors to their mountain homes. The most popular areas to visit local hill tribes include Mondulkiri and Ratanakiri Provinces in Cambodia; Luang Namtha and Muang Sing in northern Laos; Chiang Mai and Chiang Rai in northern Thailand; and Sapa and Bac Ha in northern Vietnam.

Foreign ethnographers who have carried out field research in Laos have identified anywhere from 49 to 134 different ethnic groups.

Population growth varies throughout the Mekong region. Developed Thailand embraced family planning decades ago and Vietnam has adopted a Chinese model of sorts, with a two-child policy in lowland areas, though a declining birthrate has seen the policy under review. Cambodia and Laos have the highest birth rates and large families remain the rule rather than the exception out in the countryside.

FACE IT

'Face' – or more importantly, the art of not making the locals lose face – is an important concept to understand in Asia. Face is all in Asia, and in the Mekong region it is above all. Having 'big face' is synonymous with prestige. All families, even poor ones, are expected to have big wedding parties and throw their money around like it is water in order to gain face. This is often ruinously expensive, but that is far less important than 'losing face'.

And it is for this reason that foreigners should never lose their tempers with the locals; this will bring unacceptable 'loss of face' to the individual involved and end any chance of a sensible solution to the dispute. If things aren't always going according to plan, take a deep breath, keep your cool and try to work out a solution.

Cambodian Living Arts (p194) performance, Phnom Penh, Cambodia

Chinese

Many of the great cities of the Mekong region have significant Chinese communities, and in the case of capitals like Bangkok and Phnom Penh, people of at least some Chinese ancestry may make up half the population. The Chinese are much more integrated in the Mekong region than in places like Indonesia, and continue to contribute to the economy through investment and initiative.

With one eye on history, the Vietnamese are more suspicious of the Chinese than most, even though, culturally, the Vietnamese have much in common with the Chinese. Vietnam was occupied by China for more than a thousand years and the Chinese brought with them their religion, philosophy and culture. Confucianism and Taoism were introduced and still form the backbone of Vietnamese religion, together with Buddhism.

Khmer (Cambodian)

The Khmer have inhabited Cambodia since the beginning of recorded history, around the 2nd century AD, long before the Thais and Vietnamese arrived in the southern Mekong region. Cambodia was the cultural staging post for the Indianisation of the Mekong region. Indian traders brought Hinduism and Buddhism around the 2nd century and with these came the religious languages of Sanskrit and Pali; Sanskrit forms the root of modern Khmer, Lao and Thai.

During the glory years of Angkor, Hinduism was the predominant religion, but from the 15th century Theravada Buddhism was adopted and most Khmers remain devoutly Buddhist today. Their faith was an important anchor in the struggle to rebuild their lives following the rule of the Khmer Rouge, in which it's believed as much as one-third of the Cambodian population perished.

The Cambodian and Lao people share a close bond, as Fa Ngum, the founder of the original Lao kingdom of Lan Xang (Land of a Million Elephants), was sponsored by his Khmer father-in-law.

A family in northern Laos

Kinh (Vietnamese)

Despite the Chinese view that the Vietnamese are 'the ones that got away', the Vietnamese existed in the Red River Delta area long before the first waves of Chinese arrived some 2000 years ago. The Kinh make up about 86% of the population of Vietnam. Centuries ago, the Vietnamese began to push southward in search of cultivable land and swallowed the kingdom of Champa before pushing on into the Mekong Delta and picking off pieces of a decaying Khmer empire. As well as occupying the coastal regions of Vietnam, the lowland Kinh have been moving into the mountains to take advantage of new opportunities in agriculture, industry and tourism.

Thais are given nicknames at birth, often inspired by the child's appearance, eg 'Moo' (meaning Pig) if the baby is chubby, or 'Lek' (Small).

Lao

Laos is often described as less a nation-state than a conglomeration of tribes and languages. The Lao traditionally divide themselves into four broad families – Lao Loum, Lao Thai, Lao Thoeng and Lao Soung – roughly defined by the altitude at which they live and their cultural proclivities. The Lao government has an alternative three-way split, in which the Lao Thai are condensed into the Lao Loum group. This triumvirate is represented on the back of every 1000K bill, in national costume, from left to right: Lao Soung, Lao Loum and Lao Thoeng.

Thai

Thais make up about 75% of the population of Thailand, although this group is commonly broken down into four subgroups: Central Thais who inhabit the Chao Phraya delta; the Thai Lao of northeastern Thailand; the Pak Thai of southern Thailand; and northern Thais. Each group speaks its own dialect and to a certain extent practises customs unique to its region. Politically and economically, the Central Thais are the dominant group, although they barely outnumber the Thai Lao.

Vietnam is home to 53 ethnic minority groups, mostly living in northern Vietnam. They make up about 10% of Vietnam's population of 100 million.

Minority Groups

There are many other important minority groups in the region; some were rendered stateless by the conflicts of the past, while others are recent migrants to the region, including the many hill tribes.

Cham

The Cham people originally occupied the kingdom of Champa in south-central Vietnam and their beautiful brick towers dot the landscape from Danang to Phan Rang. Victims of a historical squeeze between Cambodia and Vietnam, their territory was eventually annexed by the expansionist Vietnamese. Originally Hindu, they converted to Islam in the 16th and 17th centuries and many migrated to Cambodia.

LIFE AMONG THE MINORITIES

One of the highlights of a visit to the Mekong region is an encounter with one of the many ethnic minority groups inhabiting the mountains. Many wear incredible costumes, and so elaborate are some of these that it's easy to believe minority girls learn to embroider before they can walk.

While some of these minorities number as many as a million people, it is feared that other groups have dwindled to as few as 100. The areas inhabited by each group are often delineated by altitude, with more recent arrivals settling at a higher altitude. Each hill tribe has its own language, customs, mode of dress and spiritual beliefs. Some groups are caught between medieval and modern worlds, while others have assimilated into modern life.

Most groups share a rural, agricultural lifestyle that revolves around traditional rituals. Most hill-tribe communities are seminomadic, cultivating crops such as rice and using slash-and-burn methods, which have taken a toll on the environment. Hill tribes have among the lowest standards of living in the region and lack access to education, health care and even minimum-wage jobs. While there may be no official discrimination system, cultural prejudice against hill-tribe people ensures they remain at the bottom of the ladder. Put simply, life is a struggle for most minority people.

Tourism can bring many benefits to highland communities: cross-cultural understanding, improved infrastructure, cheaper market goods, employment opportunities and tourist dollars supporting handicraft industries. However, there are also negatives, such as increased litter and pollutants, dependency on tourist dollars, and the erosion of local values and practices. Here are some tips on how to have a positive effect when visiting minority communities:

- Where possible, hire indigenous guides – they understand taboos and traditions that might be lost on lowland guides.
- Always ask permission before taking photos of tribespeople.
- Don't show up for 15 minutes and expect to be granted permission to take photos – invest some time in getting to know the villagers first.
- Don't touch totems or sacred items hanging from trees.
- Avoid cultivating a tradition of begging, especially among children.
- Avoid public nudity and don't undress near an open window.
- Don't flirt with members of the opposite sex.
- Taste traditional wine if you are offered it, especially during a ceremony.
- Dress modestly.
- Don't buy village treasures, such as altar pieces or totems.

DIY13/SHUTTERSTOCK ©

Top Street vendor in Ho Chi Minh City (p130), Vietnam

Left Red Dzao embroidery Sapa (p81), Vietnam

Today there are small numbers of Cham in Vietnam and as many as half a million in Cambodia, all of whom continue to practise a flexible form of Islam. The Cham population has intermarried over the centuries with migrating Malay seafarers, introducing an additional ethnic background into the mix.

Hmong

The Hmong are one of the largest hill tribes in the Mekong region, spread through much of northern Laos, northern Vietnam and Thailand. As some of the last to arrive in the region in the 19th century, they were left with the highest and harshest lands from which to eke out their existence. They soon made the best of a bad deal and opted for opium cultivation, which brought them into conflict with mainstream governments during the 20th century.

Hmong groups are usually classified by their colourful clothing, including Black Hmong, White Hmong, Red Hmong and so on. The brightest group is the Flower Hmong of northwest Vietnam, who live in villages around Bac Ha. There may be as many as one million Hmong in the Mekong region, half of them living in the mountains of Vietnam.

For an in-depth look at the beauty of Angkorian-era sculpture and its religious, cultural and social context, seek out a copy of *Sculpture of Angkor and Ancient Cambodia: Millennium of Glory* (eds Helen Ibbitson Jessup and Thierry Zephir, 1997).

Dzao

The Dzao (also known as Yao or Dao) are one of the largest and most colourful ethnic groups in Vietnam and are also found in Laos, Thailand and Yunnan. The Dzao practise ancestor worship of spirits, or *ban ho* (no relation to Uncle Ho), and hold elaborate rituals with sacrifices of pigs and chickens. The Dzao are famous for their elaborate dress. Women's clothing typically features intricate weaving and silver-coloured beads and coins – the wealth of a woman is said to be in the weight of the coins she carries. Their long, flowing hair, shaved above the forehead, is tied up into a large red or embroidered turban.

Karen

The Karen are the largest hill tribe in Thailand, numbering more than 300,000. There are four distinct groups, the Skaw Karen (White Karen), Pwo Karen, Pa-O Karen (Black Karen) and Kayah Karen (Red Karen). Unmarried women wear white and kinship remains matrilineal. Most Karen live in lowland valleys and practise crop rotation.

Religion

The dominant religions of Southeast Asia have absorbed many traditional animistic beliefs of spirits, ancestor worship and the power of the celestial planets in bringing about good fortune. The Mekong region's spiritual connection to the realm of magic and miracles commands respect, even among intellectual circles. Locals erect spirit houses in front of their homes, while ethnic Chinese set out daily offerings to their ancestors, and almost everyone visits the fortune teller.

Mahayana Buddhists believe in Bodhisattvas – Buddhas who have attained nirvana but postponed their enlightenment to stay on earth to save their fellow beings.

Buddhism

The predominant religion in the Mekong region arrived in two flavours. Mahayana Buddhism (northern school) proceeded north into Nepal, Tibet, China, Korea, Mongolia, Vietnam and Japan, while Theravada Buddhism (southern school) took the southern route through India, Sri Lanka, Myanmar (Burma), Thailand, Cambodia and Laos. Every Buddhist male is expected to become a monk for a short period in his life, optimally between the time he finishes school and starts a career or marries.

Christianity

Catholicism was introduced to the region in the 16th century by missionaries. Vietnam has the highest percentage of Catholics (8% to 10% of the population) in Southeast Asia outside the Philippines.

Cao Daism

A fascinating fusion of East and West, Cao Daism (Dai Dao Tam Ky Pho Do) is a syncretic religion born in 20th-century Vietnam that contains elements of Buddhism, Confucianism, Taoism, native Vietnamese spiritualism, Christianity and Islam – as well as a dash of secular enlightenment thrown in for good measure. The term Cao Dai (meaning High Tower or Palace) is a euphemism for God. Estimates of the number of followers of Cao Daism in Vietnam vary from two million to five million.

For a virtual tour of Thai Buddhist architecture around the region, visit www.orientalarchitecture.com.

Hinduism

Hinduism ruled the spiritual lives of Mekong dwellers more than 1500 years ago, and the great Hindu empire of Angkor built magnificent monuments to their pantheon of gods. The primary representations of the one omnipresent god include Brahma (the creator), Vishnu (the preserver) and Shiva (the destroyer and reproducer).

Islam

Southeast Asians converted to Islam to join a brotherhood of spice traders and to escape the inflexible caste system of earlier Hindu empires. The Chams may be Muslims, but in practice they follow a localised adaptation of Islamic theology and law. Though Muslims usually pray five times a day, the Chams pray only on Fridays and observe Ramadan (a month of dawn-to-dusk fasting) for only three days.

Tam Giao

Over the centuries, Confucianism, Taoism and Buddhism have fused with popular Chinese beliefs and ancient Vietnamese animism to create Tam Giao (Triple Religion). When discussing religion, most Vietnamese people are likely to say that they are Buddhist, but when it comes to family or civic duties they are likely to follow the moral and social code of Confucianism, and will turn to Taoist concepts to understand the nature of the cosmos.

Taoism

Taoism originated in China and is based on the philosophy of Laotse (The Old One), who lived in the 6th century BC. Taoist philosophy focuses on contemplation and simplicity. The ideal is returning to the Tao ('the Way', or the essence of which all things are made); it also emphasises the importance of Yin and Yang (the two opposing yet complementary principles in Chinese philosophy that maintain balance in the universe).

Survival Guide

Border Crossings

During the bad old days of communism and the Cold War, there were pretty much no land borders open to foreigners in the Mekong region. Times have changed and there are now dozens of border crossings connecting the neighbouring countries of the region. Before making a long-distance trip, be aware of border closing times, visa regulations and any transport scams. Border details change regularly, so ask around or check the Lonely Planet Thorntree forums (lonelyplanet.com/thorntree).

Visa on Arrival

Visas (or in the case of Thailand, 30-day visa waivers) are available on arrival at some borders but not at others. As a rule of thumb, a visa on arrival is available entering into Cambodia, Laos and Thailand, but is not available entering into Vietnam (except for certain nationalities). However, entering Laos, visa on arrival is not available at the Paksan/Bueng Kan crossing with Thailand.

Opening Hours & Scams

Most borders are open during the core hours of 7am to 5pm or 6pm. However, some of the most popular crossings are open later in the evening. Be wary of cross-border night buses that project to arrive at the border in the middle of the night. Such buses are forced to wait around until the border opens, adding hours to the journey time.

Some of the immigration police at land border crossings have a reputation for petty extortion. Especially at remote Cambodian and Lao border stations, travellers are occasionally asked for an 'immigration fee' or an overtime surcharge – 'tea money' as it's sometimes called.

These charges typically amount to no more than US$1 or US$2, which you are best off just paying, but occasionally you might be asked for a whole lot more – either by the authorities or by shadowy touts. Be aware of the proper fees and study up on the tricks you are likely to face at the border you are crossing. The Poipet (C)/Aranya Prathet (T) border is particularly scam-ridden.

Extra charges generally occur upon entry rather than on exit.

Changing Money

There are few legal money-changing facilities at some of the more remote border crossings, so be sure to have some small-denomination US dollars handy.

Private Vehicles

The general rule is that you can get private vehicles into Cambodia, Laos and Thailand, but forget about driving into or out of Vietnam. However, some Vietnamese motorbike-tour companies do have permission to cross the border between Laos and Vietnam.

Crossing between Cambodia, Laos and Thailand, you'll want to make sure to have all of your vehicle's paperwork in order. Before setting out, check with the embassy of your target country to see if you need additional permissions and documents.

Crossings with Other Countries

Thailand/Malaysia

The main border crossings by road into Malaysia are Hat Yai (T)/Padang Besar (M) and Sungai Kolok (T)/Rantau Panjang (M).

However, due to continued violence in Thailand's Deep South, we do not recommend the Sungai Kolok (T)/Rantau Panjang (M) border. There are a few other minor crossings along this border, but a private vehicle is a necessity.

The train route into Malaysia is on the Hat Yai–Alor Setar–Butterworth route, which crosses the border at Hat Yai (T)/Padang Besar (M). On the west coast, the crossing between Satun (T) and Pulau Langkawi (M) is made by boat.

Border Crossings

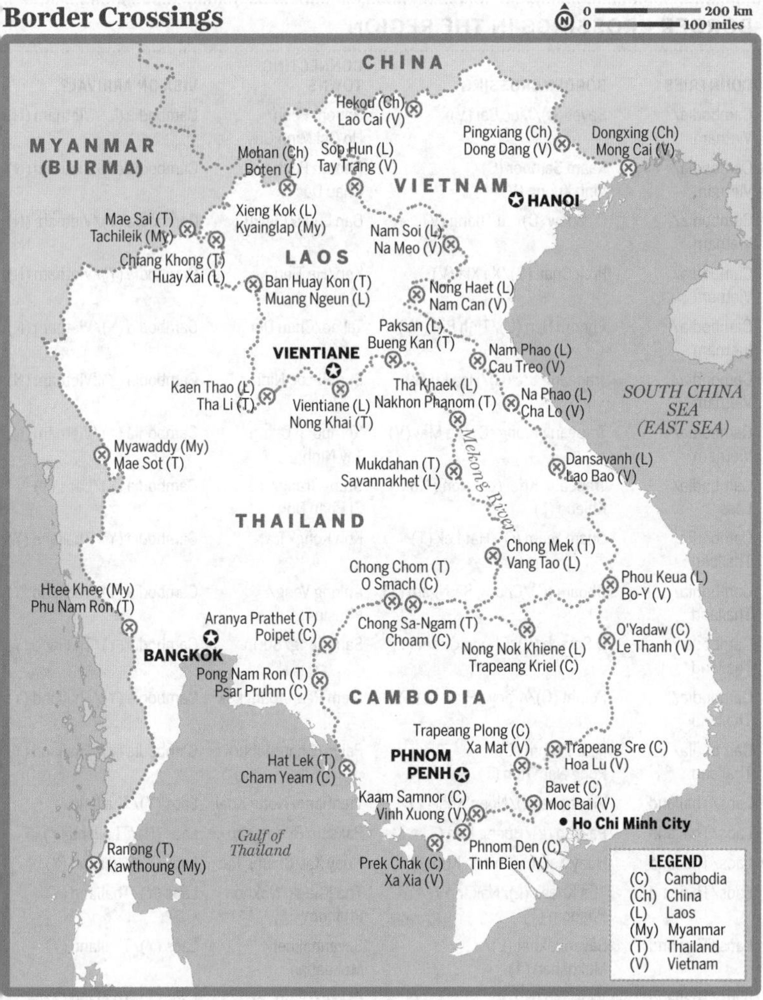

Thailand/Myanmar (Burma)

There are four legal crossings between Thailand and Myanmar: Mae Sai (T)/Tachileik (My); Ranong (T)/Kawthoung (My); Mae Sot (T)/Myawaddy (My); and Phu Nam Ron (T)/Htee Khee (My).

You'll need to procure a valid Myanmar visa in advance when entering Myanmar (although Tachileik hosts a busy border market that can be visited on a day trip from Thailand without a visa).

Vietnam/China

There are three legal crossings between northern Vietnam and China: Hekou (Ch)/Lao Cai (V), Pingxiang (Ch)/Dong Dang (V) and Dongxing (Ch)/Mong Cai (V).

Visa-on-arrival is not available in either direction at any of these borders.

Laos/China

The only border open to foreigners is the Móhān (Ch)/Boten (L) crossing. Visas on arrival are available entering Laos. You'll need to procure a Chinese visa in advance if crossing the other way.

Laos/Myanmar

The first Lao-Myanmar Friendship Bridge officially opened in May 2016, connecting Xieng Kok in Luang Namtha Province with Kyainglap in Shan State. However, the crossing here remains closed to independent foreign travellers. Check in Vientiane or Luang Namtha to see if it has opened.

BORDER CROSSINGS IN THE REGION

COUNTRIES	BORDER CROSSING	CONNECTING TOWNS	VISA ON ARRIVAL?
Cambodia/ Vietnam	Bavet (C)/Moc Bai (V)	Phnom Penh/ Ho Chi Minh City	Cambodia (Y)/Vietnam (N)
Cambodia/ Vietnam	Kaam Samnor (C)/ Vinh Xuong (V)	Phnom Penh/ Chau Doc	Cambodia (Y)/Vietnam (N)
Cambodia/ Vietnam	O'Yadaw (C)/Le Thanh (V)	Ban Lung/Pleiku	Cambodia (Y)/Vietnam (N)
Cambodia/ Vietnam	Prek Chak (C)/Xa Xia (V)	Kep/Ha Tien	Cambodia (Y)/Vietnam (N)
Cambodia/ Vietnam	Phnom Den (C)/Tinh Bien (V)	Takeo/Chau Doc	Cambodia (Y)/Vietnam (N)
Cambodia/ Vietnam	Trapeang Sre (C)/Hoa Lu (V)	Snuol/Loc Ninh	Cambodia (Y)/Vietnam (N)
Cambodia/ Vietnam	Trapeang Plong (C)/Xa Mat (V)	Kompong Cham/ Tay Ninh	Cambodia (Y)/Vietnam (N)
Cambodia/ Laos	Trapeang Kriel (C)/Nong Nok Khiene (L)	Stung Treng/ Si Phan Don	Cambodia (Y)/Laos (Y)
Cambodia/ Thailand	Cham Yeam (C)/Hat Lek (T)	Koh Kong/Trat	Cambodia (Y)/Thailand (Y)
Cambodia/ Thailand	Choam (C)/Chong Sa-Ngam (T)	Anlong Veng/ Phusing	Cambodia (Y)/Thailand (Y)
Cambodia/ Thailand	O Smach (C)/Chong Chom (T)	Samraong/Surin	Cambodia (Y)/Thailand (Y)
Cambodia/ Thailand	Poipet (C)/Aranya Prathet (T)	Siem Reap/Bangkok	Cambodia (Y)/Thailand (Y)
Cambodia/ Thailand	Psar Pruhm (C)/ Pong Nam Ron (T)	Pailin/Chanthaburi	Cambodia (Y)/Thailand (Y)
Laos/Thailand	Vientiane (L)/Nong Khai (T)	Vientiane/Nong Khai	Laos (Y)/Thailand (Y)
Laos/Thailand	Paksan (L)/Bueng Kan (T)	Paksan/Bueng Kan	Laos (N)/Thailand (Y)
Laos/Thailand	Huay Xai (L)/Chiang Khong (T)	Huay Xai/Chiang Rai	Laos (Y)/Thailand (Y)
Laos/Thailand	Tha Khaek (L)/Nakhon Phanom (T)	Tha Khaek/Nakhon Phanom	Laos (Y)/Thailand (Y)
Laos/Thailand	Savannakhet (L)/ Mukdahan (T)	Savannakhet/ Mukdahan	Laos (Y)/Thailand (Y)
Laos/Thailand	Vang Tao (L)/ Chong Mek (T)	Pakse/Ubon Ratchathani	Laos (Y)/Thailand (Y)
Laos/Thailand	Kaen Thao (L)/Tha Li (T)	Pak Lai/Loei	Laos (Y)/Thailand (Y)
Laos/Thailand	Muang Ngeun (L)/Ban Huay Kon (T)	Pak Beng/Nan	Laos (Y)/Thailand (Y)
Laos/Vietnam	Dansavanh (L)/ Lao Bao (V)	Savannakhet/ Dong Ha	Laos (Y)/Vietnam (N)
Laos/Vietnam	Phou Keua (L)/Bo Y (V)	Attapeu/Pleiku	Laos (Y)/Vietnam (N)
Laos/Vietnam	Na Phao (L)/Cha Lo (V)	Tha Khaek/Dong Hoi	Laos (Y)/Vietnam (N)
Laos/Vietnam	Nong Haet (L)/Nam Can (V)	Phonsovan/Vinh	Laos (Y)/Vietnam (N)
Laos/Vietnam	Nam Phao (L)/Cau Treo (V)	Lak Sao/Vinh	Laos (Y)/Vietnam (N)
Laos/Vietnam	Na Meo (L)/Nam Soi (V)	Sam Neua/Thanh Hoa	Laos (Y)/Vietnam (N)
Laos/Vietnam	Sop Hun (L)/Tay Trang (V)	Muang Khua/Dien Bien Phu	Laos (Y)/Vietnam (N)

Directory A–Z

Accessible Travel

Travellers with serious disabilities will likely find the Mekong region a challenging place to travel. Inconveniences include the following:

- chaotic traffic
- lack of lifts in smaller hotels
- high kerbs and uneven pavements that are routinely blocked by parked motorbikes and food stalls
- an almost complete lack of disabled-friendly public amenities, although the major international airports and newer top-end hotels and buildings include wheelchair-accessible ramps and toilets.

On the positive side, most people in the region are helpful towards foreigners, and local labour is cheap if you need someone to accompany you at all times. Few buildings have been designed with people with a disability in mind, but most guesthouses and small hotels have ground-floor rooms that are reasonably easy to access. Bus and train travel is tough, but rent a private vehicle with a driver and almost anywhere can become accessible.

Wheelchair travellers will need to undertake a lot of research before visiting Cambodia. Your best bet for advice about travelling in the country would be to contact the relevant organisation for your particular disability.

Organisations that can provide information on mobility-impaired travel:

Accessible Journeys (www.disabilitytravel.com)

Disability Rights UK (www.disabilityrightsuk.org) UK-based umbrella organisation for voluntary groups for people with disabilities.

Mobility International USA (www.miusa.org) Advises disabled travellers on mobility issues and runs an educational exchange program.

Society for Accessible Travel & Hospitality (www.sath.org)

Download Lonely Planet's free *Accessible Travel* guide from https://shop.lonelyplanet.com/categories/accessible-travel.com.

Accommodation

The Mekong region has something for everyone – from dives to the divine – and it's usually great value compared with destinations in Western countries. There's generally no need to book in advance, but if you're eyeing a popular hotel in the high season consider booking a few months earlier.

For more information, see the individual Accommodation sections for each country.

Boutiques The Mekong is the unofficial boutique-hotel capital of the world, with Luang Prabang and Siem Reap leading the charge.

Homestays Popular in rural areas across the region.

Hostels and guesthouses Abundant. A dorm bed can cost as much as a private room in a budget guesthouse.

Hotels Come in all shapes and sizes – you'll be spoilt for choice.

Camping

With the exception of the national parks in Thailand and some high-end experiences in Cambodia, Laos and Vietnam, the opportunities for general camping in this region are limited.

Homestays

A visit to a homestay is one of the best ways to experience rural culture, not to

PLAN YOUR STAY ONLINE

For more accommodation reviews by Lonely Planet authors, check out www. lonelyplanet.com. You'll find independent reviews, as well as recommendations on the best places to stay.

mention a way to ensure that your money goes directly to locals.

Homestays are well established in parts of Thailand and Vietnam, and many treks through minority areas in the far north include a night with a local family to learn about their lifestyle. Homestays are also popular in Cambodia and Laos, where they are integral components of several popular community-based tourism programs.

To get the most out of homestays take a phrasebook, photos of your family, a torch, flip-flops (thongs), a sarong and toilet paper.

Hotel Booking Tips

➡ Expect discounts of up to 50% on accommodation in touristy areas during the low season.

➡ Weekend discounts are rare outside of Bangkok and indeed weekend rates can be higher in destinations popular with local tourists.

➡ Some hotels add 25% to high-season prices over Christmas, New Year and Chinese New Year (Tet in Vietnam); advance reservations are strongly recommended during these times.

Electricity

Most countries work on a voltage of 220V to 240V at 50Hz (cycles); note that 240V appliances will happily run on 220V. You should be able to pick up adaptors in markets and electrical shops in most of the main towns and cities.

The era of sweating through the night in an unventilated shack is long gone as most areas have power these days. That said, power outages are still common in some towns and islands. Higher-end hotels will have generators to deal with blackouts and 'brownouts' (scheduled, short-lasting power shut-downs).

Solar power is becoming an increasingly common way to power resorts on Cambodian islands and in eco-lodges throughout the region.

Type A
120V/60Hz

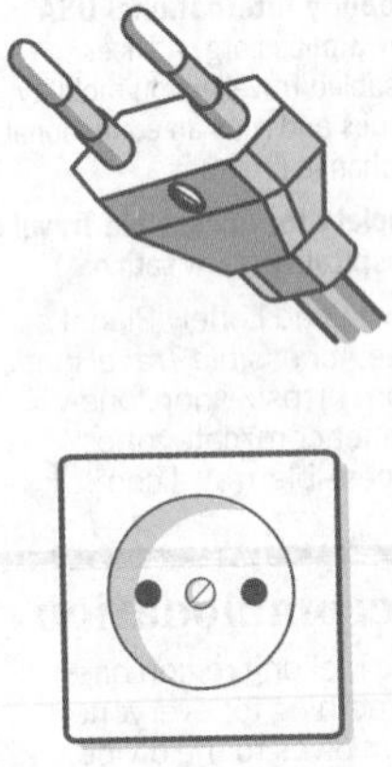

Type C
220V/50Hz

Food

This is arguably the best region in the world when it comes to sampling the local cuisine. The food of Thailand and Vietnam needs no introduction, but Laotian and Khmer cuisine are also a rewarding experience.

If there's just one dish you try, make it one of these. These are the dishes that capture the cuisine of their country in a single serving.

Cambodia *Amok* (baked fish in coconut leaves)

Laos *Láhp* (spicy salad with meat or fish)

Thailand *Đôm yam gûng* (hot-and-sour soup with shrimp)

Vietnam *Pho bo* (rice noodle soup with beef)

For more, see the individual Food & Drink sections for each country.

Insurance

A travel insurance policy to cover theft, loss and medical problems is highly recommended. Make sure your policy covers an emergency evacuation in the event of serious injury. Keep in mind that many policies do not cover more adventurous activities like ziplining, diving, rockclimbing, motorcycling and even trekking, so check the fine print.

Internet Access

You won't have trouble finding free wi-fi, at least in cities and touristy areas, and 4G connections are fast, functional and cheap at about US$1 for a few days' worth of data. Internet cafes are still an option in most cities.

Wi-fi access (and mobile-phone coverage) can be quite spotty in remote areas. This includes most national parks, particularly in Laos, and most Cambodian islands, although coverage has improved slightly on the more popular beaches.

Legal Matters

Be sure to know the national laws before unwittingly

committing a crime. If you are the victim of a crime, contact the tourist police, if available; they are usually better trained to deal with foreigners and foreign languages than the regular police force.

Travellers should note that they can be prosecuted under the law of their home country regarding age of consent, even when abroad.

Drugs

In all of the Mekong-region countries, using or trafficking drugs carries stiff punishments that are enforced, even if you're a foreigner.

While marijuana is readily available throughout the region (where it is often euphemistically associated with the term 'happy'), keep in mind that it is nonetheless illegal and you can serve jail time (or be forced to pay a huge bribe) if caught possessing it or buying it from the wrong person. Use it discreetly, and be especially wary of buying it on the street from overzealous touts or drivers.

Possession of harder drugs such as opium, heroin, amphetamines, ecstasy and hallucinogenic mushrooms carries stiffer penalties, while penalties for drug smuggling – defined as attempting to cross a border with drugs in your possession – can include execution.

LGBTIQ+ Travellers

Thailand, Cambodia and Laos have the most progressive attitudes towards homosexuality. While same-sex displays of affection are part of most Asian cultures, you should be discreet and respectful of the local culture. There is not usually a problem with same-sex couples checking into rooms throughout the region, as it is so common among travellers.

> **HAPPINESS IS A STATE OF MIND**
>
> 'Don't worry, be happy' could be the motto for the Mekong region, but in some backpacker centres the term 'happy' has taken on a completely different connotation. Seeing the word 'happy' in front of 'shake', 'pizza' or anything else does not, as one traveller was told, mean it comes with extra pineapple. The extra is usually marijuana, added in whatever quantity the shake-maker deems fit. For many travellers 'happy' is a well-understood alias, but there are others who innocently down their shake or pizza only to spend the next 24 hours floating in a world of their own.

Thailand has the most prominent gay scene, centred on Bangkok, as well as Pattaya and Phuket; all three hold annual gay pride events. Siem Reap and Phnom Penh are both very friendly places for LGBTIQ+ travellers, with plenty of gay-friendly hotels and watering holes. The small scene in Laos, centred on Vientiane and Luang Prabang, is more hidden. Hanoi and especially Ho Chi Minh City both have (small) gay nightlife scenes, but there is still plenty of social stigma.

Resources

Check out Utopia Asian Gay & Lesbian Resources (www.utopia-asia.com) for more information on gay and lesbian travel in Asia. Grindr is popular for online daters, while www.gayguide.net has country-specific information.

Maps

A good map of Indochina, including Bangkok and northeast Thailand, is the Nelles *Vietnam, Laos & Cambodia* map at a scale of 1:1,500,000.

Money

ATMs & Eftpos

- ATMs are widespread in large cities and most provincial capitals, and charge about US$5 per transaction as a rule, with withdrawal limits of about US$250 per withdrawal.
- Most banks back home charge 2% to 3% for foreign ATM withdrawals and credit-card purchases, so look for a premium account that negates such charges.

Bargaining

The art of bargaining is alive and well in the Mekong region. The general rule is that bargaining is acceptable in markets and in certain shops where the prices aren't displayed. It is also advisable to bargain for chartered transport.

Remember that it is an art, not a test of wills, and the trick is to find a price that makes everyone happy. Here are some basic 'dance moves' for bargaining for goods:

- First, ask the price, and then ask for a discount.
- If the discount isn't acceptable, offer something slightly lower – but be prepared to accept an amount in between.
- Once you counter, you can't lower your price.
- Don't start to haggle unless you're serious about buying.
- If you become angry or visibly frustrated, you've lost the game.

YOU WANT MASSAGE?

Karaoke clubs and massage parlours are ubiquitous throughout the region. Sometimes this may mean a healthy massage to ease a stiff body. However, more often than not, both these terms are euphemisms for some sort of prostitution. There may be some singing or a bit of shoulder tweaking going on, but ultimately it is just a polite introduction to something naughtier. Legitimate karaoke and legitimate massage do exist in the bigger cities, but as a general rule of thumb, if the place looks sleazy, it probably is.

When it comes to local taxis and tuk-tuks, learn the true price by asking a local or your guesthouse how much a trip should cost, then hold your ground when negotiating. If the driver won't budge, then politely decline the service and move on. Don't fight with drivers, as they are known for their tempers.

Credit & Debit Cards

Credit cards are widely accepted in the region. Thailand leads the way, where almost anything can be paid for with plastic. However, things dry up beyond major tourist centres or bigger towns, so don't rely exclusively on credit cards.

It is quite common for the business to pass on the credit-card commission (usually 3%) to the customer in Cambodia, Laos and Vietnam, so check if there is an additional charge before putting it on the plastic. Also check your monthly bills carefully in case some scamster clones your card while you are paying for something on your travels.

Tipping

Tipping is not expected in the Mekong region, but is appreciated. Upmarket hotels and restaurants often levy a 10% service charge.

Bars Not expected.

Hotels Not expected.

Guides A few dollars on day trips is sufficient, more for longer trips if the service is good.

Restaurants Leave loose change at local restaurants, 5% in smart restaurants where no service charge levied.

Taxis Not necessary, but a little extra is appreciated.

Photography

- Photography equipment and flash memory are widely available in urban areas.
- Ask for permission before taking photos of hill-tribe villagers, as many seriously object to being photographed.
- If you're after some tips, check out *Lonely Planet's Guide to Travel Photography*, written by travel photographer Richard I'Anson.

Post

Postal services are generally reliable across the region. Of course, it's always better to leave important mail and parcels for the big centres such as Bangkok and Hanoi. Poste restante is widely available throughout the region.

Public Holidays

- Chinese New Year (or Tet in Vietnam) is the one holiday common to all countries and can have a big impact on travel plans, as businesses close and all forms of transport are booked out.
- Cambodia, Laos and Thailand celebrate their own new year at the same time in the middle of April. Each country shuts down for business for at least a week, and mass water fights break out in Thailand and Laos.

Responsible Travel

Much of the Mekong region is extremely poor, so consider how you might put a little back into the countries you visit while minimising your environmental footprint:

- Stay longer, travel further and travel independently, or utilise locally based tour companies and guides that are clearly on the side of pro-poor, ecofriendly travel (just beware of 'greenwashing').
- Shun wildlife experiences that involve touching wild animals.
- Live like a local: opt for a fan instead of an air-con room; shower with cold water instead of hot.
- Try out a community-based tourism project or homestay.
- Eat at local restaurants that use locally sourced ingredients instead of imported products.
- Don't eat or drink food products made from endangered animals or plants.
- Spend money at local markets or at shops and restaurants that assist disadvantaged locals.
- Use biodegradable soap to reduce water pollution.
- Avoid single-use plastics; bring your own refillable water bottle and reusable straw.
- Choose unplugged modes of transit (walking tour over minivan tour, bicycle over motorbike, kayak over jet ski).
- Dispose of your rubbish and cigarette butts in a proper receptacle, even if the locals don't.

Safe Travel

Begging

Begging is common in many countries of the region and the tug on the shirtsleeve can become tiresome for visitors after a time. However, try to remember that many of these countries have little in the way of a social-security net. It is best to keep denominations small to avoid foreigners becoming even more of a target than they already are. Avoid giving money to children, as it is likely going straight to a 'begging pimp' or family member. Food is an option, but better still is to make a donation to one of the many local organisations trying to assist in the battle against poverty.

Drugs

The risks associated with recreational drug use and distribution have grown to the point that all visitors should exercise extreme caution, even in places that have a reputation for free and open drug use. A spell in a local prison can be truly torturous. Even worse, you could become the next in a long line of tourists who have succumbed to a bad batch of cocaine or *yaba* (homemade methamphetamines mixed with caffeine).

Noise

Remember the movie *This is Spinal Tap*? The soundtrack of the cities in this region is permanently cranked up to 11 – not just any noise, but a whole lot of noises that just never seem to stop. At night there is most often a competing cacophony from motorbikes, discos, cafes, video arcades, karaoke lounges and restaurants, although in most areas the din subsides relatively early – by 11pm or so, as few places stay open much later than that. Unfortunately, from 5am onwards an entirely new series of sounds erupts, including but not limited to monk chants, wedding music, funeral dirges, roosters, hound dogs and street vendors loudly hawking everything from duck embryos to fried crickets.

One last thing...don't forget the earplugs.

Queues

What queues? Most locals in the Mekong region don't queue, they mass in a rugby scrum, pushing towards the counter. When in Rome... This is first-seen, first-served, so take a deep breath, muscle your way to the front and wave your passport or papers as close to the counter as you can.

Scams

Every year Lonely Planet receives feedback from hapless travellers reporting that they've been scammed in this region. In most cases the scams are petty rip-offs, in which a naive traveller pays too much for a ride to the bus station, to exchange money, buy souvenirs and so on. Rip-offs are in full force at border crossings,

ELEPHANT ENCOUNTERS

Elephants have played an oversized role in the Mekong region, including in the construction of Angkor Wat and in fighting ancient wars in Thailand. More recently they were used for harvesting teak or transporting goods through mountainous terrain, but as forests have been clear-cut and roads built, the work has dried up for domesticated elephants and their mahouts.

Inevitably, elephants have been repurposed for the tourism industry, where their jobs vary from circus-like shows to elephant camps giving rides to tourists and 'mahout-training' schools. However, animal-welfare experts say that elephant rides and shows are harmful to these gentle giants, who are often overworked or abused to force them to perform, and whose backs may suffer damage from the weight of carrying heavy seats and passengers. Backlash against elephant rides has grown in recent years, and several sanctuaries have sprung up to promote more sustainable interactions, such as walking with and bathing retired and rescued elephants.

Yet even these sanctuaries are not beyond reproach, as there have been cases of sanctuaries in Thailand inadvertently (or perhaps knowingly) buying wild elephants with forged registration papers. Conscientious elephant camps are aware of the practice and have a variety of methods of circumventing fraud, but to be on the safe side you may want to consider a sanctuary that doesn't engage in the elephant trade. Mahouts, meanwhile, worry about the loss of income as the backlash against elephant rides deepens and more and more pachyderms are retired to sanctuaries.

Luckily there are positive ways to interact with elephants in the region that don't involve rides, including Elephant Valley Project (p245) in eastern Cambodia; the Elephant Conservation Center (p351) in Laos; and Thailand's ChangChill (p469). For more information, check out www.earsasia.org.

popular tourist attractions, bus and rail stations and wherever travellers might get confused.

Other common scams include having your rented bicycle or motorbike 'stolen' by someone with a duplicate key, dodgy drug deals that involve police extortion, and the notorious Filipino blackjack scam (to avoid the latter, don't play cards with friendly strangers).

Lastly, understand that third parties get commissions; if a tout tells you a certain hotel or guesthouse is closed, don't believe it – more likely the tout doesn't get a commission from that guesthouse.

Theft

Theft in this part of the world is usually by stealth rather than by force, but violent robbery isn't unheard of, especially late at night or if the victim resists. Be careful when walking alone late at night and don't fall asleep in taxis.

Other tips for avoiding theft:

- Your bling presents an easy target on beaches, so take extra care of it.
- Always be diplomatically suspicious of overfriendly locals; thieves have been known to drug travellers for easier pickings.
- Travel in groups late at night, especially after a night of carousing, to ensure safety in numbers.
- Stay *relatively* sober if you're going to be out walking alone late at night in major cities (if you're stumbling drunk, take a tuk-tuk).
- Always lock up your bicycle or motorbike and pay for parking whenever you can.

Finally, don't let paranoia ruin your trip. With just a few sensible precautions most travellers make their way across the region without incident.

INVASION OF THE BAG SNATCHERS

Drive-by theft, usually by motorcycle-riding tandems, is a regional speciality, especially in cities. There have been incidents where thieves have dragged passengers off motorbikes or bicycles, endangering lives. Shoulder bags and smartphones are particular targets. A money belt worn underneath your clothes can minimise the risk of being victimised by snatch-and-run thieves.

UXO & Landmines

The legacy of war lingers on in Cambodia, Laos and Vietnam in the form of UXO from the American bombing campaign of the early 1970s. Areas with the highest concentration of UXO include eastern Cambodia, southeastern and central Laos, and Vietnam's DMZ (Demilitarised Zone).

Cambodia suffers the additional affliction of landmines, some 4 to 6 million of them according to surveys. Many of these are located in border areas with Thailand in the north and west of the country, but it pays to stick to established trails anywhere in Cambodia.

You can learn more about the issue of landmines from the Nobel Peace Prize–winning International Campaign to Ban Landmines (www.icbl.org), or visit the websites of the Mines Advisory Group (www.maginternational.org), which specialises in clearing landmines and UXO.

Smoking

Cambodia Smoking is banned in some public places and most hotels and guesthouses offer nonsmoking rooms these days, but the rules are frequently flouted.

Laos While many people smoke in rural Laos, cities are becoming increasingly smoke-free and smoking is banned in restaurants in Vientiane and Luang Prabang.

Thailand Banned in restaurants and bars since 2008, although it still takes place in some bars.

Vietnam Smoking is widespread and official bans largely ignored, except for on air-conditioned transport and in some higher-end restaurants.

GOVERNMENT TRAVEL ADVICE

Australian Department of Foreign Affairs (www.smartraveller.gov.au)

Canadian Government Travel & Tourism Site (www.travel.gc.ca)

German Foreign Office (www.auswaertiges-amt.de)

New Zealand Ministry of Foreign Affairs (www.safetravel.govt.nz)

UK Foreign Office (www.gov.uk/foreign-travel-advice)

US State Department (www.travel.state.gov)

Telephone

Individual countries have their own codes and rules, but the following rules apply to the entire region:

- Roaming is bad for you – do not be that clueless soul who yaks their way around the world and returns home to a US$3000 phone bill. Instead, buy a local SIM card, configure it for 4G, and call home for pennies via voice-over-internet protocol (VoIP).

➡ Some mobile phones are 'locked' by your phone company back home, but most telephone shops in the Mekong region can 'unlock' them in seconds for a small charge.

➡ Mobile-phone coverage usually extends to all but the most remote areas in the Mekong region.

Time

Cambodia, Laos, Thailand and Vietnam are seven hours ahead of GMT/UTC. When it's noon in Bangkok or Hanoi, it is 9pm the previous evening in San Francisco, midnight in New York, 5am in London, 6am in Paris and 3pm in Sydney. There is no daylight saving time.

Toilets

Public toilets Fairly rare and rarely impressive. Gas stations and shopping centres usually have toilets. You may have to pay a few dong, riel, kip or baht.

Sit-down toilets Most decent hostels and all hotels from the midrange up throughout the region are equipped with Western-style 'thrones'.

Spray hoses 'Bum guns' are common across the region in private homes and in some restaurants and hotels. It's worth mastering these as sometimes they exist in lieu of toilet paper.

Squat toilets Common in public places and out in the countryside.

Toilet paper Generally to be tossed in the wastebasket and not flushed down, as it taxes local sewage systems. Seldom provided at public toilets, so carry some with you.

Tourist Information

Cambodia Tourism Ministry (www.tourismcambodia.org)

Laos National Tourism Administration (www.tourismlaos.org)

Tourism Authority of Thailand (www.tourismthailand.org)

Vietnam Tourism (https://vietnam.travel)

THE ABUSE OF INNOCENCE

The sexual abuse of children by foreign paedophiles is a serious problem in some parts of the Mekong region. Many child prostitutes are sold into the business by relatives. These sex slaves are either trafficked overseas or forced to cater to domestic demand and local sex-tourism operators. Unicef estimates that there are close to one million child prostitutes in Asia – one of the highest figures in the world.

Visitors can do their bit to fight this menace by keeping an eye out for suspicious behaviour on the part of foreigners. Don't ignore it. Try to pass on any relevant information, such as the name of the individual, to their nationality's embassy or to the local police.

Childsafe International (www.childsafe-international.org) Operates out of Cambodia and now covers Laos and Thailand as well. It aims to educate businesses and individuals to be on the lookout for children in vulnerable situations.

End Child Prostitution & Trafficking (www.ecpat.net) A global network aimed at stopping child prostitution, child pornography and the trafficking of children for sexual purposes. It has affiliates in most Western countries.

Visas

Get your visas as you go rather than all at once before you leave home; they are often easier and cheaper to get in neighbouring countries and are only valid within a certain time period, which really hinders flexibility if you're on an extended trip.

Procedures for extending a visa vary from country to country. In some cases, extensions are quite complicated, in others they're a mere formality. Remember the most important rule: treat visits to embassies, consulates and borders as formal occasions and look smart for them.

You do not need to show an onward ticket to obtain a visa or enter the countries of the Mekong region, even though some do have such rules on the book.

Volunteering

'Voluntourism' is a booming business in the Mekong region, with travel companies co-opting the idea as a new marketing angle. To avoid the bulk of your placement fees going into the pockets of third-party agencies, it's important to do your research on the hundreds of organisations that now offer volunteer work and find a suitable one that supports your skills.

Lonely Planet does not endorse any organisations that we do not work with directly, so it is essential that you do your own thorough research before agreeing to volunteer with/donate to any organisation. Volunteer consolidators like www.volunteerabroad.com can be a good starting point, but you still need to do your due diligence on any organisation you find through such sites. Scrutinise any organisation working with children (especially orphanages) carefully, as child protection is a serious concern; organisations that do not conduct

THE PERILS OF ORPHANAGE TOURISM

'Orphanage tourism' and all the connotations that come with it is a disturbing development that has brought unscrupulous elements into the world of caring for children in the Mekong. Many orphanages are scams that effectively enslave children in the name of milking dollars from oblivious tourists. In the worst cases, children are kept in miserable conditions, beaten and raped.

To be sure, there are legitimate, well-meaning orphanages in the Mekong region. But a growing body of evidence, backed by Unicef, Save the Children and Friends International, suggests that even well-run orphanages do more harm than good. Orphanages 'perpetuate the cycle of family separation,' according to ReThink Orphanages (www.rethinkorphanages.org), a coalition of international child-support groups.

So think twice before visiting, donating to, or volunteering in orphanages in the Mekong region. Friends International and Unicef joined forces to launch the 'Think Before Visiting' campaign; learn more at www.thinkchildsafe.org/thinkbeforevisiting.

background checks on volunteers should be regarded with extreme caution.

One avenue towards volunteering is to apply through a professional organisation back home that offers one- or two-year placements in the region, such as the Voluntary Service Overseas in the UK and the US Peace Corps, VSO Canada, Australian Volunteers International and New Zealand's Volunteer Service Abroad. The UN also operates its own volunteer program; details are available at www.unv.org.

Women Travellers

While travel in the Mekong region for women is generally safe, there are a few things to keep in mind.

There's no question about it: solo women make inviting targets for thieves, and countless female travellers have been the victim of bag-snatching incidents and worse in places like Phnom Penh. Women should be on guard, especially when returning home late at night or arriving in a new town at night.

While physical assault is rare, local men often consider foreign women as being exempt from their own society's rules of conduct regarding members of the opposite sex. Use common sense about venturing into dangerous-looking areas, particularly alone or at night. If you do find yourself in a tricky situation, try to extricate yourself as quickly as possible – hopping into a taxi or entering a business establishment and asking them to call a cab is often the best solution.

Work

The main opportunities for people passing through the region are teaching English (or another European language), landing a job in tourism or starting a small business such as a bar or restaurant.

Teaching English This is the easiest way to support yourself in the Mekong region. For short-term gigs, the large cities such as Bangkok, Ho Chi Minh City and Phnom Penh have a lot of language schools and a high turnover. Payaway (www.payaway.co.uk) provides a handy online list of language schools and volunteer groups looking for recruits for its regional programs.

Tourism Most of these jobs deservedly go to locals, but there are opportunities for wannabe guesthouse or hotel managers, bartenders, chefs and so on. This can be a pretty memorable way to pass a few months in a different culture. Work-for-travel platforms like Workaway (www.workaway.info) are popular in the Mekong region.

Small-business start-up There are many success stories in the region, where people came for a holiday and built an empire. That said, if you elect to go this route tread with caution: many a foreigner has been burned in the region. Sometimes it's an unscrupulous partner, other times it's the local girlfriend, or boyfriend, who changes their mind and goes it alone. Sometimes the owners themselves burn out, drinking the profits of the bar or dabbling in drugs. Do your homework regarding ownership laws and legal recourse in the event of a dispute.

The website Transitions Abroad (www.transitionsabroad.com) and its namesake magazine cover all aspects of overseas life, including landing a job in a variety of fields. The website also provides links to other useful sites and publications for those living abroad.

Transport

GETTING THERE & AWAY

Entering the Region

Most travellers arrive by air and there are also overland routes via China, Myanmar and, in Thailand's extreme south, Malaysia. There are no public sea routes into the Mekong region.

Entering Thailand, Cambodia or Laos is generally a breeze and does not require a prearranged visa; most nationalities still need a visa in advance to enter Vietnam.

Flights, cars and tours can be booked online at lonelyplanet.com/bookings.

Air

- The main points of entry by air are Bangkok, Phnom Penh, Siem Reap, Vientiane, Hanoi and Ho Chi Minh City.
- The major jumping-off points for budget flights into the Mekong region are Kuala Lumpur and Singapore.
- Bangkok is the best place to shop for onward tickets and tickets around the Mekong region.
- Note that some popular budget airlines are not covered by online travel and flight-comparison sites, so it pays to check the airline websites separately.

Airports & Airlines

INTERNATIONAL AIRPORTS

Suvarnabhumi International Airport, Bangkok (https://suvarnabhumi.airportthai.co.th/en)

Noi Bai Airport, Hanoi (www.hanoiairportonline.com)

Tan Son Nhat International Airport, Ho Chi Minh City (www.hochiminhcityairport.com)

Phnom Penh International Airport (www.cambodia-airports.aero)

Siem Reap International Airport (www.rep.aero)

Wattay International Airport, Vientiane (www.vientianeairport.com)

NATIONAL CARRIERS

Cambodia Angkor Air (www.cambodiaangkorair.com)

Lao Airlines (www.laoairlines.com)

Thai International Airways (www.thaiairways.com)

Vietnam Airways (www.vietnamairlines.com)

Land

There are two main international trains into the region:

- A daily international service between Hanoi and Beijing.
- Direct services from Singapore and Kuala Lumpur to Bangkok via Butterworth (Malaysia) and Hat Yai (Thailand).

CLIMATE CHANGE & TRAVEL

Every form of transport that relies on carbon-based fuel generates CO_2, the main cause of human-induced climate change. Modern travel is dependent on aeroplanes, which might use less fuel per kilometre per person than most cars but travel much greater distances. The altitude at which aircraft emit gases (including CO_2) and particles also contributes to their climate change impact. Many websites offer 'carbon calculators' that allow people to estimate the carbon emissions generated by their journey and, for those who wish to do so, to offset the impact of the greenhouse gases emitted with contributions to portfolios of climate-friendly initiatives throughout the world. Lonely Planet offsets the carbon footprint of all staff and author travel.

SURVIVING THE STREETS

Wherever you roam in the region, you'll have to cross some busy streets eventually, so if you don't want to wind up like a bug on a windscreen, pay close attention to a few pedestrian survival rules.

Foreigners frequently make the mistake of thinking that the best way to cross a busy street in the Mekong region is to run quickly across, but this could get you creamed. Most locals cross the street slowly – very slowly – giving the motorbike drivers sufficient time to judge their position so they can pass on either side. They won't stop or even slow down, but they *will* try to avoid hitting you. Just don't make any sudden moves.

From Vietnam you can also take local trains to the border towns of Lang Son (for Nanning, China) and Lao Cai (for Kunming, China), then pick up a Chinese train on the other side.

There are also three daily bus services from Hanoi to Nanning, involving a change of buses at the border. Reports from Nanning-bound travellers indicate that the bus is less hassle and quicker than travelling by train.

Leaving Thailand for Malaysia, an alternative rail line travels to the Malaysian east-coast border town of Sungai Kolok, but because of ongoing violence in Thailand's Deep South we don't recommend this route for travellers.

Sea

Ocean approaches to Thailand, Vietnam or Cambodia can be made aboard cargo ships plying routes around the world. Ridiculously expensive and hopelessly romantic, a trip aboard a cargo ship is the perfect chance for you to write that novel that never writes itself. Some freighter ships have space for a few noncrew members, who have their own rooms but eat meals with the crew. Prices vary depending on your departure point, but costs start at around US$100 to US$150 a day.

GETTING AROUND

Air

Airlines in the Region

Air travel is a mixed bag in the Mekong region. Some routes to/from/within Thailand are now a real bargain, as no-frills regional carriers such as Air Asia, Jetstar, Nok Air, Thai Lion Air, Thai Smile and Vietjet Air offer heavily discounted fares. However, on many other routes, there may only be one carrier and prices are high.

Flights can usually be booked online easily enough, especially for budget airlines, or you can book through one of the region's myriad travel agents.

Bicycle

Touring Southeast Asia on a bicycle has been steadily growing in popularity.

Cambodia & Laos Road conditions can make two-wheeling more challenging, but light traffic, especially in Laos, makes pedalling more pleasant than elsewhere.

Thailand Used as a base by many long-distance cyclists to head into Indochina for some challenging adventures.

Vietnam Traffic is relatively light away from National Hwy 1A; buses take bicycles and the entire coastal route is feasible, give or take a few hills.

Parts and services

International-standard bicycles and components can be bought in Bangkok and Phnom Penh, but most cyclists bring their own.

Shipping bikes Bicycles can travel by air; ask about extra charges and shipment specifications.

Boat

As roads in the region improve, boats are less a factor than they once were, but they are still popular on a few river routes; in certain particularly remote areas they remain a necessity. They are the only way to reach Cambodia's southern islands and the islands off Thailand's eastern seaboard, such as Koh Chang

Cruises

Luxury river cruises are popular along the Mekong in Laos and between Cambodia and Vietnam. Halong Bay is another popular spot for boat cruises. Companies specialising in upscale boat cruises include the following:

Compagnie Fluviale du Mekong (www.cfmekong.com)

Heritage Line (www.heritage-line.com)

Indochina Sails (☎0982 042 426; www.indochinasails.com)

Pandaw Cruises (www.pandaw.com)

Bus

Bus travel has become a great way to get around with improved roads throughout the region. Most land borders are crossed via bus; these either travel straight through the two countries with a stop for border formalities, or require a change of buses at the appropriate border towns.

➡ Thailand offers by far the most comfortable buses.

➡ Cambodia and Vietnam have a pretty impressive

network of buses connecting major cities, although these dry up in remote areas.

➡ Buses in Laos are reasonable on the busiest routes, but pretty poor elsewhere.

➡ Theft does occur on some long-distance buses; keep all valuables on your person, not in a stowed bag.

Car & Motorcycle

Hiring a self-drive car is increasingly popular in Thailand, Cambodia and Laos. Self-drive car hire is not possible in Vietnam (motorbike hire is available).

With a few notable exceptions, roads in Cambodia and Laos are empty and easy to drive. Thailand has an excellent road network with well-signposted, well-paved roads and efficient divided highways that make for quick travel times.

Laos and Cambodia offer brilliant motorbiking for experienced riders, not forgetting the incredible mountain roads of northern Vietnam. Motorbiking is still the mode of transport for many Mekong residents, so you'll find repair shops everywhere, and they're widely available for rent throughout the region.

Note that Thailand is right-hand drive, while the others are left-hand drive.

Driving Licences

If you are planning to drive a car, get an International Driving Permit (IDP) from your local automobile association before you leave your home country; IDPs are inexpensive and valid for one year.

You rarely need to show a licence to rent a motorbike in Laos, Cambodia or Vietnam (although actually driving a bike technically requires one). Hiring 250cc or larger bikes may require a licence, especially in Thailand.

However, in all four countries you almost always need to leave a passport to hire a bike. This can cause problems if you get into an accident in remote Laos or Cambodia and need to be evacuated out of the country (usually to Thailand or Vietnam) to receive adequate medical care. An alternative to leaving your passport is to leave a several-hundred-dollar deposit to cover the value of the bike.

Hire

➡ Self-drive car hire is mainly an option in Thailand, plus a few places hire out vehicles in Cambodia and Laos.

➡ Cars with drivers are available at very reasonable rates in all countries of the region.

➡ Guesthouses rent motorcycles cheaply throughout the region, usually for around US$4 to US$10 a day.

➡ Dirt bikes (250cc) are also widely available in the region and are a lot of fun if you know how to handle them; rental costs roughly US$15 to US$50 per day.

Motorcycle Safety

Before taking a hired motorbike out on the road, perform the following routine safety checks:

➡ Look at the tyres to inspect the treads.

➡ Check for oil leaks.

➡ Test the brakes.

➡ Make sure the headlights and tail lights work and that you know how to turn them on.

A decent helmet that fits is highly recommended. These can be hard to come by on the ground, so consider bringing your own if you are going to be doing a lot of two-wheeling.

Other gear-related tips to improve both safety and comfort during those long days in the saddle:

➡ If your helmet doesn't have a visor, then wear goggles, glasses or sunglasses to keep bugs, dust and other debris out of your eyes.

➡ Long trousers, long-sleeved shirts, gloves and shoes are highly recommended as protection against sunburn – and as a second skin if you fall.

➡ Pack wet-weather gear, especially in the rainy season.

Insurance

Purchasing insurance is highly recommended when you hire a motorcycle. The more reputable motorcycle-hire places will always offer insurance.

More casual rental outfits, such as guesthouses and shops, rarely offer insurance so you are responsible for anything that happens to

MOTORCYCLE PASSENGER TIPS

Most Asians are so adept at driving and riding on motorcycles that they can balance the whole family on the front bumper, or even take a quick nap as a passenger. Foreigners unaccustomed to motorcycles are not as graceful.

➡ If you're riding on the back of a motorcycle remember to relax. For balance hold on to the back bar, not the driver's waist.

➡ Tall people should keep their long legs tucked in as most drivers are used to shorter passengers.

➡ Anyone wearing a skirt (or sarong etc) should always ride side-saddle and collect longer skirts so that they don't catch in the wheel or drive chain.

FARE'S FAIR?

This is the million-dong question when using local transport: 'Am I being quoted the right fare or are they completely ripping me off?' Well, there's no easy answer, but here are some guidelines to help you navigate the maze.

Boat Fixed fares for ferries or hydrofoils, but not for small local boats or some tourist boats.

Bus and sŏrngtăaou Generally fixed, though overcharging tourists is not unheard of. Buying through a travel agent or guesthouse usually incurs a commission – anything from 5% to 100%, so watch out for predatory travel agents.

Cyclo (pedicab), motorbike taxi and tuk-tuk/remork-moto Most definitely not fixed. Any local transport prices given here are indicative; the actual price of a ride depends on the wiliness of the driver and your bargaining skills. It's best to agree on a price with your driver before setting off.

the bike – or yourself. To be absolutely clear about your liability, ask for a written estimate of the replacement cost for a similar bike.

Note that many home travel and health insurance policies exclude all cover for two-wheeled travel, while others may cover you only if you have an International Driving Permit.

Taking out insurance for a hired car is usually required. Be sure to ask the car-hire agent about liability and damage coverage.

Hitching

- Hitching is never entirely safe in any country, and we don't recommend it. Travellers who hitch should understand that they are taking a small but potentially serious risk.
- People who do choose to hitch will be safer if they travel in pairs and let someone know where they are planning to go.
- Locals do flag down private and public vehicles for a lift, but some sort of payment is usually expected.

Local Transport

In the Mekong region, anything motorised is often modified to carry passengers.

Tuk-tuk The favoured form of transportation for tourists in Thailand, Cambodia and, increasingly, Laos. In Thailand and Laos tuk-tuk (or *đúk đúk* in Thai) are high-octane three-wheeled chariots, while in Cambodia they take the form of comfy little trailers pulled by motorbikes, which are called *remork-moto* (or *remork*) instead. Thai-style tuk-tuk (auto-rickshaws) are also becoming popular in Cambodia.

Motorcycle taxi Ubiquitous in Cambodia, Thailand and Vietnam, but rarer in Laos. However, in Laos motorised *săhm lór* (three-wheelers, or motorbikes with a sidecar) are popular.

Sŏrngtăaou The main form of public transport in provincial Laos and Thailand, these are flatbed or pick-up trucks kitted out with bench seating. They generally ply fixed routes but are also usually available for private hire.

Taxis Metered taxis are common in Thai and Vietnamese cities and can be flagged down on the street easily enough. They are remarkably cheap (about US$2 for a short ride), but be on the lookout for rigged meters in Vietnam. Taxis in Laos and Cambodia are generally not metered and must be ordered by phone or through your guesthouse.

Pedicab The old-fashioned bicycle rickshaw still survives in Cambodia and Vietnam, where it's known as a *cyclo*. In Laos they are *săhm lór*, often motorised.

Public bus Bangkok, Hanoi and Ho Chi Minh City have efficient bus networks. Phnom Penh has a new system but it's rarely used by tourists.

Metro Bangkok boasts a state-of-the-art light-rail and underground system that makes zipping around town feel like time travel.

Animals Beasts of burden still make up a percentage of the local transport in very remote areas, and it is possible to ride an ox cart through remote parts of Cambodia and Laos in the wet season.

Train

Cambodia Mothballed for years, Cambodia's rail system saw limited passenger services resumed with the opening of the southern line (Phnom Penh to Sihanoukville) in 2016, followed by the opening of the northern line (Phnom Penh to Poipet on the Thai border) in 2018.

Laos Has a short link to Thailand via the Friendship Bridge to Nong Khai. This line is being extended to central Vientiane, where it will connect with a high-speed railway line being constructed from Kunming to Vientiane via Luang Prabang, scheduled for completion in 2022.

Thailand and Vietnam Both have efficient railway networks, including the option of comfortable, air-con sleeper berths.

Cross-border trains There are no cross-border trains between Mekong countries, although the Kunming–Vientiane line will change that. Thai trains serve the Thai border towns of Nong Khai (for crossing into Laos), Aranya Prathet (for crossing into Cambodia) and Ubon Ratchathani (for crossing into Laos).

Health

Travellers tend to worry about contracting infectious diseases when in the tropics, but infections are a rare cause of serious illness or death in travellers. Pre-existing medical conditions such as heart disease, and accidental injury (especially traffic accidents), account for most life-threatening problems. Becoming ill in some way, however, is relatively common. The advice given here is a general guide and does not replace the advice of a doctor trained in travel medicine.

BEFORE YOU GO

- Pack medications in their original, clearly labelled, containers.
- A letter from your physician describing medical conditions and medications, including generic names, is a good idea.
- If carrying syringes or needles, be sure to have a physician's letter stating their medical necessity.
- If taking any regular medication, bring a double supply (packed separately) in case of loss or theft.
- In most Mekong-region countries, you can buy many medications over the counter without a doctor's prescription, but it can be difficult to find some of the newer drugs.

Health Insurance

Even if you're fit and healthy, don't travel without health insurance. Hospitals are often basic, particularly in remote areas. Anyone with a serious injury or illness may require emergency evacuation to Bangkok or Hong Kong. With an insurance policy costing no more than the equivalent of a few bottles of beer a day, this evacuation is free – without an insurance policy, it will cost US$10,000 or more.

Some things to keep in mind when choosing an insurer:

- Check that the policy covers ambulance rides and emergency flights home.
- Declare any existing medical conditions, as the insurance company *will* check if the problem is preexisting and will not pay up if undeclared.
- 'Dangerous activities' such as rock climbing, scuba diving, motorcycling and even trekking sometimes require extra cover.
- If your health insurance doesn't cover you for medical expenses abroad, consider getting extra insurance.

Vaccinations

If you plan to get vaccinated before your trip, consider the following:

- Specialised travel-medicine clinics are the best source of information, as they stock all available vaccines and can give specific recommendations for each region.
- Doctors will take into account factors such as past vaccination history, length

WEBSITES

Centers for Disease Control & Prevention (www.cdc.gov) Good source of general information.

Lonely Planet (www.lonelyplanet.com) A good place to start.

MD Travel Health (www.redplanet.travel/mdtravelhealth) Travel health recommendations for every country. Updated daily.

World Health Organization (www.who.int/ith) Publishes a superb book called *International Travel & Health*, which is revised annually and is available online at no cost.

MEDICAL CHECKLIST

The following are recommended items for a personal medical kit if travelling to remote areas. Most items can easily be purchased in cities throughout the Mekong region:

- antibacterial cream, eg Muciprocin
- antibiotics for diarrhoea, such as Norfloxacin or Ciprofloxacin; for bacterial diarrhoea, Azithromycin; for giardiasis or amoebic dysentery, Tinidazole
- antifungal cream, eg Clotrimazole
- antihistamine – there are many options, eg Cetrizine for daytime and Promethazine for night
- anti-inflammatory such as Ibuprofen
- antiseptic, eg Betadine
- antispasmodic for stomach cramps, eg Buscopan
- contraceptives
- DEET-based insect repellent
- diarrhoea treatment – consider an oral rehydration solution (eg Gastrolyte), diarrhoea 'stopper' (eg Loperamide) and antinausea medication (eg Prochlorperazine)
- first-aid items such as scissors, plasters, bandages, gauze, thermometer (but not one with mercury), sterile needles and syringes, safety pins and tweezers
- Permethrin to impregnate clothing and mosquito nets
- steroid cream for allergic or itchy rashes, eg 1% to 2% hydrocortisone
- sunscreen and hat
- thrush (vaginal yeast infection) treatment, eg Clotrimazole pessaries or Diflucan tablet
- Ural or equivalent if you're prone to urine infections

of trip, activities and existing medical conditions.

- Most vaccines don't produce immunity until at least two weeks after they're given.
- Ask for an International Certificate of Vaccination (otherwise known as 'the yellow booklet'), which will list all vaccinations given.

Recommended Vaccinations

The World Health Organization (WHO) recommends the following vaccinations for travellers to the Mekong region:

Adult diphtheria and tetanus Single booster recommended if you haven't had one in the previous 10 years.

Hepatitis A Provides almost 100% protection for up to a year; a booster after 12 months provides at least another 20 years' protection.

Hepatitis B Now considered routine for most travellers. Given as three shots over six months. A rapid schedule is also available, as is a combined vaccination with hepatitis A. Lifetime protection occurs in 95% of people.

Measles, mumps and rubella (MMR) Two doses of MMR are required unless you have had the diseases. Many young adults require a booster.

Polio Only one booster is required as an adult for lifetime protection.

Typhoid Recommended unless your trip is less than a week long and only to developed cities. The vaccine offers around 70% protection, lasts for two to three years and comes as a single shot.

Required Vaccinations

The only vaccine required by international regulations is for yellow fever. Proof of vaccination is only required if you have visited a country in the yellow-fever zone within the six days before entering the Mekong region; if travelling to the Mekong region from Africa or South America, check to see if proof of vaccination is required. It's only likely to be an issue if flying directly from an affected country to a major gateway such as Bangkok.

IN VIETNAM, CAMBODIA, LAOS & NORTHERN THAILAND

Availability & Cost of Health Care

If you think you may have a serious disease, especially malaria, do not waste time – travel to the nearest quality facility to receive attention. Bangkok is a popular medical-tourism destination, with a few world-class hospitals that provide excellent care. In other Mekong capitals the best options are clinics that cater specifically to travellers and expats. These are more expensive than local medical facilities, but provide several advantages:

- They provide superior standard of care (usually).

- They liaise with insurance companies should you require evacuation.
- They understand the local system and are aware of the safest local hospitals and best specialists.

Infectious Diseases

Dengue Fever

Risk All countries; most common in cities.

Cause Mosquito-borne (day and night).

Symptoms High fever, severe headache and body ache (dengue used to be known as breakbone fever); sometimes a rash and diarrhoea.

Treatment No specific treatment, just rest and paracetamol; do not take aspirin as it increases the likelihood of haemorrhaging. See a doctor to be diagnosed and monitored.

Prevention Insect-avoidance measures (both day and night).

Hepatitis A

Risk Very common in all countries.

Cause Food- and water-borne virus.

Symptoms Infects the liver, causing jaundice (yellow skin and eyes), nausea and lethargy.

Treatment No specific treatment; just allow time for the liver to heal.

Prevention All travellers to the Mekong region should be vaccinated against hepatitis A.

Hepatitis B

Risk All countries. In some parts of the Mekong region, up to 20% of the population carry hepatitis B, and usually are unaware of this.

Cause Spread by body fluids, including sexual contact.

Long-term consequences Possible liver cancer and cirrhosis, among others.

Prevention Vaccination (it's the only STD that can be prevented by vaccination).

Hepatitis E

Risk All countries, but far less common than Hepatitis A.

Cause Contaminated food and water.

Symptoms Similar symptoms to hepatitis A.

Consequences Severe in pregnant women: can result in the death of both mother and baby.

Prevention Currently no vaccine; follow safe eating and drinking guidelines.

HIV

Risk New incidences of HIV are on the decline in all countries, but risk remains.

Cause Heterosexual sex is the main method of transmission in region.

Consequences One of the most common causes of death in people under the age of 50 in Thailand.

Malaria

Risk All countries, mainly in rural areas.

Cause Mosquito-borne parasite.

Symptoms Fever; headache, diarrhoea, cough or chills may also occur; diagnosis can only be made by taking a blood sample.

Treatment A variety of drugs taken orally or by continuous intravenous infusion.

Prevention Two-pronged strategy: mosquito avoidance and antimalarial medications. For more, see p552.

Rabies

Risk Common in most regions.

Cause Bite or lick from infected animal – most commonly a dog or monkey.

Consequences Uniformly fatal.

Treatment If an animal bites you, gently wash wound with soap and water, apply iodine-based antiseptic and immediately seek medical advice and commence postexposure treatment. If you are not prevaccinated you will need to receive rabies immunoglobulin as soon as possible.

Prevention Pretravel vaccination simplifies postbite treatment.

Schistosomiasis

Risk All countries.

Cause Tiny parasite that enters the skin after swimming in contaminated water.

Symptoms Travellers usually only get a light infection and are asymptomatic. If you are concerned, you can be tested three months after exposure.

Treatment Medications.

STDs

Sexually transmitted diseases (STDs) most common in the Mekong region include herpes, warts, syphilis, gonorrhoea and chlamydia. People carrying these diseases often have no signs of infection. Condoms will prevent gonorrhoea and chlamydia but not warts or herpes. If after a sexual encounter you develop any rash, lumps, discharge, or pain when passing urine, seek immediate medical attention. If you have been sexually active during your travels, have an STD check on your return home.

Strongyloides

Risk Common in travellers to Cambodia, Laos and Thailand.

Cause Parasite transmitted by skin contact with soil.

Symptoms Unusual skin rash called *larva currens* – a linear rash on the trunk that comes and goes. Most people don't have other symptoms until their immune system becomes severely suppressed, when the parasite can cause an overwhelming infection.

Treatment Medications.

Typhoid

Risk All countries.

Cause Spread via food and water.

Symptoms Serious bacterial infection results in high and slowly progressive fever, headache; may be accompanied by a dry cough and stomach pain. Diagnosis requires a blood test.

Treatment A course of antibiotics.

WEIGHING THE RISKS OF MALARIA

For such a serious and potentially deadly disease, there is an enormous amount of misinformation concerning malaria. You must get expert advice about whether your trip will actually put you at risk. Many parts of the Mekong region, particularly city and resort areas, have minimal to no risk of malaria, and the risk of side effects from the prevention tablets may outweigh the risk of actually getting the disease. For most rural areas in the region, however, the risk of contracting the disease far outweighs the risk of any tablet side effects. Remember that malaria can be fatal. Before you travel, seek medical advice on the right medication and dosage for you.

There are two strategies for preventing malaria: avoiding mosquito bites and taking antimalarial medication.

Mosquito Prevention

Travellers are advised to take the following steps:

- Use a DEET-based insect repellent on exposed skin. Wash off at night, as long as you are sleeping under a mosquito net. Natural repellents such as citronella can be effective, but must be applied more frequently than products containing DEET.
- Sleep under a mosquito net that is impregnated with Permethrin.
- Choose accommodation with screens and fans (if not air-conditioned).
- Impregnate clothing with Permethrin in high-risk areas.
- Wear long sleeves and trousers in light colours.
- Use mosquito coils.
- Spray your room with insect repellent before going out for your evening meal.

Antimalarials

Most people who catch malaria are taking inadequate or no antimalarial medication. The following list is not comprehensive and new treatments are constantly being developed to ward off resistance to existing medications. For up-to-date, country-specific advice on antimalarials, see www.cdc.gov/malaria.

Derivatives of Artesunate Not suitable as a preventive medication. They are useful treatments under medical supervision.

Chloroquine and Paludrine combination Limited effectiveness in most of the Mekong region. Common side effects include nausea (40% of people) and mouth ulcers. Generally not recommended.

Doxycycline Broad-spectrum antibiotic, ingested daily, that has the added benefit of helping to prevent a variety of tropical diseases, including leptospirosis, tick-borne disease, typhus and meliodosis. Potential side effects include photosensitivity (a tendency to sunburn), thrush in women, indigestion, heartburn, nausea and interference with the contraceptive pill. More serious side effects include ulceration of the oesophagus.

Lariam (Mefloquine) Weekly tablet that suits many people. Has received much bad press, some of it justified, some not. Serious side effects are rare but include depression, anxiety, psychosis and seizures. It is around 90% effective in most parts of Southeast Asia, but there is significant resistance in parts of northern Thailand, Laos and Cambodia.

Malarone Combines Atovaquone and Proguanil. Side effects are uncommon and mild, usually nausea and headache. Best tablet for scuba divers and for those on short trips to high-risk areas. Must be taken for one week after leaving the risk area.

A final option is to take no preventive tablets but to have a supply of emergency medication should you develop the symptoms of malaria. This is less than ideal, and you'll need to get to a good medical facility within 24 hours of developing a fever. If you choose this option the most effective and safest treatment is Malarone.

Prevention Vaccination recommended for all travellers spending more than one week in the Mekong region, or travelling outside of the major cities. Be aware that vaccination is not 100% effective so you must still be careful with what you eat and drink.

Rare But Be Aware

Filariasis A mosquito-borne disease that is common in the local population.

Japanese Encephalitis Viral disease transmitted by mosquitoes, typically occurring in rural areas. Rare for travellers, but vaccination recommended for those spending extended time in rural areas.

Measles Highly contagious bacterial infection, spread via coughing and sneezing. There is no specific treatment.

Meliodosis Contracted by skin contact with soil. The symptoms are very similar to TB. No vaccine, but can be treated with medications.

Opisthorchiasis (Liver Flukes) Tiny worms that are occasionally present in freshwater fish in Laos. The main risk comes from eating raw or undercooked fish. Symptoms include worms or worm eggs in the faeces. Easily treated with medication.

Tuberculosis Medical and aid workers, and long-term travellers who have significant contact with the local population should take precautions to prevent TB.

Typhus Murine typhus is spread by the bite of a flea; scrub typhus is spread via a mite. Symptoms include fever, muscle pains and a rash. Can be prevented by following general insect-avoidance measures or taking doxycycline.

Zika Virus Spread primarily by mosquitoes and sexual intercourse. No specific medicine or vaccine. Mostly found in Vietnam.

Traveller's Diarrhoea

Traveller's diarrhoea is by far the most common problem that affects travellers – between 30% and 50% of people will suffer from it within two weeks of starting their trip. In more than 80% of cases, traveller's diarrhoea is caused by bacteria (there are numerous potential culprits), and therefore responds promptly to treatment with antibiotics. Treatment will depend on your situation – how sick you are, how quickly you need to get better, where you are and so on.

Traveller's diarrhoea is defined as the passage of more than three watery bowel actions within 24 hours, plus at least one other symptom such as fever, cramps, nausea, vomiting or feeling generally unwell.

Treatment consists of staying well hydrated; rehydration solutions such as Gastrolyte are the best for this. Antibiotics such as Norfloxacin, Ciprofloxacin or Azithromycin will kill the bacteria quickly.

Loperamide is just a 'stopper' and doesn't get to the cause of the problem. It can be helpful, for example, if you have to go on a long bus ride. Don't take Loperamide if you have a fever, or blood in your stools. Seek medical attention quickly if you do not respond to an appropriate antibiotic. You should always seek reliable medical care if you have blood in your diarrhoea.

Amoebic Dysentery

Amoebic dysentery is very rare in travellers but is often misdiagnosed by poor-quality labs in the Mekong region.

Symptoms Similar to bacterial diarrhoea, ie fever, bloody diarrhoea and generally feeling unwell.

Consequences If left untreated, complications such as liver or gut abscesses can occur.

Treatment Tinidazole or Metronidazole to kill the parasite in your gut, and then a second drug to kill the cysts.

Giardiasis

Giardia lamblia is a relatively common parasite in travellers.

Symptoms Nausea, bloating, excess gas, fatigue, intermittent diarrhoea.

Treatment Tinidazole is the top choice, with Metronidazole being a second option. The parasite will eventually go away if left untreated but this can take months.

Environmental Hazards

Air Pollution

- An increasing problem (particularly vehicle emissions) in most of the Mekong region's major cities including Bangkok, Ho Chi Minh City (formerly Saigon) and Phnom Penh.
- Causes minor respiratory problems such as sinusitis, dry throat and irritated eyes.
- If you have severe respiratory problems speak with your doctor before travelling to any heavily polluted urban centres.

TAP WATER

- Never drink tap water in the region.
- Bottled water is generally safe.
- Boiling water is the most efficient method of purifying it.
- The best chemical purifier is iodine. This should not be used by pregnant women or those people who suffer with thyroid problems.
- Water filters should filter out viruses. Ensure your filter has a chemical barrier such as iodine and a small pore size, ie less than four microns.

BOX JELLYFISH

Occasionally found in the waters of Thailand, Cambodia and Vietnam, box jellyfish are extremely dangerous. Their stings are extremely painful and can even be fatal. There are two main types of box jellyfish: multi-tentacled and single-tentacled. Multi-tentacled box jellyfish are the most dangerous and a severe envenomation can kill an adult within two minutes. They are generally found along sandy beaches near river mouths and mangroves during the warmer months.

Take local advice if there are box jellies or other dangerous jellyfish around and keep out of the water.

Heat

Many parts of the Mekong region are hot and humid throughout the year, which can lead to heat exhaustion or heatstroke, especially during the first few days of your visit before you have adapted to the hot climate. Take it easy when you first arrive and stay well hydrated throughout your trip.

Insect Bites & Stings

Bedbugs Don't carry disease but their bites are very itchy. They live in the cracks of furniture and walls and then migrate to the bed at night to feed on you. Treat the itch with an antihistamine.

Lice Inhabit various parts of your body but most commonly your head and pubic area. Transmission is via close contact with an infected person. Lice can be difficult to treat and you may need numerous applications of an anti-lice shampoo, such as Permethrin. Pubic lice are usually contracted from sexual contact.

Ticks Contracted in rural areas. Commonly found behind the ears, on the belly and in armpits. If you have had a tick bite and experience symptoms such as a rash at the site of the bite or elsewhere, or fever or muscle aches, you should see a doctor. Doxycycline prevents tick-borne diseases.

Leeches Found in humid rainforest areas. Do not transmit any disease but bites are often intensely itchy for weeks afterwards and become infected easily. Apply an iodine-based antiseptic to any leech bite to help prevent infection.

Bee and wasp stings Mainly a problem for people who are allergic to them. Anyone with a serious bee or wasp allergy should carry an injection of adrenalin (eg an Epipen) for emergency treatment.

Jellyfish Mostly just irritating, not dangerous (the exception is box jellyfish). First aid for jellyfish stings involves pouring vinegar onto the affected area to neutralise the poison. Do not rub sand or water onto the stings. Take painkillers, and if you feel ill in any way after being stung seek medical advice.

Parasites

Numerous parasites are common in local populations in the Mekong region; however, most of these are rare in travellers.

➡ Two rules for avoiding parasitic infections: wear shoes and avoid eating raw food, especially fish, pork and vegetables.

➡ A number of parasites are transmitted via the skin by walking barefoot, including strongyloides, hookworm and cutaneous *larva migrans*.

Skin Problems

There are two skin problems that commonly affect travellers:

Fungal rashes These occur in moist areas that get less air, such as the groin, armpits and between the toes. Treatment involves keeping the skin dry, avoiding chafing and using an antifungal cream such as Clotrimazole or Lamisil.

Infected cuts and scratches These are common in humid climates. Take meticulous care of any cuts and scratches to prevent complications such as abscesses. Immediately wash all wounds in clean water and apply antiseptic.

Snakes

The Mekong region is home to many species of both poisonous and harmless snakes. Some rules on avoiding and treating snake bites:

➡ Assume that all snakes are poisonous and *never* try to catch one.

➡ Always wear boots and long pants if walking in an area that may have snakes.

➡ First aid in the event of a snakebite involves pressure immobilisation via an elastic bandage firmly wrapped around the affected limb, starting at the bite site and working up towards the chest. The bandage should not be so tight that the circulation is cut off, and the fingers or toes should be kept free so the circulation can be checked. Immobilise affected limb with a splint and carry the victim to medical attention.

➡ Do not use tourniquets or try to suck the venom out.

➡ Antivenin is available for most species in the urban centres of Thailand or Vietnam, and in some provincial capitals of Cambodia and Laos.

Sunburn

Just 20 or 30 minutes in the searing tropical sun can cause a nasty sunburn. Always use a strong sunscreen (at least SPF factor 30) and reapply liberally, especially after a swim.

Language

This chapter offers basic vocabulary to help you get around the countries covered in this book. Read our coloured pronunciation guides as if they were English, and you'll be understood. Some of the phrases have both polite and informal forms – these are indicated by the abbreviations 'pol' and 'inf'. The abbreviations 'm' and 'f' indicate masculine and feminine gender respectively.

KHMER

In our pronunciation guides, vowels and vowel combinations with an h at the end are pronounced hard and aspirated (with a puff of air).

The symbols are read as follows: aa as the 'a' in 'father'; a and ah shorter and harder than aa; i as in 'kit'; uh as the 'u' in 'but'; ii as the 'ee' in 'feet'; eu like 'oo' (with the lips spread flat); euh as eu (short and hard); oh as the 'o' in 'hose' (short and hard); ow as in 'glow'; u as the 'u' in 'flute' (short and hard); uu as the 'oo' in 'zoo'; ua as the 'ou' in 'tour'; uah as ua (short and hard); œ as 'er' in 'her' (more open); ia as the 'ee' in 'beer' (without the 'r'); e as in 'they'; ai as in 'aisle'; ae as the 'a' in 'cat'; ay as ai (slightly more nasal); ey as in 'prey'; o as the 'ow' in 'cow'; av like a nasal ao (without the 'v'); euv like a nasal eu (without the 'v'); ohm as the 'ome' in 'home'; am as the 'um' in 'glum'; ih as the 'ee' in 'teeth' (short and hard); eh as the 'a' in 'date' (short and hard); awh as the 'aw' in 'jaw' (short and hard); and aw as the 'aw' in 'jaw'.

Some consonant combinations in our pronunciation guides are separated with an apostrophe for ease of pronunciation, eg 'j-r' in j'rook and 'ch-ng' in ch'ngain. Also note that k is pronounced as the 'g' in 'go'; kh as the 'k' in 'kind'; p as the final 'p' in 'puppy'; ph as the 'p' in 'pond'; r as in 'rum' but hard and rolling; t as the 't' in 'stand'; and th as the 't' in 'two'.

WANT MORE?

For in-depth language information and handy phrases, check out Lonely Planet's *Southeast Asia Phrasebook*. You'll find it at **shop.lonelyplanet.com**, or you can buy Lonely Planet's iPhone phrasebooks at the Apple App Store.

Basics

Hello.	ជម្រាបសួរ	johm riab sua
Goodbye.	លាសិនហើយ	lia suhn hao-y
Excuse me./ Sorry.	សូមទោស	sohm toh
Please.	សូម	sohm
Thank you.	អរគុណ	aw kohn
Yes.	បាទ/ចាស	baat/jaa (m/f)
No.	ទេ	te

What's your name?
អ្នកឈ្មោះអី? niak ch'muah ei

My name is ...
ខ្ញុំឈ្មោះ... kh'nyohm ch'muah ...

Accommodation

I'd like a room ...	ខ្ញុំសុំបន្ទប់...	kh'nyohm sohm bantohp ...
for one person	សម្រាប់ មួយនាក់	samruhp muy niak
for two people	សម្រាប់ ពីរនាក់	samruhp pii niak

How much is it per day?
តម្លៃមួយថ្ងៃ ប៉ុន្មាន? damlay muy th'ngay pohnmaan

NUMBERS – KHMER

1	មួយ	muy
2	ពីរ	pii
3	បី	bei
4	បួន	buan
5	ប្រាំ	bram
6	ប្រាំមួយ	bram muy
7	ប្រាំពីរ	bram pii
8	ប្រាំបី	bram bei
9	ប្រាំបួន	bram buan
10	ដប់	dawp

Eating & Drinking

Do you have a menu in English?

មានមីនុយជា ភាសាអង់គ្លេសទេ? — mien menui jea piasaa awnglay te

I'm vegetarian.

ខ្ញុំតមសាច់ — kh'nyohm tawm sait

The bill, please.

សូមគិតលុយ — sohm kuht lui

beer	ប៊ីយ៉ែរ	bii-yœ
coffee	កាហ្វេ	kaa fey
tea	តែ	tai
water	ទឹក	teuk

Emergencies

Help!

ជួយខ្ញុំផង! — juay kh'nyohm phawng

Call the police!

ជួយហៅប៉ូលិសមក! — juay hav polih mao

Call a doctor!

ជួយហៅគ្រូពេទ្យមក! — juay hav kruu paet mao

Where are the toilets?

បង្គន់នៅឯណា? — bawngkohn neuv ai naa

Shopping & Services

How much is it?

នេះថ្លៃប៉ុន្មាន? — nih th'lay pohnmaan

That's too much.

ថ្លៃពេក — th'lay pek

I'm looking for the ...	ខ្ញុំរក...	kh'nyohm rohk ...
bank	ធនាគារ	th'niakia
market	ផ្សារ	p'saa
post office	«ប្រៃសណីយ៍	praisuhnii
public telephone	ទូរស័ព្ទ សាធារណៈ	turasahp saathiaranah

Transport & Directions

Where is a/the ...?

...នៅឯណា? — ... neuv ai naa

bus stop

ចំណតឡានឈ្នួល — jamnawt laan ch'nual

train station

ស្ថានីយរថភ្លើង — s'thaanii roht plœng

When does the ... leave?	...ចេញម៉ោង b"unµan?	... jein maong pohnmaan
boat	ទូក	duk
bus	ឡានឈ្នួល	laan ch'nual
train	រថភ្លើង	roht plœng
plane	យន្តហោះ	yohn hawh

LAO

Lao is a tonal language, meaning that many identical sounds are differentiated only by changes in the pitch of a speaker's voice. Pitch variations are relative to the speaker's natural vocal range, so that one person's low tone isn't necessarily the same pitch as another person's. There are six tones in Lao, indicated in our pronunciation guides by accent marks on letters: low tone (eg dęe), high (eg héu·a), rising (eg săhm), high falling (eg sôw) and low falling (eg kòw). Note that no accent mark is used for the mid tone (eg het).

The pronunciation of vowels goes like this: i as in 'it'; ee as in 'feet'; ai as in 'aisle'; ah as the 'a' in 'father'; a as the short 'a' in 'about'; aa as in 'bad'; air as in 'air'; er as in 'fur'; eu as in 'sir'; u as in 'put'; oo as in 'food'; ow as in 'now'; or as in 'jaw'; o as in 'phone'; oh as in 'toe'; ee·a as in 'lan'; oo·a as in 'tour'; ew as in 'yew'; and oy as in 'boy'.

Most consonants correspond to their English counterparts. The exceptions are đ (a hard 't' sound, a bit like 'dt') and ɓ (a hard 'p' sound, a bit like 'bp').

In our pronunciation guides, the hyphens indicate syllable breaks in words, eg àng-gít (English). Some syllables are further divided with a dot to help you pronounce compound vowels, eg kĕe·an (write).

Basics

Hello.	ສະບາຍດີ	sábai-dĕe
Goodbye.	ສະບາຍດີ	sábai-dĕe
Excuse me./ Sorry.	ຂໍໂທດ	kŏr tôht
Please.	ກະລຸນາ	ga-lú-náh
Thank you.	ຂອບໃຈ	kòrp jai
Yes./No.	ແມ່ນ/ບໍ່	maan/bor

What's your name?
ເຈົ້າຊື່ຫຍັງ — jôw seu nyăng

My name is ...
ຂ້ອຍຊື່ ... — kòy seu ...

Accommodation

hotel	ໂຮງແຮມ	hóhng háam
guesthouse	ຫໍຮັບແຂກ	hŏr hap káak

Do you have a room?
ມີຫ້ອງບໍ່ — mée hòrng bor

single room
ຫ້ອງນອນຕຽງດຽວ — hòrng nórn đĕe·ang dee·o

double room
ຫ້ອງນອນຕຽງຄູ່ — hòrng nórn đĕe·ang koo

How much ...?	... ເທົ່າໃດ	... tow dai
per night	ຄືນລະ	kéun-la
per week	ອາທິດລະ	ah-tit-la

Eating & Drinking

What do you have that's special?
ມີຫຍັງພິເສດບໍ່ — mée nyăng pi-sèt bor

I'd like to try that.
ຂ້ອຍຢາກລອງກິນເບິ່ງ — kòy yàhk lórng gin berng

I eat only vegetables.
ຂ້ອຍກິນແຕ່ຜັກ — kòy gin đaa pák

Please bring the bill.
ຂໍແຊັກແດ້ — kŏr saak daa

beer	ເບຍ	bee·a
coffee	ກາແຟ	gah-fáir
tea	ຊາ	sáh
water	ນ້ຳດື່ມ	nâm deum

Emergencies

Help!	ຊ່ວຍແດ່	soo·ay daa
Go away!	ໄປເດີ້	bai dêr

Call the police!
ຊ່ວຍເອີ້ນຕຳລວດແດ່ — soo·ay êrn đam-lòo·at daa

Call a doctor!
ຊ່ວຍຕາມຫາໝໍໃຫ້ແດ່ — soo·ay đahm hăh mŏr hài daa

I'm lost.
ຂ້ອຍຫລົງທາງ — kòy lŏng táhng

Where are the toilets?
ຫ້ອງນ້ຳຢູ່ໃສ — hòrng nâm yoo să

Shopping & Services

I'm looking for ...
ຂ້ອຍຊອກຫາ ... — kòy sòrk hăh ...

How much (for) ...?
... ເທົ່າໃດ — ... tow dai

The price is very high.
ລາຄາແພງຫລາຍ — láh-káh páang lăi

I want to change money.
ຂ້ອຍຢາກປ່ຽນເງິນ — kòy yàhk bee·an ngérn

bank	ທະນາຄານ	ta-náh-káhn
pharmacy	ຮ້ານຂາຍຢາ	hâhn kăi yah
post office	ໄປສະນີໂຮງສາຍ	bai-sá-née hóhng săi

NUMBERS – LAO

1	ໜຶ່ງ	neung
2	ສອງ	sŏrng
3	ສາມ	săhm
4	ສີ່	see
5	ຫ້າ	hàh
6	ຫກ	hók
7	ເຈັດ	jét
8	ແປດ	bàat
9	ເກົ້າ	gôw
10	ສິບ	síp

Transport & Directions

Where is the ...?
... ຢູ່ໃສ ... yòo săi

How far?
ໄກເທົ່າໃດ kại tow dại

I'd like a ticket.
ຂ້ອຍຢາກໄດ້ປີ້ kòy yàhk dâi ɓee

What time will the ... leave?
... ຈະອອກຈັກໂມງ ... já òrk ják móhng

boat	ເຮືອ	héu·a
bus	ລົດເມ	lot máir
minivan	ລົດຕູ້	lot đôo
plane	ເຮືອບິນ	héu·a bin

THAI

In Thai the meaning of a syllable may be altered by means of tones. In standard Thai there are five tones: low (eg bàht), mid (eg dee), falling (eg mâi), high (eg máh) and rising (eg săhm). The range of all tones is relative to each speaker's vocal range, so there is no fixed 'pitch' intrinsic to the language.

In our pronunciation guides, the hyphens indicate syllable breaks within words, and for ease of pronunciation some compound vowels are further divided with a dot, eg mêu·a-rai (when).

The vowel a is pronounced as in 'about', aa as the 'a' in 'bad', ah as the 'a' in 'father', ai as in 'aisle', air as in 'flair' (without the 'r'), eu as the 'er' in 'her' (without the 'r'), ew as in 'new' (with rounded lips), oh as the 'o' in 'toe', or as in 'torn' (without the 'r') and ow as in 'now'.

Note also the pronunciation of the following consonants: ɓ (a hard 'p' sound, almost like a 'b', eg in 'hip-bag'); đ (a hard 't' sound, like a sharp 'd', eg in 'mid-tone'); and r (as in 'run' but flapped; often pronounced like 'l').

Basics

Hello.	สวัสดี	sà-wàt-dee
Goodbye.	ลาก่อน	lah gòrn
Excuse me.	ขออภัย	kŏr à-pai
Sorry.	ขอโทษ	kŏr tôht
Please.	ขอ	kŏr
Thank you.	ขอบคุณ	kòrp kun
Yes.	ใช่	châi
No.	ไม่	mâi

What's your name?
คุณชื่ออะไร kun chêu à-rai

My name is ...
ผม/ดิฉัน pŏm/dì-chăn
ชื่อ... chêu ... (m/f)

Accommodation

Where's a ...?	... อยู่ที่ไหน	... yòo têe năi
campsite	ค่ายพักแรม	kâi pák raam
guesthouse	บ้านพัก	bâhn pák
hotel	โรงแรม	rohng raam
youth hostel	บ้านเยาวชน	bâhn yow-wá-chon

Do you have a ... room?	มีห้อง ... ไหม	mee hôrng ... măi
single	เดี่ยว	dèe·o
double	เตียงคู่	đee·ang kôo

Eating & Drinking

What would you recommend?
คุณแนะนำอะไรบ้าง kun náa-nam à-rai bâhng

I'd like (the menu), please.
ขอ (รายการอาหาร) หน่อย kŏr (rai gahn ah-hăhn) nòy

I don't eat (red meat).
ผม/ดิฉันไม่กิน (เนื้อแดง) pŏm/di-chăn mâi gin (néu·a daang) (m/f)

Cheers!
ไชโย chai-yoh

Please bring the bill.
ขอบิลหน่อย kŏr bin nòy

beer	เบียร์	bee·a
coffee	กาแฟ	gah-faa
tea	ชา	chah
water	น้ำดื่ม	nám dèum

Emergencies

Help!	ช่วยด้วย	chôo·ay dôo·ay
Go away!	ไปให้พ้น	ɓai hâi pón

NUMBERS – THAI

1	หนึ่ง	nèung
2	สอง	sŏrng
3	สาม	săhm
4	สี่	sèe
5	ห้า	hâh
6	หก	hòk
7	เจ็ด	jèt
8	แปด	ɓàat
9	เก้า	gôw
10	สิบ	sìp

I'm lost.
ผม/ดิฉันหลงทาง — pŏm/dì-chăn lŏng tahng (m/f)

Call the police!
เรียกตำรวจหน่อย — rêe·ak đam·ròo·at nòy

Call a doctor!
เรียกหมอหน่อย — rêe·ak mŏr nòy

I'm ill.
ผม/ดิฉันป่วย — pŏm/dì-chăn ɓòo·ay (m/f)

Where are the toilets?
ห้องน้ำอยู่ที่ไหน — hôrng nám yòo têe năi

Shopping & Services

I'd like to buy ...
อยากจะซื้อ ... — yàhk jà séu ...

How much is it?
เท่าไร — tôw-rai

That's too expensive.
แพงไป — paang ɓai

Transport & Directions

Where's ...?
... อยู่ที่ไหน — ... yòo têe năi

What's the address?
ที่อยู่คืออะไร — têe yòo keu à-rai

Can you show me (on the map)?
ให้ดู (ในแผนที่) ได้ไหม — hâi doo (nai păan têe) dâi măi

A ... ticket, please.	ขอตั๋ว ...	kŏr đŏo·a ...
one-way	เที่ยวเดียว	têe·o dee·o
return	ไปกลับ	ɓai glàp
boat	เรือ	reu·a
bus	รถเมล์	rót mair
plane	เครื่องบิน	krêu·ang bin
train	รถไฟ	rót fai

VIETNAMESE

Vietnamese is written in a Latin-based phonetic alphabet, which was declared the official written form in 1910.

In our pronunciation guides, a is pronounced as in 'at', aa as in 'father', aw as in 'law', er as in 'her', oh as in 'doh!', ow as in 'cow', u as in 'book', uh as in 'but' and uhr as in 'fur' (without the 'r'). We've used dots (eg dee·úh-ng) to separate the combined vowel sounds. Note also that d is pronounced as in 'stop', đ as in 'dog', and ğ as in 'skill'.

Vietnamese uses a system of tones to make distinctions between words – so some vowels are pronounced with a high or low pitch. There are six tones in Vietnamese, indicated in the written language (and in our pronunciation guides) by accent marks on the vowel: mid (ma), low falling (mà), low rising (mả), high broken (mã), high rising (má) and low broken (mạ). The mid tone is flat.

The variation in vocabulary between the Vietnamese of the north and the south is indicated by (N) and (S) respectively.

Basics

Hello.	*Xin chào.*	sin jòw
Goodbye.	*Tạm biệt.*	daạm bee·uht
Excuse me./ Sorry.	*Xin lỗi.*	sin lõy
Please.	*Làm ơn.*	laàm ern
Thank you.	*Cảm ơn.*	ğaảm ern
Yes.	*Vâng./Dạ.* (N/S)	vuhng/ yạ
No.	*Không.*	kawm

What's your name?
Tên là gì? — den laà zeè

My name is ...
Tên tôi là ... — den doy laà ...

Accommodation

Where's a ...?	*Đâu có ... ?*	đoh gó ...
campsite	*nơi cắm trại*	ner·ee gúhm chại
hotel	*khách sạn*	kaák sạan
guesthouse	*nhà khách*	nyaà kaák

I'd like a ...	*Tôi muốn ...*	doy moo·úhn ...
single room	*phòng đơn*	fòm dern
double room	*phòng giường đôi*	fòm zuhr·èrng đoy

How much is it per ...?	*Giá bao nhiêu một ...?*	zaá bow nyee·oo mạwt ...
night	*đêm*	đem
person	*người*	nguhr·eè

Eating & Drinking

I'd like the menu.
Tôi muốn thực đơn. doy moo·úhn tụhrk dern

What's the speciality here?
Ở đây có món gì đặc biệt? ẻr đay kó món zeè dụhk bee·ụht

I'm a vegetarian.
Tôi ăn chay. doy uhn jay

I'd like ...
Xin cho tôi ... sin jo doy ...

Cheers!
Chúc sức khoẻ! júp súhrk kwẻ

The bill, please.
Xin tính tiền. sin díng dee·ùhn

beer	*bia*	bi·a
coffee	*cà phê*	ğaà fe
tea	*chè/trà* (N/S)	jà/chaà
water	*nước*	nuhr·érk
wine	*rượu nho*	zee·oọ nyo

Emergencies

Help!
Cứu tôi! ğuhr·oó doy

Leave me alone!
Thôi! toy

I'm lost.
Tôi bị lạc đường. doi beẹ laạk đuhr·èrng

Please call the police.
Làm ơn gọi công an. laàm ern gọy ğawm aan

Please call a doctor.
Làm ơn gọi bác sĩ. laàm ern gọy baák seẽ

I'm ill.
Tôi bị đau. doy beẹ đoh

Where is the toilet?
Nhà vệ sinh ở đâu? nyaà vẹ sing ẻr đoh

Shopping & Services

I'd like to buy ...
Tôi muốn mua ... doy moo·úhn moo·uh ...

How much is this?
Cái này giá bao nhiêu? ğaí này zaá bow nyee·oo

It's too expensive.
Cái này quá mắc. ğaí này gwaá múhk

bank	*ngân hàng*	nguhn haàng
market	*chợ*	jẹr
post office	*bưu điện*	buhr·oo đee·ụhn
tourist office	*văn phòng hướng dẫn du lịch*	vuhn fòm huhr·érng zũhn zoo lịk

Transport & Directions

Where is ...?
... ở đâu? ... ẻr đoh

What is the address?
Địa chỉ là gì? đee·ụh cheẻ laà zeè

Can you show me (on the map)?
Xin chỉ giùm (trên bản đồ này). sin jeẻ zùm (chen baản dàw này)

I'd like a ... ticket.	*Tôi muốn vé ...*	doy moo·úhn vá ...
one way	*đi một chiều*	đee mạt jee·oò
return	*khứ hồi*	kúhr haw·eè

boat	*thuyền*	twee·ùhn
bus	*xe buýt*	sa beét
plane	*máy bay*	máy bay
train	*xe lửa*	sa lủhr·uh

NUMBERS – VIETNAMESE

1	*một*	mạwt
2	*hai*	hai
3	*ba*	baa
4	*bốn*	báwn
5	*năm*	nuhm
6	*sáu*	sóh
7	*bảy*	bảy
8	*tám*	dúhm
9	*chín*	jín
10	*mười*	muhr·eè

GLOSSARY

This glossary is a list of Cambodian (C), Lao (L), Thai (T) and Vietnamese (V) terms you may come across in the Mekong region.

ao dai (V) – traditional Vietnamese tunic and trousers
APEC – Asia-Pacific Economic Cooperation
apsara (C) – heavenly nymphs or angelic dancers
Asean – Association of Southeast Asian Nations

bąasĭi (L) – sometimes written as 'basi' or 'baci'; a ceremony in which the 32 khwăn are symbolically bound to the participant for health and safety
baht (T) – the Thai unit of currency
baray (C) – ancient reservoir
BE (L, T) – Buddhist Era
boeng (C) – lake
BTS (T) – Bangkok Transit System (Skytrain)
bun (L) – festival
buu dien (V) – post office

Cao Daism (V) – Vietnamese religious sect
Cham (C, V) – ethnic minority descended from the people of Champa; a Hindu kingdom dating from the 2nd century BC
chedi (T) – see stupa
Chenla (C, L, V) – Pre-Angkorian Khmer kingdom covering parts of Cambodia, Laos and Vietnam
Chunchiet (C) – ethnolinguistic minority
CPP (C) – Cambodian People's Party
cyclo (C, V) – bicycle rickshaw

devaraja (C) – god king
DMZ (V) – the misnamed Demilitarised Zone, a strip of land that once separated North and South Vietnam
dong (V) – the Vietnamese unit of currency
duong (V) – road, street; abbreviated as 'Đ'

Ecpat – End Child Prostitution & Trafficking

faràng (T) – Western, Westerner; foreigner
Funan (C, V) – first Khmer kingdom, located in Mekong Delta area

HCMC (V) – Ho Chi Minh City (Saigon)
Hoa (V) – ethnic Chinese, the largest single minority group in Vietnam

Indochina – Vietnam, Cambodia and Laos, the French colony of Indochine; the name derives from Indian and Chinese influences

Isan (T) – general term used for northeastern Thailand

jataka (C, L, T) – stories of the Buddha's past lives, often enacted in dance-drama
jumbo (L) – a motorised three-wheeled taxi, sometimes called a túk-túk

karst – limestone peaks with caves, underground streams and potholes
khao (T) – hill, mountain
khlong (T) – canal
Khmer (C) – ethnic Cambodians; Cambodian language
Khmer Rouge (C) – literally Red Khmers, the commonly used name for the Cambodian communist movement responsible for the genocide in the 1970s
khwăn (L) – guardian spirits of the body
Kinh (V) – the Vietnamese language
kip (L) – the Lao unit of currency
ko (T) – island
koh (C) – island
krama (C) – chequered scarf

lákhon (C, T) – classical dance-drama
linga (C, L, T, V) – phallic symbol

mae nam (L, T) – river
Mahayana – literally, 'Great Vehicle'; a school of Buddhism that extended the early Buddhist teachings; see also Theravada
meuang (L, T) – city
MIA (C, L, V) – missing in action, usually referring to US personnel
Montagnards (V) – highlanders, mountain people; specifically the ethnic minorities inhabiting remote areas of Vietnam
moto (C) – motorcycle taxi
Mt Meru – the mythical dwelling place of the Hindu gods, symbolised by the Himalayas
múan (L) – fun, which the Lao believe should be present in all activities
muay thai (T) – Thai boxing

nâam (L, T) – water, river
naga (C, L, T) – mythical serpent-being
NTAL (L) – National Tourism Administration of Laos
NVA (V) – North Vietnamese Army

Pali – ancient Indian language that, along with Sanskrit, is the root of Khmer, Lao and Thai
Pathet Lao (L) – literally, 'Country of Laos'; both a general term for the country and the common

name for the Lao communist military during the civil war

phansăa (T) – Buddhist lent

phnom (C) – mountain

phu (L) – hill or mountain

POW – prisoner of war

prasat (C, T) – tower, temple

psar (C) – market

quan (V) – urban district

quoc ngu (V) – Vietnamese alphabet

Ramakian (T) – Thai version of the Ramayana

Ramayana – Indian epic story of Rama's battle with demons

Reamker (C) – Khmer version of the Ramayana

remorque (C) – (or remork) a motorised three-wheeled pedicab

riel (C) – the Cambodian unit of currency

roi nuoc (V) – water puppetry

rót fai fáa (T) – Skytrain; BTS

săhmlór (T) – three-wheeled pedicab

Sanskrit – ancient Hindu language that, along with Pali, is the root of Khmer, Lao and Thai

sànùk (T) – fun

soi (L, T) – lane, small street

song (L, V) – river

Songkran (T) – Thai New Year, held in mid-April

sŏrngtăaou (L, T) – small pick-up truck with two benches in the back

SRV (V) – Socialist Republic of Vietnam (Vietnam's official name)

stung (C) – small river

stupa – religious monument, often containing Buddha relics

talat (L) – market

Tam Giao (V) – literally, 'triple religion'; Confucianism, Taoism and Buddhism fused over time with popular Chinese beliefs and ancient Vietnamese animism

Tao (V) – the Way; the essence of which all things are made

TAT (T) – Tourism Authority of Thailand

tat (L) – waterfall

Tet (V) – Lunar New Year

thâat (L) – Buddhist stupa, reliquary; also written as 'that'

thànŏn (L, T) – road, street, avenue; abbreviated as 'Th'

Theravada – a school of Buddhism found in Cambodia, Laos and Thailand; this school confined itself to the early Buddhist teachings unlike Mahayana

tonlé (C) – major river

tripitaka (T) – Buddhist scriptures

túk-túk (L, T) – motorised săhmlór

UNDP – United Nations Development Programme

UXO (C, L, V) – unexploded ordnance

VC (V) – Viet Cong or Vietnamese Communists

vihara (C) – temple sanctuary

wâi (L, T) – palms-together greeting

wat (C, L, T) – Buddhist temple-monastery

wíhăhn (T) – sanctuary, hall, dwelling

xe om (V) – motorbike taxi (also Honda om)

xich lo (V) – see cyclo

Behind the Scenes

SEND US YOUR FEEDBACK

We love to hear from travellers – your comments keep us on our toes and help make our books better. Our well-travelled team reads every word on what you loved or loathed about this book. Although we cannot reply individually to your submissions, we always guarantee that your feedback goes straight to the appropriate authors, in time for the next edition. Each person who sends us information is thanked in the next edition – the most useful submissions are rewarded with a selection of digital PDF chapters.

Visit **lonelyplanet.com/contact** to submit your updates and suggestions or to ask for help. Our award-winning website also features inspirational travel stories, news and discussions.

Note: We may edit, reproduce and incorporate your comments in Lonely Planet products such as guidebooks, websites and digital products, so let us know if you don't want your comments reproduced or your name acknowledged. For a copy of our privacy policy visit lonelyplanet.com/privacy.

OUR READERS

Many thanks to the travellers who used the last edition and wrote to us with helpful hints, useful advice and interesting anecdotes:

Sylvia Bartels, Julie Luna Bayer, Stuart Cameron, Graham Carrington, Judith Frazer, Amir Ghadimipour, Said Hajji, Nathan Highton, Moritz Isselstein, Helen Johnson, Florian Kessler, Johannes Kneitz, Alexander Kovachev, Adrian Legge, Ana Louro, Carol MacDonald, Mette Lund Møller, Ted Nixon, Dalilah Pichler, Simon Plate, Sue Ray, Sabine Rivière, Lucy and Stuart Stirland, Balt van Berkel, Jodie Wilkinson, Martin Willoughby-Thomas, Douglas Wilson, R Wolff, Esti Glustein Yudke

WRITER THANKS

Greg Bloom

The biggest thanks goes to my team on the home front: to Windi for doing more than holding down the fort, for taking care of the little 'uns while I was away and during the deadline crunch. And of course to Anna, Callie and Rocco for the smiles and comic relief. On the road, thanks to fellow writer Nick for the tips and bar-research support in Kampot. And to Joel for the yarns and Katey for the intel.

Austin Bush

I'd like to thank my DE James Smart, Angela Tinson, my co-authors Nick Ray and Bruce Evans, and the helpful people on the ground in Laos, especially Manilla, Paul Eshoo, Tek and Alex at Marvelao, Mr Somkiad at Tha Khaek's Tourism Information Centre, Amphai at Phosy Tha Lang, Inthy Deuansavanh and Ivan Scholte.

David Eimer

Thanks to all the locals and travellers who passed on tips along the way, whether knowingly or unwittingly. Special gratitude to Mr Dam in Mae Hong Son for his insights into the area and bad jokes, as well as to the Burmese guy in Chiang Saen who fixed my bike. Thanks also to the Lonely Planet office crew for their support.

Nick Ray

A huge and heartfelt thanks to the people of Vietnam, Cambodia and Laos, whose warmth, strength and spirit have made it such a fascinating region to visit over the years. Biggest thanks are reserved for my lovely wife, Kulikar Sotho, and our children, Julian and Belle, as without their support and encouragement my adventures would not be possible. Thanks also to mum and dad for giving me a taste for travel from a young age. Thanks to those in Vietnam, Cambodia and Laos who have helped shaped my experience in these countries.

Iain Stewart

Writing a book about Vietnam takes a lot of help on the ground. In HCMC, many thanks to Mark Zazula and Lu, Matt Cowan, and Mark and Duong from the Old Compass for their insider knowledge. Up and down the coastline I was helped by Neil and Caroline, Vinh Vu, Mark Wyndham, Alex Leonard, Julia Shaw and my travelling companion and son Louis Stewart.

Bruce Evans

On this trip I have to give a big shout out to the Lao people, whose friendliness made the trip so much fun, and also to my fellow authors, Nick and Austin. In addition, Vientiane expat David Wharton, Frédéric Gousset on Don Khon, Boun at Green Discovery, Yves at Noi's Bikes in Pakse, Mr Khamphan at the Attapeu tourist office, Paul Eshoo and Don Duvall.

Paul Harding

Thanks to the many people I met along the way in Thailand. In particular thanks to Steve, Apai and Pete in Pattaya, and Chris and Mike in Ko Kut. Thanks to Tanya Parker and the team at Lonely Planet. And most of all, love and thanks to Hannah and Layla for always patiently being there.

Damian Harper

Many thanks to all of those who helped along the way on what was an incredible and fascinating journey; much gratitude especially to Ben, Sophie, Kien, Binh, Hu Xuechun, Mai, Anh, Thao, Tam, Priscilla Milis, Matt Bazak, Neil, Paul Mooney, Kim, Tanya Currington, Fabienne, Justine, Thien, Hoang Nguyen, Bradley Mayhew, Truyen and Rosee. Thanks, as ever, to Daisy, Tim and Emma.

Ashley Harrell

Thanks to: co-authors for all the hard work on this book, Alana Morgan for the local expertise, Franz Betgem for the wisdom and the company, Kellyn Foxman, Ansley Luce and Erik Lokensgard for the excellent recs, Alexis Stranberg and Josh Buermann for supervising the vicious cur, and Steven Sparapani for watching me eat live shrimp and making an honest woman out of me. I love you.

Mark Johanson

Arkun (thank you) Theara Hout, Dary Sang, Virginia Brumby, Bun Puthea and Sithy Hengchan for all of your tips, help and wisdom either before or during my travels in Cambodia. A big *gracias* to my partner Felipe for enduring my long absences from home. Thanks to my parents for instilling in me a curiosity for the unknown and an insatiable thirst for travel. Also, thanks to my fellow writers Nick Ray and Greg Bloom for their invaluable insights.

Anirban Mahapatra

Sincere thanks to my resident [redacted] friends Dirk, Melva, Xavier, Roque, [redacted] Seonmi and Bruno, and my wife [redacted] of whom chipped in with valuable [redacted] insights on their favourite places [redacted] ences throughout my research. [redacted] to all my fellow writers, and to the [redacted] people of Thailand – a country of [redacted] smiles.

Bradley Mayhew

Thanks to Mr Linh for his tips on Ba Be National Park, Nguyen Van Manh in Sapa, Yom at the Doc May in Dalat and Mr Dong at Ngan Nga Bac Ha, who were all incredibly helpful with information. Cheers to QT and Jorgen in Ha Giang for all their help and first-class bike rental. Finally, cheers to Andre for a great couple of weeks riding motorbikes in the far north.

Daniel McCrohan

Massive thanks to my good friends Wez and Ketsara Hunter for helping me through this project with advice, translations, lifts and wonderful hospitality. Thanks to Wachiraphan Chaimanee and Sunti Chaimanee for help with bus timetables, to Tim Bewer for his invaluable Isan expertise and to Tanya Parker for giving me this opportunity. Love, as always, to Taotao, Dudu and Yoyo.

ACKNOWLEDGEMENTS

Climate map data adapted from Peel MC, Finlayson BL & McMahon TA (2007) 'Updated World Map of the Köppen-Geiger Climate Classification', *Hydrology and Earth System Sciences*, 11, 1633–44.

Illustrations pp94-5, pp222-3, pp408-9 and pp410-11 by Michael Weldon.

Cover photograph: Market in Hoi An, Vietnam; Keren Su/Getty Images ©

THIS BOOK

This 6th edition of Lonely Planet's *Vietnam, Cambodia, Laos & Northern Thailand* guidebook was researched and written by Greg Bloom, Austin Bush, David Eimer, Nick Ray, Iain Stewart, Bruce Evans, Paul Harding, Damian Harper, Ashley Harrell, Mark Johanson, Anirban Mahapatra, Bradley Mayhew and Daniel McCrohan.

This guidebook was produced by the following:

Senior Product Editors Kate Chapman, Sandie Kestell, Kathryn Rowan

Regional Senior Cartographers Corey Hutchison, Diana von Holdt

Product Editors Carolyn Boicos, Saralinda Turner

Assisting Editors James Appleton, Sarah Bailey, Andrea Dobbin, Rosie Nicholson, Maja Vatrić

Book Designers Lauren Egan, Virginia Moreno

Assisting Cartographers Julie Dodkins, James Leversha, Anthony Phelan, Julie Sheridan

Script Checkers Bruce Evans, Oeu Vearyda, Manivone Watson

Cover Researcher Naomi Parker

Thanks to Melanie Dankel, Mario D'Arco, Sasha Drew, Kate James, Tanya Parker, James Smart, Vicky Smith

Index

Map Pages **000**
Photo Pages **000**

Map Pages **000**
Photo Pages **000**

Map Pages **000**
Photo Pages **000**

Map Pages **000**
Photo Pages **000**

Map Pages **000**
Photo Pages **000**

Map Legend

Sights
- Beach
- Bird Sanctuary
- Buddhist
- Castle/Palace
- Christian
- Confucian
- Hindu
- Islamic
- Jain
- Jewish
- Monument
- Museum/Gallery/Historic Building
- Ruin
- Shinto
- Sikh
- Taoist
- Winery/Vineyard
- Zoo/Wildlife Sanctuary
- Other Sight

Activities, Courses & Tours
- Bodysurfing
- Diving
- Canoeing/Kayaking
- Course/Tour
- Sento Hot Baths/Onsen
- Skiing
- Snorkelling
- Surfing
- Swimming/Pool
- Walking
- Windsurfing
- Other Activity

Sleeping
- Sleeping
- Camping
- Hut/Shelter

Eating
- Eating

Drinking & Nightlife
- Drinking & Nightlife
- Cafe

Entertainment
- Entertainment

Shopping
- Shopping

Information
- Bank
- Embassy/Consulate
- Hospital/Medical
- Internet
- Police
- Post Office
- Telephone
- Toilet
- Tourist Information
- Other Information

Geographic
- Beach
- Gate
- Hut/Shelter
- Lighthouse
- Lookout
- Mountain/Volcano
- Oasis
- Park
- Pass
- Picnic Area
- Waterfall

Population
- Capital (National)
- Capital (State/Province)
- City/Large Town
- Town/Village

Transport
- Airport
- Border crossing
- Bus
- Cable car/Funicular
- Cycling
- Ferry
- Metro/MTR/MRT station
- Monorail
- Parking
- Petrol station
- Skytrain/Subway station
- Taxi
- Train station/Railway
- Tram
- Underground station
- Other Transport

Routes
- Tollway
- Freeway
- Primary
- Secondary
- Tertiary
- Lane
- Unsealed road
- Road under construction
- Plaza/Mall
- Steps
- Tunnel
- Pedestrian overpass
- Walking Tour
- Walking Tour detour
- Path/Walking Trail

Boundaries
- International
- State/Province
- Disputed
- Regional/Suburb
- Marine Park
- Cliff
- Wall

Hydrography
- River, Creek
- Intermittent River
- Canal
- Water
- Dry/Salt/Intermittent Lake
- Reef

Areas
- Airport/Runway
- Beach/Desert
- Cemetery (Christian)
- Cemetery (Other)
- Glacier
- Mudflat
- Park/Forest
- Sight (Building)
- Sportsground
- Swamp/Mangrove

Note: Not all symbols displayed above appear on the maps in this book

Bradley Mayhew

Vietnam Bradley has been writing guidebooks for 20 years now. He started travelling while studying Chinese at Oxford University, and has since focused his expertise on China, Tibet, the Himalaya and Central Asia. He is the co-writer of Lonely Planet guides to *Tibet, Nepal, Trekking in the Nepal Himalaya, Bhutan, Central Asia* and many others. Bradley has also fronted two TV series for Arte and SWR, one retracing the route of Marco Polo via Turkey, Iran, Afghanistan, Central Asia and China, and the other trekking Europe's 10 most scenic long-distance trails.

Daniel McCrohan

Northern Thailand With a Greek father, a Spanish grandfather, an Irish grandmother and a Chinese wife, Daniel has always looked beyond his English homeland for influence and inspiration. He's been travelling the world, on-and-off, for 25 years, and has been writing Lonely Planet guidebooks (42 and counting) for more than a decade. He specialises in China and India, but has travelled extensively throughout Thailand, forming a special bond over the years with Isan, a region he loves. Follow his adventures on Twitter (@danielmccrohan) or at www.danielmccrohan.com.

Iain Stewart

Vietnam Iain trained as a journalist in the 1990s and then worked as a news reporter and a restaurant critic in London. He started writing travel guides in 1997 and has since penned more than 60 books for destinations as diverse as Ibiza and Cambodia. Iain's contributed to Lonely Planet titles including *Mexico, Indonesia, Central America, Croatia, Vietnam, Bali, Lombok & Nusa Tenggara* and *Southeast Asia*. He also writes regularly for the *Independent, Observer* and *Daily Telegraph* and tweets at @iaintravel. He'll consider working anywhere there's a palm tree or two and a beach of a generally sandy persuasion. Iain lives in Brighton (UK) within firing range of the city's wonderful south-facing horizon.

Bruce Evans

Laos After travelling the hippie trail in the 1970s, Bruce lived in Thailand for more than two decades, much of that in a Buddhist monastery. When he returned to Australia he worked as an editor at Lonely Planet for many years. Since 2013 he has worked as a freelance editor and translator. He specialises in the Southeast Asia region, where he feels very much at home. This trip to Laos was his second authoring job for Lonely Planet.

Paul Harding

Northern Thailand As a writer and photographer, Paul has been travelling the globe for the best part of two decades, with an interest in remote and offbeat places, islands and cultures. He's an author and contributor to more than 50 Lonely Planet guides to countries and regions as diverse as India, Belize, Vanuatu, Iran, Indonesia, New Zealand, Iceland, Finland, Philippines, Thailand and – his home patch – Australia.

Damian Harper

Vietnam With two degrees (one in modern and classical Chinese from SOAS), Damian has been writing for Lonely Planet for more than two decades, contributing to titles as diverse as *China, Beijing, Shanghai, Vietnam, Thailand, Ireland, London, Mallorca, Hong Kong, Great Britain* and *Malaysia, Singapore & Brunei*. A seasoned guidebook writer, Damian has penned articles for numerous newspapers and magazines, including the *Guardian* and *Daily Telegraph*, and currently makes Surrey, England, his home. A self-taught trumpet novice, his other hobbies include Taekwondo, collecting modern first editions and photography, and he has had a wide variety of photographs published by Lonely Planet, *National Geographic Traveler*, AA Publishing, Insight Guides and other publishers, periodicals and publications. Follow Damian on Instagram (@damian.harper) or at www.damianharper.com.

Ashley Harrell

Northern Thailand After a brief stint selling day-spa coupons door-to-door in South Florida, Ashley decided she'd rather be a writer. She went to journalism grad school, convinced a newspaper to hire her, and started covering wildlife, crime and tourism, sometimes all in the same story. Fuelling her zest for storytelling and the unknown, she travelled widely and moved often, from a tiny NYC apartment to a vast California ranch to a jungle cabin in Costa Rica, where she started writing for Lonely Planet.

Mark Johanson

Cambodia Mark grew up in Virginia, USA, and has called five different countries home over the past decade while circling the globe reporting for British newspapers (the *Guardian*), American magazines *(Men's Journal)* and global media outlets (CNN, BBC). When not on the road, you'll find him gazing at the Andes from his current home in Santiago, Chile. Follow his adventures at www.markjohanson.com.

Anirban Mahapatra

Northern Thailand Anirban is a travel writer, photographer and filmmaker who has authored multiple editions of Lonely Planet's bestselling *India* guidebook, as well as several regional handbooks. He has written and curated Lonely Planet guidebooks on Bangladesh, Sri Lanka and Bhutan, designed content models and held author workshops for Lonely Planet and made videos and documentaries for international television networks and corporates as well as ministries under the Government of India. When not travelling the world, he lives in Kolkata and Bangkok.

OUR STORY

A beat-up old car, a few dollars in the pocket and a sense of adventure. In 1972 that's all Tony and Maureen Wheeler needed for the trip of a lifetime – across Europe and Asia overland to Australia. It took several months, and at the end – broke but inspired – they sat at their kitchen table writing and stapling together their first travel guide, *Across Asia on the Cheap*. Within a week they'd sold 1500 copies. Lonely Planet was born.

Today, Lonely Planet has offices in Tennessee, Dublin and Beijing, with a network of over 2000 contributors in every corner of the globe. We share Tony's belief that 'a great guidebook should do three things: inform, educate and amuse'.

OUR WRITERS

Greg Bloom

Cambodia Born in California and raised in the northeast United States, Greg is a freelance writer, editor, tour guide and travel planner based out of Manila and El Nido, Philippines. He got his first taste of international life at the age of 12 when he lived in Chile for a half year with his dad. He graduated from university with a degree in international development, but it was journalism that would ultimately lure him overseas. Greg began his writing career in the late '90s in Ukraine, working as a journalist and later editor-in-chief of the *Kyiv Post*, an English-language weekly. He has contributed to some 50 Lonely Planet titles, mostly in Eastern Europe and Asia. Accounts of his Lonely Planet trips over the years are at www.mytripjournal.com/bloomblogs. Greg also wrote the Plan Your Trip, Understand and Survival Guide sections.

Austin Bush

Laos Austin originally came to Thailand in 1999 as part of a language study program hosted by Chiang Mai University. The lure of city life, employment and spicy food eventually led him to Bangkok. City life, employment and spicy food have kept him there since. These days, he works as a writer and photographer, and in addition to having contributed to numerous books, magazines and websites, he has contributed text and photos to more than 20 Lonely Planet titles, including *Bangkok; the Food Book; Food Lover's Guide to the World; Laos; Malaysia, Singapore & Brunei; Myanmar (Burma); Pocket Bangkok; Thailand; Thailand's Islands & Beaches* and *The World's Best Street Food*.

David Eimer

Northern Thailand David has been a journalist and writer ever since abandoning the idea of a law career in 1990. After spells working in his native London and in Los Angeles, he moved to Beijing in 2005, where he contributed to a variety of newspapers and magazines in the UK. Since then, he has travelled and lived across China and in numerous cities in Southeast Asia, including Bangkok, Phnom Penh and Yangon. He has been covering China, Myanmar and Thailand for Lonely Planet since 2006.

Nick Ray

Cambodia, Laos, Vietnam A Londoner of sorts, Nick currently lives in Phnom Penh and has written countless guidebooks on the countries of the Mekong region. When not writing, he is often out exploring the remote parts of the region as a location scout or line producer for the world of television and film, including anything from *Tomb Raider* to *Top Gear*. The Mekong region is one of his favourite places on earth and he was excited to get back to some of its remote corners.

OVER PAGE MORE WRITERS

Published by Lonely Planet Global Limited
CRN 554153
6th edition – Oct 2021
ISBN 978 1 78701 795 5

10 9 8 7 6 5 4 3 2 1
Printed in Singapore